Yesterday:
dorm room
desk chair

Today:
political
hotseat

If you think politics is just a game, think again.

Introducing PoliSim: Political Science Simulations in American Government—where YOU have the political power to control real politics.

Using the FREE ACCESS CODE found in this textbook, enter an exclusive *Companion Website*™ featuring **PoliSim**—12 interactive simulations in American Government that put YOU in the political hotseat, a.k.a. your dorm room desk chair. Sit down, log on, and experience the power of real politics with fully animated and interactive simulations of actual political situations in American Government, politically charged situations whose outcome depends on YOU:

★ **REAL DATA:** Powered by real data, **PoliSim** challenges you with multi-level simulations that require you to make simple and complex decisions, which are best made based on information drawn from real data:
  ★ *real* election results
  ★ *real* demographics, including sex, age, education level, race, and income
  ★ *real* maps, including political persuasion (Democratic or Republican) for specific areas
  ★ *real* score cards from real Senate members showing their votes on public interest issues
  ...and much more!

★ **REAL SITUATIONS:** Experience the concepts presented in your textbook using **PoliSim**, where you will be given the political power to:
  ★ Balance the nation's budget to gain popularity in the public eye.
  ★ Spend foreign aid dollars most effectively to reduce wars, terrorism, drug trade, and brutal dictatorship, and improve the U.S. standing from an international perspective.
  ★ Pass legislation by lobbying the Senate on a realistic budget and time frame—and use provided links to real senators' websites, where you will be exposed to their real views.
  ...and much more!

Notice that many chapter openers offer you an introduction to the specific **PoliSim** experience designed to help you bring the chapter content to life; and then:

Read the text. Log on using your access code included in this new book. Follow the *Companion Website*™ links to more information. Become an informed decisionmaker who considers the impact of political decisions before you make them.

And then log on to PoliSim and feel the power.

After all, isn't that what politics is all about?

GOVERNMENT BY THE PEOPLE

NATIONAL, STATE, AND LOCAL VERSION
2001-2002 EDITION

JAMES MACGREGOR BURNS
*University of Maryland, College Park
and Williams College*

J.W. PELTASON
University of California

THOMAS E. CRONIN
Whitman College

DAVID B. MAGLEBY
Brigham Young University

DAVID M. O'BRIEN
University of Virginia

Prentice
Hall

Upper Saddle River
New Jersey 07458

Library of Congress Cataloging-in-Publication Data

Government by the people / James MacGregor Burns ... [et al]. — National, state, and
local version, 2001–2002 ed.
   p. cm.
  Includes bibliographical references and index.
  ISBN 0-13-031567-2
  1. United States—Politics and government. 2. Local government—United States. I.
Burns, James MacGregor.

JK274.G66 2002
320.473—dc21

2001034052

VP, Editorial Director: *Laura Pearson*
Senior Acquisitions Editor: *Heather Shelstad*
Development Editor and Project Manager: *Serena Hoffman*
Assistant Editor: *Brian Prybella*
Editorial Assistant: *Jessica Drew*
Director of Marketing: *Beth Gillett Mejia*
Copy Editor: *Ann Hofstra Grogg*
VP, Director of Production and Manufacturing: *Barbara Kittle*
Executive Managing Editor: *Ann Marie McCarthy*
Prepress and Manufacturing Manager: *Nick Sklitsis*
Prepress and Manufacturing Buyer: *Benjamin Smith*
Creative Design Director: *Leslie Osher*
Interior and Cover Designer: *Anne DeMarinis*
Director, Image Resource Center: *Melinda Reo*
Interior Image Specialist: *Beth Boyd*
Manager, Rights and Permissions: *Kay Dellosa*
Photo Researcher: *Linda Sykes, Abby Reip*
Manager of Production Services: *Guy Ruggiero*
Electronic Page Layout: *Joseph Lisa*
Illustrations: *Maria Piper*
Cover Art: *Corbis "American Destinations" collection*
       and S. Wanke/Picture Quest

This book was set in 10/12.5 Minion
by Prentice Hall Production Services and was
printed and bound by RR Donnelley & Sons.
The cover was printed by Phoenix Color Corp.

© 2002, 2000, 1998, 1995, 1993, 1990, 1989, 1987, 1985, 1984, 1981, 1978, 1975,
1972, 1969, 1966, 1963, 1960, 1957, 1954, 1952 by Pearson Education, Inc.
Upper Saddle River, New Jersey 07458

Printed in the United States of America
10 9 8 7 6 5 4 3 2

ISBN 0-13-093920-X (School)
ISBN 0-13-031567-2 (College)

Pearson Education LTD., *London*
Pearson Education Australia PTY, Limited, *Sydney*
Pearson Education Singapore, Pte. Ltd
Pearson Education North Asia Ltd, *Hong Kong*
Pearson Education Canada, Ltd., *Toronto*
Pearson Educación de Mexico, S.A. de C.V.
Pearson Education — Japan, *Tokyo*
Pearson Education Malaysia, Pte. Ltd
Pearson Education, *Upper Saddle River, New Jersey*

BRIEF CONTENTS

CONTENTS

FEATURES

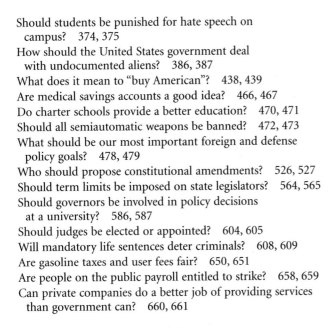

COMPARATIVE POLITICS

POLITICS ONLINE

A MESSAGE FROM THE AUTHORS

The 2000 elections were a civics lesson for all Americans. Topics like the power of the Electoral College in close elections, the appropriate role of the Supreme Court, the function of the vice-president in an evenly divided Senate, and the discovery that neither major political party would dominate the national government suddenly became dinner-table conversation. More enduring lessons for the public were that every vote can make a difference, and that elections have policy consequences. In the aftermath of the 2000 elections, debates abounded about possible constitutional changes in our electoral process and proposals to modernize how Americans vote. These are indeed interesting times to study American government and politics.

Constitutional democracy—the kind we have in the United States—is exceedingly hard to achieve, equally hard to sustain, and often hard to understand without rigorous study. Our political history has been an evolution toward an enlarged role for citizens and voters. Citizens have more rights and political opportunities in 2000 and 2002 than they had in 1800 or 1900. The framers of our Constitution warned that we must be vigilant in safeguarding our rights, liberties, and political institutions. But to do this, we must first understand these institutions and the forces that have shaped them.

Many U.S. citizens take for granted civil liberties, civil rights, free and fair elections, the peaceful transfer of power, and economic freedom and prosperity. Yet many people live in places where these freedoms are nonexistent. This is a time of testing for new democracies as well as old ones. Contempt for government and politics is being expressed in the United States and abroad, yet politics and partisan competition are the lifeblood by which free societies can achieve the ideals of government by the people.

The world we live in remains highly volatile. Although our defense policy changed with the collapse of communism and the emergence of a less powerful Russia, the world has not suddenly become a safer place in which to live. Regional strife and terrorism continue to exist. The United States has entered a period of reassessment of its role in the world, in the United Nations, in regional defense organizations like NATO, and in its economic relations with other countries.

Although we constantly turn to government and to our elected officials with problems and requests, we are critical of their shortcomings. A recurrent theme of this book is the absolute need for politics and politicians, despite the widespread tendency to criticize nearly everything political. The reality is that our political system should not be taken for granted, even as we seek ways it can be improved.

We want you to come away from reading this book with a richer understanding of American politics, government, and the job of politicans, and we hope you will participate actively in making this constitutional democracy more vital and responsive to the urgent problems of the twenty-first century.

REVIEWERS

The writing of this book has profited from the informed, professional, and often sharp, critical suggestions of our colleagues around the country. This and previous editions have been considerably improved as a result of reviews by the following individuals, for which we thank them all.

David Gray Adler, Idaho State University
James E. Anderson, Texas A&M University
David Barnum, De Paul University
Robert Bartlett, Purdue University
Robert C. Benedict, University of Utah
Thad Beyle, University of North Carolina
Robert R. Bland, University of North Texas
Gary Bryner, Brigham Young University
J. Ranson Clark, Muskingum College
Jeanne Clarke, University of Arizona
Leif Carter, University of Georgia
Morgan Chawawa, De Kalb College
Richard Chesteen, University of Tennessee
Ray Christensen, Brigham Young University

Peggy J. Connally, North Central Texas College
Elmer Cornwell, Brown University
Gary Covington, University of Iowa
Douglas Crane, Georgia Perimeter College
Richard Davis, Brigham Young University
James D. Decker, Macon College
Robert DiClerico, West Virginia University
Lois Lovelace Duke, Georgia Southern University
Pat Dunham, Duquesne University
Robert Elias, University of San Francisco
Larry Elowitz, Georgia State College
Lee Epstein, Washington University

Steven Finkel, University of Virginia
Amy Fried, Colgate University
Earl H. Fry, Brigham Young University
Mark Gibney, Purdue University
L. Tucker Gibson, Trinity University
Eugene Goss, Long Beach City College
James A. Graves, Kentucky State University
Eugene R. Grosso, Long Beach City College
Gail Harrison, Georgia Southern University
Paul Herrnson, University of Maryland
Marjorie Hershey, Indiana University
Michael J. Horan, University of Wyoming
Ronald J. Hrebenar, University of Utah
Diane P. Jennings, De Kalb College

Loch K. Johnson, University of Georgia

Bill Kelly, Auburn University

Janet M. Kelly, Clemson University

J. Landrum Kelly, Georgia Southern University

Donald F. Kettl, University of Wisconsin

Dwight Kiel, Central Florida University

Ronald F. King, Tulane University

Michael E. Kraft, University of Wisconsin

Fred A. Kramer, University of Massachusetts

William Lammers, University of Southern California

Ned Lebow, Ohio State University

James P. Lester, Colorado State University

Paul Light, Brookings Institution

William Louthan, Ohio Weslyan University

Vincent N. Mancini, Delaware County Community College

Richard Matthews, Lehigh University

Robert McCalla, University of Wisconsin

Christopher B. Mobley, De Paul University

Theodore R. Mosch, University of Tennessee-Martin

Max Neiman, University of California

David Nice, Washington State University

Richard Pacelle, University of Missouri

Glen Parker, Florida State University

Kelly D. Patterson, Brigham Young University

William A. Pelz, Elgin Community College

B. Guy Peters, University of Pittsburgh

Richard Pious, Barnard College

George Pippin, Jones County College

John Portz, Northeastern University

Pamela Rodgers, University of Wisconsin

David Rosenbloom, American University

Alan Rosenthal, Rutgers University

Henry Shockely, Boston University

Steven Shull, University of New Orleans

Christine Marie Sierra, University of New Mexico

Christopher D. Skubby, Lakeland Community College

Robert W. Small, Massasoit Community College

Gregory W. Smith, Gettysburg College

Richard Smolka, American University

Neil Snortland, University of Arkansas at Little Rock

Michael W. Sonnleitner, Portland Community College

Jacqueline Vaughn Switzer, Northern Arizona University

Thaddeus J. Tocza, University of Colorado at Boulder

Roy Thoman, West Texas A&M University

John Tierney, Boston College

Richard Valelly, Massachusetts Institute of Technology

R. Lawson Veasey, University of Arkansas

Frank L. Wilson, Purdue University

Cheryl D. Young, Texas Technical University

Joseph F. Zimmerman, State University of New York at Albany

ACKNOWLEDGMENTS

Writing this book requires teamwork—first, among the authors, who read and rewrite each other's first drafts, then with our research assistants, who track down loose ends and give us the perspective of students, and with the editors and other professionals at Prentice Hall. Important to each revision are the detailed reviews by teachers and researchers, who provide concrete suggestions on how to improve the book. We are grateful to all who helped with this edition.

Research assistants for the current edition of *Government by the People* are: Kim Spears, Charles W. Ross, Mark Pickering, Chris Rees, Eric McArutur, and Chris Fillmore at Brigham Young University; Elizabeth Schiller at University of California, Irvine, and Neil G. Kornze at Whitman College. Donna Jones and JoAnn Collins at Whitman College provided secretarial assistance. We thank the Honorable David Sills, Presiding Justice of the California Court of Appeals, Fourth District, Division Three, for his most helpful comments.

Books for major college courses like this involve state of the art teaching tools and electronic ancillaries. Highly skilled professionals produced the various supplements and media: Larry Elowitz, Regina Swopes, G. David Garson, Brian Werner, Stuart Twite, and Bryon Wolfe.

Critical to the team that produces this book is Serena Hoffman, the production editor. She knows this book and cares about it. Her commitment to this edition, while at the same time tending to important family concerns, was extraordinary. We gratefully acknowledge her important contribution. We also thank Beth Gillett Mejia, who, as political science editor, brought her boundless energy and enthusiasm to this book and the entire political science list. Our thanks, too, to Brian Prybella and Jessica Drew, who assisted Beth and later the new political science editor, Heather Shelstad, in the numerous tasks involved in publishing a book of this scope. Others at Prentice Hall we wish to thank for their continued support are Phil Miller, Charlyce Jones Owen, and Nancy Roberts.

Many skilled professionals were important to the publication of this book. They include Joseph Lisa for page layouts, Linda Sykes for photo research, Guy Ruggiero for art coordination, Maria Piper for art creation, Anne DeMarinus for interior and cover design, and Leslie Osher for design supervision.

We also want to thank you, the professors and students who use our book and who send us letters with suggestions for improving *Government by the People*. We welcome your notes, phone calls, and e-mail. Please write us care of the Political Science Editor at Prentice Hall, 1 Lake Street, Upper Saddle River, New Jersey 07458, or contact us directly:

James MacGregor Burns   Academy of Leadership, University of Maryland, College Park, MD 20742

J.W. Peltason   School of Social Sciences, University of California, Irvine, CA 92717-5700   jwpeltas@uci.edu

Thomas E. Cronin   Office of the President, Whitman College, Walla Walla, WA 99362   cronin@whitman.edu

David B. Magleby   Department of Political Science, Brigham Young University, Provo, UT 84602   david_magleby@byu.edu

David M. O'Brien   Department of Government and Foreign Affairs, University of Virginia, Charlottesville, VA 22903   dmo2y@virginia.edu

A MESSAGE FROM THE PUBLISHER

*A*lways one step ahead....

This edition marks a dynamic milestone for *Government by the People*. For 50 years *Goverment by the People*—in use in colleges and universities in every state in the nation—has been educating today's American citizens. In fact, *Government by the People* has set the standard that others strive to meet. *Government by the People* continues to innovate in response to changes in our democratic environment and changes in how the government course is taught. At Prentice Hall, we are extremely proud to continue to publish the book that always remains one step ahead of all others in its field by anticipating your needs as an educator and your students' needs as learners. This edition continues in that tradition.

Burns, Peltason, Cronin, Magleby, and O'Brien's *Government by the People, 2001–2002 Edition*, has been revised to provide you with the most current material. As we enter a political era with new leadership in office, no other book is better poised to take students from onlookers to participants in the fascinating world of American government. The gratifying success this text has enjoyed over the years results from a distinguished author team who treat each edition as a fresh challenge—and, in many ways, an entirely new book. As in the past, *Government by the People, 2001–2002 Edition*, remains one step ahead.

NEW TO THIS EDITION

- *New Co-Author:* With this edition we are honored to introduce a new member of our author team. David O'Brien of the University of Virginia joins the team to lend his knowledge to the areas of the courts, civil rights, and civil liberties. Professor O'Brien received his Ph.D. from the University of California–Santa Barbara. His research area is constitutional law, theory, and development, and he is renowned for his scholarship of the Supreme Court and judiciary processes. David O'Brien is the Leone Reeves and George W. Spicer Professor of the University of Virginia's Department of Government and Foreign Affairs. He has authored several works, including *Storm Center: The Supreme Court in American Politics*, 5th ed. (2000). Professor O'Brien is a Judicial Fellow at the Supreme Court of the United States, Russell Sage Foundation Visiting Fellow, and a Fulbright Lecturer at Oxford University.

- *Late-Breaking, Up-to-date Content:* This new edition has been thoroughly updated to reflect the happenings of the recent Election 2000. Virtually all chapters have undergone revisions to reflect events of the past two years—primarily the new leadership in Washington.

Highlights include data from the National Election Study and the latest information from the 2000 National Census. In addition, features within the text, such as A Closer Look, You Decide/Thinking It Through, We the People, and People Debate have been revised to address such important and timely issues as campaign finance reform and the Electoral College.

Finally, we continue our commitment to excellence, offering a balanced presentation with innovative treatment of political ideology and culture, political participation, voting turnout, voting behavior, and campaign financing.

These enhancements are present throughout *Government by the People, 2001–2002 Edition*. And there's more...

- *Improved Organization of Chapters:* In response to comments from reviewers and instructors, *Government by the People, 2001–2002 Edition*, now places the civil rights and civil liberty chapters *after* the explanation of the courts and judicial process. Although the chapters are self-contained and can be taught at any time during the course, this organization makes it easier to give students the background they need to understand these important topics.

- *New Chapter 13—Congressional-Presidential Relations:* This entirely new chapter examines how the president and Congress interact with each other. With the Senate almost equally divided and Republicans in the House with a very small majority, this timely topic will certainly dominate the news. Students will learn about similar periods in history and apply that knowledge to today's headlines.

- *Updated Chapter 5—The American Political Landscape:* This chapter examines social and economic diversity in American society today and some of the political consequences of living in a dynamic multicultural nation.

- *Greatly revised Chapter 11 (The Presidency), Chapter 12 (Congress), and Chapter 14 (Bureaucracy):* These chapters have been extensively revised to reflect current issues, including George W. Bush's proposed initiatives.

- *Improved Chapter 20—Making Social Policy:* This unique chapter is now updated to include current debates over welfare reform, health care, education, and crime control policies.

- *Substantially revised Chapters 19 through 21 (Policy Chapters):* These chapters have been thoroughly updated to reflect the current domestic and international policy initiatives and the priorities of the president and Congress.

New and Improved Technology

As in previous editions, *Government by the People* leads the industry in providing creative, innovative electronic solutions for your classroom. Whether in the form of tools that enable more effective communication or by providing dynamic presentation of content via the World Wide Web, Prentice Hall continues to anticipate your needs.

- **www.prenhall.com/burns**: This truly premium *Companion Website™* is available to users of *Government by the People, 2001–2002 Edition*. This website is host to more than 15 dynamic resources to support the learning or teaching of your introductory government course.

  Among the many resources included are PoliSim, Politics Online, ContentSelect (Powered by EBSCO), Documents Online (provides full text of more than 150 source documents referenced in the text), as well as an abundance of online quizzing and assessment features. Chapter summaries, practice tests, links, glossary, video tips, interactive surveys, and interactive graphics are also available on this site.

  These resources are available free by using the access code found in new copies of *Government by the People, 2001–2002, Edition*. Access to the site may also be purchased separately.

- *PoliSim: Political Science Simulations for American Government:* Entirely new, these multistep, multimedia simulations are unique to *Government by the People, 2001–2002 Edition*. A simulation for most chapters is identified on the chapter openers. Not just scripted scenarios, these fully animated, interactive simulations invite your students into the context of what they are learning, requiring them to think critically and make decisions. Available on the *Companion Website™*.

- *ContentSelect: Powered by EBSCO: Government by the People* is proud to offer access to ContentSelect with the 2001–2002 Edition. From the convenience of their computers, students and instructors can now access thousands of current and archived articles from both scholarly and contemporary journals. Available on the *Companion Website™*.

- *Politics Online:* Entirely revised since the last edition, many of these end-of-chapter sections now contain interactive exercises in addition to thought-provoking situations and applicable links. Students will be prompted to participate in a brief interactive exercise, research relevant sites, or explore government in other nations, among other activities. Students can read the material in the Politics Online box, interactive in nature, and apply their knowledge by completing these activities and conducting research.

- *CourseCompass Edition:* For instructors who would like to implement the use of course management software to organize their course and communicate with students, Prentice Hall is pleased to offer *Government by the People CourseCompass Edition*, featuring a host of organizational tools, such as gradebook management, interactive syllabus, test preparation, and pre-loaded instructional content supporting the text. Instructors can save a great deal of time preparing for lectures and managing their course. Please see your Prentice Hall representative or visit **www.prenhall.com/burns** and select the link to CourseCompass.

- *Distance Learning Solutions:* For instructors interested in creating a distance learning course, Prentice Hall offers courses in both Blackboard and WebCT, in addition to our own CourseCompass Edition. Your local Prentice Hall representative can provide you with additional details, or you can visit **www.prenhall.com/burns** for a special demonstration and additional information.

Enduring Features of the Text

Among the many attributes of *Government by the People, 2001–2002 Edition*, are the features that have consistently supported the balanced presentation of topics within the text. Each of these features has been appropriately revised to reflect those issues that are most significant in our political environment today.

- THE PEOPLE DEBATE: These two-page spreads featured throughout the text have been completely revised to address contemporary topics such as Election 2000, Campaign Finance Reform, The Electoral College, and Social Security Reform. People Debates give students a chance to participate in a pro/con debate in the text, online, and through essays and links on the *Companion Website™*.

- YOU DECIDE/THINKING IT THROUGH: This participatory question-and-answer feature is designed to strengthen students' critical thinking skills as well as introduce controversial and challenging issues and ideas about American politics. A You Decide question is presented on the left page, and on the facing page, a Thinking It Through discussion examines possible answers.

- A CLOSER LOOK: These journalistic-style boxes combine text, photos, and art on relevant issues of high student

appeal. Some of the topics include: Religion and Politics, Evaluating Bill Clinton's Presidency, The Politics of Capital Punishment, Campaign Finance Reform, and The "Don't Ask-Don't Tell" Controversy.

■ WE THE PEOPLE: These unique boxes are designed to reflect the concerns and experiences of ethnic and minority groups in American politics. Some of the topics include: Oprah Winfrey: Achieving the American Dream, Distribution of Education in the United States, Portrait of the Electorate, and Women Governors.

SUPPLEMENTS FOR THE INSTRUCTOR

In addition to the abundance of material available in the Faculty Resources section of the *Companion Website*™ (**www.prenhall.com/burns**), *Government by the People, 2001–2002 Edition*, offers instructors a wide range of instructional aids. These supplements have been completely revised, not only to incorporate material new to this edition, but also to ensure that standards of the highest quality are maintained.

■ INSTRUCTOR'S RESOURCE MANUAL WITH LECTURE OUTLINER: In addition to a new section devoted to using our *Companion Website*™, this supplement provides the following resources for each chapter of the text: summary, review of major concepts, lecture suggestions and topic outlines, suggestions for classroom discussion, and a detailed content outline for lecture planning. An electronic version is also available in the Faculty Resources section of the *Companion Website*™.
ISBN: 0-13-0933724

■ POWERPOINT GALLERY: For each chapter, the Power-Point Gallery provides electronic files for each figure and table in the text, along with pre-created PowerPoint slides ready for customization. With the use of this tool you may create a dynamic PowerPoint presentation or print your own customized 4-color transparencies. (Available in the Faculty Resources section of the *Companion Website*™.)

■ PRESENTATION PACKAGE: A new resource designed to make your presentation preparation worry free, this supplement provides detailed instructions for using our PowerPoint Gallery to create your presentation. In addition, 8½ x 11 transparency masters for every figure and table in the text are provided, ready for duplication. Finally, a collection of the most widely used, 4-color transparencies is provided for your convenience.

■ TEST ITEM FILE: Completely revised to ensure the highest level of quality and accuracy, this test item file contains over 2000 questions using multiple-choice, true/false, and essay format for covering factual, conceptual, and applied material from the text:
Basic, National, National/S/L versions: ISBN: 0-13-0326755
Brief version: ISBN: 0-13-0933686

■ PRENTICE HALL TEST MANAGER: A computerized version of the test item file, this program allows full editing of the questions and the addition of instructor-generated items. Other special features include random generation, scrambling question order, and test preview before printing. Available for both the Microsoft Windows operating system and Macintosh computers:
MAC Basic, National, National/S/L versions:
ISBN: 0-13-0326712
MAC Brief version: ISBN: 0-13-0418129
WIN Basic, National, National/S/L versions:
ISBN: 0-13-0326607
WIN Brief version: ISBN: 0-13-0418110

■ VIDEO: HOW A BILL BECOMES A LAW: This 25-minute video chronicles an environmental law in Massachusetts from its start as one citizen's concern to its passage in Washington, D.C. Students witness step-by-step the process of how a bill becomes a law. Complete with narrative and dynamic graphics:
ISBN: 0-13-0326763

■ FILMS FOR THE HUMANITIES AND SCIENCES: With a qualifying order of textbooks from Prentice Hall, you may select from a high quality library of political science videos from Films for the Humanities and Sciences. Please contact your local representative for a complete listing.

■ STRATEGIES FOR TEACHING AMERICAN GOVERNMENT: A GUIDE FOR THE NEW INSTRUCTOR: This unique guide offers a wealth of practical advice and information to help new instructors face the challenges of teaching courses in American Government. (Available in the Faculty Resources Section of the *Companion Website*™.)

SUPPLEMENTS FOR THE STUDENT

In addition to the wealth of content offered on the *Companion Website*™ (**www.prenhall.com/burns**), *Government by the People, 2001–2002 Edition*, offers the following study material to maximize students' learning potential:

■ STUDY GUIDE: In addition to a new section devoted to the *Companion Website*™, each chapter includes a detailed outline, study notes, a glossary, practice tests, Political Science Today study assignments, and data analysis worksheets that reinforce student learning. The guide was prepared by Larry Elowitz of Georgia College and State University:
Basic: ISBN: 0-13-0326674
National: ISBN: 0-13-0326682
National, State, and Local: ISBN: 0-13-0326690
Brief: ISBN: 0-13-09337A-3

■ POLITICAL SCIENCE ON THE INTERNET: EVALUATING ONLINE RESOURCES: This timely supplement provides an introduction to the Internet and the numerous political sites on the World Wide Web. Not only does it describe e-mail,

list servers, browsers, and how to document these sources, it also provides information on how to critically evaluate those sources. Furthermore, it includes addresses for the most current and useful politically-oriented websites. This 96-page supplementary book is FREE to students when shrink-wrapped with copies of *Government by the People*. ISBN: 0-13-0277584

- THE POLITICAL SCIENCE STUDENT WRITER'S MANUAL, 4TH ED.: Authored by Gregory Scott and Stephen Garrison, this comprehensive, practical writer's manual—created specifically for political science students—is designed to help students accomplish two goals: (1) improve their writing skills and strategies, and (2) learn about political science at the same time. Available to students for a discount when bundled with *Government by the People*. ISBN: 0-13-0404470

- THE WRITE STUFF: WRITING AS A PERFORMING AND POLITICAL SCIENCE ART, 2ND ED.: This brief booklet, written by Thomas E. Cronin, provides ideas and suggestions on writing style and methods in political science. Also available in the Student Resources section of the *Companion Website*™.

SUPPLEMENTARY BOOKS AND READINGS FOR AMERICAN GOVERNMENT

Each of the following books features specialized topical coverage allowing you to tailor your American Government course to suit the needs of your region or your particular teaching style. Featuring contemporary issues or timely readings, any of the following books are available for a discount when bundled with *Government by the People*. Please visit our Online Catalog at **www.prenhall.com/burns** for additional details.

American Politics: Core Arguments—Current Controversy, 2nd ed.
Peter Woolley, Fairleigh Dickenson University
Albert Papa, University of New Jersey
ISBN: 0-13-0879193 © 2002

Contemporary Readings in American Government
Mark Rozell, The Catholic University of America
John White, The Catholic University of America
ISBN: 0-13-0406457 © 2002

Issues in American Political Life: Money, Violence, and Biology, 4th ed.
Robert Thobaben, Wright State University
Donna Schlagheck, Wright State University

Charles Funderburk, Wright State University
ISBN: 0-13-0336726 © 2002

Choices: An American Government Reader—Custom Publishing
Gregory Scott, University of Central Oklahoma
Katherine Tate, University of California–Irvine
Ronald Weber, University of Wisconsin–Milwaukee
ISBN: 0-13-090399X © 2001

Civil Rights and Liberties: Provocative Questions and Evolving Answers
Harold Sullivan, The City University of New York
ISBN: 0-13-0845140 © 2001

Sense and Non-Sense: American Culture and Politics
J. Harry Wray, DePaul University
ISBN: 0-13-0833436 © 2001

21 Debated: Issues in American Politics
Gregory Scott, University of Central Oklahoma
Loren Gatch, University of Central Oklahoma
ISBN: 0-13-0219916 © 2000

Government and Politics in the Lone Star State: Theory and Practice, 4th ed.
L. Tucker Gibson, Trinity Univerity
Clay Robison, The Houston Chronicle
ISBN: 0-13-0340502 © 2002

Rethinking California: Politics and Policy in the Golden State
Matthew Cahn, California State University–Northridge
H. Eric Schockman, University of Southern California
David Shafie, Ohio University
ISBN: 0-13-4679121 © 2001

Real Politics in America series is another resource for contemporary instructional material. To bridge the gap between research and relevancy, we have launched a new series of supplemental books with the help of series editor Paul Herrnson of the University of Maryland. More descriptive than quantitative, more case study than data study, these books cut across all topics to bring students relevant details in current political science research. From exploring the growing phenomenon of direct democracy to who runs for the state legislature, these books show students that real political science is meaningful and exciting. Available for a discount when bundled with *Government by the People*. Please see your Prentice Hall representative or access **www.prenhall.com/burns** for a complete listing of titles in the series.

ABOUT THE AUTHORS

JAMES MacGREGOR BURNS

James MacGregor Burns is a Senior Scholar at the Academy of Leadership, University of Maryland, College Park, and Woodrow Wilson Professor Emeritus of Government at Williams College. He has written numerous books, including *The Power to Lead* (1984), *The Vineyard of Liberty* (1982), *Leadership* (1979), *Roosevelt: The Soldier of Freedom* (1970), *The Deadlock of Democracy: Four-Party Politics in America* (1963), and *Roosevelt: The Lion and the Fox* (1956). With his son, Stewart Burns, he wrote *A People's Charter: The Pursuit of Rights in America* (1991); with Georgia Sorenson, *Dead Center: Clinton, Gore, and the Perils of Moderation* (2000); and with Susan Dunn, *The Three Roosevelts* (2001). Burns is a past president of the American Political Science Association and winner of numerous prizes, including a Pulitzer Prize in History.

J.W. PELTASON

J.W. Peltason is a leading scholar on the judicial process and public law. He is Professor Emeritus of Political Science at the University of California, Irvine. As past president of the American Council on Education, Peltason has represented higher education before Congress and state legislatures. His writings include *Federal Courts in the Political Process* (1955), *Fifty-Eight Lonely Men: Southern Federal Judges and School Desegregation* (1961), and with Sue Davis, *Understanding the Constitution* (2000). Among his awards are the James Madison Medal from Princeton University, the Irvine Medal from the University of California, Irvine, and the American Political Science Association's Charles E. Merriam Award.

THOMAS E. CRONIN

Thomas E. Cronin is a leading student of the American presidency, leadership, and policy-making processes. He teaches at and serves as president of Whitman College. He was a White House Fellow and a White House aide and has served as president of the Western Political Science Association. His writings include *The State of the Presidency* (1980), *U.S. v. Crime in the Streets* (1981), *Direct Democracy: The Politics of Initiative, Referendum, and Recall* (1989), *Colorado Politics and Government* (1993), and *The Paradoxes of the American Presidency* (1998). Cronin is a past recipient of the American Political Science Association's Charles E. Merriam Award.

DAVID B. MAGLEBY

David B. Magleby is nationally recognized for his expertise on direct democracy, voting behavior, and campaign finance. He is Professor of Political Science at Brigham Young University and has taught at the University of California, Santa Cruz, and the University of Virginia. His writings include *Direct Legislation* (1984), *The Money Chase: Congressional Campaign Finance Reform* (1990), *Myth of the Independent Voter* (1992), and editor of *Outside Money: Soft Money and Issue Advocacy in the 1998 Congressional Elections* (2000). He was president of Pi Sigma Alpha, the national political science honor society, and has received numerous teaching awards. In 1996 he was a Fulbright Scholar at Nuffield College, Oxford University.

DAVID M. O'BRIEN

David M. O'Brien is the Leone Reaves and George W. Spicer Professor at the University of Virginia. He was a Judicial Fellow and Research Associate at the Supreme Court of the United States, a Fulbright Lecturer at Oxford University, held the Fulbright Chair for Senior Scholars at the University of Bologna, and a Fulbright Researcher in Japan, as well as a Visiting Fellow at the Russell Sage Foundation. Among his publications are *Storm Center: The Supreme Court in American Politics*, 5th ed., (2000); a two volume casebook, *Constitutional Law and Politics*, 4th ed., (2000); an annual *Supreme Court Watch*; and *To Dream of Dreams: Religious Freedom in Postwar Japan* (1996). He received the American Bar Association's Silver Gavel Award for contributing to the public's understanding of the law.

GOVERNMENT BY THE PEOPLE

NATIONAL, STATE, AND LOCAL VERSION

2001-2002 EDITION

1
CONSTITUTIONAL DEMOCRACY

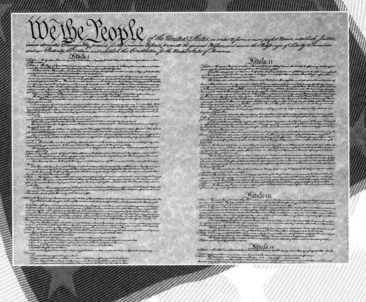

T

HE CONSTITUTIONAL DEMOCRACY WE CALL THE

UNITED STATES OF AMERICA IS ABOUT TEN GENERATIONS

OLD, YET IT IS STILL AN EXPERIMENT, STILL A WORK IN

progress. We think of it as an enduring, solid government, but in a very real sense, our constitutional political system is built on a fragile foundation. The U.S. Constitution and its crucial Bill of Rights survive not because the parchment they were written on is still with us, but because each generation of Americans respects, renews, and works at understanding the principles and values found in these precious documents.

The political and legal struggles over whether George W. Bush or Al Gore was the legitimate presidential victor in the 2000 election remind us once more about the strengths and weaknesses of our political process. Many people believe that the voting procedure in Florida and elsewhere was flawed, and the courts failed to provide non-partisan remedies. Others believe the system worked, and that this extraordinarily close presidential and congressional election created a unique opportunity to govern from the political center.

Many observers view the Supreme Court's decision in the now landmark *Bush v Gore* case as politically motivated, yet the public, weary after weeks of political haggling, wanted an end to the counts and recounts and was willing to accept George Bush as the Electoral College victor, even though Al Gore won the national popular vote.

Polls of the American people frequently ask whether Abraham Lincoln's famous description—"government of the people, by the people, for the people"—is still true today. Many say no. Moreover, people often say they do not trust their government to do the right thing. A *Wall Street Journal*/NBC poll in late 2000 found that only 28 percent of the public had "a great deal of or even quite a bit of confidence in" the federal government.[1] More than twice the percentage, in contrast, had confidence in the military and in small businesses.

We often hear people denouncing the government as if it were some alien empire. The "government," some say, is out to get us, or is corrupt, or is engaging in a conspiracy, whereas "the people" are thought to be all pure of heart. But government is not a thing. The reality is that "government" is merely a shorthand term to refer to a lot of people in our society—the people we elect and the people they appoint to promote the general welfare, provide for domestic tranquility, and secure the blessings of liberty for us.

So, too, we often refer to "the people" as if it were some abstraction. But there is no such "thing" as "the people" or "the public." The American people consist of over 285

million highly diverse people of all kinds, colors, and sizes. And it is because these people do not all think alike, or have the same values or desires, that we engage in democratic politics to decide who should make our laws and hold government offices.

Americans love their country, revere their Constitution, and respect the free enterprise system, but they often don't like the politics and politicians that are central to a functioning government. A country and its heritage are easier to admire than are the people in office at any time who tax, regulate, penalize, and sometimes even conscript us. But can government also be a force for good? Is government merely "a necessary evil"? As this book will demonstrate, constitutional government and its elected officials often do use governmental power to improve our lives, protect our freedoms, and, in general, expand our liberties.

Consider, for example, the mundane regulations you are forced to follow in this country. You can be punished if you don't drive on the right side of the road, stop at red lights, or refrain from consuming alcohol when you drive. Moreover, both you and your vehicle must be licensed by a state agency. How can you be free, you might ask, when you are subject to so many regulations and have to give up so many rights? Author Garry Wills replies:

> Actually, these rules are immensely liberating. . . . Absent the rules of the road, we would all inflict suffering not only on those hit or hurt or killed, but on those who would have to live with the thought of having been the agent of another's death. It is an act of compassion and mercy to spare both the victim and the driver that kind of misery.[2]

Thus, greater governmental power is sometimes precisely what leads to greater rights, greater freedom. But this is not always the case. We know from our early history under the king of England and from our study of other nations that governmental power can be misused and misapplied. The challenge of a constitutional democracy is that its citizens must be constantly engaged in judging whether power is being used wisely, or whether power is being used to corrupt and to cause an undesirable loss of rights, freedoms, and liberty.

CONSTITUTIONAL DEMOCRACY IS NOT A SPECTATOR SPORT

The American Republic has endured and even prospered for more than two centuries. During that time we have held—even in the midst of a civil war, depressions, and world wars—54 presidential elections (including the recent 2000 election), and we have witnessed the peaceful transfer of power from one party to another on dozens of occasions.

Few democracies have survived this long. The United States has succeeded in large part because Americans have shared a common commitment to our Constitution, to one another, and to the belief that our differences are best reconciled by debate, compromise, and voting and that elected officials govern better than do military generals, or business entrepreneurs, or professors, or religious leaders.

But as recent events remind us, there are deep divisions in the United States. Many people are concerned about the persistence of racism, about religious bigotry, about the gap in economic opportunities between rich and poor, and about the gun violence that afflicts children and minorities.

The United States appears today to be more powerful and indestructible than any nation in history. With our thriving old and new industries, colleges and universities, vast governmental institutions, unrivaled military strength, and unprecedented breakthroughs in science, technology, and medicine, this country has an aura of invincibility. "But it is built" notes John W. Gardner, "on intangibles, every beam and

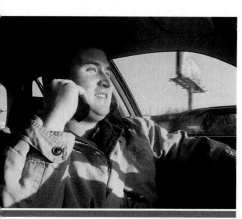

A government can regulate and restrict many of our ordinary actions, such as using cell phones. Some communities have outlawed the use of cell phones while driving because they have been found to distract drivers and cause accidents.

girder held together by mutual obligations and expectations, shared beliefs, laws and traditions, faith, caring, trust and responsibility. Weaken these beyond a certain point and the great edifice crumbles."[3]

More than any other form of government, the kind of democracy that has emerged under our Constitution requires active participation and a fine balance between faith and skepticism. Government by the people, however, does not require that *everyone* be involved in politics and policy making. Many citizens will always be too busy doing other things, and some people will always be apathetic toward politics and government. Government by the people does require a segment of the public that is attentive, interested, involved, informed, and willing, when necessary, to criticize and remove those in government.

Government by the people requires faith concerning our common human enterprise, a belief that if the people are informed and caring, they can be trusted with their own self-government and an optimism that when things begin to go wrong, the people can be relied upon to set them right. But a healthy skepticism is needed as well. Democracy requires us to question our leaders and never trust a group or institution that holds too much power. And even though constitutional advocates prize majority rule, they must remain skeptical about whether the majority is always right.

Constitutional democracy requires us to be constantly concerned about whether we are being tolerant and protective of the rights and opinions of others, and whether our democratic processes are, in fact, serving the principles of liberty, equality, and justice. Thus, the democratic faith depends on a peculiar blend of faith and skepticism when dealing with the will of the people.

Thomas Jefferson

Thomas Jefferson, one of our best-known champions of constitutional democracy, believed in the common sense of the people and in the flowering possibilities of the human spirit. Jefferson warned that every government degenerates when it is left only in the hands of the rulers. The people themselves, Jefferson wrote, are the only safe repositories of government. His was a robust commitment to popular control, to representative processes, and to accountable leadership. But he was no believer in the simple participatory democracy of ancient Greece or revolutionary France. The power of the people, too, must be restrained from time to time.

Our nation's founders set up a government that over the last two hundred years has become a government *by consent of the governed*. As Justice Robert H. Jackson wrote in a 1943 U.S. Supreme Court decision, "Authority here is to be controlled by public opinion, not public opinion by authority."[4]

Constitutional democracy is necessarily government by representative politicians. A central feature of democracy is that those who hold power do so only by winning an election. In our political system, the fragmentation of powers requires elected officials to mediate among factions, build coalitions, and work out compromises among and within the branches of our government to produce policy and action.

We expect a lot from our politicians. We expect them to operate within the rules of democracy, to be honest, humble, patriotic, compassionate, sensitive to the needs of others, well-informed, competent, fair-minded, self-confident, and inspirational. They must be candidates of all the people, not just those with money. They must not want power for itself, but lead because of their concern for the public good. And finally, they must be willing to do the job and get out when finished.

Why does such a gap persist between our image of the ideal politician and our views about actual politicians? The gap exists in part because we have unrealistic expectations. We want politicians to be perfect, to have all the answers, and to have all the correct (in our minds) values. We want politicians to solve our problems, yet we also want them to serve as scapegoats for the things we dislike about government: taxes, regulations, hard times, and limits on our freedom. It is impossible for anyone to live up to these ideals. Like all individuals, politicians live in a world in which perfection may be the goal, yet compromise, ambition, fund raising, and self-promotion are necessary.

Americans will never be satisfied with their political candidates and politicians. The ideal politician is probably a fictional entity, for the perfect official would be able to please everyone, make conflict disappear, and not ask us to make any sacrifices. Politicians become "ideal" only when they are dead.

But the love of liberty invites disagreements of ideology and values. Politicians and candidates, as well as the people they represent, have different ideas about what is best for the nation. That's why we have politics, candidates, opposition parties, heated political debates, and elections.

DEFINING DEMOCRACY

The word "democracy" is nowhere to be found in the Declaration of Independence or in the U.S. Constitution, nor was it a term used by the founders of the Republic. It is both a very old term and a new one. It was used at the time of the founding of this nation to refer to various undesirable things: mobs, lack of standards, and a system that encourages leaders to gain power by appealing to the emotions and prejudices of the rabble.

The distinguishing feature of democracy is that government derives its authority from its citizens. In fact, the word comes from two Greek words: *demos* (the people) and *kratos* (authority or power). Thus **democracy** means *government by the people*—not government by one person (a monarch, a dictator, a priest) or government by the few (an oligarchy or aristocracy).

Ancient Athens and a few other Greek cities had a **direct democracy** in which citizens came together to discuss and pass laws and select their rulers. These Greek city-states did not last. Most turned to mob rule and then resorted to dictators. Thus, when the word "democracy" came into English usage in the seventeenth century, it denoted this kind of direct democracy. It was a term of derision, a negative word, usually used to refer to mob rule.

James Madison, writing in *The Federalist*, No. 10, reflected the view of many of the framers of the U.S. Constitution when he wrote, "Such democracies [as the Greek and Roman] . . . have ever been found incompatible with personal security, or the rights of property; and have in general been as short in their lives, as they have been violent in their deaths" (*The Federalist*, No. 10, appears in the Appendix at the back of this book).

Today it is no longer possible, even if desirable, to assemble the citizens of any but the smallest towns to make their laws or to select their officials directly from among the citizenry. Rather, we have invented a system of representation. Democracy today means **representative democracy**, or, to use Plato's term, a *republic*, in which those who have governmental authority get and retain authority directly or indirectly as a result of winning free elections in which all adult citizens are allowed to participate. The framers preferred to use the term "republic" to avoid any confusion between direct democracy, which they disliked, and representative democracy, which they liked and thought secured all the advantages of a direct democracy while curing its weaknesses. Today, and in this book, *democracy* and *republic* are used interchangeably.

In defining democracy, several other terms need to be clarified. **Constitutional democracy** as used here refers to a government in which those who exercise substantial governmental powers do so as the result of winning free and relatively frequent elections. *It is a government in which there are recognized, enforced limits on the powers of all governmental officials.*

Constitutionalism is a label we apply to arrangements such as checks and balances, federalism, separation of powers, rule of law, due process, and the Bill of Rights that require our leaders to listen, think, bargain, and explain before they make laws. We then hold them politically and legally accountable for how they exercise their powers.

democracy
Government by the people, either directly or indirectly, with free and frequent elections.

direct democracy
Government in which citizens come together to discuss and pass laws and select rulers.

representative democracy
Government that derives its powers indirectly from the people, who elect those who will govern; also called a *republic*.

constitutional democracy
A government in which those who exercise governmental powers do so as a result of winning free and relatively frequent elections and are subject to recognized, enforced limits on the power of all government officials. It is the elections that make the government democratic; it is the recognized and enforced limits on power that make it constitutional.

constitutionalism
The set of arrangements such as checks and balances, federalism, separation of powers, rule of law, due process, and the Bill of Rights that requires our leaders to listen, think, bargain, and explain before they make laws. We then hold them politically and legally accountable for how they exercise their powers.

Like most political concepts, democracy encompasses many ideas and has many meanings. Democracy is a way of life, a form of government, a way of governing, a type of nation, a state of mind, and a variety of processes. We can divide these many meanings into three broad categories: democracy as a system of interacting values, a system of interrelated political processes, and a system of interdependent political structures.

Democracy as a System of Interacting Values

Today the democratic faith may be as near a universal faith as the world has. A belief in human dignity, freedom, liberty, individual rights, and other democratic values is widely shared in most corners of the world. The essence of democratic values is contained in the ideas of personal liberty, respect for the individual, equality of opportunity, and popular consent.

PERSONAL LIBERTY   Liberty has been the single most powerful value in American history. It was for "life, liberty, and the pursuit of happiness" that independence was declared; it was to "secure the Blessings of Liberty" that the Constitution was drawn up and adopted. Even our patriotic songs extol the "sweet land of liberty." The essence of liberty is *self-determination*, meaning that all individuals must have the opportunity to realize their own goals. Liberty is not simply the absence of external restraint on a person (freedom *from*); it is the individual's freedom and capacity to act positively to reach his or her goals (freedom *to*). Moreover, both history and reason suggest that individual liberty is the key to social progress. The greater the people's freedom, the greater the chance of discovering better ways of life.

RESPECT FOR THE INDIVIDUAL   Popular rule in a democracy flows from a belief that every individual has the potential for common sense, rationality, and fairness. Individuals have important rights; collectively, those rights are the source of all legitimate governmental authority and power. These concepts pervade all democratic thought. They are woven into the writings of Thomas Jefferson, especially in the Declaration of Independence: "All men . . . are endowed by their Creator with certain unalienable rights" (the Declaration of Independence appears in the Appendix). Constitutional democracies make the *person*—rich or poor, black or white, male or female—the central measure of value. The state, the union, and ideally even the corporation are measured in terms of their usefulness to individuals.

Not all political systems put the individual first. Some promote **statism**, considering the state supreme. In a modern democracy, the nation, or even the community, is less important than are the individuals who compose it.

EQUALITY OF OPPORTUNITY   The importance of the individual is enhanced by the democratic value of *equality*: "All men are created equal and from that equal creation they derive rights inherent and unalienable, among which are the preservation of liberty and the pursuit of happiness." So reads Jefferson's first draft of the Declaration of Independence, and the words indicate the primacy of the concept. Alexis de Tocqueville and other international visitors who have studied American democracy were all struck by the strength of egalitarian thought and practice in our political and social lives.

But what does equality mean? Equality for whom? For blacks as well as whites? For women as well as men? For Native Americans, descendants of the Pilgrims, and recent immigrants? And what kind of equality? Economic, political, legal, social, or some other kind of equality? Equality of opportunity? Does equality of opportunity simply mean that everyone should have the same place at the starting line? Or does it mean an effort should be made to equalize the factors that determine how well a person fares economically or socially?

"The Athenians are here, Sire, with an offer to back us with ships, money, arms, and men—and, of course, their usual lectures about democracy."

statism
The idea that the rights of the state (meaning nation) are supreme over the rights of the individual.

PEOPLE

BUSH V GORE: THE MAJORITY OPINION

In the 2000 election, for the first time in U.S. history, the Supreme Court played a decisive role in deciding who would win a presidential election when, in a 5 to 4 decision, it halted the manual recounting of ballots in Florida. After the automatic recount required under Florida law, George W. Bush's lead in the popular vote was 327 votes. The winner of Florida's 25 electoral votes would win the election. The issue before the court was whether manual recounts should proceed as ordered by the Florida Supreme Court in counties where the Gore campaign had asked for them, and what the standard of that manual recount should be. The Florida Supreme Court had not specified a standard.

Governor Bush appealed the Florida court's decision to the U.S. Supreme Court, and the majority of the justices ruled that the manual recounts violated the equal protection clause by applying different standards for counting the ballots in different counties; and that there was not time to remedy the problem before a congressional deadline of December 12 for forwarding electoral votes to the Congress. The majority argued:

> *The right to vote is protected in more than the initial allocation of the franchise. Equal protection applies as well to the manner of its exercise. Having once granted the right to vote on equal terms, the State may not, by later arbitrary and disparate treatment, value one person's vote over that of another. . . The recount mechanisms implemented in response to the decisions of the Florida Supreme Court do not satisfy the minimum requirement for non-arbitrary treatment of voters necessary to secure the fundamental right. . . The formulations of uniform rules to determine intent based on these recurring circumstances is practicable, and, we conclude, necessary. . . The want of those rules here has led to unequal evaluation of ballots in various respects. . . it is obvious that the recount cannot be conducted in compliance with the requirements of equal protection and due process without substantial additional work. . . Because it is evident that any recount seeking to meet the December 12 deadline will be unconstitutional for the reasons we have discussed, we reverse the judgment of the Supreme Court of Florida ordering a recount to proceed.* ★

The recount mechanisms implemented in response to the decisions of the Florida Supreme Court do not satisfy the minimum requirement for non-arbitrary treatment of voters.

DEBATE

BUSH V GORE: THE MINORITY DISSENT

One irony of the majority opinion is that the justices who joined it generally favored deference to state courts to set their own course. The dissent disputed the claim by the majority that U.S. Supreme Court had jurisdiction to decide this case and contended that while equal protection may have been an issue, there were alternative solutions to simply ending the recounts altogether. As Justice Stevens stated in his dissent:

The federal questions that ultimately emerged in this case are not substantial. . . The legislative power in Florida is subject to judicial review pursuant to Article V of the Florida Constitution, and nothing in Article II of the Federal Constitution frees that state legislature from the constraints in the state constitution that created it. . . It hardly needs stating that Congress, pursuant to [Section] 5 did not impose any affirmative duties upon the States that their governmental branches could "violate." Rather, [Section] 5 provides a safe harbor for States to select electors in contested elections "by judicial or other methods" established by law prior to the election day. Section 5, like Article II, assumes the involvement of the state judiciary in interpreting state election laws

and resolving election disputes under those laws. Neither [Section] 5 nor Article II grants federal judges any special authority to substitute their views for those of the state judiciary on matters of state law.

(Section 5 refers to the section of the Electoral Count Act of 1887 that provides a "safe harbor" for electoral votes receiving certification by December 12. Article II provides that "each state shall appoint, in such Manner as the Legislature thereof may direct" the electors for President and Vice President.)

Also speaking for the dissenting minority, Justice Breyer argued:

I agree that, in these very special circumstances, basic principles of fairness may well have counseled the adoption of a uniform standard to address the problem. . . Nonetheless, there is no justification for the majority's remedy, which is simply to reverse the lower court and halt the recount entirely. An appropriate remedy would be, instead, to remand this case with instructions, even at this late date, to permit the Florida Supreme Court to require recounting all undercounted votes in Florida... and to do so in accordance with a single uniform standard.★

There is no justification for the majority's remedy, which is simply to reverse the lower court and halt the recount entirely.

For further information about this debate, go to **www.prenhall.com/burns** *and click on the Debate Icon in Chapter 1.*

POPULAR CONSENT   The animating principle of the American Revolution, the Declaration of Independence, and the resulting new nation was **popular consent**, the idea that a just government must derive its powers from the *consent of the people* it governs. A commitment to democracy thus entails a community's willingness to participate and make decisions in government. These principles sound unobjectionable intellectually, but in practice they mean that certain individuals or groups may not get their way. A commitment to popular consent must involve a willingness to lose when most people vote the other way.

DEMOCRATIC VALUES IN CONFLICT   The basic values of democracy do not always coexist happily. Individualism may conflict with the collective welfare or the public good. Self-determination may conflict with equal opportunity. For example, the right of a homeowner to add another floor to her home may conflict with the right of her neighbor to have an unobstructed view. Or the right of a person to smoke an after-dinner cigar in a restaurant may conflict with the right of others not to have to breathe tobacco smoke.

Much of our political combat revolves around how to strike a balance among democratic values—how to protect the Declaration of Independence's unalienable rights of life, liberty, and the pursuit of happiness while trying to "form," as the Constitution announces, "a more perfect Union, establish Justice, insure domestic Tranquility, provide for the common defence, promote the general Welfare, and secure the Blessings of Liberty to ourselves and our Posterity" (see the Preamble to the Constitution on page 43). Over the years the American political system has moved, despite occasional setbacks, toward greater freedom and more democracy.

A strong commitment to democracy was in many ways a twentieth-century idea. Although on dozens of occasions in the past century democracies collapsed and gave way to authoritarian regimes, even more democracies triumphed. Indeed, "the global range and influence of democratic ideas, institutions, and practices has made [the twentieth century] far and away the most flourishing period for democracy."[5]

Democracy as a System of Interrelated Political Processes

Far more people dream about democracy than ever experience it, and many new democracies fail. To be successful, democratic government requires a well-defined political process as well as a stable governmental structure. To become reality, democratic values must be incorporated into a political process, most importantly in the form of free and fair elections, majority rule, freedom of expression, and the right to assemble and protest.

FREE AND FAIR ELECTIONS   Democratic government is based on free and fair elections held at intervals frequent enough to make them relevant to policy choices. Elections are one of the most important devices for keeping officials and representatives accountable.

We previously described *representative democracy* as a government in which those who have the authority to make decisions with the force of law acquire and retain this authority either directly or indirectly as the result of winning free elections in which the great majority of adult citizens are allowed to participate. Crucial to modern-day definitions of democracy is the idea that opposition political parties can exist, can run candidates in elections, and can at least have a chance to replace those who are currently holding public office. Thus *political competition and choice* are crucial to the existence of democracy.

Although all citizens should have equal voting power, free and fair elections do not imply that everyone must or will have equal political influence. Some people, because of wealth, talent, or position, have more influence than others. How much extra influence key figures should be allowed to exercise in a democracy is frequently debated. But in an election, a president or a plumber, a corporate CEO or a ditch digger, each casts only one vote.

popular consent
The idea that a just government must derive its powers from the consent of the people it governs.

MAJORITY (PLURALITY) RULE   **Majority rule**—governance according to the expressed preferences of the majority—is a basic rule of democracy. The **majority** candidate or party is the one that receives *more than half* the votes and so wins the election and takes charge of the government until the next election. In practice, however, majority rule is often **plurality** rule, in which the candidate or party with the *most* votes wins the election, even though it may not constitute a true majority of more than half the votes. About a third of our presidents have won with pluralities in the popular vote rather than majorities.[6] Once elected, officials do not have a right to curtail the attempts of political minorities to use all peaceful means to become the new majority. Even as the winners take power, the losers are at work to try to get it back at the next election.[7]

Should the side with the most votes prevail in all cases? Americans answer this question in a variety of ways. Some insist majority views should be enacted into laws and regulations. However, an effective representative democracy involves far more than simply ascertaining and applying the statistical will of most of the people. It is a more complicated and often untidy process in which the people and their agents debate, compromise, and arrive at a decision only after thoughtful deliberation.

The framers wanted to guard society against any one faction of the people acting unjustly toward any other faction of the people. The Constitution reflects their fear of tyranny by majorities, especially momentary majorities that spring from temporary passions. They insulated certain rights (such as freedom of speech) and institutions (such as the Supreme Court) from popular choice. Effective representation of the people, the framers insisted, should not be based solely on parochial interests or shifting breezes of opinion.

FREEDOM OF EXPRESSION   Free and fair elections depend on access to information relevant to voting choices. Voters must have access to facts, competing ideas, and the views of candidates. Free and fair elections require a climate in which competing, non-government-owned newspapers, radio stations, and television stations can flourish. If the government controls what is said and how it is said, there is no democracy. Without free speech there are no free and fair elections.

THE RIGHT TO ASSEMBLE AND PROTEST   Citizens must be free to organize for political purposes. Obviously, individuals can be more effective if they join with others in a party, a pressure group, a protest movement, or a demonstration. The right to oppose the government, to form opposition parties, and to have a chance of defeating incumbents is not only vital; it is a defining characteristic of a democracy.

Democracy as a System of Interdependent Political Structures

Democracy is, of course, more than values and processes. It also entails political structures that safeguard these values and processes. The Constitution and the Bill of Rights create an ingenious structure—one that both grants and checks government power. This constitutional structure is reinforced by a political system of parties, interest groups, media, and other institutions that mediate between the electorate and those who govern and thus help to maintain democratic stability.

The U.S. constitutional system has four distinctive elements: (1) *federalism*, the division of powers between the national and state governments; (2) *separation of powers* among the legislative, executive, and judicial branches; (3) *checks and balances* in which each branch is given the constitutional means, the political independence, and the motives to check the powers of the other branches; and (4) a judicially enforceable, written, explicit *Bill of Rights* that provides a guarantee of individual liberties and due process before the law.

majority rule
Governance according to the expressed preferences of the majority.

majority
The candidate or party that wins more than half the votes cast to win an election.

plurality
A candidate or party wins the most votes cast, not necessarily more than half.

Conditions Conducive to Constitutional Democracy

How do we explain the relatively small number of enduring, strong democracies? Although it is hard to specify the precise conditions that are essential for the establishment and maintenance of a democracy, here are a few things we have learned.

EDUCATIONAL CONDITIONS   The exercise of voting privileges takes some level of education on the part of the citizenry. But a word of caution: A high level of education does not cause or guarantee democratic government, as the example of Nazi Germany readily illustrates. And there are some democracies, such as India, where large numbers of people are illiterate. Still, voting makes little sense unless a considerable number of the voters can read and write and express their interests and opinions. The poorly educated and illiterate often get left out in a democracy.

ECONOMIC CONDITIONS   A relatively prosperous nation, with an equitable distribution of wealth, provides the best context for democracy. Starving people are more interested in food than in voting. Where economic power is concentrated, political power is likely to be concentrated. Well-to-do nations have a greater chance of sustaining democratic governments than do those with widespread poverty. The reality is that extremes of wealth and poverty undermine the possibilities for a healthy constitutional democracy. Thus the prospects for an enduring democracy are greater in Canada or France than in Rwanda or Russia.

Some measure of private ownership of property and a relatively favorable role for the market economy are also related to the creation and maintenance of democratic institutions. Democracies can range from heavily regulated economies with public ownership of many enterprises, such as Sweden, to those in which there is little government regulation of the marketplace. But there are no democracies with a highly centralized government-run economy and little private ownership of property, although there are many nations with a market economy and no democracy. There are no truly democratic communist states, nor have there ever been any.

SOCIAL CONDITIONS   Economic development generally makes democracy possible, yet proper social conditions are necessary to make it real.[8] In a society fragmented into warring groups that differ fiercely on fundamental issues, government by discussion and compromise is difficult, as we have seen in the Balkans. When ideologically separated groups consider the issues at stake to be vital, they may prefer to fight rather than accept the verdict of the ballot box.

In a society that consists of many overlapping associations and groupings, however, individuals are not as likely to identify completely with a single group and give their allegiance to it. For example, Joe Smith is a Baptist, an African American, a southerner, a Democrat, an electrician, and a member of the National Rifle Association, and he makes $50,000 a year. On some issues Joe thinks as a Baptist, on others as a southerner, and on still others as an African American. Sue Jones is a Catholic, a white Republican, an auto dealer, and a member of the National Organization for Women; she comes from a Polish background, and she makes $150,000 a year. Sometimes she acts as a Republican, sometimes as an American of Polish descent, and sometimes as a member of NOW. Jones and Smith differ on some issues yet agree on others. In general, the differences between them are not likely to be greater than their common interest in maintaining a democracy.[9]

Democracy is more likely to survive in a nation where the people have acquired democratic habits and are inclined to participate in social, cultural, and civic groups. Political scientist Robert Putnam calls this interest in participation **social capital**.[10] Democratic social capital is generated when there are a rich variety of associations and social institutions that bind people together. Participation in voluntary organizations such as women's groups, bowling leagues, and environmental and conservation groups help build and reinforce democratic habits of discussion, compromise,

social capital

Participation in voluntary associations that reinforce democratic and civic habits of discussion, compromise, and respect for differences.

A Closer Look

IT'S NOT EASY TO BE FREE

New democracies often fail. It is one thing to espouse democratic values, another to put them into practice. Some people believe in democracy until they lose power in an election. Or the citizens grow weary of the political wrangling that comes with democracy and long for a strong charismatic leader with simple solutions for complex problems. The struggle to convert to a market economy in Russia has produced this kind of turmoil. Leaders like Napoleon or Adolf Hitler promise to make a

country work more smoothly, often by disbanding democratic institutions. Citizens may turn to such leaders when they face economic difficulties or are under threat from a foreign power. Sectional differences can also pull apart the fabric of democracy. Parts of a country that have a distinctive racial, religious, or ethnic composition often distrust the national majority and seek guarantees or special concessions—as have French-speaking residents in Quebec and ethnic Albanians in Kosovo.

Because democracies are so difficult to sustain, comparatively few have lasted long. More than half the world's constitutions have been written in the past four decades. On the entire continent of Asia, no democracy predates World War II, when a democratic constitution was imposed on Japan. In Africa, the oldest democracy is Botswana, which has had free elections and a multiparty system since 1966.

The Map of Freedom 2000

SOURCE: *Freedom Review*, 1999–2000. © 2000 by Freedom House.

"Bowling Alone." Does this mean a decline in "social capital"?

Political scientist Robert D. Putnam has pointed to a decline in American political involvement and a decline in confidence in our political institutions. He noted that in recent decades fewer people engage in politics—voting, attending a political rally, working for a political party, or taking part in the political process in other ways. There has also been a decline in church membership and attendance, membership in labor unions, involvement in the PTA, membership in civic and fraternal organizations, volunteering for the Boy Scouts, the Red Cross, and other organizations, and membership in Lions, Elks, Shriners, and Masons.

Putnam writes, "The most whimsical yet discomforting bit of evidence of social disengagement in contemporary America that I have discovered is this: More Americans are bowling today than ever before, but bowling in organization leagues has plummeted in the last decade or so." Noting that members of bowling leagues consume three times as much beer and pizza as do those who bowl alone, he theorizes that "The broader social significance . . . lies in the social interaction and even occasionally civic conversations over beer and pizza that solo bowlers forgo." Whether or not bowling beats balloting in the eyes of most Americans—more bowl than vote—"bowling teams illustrate yet another vanishing form of *social capital*."* Do you agree with him that Americans increasingly prefer social isolation over social involvement?

*Robert D. Putnam, "Bowling Alone: America's Declining Social Capital," *Journal of Democracy* 6, no. 1 (January 1995), p. 20.

ideology
One's basic beliefs about power, political values, and the role of government—beliefs that arise out of educational, economic, and social conditions and experiences.

theocracy
Government by religious leaders, who claim divine guidance.

Articles of Confederation
The first constitution of the American states, drafted in 1777, ratified in 1781, and replaced by the present Constitution in 1789.

and respect for differences. It can "provide the social resources and the civic training that citizens need to make democracy tick."[11]

Civic and social engagement has been changing in the Internet era. Today there are more advocacy and lobbying groups, and environmental groups are plainly on the rise. Beyond the traditional Boy Scouts, Girl Scouts, the YMCA, the YWCA, and the Red Cross, there are myriad local volunteer and service groups and a vast network of youth as well as adult soccer, basketball, hockey, and snowboarding leagues. Women and minorities have been recognized and are active in many new ways. As Michael Schudson notes, if measures of civic health include "measures of political inclusion and protection for individual rights," then "Americans are unquestionably better off in the past quarter century than at any prior moment in our history."[12]

IDEOLOGICAL CONDITIONS   **Ideology** refers to basic beliefs about power, government, and political practices—beliefs that arise out of the educational, economic, and social conditions individuals experience. Out of these conditions must also develop a general acceptance of the ideals of democracy and a willingness of a substantial part of the people to agree to proceed democratically. This acceptance is sometimes called the *democratic consensus*.

THE CONSTITUTIONAL ROOTS OF THE AMERICAN EXPERIMENT

Americans often take democracy for granted. Most of us probably consider it inevitable. We take pride in our ability to make it work, yet we have essentially inherited a functioning system. Its establishment was the work of others, nine or ten generations ago. The challenge for us is not just to keep it going but to improve it and make it adapt to the challenges of our times. To do so, however, we must first understand it, and this requires systematic consideration of our democratic and constitutional roots.

The Colonial Beginnings

There were many reasons one might have expected our democratic experiment to fail. The thirteen states (formerly colonies) were independent and could have gone their separate ways. Sectional differences based on social and economic conditions, especially southern states' dependence on slavery, were an obvious problem. Religious, ethnic, and racial diversity, which challenges so many governments around the world today, existed in substantial degree in the United States during its formative years.

Given these potential problems, how did democracy survive? How did this nation establish democratic principles for its government? How did it limit potential abuses? These questions are of importance not only to Americans but to all who value freedom and democracy everywhere.

The framers of the U.S. Constitution had experience to guide them. For almost two centuries, Europeans had been sailing to the New World in search of liberty—especially religious liberty—as well as land and work. While still aboard the *Mayflower*, the Pilgrims drew up a compact to protect their religious freedom and to make possible "just and equal laws." In the American colonies, editors found they could speak freely in their newspapers, dissenters could distribute leaflets, and agitators could protest in taverns or in the streets.

But the picture of freedom in the colonies was a mixed one. The Puritans in Massachusetts soon established a **theocracy**, a system of government in which religious leaders claimed divine guidance and in which not all religious sects were granted religious liberty. Dissenters were occasionally chased out of town, and some printers were beaten and had their shops closed. In short, the colonists were struggling with the balance of unity and diversity, stability and dissent, order and liberty. Puritans continued to worry "about what would maintain order in a society lacking an estab-

lished church, an attachment to place, and the uncontested leadership of men of merit."[13] Nine of the thirteen colonies eventually set up a state church. Throughout the 1700s Puritans in Massachusetts barred certain men from voting on the basis of church membership. To the Anglican establishment in Virginia, campaigns for toleration were in themselves subversive. Women and slaves could not vote at all.

The Rise of Revolutionary Fervor

As resentment against British rule mounted during the 1770s and revolutionary fervor rose, Americans became determined to fight the British to win their rights and liberties. A year after the fighting broke out in Massachusetts, the Declaration of Independence proclaimed in ringing tones that all men are created equal, endowed by their Creator with certain unalienable rights; that among them are "life, liberty, and the pursuit of happiness"; that to secure those rights governments are instituted among men; and that whenever a government becomes destructive of those ends, it is the right of the people to alter or abolish it. (Read the full text of the Declaration of Independence in the Appendix.)

We have all heard these great ideals so often that we take them for granted. Revolutionary leaders did not. They were deadly serious about these rights and willing to fight and pledge their lives, fortunes, and sacred honor for them. Bills of rights in the new state constitutions guaranteed free speech, freedom of religion, and the natural rights to life, liberty, and property. All their constitutions spelled out the rights of persons accused of crime, such as knowing the nature of the accusation, being confronted by their accusers, and receiving a timely and public trial by jury.[14] Moreover, these guarantees were in *written* form, a sharp contrast to the unwritten British constitution.

Toward Unity and Order

As the war against the British widened, the need arose for a stronger central government that could pull the colonies together and conduct a revolutionary war. For a time the Continental Congress, which had led the way toward revolution, tried to direct hostilities against the British, but it took a man of George Washington's iron resolve to unify and direct the war effort. Sensing the need for more unity, Congress established a new national government under a written document called the **Articles of Confederation**. At first hardly worthy of the term "government," the Articles were not approved by all the state legislatures until 1781, after Washington's troops had been fighting for six years.

This new Confederation was a move toward a stronger central government, but a limited and inadequate one. Having fought a war against a strong central government in London, Americans were understandably reluctant to create another one, so the Articles established a fragile league of friendship rather than a national government. From 1777 to 1788, Americans made progress under this Confederation, but with the end of the war in 1783, the sense of urgency that had produced unity began to fade. Conflicts between creditors and debtors within the states grew intense. Foreign threats continued; territories ruled by England and Spain surrounded the new nation, which—internally divided and lacking a strong central government—made a tempting prize.

As pressures on the Confederation mounted, many leaders became convinced it would not be enough merely to revise the Articles of Confederation. To create a union strong enough to deal with internal diversity and factionalism as well as to resist external threats, a stronger central government was needed.

In September 1786, under the leadership of Alexander Hamilton, those who favored a truly national government took advantage of the **Annapolis Convention**—a meeting in Annapolis, Maryland, on problems of trade and navigation attended by delegates from five states—to issue a call for a convention that would have full authority to consider basic amendments to the Articles of Confederation. The delegates in Annapolis asked the legislatures of all the states to appoint

Thinking It Through...

While more Americans may be bowling alone, what about the growth of new organizations such as the Sierra Club, the National Organization for Women, the American Association of Retired Persons, and so on? Doesn't that show a counter trend? Putnam found that the vast majority of the members of these associations only write a check or read a newsletter; few ever attend meetings or have any connection to other members. He acknowledges the growth of "support groups" as offsetting the erosion of conventional civic organizations.

Americans still rank high compared with other countries in social capital, but if there has been a deterioration in social capital, it could have consequences for the stability of our political system. What has caused this decline? Putnam discounts the movement of women into the labor force or the increasing mobility of our population as causes of this decline, but suggests that television—and, it may be assumed, the computer—have made our communities wider but shallower.

But other scholars such as Everett C. Ladd say there has not been a serious decline in social involvement. Anyone living and working on an American college campus certainly finds active student participation in all kinds of organizations and associations. Others challenge Putnam's conclusion that television is responsible for this decline in political participation. The growth of radio talk shows, C-SPAN, CNN, all-news cable channels, and Internet chat groups may be new ways to build social capital. And the major increase in community service, volunteering, and charitable giving also raises doubts about Putnam's claims.

Do you think Putnam's arguments are convincing? How would you gather evidence to test his hypothesis? You might begin with a look at Theda Skocpol and Morris Fiorina, eds., *Civic Engagements in American Democracy* (Brookings/Russell Sage, 1999) and Pippa Norris, "Does Television Erode Social Capital? A Reply to Putnam," *P.S.: Political Science & Politics* 29 (September 1996), pp. 474–79. See also Everett Carll Ladd, *The Ladd Report* (Free Press, 1999) and Michael Schudson, *The Good Citizen: A History of American Civic Life* (Harvard University Press, 1998).

commissioners to meet in Philadelphia on the second Monday of May 1787, "to devise such further provisions as shall appear to them necessary to render the Constitution of the Federal Government adequate to the exigencies of the Union." The convention they called for became the **Constitutional Convention**.

For a short time all was quiet. Then, late in 1786, messengers rode into George Washington's plantation at Mount Vernon with the kind of news he and other leaders had dreaded. Farmers in western Massachusetts, crushed by debts and taxes, were rebelling against foreclosures, forcing judges out of their courtrooms, and freeing debtors from jails. Washington was appalled. "What, gracious God, is man?" he exclaimed. Ten years before, he had been leading Americans in a patriotic war against the British, and now Americans were fighting Americans!

Not all Americans reacted as Washington did to what became known as **Shays' Rebellion** after Daniel Shays, its leader. When Abigail Adams, the politically knowledgeable wife of John Adams, sent news of the rebellion to Thomas Jefferson, the Virginian replied, "I like a little rebellion now and then," noting also that the "tree of liberty must be refreshed from time to time with the blood of patriots and tyrants. It is its natural manure."[15]

Shays' Rebellion petered out after the farmers attacked an arsenal and were cut down by cannon fire. Yet this "little rebellion" sent a stab of fear into the established leadership. It also acted as a catalyst. The message now was plain: Action must be taken to strengthen the machinery of government. Seven states appointed commissioners to attend a convention in Philadelphia to strengthen the Articles of Confederation. Congress finally issued a cautiously worded call to all the state legislatures to appoint delegates for the "sole and express purpose of revising the Articles of Confederation." The suspicious congressional legislators specified that no recommendation would be effective unless approved by Congress and confirmed by all the state legislatures, as provided by the Articles.

THE CONSTITUTIONAL CONVENTION, 1787

The delegates who assembled in Philadelphia that May had to establish a national government powerful enough to prevent the young nation from dissolving but not so powerful it would crush individual liberty. What these men did continues to have a major impact on how we are governed. It also provides an outstanding lesson in political science for the world.

The Delegates

Seventy-four delegates were appointed by the various states, but only 55 arrived in Philadelphia. Of these, approximately 40 took a real part in the work of the convention. It was a distinguished gathering. Many of the most important men of the nation were there: successful merchants, planters, bankers, lawyers, and former and present governors and congressional representatives (39 of the delegates had served in Congress). Most had read the classics of political thought. Most had participated vigorously in the practical task of constructing local and state governments. Many had also worked hard to create and direct the national Confederation of the states. And 8 of the 56 signers of the Declaration of Independence were present at the Constitutional Convention.

The convention was as representative as most political gatherings at the time: the participants were all white male landowners. These well-read, well-fed, well-bred, and often well-wed delegates were mainly state or national leaders, for in the 1780s ordinary people were not likely to participate in politics. (Even today farm laborers, factory workers, and truck drivers are seldom found in Congress, although a haberdasher, a peanut farmer, and a movie actor have made their way to the White House.)

Annapolis Convention
A convention held in September 1786 to consider problems of trade and navigation, attended by five states and important because it issued the call to Congress and the states for what became the Constitutional Convention.

Constitutional Convention
The convention in Philadelphia, May 25 to September 17, 1787, that framed the Constitution of the United States.

Shays' Rebellion
Rebellion by farmers in western Massachusetts in 1786–87, protesting mortgage foreclosures; led by Daniel Shays and important because it highlighted the need for a strong national government just as the call for a Constitutional Convention went out.

Although active in the movement to revise the Articles of Confederation, George Washington had been reluctant to attend the convention. He accepted only when persuaded that his prestige was needed for its success. He was selected unanimously to preside over the meetings. According to the records, he spoke only twice during the deliberations, yet his influence was felt in the informal gatherings as well as during the sessions. Everyone understood that Washington favored a more powerful central government led by a president. The general expectation that George Washington would likely be the first president played a crucial role in the creation of the presidency. "No one feared that he would misuse power. . . . His genuine hesitancy, his reluctance to assume the position only served to reinforce the almost universal desire that he do so."[16]

The proceedings of the convention were kept secret. To encourage everyone to speak freely, delegates were forbidden to discuss the debates with outsiders. It was feared that if a delegate publicly took a firm stand on an issue, it would be harder for him to change his mind after debate and discussion. The delegates also knew that if word of the inevitable disagreements got out, it would provide ammunition for the many enemies of the convention. There were critics of this secrecy rule, but without it, agreement might not have been possible.

Consensus

The Constitutional Convention is usually discussed in terms of its three famous compromises: the compromise between large and small states over representation in Congress, the compromise between North and South over the regulation and taxation of foreign commerce, and the compromise between North and South over the counting of slaves for the purpose of taxation and representation. There were many other important compromises; yet on many significant issues, most of the delegates were in agreement.

Although a few delegates might have privately favored a limited monarchy, all supported a republican form of government based on elected representatives

WE THE PEOPLE

The Framers: Hamilton and Madison

In the Constitution the framers offered perhaps the most brilliant example of collective intellectual genius—of combining both theory and practice—in the history of the Western world. How could a country 70 times smaller in population than it is today produce several dozen men of genius in Philadelphia, and probably another hundred or so equally talented political thinkers who did not attend? The lives of two prominent delegates, Alexander Hamilton and James Madison, help explain the origins of this collective genius.

Alexander Hamilton had been the engineer of the Annapolis Convention, and as early as 1778 he had been urging that the national government be made stronger. Hamilton had come to the United States from the West Indies and while still a college student had won national attention for his brilliant pamphlets in defense of the Revolutionary cause. During the war he served as General Washington's aide, and his experiences confirmed his distaste for a Congress so weak it could not even supply the Revolution's troops with enough food or arms.

James Madison was only 36 years old at the time of the convention, yet he was one of its most learned members. He had helped frame Virginia's first constitution and had served both in the Virginia Assembly and in the Continental Congress. Madison was also a leader of those who favored the establishment of a stronger national government.

Like most of the other framers, Hamilton and Madison were superbly educated. Both had extensive private tutoring—a one-to-one teacher-student ratio. Like scores of other thinkers of the day, both combined extensive practical experience with their schooling. Both were active in their political and religious groups; both took part in political contests and electoral struggles; both helped build political coalitions.

Both men were "moral philosophers" as well as political thinkers. They had strong views on the supreme value—liberty—as well as on current issues. Instead of simply sermonizing about liberty, they analyzed it; they debated what kind of liberty, how to protect it, how to expand it.

James Madison

Alexander Hamilton

of the people. This was the only form seriously considered and the only form acceptable to the nation. Equally important, all the delegates opposed arbitrary and unrestrained government.

The common philosophy accepted by most of the delegates was that of *balanced government.* They wanted to construct a national government in which no single interest would dominate. Because most of the delegates represented citizens who were alarmed by the tendencies of desperate farmers to interfere with the property rights of others, they were primarily concerned with balancing the government in the direction of protection for property and business.

Benjamin Franklin, the 81-year-old delegate from Pennsylvania, favored extending the right to vote to all white males, but most of the delegates believed that owners of land were the best guardians of liberty. James Madison feared that those without property, if given the right to vote, might combine to deprive property owners of their rights. Delegates agreed in principle on limited voting rights, but differed over the kind and amount of property one must own in order to vote. Because states were in the process of relaxing qualifications for the vote, the framers recognized they would jeopardize approval of the constitution if they made the qualifications to vote in federal elections more restricted than those of the states. As a result, each state was left to determine the qualifications for electing members of the House of Representatives, the only branch of the national government that was to be elected directly by the voters.

Within five days of its opening, the convention—with only the Connecticut delegates dissenting—voted that "a national government ought to be established consisting of a supreme legislative, executive, and judiciary." This decision to establish a supreme national government profoundly altered the nature of the union from a loose confederation of states to a truly national government.

Few dissented from proposals to give the new Congress all the powers of the old Congress plus all other powers necessary to ensure that the harmony of the United States would not be challenged by state legislation. The framers agreed that a strong executive, which had been lacking under the Articles of Confederation, was necessary to provide energy and direction. An independent judiciary was also accepted without much debate. Other issues, however, sparked considerable conflict.

Representing different constituencies and different ideologies, the Constitutional Convention devised a totally new form of government that provided for a central government strong enough to rule but still responsible to its citizens and to the member states.

Conflict and Compromise

There were serious differences among the various delegates, especially between those from the large and small states. One of the most contentious issues was how to distribute the land extending westward to the Mississippi, land that had been secured through the Revolution. Several large states asserted claims to these western lands, but small states generally objected. The large states also favored a strong national government (which they expected they could dominate), while delegates from small states were anxious to avoid being dominated.

This tension surfaced in the first discussions of representation in Congress. Franklin favored a single-house national legislature, but most states had had two-chamber legislatures since colonial times, and the delegates were used to the system. **Bicameralism**—the principle of the two-house legislature—reflected delegates' belief in the need for balanced government. The Senate, the smaller chamber, would represent the states, and to some extent the aristocracy, and offset the larger, more democratic House of Representatives.

THE VIRGINIA PLAN   The Virginia delegation took the initiative. They had met during the delay before the convention, and as soon as the convention was organized, they presented 15 resolutions. These resolutions, the **Virginia Plan**, called for a strong central government with a legislature composed of two chambers. The members of the more representative chamber were to be elected by the voters; those of the smaller and more aristocratic chamber were to be chosen by the larger chamber from nominees submitted by the state legislatures. Representation in both houses would be based on either wealth or numbers, which would give the wealthier and more populous states—Massachusetts, Pennsylvania, and Virginia—a majority in the national legislature.

The Congress thus created was to be given all the legislative power of its predecessor under the Articles of Confederation, as well as the right "to legislate in all cases in which the separate States are incompetent." Further, it was to have the authority to veto state legislation that conflicted with the proposed constitution. The Virginia Plan also called for a national executive with extensive jurisdiction who would be chosen by the legislature. A national Supreme Court, along with the executive, was to have a qualified veto over acts of Congress.

THE NEW JERSEY PLAN   The Virginia Plan dominated the discussion for the first few weeks. But by June 15 additional delegates from the small states arrived, and they began a counterattack. They rallied around William Paterson of New Jersey, who presented a series of resolutions known as the **New Jersey Plan**. Table 1–1 outlines the key features of both plans. Paterson did not question the need for a strengthened central government, yet he was concerned about how this strength might be used. The New Jersey Plan would give Congress the right to tax and regulate commerce and to coerce states, and it would retain the single-house unicameral legislature (as under the Articles of Confederation) in which each state, regardless of size, would have the same vote.

The New Jersey Plan contained the germ of what eventually came to be a key provision of our Constitution: the *supremacy clause*. The national Supreme Court was to hear appeals from state judges, and the supremacy clause would require all judges—state and national—to treat laws of the national government and the treaties of the United States as superior to the constitutions and laws of each of the states.

To adopt the Virginia Plan—which would create a powerful national government dominated by Massachusetts, Pennsylvania, and Virginia and eliminate the states as important units of government—would guarantee that many of the other states would reject the new constitution. Still, large states resisted, and for a time the

"Remember, gentlemen, we aren't here just to draft a constitution. We're here to draft the best damn constitution in the world."

bicameralism
The principle of a two-house legislature.

Virginia Plan
Proposal at the Constitutional Convention made by the Virginia delegation for a strong central government with a bicameral legislature, the lower house to be elected by the voters and the upper chosen by the lower.

New Jersey Plan
Proposal at the Constitutional Convention made by William Paterson of New Jersey for a central government with a single-house legislature in which each state would be represented equally.

TABLE 1–1 The Virginia and New Jersey Plans

Virginia Plan	New Jersey Plan
Legitimacy derived from citizens, based on popular representation	Derived from states, based on equal votes for each state
Bicameral legislature	Unicameral legislature
Executive size undetermined, elected and removable by Congress	More than one person, removable by state majority
Judicial life-tenure, able to veto state legislation	No power over states
Legislature can override state laws	Government can compel obedience to national laws
Ratification by citizens	Ratification by states

convention was deadlocked. Small states believed all states should be represented equally in Congress, especially in the smaller "upper house" if there were to be two chambers. Large states insisted representation in both houses be based on population or wealth and that national legislators be elected by voters rather than by state legislatures. Finally, a Committee of Eleven was elected to devise a compromise. On July 5 it presented its proposals.

THE CONNECTICUT COMPROMISE   Because of the prominent role of the Connecticut delegation in constructing this plan, it has since been known as the **Connecticut Compromise**. It called for one house in which each state would have an equal vote and a second house in which representation would be based on population and in which all bills for raising or appropriating money would originate. This proposal was a setback for the large states, which agreed to it only when the smaller states made it clear this was their price for union. After equality of state representation in the Senate was accepted, most objections to a strong national government dissolved.

NORTH-SOUTH COMPROMISES   Other issues split the delegates North and South. Southerners were afraid a northern majority in Congress might discriminate against southern trade. They had some basis for this concern. John Jay, secretary of foreign affairs for the Confederation, had proposed a treaty with Great Britain that would have given advantages to northern merchants at the expense of southern exporters. To protect themselves, the southern delegates insisted a two-thirds majority be required in the Senate before presidents could ratify treaties.

Differences between the North and South were also evident on the issue of representation in the House of Representatives. The question was whether to count slaves for purposes of apportioning seats in the House. The South wanted to count slaves, thereby enlarging its number of representatives; the North resisted. After heated debate, the delegates agreed on the **three-fifths compromise**. Each slave would be counted as three-fifths of a free person for the purposes of apportionment in the House and of direct taxation; this fraction was chosen because it maintained a balance of power between the North and South. The issue of "balance" would recur in the early history of our nation as territorial governments were established and territories applied for statehood.

OTHER ISSUES   Delegates found other issues to argue about. Should the national government have lower courts, or would one federal Supreme Court be enough? This

Connecticut Compromise
Compromise agreement by states at the Constitutional Convention for a bicameral legislature with a lower house in which representation would be based on population, and upper house in which each state would have two senators.

three-fifths compromise
Compromise agreement between northern and southern states at the Constitutional Convention in which the slave population would be counted at three-fifths for determining direct taxation and representation in the House of Representatives.

issue was resolved by postponing the decision. The Constitution states that there shall be one Supreme Court and that Congress may establish lower courts.

How should the president be selected? For a long time the convention accepted the idea that the president should be chosen by Congress, but the delegates feared Congress would dominate the president, or vice versa. Election by the state legislatures was rejected because the delegates distrusted the state legislatures. Finally, the Electoral College system was devised. This was perhaps the most novel and contrived contribution of the delegates, and has long been one of the most criticized provisions in the Constitution.[17] (Consult Article II, Section 1, of the Constitution.)

After three months the delegates stopped debating. On September 17, 1787, they assembled for an impressive ceremony of signing the document they were recommending to the nation. All but three of those still present signed; others who opposed the general drift of the convention had already left. Their work well done, delegates adjourned to the nearby City Tavern to celebrate.

According to an old story, Benjamin Franklin was confronted by a woman as he left the last session of the convention.

"What kind of government have you given us, Dr. Franklin?" she asked. "A Republic or a Monarchy?"

"A Republic, Madam," he answered, "if you can keep it."

To Adopt or Not to Adopt?

The delegates had gone far. Indeed they had wholly disregarded Congress's instruction to do no more than revise the Articles. They had ignored Article XIII of the Articles of Confederation, which declared the Union to be perpetual and prohibited any alteration of the Articles unless agreed to by Congress and by *every one of the state legislatures*—a provision that had made it impossible to amend the Articles. The convention delegates, however, boldly declared that their newly proposed Constitution should go into effect when ratified by popularly elected conventions in nine states.

They turned to this method of ratification for practical considerations as well as for reasons of securing legitimacy for their newly proposed government. Not only were the delegates aware that there was little chance of winning approval of the new Constitution in all state legislatures; many also believed the Constitution should be ratified by an authority higher than a legislature. A constitution based on approval *by the people* would have higher legal and moral status. The Articles of Confederation had been a compact of state governments, but the Constitution was based on "We the People." Still, even this method of ratification would not be easy. The nation was not ready to adopt the Constitution without a thorough debate.

Federalists versus Antifederalists

Supporters of the new government, by cleverly appropriating the name **Federalists**, took some of the sting out of charges they were trying to destroy the states and establish an all-powerful central government. By calling their opponents **Antifederalists**, they pointed up the negative character of the arguments of those who opposed ratification.

The split was in part geographic. Seaboard and city regions tended to be Federalist strongholds; backcountry regions from Maine (then a part of Massachusetts)

Note: It took about 15 years to win independence, form an interim government that tried to govern, fashion a "more perfect union," and actually get a national government, with functioning legislative, executive, and judicial branches.

Federalists
Supporters of ratification of the Constitution whose position promoting a strong central government was later voiced in the Federalist party.

Antifederalists
Opponents of ratification of the Constitution and of a strong central government generally.

Challenges for Our Constitutional Democracy

1. *"All men are created equal"*: What kinds of equality are—and should be—protected by the Constitution, and by what means?

2. *"Government by the people"*: Does the evolving constitutional system, including political parties and interest groups, strengthen fair and effective representation of the people?

3. *Federalism*: Does the Constitution provide an efficient and realistic balance between national and state power?

4. *Checks and balances*: Does the constitutional separation of powers between the president and Congress lead too often to gridlock and stalemate?

5. *Minority rights*: Does the Constitution adequately protect the rights of women, African Americans, Native Americans, Hispanic Americans, other ethnic groups, and recent immigrants?

6. *Suspects' rights*: Can representative government uphold the rights of the criminally accused and yet protect its citizens?

7. *Individual liberties*: Are individual liberties adequately protected in the Constitution? Do big government and big business diminish the freedom of the individual?

8. *The judicial branch*: Is it too powerful? Are the federal courts exceeding their proper powers as interpreters of the Constitution?

9. *War and peace*: What are the responsibilities of the United States as the only superpower?

10. *Constitutional responsibilities*: Are Americans participating adequately in our democratic system? Do citizens have the social capital and understanding of our governmental processes to be heard and to make a difference?

The Federalist

Series of essays promoting ratification of the Constitution, written by Alexander Hamilton, John Jay, and James Madison in 1787 and 1788.

through Georgia, inhabited by farmers and other relatively poor people, were generally Antifederalist. But as in most political contests, no single factor completely accounted for the division between Federalists and Antifederalists. Thus in Virginia the leaders of both sides came from the same general social and economic class. New York City and Philadelphia strongly supported the Constitution, yet so did predominantly rural New Jersey.

The great debate was conducted through pamphlets, papers, letters to the editor, and speeches. The issues were important, but with few exceptions the argument about the merits of the Constitution was carried on in a quiet and calm manner. Out of the debate came a series of essays known as **The Federalist**, written by Alexander Hamilton, James Madison, and John Jay to persuade the voters of New York to ratify the Constitution. *The Federalist* is still, said Charles Beard, "widely regarded as the most profound single treatise on the Constitution ever written and as among the few masterly works in political science produced in all the centuries of history."[18] (Three of the most important *Federalist* essays, Nos. 10, 51, and 78, are found in the Appendix of this book. We urge you to read them.) The great debate stands even today as an outstanding example of free people using public discussion to determine the nature of their fundamental laws.

The Antifederalists' most telling criticism of the proposed Constitution was its failure to include a bill of rights.[19] The Federalists believed a bill of rights was unnecessary because the proposed national government had *only* the specific powers delegated to it by the states and the people. Thus there was no need to specify that Congress could not, for example, abridge freedom of the press because the states and the people had not given it power to regulate the press. Moreover, the Federalists argued, to guarantee some rights might be dangerous, because it would then be thought that rights not listed could be denied. The Constitution already protected some important rights—trial by jury in federal criminal cases, for example. Hamilton and others also insisted that paper guarantees were weak supports on which to depend for protection against governmental tyranny.

The Antifederalists were unconvinced. If some rights were protected, what could be the objection to providing constitutional protection for others? Without a bill of rights, what was to prevent Congress from using one of its delegated powers to abridge free speech? If bills of rights were needed in state constitutions to limit state governments, why was a bill of rights not needed in the national constitution to limit the national government? This was a government farther from the people, they contended, with a greater tendency to subvert natural rights.

The Politics of Ratification

The absence of a bill of rights in the proposed constitution dominated the struggle over its adoption. In taverns and church gatherings and newspaper offices up and down the eastern seaboard, people were muttering, "No bill of rights—no constitution!" This feeling was so strong that some Antifederalists, who were far more concerned with states' rights than individual rights, joined forces with bill of rights advocates in an effort to defeat the proposed Constitution.

The Federalists were first to begin the debate over the Constitution that opened as soon as the delegates left Philadelphia in mid-September 1787. The Fed-

eralists' tactic was to secure ratification in as many states as possible before the opposition had time to organize. The Antifederalists were handicapped. Most newspapers were owned by supporters of ratification. Moreover, Antifederalist strength was concentrated in rural areas, which were underrepresented in some state legislatures and difficult to arouse to political action. The Antifederalists needed time to perfect their organization and collect their strength, while the Federalists, composed of a more closely knit group of leaders throughout the colonies, moved in a hurry.

In most of the small states, now satisfied by equal Senate representation, ratification was gained without difficulty. Delaware was the first state to ratify, and by early 1788, Pennsylvania, New Jersey, Georgia, and Connecticut had also ratified (see Table 1–2). Reports were coming in from Massachusetts, however, that opposition was broadening. The position of such key leaders as John Hancock and Samuel Adams was in doubt. The debate in the ratifying convention in Boston pitched some of the most polished Federalist speakers against an array of eloquent but plainspoken Antifederalists. The debate raged for most of January 1788 into February. At times it looked as though the Constitution would lose, as Antifederalists raised the cry of "Why no bill of rights?" and other objections. But in the end the Constitution was narrowly ratified in Massachusetts, by 187 to 168.

The struggle over ratification continued through the spring of 1788. By June 21, Maryland, South Carolina, and New Hampshire had ratified, putting the Constitution over the top in the number (nine) required for ratification. But two big hurdles remained: Virginia and New York. It would be impossible to begin the new government without the consent of these two major states. Virginia was crucial. As the most populous state, the home of Washington, Jefferson, and Madison, it was a link between North and South. The Virginia ratifying convention rivaled the Constitutional Convention in the caliber of its delegates. Madison, who had only recently switched to favoring the bill of rights after saying earlier it was unnecessary, captained the Federalist forces. The fiery Patrick Henry led the opposition. In an epic debate, Henry cried that liberty was the issue: "Liberty, the greatest of earthly possessions . . . that precious jewel!" But Madison quietly rebutted him and then played his trump card, a promise that a bill of rights embracing the freedoms of religion and speech and assembly would be added to the Constitution as the first order of business once the new government was established. At a critical moment, Washington himself tipped the balance with a letter urging ratification. News of the Virginia vote, 89 for the Constitution and 79 opposed, was rushed to New York.[20]

The great landowners along New York's Hudson River, unlike their southern planter friends, were opposed to the Constitution. They feared federal taxation of their holdings, and they did not want to abolish the profitable tax New York had been levying on trade and commerce with other states. When the convention assembled, the Federalists were greatly outnumbered, but they were aided by Alexander Hamilton's strategy and skill and by word of Virginia's ratification. New York approved by a margin of three votes. Although North Carolina and Rhode Island still remained outside the Union (the former ratified in November 1789, and the latter six months later), the new nation was created. In New York, a few members of the old Congress assembled to issue the call for elections under the new Constitution. Then they adjourned without setting a date for reconvening.

TABLE 1–2 Ratification of the U.S. Constitution

State	Date
Delaware	December 7, 1787
Pennsylvania	December 12, 1787
New Jersey	December 18, 1787
Georgia	January 2, 1788
Connecticut	January 9, 1788
Massachusetts	February 6, 1788
Maryland	April 28, 1788
South Carolina	May 23, 1788
New Hampshire	June 21, 1788
Virginia	June 25, 1788
New York	July 26, 1788
North Carolina	November 21, 1789
Rhode Island	May 29, 1790

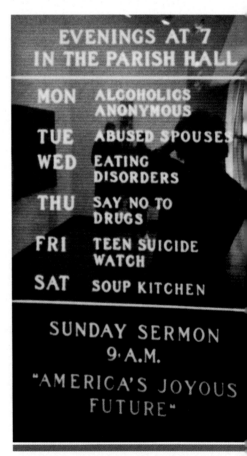

Despite the many serious problems facing our country, a spirit of optimism is still evident in our hopes for the future, as this church bulletin testifies.

POLITICS ONLINE

The Internet and Your Study of Political Science

Students of political science today have instant access to documents, journal articles, video, scholarly indexes, statistical data bases, and other resources that formerly took a trip to the library and hours of work to access. Your study of this subject, and any subject for that matter, is made much more accessible to you through the World Wide Web. Original documents, library catalogs, news reports, and research by public and private agencies are now at your fingertips and often free of charge.

One of the purposes of this Politics Online feature at the end of each chapter is to show you how you can use the Web to assist you in your study of political science and American government. Often in these boxes, we will also present an interesting example of how the Internet and related technology impact politics. Additionally, our publisher has invested heavily in web-based resources intended to reinforce key concepts and give you a chance to apply what you have learned through simulations and activities. In some chapters, we will invite you to explore your own ideology or assess how much you are investing in Social Security.

Many college students today are skilled in navigating the Web but can get lost in the enormous amount of information available. Politics Online will introduce you to relevant and interesting content you might not have known was there. Because websites are constantly changing, the place to start will always be the website for this book:
www.prenhall.com/burns

Politics Online will also demonstrate how the Internet impacts politics; how it is used by citizens, politicians, and government agencies; and some of the policy challenges it poses. Examples of this last category include e-mail privacy, sales taxes on Internet transactions, and pornography on the Internet.

Take, for example, the question of the extent to which the world's governments are democratic. In June 2000, 100 countries signed the Warsaw Declaration promoting democracy. To read this declaration and get a list of electoral democracies, go to:
www.fordemocracy.net.

We welcome your feedback on these boxes and hope they are helpful in opening up this remarkable resource, not only for this class but for other classes and in your future as an active citizen.

SUMMARY

1. Americans have long been skeptical of politicians and politics. Yet politics is a necessary activity for a democracy. Indeed politics and politicians are indispensable to making our system of separated institutions and checks and balances work.

2. "Democracy" is an often misused term, and it has many different meanings. We use it here to refer to a system of interacting values, interrelated political processes, and interdependent political structures. The vital principle of democracy is that a just government must derive its powers from the consent of the people and that this consent must be regularly renewed at free and fair elections.

3. Stable constitutional democracy is encouraged by various conditions, such as an educated citizenry, a healthy economy, and overlapping associations and groupings within a society in which major institutions interact to create a certain degree of consensus.

4. There has recently been some concern about a decline in *social capital*—the experiences people gain in working together in community groups. Lessons about compromise, accommodation, and participation are important building blocks for democracy. Some say we have a decline in civic engagement while others see a healthy level of voluntary and char-

itable engagement that is making our communities and nation better.

5. Constitutionalism is a general label we apply to arrangements such as checks and balances, federalism, separation of powers, rule of law, due process, and the Bill of Rights that force our leaders and representatives to listen, think, bargain, and explain before they act and make laws. A constitutional government enforces recognized and regularly applied limits on the powers of those who govern.

6. Democracy developed gradually. A revolution had to be fought before a system of representative democracy in the

United States could be tried and tested. It took several years before a national constitution could be written, and almost another year to be ratified. It took still another two years before a Bill of Rights could be adopted and ratified. It has taken more than two hundred years for democratic institutions to be refined and for systems of competition and choice to be hammered out. Democratic institutions such as free and fair elections and equal protection of the laws in the United States are still a work in progress, still in the process of being refined and improved.

KEY TERMS

democracy 4
direct democracy 4
representative democracy 4
constitutional democracy 4
constitutionalism 4
statism 5
popular consent 8

majority rule 9
majority 9
plurality 9
social capital 10
ideology 12
theocracy 12
Articles of Confederation 12

Annapolis Convention 14
Constitutional Convention 14
Shays' Rebellion 14
bicameralism 17
Virginia Plan 17
New Jersey Plan 17
Connecticut Compromise 18

three-fifths compromise 18
Federalists 19
Antifederalists 19
The Federalist 20

FURTHER READING

BERNARD BAILYN, ED., *The Debate on the Constitution: Federalist and Antifederalist Speeches, Articles, and Letters During the Struggle over Ratification*, 2 vols. (Library of America, 1993).

LANCE BANNING, *The Sacred Fire of Liberty: James Madison and the Founding of the Federal Republic* (Cornell University Press, 1995).

ROBERT A. DAHL, *On Democracy* (Yale University Press, 1998).

ALEXANDER HAMILTON, JAMES MADISON, AND JOHN JAY, *The Federalist Papers*, ed. Clinton Rossiter (New American Library, 1961). Also in several other editions.

SAMUEL P. HUNTINGTON, *The Third Wave: Democratization in the Late Twentieth Century* (University of Oklahoma Press, 1991).

EVERETT CARLL LADD, *The Ladd Report: Startling New Research Shows How an Explosion of Voluntary Groups, Activities and Charitable Donations Is Transforming Our Towns and Cities* (Free Press, 1999).

AREND LIJPHART, *Patterns of Democracy: Government Forms and Performance in Thirty-Six Countries* (Yale University Press, 1999).

DREW R. MCCOY, *The Last of the Fathers: James Madison and the Republican Legacy* (Columbia University Press, 1989).

RICHARD B. MORRIS, *Witnesses at the Creation: Hamilton, Madison, and Jay and the Constitution* (Holt, Rinehart and Winston, 1985).

PIPPA NORRIS, ED., *Critical Citizens: Global Support for Democratic Institutions* (Oxford University Press, 1999).

ROBERT D. PUTNAM, *Bowling Alone: The Collapse and Revival of American Community* (Simon & Schuster, 2000).

ROBERT D. PUTNAM, *Making Democracy Work: Civic Traditions in Modern Italy* (Princeton University Press, 1993).

JACK N. RAKOVE, *Original Meanings: Politics and Ideas in the Making of the Constitution* (Vintage Books, 1997).

MICHAEL SCHUDSON, *The Good Citizen: A History of American Civic Life* (Harvard University Press, 1998).

THEDA SKOCPOL AND MORRIS P. FIORINA, EDS., *Civic Engagement in American Democracy* (Brookings/Russell Sage, 1999).

ALEXIS DE TOCQUEVILLE, *Democracy in America*, 2 vols., 1835 (Vintage, 1955).

SIDNEY VERBA, KAY LEMAN SCHOLZMAN, AND HENRY E. BRADY, *Voice and Equality: Civic Volunteerism in American Politics* (Harvard University Press, 1995).

GARRY WILLS, *A Necessary Evil: A History of American Distrust of Government* (Simon & Schuster, 1999).

GORDON S. WOOD, *The Creation of the American Republic, 1776–1787* (University of North Carolina Press, 1969).

See also the *Journal of Democracy* (Johns Hopkins University Press).

2 THE LIVING CONSTITUTION

THE CONSTITUTION OF THE UNITED STATES, THE WORLD'S OLDEST WRITTEN CONSTITUTION, IS ONE OF THE SHORTEST. THE ORIGINAL, UNAMENDED CONSTITUTION, WHICH went into effect in 1789, contains just 4,543 words, yet it established the framers' experiment in free-government-in-the-making that each generation reinterprets and renews. The Constitution remains a document Americans revere. Optimists read it as expressing their hopes; pessimists put faith in its protections against tyranny and other abuses.

Why, after more than two hundred years, have we not written another constitution—let alone two, three, or more, as have other countries around the world? Part of the answer is the widespread acceptance of the Constitution by optimists and pessimists alike. But also part of the reason the Constitution endures is because of its brilliant structure for limited government and because the framers built into the document the capacity for adaptability and flexibility.

As the Constitution won the support of citizens of the early years of the Republic, it took on the aura of **natural law**—law that defines right from wrong, law that is higher than human law. "The [Founding] Fathers grew ever larger in stature as they receded from view; the era in which they lived and fought became a Golden Age; in that age there had been a fresh dawn for the world, and its men were giants against the sky."[1] This early Constitution worship helped bring unity to the diverse new nation. Like the Crown in Great Britain, the Constitution became a symbol of national loyalty, evoking both emotional and intellectual support from Americans, regardless of their differences. The framers' work became part of the American creed and culture.[2] It stood for liberty, equality before the law, limited government—indeed, for just about whatever anyone wanted to read into it.

Even today, Americans generally revere the Constitution, yet many do not know what is in it. A poll by the National Constitution Center found that nine out of ten Americans are proud of the Constitution and feel it is important to them. However, a third think the Constitution establishes English as the country's official language. One in six believes the Constitution establishes America as a Christian nation. Only one out of four could name a single First Amendment right. Although two out of three knew that the Constitution creates three branches of the national government, only one in three could name all three branches.[3]

The Constitution, however, is more than a symbol. It is a *supreme and binding law that both grants and limits powers.* "In framing a government which is to be administered

CHAPTERMEDIA

POLITICS ONLINE
What's Happening to the Constitution?
www.prenhall.com/burns

"And there are three branches of government, so that each branch has the other two to blame everything on."

© Tribune Media Services. All rights reserved. Reprinted with permission.

by men over men," wrote James Madison in *The Federalist*, No. 51, "the great difficulty lies in this: you must first enable the government to control the governed; and in the next place oblige it to control itself." (See *The Federalist*, No. 51, in the Appendix of this book, or go on the Web to **http://www.mcs.net/knautzer/fed/fedpaper.html.**) The Constitution is both a positive instrument of government, which enables the governors to control the governed, and a restraint on government, which enables the ruled to check the rulers.

In what ways does the Constitution limit the power of the government? In what ways does it create governmental power? How has it managed to serve as a great symbol of national unity and at the same time a somewhat adaptable and changing instrument of government? The secret is an ingenious separation of powers and a system of checks and balances that check power with power.

CHECKING POWER WITH POWER

It may seem strange to begin by stressing the ways in which the Constitution *limits* governmental power, but you must keep in mind the dilemma the framers faced. They wanted a stronger and more effective national government than they had under the Articles of Confederation; at the same time, they were keenly aware that the people would not accept too much central control. Efficiency and order were important concerns, but they were not as important as liberty. The framers wanted to ensure domestic tranquillity and prevent future rebellions, but they also wanted to forestall the emergence of a homegrown King George III. Accordingly, they allotted certain powers to the national government and reserved the rest for the states, thus establishing a system of *federalism* (whose nature and problems we take up in Chapter 3). Even this was not enough. They believed they needed additional means to limit the national government.

The most important way they devised to make public officials observe the constitutional limits on their powers was through *free and fair elections*; voters would be able to throw out of office those who abuse power. Yet the framers were not willing to depend solely on political controls, because they did not fully trust the people's judgment. "Free government is founded on jealousy, and not in confidence," said Thomas Jefferson. "In questions of power, then, let no more be heard of confidence in man, but bind him down from mischief by the chains of the Constitution."[4]

Even more important, the framers feared that a majority might deprive minorities of their rights. "A dependence on the people is, no doubt, the primary control on the government," Madison admitted in *The Federalist*, No. 51, "but experience has taught mankind the necessity of auxiliary precautions." What were these "auxiliary precautions" against popular tyranny?

Separation of Powers

The first step was the **separation of powers**, that is, the distribution of constitutional authority among the three branches of the national government. In *The Federalist*, No. 47, Madison wrote, "No political truth is certainly of greater intrinsic value, or is stamped with the authority of more enlightened patrons of liberty, than that . . . the accumulation of all powers, legislative, executive, and judiciary, in the same hands . . . may justly be pronounced the very definition of tyranny."[5] Chief among the "enlightened patrons of liberty" to whose authority Madison was appealing were John Locke and Montesquieu, whose works were well known to most educated Americans.

The intrinsic value of the principle of dispersion of power does not by itself account for its inclusion in our Constitution. Such dispersion of power had been the general practice in the colonies for more than one hundred years. Only during the Revolutionary period did some of the states concentrate authority in the hands of the legislature, and that unhappy experience confirmed the framers' belief in the merits of separation of powers. Many attributed the evils of state government and the lack of

natural law
God's or nature's law that defines right from wrong and is higher than human law.

separation of powers
Constitutional division of powers among the legislative, executive, and judicial branches, with the legislative branch making law, the executive applying and enforcing the law, and the judiciary interpreting the law.

energy in the central government to the fact that there was no strong executive both to check legislative abuses and to give energy and direction to administration.

Still, separating power was not enough. There was always the danger—from the framers' point of view—that different officials with different powers might pool their authority and act together. Separation of powers by itself might not prevent governmental branches and officials from responding to the same pressures—from the demand of an overwhelming majority of the voters to suppress an offensive book, for example, or to impose confiscatory taxes on rich people. If separating power was not enough, what else could be done?

Checks and Balances: Ambition to Counteract Ambition

The framers' answer was a system of **checks and balances**. "The great security against a gradual concentration of the several powers in the same department," wrote Madison in *The Federalist*, No. 51, "consists in giving to those who administer each department the necessary constitutional means and personal motives to resist encroachments of the others: . . . Ambition must be made to counteract ambition." Each branch therefore has a role in the actions of the others (see Figure 2–1). Congress enacts laws, but the president can veto them. The Supreme Court can declare

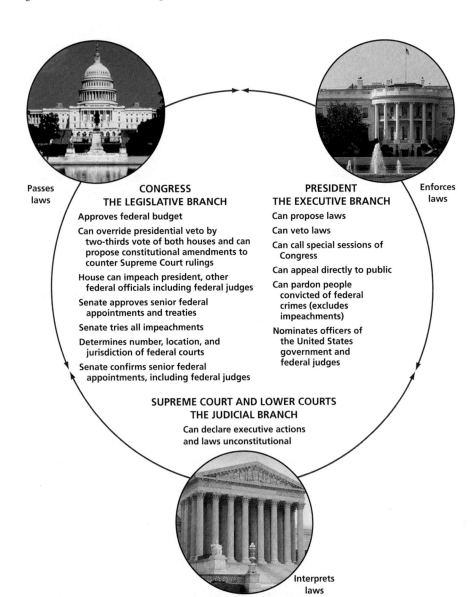

Passes laws

CONGRESS
THE LEGISLATIVE BRANCH

Approves federal budget

Can override presidential veto by two-thirds vote of both houses and can propose constitutional amendments to counter Supreme Court rulings

House can impeach president, other federal officials including federal judges

Senate approves senior federal appointments and treaties

Senate tries all impeachments

Determines number, location, and jurisdiction of federal courts

Senate confirms senior federal appointments, including federal judges

PRESIDENT
THE EXECUTIVE BRANCH

Can propose laws

Can veto laws

Can call special sessions of Congress

Can appeal directly to public

Can pardon people convicted of federal crimes (excludes impeachments)

Nominates officers of the United States government and federal judges

Enforces laws

SUPREME COURT AND LOWER COURTS
THE JUDICIAL BRANCH

Can declare executive actions and laws unconstitutional

Interprets laws

FIGURE 2–1 The Separation of Powers and Checks and Balances

checks and balances
Constitutional grant of powers that enables each of the three branches of government to check some acts of the others and therefore ensure that no branch can dominate.

THE Ecercise of Checks and Balances, 1789–2000

vetoes The president has vetoed more than 2,500 acts of Congress. Congress has overridden presidential vetoes more than 100 times.

judicial review The Supreme Court has ruled 155 congressional acts or parts thereof unconstitutional. Its 1983 decision on legislative vetoes (*INS v Chadha*) affects another 200 provisions.

impeachment The House of Representatives has impeached 17 federal officials, 2 presidents, and 15 federal judges; of these, the Senate has convicted 7 judges but has not convicted a president.

confirmation The Senate has refused to confirm 9 cabinet nominations, and many other cabinet and subcabinet appointments were withdrawn because of likely Senate rejection.

For Internet resources on the Constitution, see our home page: **www.prenhall.com/burns**

laws passed by Congress and signed by the president unconstitutional, but the president appoints the justices and all the other federal judges with the Senate's approval. The president administers the laws, but Congress provides the money. Moreover, the Senate and the House of Representatives have an absolute veto over each other in the enactment of a law, because both houses must approve bills.

Not only does each branch have some authority over the others, but each is politically independent of the others. Voters in each local district choose members of the House; voters in each state choose senators; the president is elected by all voters. With the consent of the Senate, the president appoints federal judges, who remain in office until they retire.

The framers also ensured that a majority of the voters could win control over only part of the government at one time. Although in an off-year (nonpresidential) election a new majority might take control of the House of Representatives, the president would still have at least two years to go, and senators stay on for six years. Finally, independent federal courts, which have developed their own powerful checks, were also provided.

Modifications of Checks and Balances

Distrustful of both the elites and the masses, the framers deliberately *built inefficiency into our political system.* They designed the decision-making process so that the national government can act decisively only when there is a consensus among most of the interest groups and after all sides have had a chance to have their say. Even though the fragmentation of political power written into the Constitution remains, several developments have modified the way the system of checks and balances works.

THE RISE OF NATIONAL POLITICAL PARTIES   Political parties can serve as unifying factors—at times drawing together the president, senators, representatives, and sometimes even judges behind common programs. When parties do this they help bridge the separation of powers. Yet parties can be splintered and weakened by having to work through a system of fragmented governmental power, so they never become strong or cohesive. Moreover, when one party controls the Congress and the other the White House (**divided government**), as has generally been the case since the end of World War II, the parties may intensify checks and balances rather than moderate them, to the point that action on some important issues may be difficult.[6]

Divided government may lead to so much competition between the legislative and executive branches that we find "each institution protecting and promoting itself through a broad interpretation of its constitutional and political status, even usurping the other's power when the opportunity presents itself."[7] Thus we have had battles over presidential impoundment of funds appropriated by Congress, budget gridlock, and unseemly and angry confirmation hearings for the appointment of justices of the Supreme Court. Divided government also makes it difficult for the voters to hold anybody or any party accountable. "Presidents blame Congress . . . while members of Congress attack the president. . . . Citizens genuinely cannot tell who is to blame."[8]

Yet when all the shouting dies down, political scientist David R. Mayhew concludes, there have been just as many congressional investigations and just as much important legislation passed when one party controls Congress and another controls the presidency as when the same party controls both branches.[9] And Charles Jones, a noted scholar of Congress and the presidency, adds that not only is divided government not that important in determining how our government responds to crises, but divided government is precisely what the voters appear to have wanted through much of our history.[10]

Bill Clinton's first term as president confirmed Jones's thesis. There was more major legislation signed into law during his second two years (104th Congress,

divided government
Governance divided between the parties, especially when one holds the presidency and the other controls one or both houses of Congress.

1995–97) when Republicans controlled both houses, than during his first two years (103d Congress, 1993–95), when Democrats controlled Congress. During Clinton's second term (1996–2000), however, there was continual partisan conflict between the Republican-controlled Congress and the Democratic White House. Congressional committees spent most of their time investigating allegations of misconduct on the part of the president and members of his cabinet.

EXPANSION OF THE ELECTORATE AND CHANGES IN ELECTORAL METHODS   The framers wanted the president to be chosen by the Electoral College—wise, independent citizens free from popular passions and hero worship—rather than by ordinary citizens. Almost from the beginning, however, that is not the way the Electoral College worked. Rather, voters actually select the president, because presidential electors chosen by the voters are pledged in advance to cast their electoral votes for their party's candidates for president and vice president.

The kind of "people" entitled to vote has expanded from white property-owning males to all citizens over 18 years of age. During the past century, American states have expanded the role of the electorate by adopting **direct primaries** in which the voters elect party nominees for the House and Senate and even for president; by permitting the voters in about half the states to propose and vote on laws (**initiatives**); by allowing voters to reconsider actions of the legislature (**referendums**) and even to remove elected state and local officials from office (**recall**). And with the passage of the Seventeenth Amendment, senators are no longer elected by state legislatures but are chosen directly by the people.

ESTABLISHMENT OF AGENCIES DELIBERATELY DESIGNED TO EXERCISE LEGISLATIVE, EXECUTIVE, AND JUDICIAL FUNCTIONS   When the national government began to regulate the economy, it issued detailed rules on such complex matters as railroad safety, bank and stock-exchange practices, employment conditions, union negotiations, and automobile emissions. It was impossible to assign these regulatory responsibilities without providing the power to make and apply rules and to decide disputes. Beginning in 1887, Congress created *independent regulatory commissions* such as the Interstate Commerce Commission (which went out of business in 1995, although many of its functions were transferred to the Surface Transportation Board within the Department of Transportation) and the Federal Communications Commission. More recently it established *independent executive agencies* such as the Environmental Protection Agency.

CHANGES IN TECHNOLOGY   The system of checks and balances operates differently today from the way it did in 1789. Back then there were no televised congressional committee hearings, no electronic communications, no *Larry King Live* or *Rush Limbaugh* talk shows, no *New York Times, Wall Street Journal,*

THE JAPANESE CONSTITUTION

The Japanese Constitution of 1947 created a parliamentary democracy and established the power of American-style judicial review. Although drafted in part by the United States and the Allied Occupation Forces after World War II, the Japanese Constitution was made easier to amend than ours. A proposed amendment needs only to be passed by a two-thirds majority of both houses of Japan's parliament and then be ratified by a majority vote of the people in a national referendum. Yet it has never been amended.

What explains the reluctance of the Japanese to amend their constitution? Part of the explanation may be that the Japanese Constitution goes well beyond our Bill of Rights to include a broad range of economic and social rights, so that progressive Japanese vigorously oppose changing it. Opposition also comes from older Japanese who remember World War II and revere their "Peace Constitution," while younger generations tend to be indifferent and more concerned with economic matters.

Another explanation is that the Japanese have learned to reinterpret controversial provisions of their constitution, as have Americans, in ways that make formal amendments unnecessary. For example, although Article 9 of the Japanese Constitution forbids the maintenance of "land, sea, and air forces," and includes a renunciation of war, the Japanese have interpreted Article 9 to permit them to maintain "self-defense forces," thus making it less urgent to change the constitution. Japan now ranks among the top five countries in terms of military spending and looks toward a larger role in international peacekeeping missions.

For more information on the Japanese Constitution, go on the Internet to **www.home.ntt.com/jap/constitution/ english-constitution.html**

direct primary
Election in which voters choose party nominees.

initiative
Procedure whereby a certain number of voters may, by petition, propose a law or constitutional amendment and have it submitted to the voters.

referendum
Procedure for submitting to popular vote measures passed by the legislature or proposed amendments to a state constitution.

recall
Procedure for submitting to popular vote the removal of officials from office before the end of their term.

THE EUROPEAN UNION

The European Union was formed after World War II to promote economic integration. Through a series of treaties, the union has grown to include 15 countries in Western Europe. One of the most important institutions created by the union is the European Court of Justice (ECJ). The ECJ has the power to declare national laws invalid when they conflict with treaty obligations and has created a uniform system of law that takes precedence over national laws and constitutions.

The member states of the European Union have also signed the European Convention of Human Rights, which establishes a long list of civil liberties. They are subject to the jurisdiction of the European Court of Human Rights, which resolves allegations of human rights abuses and enforces the Convention on Human Rights. This court has interpreted its powers broadly and has asserted its right to invalidate national laws that contravene obligations that the nations accepted in signing the convention.

For the most part, the issues coming before the ECJ have been economic and commercial in nature, but it has struck down laws based on gender discrimination and advanced the right to equal pay for equal work. Critics of the ECJ complain that it has become too activist and compare it to the U.S. Supreme Court in the early nineteenth century under Chief Justice John Marshall, whose rulings striking down state trade barriers promoted the growth of our unified economy.

Even with these trends toward more active judicial review in the European Union, courts in the United States continue to exercise the power of judicial review more frequently and more broadly than do the newer constitutional and supranational courts.

For more information on the European Union go on the Internet to these addresses:

www.userpage.chemie.fu-berlin.de/ adressen/eu.html

lib.berkeley.edu/gssi/eugde.html

The ECJ maintains a site at europa.eu.int/ cj/en/ containing recent decisions and other information.

USA Today, CNN, or C-SPAN, no nightly news programs with national audiences, no presidential press conferences, and no live coverage of wars and of Americans being held hostage in foreign lands. Nuclear bombs, television, computers, cellular telephones, fax machines, the World Wide Web—these and other innovations create conditions today that are very different from those of two centuries ago. We also live in a time of instant polls that tell us what people are thinking about public issues.

In some ways these new technologies have added to the powers of presidents by permitting them to appeal directly to millions of people and giving them immediate access to public opinion. And these new technologies have also added leverage to organized interests by making it easy for them to target thousands of letters and calls at Congress, to organize letters to the editor, and to stage media events. New technologies have also given greater independence and influence to nongovernmental agencies such as the press. They have made it possible for rich people like Ross Perot and Steve Forbes and religious leaders like Pat Robertson, who have access to large resources, to bypass political parties and carry their message directly to the electorate.

THE EMERGENCE OF PRESIDENTIAL POWER   Today problems anywhere in the world—Israel, Kosovo, North Korea, and Iraq—often become crises for the United States. The need to deal with perpetual emergencies has concentrated power in the hands of the chief executive and the presidential staff. The president's role as the most significant player on the world stage and media coverage of summit conferences with foreign leaders enhance his status. Headline-producing events give the president a visibility no congressional leader can achieve. The office of the president has on occasion served to modify the system of checks and balances and provide some measure of national unity. Drawing on constitutional, political, and emergency powers, the president is sometimes able to overcome the restraints imposed by the Constitution on the exercise of governmental power—to the applause of some and the alarm of others.

JUDICIAL REVIEW AND THE "GUARDIANS OF THE CONSTITUTION"

Judges have become so important in our system of checks and balances that they deserve special attention. Judges did not claim the power of **judicial review**— the power of a court to refuse to enforce a law or a government regulation that in the opinion of the judges conflicts with the Constitution—until some years after the Constitution was in operation. From the beginning, however, judges were expected to restrain legislative majorities. "The independence of judges," wrote Alexander

judicial review
The power of a court to declare unconstitutional a law or a government regulation that in the opinion of the judges conflicts with the Constitution.

Hamilton in *The Federalist*, No. 78 (which appears in the Appendix), "may be an essential safeguard against the effects of occasional ill humors in the society."

Judicial review is a contribution of the United States to the art of government, a contribution that has been adopted at an increasing rate by other nations. In Japan, Germany, France, Italy, and Spain, constitutional courts are responsible for reviewing laws referred to them to ensure constitutional compliance, including compliance with the charter of rights that is now part of these constitutions.[11] The Canadian Constitution allows either a provincial legislature or the national parliament to override certain sections of the Charter of Rights for a renewable period of six years.[12] (See also the box on the growth of judicial review within the European Union.)

Origins of Judicial Review

The Constitution says nothing about who should have the final word in disputes that might arise over its meaning. Whether the delegates to the Constitutional Convention of 1787 intended to give the courts the power of judicial review is a question long debated. The framers clearly intended that the Supreme Court have the power to declare *state* legislation unconstitutional, but whether they intended to give it the same power over *congressional* legislation is not clear. Why then didn't the framers specifically provide for judicial review? Probably because they believed the power could be inferred from certain general provisions.

The Federalists—those who urged ratification of the Constitution and controlled the national government until 1801—generally supported a strong role for federal courts and favored judicial review. Their opponents, the Jeffersonian Republicans (called Democrats after 1832), were less enthusiastic. In the Kentucky and Virginia Resolutions (1798, 1799), Jefferson and Madison (who by this time had left the Federalist camp) came close to the position that state legislatures—and not the Supreme Court—had the ultimate power to interpret the Constitution. These resolutions seemed to question whether the Supreme Court even had final authority to review state legislation, something about which there had been little doubt.

When the Jeffersonians defeated the Federalists in the election of 1800, it was still undecided whether the Supreme Court would actually exercise the power of judicial review. Logical reasons to support such a doctrine were at hand, and some precedents could even be cited; nevertheless judicial review was not an established power. Then in 1803 came *Marbury v Madison*, one of the most famous Supreme Court decisions of all time.[13]

Marbury versus Madison

The election of 1800 marked the rise to power of the Jeffersonian Republicans. President John Adams and fellow Federalists did not take their defeat easily. Indeed, they were greatly alarmed at what they considered to be the "enthronement of the rabble." Yet there was nothing much they could do about it before leaving office—or was there? The Constitution gives the president, with the consent of the Senate, the power to appoint federal judges to hold office during "good Behaviour." With the judiciary in the hands of good Federalists, thought Adams and his associates, they could stave off the worst consequences of Jefferson's victory.

The outgoing Federalist Congress then created dozens of new federal judicial posts. By March 3, 1801, Adams had appointed and the Senate had confirmed loyal Federalists to all these new positions. Adams signed the commissions and turned them over to John Marshall, his secretary of state, to be sealed and delivered. Marshall had just received his own commission as chief justice of the United States, but he was continuing to serve as secretary of state until Adams's term as president expired. Working right up until nine o'clock on the evening of March 3, Marshall sealed, but was unable to deliver, all the commissions. The only ones left were for the justices of the peace for the

Chief Justice John Marshall (1755–1835), our most influential Supreme Court justice. Appointed in 1801, Marshall served until 1835. Earlier he had been a staunch defender of the U.S. Constitution at the Virginia ratifying convention, a member of Congress, and a secretary of state. He is one of those rare people who served in all three branches of government.

Supreme Court Justice Thurgood Marshall

I do not believe that the meaning of the Constitution was forever "fixed" at the Philadelphia Convention. Nor do I find the wisdom, foresight, and sense of justice exhibited by the framers particularly profound. To the contrary, the government they devised was defective from the start, requiring several amendments, a civil war, and momentous social transformation to attain the system of constitutional government, and its respect for the individual freedoms and human rights, that we hold as fundamental today. When contemporary Americans cite "The Constitution," they invoke a concept that is vastly different from what the framers barely began to construct two centuries ago.

For a sense of the evolving nature of the Constitution we need look no further than the first three words of the document's preamble: "We the People." When the Founding Fathers used this phrase in 1787, they did not have in mind the majority of America's citizens. "We the People" included, in the words of the framers, "the whole Number of free Persons." On a matter so basic as the right to vote, for example, Negro slaves were excluded, although they were counted for representational purposes—at three-fifths each. Women did not gain the right to vote for over a hundred and thirty years.

These omissions were intentional. The record of the framers' debates on the slave question is especially clear: the Southern states acceded to the demands of the New England states for giving Congress broad power to regulate commerce, in exchange for the right to continue the slave trade. . . .

And so we must be careful, when focusing on the events which took place in Philadelphia two centuries ago, that we not overlook the momentous events which followed, and thereby lose our proper sense of perspective. . . . If we seek, instead, a sensitive understanding of the Constitution's inherent defects, and its promising evolution through 200 years of history, the celebration of the "Miracle at Philadelphia" will, in my view, be a far more meaningful and humbling experience. We will see that the true miracle was not the birth of the Constitution, but its life, a life nurtured through two turbulent centuries of our own making, and a life embodying much good fortune that was not.

SOURCE: Remarks of Thurgood Marshall at the Annual Seminar of the San Francisco Patent and Trademark Law Association (Maui, Hawaii, May 16, 1987). It appears in David M. O'Brien, ed., *Judges on Judging* (Chatham House, 1997), pp. 195–200.

District of Columbia. The newly appointed chief justice left these commissions for his successor to deliver.

This "packing" of the judiciary angered Jefferson, now inaugurated as president. When he discovered that some of the commissions were still lying on a table in the Department of State, he instructed a clerk not to deliver them. Jefferson could see no reason why the District needed so many justices of the peace, especially Federalist justices.[14]

Among the commissions not delivered was one for William Marbury. After waiting in vain, Marbury decided to seek action from the courts. Searching through the statute books, he came across Section 13 of the Judiciary Act of 1789, which authorized the Supreme Court "to issue writs of *mandamus*." A **writ of mandamus** is a court order directing an official, such as the secretary of state, to perform a duty about which the official has no discretion, such as delivering a commission. So, thought Marbury, why not ask the Supreme Court to issue a writ of mandamus to force James Madison, the new secretary of state, to deliver the commission? Marbury and his companions went directly to the Supreme Court, and, citing Section 13, they made the request.

What could Marshall do? If the Court issued the writ, Madison and Jefferson would probably ignore it. The Court would be powerless, and its prestige, already low, might suffer a fatal blow. On the other hand, by refusing to issue the writ, the judges would appear to support the Jeffersonian Republicans' claim that the Court had no authority to interfere with the executive. Would Marshall issue the writ? Most people thought so; angry Republicans even threatened impeachment if he did so.

On February 24, 1803, the Supreme Court delivered its opinion. The first part was as expected. Marbury was entitled to his commission, said Marshall, and Madison should have delivered it to him. Moreover, the proper court could issue a writ of mandamus, even against so high an officer as the secretary of state.

Then came the surprise. Section 13 of the Judiciary Act seems to give the Supreme Court original jurisdiction in cases such as that in question. But Section 13, said Marshall, is contrary to Article III of the Constitution, which gives the Supreme Court original jurisdiction only when an ambassador or other foreign minister is affected or when a state is a party. Even though this is a case of original jurisdiction, Marbury is neither a state nor a foreign minister. If we follow Section 13, wrote Marshall, we have jurisdiction; if we follow the Constitution, we have no jurisdiction.

Marshall then posed the question in a more pointed way: Should the Supreme Court enforce an unconstitutional law? Of course not, he concluded. *The Constitution is the supreme and binding law,* and the courts cannot enforce any action of Congress that conflicts with it. Thus by limiting the court's power to what is granted in the Constitution, Marshall gained the much more important power to declare laws passed by Congress unconstitutional. It was a brilliant move.

Marbury v Madison might have been interpreted by subsequent generations in a very limited way. It could have been interpreted to mean that the Supreme Court had the right to determine the scope of its own powers under Article III, but Congress and the president had the authority to interpret their own powers under Articles I and II. But over the decades, building on Marshall's precedent, the Court has taken the commanding position as the authoritative interpreter of the Constitution.

Several important consequences follow from the acceptance of Marshall's argument that judges are the official interpreters of the Con-

THE BRITISH AND AMERICAN SYSTEMS: A STUDY IN CONTRASTS

Our political system is based on the Constitution; Britain has no such single document. Yet both systems are "constitutional" in the sense that the rulers are subject to well-defined restraints. Parliament is the guardian of the British constitution. In the United States it is the courts—ultimately the Supreme Court—that are the keepers of the constitutional conscience, not Congress or the president. The limitations in our written Constitution and the practices in the unwritten British constitution rest on underlying national values and attitudes to toward government.

In the British system, voters elect members of the House of Commons from districts, much as we elect members of our House of Representatives. Like us, the party with the most votes in a district wins the seat, so that even with three or more parties, a plurality of the popular vote usually results in a majority of the parliamentary seats. So long as the parliamentary majority stays together, it can enact into law the ruling party's program.

Leaders of the majority party in the House of Commons serve as executive ministers who collectively form the cabinet, with the prime minister at its head. The majority selects the prime minister. If the ruling party loses the support of the majority in the Commons on a major issue, it must resign or call for new elections. Formerly, the House of Lords could check the Commons, but it is now almost powerless.

The House of Commons, when it chooses to act, has almost complete constitutional power. There is no high court with the power to declare acts of Parliament unconstitutional, and the prime minister cannot veto them, although he or she may ask the Crown to dissolve Parliament and call new elections.

In British politics, parties are cohesive and disciplined; party members vote together and support their parliamentary leaders. In Britain the party that wins an election has a very good chance of seeing its policies enacted. By contrast, our system depends on the agreement of

American System of Separation of Powers

House of Representatives Two-year term | Senate Six-year term | Judges Life-term | President Four-year term

Electors

Ballot

Ballot

Voter

British Parliamentary System of Concentration of Responsibility

Prime Minister

Cabinet
Cabinet members serve at the pleasure of the Prime Minister or until the House of Commons is dissolved

Crown (Figurehead)

Judges
Life term
(No power of judicial review)

Speaker

House of Commons
Five-year terms unless dissolved earlier by the Prime Minister

Majority Party | Minority Party

House of Lords
Life terms
(Little power)

Ballot

A Comparison of the British and American Systems

many elements of society. The party that wins a presidential or congressional election or even one that controls both these branches may still have a tough time carrying out its campaign promises.

In recent years the British system has been substantially modified. In addition to introducing elements of federalism by providing for regional parliaments in Scotland and Wales, the House of Lords has been stripped of its hereditary peers, peers who served as a result of hereditary titles. The House of Lords can still

delay implementation of acts of the House of Commons, but it now consists only of people appointed by the prime minister for their accomplishments in the arts, business, and public service.

In October 2000, England made the European Convention on Human Rights part of domestic law, giving ordinary citizens their first American-style bill of rights. Civil libertarians praised the move as the most important change to the British constitutional system in more than 300 years.

Impeachment of presidents: Charges against Andrew Johnson failed to receive the necessary two-thirds vote in the Senate; President Richard Nixon resigned when it became clear that the House of Representatives was prepared to pass articles of impeachment; the House passed two of the four articles of impeachment against Bill Clinton, but the Senate could not muster the two-thirds majority needed to convict.

writ of mandamus
Court order directing an official to perform an official duty.

impeachment
Formal accusation against a public official and the first step in removal from office.

stitution. The most important is that people can challenge laws enacted by Congress and approved by the president. Simply by bringing a lawsuit, those who lack the clout to get a bill through Congress can often secure a judicial hearing. And organized interest groups often find that goals unattainable by legislation can be achieved by litigation. Litigation thus supplements, and at times takes precedence over, legislation as a way to make public policy.[15]

THE CONSTITUTION AS AN INSTRUMENT OF GOVERNMENT

As careful as the Constitution's framers were to limit the powers they gave the national government, the main reason they had assembled in Philadelphia was to create a stronger national government. Having learned that a weak central government was a danger to liberty, they wished to establish a national government within the framework of a federal system with enough authority to meet the needs of all time. They made general grants of power, leaving it to succeeding generations to fill in the details and organize the structure of government in accordance with experience.

Hence our formal, written Constitution is only the skeleton of our system. It is filled out in numerous ways that must be considered part of our constitutional system in its larger sense. In fact, it is primarily through changes in the informal, unwritten Constitution that our system is kept up to date. These changes are found in certain basic statutes and historical practices of Congress, presidential practices, and decisions of the Supreme Court.

Congressional Elaboration

Because the framers gave Congress authority over many of the structural details of the national government, it is not necessary to amend the Constitution every time a change is needed. Rather, Congress can create legislation to meet the need. Examples of congressional elaboration appear in such legislation as the Judiciary Act of 1789, which laid the foundations of our national judicial system; in the laws establishing the organization and functions of all federal executive officials subordinate to the president; and in the rules of procedure, internal organization, and practices of Congress.

Impeachment and Removal Power

A dramatic example of congressional elaboration of our constitutional system is the use of the impeachment and removal power. An **impeachment** is a formal accusation against a public official and the first step in removal from office. Constitutional language defining the grounds for impeachment is sparse. Look at your copy of the Constitution, and note that Article II (the Executive Article) calls for removal of the president, vice-president, and all civil officers of the United States on impeachment for, and conviction of, "Treason, Bribery, or other High Crimes and Misdemeanors." It is up to Congress to give meaning to that language.

Article I (the Legislative Article) gives the House of Representatives the sole power to initiate impeachments and the Senate the sole power to try impeachments. In the event the president is being tried, the chief justice of the United States presides, as Chief Justice William H. Rehnquist did in the impeachment of President Bill Clinton. Article I also requires conviction on impeachment charges to have the agreement of two-thirds of the senators present. Judgments shall extend no further than removal from office and disqualification from holding any office under the United States, but a person convicted shall also be liable to indictment, trial, judgment, and punishment according to the law. Article I also exempts cases of impeachment from the president's pardoning power. Article III (the Judicial Article) exempts cases of impeachment from the jury trial requirement. That is all the relevant constitutional language about impeachment. We must look to history to answer most questions about the proper exercise of these powers.[16]

Fortunately, past experience has triggered few acute constitutional disputes about the interpretation of impeachment procedures, so there is little history to go on. The House of Representatives has investigated 67 individuals for possible impeachment and has impeached 17 (2 presidents and 15 federal judges). The Senate has convicted only seven, all federal judges.

Presidential Practices

Although the formal constitutional powers of the president have not changed, the office is dramatically more important and more central today than it was in 1789. Vigorous presidents—George Washington, Thomas Jefferson, Andrew Jackson, Abraham Lincoln, Theodore Roosevelt, Woodrow Wilson, Franklin Roosevelt, Harry Truman, Lyndon Johnson, Bill Clinton—have boldly exercised their political and constitutional powers, especially during times of national crisis. Their presidential practices have established important precedents, building the power and influence of the office.

A major practice involves **executive orders**, which carry the full force of law. They may make major policy changes, such as withholding federal contracts from businesses engaging in racial discrimination, or they may simply be formalities, such as the presidential proclamation of Earth Day.

Other practices include **executive privilege** (the right to confidentiality of executive communications, especially those that relate to national security), **impoundment** by a president of funds previously appropriated by Congress, the right to send our armed forces into hostilities, and, most important, the right to propose legislation and work actively to secure its passage by Congress. President Clinton requested a federal judge to extend executive privilege to two of his advisers to prevent testimony before the grand jury investigating his relationship with White House intern Monica Lewinsky, but the request was denied.

Foreign and economic crises as well as nuclear age realities have expanded the president's role: "When it comes to action risking nuclear war, technology has modified the Constitution: the President, perforce, becomes the only such man in the system capable of exercising judgment under the extraordinary limits now imposed by secrecy, complexity, and time."[17] The presidency has also become the pivotal office for regulating the economy and protecting the general welfare. Plainly, the president has become our chief legislator as well as our chief executive.

Custom and Usage

Custom and usage round out our governmental system. The development of structures outside the formal Constitution—such as national political parties and the extension of the suffrage within the states—has democratized our Constitution. Examples of custom and usage are televised press conferences and presidential and vice-presidential debates. Through such developments, the president has become responsive to the people and has a political base different from that of Congress. Consequently, the constitutional relationship between the branches today is considerably different from that envisioned by the framers.

Judicial Interpretation

As discussed earlier, judicial interpretation of the Constitution, especially by the Supreme Court, has played an important part in keeping the constitutional system up to date. As social and economic conditions have changed and new national demands have developed, the Supreme Court has changed its interpretation of the Constitution accordingly. Because the Constitution adapts to changing times, it does not require frequent formal amendment. The advantages of this flexibility may be appreciated by comparing the national Constitution with the rigid and often overly specific state constitutions. Many state constitutions are so detailed

executive order
An order issued by a president that has the force of law.

executive privilege
The right to confidentiality of executive communications, especially those that relate to national security.

impoundment
Presidential refusal to allow an agency to spend funds authorized and appropriated by Congress.

Leaving aside the first ten amendments (the Bill of Rights), the power of constitutional amendment has served a number of purposes:

To Add or Subtract National Government Power

The Eleventh took some jurisdiction away from the national courts.

The Thirteenth abolished slavery and authorized Congress to legislate against it.

The Sixteenth enabled Congress to levy an income tax.

The Eighteenth authorized Congress to prohibit the manufacture, sale, or transportation of liquor.

The Twenty-first repealed the Eighteenth and gave states the authority to regulate liquor sales.

The Twenty-seventh limited the power of Congress to set members' salaries.

To Expand the Electorate and Its Power

The Fifteenth extended the suffrage to all male African Americans.

The Seventeenth took the right to elect their United States senators away from state legislatures and gave it to the voters in each state.

The Nineteenth extended suffrage to women.

The Twenty-third gave voters of the District of Columbia the right to vote for president and vice-president.

The Twenty-fourth prohibited any state from taxing the right to vote (the poll tax).

The Twenty-sixth extended the suffrage to otherwise qualified persons 18 years of age or older.

To Reduce the Electorate's Power

The Twenty-second took away from the electorate the right to elect any person to the office of president for more than two full terms.

To Limit State Government Power

The Thirteenth abolished slavery.

The Fourteenth granted national citizenship and prohibited states from abridging privileges of national citizenship; from denying persons life, liberty, and property without due process; and from denying persons equal protection of the laws. This amendment has come to be interpreted as imposing restraints on state powers in every area of public life.

To Make Structural Changes in Government

The Twelfth corrected deficiencies in the operation of the Electoral College that were revealed by the development of a two-party national system.

The Twentieth altered the calendar for congressional sessions and shortened the time between the election of presidents and their assumption of office.

The Twenty-fifth provided procedures for filling vacancies in the vice-presidency and for determining whether presidents are unable to perform their duties.

that they tie the hands of the public officials and must be amended or replaced frequently.

CHANGING THE LETTER OF THE CONSTITUTION

The idea of a constantly changing system disturbs many people. How, they contend, can you have a constitutional government when the Constitution is constantly being twisted by interpretation and changed by informal methods? This view fails to distinguish between two aspects of the Constitution. As an expression of *basic and timeless personal liberties*, the Constitution does not, and should not, change. For example, a government cannot destroy free speech and still remain a constitutional government. In this sense the Constitution is unchanging. But when we consider the Constitution as an *instrument of government* and a positive grant of power, we realize that if it does not grow with the nation it serves, it will soon be ignored.

The framers could never have conceived of the problems facing the government of a large, powerful and wealthy nation of over 285 million people at the beginning of the twenty-first century. Although the general purposes of government remain the same—to establish liberty, promote justice, ensure domestic tranquillity, and provide for the common defense—the powers of government that were adequate to accomplish these purposes in 1787 are simply insufficient more than two hundred years later. Through its remarkable adaptability, our Constitution has survived democratic and industrial revolutions, the turmoil of civil war, the tensions of major depressions, and the dislocations of world wars.

The framers knew that future experiences would call for changes in the text of the Constitution and that some means for formal amendment was necessary. In Article V they gave responsibility for amending the Constitution to Congress and to the states. The president has no formal authority over constitutional amendments; presidential veto power does not extend to them, although presidential political influence is often crucial in getting amendments proposed and ratified. Nor may governors veto ratification of amendments by either state legislatures or state ratifying conventions.

Proposing Amendments

The first method for proposing amendments—and the only one used so far—is *by a two-thirds vote of both houses of Congress.* Dozens of resolutions proposing amendments are introduced in every session. Thousands have been introduced since 1789, but few make any headway. Throughout our history Congress has proposed only 31 amendments, of which 27 have been ratified—including the Twenty-seventh, which was originally part of the Bill of Rights but took more than two hundred years for ratification (see Figure 2–2).

In recent decades there has been a flurry of congressional attempts at constitutional amendments.[18] None has been formally proposed by both chambers; many are currently under consideration. One given serious consideration is the Balanced Budget Amendment. Such an amendment has several times secured the two-

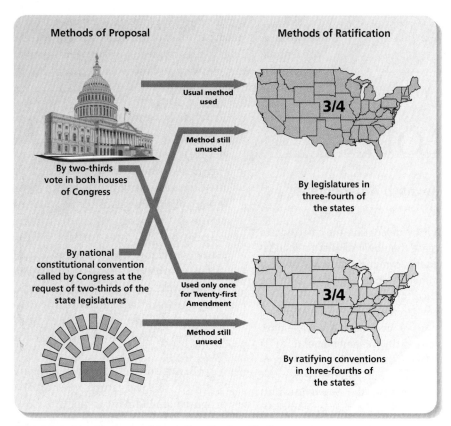

FIGURE 2–2 Four Methods of Amending the Constitution

thirds vote needed in the House, but failed to do so in the Senate. Republicans tend to favor it; most Democrats oppose it. The fact that, as a result of good economic times and some fiscal restraint, the budget actually started to generate a surplus for the first time in decades has reduced the pressure to pass a Balanced Budget Amendment. Nevertheless, in view of strong public support for it, this debate is likely to continue.

Why has proposing amendments to the Constitution become so popular? In part because interest groups unhappy with Supreme Court decisions seek to overturn them. In part because groups frustrated by their inability to get things done in Congress hope to bypass Congress. And in part because scholars or interest groups (not necessarily mutually exclusive categories) seek to change the procedures and processes of government to make the system more responsive.[19]

The second method for proposing amendments—*a convention called by Congress* at the request of the legislatures in two-thirds of the states—has never been used. This method presents some difficult questions.[20] First, can state legislatures apply for a convention to propose specific amendments on one topic, or must they request a convention with full powers to revise the entire Constitution? How long do state petitions remain alive? How should delegates be chosen? How should such a convention be run? Congress has considered bills to answer some of these questions but has not passed any, in part because most members do not wish to encourage a constitutional convention for fear that once in session it might propose amendments on any and all topics.

Under Article V of the Constitution, Congress could call for such a convention without the concurrence of the president. Under most proposals, each state would have as many delegates to the convention as it has representatives and senators in Congress. Finally—a crucial point—the convention would be limited to

WE THE PEOPLE

Gregory Watson and the Twenty-seventh Amendment

In March 1982, Gregory Watson, a student at the University of Texas writing a paper on the Equal Rights Amendment, came across an amendment proposed in 1789 as part of the Bill of Rights that would prohibit a pay raise for members of Congress until the intervention of an election for members of the House. He found that only 6 of the original 13 states had ratified it, and that during the intervening years only 3 more states had done so.

Watson decided to start a ratification movement. He got some publicity for his efforts and, with the help of Texas Republican State Representative Don Mielke, persuaded 6 more state legislatures to ratify this long-forgotten proposed amendment. (By the way, Watson got only a C on his paper, although he is credited with influencing 26 state legislatures to ratify the Twenty-seventh Amendment.)*

After members of Congress tried unsuccessfully in 1989 to avoid public anger by delegating their decision to increase their own salaries to an independent commission, anti-Congress sentiment began to grow, and the ratification movement picked up steam. On May 7, 1992, the Michigan legislature became the thirty-eighth state to ratify the amendment.

The first reaction of some congressional leaders was to question this action because the Supreme Court had made it clear that amendments must be ratified within a "reasonable time." However, when members of Congress realized that the issue could be used against them in the next election, they declared the Twenty-seventh Amendment to be "valid as part of the Constitution of the United States." The vote was 99 to 0 in the Senate, 414 to 3 in the House.

*Ruth Ann Strickland, "The Twenty-seventh Amendment and Constitutional Change by Stealth," *P.S.: Political Science and Politics* (December 1993), p. 720.

considering only the subject specified in the state legislative petitions and described in the congressional call for the convention. Scholars are divided, however, on whether Congress has the authority to limit what a constitutional convention might propose.[21]

Ratifying Amendments

After an amendment has been proposed, it must be ratified by the states. Again, two methods are provided by the Constitution: approval by the legislatures in three-fourths of the states or approval by specially called ratifying conventions in three-fourths of the states (see Figure 2–3). Congress determines which method is used. All amendments except one—the Twenty-first (to repeal the Eighteenth, the Prohibition Amendment)—have been submitted to the state legislatures for ratification.

Seven state constitutions specify that their state legislatures must ratify a proposed amendment to the U.S. Constitution by majorities of three-fifths or two-thirds of each chamber. Although a state legislature may change its mind and ratify an amendment after it has voted against ratification, the weight of opinion is that once a state has ratified an amendment, it cannot "unratify" it.[22]

The Supreme Court has said that ratification must take place within a "reasonable time." When Congress proclaims an amendment to be part of

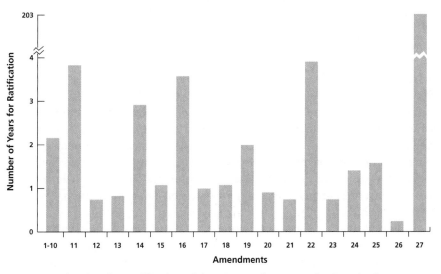

FIGURE 2-3 The Time for Ratification of the 27 Amendments to the Constitution

the Constitution, it must decide whether the amendment has been ratified within a reasonable time so that it is "sufficiently contemporaneous to reflect the will of the people."[23] However, Congress approved ratification of the Twenty-seventh Amendment, which had been before the nation for almost 203 years, so there seems to be no limit to what it will consider to be a "reasonable time." Because of the experience with the Twenty-seventh Amendment, Congress will probably continue the current practice of stipulating in the text of a proposed amendment that the necessary number of states must ratify it within seven years from the date of submission by Congress. In fact, ratification ordinarily takes place rather quickly.[24]

Ratification Politics

The failure of the Equal Rights Amendment to be ratified provides a vivid example of the pitfalls of ratification. First introduced in 1923 and frequently thereafter, the Equal Rights Amendment (ERA) did not get much support until the 1960s. An influential book by Betty Friedan, *The Feminine Mystique* (1963), challenged stereotypes about the role of women. The National Organization for Women (NOW), formed in 1966, made passage of ERA its central mission. By the 1970s the ERA had overwhelming support in both houses of Congress and in both national party platforms; not until 1980 did one party (the Republican) adopt a stance of neutrality. Every president from Harry Truman to Ronald Reagan, and many of their wives, endorsed the amendment. More than 450 organizations with a total membership of more than 50 million were on record in support of the ERA.[25]

Soon after passage of the amendment by Congress in 1972 and submission to the states, many legislatures ratified it quickly—sometimes without hearings—and by overwhelming majorities. By the end of 1972, 22 states had ratified the amendment, and it appeared that the ERA would soon become part of the Constitution.[26] Then the opposition organized under the articulate leadership of Phyllis Schlafly, a prominent spokesperson for conservative causes, and the ERA became controversial.

Opponents argued that "women would not only be subject to the military draft but also assigned to combat duty. Full-time housewives and mothers would be forced to join the labor force. Further, women would no longer enjoy existing advantages under state domestic relations codes and under labor law."[27] The ERA also became embroiled in the controversy over abortion. Many opponents contended that its ratification would jeopardize the power of states and Congress to regulate abortion and would compel public funding of abortions.[28]

After the ERA became controversial, state legislatures held lengthy hearings, and floor debates became heated. Legislators hid behind parliamentary procedures and avoided making a decision for as long as possible. Opposition to ratification arose chiefly in the same cluster of southern states that had opposed ratification of the Nineteenth Amendment, which gave women the vote. As the opposition grew more active, proponents redoubled their efforts.

In the autumn of 1978 it appeared that the ERA would fall three short of the necessary number of ratifying states before the expiration of the seven-year limit on March 22, 1979. After an extended debate, and after voting down provisions that would have authorized state legislatures to change their minds and rescind prior ratification, Congress, by a simple majority vote, extended the time limit until June 30, 1982. Nonetheless, by the final deadline the amendment was still three states short.

The framers intended that amending the Constitution should be difficult. The ERA ratification battle demonstrated how well they planned.

The Equal Rights Amendment

Proposed March 22, 1972. Died June 30, 1982, three state legislatures short of the thirty-eight needed for ratification.

Section 1. Equality of rights under the law shall not be denied or abridged by the United States or by any State on account of sex.

Section 2. The Congress shall have power to enforce, by appropriate legislation, the provisions of this article.

Section 3. This amendment shall take effect two years after the date of ratification.

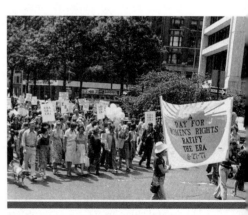

People came from every state of the union to march in support of passage of the Equal Rights Amendment.

POLITICS ONLINE

What's Happening to the Constitution?

For obvious reasons, students and teachers of American government tend to focus on the 27 amendments that have been ratified and incorporated into our constitutional framework. Aside from a few notable exceptions—like the Equal Rights Amendment (ERA), a balanced-budget amendment, or a right-to-life amendment, we hear little about proposed changes that failed to qualify or are now under consideration.

The topics of some of these unsuccessful amendments can inform us about moods and trends that have shaped American politics. We have rejected amendments limiting the size of the House of Representatives, prohibiting U.S. citizens from receiving gifts or titles from foreign powers, and allowing Congress to regulate child labor. Within the last decade, Congress has entertained amendment proposals ranging from establishing the right to a home, to lowering the voting age to 16 to establishing a new method for amending the Constitution. To review a list of proposed constitutional amendments, visit:

www.usconstitution.net/constam.html

As you consider the list of pending or unsuccessful amendments, ask yourself how our government would be different if they had been adopted. Of the amendments under consideration now, are there any you strongly support or oppose? If so, you might look into how you can become involved in the ratification process.

SUMMARY

1. Our Constitution both grants and limits powers. The framers established a government by the people. Yet the framers were suspicious of people, especially of those having political power, so they separated and distributed the powers of the newly created national government in a variety of ways.

2. The framers were also concerned to create a national government strong enough to solve national problems. Thus they gave the national government substantial grants of power, but these grants were made with such broad strokes that it has been possible for the constitutional system to remain flexible and adapt to changing conditions.

3. Judicial review is the power of the courts to strike down acts of Congress, the executive branch, and the states as unconstitutional. It is one of the unique features of the U.S. constitutional system.

4. The constitutional system has been modified over time, adapting to new conditions through congressional elaboration, presidential practices, custom and usage, and judicial interpretation.

5. Although adaptable, the Constitution itself needs to be altered from time to time, and the framers provided a procedure for its amendment. An amendment must be both proposed and ratified: proposed by either a two-thirds vote in each chamber of Congress or by a national convention called by Congress on petition of the legislatures in two-thirds of the states; ratified either by the legislatures in three-fourths of the states or by specially called ratifying conventions in three-fourths of the states.

6. The Constitution has been formally amended 27 times. The usual method has been proposal by a two-thirds vote in both houses of Congress and ratification by the legislatures in three-fourths of the states.

KEY TERMS

natural law 26
separation of powers 26
checks and balances 27
divided government 28

direct primary 29
initiative 29
referendum 29
recall 29

judicial review 30
writ of mandamus 34
impeachment 34
executive order 35

executive privilege 35
impoundment 35

FURTHER READING

BRUCE A. ACKERMAN, *We the People* (Harvard University Press, Belknap Press, 1993).

LANCE BANNING, *The Sacred Fire of Liberty: James Madison and the Founding of the Federal Republic* (Cornell University Press, 1995).

RICHARD B. BERNSTEIN, *Amending America: If We Love the Constitution So Much Why Do We Keep Trying to Change It?* (Time, 1993).

JAMES BRYCE, *The American Commonwealth* (Macmillan, 1889), vols. 1 and 2.

JAMES MACGREGOR BURNS, *The Vineyard of Liberty* (Knopf, 1982).

GERHARD CASPER, *Separation Powers: Essays on the Founding Period* (Harvard University Press, 1997).

ROBERT LOWRY CLINTON, *"Marbury v. Madison" and Judicial Review* (University Press of Kansas, 1989).

NEIL H. COGAN, *The Complete Bill of Rights: The Drafts, Debates, Sources, and Origins* (Oxford University Press, 1997).

LOUIS FISHER, *Constitutional Conflicts Between Congress and the President*, 4th ed. (University Press of Kansas, 1997).

MICHAEL KAMMEN, *A Machine That Would Go of Itself: The Constitution in American Culture* (Alfred A. Knopf, 1986).

BARBARA B. KNIGHT, *Separation of Powers in the American Political System* (George Mason University Press, 1989).

PHILIP B. KURLAND AND RALPH LERNER, *The Founders' Constitution*, 5 vols. (University of Chicago Press, 1987).

DAVID E. KYVIG, *Explicit and Authentic Acts: Amending the U.S. Constitution, 1776–1995* (University Press of Kansas, 1996).

LIBRARY OF CONGRESS, CONGRESSIONAL RESEARCH SERVICE, *The Constitution of the United States of America: Analysis and Interpretation*, Senate Document 100-9 (U.S. Government Printing Office, 1991). Updated on the Web at http://www.findlaw.com/case_code

J. W. PELTASON AND SUE DAVIS, *Understanding the Constitution*, 15th ed. (Harcourt College Division, 2000).

WILLIAM H. REHNQUIST, *Grand Inquests: The Historic Impeachments of Justice Samuel Chase and President Andrew Johnson* (Morrow, 1992).

JOHN R. VILE, *Encyclopedia of Constitutional Amendments, Proposed Amendments, and Amending Issues, 1789–1995* (ABC-CLIO, 1996).

On Reading the Constitution

More than two hundred years after its ratification, our Constitution remains the operating charter of our republic. It is neither self-explanatory nor a comprehensive description of our constitutional rules. Still, it remains the starting point. Many Americans who swear by the Constitution have never read it seriously, although copies can be found in the back of most American government and American history textbooks.

Justice Hugo Black, who served on the Supreme Court for 34 years, kept a copy of the Constitution with him at all times. He read it often. Reading the Constitution would be a good way for you to begin (and then reread again to end) your study of the government of the United States. Thus, we have included a copy of it at this point in the book. Please read it carefully.

The Constitution of the United States

The Preamble

We the People of the United States, in Order to form a more perfect Union, establish Justice, insure domestic Tranquility, provide for the common defense, promote the general Welfare, and secure the Blessings of Liberty to ourselves and our Posterity, do ordain and establish this Constitution for the United States of America.

Article I—The Legislative Article

Legislative Power

Section 1   All legislative Powers herein granted shall be vested in a Congress of the United States, which shall consist of a Senate and House of Representatives.

House of Representatives: Composition; Qualifications; Apportionment; Impeachment Power

Section 2   The House of Representatives shall be composed of Members chosen every second Year by the People of the several States, and the Electors in each State shall have the Qualifications requisite for Electors of the most numerous Branch of the State Legislature.

No Person shall be a Representative who shall not have attained to the Age of twenty five Years, and been seven Years a Citizen of the United States, and who shall not, when elected, be an Inhabitant of that State in which he shall be chosen.

Representatives and direct Taxes[1] shall be apportioned among the several States which may be included within this Union, according to their respective Numbers, *which shall be determined by adding to the whole Number of free Persons, including those bound to Service for a Term of Years, and excluding Indians not taxed, three fifths of all other Persons.*[2] The actual Enumeration shall be made within three Years after the first Meeting of the Congress of the United States, and within every subsequent Term of ten Years, in such Manner as they shall by Law direct. The Number of Representatives shall not exceed one for every thirty Thousand, but each State shall have at least one Representative; and until each enumeration shall be made, the State of New Hampshire shall be entitled to chuse three, Massachusetts eight, Rhode-Island and Providence Plantations one, Connecticut five, New-York six, New Jersey four, Pennsylvania eight, Delaware one, Maryland six, Virginia ten, North Carolina five, South Carolina five, and Georgia three.

When vacancies happen in the Representation from any State, the Executive Authority thereof shall issue Writs of Election to fill such Vacancies.

The House of Representatives shall chuse their Speaker and other Officers; and shall have the sole Power of Impeachment.

Senate Composition: Qualifications, Impeachment Trials

Section 3   The Senate of the United States shall be composed of two Senators from each State, *chosen by the Legislature thereof,*[3] for six Years; and each Senator shall have one Vote.

Immediately after they shall be assembled in Consequence of the first Election, they shall be divided as equally as may be into three Classes. The Seats of the Senators of the first Class shall be vacated at the Expiration of the second Year, of the second Class at the Expiration of the fourth Year, and of the third Class at the Expiration of the sixth Year, so that one third may be chosen every second Year; *and if Vacancies happen by Resignation, or otherwise, during the Recess of the Legislature of any State, the Executive thereof may make temporary Appointments until the next Meeting of the Legislature, which shall then fill such Vacancies.*[4]

No person shall be a Senator who shall not have attained to the Age of thirty Years, and been nine Years a Citizen of the United States, and who shall not, when elected, be an inhabitant of that State for which he shall be chosen.

The Vice President of the United States shall be President of the Senate, but shall have no Vote, unless they be equally divided.

The Senate shall chuse their other Officers, and also a President pro tempore, in the Absence of the Vice President, or when he shall exercise the Office of President of the United States.

The Senate shall have the sole Power to try all Impeachments. When sitting for that Purpose, they shall be on Oath or Affirmation. When the President of the United States is tried, the Chief Justice shall preside: And no Person shall be convicted without the Concurrence of two thirds of the Members present.

Judgment in Cases of Impeachment shall not extend further than to removal from Office, and disqualification to hold and enjoy any Office of honor, Trust or Profit under the United States; but the Party convicted shall nevertheless be liable and subject to Indictment, Trial, Judgment and Punishment, according to law.

Congressional Elections: Times, Places, Manner

Section 4   The Times, Places and Manner of holding Elections for Senators and Representatives, shall be prescribed in each State by the Legislature thereof; but the Congress may at any time by Law make or alter such Regulations, except as to the Places of chusing Senators.

The Congress shall assemble at least once in every Year, *and such Meeting shall be on the first Monday in December, unless they shall by Law appoint a different Day.*[5]

---

[1]Modified by the 16th Amendment
[2]Replaced by Section 2, 14th Amendment

[3]Repealed by the 17th Amendment
[4]Modified by the 17th Amendment
[5]Changed by the 20th Amendment

Powers and Duties of the Houses

Section 5   Each House shall be the Judge of the Elections, Returns and Qualifications of its own Members, and a Majority of each shall constitute a Quorum to do Business; but a smaller Number may adjourn from day to day, and may be authorized to compel the Attendance of absent Members, in such Manner, and under the Penalties as each House may provide.

Each House may determine the Rules of its Proceedings, punish its Members for disorderly Behaviour, and, with the Concurrence of two thirds, expel a Member.

Each House shall keep a Journal of its Proceedings, and from time to time publish the same, excepting such Parts as may in their Judgment require Secrecy; and the Yeas and Nays of the Members of either House on any question shall, at the Desire of one fifth of those Present, be entered on the Journal.

Neither House, during the Session of Congress, shall, without the Consent of the other, adjourn for more than three days, nor to any other place than that in which the two Houses shall be sitting.

Rights of Members

Section 6   The Senators and Representatives shall receive a Compensation for their Services, to be ascertained by Law, and paid out of the Treasury of the United States. They shall in all Cases, except Treason, Felony and Breach of the Peace, be privileged from Arrest during their Attendance at the Session of their respective Houses, and in going to and returning from the same; and for any Speech or Debate in either House, they shall not be questioned in any other Place.

No Senator or Representative, shall, during the time for which he was elected, be appointed to any civil Office under the Authority of the United States, which shall have been created, or the Emoluments whereof shall have been encreased during such time; and no Person holding any Office under the United States, shall be a Member of either House during his Continuance in Office.

Legislative Powers: Bills and Resolutions

Section 7   All Bills for raising Revenue shall originate in the House of Representatives; but the Senate may propose or concur with Amendments as on other Bills.

Every Bill which shall have passed the House of Representatives and the Senate, shall, before it becomes a Law, be presented to the President of the United States; if he approve he shall sign it, but if not he shall return it, with his Objections to that House in which it shall have originated, who shall enter the Objections at large on their Journal, and proceed to reconsider it. If after such Reconsideration two thirds of that House shall agree to pass the Bill, it shall be sent, together with the Objections, to the other House, by which it shall likewise be reconsidered, and if approved by two thirds of that House, it shall become a Law. But in all such Cases the Votes of both Houses shall be determined by yeas and Nays, and the Names of the Persons voting for and against the Bill shall be entered on the Journal of each House respectively. If any Bill shall not be returned by the President within ten Days (Sundays excepted) after it shall have been presented to him, the Same shall be a Law, in like Manner as if he had signed it, unless the Congress by their Adjournment prevent its Return, in which Case it shall not be a Law.

Every Order, Resolution, or Vote to which the Concurrence of the Senate and House of Representatives may be necessary (except on a question of Adjournment) shall be presented to the President of the United States; and before the Same shall take Effect, shall be approved by him, or being disapproved by him, shall be repassed by two thirds of the Senate and House of Representatives, according to the Rules and Limitations prescribed in the Case of a Bill.

Powers of Congress

Section 8   The Congress shall have Power To lay and collect Taxes, Duties, Imposts and Excises, to pay the Debts and provide for the common Defence and general Welfare of the United States; but all Duties, Imposts and Excises shall be uniform throughout the United States.

To borrow Money on the Credit of the United States;

To regulate Commerce with foreign Nations, and among the several States, and with the Indian Tribes;

To establish an uniform Rule of Naturalization, and uniform Laws on the subject of Bankruptcies throughout the United States;

To coin Money, regulate the Value thereof, and of foreign Coin, and fix the Standard of Weights and Measures;

To provide for the Punishment of counterfeiting the Securities and current Coin of the United States;

To establish Post Offices and post Roads;

To promote the Progress of Science and useful Arts, by securing for limited Times to Authors and Inventors the exclusive Right to their respective Writings and Discoveries;

To constitute Tribunals inferior to the supreme Court;

To define and punish Piracies and Felonies committed on the high Seas, and Offences against the Law of Nations;

To declare War, grant Letters of Marque and Reprisal, and make Rules concerning Captures on Land and Water;

To raise and support Armies, but no Appropriation of Money to that Use shall be for a longer Term than two Years;

To provide and maintain a Navy;

To make Rules for the Government and Regulation of the land and naval Forces;

To provide for calling for the Militia to execute the Laws of the Union, suppress Insurrections and repel Invasions;

To provide for organizing, arming, and disciplining, the Militia, and for governing such Part of them as may be employed in the Service of the United States, reserving to the States respectively, the Appointment of the Officers, and the Authority of training the Militia according to the discipline prescribed by Congress;

To exercise exclusive Legislation in all Cases whatsoever, over such District (not exceeding ten Miles square) as may, by Cession of particular States, and the Acceptance of Congress, become the Seat of the Government of the United States, and to exercise like Authority over all Places purchased by the Consent of the Legislature of the State in which the Same shall be, for the Erection of Forts, Magazines, Arsenals, dock-Yards, and other needful Buildings;—And

To make all Laws which shall be necessary and proper for carrying into Execution the foregoing Powers, and all other Powers vested by this Constitution in the Government of the United States, or in any Department or Officer thereof.

Powers Denied to Congress

Section 9   The Migration of Importation of such Persons as any of the States now existing shall think proper to admit, shall not be prohibited by the Congress prior to the Year one thousand eight hundred and eight, but a Tax or Duty may be imposed on such Importation, not exceeding ten dollars for each Person.

The privilege of the Writ of Habeas Corpus shall not be suspended, unless when in Cases of Rebellion or Invasion the public Safety may require it.

No Bill of Attainder or ex post facto Laws shall be passed.

No Capitation, or other direct, Tax shall be laid, unless in Proportion to the Census or Enumeration herein before directed to be taken.[6]

No Tax or Duty shall be laid on Articles exported from any State.

No Preference shall be given by any Regulation of Commerce or Revenue to the Ports of one State over those of another; nor shall Vessels bound to, or from, one State, be obliged to enter, clear, or pay Duties in another.

---

[6]Modified by the 16th Amendment

No Money shall be drawn from the Treasury, but in Consequence of Appropriations made by Law; and a regular Statement and Account of the Receipts and Expenditures of all public Money shall be published from time to time.

No Title of Nobility shall be granted by the United States; And no Person holding any Office of Profit or Trust under them, shall, without the Consent of Congress, accept of any present, Emolument, Office, or Title, of any kind whatever, from any King, Prince, or foreign State.

Powers Denied to the States

Section 10 No State shall enter into any Treaty, Alliance, or Confederation; grant Letters of Marque and Reprisal; coin Money; emit Bills of Credit; make any Thing but gold and silver Coin a Tender in Payment of Debts; pass any Bill of Attainder, ex post facto Law, or Law impairing the Obligation of Contracts, or grant any Title of Nobility.

No State shall, without the Consent of the Congress, lay any Imposts or Duties on Imports or Exports, except what may be absolutely necessary for executing its inspection Laws: and the net Produce of all Duties and Imposts, laid by any State on Imports or Exports, shall be for the Use of the Treasury of the United States; and all such Laws shall be subject to the Revision and Controul of the Congress.

No State shall, without the Consent of Congress, lay any Duty of Tonnage, keep Troops, or Ships of War in time of Peace, enter into any Agreement or Compact with another State, or with a foreign Power, or engage in War, unless actually invaded, or in such imminent Danger as will not admit of Delay.

ARTICLE II—THE EXECUTIVE ARTICLE

Nature and Scope of Presidential Power

Section 1 The executive Power shall be vested in a President of the United States of America. He shall hold his Office during the Term of four Years and, together with the Vice President, chosen for the same Term, be elected as follows:

Each State shall appoint, in such Manner as the Legislature thereof may direct, a Number of Electors, equal to the whole Number of Senators and Representatives to which the State may be entitled in the Congress: but no Senator or Representative, or Person holding an Office of Trust or Profit under the United States, shall be appointed an Elector.

The Electors shall meet in their respective States, and vote by Ballot for two Persons, of whom one at least shall not be an Inhabitant of the same State with themselves. And they shall make a List of all the Persons voted for, and of the Number of Votes for each; which List they shall sign and certify, and transmit sealed to the Seat of the Government of the United States, directed to the President of the Senate. The President of the Senate shall, in the Presence of the Senate and House of Representatives, open all the Certificates, and the Votes shall then be counted. The Person having the greatest Number of Votes shall be the President, if such Number be a Majority of the whole Number of Electors appointed; and if there be more than one who have such Majority and have an equal Number of Votes, then the House of Representatives shall immediately chuse by Ballot one of them for President; and if no person have a Majority, then from the five highest on the List the said House shall in like Manner chuse the President. But in chusing the President, the Votes shall be taken by States, the Representation from each State having one Vote; A quorum for this Purpose shall consist of a Member or Members from two thirds of the States, and a Majority of all the States shall be necessary to a Choice. In every Case, after the Choice of the President, the person having the greatest Number of Votes of the Electors shall be the Vice President. But if there should remain two or more who have equal Vote, the Senate shall chuse from them by Ballot the Vice President.[7]

The Congress may determine the Time of chusing the Electors, and the Day on which they shall give their Votes; which Day shall be the same throughout the United States.

No Person except a natural born Citizen, or a Citizen of the United States, at the time of the Adoption of this Constitution, shall be eligible to the Office of President; neither shall any Person be eligible to that Office who shall not have attained to the Age of thirty five Years, and been fourteen Years a Resident within the United States.

In Case of the Removal of the President from Office, or of his Death, Resignation, or Inability to discharge the Powers and Duties of the said Office, the same shall devolve on the Vice President, and the Congress may by Law provide for the Case of Removal, Death, Resignation, or Inability, both of the President and Vice President, declaring what Officer shall then act as President, and such Officer shall act accordingly, until the Disability be removed, or a President shall be elected.[8]

The President shall, at stated Times, receive for his Services, a Compensation, which shall neither be encreased nor diminished during the Period of which he shall have been elected, and he shall not receive within that Period any other Emolument from the United States, or any of them.

Before he enter on the Execution of his Office, he shall take the following Oath or Affirmation:—"I do solemnly swear (or affirm) that I will faithfully execute the Office of President of the United States, and will to the best of my Ability, preserve, protect and defend the Constitution of the United States."

Powers and Duties of the President

Section 2 The President shall be the Commander in Chief of the Army and Navy of the United States, and of the Militia of the several States, when called into the actual Service of the United States, he may require the Opinion, in writing, of the principal Officer in each of the executive Departments, upon any Subject relating to the Duties of their respective Offices, and he shall have the Power to grant Reprieves and Pardons for Offences against the United States, except in Cases of Impeachment.

He shall have Power, by and with the Advice and Consent of the Senate to make Treaties, provided two thirds of the Senators present concur; and he shall nominate, and by and with the Advice and Consent of the Senate, shall appoint Ambassadors, other public Ministers and Consuls, Judges of the supreme Court, and all other Officers of the United States, whose Appointments are not herein otherwise provided for, and which shall be established by Law: but the Congress may by Law vest the Appointment of such inferior Officers, as they think proper, in the President alone, in the Courts of Law, or in the Heads of Departments.

The President shall have Power to fill up all Vacancies that may happen during the Recess of the Senate, by granting Commissions which shall expire at the End of their next Session.

Section 3 He shall from time to time give to the Congress Information of the State of the Union, and recommend to their Consideration such Measures as he shall judge necessary and expedient; he may, on extraordinary Occasions, convene both Houses, or either of them, and in Case of Disagreement between them, with Respect to the Time of Adjournment, he may adjourn them to such Time as he shall think proper; he shall receive Ambassadors and other public Ministers; he shall take Care that the Laws be faithfully executed, and shall Commission all the Officers of the United States.

Section 4 The President, Vice President and all civil Officers of the United States, shall be removed from Office on Impeachment for, and Conviction of, Treason, Bribery, or other High Crimes and Misdemeanors.

ARTICLE III—THE JUDICIAL ARTICLE

Judicial Power, Courts, Judges

Section 1 The judicial Power of the United States, shall be vested in one supreme Court, and in such inferior Courts as the Congress may from time to time ordain and establish. The Judges, both the supreme and inferior Courts,

---

[7]Changed by the 12th and 20th Amendments

[8]Modified by the 25th Amendment

shall hold their Offices during good Behaviour, and shall, at stated Times, receive for their Services, a Compensation, which shall not be diminished during their Continuance in Office.

Jurisdiction

Section 2   The judicial Power shall extend to all Cases, in Law and Equity, arising under this Constitution, the Laws of the United States, and Treaties made, or which shall be made, under their Authority;—to all Cases affecting Ambassadors, other public Ministers and Consuls;—to all Cases of admiralty and maritime Jurisdiction;—to Controversies to which the United States shall be a Party;—to Controversies between two or more States; *between a State and Citizens of another State;*[9]—between Citizens of different States;—between Citizens of the same State claiming Lands under Grants of different States, and between a State, or the Citizens thereof, and foreign States, Citizens, or Subjects.

In all Cases affecting Ambassadors, other public Ministers and Consuls, and those in which a State shall be Party, the supreme Court shall have original Jurisdiction. In all the other Cases before mentioned, the supreme Court shall have appellate Jurisdiction, both as to Law and Fact, with such Exceptions, and under such Regulations as Congress shall make.

The Trial of all Crimes, except in Cases of Impeachment, shall be by Jury; and such Trial shall be held in the State where the said Crimes shall have been committed; but when not committed within any State, the Trial shall be at such Place or Places as the Congress may by Law have directed.

Treason

Section 3   Treason against the United States, shall consist only in levying War against them, or in adhering to their Enemies, giving them Aid and Comfort. No Persons shall be convicted of Treason unless on the Testimony of two Witnesses to the same overt Act, or on Confession in open Court.

The Congress shall have Power to declare the Punishment of Treason, but no Attainder of Treason shall work Corruption of Blood, or Forfeiture except during the Life of the Person attainted.

ARTICLE IV—INTERSTATE RELATIONS

Full Faith and Credit Clause

Section 1   Full Faith and Credit shall be given in each State to the public Acts, Records, and judicial Proceedings of every other State. And the Congress may by general Laws prescribe the Manner in which such Acts, Records and Proceedings shall be proved, and the Effect thereof.

Privileges and Immunities; Interstate Extradition

Section 2   The Citizens of each State shall be entitled to all Privileges and Immunities of Citizens in the several States.

A person charged in any State with Treason, Felony or other Crime, who shall flee from Justice, and be found in another State, shall on Demand of the executive Authority of the State from which he fled, be delivered up, to be removed to the State having jurisdiction of the Crime.

No person held to Service or Labour in one State, under the Laws thereof, escaping into another, shall, in Consequence of any Law or Regulation therein, be discharged from such Service or Labour, but shall be delivered up on Claim of the Party to whom such Service or Labour may be due.[10]

Admission of States

Section 3   New States may be admitted by the Congress into this Union; but no new State shall be formed or erected within the Jurisdiction of any other State; nor any State to be formed by the Junction of two or more States, or Parts of States, without the Consent of the Legislatures of the States concerned as well as of the Congress.

The Congress shall have Power to dispose of and make all needful Rules and Regulations respecting the Territory or other Property belonging to the United States; and nothing in this Constitution shall be so construed as to Prejudice any Claims of the United States, or of any particular State.

Republican Form of Government

Section 4   The United States shall guarantee to every State in this Union a Republican Form of Government, and shall protect each of them against Invasion; and on Application of the Legislature, or of the Executive (when the Legislature cannot be convened) against domestic Violence.

ARTICLE V—THE AMENDING POWER

The Congress, whenever two thirds of both Houses shall deem it necessary, shall propose Amendments to this Constitution, or, on the Application of the Legislatures of two thirds of several States, shall call a Convention for proposing Amendments, which, in either Case, shall be valid to all Intents and Purposes, as Part of this Constitution, when ratified by the Legislatures of three fourths of the several States, or by Conventions in three fourths thereof, as the one or the other Mode of Ratification may be proposed by the Congress; Provided that no Amendment which may be made prior to the Year One thousand eight hundred and eight shall in any Manner affect the first and fourth Clauses in the Ninth Section of the first Article; and that no State, without its Consent, shall be deprived of its equal Suffrage in the Senate.

ARTICLE VI—THE SUPREMACY ARTICLE

All Debts contracted and Engagements entered into, before the Adoption of this Constitution, shall be as valid against the United States under the Constitution, as under the Confederation.

This Constitution, and the Laws of the United States which shall be made in Pursuance thereof; and all Treaties made, or which shall be made, under the Authority of the United States, shall be the supreme Law of the Land; and the Judges in every State shall be bound thereby, any Thing in the Constitution or Laws of any State to the Contrary notwithstanding.

The Senators and Representatives before mentioned, and the Members of the several State Legislatures, and all executive and judicial Officers, both of the United States and of the several States, shall be bound by Oath or Affirmation, to support this Constitution; but no religious Test shall ever be required as a Qualification to any Office or public Trust under the United States.

ARTICLE VII—RATIFICATION

The Ratification of the Conventions of nine States, shall be sufficient for the Establishment of this Constitution between the States so ratifying the Same.

Done in Convention by the Unanimous Consent of the States present the Seventeenth Day of September in the Year of our Lord one thousand seven hundred and Eighty seven and of the Independence of the United States of America the Twelfth *In Witness whereof We have hereunto subscribed our Names.*

AMENDMENTS

The Bill of Rights

[The first ten amendments were ratified on December 15, 1791, and form what is known as the "Bill of Rights."]

AMENDMENT 1—RELIGION, SPEECH, ASSEMBLY, AND POLITICS

Congress shall make no law respecting an establishment of religion, or prohibiting the free exercise thereof; or abridging the freedom of speech, or of the press; or the right of the people peaceably to assemble, and to petition the government for a redress of grievances.

---

[9]Modified by the 11th Amendment
[10]Repealed by the 13th Amendment

AMENDMENT 2—MILITIA AND THE RIGHT TO BEAR ARMS

A well regulated Militia, being necessary to the security of a free State, the right of the people to keep and bear Arms, shall not be infringed.

AMENDMENT 3—QUARTERING OF SOLDIERS

No Soldier shall, in time of peace be quartered in any house, without the consent of the Owner, nor in time of war, but in manner to be prescribed by law.

AMENDMENT 4—SEARCHES AND SEIZURES

The right of the people to be secure in their persons, houses, papers, and effects, against unreasonable searches and seizures, shall not be violated, and no Warrants shall issue, but upon probable cause, supported by Oath or affirmation, and particularly describing the place to be searched, and the persons or things to be seized.

AMENDMENT 5—GRAND JURIES, SELF-INCRIMINATION, DOUBLE JEOPARDY, DUE PROCESS, AND EMINENT DOMAIN

No person shall be held to answer for a capital, or otherwise infamous crime, unless on a presentment or indictment of a Grand jury, except in cases arising in the land or naval forces, or in the Militia, when in actual service in time of War or public danger; nor shall any person be subject for the same offence to be twice put in jeopardy of life or limb; nor shall be compelled in any criminal case to be a witness against himself, nor be deprived of life, liberty, or property, without due process of law; nor shall private property be taken for public use, without just compensation.

AMENDMENT 6—CRIMINAL COURT PROCEDURES

In all criminal prosecutions, the accused shall enjoy the right to a speedy and public trial, by an impartial jury of the State and district wherein the crime shall have been committed, which district shall have been previously ascertained by law, and to be informed of the nature and cause of the accusation; to be confronted with the witnesses against him; to have compulsory process for obtaining Witnesses in his favor, and to have the Assistance of Counsel for his defense.

AMENDMENT 7—TRIAL BY JURY IN COMMON LAW CASES

In Suits at common law, where the value in controversy shall exceed twenty dollars, the right of trial by jury shall be preserved, and no fact tried by a jury shall be otherwise re-examined in any Court of the United States, than according to the rules of the common law.

AMENDMENT 8—BAIL, CRUEL AND UNUSUAL PUNISHMENT

Excessive bail shall not be required, nor excessive fines imposed, nor cruel and unusual punishments inflicted.

AMENDMENT 9—RIGHTS RETAINED BY THE PEOPLE

The enumeration in the Constitution, of certain rights, shall not be construed to deny or disparage others retained by the people.

AMENDMENT 10—RESERVED POWERS OF THE STATES

The powers not delegated to the United States by the Constitution, nor prohibited by it to the States, are reserved to the States respectively, or to the people.

AMENDMENT 11—SUITS AGAINST THE STATES
[Ratified February 7, 1795]

The Judicial power of the United States shall not be construed to extend to any suit in law or equity, commenced or prosecuted against one of the United States by Citizens of another State, or by Citizens or Subjects of any Foreign State.

AMENDMENT 12—ELECTION OF THE PRESIDENT
[Ratified June 15, 1804]

The Electors shall meet in their respective states, and vote by ballot for President and Vice-President, one of whom, at least, shall not be an inhabitant of the same state with themselves; they shall name in their ballots the person voted for as President, and in distinct ballots the person voted for as Vice-President, and they shall make distinct lists of all persons voted for as President, and of all persons voted for as Vice-President, and of the number of votes for each, which lists they shall sign and certify, and transmit sealed to the seat of the government of the United States, directed to the President of the Senate;—The President of the Senate shall, in presence of the Senate and House of Representatives, open all the certificates and the votes shall then be counted;—The person having the greatest number of votes for President, shall be the President, if such number be a majority of the whole number of Electors appointed; and if no person have such majority, then from the persons having the highest numbers not exceeding three on the list of those voted for as President, the House of Representatives shall choose immediately, by ballot, the President. But in choosing the President, the votes shall be taken by states, the representation from each state having one vote; a quorum for this purpose shall consist of a member or members from two-thirds of the states, and a majority of all states shall be necessary to a choice. And if the House of Representatives shall not choose a President whenever the right of choice shall devolve upon them, *before the fourth day of March next following*, then the Vice-President shall act as President, as in the case of the death or other constitutional disability of the President.[11] The person having the greatest number of votes as Vice-President, shall be the Vice-President, if such a number be a majority of the whole numbers of Electors appointed, and if no person have a majority, then from the two highest numbers on the list, the Senate shall choose the Vice-President; a quorum for the purpose shall consist of two-thirds of the whole number of Senators, and a majority of the whole number shall be necessary to a choice. But no person constitutionally ineligible to the office of President shall be eligible to that of Vice-President of the United States.

AMENDMENT 13—PROHIBITION OF SLAVERY
[Ratified December 6, 1865]

Section 1 Neither slavery nor involuntary servitude, except as a punishment for crime whereof the party shall have been duly convicted, shall exist within the United States, or any place subject to their jurisdiction.

Section 2 Congress shall have power to enforce this article by appropriate legislation.

AMENDMENT 14—CITIZENSHIP, DUE PROCESS, AND EQUAL PROTECTION OF THE LAWS
[Ratified July 9, 1868]

Section 1 All persons born or naturalized in the United States, and subject to the jurisdiction thereof, are citizens of the United States and of the State wherein they reside. No State shall make or enforce any law which shall abridge the privileges or immunities of citizens of the United States; nor shall

---

[11]Changed by the 20th Amendment

any State deprive any person of life, liberty, or property, without due process of law; nor deny to any person within its jurisdiction the equal protection of the laws.

Section 2 Representatives shall be apportioned among the several States according to their respective numbers, counting the whole number of persons in each State, excluding Indians not taxed. But when the right to vote at any election for the choice of electors for President and Vice President of the United States, Representatives in Congress, the Executive and Judicial officers of a State, or the members of the Legislature thereof, is denied to any of the male inhabitants of such State, being twenty-one[12] years of age, and citizens of the United States, or in any way abridged, except for participation in rebellion, or other crime, the basis of representation therein shall be reduced in the proportion which the number of such male citizens shall bear to the whole number of male citizens twenty-one years of age in such State.

Section 3 No person shall be a Senator or Representative in Congress, or elector of President and Vice President, or hold any office, civil or military, under the United States, or under any State, who, having previously taken an oath, as a member of Congress, or as an officer of the United States, or as a member of any State legislature, or as an executive or judicial officer of any State, to support the Constitution of the United States, shall have engaged in insurrection or rebellion against the same, or given aid or comfort to the enemies thereof. But Congress may by a vote of two-thirds of each House, remove such disability.

Section 4 The validity of the public debt of the United States, authorized by law, including debts incurred for payment of pensions and bounties for services in suppressing insurrection or rebellion, shall not be questioned. But neither the United States nor any State shall assume or pay any debt or obligation incurred in aid of insurrection or rebellion against the United States, or any claim for the loss or emancipation of any slave; but all such debts, obligations and claims shall be held illegal and void.

Section 5 The Congress shall have power to enforce, by appropriate legislation, the provisions of this article.

AMENDMENT 15—THE RIGHT TO VOTE
[Ratified February 3, 1870]

Section 1 The right of citizens of the United States to vote shall not be denied or abridged by the United States or by any State on account of race, color, or previous condition of servitude.

Section 2 The Congress shall have power to enforce this article by appropriate legislation.

AMENDMENT 16—INCOME TAXES
[Ratified February 3, 1913]

The Congress shall have power to lay and collect taxes on incomes, from whatever source derived, without apportionment among the several States, and without regard to any census or enumeration.

AMENDMENT 17—DIRECT ELECTION OF SENATORS
[Ratified April 8, 1913]

The Senate of the United States shall be composed of two Senators from each State, elected by the people thereof, for six years; and each Senator shall have one vote. The electors in each State shall have the qualifications requisite for electors of the most numerous branch of the State legislatures.

When vacancies happen in the representation of any State in the Senate, the executive authority of such State shall issue writs of election to fill such vacancies: *Provided*, That the Legislature of any State may empower the executive thereof to make temporary appointment until the people fill the vacancies by election as the legislature may direct.

This amendment shall not be so construed as to affect the election or term of any Senator chosen before it becomes valid as part of the Constitution.

AMENDMENT 18—PROHIBITION
[Ratified January 16, 1919. Repealed December 5, 1933 by Amendment 21]

Section 1 After one year from the ratification of this article the manufacture, sale, or transportation of intoxicating liquors within, the importation thereof into, or the exportation thereof from the United States and all territory subject to the jurisdiction thereof for beverage purposes is hereby prohibited.

Section 2 The Congress and the several states shall have concurrent power to enforce this article by appropriate legislation.

Section 3 This article shall be inoperative unless it shall have been ratified as an amendment to the Constitution by the legislatures of the several states, as provided in the Constitution, within seven years from the date of the submission hereof to the States by the Congress.[13]

AMENDMENT 19—FOR WOMEN'S SUFFRAGE
[Ratified August 18, 1920]

The right of the citizens of the United States to vote shall not be denied or abridged by the United States or by any State on account of sex.

Congress shall have power, by appropriate legislation, to enforce the provision of this article.

AMENDMENT 20—THE LAME DUCK AMENDMENT
[Ratified January 23, 1933]

Section 1 The terms of the President and Vice President shall end at noon on the 20th day of January, and the terms of the Senators and Representatives at noon on the 3rd day of January, of the years in which such terms would have ended if this article had not been ratified; and the terms of their successors shall then begin.

Section 2 The Congress shall assemble at least once in every year, and such meeting shall begin at noon on the 3rd day of January, unless they shall by law appoint a different day.

Section 3 If, at the time fixed for the beginning of the term of the President, the President elect shall have died, the Vice President elect shall become President. If a President shall not have been chosen before the time fixed for the beginning of his term, or if the President elect shall have failed to qualify, then the Vice President elect shall act as President until a President shall have qualified; and the Congress may by law provide for the case wherein neither a President elect nor a Vice President elect shall have qualified, declaring who shall then act as President, or the manner in which one who is to act shall be selected, and such person shall act accordingly until a President or Vice President shall have qualified.

Section 4 The Congress may by law provide for the case of the death of any of the persons from whom the House of Representatives may choose a President whenever the right of choice shall have developed upon them, and for the case of the death of any of the persons from whom the Senate may choose a Vice President whenever the right of choice shall have devolved upon them.

---

[12]Changed by the 26th Amendment

[13]Repealed by the 21st Amendment

Section 5 Sections 1 and 2 shall take effect on the 15th day of October following the ratification of this article.

Section 6 This article shall be inoperative unless it shall have been ratified as an amendment to the Constitution by the legislatures of three-fourths of the several States within seven years from the date of its submission.

AMENDMENT 21—REPEAL OF PROHIBITION
[Ratified December 5, 1933]

Section 1 The eighteenth article of amendment to the Constitution of the United States is hereby repealed.

Section 2 The transportation or importation into any State, Territory, or Possession of the United States for delivery or use therein of intoxicating liquors, in violation of the laws thereof, is hereby prohibited.

Section 3 This article shall be inoperative unless it shall have been ratified as an amendment to the Constitution by conventions in the several States, as provided in the Constitution, within seven years from the date of the submission hereof to the States by the Congress.

AMENDMENT 22—NUMBER OF PRESIDENTIAL TERMS
[Ratified February 27, 1951]

Section 1 No person shall be elected to the office of the President more than twice, and no person who has held the office of President, or acted as President, for more than two years of a term to which some other person was elected President shall be elected to the Office of the President more than once. But this Article shall not apply to any person holding the office of President when this article was proposed by the Congress, and shall not prevent any person who may be holding the office of President, or acting as President, during the term within which this Article becomes operative from holding the office of President or acting as President during the remainder of such term.

Section 2 This Article shall be inoperative unless it shall have been ratified as an amendment to the Constitution by the legislatures of three-fourths of the several states within seven years from the date of its submission to the States by the Congress.

AMENDMENT 23—PRESIDENTIAL ELECTORS FOR THE DISTRICT OF COLUMBIA
[Ratified March 29, 1961]

Section 1 The District constituting the seat of Government of the United States shall appoint in such manner as the Congress may direct:

A number of electors of President and Vice President equal to the whole number of Senators and Representatives in Congress to which the District would be entitled if it were a State, but in no event more than the least populous State; they shall be in addition to those appointed by the States, but they shall be considered, for the purposes of the election of President and Vice President, to be electors appointed by a State; and they shall meet in the District and perform such duties as provided by the twelfth article of amendment.

Section 2 The Congress shall have power to enforce this article by appropriate legislation.

AMENDMENT 24—THE ANTI-POLL TAX AMENDMENT
[Ratified January 23, 1964]

Section 1 The right of citizens of the United States to vote in any primary or other election for President or Vice President, for electors for President or Vice President, or for Senator or Representative in Congress, shall not be denied or abridged by the United States or any State by reason of failure to pay any poll tax or other tax.

Section 2 The Congress shall have power to enforce this article by appropriate legislation.

AMENDMENT 25—PRESIDENTIAL DISABILITY, VICE PRESIDENTIAL VACANCIES
[Ratified February 23, 1967]

Section 1 In case of the removal of the President from office or his death or resignation, the Vice President shall become President.

Section 2 Whenever there is a vacancy in the office of the Vice President, the President shall nominate a Vice President who shall take the office upon confirmation by a majority vote of both houses of Congress.

Section 3 Whenever the President transmits to the President pro tempore of the Senate and the Speaker of the House of Representatives his written declaration that he is unable to discharge the powers and duties of his office, and until he transmits to them a written declaration to the contrary, such powers and duties shall be discharged by the Vice President as Acting President.

Section 4 Whenever the Vice-President and a majority of either the principal officers of the executive departments, or of such other body as Congress may by law provide, transmit to the President pro tempore of the Senate and the Speaker of the House of Representatives their written declaration that the President is unable to discharge the powers and duties of his office, the Vice President shall immediately assume the powers and duties of the office as Acting President.

Thereafter, when the President transmits to the President pro tempore of the Senate and the Speaker of the House of Representatives his written declaration that no inability exists, he shall resume the powers and duties of his office unless the Vice President and a majority of either the principal officers of the executive departments, or of such other body as Congress may by law provide, transmit within four days to the President pro tempore of the Senate and the Speaker of the House of Representatives their written declaration that the President is unable to discharge the powers and duties of his office. Thereupon Congress shall decide the issue, assembling within forty-eight hours for that purpose if not in session. If the Congress, within twenty-one days after receipt of the latter written declaration, or, if Congress is not in session, within twenty-one days after Congress is required to assemble, determines by two-thirds vote of both houses that the President is unable to discharge the powers and duties of his office, the Vice President shall continue to discharge the same as Acting President; otherwise, the President shall resume the powers and duties of his office.

AMENDMENT 26—EIGHTEEN-YEAR-OLD VOTE
[Ratified July 1, 1971]

Section 1 The right of citizens of the United States, who are eighteen years of age, or older, to vote shall not be denied or abridged by the United States or by any State on account of age.

Section 2 The Congress shall have power to enforce this article by appropriate legislation.

AMENDMENT 27—CONGRESSIONAL SALARIES
[Ratified May 7, 1992]

No law, varying the compensation for the services of the Senators and Representatives, shall take effect, until an election of Representatives shall be intervened.

3

AMERICAN FEDERALISM

S INCE THE FOUNDING OF THE REPUBLIC, THE RELATIONSHIP OF THE NATIONAL GOVERNMENT TO THE STATES HAS BEEN DEBATED.[1] IN 1787 THE FEDERALISTS defended the creation of a strong national government, whereas the Antifederalists warned that a strong national government would overshadow the states. More recently, Republicans have led the charge against big government, urging the return of many functions to the states—a **devolution revolution**.[2] They had some success when President Bill Clinton agreed to turn over more responsibilities for welfare to the states and to put the brakes on the growth of the national government.

Federalism has recently emerged as a hot topic in other countries as well. Within the European Union, member states have given up some authority over economic regulation and have agreed to a common currency (the euro).[3] The Association of South East Asian Nations (ASEAN) is another example of countries joining together to compete effectively in the global economy. In contrast, the former Soviet Union—a highly centralized government that was federal in name only—broke apart into 15 independent nations. Now Russia (or more precisely, the Russian Federation) is redefining relationships with its 21 autonomous republics, conceding them more autonomy while trying to preserve its territorial integrity and economic power. The pressures of international economic competition are driving these developments.

Heightened interest in federalism also comes from demands for greater local self-governance for ethnic nationalities. The Canadian federal system strains under the demands of the French-speaking province of Quebec for special status and even independence. In the United Kingdom, devolution is occurring in Scotland and Wales, which have recently established their own parliaments. Belgium, Italy, and Spain are devolving powers from their central governments to regional governments. Central European nations have divided and subdivided over ethnic tensions, some of which have culminated in ethnic cleansing and war.

In contrast to these countries, the United States has had a relatively peaceful experience with the shifting balances of power under federalism. From the New Deal in the 1930s to today, there has been a drift of power and responsibility from the states to the national government. Although presidents from Richard Nixon to Bill Clinton slowed the growth of the national government, it was not until the late 1990s that the Republican-controlled Congress sought major reforms that heated the debate over federalism. As with welfare reform in 1996, Congress promoted decentralization in education with

CHAPTER MEDIA

 POLITICS ONLINE
Should Internet Sales Be Taxed?
www.prenhall.com/burns

the Educational Flexibility Partnership Demonstration Act of 1999, authorizing the secretary of education to grant states waivers from federal rules setting educational goals. Still, in spite of such moves toward decentralization, Congress continues to expand federal law by making federal crimes such offenses as car-jacking and church-burning, even though they are already state and local crimes.

After more than half a century, the Supreme Court is now placing some constraints on congressional powers in the name of federalism.[4] Like Congress, however, the Court's recent record on federalism is mixed. In spite of rulings in 1999 holding that Congress may not authorize individuals to sue states to enforce federal laws,[5] the Court ruled that state welfare programs may not restrict benefits to new residents to what they would have received in the states from which they moved[6] and that Congress may restrict states from selling drivers' personal information.[7]

devolution revolution
Movement beginning with the 1994 congressional elections to transfer functions and responsibilities from the national government to the states; for example, for providing welfare.

At the official opening of Scotland's parliament on July 1, 1999, Queen Elizabeth was presented with the Scottish crown. The 129-member assembly is Scotland's first parliament in nearly 300 years.

Debates over federalism resemble those over whether "the glass is half-empty or half-full."[8] People who think they can get more of what they want from the national government usually advocate national action. Those who view states as more responsive and accountable argue for decentralization. Although Republicans generally favor action at the state level and Democrats tend to support action by the national government, neither are consistent in their positions on the balance of power between the national government and the states. It depends on the issue at stake.

This chapter begins by defining federalism and discussing its advantages. We look next at the constitutional basis for our federal system. Then we see how court decisions and political developments have shaped, and continue to shape, federalism in the United States.

DEFINING FEDERALISM

Scholars argue and wars have been fought about what federalism means. Our own Civil War was one such war. One scholar counted 267 definitions.[9]

- *Dual federalism* views the Constitution as giving a limited list of powers—primarily foreign policy and national defense—to the national government, leaving the rest to sovereign states. Each level of government is dominant within its own sphere. The Supreme Court serves as the umpire between the national government and the states in disputes over which level of government has responsibility for a particular activity. During our first hundred years, dual federalism was the favored interpretation given by the Supreme Court.

- *Cooperative federalism* stresses federalism as a system of intergovernmental relations in delivering governmental goods and services to the people and calls for cooperation among various levels of government.

- *Marble cake federalism*, a term coined by political scientist Morton Grodzins, conceives of federalism as a marble cake in which all levels of government are involved in a variety of issues and programs, rather than a layer cake, or dual federalism, with fixed divisions between layers or levels of government.[10]

- *Competitive federalism*, a term created by political scientist Thomas R. Dye, views the national government, 50 states, and thousands of other units as competing with each other over ways to put together packages of services and taxes. Applying the analogy of the marketplace, Dye emphasizes that at the state and local levels we have some choice about which state and city we want "to use," just as we have choices about what kind of automobile we drive.[11]

- *Permissive federalism* implies that although federalism provides "a sharing of power and authority between the national and state government, the states' share rests upon the permission and permissiveness of the national government."[12]

- *New federalism*, favored by Richard Nixon, Ronald Reagan, and former president George Bush, emphasizes their position that many of the fiscal resources and responsibilities of the federal government should be returned to the states in the form of large block grants and revenue sharing.

Federalism, as we define it here, is a form of government in which a constitution distributes powers between a central government and subdivisional governments—usually called states, provinces, or republics—giving to both the national government and the regional governments substantial responsibilities and powers, including the power to collect taxes and to pass and enforce laws regulating the conduct of individuals.

The mere existence of both national and state governments does not make a system federal. What is important is that a *constitution divides governmental powers between the national government and the subdivisional governments*, giving clearly defined functions to each. Neither the central nor the subdivisional government

federalism
Constitutional arrangement whereby power is distributed between a central government and subdivisional governments, called states in the United States. The national and the subdivisional governments both exercise direct authority over individuals.

TABLE 3–1 **Number of Governments**	
U.S. government	1
States	50
Counties	3,043
Municipalities	19,279
Townships or towns	16,656
School districts	14,422
Special districts	31,555
Total	85,006

Source: U.S. Bureau of the Census, *Statistical Abstract of the United States, 1998* (Government Printing Office, 1998).

receives its powers from the other; both derive them from a common source—the constitution. No ordinary act of legislation at either a national or a state level can change this constitutional distribution of powers. Both levels of government operate through their own agents and exercise power directly over individuals.

The number of federal nations is not large. Only 21 of the approximately 185 nation-states claim to be federal. But, they "cover more than half of the land surface of the globe, and include almost half of the world's population."[13] Federalism thus appears well suited for large countries with large populations.

Constitutionally, the federal system of the United States consists of only the national government and the 50 states. "Cities are not," the Supreme Court reminded us, "sovereign entities." But in a practical sense, we are a nation of about 85,000 governmental units—from the national government to the school board district (see Table 3–1). This does not make for a tidy, efficient, easy-to-understand system; yet, as we shall see, it has its virtues.

Alternatives to Federalism

Among the alternatives to federalism are **unitary systems** of government, in which a constitution vests all governmental power in the central government. The central government, if it so chooses, may delegate authority to constituent units, but what it delegates it may take away. England, France, Israel, and the Philippines have unitary governments. In the United States, state constitutions usually create this kind of relationship between the state and its local governments.

At the other extreme are **confederations**, in which sovereign nations by a constitutional compact create a central government but carefully limit the power of the central government and do not give it the power to regulate the conduct of individuals directly. The central government makes regulations for the constituent governments, but it exists and operates only at their direction. The 13 states under the Articles of Confederation operated in this manner, as did the southern Confederacy during the Civil War (see Figure 3–1). The European Union is another example.[14]

Why Federalism?

In 1787, federalism was an obvious choice. Confederation had been tried but proved unsuccessful. A unitary system was out of the question because most people were too deeply attached to their state governments to permit subordination to central rule. Federalism was, and still is, thought to be ideally suited to the needs of a heterogeneous people spread over a large continent, suspicious of concentrated power, and desiring unity but not uniformity. Federalism offered, and still offers, many advantages for such a people.

FEDERALISM CHECKS THE GROWTH OF TYRANNY   Although in the rest of the world federal forms have not been notably successful in preventing tyranny, and many unitary governments are democratic, Americans tend to associate freedom with federalism.[15] As James Madison pointed out in *The Federalist*, No. 10: If "factious leaders . . . kindle a flame within their particular states," national leaders can check the spread of the "conflagration through the other states" (*The Federalist*, No. 10, appears in the Appendix of this book). Moreover, when one political party loses control of the national government, it is still likely to hold office in a number of states. It can then regroup, develop new policies and new leaders, and continue to challenge the party in power at the national level.

Such diffusion of power creates its own problems. It makes it difficult for a national majority to carry out a program of action, and it permits those who control state governments to frustrate the policies enacted by Congress and administered by federal agencies. To the framers, these obstacles were an advantage. They

unitary system
A constitutional arrangement in which power is concentrated in a central government.

confederation
A constitutional arrangement in which sovereign nations or states, by compact, create a central government but carefully limit its power and do not give it direct authority over individuals.

Government Under the Artic es of Confederation: 1781–1788

The People

The People

Central Goverment

The People

The People

The confederation was a union of states. The central government received power from the states and had no direct authority over the people.

Government Under U.S. Constitution (Federation): 1789–

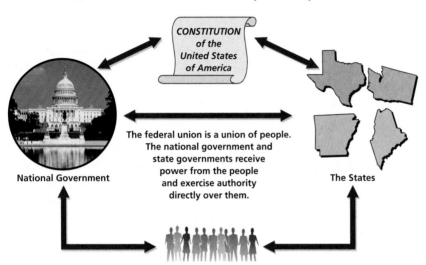

CONSTITUTION
of the
United States
of America

National Government

The States

The federal union is a union of people. The national government and state governments receive power from the people and exercise authority directly over them.

FIGURE 3–1 A Comparison of Federalism and Confederation

feared that a single-interest group might capture the national government and attempt to suppress the interests of others. Of course the size of the nation and the many interests within it are the greatest obstacles to the formation of a single-inter-est majority—a point often overlooked today but emphasized by Madison in *The Federalist*, No. 10. If such a majority were to occur, having to work through a federal system would check its power.

FEDERALISM ALLOWS UNITY WITHOUT UNIFORMITY   National politicians and parties do not have to iron out every difference on every issue that divides us, whether it be abortion, same-sex marriages, gun control, capital punishment, welfare financing, or assisted suicide. Instead, these issues are debated in state legislatures, county courthouses, and city halls. But this advantage of federalism is becoming less significant as many local issues become national and as events in one state immedi-ately affect policy debates at the national level.

FEDERALISM ENCOURAGES EXPERIMENTATION   Supreme Court Justice Louis Brandeis pointed out that state governments provide great "laboratories" for public policy experimentation, with states serving as proving grounds. If they adopt programs that fail, the negative effects are limited; if programs succeed, they can be

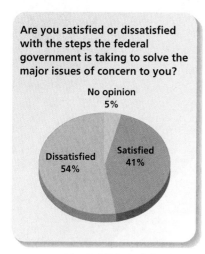

Are you satisfied or dissatisfied with the steps the federal government is taking to solve the major issues of concern to you?

No opinion 5%

Dissatisfied 54%

Satisfied 41%

FIGURE 3–2 The Public's Satisfaction with Government

SOURCE: Gallup Poll, August 24, 2000. For more information on trends in public opinion, go to: gallup.com/poll/releases.

express powers
Powers specifically granted to one of the branches of the national government by the Constitution.

implied powers
Powers inferred from express powers that allow Congress to carry out its functions.

necessary and proper clause
Clause of the Constitution setting forth the implied powers of Congress. It states that Congress, in addition to its express powers, has the power to make all laws necessary and proper for carrying out all powers vested by the Constitution in the national government.

inherent powers
Those powers of the national government in the field of foreign affairs that the Supreme Court has declared do not depend upon constitutional grants but rather grow out of the very existence of the national government.

adopted by other states and by the national government. Georgia, for example, was the first state to permit 18-year-olds to vote; Wisconsin has experimented with putting welfare recipients to work; California has pioneered air pollution control programs; Oregon and Hawaii are creating new systems for the delivery of health care; Nevada is the only state, so far, to legalize statewide gambling, but aspects of legalized casino gambling are now found in more than half the states. Not all innovations, even those considered successful, are widely adopted. Nebraska is the only state to have a unicameral legislature, although in recent years such a change has been discussed, not too seriously, in both Minnesota and California.

FEDERALISM KEEPS GOVERNMENT CLOSER TO THE PEOPLE   By providing numerous arenas for decision making, federalism involves many people and helps keep government closer to the people. Every day thousands of Americans are busy serving on city councils, school boards, neighborhood associations, and planning commissions. Since they are close to the issues and have firsthand knowledge of what needs to be done, they may be more responsive to problems than the experts in Washington.

We should be cautious, however, about generalizing that state and local governments are necessarily "closer to the people" than is the national government. True, more people are involved in local and state politics than in national affairs, and confidence in state governments has gone up while respect for national agencies has diminished. A majority of the public appears to be dissatisfied with the federal government's responses to major issues (see Figure 3–2). Yet national and international affairs are more often on people's minds than are state or local politics. Fewer voters participate in state and local elections than in congressional and presidential elections.

THE CONSTITUTIONAL STRUCTURE OF AMERICAN FEDERALISM

Dividing powers and responsibilities between the national and state governments has resulted in thousands of court decisions, hundreds of books, and endless speeches to explain—and even then the division lacks precise definition. Nonetheless, a basic understanding of how the Constitution divides these powers and responsibilities and of what obligations are imposed on each level of government is helpful (see Table 3–2).

The formal constitutional framework of our federal system may be stated relatively simply:

1. The national government has only those powers delegated to it by the Constitution (with the important exception of the inherent power over foreign affairs).
2. Within the scope of its operations, the national government is supreme.
3. The state governments have the powers not delegated to the central government, except those denied to them by the Constitution and their state constitutions.
4. Some powers are specifically denied to both the national and state governments; others are specifically denied only to the states; still others are denied to the national government, but not the states.

Powers of the National Government

The Constitution, chiefly in the first three articles, delegates legislative, executive, and judicial powers to the national government. In addition to these **express powers**, such as the power to appropriate funds, Congress has assumed constitutionally **implied powers**, such as the power to create banks, which are inferred from express powers. The constitutional basis for the implied powers of Congress is the **necessary**

and proper clause (Article I, Section 8, Clause 18). This clause gives Congress the right "to make all Laws which shall be necessary and proper for carrying into Execution the foregoing Powers, and all other Powers vested . . . in the Government of the United States."

In the field of foreign affairs the Constitution gives the national government **inherent powers**. The national government has the same authority to deal with other nations as if it were the central government in a unitary system. Such inherent powers do not depend on specific constitutional provisions. For example, the government of the United States may acquire territory by purchase or by discovery and occupation, though no specific clause in the Constitution allows such acquisition. Even if the Constitution were silent about foreign affairs—which it is not—the national government would still have the power to declare war, make treaties, and appoint and receive ambassadors.

Together, these express, implied, and inherent powers create a flexible system that allows the Supreme Court, Congress, the president, and the people to expand the central government's powers to meet the needs of a modern nation in a global economy. This expansion of central government functions rests on four constitutional pillars.

These four constitutional pillars—*the national supremacy article, the war power, the commerce clause, and most especially, the power to tax and spend for the general welfare*—have permitted a tremendous expansion of the functions of the national government, so much so that, despite the Supreme Court's recent declaration that some national laws exceed Congress's constitutional powers, the national government has, in effect, almost full power to enact any legislation that Congress deems necessary, so long as it does not conflict with those provisions of the Constitution designed to protect individual rights and the powers of the states.

THE NATIONAL SUPREMACY ARTICLE One of the most important pillars is found in Article VI of the Constitution: "This Constitution, and the Laws of the United States which shall be made in Pursuance thereof; and all Treaties made . . . under the Authority of the United States, shall be the supreme Law of the Land; and the Judges in every State shall be bound thereby; any Thing in the Constitution or Laws of any State to the Contrary notwithstanding." All officials, state as well as national, swear an oath to support the Constitution of the United States. States may not override national policies; this restriction also applies to local units of government since they are agents of the states. National laws and regulations of federal agencies *preempt* the field, so that conflicting state and local rules and regulations are unenforceable.

An Expanding Nation

A great advantage of federalism—and part of the genius and flexibility of our constitutional system—has been the way in which we acquired territory and extended rights and guarantees by means of statehood, commonwealth, or territorial status, and thus grew from 13 to 50 states, plus territories.

Louisiana Purchase	1803
Florida	1819
Texas	1845
Oregon	1846
Mexican Cession	1848
Gadsden Purchase	1853
Alaska	1867
Hawaii	1898
Philippines	1898–1946
Puerto Rico	1899
Guam	1899
American Samoa	1900
Canal Zone	1904–2000
U.S. Virgin Islands	1917
Pacific Islands Trust Territory	1947

TABLE 3–2 The Federal Division of Powers

Types of Powers Delegated to the National Government	Some Powers Reserved for the States	Some Concurrent Powers Shared by the National and State Governments
■ Express powers stated in Constitution ■ Implied powers that may be inferred from express powers ■ Inherent powers that allow the nation to present a united front to foreign powers	■ To create a republican form of government ■ To charter local governments ■ To conduct elections ■ To exercise all powers not delegated to the national government or denied to the states by the Constitution	■ To tax citizens and businesses ■ To borrow and spend money ■ To establish courts ■ To pass and enforce laws ■ To protect civil rights

THE WAR POWER   The national government is responsible for protecting the nation from external aggression and, when necessary, for waging war. In today's world, military strength depends not only on troops in the field but also on the ability to mobilize the nation's industrial might as well as to apply scientific and technological knowledge to the tasks of defense. The national government has the power to do whatever is necessary and proper to wage war successfully. Thus the national government has the power to do almost anything not in direct conflict with constitutional guarantees.

THE POWER TO REGULATE COMMERCE   Congressional authority extends to all commerce that affects more than one state. Commerce includes the production, buying, selling, renting, and transporting of goods, services, and properties. The **commerce clause** (Article I, Section 8, Clause 3) packs a tremendous constitutional punch; it gives Congress the power "to regulate Commerce with foreign Nations, and among the several States, and with the Indian Tribes." In these few words the national government has been able to find constitutional justification for regulating a wide range of human activity, since very few aspects of our economy today affect commerce in only one state and are thus outside the scope of the national government's constitutional authority.[16]

The commerce clause can also be used to sustain legislation that goes beyond commercial matters. When the Supreme Court upheld the 1964 Civil Rights Act forbidding discrimination because of race, religion, or national origin in places of public accommodation, it said: "Congress's action in removing the disruptive effect which it found racial discrimination has on interstate travel is not invalidated because Congress was also legislating against what it considers to be moral wrongs."[17] Discrimination restricts the flow of interstate commerce; therefore, Congress could legislate against discrimination. Moreover, the law could be applied even to local places of public accommodation because local incidents of discrimination have a substantial and harmful impact on interstate commerce, though the Court has recently limited congressional powers to address such harms.[18]

THE POWER TO TAX AND SPEND   Congress lacks constitutional authority to pass laws solely on the ground that they will promote the general welfare, but it may raise taxes and spend money for this purpose. Congress, for example, lacks the power to regulate education or agriculture directly, yet it does have the power to appropriate money to support education or to pay farm subsidies. By attaching conditions to its grants of money, Congress may thus regulate what it cannot directly control by law.

When Congress puts up the money, it determines how the money will be spent. By withholding or threatening to withhold funds, the national government can influence or control state operations and regulate individual conduct. For example, Congress has stipulated that federal funds should be withdrawn from any program in which any person is denied benefits because of race, color, national origin, sex, or physical handicap. Congress has also used its power of the purse to force states to raise the drinking age to 21 by tying such a condition to federal dollars for highways.

Congress frequently requires states to do certain things—for example, provide services to indigent mothers and clean up the air and water. These requirements are called **federal mandates**. Often, Congress does not supply the funds required to carry out these mandates, and its failure to do so has become an important issue as states face growing expenditures with limited resources.

Powers of the States

The Constitution *reserves for the states all powers not granted to the national government*, subject only to the limitations of the Constitution. Powers not given exclusively to the national government by provisions of the Constitution or by judicial interpretation may be exercised concurrently by the states, as long as there is no conflict with

commerce clause
The clause (Article I) in the Constitution that gives Congress the power to regulate commerce among the states, with other nations, and with the Indian tribes. This clause provides the constitutional basis for most national regulations of our economy, as well as for much civil rights legislation.

federal mandate
A requirement imposed by the federal government as a condition of receipt of federal funds.

national law. Such **concurrent powers** with the national government include the power to levy taxes and regulate commerce internal to each state.

In general, a state may levy a tax on the same item as the national government does, but a state cannot, by a tax, "unduly burden" commerce among the states, interfere with a function of the national government, complicate the operation of a national law, or abridge the terms of a treaty of the United States. Where Congress has not preempted the field, states may regulate interstate businesses, provided these regulations do not cover matters requiring uniform national treatment or unduly burden interstate commerce.

Who decides what matters require "uniform national treatment" or what actions might place an "undue burden" on interstate commerce? Congress does, subject to final review by the Supreme Court. When Congress is silent or does not clearly state its intentions, the courts—ultimately the Supreme Court—decide if there is a conflict with the national Constitution or if there has been federal preemption by law or regulation.

CONSTITUTIONAL LIMITS AND OBLIGATIONS   To make federalism work, the Constitution imposes certain restraints on both the national and the state governments. States are prohibited from:

1. Making treaties with foreign governments
2. Authorizing private persons to prey on the shipping and commerce of other nations
3. Coining money, issuing bills of credit, or making anything but gold and silver coin legal tender in payment of debts
4. Taxing imports or exports
5. Taxing foreign ships
6. Keeping troops or ships in time of peace (except the state militia, now called the National Guard)
7. Engaging in war, unless invaded or in such imminent danger as will not admit of delay

The national government, in turn, is required by the Constitution to refrain from exercising its powers, especially its powers to tax and to regulate interstate commerce, in such a way as to interfere substantially with the states' abilities to perform their responsibilities. Today, the protection states have from intrusions by the national government comes primarily from the political process—because senators and representatives elected from the states participate in the decisions of Congress. However, the Court has held that Congress may not command states to enact laws to comply with, and state employees to enforce, unfunded federal mandates; for example, Congress may not require local law enforcement officials to make background checks prior to handgun sales.[19] It has also ruled that the Eleventh Amendment guarantee of states' sovereign immunity from lawsuits forbids state employees from suing states in federal and state courts in order to force state compliance with federal employment laws.[20] While Congress may not use those sticks, it may offer the carrot of federal funding if states comply with national policies, such as establishing a minimum drinking age or setting 55-mile-an-hour speed limits.

The Constitution also requires the national government to guarantee to each state a "Republican Form of Government." The framers used this term to distinguish a republic from a monarchy, on the one side, and from a pure, direct democracy, on the other. Congress, not the courts, enforces this guarantee and determines what is or is not a republican form of government. By permitting the congressional delegation of a state to be seated in Congress, Congress acknowledges that the state has the republican form of government guaranteed by the Constitution.

concurrent powers
Powers the Constitution gives to both the national and state governments, such as the power to levy taxes.

SAME-SEX MARRIAGES AND THE FULL FAITH AND CREDIT CLAUSE

The full faith and credit clause has become part of a national debate because one state now recognizes same-sex unions. In April 2000 Vermont enacted a law recognizing "civil unions," granting same-sex couples the same rights and protections of married couples. It was the first state to do so. As a result, same-sex couples were entitled to 300 state benefits, ranging from health care and inheritance rights to property transfers. However, in March 2001 the Vermont House of Representatives reversed course and passed a bill outlawing same-sex marriages.

Same-sex partnerships are legally recognized in several European countries, including Belgium, Denmark, France, Hungary, Luxembourg, Norway, and Sweden. However, such unions are banned in 32 states. Congress passed and President Bill Clinton signed the Defense of Marriage Act of 1996, which relieves states of any obligation to recognize same-sex marriages even if they are recognized in other states, and stipulates that the national government recognizes only heterosexual marriages for federal benefits such as Social Security.

The Defense of Marriage Act may well be challenged in the courts for going beyond the power of Congress to provide states with an exemption from their constitutional obligation under the full faith and credit clause. Those supporting the

Gay couples renew their vows to each other in this ceremony in San Francisco's Metropolitan Community church.

act point to the Constitution, which gives Congress the responsibility for prescribing the manner in which states are to comply with the clause.

The Supreme Court has not addressed the issue squarely, and precedents provide no clear answer. It is the view of one authority that in light of recent Court rulings showing the present Court's tilt toward states' rights and "the fact that marriage has traditionally been an almost exclusive sphere of state authority, the Court would likely maintain the noncentralized and dual nature of American domestic relations that exist today, and allow the states to decide whether to recognize same-sex marriages."*

*John P. Feldmeier, "Federalism and Full Faith and Credit: Must States Recognize Out-of-State Same-Sex Marriages?" *Publius* 25, no. 4 (Fall 1995), p. 126. See also "Special Report, Shades of Gay," *Newsweek*, March 20, 2000.

In addition, the national government is obliged by the Constitution to protect states against *domestic insurrection*. Congress has delegated to the president the authority to dispatch troops to put down such insurrections when so requested by the proper state authorities. If there are contesting state authorities, the president decides which is the proper one. The president does not have to wait, however, for a request from state authorities to send federal troops into a state to enforce federal laws.

Interstate Relations

Three clauses in the Constitution, taken from the Articles of Confederation, require states to give full faith and credit to each other's public acts, records, and judicial proceedings; to extend to each other's citizens the privileges and immunities of their own citizens; and to return persons who are fleeing from justice.

FULL FAITH AND CREDIT   The **full faith and credit clause** (Article IV, Section 1), one of the more technical provisions of the Constitution, requires state courts to enforce the civil judgments of the courts of other states and accept their public records and acts as valid. It does not require states to enforce the criminal laws of other states; in most cases, for one state to enforce the criminal laws of another would raise constitutional issues. The clause applies especially to enforcement of judicial settlements and court awards.

INTERSTATE PRIVILEGES AND IMMUNITIES   Under Article IV, Section 2, states must extend to citizens of other states the privileges and immunities granted to their own citizens, including the protection of the laws, the right to engage in peaceful occupations, access to the courts, and freedom from discriminatory taxes. Because of this clause, states may not impose unreasonable residency requirements, that is, withhold rights to American citizens who have recently moved to the state and thereby have become citizens of that state. For example, a state may not set unreasonable time limits to withhold state-funded medical benefits from new citizens or to keep them

FEDERALISM
IN COMPARATIVE PERSPECTIVE

There is no single model for dividing authority between national and state governments or for power sharing in intergovernmental relations. The federal systems in Canada, Germany, and Switzerland are illustrative.

Canada combines a federal system with a parliamentary form of government that has authority to legislate on all matters pertaining to "peace, order, and good government." The system was established in 1867, in part to prevent conflicts similar to those between the states that led to the American Civil War. In each of the ten provinces, the lieutenant governor is appointed on the advice of the prime minister and must approve any provincial law before it goes into effect. The legislative powers of the provinces are thus checked and limited. However, the provinces retain residual powers, and unlike the U.S. Supreme Court, the Canadian judiciary has generally encouraged decentralization in recognition of its multicultural society. Thus, Canadian provinces exercise greater power and the national government is weaker than in the United States. In addition, the special status claimed by French-speaking Quebec has led to intergovernmental relations that alternate between periods of centralization and decentralization.

The Federal Republic of Germany, whose Basic Laws of 1949 became the constitu-

tion with the reunification of East and West Germany in 1990, is often referred to as an example of cooperative federalism. Its 16 states, or Länder, exercise a great deal of power, far more than states do in the United States. The central government has a president and a bicameral parliament composed of an upper house, the Federal Council, and a lower house, the National Assembly, as well as an independent judiciary. The central government has exclusive authority over foreign affairs, money, immigration, and telecommunications. But the Länder retain residual powers over all other matters and have concurrent powers over civil and criminal law, along with matters related to education, health, and the public welfare. Moreover, national legislation does not become law unless approved by a majority of the Federal Council, whose members are selected by legislatures in the Länder, not by popular elections.

Switzerland established a confederation on the basis of regional governments (cantons). The cantons reflect the ethnic and linguistic differences of their German-, French-, and Italian-speaking populations. All three languages are officially recognized by the central government. But of the 22 cantons, there are 18 that are unilingual, 3 that are bilingual, and 1 trilingual. They exercise most lawmaking powers and are represented in the National Council, a bicameral legislature, and the Council of States.

from voting. How long a residency requirement may a state impose? A day seems about as long as the Court will tolerate to withhold welfare payments or medical care, 50 days or so for voting privileges, and one year for eligibility for in-state tuition for state-supported colleges and universities.

Financially independent adults who move into a state just before enrolling in a state-supported university or college may be required to prove that they have become citizens of that state and intend to remain after finishing their schooling by supplying such evidence of citizenship as tax payments, a driver's license, car registration, voter registration, and a continuous, year-round off-campus residence. Students who are financially dependent on their parents remain citizens of the state of their parents.

EXTRADITION   In Article IV, Section 2, the Constitution asserts that when individuals charged with crimes have fled from one state to another, the state to which they have fled is to deliver them to the proper officials upon the demand of the executive authority of the state from which they fled. This process is called **extradition**. "The obvious objective of the Extradition Clause," the courts have claimed, "is that no State should become a safe haven for the fugitives from a sister State's criminal justice system."[21] Congress has supplemented this constitutional provision by making the governor of the state to which fugitives have fled responsible for

full faith and credit clause
Clause in the Constitution requiring each state to recognize the civil judgments rendered by the courts of the other states and to accept their public records and acts as valid documents.

extradition
Legal process whereby an alleged criminal offender is surrendered by the officials of one state to officials of the state in which the crime is alleged to have been committed.

returning them. Despite their constitutional obligation, governors of asylum states have on occasion refused to honor a request for extradition.

INTERSTATE COMPACTS The Constitution also requires states to settle disputes with one another without the use of force. States may carry their legal disputes to the Supreme Court, or they may negotiate **interstate compacts**. Interstate compacts often establish interstate agencies to handle problems affecting an entire region. Before most interstate compacts become effective, congressional approval is required. After a compact has been signed and approved by Congress, it becomes binding on all signatory states, and its terms are enforceable by the federal judiciary. A typical state may belong to 20 compacts dealing with such subjects as environmental protection, crime control, water rights, and higher education exchanges.[22]

THE ROLE OF THE FEDERAL COURTS: UMPIRES OF FEDERALISM

Although the political process ultimately decides how power will be divided between the national and the state governments, the federal courts—and especially the Supreme Court—have often been called on to umpire the ongoing debate about which level of government should do what, for whom, and to whom. This role for the courts was claimed in the celebrated case of *McCulloch v Maryland*.

McCulloch versus Maryland

In *McCulloch v Maryland* (1819), the Supreme Court had the first of many chances to define the division of power between the national and state governments.[23] The state of Maryland had levied a tax against the Baltimore branch of the Bank of the United States, a semipublic agency established by Congress. James William McCulloch, the cashier of the bank, refused to pay on the grounds that a state could not tax an instrument of the national government.

Maryland was represented before the Court by some of the country's most distinguished lawyers, including Luther Martin, who had been a delegate to the Constitutional Convention. Martin said the power to incorporate a bank was not expressly delegated to the national government in the Constitution. He maintained that the necessary and proper clause gives Congress only the power to choose those means and to pass those laws absolutely essential to the execution of its expressly granted powers. Because a bank is not absolutely necessary to the exercise of any of its delegated powers, Congress had no authority to establish it. As for Maryland's right to tax the bank, the power to tax is one of the powers reserved to the states; they may use it as they see fit.

The national government was represented as well by distinguished counsel, including Daniel Webster. Webster conceded the power to create a bank is not one of the express powers of the national government. However, the power to pass laws necessary and proper to carry out Congress's express powers is specifically delegated to Congress. Therefore, Congress may incorporate a bank as an appropriate, convenient, and useful means of exercising the granted powers of collecting taxes, borrowing money, and caring for the property of the United States. Although the power to tax is reserved to the states, Webster argued that states cannot interfere with the operations of the national government. The Constitution leaves no room for doubt; in cases of conflict between the national and state governments, the national government is supreme.

Speaking for a unanimous Court, Chief Justice John Marshall rejected every one of Maryland's contentions. He summarized his views on the powers of the national government in these now-famous words: "Let the end be legitimate, let it be within the scope of the Constitution, and all means which are appropriate, which are plainly adapted to that end, which are not prohibited, but consist with the letter and

interstate compact
An agreement among two or more states. The Constitution requires that most such agreements be approved by Congress.

national supremacy
Constitutional doctrine that whenever conflict occurs between the constitutionally authorized actions of the national government and those of a state or local government, the actions of the federal government take priority.

preemption
The right of a federal law or regulation to preclude enforcement of a state or local law or regulation.

centralists
Those who favor national action over action at the state and local levels.

decentralists
Those who favor state or local action rather than national action.

spirit of the constitution, are constitutional." Having thus established the doctrine of *implied national powers*, Marshall set forth the doctrine of **national supremacy**. No state, he said, can use its taxing powers to tax a national instrument. "The power to tax involves the power to destroy. . . . If the right of the States to tax the means employed by the general government be conceded, the declaration that the Constitution, and the laws made in pursuance thereof, shall be the supreme law of the land, is empty and unmeaning declamation."

The long-range significance of *McCulloch v Maryland* in providing support for the developing forces of nationalism and a unified economy cannot be overstated. The arguments of the states' righters, if they had been accepted, would have strapped the national government in a constitutional straitjacket and denied it powers needed to handle the problems of an expanding nation.

Federal Courts and the Role of the States

The authority of federal judges to review the activities of state and local governments has expanded dramatically in recent decades because of modern judicial interpretations of the Fourteenth Amendment, which forbids states to deprive any person of life, liberty, or property without *due process of the law;* nor can states deny to any person the *equal protection of the laws* and congressional legislation enacted to implement this amendment. Almost every action by state and local officials is now subject to challenge before a federal judge as a violation of the Constitution or of federal law.

Preemption occurs when a federal law or regulation takes precedence over enforcement of a state or local law or regulation. State and local laws are preempted not only when they conflict directly with federal laws and regulations, but also if they touch a field in which the "federal interest is so dominant that the federal system will be assumed to preclude enforcement of state laws on the same subject."[24] Examples of federal preemption include laws regulating hazardous substances, water quality, and clean air standards, and many civil rights acts, most especially the Civil Rights Act of 1964 and the Voting Rights Act of 1965.

Over the years federal judges, under the leadership of the Supreme Court, have generally favored the powers of the federal government over the states. In spite of the Supreme Court's recent bias in favor of state over national authority, few would deny the Supreme Court the power to review and set aside state actions. As Justice Oliver Wendell Holmes of the Supreme Court once remarked: "I do not think the United States would come to an end if we lost our power to declare an Act of Congress void. I do think the Union would be imperiled if we could not make that declaration as to the laws of the several States."[25]

The Great Debate—Centralists versus Decentralists

From the beginning of the Republic there has been an ongoing debate about the "proper" distribution of powers, functions, and responsibilities between the national government and the states. Did the national government have the authority to outlaw slavery in the territories? Did the states have the authority to operate racially segregated schools? Could Congress regulate labor relations? Does Congress have the power to regulate the sale and use of firearms? Does Congress have the right to tell states how to clean up air and water pollution? The debates in the past and those today are frequently phrased in constitutional language, with appeals to the great principles of federalism. But they are also arguments over who gets what, where, and how.

During the Great Depression of the 1930s, the nation debated whether Congress had the constitutional authority to enact legislation on agriculture, labor, education, housing, and welfare. Only 40 years ago some legislators and public officials—as well as some scholars—questioned the constitutional authority of Congress to legislate against racial discrimination. The debate continues between **centralists**, those who favor national action, and **decentralists**, those who favor action at the state and local levels.

Thinking It Through . . .

The great debate about which level of government can best perform functions continues to rage. The Republican party started its history as the party of the National Union, while the Democrats were then the champion of states' rights, but for the past several decades there has been a switch. After winning majority status in Congress in 1994, Republicans led the charge on Washington, demanding the return of functions back to the states. Democrats tend to be reluctant about removing all federal standards, especially with respect to regulation of the environment and of the workplace, and they tend to be in favor of providing minimum standards for programs, especially welfare and health care.

Centralists' Arguments

1. State and local officials tend to be less competent than national officials.

2. State and local officials tend to be concerned only with the interests of their own areas.

3. State and local governments are unable or unwilling to raise taxes needed to carry out vital government functions.

4. State and local governments are more apt to reflect local racial and ethnic biases as well as the biases of dominant local industries.

5. State and local governments are afraid to regulate industries for fear the industries will move elsewhere.

Decentralists' Arguments

1. Increased urbanization has made states more responsive to the needs of city people.

2. In recent years state and local governments have shown greater willingness to raise taxes than the national government.

3. State and local governments have become as sensitive to the needs of the poor and minorities as is the national government.

4. State and local governments have reformed and modernized and thus become more effective governments.

THE DECENTRALIST POSITION   Among those favoring the decentralist or states' rights interpretation were the Antifederalists, Thomas Jefferson, John C. Calhoun, the Supreme Court from the 1920s to 1937, and more recently, Ronald Reagan, George Bush, the Republican leaders of Congress, Chief Justice William H. Rehnquist, and Justices Antonin Scalia, Clarence Thomas, and Sandra Day O'Connor.

Most decentralists contend the Constitution is a treaty among sovereign states that created the central government and gave it very limited authority. As Justice Clarence Thomas, an ardent decentralist, wrote in a dissenting opinion supporting the argument that a state has the power to impose term limits on members of Congress, "The ultimate source of the Constitution's authority is the consent of the people of each individual State, not the consent of the undifferentiated people of the Nation as a whole."[26] Thus the national government is little more than an agent of the states, and every one of its powers should be narrowly defined. Any question about whether the states have given a particular function to the central government or have reserved it for themselves should be resolved in favor of the states.

Decentralists hold that the national government should not interfere with activities reserved for the states. The Tenth Amendment, they claim, makes this clear: "The powers not delegated to the United States by the Constitution, nor prohibited by it to the States, are reserved to the States respectively, or to the people." Decentralists insist state governments are closer to the people and reflect the people's wishes more accurately than does the national government. The national government, they add, is inherently heavy-handed and bureaucratic; to preserve our federal system and our liberties, central authority must be kept under control.

THE CENTRALIST POSITION   The centralist position has been supported by Chief Justice John Marshall, Abraham Lincoln, Theodore Roosevelt, Franklin Roosevelt, and throughout most of our history by the Supreme Court.

Centralists reject the whole idea of the Constitution as an interstate compact. Rather, they view the Constitution as a supreme law established by the people. The national government is an agent of the people, not of the states, because it was the people who drew up the Constitution and created the national government. They intended the central government's powers to be defined by the national political process and that it should be denied authority only when the Constitution clearly prohibits it from acting.

Centralists argue that the national government is a government of all the people, whereas each state speaks only for some of the people. Although the Tenth Amendment clearly reserves powers for the states, it does not deny the national government the authority to exercise, to the fullest extent, all of its powers. Moreover, the supremacy of the national government restricts the states, because governments representing part of the people cannot be allowed to interfere with a government representing all of them.

The Supreme Court and the Role of Congress

From 1937 until the 1990s the Supreme Court essentially removed federal courts from what had been their traditional role of protecting states from acts of Congress. The Supreme Court broadly interpreted the commerce clause to allow Congress to do whatever Congress thought necessary and proper to promote the common good, even if the federal laws and regulations infringed on the activities of state and local governments. In 1985 the Supreme Court went so far as to tell the states that they should look to the political process to protect their interests, not to the federal courts.[27]

In the last decade, however, the Supreme Court signaled that federal courts should no longer remain passive in resolving federalism issues.[28] In 1995 the Court declared that a state could not impose term limits on its members of Congress, but it did so only by a 5 to 4 vote. Justice John Paul Stevens, writing for the majority,

built his argument on the concept of the federal union as espoused by the great Chief Justice John Marshall, as a compact among the people, with the national government serving as the people's agent. By contrast, Justice Clarence Thomas, writing for the dissenters, espoused a view of federalism not heard from a justice of the Supreme Court since prior to the New Deal. He interpreted the Tenth Amendment as requiring the national government to justify its actions in terms of an enumerated power and granting to the states all other powers not granted to the national government.[29]

The Court also declared that the clause in the Constitution empowering Congress to regulate commerce with the Indian tribes did not give Congress the power to authorize federal courts to hear suits against a state brought by Indian tribes.[30] The effect of this decision goes beyond Indian tribes. As a result, except to enforce rights stemming from the Fourteenth Amendment, which the Court explicitly acknowledged to be within Congress's power, Congress may no longer authorize individuals to bring legal actions against states in order to force their compliance with federal law in either federal or state courts.[31]

Building on those rulings, the Court continues to press ahead with its "constitutional counterrevolution"[32] in returning to an older vision of federalism not embraced since the constitutional crisis over the New Deal in the 1930s. Among other recent rulings,[33] the Court struck down the Violence Against Women Act, which had given women who are victims of violence the right to sue their attackers for damages.[34] Congress had found that violence against women annually costs the national economy $3 billion, but the Court held that Congress exceeded its powers in enacting the law and intruded on the powers of the states.

These Supreme Court decisions—most of which split the Court 5 to 4 along ideological lines, with the conservative justices favoring states' rights—may presage a major shift in the Court's interpretation of the constitutional nature of our federal system. Chief Justice Rehnquist, joined by Justices Scalia, Thomas, O'Connor, and frequently Justice Anthony M. Kennedy, veered the Court back to a decentralist position. President Clinton's two appointees, Justices Ruth Bader Ginsburg and Stephen Breyer, joined by Justices David Souter and John Paul Stevens, are resisting this movement back to a states' rights interpretation of our federal system. Consequently, federalism issues are likely to come up in future Supreme Court confirmation hearings, and the outcome of presidential elections—which determine who gets appointed to the Supreme Court—could well determine how these and other federalism issues will be decided.

REGULATORY FEDERALISM, FEDERAL GRANTS, AND FEDERAL MANDATES

Congress authorizes programs, establishes general rules for how the programs will operate, and decides whether and how much room should be left for state or local discretion. Most important, Congress appropriates the funds for these programs and, until recently, has had deeper pockets than even the richest states. One of Congress's most potent tools for influencing policy at the state and local levels has been federal grants.

Federal grants serve four purposes, the most important of which is the fourth:

1. To supply state and local governments with revenue.

2. To establish minimum national standards for such things as highways and clean air.

3. To equalize resources among the states by taking money from people with high incomes through federal taxes and spending it, through grants, in states where the poor live.

4. To attack national problems yet minimize the growth of federal agencies.

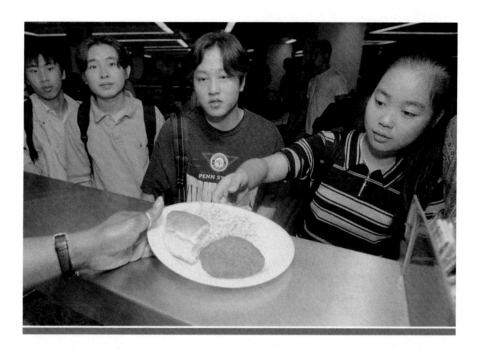

Types of Federal Grants

Three types of federal grants are currently being administered: categorical-formula grants, project grants, and block grants (or sometimes called flexible grants). From 1972 to 1987 there was also **revenue sharing**—federal grants to state and local governments to be used at their discretion and subject only to very general conditions. But when budget deficits soared in the second Reagan administration (1985–89) and there was no revenue to share, revenue sharing was terminated—to the states in 1986 and to local governments in 1987.

CATEGORICAL-FORMULA GRANTS   Congress appropriates funds for specific purposes, such as school lunches or the building of airports and highways. These funds are allocated by formula and are subject to detailed federal conditions, often on a matching basis; that is, the local government receiving the federal funds must put up some of its own dollars. Categorical grants, in addition, provide federal supervision to ensure that the federal dollars are spent as Congress wants. There are hundreds of grant programs, but two dozen, including Medicaid, account for more than half of total spending for categoricals.

PROJECT GRANTS   Congress appropriates a certain sum, which is allocated to state and local units and sometimes to nongovernmental agencies, based on applications from those who wish to participate. Examples are grants by the National Science Foundation to universities and research institutes to support the work of scientists or grants to states and localities to support training and employment programs.

BLOCK GRANTS   These are broad grants to states for prescribed activities—welfare, child care, education, social services, preventive health care, and health services—with only a few strings attached. States have great flexibility in deciding how to spend block grant dollars, but when the federal funds for any fiscal year are gone, there are no more matching federal dollars.

The Politics of Federal Grants

Republicans "have consistently favored fewer strings, less federal supervision, and the delegation of spending discretion to the state and local governments."[35] Democrats have generally been less supportive of broad discretionary block grants, favoring instead more detailed, federally supervised spending. The Republican-controlled Congress in the 1990s gave high priority to the creation of block grants, but it ran

revenue sharing
Program from 1972 to 1987 whereby federal funds were provided to state and local governments to be spent largely at the discretion of the receiving governments, subject to very general conditions.

into trouble by trying to lump together welfare, school lunch and breakfast programs, prenatal nutrition programs, and child protection programs in one block grant.

With President Clinton's enthusiastic support, however, the Republicans succeeded in making a major change in federal-state relations—a devolution of responsibility for welfare from the national government to the states. The Personal Responsibility and Work Opportunity Reconciliation Act of 1996 put an end to the 61-year-old program of Aid to Families with Dependent Children (AFDC), a federal guarantee of welfare checks for all eligible mothers and children. The 1996 act substituted for AFDC a welfare block grant to each state, with caps on the amount of federal dollars that the state will receive. It also put another big federal child care program into another block grant—Child Care and Development Block Grant (CCDBG).

Welfare block grants give states flexibility in how they provide for welfare, but no federal funds can be used to cover recipients who do not go to work within two years, and no one can receive federally supported benefits for more than five years. In order to slow down "the race to the bottom" in which states may try to make themselves "the least attractive state in which to be poor,"[36] Congress also stipulated that in order for states to receive their full share of federal dollars, they must continue to spend at least 75 percent of what they had been spending on welfare.

The battle over the appropriate level of government to control funding and to exercise principal responsibility for social programs tends to be cyclical. As one scholar of federalism explains, "Complaints about excessive federal control tend to be followed by proposals to shift more power to state and local governments. Then, when problems arise in state and local administration—and problems inevitably arise when any organization tries to administer anything—demands for closer federal supervision and tighter federal controls follow."[37]

Federal Mandates

Fewer federal dollars do not necessarily mean fewer federal controls. On the contrary, the federal government has imposed mandates on states and local governments, often without providing federal funds. State and local officials complained, and protests from state and local officials against unfunded federal mandates were effective. Congress, with President Clinton's support, passed the Unfunded Mandates Reform Act of 1995. The act requires the Congressional Budget Office (CBO) and federal agencies to issue reports about the impact of unfunded mandates. The act also imposed some mild constraints on Congress itself. A congressional committee that approves any legislation containing a federal mandate must draw attention to the mandate in its report and describe its cost to state and local governments. If the committee intends any mandate to be partially unfunded, it must explain why it is appropriate for the cost to be borne by state and local government.

Whether the Unfunded Mandates Reform Act significantly slows down federal mandates remains to be seen. So far it has had little effect. The Americans with Disabilities Act (1990), for example, called on state and local governments to build ramps and alter curbs—renovations that are costing millions. Environmental Protection Agency regulations require states to build automobile pollution-testing stations and take other actions to reduce pollution, but without corresponding federal dollars. Still, state officials praise the law for increasing congressional awareness of unfunded mandates. It has forced members of Congress to take into account how a bill would affect state and local governments, and to check with the Congressional Budget Office to avoid exposing a bill to procedural objections that could slow down or even block its passage.[38]

THE POLITICS OF FEDERALISM

The formal structures of our federal system have not changed much since 1787, but the political realities, especially during the last half-century, have greatly altered how federalism works. To understand these changes, we need to look at some of the trends that continue to fuel the debate about the meaning of federalism.

Direct Orders In a few instances, federal regulation takes the form of direct orders that must be complied with under threat of criminal or civil sanction. An example is the Equal Employment Opportunity Act of 1972, barring job discrimination by state and local governments because of race, color, religion, sex, and national origin.

Cross-cutting Requirements The first and most famous of these requirements (so called because a condition on one federal grant is extended to all activities supported by federal funds, regardless of their source) is Title VI of the 1964 Civil Rights Act, which holds that no person may be discriminated against in the use of federal funds because of race, color, or national origin. Other laws extend these protections to persons because of gender or handicapped status. More than 60 cross-cutting requirements concern the environment, historic preservation, contract wage rates, access to governmental information, the care of experimental animals, the treatment of human subjects in research projects, and so on.

Cross-over Sanctions These sanctions permit the use of federal dollars in one program to influence state and local policy in another. One example is a 1984 act that threatened to reduce federal highway aid by up to 15 percent for any state that failed to adopt a minimum drinking age of 21 by 1987.

Total Preemption This kind of control rests not on the national government's power to spend but on its powers under the supremacy and commerce clauses to preempt conflicting state and local activities. Building on this constitutional authority, federal law in certain areas just preempts state and local governments from the field. "There are fourteen types of total preemption laws, ranging from ones removing all regulatory powers from the states to ones authorizing states to cooperate in enforcing a statute."*

Partial Preemption In these instances, federal law establishes basic policies but requires states to administer them. Some programs give states an option not to participate, but if a state chooses not to do so, the national government then steps in and runs the programs. Even worse from the state's point of view is *mandatory partial preemption*, in which the national government requires the state to act on peril of losing other funds but provides no funds to support the state action. The Clean Air Act of 1990 is an example of mandatory partial preemption; the federal government set national air quality standards and required states to devise plans and pay for their implementation and enforcement.** Medicaid is another example of the national government providing some funds but mandating states to provide services that cost more than the federal funds cover.

*Joseph F. Zimmerman, "Congressional Regulation of Subnational Governments," *P.S.: Political Science and Politics* 26 (June 1993), p. 179.

**Mel Dubnick and Alan Gitelson, "Nationalizing State Policies," in *The Nationalization of State Government*, ed. Jerome J. Hanus (D.C. Heath, 1981), pp. 56–57.

The Growth of Big Government

Over the past two centuries there has been a drift of power to the national government. "No one planned the growth, but everyone played a part in it."[39] How did this shift come about? For a variety of reasons. One is that many of our problems have become national in scope. Much that was local in 1789, in 1860, or in 1930 is now national—even global. State governments could supervise the relations between small merchants and their few employees, but only the national government can supervise relations between multinational corporations and their thousands of employees, many organized in national unions.

As industrialization proceeded, powerful interests made demands on the national government. Business groups called on the government for aid in the form of tariffs, a national banking system, subsidies to railroads and the merchant marine, and uniform rules relating to the environment. Farmers learned that the national government could give more aid than the states, and they too began to demand help. By the beginning of this century, urban groups in general and organized labor in particular pressed their claims. Big business, big agriculture, and big labor all added up to big government.

The growth of the national economy and the creation of national transportation and communications networks altered people's attitudes toward the national government. Before the Civil War, the national government was viewed as a distant, even foreign, government. Today, in part because of television and the Internet, most people identify as closely with Washington as with their state capitals. People are apt to know more about the president than about their governor, more about their national senators and representatives than about their state legislators, or even about the local officials who run their cities and schools.

The Great Depression of the 1930s stimulated extensive national action on welfare, unemployment, and farm surpluses. World War II brought federal regulation of wages, prices, and employment, as well as national efforts to allocate resources, train personnel, and support engineering and inventions. After the war the national government helped veterans obtain college degrees and inaugurated a vast system of support for university research. The United States became the most powerful leader of the free world, maintaining substantial military forces even in times of peace. The Great Society programs of the 1960s poured out grants-in-aid to states and localities. City dwellers who had migrated from the rural South to northern cities began to seek federal funds for— at the very least—housing, education, and mass transportation.

Although economic and social conditions created many of the pressures for expansion of the national government, so did political claims. Until federal budget deficits became a hot issue in the 1980s and early 1990s, members of Congress, presidents, federal judges, and federal administrators actively promoted federal initiatives. With the return of more balanced federal budgets, it will be interesting to see if Congress returns to active promotion of federal programs. True, when there is widespread conflict about what to do—how to reduce the federal deficit, adopt a national energy policy, reform Social Security, provide health care for the indigent—Congress waits for a national consensus. But when an organized constituency wants something and there is no counterpressure, Congress "responds often to everyone, and with great vigor."[40] Once established, federal programs generate groups with vested interests in promoting, defending, and expanding them. Associations are formed and alliances are made. "In a word, the growth of government has created a constituency of, by, and for government."[41]

The politics of federalism are changing, however, and Congress is being pressured to reduce the size and scope of national programs. At the same time, the cost of entitlement programs such as Social Security and Medicare are going up because there are more older people and they live longer. These programs have widespread public support, and to cut them is politically risky. "With all other options disappearing, it is politically tempting to finance tax cuts by turning over to the states many of the social programs . . . that have become the responsibility of the national government."[42]

The Devolution Revolution—A Revolution or Just Rhetoric?

The Republican sweep of the Congress in the 1994 elections carried with it a pledge to return many functions, most especially welfare, back to the states. President Clinton appeared to agree with the general tone of the Republicans. In his 1996 State of the Union Address, he proclaimed, "The era of big government is over." However, he tempered his comments by saying, "But we cannot go back to the time when our citizens were left to fend for themselves." Congress and the president came together for a major overhaul of welfare and, to a lesser degree, education. Congress also freed the states to set their own highway speed limits, changed the Safe Drinking Water Act to allow states to operate certain programs, and gave states a greater role over how federal rural development funds can be used.

Yet despite these shifts, recent Congresses, like their predecessors, have increased the authority of the national government in many areas. "Legislation cleared by the first Republican majority in four decades established national criteria for state-issued driver's licenses, ended state registration of mutual funds, created national food safety standards, nullified state laws that had restricted telecommunications competition, and extended federal criminal penalties to cover certain violent crimes."[43] Legislators made a host of offenses federal crimes, including car-jacking and stalking, and federalized the crime of rape committed while car-jacking. Appropriation bills pressured states to keep criminals behind bars by threatening to take grants away from states that failed to meet federal standards. As one reporter concluded, "The 'Devolution' promised by Congressional Republicans . . . has mostly fizzled. Instead of handing over authority to state and local governments, they're taking it away."[44]

THE FUTURE OF FEDERALISM

In 1933, during the Great Depression with state governments helpless, one writer stated, "I do not predict that the states will go, but affirm that they have gone."[45] Those prophets of doom were wrong. States are stronger than ever. During recent decades state governments have undergone a major transformation. Most have improved their governmental structures, taken on greater roles in funding education and welfare, launched programs to help distressed cities, and—despite new constitutional limitations—expanded their tax bases. Able men and women have been attracted to many governorships. "Today, states, in formal representational, policy making, and implementation terms at least, are more representative, more responsive, more activist, and more professional in their operations than they ever have been. They face their expanded roles better equipped to assume and fulfill them."[46]

Until the civil rights revolution of the 1960s, segregationists had feared that national officials would work for racial integration. Thus they praised local government, emphasized the dangers of centralization, and argued that the protection of civil rights was not a proper function of the national government. As one political scientist observed, "Federalism has a dark history to overcome. For nearly two hundred years, states' rights have been asserted to protect slavery, segregation, and discrimination."[47]

Today the politics of federalism, even with respect to civil rights, is more complicated than in the past. The national government is not necessarily more favorable to the claims of minorities than are state or city governments. When the Supreme

Court did not extend marital privacy rights to gays and lesbians, Vermont and some other state courts interpreted their state constitutions to provide more protection for these rights than does the U.S. Constitution. However, other states are passing legislation that would eliminate such protections.

As states more actively regulate the economy and as state attorneys general prosecute anticompetitive business practices, as they did in joining the suit against Microsoft in 2000, business interests have been arguing that conflicting state regulations are unduly burdening interstate commerce. They are asking for preemptive federal regulation, barring state taxes on e-commerce, for instance, in order to save them not only from stringent state regulations but from having to adjust to 50 different state laws. "One national dumb rule is better than 50 inconsistent rules of any kind," says a lawyer who represents trade groups in the food industries and medical devices.[48]

The national government is not likely to retreat to a pre-1930 posture or even a pre-1960 one. The underlying economic and social conditions that generated the demand for federal action have not been altered substantially. On the contrary, in addition to such traditional issues as helping people find jobs and preventing inflation and depressions—which still require national action—countless new issues have been added to the national agenda by the growth of a global economy based on e-commerce, an information explosion, and advancing technologies.

Most Americans have strong attachments to our federal system—in the abstract. They remain loyal to their states and show a growing and healthy skepticism about the national government. Some evidence suggests, however, that the anti-Washington sentiment "is 3,000 miles wide but only a few miles deep."[49] The fact is that Americans are pragmatists and are prepared to use whatever level of government—national, state, or local—necessary to meet their needs and new challenges.

POLITICS ONLINE

Should Internet Sales Be Taxed?

People can now buy virtually anything over the Internet; from groceries to automobiles to airline tickets, consumers find using their personal computer preferable to other forms of shopping. E-commerce is clearly a powerful new form of doing retail business. One problem e-commerce poses for government is that it makes collecting sales tax difficult. Conventional retail businesses collect sales taxes at the point of sale and forward those revenues to the government. Internet sales are generally not taxed, the exception being firms that operate a conventional retail business in the home state of the consumer. Hence, if a consumer purchased a book from *Amazon.com,* she would not pay sales tax, but if she purchased the same book via the Internet from the Barnes & Noble website, she would have to pay sales tax if her state had a Barnes & Noble store.

Conventional retail businesses have understandably cried "foul" to the non-taxable advantage enjoyed by many of their e-commerce competitors. Some state and local officials, like Utah Governor Mike Leavitt, have taken the lead in demanding tax fairness across the two types of retail business. On the other side of the issue are the Internet merchants, whose mantra is: "No Internet Taxes." Virginia Governor James Gilmore has been the leader of this group.

A national commission on this topic ended up so badly divided on what policy to recommend to Congress that it issued no formal recommendation, only majority and minority reports. We have archived the majority and minority report at:
www.prenhall.com/burns for this chapter.

For additional information on these issues go to:
www.ecomercetax.com.

SUMMARY

1. A federal system checks the growth of tyranny, allows unity without uniformity, encourages experimentation, and keeps government closer to the people.

2. Alternatives to federal systems are unitary systems in which all constitutional power is vested in the central government, and confederations, which are loose compacts among sovereign states.

3. The national government has the constitutional authority, stemming primarily from the national supremacy clause, from the war powers, and from its powers to regulate commerce among the states to tax and spend, to do what Congress thinks is necessary and proper to promote the general welfare and to provide for the common defense. These constitutional pillars have permitted tremendous expansion of the functions of the federal government.

4. States must give full faith and credit to each other's public acts, records, and judicial proceedings; extend to each other's citizens the privileges and immunities it gives its own; and return fugitives from justice.

5. The federal courts umpire the division of power between the national and state governments.

6. Today debates about federalism are less often about its constitutional structure than over whether action should come from the national or state and local levels. Recent Supreme Court decisions favor a decentralist position and may presage a major shift in the Court's interpretation of the constitutional nature of our federal system.

7. The major instruments of federal intervention in state programs have been various kinds of financial grants-in-aid, of which the most prominent are categorical-formula grants, project grants, and block grants. The national government also imposes federal mandates and controls some activities of state and local governments by other means.

8. Over the past 220 years there has been a drift of power to the national government, but recently Congress has been pressured to reduce the size and scope of national programs and to shift some existing programs back to the states. While responsibility for welfare has been turned over to the states, the authority of the national government has increased in many areas.

KEY TERMS

devolution revolution 52
federalism 53
unitary system 54
confederation 54
express powers 56

implied powers 56
necessary and proper clause 56
inherent powers 56
commerce clause 58
federal mandate 58

concurrent powers 59
full faith and credit clause 61
extradition 61
interstate compact 62
national supremacy 62

preemption 62
centralists 62
decentralists 62
revenue sharing 66

FURTHER READING

SAMUEL H. BEER, *To Make a Nation: The Rediscovery of American Federalism* (Harvard University Press, 1993).

MICHAEL BURGESS, *Federalism and the European Union: Building of Europe, 1950–2000* (Routledge, 2000).

CENTER FOR THE STUDY OF FEDERALISM, *The Federalism Report* (published quarterly by Temple University; this publication notes research, books and articles, and scholarly conferences).

CENTER FOR THE STUDY OF FEDERALISM, *Publius: The Journal of Federalism* (published quarterly by Temple University; one issue each year is an "Annual Review of the State of American Federalism").

TIMOTHY J. CONLAN, *From New Federalism to Devolution: Twenty-five Years of Intergovernmental Reforms* (Brookings Institution, 1998).

MARTHA DERTHICK, ed., *Dilemmas of Scale in America's Federal Democracy* (Cambridge University Press, 1999).

THOMAS R. DYE, *Politics in States and Communities*, 10th ed. (Prentice Hall, 2000).

DANIEL J. ELAZER AND JOHN KINCAID, *The Covenant Connection: From Federal Theology to Modern Federalism* (Lexington Books, 2000).

JOHN FEREJOHN AND BARRY WEINGAST, *The New Federalism: Can the States Be Trusted?* (Hoover Institute Press, 1998).

MICHAEL GREVE, *Real Federalism: Why It Matters, How It Could Happen* (American Enterprise Institute, 1999).

ELLIS KATZ AND G. ALAN TARR, eds., *Federalism and Rights* (Roman & Littlefield, 1996).

PAUL E. PETERSON, *The Price of Federalism* (Brookings Institution, 1995).

PAUL J. POSNER, *The Politics of Unfunded Mandates: Whither Federalism* (Georgetown University Press, 1998).

MARTIN REDISH, *The Constitution as Political Structure* (Oxford University Press, 1995).

WILLIAM H. RIKER, *The Development of American Federalism* (Academic Publishers, 1987).

ROBERT C. VIPOND, *Liberty and Community: Canadian Federalism and the Failure of the Constitution* (State University of New York Press, 1991).

DAVID B. WALKER, *The Rebirth of Federalism: Slouching Toward Washington* (Chatham House, 1995).

JOSEPH F. ZIMMERMAN, *Contemporary American Federalism: The Growth of National Power* (Praeger, 1992).

4

POLITICAL CULTURE AND IDEOLOGY

P OLITICAL CULTURE IS THE UNDERLYING BELIEFS, ASSUMPTIONS, ATTITUDES, AND PATTERNS OF BEHAVIOR PEOPLE HAVE TOWARD GOVERNMENT AND POLITICS. THE specifics of a political culture can be discovered not only by what people believe and say, but also by how they behave. Political culture relates to such fundamental issues as who may participate in political decisions, what rights and liberties citizens have, how decisions are made, as well as how people view politicians and government generally. Some elements of our political culture—like our fear of concentrated power and our concern with individual liberty—have remained constant over time. In other respects, our political culture has changed to give more people the right to vote and to allow all citizens to participate in a wider range of political activities. For example, citizens now vote in party primaries to select nominees for office, whereas previously, party leaders determined who would stand for office.

Does it make a difference to our political culture how we participate in politics? The answer is yes. Contrast primary elections, in which individuals cast ballots on election day at voting places, with political caucuses, in which participants attend a meeting and listen to their neighbors making speeches about the candidates and issues of concern. The idea of people coming together, listening to each other, exchanging ideas, learning to appreciate each other's differences, and defending their opinions is thought to build community and relationships in ways that do not happen when citizens cast ballots. Even more impersonal are elections where voters cast ballots over the Internet.

Other places where citizens deliberate together include town council meetings, community groups, the PTA, labor unions, or business associations. Because of a decline of public participation in these institutions, some social scientists believe there has been a loss of the skills and learned behaviors people develop in such settings. Harvard professor Robert Putnam has defined **social capital** as "features of social organization such as networks, norms, and social trust that facilitate coordination and cooperation for mutual benefit."[1] But as we noted in Chapter 1, not all political scientists agree with Putnam's assessment of declining social capital.

The social capital debate has rekindled an interest in the nature and viability of the American political culture and an examination of how it is changing. Americans have conflicting ideas and beliefs about the proper role of government and where and how political power should be exercised. In this chapter, we look at the political culture that unites us as well as the ideologies that sometimes divide us.

CHAPTER MEDIA

POLITICS ONLINE
What's My Ideology?
www.prenhall.com/burns

PoliSim
What Do You Believe?
www.prenhall.com/burns

social capital

Participation in voluntary organizations that reinforce democratic and civic habits of discussion, compromise, and respect for differences.

political culture

The widely shared beliefs, values, and norms concerning the relationship of citizens to government and to one another.

natural rights

The rights of all people to dignity and worth; also called *human rights.*

THE AMERICAN POLITICAL CULTURE

Political scientists use the term **political culture** to refer to the widely shared beliefs, values, and norms concerning the relationship of citizens to government and to one another. American democratic values include liberty, equality, individualism, democracy, justice, the rule of law, nationalism, optimism, and idealism. There is no definitive list of American political values, however, for as we noted in Chapter 1, these widely shared democratic values overlap and sometimes conflict.

Shared Values

Before the American and French Revolutions, discussions about individual liberty, freedom, equality, private property, limited government, and popular consent were not widespread. Europe had been dominated by aristocracies, had experienced centuries of political and social inequality, and had been ruled by governments that were often arbitrary in their exercise of power. Liberal political philosophers rebelled against these traditions and proclaimed the principles of classical liberalism. They claimed individuals have certain **natural rights**—the rights of all people to dignity and worth—and that government, as a primary threat to those rights, must be limited and controlled. During this same period, the economic system was changing to a free market system. People began to think they could improve their lot in life and own property. Radical new ideas like these influenced the thinking of the founders of our nation.

LIBERTY   Americans have always been united by a commitment to liberty or freedom. No value in the American political culture is more revered. "We have always been a nation obsessed with liberty. Liberty over authority, freedom over responsibility, rights over duties—these are our historic preferences," wrote the late Clinton Rossiter, a noted political scientist. "Not the good man, but the free man has been the measure of all things in this sweet 'land of liberty'; not national glory but individual liberty has been the object of political authority and the test of its worth."[2]

EQUALITY   Jefferson's famous words in the Declaration of Independence express the primacy of our views of equality: "We hold these truths to be self-evident, that all men are created equal, that they are endowed by their Creator with certain unalienable rights, that among these are life, liberty, and the pursuit of happiness." Americans have always believed in social equality. In contrast to Europeans, our nation shunned aristocracy, and our Constitution explicitly bans titles of nobility.

Equality also refers to *political equality*, the idea that every individual has a right to equal protection under the law and equal voting power. Although political equality has always been a goal, it has not always been a reality. African Americans, Native Americans, and women have been denied political equality in the past.

Equality encompasses the idea of equality of opportunity, especially with regard to improving our economic status. Americans believe that social background should not limit our opportunity to achieve to the best of our ability, nor should race, gender, or religion. The nation's commitment to public education programs like Head Start for underprivileged preschool children, state support for public colleges and universities, and federal financial aid for higher education reflect this belief in equality.

INDIVIDUALISM   The United States is characterized by a persistent commitment to the individual. Under our system of government, individuals have both rights and responsibilities. Concern for preserving individual freedom of choice and what lim-

its, if any, to place on individual choice generate intense political conflict. The debate over legalized abortion is often framed in these terms. Although Americans agree with individual rights and freedoms, they also understand that rights can conflict with other rights or with the government's need to maintain order.

POWER TO THE PEOPLE   Americans have faith in the common sense of the ordinary person. We prefer action to reflection. We are often anti-expert and sometimes anti-intellectual. The emphasis on practicality and common sense has become part of our image. Poets like Walt Whitman and Carl Sandburg and storytellers like Mark Twain, Will Rogers, Eudora Welty, and Garrison Keillor have helped shape this tradition. This reverence for the common person helps explain our ambivalence toward power, politics, and government authority. In the United States, government is often viewed as a necessary evil.

DEMOCRATIC CONSENSUS   The most important feature that binds us together is the **democratic consensus**, a fairly widespread agreement on fundamental principles of governance and the values that undergird them. We are a people from many different cultural and ethnic backgrounds, histories, and religions. Despite these differences, our political culture includes widely shared attitudes and beliefs about principles of government, procedures, documents, and institutions. Americans have strong opinions about who has power to do what, how people acquire power, and how they are removed from power. These are fundamental "rules of the game" in which widespread consensus is important.

We believe in **majority rule**—governance according to the expressed preferences of the majority at regular elections. Yet we also believe that people in the minority should be free to try to win majority support for their opinions. Despite the fact that large numbers of Americans lack strong party attachments, we favor a two-party system. Our institutions are based on the principle of representation and consent of the governed. We believe in **popular sovereignty**—that ultimate power resides in the people. Government, from this perspective, exists to serve the people rather than the other way around. The means by which the government learns the will of the people is through *elections*, perhaps the most important expression of popular consent. But there are instances when popular sovereignty and majority rule must be limited by other fundamental rights, as in the case of referenda limiting civil rights.[3] Examples include California's 1964 vote to permit people to discriminate in the sale of residential housing and 1996 vote to overturn affirmative action.

Many of the limits on government are specified in the Constitution and the Bill of Rights. The Constitution is revered as a national symbol, yet we often differ over the precise meaning of the framers' original intentions. We honor many of these rights more in the abstract than in the particular. More than half of us, for instance, think that books with dangerous ideas should be banned from public school libraries (see Table 4–1). Intolerance of dissenting or offensive views is amply demonstrated in many public opinion polls and is observed on college and university campuses. Still, Americans can ordinarily be characterized as affirming support for democratic and constitutional values.

JUSTICE AND THE RULE OF LAW   Inscribed over the entrance to the U.S. Supreme Court are the words "Equal Justice Under Law." The rule of law means that government is based on a body of law applied equally and by just procedures, as opposed to rule by an elite in which the whims of those in power decide policy or resolve disputes. Chief Justice John Marshall succinctly summarized this principle: "The government of the United States has been emphatically termed a government of laws, not of men."[4] Americans believe strongly in the principle of fairness: all individuals are entitled to the same legal rights and protections.

democratic consensus
Widespread agreement on fundamental principles of democratic governance and the values that undergird them.

majority rule
Governance according to the expressed preferences of the majority.

popular sovereignty
A belief that ultimate power resides in the people.

WHERE WE LEARN THE AMERICAN POLITICAL CULTURE

The Family

One of the important sources of political culture in the United States and in other nations as well is the family. Children are taught from an early age what it means to be an American. They are curious about why people vote, what the president does, and whether Grandpa fought in World War II. The questions may vary somewhat from family to family, but the themes of authority, freedom, equality, liberty, and partisanship are common. Families are the most important reference groups, and compared to families in other cultures, American families are much more egalitarian.

The Schools

Public schools are another source of the American political culture. Children and teachers often begin the school day by saluting the flag, reciting the Pledge of Allegiance, or singing the National Anthem. Teaching American political and economic values is part of the curriculum. Not only are values taught in American history classes, but they are put into practice in school elections and newspapers and in encouraging students to participate in small-scale economic ventures.

Colleges and universities also play a role in fostering the American political culture. Students who attend college are often more confident than other persons in dealing with bureaucracy and politics generally, more likely to participate in politics and vote, and more knowledgeable about government. Many states

require students at state colleges and universities to take courses in American government or state government, in part to instill a sense of civic duty while imparting knowledge about state and national governments.

Religious and Civic Organizations

Religious freedom and diversity have played a part in the formation and maintenance of the American political culture. American churches, synagogues, and mosques have long fostered a common understanding of right and wrong. Freedom, including freedom of religion, individualism, pluralism, and civic duty, have all been fostered by churches. As churches do not all take the same positions on political issues, their impact is sometimes mitigated, but they have been important to such major social and political movements as abolition of slavery, expansion of civil

rights, and opposition to war. Civic organizations like the Boy Scouts, 4-H, League of Women Voters, Rotary Club, and Chamber of Commerce encourage citizen participation and pride in community and nation.

The Mass Media

In modern times the mass media have taken over some functions previously performed by the family. By the time they are adults, children will probably have spent more time watching television than in conversation with their parents. They may have had more political instruction from MTV than from their parents or their schools.

Political Activities

Finally, Americans educate each other about political values in the workplace, at the PTA meeting, or in more expressly political activities.

TABLE 4–1 It Depends on What You Mean by Rights and Freedoms

	Agree	Disagree	Don't Know*
Freedom of speech should apply to groups such as communist and the Ku Klux Klan.	57%	39%	4%
There has been real improvement in the position of African Americans.	53	38	9
Books that contain dangerous ideas should be banned from public school libraries.	55	43	2
Affirmative action programs to help African American women get better jobs and education should be continued.	65	31	4
The police should be allowed to search the houses of known drug dealers without a court order.	45	53	2
School boards ought to have the right to fire teachers who are known homosexuals.	33	62	4

SOURCE: The Pew Research Center for the People and the Press, *Retro-Politics—The Political Typology*, November 14, 1999.

*Includes those who said "neither."

For government to adhere to the rule of law, its policies and laws should follow these five rules:

- *Generality*: Laws should be stated generally, not singling out any group or individual.
- *Prospectivity*: Laws should apply to the future, not punish something someone did in the past.
- *Publicity*: Laws cannot be kept secret and then enforced.
- *Authority*: Valid laws are made by those with legitimate power, and the people legitimate that power through some form of popular consent.
- *Due Process*: Laws must be enforced impartially with fair processes.

NATIONALISM, OPTIMISM, AND IDEALISM Americans are highly nationalistic, sharing a sense of values and identity. We are proud of our past and our role in the world today. We are optimistic, though more about people than about government. We believe in opportunity, choice, individualism, and most of all, in freedom to improve ourselves and to achieve success with as little interference as possible from others or from government. As Table 4–2 indicates, U.S. citizens are more satisfied with their democratic government than are citizens of other countries.

We know our system is not perfect. We often grumble that elected officials have lost touch with us, we are disgusted by scandals, and we are impatient with the slowness of the system to solve problems like health care, crime, drug abuse, and campaign finance. Yet we have an abiding faith in government by the people. Despite the dissatisfactions, a remarkable belief persists that this nation is better, stronger, and more virtuous than other nations. Like every country, the United States has interests and motives that are selfish as well as generous, cynical as well as idealistic. Still, our support of human needs and rights throughout the world is evidence of an enduring idealism.

TABLE 4–2 Satisfaction with the Way Democracy Works

	Satisfied	Dissatisfied
United States	64%	27%
Canada	62	24
Germany	55	27
Iceland	54	23
Thailand	54	27
Costa Rica	52	25
Chile	43	31
France	43	32
Dominican Republic	40	38
United Kingdom	40	43
Japan	35	32
India	32	43
Spain	31	30
Venezuela	28	59
Taiwan	25	18
Hungary	17	50
Mexico	17	67
China	na	na

SOURCE: "People Throughout the World Largely Satisfied with Personal Lives," *Gallup Poll Monthly*, June 1995, p. 6.

WE THE PEOPLE

Oprah Winfrey: Achieving the American Dream

Is the American Dream a reality? If you don't think so, ask Oprah Winfrey. Born in Kosciusko, Mississippi, in 1954 to parents who never married, Oprah had a less than ideal childhood. At age six, she moved from her grandmother's farm in Mississippi to live with her mother in Wisconsin. At age twelve a family member sexually molested her. Later she attempted to run away from home. To avoid being put in a detention center, she was sent to live with her father in Nashville.

Under her father's direction, Oprah began to straighten out her life. She enrolled in Tennessee State University but dropped out during her sophomore year to become the first African-American anchor for Nashville's WTVF-TV. She moved to Baltimore to anchor a TV news broadcast and was later fired. But she found her niche as host of a Baltimore morning talk show. Building on this success, she moved to Chicago and hosted *A.M. Chicago*, which was later syndicated as *The Oprah Winfrey Show*.

Today Oprah Winfrey is a household name, and for many, a household personality. She has amassed a net worth of over a half a billion dollars, owns her own production company, and has her own women's magazine. She has starred in several films and was nominated for an Academy Award for her role in *The Color Purple*. She has even been

Coming from humble beginnings, Oprah Winfrey—television host, movie actress, and one of the highest paid people in the country—epitomizes the American Dream.

active in the political arena. In 1994, Bill Clinton signed into law the "Oprah Bill," federal legislation to protect children from abuse.

SOURCES: Deborah Tannen, "The T.V. Host Oprah Winfrey" (http://www.time.com/time/time100/artists/profile/winfrey.html); "Oprah Winfrey: The Real Story," *Bibliobytes, 2000* (http://www.bb.com/looptestlive.cfm?BOOKID=1581&StartRow=1).

The American Dream

Many of our political values come together in the **American Dream**, a complex set of ideas holding that the United States is a land of opportunity, and that individual initiative and hard work can bring economic success. Whether realized or not, this American Dream speaks to our most deeply held hopes and goals. The essence of the American Dream can be found in our enthusiasm for **capitalism**, an economic system characterized by private property, competitive markets, economic incentives, and limited government involvement in the production and pricing of goods and services.

The concept of *private property* enjoys extraordinary popularity in our political culture. In many European democracies, the state owns and operates transportation systems, the media, and other businesses that are privately owned and operated in the United States, although there has been some privatization of communications systems like telephone companies and broadcast media. Americans cherish the dream of acquiring property. Moreover, most Americans believe that those who own property have the right to decide how to use it.

The right to private property is just one of the economic incentives that cement our support for capitalism and fuel the American Dream. This is the land of opportunity for the enterprising. Here the competitive, practical go-getter can make a fortune, build a dream home, and retire early. We assume that people who have more ability or work extremely hard will get ahead, earn more, and enjoy economic rewards. We also believe people should be able to pass most of what they have accumulated along to their children and relatives. Even the poorest Americans generally oppose high inheritance taxes or limits on how much someone can earn.

Americans believe the free market system gives almost everyone a fair chance, that capitalism is necessary, and that freedom depends on it. We reject communism and socialism—a rejection fortified in recent years as most communist nations shifted toward capitalism. In the United States, individuals and corporations have acquired wealth and, at the same time, exercised political clout. Their power has, in turn, bred some resentment.

The conflict in values between a *competitive economy*, in which individuals reap large rewards for their initiative and hard work, and an *egalitarian society*, in which

everyone earns a decent living, carries over into politics. How the public resolves this tension changes over time and from issue to issue.

As important as the American Dream is to the national consciousness, Americans know it remains unfulfilled. An underclass persists in the form of impoverished families, ill-nourished and poorly educated children, and people living on the streets.[5] Many cities are actually two cities, where some live in luxury while others live in squalor. The gap between rich and poor has grown in recent years, and a sharp difference between white and black income persists tenaciously.[6] For more people than we want to admit, chances for success still depend on the family you were born in, the neighborhood you grew up in, or the college you attended.

Political and Economic Change

Political values are clearly affected by historical developments and by economic and technological growth. The Declaration of Independence and the Constitution identified such important political values as individual liberty, property rights, and limited government.[7] Early in our history we emphasized separation of powers, checks and balances, states' rights, and the Bill of Rights. It took an additional generation or two before we also began to take seriously the expansion of suffrage and competitive nominations and elections. Notions of political equality and effective participation emerged during the presidency of Andrew Jackson and matured in the course of the nineteenth century. By the end of the nineteenth century, populists and suffragists turned ideals into action and formed large-scale movements to achieve more democratic forms of participation and more responsive forms of governance.

THE INDUSTRIAL TRANSFORMATION   By 1900, the agrarian society the framers knew had been largely replaced by industrial capitalism and the growth of large corporations. With these changes, ideology was irreversibly transformed. Large privately owned corporations changed the economic order, including changes in the role of government and how people viewed each other. No one captures the implications of this shift better than political scientist Robert A. Dahl:

> One of the consequences of the new order has been a high degree of inequality in the distribution of wealth and income, and far greater inequality than had ever been thought likely or desirable under an agrarian order by Democratic Republicans like Jefferson and Madison, or had ever been thought consistent with democratic or republican government in the historic writings on the subject from Aristotle to Locke, Montesquieu, and Rousseau. Previous theorists and advocates had, like many of the framers of our own Constitution, insisted that a republic could exist only if the citizen body continued neither rich nor poor. Citizens, it was argued, must enjoy a rough equality of conditions.[8]

The success of the American industrial economy led to the accumulation of great wealth in the hands of a few—the robber barons or tycoons. Many had taken great risks or earned their fortunes through inventions and efficient production practices. But as disparities of income grew, so did disparities in political resources. Economic resources can be converted into political resources, like time to spend on politics and money to contribute to parties and candidates.[9]

At the turn of the century, the rise of the large corporation and the concentration of individual wealth in the United States created divisions and resentment. Muckraking journalists charged that the huge corporations had become **monopolies**, using their dominance of their industry to exploit workers and limit competition. Unsafe work conditions led to some regulation of the workplace by the states, but only the national government, it seemed, had the power to ensure fair treatment in the marketplace. This sentiment not only gave rise to the nation's first **antitrust legislation**—federal laws that try to prevent monopolies from dominating an industry and restraining trade—but also sowed the idea that government could—and

American Dream
The widespread belief that individual initiative and hard work can bring economic success, and that the United States is a land of opportunity.

capitalism
An economic system characterized by private property, competitive markets, economic incentives, and limited government involvement in the production and pricing of goods and services.

monopolies
Large corporations or firms that dominate their industries and are able to artificially fix prices and discourage competition.

antitrust legislation
Federal laws (starting with the Sherman Act of 1890) that try to prevent monopolies from dominating an industry and restraining trade.

should—as the Constitution asserts, "promote the general Welfare" by regulating working conditions, product safety, and labor-management disputes.

THE GREAT DEPRESSION AND THE NEW DEAL   Much of our thinking about the role of government in a capitalistic system was shaped by the Great Depression of the 1930s and the near collapse of the capitalistic system. Unrestrained capitalism and an unregulated market were faulted as causes of the Depression. The collapse of the stock market, massive unemployment, and a failed banking system brought the nation to the brink of disaster. There was no unemployment compensation, no guarantee on bank savings, no federal regulation of the securities exchanges, no Social Security. Americans turned to government to improve the lot of millions of jobless and homeless citizens. Beginning with Franklin D. Roosevelt's New Deal, the idea gradually gained widespread acceptance that government should use its powers and resources to ensure some measure of equal opportunity and social justice.

Roosevelt's State of the Union Address in 1944 outlined a "Second Bill of Rights" for all citizens in which he declared that this nation must make a firm commitment to "economic security and independence." Included in his Second Bill of Rights were:

- The right to a useful and remunerative job in the industries, shops, farms, or mines of the nation
- The right to earn enough to provide adequate food and clothing and recreation
- The right of every farmer to raise and sell his products at a return that would give him and his family a decent living
- The right of every businessman, large and small, to trade in an atmosphere of freedom from unfair competition and domination by monopolies at home or abroad
- The right of every family to a decent home
- The right to adequate medical care and the opportunity to achieve and enjoy good health
- The right to adequate protection from the economic fears of old age, sickness, accident, and unemployment
- The right to a good education.[10]

Roosevelt's policies and later efforts by John F. Kennedy and Lyndon Johnson in the 1960s to pass civil rights and voting rights legislation and launch a War on Poverty defined the ideological and political fights in the last half of the twentieth

Breadlines like this provided handouts of food to thousands of unemployed and destitute people during the Great Depression.

TABLE 4–3 Attitudes on Business and Welfare			
	Agree	Disagree	Don't Know*
There is too much power concentrated in the hands of a few big companies.	74%	25%	1%
Business corporations make too much profit.	56	38	6
Regulation of business does more harm than good.	55	37	8
It is the responsibility of the government to take care of people who can't take care of themselves.	62	35	3
The government should help more needy people even if it means going deeper into debt.	49	47	4
The government should guarantee every citizen enough to eat and a place to sleep.	64	33	2

SOURCE: The Pew Research Center for the People and the Press, *Retro-Politics—The Political Typology*. November 14, 1999.

*Includes those who said "neither."

century. Modern-day liberalism and conservatism turn, in large measure, on how much one believes in Roosevelt's Second Bill of Rights and how much government assistance one thinks is owed to minorities, women, and others who have suffered discrimination or have been left behind by the industrial or technological revolutions of the twentieth century.

Today, free enterprise is no longer unbridled. Government regulations, antitrust laws, job safety regulations, environmental standards, and minimum wage rates all balance the freedom of enterprise against the rights of individuals. Most people today support a semiregulated or mixed free enterprise system that checks the worst tendencies of capitalism, but they reject excessive government intervention (see Table 4–3). Much of American politics centers on how to achieve this balance.

Currently, liberals and conservatives agree that some governmental intervention is necessary to assist those who fail in the competition for education and economic prosperity. In the 2000 elections, presidential candidates of both major parties debated the precise role and extent of government involvement in this area: Al Gore's campaign promised to provide health care to all Americans; George W. Bush's theme of "compassionate conservatism" would rely more on private charities to attend to human needs.

IDEOLOGY AND ATTITUDES ABOUT THE ROLE OF GOVERNMENT

deology refers to a person's ideas or beliefs about political values and the role of government. It includes the views people have about how government should work and how it actually works. Ideology links our basic values to the day-to-day operations or policies of government.

Two major schools of political ideology dominate American politics: *liberalism* and *conservatism*. Three lesser, but more defined, schools of thought, *socialism*, *environmentalism*, and *libertarianism*, also help define the spectrum of ideology in the United States. Table 4–4 provides a general distribution of political ideology in the United States.

Liberalism

In the seventeenth and eighteenth centuries, classical liberals fought to minimize the role of government. They stressed individual rights and perceived government as the primary threat to rights and liberties. Classical liberals favored *limited government* and sought ample protections from governmental harassment. Over time, the emphasis on individualism remained constant, but the perception of the need for government changed.

ideology
One's basic beliefs about political values and the role of government.

TABLE 4–4 Differences in Political Ideology

	Conservative	Moderate	Liberal
Sex			
Male	39%	45%	16%
Female	25	55	20
Race			
White	34	46	20
Black	10	78	12
Age			
18–34	19	58	24
35–45	37	44	18
46–55	35	44	21
56–64	36	55	10
65+	32	52	16
Religion			
Protestant	37	51	12
Catholic	25	55	20
Jewish	18	64	18
Education			
Less than high school	11	80	9
High school diploma	23	66	11
Some college	32	43	25
Bachelor's degree	44	34	21
Advanced degree	41	39	20
Party			
Democrat	15	54	31
Independent	26	58	16
Republican	71	24	6

Source: Center for Political Studies, University of Michigan, *American National Election Study*, 2000.

Note: We have combined with the moderates persons who do not know their ideology or had not thought much about it. For party identification, we have combined Independent leaners with their respective parties. Rows may not add up to 100 percent due to rounding.

Today liberals view government as protecting individuals from being abused by a variety of forces, such as market vagaries, business decisions, and discriminatory practices.

CONTEMPORARY LIBERALS   In its current American usage, **liberalism** refers to a belief in the positive uses of government to bring about justice and equality of opportunity. Modern-day liberals wish to preserve the rights of the individual and the right to own private property, yet they are willing to have the government intervene in the economy to remedy the defects of capitalism. Liberals seek protection against inadequate or deficient health care, housing, and education. They generally believe in affirmative action programs, workers' health and safety protections, tax rates that rise with income, and unions' right to organize and strike.

On a more philosophical level, liberals generally believe in the possibility of progress. They believe that the future will be better, that obstacles can be overcome. This positive set of beliefs may explain their willingness to trust government programs. Liberals contend that modern technology and industrialization cry out for government programs to offset the loss of liberties suffered by the poor and the weak. Liberals such as Bill Bradley, Edward Kennedy, Hillary Rodham Clinton, and Jesse Jackson frequently stress the need for an involved and affirmative government.

liberalism

A belief in the positive uses of government to bring about justice and equality of opportunity.

Liberals charge that conservatives usually act in self-interest and follow the maxim, "Let the government take care of the rich, and the rich in turn will take care of the poor." Liberals, on the other hand, prefer that government take care of the weak, for the strong can always take care of themselves. "We have rejected the discredited theory that the fortunes of the nation should be in the hands of a privileged few," said President Harry Truman. "Instead, we believe that our economic system should rest on a democratic foundation and that wealth should be created for the benefit of all. . . . Every segment of our population and every individual has a right to expect from his government a fair deal."[11]

The liberal view holds all people equal. Equality of opportunity is essential, and to achieve that end, discriminatory practices must be eliminated. Some liberals favor the reduction of great inequalities of wealth that make equality of opportunity impossible. Most favor a certain minimum level of income. Rather than placing a cap on wealth, they want a floor placed beneath the poor. In short, liberals seek to lessen the impact of great inequalities of wealth and work to extend opportunities to all, regardless of their economic standing.

CRITICISMS OF LIBERALISM   Critics of liberalism say liberals place too much reliance on governmental solutions, higher taxes, and bureaucracy. These opponents argue that somewhere along the line liberals forgot that government, to serve our best interests, has to be limited. Power tends to corrupt, and too much dependence on government can corrupt the spirit, undermine self-reliance, and make people forget those cherished personal freedoms and property rights our Republic was founded to secure and protect. Too many governmental regulations and too much taxation tend to undermine the self-help ethic that "made America great." In short, critics of liberalism contend that the welfare and regulatory state pushed by liberals will ultimately destroy individual initiative, the entrepreneurial spirit, and the very engine of economic growth that might lead to true equality of economic opportunities.

In recent elections, Republicans have made liberalism a villain and positioned their own candidates more in the mainstream. George Bush, in 1988, consistently referred to Michael Dukakis as from the "liberal Democratic party." Bill Clinton was careful not to label his program as liberal, focusing on the need for economic growth, jobs, and a lower budget deficit. He insisted he was a "New Democrat." Al Gore positioned himself in the tradition of Clinton as a centrist, not a liberal, but George W. Bush charged that Gore was an advocate of big government.

The movement to the center by some Democrats and the conventional wisdom that liberal or progressive approaches are in decline is disputed by political commentator E. J. Dionne, Jr., whose book on how progressives can regain power is aptly titled *They Only Look Dead*. Dionne contends that the current political upheaval should be defined less as a revolt against *big* government than as a rebellion against *bad* government—government that has proven ineffectual in grappling with the political, economic, and moral crises that have shaken the country. Dionne challenges the claims that big government is bad or even over. Pointing to past progressive or liberal successes, Dionne contends Americans want a government that eases economic transitions, helps "preserve a broad middle class," and "expands the choices available to individuals."[12]

The popularity of liberalism and conservatism and the importance of particular issues change with world events. We were preoccupied with budget deficits until the budget surpluses of recent years. With the end of the cold war, we became more concerned about domestic policy than about foreign policy. But we live in a global economy in which our jobs and economic progress are linked to our neighbors and

Is Government a Necessary Evil or a Force for Good?

In his provocative book *A Necessary Evil: A History of American Distrust of Government*, historian Garry Wills explores the tension between widespread anti-government attitudes and the tendency of Americans to turn to government to solve problems. Hostility to government is deeply rooted and longstanding. In recent years it has been manifested in the tax revolt of the late 1970s and early 1980s, the movement to limit the number of terms legislators can serve in the 1980s and 1990s, and in the opposition to gun controls in the last two decades.

Wills identifies the following values as the core of anti-government hostility: the belief that government should be kept to a minimum; that local government is preferred to higher levels; that politicians should be amateur, spontaneous, voluntary, religious, and rotational.[*] Moreover, there is a tendency of the anti-government attitudes to cling together—take one and you are likely to end up with most or all of them.[**] Wills asserts that those who see government as a force for good believe that government is sometimes a positive good, and that good government is, among other things, expert, authoritative, efficient, secular, progressive, and regulatory.[***]

[*]Garry Wills, *A Necessary Evil: A History of American Distrust of Government* (Simon & Schuster, 1999, pp. 17–18.

[**]Ibid. p. 20.

[***]Ibid. p. 18.

Gary Bauer represented the strongly conservative position in the candidate debates for the Republican presidential nomination.

to other countries around the world. The net effect of these changes is that our national government, while focusing on domestic issues like health care and education, must also deal with international matters.

Conservatism

Private property rights and belief in free enterprise are cardinal attributes of contemporary **conservatism**. In contrast to liberals, conservatives want to keep government small, especially the national government, except in the area of national defense. However, because conservatives take a more pessimistic view of human nature than liberals do, they maintain that people need strong leadership institutions, firm laws, and strict moral codes to keep their appetites under control. Government, they think, needs to ensure order. Conservatives also believe that those who fail in life are in some way the architects of their own misfortune and must bear the main responsibility for solving their own problems. Conservatives prefer the status quo and desire change only in moderation.

TRADITIONAL CONSERVATIVES   Traditional conservatives are emphatically pro-business. They oppose higher taxes and resist all but the most necessary antitrust, trade, and environmental regulations on corporations. The functions of government should be to encourage family values, protect the nation from foreign enemies, preserve law and order, enforce private contracts, foster competitive markets, and encourage free and fair trade. Traditional conservatives favor dispersing power broadly throughout the political and social systems to avoid concentration of power at the national level. They favor having the market, rather than the government, provide services.

Until recent decades, conservatives opposed the New Deal programs of the 1930s, the War on Poverty in the 1960s, and most aggressive civil rights and affirmative action programs. Human needs, they say, can and should be cared for by families and charities. Conservatives put their faith in the private sector and consider social justice to be essentially an economic question. They dislike the tendency to turn to government, especially the national government, for solutions to societal problems. Government social activism, they say, has been expensive and counterproductive. They prefer private giving and individual voluntary efforts targeted at social and economic problems rather than government programs.

In the 2000 presidential campaign, George W. Bush attempted to build upon the successes of churches and other organizations in providing assistance to needy individuals, while at the same time trying to avoid the image of outright hostility to all government aid. Bush said early in his campaign, "Too often, my party has confused the need for a limited government with a disdain for government itself. . . . That love [of our country] is undermined by sprawling, arrogant, aimless government. It is restored by focused and effective and energetic government."[13]

SOCIAL CONSERVATIVES   Some conservatives focus less on economics and more on morality and lifestyle. Social conservatives favor strong governmental action to protect children from pornography and drugs. They want stringent limitations on abortions. This brand of conservatism—sometimes called the New Right, ultraconservatism, or even the Radical Right—emerged in the 1980s. The New Right shares traditional conservative's love of freedom and backs an aggressive effort to defend America's interests abroad. It favors the return of organized prayer in public schools and opposes policies like job quotas, busing, and tolerance of homosexuality. In sum, a defining characteristic of the New Right is a strong desire to impose various *social controls*.

A very active New Right or Religious Right group that supports social conservatism is the Christian Coalition, founded by Pat Robertson, a minister who sponsors a nightly cable television program. The Coalition has become a major political force. Although ostensibly working in a bipartisan fashion, it is more at

conservatism

A belief that limited government ensures order, competitive markets, and personal opportunity.

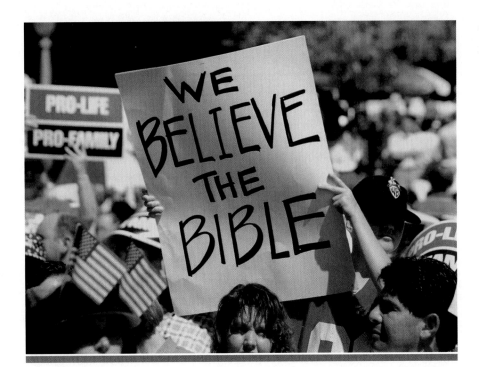

A growing force in recent years is the Religious Right. They are active in local school boards and town councils as well as in national elections.

home in the Republican party. The Coalition lobbies for and funds candidates who are pro-family, anti-abortion, anti-gay. It favors a constitutional amendment that would guarantee the rights to prayer in public schools and religious symbols in public places. It works at all levels of government and especially targets candidates who have voted for abortion rights legislation.

Some conservatives are uncomfortable with the close association between the Republican party and the Christian Coalition. Former U.S. senator Warren Rudman, of New Hampshire, has observed, "Politically speaking, the Republican Party is making a terrible mistake if it appears to ally itself with the Christian right. There are some fine, sincere people in its ranks, but there are also enough anti-abortion zealots, would-be censors, homophobes, bigots, and latter-day Elmer Gantrys to discredit any party that is unwise enough to embrace such a group."[14] Rudman's statement was later used to justify phone calls by Reverend Pat Robertson to Christian Coalition members urging them to vote for George W. Bush in the 2000 South Carolina and Michigan primaries instead of for John McCain, whose campaign Rudman was managing.[15]

CRITICISMS OF CONSERVATISM   Not everyone agreed with Ronald Reagan's statement that "government is the problem." Indeed, critics of conservatism before and during the Reagan-Bush era saw hostility to government as counterproductive and inconsistent. Conservatives, they argued, have a selective opposition to government. They want more government when it serves their needs—regulating pornography and abortion, for example—but are opposed to it when it serves somebody else's.

Conservatives place great faith in the market economy—critics would say too much faith. This posture often puts conservatives at odds with labor unions and consumer activists and in close alliance with businesspeople, particularly large corporations. Hostility to regulation and a belief in competition leads them to push for deregulation. This approach has not always had the intended positive effects, as the collapse of many savings and loan companies in the 1980s and the energy crisis in California in the early 2000s revealed.[16] Conservatives counter that relying on market solutions and encouraging the free market are still the best course of action in most policy areas.

The policy of the Reagan years of lowering taxes was consistent with the conservative hostility to big government. Many conservatives embraced the idea that if

Bernard Sanders, a self-described Social-ist, represents Vermont in the U.S. House of Representatives as an Independent.

we lower taxes on the rich, their increased economic activity will "trickle down" to the poor. This view was criticized by many Democrats, who pointed out that the growth in income and wealth in the 1980s was largely concentrated among the well-to-do.[17] They also pointed out that government spending, especially for defense, tripled the deficit during the 1980s when conservatives were in control.

Conservatives are also criticized for their failure to acknowledge and endorse policies that deal with racism and sexism in the United States. Their opposition to the civil rights laws in the 1960s and to affirmative action more recently are examples of this perspective. Not only have conservatives opposed new laws in these areas; they have hampered the activity of the executive branch when in power and have sought to limit the activity of the courts in these matters as well.

The selective application of government by liberals and social conservatives demonstrates the lack of consistency in both groups. Liberals favor vigorous governmental programs to help the poor but oppose governmental intrusion into citizens' private lives, while social conservatives preach less government except in promoting proper conduct.

Socialism

Socialism is an economic and governmental system based on public ownership of the means of production and exchange. Karl Marx once described socialism as a transitional stage of society between capitalism and communism. In a capitalist system, the means of production and most property are privately owned; in a communist system, property is controlled by the state in common for all the people. In the ultimate communist country, justice is achieved by having participants determine their own needs and take what is appropriate from the common product of society. Marx's dictum was, "From each according to his ability, to each according to his needs." Some aspects of socialism have been combined with democracy, as in Sweden. Communist countries like Cuba are ruled by one party, the Communist party.

In one of the most dramatic transformations in recent times, Russia, its sister republics, and its former European satellites abandoned communism and are attempting to establish free markets. These countries had previously rejected capitalism, opting for state ownership and centralized government planning of the economy. But by the end of the twentieth century, the disparities in economic well-being between capitalist and communist nations produced a tide of political and economic reform that left communism intact in only a few countries, such as Cuba and China.

American socialists—of whom there are only a few prominent examples—favor a greatly expanded role for the government. They would nationalize certain industries, institute a public jobs program so that all who want work would be put to work, place a much steeper tax burden on the wealthy, and drastically cut defense spending.[18] Most of the democracies of Western Europe are more influenced by socialist ideas than we are in the United States, but they remain, like the United States, largely market economies. Many countries appear to be turning to market solutions for problems once assumed to be the responsibility of government. Some of the most important debates of the next century are going to be about what is the proper role of government and what the market can do better.[19]

Debates about communist expansionism are increasingly dated and irrelevant in American politics. There is little fear today that the United States will become communist, and the communist threat around the world is greatly diminished. But people of varying ideologies do indeed worry about whether the United States is maintaining adequate military strength or losing ground in the global economy.

Environmentalism

Preoccupation with the environment and related matters is **environmentalism,** an ideology that has taken root in several democracies in recent decades. The so-called "Green movement" has elected members of parliament in Finland, Germany,

socialism

An economic and governmental system based on public ownership of the means of production and exchange.

environmentalism

An ideology that is dominated by concern for the environment but also promotes grass-roots democracy, social justice, equal opportunity, nonviolence, respect for diversity, and feminism.

Switzerland, Sweden, Luxembourg, Austria, and the Netherlands and is part of the liberal-left coalition governing Germany today. In the United States, the Green party emphasizes such values as grass-roots democracy, social justice, equal opportunity, nonviolence, respect for diversity, and feminism. In these areas environmentalism is little different from liberalism, but it is in their emphasis on ecology and the environment that "greens" are distinct.

The website of the U.S. Green party says, "We must practice agriculture which replenishes the soil; move to an energy-efficient economy; and live in ways that respect the integrity of natural systems."[20] Ralph Nader, the presidential standard-bearer for the Green party in 2000, enhanced the visibility of the party but still won less than 3 percent of the vote.

Harry Browne, Libertarian candidate for president in 1996 and 2000, was on the ballot in all 50 states but received less than 1 percent of the total vote.

Libertarianism

Libertarianism is an ideology that cherishes individual liberty and insists on sharply limited government. It carries some overtones of anarchism, of the classical English liberalism of the past, and of a 1930s-style conservatism. The Libertarian party has gained a small following among people who believe that both liberals and conservatives lack consistency in their attitude toward the power of the national government.

Libertarians preach opposition to just about all government programs. They favor massive cuts in government spending and an end to the Federal Bureau of Investigation, the Central Intelligence Agency, and most regulatory commissions. They oppose participation in the United Nations and favor a defense establishment that would defend the United States only if directly attacked. They oppose *all* government regulation, including, for example, mandatory seat-belt and helmet laws. Unlike conservatives, libertarians would repeal laws that regulate personal morality, including abortion, pornography, prostitution, and recreational drugs.

A Libertarian party candidate for president has been on the ballot in all 50 states in recent presidential elections, although never obtaining more than 1 percent of the vote. The Libertarian candidate for president in 2000, Harry Browne, ran on a platform that emphasized freedom from government. The 2000 Libertarian platform was committed to a smaller government, limited by the Constitution's specifications, and proposed immediate and complete removal of the federal government from education, energy, regulation, crime control, welfare, housing, transportation, health care, and agriculture; repeal of the income tax and all other direct taxes; decriminalization of drugs and pardons for prisoners convicted of nonviolent drug offenses; and withdrawal of overseas military forces. Libertarian positions are rarely timid; at the very least, they prompt intriguing political debates.[21]

A Word of Caution

Political labels have different meanings across national boundaries as well as over time. To be a liberal in certain European nations is to be on the right; to be a liberal in the United States is to be on the left. In recent elections, the term "liberal"—which back in Franklin Roosevelt's day had been popular—became "the L-word," a label most politicians sought to avoid.

But liberalism is more than a label. On big questions—such as the role of government in the economy, in promoting equality of opportunity, and in regulating the behavior of individuals or businesses—real differences separate conservative and liberal groups. This does not mean, however, that people who are conservative in one area are necessarily conservative in another, or that liberals always hold similar views.

It is important to appreciate that ideology both causes events and is affected by them. Just as the Great Depression resulted in a tidal wave of ideological change, so did our involvement in World War II, Korea, and Vietnam, each in its own way. World War II, with its positive example of how government can work to defend freedom, strengthened positive views about the role of the national government. The Vietnam War probably had the opposite effect, producing disillusionment with government.

libertarianism
An ideology that cherishes individual liberty and insists on a sharply limited government, promoting a free-market economy, a noninterventionist foreign policy, and an absence of regulation in the moral and social spheres.

CONSERVATIVE MANIFESTO

Pete DuPont

Former governor of Delaware and Republican presidential candidate Pete DuPont is a strong advocate for what he calls "contemporary conservatism." According to DuPont, conservatives are troubled by the inability of many individuals to accept the responsibility that living independently and morally in a free society entails.

Pointing to the Declaration of Independence, which states that "that all men are created equal, that they are endowed by their creator with certain unalienable rights," DuPont asserts that people receive their rights from God rather than from government. The problem is that today's government has unnecessarily restricted rights and freedoms by regulating the economy and replacing private initiative with publicly financed social programs. These actions have encouraged many individuals to abandon responsibility for their own welfare in favor of dependence upon government programs. DuPont asserts that, "Even in America, amidst the greatest success of political and economic freedom in the history of the world, generations of central social and economic planning have finally fostered a new culture—a culture of dependency, rampant crime, single parenthood, broken families, tribal-like group competition, and a turn away from personal responsibility."

Human beings, in the conservative view, are competitive and individualistic. Like many conservatives, DuPont applauds the open marketplace in which people can establish their own businesses

and compete freely to build enterprises that contribute to the general welfare of society. Conservatives enjoy the exhilaration of risk and competition. They find personal dignity in facing adversity with courage and overcoming obstacles with determination. They find personal irresponsibility and immorality to be the two most negative features of human nature. Irresponsible people rely on government or private handouts or resort to crime to meet their needs; immoral people have extramarital affairs and desert their families in their pursuit of pleasure.

What, then, is the conservative vision of the good society? DuPont repeatedly emphasizes strength as he identifies explicit principles for creating a prosperous and just society. Conservatives would: (1) strengthen our national defense by increasing the military forces and improving technology; (2) strengthen law enforcement by building more prisons, reinvigorating drug enforcement programs, and reaffirming the public's right to own firearms; (3) strengthen our economy by reducing taxes, minimizing government regulation of business, abolishing affirmative action programs, and paring down social programs such as health and welfare subsidies; (4) strengthen families by making divorce and abortion more difficult and allowing families to select the schools their children will attend.)★

SOURCE: "Conservative Manifesto," *National Review* 46, March 21, 1994, pp. 32-38.

> **Conservatives are troubled by the inability of many individuals to accept the responsibility that living independently and morally in a free society entails.**

DEBATE

WHY I'M STILL LEFT

Mitchell Cohen

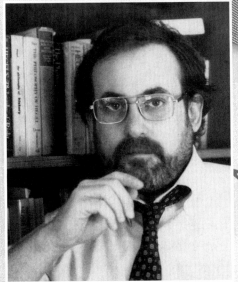

Mitchell Cohen, an editor of *Dissent* magazine, offers a different vision: one of American liberalism (or "social democracy," as he calls it). He explains that he uses the word "left" in order to identify with three "entwined" ideas: "liberty, equality, and solidarity." Conservatives, he says, have distorted what it means to be "liberal" or "left" and have tried to give these words negative connotations. Cohen maintains that at the heart of leftist values are democracy and social justice. This does not mean creating a utopia in which all people are forced to be equal. It does, however, include "siding with working people and the dispossessed, especially against private economic power." He hopes to convince people that "democracy ought to pervade socioeconomic in addition to political domains of life so that. . .the conditions for the freedom of one would be the conditions for the freedom of all."

Cohen insists that when conservatives claim that all people are equally free to pursue opportunity in our society, this is a myth. Citizens don't begin life at the same starting place. Our "free market" economy is in fact highly undemocratic because of the power of corporations and the advantages enjoyed by the upper social strata. People are not actually born with equal resources. We are born into a world in which some possess considerable advantages and many others are at a disadvantage. Cohen writes (following philosopher John Rawls) that "Our parents are a matter of chance, not choice. Unless you can be said to have rated your progenitors, why should advantages or disabilities that attend accidents of birth be translated into social privileges?" He points to national income data that indicates that the top 20 percent of the population has nine times as much wealth as the bottom 20 percent. This imbalance, he believes, is inherently unjust.

Cohen also thinks that conservatives are too one-sided when they say that people are competitive, "rugged individualists" by nature. Cohen argues that we are "social individuals" who want freedom, but who also feel solidarity with other human beings. So while Cohen believes markets are an important part of economic life, he also contends that they need to be regulated on behalf of broader human values. Cohen advocates an "equality-friendly society" and "social citizenship." He wants to ensure equal access to education and health care and to restrain the power of large corporations. According to Cohen, a healthy political democracy requires economic democracy.)★

SOURCE: Mitchell Cohen, "Why I'm Still Left," *Dissent* 44 (Spring 1997).

> We are "social individuals" who want freedom, but who also feel solidarity with other human beings.

For further information about this debate, go to **www.prenhall.com/burns** *and click on the Debate Icon in Chapter 4.*

The antigovernment sentiment in recent presidential elections is undoubtedly related to Vietnam, the Watergate scandal, and allegations of sexual misconduct by political leaders.

IDEOLOGY AND THE AMERICAN PEOPLE

Ideological controversy today centers on how we can improve schools, encourage a stronger work ethic, and stop the flow of drugs into the country; whether to permit openly gay people into the military or sanction same-sex marriages; and the best ways to instill moral values, build character, and encourage cohesive and lasting families.

Despite the twists and turns of American politics, the distribution of ideology in the nation has been remarkably consistent (see Figure 4–1). Conservatives out-number liberals, but the proportion of conservatives did not increase substantially with the decisive Republican presidential victories of the 1980s or congressional victories of the 1990s.

Another important fact about ideology in the United States is that few people see themselves as extremists. In 2000 only 2 percent of the population saw themselves as extreme conservatives, and the same percent saw themselves as extreme liberals (see Figure 4–2). These percentages have changed very little over time. The tendency toward muted ideology is also demonstrated by the fact more people consider themselves *slightly* liberal or *slightly* conservative than liberal or conservative. Despite claims by ideological factions in both parties to move to the right or move to the left, there are simply more votes in the middle.[22]

Both major parties targeted moderate or centrist voters in the 2000 presidential election, as reflected in the stands of the candidates on key issues, including their efforts to minimize ideological battles at the conventions. Governor Tommy Thompson of Wisconsin, who chaired the Republican Platform Committee, stated that their more conservative partisans did not push their issues because "they want to win."[23] Democrats adopted a similar strategy. For example, they stressed the need to limit violence and sexuality in video games sold to children. This move to the center by both parties does not mean that there are not liberal and conservative wings in both parties, with the liberal wing more powerful in the Democratic party and the conservative wing more powerful in the Republican party. (We analyze party identification in greater detail in Chapter 7.)

For those who have a liberal or conservative preference, ideology provides a lens through which to view politics. It helps simplify the complexities of politics,

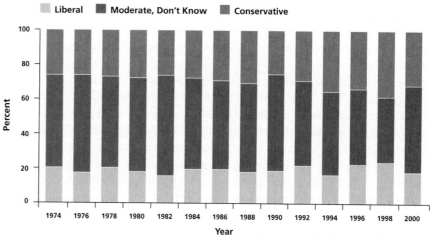

FIGURE 4–1 Ideology over Time

SOURCE: Center for Political Studies, University of Michigan, National Election Study Cumulative Data File, 1952–1992; *1994, 1996, 1998, and 2000 National Election Study.*

policies, personalities, and programs. An ideology may be an accurate or an inaccurate description of reality, yet it is still the way a person thinks about people, power, and society. However, most Americans do not organize their attitudes systematically. A voter may want increased spending for defense but vote for the party that is for reducing defense spending because he or she has always voted for that party or prefers its stand on the environment. Or a person may favor tax cuts and balancing the budget while at the same time be unwilling to see government programs cut back substantially.

Consistency among various attitudes and opinions is often relatively low. Much of the time people view political issues as isolated matters and do not apply an overall standard of performance in evaluating parties or candidates. Indeed, many citizens find it difficult to relate what happens in one policy situation to what happens in another. This problem becomes worse as government gets into more and more policy areas. Hence, many people, not surprisingly, have difficulty finding candidates who reflect their ideological preferences across a range of issues.

The absence of widespread and solidified liberal and conservative positions in the United States makes for politics and policy-making processes that are markedly different from those in many European and other nations. Policy making in this country is characterized more by coalitions of the moment than by fixed alignments that pit one set of ideologies against another. Our politics is marked more by moderation, pragmatism, and accommodation than by a prolonged battle among two, three, or more competing philosophies of government. Elsewhere, especially in countries where a strong Socialist or Christian Democratic party exists, things are different.

This does not, however, mean that policies or ideas are not elements in American politics. There has been, for instance, a shift to strongly partisan and ideological voting in the House of Representatives. Part of the explanation for the increasing importance of ideology in Congress is Republican gains in the South, with remaining southern Democrats becoming more liberal; in other parts of the country where moderate Republicans were once successful, liberal Democrats now hold many seats.

FIGURE 4–2 **Ideology Curve**

SOURCE: Center for Political Studies, University of Michigan, *2000 National Election Study*.

IDEOLOGY AND TOLERANCE

Is there a connection between the ideologies of liberalism and conservatism and support for civil liberties and tolerance for racial minorities? Some political scientists assert that conservatives are generally less tolerant than liberals. This view is stoutly contested by conservatives, who have charged liberals with trying to impose a "politically correct" position on universities and the media. Liberals are usually more tolerant of dissent and the expression of unorthodox opinions. However, liberals, too, can be intolerant—of anti-abortion forces, for example, or the National Rifle Association, or the views of Pat Robertson.

Most liberals are strongly opposed to crime and lawbreaking, yet they are as concerned about the roots or causes of crime as they are about the punishment of criminals. Perhaps for this reason, liberals exhibit somewhat greater concern than conservatives for the rights of the accused and are more willing to expand the rights of due process. Conservatives usually take a harder line and, in recent years, have won widespread popular support for their greater concern for the victims of crime than for the rights of the accused.

Such differences are most evident in the responses of liberals and conservatives to questions of civil rights and civil liberties. In the area of free speech, conservatives are usually seen as less willing to permit speech that is out of the political or cultural mainstream. Perhaps conservatives are less tolerant because those who claim to be exercising the right of free speech often attack established values. Liberals favor limiting speech in areas like cigarette advertising or campaign spending.[24]

Conservatives believe that the United States has become too permissive. Many conservatives, especially in the New or Religious Right, are highly critical of

homosexuals, drug users, prostitutes, unwed mothers, and pornographers. They worry about what they claim has been a decline in moral standards and, interestingly, call on government to help reverse these trends. Liberals, on the other hand, generally accept nonconformity in conduct and opinion as an inescapable by-product of freedom.[25] In this regard, liberals are like libertarians.

Ideologies have consequences. It is these sharp cleavages in political thinking that stir opposing interest groups into action. Groups such as the Christian Coalition, the American Civil Liberties Union, Amnesty International, Mothers Against Drunk Driving, Queer Nation, and countless others promote their views of what is politically desirable. It is also these differences in ideological perspectives that reinforce party loyalties and divide us at election time. Policy fights in Congress, between Congress and the White House, and during judicial confirmation hearings also have their roots in our uneasily coexisting ideological values.

Our hard-earned rights and liberties are never entirely safeguarded; they are fragile and are shaped by the political, economic, and social climate of the day. In later chapters we examine the interest groups and political parties that are battling to advance their values and compete in the American political culture. But before turning to those topics, we examine the social and economic diversity of the American political landscape in Chapter 5 and see why agreement on shared democratic values is all the more remarkable.

POLITICS ONLINE

What's My Ideology?

Ideology is typically arrayed on a continuum from left to right, liberal to conservative. As we have noted in this chapter, there are several different dimensions on which people can classify themselves: economic policy, civil rights and liberties, foreign and defense policy, and lifestyle issues. Most people are moderate in their overall positions, and some do not even think in these terms.

At the www.prenticehall.com/burns site for this chapter, we have prepared a set of questions for you to answer that will give you a sense of your ideology for each of the four issue dimensions. Depending on which issue dimension you think most important, the exercise will also calculate an overall score for you. As you complete the self-assessment, do not hesitate to evaluate the extent to which the items capture the liberal/conservative concept.

Once you have used the questions to classify yourself, you may want to read more about different ideological perspectives. For example, libertarians may be a group you want to know more about; a useful website for to learn more about libertarians is:
www.lp.org.

There are a host of websites that advocate conservative positions; some you might find interesting include:
www.conservativedigest.net and ww.aei.org.

For a more liberal perspective, you can go to:
www.prospect.org or www.trunleft.com/ligeral.html.

SUMMARY

1. The United States, like every other nation or society, has a distinctive political culture. It consists of a widely held set of fundamental political values and accepted processes and institutions that help us manage conflict and resolve problems. In the United States, there is, at least in the abstract, respect for the Constitution, the Bill of Rights, a two-party system, and the right to elect officials on the basis of majority rule. Our belief in social equality has fostered acceptance of the

notion that government should guarantee equality of opportunity through programs like education and job training.

2. Americans share a widespread commitment to classical liberalism, which embraces the importance of individual liberty, equality, individualism, power to the people, private property, limited government, nationalism, optimism, idealism, the democratic consensus, and justice and the rule of law. They also believe that the American Dream should be something we can all pursue.

3. American political values have been affected by the industrial transformation, the development of large corporations and other large institutions, the Great Depression, and a global economy.

4. The sources of the American political culture include the family, schools, religious and civic organizations, the mass media, and political activities.

5. Two broad schools of thought are important in American politics today: liberalism, a belief in the positive uses of government to bring about justice and equality of opportunity; and conservatism, a belief that limited government ensures order, competitive markets, and personal opportunity. Socialism, environmentalism, and libertarianism also attract a following in America.

6. Most Americans are nonideological and are guided primarily by moderate pragmatism. Few Americans are extremists.

7. Ideological orientation has a bearing on how tolerant we are of the views and conduct of others. Liberals tend to be more permissive, whereas conservatives generally favor tradition, stability, and greater levels of "law and order." These differences have consequences for electoral contests and policy development in our political system.

KEY TERMS

social capital 74
political culture 74
natural rights 74
democratic consensus 75

majority rule 75
popular sovereignty 75
American Dream 79
capitalism 79

monopolies 79
antitrust legislation 79
ideology 81
liberalism 82

conservatism 84
socialism 86
environmentalism 86
libertarianism 87

FURTHER READING

WILLIAM F. BUCKLEY AND CHARLES R. KESLER, *Keeping the Tablets: Modern American Conservative Thought* (Harper & Row, 1988).

JAMES W. CEASER, *Reconstructing America: The Symbol of America in Modern Thought* (Yale University Press, 1997).

E. J. DIONNE, JR., *They Only Look Dead: Why Progressives Will Dominate the Next Political Era* (Simon & Schuster, 1996).

JOHN EHRMAN, *The Rise of Neoconservatism: Intellectuals and Foreign Affairs, 1945–1994* (Yale University Press, 1995).

JEAN BETHKE ELSHTAIN, *Democracy on Trial* (Basic Books, 1995).

DAVID FRUM, *What's Right: The New Conservative Majority and the Remaking of America* (Basic Books, 1996).

AMY GUTMANN AND DENNIS THOMPSON, *Democracy and Disagreement: Why Moral Conflict Cannot Be Avoided in Politics, and What Should Be Done About It* (Harvard University Press, 1996).

LOUIS HARTZ, *The Liberal Tradition in America* (Harcourt Brace, 1955).

LAWRENCE E. HARRISON AND SAMUEL P. HARRINGTON, EDS., *Culture Matters: How Values Shape Human Progress* (Basic Books, 2000).

IRVING KRISTOL, *Neoconservatism: The Autobiography of an Idea* (Free Press, 1995).

HERBERT MCCLOSKY AND JOHN ZALLER, *The American Ethos: Public Attitudes Toward Capitalism and Democracy* (Harvard University Press, 1984).

CHARLES MURRAY, *What It Means to Be a Libertarian: A Personal Interpretation* (Broadway Books, 1997).

JOHN J. SCHWARZMANTEL, *The Age of Ideology: Political Ideologies from the American Revolution to Post-Modern Times* (New York University Press, 1998).

ALEXIS DETOCQUEVILLE, *Democracy in America* (Knopf reprint, 1994).

GARRY WILLS, *A Necessary Evil: A History of American Distrust of Government* (Simon & Schuster, 1999).

J. HARRY WRAY, *Sense and Nonsense: American Culture and Politics* (Prentice Hall, 2001).

DANIEL YERGIN AND JOSEPH STAINSLAW, *The Commanding Heights: The Battle Between Government and the Marketplace That Is Remaking the Modern World* (Simon & Schuster, 1998).

5

THE AMERICAN POLITICAL LANDSCAPE

THE UNITED STATES IS A NATION OF IMMIGRANTS.
WE CELEBRATE OUR IMMIGRANT PAST AND PROUDLY
RECITE THE WORDS OF EMMA LAZARUS INSCRIBED AT THE BASE
of the Statue of Liberty: "Give me your tired, your poor, your huddled masses yearning
to breath free." And yet our borders are not open to all who wish to come here, and
immigration is limited, with specific numbers of immigrants allowed to enter from each
country each year. Hundreds of thousands avoid these limitations by crossing our borders illegally, seeking employment, refuge, and freedom.

The number of these illegal immigrants, as well as U.S. immigration policy generally, were the focus of television and newspaper ads in the 2000 Iowa caucuses, the South
Carolina presidential primary, and some congressional contests. One group, the Federation for American Immigration Reform (FAIR), ran a television commercial about
Storm Lake, Iowa, in the weeks leading up to the Iowa caucuses in January 2000. The
commercial claimed that rising crime rates, increased costs for bilingual education, and
increased public health care costs could be traced to the rise in immigrants who work in
the town's meat-packing plants. FAIR was one of five anti-immigration groups that
joined together in mounting an advertising campaign in 2000 on problems immigrants
pose for our country. But the anti-immigration groups did not have much impact in the
Iowa caucuses, in part because Iowa faces a net out-migration of population and needs
the immigrants to fill jobs like the meat-packing jobs in Storm Lake. Elected officials in
Iowa came out against the anti-immigration groups and strongly criticized the Storm
Lake ad. Presidential candidates opposed the limits on immigration proposed. For
instance, George W. Bush stated, "Family values don't stop at the Rio Grande. My
administration will reform the INS, and make it worthy of a nation of immigrants."[1]

Disagreements about admission of aliens into this country and about their rights
and privileges have been featured in political campaigns for the last two hundred years.
In 1994 Californians passed a controversial ballot initiative, Proposition 187, restricting
public services to illegal immigrants. Even though a federal judge found portions of the
proposition unconstitutional, the furor about Proposition 187 demonstrated the intense
feelings on both sides of the issue, especially in a border state like California.

Albert Einstein once said few people are capable of expressing opinions that
differ much from the prejudices of their social upbringing.[2] This **ethnocentrism**—
selective perception based on individual background, attitudes, and biases—is not
uncommon, even among college students, who often assume that others share their

CHAPTERMEDIA

 POLITICS ONLINE
Who Are My Neighbors?
www.prenhall.com/burns

 POLISIM
The Great American Divide
www.prenhall.com/burns

The Census Bureau, which conducts the once-a-decade count of all persons in the United States, proposed using random sampling rather than attempting to count all households in the 2000 census. Republicans opposed sampling because they considered it unreliable. The proposed sample approach would contact 90 percent of the households in a census tract consisting of roughly 1,700 individuals. The bureau would then check the accuracy of the sample by surveying 750,000 households throughout the nation and adjusting the final total accordingly.

The sample approach responds to complaints about the flawed 1990 census, which cost $2.6 billion (a 400 percent increase over the cost of the 1980 census) and failed to account for 10 million people and double-counted 6 million others, according to a study by the National Academy of Sciences. Do you think that sampling is a fair and effective solution?

ethnocentrism
Selective perception based on individual background, attitudes, and biases that leads one to believe in the superiority of one's nation or ethnic group.

political socialization
The process by which we develop our political attitudes, values, and beliefs.

demographics
The study of the characteristics of populations.

political predisposition
A characteristic of individuals that is predictive of political behavior.

reinforcing cleavages
Divisions within society that reinforce one another, making groups more homogeneous or similar.

cross-cutting cleavages
Divisions within society that cut across demographic categories to produce groups more heterogeneous or different.

economic opportunities, social attitudes, sense of civic responsibility, and self-confidence. In this chapter we consider to what extent our social environment explains, or at least shapes, our opinions and prejudices. We also look at our diversity as Americans and the implications of geographic, social, and economic divisions for politics and government. Specifically, this chapter explores the effects of regional or state identity on political perspectives; the implications of differences in race, ethnicity, gender, family structure, religion, wealth and income, occupation, and social class for opinions and voting choices; and the relationship between age and education and political participation.

A LAND OF DIVERSITY

Most nations consist of groups of people who have lived together for hundreds of years and who speak the same language, hold the same concept of deity, and share a common history. Most Japanese citizens are Japanese in the fullest sense of the word, and it is generally the same in Germany, Sweden, Saudi Arabia, China, and France. The United States is different. We have attracted the poor and oppressed, the adventurous and the talented, from all over the world, and we have been more open to accepting these people than have other nations.

One reason so many people want to come to the United States is that it holds a promise of religious, political, and economic freedom. It is also a place of opportunity for the enterprising. Our economic system has provided widespread (but not universal) opportunity for individuals to improve their economic standing. The American Dream—that everyone can "make it"—is widely shared.

Some elements of our diversity have political significance. For example, sectional differences persist between the South and the rest of the country. Many Americans retain an identity with the native land of their ancestors, even after three or four generations. Holding onto such differences is often the result of socialization in families, churches, and other closely knit groups. **Political socialization** is the process by which parents and others teach children about political values, beliefs, and attitudes. This teaching occurs in the home, on the playground, in school, and in the neighborhood. In addition to fostering group identities, political socialization strongly influences how individuals see politics and which political party they prefer. Because where we live and who we are in terms of our age, education, religion, and occupation affect how we vote, many who study voting and make predictions about it do so in terms of these and other factors, referred to as **demographics**. A **political predisposition** is a characteristic of individuals that is predictive of political behavior. Although demographics can be important, there are large individual differences within socioeconomic and demographic categories.

When social and economic differences coincide, they reinforce each other and make the differences between groups more important. Social scientists call these differences **reinforcing cleavages;** where they occur, political conflict becomes more intense and there is greater polarization in society. In Italy, for example, the regional divide between North and South is reinforced by the tendency of the North to lean toward the Socialist or Communist parties and the South to be Christian Democratic and Catholic in orientation. Nations can also have **cross-cutting cleavages**, instances where differences do not reinforce each other. To illustrate, if all the rich individuals in a society are of one religion and the poor another, we would have reinforcing cleavages, and political conflict would be intensified. But if there are both rich and poor in all religions, and if people sometimes vote on the basis of their religion and sometimes on the basis of their wealth, then we would say the divisions are cross-cutting. American diversity has generally been more of the cross-cutting type than the reinforcing type, lessening political conflict because individuals have multiple allegiances.

In some societies, politics centers largely upon passions over economic and religious differences. Although socioeconomic differences are important to under-

standing American government and politics, they are not as central to the form and structure of politics as religion is in Bosnia or tribal identity in Rwanda. In Northern Ireland, the religious differences between Catholics and Protestants produced centuries of violent division that is yet to be resolved.

Despite the fact that America has been more hospitable to people from different religions, classes, or races than almost any other nation in the world, we often prefer to associate only with people "like us" and are suspicious of people "like them." From hostility toward different religions in the early colonies, to the anti-immigration movements of the late 1800s and early 1900s, to the various anti-immigration and anti–civil rights ballot initiatives of the 1990s, Americans have exhibited ethnocentrism, and for much of our history, minorities have been excluded from full participation in American political and economic life.

Geography and National Identity

The United States is a geographically large and historically isolated country. The French commentator Alexis de Tocqueville observed in 1835 that the country had no major political or economic powers on its borders "and consequently no great wars, financial crises, invasions, or conquests to fear."[3] Geographic isolation from the major powers of the world during our government's formative period helps explain American politics. The Atlantic Ocean served as a barrier to foreign meddling, giving us time to establish our political tradition and develop our economy. The western frontier provided room to grow and avoid some of the social and political tensions that Europe experienced. Two great oceans also reinforced our sense of isolation from Europe and foreign alliances. This reluctance to become involved in foreign wars and controversies still arises in debates over foreign policy.

In our entire history we have fought only one foreign enemy on our own soil—England in the War of 1812. (The war against Mexico of 1846–48 was fought almost entirely on Mexican land, some of which later became American land as a result of the war. The only other war fought on our soil was, of course, the Civil War.) In contrast, Poland has been invaded repeatedly and was partitioned by Austria, Prussia, and Russia in the eighteenth century and by Nazi Germany and the Soviet Union in the twentieth century. The difference is explained largely by location: Poland was surrounded by Europe's great powers. Had the United States been closer to Europe, it might have been overrun like

Part of our national identity is bound up with the physical isolation and hardship many families endured as pioneers.

Evidence of the persistent racial divide in this country was brought out by the dispute over the flag of the Confederacy (bottom flag) flying over the South Carolina capitol building. After bitter debate between descendents of slave-owning families and descendents of slaves, the flag was relocated near a small statue on the capitol grounds.

Poland, and our Constitution and institutions repeatedly changed or eliminated to suit the victorious invaders. Having powerful and aggressive neighbors makes it difficult for relatively weak nations to nurture democracy.

The United States is a large country. Its land mass exceeds that of all but three nations in the world. In contrast, India has a population more than three times larger than that of the United States on a land mass one-third the size. Geographic space gave the expanding population of the United States room to spread out. This possibility meant that some of the political conflicts arising from religion, social class, and national origin were diffused because groups could isolate themselves from one another. (See James Madison, *The Federalist*, No. 10, in the Appendix, for the "large republic" idea.) Moreover, the large and accessible land mass helped foster the perspective that the United States had a **manifest destiny** to be a continental nation reaching from the Atlantic to the Pacific oceans. This notion that the United States was "destined" to expand across the continent was used to justify taking land occupied by Native Americans and Mexicans, especially the land acquired following victory in the Mexican-American War.

The United States is also a land of abundant natural resources. We have rich farmland, which not only feeds our population but makes us the largest exporter of food in the world.[4] We are rich in such natural resources as coal, iron, uranium, and precious metals. All these resources enhance economic growth, provide jobs, and stabilize government. "The physical causes, unconnected with laws, which can lead to prosperity are more numerous in America than in any other country at any other time in history," observed Alexis de Tocqueville. "In the United States not legislation alone is democratic, for Nature herself seems to work for the people."

Geography also helps explain our diversity. Parts of the United States are wonderfully suited to agriculture, others to mining or ranching, and still others to shipping. These differences produce different regional economic concerns, which in turn influence politics. For instance, a person from the agricultural heartland may have a perception of foreign trade different from that of an automobile worker in Detroit. But if that automobile worker is African American, this fact may be more important to her politics than what she does or where she lives. To understand American politics, we must appreciate these differences and their relative importance.

Sectional Differences

Unlike many other countries, geography in the United States does *not* define an ethnic or religious division. All the Serbs in the United States do not live in one place, all French-speaking Catholics in another, and all German immigrants in another. Sectional differences in the United States are primarily geographic, not ethnic or religious.

The most distinct section of the United States remains the South, although the South's differences are diminishing. From the beginning of the Republic, the agricultural South differed from the North, where commerce and manufacturing were more significant. But the most important difference between the regions was the institution of slavery. Northern opposition to slavery, which grew increasingly intense by the middle of the nineteenth century, reinforced the sectional economic interests. The eleven Confederate states, by virtue of their decision to secede from the Union, reinforced a common political identity, and after the Civil War sectional differences were strengthened by the policy of Reconstruction and the problems of race relations.

Sectional differences have moderated in the last few decades. The South is becoming less distinct from the rest of the United States. A large in-migration has diminished the sense of regional identity, and the South has undergone tremendous economic change. The civil rights revolution gave African Americans the right to vote, opened up new educational opportunities, and helped to integrate the South into the national economy. African Americans still lag behind whites in voter registration, but the gap is now no wider in the South than elsewhere and is explained more by differences in education than by race.[5] In economic terms, the South, as a

manifest destiny
A notion held by nineteenth-century Americans that the United States was destined to rule the continent, from the Atlantic to the Pacific oceans.

region, still falls below the rest of the country in per capita income and education, but much less so than 50 years ago. The religious and moral conservatism of the South remains notable.

Until the 1970s, political observers spoke of the "solid South"—a region that voted for Democrats at all levels. The reason for the connection between the South and Democrats is simple: "The Civil War made the Democratic party the party of the South, and the Republican party, the party of the North."[6] The Democratic "solid South" was to remain a fixture of American politics for more than a century. Since 1968 that has changed dramatically, first at the presidential level and increasingly at the state and local levels. As two respected observers of the region comment, "The fall of the South as an assured stronghold of the Democratic party in presidential elections is one of the most significant developments in modern American politics."[7] The political alignment has shifted as African Americans have been enfranchised and become overwhelmingly Democrats, and many whites have become Republicans. In 1992 and 1996, even with two southerners (Bill Clinton and Al Gore) on the ticket, Democrats won only four of the eleven former Confederate states. In 2000, George W. Bush carried all 11 southern states, including Al Gore's home state of Tennessee.

What explains this dramatic reversal? Part of the explanation is that the Democrats' advocacy of aggressive action on civil rights in the 1960s alienated some southern whites. In addition, the debate within the Democratic party over Vietnam policy in the late 1960s and 1970s was "perceived by many southern voters as unpatriotic."[8] Republican presidential candidates have more recently emphasized family values, opposition to taxes, and law-and-order issues that appeal to conservative southern voters.

Republican success at the presidential level was slow to affect contests for Congress and state legislatures. Yet in recent years, Republicans had more than half of southern votes for the U.S. House of Representatives (see Table 5–1), and by 2000 they had seven of the eleven governorships in the former Confederate states. In the state legislatures of several southern states, remnants of the old "solid South" remain, but Republicans have made major inroads, and politics in the region is now much more competitive.

Another sectional division is the *sun belt*—the eleven former Confederate states plus New Mexico, Arizona, and the southern half of California. Sun belt states are growing much more rapidly than the rest of the country. Population shifts during the 1990s meant these states gained 12 seats in the House of Representatives after the 2000 census: Arizona, California, Colorado, Florida, Georgia, Nevada, North Carolina, and Texas.[9] Moreover, population growth in the South and West is occurring in different age groups. In the South, growth is largest among those over 65; in the West, it is younger persons who provide the growth. Sun belt states have also experienced greater economic growth as industries headed south and southwest, where land is cheaper and more abundant, and where labor is cheaper as well (see Figure 5–1).

State and Local Identity

Different states have different political traditions. Mention Wyoming, Mississippi, Oregon, New York, or Kansas, and it brings to mind a certain type of politics. The same is true for many other states. Like most stereotypes, these images are often misleading, yet they reflect the fact that there is a sense of identity to states as political units that goes beyond demographic characteristics and is supported by recent

TABLE 5–1 Voting Patterns in the Eleven Former Confederate States

Republican for President	
1980	50%
1984	62
1988	59
1992	43
1996	46
2000	54

Republican Vote for U.S. Representatives	
1980	40%
1982	39
1984	42
1986	41
1988	42
1990	43
1992	48
1994	58
1996	53*
1998	58
2000	53

Republican Share of State Legislators		
	House	Senate
1980	18%	17%
1982	22	14
1984	23	17
1986	24	20
1988	27	24
1990	28	26
1992	31	31
1994	37	37
1996	44	44
1998	42	40
2000	44	42

Source: U.S. Bureau of the Census, *Statistical Abstract of the United States,* 1993–2000. For 2000, www.cnn.com/elections/2000/results and *Congressional Quarterly Weekly Report,* November 11, 2000, pp. 2694–2703; and Todd Edwards, telephone interview, The Council of State Governments, Southern Office, 12/22/00.

*The 1996 Texas runoff elections are not included.

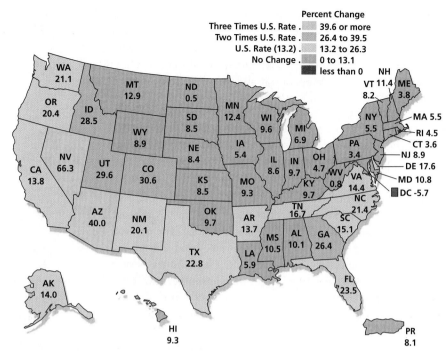

FIGURE 5–1 Percent Change in Resident Population, 1990-2000

SOURCE: U.S. Bureau of the Census home page: www.census.gov/population/cen2000/tab01.

empirical evidence. States have distinctive political cultures that affect public opinion and policy outcomes.[10] These state identities are reinforced by our electoral rules
and other laws.

In American politics today, one state—California—stands out. More than one
out of eight Americans is a Californian.[11] In terms of economic and political importance, California is in a league by itself; its 53 members of the House of Representatives exceed the total number of representatives from the smallest 20 states. Securing California's electoral votes is key for any presidential candidate.[12] In 2004,
California will have 55 electoral voters.

WHERE WE LIVE

Most Americans, 80 percent of them, now live in central cities and their suburbs—what the Census Bureau calls *metropolitan areas*.[13] During the early
twentieth century, the movement of population was from rural areas to central cities,
but the movement since the 1950s has been from the central cities to their suburbs.
Today the most urban state is California (93 percent of its population lives in cities
or suburbs). Vermont is the least urban, with only 32 percent living in cities or suburbs.[14] Regionally, the West and Northeast are the most urban, the South and Midwest the most rural.

People move from cities to the suburbs for many reasons—better housing, new
transportation systems that make it easier to get to work, the desire for cleaner air
and safer streets. Another reason is *white flight*, the movement of whites away from
the central cities so that children can avoid being bused for racial balance and attend
generally better schools. White, middle-class migration to the suburbs means that
American cities have become increasingly poor, increasingly African American, and
increasingly Democratic. More than half of all African Americans now live in central
cities, as opposed to only about one-quarter of whites, and the poverty level among
blacks living in central cities is higher than whites living in the same cities.[15] The proportions are very nearly reversed for suburbs, where more than half of all white

Americans reside. Almost one-third of African Americans live in the suburbs, up from one-fifth in 1980.[16] In large cities such as Washington, D.C., Detroit, Baltimore, Atlanta, and New Orleans, the city population is now more than 50 percent African American (see Table 5–2). Hispanics constitute roughly two-thirds of the population of El Paso, Texas, Santa Ana, California, and Miami, Florida.[17]

As these population shifts occur, the tax base of cities declines because the richer people have moved to the suburbs. At the same time, service needs in the cities increase as the less-affluent remaining population must pay for education, police protection, and health care. Older suburban cities now face the same problems as the inner cities, as they too suffer from out-migration to newer cities and towns. High-tech and professional service companies frequently relocate to the suburbs to avoid traffic congestion and to be closer to the bedroom communities of their workers. Political boundaries, which define local governments and delineate responsibility for services, create understandable tensions among cities, suburbs, and rural areas. Tax revenues, legislative representation, zoning laws, and governmental priorities are hotly contested issues in most metropolitan areas.

TABLE 5–2	Cities with Populations of 100,000 or More That Are at Least 50 Percent African American, 2000	
City	Population	Percent African American
Atlanta, GA	416,474	61.4%
Baltimore, MD	651,154	64.3
Birmingham, AL	242,820	73.5
Detroit, MI	951,270	81.6
Gary, IN	102,746	84
Jackson, MS	184,256	70.6
Memphis, TN	650,100	61.4
Newark, NJ	273,546	53.5
New Orleans, LA	484,674	67.3
Richmond, VA	197,790	57.2
Savannah, GA	131,510	57.1
Washington, D.C.	572,059	60.0

SOURCE: 2000 U.S. Census: www.census.gov/population/cen2000/phc-t6/tab05.pdf; release date April 2, 2001 Table 5.

WHO WE ARE

Sectional distinctions are less prominent today than they were a century or even a half century ago. Today Americans are more likely to define themselves by a number of characteristics, each of which may influence how they vote or think about various candidates, issues, or policies.

Race and Ethnicity

Racial and ethnic differences have always had political significance. **Race** can be defined as a grouping of human beings with common genetic characteristics. **Ethnicity** is a social division based on national origin, religion, and language, often within the same race, and includes a sense of attachment to that group. In the United States, race and ethnicity issues focus on African Americans, Asian Americans, and Hispanics.

There are more than 34 million African Americans in the United States, roughly 13 percent of the population. Asian Americans constitute just under 4 percent of the population, and Native Americans just under 1 percent. Most American Hispanics are classified as white by the Census Bureau, although Hispanics can be of any race. Hispanics are the fastest growing ethnic group; the Census Bureau estimates that there are 28 million American Hispanics, constituting over 10 percent of the population.[18] Because of differences in immigration and birth rates, whites in America will have declined to just under three-quarters of the population by the year 2050.

AFRICAN AMERICANS   Most people came to this country of their free choice in search of freedom and opportunity. African Americans came as slaves. Although they were freed as a result of the Civil War, racial divisions continue as one of the enduring issues of American politics. Until 1900, more than 90 percent of all African Americans lived in the South; by the end of the twentieth century, the figure was 54 percent.[19] Many African Americans left the South hoping to improve their lives by settling in the large cities of the Northeast, Midwest, and West. The reality for many was urban poverty. More recently, some African Americans have been returning to the South, especially to its urban areas.

In economic terms, most African Americans are worse off than most whites in the United States. African American median family income is close to $30,000, compared to more than $49,000 for whites.[20] More than one-quarter of African American incomes are below the poverty level, compared to 11 percent of whites.[21] Poverty

race
A grouping of human beings with common characteristics presumed to be transmitted genetically.

ethnicity
A social division based on national origin, religion, language, and often race.

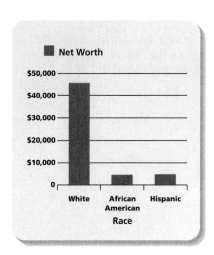

FIGURE 5–2 Wealth Distribution in the United States by Race, 1995.

SOURCE: U.S. Bureau of the Census, www.census.gov/hhes/www/wealth/wlth93f.html.

among Native Americans and Alaskan Natives has averaged 26 percent in recent years, a proportion quite similar to that found among African Americans and Hispanics.[22] However, many African Americans have recently become relatively prosperous; 21 percent of African American households have earnings of over $50,000, a proportion still only half that for whites.[23] Some African Americans, like Shaquille O'Neal and Oprah Winfrey, have risen to top earnings in their professions.

Another way to measure economic well-being is in terms of assets or wealth. *Wealth* encompasses the things of economic value (savings, stocks, property), as compared to *income*, which is how much money you make from your job or investments. As a group, African Americans' net wealth is only one-tenth that of whites, and Hispanics have only slightly more wealth than African Americans (see Figure 5–2).[24] As a result, most African Americans and Hispanics have fewer resources to fall back on in hard times, and they are less likely to have the savings to help a child pay for college.[25]

Middle-class African Americans, a growing category, are role models for the young of all races, yet their comparatively small number serves as a reminder that most African Americans remain behind whites in an economy that relies more and more on education and job skills. About 25 percent of whites graduate from college, whereas only about 15 percent of African Americans do.[26] Among 18-to-21-year-old high school graduates, 46 percent of whites go on to college, but only 33 percent of African Americans do.[27]

Finally, the African American population is much younger than the white population; the median age for whites in 1999 was 36.3, compared to 29.5 for African Americans.[28] The combination of a younger African American population, a lower level of education, and their concentration in economically hard-pressed urban areas has resulted in a much higher unemployment rate for young African Americans. Unemployment, in turn, can lead to social problems like crime, drug and alcohol abuse, and family dissolution.

African Americans had little political power until after World War II. Owing their freedom from slavery to the "party of Lincoln," most African Americans initially identified with the Republicans, but this loyalty started to change with Franklin Roosevelt, who insisted on equal treatment for African Americans in his New Deal programs.[29] After World War II, African Americans came to see the Democrats as the party of civil rights. The 1964 Republican platform position on civil rights espoused *states' rights*—then the creed of southern segregationists—in what appeared to be an effort to win the support of southern white voters. Virtually all African Americans voted for Lyndon Johnson in 1964, and in presidential elections between 1964 and 1996, their Democratic vote averaged 85 percent.[30]

Recently, African Americans have become much more important politically because of their increased voter participation and their concentrated population. African Americans constitute only .3 percent of the population in Montana and .6 percent of South Dakota, but 36 percent of Mississippi, 32 percent of Louisiana, and 30 percent of South Carolina.[31] Southern senators and representatives cannot afford to ignore the African American vote.[32] Evidence of growing African American political power is the dramatic increase in the number of African American state legislators, which rose from 168 in 1970 to 579 in 1998.[33] Mississippi has 45 African American state legislators, the most of any state. Alabama, Georgia, South Carolina, Maryland, and Louisiana all have over thirty.[34]

HISPANICS/LATINOS   Latinos are not a monolithic group, and while they share a common linguistic heritage, they often differ from one another, depending on which country they emigrated from. Cuban Americans, for instance, tend to be Republicans, while Mexican Americans and Puerto Ricans are disproportionately Democrats.[35] Latinos are politically important in a growing number of states. Nearly two-thirds of Cuban immigrants live in Florida, especially greater Miami; Puerto Rican immigrants are concentrated in or around New York City; and Mexican American immigrants in

the southwest and California. Almost 11 million Hispanics live in California.[36]

Cuban Americans are more in the upper-middle income levels, while Puerto Rican Americans and Mexican Americans are generally in lower and lower-middle income categories.[37] A recent study found differences among Latinos of Mexican, Puerto Rican, and Cuban descent in partisanship, ideology, and rates of participation, but widespread support for a liberal domestic agenda, including increased spending on health care, crime and drug control, education, the environment, child services, and bilingual education.[38]

Given the overall growth of the Latino population, it is not surprising that both major parties are aggressively cultivating Latino candidates. Three Latinos, all from New Mexico, have won election to the U.S. Senate. Several Hispanics have been cabinet members: Manuel Lujan (Secretary of Interior), Laura F. Cavazos (Secretary of Education), Henry G. Cisneros (Secretary of HUD), Frederico Peña (Secretary of Transportation), and Bill Richardson (Secretary of Energy). In the George W. Bush administration, Mel Martinez is Secretary of Housing and Urban Development.

ASIAN AMERICANS   Asian Americans are classified together by the Census Bureau for statistical purposes, but there are significant differences among them in culture, language, and political experience in the United States. Asian Americans include persons of Chinese, Japanese, Korean, Vietnamese, Filipino, and Thai origin, as well as persons from the Pacific Islands.

The United States is home to 10.6 million Asian Americans and Pacific Islanders, residing primarily in the western states, especially Hawaii, California, and Washington.[39] The numbers of Asian Americans grew during the 1970s and 1980s, largely as a result of Southeast Asian immigration. Immigrants from Asia have climbed to one of four of all foreign-born persons now living in the United States, and the Philippines was surpassed only by Mexico as the country of birth for foreign-born persons living in this country.[40]

Many Asian Americans have done well both economically and educationally. More than two out of every five Asian Americans have graduated from college, compared to one out of every four white Americans and one in seven African Americans.[41] Asian Americans are becoming more politically important and visible in politics. In 1996, Washington elected the first Chinese American governor of a state in the continental United States—Gary Locke. He was reelected in 2000.

THE TIES OF ETHNICITY   Except for Native Americans, all Americans are immigrants or are descended from immigrants. Early settlers were generally English-speaking Protestants; even today, people of English, Scottish, and Welsh background are the largest "ethnic" group in the United States. Irish immigrants, largely Catholics, started coming before the potato famine in the 1840s and came in larger numbers after it. Upon their arrival, they experienced economic exploitation and religious bigotry. The Irish American response was to retreat among themselves, forming a strong ethnic consciousness. Other ethnic groups that followed—Italians, Greeks, Chinese—each experienced a similar cycle: flight from their homeland and happy arrival here, then discrimination, exploitation, residential clustering, and the formation of a strong group identity.

The largest number of immigrants came between 1900 and 1924, when 17.3 million people relocated to the United States—by far the largest immigration to one country in any quarter-century in human history. From 1991 to 1997, there were more than 6.9 million immigrants,[42] primarily from the Caribbean and Mexico, and from Asian countries such as the Philippines, Vietnam, and China. The foreign-born proportion of the U.S. population has increased in recent years, rising from 14 million in

What's My Name?

The terms "Latino" and "Chicano" are preferred to "Hispanic" by some persons of Spanish-speaking descent to disassociate themselves from Spain, a colonial power against which their ancestors fought wars of independence. "Hispanic" is the term most widely used by government agencies and the media, while "Latino" appears more popular among leaders of the group. "Chicano" is often associated with the politically active Mexican American movement of the 1960s and 1970s. Most Mexican Americans, Puerto Rican Americans, and Cuban Americans prefer to be called American rather than Latino or Hispanic.

SOURCE: Richard Santillan and Carlos Munoz, Jr., "Latinos and the Democratic Party," in *The Democrats Must Lead*, ed. James MacGregor Burns, William Crotty, Lois Lovelace Duke, and Lawrence D. Longley (Westview Press, 1992), pp. 182–83; Rodolfo O. de la Garza, Louis DeSipio, F. Chris Garcia, John Garcia, and Angelo Falcon, *Latino Voices: Mexican, Puerto Rican, and Cuban Perspectives on American Politics* (Westview Press, 1992), p. 13.

1980 to nearly 26 million in 1998, the largest number of foreign-born in U.S. history.[43] Recently the proportion of Asian and Mexican immigrants has pulled even with or surpassed the number of Europeans.

Having large numbers of immigrants can pose challenges to any political and social system. Immigrants are often a source of social conflict as they compete with more established groups for jobs, rights, political power, and influence.

WE THE PEOPLE

Percentage of the Population by Race and Origin

	1990	2000	2025	2050
White	83.9%	82.1%	78.3%	74.8%
African American	12.3	12.9	14.2	15.4
American Indian, Inuit, Aleut	0.8	0.9	1.0	1.1
Asian and Pacific Islander	3.0	4.1	6.6	8.7
Hispanic	9.0	11.4	17.6	24.5

SOURCE: U.S. Bureau of the Census, *Statistical Abstract of the United States, 1999* (Government Printing Office, 1999), p. 18.

Percentages do not equal 100 percent because Hispanics can be of any race. Figures for 2000, 2025, and 2050 are projections.

Gender

For most of U.S. history, politics and government were men's business. As will be discussed in greater detail in Chapter 17, women first gained the right to vote primarily in the western territories, beginning with Wyoming in 1869 and Utah in 1870, and then in Colorado and Idaho before the turn of the century.[44] The right was not extended nationally until 1920 with passage of the Nineteenth Amendment. The fears of some opponents of *women's suffrage* (the right to vote)—that women would form their own party and vote largely for women or fundamentally alter our political system—have not been realized. During Susan B. Anthony's suffrage campaign, Jonas H. Upton, editor of the *Democratic Salem Monitor* in Salem, Oregon, contended that women, if given the right to vote, would combine to vote for war because they were exempt from the draft.[45] Others said women would unite to vote for prohibition.[46]

For a half-century after gaining the right to vote, American women voted at a lower rate than women in other Western democracies.[47] But in the past 20 years, women have voted at nearly the same rate as men. Since women outnumber men, there are more female than male voters. Women have chosen to work within the existing political parties and do not overwhelmingly support female candidates, especially if they must cross parties to do so.

WOMEN IN POLITICS The women's movement in American politics encompasses a comprehensive agenda, including voting and political rights as well as extending the basic liberties of the Bill of Rights and Fourteenth Amendment. In addition to rights and liberties, women seek equal opportunity, education, jobs, skills, and respect in what has been a male-dominated system.[48]

Since 1917, less than 6 percent of representatives in the U.S. House have been women, but the number of women in the House of Representatives and U.S. Senate reached new highs in the 1990s. Following the 2000 elections, there were 3 female governors, 13 women serving in the Senate, and 58 in the U.S. House of Representatives. The number of female officeholders is rising in part because women are increasingly running in contests with no incumbent running.[49]

Is there a **gender gap**? Do women vote differently from men? Women have typically divided their vote between the two major political parties. However, in recent elections women have been more likely than men to vote for Democratic presidential candidates (see Figure 5–3). In the 2000 presidential election, Al Gore's share of the vote among women was 12 percent higher than among men.[50]

Women are more likely to oppose violence in any form—death penalty, new weapons systems, or the possession of handguns. Women, as a group, are more compassionate than men and are more likely to favor government that provides

FIGURE 5–3 Gender and the Vote for President, 2000

gender gap

The difference between the political opinions or political behavior of men and of women.

health insurance and family services. Women generally are more concerned than men about women's rights—enforcement of child support, punishment for sexual abuse and rape, and equal treatment in the legal system. They also identify work and family issues such as day-care, prenatal and postnatal leave, and equal treatment in the workplace as important.[51] Other gender issues, some of them focal points in recent elections, include reproductive rights, restrictions on pornography, gun control, and sexual harassment.[52]

There are serious income inequalities between men and women. About 64 percent more women than men work at or below the minimum wage.[53] Because an increasing number of women today are the sole breadwinners for their families, the implications of this low income level are significant. Women earn on average less than men for the same work. Even among college graduates ages 25–34, women earn an average of 80 cents for every dollar earned by men of the same age and education. After controlling for characteristics such as job experience, education, occupation, and other measures of productivity, studies show that wage discrimination is somewhere between 89 to 98 cents on every dollar.[54] As age increases, the earnings gap widens. Increasing women's income is an important issue to the women's movement.

Sexual Orientation

Differences in sexual orientation have become important politically in recent years. The movement for expanded rights for gays and lesbians traces its roots to 1969, when New York City police raided the Stonewall Inn in Greenwich Village. Precise data on the number of homosexuals in the United States are in dispute. The gay and lesbian community talk in terms of 10 percent; other estimates come in much lower.[55] One source estimates that 2.8 percent of men and 1.4 percent of women identified themselves as homosexual or bisexual.[56] Regardless of its overall size, the homosexual community has become important politically in several cities, most notably San Francisco. Both parties have gay members of Congress.

In 2000 Vermont became the first state to enact legislation granting gay and lesbian couples "civil union" status, which in many respects is like marriage. Prior to this law taking effect, the Vermont Supreme Court had ruled that denying gay couples the same rights and benefits as heterosexual couples is unconstitutional. The legislation became an issue in the Vermont 2000 elections, and court challenges are also likely to arise.

The political agenda for gay and lesbian advocacy groups includes fighting discrimination, including the military's "Don't ask, Don't tell" policy. On some fronts the groups have been successful. In several cities and among some employers, gays and lesbians have been able to secure health care and other benefits for domestic partners. Antidiscrimination statutes protecting sexual orientation in housing and employment have been passed in several cities and states. Groups like the Human Rights Campaign are visible advocates of limiting restrictions based on sexual orientation. Hate crimes against gays and lesbians have led the Senate to include sexual orientation in federal hate crimes legislation.[57]

Conservative groups have, however, largely been successful in banning same-sex marriage in a series of statewide ballot initiatives. Among the groups who have been active in the protest movement have been conservative Christians, Catholics, and Mormons. The courts have also been drawn into the battle over sexual orientation. In a 5-to-4 decision, the Supreme Court upheld the right of the Boy Scouts of America to bar homosexuals from leadership positions, as well as general membership, in its organization.[58] As the Boy Scouts controversy illustrates, policies relating to sexual orientation are among the most contentious in our society.

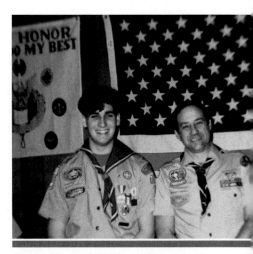

The Boy Scouts do not permit homosexuals to be scout leaders. James Dale, an Eagle Scout who is gay, lost his lawsuit because the court said the Boy Scouts are a private association and can exclude gays.

FAMILY STRUCTURE

Over the past half-century the typical American family has been transformed from a "traditional family" (mother and father married with children in the home) to a variety of living arrangements and varying family structures. Today, Americans are much more likely to approve of premarital sex than in the early 1970s. And at some point in their lives, over half of Americans will *cohabit* (live with someone of the opposite sex to whom they are not married). Cohabitation raises public policy questions such as whether the live-in partner is eligible for employment benefits and welfare payments. Contraception is widely used and accepted, and yet one-third of all births are now illegitimate. These children will often be in need of social services and financial assistance.

People now marry later in life, with men marrying at average age 26 and women at 24.[59] Yet marrying later has not improved the chances of avoiding divorce. The average marriage today lasts only about 7.2 years. Before World War II, only 9 out of every 1,000 marriages ended in divorce; from 1950 to 1994 the divorce rate nearly doubled; today about one-half of all marriages are estimated to end in divorce.[60]

Divorce is one reason why many women go to work and why the number of households headed by women has risen. Attitudes about the role of women in marriage and the family have also changed. In 1972, one-third of Americans thought a woman's place is in the home (meaning she should not work outside the home), but in 1996, only one-sixth of all Americans felt this way.[61]

Religion

In many parts of the world, religious differences are a source of violent conflict. In Iraq and Turkey the Kurdish people have been subjected to expulsion and even to genocide. The war in Bosnia-Herzegovina was a religious and ethnic battle among Muslims, Serbs, and Catholics, as was the war between Serbs and Muslims in Kosovo. Countries like Afghanistan, Israel, Lebanon, India, and Sri Lanka have also experienced intense religious conflict. Jews have often been the target of religious discrimination and persecution (anti-Semitism), including the Holocaust, during which an estimated 6 million Jews were murdered.[62] The United States has not been immune, despite its principle of religious freedom. In 1838, Governor Lilburn W. Boggs of Missouri issued an extermination order against the Mormons.[63]

Our government is founded on the premise that religious liberty is more likely when there is not one predominant or official faith, which is why the framers of our Constitution did not sanction a national church. In fact, James Madison wrote in *The Federalist*, No. 51, "In a free government the security for civil rights must be the same as that for religious rights. It consists in the one case in the multiplicity of interests, and in the other in the multiplicity of sects" (see the Appendix).

The absence of an official American church does not mean that religion is unimportant in American politics; indeed, there were established state churches in this country until the 1830s. Some contend that "the root of American political and social values . . . is the distinctive Puritanism of the early New England settlers."[64] Politicians frequently refer to God in their speeches or demonstrate their piety in other ways. Democratic Vice-presidential candidate Joe Lieberman created some controversy in the 2000 campaign by his frequent references to deity and religion.

Many Americans take their religious beliefs seriously, more so than people of other industrial democracies.[65] Nearly two-thirds of Americans attend houses of worship several times a year, more than half attend a church or synagogue at least once a month, and more than one-third attend nearly every week.[66] Religion, like ethnicity, is a *shared identity*. People identify themselves as Baptist, Catholic, or Buddhist. Sometimes church attendance or nonattendance is more important than differences between religions in explaining attitudes. "Among both Catholics and Protestants, opposition to abortion increases with frequency of church attendance,

RELIGION AND POLITICS

At one time we thought a Catholic could not be elected president. With the election of 1960 that issue was resolved. John F. Kennedy directly confronted the question of whether a Catholic would put aside religious teachings if they conflicted with constitutional obligations. He said, "I am not the Catholic candidate for President. I am the Democratic party's candidate for President who happens also to be Catholic. I do not speak for my church on public matters, and the church does not speak for me." Nevertheless, today it is still the case that a candidate's religion may become an issue if religious convictions on sensitive issues such as abortion threaten to conflict with public obligations.

Religion can be an important catalyst for social change, as the Catholic church was in the overthrow of communism in Central Europe and the leadership of the black church was instrumental in the American civil rights movement. As writer Taylor Branch explains, the black church "served not only as a place of worship but also as a bulletin board to a people who owned no organs of communication, a credit union to those without banks, and even a kind of people's court."[*] African American ministers, like the Reverend Martin Luther King, Jr., became leaders of the civil rights movement; others, like the Reverend Jesse Jackson, have run for national office. Hence religion can be important not only as a source of personal values and attitudes but as a means of political activity and organization.

More recently there has been an increase in political activity among fundamentalist Christians. Led by ministers like Jerry Falwell and Pat Robertson, they have supported political organizations such as the Moral Majority and Christian Coalition. For the past two decades, they have sought to influence the national agenda, and Robertson taped telephone endorsements for George W. Bush in 2000. They also focus their attention at the local level—school boards, city councils, mayorships, and local GOP leadership.[**] Their agenda includes the return of school prayer, the outlawing of abortion, restrictions on homosexuals, and opposition to gun control.

In the 2000 presidential election, religion and deity were frequently raised by Joe Lieberman, Al Gore's running mate. Lieberman, the first Jewish candidate for vice president, was criticized by some for his frequent references to God and religion.[***] One of President Bush's first actions was to propose government use of churches to deliver social services, his "faith-based" initiative.

[*]Taylor Branch, *Parting the Waters: America in the King Years, 1954–63* (Simon & Schuster, 1988), p. 3.

[**]Kevin Lange, "An Energized Religious Right? Strategies for the Clinton Era," *Christian Century* 110 (February 17, 1993), pp. 177–79.

[***]Janine Zacharia, "The Role of God in U.S. Elections," *Jerusalem Post*, September 7, 2000, p. 6.

President John F. Kennedy

Pat Robertson

Joseph Lieberman

but the percentages expressing pro-choice and pro-life sentiments are almost identical for the Catholic and Protestant groups."[67]

One defining characteristic of religion in the United States is the tremendous variety of denominations. About half the people in the United States describe themselves as Protestant (see Figure 5–4). The largest Protestant denomination is Baptist, followed by Methodists, Lutherans, Presbyterians, and Episcopalians. Because

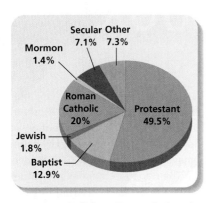

FIGURE 5–4 Religious Groups in America

SOURCE: "Largest Religious Groups in the United States of America" (www.adherents.com/relUSA.htm).

Protestants are divided among so many different churches, Catholics have the largest single membership in the United States, constituting more than one-quarter of the population. Jews constitute less than 2 percent of the population. Followers of Islam number more than 500,000.[68] Protestants came to the United States first; most Catholics and Jews immigrated after the 1840s. It was not until 1960, however, that Americans elected a Catholic president.

Religion is important in American politics in part because of the concentrations of people of particular religions in a few states. Catholics, as noted, make up about one-quarter of the U.S. population, yet they are more than 50 percent of the population of Rhode Island, Massachusetts, and Connecticut. Baptists represent 19 percent of the U.S. population, yet they are more than 50 percent of the population of Mississippi, Alabama, and Georgia. Mormons are only 2 percent of the U.S. population, yet they are more than 70 percent of the population of Utah. The South is the most Protestant—61 percent. The state of New York has the highest percentage of Jews, 7 percent; New York City is 14 percent Jewish.

In recent presidential elections, a majority of Protestants voted Republican, while majorities of Catholics and Jews voted Democratic.[69] The perception among many Catholics and Jews that the Democratic party is more open to them helps explain the strength of their Democratic identification. Democrats won the loyalty of many Catholics by their willingness to nominate Al Smith for the presidency in 1928 and John Kennedy in 1960. Jewish voter identification with the Democratic party was reinforced by Al Gore's selection of Joe Lieberman, an Orthodox Jew, to be his running mate in 2000. Southern Protestants have been Democrats for different reasons, having largely to do with the sectional issues discussed earlier. Religious groups vary in their rates of participation. Jews have the highest rate of reported voter turnout, 85 percent in 1996, while those who claim no religious affiliation have the lowest, 65 percent. Catholics voted at a slightly higher rate than Protestants.[70]

Religion can be related to other politically important characteristics. For instance, Jews are the most prosperous and best educated of any ethnic or religious group. More than 46 percent of Jewish adults graduated from college, compared to 22 percent of Protestants and 20 percent of Catholics.[71] In this example, as in others, religion is a cross-cutting cleavage in American politics; the differences do not reinforce one another. On the basis of income and education, Jews predictably should be Republicans, but 66 percent of American Jews are Democrats.[72] Similarly, southern Protestants should predictably be heavily Republican, but many are Democrats.

Wealth and Income

The United States is a wealthy nation. Compared to other nations, our purchasing power is higher than that of any other advanced democracy.[73] Indeed, to some knowledgeable observers, "the most striking thing about the United States has been its phenomenal wealth."[74] Most Americans lead comfortable lives. They eat and live well and have first-class medical care. But the unequal distribution of wealth and income still results in important political divisions and conflicts.

Wealth (total value of possessions) is more concentrated than income (annual earnings). The wealthiest families hold most of the property and other forms of wealth like stocks and savings. Traditionally, one of the problems with concentrated wealth has been that it fosters an aristocracy. Thomas Jefferson sought to break up the "aristocracy of wealth" by changing from laws based on *primogeniture* (the eldest son's exclusive right to inherit his father's estate) to laws that encouraged people to divide their estates equally among all their children, the result being smaller land-holding. Jefferson sought to foster an "aristocracy of virtue and talent" through a public school system open to all for primary grades and for the best students through the university level.[75]

Education has been one of the most important means for Americans to achieve economic and social mobility. Those who have gone to college earn more than those

gross domestic product (GDP)
An estimate of the total output of all economic activity in the nation, including goods and services.

who have not, and those from wealthier families are more inclined to get an education. Most college students come from the top quarter of American families in
income—those earning $50,000 a year or more. In fact, students from these families
graduate from college at nearly twice the rate as those from the bottom 75 percent of
the socioeconomic ladder.[76]

"The most common and durable source of factions has been the various and
unequal distribution of property," wrote James Madison in *The Federalist*, No. 10
(reprinted in the Appendix). He continued, "Those who hold, and those who are
without property, have ever formed distinct interests in society." Madison was right.
Economic differences often lead to conflict, and Americans remain divided politically
along economic lines. Aside from race, income may be the single most important factor in explaining views on issues, partisanship, and ideology. Most rich people are
Republicans, and most poor people are Democrats, and this has been true since at
least the Great Depression of the 1930s. In terms of income, the Northeast is the most
prosperous region and the South the least prosperous.

Income has been rising in the United States. Even after adjusting for inflation,
income doubled in the period between the 1950s and the 1970s. Since then, inflation-
adjusted income has gone up and down, but the steady rise seen earlier has not
occurred (see Figure 5–5).[77] Economists debate the causes for this change; some cite
higher energy costs, low levels of personal savings, and the worldwide slowdown in
productivity growth.[78]

Despite the general rise in income in the last quarter-century, roughly one
in every ten Americans still comes from a family whose income is below the
poverty line. In 1999 the official poverty level for a family of four was an income
below $17,184.[79] Families headed by a female are three times more likely to fall
below the poverty line than families headed by men, and nearly 35 percent of all
households headed by females fall below the poverty line.[80] Close to 22 percent of
the poor are children under 18 years of age, and many appear to be trapped in a
cycle of poverty (see Figure 5–6). Both African Americans and Hispanics are
nearly three times as likely to be poor than whites.[81]

The definition of poverty is itself political. It identifies persons who cannot
meet a minimum standard in such basics as housing, food, and medical care. Regardless of how one defines poverty, however, the poor are a minority who lack political
power. The poor vote less than wealthier groups and are less confident and organized
in dealing with politics and government. During the last two decades there has been
increasing inequality between rich and poor, a trend quite different from the 1960s,
when the gap between rich and poor narrowed.[82] Although the gap did begin to
decrease under the first Bush administration (1989–93), over the past decade
inequality between rich and poor has again been on the rise.[83]

The distribution of income within a society can have important consequences
for democratic stability. If there is a perception that only the few at the top of the economic ladder can hope to earn enough for an adequate standard of living, then
domestic unrest and revolution may follow. Income is related to participation in politics. Poor people who need the most help from government are the least likely to
participate. They are also the most likely to favor social welfare programs.

Occupation

Americans at the time of Jefferson and for several generations after worked primarily in agriculture, but by the end of World War I, the United States had become the
world's leading industrial nation. This dramatic transformation also resulted in the
expansion of American cities, as workers moved to find jobs. Labor conditions,
including child labor practices, became important political issues. The invention and
application of technology, combined with abundant natural and human resources,
meant that the U.S. **gross domestic product (GDP)** rose, after adjusting for inflation,
by more than 565 percent in real terms over the period from 1929 to 1998.[84]

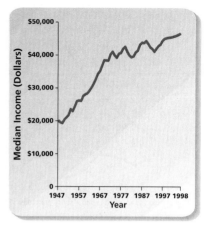

**FIGURE 5–5 Median Family Income,
1947–1998**

SOURCE: U.S. Bureau of the Census home page:
www.census.gov/hhes/income/histinc/f06.html;
www.census.gov/hhes/poverty/ poverty98/
pv98est1.html.

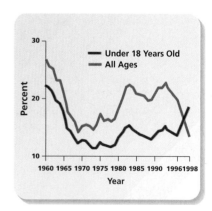

**FIGURE 5–6 Percentage of Americans
Living in Poverty, by Age,
1960–1998**

SOURCE: U.S. Bureau of the Census
(www.census.gov/prod/3/97pubs/p60-198.pdf).

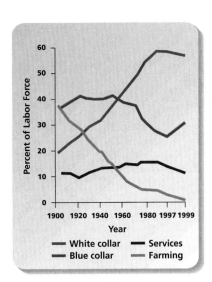

FIGURE 5–7 Occupational Groups, 1900–1999

Sources: U.S. Department of Labor, *Employment and Earnings*, vol. 43, no. 1 (Government Printing Office, 1996), p. 30; U.S. Department of Labor, *Employment and Earnings* 44, no. 1 (1997), p. 31; U. S. Department of Labor, *Employment and Earnings*, vol. 47, no. 1 (Government Printing Office, 2000), p.31.

The United States several years ago entered what Daniel Bell, a noted sociologist, labeled the "post-industrial phase of our development." "A post-industrial society, being primarily a technical society, awards less on the basis of inheritance or property . . . than on education and skill."[85] *Knowledge* is the organizing device of the postindustrial era. Postindustrial societies have greater affluence and a class structure less defined along traditional labor versus management lines.

The changing dynamics of the American labor force can be seen in Figure 5–7, which shows the percentage of the U.S. labor force in various occupations. There has been tremendous growth in the white-collar sector of our economy. This sector includes managers, accountants, and lawyers, as well as professionals and technicians in such rapid growth areas as computers, communications, finance, insurance, and research. This shift has been accompanied by a dramatic decline in the number of people engaged in agriculture and a more modest decline in the number of people in manufacturing (blue collar). Today only one in five working Americans produces goods, and only 2 percent work on farms.[86] Governments are among the biggest employers in this country. More than one-sixth of our gross domestic product is produced by federal, state, and local governments.[87]

Women and racial minorities have distinct occupational patterns. Women are much less likely than men to work in blue-collar jobs and more likely to work in clerical positions (30 percent) or in the service sector (15 percent).[88] As noted earlier, women generally earn less than men of the same age and education. Occupations in which women predominate, like teaching and clerical work, are generally lower paying than industrial or management jobs. And as women advance in their careers, especially in management, they encounter a barrier to advancement that has been labeled the "glass ceiling."

Social Class

Many observers have questioned why Americans do not divide themselves into social classes as Europeans do. American workers have not formed their own political party, nor does class seem to dominate our political life. Marxist categories of *proletariat* (those who sell their labor) and *bourgeoisie* (those who own or control the means of production) are far less important here than they are in Europe. Still, we do have social classes and what social scientists call **socioeconomic status (SES)**—a division of the population based on occupation, income, and education.

Most Americans, when asked what class they belong to, say "middle class." Very few see themselves as lower class or upper class. But what constitutes "middle class" is highly subjective. For instance, some individuals perform working-class tasks (such as plumbing), but their income is middle class or even upper middle class. A school teacher's income is below that of many working-class jobs, but in terms of status, the job ranks at least with middle-class fields. In many other industrial democracies, large proportions of the population think of themselves as working class instead of middle class.[89] In England, nearly three out of five persons see themselves as working class.[90] But to many Americans there is something undesirable about the label "working class."

One explanation for Americans' responses may be the elements of the American Dream that involve upward mobility. Or their responses may reflect the hostility many feel toward organized labor. In any case, compared to many countries, class divisions in the United States are less defined and less important to politics. As political scientist Seymour Martin Lipset has written, "The American social structure and values foster an emphasis on competitive individualism, an orientation that is not congruent with class consciousness, support for socialist or social democratic parties, or a strong union movement."[91]

Age

Americans are living longer, a phenomenon called the "graying of America" (Figure 5–8). Moreover, given the size of the population, fewer babies are being born. This demographic change is having important consequences; it has increased the

socioeconomic status (SES)

A division of population based on occupation, income, and education.

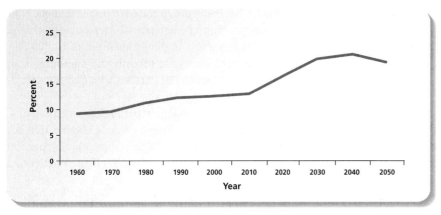

FIGURE 5–8 Percent of Population over Age 65, 1960–2050

SOURCE: U.S. Bureau of the Census, "Aging in the United States, Past Present and Future," at www.census.gov/ipc/prod/97agewc.pdf.

demand for medical care, retirement benefits, and a host of other age-related services. Persons over the age of 65 constitute less than 13 percent of the population yet account for 31 percent of the total medical expenditures.[92]

Older Americans have political concerns, and they vote. Past legislative victories have changed the lives of older citizens. For instance, the poverty rate among this group dropped from 35 percent in 1959 to 10 percent in 1997, a change partly due to improved medical benefits passed during the 1960s.[93] As a group, older Americans fight to ensure that Social Security is protected; they value Medicare and favor prescription drug coverage. Despite their desire for services that benefit themselves, they also favor tax cuts.

In recent presidential elections, less than one-third of all 18-to-20 year-olds voted; in contrast, 70 percent of those 65 and older turned out to vote.[94] Their vote is especially important in western states and in Florida, the state with the largest proportion of people over 65. The "gray lobby" not only votes in large numbers but also has four other political assets not found in other age groups that make it politically powerful: disposable income, discretionary time, a clear focus on issues, and effective organization. When older Americans compete for their share of the budget pie, the young, minorities, and the poor often lose out. Al Gore, by championing Social Security, secured a majority of the vote of those over age 60.[95]

Age is important to politics in two additional ways: life cycle and generational. *Life-cycle effects* have shown that as people become middle-aged, they become more politically conservative, less mobile, and more likely to participate in politics. As they age further and rely more on the government for services, they tend to grow more liberal.[96]

There are also *generational effects* in politics that arise when a particular generation has had experiences that make it politically distinct. An example is the experience of those who lived through the Great Depression of the 1930s, which shaped their lifelong views of parties, issues, and political leaders. Some members of this generation saw Franklin Roosevelt as the leader who saved the country by pulling it out of the Depression; others felt he sold the country down the river by launching too many government programs. More recently, the baby boomers shared a common and distinctive political experience. These Americans came of age politically in the 1960s and 1970s during the civil rights movement and the Vietnam War.

Education

Education has long been linked to citizenship and civic virtue. Differences in education affect not only economic well-being but political participation and involvement. Thomas Jefferson wrote of education, "Enlighten the people generally, and tyranny and oppressions of body and mind will vanish like evil spirits at the dawn of day."[97]

"It's like this. If the rich have money, they invest. If the poor have money, they eat."

The vast majority of people in the United States are educated in public schools. Nine out of every ten students in kindergarten through high school attend public schools, and nearly four out of five students in college are in public institutions.[98]

Many people are surprised to learn that only recently did the number of college graduates in America surpass the number of persons who had not graduated from high school.[99] Just over half of all Americans have not gone to college, though many college students assume that the college experience is widely shared. The proportion of whites who are college graduates is nearly double that for African Americans and more than double that for Hispanics; roughly 24 percent of African Americans and nearly half of all Hispanics stopped their schooling before completing high school[100] (Table 5–3).

Education is one of the most important variables in predicting political participation, confidence in dealing with government, and awareness of issues. Education is also related to the acquisition of democratic values. Those who have failed to learn the prevailing norms of American society are far more likely to express opposition to democratic and capitalist ideals than those who are well educated and politically knowledgeable.[101]

UNITY IN A LAND OF DIVERSITY

As remarkable as American diversity is, the existence of a strong and widely shared sense of national unity and identity may be even more remarkable. Writing about the United States some years ago, a famous reporter, John Gunther, summarized his insights from extensive travels:

> Whoever invented the motto E Pluribus Unum [out of many one] has given the best three-word description of the United States ever written. The triumph of America is the triumph of a coalescing federal system. Complex as the nation is almost to the point of insufferability, it interlocks. Homogeneity and diversity— these are the stupendous rival magnets. . . . Think of the United States as an

TABLE 5–3 Distribution of Education in the United States					
	Population (1,000)	Not a high school graduate	High school graduate	Bachelor's degree	Advanced degree
Age					
25 to 34 years old	39,354	11.9%	31.9%	21.3%	6.2%
35 to 44 years old	44,462	12.0	34.0	18.3	8.0
45 to 54 years old	34,058	13.0	32.1	17.5	11.3
55 to 64 years old	22,255	20.5	37.3	13.0	9.2
65 to 74 years old	17,873	28.9	36.4	10.0	6.6
75 years old or over	14,209	38.0	33.2	8.1	4.4
Sex					
Male	82,376	17.2	32.3	17.1	9.4
Female	89,835	17.1	35.2	15.8	6.6
Race					
White	145,078	16.3	33.9	16.8	8.1
Black	19,376	24.0	36.0	10.3	4.4
Hispanic	16,044	44.5	26.8	7.8	3.2
Other	7,756	16.5	25.5	24.7	12.8

SOURCES: U.S. Bureau of the Census, *Current Population Reports*, P20–513 (Government Printing Office, 1999); U.S. Bureau of the Census, *Statistical Abstract of the United States, 1999* (Government Printing Office, 1999), p. 170.

immense blanket or patchwork quilt solid with different designs and highlights. But, no matter what colors burn and flash in what corners, the warp and woof, the basic texture and fabric is the same from corner to corner, from end to end.[102]

Social scientists sometimes speak of the *melting pot*, meaning that as minorities, especially ethnic groups, associate with other groups, they are assimilated into the rest of American society and come to share democratic values like majority rule, individualism, and the notion that America is the land of opportunity. The melting pot idea has been criticized as assuming that differences between groups are to be discouraged. In its place, critics propose the notion of the *salad bowl*, in which "though the salad is an entity, the lettuce can still be distinguished from the chicory, the tomatoes from the cabbage."[103]

As we have seen, important differences persist among groups, and in that sense the salad bowl analogy is accurate. Divisive issues like immigration, affirmative action, and programs for the poor have reinforced our differences. But in another way, our society has achieved a unity of commitment to democratic values and processes—a political culture that is, at least in part, a consequence of such elements of the melting pot theory as public schools, a common language, and hope for a better life for one's children. Ethnic divisions in the United States pose challenges to the institutions and processes of government, yet the public has generally accepted diversity in political appointments, government jobs and contracts, and other aspects of policy. This acceptance is in sharp contrast to the violent ethnic conflicts in other parts of the world. But we are still seeking the appropriate balance among recognition, preservation, and representation of ethnic groups and the needs for assimilation, common commitments, and a shared identity.

POLITICS ONLINE

Who Are My Neighbors?

We live in a diverse country. Some call it a melting pot; others call it a salad bowl or a patchwork quilt. Many different personal characteristics and associations distinguish people from one another: race, religion, ethnicity, gender, socioeconomic status, age, occupation, education, political ideology, and state or city of origin. As this chapter has demonstrated, these personal differences can often be important to politics. Although we may appreciate the importance of differences, we tend to know our own group's identities best, and we often project our own experience onto others (ethnocentrism). Once each decade, we get a chance to learn a lot more about social and economic differences through the census. The 2000 census gathered data on as many residents as it could find. You can access the census data at: www.census.gov.

A picture of the changing mosaic of the American people emerges out of the census data. *Indivisible: Stories of an American Community* is a project by Duke University and the Pew Charitable Trusts that gives you a glimpse of some of your neighbors. Photographers and interviewers recorded stories and snapshots of people who live in places ranging from Delray Beach, Florida, to Yaak Valley, Montana. To catch a glimpse of some of your neighbors, visit their website at: www.indivisible.org. Listen to their stories, learn who they are, how they live, how they are different from you, as well as what you have in common with them, and how they're trying to better our communities.

If you want to learn more about segments of the community more specifically, visit individual websites. For example, a good website for Latinos is: faclon.cc.ukans.edu/~droy/.

For Catholics or Mormons you can go to: www.catholic.net; or www.lds.org.

Use the search engine at www.prenhall.com/burns and you are likely to find links to groups that will help you learn more about them.

SUMMARY

1. The character of a political society and its social environment are important to understanding our politics and government.

2. As a nation of immigrants, Americans are more diverse than the citizens of most other nations. Diversity in race and ethnicity are reflected in different family structures and religions. The nation's citizens also differ in wealth and income, occupation, social class, age, and education. Divisions by gender and sexual orientation have recently become more important. This diversity is often significant in our politics, though most divisions cut across demographic categories, rather than reinforcing them.

3. Geography, room to grow, abundant natural resources, wealth, and relative isolation from "foreign entanglements" help to explain American politics and traditions, including the notions of manifest destiny, ethnocentrism, and isolationism.

4. Until recently, the South was a very distinct region in the United States, in large part because of its agricultural base and the issue of slavery and race relations. With in-migration and the impact of the civil rights movement, it is no longer solidly Democratic. Recently the most significant migration has been from cities to suburbs. Today large cities are increasingly poor, African American, and Democratic, surrounded by suburbs that are primarily middle class, white, and Republican.

5. Race has been among the most important of the differences in our political landscape. Although we fought a civil war over freedom for African Americans, racial equality was largely postponed until the latter half of the twentieth century. Race remains an important issue in our politics and government. Ethnicity, including the rising numbers of Hispanics, continues to be a factor in politics.

6. Gender is important in American politics. Women have gradually acquired political rights. They now play important roles in our government, and they differ from men in their attitudes on some issues. Sexual orientation policies are among the most contentious in our society.

7. Since World War II, attitudes toward sexuality, marriage, and family have changed in important ways. The use of birth control and contraception has risen, as has abortion and the number of illegitimate births. People cohabit at much higher rates, and those who marry are older. Divorce has also become much more commonplace. Changing family structures and attitudes affect our tax policies, child care, parental leave, and gender equality. They are also important political issues.

8. The U.S. has a large variety of religious denominations and these differences help explain public opinion and political behavior. Important differences also exist between those who are religious and those who are not.

9. While the United States is a land of wealth with a large middle class, not everyone has an adequate share in the American economic success. Poverty has grown over the past two decades, and it is most concentrated among African Americans, Native Americans, Hispanics, and single-parent households. Women as a group continue to earn less than men, even in the same occupations. Differences in income and wealth remain important.

10. America has shifted from an agricultural to an industrial to a postindustrial society, with consequences for occupations and politics. Governments are a major source of employment. Social class is less important in America than in other industrialized democracies.

11. Age and education are important to understanding American politics. Older citizens participate much more than young voters and are a potent political force. Education not only opens up economic opportunities in America but also explains many important aspects of political participation.

12. Despite our diversity, Americans share an important unity. We are united by our shared commitment to democratic values, economic opportunity, the work ethic, and the American Dream.

KEY TERMS

ethnocentrism 96
political socialization 96
demographics 96
political predisposition 96

reinforcing cleavages 96
cross-cutting cleavages 96
manifest destiny 98
race 101

ethnicity 101
gender gap 104
gross domestic product (GDP) 108

socioeconomic status (SES) 110

FURTHER READING

DOUGLAS L. ANDERSON, RICHARD BARNETT, AND DONALD BOGUE, *The Population of the United States*, 3d ed. (Free Press, 1996).

DAVID H. BENNETT, *The Party of Fear* (University of North Carolina Press, 1990).

EARL BLACK AND MERLE BLACK, *The Vital South: How Presidents Are Elected* (Harvard University Press, 1992).

URIE BRONTENBRENNER ET AL., *The State of Americans: The Disturbing Facts and Figures on Changing Values, Crime, the Economy, Poverty, Family, Education, the Aging Population, and What They Mean for Our Future* (Free Press, 1996).

DAVID T. CANON, *Race, Redistricting, and Representation: The Unintended Conse-*

quinces of *Black Majority Districts* (University of Chicago Press, 1999).

RODOLFO O. DE LA GARZA, LOUIS DESIPIO, F. CHRIS GARCIA, JOHN GARCIA, and ANGELO FALCON, *Latino Voices: Mexican, Puerto Rican, and Cuban Perspectives on American Politics* (Westview Press, 1992).

LOIS LOVELACE DUKE, ED., *Women in Politics: Outsiders or Insiders?* 2d ed. (Prentice Hall, 1995).

SARAH H. EVANS, *Born for Liberty: A History of Women in America* (Free Press, 1989).

GEOFFREY FOX, *Hispanic Nation: Culture, Politics and the Constructing of Identity* (Birch Lane Press, 1996).

DONALD R. KINDER AND LYNN M. SANDERS, *Divided by Color: Racial Politics and Democratic Ideals* (University of Chicago Press, 1996).

SEYMOUR MARTIN LIPSET, *Continental Divide: The Values and Institutions of the United States and Canada* (Routledge, 1990).

NANCY E. MCGLEN AND KAREN O'CONNOR, *Women, Politics, and American Society,* 2d ed. (Prentice Hall, 1998).

PETER NABOKOV, ED., *Native American Testimony: A Chronicle of Indian-White Relations from Prophecy to the Present, 1492–1992* (Viking, 1991).

KEVIN PHILLIPS, *The Politics of Rich and Poor: Wealth and the American Electorate in the Reagan Aftermath* (Random House, 1990).

STEVEN J. ROSE, *Social Stratification in the United States: The American Profile Poster Revised and Expanded* (New Press, 1992).

ARTHUR M. SCHLESINGER, JR., *The Disuniting of America* (W. W. Norton, 1992).

JEFFREY M. STONECASH, *Class and Party in American Politics* (Westview Press, 2000).

STUDS TERKEL, *Race: How Blacks and Whites Think and Feel About the American Obsession* (W. W. Norton, 1992).

ALEXIS DE TOCQUEVILLE, *Democracy in America,* ed. J. P. Mayer, trans. George Lawrence (Doubleday and Company, 1969).

KENNETH D. WALD, *Religion and Politics in the United States,* 3d ed. (CQ Press, 1996).

6

INTEREST GROUPS: THE POLITICS OF INFLUENCE

D URING THE FINAL DAYS OF THE 2000
REPUBLICAN PRESIDENTIAL PRIMARY IN NEW YORK, A
GROUP CALLED REPUBLICANS FOR CLEAN AIR BEGAN RUNNING
television commercials attacking the environmental record of Arizona Senator John
McCain. The estimated cost of the advertising buy was approximately $2 million in New
York alone, with additional money spent in California and Ohio. The coincidence of the
harsh negative attack on McCain, coming at a time when George W. Bush was on the
defensive about his environmental record, raised suspicions about the group paying for
the ads. Finding out who these Republicans for Clean Air really were took intense investigative efforts by national media organizations.[1] Days after the ads started running,
Sam Wyly, a wealthy Texas businessman whose brother was a major contributor to
George W. Bush, issued a press release admitting he had paid for the ads.

Wyly was not the only person to hide behind an unidentified group in order to
campaign for or against presidential candidates in 2000. A group named Keep It Flying,
PAC sent out an estimated 200,000 letters to voters shortly before the South Carolina
Republican primary incorrectly claiming McCain opposed flying the Confederate flag
over the South Carolina state capitol. The letter quoted George W. Bush's wife, Laura, as
having positive views on the Confederate flag and urging support for her husband. Who
was Keep It Flying, PAC? After months of research, *The Wall Street Journal* reported that
Richard Towell Hines, a native of South Carolina with close ties to George W. Bush and
now a Washington, D.C. lobbyist whose major client is the Cambodian government,
headed the group.[2]

Group-sponsored activity in recent elections has also included groups with
names you will likely recognize: the Christian Coalition, American Federation of
Labor–Congress of Industrial Organizations (AFL-CIO), National Education Association, National Abortion and Reproductive Rights Action League (NARAL), National
Right To Life, and the Sierra Club. All these interest groups—dedicated to advancing
specific interests through the political process—have run ads on television and radio
and mounted telephone or mail campaign efforts in recent election cycles. When
groups run ads that do not do not use words like "vote for" or "vote against," the U.S.
Supreme Court defines these communications as **issue advocacy**. As such, they are not
subject to the same disclosure requirements or contribution limitations as contributions to candidates. Groups can engage in issue advocacy in addition to the money they
contribute to candidates and parties through their political action committees (PACs)

CHAPTER MEDIA

POLITICS ONLINE
In Whose Interest?
www.prenhall.com/burns

PoliSim
Lobbying America
www.prenhall.com/burns

117

and through contributions to political parties.[3] Much of this election activity is done late in the campaign and in ways designed to avoid media scrutiny.

How interest groups compete for influence, the role they play in elections, and how to limit their "mischiefs" are the subjects of this chapter. We begin by discussing the types of interest groups and the roles they play. Then we turn to one of their most important activities—lobbying. Finally, we examine the problems interest groups pose and ways to regulate them.

INTEREST GROUPS PAST AND PRESENT— THE "MISCHIEFS OF FACTION"

What we call interest groups today, founding father James Madison called **factions**. (Madison also thought of political parties as factions.) For Madison and the other framers of the Constitution, the daunting problem was how to establish a stable and orderly constitutional system that at the same time would respect the liberty of free citizens and prevent the tyranny of the majority or of a single dominant interest. As a good practical politician and a brilliant theorist, Madison offered both a diagnosis and a solution in *The Federalist*, No. 10 (reprinted in the Appendix). He began with a basic proposition: "The latent causes of faction are thus sown in the nature of man." Acknowledging that Americans live in a maze of group interests, Madison went on to argue that the "most common and durable source of factions has been the various and unequal distribution of property."

A Nation of Interests

As we noted in Chapter 5, some Americans identify with groups distinguished by race, gender, ethnic background, age, occupation, and sexual orientation. Others form groups based on issues like gun control or tax reduction. When such associations seek to influence government in some way, they are **interest groups**.

Interest groups are sometimes called "special interests." Politicians and the media often use this term in a pejorative way. What makes an interest group a "special" one? The answer is highly subjective. One person's special interest is another's national interest. Some interest groups claim to speak for the "public interest," yet so-called public interest groups like Common Cause or the Center for Responsive Politics support policies that not everyone agrees with. Politics is best seen as a clash among interests with differing concepts of what is in the public interest rather than a battle between the special interests on one side and "the people" on the other.

When political scientists call something an "interest group" or a "special interest," they are not calling it names. These are analytic terms to describe a group that speaks for some but not all of us. Much of our politics focuses on what is in the national interest. In a democracy there are many interests and many organized interest groups. The democratic process exists to decide among those national interests. Part of the politics of interest groups is to persuade the public that your group's interest is better, broader, more beneficial, and more general, and at the same time label groups that oppose yours as "special interests." For this reason we use the neutral term "interest groups."

Social Movements

Interest groups sometimes have their beginnings as movements. A **movement** consists of a large body of people who are interested in a common issue, idea, or concern that is of continuing significance and who are willing to take action on that issue. Examples include the abolitionist, temperance, civil rights, environmental, antitax, animal rights, and women's rights movements. Each movement represents groups who have felt "left out" of government. Such groups often arise at the grass-roots level and evolve into national groups. Movements tend to see their causes as morally right and the positions of the opposition as morally wrong.

---

issue advocacy
Unlimited and undisclosed spending by an individual or group on communications that do not use words like "vote for" or "vote against," although much of this activity is actually about electing or defeating candidates.

faction
A term used by James Madison and other founders of this country to refer to political parties as well as what we now call special interests or interest groups.

interest group
A collection of people who share some common interest or attitude and seek to influence government for specific ends. Interest groups usually work within the framework of government and employ tactics such as lobbying to achieve their goals.

movement
A large body of people interested in a common issue, idea, or concern that is of continuing significance and who are willing to take action on that issue. Movements seek to change attitudes or institutions, not only policies.

To a marked degree, our Constitution protects the liberties and independence of movements. The Bill of Rights guarantees movements—whether popular or unpopular—free assembly, free speech, and due process. Hence militants do not have to engage in terrorism or other extreme activities in the United States, as they do in some countries, and they need not fear persecution for demonstrating peacefully. In a democratic system that restricts the power of those in authority, movements have considerable room to operate *within* the constitutional system.

TYPES OF INTEREST GROUPS

Interest groups vary widely. Some are formal associations or organizations; others have no formal organization. Some are organized primarily to lobby for limited goals such as securing wage increases, conducting research, or broadly influencing public opinion by publishing reports and mass mailings.

Interest groups can be categorized into several broad types: (1) economic, including both business and labor, (2) ideological or single-issue, (3) public interest, (4) foreign policy, and (5) government itself. Obviously these categories are not mutually exclusive. The varied and overlapping nature of interest groups in the United States has been described as *interest group pluralism*, meaning that competition among open, responsive, and diverse groups helps preserve democratic values and limits the concentration of power in any single group.

Most Americans' interests are represented by a number of interest groups, some of which they are aware of and others of which they may not be and often with which they differ. For instance, older citizens may not be aware that the American Association of Retired Persons (AARP) claims to represent their interests. Others may not know that when they join the American Automobile Association (AAA), they not only purchase travel assistance and automobile towing when needed but also join a group that lobbies Congress and the Federal Highway Administration on behalf of motorists.

Economic Interest Groups

There are thousands of economic interests: agriculture, consumers, plumbers, northern businesses, southern businesses, labor unions, the airplane industry, landlords, truckers, bond holders, property owners, and so on and on.

BUSINESS   The most familiar business institution is probably the large corporation. Corporations range from small one-person enterprises to large multinational entities. Large corporations—General Motors, AT&T, Microsoft, Coca-Cola, McDonald's, Amazon, and other large companies—exercise considerable political influence, as do hundreds of smaller corporations. Corporate power and the implications of a changing domestic and global economy make business practices important political issues.

TRADE AND OTHER ASSOCIATIONS   Businesses with similar interests in government regulations and other issues join together as trade associations, which are as diverse as the products and services they provide. In addition, businesses of all types are organized into large, nationwide associations such as the Conference Board, the National Association for the Self-Employed, the Business Higher-Education Forum, and the Chamber of Commerce.

The broadest business trade association is the Chamber of Commerce of the United States. Organized in 1912, the Chamber is a federation of several thousand local Chambers of Commerce representing tens of thousands of business firms. Loosely allied with the Chamber on most issues is the National Association of Manufacturers, which, since its founding in the wake of the depression of 1893, has tended to speak for the more conservative elements of American business.

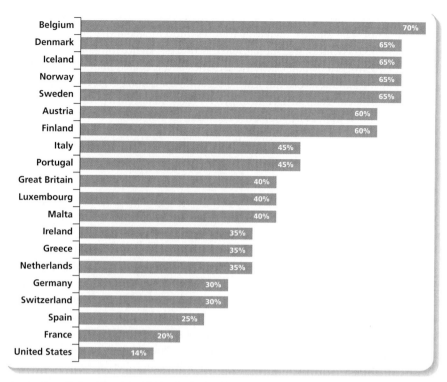

FIGURE 6–1 Union Membership in the United States Compared to Other Countries (Estimated Percentage of the Work Force)

SOURCE: *The World Almanac and Book of Facts, 2000*; based on data from Dr. Henri J. Wamenhoven, *Western Europe*, 5th ed. (Dushkin/McGraw-Hill, 1997), p. 46.

LABOR   Workers' associations have a range of interests, from professional standards to wages and working conditions. Labor unions are one of the most important groups representing workers. The American work force is the least unionized of almost any industrial democracy (Figure 6–1).

Probably the oldest unions in the United States were farm organizations. The largest farm group now is the American Farm Bureau Federation, which is especially strong in the corn belt. Originally organized around government agents who helped farmers in rural counties, the federation today is almost a semigovernmental agency, but it retains full freedom to fight for such goals as price supports and expanded credit. Other farm organizations are based on the interests of producers of specific commodities, such as the American Soybean Association.

Throughout the nineteenth century, workers organized political parties and local unions. Their most ambitious effort at national organization, the Knights of Labor, claimed 700,000 members. By the beginning of the twentieth century, the American Federation of Labor (AFL), a confederation of strong and independent-minded national unions mainly representing craft workers, was the dominant organization. During the ferment of the 1930s, unions more responsive to industrial workers broke away from the AFL and formed a rival national organization organized by industry, the Congress of Industrial Organizations (CIO). In 1955 the AFL and CIO reunited in the organization that exists today.

For some years the Committee on Political Education (COPE) of the AFL-CIO was one of the most respected—and most feared—political organizations in the country. In the Kennedy-Johnson years it won a reputation for political effectiveness. It encouraged and supervised grass-roots political activity, and at the national level it prepared and adopted a detailed platform that spelled out labor's position on issues. Labor contributed money to candidates, ran registration and get-out-the-vote campaigns, and otherwise supported its favorites. In recent elections COPE has had a fair,

but not spectacular, record of wins for its endorsed House and Senate candidates.[4] Labor unions invested heavily in the fight against the North American Free Trade Agreement (NAFTA), claiming it would cost jobs. Labor's defeat in this battle was compounded by the 1994 election, which put Republicans in charge of Congress, and the 2000 election, which put the GOP in charge of Congress and the White House.

In recent elections the AFL-CIO has mounted vigorous campaigns to elect a Democratic majority in Congress and to keep the White House Democratic. Some foes of labor have proposed legislation and ballot initiatives called "paycheck protection," which would require annual authorization by union members for portions of their dues to be used for political purposes. Labor unions have successfully defeated these measures.

Unions have been effective in communicating with their members and organizing them for political purposes. In the 1998 elections and again in 2000, unions sent mailings to their members, organized get-out-the-vote drives, and paid for television advertising. The voter identification and mobilization done by the AFL-CIO for Al Gore in the Iowa caucuses and New Hampshire primary were important to his victories in those states. The strong labor backing of Gore continued through the general election and was also aimed at key congressional contests.

Union membership is optional in states whose laws permit the **open shop**, in which union membership cannot be required as a condition of employment. In states with the **closed shop**, union membership may be required as a condition of employment if most employees so vote. In both cases, the unions conduct negotiations with management, and the benefits the unions gain will be shared with all workers. In open shop states many workers choose not to affiliate with a union, as they can secure the same benefits without incurring the costs associated with union membership, a condition referred to as the **free rider**.

The AFL-CIO speaks for about 80 percent of unionized labor, but unions represent only about 13 percent of the nation's work force (see Figure 6–2).[5] The decline in the proportion of the work force belonging to unions is explained in part by the

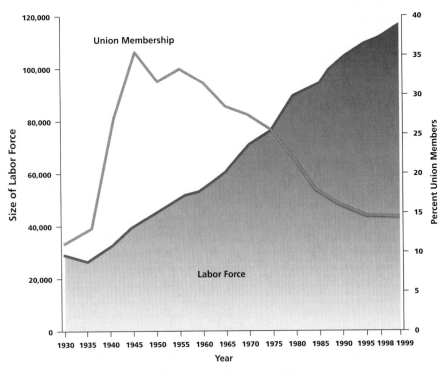

FIGURE 6–2 Labor Force and Union Membership, 1930–1999

Source: *The World Almanac and Book of Facts, 2000.* Copyright © 1999 Primedia Reference, Inc. Reprinted with permission; all rights reserved. U.S. Bureau of Labor Statistics, www.stats.bls.gov/ news.release/union2.toc.htm.

open shop
A company with a labor agreement whereby union membership cannot be required as a condition of employment.

closed shop
A company with a labor agreement whereby union membership is a condition of employment.

free rider
An individual who does not join an interest group representing his or her interests, yet receives the benefit of the influence the group achieves.

shift from an industrial to a service economy. Dwindling membership limits organized labor's political and lobbying muscle, and its prospects for increasing influence in the future are dim. Recently there has been growth in public sector unions, however, and even some doctors have unionized.

Traditionally identified with the Democratic party, unions have not enjoyed a close relationship with Republican administrations. Given labor's limited resources, one option for unions is to form temporary coalitions with consumer, public interest, liberal, and sometimes even with industry groups—especially on issues related to foreign imports. But labor pays a price for such collaboration. It must water down or give up some of its own goals. Few of labor's recent legislative initiatives have been successful, and with Reagan and Bush appointees in the majority, labor faces a much less sympathetic Supreme Court.

PROFESSIONAL ASSOCIATIONS   Professional people have organized some of the strongest unions in the nation. Some are well known, such as the American Medical Association and the American Bar Association. Others are divided into many subgroups. Teachers, for example, are organized into large groups such as the National Education Association, the American Federation of Teachers, the American Association of University Professors, and also into subgroups based on specialties, such as the Modern Language Association and the American Political Science Association.

Government, especially on the state level, regulates many professions. Lawyers, for example, are licensed by states, which, often as a result of pressure from lawyers themselves, have set up certain standards of admission to the state bar. Professional associations also use the courts to pursue their agenda. In the area of medical malpractice, for example, doctors lobby hard for limited liability laws, while the trial lawyers association resists such efforts. Teachers, hair stylists, and marriage therapists work for legislation or regulations of concern to them. It is not surprising, then, that among the largest donors to political campaigns through political action committees are those representing professional associations such as the American Medical Association and the American Realtors Association (see Table 6–1). Professional associations, in addition to lobbying legislative bodies, use the courts to pursue their agendas.

Ideological or Single-Issue Interest Groups

Ideological groups behave very much like economic interest groups, although they may not be driven by a desire to make money. Some of these groups are *single-issue groups*, often highly motivated and seeing politics primarily as a means to pursue

TABLE 6–1 PACs That Gave the Most to Federal Candidates (1996–2000) (contributions in millions of dollars)

	2000	1998	1996
Realtors Political Action Committee	$3.42	$2.47	$2.10
Association of Trial Lawyers of America Political Action Committee	2.66	2.43	2.36
American Federation of State, County, and Municipal Employees	2.58	2.37	2.50
Dealers Election Action Committee of the National Automobile Dealers	2.50	2.10	2.35
Democrat Republican Independent Voter Education Committee	2.50	2.18	2.61
International Brotherhood of Electrical Workers Committee on Political Action	2.46	1.88	2.08
Machinists Non-Partisan Political League	2.18	1.64	2.00
United Auto Workers Voluntary Community Action Program	2.16	1.92	2.47
Service Emplyees International Union Politcal Acton Committee	2.15	1.30	.82
American Medical Association Political Action Committee	1.95	2.34	2.32

Source: Federal Election Commission, "PAC Activity Increases in 1995–96 Election Cycle," press release, April 22, 1997, p. 19; FEC/Info: Political Action Committee and Party Committee home page: www.fecinfo.htm.

their one issue. Such groups are often adamant about their position and unwilling to negotiate compromises. Right-to-life and pro-choice groups on abortion fit this description, as does the National Rifle Association.

Countless groups have organized around other specific issues, such as civil liberties, environmental protection, nuclear energy, and nuclear disarmament.[6] Such associations are not new. The Anti-Saloon League of the 1890s was single-mindedly devoted to barring the sale and manufacture of alcoholic beverages, and it did not care whether legislators were drunk or sober, as long as they voted dry. One of the best-known ideological groups today is the American Civil Liberties Union (ACLU), with roughly one-quarter million members committed to the protection of civil liberties.[7] Ideological religious groups are thriving in the otherwise pragmatic, pluralistic politics of today; examples include the Christian Coalition, which distributes Voter Guides the Sunday before the election.

Public Interest Groups

Out of the political ferment of the 1960s came groups that make a specific claim to promote "the public interest." For example, Common Cause, founded in 1970 by independent Republican John W. Gardner and later led by noted Watergate prosecutor Archibald Cox, campaigns for electoral reform and for making the political process more open. Its Washington staff raises money through direct mail campaigns, oversees state chapters, issues a flood of research reports and press releases on current issues, and lobbies on Capitol Hill and in major government departments.

Ralph Nader started a conglomerate of consumer organizations that investigates and reports on governmental and corporate action—or inaction—relating to consumer interests. Public Interest Research Groups (PIRGs) founded by Nader are among the largest interest groups in the country. PIRGs have become important players on Capitol Hill and in several state legislatures, promoting environmental issues, safe energy, consumer protection, and good government. Nader ran for president in 2000 as the nominee of the Green party. He received 3 percent of the popular vote.

A specific type of public interest group is the tax-exempt public charity. Examples include the American Heart Association, the Girl Scouts, and the American Cancer Society. These organizations must meet certain conditions, such as educational or philanthropic objectives, to qualify for this preferred status. Not only are public charities tax exempt, but donations to these organizations are tax deductible, and the

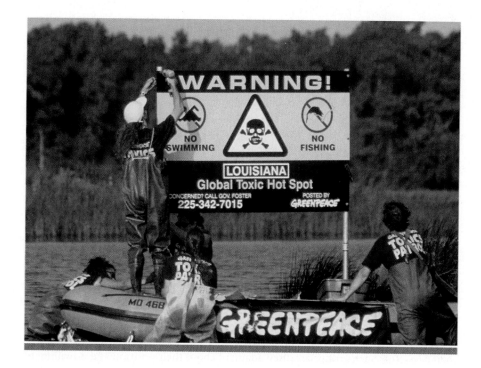

Environmental interest groups such as Greenpeace stage protests and even form political parties to protest the destruction of the beauty and safety of our natural resources.

organizations are not required to disclose information about their donors publicly. These organizations cannot participate in elections or support candidates, nor can they benefit an individual or small group. Despite these limitations, tax-exempt charitable organizations have been very active in voter registration efforts and in advertising campaigns designed to influence public opinion.

Foreign Policy Interest Groups

Domestic policy is not the only matter of concern to interest groups. More and more groups are organizing to promote or oppose certain foreign policies. Among the most prestigious foreign affairs groups is the Council on Foreign Relations in New York City. Other groups, devoted to narrower areas of American foreign policy, exert pressure on members of Congress and the president to enact specific policies. For example, interest group pressure influenced U.S. policy toward South Africa and played a role in South Africa's decision to abandon apartheid. Groups ranging from student organizations to national lobbies like the American Committee on Africa urged divestment, sanctions, or other policy measures that ultimately promoted change in South Africa from the outside.

The American-Israel Political Action Committee (AIPAC) has more than 50,000 members and has been very successful. Because AIPAC's primary focus is lobbying and not distributing campaign funds, it is not required to disclose where its money comes from or goes. Included in the long list of AIPAC lobbying successes are enactment of aid packages to Israel, passage of the 1985 United States-Israel Free Trade Agreement, and emergency assistance to Israel in the wake of the 1992 Gulf War. Its counterpart, the National Association of Arab Americans, lobbies for action in support of Arab causes and hosted events at both parties' 2000 national conventions. Efforts to secure a negotiated settlement between Palestine and Israel have meant that American interest groups on both sides of the dispute remain visible and important.

Government Interest Groups

Governments are themselves important interest groups. Many cities and most states retain Washington lobbyists, and cities also hire lobbyists to represent them at the state legislature. Governors are organized through the National Governors Associa-

A NEW MOVEMENT—OPPOSITION TO INTERNATIONAL TRADE AND GLOBALIZATION

Leaders such as Mahtma Gandhi and Martin Luther King have preached the use of "civil disobedience" to achieve governmental change. Civil disobedience is a peaceful, nonviolent demonstration against policy. Groups or movements trying to attract the attention of both the media and elected officials in support of their cause have often used civil disobedience tactics. As our own civil rights movement demonstrated, civil disobedience can be effective. A recent example of a movement that sought to use protest demonstrations to achieve its aims is the diverse set of interest groups that together assembled an estimated 10,000 protesters in Seattle, Washington, December 11–13, 1999, to oppose the labor, environmental, and trade practices fostered by the World Trade Organization (WTO). Though some groups, such as the AFL-CIO, applied for and were granted protest permits from the local government, other groups took a more confrontational approach.

What started out as a peaceful protest turned into riots. Peaceful groups like Public Citizen and the AFL-CIO were soon brushed aside by more violent protesters like the Ruckus Society and Direct Action Network. Vandals abandoned any pretense of peaceful protest by smashing store windows, and spray-painting the anarchist symbol of an "A" in a circle on buildings. The Seattle police, unable to control the situation and fearful they would be unable to protect delegates from 135 countries, used riot-control tactics like tear gas, rubber bullets, and pepper spray. They also arrested more than 400 protesters, many claiming to have committed no criminal act. Newspapers and television

Thousands of protesters from a great diversity of interest groups took over the streets of Seattle during the World Trade Organization meeting and caused much damage. The police battled back with tear gas and pepper spray.

around the world showed the confrontations, arrests, and destruction.

In the days and weeks that followed, the tactics of the protesters and the police were debated. By most accounts, the protests led to an abrupt ending to the meeting, and despite high hopes of important progress on international trade issues before the meeting, no new agreements were reached. More broadly, the protesters succeeded in forcing globalization and the negative consequences of increased international trade onto the political agenda. Before the protests in Seattle, it is doubtful many people had ever heard of the WTO or the concept of globalization.

Some of the same groups who protested in Seattle were also part of later demonstrations in Washington, D.C., aimed at the World Bank. This time the police were better prepared, and there were far fewer arrests and little damage to buildings. Whether those concerned about globalization and adverse consequences of international trade are able to turn protest into policy remains to be seen. But the use of protest demonstrations to force issues onto the agenda has once again been demonstrated.

SOURCES: Kim Murphy, "Anarchists Deployed New Tactics in Violent Seattle Demonstrations," *The Los Angeles Times*, December 16, 1999, p. A3; Marc Cooper, "Street Fight in Seattle," *The Nation*, December 20, 1999, pp. 3–4; Kenneth Klee, "The Siege of Seattle," *Newsweek*, December 13, 1999, p. 30.

---

tion, cities through the National League of Cities, and counties through the National Association of Counties.

Government employees form a large and well-organized group. The National Education Association (NEA), for example, claims more than 2.3 million members.[8] Public employees are also important to organized labor, and they are the fastest growing unions.

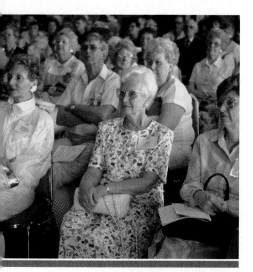

The American Association of Retired Persons (AARP) is a very large and effective interest group that influences legislation favoring the elderly.

Other Interest Groups

Americans are often emotionally and financially involved in a variety of groups: veterans groups such as American Legion or Veterans of Foreign Wars; nationality groups such as the multitude of German, Irish, Hispanic, and Korean organizations; or religious organizations such as the Knights of Columbus or B'nai B'rith. More than 150 nationwide organizations are based on national origin alone. In recent years there has been a virtual explosion in the number and variety of interests and associations. This is especially true for environmental groups (see Table 6–2).

CHARACTERISTICS AND POWER OF INTEREST GROUPS

Groups vary in their goals, methods, and power. Among the most important group characteristics are size, resources, cohesiveness, leadership, and techniques.

Size and Resources

Obviously size is important to political power; an organization representing five million voters has more influence than one speaking for five thousand. Perhaps even more important than size is the extent to which members are actively involved and fight for policy objectives. Often people join an organization for reasons that have little to do with its political objectives. They may want to secure group insurance, take advantage of travel benefits, participate in professional meetings, or get a job.

How do associations motivate potential members to join them? Organizations must provide incentives, material or otherwise, that are compelling enough to attract the potential free rider.[9] Unions are organized not just for lobbying but also to perform other important services for their members. They derive much of their strength from their negotiating position with corporations, which they use to obtain wage increases or improved safety standards. Similarly, the AARP, in addition to lobbying against Social Security cuts and speaking out on other issues of concern to older citizens, offers incentives such as a free subscription to its magazine, *Modern Maturity*, and member discounts at certain hotels. This combination of size and strength sets these groups apart from other large organizations in their effectiveness, as members derive numerous benefits from joining.

TABLE 6–2 Some Environmental Groups and How They Do Business

Group	Membership	Issues	Activities
Greenpeace USA	240,000	Oceans, global warming, genetically engineered foods	Media events; mass mailings; grass-roots activity; does not lobby government
Natural Resources Defense Council	400,000	Resources, energy, pollution	Lobbying; litigation; a watchdog; its scientists compete with experts from agencies and industry
Sierra Club	550,000	Wilderness, pollution, endangered species	Grass-roots action; media; hierarchy of 55 chapters and 400 local groups
Wilderness Society	200,000	Strictly public lands	Headquarters in Washington, D.C., with eight regional offices; mostly an analysis and advocacy group

SOURCE: www.sierraclub.org; www.greenpeace.org; www.wilderness.org; www.nrdc.org

While the size of an interest group is often important, so, too, is its *spread*—the extent to which membership is concentrated or dispersed. Automobile manufacturing is concentrated in Michigan and a few other states, and as a result the auto industry's influence does not have the same spread as that of the American Medical Association, which has an active chapter in virtually every congressional district. An association consisting of three million supporters concentrated in a few states will usually have less influence than another group consisting of three million supporters spread out in a large number of states.

Interest groups also differ in the extent to which they preempt a policy area or share it with other groups. Doctors and the AMA have effectively preempted the health care policy area because they play such an important role in the delivery of health care. But in the transportation policy area, railroads must compete with interstate trucking and even airfreight companies.

Groups also differ in their *resources*, which include money, volunteers, expertise, and reputation. Some groups can influence many centers of power—both houses of Congress, the White House, federal agencies, the courts, and state and local governments—while others cannot.

Cohesiveness

Usually a mass-membership organization is made up of three types of members: (1) a relatively small number of formal leaders who may hold full-time, paid positions or devote much time, effort, and money to the group's activities; (2) people intensely involved in the group who identify with the group's aims, attend meetings, faithfully pay dues, and do a lot of the legwork; (3) people who are members in name only, do not participate actively, and cannot be depended on to vote in elections or otherwise act as the leadership wants.[10] In a typical large organization, for every top leader there might be a few hundred hard-core activists and thousands of essentially inactive members.

Another factor in group cohesiveness is its *organizational structure*. Some associations have a strong formal organization; others are local organizations that have joined together in a loose state or national federation in which they retain a measure of separate power and independence. Separation of powers may be found as well: the national assembly of an organization establishes, or at least ratifies, policy; an executive committee meets more frequently; a president or director is elected to head and speak for the group; and permanent paid officials form the organization's bureaucracy.

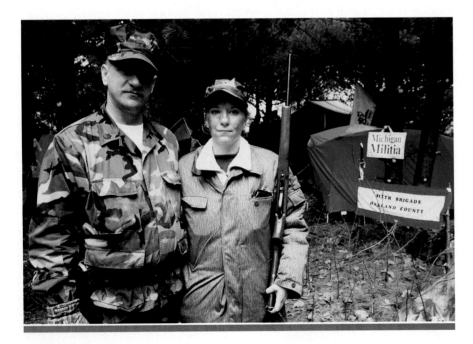

Militia groups have sprung up in many parts of the country. They generally object to gun control laws and tend to be suspicious of government.

Power may be further divided between the organization's main headquarters and its Washington office. An organization of this sort tends to be far less cohesive than a centralized, disciplined group such as the army or some trade unions.

Leadership

Closely related to cohesion is the nature of the leadership. In a group that embraces many attitudes and interests, leaders may either weld the various elements together or sharpen their disunity. The leader of a national business association, for example, must tread cautiously between big business and small business, between exporters and importers, between chain stores and corner grocery stores, and between the producers and the sellers of competing products. The group leader is in the same position as a president or a member of Congress; he or she must know when to lead followers and when to follow them.

Techniques

Interest groups seeking to wield influence choose from a variety of political weapons and targets. They present their case to both houses of Congress, the White House staff, state and local governments, and federal agencies and departments. They also become involved in litigation. Other techniques include election activities, establishing political parties, and lobbying.

PUBLICITY AND MASS MEDIA APPEALS   Interest groups exploit the communications media—television, radio, newspapers, leaflets, signs, direct mail, and word of mouth—to influence voters during elections and to motivate constituents to contact their representatives between elections. Business enjoys a special advantage in this arena, and businesspeople have the money and staff to use propaganda machinery. As large-scale advertisers, they know how to deliver their message effectively or can find an advertising agency to do it for them. But organized labor is also effective in communicating with its membership through shop stewards, mail, and phone calls.

As people communicate more and more via e-mail, this technology will become an important means of political mobilization. John McCain effectively used e-mail in the 2000 primary campaign to turn out crowds in New Hampshire; after his big win in that state, he was able to raise campaign funds nationally. Candidates at all levels used e-mail for fund raising and to motivate supporters. E-mail will likely become part of political communication at the workplace, as management communicates information to its workers about the candidates and ballot issues.

MASS MAILING   One means of communication that has increased the reach and effectiveness of interest groups is computerized and targeted mass mailing.[11] Prior to computers, interest groups had to cull from telephone directories and other sources lists of people to contact, and managing these lists was time consuming. As a result, some groups sent out mailings indiscriminately. Today the computer permits easy data storage and efficient management of mailing lists. Mass mailing is now used by all kinds of interest groups. Today's technology can produce personalized letters targeted to specific groups, like the South Carolina "Keep It Flying" letter shown in Figure 6–3. Such targeted direct mail can also appeal to people who share a common concern, such as environmental groups.

INFLUENCE ON RULE MAKING   Organized groups have ready access to the executive and regulatory agencies that write the rules implementing laws passed by Congress. Government agencies publish proposed regulations in the *Federal Register* and invite responses from all interested persons before the rules are finalized. (The *Federal Register* is published every weekday. You can find it in your school, public library, or on the Internet at www.access.gpo.gov.) Well-staffed associations and corporations peruse the *Register*, ever alert for actions that will affect their interests.

Federal Register

This official document, published every weekday, lists new and proposed regulations of executive departments and regulatory agencies.

Keep It Flying

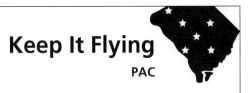

PAC

February 11, 2000

Dear Friend:

The NAACP has demanded that the Confederate Flag that flies over the South Carolina State House be taken down—calling it an "ugly symbol of racism" and even comparing it to the Nazi swastika.

The Confederate Flag flies over the State House to honor South Carolina's heritage. And the NAACP is just plain wrong to compare it to the swastika.

The liberal Democrats in the State Legislature have announced they will introduce a bill in the next few days to have the flag taken down. I hope you will help us keep it flying by doing three things today:

1. Display the enclosed "Keep the Flag! Dump Hodges!" sticker.

2. Call your State Senator or Representative and urge him or her to "Keep It Flying." The telephone number is 803-734-3000.

3. Send a contribution to Keep It Flying to help us rally grassroots supporters to "Keep It Flying."

Make no mistake: This fight isn't about whether the flag will fly over the State House or at another place of honor. The flag's opponents don't want it to fly at all. Anywhere.

Please act today. Remember: The liberal Democrats will introduce their legislation any day to take down the flag.

1. Call your State Representative or State Senator (803-734-3000). When the politicians hear from people across South Carolina, we will win.

2. Display the enclosed "Keep the Flag! Dump Hodges!" sticker.

3. Send a contribution to Keep It Flying. We need your contribution in the next few days to keep our TV and radio ads on the air. Please give $25, $50, $100—or if you can afford it, $250, $500, $1000.

Working together, we can win this fight. And keep the Confederate Flag flying to honor our heritage.

Yours truly,

John Brannen, Chairman
Keep It Flying PAC

P.S. Governor Hodges, the NAACP, Al Gore, and Bill Clinton all want to take down the Confederate Flag flying over the Senate House. Join us today to stop them.

FIGURE 6–3 A Sample of an Interest Group Mailing.

SOURCE: Data Archive, "Getting Inside the Outside Campaign," David B. Magleby, ed. (Brigham Young University, Center for the Study of Elections and Democracy).

WE THE PEOPLE

Bernadette Budde, Senior Vice President, BIPAC

Thirty years ago, fresh out of Marquette University, Bernadette Budde started as a researcher for the Business and Industrial Political Action Committee (BIPAC). In college she had majored in journalism and wanted to be a newspaper reporter, but finding a reporter's low pay discouraging and not wanting to face "no news" days, she decided instead to go to Washington and find a job doing something related to government.

Her first assignment at BIPAC was typing numerous letters and checks perfectly, a task she did not enjoy. Her drive and ingenuity helped her move on to more analytic and strategic duties. Today she is one of the most respected PAC managers in the country. Her job is to decide which candidates BIPAC will support and with how much money. In the course of making these decisions, she interviews candidates and asks pointed questions about issues of importance to the business community.

In the 2000 election cycle, BIPAC contributed $226,000 to con-gressional candidates. While this is a relatively small sum compared to other donors, a contribution from BIPAC signals the business community at large that a candidate is a good investment. An early contribution from BIPAC can help secure contributions from larger business groups like the U.S. Chamber of Commerce and the Business Roundtable.

Budde's success is due in large measure to her ability to survey the political landscape and find new approaches. The traditional wisdom for PACs is to give money to incumbents and stay out of primaries, But Budde played a leading role in BIPAC's effort to mobilize pro-business voters in 2000, in much the same way that unions do. The effort was called "Project 2000" and provided businesses with a web-based "tool kit" that included voter registration forms and rules, candidates' voting records in a format ready for a customized voting guide, templates to create newsletters for employees, and get-out-the-vote materials. You can find these materials at **www.politikit.com.**

Lobbyists prepare written responses to the proposed rules, draft alternative rules, and appear at the hearings to make their case. These lobbyists seek to be on good terms with the staff of the agencies so that they can learn what rules are being considered long before they are released publicly and thus have input in the early stages. Administrative rules are defined over time through legal cases and agency modifications, so even if an interest group fails to get what it wants, it can fight the rules in court or press for a reinterpretation when the agency leadership changes hands.

Finally, an interest group can seek to modify rules it does not like by pressuring Congress to change the legal mandate for the agency or have the agency's budget reduced, making enforcement of existing rules difficult. In short, interest groups and lobbyists never really quit fighting for their point of view.

LITIGATION   When groups find the political channels closed to them, they may turn to the courts.[12] The Legal Defense and Education Fund of the National Association for the Advancement of Colored People (NAACP), for example, initiated and won numerous court cases in its efforts to get rid of racial segregation and to protect the right to vote for African Americans. Urban interests and environmental groups, feeling underrepresented in state and national legislatures, turned to the courts to influence the political agenda.[13] Women's groups—such as the National Organization for Women and the American Civil Liberties Union's Women's Rights Project—also used the courts to pursue their objectives.[14] Conservative religious groups like the Washington Legal Foundation or groups identified with the Religious Right also actively used litigation as a strategy to pursue their objectives.[15]

In addition to initiating lawsuits, associations can gain a forum for their views in the courts by filing ***amicus curiae* briefs** (literally "friend of the court" briefs) in cases in which they are not direct parties. Despite the general impression that associations achieve great success in the courts, groups are no more likely than individuals to win their cases at the district court level.[16]

ELECTION ACTIVITIES   Although nearly all large organizations say they are nonpolitical, almost all are politically involved in some way. What they usually mean when they say they are nonpolitical is that they are *nonpartisan.* A distinguishing feature of organized interest groups is that they often try to work through *both* parties.

Labor usually favors Democrats. The AFL-CIO has supported every Democratic candidate for president since the New Deal, although the Teamsters Union has often endorsed Republicans. In 2000 the Teamsters joined most other unions in backing Al

***amicus curiae* brief**

Literally, "friend of the court" brief, this document is filed by an individual or organization to present arguments in addition to those presented by the immediate parties to the case.

Gore. Business groups generally endorse the incumbent but favor Republicans when no incumbent is running.

Some organizations are prevented from taking a firm position by the diversity of their members. A local retailers' group, for example, might be composed equally of Republicans and Democrats, and many of its members might refuse to openly support a candidate for fear of losing business.

Ideological groups target certain candidates, seeking to change the candidate's positions or, failing that, to influence voters to vote against that candidate. Americans for Democratic Action and the American Conservative Union publish ratings of members of Congress's voting record on liberal and conservative issues, as do the U.S. Chamber of Commerce and the AFL-CIO, among others.

How effective is electioneering by interest groups? In general, the mass-membership organizations' power to mobilize their full strength in elections has been exaggerated in the press. Too many cross-pressures are operating in the pluralistic politics of the United States for any one group to assume a commanding role. Some groups reach their maximum influence only by allying themselves closely with one of the two major parties. They may place their members on local, state, and national party committees and help send them to party conventions as delegates, but such alliances mean losing some independence.

FORMING A POLITICAL PARTY   Another interest group strategy is to form a political party. These parties are organized less with the intent to win elections than to *publicize a cause.* The Free Soil party was formed in the mid-1840s to work against the spread of slavery into the territories, and the Prohibition party was organized two decades later to ban the sale of liquor. Farmers have formed a variety of such parties. More often, however, interest groups prefer to work through existing parties. Today environmental groups and voters for whom the environment is a central issue must choose between supporting the Green party, which has yet to elect a person to federal office, and one of the two major parties. In a New Mexico congressional special election in 1997, the Green party candidate won 17 percent of the vote, helping elect a Republican to the seat. In the 1998 election, environmental groups campaigned aggressively for the Democrat, who obtained 53 percent of the vote, while all minor parties combined only got 4 percent.[17] In the 2000 presidential election, most environmental groups supported Al Gore over Green party nominee Ralph Nader.

COOPERATIVE LOBBYING   Often like-minded groups join together as cooperative groups. In 1987 the Leadership Conference on Civil Rights and People for the American Way brought together many groups in the battle to defeat the nomination of outspoken federal judge Robert Bork to the U.S. Supreme Court.[18] Different types of environmentalists work together, as do consumer and ideological groups on the right and on the left. Women continue to be represented by a large variety of groups that reflect diverse interests, but the larger the coalition, the greater the chance that members may divide over such issues as abortion.

Another example is the Food Group, a 30-year-old informal conference group in Washington that has represented more than 60 business and trade associations. In addition, it spawned an Information Committee on Federal Food Regulations to fight "truth-in-packaging" legislation. Although the Food Group has been fairly effective, it does run into the predictable problem of differences among its constituents over goals and priorities and has found it difficult to put strong and unified pressure on Congress and government agencies.

THE INFLUENCE OF LOBBYISTS

The terms "lobbying" and "lobbyist" were not generally used until around the middle of the nineteenth century in the United States. The root in these words refers to the lobby or hallway outside House and Senate chambers in the U.S.

Capitol. It was also used to refer to hotel lobbies in Washington where petitioners and agents of influence congregated. Thus a senator coming out of the Senate chamber might be accosted politely by several lobbyists seeking to influence his vote on some measure. Or a president might be dining at the Willard Hotel, a few blocks from the White House, and make reference to the number of "lobbyists" hanging around in the hotel lobby. The noun "lobby" has been turned into a verb in this political context. Thus "to lobby" is to seek to influence legislators and government officials, and we call this **lobbying** even if there is no lobby in sight.

Despite their negative public image, lobbyists perform useful functions for government. They provide information for the decision makers of all three branches of government, they help educate and mobilize public opinion, they help prepare legislation and testify before legislative hearings, and they contribute a large share of the costs of campaigns. Yet many people are concerned that lobbyists have too much influence on government and add to legislative gridlock by being able to stop action on pressing problems.

Who Are the Lobbyists?

The typical image is that of powerful, hard-nosed lobbyists who skillfully employ a combination of knowledge, persuasiveness, personal influence, charm, and money to influence legislators and bureaucrats. **Lobbyists** are the employees of associations who try to influence policy decisions and positions in the executive and especially in the legislative branches of our government. They are experienced in the ways of government, often having been public servants before going to work for an organized interest group, association, or corporation. They might start as staff in Congress, perhaps on a congressional committee. Later, when their party wins the White House, they gain an administration post, often in the same policy area as their congressional committee work. After a few years in the administration, they are ready to make the move to lobbying, either by going to work for one of the interests they dealt with while in the government or by obtaining a position with a lobbying firm.

Moving from a government job to one with an interest group is quite common, a practice called the **revolving door**. Despite the fact that it is illegal for former government employees to directly lobby the agency from which they came, their contacts made during government service are helpful to interest groups. Many former members of Congress make use of their congressional experience as full-time lobbyists.

The revolving-door tendency between government and interest groups produces networks of people who care about certain issues. These networks have been

Personal contact and access to decision makers continue to be key elements of lobbying today, as they were at the time of President Grant's administration.

called **iron triangles**—meaning mutually supporting relationships among interest groups, congressional committees and subcommittees, and the government agencies that share a common policy concern. Sometimes these relationships become so strong and mutually beneficial that the issue network becomes very powerful. Retired military officers, for example, can go to work for defense contractors after leaving the military, although they are banned for life from selling Department of Defense contracts. This restriction does not preclude them from providing advice to corporations on how best to compete for defense projects.

Legal and political skills, along with specialized knowledge, have become so crucial in executive and legislative policy making as to become a form of power in themselves. Elected representatives increasingly depend on their staffs for guidance, and these issue specialists know more about Section 504 or Title IX or the amendment of 1972—and who wrote that amendment and why—than most political and administrative leaders, who are usually generalists. It is in this gray area of policy making that many interest groups and lobbyists play a vital role, as people move freely from congressional or agency staff to association staff and perhaps back again. These groups of experts are sometimes called *issue networks*.

What Do Lobbyists Do?

Thousands of lobbyists are active in Washington, but few are as glamorous or as unscrupulous as the media suggest, nor are they necessarily influential. One limit on their power is the competition among interest groups. Rarely does any one group have a policy area all to itself. For example, transportation policy involves airplanes, trucks, cars, railroads, consumers, suppliers, state and local governments—the list goes on and on.

To members of Congress, the single most important thing lobbyists provide is money for their next reelection campaign. "Reelection underlies everything else," writes political scientist David Mayhew.[19] Money from interest groups has become instrumental in this driving need of incumbents. Interest groups also provide volunteers for campaign activity. In addition, their failure to support the opposition can enhance an incumbent's chances of being reelected.

Some people defend lobbyists as a kind of "third house" of Congress. Whereas the Senate and House are set up on a geographical basis, lobbyists represent people on the basis of interests and money. Small but important groups can sometimes get representation in the "third house" when they cannot get it in the other two. In a nation of vast and important interests, this kind of functional representation, if it is not abused, can be a useful supplement to geographical representation.

Beyond their central role in campaigns and elections, interest groups provide another essential commodity to legislators: information of two important types, political and substantive. The *political information* provided by lobbyists includes such matters as who supports or opposes legislation and how strongly they feel.[20] *Substantive information* such as the impact of proposed laws might not be available from any other source. Lobbyists often provide technical assistance on the drafting of bills and amendments, identify persons to testify at legislative hearings, and formulate questions to ask of administration officials at oversight hearings.

MONEY AND POLITICS

A **political action committee (PAC)** is the political arm of an interest group that is legally entitled to raise funds on a voluntary basis from members, stockholders, or employees in order to contribute funds to favored candidates or political parties. PACs link two vital techniques of influence—giving money and other political aid to politicians and persuading officeholders to act or vote "the right way" on issues. Thus PACs are the means by which interest groups seek to influence which legislators are elected and what they do once they take office.[21] PACs can be

lobbying
Activities aimed at influencing public officials, especially legislators, and the policies they enact.

lobbyist
A person who is employed by and acts for an organized interest group or corporation to try to influence policy decisions and positions in the executive and legislative branches.

revolving door
The employment cycle in which individuals work, in turn, for governmental agencies regulating interests and then for the interest groups or businesses with the same policy concern.

iron triangle
A mutually supporting relationship among interest groups, congressional committees and subcommittees, and government agencies that share a common policy concern.

political action committee (PAC)
The political arm of an interest group that is legally entitled to raise funds on a voluntary basis from members, stockholders, or employees in order to contribute funds to favored candidates or political parties.

You Decide . . .

Should PACs be abolished?

As a new member of Congress who almost lost to a candidate supported by PACs in the last election, you are urged by your local newspaper and some constituents to take a bold step and introduce legislation to abolish all PACs. If such legislation were introduced, how would you defend it?

categorized according to the type of interest they represent: corporations, trade and health organizations, labor unions, ideological organizations, and others.

The Growth of PACs

Ironically, considering that the explosion of PACs has occurred mainly in the business world, it was organized labor that invented this device. In the 1930s, John L. Lewis, president of the United Mine Workers, set up the Non-Partisan Political League as the political arm of the newly formed Congress of Industrial Organizations. When the CIO merged with the American Federation of Labor, the new labor group established the Committee on Political Education (COPE), whose activities we have already described. This unit came to be the model for most political action committees: "From the outset, national, state, and local units of COPE have not only raised and distributed funds, but have also served as the mechanism for organized and widespread union activity in the electoral process, for example, in voter registration, political education, and get-out-the-vote drives."[22] Some years later, manufacturers formed the Business-Industry Political Action Committee, but this committee played a limited role in the 1960s.

The 1970s brought a near revolution in the role and influence of PACs, ironically as the result of post-Watergate reforms. The number of PACs increased dramatically, from about 150 to nearly 4,000 today. Corporations and trade associations contributed most to this growth; today their PACs constitute the majority of all PACs. Labor PACs, on the other hand, increased only slightly in number, representing less than 10 percent of all PACs. But the increase in the number of PACs is less important than the intensity of recent PAC participation in elections and in lobbying.

How PACs Invest Their Money

PACs take part in the entire election process, but their main influence lies in their capacity to contribute money to candidates. Candidates today need a lot of money to wage their campaigns. It is no longer uncommon for House candidates to spend more than a million dollars, and for many senators or would-be senators to spend ten times that amount.[23] And as PACs contribute more, their influence grows. What

bundling
A tactic of political action committees whereby they collect contributions from like-minded individuals (each limited to $2,000) and present them to a candidate or political party as a "bundle," thus increasing their influence.

soft money
Unlimited contributions to a state or local political party for party-building purposes.

Labor PACs tend to favor Democratic candidates, as did these fire fighters.

counts is not only the amounts they give but to whom they give. PACs give to the most influential incumbents, to committee chairs, party leaders and whips, and to the Speaker. PACs give not only to the majority party but to key incumbents in the minority party as well, because they understand that today's minority could be tomorrow's majority.

PACs, like individuals, are limited by law in the amount of money they can contribute to any single candidate in an election cycle. The Federal Election Campaign Act of 1971 limits PACs to $5,000 per election or $10,000 per election cycle (primary and general elections). Individuals have a limit of $2,000 per candidate per election cycle. PACs have found some creative ways around this limit. They can host fund-raisers attended by other PACs to boost their reputation with the candidate, or they can collect money from several persons and give it to the candidate as a bundle. Through **bundling**, PACs and interested individuals can increase their clout with elected officials. PACs are not limited in how much they can give the political parties for "party building" purposes. Some of the largest PAC soft money contributors in the 2000 election cycle included several labor unions, AT&T, Philip Morris, and Microsoft.[24]

The Effectiveness of PACs

The strong tendency of PACs to give to incumbents has meant that challengers face real difficulties in getting their campaigns funded. Challengers have to rely more on individual contributors, and PACs can give five times as much to a candidate as can individuals. Moreover, PACs can help friendly incumbents with **soft money** contributions (unlimited contributions to political parties to be used for party building).

In highly competitive races, interest groups mount *issue advocacy* campaigns to help elect or defeat candidates. These campaigns are highly professional, often negative, and can be substantial in scope. Moreover, interest group electioneering includes all modes of communication with voters—phone calls, mail, personal contact, e-mail, radio commercials, and television. Groups—and even individuals—sometimes run their campaigns hiding behind phony names like Citizens for Good Sense, or the Foundation for Responsible Government, or Republicans for Clean Air or Keep It Flying. Mailings and ads by groups with names like these make it difficult for voters to evaluate the source of the communications. Voters assume that candidates are responsible for the tone and content of campaigns, but the growth in issue advocacy campaigns raises doubts about the validity of that assumption.

How much does PAC money influence election outcomes, legislation, and representation? One critic has written, "When politicians start to see a dollar sign behind every vote, every phone call, every solicitation, those other factors sometimes weighed during governance, like the public good and equal access to government, become less and less important."[25] In this area, as in others, money obviously talks. But it is easy to exaggerate that influence. While a candidate may receive a great amount of PAC money, only a fraction of that total comes from any single interest. In addition, it is debatable how much campaign contributions affect election outcomes and uncertain that winning candidates will be willing and able to "remember" their financial angels or that the money in the end produces a real payoff in legislation.

Much depends, however, on the context in which money is given and received. Many campaigns—especially state and local campaigns—are small-scale undertakings in which a big contribution makes a difference. Amid all the murk of campaigning, a candidate may feel grateful for so tangible and convertible a contribution as money. Studies demonstrate a significant relationship between the frequency of lobbying contacts and favorable treatment in the Ways and Means and House Agriculture Committees. Campaign contributions were found to predict lobbying patterns.[26]

Campaign fund raisers such as this one often charge donors $1,000 a plate for the privilege of meeting the candidates and mingling with influential policy makers.

Thinking It Through . . .

As an incumbent, your self-interest would dictate that you oppose a ban on PACs because you stand to benefit from them and your challengers do not. PAC contributions provide a major advantage to you and a huge obstacle to most challengers. This is why many incumbents who ran against PACs in their first race suddenly discover, once elected, that PACs are not all bad. Defenders of PACs label PAC contributions an important form of participation. They argue that such contributions are constitutionally protected. Or they point to a PAC from their district that has supported them and claim that PACs are merely groups of constituents.

If you want to stand by your original opposition to PACs and win others to your point of view, you will need to find a way to substitute "untainted" money like public financing of elections for what you see as "tainted" PAC money. You will have to overcome an intense lobbying effort by PACs to defend what they have been doing. Your best argument against them is that they give so heavily to incumbents (especially incumbents on committees that deal with their concerns) that they make competitive elections unlikely.

CURING THE MISCHIEFS OF FACTION— TWO HUNDRED YEARS LATER

If James Madison were to return today, he would not be surprised by the existence of interest groups, nor would he be surprised by the variety of interest groups. He might be surprised, however, by the varied weapons of group influence, the deep involvement of interest groups in the electoral process, and the vast number of lobbyists in Washington and the state capitals. And doubtless Madison, were he alive today, would still be concerned about the power of faction, especially its tendency toward instability and injustice.

Concern about the evils of interest groups has been a recurrent theme throughout U.S. history. President Ronald Reagan in his Farewell Address warned of the power of "special interests,"[27] and President Dwight Eisenhower used his Farewell Address to warn against the military-industrial complex.

Single-interest groups organized for or against particular policies—abortion, handgun control, tobacco subsidies, animal rights—have aroused much concern in recent years. "It is said that citizen groups organizing in ever greater numbers to push single issues ruin the careers of otherwise fine politicians who disagree with them on one emotional issue, paralyze the traditional process of governmental compromise, and ignore the common good in their selfish insistence on getting their own way."[28] But which single issues reflect narrow interests? Women's rights—even a specific issue such as sexual harassment—are hardly "narrow," women's rights leaders contend, because they would help over half the population. Peace groups, too, claim that they represent the whole population, as do those who support prayer in schools. These issues may seem quite different from those related to subsidies to dairy farmers, for example.

What should be done about factions—if anything? For decades Americans have tried to find ways to keep interest groups in check. They have agreed with James Madison that the "remedy" of outlawing factions would be worse than the disease. It would be absurd to abolish liberty simply because it nourished faction. And the existence and activity of interest groups and lobbies are solidly protected by the Constitution. But by safeguarding the value of liberty, have Americans allowed interest groups to threaten equality, the second great value in our national heritage? The question remains: How can interest groups be regulated in a way that does not threaten their constitutional liberties?

Federal and State Regulation

Americans have generally responded to this question by seeking to regulate lobbying in general and political money in particular. Concern over the use of money—especially corporate funds—to influence politicians goes back well over a century, to the Crédit Mobilier scandals during the administration of Ulysses S. Grant. During the "progressive" first two decades of the twentieth century, Congress legislated against corporate contributions in federal elections and required disclosure of the use of the money.

In 1925, responding to the Teapot Dome scandal during Warren G. Harding's administration, Congress passed the Federal Corrupt Practices Act. It required disclosure reports, both before and after elections, of receipts and expenditures by Senate and House candidates and by political committees that sought to influence federal elections in more than one state. Note that these were *federal* laws applying to *federal* elections; regulation of state lobbying and elections was left to the states.

Federal legislation, including the 1925 Federal Corrupt Practices Act and the 1946 Federal Regulation of Lobbying Act, was not very effective. It was, in fact, largely unenforced. Many candidates filed incomplete reports or none at all. The reform mood of the 1960s brought basic changes. The upshot was the Federal Election Campaign Act (FECA) of 1971, which supplanted the earlier legislation.

FECA, which has been amended three times, establishes reporting or disclosure requirements for all candidates for the U.S. House of Representatives, the Senate, and the presidency, as well as their political parties and campaign committees. It also requires disclosure of the amounts spent to influence federal elections by others, including individuals and political action committees. The act established partial public financing for presidential candidates, financed by a voluntary check-off on federal income tax forms. *Spending by candidates* is not limited, but *contributions* to these candidates and to presidential candidates are limited. Two candidates for president in 2000, Steve Forbes and George W. Bush, turned down the federal matching funds and state-by-state limits in the primaries, a move likely to be copied by wealthy or well-funded candidates in the future.

There have been notable problems with the act, including an ineffective Federal Election Commission. The act has had its critics, and Congress has frequently debated reforming campaign financing. (We discuss these reform proposals in greater detail in Chapter 9.) There have also been significant attempts to regulate interest-group activity in elections at the state level. Some states, like Maine, Wisconsin, Minnesota, and Hawaii, provide for public financing of state offices and state legislative races; others, like Michigan, New Jersey, and Massachusetts, provide partial public financing of gubernatorial elections; a dozen more help underwrite parties with public funds.[29]

During President Bill Clinton's first term, Congress passed the first major overhaul of lobbying laws since 1946. Under the Lobbying Disclosure Act of 1995, the definition of lobbyist was significantly expanded to include part-time lobbyists, those who deal with congressional staff or executive branch agencies, and those who represent foreign-owned companies and foreign entities. This act was expected to increase the number of registered lobbyists anywhere from three to ten times its current level.[30] The act also included specific disclosure requirements and information requirements.

Just six months before leaving office, President Clinton signed into law legislation expanding disclosure requirements by interest groups running issue ads. Some groups had previously been able to avoid disclosure because they fell outside the disclosure requirements of either the Federal Election Commission or the Internal Revenue Service. An example previously discussed, Republicans for Clean Air, attacked Senator McCain's environmental record in the 2000 primaries. The new law will have only a minor impact, as interest groups desiring to engage in issue advocacy can continue to do so, hiding behind vague names like Foundation for Responsible Government, or Coalition to Make Our Voices Heard—two groups that have run ads in recent election cycles. These advertisements generally attack one candidate or praise another, and they are difficult to distinguish from candidate or party ads. But to limit them, as some reformers propose, means some wider limitation on freedom of speech.

Interest group issue advocacy ads as well as party ads paid for by soft money permit the interest group or party to circumvent the contribution limits and some of the disclosure requirements imposed on candidates. This strategic advantage has made issue advocacy and soft money increasingly important in competitive election contests. Interest groups are a major donor of soft money to the parties and also the primary donor to candidates. Under current rules, the same interest group may invest in elections through hard money (limited and disclosed) to candidates, soft money to the parties, and issue advocacy.

The Effects of Regulation

What have been the effects of past reforms on interest groups? Ironically, one has been to increase the number and importance of such groups. The strategy of the 1971 law was to authorize direct and open participation by both labor and corporate organizations in elections and lobbying in the hopes that a visible role for interest-group activity, backed by effective enforcement, would be constitutional under the First Amendment. The 1971 act allowed unions and corporations to communicate on political matters to members or stockholders, to conduct registration and get-out-the-vote drives, and to spend union and company funds to set up "separate segregated funds" (PACs) to use for political purposes.

Corporations, trade associations, and unions made PACs a central part of their government relations strategy. But what changed the rules of the game for corporate interests was passage in 1974 of limits on individual contributions, something not part of the 1971 act. An explosion of corporate PACs followed this 1974 amendment.[31] In 1978 there was little difference in the level of campaign activity of PACs representing corporations, labor unions, or trade associations.[32] But that has changed, with corporate PACs spending more than the others, and ideological PACs at roughly half the level of spending of trade and labor PACs. In the 1997–98 election cycle, corporate PACs spent $137.6 million, labor PACs spent $98.2 million, and trade PACs spent $114.4 million.[33]

The three major types of PACs all substantially expanded their contributions to candidates in 1999–2000. Labor PACs saw the greatest increase in spending, climbing to $126 million, or a 28 percent increase over 1997–98. Trade association PACs exceeded their past cycle contributions by $23 million, for a total of $114 million. Corporate PACs again led all PACs in contributions in 1999–2000, giving nearly $162 million, a 17 percent increase over 1997–98.

With each successive election cycle, PACs spend more money. Most of this money goes to incumbents, especially committee chairs and party leaders. The result, labor leaders contend, has been a greater imbalance than ever between the political action and power of a relatively small number of corporate executives and stockholders, on the one hand, and the labor unions on the other.

A centerpiece of past efforts to regulate interest-group activity was *disclosure* of how politicians fund their campaigns. Until the 1996 election cycle, with the important exception of soft money, we had a much better idea of how much money candidates raised and how they spent it. Without disclosure, much of what we have written here about PACs, for instance, would not be public knowledge. Disclosure permits the press and public to assess the implications of how candidates finance their campaigns. The growth of soft money and the advent of issue advocacy by interest groups now means that we know less and less about how campaigns are financed. Groups and individuals can avoid disclosure, and the public remains uninformed about who is trying to influence their vote.

Candidates and some appointed officials must also disclose their personal finances, permitting voters and the press to see what investments and resources candidates have that may affect their ability to be impartial. Such public disclosure of personal worth, the value of property owned, and outstanding debts no doubt discourages some persons from entering public life, but it also makes officeholders accountable for certain obligations and actions once they enter office.

IS REFORM POSSIBLE?

Will Congress reform the PACs and campaign finance in general? Not only is reform itself complex and difficult, but it is doubtful that most members of Congress really want reform. Many members of Congress thrive on the present arrangements, and the leaders and members of both parties actually compete for

Donor	Republicans	Democrats	Total
Philip Morris Co. (tobacco)	$2,517,518	$ 481,518	$2,999,036
Joseph E. Seagram & Sons/MCA (liquor, music)	$ 685,145	$1,180,700	$1,865,845
RJR Nabisco (tobacco)	$1,188,175	$ 253,403	$1,441,578
Walt Disney Co. (entertainment)	$ 296,450	$ 997,050	$1,293,500
Atlantic Richfield Co.* (oil, gas)	$ 766,506	$ 486,372	$1,252,878
Communications Workers of America* (labor union)	$ 0	$1,128,425	$1,128,425

SOURCE: Common Cause home page: www.commoncause.org/cgi-bin/ccause/soft_money.pl.

*Includes contributions from subsidiaries and/or executives.

PAC dollars (see Table 6–3). Although Republicans have generally received the larger amounts, Democrats in recent election cycles put pressure on the pharmaceutical and insurance industries to give more to Democratic candidates because Democrats might emerge from the election as the majority party, controlling all committee chairmanships and managing the floor of the House, Senate, or both.[35] One reason members of Congress become entrenched in their seats is that PACs fund them. Some of them are reluctant to give up such a cozy relationship. Thus the real question may not be whether Congress can reform the interest-group lobbies, but whether Congress can reform itself.

While PACs help secure incumbent victories with campaign contributions and their general tendency not to support challengers, interest groups also increasingly contribute soft money to the parties, who in turn spend this money to help elect or defeat candidates in competitive contests. This dual-track strategy is relatively new and, in the instance of some interest groups, substantial. For example, pharmaceutical industry PACs donated an estimated $5.2 million to federal candidates in 2000; they also gave another $15.2 million in soft money to the political parties.[36] The pharmaceutical industry exemplifies another recent development—the willingness of groups to spend money on issue advocacy. Beginning in 1999, the pharmaceutical industry contributed heavily to a group named "Citizens for Better Medicare," which reported it would spend $40 million in issue advertising in 2000.[37] Some of their ads ran in states with competitive Senate races, like Montana and Michigan.[38] This issue advocacy is unsettling to incumbents because it is unlimited and often not disclosed.

Interest groups and wealthy individuals have underwritten the dramatic surge in party soft money in recent elections. With control of the executive and legislative branches now so tenuous, both parties have turned up the pressure on interested groups and individuals to give large sums to win the battle for the White House or control of Congress, and groups and individuals responded vigorously. Probably the most conspicuous soft money fund raiser was Bill Clinton; George W. Bush waited only a few months into his new presidency before he started raising soft money for the Republicans.

The combination of issue advocacy and soft money spending invested in competitive races were factors in the Senate vote to pass campaign finance reform in 2001. The McCain-Feingold-Cochran legislation included a soft money ban as well as limits on issue advocacy and requirements for greater disclosure of groups

supporting issue advocacy. Passage of the bill depended on whether the House would enact similar legislation, whether the House and Senate could agree on an identical bill, and whether President Bush would sign such a bill. The lengthy Senate debate and the ability of John McCain to mobilize media coverage of the issue enhanced its visibility and made passage more likely.

Strengthening the political parties might be another way to reduce the power of special interests. If campaign contributions were directed more to parties than to candidates, then candidates would be more accountable to the parties and less tied to any particular interest. Parties are also more likely to invest in challengers than are PACs. Finally, because parties must seek to broaden their appeal, they cannot risk becoming captive of a particular narrow interest. Yet politicians and the interest groups that finance their campaigns strongly favor the current system. This mutually beneficial system is likely to continue until public pressure for change increases.

POLITICS ONLINE

In Whose Interest?

One of the ways interest groups try to win friends and gain access to members of Congress is through campaign contributions, typically through their political action committee (PAC). There are over 4,000 political action committees registered with the Federal Elections Commission. You can access a list of most PACs by industry at:
www.opensecrets.org/pacs/index.asp.

Interest groups can attempt to influence the outcome of elections by spending money for or against a candidate through independent expenditures. The Supreme Court in *Buckley v Valeo* said that groups could not be limited in how much they spent to elect or defeat a candidate, so long as that expenditure was independent of the candidate or party campaigns. One group that engages in independent expenditures is the National Rifle Association (NRA). To learn how much they and other groups spend in this way, go to:
www.nra.org.

Since 1996, interest groups have found a new way to influence elections—issue advocacy—which permits them to spend unlimited and undisclosed amounts of money so long as they avoid using the words "Vote for—," as discussed earlier in this chapter. In 2000, money raised by interest group activity, combined with national political party activity, surpassed candidate activity. Many of these groups, in an effort to hide the identity of their donors and the goals of their group, take on innocuous names like Citizens for Good Common Sense, American Family Voices, and Americans for Hope, Growth, and Opportunity. Who are these groups? What do they advocate? Where do they get their money? In whose interest do they work?

During the 2000 election, The Annenberg Public Policy Center of the University of Pennsylvania tracked broadcast issue ads and the groups that paid for them. From this information, they compiled a database of groups and their activities. Visit the group index at: www.appcpenn.org/issueads/gindex.htm, and click on a specific group to find out who they are, who they represent, and what they did to influence the 2000 election. This site also contains links to many groups' home pages.

SUMMARY

1. Interest groups exist to make demands on government. The dominant interest groups in the United States are economic or occupational, but a variety of other groups—ideological, public interest, foreign policy, government itself, as well as ethnic, religious, and racial—have memberships that cut across the big economic groupings; thus their influence is both reduced and stabilized.

2. Movements of large numbers of people who are frustrated with government policies have always been with us in the United States. Blacks, women, and the economic underdogs have at various times organized themselves into movements.

3. Elements in interest-group power include size, resources, cohesiveness, leadership, and techniques, especially the ability to contribute to candidates and political parties as well as the ability to fund lobbyists. But the actual power of an interest group stems from the manner in which these elements relate to the political and governmental environment in which the interest group operates.

4. For many decades, interest groups have engaged in lobbying, but these efforts have become far more significant as groups become more deeply involved in the electoral process, especially through the expanded use of political action committees (PACs). Interest groups also take their messages directly to the public through mass mailings and advertising campaigns. Other interest group techniques include influencing rule making, litigation, election activities, and cooperative lobbying.

5. Concern for PACs centers on their ability to raise money and spend it on elections on behalf of endorsed candidates, typically incumbents. This concern has led to proposals to ban PACs or more strictly limit their activities. Yet their existence and rights are protected by the First Amendment.

6. Reforms of interest-group excess often include regulations that seek fairness, disclosure, and balance between interest groups. All reform efforts must operate so as not to take away basic constitutional rights of individuals. The key issue today in "controlling factions" is whether to allow groups to proliferate and so balance each other, to try to regulate groups, or to seek reforms outside the groups by fostering balanced power in political parties or elsewhere.

KEY TERMS

issue advocacy 118
faction 118
interest group 118
movement 118
open shop 121

closed shop 121
free rider 121
Federal Register 128
amicus curiae brief 130
lobbying 133

lobbyist 133
revolving door 133
iron triangle 133
political action committee
   (PAC) 133

bundling 134
soft money 134

FURTHER READING

JEFFREY M. BERRY, *The Interest Group Society*, 3d ed. (Longman, 1997).

JEFFERY H. BIRNBAUM, *The Lobbyists: How Influence Peddlers Get Their Way in Washington* (Times Books, 1992).

WILLIAM P. BROWNE, *Groups, Interests, and Public Policy* (Georgetown University Press, 1998).

ALLAN J. CIGLER AND BURDETT A. LOOMIS, EDS., *Interest Group Politics*, 5th ed. (Congressional Quarterly Press, 1998).

ALLEN D. HERTZKE, *Representing God in Washington: The Role of Religious Lobbies in the American Polity* (University of Tennessee Press, 1988).

RONALD J. HREBENAR, *Interest Group Politics in America* (M. E. Sharpe, 1997).

MANCUR OLSON, *The Logic of Collective Action* (Harvard University Press, 1965).

MARK P. PETRACCA, ED., *The Politics of Interests: Interest Groups Transformed* (Westview Press, 1992).

DAVID VOGEL, *Kindred Strangers: The Uneasy Relationship Between Politics and Business in America* (Princeton University Press, 1996).

JACK L. WALKER, JR., *Mobilizing Interest Groups in America: Patrons, Professions, and Social Movements* (University of Michigan Press, 1991).

CLYDE WILCOX, *Risky Business? PAC Decision Making in Congressional Elections* (M. E. Sharpe, 1994).

JOHN R. WRIGHT, *Interest Groups and Congress: Lobbying Contributions and Influence* (Allyn and Bacon, 1996).

7

POLITICAL PARTIES: ESSENTIAL TO DEMOCRACY

S OME YEARS AGO A COMMUNITY COLLEGE DISTRICT

IN LOS ANGELES HELD A NONPARTISAN ELECTION IN

WHICH ANY REGISTERED VOTER COULD RUN IF HE OR SHE PAID
the $50 filing fee and gathered 500 valid signatures on a petition. One hundred and
thirty-three candidates ran, and each voter could cast up to seven votes in the election.
Political parties were not allowed to nominate candidates, and party labels did not
appear on the ballot to help orient voters to the candidates.[1]

How did people vote in an election without parties? Candidates were listed alpha-
betically, and those whose names began with the letters A to F did better than those later
in the alphabet. Being well known helped. Endorsements by *The Los Angeles Times* also
influenced the outcome, as did campaigning by a conservative group. A Mexican-American surname also helped. In this election an important voting cue was absent: incumbency.
Because the board of trustees was newly created, none of the candidates were incumbents.

Rarely are American voters faced with such unorganized and plentiful choices,
because parties give structure to national and state elections. E. E. Schattschneider, a
noted political scientist, once said, "The political parties created democracy, and modern democracy is unthinkable save in terms of the parties."[2] This provocative statement
is true, but such a favorable evaluation of political parties runs counter to a long-
standing and deep-seated American fear and distrust of them. Experience has taught
us that free people create political parties to promote their own goals. Parties are a consequence of freedom, as we learned again with the fall of communism in Eastern
Europe. Even though our founders hoped to discourage them, political parties quickly
became an integral part of our political system.

Elections serve the vital task of deciding who can legitimately exercise political
power, and parties are an integral part of making national and state elections work. We
take for granted the peaceful transfer of power from one elected official to another, from
one party to another, yet in new democracies the transfer of power following an election is often problematic. Parties serve many functions, including an important one of
narrowing the choices for voters.[3] They are both a consequence of democracy and an
instrument of it. Parties need not be strong and cohesive like those in Britain and
Europe, but without some kind if party system, democracies are not likely to survive.

This chapter begins by examining the purposes parties serve that make them so
vital to the functioning of democracy. We then examine the evolution of American
political parties. Although American political parties have changed over time, they

CHAPTERMEDIA

 POLITICS ONLINE
What's Your Party?
www.prenhall.com/burns

POLISIM
The Political Horizon
www.prenhall.com/burns

remain important in three different settings: as institutions, in government, and in the electorate. It is important to understand how parties facilitate democracy in all three settings. Finally, we turn to a discussion of the strength of parties today and the prospects for party reform and renewal.

WHAT PARTIES DO FOR DEMOCRACY

Party Functions

Amerian political parties serve a variety of political and social functions, some obvious and some not so obvious. They perform some functions well and others not so well, and how they perform them differs from place to place and time to time.

ORGANIZE THE COMPETITION   One of the most important functions of parties is to organize the competition by choosing candidates to run under their label. Parties recruit and nominate candidates for office; they register and activate voters; they help candidates by training them, raising money for them, providing them with research and voter lists, and enlisting volunteers to work for them.[4] Recently campaign consultants rather than party officials have taken over some of these responsibilities; we explore this topic at some length in Chapter 8.

The ability of parties to influence the selection of candidates varies by the type of nominating system used in the state. A few states use a *caucus or convention system*, which permits party leaders to play a role in the selection of nominees. Other states utilize *primary elections*. As more and more states use primary elections, the ability of party leaders to influence who runs under their party label is reduced. Candidates with little party experience but with well-known names or ample personal funds can often win in a primary over a person with a known track record of prior party service or success in a less visible office.

A party's ability to organize the competition is also influenced by how states organize their ballots. In many states, candidates are listed in party columns—the **party column ballot**—which makes it easier for voters to vote a *straight ticket* for all the party candidates. Straight-ticket voting is also more likely in voting systems that permit flipping one switch or punching one chad to vote for all candidates from one party. Other states organize the ballot by office—the **office block ballot**—which makes straight-ticket voting harder. Even though many voters cast votes for candidates in more than one party, the party label of a candidate means something to most voters and is important in their voting decision.

Local and judicial elections in most states are **nonpartisan**, which means no party affiliation is indicated. Such systems make it more difficult for political parties to operate—precisely the reason why many jurisdictions have adopted this reform. Proponents of nonpartisan local and judicial elections contend that party affiliation is not important to being a good judge or school board member.

UNIFY THE ELECTORATE   Parties are often accused of creating conflict, but the fact is that they actually help unify the electorate and moderate conflict. There is a strong incentive in both parties to fight out their differences inside the party but then come together to take on the opposition. Moreover, in order to win elections, parties need to reach out to voters outside their party and gain their support. This action also helps unify the electorate, at least into the two large national political parties in our system.

Parties have great difficulty building coalitions when faced with controversial issues like abortion or gun control. Not surprisingly, candidates and parties generally try to avoid defining themselves or the election in single-issue terms. Rather, they hope that if voters disagree with them on one issue, they will still support them because they agree with them on other issues.

party column ballot
Ballot in which all candidates are listed under their party designations, making it easy for voters to cast votes for all the candidates of one party.

office block ballot
Ballot in which all candidates are listed under the office for which they are running.

nonpartisan
A local or judicial election in which party affiliation is not listed on ballots.

HELP ORGANIZE GOVERNMENT   Although American political parties are not as cohesive as those in England and most European democracies, parties are important when it comes to organizing our state and national governments. Congress is organized along party lines. The political party with the most votes in each chamber elects the officers of that chamber, selects the chair of each committee, and has a majority on all the committees. State legislatures, with the notable exception of Nebraska, are also organized along party lines.

Following the 2000 election, the U.S. Senate was evenly split between Republicans and Democrats, and the Republicans could have relied on Vice-President Cheney to cast a tie-breaking vote on which party would chair all committees. Instead, leaders of both parties negotiated a power-sharing arrangement in which Republicans chair all committees, but membership on committees is evenly split, with both parties having the same allocation of staff on all committees.[5]

The party that controls the White House, the governor's mansion, or city hall gets **patronage**, which means it can select party members as public officials or judges. Such appointments are limited only by civil service regulations that restrict patronage typically to the top posts, but these posts number about 4,000 in the federal government and are also numerous at the state and local levels. Patronage provides an incentive for people to become involved in politics and gives the party leaders loyal partisans in key positions to help them achieve their policy objectives.

TRANSLATE PREFERENCE INTO POLICY   One of the great strengths of our democracy is that even the party that wins an election usually has to moderate what it does in order to win reelection. For that reason, public policy does not change dramatically with each election. Nonetheless, the party that wins the election has a chance to enact its policies and implement its campaign promises.

American parties have had only limited success in setting the course of national policy, especially when compared with traditionally strong European parties. The European model of party government, which has been called a *responsible party system*, assumes that parties discipline their members through their control over nominations and campaigns. Officeholders in such party-centered systems are expected to act according to party wishes or they will not be allowed to run again under the party label. Moreover, candidates run on fairly specific party platforms and are expected to implement those policies if they win control in the election.

Because American parties do not control nominations, they are unable to discipline members who express views contrary to those of the party. The American system is *candidate centered*; politicians are nominated largely on the basis of their qualifications and personal appeal, not party loyalty. In fact, it is more correct to say that in most contests we have candidate politics rather than party politics. As a consequence, party leaders cannot guarantee passage of their program, even if they are in the majority. But in recent years parties have come to play an important role in competitive federal elections through their **soft money** expenditures. Soft money comes from unlimited contributions to the political parties from individuals, corporations, labor unions, and political action committees (PACs) for "party building" purposes, but it has come to be used for candidate promotion. Because such contributions are unlimited, parties put a premium on large donors.[6]

In our Congress, most, but not all, Democrats vote together, as do most, but not all, Republicans. And then there are times, rather unusual but not unprecedented, when a president of one party receives more congressional votes from the opposing party than from his own, as President Bill Clinton did in 2000 on legislation granting China permanent normal trade relations status with the United States.[7]

PROVIDE LOYAL OPPOSITION   Parties provide a loyal opposition. After a polite interval following an election—**the honeymoon**—the opposition party begins to criticize the party that controls the White House, especially when the opposition

patronage
The dispensing of government jobs to persons who belong to the winning political party.

soft money
Money contributed for party-building purposes that does not have to be disclosed under federal law.

honeymoon
A period at the beginning of a new president's term in which the president enjoys generally positive relations with the press and Congress, usually lasting about six months.

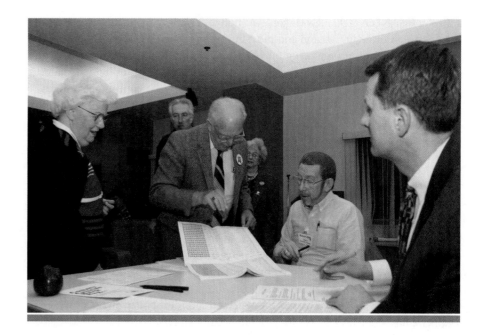

A precinct caucus in Des Moines, Iowa, discusses and votes on delegates to represent their choice for president.

party controls one or both houses of Congress.[8] The length of the honeymoon depends in part on how contentious the agenda of the new administration is and on the leadership skills of the new president. Early success in enacting policy can prolong the honeymoon; mistakes or controversies can shorten it.

The Nomination of Candidates

From the beginning, parties have been the mechanism by which candidates for public office are chosen. Massachusetts used the earliest method of nominating candidates—the **caucus**, a closed meeting of local leaders. The caucus played an important part in pre-Revolutionary politics. Elected officials organized themselves into groups or parties and together selected candidates to run for higher office, including the presidency. This method of nomination operated for several decades after the United States was established.

As early as the 1820s, however, charges of "secret deals" and "smoke-filled rooms" were made against this method. Moreover, it was not representative of people from areas where a party was in a minority or nonexistent, as only officeholders took part in the caucus. Efforts were made to make the caucus more representative of rank-and-file party members. The *mixed caucus* brought in delegates from districts in which the party had no elected legislators.

Then, during the 1830s and 1840s, a system of **party conventions** was instituted. Delegates, usually chosen directly by party members in towns and cities, selected the party standard-bearers, debated and adopted a platform, and built party spirit by celebrating noisily. But the convention method soon came under criticism that it was subject to control by the party bosses and their machines.

To involve more voters and reduce the power of the bosses to pick party nominees, states adopted the **direct primary**, in which people could vote for the party's nominees for office. Primaries spread rapidly after Wisconsin adopted them in 1905—in the North as a Progressive era reform and in the South as a way to bring democracy to a region that had seen no meaningful general elections since the end of Reconstruction due to one-party rule by the Democrats. By 1920 direct primaries were used for some offices in almost all states.

Today the direct primary is the typical method of picking party candidates. Primaries vary significantly from state to state. They differ in terms of: (1) who may run in a primary and how one qualifies for the ballot; (2) whether the party organization

caucus
A meeting of local party members to choose party officials and/or candidates for public office and to decide the platform.

party convention
A meeting of party delegates to pass on matters of policy and in some cases to select party candidates for public office.

direct primary
Election open to all members of the party in which voters choose the persons who will be the party's nominees in the general election.

can or does endorse candidates before the primary; (3) who may vote in a party's primary—that is, whether a voter must register with a party in order to vote; and (4) how many votes are needed for nomination—a plurality, a majority, or some other number determined by party rule or state law. The differences among primaries are not trivial; they have an important impact on the role played by party organization and on the strategy used by candidates.

In states with **open primaries**, any voter, regardless of party, can participate in whichever primary he or she may choose. This kind of primary permits **crossover voting**—Republicans and Independents helping to determine who the Democratic nominee will be, and vice versa. Other states use **closed primaries**, in which only persons already registered in a party may participate. Some states, like Washington and California, experimented with *blanket primaries* in which all voters could vote for any candidate, regardless of party. In 2000, blanket primaries were declared unconstitutional by the U.S. Supreme Court, in part because they permit people who have "expressly affiliated with a rival" party to have a vote in the selection of a nominee from a different party.[9]

Direct primaries were introduced to reduce the influence of party leaders, which they have done, but many critics believe that this change has had more undesirable than desirable consequences. Party leaders now have less influence over who gets to be the party's candidate, and candidates are less accountable to the party both during the election and after it. Along with modern communications and fund-raising techniques, direct primaries have diminished the influence of leaders of political parties.

The rise of direct primaries has not meant the death of caucuses or conventions. In some states local caucuses choose delegates to attend regional meetings, which in turn select delegates to state and national conventions, where they nominate party candidates for offices. The Iowa caucuses, in which roughly one hundred thousand Iowans in each major party participate, are highly publicized as the first important test of potential presidential nominees.[10]

In a few states, conventions still play a role in the nominating process. In Connecticut, for example, convention choices become the party nominees unless they are challenged. Candidates who attain at least 15 percent of the vote in the convention have an automatic right to challenge, but they do not always exercise this right.[11] In Utah, if a candidate gets 60 percent of the delegate vote at the convention, there is no primary. Should no candidate reach 60 percent, only the top two candidates are listed on the primary ballot. In other states, convention nominees are designated as such on the primary ballot; they may or may not receive help from the party organization. Conventions are also used to invigorate the party faithful by enabling them to meet with their leaders.

In most states candidates can get their names on the ballot as an Independent or minor party candidate by securing the required number of signatures on a nomination petition. This is hard to do, but it can be done, as Ross Perot demonstrated in 1992. He spent his own money to build an organization of volunteers who put his name on the ballot in all 50 states. Minor party gubernatorial candidates like the Minnesota Reform party's Jessie Ventura in 1998 or the Green party's presidential candidate Ralph Nader in 2000 secured their nominations through their existing parties. However, in 2000 Nader did not appear on the ballot in seven states.[12]

Party Systems

Although we have many minor parties, only the two major parties have much of a chance to win elections. Ours is a two-party system; most other democracies have a multiparty system. Multiparty systems are almost always found in countries that have a parliamentary government, in contrast to our presidential system. This is, however, not always true. For example, England has a parliamentary system but also a strong two-party system.

Parliamentary systems usually have a *head of the nation*, often called the president, but they also have a *head of the government*, often called the prime minister or

open primary
A primary in which any voter, regardless of party, may vote.

crossover voting
A member of one party voting for a candidate of another party.

closed primary
A primary in which only persons registered in the party holding the primary may vote.

ISRAEL'S COALITION GOVERNMENT

Israel has a multiparty system. Though Israelis vote for prime minister and parliament separately, the prime minister must still have the support of the majority of the members of parliament. If he doesn't, he is in danger of facing a parliamentary vote of no confidence. A vote of no confidence leads to new elections for prime minister and parliament. Because there are many parties, it is difficult—if not impossible—for any one party to gain a majority of the seats in the Knesset, the Israeli parliament. Usually one party can only get a plurality of the seats. A party with only a plurality of seats must form a coalition with other parties in order to rule. Certain concessions must be made to those parties to convince them to join. If the ruling party loses the support of its coalition partners, the prime minister and his party must form a new coalition or their government will be toppled by a parliamentary vote of no confidence.

In July 2000, three religious or rightist parties withdrew from Prime Minister Ehud Barak's coalition government in protest over the peace talks with the Palestinians. This left Barak without a parliamentary majority. Though he survived the subsequent vote of no confidence, he was forced into forming a new coalition government. This effort even led to talks of forming a unity party with

the Likud party. The Likud party leader, Ariel Sharon, was one of Barak's most outspoken critics. Sharon demanded that if his party were to join a unity government with Barak, it must have a veto over any future concessions in peace talks. These negotiations were ultimately unfruitful, and in a surprise move in November, Barak exercised his authority to call an early election for prime minister. On February 6, 2001, Ariel Sharon soundly defeated Ehud Barak. Now Sharon had to form a coalition government in a limited amount of time.

It is not clear what effect these developments will have on peace talks with the Palestinians. Sharon and the Likud party are much more reluctant to make concessions to the Palestinians than Barak and his government were, but to form a government, they must still make concessions to other parties. The peace policy they ultimately pursue may be a reflection of the concessions they must make to form a coalition government.

Source: John Kifner, "Barak Seems in Position to Survive Vote in Parliament," *The New York Times*, July 31, 2000, p. A8; Joel Greenberg, "Barak and Sharon Open Talks on Forming a Coalition," *The New York Times*, October 24, 2000, p. A18; and Deborah Sontag, "Barak Declares Early Elections, in Surprise Move," *The New York Times*, November 29, 2000, p. A1.

chancellor, who is the leader of one of the larger parties in the legislature. In democracies with multiparty systems, such as Israel and Italy, because no one party has a majority of the votes, *coalition* governments are necessary. Minor parties can gain concessions—positions in a cabinet or support of policies they want implemented—in return for their participation in a coalition. Major parties need the minor parties and are therefore willing to bargain. Thus the multiparty system favors the existence of minor parties by giving them incentives to persevere.

In some multiparty parliamentary systems, parties run slates of candidates for legislative positions, and winners are determined by **proportional representation**, in which the parties receive a proportion of the legislators corresponding to their proportion of the vote. In our **winner-take-all** system, only the candidate with the most votes in a district or state takes office. Because a party does not gain anything by finishing second, minor parties in a two-party system can rarely overcome the assumption that a vote for them is a wasted vote.[13] Even if a third-party candidate can keep either major party candidate from receiving more than 50 percent (a *majority*) of the vote, the candidate with the most votes (a *plurality*) wins.

In multiparty systems, parties at the extremes are apt to have more influence than in our two-party system, and their legislatures more accurately reflect the full range of the views of the electorate. Political parties in multiparty systems can be more doctrinaire than ours because they do not have to appeal to masses of people. Even though parties that do not become part of the governing coalition may have little to say in setting government policy, they survive because they appeal to some voters. Under such a system, an incentive exists for third, fourth, or additional parties to run because they may win some seats. In contrast, our two-party system tends to create *centrist* parties that appeal to moderate elements and suppress the views of extremists in the electorate. Moreover, once elected, our parties do not form as cohesive a voting block as do ideological parties in multiparty systems.

Multiparty parliamentary systems make governments unstable, as coalitions form and collapse. In addition, swings in policy when party control changes can be quite dramatic. In contrast, two-party systems produce governments that tend to be stable and centrist, and as a result, policy changes occur incrementally.

Minor Parties: Persistence and Frustration

Although we have a primarily two-party system in the United States, we also have **minor parties**, sometimes called *third parties*. Those that arise around a candidate usually disappear when the charismatic personality does. Examples of such parties

proportional representation
An election system in which each party running receives the proportion of legislative seats corresponding to its proportion of the vote.

winner-take-all
An election system in which the candidate with the most votes wins.

minor party
A small political party that rises and falls with a charismatic candidate or, if composed of ideologies on the right or left, usually persists over time; also called a *third party*.

are Theodore Roosevelt's Bull Moose party and George Wallace's American Independent party. Wallace's party polled more than 13 million votes and won 46 electoral votes in 1968. Ross Perot won 19 million votes, for 19 percent of the total vote in 1992. He did only about half as well in 1996, despite the fact that he had organized a political party. Without Ross Perot to lead it, the Reform party was badly divided in 2000 and its presidential candidate, Pat Buchanan, failed to reach 1 percent of the national popular vote. More visible than the Reform party was the Green party, which mounted a major effort to reach 5 percent of the popular vote for presidential candidate Ralph Nader and thereby qualify the party for federal funding in the 2004 elections. The effort failed. The Green party mustered only 3 percent of the popular vote.

Minor parties that are organized around an *ideology* usually persist over a longer time than do those built around a particular leader. Communist, Prohibition, Libertarian, or Green parties are of the ideological type. Minor parties of both types come and go, and there are usually several minor parties running in any given election.[14] Some parties arise around a single issue, like the States' Rights party that split with the Democratic party in 1948 over President Harry Truman's civil rights policies.

Minor parties have had an indirect influence in our country by drawing attention to controversial issues and by organizing such groups as the antislavery and the civil rights movements. However, they have never won the presidency or more than a handful of congressional seats (see Table 7–1).[15] They have never shaped national policy from *inside* the government, and their influence on national policy and on the platforms of the two major parties has been limited.[16]

Minor parties have been criticized by major parties as "spoilers," diverting votes away from the major party candidate and costing that candidate the election. Green party candidate Ralph Nader was accused of doing this to Al Gore in 2000. Interest groups identified with environmental issues ran ads urging voters not to waste their vote on Nader, who could not win the election.

CANADA'S MULTIPARTY SYSTEM

In contrast to the two-party system found in the United States, Canada has a multiparty system. Following the general elections of 1997, the Liberal party, led by Jean Chrétien, formed Canada's government. In addition, seats were allocated in the House of Commons, Canada's preeminent legislative chamber, to the Progressive Conservative party, the New Democratic party, the Reform party, and the Bloc Québécois. Either the Liberals or the Progressive Conservatives have dominated the national political landscape since Canada became a sovereign nation in 1867, and both parties are basically centrist.

The New Democrats, which have formed several provincial governments in recent years, believe in social democracy and support a strong governmental role in the economy, an extensive social welfare system, and Canada's withdrawal from both the North Atlantic Treaty Organization (NATO) and the North American Free Trade Agreement (NAFTA). They are outspoken about too much American influence over Canada. The Reform party receives most of its support from voters in Canada's western provinces and believes in a limited governmental role in the economic sector and cordial relations with the United States. The Bloc Québécois's primary mission is to promote Quebec's independence from Canada through democratic means. All of Canada's major parties are to the left of the Democratic and Republican parties in the United States, and Canadians in general are much more supportive than Americans of a major governmental role in the economic and social welfare sectors.

Because of the multiplicity of parties, Canadian voters have more options in linking their own policy preferences to specific party platforms. On the other hand, the multiparty system may occasionally result in a minority government, meaning that no party controls a majority of the seats in parliament. This can make governing a much more precarious process. In addition, Canada's multiparty system has accentuated regional biases and preferences within this vast northern nation, complicating efforts to promote national unity and a national vision of Canada's future.

A BRIEF HISTORY OF AMERICAN POLITICAL PARTIES

Our First Parties

To the founders of the young Republic, parties meant bigger, better organized, and fiercer factions, and they did not want that. Benjamin Franklin worried about the "infinite mutual abuse of parties, tearing to pieces the best of characters." In his Farewell Address, George Washington warned against the "baneful effects of the Spirit of Party." And Thomas Jefferson said, "If I could not go to heaven but with a party, I would not go there at all."[17]

Ross Perot, organizer of the Reform party and its presidential candidate in 1992 and 1996.

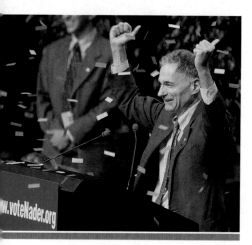

Green party presidential candidate in 2000, Ralph Nader.

How, then, did parties get started? Largely out of practical necessity. The same early leaders who so frequently stated their opposition to political parties also recognized the need to organize officeholders who shared their views so that government could act. To get its measures passed by Congress, the Washington administration had to fashion a coalition among factions. This job fell to Treasury Secretary Alexander Hamilton, who built an informal Federalist party, while Washington stayed "above politics."

Secretary of State Jefferson and other officials, many of whom despised Hamilton and his aristocratic ways as much as they opposed the policies he favored, were uncertain about how to deal with these political differences. Their overriding concern was the success of the new government; personal loyalty to Washington was a close second. Thus Jefferson stayed in the cabinet, despite his opposition to administration policies, during most of Washington's first term. When he left the cabinet at the end of 1793, many who joined him in opposition to the administration's economic policies remained in Congress, forming a group of legislators opposed to Federalist fiscal policies and eventually to Federalist foreign policy, which appeared "soft on Britain." This party was later known as Republicans, then as Democratic-Republicans, then as Democrats.[18]

Realigning Elections

American political parties have evolved and changed over time, but some underlying characteristics have been constant. Historically, we have had a two-party system with minor parties. Our parties are moderate and accommodative, meaning that they are open to people with diverse outlooks. Political scientist V. O. Key and others argue that our party system has been shaped in large part by **realigning elections**, turning points that define the agenda of politics and the alignment of voters within parties during periods of historic change in the economy and society. Realigning elections are characterized by intense electoral involvement by the voters, disruptions of traditional voting patterns, changes in the relations of power within the community, and the formation of new and durable electoral groupings. They have occurred cyclically, not randomly. These elections tend to coincide with expansions of the suffrage or changes in the rate of voting.[19] We focus here on four realigning elections: 1824, 1860, 1896, and 1932.

TABLE 7–1 Minor Parties in the United States

Year	Party	Candidate	Percent of Vote	Electoral Vote
1832	Anti-Masonic	William Wirt	8%	7
1856	American (Know-Nothing)	Millard Fillmore	22	8
1860	Democratic (Secessionist)	J.C. Breckinridge	18	72
1860	Constitutional Union	John Bell	13	39
1892	People's (Populist)	James B. Weaver	9	22
1912	Bull Moose	Theodore Roosevelt	27	88
1912	Socialist	Eugene V. Debs	6	0
1924	Progressive	Robert M. La Follette	17	13
1948	States' Rights (Dixiecrat)	Strom Thurmond	2	39
1948	Progressive	Henry A. Wallace	2	0
1968	American Independent	George C. Wallace	14	46
1980	National Unity	John Anderson	7	0
1992	United We Stand, America	Ross Perot	19	0
1996	Reform	Ross Perot	9	0
2000	Reform	Pat Buchanan	0	0
2000	Green	Ralph Nader	3	0

1824: ANDREW JACKSON AND THE DEMOCRATS Party politics was invigorated following the election of 1824, in which the leader in the popular vote—the hero of the battle of New Orleans, Democrat Andrew Jackson—failed to achieve the necessary majority of the Electoral College and was defeated by John Quincy Adams in the runoff election in the House of Representatives. Jackson, brilliantly aided by Martin Van Buren, a veteran party builder in New York State, later knit together a winning combination of regions, interest groups, and political doctrines to win the presidency in 1828. The Whigs succeeded the Federalists as the opposition party. By the time Van Buren followed Jackson in the White House in 1837, the Democrats had become a large, nationwide movement with national and state leadership, a clear party doctrine, and grass-roots organization. The Whigs were almost as strong; in 1840 they put their own man, General William Henry Harrison ("Old Tippecanoe") into the White House. A two-party system had been born, and we have had that two-party system ever since—one of few such systems worldwide.

1860: THE CIVIL WAR AND THE RISE OF THE REPUBLICANS Out of the crisis over slavery evolved a new party: the second Republican party—ultimately the "Grand Old Party" (GOP).[20] Abraham Lincoln was elected in 1860 with the support not only of financiers, industrialists, and merchants, but also of large numbers of workers and farmers. For 50 years after 1860, the Republican coalition won every presidential race except for Grover Cleveland's victories in 1884 and 1892. The Democratic party survived with its durable white male base in the South.

1896: A PARTY IN TRANSITION The Republican party's response to industrialization and hard times for farmers transformed it in the late 1800s. A combination of western and southern farmers and western mining interests sought an alliance with workers in the East and Midwest to "recapture America from the foreign moneyed interests responsible for industrialization. The crisis of industrialization squarely placed an agrarian-fundamentalist view of life against an industrial-progress view."[21] This realignment of 1896 differs from the others, however, in that the party in power did not change hands. In that sense it was a *converting realignment* because it reinforced the Republican majority status that had been in place since 1860.[22]

The Progressive era, the first two decades of the twentieth century, was a period of political reform led by the Progressive wing of the Republican party. Much of the agenda of the Progressives focused on the corrupt political parties. Civil service reforms shifted some of the patronage out of the hands of party officials. The direct primary election took control of nominations from party leaders and gave it to the rank-and-file. And in a number of cities, nonpartisan governments were instituted, totally eliminating the role of a party. With the ratification of the Seventeenth Amendment to the Constitution in 1913, U.S. senators came to be popularly elected. Women obtained the right to vote when the Nineteenth Amendment was ratified in 1920. Thus within a short time, the electorate changed, the rules changed, and even the stakes of the game changed. Democrats were unable to build a durable winning coalition during this time and remained the minority party until the early 1930s, when the Hoover administration was overwhelmed by the Great Depression.

1932: FRANKLIN ROOSEVELT AND THE NEW DEAL ALIGNMENT The 1932 election was a turning point in American politics. In the 1930s the United States faced a devastating economic collapse. Between 1929 and 1932, the gross national product fell over 10 percent per year, and unemployment rose from 1.5 million to more than 15

Minor Parties

- **The Natural Law party** was started at the Mahirishi International University in Fairfield, Iowa, with the stated purpose to "bring the light of science into politics." The party's platform includes preventive health care and sustainable agriculture without pesticides; it favors using renewable energy to reduce pollution and create national energy self-sufficiency and advocates transcendental meditation as a solution to major health and crime problems, as well as a foreign policy tool. The Natural Law party also wants a 10 percent flat tax by 2002. The party had more than 700 candidates running for office in 1996.

- **The Libertarian party** places heavy emphasis on individual liberties, personal responsibility, and freedom from government. Its agenda calls for an end to the federal government's role in education and crime control. Libertarians believe the income tax is the "biggest intrusion into the lives of the American people," and they perceive Social Security as a "fraudulent scheme." They think the United States should wash its hands of foreign involvement—bring all U.S. troops home and only maintain sufficient military for our own defense. About 1,000 Libertarians ran for office in 1996.

- **The Green party** takes its name from other pro-environment parties throughout Europe. In the United States, the Greens not only embrace pro-environment positions but are committed to social justice, decentralization, respect for diversity, community-based economics, nonviolence, feminism, ecological wisdom, grass-roots democracy, and personal and global responsibility. Their 1996 and 2000 presidential candidate, Ralph Nader, called for public campaign financing, greater environmental protection, and affordable housing.

realigning election
An election during periods of historic change in the economy and society that proves to be a turning point, redefining the agenda of politics and the alignment of voters within parties.

laissez-faire

Doctrine opposing governmental interference in economic affairs beyond what is necessary to protect life and property.

Keynesian economics

Economic principles based on the principles advocated by John Maynard Keynes: increasing government spending during business slumps and curbing spending during booms.

million, with millions more working only part-time. Herbert Hoover and the Republican majority in Congress had responded to the Depression by arguing that the problems with the economy were largely self-correcting and that their long-standing policy of *laissez-faire*, a hands-off approach to the economy, was appropriate.

Voters wanted more. Franklin D. Roosevelt and the Democrats were swept into office in 1932 by a tide of anti-Hoover and anti-Republican sentiment. Roosevelt rode this wave and labeled his response to the Depression the New Deal. He rejected *laissez-faire* economics and instead relied on **Keynesian economics,** which asserted that government could influence the direction of the economy through fiscal and monetary policy. After a century of sporadic government action, the New Dealers stepped in and fundamentally altered the relationship between government and society.

The central issue on which the Republicans and Democrats disagreed in this New Deal period was the role of government regarding the economy. Roosevelt Democrats argued that the government had to take action to pull the country out of the Depression, but Republicans objected to enlarging the scope of government activity and intruding it into the economy. This basic disagreement about whether the national government should play an active role in regulating and promoting our economy remains one of the most important divisions between the Democratic and Republican parties today, although, with time, the country and both parties accepted many of the New Deal programs.

For the two decades following the 1932 election, the Republican party was relegated to watching the majority Democrats—a new coalition of union households, immigrant workers, and people hurt by the Great Depression—implement their domestic policies. During World War II, both parties cooperated in embracing a bipartisan foreign policy.

We have gone a long time since the last critical or realigning election. You will note that each realignment lasted roughly 36 years, or a couple of generations. Some political scientists anticipated that we were ripe for such an election in 1968–1972, but it did not happen. Now, as memories of the New Deal fade and the agenda of American politics shifts, the alignments of the 1930s and 1940s hold less and less relevance. Yet, to a surprising degree, the parties are stable and closely competitive, as the 2000 elections demonstrated. Whether one party can seize the agenda of politics and fashion itself as the new majority party is one of the interesting political questions for the future.

Divided Government

Major shifts in the demographics of the parties have occurred in recent decades. The once "Solid South" that Democrats could count on to bolster their legislative majorities and help win the White House has now become the "Solid Republican South" in presidential and increasingly in congressional elections as well. Republican congressional leaders—House Majority Leader Dick Armey and Whip Tom DeLay, both of Texas, and Senate Minority Leader Trent Lott of Mississippi—came from states that once rarely elected Republicans. Further evidence of partisan change in the South is the fact that Vice-President Al Gore did not carry his home state of Tennessee in the 2000 presidential race and was also defeated in President Bill Clinton's home state of Arkansas. This shift in the South is explained by the movement of whites out of the Democratic party, largely as a result of the party's position on civil rights. The rise of the Republican South reinforced the shift to conservatism in the Grand Old Party. And as the South became more Republican, the Northeast became more Democratic and is increasingly the home of the Democratic party. This shift, combined with the diminished ranks of conservative southern

Democrats, made the Democratic party, especially the congressional Democrats, more unified and more liberal than in the days when many of its congressional members had "safe" southern seats.

Since 1953 we have had **divided government**, with one party controlling the Congress and the other the White House, twice as often as we have had one party in control of both legislative and executive branches. Until the 1994 election, Republican strength had been in presidential elections, where they often won with landslide margins. Part of the explanation was their ability to attract popular candidates like Dwight Eisenhower and Ronald Reagan, but Republicans also reaped the rewards of Democratic party divisiveness and generally weaker Democratic presidential candidates. Further evidence that voters are inclined to favor divided government came in the 1990s, when voters elected a Republican congressional majority in 1994 and then retained it in 1996 and 1998.

Republican victories in presidential elections between 1952 and 1992 were achieved with the support of some elements of Roosevelt's New Deal coalition. New Deal programs that benefited these voters had expanded the middle class and made possible the conservative "hold onto what we've got" thinking of voters in the 1980s, 1990s, and 2000. One way to interpret the closeness of the 2000 national elections is that the country is evenly divided, and while the election put Republicans in charge of both houses of Congress and the White House, their majorities are so slim that they effectively mean divided government.

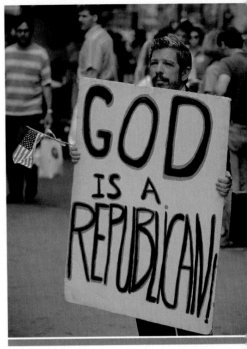

Religion is sometimes linked to partisanship. In reality, devoutly religious people are found in both major parties.

The 2000 Elections–Into the New Century

Neither party could claim a mandate after the tightly contested 2000 elections, which resulted in a 50–50 partisan tie in the U.S. Senate, a slim Republican majority in the U.S. House, and a presidential contest whose outcome was unresolved for weeks as ballots were recounted in Florida. Although the outcome was essentially a tie, the breakdown of the vote was anything but random. The 2000 presidential results and exit polls demonstrated a divided nation. Al Gore carried the Northeast and Pacific states and a few urban states in the nation's midsection. George W. Bush carried the South and interior of the country, minus a few states like New Mexico. Demographically, the Democrats received large majorities of votes from African Americans, Hispanics, union households, Jews, and gays. Republicans did well among white males, religious conservatives, and higher income voters.[23] People's positions on most issues in the 2000 election were not as strongly held as on issues in the past, like Vietnam, civil rights, or the Great Society, but there were clear differences between Democratic and Republican voters on tax cuts, school vouchers, and privatization of Social Security.

AMERICAN PARTIES TODAY

Americans are largely indifferent about political parties. If anything, most people are critical or even fearful of the major parties. Parties are, in a word, distrusted. Some see parties as corrupt institutions, interested only in the spoils of politics. Critics charge that the parties evade the issues; they fail to deliver on their promises; they have no new ideas; they follow public opinion rather than lead it; or they are just one more special interest.

Still, Americans understand that parties are necessary. They want party labels kept on the ballot, at least for congressional and presidential elections as well as those for statewide offices. Most voters think of themselves as Democrats or Republicans, and typically vote for candidates from their party. They even contribute millions of dollars to the two major parties. Far more individual contributions go to the Republicans than to the Democrats.[24] Thus Americans appreciate, at least vaguely, that you cannot run a big democracy without parties.

Both the Democratic and Republican parties are moderate in their policies and leadership.[25] Successful party leaders must be diplomatic; to win presidential

divided government
Governance divided between the parties, especially when one controls the White House and the other controls Congress.

Jim Nicholson, Republican National Committee chair.

elections and congressional majorities, they must find a middle ground among more or less hostile groups. Members of the House of Representatives, in order to be elected and reelected, have to appeal to a majority of the voters from their own district. As more House districts have become "safe" for incumbents, the House of Representatives has become the home of partisan ideological clashes to a greater extent than the Senate or the White House.

Although each party usually takes its extremist supporters more or less for granted and seeks out the voters in the middle, both parties retain some ideological diversity. The Democratic umbrella encompasses the conservative Coalition for a Democratic Majority, the moderate Democratic Leadership Council (dominated by an array of southern governors and senators), and the liberal Americans for Democratic Action. The Democratic coalition embraces activists in the civil rights and other liberal-left movements. Republicans, while more homogeneous, have their contentious factions as well. On the more conservative side are the Religious Right, staunch supporters of the right to bear arms, and antitax activists.

Among Republicans the split has been between more liberal northeastern Republicans like Governors Christine Todd Whitman of New Jersey (now director of the Environmental Protection Agency) and Tom Ridge of Pennsylvania, and the dominant conservative wing. Democratic Senator Joseph Lieberman from Connecticut, known for his willingness to consider school vouchers and his concerns about affirmative action, had to reconcile with more liberal Democratic party activists after being selected by Al Gore to be his running mate in 2000.

Parties as Institutions

Political parties are organizations that seek political power by electing people to office so that their positions and philosophy become public policy. Like other institutions of American government—Congress, the presidency, and the courts—parties have rules, procedures, and organizational structure, and they make policy. What are the institutional characteristics of political parties?

NATIONAL PARTY LEADERSHIP   The supreme authority in both major parties is the **national party convention**, which meets every four years to nominate candidates for president and vice-president, to ratify the party platform, and to adopt rules. The delegates have only four days in which to accomplish their business, but many key decisions have been made ahead of time.

In charge of the national party is the *national committee*. In recent years both parties have strengthened the role of the national committee and enhanced the influence of individual committee members. The committees are now more representative of the party rank-and-file. But in neither party is the national committee the center of party leadership.

Each major party has a *national chair* as its top official. The national committee formally elects the chair, but in reality it is the choice of the presidential nominee. Even though he or she serves as a liaison between the party and the White House, the chair actually serves at the pleasure of the president and does the president's bidding. The chair of the party without an incumbent president has considerable independence, yet works closely with the party's congressional leadership. The national committee often elects a new head after electoral defeats. Although chairs are the heads of their national party apparatus, they remain largely unknown to the voters. The chair may play a major role in running the national campaign; after the election, the power of the national chair of the victorious party tends to dwindle.

National party organizations are often agents of an incumbent president in securing his renomination. When there is not an incumbent president seeking reelection, the national party committee is generally neutral until the nominee is selected. Although heated primary contests often preclude having a united party in the general election, national parties are helpless to prevent them.[26]

political party
An organization that seeks political power by electing people to office so that its positions and philosophy become public policy.

national party convention
The national meeting of delegates elected in primaries, caucuses, or state conventions who assemble once every four years to nominate candidates for president and vice-president, ratify the party platform, elect officers, and adopt rules.

In addition to the national party committees, there are also congressional and senatorial *campaign committees*. Senatorial campaign committees are composed of senators chosen for two-year terms by their fellow party members in the Senate; congressional campaign committees are chosen in the same manner by the House. Chairs of campaign committees are nominated by their party leadership and typically ratified by their party caucus. They have a lot of say about which candidates get campaign funds. In recent years congressional campaign committees have become much more active—recruiting candidates, training them, and assisting with campaign finance.[27]

The chair of the Republican House campaign committee is elected by the House Republican Conference after each congressional election (**www.nrcc.org/ about/overview.htm**). A similar process is used to elect the chair of the National Republican Senatorial Committee. For more information on the process in the Democratic party, see **www.takebackthehouse.com/about/index.cfm** for information on the House and **www.dscc.org/2000revised/bobtorricelli.htm** for information on the Senate.

In the 1998 and 2000 elections, congressional campaign committees, following the lead of the national party committees in previous presidential elections, raised unprecedented amounts of soft money, contributions intended to support party activity in general, not a specific candidate. The soft money reform was enacted by Congress following the 1976 election, in which both parties complained that they did not have enough money for generic party activities like billboard advertising and get-out-the-vote drives. Amendments to the Federal Election Campaign Act and the interpretations of this legislation by the Federal Election Commission permitted unlimited contributions to the parties by individuals and PACs for these purposes. Over time both parties have found ways to spend soft money to promote the election or defeat of specific candidates, effectively circumventing the campaign finance reform rules. This is why banning soft money has become such a dedicated cause for Arizona Senator John McCain, a co-sponsor of the McCain-Feingold campaign finance reform legislation that finally passed the U. S. Senate in 2001.

Today soft money is spent in the most competitive races where it makes the biggest difference. The party committee leaders who make these allocations have grown in power as the amount of soft money raised has grown. Party committee leaders effectively used the close party balance, especially in the House of Representatives, to justify their soft money spending decisions.

What are the implications of this surge in soft money in presidential and congressional elections? First, because soft money contributions are unlimited, the priority given to raising soft money has elevated the importance of the large contributor. Although the reforms had lessened the power of wealthy individuals because they could give only $50,000 in total political contributions to candidates or parties in a two-year period, with the soft money loophole, such individuals can now give unlimited amounts. Parties rely heavily on these large donors.

A second implication is that those who allocate soft money are now very influential because they can contribute more money to a race than a candidate could have raised in months of fund raising. Decisions about which races will be targets for soft money spending are critical in an election outcome.

PARTIES AT THE GRASS ROOTS   The two major parties are decentralized, organized around elections in states, cities, or congressional districts. Like the government itself, they have national, state, and local organizations. Party organization at the state and local levels is structured much like the national level. Each state has a *state committee* headed by a *state chair*. State law determines the composition of the state committees and sets rules regulating them. Members of state committees are usually elected from local areas. Party auxiliaries such as the Young Democrats or the Federation of Republican Women are sometimes represented as well. In many states these committees are dominated by governors, senators, or coalitions of locally

Democratic Congressional Campaign Committee chair Nita Lowey of New York.

Republican Senatorial Campaign Committee chair Bill Frist of Tennessee.

A Closer Look

PARTY PLATFORMS

The typical party platform—the official statement of party policy—is often a vague and ponderous document that hardly anyone reads. Platforms are ambiguous by design, giving voters few obvious reasons to vote against the party. This generalization about party platforms does not mean that political parties do not stand for anything. Thus most business and professional people believe the Republican party best serves their interests, while working people tend to look to the Democrats to speak for them. The proportion of voters discerning important differences between the parties increased sharply in recent years, as the parties became more polarized.[*]

Many politicians contend that platforms rarely help elect anybody, but platform positions can hurt a presidential candidate. Because the platform-writing process is not always controlled by the nominee, it is possible for presidential candidates to disagree with their own party platform. But the platform-drafting process gives partisans, especially those motivated by particular issues, an opportunity to express their views, and it serves to identify the most important values and principles upon which the two parties are based. Once elected, politicians are rarely reminded of what their platform position was on a given issue. One major exception to this was former President George Bush's promise not to raise taxes if elected in 1988 with his memorable "Read my lips—no new taxes." He was forced to eat those words when taxes were raised.

Party platforms in 2000 were carefully controlled by the Gore and Bush campaigns. The Republican platform reflected Bush's compassionate conservative themes, but Bush was criticized for not softening the party position on abortion.[**] The Bush campaign decided not to risk a convention fight by removing the plank, preferring to present an image of a unified party, and pro-choice Republicans at the convention did not challenge the platform language. Vice-President Gore tried to reinforce centrist themes in his party's platform. For example, the Democratic platform included the death penalty as a means of fighting crime. In part because Al Gore and George W. Bush so thoroughly dominated the nomination process, neither party platform became the subject of attack from the opposing party.

Differences between 2000 Democratic and Republican platforms are highlighted below, and the platforms in their entirety are available at www.democrats.org/hq/resources/platfom,/platform..html and www.rnc.org/2000/2000.

[*]See Bruce E. Keith, David B. Magleby, Candice J. Nelson, Elizabeth Orr, Mark C. Westlye, and Raymond E. Wolfinger, *The Myth of the Independent Voter* (University of California Press, 1992), p. 148.

[**]Richard Benedetto, "Bush's Influence on Platform Results in 'More Upbeat' Tone," *USA Today*, July 31, 2000, p. A6.

Key Party Differences: Excerpts from Republican and Democratic Party Platforms, 2000

Democrats	Republicans
Abortion	
Support the right of every woman to choose, consistent with *Roe v. Wade*, and regardless of ability to pay. Individual—not government—can best take responsibility for making the most difficult and intensely personal decisions regarding reproduction.	Support a human life amendment to the Constitution and endorse legislation to make clear that the 14th Amendment's protections apply to unborn children. Oppose using public revenues for abortion and will not fund organizations which advocate it.

elected business and ethnic leaders. State chairs are normally elected by the state committees, although approximately one-quarter are chosen at state conventions. When the party controls the governorship, chairs are often agents of the governor, but some can remain independent.[28]

Some powerful state parties have developed in recent years. Despite much state-to-state variation, the trend is toward stronger state organizations, with Republicans typically much better funded.[29] In some states, third and fourth parties play a role in local elections. New York, for instance, has both a Liberal party and a Conservative party in addition to Democratic and Republican parties. The role minor parties play in statewide elections can be important, even though they rarely win office themselves.

Below the state committees are *county committees*, which vary widely in function and power. The key role of these committees is recruiting candidates for such offices as county commissioner, sheriff, and treasurer. The recruiting job often involves finding a candidate for the office, not deciding among competing contenders. For a party that rarely wins an election, the county committee has to struggle to find

Democrats	Republicans

Campaign Finance Reform

Proposes tough new lobbying reform, publicly guaranteed TV time for debates and advocacy by candidates, a crackdown on special interest issue ads, and a public-private, nonpartisan Democracy Endowment which will raise money from Americans and finance Congressional elections—with no other contributions allowed to candidates who accept the funding.

Enact 'Paycheck Protection,' ensuring that no union member is forced to contribute to anybody's campaign. Preserve the right of every individual and all groups to express their opinions and advocate their issues.

Foreign Policy and Military Deployment

"We cannot be the world's policemen, and we must be discriminating in our approach. But where the stakes are high, when nothing short of military engagement can secure our national interest, when we have the military forces available and have made our best efforts to join with allies, and cost is proportionate to the objective, we must be ready to act."

"The military is not a civilian police force or a political referee. . . A Republican president will identify and pursue vital American national interests, build and secure the peace. Republicans know what it takes to accomplish this: robust military forces, strong alliances, expanding trade, and resolute diplomacy."

Missile Defense

Support the development of the technology for a limited national missile defense system. Any such system is compatible with the Anti-Ballistic Missile Treaty.

Favor deploying an effective missile defense . . . at the earliest possible date, and designed to protect all 50 states. America's deployed forces overseas, and our friends and allies . . . will seek a negotiated change in the Anti-Ballistic Missile (ABM) Treaty.

School Choice

Favor public schools that compete with one another and are held accountable for results. Oppose private school vouchers.

Expand parental choice and encourage competition by providing parents with information on their child's school, increasing the number of charter schools, and expanding education savings accounts.

Gun Control

Favor mandatory child safety locks, to protect our children, a photo license ID, a full background check, and a gun safety test to buy a new handgun.

Support background checks. Oppose federal licensing of law-abiding gun owners and national gun registration.

Status of Gays

Support continued efforts . . . to end workplace discrimination against gay men and lesbians.

Support the traditional definition of 'marriage' as the legal union of one man and one woman.

SOURCE: *The New York Times*, August 14, 2000.

someone willing to run. When those seeking it value the job, however, primaries, not the party leaders, usually decide the winner.[30] Many county organizations maintain a significant level of activity, distributing campaign literature, organizing telephone campaigns, putting up posters and lawn signs, and canvassing door-to-door. Other county committees do not function at all, and many party leaders are just figureheads.

In recent elections the campaign efforts of state and county organizations have been aided by financial assistance from the party's national committee, which has distributed millions of dollars in soft money. In many instances broadcast ads paid for with soft money do not even mention the party.[31]

It is not clear that soft money helps build stronger parties at the state and local level. Some soft money spending may enhance such party activities as building a list of active partisans in the state or district, improving the computer technology of the party offices, or secondary benefits when party supporters are mobilized for a U.S. Senate or U.S. House race. But for most soft money spending, state parties simply become local bank accounts for candidate endorsements.

American government may be intensely partisan—some think much too partisan. In Congress the two parties have been locked in battle over legislation, investigations, and budget priorities. When legislators become intensely partisan, they become more concerned with advancing their own party's fortunes in the next election than with finding an acceptable compromise that would serve the public. And when there is divided government, with a governor or president from a party different from the legislative majority, that difference often leads to gridlock. Finally, partisanship in judicial or executive branch appointments means that qualified people may be excluded from consideration on the basis of party affiliation.

Would we be better off if we did not have political parties? Is intense partisanship destroying our political system?

party registration

The act of declaring party affiliation; required by some states when one registers to vote.

One possible benefit of soft money would be strengthening parties at the grassroots level. At the base of the party pyramid—at the city, town, ward, and precinct level—strong local party organization is rare. Most local committees are poorly financed and inactive except during the few weeks before election day.[32] In a few places, local ward and precinct leaders still do favors for constituents, from getting more police patrols in a neighborhood, to organizing clambakes, or obtaining horse-racing passes in a state like Arkansas.

Parties in Government

Political parties are central to the operation of government in the United States. Party organizations play a more important role after the election in the operation of government than they play in the elections.

IN THE LEGISLATIVE BRANCH   Members of Congress take their partisanship seriously, at least while they are in Washington. Their power and influence are determined by whether their party is in control of the House or Senate; they also have a stake in which party controls the White House. The chairs of all standing committees in Congress come from the majority party, as do the presiding officials of both chambers. Members of both houses sit together with fellow partisans on the floor and in committee, leading to the expression often heard in floor debate, "the other side of the aisle."

In the wake of the tie in the U.S. Senate following the 2000 elections, with each party having 50 members, the Democrats suggested a power-sharing arrangement, including the possibility of co-chairs for some or all committees. The two parties agreed to equal membership and staff on all committees, but all chairs are Republicans.

Members of congressional staffs are also partisan. From the volunteer intern to the senior staffer, members of Congress expect their staff to be loyal first to them and then to their party. Should you decide to go to work for a representative or senator, you would be expected to identify yourself with that person's party, and you would have some difficulty working for the other party later. Employees of the House and Senate—from elevator operators to the Capitol Hill police and even including the chaplain—hold patronage jobs. With few exceptions, such jobs go to persons from the party that has a majority in the House or the Senate.

IN THE EXECUTIVE BRANCH   Presidents select almost all senior White House staff and cabinet members from their own party. However, it is not unusual for them to choose one or two advisers or cabinet members from the opposition party. Presidents, however, typically surround themselves with advisers who have campaigned with them and proven their party loyalty.

Partisanship is also important in presidential appointments to the highest levels of the federal bureaucracy. The party that wins the White House has more than 4,000 noncareer positions to fill.[33] Included in these positions are cabinet-level appointments and ambassadorships around the world. Party commitment, including making campaign contributions, is expected of those who seek these positions.

IN THE JUDICIAL BRANCH   The judicial branch of the national government, with its lifetime tenure and political independence, is designed to operate in an expressly nonpartisan manner. Judges, unlike Congress, do not sit together by political party. But the appointment process for judges has been partisan from the beginning. The landmark case establishing the principle of judicial review, *Marbury v Madison* (1803), concerned the efforts of one party to stack the judiciary with fellow partisans before leaving office.[34] Today party identification remains an important consideration in the naming of federal judges. While the party of a judicial nominee is not called for on any form, those responsible for

screening and evaluating candidates certainly take party and ideology into account. Appointees must be acceptable to certain power centers in the party. For example, Republicans in the Ronald Reagan and George Bush administrations insisted on conservative judges; Bill Clinton, although nominating Democrats, gave more emphasis to gender and race than to ideology in selecting judges.

STATE AND LOCAL LEVELS   The importance of party in the operation of local government varies among states and localities. In some states, such as New York and Illinois, local parties play an even stronger role than they do at the national level. In others, such as Nebraska, parties play almost no role. In Nebraska, the state legislature is expressly nonpartisan, though factions perform like parties and still play a role. Parties are likewise unimportant in the government of most city councils. But in most states and many cities, parties are important to the operation of the legislature, governor, or mayor. Judicial selection in most states is also a partisan matter. Much was made by the Bush campaign of the fact that six of the seven Florida Supreme Court justices deciding the 2000 ballot-counting cases were Democrats. And the U.S. Supreme Court's decision on the Florida count was also said to be partisan.

Parties in the Electorate

Political parties would be of little significance if they did not have meaning to the electorate. Adherents of the two parties are drawn to them by a combination of factors: stand on issues; personal or party history; religious, racial, or social peer grouping; attractiveness of candidates. The emphases among these factors change over time, but they are remarkably consistent with those identified by political scientists more than 40 years ago.[35]

PARTY REGISTRATION   For citizens in most states, "party" has a particular legal meaning—**party registration**. At the time voters register to vote in these states, they are asked to state their party preference. They then become registered Democrats, Republicans, Libertarians, or whatever. Voters can subsequently change their party registration. The purpose of party registration is to limit the participants in primary elections to members of that party and to make it easier for parties to contact people who might vote for their party.

PARTY ACTIVISTS   This group tends to fall into three broad categories: party regulars, candidate activists, and issue activists. *Party regulars* place the party first. They value winning elections and understand that compromise and moderation may be necessary to reach that objective. They also realize that it is important to keep the party together as much as possible, because a fractured party only helps the opposition.

Candidate activists are followers of a particular candidate who see the party as the means to place their candidate in power. Candidate activists are often not concerned with the other operations of the party—with nominees for other offices or with raising money for the party. For example, people who supported Pat Buchanan in his unsuccessful run for the presidency as a Reform party candidate in 2000 would be classified as candidate activists. Buchanan, a former television commentator and unsuccessful Republican candidate for the Republican nomination in 1996, built a personal following. Reform party members who traced their roots in the party to Ross Perot were so disaffected from Buchanan that they split from him and nominated their own candidate for president. Buchanan fared poorly in the 2000 election, getting less than 1 percent of the vote and as a result losing millions of dollars in federal subsidies for the 2004 elections. The federal subsidy from Perot's 8 percent vote total in 1996 largely funded the Buchanan 2000 campaign.[36]

Issue activists wish to push the parties in a particular direction on a single issue or narrow range of issues: abortion, taxes, school prayer, the environment, or civil

Thinking It Through . . .

It is naive to believe that the removal of parties will negate conflict, self-interest, or ambition. A political system without parties would be a society without the means to deal with disagreements over policies, economics, or social values. Americans expect legislators to be partisan, to be contentious, and to make the most of partisan opportunities. Divided government may be inefficient, but that clearly has not bothered voters, who routinely elect legislators from one party and governors or presidents from another. Finally, people with judicial or administrative ambitions understand the role that parties play in appointments, giving them an incentive to get involved in a party. This is not all bad because, as we have seen, it is possible for idealistic individuals to redefine and reshape a party.

WE THE PEOPLE

Portrait of the Electorate

	Republican	Democrat	Independent
Sex			
Male	**41**	**49**	**10**
Female	35	54	11
Race			
White	42	47	11
Black	7	86	7
Hispanic	32	60	8
Age			
18–34	40	49	11
35–45	42	46	12
46–55	37	52	11
56–64	32	61	6
65+	31	58	10
Income			
Less than $10,000	34	54	12
$10,000–$19,999	29	62	9
$20,000–$29,999	35	53	12
$30,000–$39,999	32	54	14
$40,000–$59,999	37	53	10
$60,000+	48	42	10
Religion			
Protestant	41	51	8
Catholic	38	52	10
Jewish	18	82	0
Ideology			
Liberal	14	81	5
Moderate/Don't know	30	56	15
Conservative	67	28	5
Region			
Northeast	36	48	16
North-central	38	53	9
South	39	51	10
West	35	56	9
Total	**37**	**52**	**11**

SOURCE: *2000 American National Election Study*, Center for Political Studies, University of Michigan.

rights. To issue activists, the party platform is an important battleground because they seek party endorsement for their position. Issue activists are also often candidate activists if they can find a candidate willing to embrace their position.

Both issue activists and candidate activists insist on making their "statement" regardless of the electoral consequences. They prefer to lose the election rather than compromise. Party activists thus include a diverse group of people who come to the political party with different objectives. It is not surprising, then, that some of the most interesting politics you will observe are over candidate selection and issue positions within the political parties. Fights over strategy and party position are conducted in open meetings and under democratic procedures. Political parties foster democracy not only by competition *between* the parties but *within* the parties as well.

Party Identification

Most Americans are mere spectators of party activity. They lack the partisan commitment and interest needed for active party involvement. This is not to say that parties are irrelevant or unimportant to them. For them, partisanship is what political scientists call **party identification**—an informal and subjective affiliation with a political party that most people acquire in childhood, a standing preference for one party over another.[37] This type of voter may sometimes vote for a candidate from the other party, yet in the absence of a compelling reason to do otherwise, most will vote according to their party identification. Peers and early political experiences reinforce party identification, generally acquired from parents. It is part of the political socialization process described in Chapter 4.

Party identification is the single best predictor of how people will vote. Unlike candidates and issues, which come and go, party identification is a long-term element in voting choice. The strength of party identification is also important in predicting participation and political interest. Strong Republicans and Strong Democrats participate more actively in politics than any other groups and are generally more knowledgeable and informed. Pure Independents are just the opposite; they vote at the lowest rates and have the low-

est levels of interest and awareness of any of the categories of party identification. This evidence runs counter to the notion that persons who are
strong partisans are unthinking party adherents.[38]

Partisan Realignment and Dealignment

The current system of party identification is built upon a foundation of
the New Deal and the critical election of 1932, events that took place
nearly 70 years ago. How can events so removed from the present still be
important in shaping our party system? When will there be another
realignment—an election that dramatically changes the voters' partisan
identification? Or has such a realignment already occurred, a question
frequently debated in the literature of political science. Most scholars
believe we have not experienced any major realignment since 1932.[39]
Partisan identification for the past four decades has been stable, and
while new voters have been added to the electorate—minorities and 18-
to-21-year-olds—the basic character of the party system has not
changed dramatically. Table 7–2 presents the party identification breakdown for the period from the 1950s to 2000.

Possible evidence of a voting realignment came in the early 1980s,
when Republicans won several close Senate elections and gained a majority in that body. Democrats, however, won back the Senate in 1986, and
until 1994 they appeared to have a permanent majority in the House. All
that changed with the 1994 election, as Republicans were swept into
office on a tidal wave of victories. Republicans made major inroads in the
South and strengthened their share of the vote among white males.

The 1998 election gave the Democrats renewed hope that they
could regain control of Congress, or at least the House of Representatives, in the 2000 elections. Overcoming their worst fears that the
Clinton–Monica Lewinsky scandal would enlarge Republican majorities in the Senate and House, the Democrats effectively mobilized their core voters
and actually picked up five seats in the House of Representatives. Allies of the
Democratic party like organized labor were also encouraged by gains they saw in
1998. Republicans were disheartened by the congressional election outcome but
pointed to their strength in several key governorships as cause for optimism.

The 2000 presidential and congressional elections were exceedingly close. The
Republicans narrowly held onto their majority in the House in 2000, and the parties
were evenly divided in the Senate after the election. While losing the White House to
the Republicans through the Electoral College vote, Democrats see the 2002 election
as their opportunity to regain the majority in both houses of Congress. The historic

Party Identification

Party identification is measured by the answers to the
following questions:

*Generally speaking, in politics do you usually think
of yourself as a Republican, a Democrat, an Independent, or what?*

Persons who answer Republican or Democrat to this
question are then asked:

*Would you call yourself a strong or a not very
strong Republican/Democrat?*

Persons who answered Independent to the first
question are asked this follow-up question:

*Do you think of yourself as closer to the Republican
or the Democratic party?*

Persons who do not indicate Democrat, Republican,
or Independent to the first question rarely exceed 2
percent of the electorate and include those who are
apolitical or who identify with one of the minor political parties. Because of their consistently small numbers, they are typically not important to election outcomes. In a close race, like the 2000 presidential
contest, Green party supporters became an important
target for both Al Gore and Ralph Nader.

Party identification questionnaires produce seven
categories of persons: Strong Democrats, Weak
Democrats, Independent-leaning Democrats, Pure
Independents, Independent-leaning Republicans, Weak
Republicans, and Strong Republicans. Over the nearly
50-year period during which political scientists have
been conducting such surveys, the partisan preferences
of the American public have been remarkably stable.

party identification
An informal and subjective affiliation
with a political party that most people
acquire in childhood.

TABLE 7–2 Party Identification, 1950s to 2000

Decade	Strong Democrat	Weak Democrat	Independent-Leaning Democrat	Independent	Independent-Leaning Republican	Weak Republican	Strong Republican	Apolitical
1950s*	23%	23%	8%	7%	7%	15%	13%	4%
1960s	22	25	8	10	7	15	12	2
1970s	17	24	12	14	10	14	9	2
1980s	18	26	11	12	11	14	11	2
1990s	18	19	13	10	12	15	13	1
2000	19	15	14	11	13	12	13	2

SOURCE: American National Election Studies, Center for Political Studies, University of Michigan.

Note: Data may not sum to 100% due to averaged data.

*1950s percentages based on years 1952, 1956, 1958.

dealignment

Change in the composition of the electorate or its partisan preferences that points to a rejection of both major parties and a rise in the number of Independents.

pattern of the president's party losing seats in a midterm election works to their favor, and several of their key constituencies may be motivated to vote in large numbers in 2002 because of the perception of unfairness in the counting of Florida's presidential ballots and charges that election officials and procedures discriminated against minority voters.

In presidential voting, Republicans have done well, winning six of the last nine presidential elections, although they lost the popular vote in 2000. Bill Clinton's victories in 1992 and 1996 demonstrated, however, that Democrats could still assemble a winning coalition. But, as discussed previously, the 2000 presidential vote showed an evenly divided nation. Whether one party can expand its support to make it dominant remains an open question, especially in light of the strong feelings many people had about how the winner was determined in the Florida presidential contest.

Recent national elections can thus be characterized as a period in which voters have not demonstrated a consistent preference for one party over the other. In a time of such electoral volatility and low turnout, the winners and losers are determined by the basics of politics: who turns out their vote, who strikes a theme that motivates voters to participate, or who does a better job in communicating with the voters. Party identification remains important for those voters who come out to vote, and strength of partisanship remains positively correlated with turnout.

There are few signs of realignment, but there are signs of disengagement. Some think that, instead of a realignment, we are experiencing the rejection of partisanship in favor of becoming Independents, and there has indeed been an increase in the number of persons who characterize themselves as Independents. Journalist Hedrick Smith expresses a widespread view: "The most important phenomenon of American politics in the past quarter century has been the rise of independent voters who have at times outnumbered Republicans."[40]

The **dealignment** argument—that people have abandoned both parties to become Independents—would be more persuasive were it not that two-thirds of all Independents are really partisans in their voting behavior and attitudes. One-third of those who claim to be Independents lean toward the Democratic party and vote Democratic election after election. Another third of Independents lean toward Republicans and just as predictably vote Republican. The remaining third, who appear to be genuine Independents and who do not vote predictably for one party, turn out to be people with little interest in politics. Despite the reported growth in Independents, there were proportionately about the same number of Pure Independents now as there were in 1956.[41] There are, in short, at least three types of Independents, and most of them are predictably partisan. Table 7–3 summarizes voting behavior in contests for president in 1992, 1996, and 2000, and for U.S. House of Representatives since 1994.

Why has realignment moved so slowly? Why aren't all conservatives now happily ensconced in the Republican party and all liberals gladly lodged in the Democratic party? Americans do not casually cross party lines. If you grew up in a conservative New Hampshire family whose forebears voted Republican for a century, you are pretty much conditioned to stay with the GOP. Even if that party took a direction you disliked, you might continue to register as a Republican but quietly vote Democratic to avoid friction in the family. Or if you come from a "yellow dog" Democratic family in Texas (meaning your family would vote for a "yellow dog" before it would vote for a Republican), you might continue to vote for Democrats locally even though you disliked various Democratic candidates for president or senator. Evidence indicates that this pattern is common throughout the South.

TABLE 7–3 Voting Behavior of Partisans and Independents, 1992–2000

| | Percent Democratic Vote | | | | | | |
| | President | | | U.S. House | | | |
	1992	1996	2000	1994	1996	1998	2000
Strong Democrats	93%	96%	97%	88%	87%	77%	90%
Weak Democrats	68	82	89	73	70	57	73
Independent-leaning Democrats	70	76	72	68	69	63	73
Pure Independents	41	35	44	55	41	41	50
Independent-leaning Republicans	11	20	13	25	21	24	26
Weak Republicans	14	20	14	21	21	25	18
Strong Republicans	3	5	2	7	3	7	12

SOURCE: *American National Election Study*, Center for Political Studies, University of Michigan.

Another reason for slow realignment is the local nature of the parties. For decades, conservative Democrats in the South have been voting for Republican candidates for president—not only George W. Bush and Ronald Reagan but also Richard Nixon and even Dwight Eisenhower—without changing their identification from the Democratic party to the Republican. Why? Partly because they still see themselves as Democrats, but also because the Democratic party remains stronger at the state and local level in many southern states. So if candidates and voters want to have an impact on local politics, in which the only meaningful elections may be in the Democratic primaries, they retain their Democratic affiliation.

ARE THE POLITICAL PARTIES DYING?

Critics of the American party system make three allegations against it: (1) parties do not take meaningful and contrasting positions on issues; (2) party membership is essentially meaningless; and (3) parties are so concerned with accommodating those on the middle of the ideological spectrum that they are incapable of serving as an avenue for social progress. Are these statements accurate, and if accurate, are they important?

Some fear parties are so meaningless they may be mortally ill, or at least in a severe decline. They point first to the long-run adverse impact on political parties of the Progressive reforms early in this century, reforms that robbed party organizations of their control of the nomination process by allowing masses of independent and "uninformed" voters to enter the primaries and nominate candidates who might not be acceptable to party leaders. They also point to the spread of nonpartisan elections in cities and towns and the staggering of national, state, and local elections that made it harder for parties to influence the election process.

Legislation limiting the viability and functions of parties was bad enough, say the party pessimists, but parties suffer from additional ills. The rise of television and electronic technology and the parallel increase in the number of campaign, media, and direct-mail consultants have made parties less relevant in educating, mobilizing, and organizing the electorate. Television, radio, the Internet, and telephones have strengthened the role of candidates and lessened the importance of parties. (See Chapter 10 for more on the media in this role.)

Advocates of strong parties concede that parts of this diagnosis may be correct: the demise of political machines at the local level, the decline in strong partisan affiliations, the weakness of grass-roots party membership. Yet they also see signs of party revival, or at least the persistence of party. The national party organizations—the national committees and the congressional and senatorial campaign committees—are significantly better funded than they were in earlier days; they even own permanent,

PEOPLE

Campaign contributions from a single source that run to the hundreds of thousands, or millions, of dollars are not healthy to a democracy.

SOFT MONEY IS BUYING OUR GOVERNMENT

Senator John McCain

For fifteen years Congress debated campaign finance reform, which passed the House only to die in the Senate. Early in 2001, Senate Majority Leader Trent Lott allotted two weeks for debate on the McCain Feingold campaign finance legislation. The number of debate amendments and its early scheduling were in part due to the persistence of Arizona Senator John McCain (R), a cosponsor of the bill and the nation's most visible campaign finance reform advocate.

The many sponsors of this legislation have but one purpose: to enact fair bipartisan campaign finance reform that seeks no special advantage for one party or another, but that helps change the public's widespread belief that politicians have no greater purpose than their own re-election, and to that end we will respond disproportionately to the needs of those interests that can best finance our ambition, even if those interests conflict with the public interest and with the governing philosophy we once sought office to advance.

Most Americans believe that we would let this nation pay any price, bear any burden, for the sake of securing our own ambitions, no matter how injurious the effect might be to the national interest.

Why can't we all agree to this very simple, very obvious truth that campaign contributions from a single source that run to the hundreds of thousands, or millions, of dollars are not healthy to a democracy?

Is that not self-evident? It is to the people. It is to the people.

Some will argue that there isn't too much money in politics. They will argue there's not enough; they will argue that soft money, the huge unregulated revenue stream into political party coffers, is necessary to ensure the strength of the two-party system.

I find this last point hard to understand, considering that in the 15 years or so that soft money has become the dominant force in our elections, the parties have grown appreciably weaker as independents become the fastest growing voter registration group in the country. . . .

Some will argue that the First Amendment of the Constitution renders unlawful any restriction on the right of anyone to raise unlimited amounts of money for political campaigns. Which drafter of the Constitution believed or anticipated that the First Amendment would be exercised in political campaigns by the relatively few at the expense of many. ★

SOURCE: *The Congressional Record*, March 19, 2001.

DEBATE

SOFT MONEY IS FREEDOM OF SPEECH

Senator Mitch McConnell

The leading opponent of campaign finance reform, Senator Mitch McConnell, led the opposition in the 2001 debate. McConnell chaired the National Republican Senatorial Committee for the 1997–98 and 1999–2000 election cycles, a job in which he raised millions in soft money—money which is restricted under new reforms.

The real problem is not that there's too much money in politics; there's too little money in politics, particularly hard money, which is all limited and disclosed, directly given to parties and candidates to expressly advocate the election or defeat of a candidate. And yet nobody on the so-called reform side is trying to deal with the single biggest problem we have.

Now, the only way to really get at the core of this problem if senators believe that the influence of money in politics is so pernicious is to change the First Amendment. You have to go right to the core of the problem.

It's important to get the record straight about nonfederal money. The average soft money contribution to the Republican Senatorial Committee last cycle was $520. That's less than one-tenth of 1 percent of the money that the Republican Senatorial Committee raised.

If you look over at the Republican National Committee and the Republican Senatorial Committee, the largest contribution either of us got during the course of the year was $250,000. Admittedly that's a very large contribution. But any one of those $250,000 contributions would have represented less than one-half of 1 percent of the total money raised by either the senatorial committee or the Republican National Committee.

Each of those interests who care about what we're doing here, who believe that it may have an impact on their business or their interest, cannot be constitutionally restricted from speaking. Maybe some court somewhere would let us completely federalize the national parties, completely eliminate their ability to operate in state and local races in federal dollars. Maybe some court would let us do that. But no court in America, no federal court in America, is going to let us quiet the voices of all these interests who have a perfect right to go out and engage in issue advocacy up to and including the day of the election. There isn't a serious person who knows anything about the First Amendment who believes that we could do that. ★

SOURCE: *The Congressional Record*, March 19, 2001.

The real problem is not that there's too much money in politics; there's too little money in politics.

For further information about this debate, go to **www.prenhall.com/burns** *and click on the Debate Icon in Chapter 7.*

modern headquarters buildings in Washington, D.C., located a few blocks from the U.S. Capitol. Moreover, the parties are more capable of providing assistance to candidates and to state and local party organizations because of their strong financial base from political contributions. They have defined their role as providing expertise to those who need it but cannot otherwise obtain it. Optimists hope these services will give the national parties some leverage over the positions that candidates and officeholders take on party issues.[42]

Since the first years of the Reagan administration, both the Republican and Democratic parties have demonstrated a remarkable cohesiveness in Congress on issues of importance. This trend can be measured by the *party unity score*, defined as the percentage of members of a party who vote together on roll call votes in Congress on which a majority of the members of one party vote against a majority of the members of the other party. Clinton had higher party unity scores from his party in 1993 than any party gave its president in the past 40 years; 85 percent of the Democrats voted together, while 84 percent of the Republicans voted together.[43] During the Republican-controlled 105th Congress (1997–98) as well as during the first half of the 106th Congress (1999), House and Senate Republicans voted together 86 percent of the time—a new all-time high. Democrats were only slightly less united.[44] Thus, while rank-and-file voters do not display strong partisan ties, party organizations and the party in government do show significant signs of strength.[45]

Reform Among the Democrats

After the 1968 election, the Democrats, responding to the disarray during their Chicago convention and disputes about the fairness of delegate selection procedures, agreed to a series of reforms. They put in place a process that led to greater use of direct primaries for the selection of delegates to the national convention and greater representation of younger voters, women, and minorities as elected delegates. Another reform was the abolition of the rule that a winner of a state's convention or primaries got all the state's delegates (the *unit rule*). This rule was replaced by a system of *proportionality* in which candidates won delegates in rough proportion to the votes they received in the primary election.

Chicago's mayor Richard Daley, father of the current mayor of Chicago, and many other party stalwarts argued that these reforms would make the party reflective of the views of college professors and intellectuals, and not working-class people, unionists, the elderly, and elected officials. Responding to this criticism, the party created "superdelegate" positions for elected officials and party leaders.

Reform Among the Republicans

Republicans have not been immune to criticism that their party conventions and party procedures were keeping out the rank-and-file. They did not make changes as drastic as those made by the Democrats, but they did give the national committee more control over presidential campaigns, and state parties were urged to encourage broader participation by all groups, including women, minorities, youth, and the poor.

The Republican party entered the 1980s with a party organization far superior to that of the Democrats. The GOP emphasized grass-roots organization and membership recruitment. Seminars were held to teach Republican candidates how to make speeches and hold press conferences, and weekend conferences were organized for training young professionals. Both parties now conduct training sessions for candidates on campaign planning, advertising, fund raising, using phone banks, recruiting volunteers, and campaign scheduling.[46]

Soft Money and Stronger Parties

Parties can spend unlimited and largely undisclosed amounts of soft money, but the candidate who benefits can deny any role in the message. Our election system lacks candidate accountability for the content and tone of the campaign. Account-

ability is also diminished by the large amounts of money spent by interest groups supporting one candidate or opposing another. Some of the largest soft money donors in the 2000 election cycle included the American Federation of State, County, Municipal Employees (AFSCME), which gave nearly $4.5 million in soft money to the Democrats, and AT&T, which gave over $2 million to the Republicans and over $1 million to the Democrats. Unions like AFSCME give most of their money to Democratic candidates and party committees. Unions were concerned in 2000 that if Republicans continued to hold both houses of Congress and won the White House, they would confront a national government controlled by Republicans for the first time in nearly 50 years. To avoid this, unions not only contributed to candidates but gave millions in soft money as well. Corporations like AT&T pursued a more bipartisan soft money strategy; this was a way of hedging their bet on who would win the election and ensuring friends in whichever party won. The volume of giving by labor and business entities shows how much soft money is now at play in national elections. If the system is not changed, we will certainly see more expensive campaigns and increasingly negative campaigning.

Despite their limitations, political parties have shown resilience. We have had Democrats and Republicans as the major parties in some form now for nearly 150 years. One reason for their resilience is they continue to serve a vital function in our constitutional democracy. Another reason is that our election rules clearly favor two parties. They do this through the winner-takes-all rule, which, unlike proportional representation, leaves the party with fewer votes no share of representation in that district or statewide race. This rule has served to moderate our major parties and makes it difficult to build minor parties into organizations that can win an election. State legislatures, generally under the control of a major party, have also strengthened the position of major parties over minor parties. As a result, we are likely to continue with the two parties we have for some time to come.

POLITICS ONLINE

What's Your Party?

Party identification is measured by political scientists by asking people the following question: Generally speaking, in politics do you consider yourself to be a Democrat, Republican, Independent, or what? As we have shown in this chapter, this measure of partisanship is a quite reliable predictor of voting behavior, and even Independents who lean towards a party are likely to vote for the party they lean towards. You might try out these questions on some friends or neighbors and see how often party leaners typically vote for the party towards which they lean. For the wording of the questions and the national data over time go to: www.prenhall.com/burns for Chapter 7.

Less academic but often fun ways to measure the degree to which you fit one party profile or another can be found on the Web. Often these quizzes will assess your party compatibility score. One example of such a site is: www.3pc.net/matchmaker/quiz.html. Among the categories covered are taxes, abortion policy, the role of the federal government, and government regulation in a variety of ways.

This kind of fun quiz does give you a sense of what some people see as differences between the national parties. One problem with quizzes like these is that they are not sensitive to differences between the party traditions in the states. Hence, Rhode Island Republicans are very different from Idaho Republicans, but these differences are lost in a national quiz like this. To see the differences, you might check out the websites of different state parties, looking for state party platforms or other position statements. The websites are: for the Republicans, www.rnc.org; for the Democrats: www.democrats.org; for the Green party: www.greenparties.org; and for the Libertarians: www.lp.org. Each party website has links to state parties.

SUMMARY

1. Political parties are essential to democracy—simplifying voting choices, organizing the competition, unifying the electorate, helping to organize government by bridging the separation of powers and fostering cooperation among branches of government, translating public preferences into policy, and providing loyal opposition.

2. Political parties help structure voting choice by nominating candidates to run for office. Before the advent of direct primaries, in which voters determine the party nominees, the parties had more control of who ran under their label. States determine the nomination rules. While most states employ the direct primary, some use a caucus or mixed caucus system where more committed partisans have a larger role in the decision of who gets nominated.

3. American parties are moderate. Bringing factions and interests together, they are broad enough to win the presidency and other elections. Third parties have been notably less successful. One reason for this is our single-member district, winner-take-all election rules. In systems with proportional representation or multimember districts, there is a greater tendency for more parties and the need to assemble governing coalitions across parties.

4. American parties have experienced critical elections and realignments. Most political scientists agree the last realignment occurred in 1932. In recent years, there has been divided government and an increase in the number of persons who call themselves Independents. This trend is sometimes called dealignment, but most Independents are closet partisans who vote for the party toward which they lean.

5. For the last 50 years, it has been routine to have divided government, with one party in control of the presidency and the other in control of one or both houses of Congress. Because of the partisan shift in the South toward Republicans, Republicans won control of the White House, often with Democrats controlling one or both houses of Congress. Successful presidents have found ways to cope with divided government and enact important parts of their agenda.

6. Parties are governed by their national and state committees, and the focal point of party organization is the national and state party chairs. When the party controls the executive branch of government, the executive (governor or president) usually has a determining say in selecting the party chair. With the rise of soft money in recent elections, parties now have more resources to spend on politics.

7. Party platforms are vague and generalized by design, giving the other party and voters little to oppose.

8. Parties are vital in the operation of government. They are organized around elected offices at the state and local levels. Congress is also organized around parties, and judicial and many executive branch appointments are based in large part on partisanship.

9. Parties are also active in the electorate, seeking to organize elections, simplify voting choices, and strengthen party identification.

10. Frequent efforts have been made to reform our parties. The Progressive movement saw parties, as then organized, as an impediment to democracy and pushed direct primaries as a means to reform them. Following the 1968 election, the Democratic party took the lead in pushing primaries and stressing greater diversity in those elected as delegates. Republicans have also encouraged broader participation, and they have improved party structure and finances.

11. Compared to some European parties, ours remain organizationally weak. There has been some party renewal in recent years as party competition has grown in the South and the parties themselves have initiated reforms.

KEY TERMS

FURTHER READING

JOHN H. ALDRICH, *Why Parties? The Origin and Transformation of Party Politics in America* (University of Chicago Press, 1995).

PAUL ALLEN BECK, *Party Politics in America,* 8th ed. (Longman, 1997).

JOHN F. BIBBY, *Politics, Parties, and Elections in America,* 3d ed. (Nelson-Hall, 1996).

DAVID BOAZ, *Libertarianism: A Primer* (Free Press, 1998).

MARY C. BRENNAN, *Turning Right in the Sixties: The Conservative Capture of the GOP* (University of North Carolina Press, 1995).

STEPHEN C. CRAIG, ED., *Broken Contract: Changing Relationships Between Ameri-*

cans and Their Government (Westview Press, 1996).

Leon Epstein, *Political Parties in the American Mold* (University of Wisconsin Press, 1986).

Jeff Faux, *The Party's Not Over: A New Vision for Democrats* (Basic Books, 1996).

J. David Gillespie, *Politics at the Periphery: Third Parties in Two-Party America* (University of South Carolina Press, 1993).

John C. Green and Daniel M. Shea, eds., *The State of the Parties: The Changing Role of Contemporary American Parties*, 2d ed. (Rowman and Littlefield, 1996).

Paul S. Herrnson, *Party Campaigning in the 1980s: Have the National Parties Made a Comeback as Key Players in Congressional Elections?* (Harvard University Press, 1988).

Paul S. Herrnson and John C. Green, eds., *Multiparty Politics in America* (Rowman and Littlefield, 1997).

William J. Keefe, *Parties, Politics, and Public Policy in America*, 8th ed. (Congressional Quarterly Press, 1998).

Bruce E. Keith, David B. Magleby, Candice J. Nelson, Elizabeth Orr, Mark C. Westlye, and Raymond E. Wolfinger, *The Myth of the Independent Voter* (University of California Press, 1992).

G. Calvin Mackenzie, *The Irony of Reform: Roots of American Political Disenchantment* (Westview Press, 1996).

L. Sandy Maisel, ed., *The Parties Respond: Changes in American Parties and Campaigns*, 3d ed. (Westview, 1998).

William G. Mayer, *The Divided Democrats: Ideological Unity, Party Reform, and Presidential Elections* (Westview, 1996).

Sidney M. Milkis, *The President and the Parties: The Transformation of the American Party System Since the New Deal* (Oxford University Press, 1993).

Warren E. Miller and J. Merrill Shanks, *The New American Voter* (Harvard University Press, 1996).

Kelly D. Patterson, *Political Parties and the Maintenance of Liberal Democracy* (Columbia University Press, 1996).

Steven J. Rosenstone, Roy L. Behr, and Edward H. Lazarus, *Third Parties in America: Citizen Response to Major Party Failure*, 2d ed. (Princeton University Press, 1996).

James Sundquist, *Dynamics of the Party System: Alignment and Realignment of Political Parties in the United States*, rev. ed. (Brookings, 1983).

Martin P. Wattenberg, *The Decline of American Political Parties, 1952–1992* (Harvard University Press, 1994).

John K. White and Daniel M. Shea, *New Party Politics: From Jefferson and Hamilton to the Information Age* (Bedford/St. Martin's, 2000).

8

PUBLIC OPINION, PARTICIPATION, AND VOTING

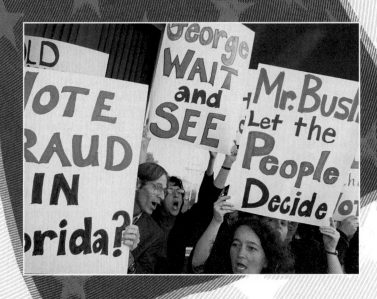

U NDECIDED OR "SWING VOTERS" GOT A LOT OF ATTENTION IN 2000 IN STATES OR DISTRICTS WITH COMPETITIVE CONTESTS FOR PRESIDENT, U.S. SENATE, OR U.S. HOUSE. Because so much was at stake in the 2000 elections—no incumbent running for president, and Republicans holding only a narrow majority in both houses of Congress—the candidates, parties, and interest groups made voter registration and turnout high priorities. Voters who had already made up their minds were bombarded with postcards reminding them to vote and phone calls reminding them it was election day and that their vote was needed. For example, the National Abortion and Reproductive Rights Action League (NARAL) made phone calls to pro-choice women under 40 years of age with a recorded message from Sarah Jessica Parker of HBO's *Sex and the City*, reminding them of the importance of electing pro-choice candidates.[1]

Candidate preferences and issue positions of possible voters are discovered by interviewing them on the telephone or in person, a process called a *canvas*. If these voters are undecided, they receive numerous pieces of mail and telephone calls aimed at persuading them to support one candidate over another. Mailings emphasize the stand of the candidate on such issues as Social Security, education, and prescription drug benefits. Interest groups and political parties send out similar persuasion pieces to undecided voters, often reinforcing the same themes as do the candidates. For example, in the U.S. House race in Washington's Second Congressional District, parties and interest groups sent out a total of 78 different mailings. In California's Twenty-seventh Congressional District—the most expensive U.S. House race in the country—parties and interest groups sent 71 different mailers on top of 45 different pieces of mail from the candidates' own campaigns.[2] No single household received all this mail; most of it was sent to voters who were for some reason thought to be persuadable. Consultants used all kinds of creative strategies like sending oversized mail and even a pop-up mailer like a children's book.

Some voters received conflicting messages. For instance, Michigan voters who were union members as well as gun owners received many communications from the National Rifle Association urging them to vote Republican, at the same time that their union was pushing a vote for the Democrats. In such cases, how do voters respond? Is a contact by telephone more persuasive than a piece of mail? Is the recorded voice of Sarah Jessica Parker more likely to get a person to vote than a live voice from someone calling from a telemarketing firm?

CHAPTERMEDIA

 POLITICS ONLINE
Who Votes? Why Not You?
www.prenhall.com/burns

 POLISIM
The Spin Effect
www.prenhall.com/burns

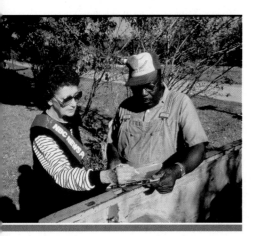

In addition to polls conducted by Gallop, Pew, and other such organizations, newspapers and TV networks conduct polls on election preferences and numerous other subjects.

What we learned from the 2000 election is that a few hundred votes can determine an election outcome. Candidates cannot take any votes for granted, so in close contests, voter mobilization is critical. In this chapter we look at the nature of public opinion, how to measure it, the factors that affect the formation of opinions, the nature and level of political participation in the United States, and why people vote as they do.

PUBLIC OPINION

All governments in all nations must be concerned with public opinion. In nondemocratic nations unrest and protest can topple them. And in a constitutional democracy, citizens can express opinions in a variety of ways, including demonstrations, letters to newspaper editors, and voting in free and regularly scheduled elections. Elected officials refer often to public opinion as the basis for their policy-making decisions. In short, democracy and public opinion go hand in hand.

What Is Public Opinion?

Everybody talks about "public opinion." Everybody claims to speak for "the public." But social scientists use the term more precisely: we define **public opinion** as the distribution of individual preferences for, or evaluations of, a given issue, candidate, or institution within a specific population. *Distribution* means the proportion of the population that holds a particular opinion, as compared to people with opposing opinions or those with no opinion at all. For instance, final pre-election polls in 2000 by the Gallup Organization found that among potential voters, 48 percent reported they would vote for George W. Bush, 46 percent for Al Gore, and 4 percent for Ralph Nader.[3] The actual vote was Bush 48 percent, Gore 48 percent, and Nader 3 percent.[4]

TAKING THE PULSE OF THE PEOPLE   *Proper sampling* is based on randomly selecting people to survey. *Random sampling* means that every individual has an equal chance of being selected. The sample of randomly selected respondents should be appropriate for the questions being asked. For instance, a survey of 18-to-24-year-olds should not be done solely among college students, since roughly three-quarters of this age group do not attend college. Even with proper sampling, surveys have a *margin of error*, meaning the sample accurately reflects the population within a certain percentage—usually plus or minus 3 percent for a sample of at least 1,500 individuals.

The art of asking questions is also important to scientific polling. The wording of questions can influence the answers. Question order can also alter the responses. Good questions have been pretested to be sure that the way the question is asked does not bias how it is answered. They should be delivered by trained and professional interviewers, who read the questions exactly as written and without any intonation in their voices. Questions can be worded in different ways to measure factual knowledge, opinions, the intensity of opinion, or views on hypothetical situations. Sometimes *open-ended questions* are asked that permit respondents to answer in their own words rather than in set categories.

Thorough analysis and reporting of the results as well as random sampling and clearly worded questions are required of scientific polls. Scientific polls inform the public of the sample size, the margin of expected statistical error for a standard question, and when and where the poll was conducted. It is also important to realize that public opinion can change and that most polls are really snapshots of opinion at a point in time rather than moving pictures of opinions over time.

Individual preference means that when we measure public opinion, we are asking *individuals*—not groups, elected officials, or journalists—about their opinions. The *universe* or *population* is the relevant group of people for the question. When a substantial percentage of a sample agree on an issue—for example, that we should honor the American flag—there is a *consensus*. But on most issues, opinions are divided. When a large portion of opposing sides feels intensely about an issue, voters are said to be *polarized*. Vietnam in the 1960s and currently abortion are polarizing issues (see Table 8–1).

TABLE 8–1 How Opinions Differ on Abortion

| | Percent saying abortion should be | | | |
	Legal under any circumstances	Legal under certain circumstances	Illegal under all circumstances	Don't know
Total Adults	28%	51%	19%	2%
Age				
18–29	25	58	17	—
30–49	27	55	17	1
50–64	22	63	14	1
65+	13	64	21	2
Sex				
Men	21	62	16	1
Women	24	56	18	2
Education				
High school graduate or less	18	61	19	2
Some college	22	61	15	2
College graduate	35	47	18	—
Postgraduate	33	55	11	1
Race				
White	22	60	17	1
Nonwhite	25	55	18	2
Black	21	55	23	1
Religion				
Protestant	21	61	17	1
Catholic	23	57	19	1
Political Philosophy				
Liberal	35	55	9	1
Moderate	27	59	13	1
Conservative	11	63	26	—
Party Identification				
Republican	18	62	19	1
Democrat	27	57	15	1
Independent	25	55	19	1
Income				
Less than $20,000	17	57	25	1
$20,000–$29,999	21	59	19	1
$30,000–$49,999	24	59	15	2
More than $50,000	29	60	10	1

SOURCE: Data for total adults and for sex are from a national survey by the Gallup Organization, May 2000 and January 1998; other data are from the Gallup Organization, January 1992.

Note: Figures may not add up to 100 percent due to rounding.

public opinion
The distribution of individual preferences for, or evaluations of, a given issue, candidate, or institution within a specific population.

"It should be 'yes' or 'no' or 'undecided'—we don't accept a 'don't give a damn' answer!"

Cartoon Features Syndicate.

INTENSITY   The factor called *intensity* produces the brightest and deepest hues in the fabric of public opinion. The fervor of people's beliefs varies greatly. For example, some individuals mildly favor gun control legislation and others mildly oppose it; some people are emphatically for or against it, and some have no interest in the matter at all; still others may not even have heard of it. Intensity is typically measured by asking people how strongly they feel about an issue or about a politician. Such a question is often called a *scale*.

LATENCY   *Latency* refers to political opinions that exist merely as a potential; they may not have crystallized, yet they are still important, for they can be aroused by leaders and converted into political action. Latent opinions set rough boundaries for leaders who know that if they take certain actions, they will trigger either opposition or support from millions of people. If leaders have some understanding of latent opinions—people's unexpressed wants, needs, and hopes—they will know how to mobilize them and draw them to the polls on election day. Many who lived in communist Poland, East Germany, Czechoslovakia, or Yugoslavia must have had latent opinions favorable to democracy—opinions supporting majority rule, freedom, and meaningful elections. The speed with which these countries embraced democratic reforms was possible when leaders encouraged widespread expression of such ideas.

SALIENCE   By *salience* we mean the extent to which people believe issues are relevant to them. Most people are more concerned about personal issues like paying their bills and keeping their jobs than about national issues, but if national issues somehow threaten their security or safety, salience of national issues rises sharply.

The saliency of issues may change over time. During the Great Depression of the 1930s, Americans were concerned mainly about jobs, wages, and economic security. By the 1940s, foreign affairs came to the fore. In the 1960s, problems of race and poverty aroused intense feeling. In the 1970s, Vietnam and then Watergate riveted people's attention. By the early 2000s, concern about drugs, crime, health care, education, and the state of the environment had become salient issues.

How Do We Get Our Political Opinions and Values?

No one is born with political views. We learn them from many teachers. The process by which we develop our political attitudes, values, and beliefs is called **political socialization**. This process starts in childhood, and the family and the schools are probably the two most important political teachers. Children learn the content of our culture in childhood and adolescence but reshape it as they mature.[5] Socialization lays the foundation for political beliefs, values, ideology, and partisanship.

A common element of political socialization in all cultures is *nationalism*, a consciousness of the nation-state and of belonging to that entity. Robert Coles describes it this way:

> As soon as we are born, in most places on this earth, we acquire a nationality, a membership in a community. . . . A royal doll, a flag to wave in a parade, coins with their engraved messages—these are sources of instruction and connect a young person to a country. The attachment can be strong, indeed even among children yet to attend school, wherever the flag is saluted, the national anthem sung. The attachment is as parental as the words imply—homeland, motherland, fatherland. . . . Nationalism works its way into just about every corner of the mind's life.[6]

The sources of our views are immensely varied in the pluralistic political culture of the United States. Political attitudes may stem from religious, racial, gender, ethnic, or economic beliefs and values. But we can make at least one generalization safely: We form our attitudes in *groups*, and not only in groups such as schools and social organizations, but especially in close-knit groups like the family. When we

political socialization

The process by which we develop our political attitudes, values, and beliefs.

identify closely with the attitudes and interests of a particular group, we tend to see politics through the "eyes" of that group.[7]

Group affiliation does not necessarily mean that individual members do not think for themselves. Each member brings his or her own emotions, feelings, memories, and resistance to groups. The extent to which people are captive to groups is indeed a running argument among scholars from different disciplines. Sociologists tend to emphasize the pervasive influence of groups over their members. Psychologists focus more on the developmental stages within individuals that prompt them to be joiners or loners. Political scientists have traditionally tended to agree more with the sociological approach.[8] Political psychologists seek to combine both approaches.

Children in the United States tend at an early age to adopt common values that provide continuity with the past and legitimize the American political system. Young children know what country they live in, and their loyalty to the nation develops early. Although the details of our political system may still elude them, most young Americans acquire a respect for the Constitution and for the concept of participatory democracy, as well as an initially positive view of the most visible figure in our democracy—the president.

FAMILY   American children typically show political interest by the age of ten, and by the early teens their interest may be fairly high. Consider your own political learning process. You probably formed your picture of the world by listening to a parent at dinner or by absorbing the tales your older brothers and sisters brought home from school. Perhaps you heard about politics from grandparents, aunts, and uncles. You, in turn, influenced your family, if only by bringing some of your own hopes and problems home from school. What we first learn in the family is not so much specific political opinions as basic *attitudes* that shape our opinions—attitudes toward our neighbors, political parties, other classes or types of people, particular leaders (especially presidents), and society in general.

Studies of high school students indicate a high correlation between the political party of the parents and the partisan choice of their children. This relatively high degree of correspondence continues throughout life. Such a finding raises some interesting questions: Does the direct influence of parents create the correspondence? Or does living in the same social environment—neighborhood, church, socioeconomic group—equally influence parents and children? The answer is *both*, and one influence often strengthens the other. For example, a daughter of Democratic parents growing up in a small southern town with strong Democratic leanings will be affected by friends, by other adults, and perhaps by youngsters in a church group, all of whom may reinforce the attitudes of her parents.[9] What happens when a young person's parents and friends disagree? Young people tend to go along with parents rather than friends on party affiliation, with friends rather than parents on issues like the death penalty or gun control, and somewhere in between in their actual votes in presidential elections.[10]

SCHOOLS   Schools also mold young citizens' political attitudes. American schools see part of their purpose as preparing students to be citizens and active participants in governing their communities and nation. At an early age, schoolchildren begin to pick up specific political values and acquire basic attitudes toward our system of government. Education, like the family, prepares Americans to live in society.

From kindergarten through college, students generally develop political values that will enhance their citizenship and legitimize the American political system. In their study of American history, they are introduced to our nation's heroes and heroines, the important events in our history, and the ideals of our society. Other aspects of the their experience, such as the daily Pledge of Allegiance, usually reinforce respect of country. Children also gain practical experience in the workings of

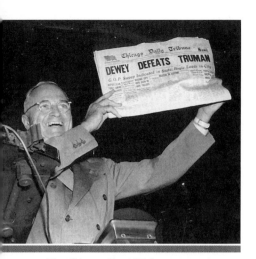

The Chicago Herald Tribune was so sure of its polling data in the 1948 election, they predicted a win for Republican Thomas Dewey before the results were final. A victorious Harry Truman displays the mistaken headline.

democracy through elections for class or school officers and student government. In some high schools and colleges, the state legislature or college trustees have made courses in U.S. history or American government a graduation requirement.

Do school influences give young people greater faith in political institutions? Yes and no. A classic study examined civics texts and students' attitudes in three Boston communities—one upper-middle class, one lower-middle class, and one working class. The textbooks in all three communities stressed the right of citizens to try to influence government, but only the texts used in the upper-middle-class community stressed politics as conflict and as a process for resolving differing group demands. Edgar Litt, a political scientist, concluded that the lower-middle-class students were learning that government was a process carried out by institutions on their behalf, while the upper-middle-class students were learning that the political process was something they could influence.[11]

The debate about whether there is peer pressure on college campuses to conform to certain acceptable ideas—*political correctness (PC)*—highlights the role higher education can play in shaping attitudes and values. How does college influence political opinions? One study suggests that college students are more likely to be knowledgeable about politics, more in favor of free speech, and more likely to talk and read about politics.[12] Is this the influence of the professors, the curriculum, the students, or the party leadership in the White House? It is difficult to generalize. Parents sometimes fear professors have too much influence on their college-age children; however, most professors doubt they have significant influence over the political views of their students.

MASS MEDIA   Like everybody else, young people are exposed to a wide range of media—school newspapers, national newspapers, the Internet, movies, television—all of which influence what they think. They, like adults, pick and choose the media with which they agree, so their exposure is *selective*. The mass media also serve as agents of socialization by providing a link between individuals and the values and behavior of others. When people watch, listen, and read, they discover which values and role models are considered important. News broadcasts present information about our society; events that get intensive media coverage often focus our attention on certain issues. For example, the hours of TV coverage of the presidential vote count in Florida in 2000 directed widespread attention to voting systems and the Electoral College.

OTHER INFLUENCES   Religious, ethnic, and racial attitudes also shape opinions, both within and outside the family. Generalizations about how people vote are useful, but we have to be careful about stereotyping people. True, Jewish families tend to be more liberal on both economic and noneconomic issues than either Catholics or Protestants, but there are lots of conservative Jewish families and lots of liberal Catholic and Protestant ones. It is dangerous to assume that because we know a person's religious affiliation or ethnic background we can know his or her political opinions.

Stability and Change in Public Opinion

Adults are not simply the sum of all their early experiences, but most of us do not change our opinions very often. Even if the world around us changes rapidly, we are slow to shift our loyalties or to change our minds about things that matter to us. In general, people who remain in the same place, in the same occupation, and in the same income group throughout their lives tend to have stable opinions. But people carry their attitudes with them, and families who move from cities to suburbs often retain their big-city attitudes long after they have moved. Political analysts are becoming more interested in the ways in

which adults modify their views. A major factor may be a harsh experience—a war, economic depression, or loss of a job—that shocks people out of their existing attitudes.

Some of our political opinions change very little because they are part of our core values. Thus our views on abortion, the death penalty, and doctor-assisted suicide remain relatively stable over time. On issues that are less central to our values, such as our view of how a president is performing his job, opinions can show substantial change over time. On many issues, public opinion can change once the public learns more about the issue or perceives there is another side to the question. It is on these issues that politicians can help shape attitudes.

Public Opinion and Public Policy

For much of human history it has been difficult to measure public opinion. "What I want," Abraham Lincoln once said, "is to get done what the people desire to be done, and the question for me is how to find that out exactly." Politicians in our day do not face the uncertainty about public opinion faced by Lincoln. Modern polling tells them what public opinion is on all major policy issues. In addition to polls the politicians commission, they can turn to public or media polls. More than 80 percent of newspapers and half of all television stations conduct or commission their own polls.[13]

Here are some examples of how public opinion can shape policy and in turn how policies shape opinion. During the Vietnam War, antiwar demonstrations on college campuses spread to cities all over the country. "Public opinion had a substantial impact on the rate of troop withdrawals."[14] In the Persian Gulf War, opposition to the use of U.S. forces was greatly reduced after a few days of success in the air and ground war. When American forces were dispatched to Somalia in Operation Restore Hope in January 1993, 79 percent approved of the use of troops to ensure the delivery of humanitarian aid, food, and medical provisions. But when U.S. soldiers were killed and dragged through the streets of Mogadishu, support fell to only 17 percent in October of the same year.[15]

Typically, elected officials seek to follow public opinion. Winning reelection is a strong motive for members of Congress.[16] "Legislators show greater attention to public opinion as election day looms," and the closeness of the fit between constituent opinion and roll call voting reflects that connection.[17] Candidates use polls to determine where to campaign, how to campaign, and even whether to campaign. In the years and months preceding a national convention, politicians watch the polls to determine who among the hopefuls has political appeal.

Surely polls are no substitute for elections. Faced with a ballot, voters must translate their opinions into concrete decisions. They must decide what is important and what is not. Democracy is more than the expression of views, more than a simple mirror of opinion. It also involves choosing among leaders, taking sides on certain issues, and selecting the governmental actions that may follow. Democracy is the thoughtful participation of people in the political process. It means using heads as well as counting them. Elections, with all their failings, still establish the link between the many voices of "We the People" and the selection of their leaders.

Awareness and Interest

For most people, politics is of secondary importance to earning a living, raising a family, and having a good time; some Americans are more concerned about which team wins the Super Bowl than they are about who wins the school board elections,

These college students feel responsible to vote and line up on campus to fill out absentee ballots.

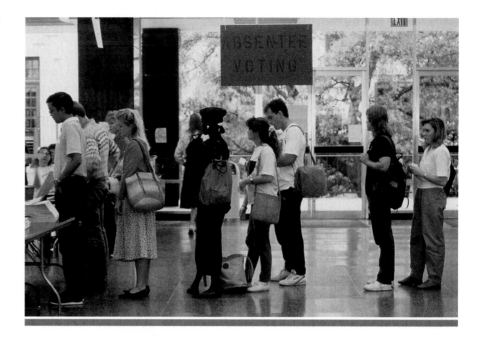

who gets to be mayor, or even who gets to be president of the United States. Most people find politics complicated and difficult to understand. And they should, for democracy *is* complicated and difficult to understand. But it helps to understand the mechanics and structures of our government: how the government operates, how the Electoral College works, how many chambers there are in Congress, the length of terms for the president and for members of the Senate and House of Representatives, for example.

Details about how the government works are typically best known by younger adults, who remember learning them in school. The general adult public, however, fares poorly when quizzed about their elected officials. Just over a quarter of Americans are able to recall the name of their member of Congress, and only 60 percent can name even one of their U.S. senators.[18] With so many voters not knowing who represents them in Congress, it is not surprising that "on even hotly debated congressional issues, few people know where their Congress member stands."[19]

Although the public's knowledge of institutional and candidate issues is poor, its knowledge of important public policy issues is worse. In 1982, after years of debate over ratification of the Equal Rights Amendment, nearly one-third of the adults in the United States indicated they had never heard of it. In late August 1993, several weeks before the vote in Congress on the North American Free Trade Agreement (NAFTA), six out of ten Americans reported they were not following the NAFTA story at all.[20]

Fortunately, not all Americans are uninformed or uninterested. About 25 percent of the public are interested in politics most of the time. They are the **attentive public**, people who know and understand how the government works. They vote in most elections, read a daily newspaper, and "talk politics" with their families and friends. They tend to be better educated and more committed to democratic values than are other Americans.

At the opposite end of the spectrum are *nonvoters*, people who are rarely interested in politics or public affairs and who rarely vote. About 35 percent of Americans have indicated that they have little interest in politics or are only occasionally interested.[21] A subset of this group might be called *political know-nothings*. These individuals not only avoid political activity but also have little interest in government and limited knowledge about it.

attentive public

Those who follow public affairs carefully.

Between the attentive public and the nonvoters are the *part-time citizens*, roughly 40 percent of the American public. These individuals participate selectively in elections, voting in presidential elections but usually not in others. Politics and government do not greatly interest them; they pay only minimal attention to the news, and they rarely discuss candidates or elections with others.

Democracy can survive even when a large number of citizens are passive and uninformed, as long as a substantial number of people serve as opinion leaders and are interested and informed about public affairs. Obviously, these activists will have much greater influence than their less active fellow citizens.

PARTICIPATION: TRANSLATING OPINIONS INTO ACTION

Americans influence their government's actions in several different ways, many of which are protected by the Constitution. They vote in elections, join interest groups, go to political party meetings, ring doorbells, call friends urging them to vote for issues or candidates, sign petitions, write letters to the editors of newspapers, and make calls to radio talk shows.

Protest is also a form of political participation. Our political system is remarkably tolerant of protest that is not destructive or violent; boycotts, picketing, sit-ins, and marches are all legally protected. Rosa Parks and Martin Luther King, Jr., used the peaceful breaking of the law to protest what they saw as unfair laws. The number of Americans who participate in protests is small, but the impact of their actions in shaping public opinion can be substantial.

A distinguishing characteristic of a democracy is that citizens can influence government decisions by participating in politics. In totalitarian societies, participation is very limited, forcing people who want to influence government to resort to violence or revolution. When the citizens of Belgrade turned out night after night to protest the nullification of their election, they forced Slobodan Milosevic to permit the victorious candidate, Vojislav Kostunica, to take power. But protests and demonstrations are not always peaceful or successful. The protest of Chinese students in Tiananmen Square failed to stop the onslaught of tanks and the repression that followed. Americans sometimes forget that our democracy was born of revolution, but that maintaining a constitutional democracy is also difficult and demands public participation.

Even in an established democracy, people may feel so strongly about an issue that they would rather fight than accept the verdict of an election. The classic example is the American Civil War. Following the election of 1860, in which an antislavery candidate who did not receive a single electoral vote from a slave state won the presidency, the South took up arms. The ensuing war marked the breakdown of democracy. Examples in our own time include antiabortion groups that use violence to press their political agenda and militia groups that arm themselves for battle against government restrictions.

Large numbers of Americans routinely participate in such rituals of democracy as singing the National Anthem or reciting the Pledge of Allegiance. They communicate their views about government and politics to their representatives in Washington and the state capitol. They serve as jurors in courtrooms and enlist in the military. They express concern about the involvement of American military forces in foreign hostilities. They complain about taxes and government regulations. And each year millions of Americans visit Washington, D.C., and other historic sights.

Street demonstrations in Belgrade, Yugoslavia, finally forced Slobodan Milosevic to concede defeat and permit the victorious candidate, Vojislav Kostunica, to take power. He was later taken into custody.

TABLE 8-2 Political Participation and Awareness in the United States	
Vote in presidential elections	49%
Vote in congressional elections	34
Know name of U.S. representative	28
Sign a petition	48
Write U.S. representative or state representative	30
Vote in local elections	10–30
Try to persuade vote of others	19
Display campaign button, sticker, or sign	7
Attend dinner, meeting, or rally for candidate	5
Contribute to candidate	4
Contribute to party	4

SOURCES: U.S. Bureau of the Census, *Statistical Abstract of the United States, 1998* (Government Printing Office, 1998), p. 297; 1998 American National Election Study, Center for Political Studies, University of Michigan.

For most people, politics is a private activity. Some books on manners still consider it impolite to discuss politics at dinner parties. To say that politics is private does not mean people do not have opinions or will not discuss them when asked by others, including pollsters. But often politics is avoided in discussions with neighbors, work associates, even friends and family, as too divisive or upsetting. Typically, less than one person in four attempts to influence how another person votes in an election. An even smaller number actually work for a candidate or party. Only one in 20 people make a contribution to a candidate, and only one in six designate three dollars of their taxes to the fund that pays for presidential general elections (see Table 8–2).[22]

Few individuals attempt to influence others by writing letters to elected officials or to editors of newspapers for publication. Even smaller numbers participate in protest groups or activities. Despite the small number of persons who engage in these activities, it would be a mistake to assume that small numbers of individuals cannot make a difference to politics and government. An individual or small group can generate media interest in an issue and expand the impact. Peaceful protests for civil rights, about environmental issues, and both for and against abortion have generated public attention and even changed opinions.

Voting

Americans' most typical political activity is voting. The United States is a constitutional democracy with more than 200 years of free and frequent elections and a tradition of the peaceful transfer of power between competing groups and parties.

Originally the Constitution left it to the individual states to determine the crucial question of who could vote, and the qualifications for voting differed considerably from state to state. All states except New Jersey barred women from voting, many did not permit African Americans to vote, and until the 1830s, property ownership was often a requirement. By the time of the Civil War, the franchise had been extended to all white male citizens in every state. Since that time, eligibility standards for voting have been expanded by legislation and constitutional amendments:

1870 Fifteenth Amendment forbade states from denying the right to vote because of "race, color, or previous condition of servitude."

1920 Nineteenth Amendment gave women the right to vote.

1924 Congress granted Native Americans citizenship and voting rights.

1961 Twenty-third Amendment permitted District of Columbia residents to vote in federal elections.

1964 Twenty-fourth Amendment prohibited the use of poll taxes in federal elections.

1965 Voting Rights Act removed restrictions that kept blacks from voting.

1971 Twenty-sixth Amendment extended the vote to citizens age 18 and older.

The civil rights movement in the 1960s, which made voting rights a central issue, secured adoption of the Twenty-fourth Amendment and passage of the 1965 Voting Rights Act. The Voting Rights Act banned literacy tests, eased registration requirements, and provided for the replacement of local election officials with federal registrars in areas where the denial of the right to vote had been most blatant. Its passage resulted in a dramatic expansion of African American registration and voting. Once African Americans were permitted to register to vote, "the focus of

voting discrimination shifted . . . to preventing them from winning elections."[23] In southern legislative districts where African Americans are in the majority, however, there has been a "dramatic increase in the proportion of African American legislators elected"[24] (see Figure 8–1).

Registration

One peculiarly American legal requirement—**voter registration**—discourages voting. Most other democracies have automatic voter registration. Average turnout in the United States is more than 30 percentage points lower than in countries like Australia, Austria, Belgium, Denmark, Germany, and Italy; only Switzerland has lower average turnout.[25] This was not always the case. In fact, in the 1800s, turnout in the United States was much like that of Europe today. Turnout began to drop significantly around the turn of the century, in part as a result of election reform (see Figure 8–2).

American elections in the 1800s were different from those of today. Ballots were prepared by the parties, often using different colors of paper that allowed party officials to monitor how people had voted. In some areas charges of multiple voting generated a reform movement that substituted the **Australian ballot**, a secret ballot printed by the state, and initiated voter registration to reduce multiple voting and limit voting to those who had previously established their eligibility.

Registration laws vary by state, but in every state except North Dakota registration is required in order to vote. Three states permit election-day voter registration. The most important provision regarding voter registration may be the closing date. A few years ago it was not uncommon for closing dates to be six months before the election; now, by federal law, no state can stop registration more than 30 days before a federal election.[26] Voter registration places a responsibility on voters to take an extra step—usually filling out a form at the county courthouse, when renewing a driver's license, or with a roving registrar—some days or weeks before the election. Other important provisions include places and hours of registration.[27]

Motor-Voter

The burdens of voter registration were eased a bit when, on May 20, 1993, President Bill Clinton signed the National Voter Registration Act—called the "Motor-Voter" bill because it allows people to register to vote while applying for or

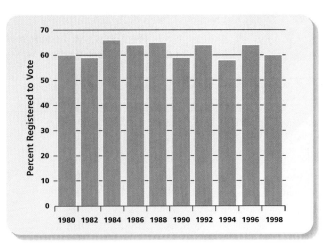

FIGURE 8–1 Percent of African American Registered Voters, 1980–1998

SOURCE: U.S. Bureau of the Census, *Statistical Abstract of the United States, 1999* (Government Printing Office, 1999), p. 300.

FIGURE 8–2 Voter Turnout in Presidential Elections, 1800–2000

SOURCE: Howard W. Stanley and Richard G. Niemi, *Vital Statistics on American Politics, 1999–2000* (Congressional Quarterly Press, 2000). See also www.infoplease.com/ipa/A0781453.html.

voter registration
System designed to reduce voter fraud by limiting voting to those who have established eligibility by submitting the proper form.

Australian ballot
A secret ballot printed by the state.

REGISTRATION AND VOTING IN THE WORLD'S DEMOCRACIES

	Turnout as percent of eligible vote	Compulsion penalties*	Automatic registration**
Australia	94%	Yes	No
Austria	91	No	Yes
Belgium	93	Yes	Yes
Canada	76	No	Yes
Denmark	86	No	Yes
Finland	78	No	Yes
France	66	No	No
Germany	84	No	Yes
Greece	85	Yes	Yes
Ireland	69	No	Yes
Israel	80	No	Yes
Italy	91	Yes	Yes
Japan	71	No	Yes
Netherlands	86	No	Yes
New Zealand	87	No	No
Norway	84	No	Yes
Spain	71	No	Yes
Sweden	86	No	Yes
Switzerland	46	No	Yes
United Kingdom	75	No	Yes
United States	53	No	No

SOURCES: Thomas T. Mackie and Richard Rose, *The International Almanac of Electoral History*, 3d ed. (Congressional Quarterly Press, 1991); G. Bingham Powell, Jr., "American Voter Turnout in Comparative Perspective," *American Political Science Review* 80 (March 1986), p. 38. Iceland, Luxembourg, Malta, and Portugal were not included in the Powell study and were therefore omitted from this table.

*Compulsion penalties are fines or other possible state actions against nonvoters.

**Automatic registration utilizes other forms of citizen identification like a driver's license.

renewing a driver's license. Offices that provide welfare and disabled assistance can also facilitate voter registration. States have the option to include public schools, libraries, and city and county clerks' offices as registration sites. The law also requires states to allow registration by mail using a standardized form. Motor-Voter requires a questionnaire be mailed to registered voters every four years to purge for death and change of residence, but forbids purging for any other reasons, such as nonvoting.

The law has been successful, at least in terms of numbers of new voters registered.[28] Early data on the impact of Motor-Voter suggest that neither Democrats nor Republicans are the primary beneficiaries because most who have registered claim to be Independent.[29] Yet even with the increase in registration, Motor-Voter does not appear to have increased turnout.[30]

Turnout

Americans hold more elections for more offices than do citizens of any other democracy. In part because there are so many elections, American voters tend to pick and choose which elections to vote in. Americans elect officeholders in *general elections*, determine party nominees in *primary elections*, and replace senators who have died or left office in *special elections*.

Elections held in years when the president is on the ballot are called *presidential elections*, elections held midway between presidential elections are called *midterm elections*, and elections held in odd-numbered calendar years are called *off-year elections*. Midterm elections (like the one in 2002) elect about one-third of the U.S. Senate, all members of the House of Representatives, and most governors and other statewide officeholders as well as large numbers of state legislators. Many local elections to elect city councils and mayors are held in the spring of odd-numbered years.

Turnout—the proportion of the voting-age public that votes—is highest in presidential general elections (see Figure 8–3). Turnout is higher in general elections than in primary elections and higher in primary elections than in special elections. Turnout is higher in presidential general elections than in midterm general elections, and higher in presidential primary elections than in midterm primary elections.[31] Turnout is higher in elections in which candidates for federal office are on the ballot (U.S. senator, member of the House of Representatives, president) than in state elections in years when there are no federal contests. Some states elect their governor and other state officials in odd-numbered years to separate state from national politics. The result is generally lower turnout. Finally, local or municipal

turnout

The proportion of the voting-age public that votes.

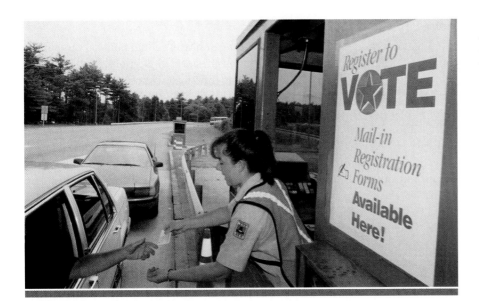

In an effort to make registration easier, states have made registration forms available at motor vehicle stations, schools, public buildings, and even highway tollbooths.

elections have lower turnout than state elections, and municipal primaries have even lower rates of participation.

Turnout peaked in 1960 at more than 65 percent of persons over 21 years of age, but it has since declined to 36 percent in 1998, and 51 percent in 2000.[32] Turnout should have gone up since 1960 because the Voting Rights Act of 1965 added large numbers of African Americans to the pool of registered voters. Women, another historically underrepresented group, have also increased their voting levels.[33] Finally, our electorate has grown richer and more educated since the 1960s, and since wealth and education are related to voting, we should have seen an increase instead of a decrease in voting. However, 85 million of eligible Americans failed to vote in recent presidential elections; the nonvoting figures are even higher for congressional, state, county, and local elections.[34]

Who Votes?

The extent of voting varies widely among different groups. The level of education especially helps predict whether people will vote; as education increases, so does the propensity to vote. "Education increases one's capacity for understanding complex and intangible subjects such as politics," according to one study, "as well as encouraging the ethic of civil responsibility. Moreover, schools provide experience dealing with a variety of bureaucratic problems, such as coping with requirements, filling out forms, and meeting deadlines."[35] Race and ethnic background are linked with different levels of voting, in large part because they correlate with education. Blacks in general turn out at lower rates than whites. However, women, another historically underrepresented group, increased their voting levels to the point where since 1984 more women than men vote.[36]

Income and age are also important factors. Those with higher family incomes are more likely to vote than those with lower incomes. Income, of course, corresponds to occupation, and those with higher-status careers are more likely to vote than those with lower-status jobs. Poor people are less likely to feel politically involved and confident, and their social norms tend to deemphasize politics.[37] Older people, unless they are very old and infirm, are more likely to vote than younger people. Women's recent higher turnout is generally attributed to increasing levels of education and employment.

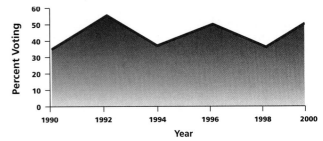

FIGURE 8–3 Voter Turnout in Presidential and Midterm Elections, 1990–2000

SOURCES: U.S. Bureau of the Census, *Statistical Abstract of the United States, 1998* (Government Printing Office, 1998), p. 97; Louis V. Gerstner, "Next Time, Let Us Boldly Vote As No Democracy Has Before," *USA Today*, November 16, 1998, p. A15. For 2000 data, www.infoplease.com/ipa/A0781453.html.

League of Women Voters

This poster, published by the League of Women Voters, urged women to use the vote the Nineteenth Amendment had given them.

TABLE 8–3 Why People Don't Vote	
Not registered to vote	35%
Didn't have time to go	6
No campaign or organization contacted them	6
Was not convenient	24
Not interested in the candidates	22
Election just didn't seem important	10
Too young at the time	1
Other	2
Not sure	8

SOURCE: Roper Center at University of Connecticut, February 1997, Public Opinion Online, Question ID (Ushare.97govn, rf03b).

Note: Results add up to more than 100 percent due to multiple responses.

How Serious Is Nonvoting?

Although Americans can hardly avoid reading or hearing about political campaigns, roughly 85 million Americans fail to vote in presidential elections. Who are they? Why don't they vote? Is the fact that so many Americans choose not to vote a cause for alarm? If so, what can we do about it?

The simplest explanation for low turnout is that people are lazy, but there is more to it than that. Of course, some people are apathetic, but the vast majority of Americans are not. Paradoxically, we compare favorably with other nations in political interest and awareness, but for a variety of institutional and political reasons, we fail to convert these qualities into votes (see Table 8–3).

The difficulty of voting in the United States, the cost in time and effort, is higher than in other democracies. In our system, individuals are required to register to vote, and they must make sense of a range of political alternatives that do not necessarily meet their interests.

Another factor in the decline of voter turnout since the 1960s is the Twenty-sixth Amendment, which lowered the voting age to 18. It increased the number of eligible voters, but that group is the least likely to vote. With ratification of the amendment in 1971, turnout fell from 62 percent in 1968 to 57 percent in 1972.[38] The effect of adding this low turnout group to the electorate has been to lower the overall turnout rate.

Some political scientists argue that nonvoting is not a critical problem. "Nonvoting is not a social disease," contends Austin Ranney, a noted scholar of politics. He points out that legal and extralegal denial of the vote to African Americans, women, Hispanics, persons over 18, and other groups has now been outlawed, so nonvoting is voluntary. He quotes the late Senator Sam Ervin of North Carolina: "I don't believe in making it easy for apathetic, lazy people to vote."[39]

Those who argue that nonvoting is a critical problem cite the "class bias" of those who do vote. The social makeup and attitudes of nonvoters are significantly different from those of voters and hence greatly distort the representative system. "The very poor . . . have about two-thirds the representation among voters than their numbers would suggest." Thus the people who need help the most from the government lack their fair share of electoral power to obtain it. And, it is argued, this situation is growing worse.[40]

Low voting, according to those who see a class bias in voting, reflects "the underdevelopment of political attitudes resulting from the historic exclusion of low-income groups from active electoral participation." In short, part of the problem of nonvoting among low-income, less-educated people is their failure to be conscious of their interests. Dynamic leadership or strong party organization, or both, would not only attract the poor to the polls but also make clear their "class grievances and aspirations."[41]

Others reject this class-bias argument. They admit nonvoters are demographically different, yet they cite polls showing that nonvoters' attitudes are not much different from voters' attitudes. One study, comparing the party identification of voters with that of all Americans, found the proportion of Democrats was nearly identical (51.4 percent of all citizens and 51.3 percent of voters), while Republicans as voters were slightly overrepresented (36 percent of citizens and 39.7 percent of voters). All other political differences are considered to be much smaller than this 3.7 percent gap. Further, voters are not "disproportionately hostile" to social welfare policies.[42]

What effect might increased voter turnout have in national elections? It might make a difference, since there are partisan differences between different demographic groups, and candidates would have to adjust to the demands of an expanded electorate. A noted political scientist, while acknowledging that no political system could achieve 100 percent participation, pointed out that the entire balance of power in the political system could be overturned if the large nonvoter population decided to vote.[43] However, others argue that the difference may not be as pronounced. Nonvoters are not more in favor of government ownership or control of industry, and they are not more egalitarian. Nonvoters are, however, more inclined to favor additional spending on welfare programs.[44]

Another way to think of low voter turnout is to see it as a sign of approval with things as they are, whereas high voter turnout would signify disapproval and widespread desire for change. Even on the subject of how to interpret low turnout there is disagreement.

VOTING CHOICES

Why do people vote as they do? Political scientists have identified three main elements of the voting choice: party identification, candidate appeal, and issues. These elements often overlap.

WE THE PEOPLE

Voter Turnout by Demographic Factors

	1992	1994	1996	1998
Sex				
Men	60.2%	44.4%	52.8%	41.4%
Women	62.3	44.9	55.5	42.4
Race				
White	63.6	46.9	56.0	46.5
Black	54.0	37.0	50.6	40
Hispanic	28.9	19.1	26.7	20
Education				
Some high school	41.2	27.0	33.8	24.6
High school graduate	57.5	40.5	49.1	37.1
Some college	68.7	49.1	60.5	46.2
College graduate	81.0	63.1	73.0	57

SOURCE: U.S. Bureau of the Census, *Statistical Abstract of the United States, 2000* (Government Printing Office, 2000), p. 290.

Voting on the Basis of Party

Party identification is the subjective sense of identification or affiliation that a person has with a political party, (see Chapter 7). Party identification often predicts a person's stand on issues. It is part of our national mythology that Americans vote for the person and not the party, but, as you will see, the person we vote for is most often from the party we prefer.

Partisanship is typically acquired in childhood or adolescence as a result of the socialization process in the family, then reinforced by peer groups in adolescence. In the absence of reasons to vote otherwise, people depend on party identification to simplify their voting choices. Party identification is not the same as party registration; it is not party membership in the sense of being a dues-paying, card-carrying member, as in some European parties. Rather, it is a psychological sense of attachment to one party or another.

There has been a dramatic increase in the number of Independents since the mid-1970s. Nominally there are more Independents in the electorate today than Republicans. But two-thirds of all Independents are, in fact, partisans in their voting behavior. Independent-leaning Democrats are predictably Democratic in their voting behavior, and Independent-leaning Republicans vote heavily Republican. Independent-leaners are thus very different from each other and

party identification
An informal and subjective affiliation with a political party that most people acquire in childhood.

A Closer Look

PROBLEMS COUNTING BALLOTS AND ADMINISTERING ELECTIONS

The chaos in the counting of ballots in Florida in the 2000 election surprised many Americans, who assumed that vote counting is simple and precise. They were wrong. The problems were not isolated to Florida's clogged voting machines, defective punch cards, and inconsistent standards for dealing with problems. Ballots were misplaced in New Mexico, voting machines broke down in several states, people's names were incorrectly purged from voting lists, and long lines of people waiting to vote led to court challenges in many states. In the weeks and months following the election, at least half the states launched efforts to study the problems and propose solutions; in addition, national commissions, advisory groups, and experts undertook extensive analyses of our voting procedures.

Most people agree that many communities need new voting equipment, and that the antiquated and flawed punch card technology used by "roughly 30 percent of the nation's voters" must be abandoned.* Whether jurisdictions adopt the less expensive optically scannable ballots or more expensive high-tech computer systems will depend in part on how much money Congress is willing to provide. Estimates vary, but the cost could be as high as $6.5 billion, depending on which new voting system is adopted.

The National Association of Secretaries of State—the state officials charged with election administration—issued recommendations that included: better pay

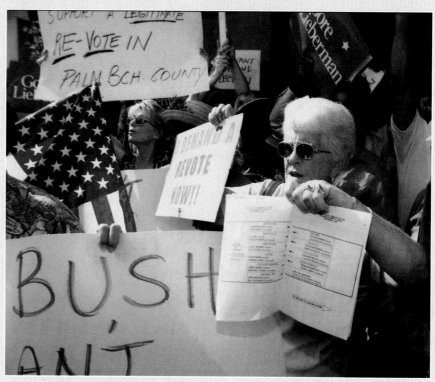

Angry voters in Palm Beach County protested that the "butterfly ballot" caused them to vote incorrectly and demanded an opportunity to vote over again, but were not allowed to do so.

for poll workers; aggressive voter education on matters like how to ask for a second ballot if the first is spoiled; equal access to balloting for minorities, poor, and elderly voters; maintaining up-to-date voter lists; ensuring the integrity of absentee ballots; and providing federal money to local communities to upgrade their voting systems.**

The debate over electoral reform growing out of the 2000 election is not limited to machines and ballots but includes standards for recounts, ways to ensure the process is open to all citizens, and concerns about the news media projecting winners before the polls close.

*Robert Tanner, "Ballot Reforms Are Slow in Coming, Despite Hundreds of Ideas, Studies," *Deseret News*, March 4, 2001, p. A3.

**Katharine Q. Seelye, "Panel Suggests Election Changes That Let States Keep Control," *The New York Times*, February 5, 2001, p. A16.

---

from the Pure Independents. Pure Independents have the lowest rate of turnout but generally do side with the eventual winner in presidential elections. These data on Independents only reinforce the importance of partisanship as an explanation of voting choice, because when we consider Independent-leaning Democrats and Independent-leaning Republicans as Democrats and Republicans respectively, there were only 11 percent Pure Independents or others without a party in 2000, and the average for the period 1952–2000 was only 11 percent.[45]

Although party identification has fluctuated somewhat in the past 40 years, it remains more stable than attitudes about issues or political ideology. Fluctuations in

party identification appear to come in response to economic conditions and political performance, especially of the president. The more information voters have about their choices, the more likely they are to defect from their party and vote for a candidate from the other party.

Permission of Harley Schwadron.

Voting on the Basis of Candidates

While long-term party identification is important, it is clearly not the only factor in voting choices; otherwise the Democrats would have won every presidential election since the last realignment in 1932. In fact, since 1952, Republicans have been more successful in winning the White House than Democrats. The answer to this puzzle is largely found in a second major explanation of voting choice—candidate appeal.

The elections of the 1980s marked a critical threshold in the emergence of the candidate-centered era in American electoral politics. This change in focus from parties to candidates is an important historical trend that has been gradually taking place over the last several decades.[46]

Candidate appeal often involves an assessment of a candidate's character. Is the candidate honest? Is the candidate consistent? Is the candidate dedicated to "family values"? Does the candidate have religious or spiritual commitments? The press in recent elections has sometimes played the role of "character cop," asking questions about private lives and lifestyles. The press asks these questions because voters are interested in a political leader's background—perhaps even more interested in personal character than in a political position on hard-to-understand health care or regulatory policy issues.

Ronald Reagan's effort to generate positive candidate appeal was successful. Carter had hoped that Reagan would behave more like Barry Goldwater, who in his acceptance speech in 1964 had said, "Extremism in the defense of liberty is no vice. . . . Moderation in the pursuit of justice is no virtue."[47] Lyndon Johnson, Goldwater's opponent, benefitted from public perception that Goldwater and those who nominated him were out of the mainstream of American politics.

Like Barry Goldwater in 1964, George McGovern, who ran as the Democrat in 1972, was a candidate with negative appeal. Many of his supporters, by their dress and manner, appeared out of the mainstream of American politics. McGovern raised doubts about his judgment and leadership by how he handled his choice of a vice-president. McGovern named Missouri Senator Tom Eagleton as his running mate, only to discover that Eagleton had once been hospitalized for emotional exhaustion and depression and received electric shock therapy. McGovern initially stood behind Eagleton, but as press coverage and criticism of McGovern's lack of investigation into Eagleton's past grew, McGovern dropped Eagleton and named a new running mate, Sargent Shriver. In the end, "only about one-third of the public thought McGovern could be trusted as president."[48]

Candidate appeal or the lack of it—in terms of leadership, experience, good judgment, integrity, competence, strength, and energy—is often more important than party or issues. Dwight Eisenhower had great candidate appeal. He was a five-star general, a legendary hero of the Allied effort in World War II. His unmilitary manner, his moderation, his personal charm, and his lack of a strong party position made him appealing across the ideological spectrum. Ronald Reagan generated positive candidate appeal, in part by asserting characteristics the public found lacking in Jimmy Carter—leadership and strength. Neither George W. Bush nor Al Gore were able to convey a vision that lead to decisive victory in 2000. Bush was seen as more "likeable" and Gore as more "competent." But both candidates had liabilities. Bush

You Decide...

fought the image of not being up to the job and Gore tried to make himself more likeable.

Increasingly, campaigns today focus on the negative elements of candidates' history and personality. Opponents and the media are quick to point out the limitations or problems of any given candidate. The political parties and interest groups did most of the attacking in 2000. Bush was attacked for his stand on abortion, his lack of support for hate crime legislation, his environmental record, and his competence.[49] Gore was attacked for the 1996 fund-raising scandals, his misstatement about inventing the Internet, and his position on gun control.[50] Voters indicated that the candidate quality that mattered most was "honest/trustworthy," which one in four voters mentioned. For these voters, Bush was preferred by 80 percent over Gore, Nader, and Buchanan. All other candidate attributes—"understands issues," "cares about people," "has experience," "strong leader," and "good judgment" were mentioned by 12 to 15 percent of voters as the quality that mattered most. For voters who saw understanding issues as most important, Gore got 75 percent of the vote. Gore also was the preferred candidate for voters who valued "cares about people" and "has experience," where he got 63 and 82 percent, respectively of the vote. Bush got nearly two-thirds of the vote of respondents who said strong leadership mattered most; among the 2 percent who said "likeable" was the candidate quality that mattered most, Bush got 82 percent of the vote.[51]

Voting on the Basis of Issues

Most political scientists agree that issues, while important, are not as central to the decision process as party identification and candidate appeal.[52] Part of the reason is that candidates often intentionally obscure their positions on issues—an understandable strategy.[53] Richard Nixon said he had a plan to end the Vietnam War in 1968, clearly the most important issue in that year, but he would not reveal the specifics of that plan. By not detailing his plan, he stood to gain votes from those who wanted a more aggressive war effort as well as those who wanted a cease-fire.

For issue voting to become of major significance, the issue must be important to a substantial number of voters, opposing candidates must take opposing stands on the issues, and voters must know these positions and vote accordingly. Rarely do candidates focus on only one issue. Voters often will agree with one candidate on one issue and with the opposing candidate on another. In such an instance, issues will likely not be the determining factor. But lack of interest by voters in issues does not mean candidates can take any issue position they wish.[54]

More likely than *prospective issue voting* (voting based on what a candidate pledges to do in the future about an issue if elected) is *retrospective issue voting* (holding incumbents, usually the president's party, responsible for past performance on issues such as the economy or foreign policy).[55] In times of peace and prosperity, voters will reward the incumbent; if the nation falls short on either, voters will elect the opposition.

But good economic times do not always lead to the retention of an administration, as Al Gore learned in 2000. Part of Gore's problem in 2000 was that only half of the public saw their family's financial situation as having gotten better. Of these voters, Gore received 61 percent of the vote.[56] But his inability to effectively claim credit for the good economic times hurt him, especially when Republicans contended that it was the American people, not the government, that produced the strong economy.

The state of the economy is often the central issue in midterm elections as well as presidential ones. Several studies have found a positive relationship between the

state of the economy and "out" party gains and "in" party losses in congressional seats.[57] Political scientists have been able to locate the sources of this effect in individual voter's decision making. Voters tend to vote against the party in power if they perceive a decline or standstill in their personal financial situations.[58] Voters see responsibility for the economy resting with the president and Congress more than with governors or local officials.[59]

Despite generally good economic news and success in lowering the federal budget deficit, Democrats suffered a substantial defeat in 1994. Why? Part of the explanation lies in Bill Clinton's low approval ratings. The public continued to have doubts about his leadership. Clinton, who had won election in 1992 on the theme of change, found that he and Democrats in Congress were targets of the same voter frustrations they had directed at the Republicans. Republicans in Congress had used the filibuster and other tactics to defeat much of the Clinton agenda and then succeeded in arguing that Congress was in need of wholesale change. Newt Gingrich captured the "change" theme in 1994 by presenting the Contract with America, which included a commitment to a Balanced Budget Amendment, term limits for members of Congress, and other reforms. This strategy kept Democrats off balance and enabled Republicans to take advantage of voter anger.

Democrats focused the 1998 midterm election on four issues: Social Security, education, health care, and the environment. In contrast, the Republicans wanted to emphasize the accomplishments of the 105th Congress and the reasons to return that Congress to power. The Republican party also decided to raise the impeachment issue late in the campaign. Exit polls demonstrated that this strategy did not resonate well with voters, who wanted to move beyond the impeachment debate. The Democrats' emphasis on concrete issues, when combined with strong candidates in the relative few competitive races, helped them surprise even themselves by picking up a net gain of five House seats. This reinforced the sense that both parties would have a lot to gain or lose in the 2000 elections.

Republicans in 2000 worked hard to deny Democrats the kind of issue advantage they enjoyed in 1998. They had their own plans to privatize Social Security, foster better public schools, and provide prescription drugs for seniors. Democrats complained that Republicans were stealing their issues, something Republicans accused Bill Clinton of doing in 1996 with welfare reform. While Democrats retained an advantage on most issues in 2000, it was not enough for them to win in the Electoral College or secure a majority in either congressional chamber.

The bitterness and partisanship of the protracted ballot counting controversy in Florida following the 2000 vote, which was brought to an end by the Supreme Court, provides the Democrats with an issue for the future. The claim that the election was unfairly decided and that not all the votes were officially counted is one that Democrats may find still rankles many voters. Moreover, the fact that the greatest number of *undervotes* (what happens when a punch card ballot is not read by a card reader) occurred in counties with large minority group populations may help them mobilize those constituencies in future elections.

The 2000 presidential election was exceedingly close. Voters and political gurus learned anew the importance of just a few votes. Bush strategists may regret they had not mobilized Republicans, even in safe states, so their candidate could have won the popular vote. And had Gore carried his home state of Tennessee, or Clinton's home state of Arkansas, he would be president. Both parties, no doubt, will cite the 2000 election as a reason never to take votes for granted and to do all possible to get out their supporters.

Thinking It Through...

One of the problems with making elections more frequent is that voters will get fed up. Americans already vote more frequently and for more offices than citizens of any other democracy do. Asking them to make voting choices even more frequently could result in lower turnout and less rational consideration. Many voters may be unaware an election is going on. Yet the advantage of the vote-by-mail system employed by Oregon and some cities and counties is that it increases turnout, at least initially. What political scientists dispute is whether such increases in participation will continue when the novelty wears off.

Some critics of voting by mail or electronic democracy worry about fraud. Even when voters are required to sign their mailed-in ballots, the possibility for forgery still exists. Also voting by mail or computer has the possibility of allowing people to pressure or harass voters. Another concern is late returns, as occurred in 2000.

Another criticism is that mail and electronic voting could be skewed toward participation by better-educated and higher-income voters, who routinely pay their bills by mail, make purchases on their computer, and own a personal computer with Internet access. Advocates of these new voting procedures contend that voters who do not own computers can drop off their ballots in some public building, and that eventually computers will be available widely enough that access will not be a problem.

However, if voting can be made easier and more convenient, why not do it? If the integrity of the vote can be protected and the new ways of voting become widely accessible, then such changes are probably inevitable.

SOURCES: David B. Magleby, "Participation in Mail Ballot Elections," *Western Political Quarterly* 40 (March 1987), pp. 79–91; Michael W. Traugott, "An Evaluation of Voting by Mail in Oregon," paper prepared for workshop co-sponsored by the University of Michigan and the League of Women Voters, Washington, D.C., August 27, 1997.

POLITICS ONLINE

Who Votes? Why Not You?

You have a wide variety of elections and political process you can engage in if you are registered to vote. You can sign a petition to place a proposed law on the ballot if you live in a state that allows initiatives. You can vote in as many as four or more federal, state, or local elections per year in many localities. To get a sense of the different levels of participation in America, go to the website for this book and Chapter 8 at:

www.prenhall.com/burns.

The age cohort that is least likely to vote is 18–24-year-olds. There are several reasons for this, including the higher mobility of this age group. When you move often, it becomes a hassle to register to vote, especially if you have to do so in person. Many states have moved to simplify and streamline voter registration, and some even permit you to register online. To register to vote, you can go to the Federal Elections Commission website at: www.fec.gov.votregis/vr.htm, where you will find a National Mail Voter Registration form that can be downloaded and returned. Most states accept this form. The site also has links to learn about how to register in your state. State registration requirements are found at:

www.fec.gov/pages/voteinst.htm.

Elections have consequences. As the 2000 election demonstrated, elections can be decided by a few votes. Close elections were not limited to the presidential race. Some House and Senate races went into recounts, and the same is likely to happen in 2002 and 2004. Make use of the resource of the Web to learn how to register to vote, and then exercise your franchise.

SUMMARY

1. Public opinion is a complex combination of views and attitudes individuals acquire through various influences from childhood on. Public opinion takes on qualities of intensity, latency, consensus, or polarization—each of which is affected by people's feelings about the salience of issues.

2. The American public has a generally low level of interest in politics, and most people do not follow politics and government closely. The public's knowledge of political issues is poor.

3. Those Americans who are interested in public affairs can participate by voting, joining interest groups and political parties, working on campaigns, writing letters to newspaper editors or elected officials, attempting to influence how another person will vote, or even protesting.

4. Better educated, older, and party- and group-involved people tend to vote more; the young tend to vote the least. Voter turnout tends to be higher in national than in state and local elections, and higher in presidential than in midterm elections.

5. Party identification remains an important element in the voting choice of most Americans. It represents a long-term attachment and is a "lens" through which voters view candidates and issues as they make their voting choices. Candidate appeal, including character and record, is another key factor in voter choice. Voters decide their vote less frequently on the basis of issues.

KEY TERMS

public opinion 173
political socialization 174

attentive public 178
voter registration 181

Australian ballot 181
turnout 182

party identification 185

FURTHER READING

JOSEPH A. AISTRUP, *The Southern Strategy Revisited: Republican Top-Down Advancement in the South* (University of Kentucky Press, 1996).

HERBERT ASHER, *Polling and the Public: What Every Citizen Should Know*, 3d ed. (Congressional Quarterly Press, 1995).

EARL BLACK AND MERLE BLACK, *The Vital South: How Presidents Are Elected* (Harvard University Press, 1992).

M. MARGARET CONWAY, *Political Participation in the United States*, 4th ed. (Congressional Quarterly Press, 2000).

ROBERT S. ERIKSON AND KENT L. TEDIN, *American Public Opinion: Its Origins, Content and Impact*, 5th ed. (Allyn and Bacon, 1995).

WILLIAM H. FLANIGAN AND NANCY H. ZINGALE, *Political Behavior of the American Electorate*, 10th ed. (Congressional Quarterly Press, 1998).

JOHN G. GEER, *From Tea Leaves to Opinion Polls: A Theory of Democratic Leadership* (Columbia University Press, 1996).

ROBERT HUCKFELDT AND JOHN SPRAGUE, *Citizens, Politics, and Social Communication: Information and Influence in an Election Campaign* (Cambridge University Press, 1995).

LAWRENCE R. JACOBS AND ROBERT Y. SHAPIRO, *Politicians Don't Pander: Political Manipulation and the Loss of Democratic Responsiveness* (University of Chicago Press, 2000).

BRYAN D. JONES, *Reconceiving Decision-Making in Democratic Politics: Attention, Choice and Public Policy* (University of Chicago Press, 1994).

BRUCE E. KEITH, DAVID B. MAGLEBY, CANDICE J. NELSON, ELIZABETH ORR, MARK C. WESTLYE, AND RAYMOND E. WOLFINGER, *The Myth of the Independent Voter* (University of California Press, 1992).

V. O. KEY, JR., *Public Opinion and American Democracy* (Alfred A. Knopf, 1961).

ANTHONY KING, *Running Scared: Why America's Politicians Campaign Too Much and Govern Too Little* (Free Press, 1997).

PHILIP A. KLINKNER, ED., *Midterm: The Elections of 1994 in Context* (Westview Press, 1996).

WARREN E. MILLER AND J. MERRILL SHANKS, *The New American Voter* (Harvard University Press, 1996).

MICHAEL NELSON, ED., *The Elections of 1996* (Congressional Quarterly Press, 1997).

RICHARD G. NIEMI AND HERBERT F. WEISBERG, *Classics in Voting Behavior* (Congressional Quarterly Press, 1993).

RICHARD G. NIEMI AND HERBERT F. WEISBERG, *Controversies in Voting Behavior*, 3d ed. (Congressional Quarterly Press, 1993).

BENJAMIN I. PAGE AND ROBERT Y. SHAPIRO, *The Rational Public: Fifty Years of Trends in Americans' Policy Preferences* (University of Chicago Press, 1992).

FRANK R. PARKER, *Black Votes Count: Political Empowerment in Mississippi After 1965* (University of North Carolina Press, 1990).

GERALD M. POMPER, ED., *The Election of 1996: Reports and Interpretations* (Chatham House, 1997).

SAMUEL L. POPKIN, *The Reasoning Voter: Communication and Persuasion in Presidential Campaigns* (University of Chicago Press, 1991).

JACOB SHAMIR AND MICHAL SHAMIR, *The Anatomy of Public Opinion* (University of Michigan Press, 2000).

SUSAN J. TOLCHIN, *The Angry American: How Voter Rage Is Changing the Nation* (Westview Press, 1996).

JOHN ZALLER, *The Nature and Origins of Public Opinion* (Cambridge University Press, 1992).

See also *Public Opinion Quarterly, American Journal of Political Science*, and *American Political Science Review*.

CAMPAIGNS AND ELECTIONS: DEMOCRACY IN ACTION

9

S OME CYNICS CONTEND THAT ELECTIONS DO NOT MATTER AND THERE IS LITTLE POINT IN VOTING. STRONG EVIDENCE TO THE CONTRARY COMES FROM THE 2000 ELECTIONS, in which Al Gore won the popular vote by 539,947 votes, or only slightly more than 180 votes per county! The contest was especially close in Florida and New Mexico, where the margins were 193 and 366 votes respectively. The contest for the presidency was not the only one that required recounts; in Washington State, Maria Cantwell was elected to the U.S. Senate by 2,229 votes—less than 1 percent of the vote. In Michigan, Mike Rogers won election to the House by 88 votes. In the 2000 election, you could truthfully say that every vote counted.

Although several contests were close, the attention of the nation in the days and weeks after the election was focused on Florida, where the counting and recounting of ballots, the legitimacy of some absentee ballots, and problems with punchcard ballots all ended up in court. At issue in Florida was whether partially punched ballots were valid. Experts debated in the media and testified in court about "dangling chads" (when part of the card is not fully detached) and "pregnant" or "dimpled chads," which show a depression from the stylus used by the voter but are not detached. This confusion meant the officials doing the recount would hold up the punch cards to see if they could see light through the ballot at the spot of the "dimple."

How could it be that in the United States, with computers in every high school, voting technology is so antiquated? The answer in part is that American elections, even presidential elections, are largely governed by *state* law and administered by *local* election officials—typically county clerks. Consequently, the mode of voting can vary from county to county. As a result of the nation's attention being focused on the Florida elections, governments at all levels have started to look for ways to improve voting and election procedures.

In the United States, citizens vote more often and for more offices than citizens of any other democracy. We hold thousands of elections for everything from community college directors to county sheriffs. About half a million persons hold elected state and local offices.[1] In 2000 we elected a president, a vice-president, 33 U.S. senators, all 435 members of the U.S. House of Representatives, 11 governors, plus dozens of treasurers, secretaries of state, and, in most states, judges.

In addition to electing people, voters in 27 states vote on laws or constitutional amendments proposed by initiative petitions or on popular referendums put on the

CHAPTER MEDIA

 POLITICS ONLINE
Who Donates to Which Campaigns in Your Neighborhood?
www.prenhall.com/burns

POLISIM
Election in Action
www.prenhall.com/burns

Important Factors in Winning an Election

Uncontrollable Factors

- Incumbent running
- Strength of party organization
- National tides or landslide possibility
- Socioeconomic makeup of district

Organizational Factors

- Registration drives
- Fund-raising machinery
- Campaign organization
- Volunteers
- Media campaign
- Direct-mail campaign efforts
- Get-out-the-vote efforts

Candidate's Personal Leadership Factors

- Personal appeal
- Knowledge of issues
- Speaking and debating ability
- Commitment and determination
- Ability to earn free, positive media coverage

ballot by petition. In all states except Delaware, voters must approve all changes in the state constitution.

In this chapter we explore our election rules. We note four important problems: the lack of competition for some offices, the complexities of nominating presidential candidates, the distortions of the Electoral College, and the influence of money in our elections. We also discuss proposed reforms in each of these areas.

ELECTIONS: THE RULES OF THE GAME

The rules of the game—the electoral game—make a difference. Although the Constitution sets certain conditions and requirements, most electoral rules remain matters of state law.

Regularly Scheduled Elections

In our system, elections are held at fixed intervals that cannot be changed by the party in power. It does not make any difference if the nation is at war, as we were during the Civil War, or in the midst of a crisis, as in the Great Depression; when the calendar calls for an election, the election is held. Elections for members of Congress occur the first Tuesday after the first Monday in November of even-numbered years. Although there are some exceptions (special elections or peculiar state provisions), participants know *in advance* just when the next election will be. In many parliamentary democracies, such as Great Britain and Canada, the party in power calls elections at a time of its choosing.

Fixed, Staggered, and Sometimes Limited Terms

Our electoral system is based on *fixed terms*, meaning that the length of a term in office is specified, not indefinite. The Constitution has set the term of office for the U.S. House of Representatives at two years, the Senate at six years, and the presidency at four years.

Our system also has *staggered terms* for some offices; not all offices are up for election at the same time. All House members are up for election every two years, but only one-third of the senators are up for election at the same time. Since presidential elections occur two or four years into a senator's six-year term, senators can run for the presidency without fear of losing their seat. But if their Senate term expires the same year as the presidential election, the laws of many states require them to give up their Senate seat to run for president or vice-president or any other position. An example of a state that permits a candidate to stand for election to two offices is Connecticut, where Joe Lieberman was reelected to the U.S. Senate in 2000 while being narrowly defeated in his race for vice-president. Had he been victorious in both campaigns, he would have resigned his Senate seat.

Term Limits

The Twenty-second Amendment to the Constitution, adopted in 1951, limits presidents to two terms. Knowing that a president cannot run again changes the way members of Congress, the voters, and the press regard the president. A politician who cannot, or has announced he or she will not, run again is called a "lame duck." Efforts to limit the terms of other politicians have become a major issue in several American states. The most frequent targets have been state legislators. One consequence of term limits is more lame ducks.

Term limits are popular. Voters in 22 states have enacted them for their state legislature, and even more states limit the term of governors.[2] Three-fourths of all voters favor term limits (9 out of 10 strong Republicans and 7 out of 10 strong Democrats).[3] Still, despite their popularity, proposals for term limits have repeatedly lost when they have come to a vote in recent sessions of Congress.

The Supreme Court, by a vote of 5 to 4, declared that a state does not have the constitutional power to impose limits on the number of terms for which its members of the U.S. Congress are eligible, either by amending its own constitution or by state law.[4] Congress has refused to propose a constitutional amendment to impose a limit on congressional terms.

Winner-Takes-All

An important feature of our electoral system is the **winner-takes-all** rule.[5] In most American electoral settings, the candidate with the most votes wins. The winner does not need to have a *majority* (more than half the votes cast); in a multicandidate race, the winner may have only a *plurality* (the largest number of votes). In 2000, three senators and seven House members were elected by pluralities.

Most American electoral districts are **single-member districts**, meaning that in any district for any given election—senator, governor, U.S. House, state legislative seat—the voters choose *one* representative or official.[6] When a single-member-district system is combined with the winner-takes-all rule, minor parties find it hard to win. For example, even if a third party gets 25 percent of the vote in several districts, it still gets no seats.

The single-member-district and winner-takes-all system is different from a **proportional representation** system, in which political parties secure legislative seats and power in proportion to the number of votes they receive in the election. Let's assume a hypothetical state has three representatives up for election. In each of the three contests, the Republican defeats the Democrat, but in one district by only a narrow margin. If you add up the statewide vote, the Republicans get 67 percent and the Democrats 33 percent. Under our single-member-district and winner-takes-all system, the Republicans get all three seats. But under a system of proportional representation, in which the three seats represent the whole state, the Democrats would receive one seat because they got roughly one-third of the vote in the entire state. Proportional representation thus rewards minor parties and permits them to participate in government. Countries that practice some form of proportional representation include Germany, Israel, and Japan.

The Electoral College

We elect our president and vice-president not by a national vote, but by an indirect device known as the **Electoral College**. The framers of the U.S. Constitution devised this system because they did not trust the choice of president to a direct vote of the people. Under this system each state has as many electors as it has representatives and senators. Thus California will have 55 electoral votes and Vermont 3 for the election of 2004.

Each state legislature is free to determine how its electors are selected. Each party nominates a slate of electors, usually longtime party workers. They are expected to cast their electoral votes for the party's candidates for president and vice-president. In our entire history, no "faithless elector"—an elector who does not vote for his state's popular vote winner—has ever cast the deciding vote. There were no faithless electors in 2000, but one elector from the District of Columbia abstained.

The Twelfth Amendment requires electors to vote separately for president and vice-president. To demonstrate how this works, if you voted for the Republican candidate in 2000, you actually voted for the Republican slate of electors pledged to support George W. Bush for president and Dick Cheney for vice-president.

Candidates who win a plurality of the popular vote in a state secure all that state's electoral votes, except in Nebraska and Maine, which allocate electoral votes to the winner in each congressional district plus two electoral votes for the winner of the state as a whole. Winning electors go to their state capital on the first Monday after the second Wednesday in December to cast their ballots. These ballots are then sent to Congress, and early in January, Congress formally counts the ballots and

winner-takes-all
An election system in which the candidate with the most votes wins.

single-member district
An electoral district in which voters choose one representative or official.

proportional representation
An election system in which each party receives the proportion of legislative seats corresponding to its proportion of the vote.

Electoral College
The electoral system used in electing the president and vice-president, in which voters vote for electors pledged to cast their ballots for a particular party's candidates.

The Electoral Commission of 1877 met in secret session to decide the controversial presidential election between Rutherford B. Hayes and Samuel Tilden. After many contested votes the presidency was eventually awarded to Hayes.

He went on way too long.

declares to the world what everybody already knows—who won the election for president and vice-president.

It takes a majority of the electoral votes to win. If no candidate gets a majority of the electoral votes for president, the House chooses among the top three candidates, with each state delegation having one vote. If no candidate gets a majority of the electoral votes for vice-president, the Senate chooses among the top two candidates, with each senator casting one vote.

When there are only two major candidates for the presidency, the chances of an election being thrown into the House are remote. But twice in our history the House has had to act: in 1800, before the Twelfth Amendment was written, the House had to choose in a tie vote between Thomas Jefferson and Aaron Burr; in 1824 the House picked John Quincy Adams over Andrew Jackson and William Crawford. Henry Clay, who was forced out of the race when he came in fourth in the Electoral College, threw his support behind Adams. When Adams was elected, he made Clay his secretary of state. The 1824 vote in the House was especially contentious. Jackson, winner of the popular vote, was passed over when the vote went to the House. This outcome infuriated Jackson, who won the Electoral College vote by a wide margin four years later.

As we were reminded in 2000, our Electoral College system makes it possible for a presidential candidate to receive the most popular votes, as Al Gore did, and not get enough electoral votes to be elected president. Al Gore won the popular vote by over 500,000 votes but lost the Electoral College 271 to 266.[7] This also happened in 1824, when Andrew Jackson won 12 percent more of the vote than John Quincy Adams; in 1876, when Samuel Tilden received more popular votes than Rutherford B. Hayes; and in 1888, when Benjamin Harrison won in the Electoral College although Grover Cleveland received more popular votes. It almost happened in 1960 and 1976, when the shift of a few votes in a few key states could have resulted in the election of a president without a popular majority. In a year with a serious minor party candidate, the result could be the election of a president without a plurality of the vote, as happened in 2000, when the Green party took enough votes away from Al Gore to have made the difference in Florida and New Hampshire.

In two of the four elections in which winners of the popular vote did not become president, the Electoral College did not decide the winner. The 1824 election was decided by the U.S. House of Representatives. In 1876 the electoral vote in three southern states and Oregon was disputed, resulting in an Electoral Commission deciding how those votes should be counted. In 1888 and 2000 the Electoral College awarded the presidency to the candidate with fewer popular votes.[8]

Concern about the Electoral College is renewed every time there is a serious third-party candidate for the presidency. Even a candidate like Green party candidate Ralph Nader, who got less than 5 percent of the popular vote in 2000, prompted pre-election discussions about his impact on the Electoral College vote. People began to ask: Which Congress casts the vote, the one serving during the election or the newly elected one? The answer is the new one, the one elected in November and taking office the first week in January. Since each state has one vote in the House, what happens if a state's delegation is tied in its vote, 2 to 2 or 3 to 3? Then its vote does not count. Would it be possible to have a president of one party and a vice-president of another? Yes, if the election were thrown into the House and Senate, and each chamber were controlled by a different party.

The Electoral College sharply influences presidential politics. To win a presidential election, a candidate must appeal successfully to the big states of California, Texas, Ohio, and Illinois.[9] California's electoral vote of 54 in 2000 exceeded the combined electoral votes of the 14 least populous states plus the District of Columbia. The map inside the front cover of this book provides a visual comparison of state size based on electoral votes.

Presidential candidates do not ordinarily waste time campaigning in a state unless they have at least a fighting chance of carrying that state; nor do they waste time in a state in which their party is a sure winner. Richard Nixon in 1960 was the last candidate to campaign in all 50 states, but he lost valuable time traveling to and from Alaska, while John Kennedy focused on the more populous states in which he had a chance to win. The contest usually narrows down to the medium-sized and big states, where the balance between the parties tends to be fairly even.

RUNNING FOR CONGRESS

How candidates run for Congress depends on the nature of their district or state, on whether candidates are incumbents or challengers, on the strength of their personal organization, on how well-known they are, and on how much money they have to spend on their campaign. We can, however, note several similarities in House and Senate elections.

First, most congressional elections are not close. In districts where most people belong to one party or where incumbents are popular and enjoy fund-raising and other campaign advantages, there is often little competition.[10] Those who believe competition is essential to constitutional democracy are concerned that so many officeholders have **safe seats**. When officeholders do not have to fight to retain their seat, elections are not performing their proper role.[11]

Competition is more likely when funding is adequate for both candidates, which is not often the case in U.S. House elections. Elections for governor and for the U.S. Senate are more seriously contested and adequately financed than those for the U.S. House of Representatives.

Presidential popularity affects both House and Senate elections during presidential election years as well as midterm elections. The impact of presidential popularity in a presidential election is the **coattail effect**, the boost candidates from the president's party get from a popular presidential candidate running in the same election. But winning presidential candidates do not always provide such a boost. The Republicans suffered a net loss of six House seats in 1988, even though George Bush won the presidency, and the Democrats suffered a net loss of ten house seats in 1992 when Bill Clinton won the presidential election. Democrats fared better in 1996, picking up a net gain of nine house seats. There were no discernible coattails in the 2000 elections. Overall, "measurable coattail effects continue to appear," according to congressional elections scholar Gary Jacobson, but they are "erratic and usually modest" in their impact.[12]

safe seat
An elected office that is predictably won by one party or the other.

coattail effect
The boost candidates of the president's party receive in an election because of the president's popularity.

In midterm elections, presidential popularity and economic conditions have long been associated with the number of House seats a president's party loses.[13] These same factors are associated with how well the president's party does in Senate races, but the association is not as strong.[14] Figure 9–1 shows the number of seats in the House of Representatives and U.S. Senate gained or lost by the party controlling the White House in midterm elections since 1938. Republicans did better in 1994 than in any midterm election since 1946, picking up 53 seats. The Republican tide was not limited to the House but included a net gain of nine Senate seats.[15] In each of these elections until 1998, the party controlling the White House lost seats in the House. The range of losses, however, is quite wide, from a low of 4 seats for the Democrats in 1962 to a high of 71 seats for the Democrats in 1938. The robust economy and President Bill Clinton's high job approval ratings contributed to the success of the Democrats in the 1998 elections.

When presidential landslides occur, as they did with Lyndon Johnson in 1964, the victorious party is especially vulnerable and likely to lose seats in the next midterm election, as the Democrats did in 1966. Given the historic pattern of the president's party losing seats and the close party balance resulting from the 2000 elections, Democrats believe they are well positioned in 2002 to recapture control of both houses of Congress.

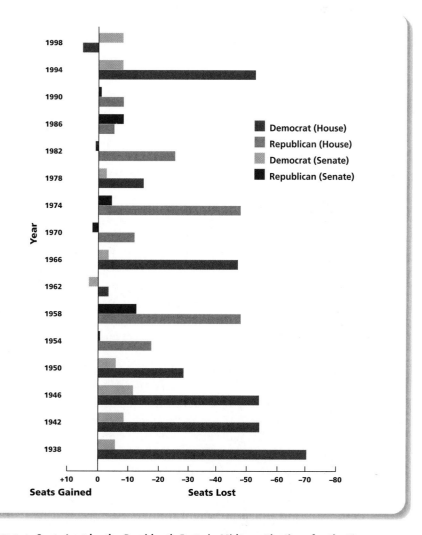

FIGURE 9–1 Seats Lost by the President's Party in Midterm Elections for the House of Representatives and the Senate (1938–1998)

The House of Representatives

Every two years, as many as 1,000 candidates—including approximately 400 incumbents—campaign for Congress. After deciding to take the plunge, candidates must first plan a primary race, unless they face no opponents for their party nomination. Incumbents are rarely challenged for renomination from within their own party, and when they are, the challenges are seldom serious. In the 1990s, for example, on average only two House incumbents were denied renomination each election cycle. Challengers from other parties running against entrenched incumbents rarely encounter opposition in their own party.[16]

MOUNTING A PRIMARY CAMPAIGN   The first step for would-be challengers is to raise hundreds of thousands of dollars to mount a serious campaign. This requires asking friends and acquaintances as well as interest groups for money. Parties can sometimes help, but they shy away from giving money in primary contests. The party organization usually stays neutral until the nomination is decided.

The second step is to build a *personal organization*. A candidate can build an organization while holding another office, such as a seat in the state legislature, or by serving in civic causes, helping other candidates, and being conspicuous without being controversial.

The next steps are to hire campaign managers and technicians, buy television and other advertising, conduct polls, and pay for a variety of activities. All these things depend on raising funds, which most candidates find difficult before they have secured the nomination.

A candidate's main hurdle is gaining visibility. Candidates work hard to be mentioned by the media. In large cities with many simultaneous campaigns, congressional candidates are frequently lost in media "noise," and in rural areas the press often plays down political news. Candidates rely on personal contacts, on hand shaking and door-to-door campaigning, and on identifying likely supporters and courting their favor—the same techniques used in campaigns for lesser offices. The turnout in primaries tends to be low, except in campaigns in which large sums of money are expended on advertising.

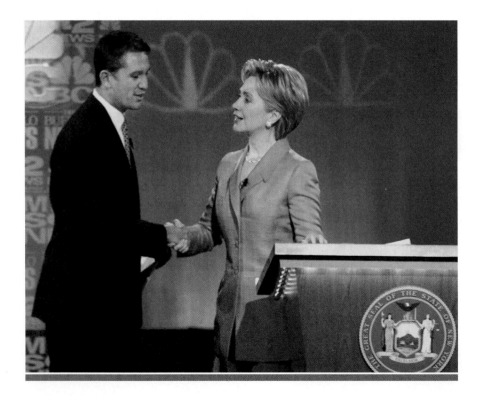

New York U.S. Senate Republican candidate Rick Lazio shakes hands with Democratic candidate Hillary Rodham Clinton in their first televised debate. Here Lazio is challenging Clinton not to use soft money in their race.

"My former opponent is supporting me in the general election. Please disregard all the things I said about him in the primary."

Dunagin's People. Tribune Media Services.

CAMPAIGNING FOR THE GENERAL ELECTION   As we have mentioned, most incumbent members of Congress win reelection.[17] Since 1970, over 95 percent of incumbent House members seeking reelection have won, and in 2000, 98 percent of incumbent House members running for reelection were successful[18] (see Figure 9–2). Incumbents outspent their challengers roughly 3 to 1; in the Senate the difference was closer to 1.75 to 1.[19] Most challengers spend little money, run campaigns that are not significantly more visible than primary campaigns, contact few voters, and lose badly.

Serious challengers in House races are hard to find. Many are scared away by the prospect of having to raise close to a million dollars in campaign funds; others realize the district has been drawn with fewer persons from their party than the incumbent's; and some do not want to face the media scrutiny that comes with a serious race for Congress. Nonetheless, in each election a few challengers mount serious challenges because of the incumbent's perceived vulnerability, the challengers' own wealth, party, or political action committee efforts, or a combination of factors.

Why is keeping a House seat so much easier than gaining it? Incumbents have a host of advantages that help them gain reelection. These "perks" include free mailings to constituents (the *franking* privilege), the free use of broadcast studios to record radio and television tapes to be sent to local media outlets, and perhaps most important of all, a large staff to perform countless favors for constituents and send a stream of press reports and mail back to the district.[20] Representatives also try to win committee posts, even on minor committees, that relate to the needs of their districts and build connections with constituents.[21]

If incumbents win so often, how do we get any significant turnover in the House of Representatives? Turnover comes when incumbents die, decide to retire, or seek some other office. *Redistricting*, which happens once each decade, often promotes some turnover, as it will in 2002, when incumbents are forced to run in new districts. More than one-third of the U.S. House retired between 1992 and 1996. This amount of turnover was unusual and included some members who were disillusioned by partisan bickering.

These retirements and redistricting create *open seats*, which can result in more competitive elections. Potential candidates, as well as political action committees and political party committees, all watch open seat races closely. But as noted, most races have incumbents and most incumbents win, lending credibility to the charge that we have a "permanent Congress."

FIGURE 9–2 U. S. House Incumbents Reelected in 1946–2000

Sources: Federal Election Commission, press release, April 14, 1997, pp. 32–51; "House Membership in the 106th Congress," *Congressional Quarterly Weekly Report*, November 7, 1998, p. 3010; *Congressional Quarterly Weekly Report*, November 11, 2000, p. 2652.

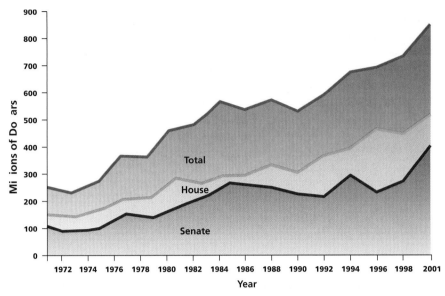

FIGURE 9–3 Rising Campaign Costs (General Elections)

SOURCE: Federal Election Commission: ftp.fcc.gov/fec.

The Senate

Running for the Senate is big-time politics. The six-year term and the national exposure make a Senate seat a glittering prize, so competition is usually intense. Senate campaigns generally feature state-of-the-art campaign technology; a race normally costs millions of dollars[22] (see Figure 9–3). The essential tactics are to raise lots of money, get good people involved, make as many personal contacts as possible (especially in the states with smaller populations), avoid giving the opposition any positive publicity, and have a simple campaign theme. Incumbency is an advantage for senators, although not as much as for representatives.[23] Incumbent senators are widely known, but so are their opponents, who often raise and spend significant amounts of money.[24]

When one party controls the Senate by only a few seats, as has been the case in recent years, more good candidates run, and the number of competitive elections increases. The cost of Senate campaigns can vary greatly. California has 69 times the number of potential voters as Wyoming;not surprisingly, running for a seat from Wyoming is much cheaper than a seat from California. As a result, interest groups and parties direct more money to competitive races in small states when the stakes for control of the Senate are high.[25]

RUNNING FOR PRESIDENT

Presidential elections are major media events, with candidates seeking as much positive television coverage as possible and trying at the same time to avoid negative coverage. The formal campaign has three stages: winning the nomination, campaigning at the convention, and mobilizing support in the general election.

Stage 1: The Nomination

Presidential hopefuls must make a series of critical tactical decisions. The first is when to start campaigning. For the presidential election of 2000, some candidates, like Steve Forbes and Lamar Alexander, began almost as soon as the 1996 presidential election was over. Early decisions are increasingly necessary for candidates to raise the money and assemble an organization. Campaigning begins well before any actual declaration of candidacy, as candidates try to line up supporters to win caucuses or primaries in key states and to raise money for their nomination effort.

One of the hardest jobs for candidates and their strategists is calculating how to deal with the complex maze of presidential primaries and caucuses that constitutes the delegate selection system. The system for electing delegates to the national party convention varies from state to state and often from one party to the other in the same state. Although the process is influenced somewhat by federal regulation of campaign financing and national party rules, within broad limits states can set up the systems they prefer.

PRESIDENTIAL PRIMARIES   State presidential primaries, unknown before 1900, have become the main method of choosing delegates to the national convention. Today more than three-fourths of the states use presidential primaries. In 2000, 84 percent of the Democratic delegates and 89 percent of the Republican delegates were chosen in the primaries.[26] The rest of the delegates were chosen by party caucuses or conventions.

Voters in states like Iowa and New Hampshire, which are the first states to pick delegates, bask in media attention for weeks and even months before they cast the first ballots in the presidential sweepstakes. Because these early contests have had the effect of limiting the choices of voters in states that come later in the process, there has been a tendency for states to move their primaries up. This process is called "front loading." California, which traditionally held its primary in June, moved it to March in 2000 so that its voters would play a more important role in selecting the nominee. Other states did the same thing. On March 7, 16 states had primaries, forcing candidates to pick and choose where they would campaign aggressively. In effect, the 2000 primary season was compressed into several weeks of intense activity in the spring of 2000.

Presidential primaries have two main features: a *beauty contest*, or popularity vote in which voters indicate which candidate they prefer but do not actually elect delegates to the convention, and *actual voting* for delegates pledged to a candidate. Candidates may win the beauty contest and find their opponents doing better in actual delegates elected because they failed to put a full slate of delegates on the ballot or because local notables were listed on the ballot as delegates pledged to another candidate. Different combinations of these two features have produced the following systems:

1. *Proportional representation:* Delegates to the national convention are allocated on the basis of the votes candidates win in the beauty contest. This system has been used in most of the states, including several of the largest ones. The Democrats now mandate a proportional representation rule for all their primaries.[27] In some states Republicans use this same system, but Republicans are much more varied in their delegate selection processes.[28]

2. *Winner-takes-all:* In some states there is a winner-takes-all rule that whoever gets the most votes wins all that state's delegates, as George W. Bush did in the California Republican primary in 2000. To win all the delegates of a state like California is an enormous bonus to a candidate. Republicans still use the winner-takes-all system at the state level, and in 1996 about half of all states used this rule at either the state or congressional district levels.

3. *Delegate selection:* In several states, large and small, voters choose delegates who may or may not have pledged how they will vote in the national party convention. The names of the presidential hopefuls do not appear separately on the ballot, and there is no declared presidential preference. Under this arrangement, delegates are free to exercise their independent judgment at the convention. Only Republicans use this system; in 2000 it was used most prominently in New York and Illinois.

4. *Delegate selection and separate presidential poll:* In several states voters decide twice: once to indicate their choice for president, and again to choose delegates pledged, or at least favorable, to a presidential candidate.[29]

CAUCUSES AND CONVENTIONS   A **caucus** is a meeting of party members and supporters of various candidates. About a dozen states use a caucus and/or convention system for choosing delegates.[30] Each state's parties and legislature regulate them. The caucus or convention is the oldest method of choosing delegates and differs from the primary system because it centers on the party organization.

Delegates who will attend the national party conventions are chosen by delegates to state or district conventions, who themselves are chosen earlier in county, precinct, or town caucuses. The process starts at local meetings open to all party members, who discuss and take positions on candidates and issues and elect delegates to represent their views at the next level. This process is repeated until national nominating convention delegates are chosen by conventions of delegates throughout a district or state.

The best-known example of a caucus is in Iowa, because Iowa has held the earliest caucuses in the most recent presidential nominating contests. Every January or February in a presidential election year, Iowans have the opportunity to attend Republican and Democratic precinct meetings. Large numbers of voters attend these small town meetings and have a chance to meet and exchange views on issues and candidates, rather than merely pulling a lever in a voting booth or placing an X on a ballot.

Presidential hopefuls face a dilemma: to get the Republican nomination you have to appeal to the more intensely conservative Republican partisans, those who vote in primaries and support campaigns. Democratic hopefuls have to appeal to the liberal wing of their party as well as minorities, union members, and environmental activists. But to win the general election, candidates have to win support from moderates and pragmatic voters, many of whom do not vote in the primaries. If candidates get out too far from the moderates in their nomination campaign, they risk being labeled extreme in the general election.

STRATEGIES   Strategies for gaining delegates to the national convention have changed over the years. Some candidates think it wise to skip some of the earlier contests and enter first in states where their strength lies. John McCain pursued such a strategy in 2000, ignoring Iowa and concentrating on New Hampshire. Most candidates choose to run hard in Iowa and New Hampshire, hoping that early showings in these states, which receive a great deal of media attention, will move them into the spotlight for later efforts.

During this early phase, especially important is the ability of candidates to manage the media's expectations of their performance. Lyndon Johnson actually won the New Hampshire primary in 1968, but because Eugene McCarthy did better than the press had predicted, McCarthy was interpreted as the "winner."

Winning in the primaries thus becomes a game of expectations, and candidates may intentionally downplay their expectations so that "doing better than expected" might generate momentum for their campaign. John McCain's surprise victory in New Hampshire in 2000 generated a lot of free publicity and garnered campaign contributions via the Internet.[31] As the race moved to more friendly turf for George W. Bush in South Carolina, Bush won. Al Gore's early victories in Iowa and New Hampshire knocked Bill Bradley out of the race and effectively gave Gore the Democratic nomination.

Stage 2: The Convention

The delegates elected in primaries, caucuses, or state conventions assemble at their **national party convention** in the summer before the election to pick the party's presidential and vice-presidential candidates. In the past, delegates arrived at national nominating conventions with differing degrees of commitment to presidential candidates; some delegates were pledged to no candidate at all, others to a specific candidate for one or two ballots, and others firmly to one candidate only. Recent conventions have merely ratified decisions already made in the primaries and

caucus
A meeting of local party members to choose party officials and/or candidates for public office and to decide the platform.

national party convention
The national meeting of delegates elected in primaries, caucuses, or state conventions who assemble once every four years to nominate candidates for president and vice-president, ratify the party platform, elect officers, and adopt rules.

Every four years since 1856 both major parties have held conventions to nominate candidates for president and vice-president. Conventions bring together delegates from the state parties to represent the wishes of their voters. Successful conventions build party unity, mobilize support for the party nominees, and capture the interest and attention of the nation. Conventions also decide on rules and regulations governing the party, settling controversies surrounding delegate selection (credentials) and party platforms.

The 1968 Democratic National Convention will long be remembered for the more than ten thousand protesters who came to Chicago to oppose the war in Vietnam. Security concerns were high because earlier in 1968 Martin Luther King, Jr. and Robert Kennedy had been assassinated. Televised images of Chicago police using tear gas and night sticks to disperse the crowd not only hurt the Democrats in 1968 but meant neither party held a convention in Chicago for the next 28 years.

The intense battle in the streets of Chicago carried over onto the convention floor as delegates debated the Vietnam plank of the party platform into the early hours of the morning. Civil rights issues nearly tore the Democratic party apart as some southern states still had all-white delegations to the convention. African American delegates sought recognition, and the convention voted to seat some of them over the protest of the white delegates. The party remained badly divided after the Chicago convention and later changed its rules to encourage greater diversity in delegations and more extensive use of direct primaries.

Who attends conventions? Delegates come from all walks of life, yet many are former party leaders or public officials. Republican delegates are more likely to be male than their Democrat counterparts. Aside from the candidates and delegates, the most important people at the conventions are journalists and TV reporters. Thousands from all over the world view these festivities. The parties have an interest in getting a positive "spin" out of the convention, so they work hard to manage the news coverage. Reporters, on the other hand, have an interest in stirring up controversy.

Because the choice of the party nominees has been decided well before the convention, there has been relatively little controversy on the floor of the conventions in recent years. The parties have turned to theatrics and celebrities in an effort to boost the audience watching the televised conventions. They have also shortened the proceedings on network television coverage to only a few hours in the evening. Even with these changes, audience share continued to drop in 2000.

caucuses, in part because delegates are required to pledge themselves to a specific presidential hopeful (in the Democratic party), or because one candidate has been able to amass a majority of delegates. And because of reforms encouraging delegates to stick with the person to whom they are pledged, there has been no room to maneuver at conventions. National party conventions used to be events of high excitement because they determined who would be the party nominee, but in every election since the Republican convention of 1948 and the Democratic convention of 1952, the party primaries have decided who would be the nominee.

As recently as 1988, Democratic and Republican national conventions were given gavel-to-gavel coverage by the major networks, meaning that from the beginning of the first night to the end of the fourth night, millions of people watched. Now the major networks leave comprehensive coverage to C-SPAN and CNN. National nominating conventions have ceased to dominate the national news, for the very good reason that they are no longer the place where candidates are selected.[32] The long-term trend of declining viewership and reduced hours of coverage has altered the parties' strategies. In 2000 the parties featured their most important speakers and highlighted their most important messages in the limited time given them by the networks.

Conventions follow standard rules, routines, and rituals. Usually the first day is devoted to a keynote address and other speeches touting the party and denouncing the opposition; the second day to committee reports, including party and convention rules and the party platform; the third day to presidential balloting; and the fourth to choosing the vice-presidential nominee and winding up with the presidential candidate's acceptance speech.[33]

Both party conventions in 2000 lacked drama. Gone were struggles over the adoption of the platform. For decades the parties have not fought over credentials—that is, over which delegates should be seated. The matter had been in dispute when southern states sent all-white delegations to the Democratic convention. The big news event of the 2000 conventions was Vice-President Gore's prolonged kiss with his wife Tipper before his acceptance speech.

THE PARTY PLATFORM Delegates to the national party conventions decide upon the platform, a statement of party perspectives on public policy. Why does anyone care what is in the party platform? Critics have long pointed out that the party platform is binding on no one and is more likely to hurt than help a candidate. But presidential candidates as well as delegates take the platform seriously because it defines the direction a party wants to take. Also, despite the charge that the platform is ignored, most presidents make an effort to implement it.[34] Neither party had a platform fight in 2000.

THE VICE-PRESIDENTIAL NOMINEE The choice of the vice-presidential nominee generates widespread attention. Rarely does a person actually "run" for the vice-presidential nomination because only the president's "vote" counts. But there is a good deal of maneuvering to capture that one vote. Sometimes the choice of a running mate is made at the convention—not a time conducive to careful and deliberate thought. More often the choice is made before the convention, and the announcement is timed to enhance media coverage and momentum going into the convention. The last time a presidential candidate left the choice of vice-president to the delegates was for the Democrats in 1956.

The hoopla and excitement of the national convention reach a nationwide audience on TV.

Traditionally the presidential nominee chooses a running mate who will "balance the ticket." Democratic presidential nominee Walter Mondale raised this tradition to a dramatic new height in 1984 by selecting a woman, Representative Geraldine A. Ferraro, to run with him. Mondale's bold decision was an effort to strengthen his appeal to women voters. But presidential candidates can also ignore the idea of a balanced ticket, as George W. Bush did when he chose another Texan from the oil industry to be his running mate. Dick Cheney moved his official residence to Wyoming and registered to vote there so that if the Bush-Cheney ticket won the popular vote in Texas, Republican Texas electors could vote for him, since the Constitution (Article II, Section 1) prohibits electors from voting for more than one person for president and vice-president from their own state.

THE VALUE OF CONVENTIONS   Why do the parties continue to have conventions if the nominee is known in advance and the vice-presidential nominee is the choice of one person? What role do conventions play in our system? For the parties, they are a time of "coming together" to endorse a party program and to build unity and enthusiasm for the fall campaign. For candidates as well as other party leaders, conventions are a chance to capture the national spotlight and further their political ambitions. For nominees, they are an opportunity to define themselves in positive ways. The potential is there to heal wounds festering from the primary campaign and move into the general election united, but the potential is not always achieved. Conventions can be potentially divisive, as the Republicans learned in 1964 when conservative Goldwater delegates loudly booed New York Governor Nelson Rockefeller, and as the Democrats learned in 1968 when the convention spotlighted divisions within the party over Vietnam as well as ugly battles between police and protesters near the convention hotels.

NOMINATION BY PETITION   There is a way to run for president of the United States that avoids the grueling process of primary elections and conventions—if you are rich enough or well known enough. John Anderson in 1980 and H. Ross Perot in 1992 met the various state petition requirements or paid the $500 filing fee in Louisiana and made it onto the ballot in all 50 states. In 2000, the petition process was as simple as submitting the signatures of 200 registered voters in Washington State, or as difficult as getting the signatures of 2 percent of voters who voted in the last election in North Carolina (52,000 signatures).[35] Patrick Buchanan, candidate of the Reform party, was able to get his name on the ballot in all but one state and

the District of Columbia, and Ralph Nader, candidate of the Green party, in all but seven states.[36]

Stage 3: The General Election

The national party convention adjourns immediately after the presidential and vice-presidential candidates deliver their acceptance speeches to the delegates and the national television audience. Traditionally, the time between the conventions and Labor Day was a time for resting, binding up convention wounds, gearing up for action, and planning campaign strategy. In recent elections, however, the candidates have not paused after the convention but left the convention engaging in all-out campaigning.[37]

PRESIDENTIAL DEBATES   Televised presidential debates are a major feature of presidential elections. The 1960 debate between John Kennedy and Richard Nixon boosted Kennedy's campaign and elevated the role of television in national politics.[38] In 1976, President Gerald Ford debated Jimmy Carter and mistakenly said that each country in Eastern Europe "is independent, autonomous, it has its own territorial integrity, and none was under Soviet domination." That mistake damaged his credibility. Ronald Reagan's performance in the 1980 and 1984 debates confirmed the public view of him as decent, warm, and dignified. Bill Clinton's skirmishes with George Bush in 1992 and Bob Dole in 1996 showed him to be a skilled performer.

Each of the 2000 debates had a different format, one of which had voters asking George W. Bush and Al Gore questions. The debates did not result in large numbers of voters changing their minds about the candidates; rather, they reinforced voters' prior choices. Al Gore had the advantage of previous debate experience but was seen by critics and even some of his supporters as too aggressive in the first debate—asking for more time to answer charges and adopting a confrontational attitude. In the second debate he was more restrained, probably too much so. George W. Bush avoided any serious mistakes and met or exceeded expectations. As Tom Shales, media critic at *The Washington Post,* reported: George W. Bush "did not make any outrageous goofs, gaffes or bloopers and so the debate will go down as a plus for him."[39]

Since 1988, a nonpartisan Commission on Presidential Debates has sponsored and produced the presidential and vice-presidential debates. The commission includes representatives from such neutral groups as the League of Women Voters. Before the commission became involved, there was often a protracted debate about debates. No detail seemed too small to the candidate managers—whether the candidates will sit or stand, whether they will be able to ask each other questions,

 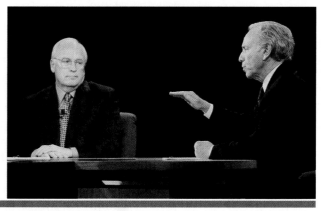

Presidential debates give candidates an opportunity to show how quickly and accurately they can respond to questions and outline their goals. In the debates of the 2000 elections, many viewers felt that the vice-presidential candidates, Dick Cheney and Joseph Lieberman, were more effective than the presidential candidates.

whether they will be allowed to bring notes, and whether the questions will be posed by a single journalist or by a panel of reporters or by a sample of citizens. By negotiating in advance many of the contentious details and arranging for debate locations, the commission now facilitates the presidential and vice-presidential debates. In 2000, George W. Bush proposed alternative formats and locations, only to back down as it appeared he was avoiding debates.

Ralph Nader, the Green party candidate in 2000, charged that the commission had a bias in favor of the two major parties when he and Reform party candidate Pat Buchanan were excluded from the debates. But Nader and Buchanan failed to meet the Commission's criteria for inclusion of minor parties; neither had an average of 15 percent or higher in the five major polls used by the commission for this purpose. The other criteria for minor party candidate inclusion in debates are that the candidate be legally eligible and be on the ballot in enough states to be able to win at least 270 electoral votes.[40] In 1992 Ross Perot and his running mate, James Stockdale, had been included in the presidential and vice-presidential debates, which generated large viewing audiences, averaging more than 80 million for each debate. The issue of excluding minor party candidates remains contentious. Including them takes time away from the major party candidates, especially if two or more minor party candidates are invited. Including them may also reduce the likelihood of both major party candidates participating. But excluding them raises issues of fairness and free speech.

Although some critics are quick to express their dissatisfaction with presidential candidates for being so concerned with makeup and rehearsed answers, and although the debates have not significantly affected the election outcomes, they have provided important opportunities for candidates to distinguish themselves and for the public to weigh their qualifications. Candidates who do well in these debates are at a great advantage. They have to be quick on their feet, well rehearsed, and project a positive image. But these are not necessarily the qualities that make for a successful presidency.

Although each election is unique, politicians, pollsters, and political scientists have collected enough information to agree broadly on a number of basic factors they believe affect election outcomes. Whether the nation is prosperous probably has the most to do with who wins a presidential election, but, as we have noted, most voters vote on the basis of party and candidate appeal.[41] Who wins depends on voter turnout. The Democrats' advantage in number of people who identify themselves as Democrats is mitigated by the higher voter turnout among Republicans. Republicans also usually have better access to money, which means they can put on more television ads in more places and more often. In 2000, the Democrats achieved financial parity with the Republicans and more effectively targeted resources to key Senate races.[42]

MONEY IN AMERICAN ELECTIONS

Election campaigns cost money, and the methods of obtaining the money have long been controversial. Campaign money can come from a candidate's own wealth, political parties, interested individuals, or interest groups. Money is contributed to candidates for a variety of reasons, ranging from altruism to self-interest. Individuals or groups, in hopes of influencing the outcome of an election and subsequently influencing policy, give **interested money**. Concern about campaign finance stems from the possibility that candidates, in their pursuit of campaign funds, will decide it is more important to represent their contributors than their conscience or the voters. The potential corruption that results from politicians' dependence on interested money concerns many observers of American politics.

Scandals about money influencing policy are not new. In 1925, responding to the Teapot Dome scandal in which a cabinet member was convicted of accepting bribes, Congress passed the Corrupt Practices Act, which required disclosure of campaign funds but was "written in such a way as to exempt virtually all of them [members of Congress] from its provisions."[43]

interested money
Contributions by individuals or groups in hopes of influencing the outcome of an election and subsequently influencing policy.

THE SOFT MONEY LOOPHOLE IN JAPAN

The Japanese strategy to combat corruption and money politics has been to create some of the most stringent campaign regulations in the world:

- Door-to-door campaigning is banned.

- Candidates may not run campaign advertisements in the media although parties may.

- Each campaign may produce only two versions of its campaign brochure, and only a limited number may be distributed; the number varies according to the number of registered voters in a district.

- Campaign posters are allowed only on government-provided poster boards that are set up in several locations across a district during the campaign.

- Direct mailing of campaign literature is not allowed except for a specified number of government-provided campaign postcards.

- The number of campaign offices, employees, and vehicles is restricted by law.

These regulations should make it impossible for candidates to raise and spend large sums of money in a campaign, but Japanese candidates have found a giant loophole in these restrictions by avoiding "official" campaign activities. A candidate will go door-to-door or mail out literature to voters or put up posters *before* the official campaign period. In these precampaign activities, the candidates will be very careful never to mention the upcoming election, so their efforts are not covered by law.

Attempts to limit these activities have run into constitutional concerns. If a campaign has not begun and a person has not declared his or her candidacy, how can the Japanese government restrict the right of a citizen to hold meetings, discuss issues with people, mail information to people, or put up posters? In a similar manner, concern for free speech led to the soft money loophole in U.S. campaign restrictions.

The 1972 Watergate scandal—an illegal break-in of Democratic party headquarters by persons associated with the Nixon campaign to steal campaign documents and plant listening devices—led to discoveries by news reporters and congressional investigators that large amounts of money from corporations and individuals were "laundered" in secret bank accounts outside the country for political and campaign purposes. Nixon's 1972 campaign spent more than $60 million, more than twice what it had expended in 1968. Investigators discovered that wealthy individuals made large contributions to influence the outcome of the election or secure ambassadorships and administrative appointments.

In the early 1990s, Charles Keating and his failed Lincoln Savings and Loan spotlighted the possibility that undue influence comes with large contributions. Keating had asked five U.S. senators, all of whom had received substantial campaign contributions or other "perks" from him, to intervene on his behalf with federal bank regulators looking into his savings and loan business. These senators came to be called the Keating Five. One of the Senators was John McCain, who has since become a strong advocate of campaign finance reform.

The high costs of television advertising diminish the ability of challengers to mount visible campaigns, resulting in declining competition. Incumbents have a substantial advantage in raising interested money from wealthy individuals and political action committees (PACs). Hence it is not only the source of campaign money that is a problem but the pattern of unequal distribution as well.

During the 2000 presidential nomination battles, the Republican candidate John McCain and Democratic candidates Al Gore and Bill Bradley stressed campaign finance reform. McCain, more than any candidate, emphasized the role of large donors to both parties and the negative influences these individuals and groups have on the political process. Vice-President Gore inherited the negative publicity of the Clinton administration's fund-raising tactics, which included rewarding large donors with overnight stays in the White House and invitations to policy discussions. More incriminating, Gore had participated in a fund raiser at a Buddhist temple in 1996 at which illegal campaign contributions were made. This incident was fodder for ads against Gore by the Republican party in the general election. George W. Bush, after losing the New Hampshire primary, emphasized his own commitment to political reform with the slogan, "Reformer with Results"; still, he resisted endorsing any particular campaign finance reform agenda.

Efforts to Reform

Reformers have tried three basic strategies to prevent abuse in political contributions: (1) imposing limitations on giving, receiving, and spending political money; (2) requiring public disclosure of the sources and uses of political money; and (3) giving governmental subsidies to presidential candidates, cam-

paigns, and parties. Recent campaign finance laws have tended to use all three strategies.

THE FEDERAL ELECTION CAMPAIGN ACT   In 1971 Congress passed two significant laws dealing with campaign funding. The Federal Election Campaign Act (FECA) limited amounts that candidates for federal office can spend on advertising, required the disclosure of the sources of campaign funds as well as how they are spent, and required political action committees to register with the government and report all major contributions and expenditures. This 1971 law also provided a checkoff that allowed taxpayers to contribute $1 to a fund to subsidize presidential campaigns by checking a box on their income tax form. The checkoff option is now $3.

In 1974 Congress passed and President Gerald Ford signed the most sweeping campaign reform measure in U.S. history. These amendments to the Federal Election Campaign Act established somewhat more realistic limits on contributions and spending, tightened disclosure, and provided for public financing of presidential campaigns.

The 1974 law was extensively amended after the 1976 *Buckley v Valeo* decision, which overturned several of its provisions on grounds that they violated the First Amendment.[44] The *Buckley* decision emphasized limitations on contributions and full and open disclosure of all fund-raising activities by candidates for federal office, as well as the system of public financing for presidential elections.[45] The Supreme Court made a distinction between campaign spending and campaign contributions, holding that the First Amendment protects spending; therefore, legislatures may not limit how much of their own money people spend on elections, but Congress may limit how much people contribute to somebody else's campaign. Later modifications of the law and court interpretations sought to encourage volunteer activities and party building by permitting national political parties, corporations, labor unions, and individuals to give unlimited amounts, called **soft money**, to state parties, provided the funds are used for party-building purposes.

The public subsidy of presidential candidates has started to break down. Until 2000, presidential candidates (except wealthy self-financed candidates) accepted the voluntary limitations that come with partial public financing of presidential campaigns. George W. Bush, who raised more than $125 million for his campaign,[46] declined federal matching funds in the 2000 primaries, but accepted the federal subsidy of $67.5 million for the general election and with it the limits on how much his campaign could spend. Whether future candidates will also pass up some federal funds depends on how well funded their opponents are and their own ability to raise money. Beyond the problem of candidates passing up the federal funds, the number of taxpayers checking the campaign subsidy on their income tax forms has been declining, although enough did so to cover all the costs of the 2000 elections.[47]

The Unsolved Problem of Soft Money

The most serious problem with the presidential campaign finance system is soft money—funds given to state and local parties by political parties, individuals, or political action committees ostensibly for party-building registration drives, mailings, and advertising, which do not specify a candidate by name. No limits are set on the amount of such contributions. The money is called "soft" because federal law does not limit how much individuals or groups can contribute or how much parties can spend. Although soft money is supposed to benefit only parties, it is used by the parties to influence the election of federal candidates. Both parties have made raising

The Federal Election Campaign Act (1971) and Amendments (1974)

- Establishes a Federal Election Commission appointed by the president with the advice and consent of the Senate to regulate the campaign financing of candidates for president, senator, and representative.

- Provides for public financing of presidential general election campaigns with funds from the income tax checkoff.

- Provides for partial public financing on a matching basis of presidential nominating campaigns.

- Provides for subsidies to the two national parties for their convention expenses and to any minor party that polled 5 percent of the total vote in the previous presidential election.

- Limits spending by candidates for presidential nominations (on a state-by-state basis and in total) and in the presidential general elections for those candidates who accept public funding.

- Limits the amounts that national parties may spend on presidential campaigns and on individual congressional and senatorial campaigns.

- Sets a limit of $1,000 on the amount that any individual can give to a candidate for the U.S. Senate or for the U.S. House of Representatives in the primary election; a limit of $1,000 per candidate in the general election; and a limit of $5,000 per candidate per election ($5,000 in primary and $5,000 in general election) for political action committees.

- Sets an overall limitation of $25,000 on the amount that any individual can donate to all candidates for federal office in an election cycle; no similar limitation applicable to political action committees.

- Sets no limit on the amount of their own money candidates can spend on their campaign.

- Sets no limit on the amount that individuals or groups can spend independently.

soft money
Money contributed to a state or local party for party-building purposes that does not have to be disclosed under federal law.

When Is an issue ad an election ad?

Political ads have many different purposes: some are about issues, attempting to persuade the audience to a point of view; others are about a candidate's qualifications; and still others are about both issues and candidates. But does the content of an advertisement indicate the ad's purpose?

Assume it is a few weeks before an election, and you are watching an ad on TV or listening to one on the radio. Ask yourself if what you are seeing or hearing is only about issues, or if it is about electing or defeating a candidate. Does it:

Show an image or likeness of a candidate?

Mention a candidate by name?

Mention an election?

Use words like "vote for," "vote against," "support. . . ."?

Is it shown in the weeks before an election?

Defining characteristics like these are important because they can determine whether this is an "issue advertisement." As the current law states, only if an ad uses a candidate's name and words like "vote for" or "vote against" is it about electing or defeating a candidate and therefore subject to limitations or regulation.

issue advocacy
Commercial advertising on radio and television advocating a particular position on an issue, paid for by interest groups and designed to influence voters' choices on election day.

independent expenditures
Money spent by individuals or groups not associated with candidates to elect or defeat candidates for office.

soft money a high priority. Soft money spending has risen dramatically. All national party committees combined raised over $487 million of soft money in the 1999–2000 election cycle, up from $78 million in 1991–1992[48] (see Figure 9–4).

Soft money has brought back the large donors as major players in campaign finance. It has also strengthened the power of the national party committees, which allocate the money to state parties and indirectly to candidates. In 2000, national and congressional party committees spent nearly one-half billion dollars in soft money; Democratic party soft money spending pulled even with the Republicans. In the past, soft money had been more important in presidential than in congressional contests, but that changed in a dramatic way with the 1998 and 2000 congressional elections. The most dramatic growth in 2000 came among Senate Democrats, who raised only $372,000 in soft money in 1994 but raised $63 million in 1999–2000—a surge in spending that helped Senate Democrats pick up a net gain of four Senate seats, resulting in a 50 to 50 Senate. Figure 9–4 plots the surge in soft money funds for the four congressional campaign committees.

ISSUE ADVOCACY ADVERTISING   The 1996 election saw a surge in a campaign activity called **issue advocacy**. Money spent on issue advocacy ads is unlimited because it presumably deals with issues, not candidates. Issue ad spending in some U.S. House races has exceeded $1 million in recent elections; for example, in 2000, one group, the Alliance for Quality Nursing Home Care, spent more than $1 million on issue ads in the Delaware U.S. Senate race.[49] In the 1998 and 2000 elections, businesses, labor unions, health maintenance organizations, the Sierra Club, the League of Conservation Voters, the Business Roundtable, pro- and anti-gun groups, pro- and anti-abortion groups, and the pharmaceutical industry ran issue ads (see Table 9–1). These ads not only help the candidate interest groups prefer or punish the candidate they oppose; they also force candidates to discuss the interest group's agenda. While these ads do not specifically say to vote for or against a candidate, they do contain candidates' images and names.

The use of issue ads and the growth in soft money mean that competitive congressional elections are shifting from candidate-centered elections to party- and interest group-centered campaigns.[50] Soft money spending combined with interest group issue advocacy spending exceeded the candidate campaigns in radio and television advertising by a margin of 2 to 1 in 17 of the most competitive congressional races of 2000.[51] Parties and interest groups also spend large sums of money on mail

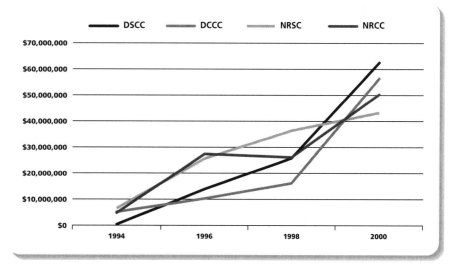

FIGURE 9–4 Congressional Campaign Committee Soft Money Spending, 1994–2000

Source: Federal Election Commission, "Party Fundraising Escalates," press release, January 12, 2001, at fecweb1.fec.gov/press/011201partyfunds.htm.

and on the telephone. For example, in some congressional races in 2000, targeted voters received as many as 12 pieces of political mail per day as election day approached.[52]

One of the problems with issue ads is accountability. Since these interest groups are not required to disclose how much they spend or how they raise their money, voters have a hard time knowing the source of the funds. Ads by these groups also tend to be more negative. Often candidates get blamed for the attacks made by these groups because voters assume the ads are run by the candidates. Finally, because of the amounts of money involved and the negative tone of the communications, issue advocacy has reinforced cynicism and alienation among voters.

Some senators have proposed requiring disclosure of the identity of groups doing issue advertising in the 30 to 60 days before congressional and presidential elections; they define issue advertising as communication that mentions a candidate by name or shows the image or likeness of a candidate.

Defenders of issue ads point to recent ad campaigns that focused on legislation, like those mounted by tobacco companies in 1998 to defeat a tobacco tax in the Senate or ads run by insurance companies attacking the Clinton health care plan in 1994. Because issue advocacy ostensibly lacks a campaign or election referent, it is likely to be protected as free speech. Drawing a distinction between genuine issue advocacy and election issue advocacy is not easy, but election issue ads occur in the weeks before an election and frequently have the image of a candidate or mention the candidate by name.[53]

CANDIDATES' PERSONAL WEALTH   Campaign finance legislation cannot constitutionally restrict rich candidates—the Rockefellers, the Kennedys, the Perots—from giving heavily to their own campaigns. Big money makes a big difference, and wealthy candidates can afford to spend big money. In presidential politics, this advantage can be most meaningful in the period before the primaries begin. There may be no constitutional way to limit how much money people can spend on their own campaigns. The 2000 New Jersey U.S. Senate race set new records for a candidate spending personal wealth in an election. Wall Street investment banker John Corzine, a newcomer to elections, spent a total of $60 million, with $35 million of it spent in the primary alone.[54]

INDEPENDENT EXPENDITURES   Current finance laws do not constrain **independent expenditures** by groups or individuals who are separate from political candidates. This loophole has been permitted by the Supreme Court on free speech grounds. Groups sympathetic to, but independent of, candidates are allowed to raise and spend unlimited funds to help elect them or to defeat their opponents. For example, in 1984 Michael Goland, a Californian, spent $1,100,740 as an independent expenditure to defeat Illinois Senator Charles Percy.[55] As long as there is no collusion between the independent spender and the candidate, an individual or PAC can spend an unlimited amount of money for or against a candidate.

Issue ads have largely replaced independent expenditures in recent election cycles because interest groups can spend the same amount of money without having to disclose the activity. Some groups like the National Rifle Association and National Education Association continue to use independent expenditures, however, perhaps because they want to urge voters to "vote for" or "vote against" specific candidates, words you cannot include in an issue ad.

Consequences of Current Campaign Financing

The problems with federal election fund raising are easy to identify: dramatically escalating costs, a growing dependence on PAC money, decreasing visibility and competitiveness of challengers (especially in the House), the ability of

TABLE 9–1 Top Ten Issue Advertisers, 2000 (in millions)	
Citizens for Better Medicare	$64
AFL-CIO	$45
Coalition to Protect America's Health Care	$30
National Rifle Association	$25
U.S. Chamber of Commerce	$15
Planned Parenthood Action Fund	$14
Business Roundtable	$13
Federation for American Immigration Reform	$12
NAACP National Voter Fund	$11
Americans for Job Security	$10

SOURCES: Data from David B. Magleby, ed., *Election Advocacy: Soft Money and Issue Advocacy in the 2000 Congressional Elections* (Center for the Study of Elections and Democracy, Brigham Young University, 2001); Erika Falk, "Issue Advocacy Advertising Through the Presidential Primary: 1999–2000 Election Cycle," Annenberg Public Policy Center, press release, September 20, 2000.

NOTE: The numbers estimate total spending: issue advocacy and express advocacy. However, a large proportion of the totals were issue advocacy.

Thinking It Through . . .

Based on a distinction in the *Buckley v Valeo* Supreme Court decision, communications that do not use words such as "vote for" or "vote against" are considered issue ads, which are not subject to the same disclosure rules as ads that are about electing or defeating a candidate. But in the context of an election, it is possible to convey a positive or negative election message without using these words. Some of these ads end by telling viewers to "Call" or "Write" the candidate to express support or opposition. But the real intent of the message is to get the audience to vote for or against a candidate.

Research on the types of ads run in election cycles have found that less than 10 percent were only about issues and not about candidates. Research also shows that people do not think it necessary to use words like "vote for" in order to convey an election message, but that even showing the candidate's image is enough to convey that the ad is about electing or defeating a candidate.

Opponents to limiting or prohibiting issue ads point out that Congress is often in session until a few days before an election, and interest groups need to be able to inform the public about important issues that are being considered. To limit issue ads during this period may stifle the free speech of groups with a more legislative than electoral agenda.

A Closer Look

CAMPAIGN FINANCE REFORM

For several years Congress has considered campaign finance reform. However, due to a presidential veto, the lack of action by one house or the other, or the use of legislative obstructions, only minor changes have been enacted. Despite scandals involving the president and members of Congress that resulted in protracted legislative hearings and numerous editorials, Congress failed to pass changes in our campaign finance laws.

The most visible advocate of reform is Arizona Senator John McCain, who, ironically, was part of a scandal involving campaign contributions by Charles Keating, owner of a failed Savings and Loan. McCain made campaign finance reform a theme of his 2000 presidential campaign, forcing his rival, George W. Bush, to characterize himself as a "reformer with results." Although he lost the nomination to Bush, McCain continued to beat the campaign finance

reform drum and was successful in getting Senate leadership to schedule an early debate and vote on his bill, the McCain–Feingold–Cochran bill.

President Bush did not make campaign finance reform a high priority in his new administration. Bush's own proposal included what some saw as a "poison pill" for the bill, a requirement that union members must sign-off annually for their political contributions to their unions.

The 2000 elections resulted in a U.S. Senate more supportive of campaign finance reform and without enough votes for its opponents to sustain a filibuster. The result was passage of McCain-Feingold-Cochran by a vote of 59 to 41. The Senate version of the bill closely resembled versions of the legislation that had passed the House in 1998 and again in 1999.

Opponents of the legislation in the House sought to delay consideration of the bill. If the bill passed, opponents

In the opening weeks of the 2001 session, Senators John McCain and Russ Feingold kept up the fight for campaign finance reform that had failed to gain Senate approval in 1997 and 1998 but was successful in 2001.

hoped to force a conference committee that which would either kill the bill or force the Senate to reconsider and possibly reject it. President Bush was noticeably noncommittal as to whether or not he would sign the Senate version of the bill.

---

wealthy individuals to fund their own campaigns, and the danger of large contributions altering election outcomes. These problems are exacerbated by soft money and issue advocacy, which have moved to the top of the agendas of campaign finance reformers.

RISING COSTS OF CAMPAIGNS The American ideal that anyone—a person from humble beginnings or of modest wealth—should be able to run for public office is quickly becoming impossible. And rising costs mean incumbents spend more time raising funds and therefore less time legislating and representing their districts. Since the Federal Election Campaign Act became law in 1972, total expenditures by candidates for the House of Representatives have more than doubled after controlling for inflation, and they have risen even more in Senate elections (see Table 9–2). Television advertising is expensive, limiting the field of challengers to those who can spend more than a year raising money.

DECLINING COMPETITION Unless something is done to help finance challengers, incumbents will continue to have the advantage in seeking reelection. Challengers in both parties are typically underfunded. House Democratic challengers averaged $168,650 in spending in 2000.[56] In today's expensive campaigns, candidates are invisible if they can spend only two or three hundred thousand dollars.

The high cost of campaigns dampens competition by discouraging individuals from running for office. Potential challengers look at the fund-raising advantages enjoyed by incumbents—at incumbents' campaign war chests, which sometimes

A candidate's personal fortune has played a big role in recent elections. Jon Corzine's $60 million investment won him the New Jersey seat in the U.S. Senate in 2000.

TABLE 9–2 Average Campaign Expenditures of Candidates for the House of Representatives, 1988–2000 General Election (1998 Dollars in Thousands)

	Incumbent	Challenger	Open Seat
Republican			
1988	$563.8	$138.4	$1123.5
1990	496.5	138.2	1036.8
1992	617.7	219.3	727.5
1994	506.4	263.1	1111.8
1996	766.9	219.6	653.5
1998	668.9	245.1	709.2
2000	883.0	310.1	1200.0
Democrat			
1988	$493.6	$198.1	$616.0
1990	501.3	137.8	667.8
1992	702.6	186.8	560.2
1994	665.0	174.2	639.6
1996	593.7	307.9	652.5
1998	539.5	232.9	709.8
2000	735.7	454.0	1100.0

SOURCES: Federal Election Commission, "Congressional Fundraising and Spending Up Again in 1996," press release, April 14, 1997, p. 13; Federal Election Commission, "1998 Congressional Financial Activity Declines," press release, December 29, 1998, p. 5; ftp.fec.gov/fec.

have $1 million before the campaign even starts, and at the time it will take for them to raise enough money to launch a minimal campaign—and they decide to direct their energies elsewhere. Moreover, unlike incumbents, who are being paid while campaigning and fund raising, most challengers have to support themselves and their families for the duration of the campaign, which for the House and Senate is roughly two years.

INCREASING DEPENDENCE ON PACS AND WEALTHY DONORS   Where does the money come from to finance these expensive election campaigns? For most House incumbents the answer is political action committees (PACs), which we discussed in Chapter 6 as well. In 2000, for instance, 191 of the 408 incumbents seeking reelection raised more money from PACs than from individuals[57] (see Figure 9–5). Senators get a smaller percentage of their campaign funds from PACs, but because they spend so much more, they need to raise even more money from PACs than House incumbents do. Challengers receive little from PACs because PACs do not want to offend politicians in power.

To be sure, PACs and individuals give political money for many reasons. Most of them want certain laws to be passed or repealed, certain funds appropriated, or certain administrative decisions rendered. At a minimum, they want access to office-holders, a chance to talk with members before key votes.

Defenders of PACs point out that there is no demonstrable relationship between contributions and legislators' votes. But influence in the legislative process depends on access to staff and members of Congress, and most agree that campaign contributions give donors unusual access. PACs influence the legislative process in other ways as well. Their access helps them structure the legislative agenda with friendly legislators and influence the drafting of legislation or amendments to existing bills. These are all advantages that others do not have.

FIGURE 9–5 PAC Money Favors Incumbents

SOURCE: Federal Election Commission; ftp.fec.gov/fec.

IMPROVING ELECTIONS

A combination of party rules and state laws determines how we choose nominees for president. Reformers agree that the current process is flawed but disagree over which aspects require change.

Concern over how we choose presidents now centers on four issues: (1) the number, timing, and representativeness of presidential primaries; (2) the role of the Electoral College, including the possibility that a presidential election might be thrown into the House of Representatives;[58] (3) how we vote; and (4) campaign finance reform.

Reforming Presidential Primaries

Presidential primaries open the nominating process to more voters than do caucus or convention methods for selecting presidential candidates. Today the media play up the primary in every important state, and voters follow the races in other states as well as their own. In so doing, they can judge the candidates' political qualities: their abilities to organize campaigns, communicate through the media, stand up under pressure, avoid making mistakes (or recover if they do make them), adjust their appeals to shifting events and to different regions of the country, control their staffs as well as utilize them, and be decisive, articulate, resilient, humorous, informed, and ultimately successful in winning votes. In short, supporters claim, primaries test candidates on the very qualities they must exhibit in the presidency.[59]

Critics of primaries grant that more voters take part in primaries than in the caucus and convention methods of choosing delegates, but they question the quality of the participation. For one thing, supporters of the different candidates have no opportunity to deliberate together in public. Voters in caucuses can argue and persuade one another in small meetings; voters in primaries must depend largely on the news media and advertising for their information and basis for judgment. Voters in primaries tend to be more influenced by candidates' personalities and media skills than their positions on vital issues.[60]

Participation in primaries has been low in recent years (see Figure 9–6). In the 2000 primaries, turnout was generally under 18 percent of the voting-age population, and it declined as the primary season progressed and the field of candidates narrowed.[61] Low levels of turnout in primaries open the possibility that extreme groups will have a

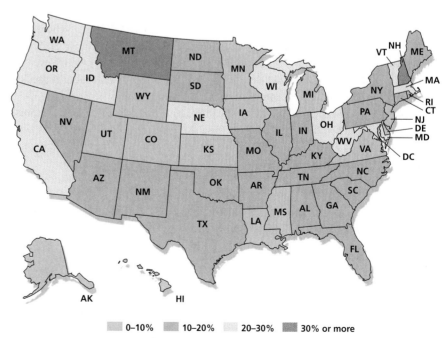

0–10%   10–20%   20–30%   30% or more

FIGURE 9–6 **Voter Turnout in the 2000 Presidential Primaries**

disproportionate say; the "selectorate" replaces the electorate. In addition, candidates are forced to appeal to highly motivated voters, usually from the conservative wing of the Republican party and the liberal wing of the Democratic party.

For many years the primary season was criticized for being too long.[62] Some states, by virtue of coming early in the process, had a disproportionate say in determining the nominee and therefore were more influential with presidents. Several states moved up their primary dates in 2000 so that 48 percent of the Republican and 37 percent of the Democratic delegates were selected by March 7.[63] Not surprisingly, Al Gore and George W. Bush had their nominations locked up by this date. States that came later in the process found the nominee had already been selected.

Finally, some critics question whether primaries test the qualities needed to be president. To win "the media game," candidates must be witty, resourceful, attractive, and articulate—not necessarily the most important qualities to be a good president. Thomas Jefferson, Abraham Lincoln, and Harry Truman were able presidents, but they did not have great "media appeal." Critics are disturbed by the gap between the qualities required to carry primary contests and the qualities needed to govern: to organize an administration, get support on issues, make hard decisions, and deal with congressional leaders, governors, and mayors.

Reforming the Nominating Process

What would the critics substitute for state presidential primaries? Some argue in favor of a *national presidential primary* that would take the form of a single nationwide election, probably held in May or September, or separate state primaries held in all the states on the same day. Supporters contend that a one-shot national presidential primary (though a runoff might be necessary) would be simple, direct, and representative. It would cut down the wear and tear on candidates, and it would attract a large turnout because of intensive media coverage. Opponents argue that such a reform would make the present system even worse. It would enhance the role of showmanship and gamesmanship; and, being enormously expensive, it would hurt the chances of candidates who lack strong financial backing.[64]

A more modest proposal is to hold *regional primaries*, possibly at two- or three-week intervals across the country. Regional primaries might bring more coherence to the process, encourage more emphasis on issues of regional concern, and also cut down on wear and tear. But such primaries would retain most of the disadvantages of the present system—especially the emphasis on money and media. Clearly, they would give an advantage to candidates from whatever region held the first primary, and this advantage would encourage regional candidates and might increase polarization among sections of the country.

A different proposal is to drastically reduce the number of presidential primaries and make more use of the caucus system. The turnout of voters in the Iowa caucuses in recent elections shows that participation can be high, and the time participants spent discussing candidates and issues shows that such participation can be thoughtful and informed. In caucus states, candidates are less dependent on the media and more dependent on convincing political activists. By centering delegate selection in party meetings, the caucus system would also, some say, enhance the role of the party.[65]

Still another idea—used by Colorado for nominations to state offices and by Utah for nominations to federal and state office—would turn the process around. Beginning in May, local caucuses and then state conventions would be held in every state. They would then send delegates—a certain percentage of whom would be unpledged to any presidential candidate—to the national party conventions, which would be held in the summer. The national conventions would select two or three candidates to compete in a national primary to be held in September. In this plan, voters registered by party would be allowed to vote for their party nominee in the September primaries.[66]

PEOPLE

It counts some votes as more important than others, according to the state in which they are cast.

THE ELECTORAL COLLEGE IS NOT FAIR

Lawrence D. Longley

Long before the curent controversy surrounding who won the 2000 presidential election, Americans have debated whether to abolish the Electoral College and what to replace it with. George W. Bush was the first candidate since Benjamin Harrison in 1888 to loose the popular vote but win office through the Electoral College. The failure of the popular vote winner to gain office in 2000 makes the debate over reform of the Electoral College a more salient issue.

Professor Lawrence D. Longley, in testimony before Congress, points out the unfair effects of the Electoral College:

The Electoral College means of presidential election is of great significance, even when it produces a clear decision. The Electoral College is not a neutral and fair counting device for tallying popular votes cast for President in the form of electoral votes. Instead, it counts some votes as more important than others, according to the state in which they are cast. As a result, these distortions of popular preferences greatly influence candidate strategy: certain key states, their voters, parochial interests, political leaders, and unique local factions, are favored.

The Electoral College election of the President also discriminates among types of candidates. Independent or third-party contenders with a regional following have great opportunities for Electoral College significance, while independent or third-party candidates with broad-based but nationally distributed support may find themselves excluded from winning any Electoral College votes. Even without receiving electoral votes, however, such candidates can prove decisive in terms of swinging large blocs of electoral votes from one major party candidate to the other.

Finally, the Electoral College can reflect inaccurately the popular will because of the action of faithless electors—individual electors who vote differently in the electoral college from the expectations of those who elected them. ★

SOURCE: Statement of Lawrence D. Longley, Professor of Government at Lawrence University, before the U.S. Senate Committee on the Judiciary Subcommittee on the Constitution, July 21-22, 1992.

DEBATE

THE ELECTORAL COLLEGE FORMS A CONSENSUS

Senator Patrick Moynihan

It is easier to point out the limitations of the Electoral College than it is to come up with a process that does not also have significant problems. The most frequently proposed reform—eliminate the Electoral College and elect the popular vote winner—has the disadvantage of placing the entire country into a position where recounts might be necessary. Indeed, if the automatic recount provisions in most states had been in place in 2000, all ballots would have had to be recounted. As former Senator Patrick Moynihan articulated, there are other problems with proposed reforms as well:

> There is no fact more singular about our Constitution than its durability. . . No other large industrial . . . nation has anything like our experience of a sustained and stable government under a written constitution basically unchanged from its original construction. . . I would stress . . . the idea that the Founding Fathers had learned from history . . . the representation directly and indirectly of people and States. . . a principle that involved not just one majority, but in the most important sense, many majorities.
>
> Dr. Judith Best . . . has spoken at length . . . on the principle of concurrent

majorities. . . She said, " . . . the principle of concurrent majority is, has been, and was intended to be the American idea of democracy because the size of the popular vote is not sufficient to maintain liberty." . . . The Electoral College requires the assembly of . . . concurrent majorities—in one part of the country and another part of the country, and yet another part, all defined in terms of several States. It has as its extraordinary ability the formation of consensus as between widely differing regions, political purposes and styles, and political agendas. It has as its purpose and function the narrowing of differences. . .

> . . . the proposal before us [direct election of the president], in the guise of perfecting an alleged weakness in the Constitution, proposes the most radical transformation in our constitutional system that has ever been considered. I remarked that the Founders devised our system with the idea of a network of concurrent majorities which would be required to exercise power. The fundamental thrust of this measure . . . would be to abolish that principle of concurrent majority. ★

SOURCE: Senator Daniel Patrick Moynihan (D., NY) on the floor of the United States Senate, June 27, 1979; Judith A. Best, *The Choice of the People?* (Rowman & Littlefield Publishers, Inc., 1996), pp. 85-86; 151-159.

It has as its purpose and function the narrowing of differences.

For further information about this debate, go to **www.prenhall.com/burns** *and click on the Debate Icon in Chapter 9.*

Reforming the Electoral College

The Florida ballot counting and recounting at the close of the 2000 election and the fact that the popular vote winner did not become president prompted a national debate on the Electoral College. The most frequently proposed reform of the Electoral College system is *direct popular election* of the president. Presidents would be elected directly by the voters, just as governors are, and the Electoral College and individual electors would be abolished. Such proposals usually provide that, if no candidate receives at least 40 percent of the total popular vote, a *runoff election* would be held between the two contenders with the most votes. Supporters argue that direct election would give every voter the same weight in the presidential balloting in accordance with the one-person, one-vote doctrine. Winners would take on more legitimacy because their victories would reflect the will of the voters.

Opponents contend that the plan would further undermine federalism, that it would encourage unrestrained majority rule and hence political extremism, and that it would hurt the smaller states, which would lose some of their present influence. Others fear that the plan would make presidential campaigns more remote from the voters; candidates might stress television and give up their forays into shopping centers and city malls.[67] Some also fear that the plan would increase the reliance of presidential campaigns on television.

From time to time, Congress considers proposals for a constitutional amendment to elect presidents directly. Such proposals, however, seldom get far because of the strong opposition of various interests that believe they may be disadvantaged by such a change, especially small states and minority groups whose role is enlarged by the Electoral College. Groups such as African Americans and farmers, for example, fear they might lose their swing vote power—their ability to make a difference in key states that may tip the Electoral College balance.

Another alternative to the Electoral College is sometimes called the National Bonus Plan. This plan adds to the current 538 Electoral College members another 102 electoral votes, to be awarded on a winner-takes-all basis to the candidate with the most votes, so long as that candidate received over 40 percent of the popular vote. This system would avoid elections being thrown into the House of Representatives and would help the popular vote winner take over the White House. The most serious liabilities of the plan are that it is complicated and requires a run-off election if there is no winner.

Finally, some states have already modified the Electoral College, adopting a district system in which the candidate who carries each congressional district gets that electoral vote, and the candidate who carries the state gets the state's two additional electoral votes. This quasi-proportional representation system has been used in Maine and Nebraska. It has the advantage of not shutting out a candidate who is strong in some areas of a state but not others, but otherwise it does not address the larger concerns with the Electoral College.

The failure of attempts to change the system of elections points to an important conclusion about procedural reform: Americans normally do not focus on procedures. Only after an Electoral College crisis like we experienced in 2000 is any significant change likely. As the crucial importance of ballot counts dragged on, citizens focused on actual problems with the electoral system, not on hypothetical problems discussed by political scientists and democratic theorists.

Reforming How We Vote

The 2000 presidential election ended with a month-long controversy over ballots and how to count them. While Florida became the focal point of national and international attention with its problems with punch-card ballots, dangling chads, voter confusion over ballot formats, and when to count or not count absentee ballots, such problems are common to most, if not all, states. As we noted earlier in this chapter, election administration is a state and local matter, and election law is constitutionally assigned to the individual states.

While technology could eliminate some of these problems by making electronic voting possible, the question of who would pay the costs of converting to new voting systems stands in the way of change. Improving election administration has not been high on the budget priorities of counties in Florida or most other states. Most observers agree that it will take a substantial infusion of money from the national government to fund new and improved voting systems.

As the country debates new voting systems, it is likely that state legislatures and Congress will debate permitting people to vote via the Internet. The argument will be that if people can make purchases over the Internet, why not let them vote electronically as well. Some states have experimented with "e-voting" on a small scale in presidential primaries in 2000. A shift to e-voting is in some respects an extension of the Oregon vote-by-mail experience since 1996. Yet critics worry that important elements of community and democracy are lost when people do not vote collectively at the schoolhouse or fire station. Another concern with e-voting is that it may encourage a proliferation of elections. If we can vote from home, why not vote on more things and more often? E-voting could foster a political culture of more and more ballot referenda.

CAMPAIGN FINANCING IN BRITAIN AND CANADA

U.S. election campaigns go on for months or even years and are very expensive. In contrast, Canadian general election campaigns are limited by law to about five weeks. Public opinion polls cannot be published during the last three days of a campaign, and the media are prohibited by law from reporting results from earlier time zones on the evening of the election in any district where voting is still taking place.

Expenditures are strictly limited for Canadian political parties and individual candidates. During the 1997 general election campaign to fill the 301 seats in the House of Commons, political parties that fielded candidates in all districts were limited by law to spending no more than approximately $8 million each for the entire election, and individual candidates could spend from about $35,000 to $45,000, depending on the number of voters per district. In return, media outlets were required to sell a certain amount of airtime to the parties, and national and regional television and radio networks had to donate some free airtime to these parties. If individual candidates received more than 15 percent of the vote in their districts, the government reimbursed 50 percent of their election-related expenses. Political parties receiving at least 2 percent of the national vote or at least 5 percent of the votes cast in electoral districts where they ran candidates were reimbursed 22.5 percent of their expenses.

In the June 1997 Canadian elections, 1,672 candidates ran for office, and 10 political parties received registered status. Total spending by the parliamentary candidates and political parties was approximately $70 million—much less than the $29 million spent by candidates in the United States seeking seats in the House of Representatives and the $128 million spent by candidates seeking seats in the Senate during the 1996 election campaign.

British general elections also offer an interesting contrast to elections in the United States. The election campaign lasts only three weeks. Candidates for the House of Commons, the most critical election in Britain, are allowed to raise and spend only $15,000. If they spend more, they are disqualified. Each candidate gets the same amount of free airtime, and each candidate is allowed one free election leaflet mailed to each voter in the constituency. About 75 percent of voters turn out, and about 95 percent of eligible voters are registered to vote. At the voting booth, the voter is handed a slip of paper with the names of three or four candidates for the House of Commons. No other offices or ballot questions are presented at the same time.

SOURCE: Adapted from Dudley Fishburn (a candidate for Parliament in 1992), "British Campaigning—How Civilized!" *The New York Times*, April 14, 1992, p. 25.

Reforming Campaign Finance

Although campaign finance reform is not a pressing concern to most citizens, large majorities of Americans think we need to reform the way we fund elections. The issues we have been discussing—soft money, issue advocacy, personal wealth, PAC contributions—are all examples of the need for reform. Why, then, has Congress been so slow to reform campaign finance? One reason is that the current members of Congress got elected with the current system, and they perceive the status quo to benefit them. Another reason is that the same interests who invest millions in funding campaigns also like things to stay as they are.

But campaign finance reform faces more fundamental problems as well. The courts and civil liberties groups have defined campaign money as political speech, and limitations on political speech face substantial constitutional hurdles. In a sense, the continuing debate about reforming presidential nominations, the Electoral College, how we vote, and how we fund elections can be taken as indications that elections and voting matter. The involvement of all the branches of government—legislative, executive, and judicial—in the outcome of the 2000 election and the nationwide interest in following the convoluted steps leading to the final decision reinforce the need to understand and take part in our democratic election procedures.

POLITICS ONLINE

Who Donates to Which Campaigns in Your Neighborhood?

The 2000 election set new records in all types of political money. Hard money—the limited and disclosed money individuals and PACs can give candidates—reached new highs. To see how much growth there has been in PAC giving, go to: www.prenhall.com/burns and click on the link to Chapter 9. You will find an interactive graph that lists PAC growth by sector.

One very successful fund raiser was George W. Bush. He formed what he called the Pioneers, a group of wealthy friends and supporters who each agreed to raise $100,000 for him. They did this by recruiting ten people to each give $1,000 and they in turn found ten more donors. By March 2000, the Pioneers had raised $180 million for Bush.

Individuals are limited in what they can give federal candidates and national parties; unlimited soft money is the exception to this rule. Soft money is presumably intended for non-candidate campaigning or party building. But the reality, as we demonstrated in this chapter, is that most soft money is spent to help elect or defeat a specific candidate.

Both national party committees and their respective congressional campaign committees made raising soft money a high priority in 2000. The committee that saw the most dramatic increase was the Democratic Senatorial Campaign Committee (DSCC); they raised $65 million in soft money in 1999 and 2000. Overall, all party committees together raised nearly $500 million.

Only a small percentage of Americans contribute money to a candidate or party. Who are these relatively few people who donate to parties and candidates? To which candidates, parties, or PACs did they contribute? Did they donate hard or soft money? Do any of these donors live in your neighborhood? Do you know any of them?

To answer these questions, visit: www.opensecrets.org. This site is maintained by the Center for Responsive Politics; they keep a watch on who donates to whom and how much. Punch in a zip code on the right-hand side of the screen and find out who donates money during an election cycle. (Only donations over $200 are reported).

SUMMARY

1. American elections, even presidential elections, are largely governed by state law and administered by local election officials. Following the 2000 elections, governments at all levels have begun to look for ways to improve the system.

2. Our electoral system is based on winner-takes-all rules, with typically single-member-district or single-officeholder arrangements. These rules encourage a moderate, two-party system. That we have fixed and staggered terms of office adds predictability to our electoral system.

3. The Electoral College is the means by which presidents are actually elected. To win a state's electoral votes, a candidate must have a plurality of votes in that state. Except in two states, the winner takes all. Thus candidates cannot afford

to lose the popular vote in the most populous states. The Electoral College also gives disproportionate power to the largest states and has the potential for defeat of the popular vote winner.

4. Many congressional, state, and local races are not seriously contested. The extent to which a campaign is likely to be hotly contested varies with the importance of the office and the chance a challenger has of winning. Senate races are more likely to be contested, though most incumbents win.

5. The race for the presidency actually takes place in three stages: winning enough delegate support in presidential primaries and caucuses to secure the nomination, campaigning at the national party convention, and mobilizing voters for a win in the Electoral College.

6. Even though presidential nominations today are usually decided weeks or months before the national party conventions, these conventions still have an important role in setting the parties' direction, unifying their ranks, and firing up enthusiasm. Speakers who are highlighted are positioned to pursue nominations in future years.

7. Because large campaign contributors are suspected of improperly influencing public officials, Congress has long sought to regulate political contributions. The main approaches to reform have been: (1) imposing limitations on giving, receiving, and spending political money; (2) requiring public disclosure of the sources and uses of political money; and (3) giving governmental subsidies to presidential candidates,

campaigns, and parties, including incentive arrangements. Present regulation includes all three approaches.

8. Loopholes in federal law—including soft money, issue advocacy, and independent expenditures—and rising costs of campaigns have led to declining competition for congressional seats and increasing dependence on PACs and wealthy donors.

9. The present presidential selection system is under criticism because of its length and expense, because of uncertainties and biases in the Electoral College, and because it seems to test candidates for media skills less needed in the White House than the ability to govern, including the capacity to form coalitions and make hard decisions.

10. Reform efforts center on presidential primaries and the Electoral College as well as on voting methods and campaign finance.

KEY TERMS

winner-takes-all 195
single-member district 195
proportional representation 195

Electoral College 195
safe seat 197
coattail effect 197

caucus 203
national party convention 203
interested money 207

soft money 209
issue advocacy 210
independent expenditures 210

FURTHER READING

R. MICHAEL ALVAREZ, *Information and Elections* (University of Michigan Press, 1998).

LARRY M. BARTELS, *Presidential Primaries and the Dynamics of Public Choice* (Princeton University Press, 1988).

LARRY M. BARTELS AND LYNN VAVRECK, EDS., *Campaign Reform: Insights and Evidence* (University of Michigan Press, 2000).

JUDITH A. BEST, *The Choice of the People? Debating the Electoral College* (Rowman and Littlefield, 1996).

EARL BLACK AND MERLE BLACK, *The Vital South: How Presidents Are Elected* (Harvard University Press, 1992).

ANDREW E. BUSH, *Horses in Midstream: U.S. Midterm Elections and Their Consequences, 1894–1998* (University of Pittsburgh Press, 2000).

ALAN EHRENHALT, *The United States of Ambition: Politicians, Power, and the Pursuit of Office* (Times Books, 1991).

THOMAS FERGUSON, *Golden Rule: The Investment Theory of Party Competition and the Logic of Money-Driven Political Systems* (University of Chicago Press, 1995).

LINDA L. FOWLER AND ROBERT D. MCCLURE, *Political Ambition: Who Decides to Run for Congress* (Yale University Press, 1989).

THOMAS GAIS, *Improper Influence: Campaign Finance Law, Political Interest Groups, and the Problem of Equality* (University of Michigan Press, 1996).

PAUL GRONKE, *The Electorate, the Campaign, and the Office: A Unified Approach to Senate and House Elections* (University of Michigan Press, 2000).

PAUL S. HERRNSON, *Congressional Elections: Campaigning at Home and in Washington*, 3d ed. (Congressional Quarterly Press, 2000).

GARY C. JACOBSON, *The Politics of Congressional Elections*, 4th ed. (Longman, 1997).

MARION R. JUST, ANN N. CRIGLER, DEAN E. ALGER, TIMOTHY E. COOK, MONTAGUE KERN, AND DARREL M. WEST, *Crosstalk: Citizens, Candidates and the Media in a Presidential Campaign* (University of Chicago Press, 1996).

KIM F. KAHN AND PATRICK J. KENNEDY, *The Spectacle of U.S. Senate Campaigns* (Princeton University Press, 1999).

JOHN KESSEL, *Presidential Campaign Politics*, 4th ed. (Brooks Cole, 1992).

JONATHAN S. KRASNO, *Challengers, Competition, and Reelection: Comparing Senate and House Elections* (Yale University Press, 1994).

ROBERT D. LOEVY, *The Flawed Path to the Presidency, 1992: Unfairness and Inequality in the Presidential Selection Process* (State University of New York Press, 1994).

DAVID LUBLIN, *The Paradox of Representation: Racial Gerrymandering and Minority Interests in Congress* (Princeton University Press, 1997).

DAVID B. MAGLEBY AND CANDICE J. NELSON, *The Money Chase: Congressional Campaign Finance Reform* (Brookings Institution, 1990).

NELSON W. POLSBY AND AARON B. WILDAVSKY, *Presidential Elections: Contemporary Strategies of American Politics*, 9th ed. (Chatham House, 1995).

GERALD M. POMPER ET AL., *The Election of 1992* (Chatham House, 1993).

SAMUEL L. POPKIN, *The Reasoning Voter: Communication and Persuasion in Presidential Campaigns* (University of Chicago Press, 1991).

FRANK J. SORAUF, *Inside Campaign Finance: Myths and Realities* (Yale University Press, 1992).

JAMES A. THURBER AND CANDICE J. NELSON, EDS., *Campaign Warriors: Political Consultants in Elections* (Brookings Institution Press, 2000).

JAMES A. THURBER AND CANDICE J. NELSON, EDS., *Campaigns and Elections American Style* (Westview Press, 1995).

STEPHEN J. WAYNE, *The Road to the White House, 2000: The Politics of Presidential Elections* (St. Martin's Press, 2000).

See also *Public Opinion Quarterly, American Journal of Politics,* and *American Political Science Review.*

THE MEDIA AND AMERICAN POLITICS

10

Election night, November 7, 2000, saw the
television networks project Al Gore as the winner
in Florida at 7:50 p.m. (Eastern Standard Time), only to
have that projection withdrawn. At 2:16 A.M. (Eastern Standard Time), Fox News projected George W. Bush as winning Florida and the presidency. Within minutes of Fox
calling Florida for Bush, the other networks followed. The reality was that Florida was
too close to call, and no network should have called the race. In the days and weeks after
the election, the Voter News Service, which conducts exit polls for the broadcast networks and some newspapers, admitted that its Florida sample was flawed, that it under-
estimated the Florida absentee vote, and that it relied on incomplete actual vote totals.[1]
The mistaken projections by the networks were embarrassing. Tom Brokaw of NBC
said, "That's not 'an egg' on our faces; that's 'an omelette.'"[2]

Projecting Gore as having carried Florida before the polls had closed in western
Florida prompted Republicans to charge that the networks had depressed turnout in
this more Republican part of the state. Since the 1980 election, the networks generally
followed the practice of not calling a state before the polls close in that state, and the
embarrassment of the 2000 election night will likely reinforce that practice in the future.

Executives at Fox News, the first to call Florida for Bush, were on the defensive not
only for their mistaken call, but because Governor Bush's cousin John Ellis was in charge
of the analysts that called the state, placing him in a clear conflict of interest. Also troubling were reports that Mr. Ellis was on the phone with both Governor George W. Bush
and Governor Jeb Bush throughout the evening, presumably sharing exit poll data with
his cousins.

Election night projections were not the only media controversy in the 2000 elections. Republicans charged a clear media bias in favor of Democrats, especially Al
Gore. Republican Representative Billy Tauzin, who chairs the House Commerce Subcommittee on Telecommunications, believed that election night coverage was biased
toward Gore and suggested that networks were reluctant to call states for Bush in hopes
that voters for Bush would be discouraged and not vote.[3]

The public had a different view of media bias in coverage of the 2000 presidential election; 65 percent said the media were fair in their treatment of Bush, while
74 percent gave the same response for Gore. Democrats and Republicans had similar views of fairness of the media toward Gore, but Republicans were far less likely
than Democrats to say the media were fair toward Bush (48 percent for Republicans

CHAPTER MEDIA

 POLITICS ONLINE

*How to Be Your Own
News Filter*
www.prenhall.com/burns

compared to 75 percent for Democrats). Democrats thought journalists favored Bush and Gore in roughly the same proportions, while Republicans overwhelmingly thought reporters favored Gore.[4]

Media coverage of the 2000 election and its aftermath in Florida demonstrated the public's tremendous appetite for instant news and analysis. Americans spend on average an hour a day consuming news. As people grow older, they devote even more time to the news.[5] Despite the fact that Americans have many news sources to choose from, people are quick to criticize the media. James Fallows, a journalist himself, begins his book on the media by saying: "Americans have never been truly fond of their press. Through the last decade, however, their disdain for the media establishment has reached new levels. Americans believe that the news media have become too arrogant, cynical, scandal-minded, and destructive."[6]

How often have you or your friends blamed the media for being biased, criticized the frenzy that surrounds a particular story, or denounced the "if it bleeds it leads" mentality of nightly television news? Yet the content and style of news coverage is driven by market research in which viewers and readers are asked what they want to see reported and how they want it presented. Advertising revenue is closely linked to the number of readers or viewers a media outlet has.

Media bashing has become something of a national pastime. People often blame the media for many of our ills—for increasing tension between the races, biased attacks upon public officials, sleaze and sensationalism—and for being more interested in making money than in conveying information. Many in the media even agree with these charges.[7] But complaints about the media may simply be a case of criticizing the messenger in order to avoid dealing with the message. Comments like, "It is the media's fault that we have lost our social values," or "The media's preoccupation with the private lives of politicians turns Americans off to politics," are overly broad assertions. Americans tend to blame far more problems on the media than they deserve.

THE INFLUENCE OF THE MEDIA ON POLITICS

The media, in particular the print media, have been called "the other government," "the fourth estate," and "the fourth branch of government."[8] Evidence that the media influence our culture and politics is plentiful. Before we can examine that influence, however, we must define some terms. The **mass media**—that is, newspapers and magazines, radio, television (broadcast, cable, and satellite), films, recordings, books, and electronic communication—are the means of communication that reach the mass public.[9] The **news media** are that part of the mass media that emphasizes the news, although the distinctions between entertainment and news are sometimes blurred. News programs often have entertainment value, and entertainment programs often convey the news. Programs in this latter category include TV newsmagazines such as *60 Minutes, 20/20, Dateline*, and talk shows with hosts like Larry King, Oprah Winfrey, Chris Matthews, and Geraldo Rivera.

By definition, the mass media disseminate messages to a large and often heterogeneous audience. Because they must have broad appeal, their messages are often simplified, stereotyped, and predictable. The mass media are big business and make money by appealing to large numbers of people. But do large audiences equal political clout? Two factors are important in answering this question: the media's pervasiveness and their role as a linking mechanism between politicians and government officials and the public.

Where do Americans get their news? Until 1960 most people got their news from newspapers. Today they rely primarily on television, although many people use several sources. Whenever there is a crisis—say the capture of Elian Gonzalez by immigration officials, or the impeachment of President Bill Clinton—or a major news event, such as the Florida presidential election recount controversy, many people are glued to their TV sets.

mass media
Means of communication that reach the mass public. The mass media include newspapers and magazines, radio, television (broadcast, cable, and satellite), films, recordings, books, and electronic communication.

news media
That part of the mass media that emphasizes the news.

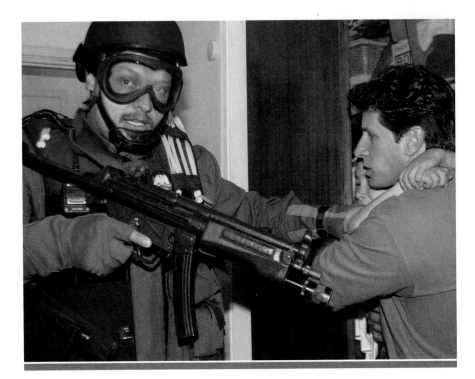

Today the Internet is becoming an increasingly important source of news for Americans, taking its place alongside print, radio, and television. The number of Americans going online for news is growing dramatically and promises to become even more important as candidates and issue advocates pay increasing attention to the Web as a way to get their messages to the voting public.[10]

The Pervasiveness of Television

Perhaps more than any other invention, television has changed the character of American politics. The average American watches 4.3 hours per day, and most homes have at least two sets.[11] While television is primarily an entertainment medium, most Americans use it for news as well. Most Americans watch some kind of television news network on a daily basis. Television provides instant news from around the country and the globe, permitting citizens and leaders alike to observe, firsthand, a refugee crisis in Indonesia or a hostage situation in Sierra Leone. This instant coverage increases the pressure on world leaders to respond quickly to crises, permits terrorists to gain widespread coverage of their actions, and elevates the role played by the president in both domestic and international politics.

Perhaps the single biggest change in American electoral politics in the last half century is that most voters now rely on television commercials for information about candidates and issues. Although candidate debates and speeches generate news coverage, the more pervasive battleground is radio and TV advertisements. As a result, electoral campaigns now focus on image and slogans rather than on substance. Successful candidates must be able to communicate with voters through this medium. To get their message across to TV audiences, politicians increasingly communicate with citizens through "sound bites"—10-to-45-second statements for the television or radio news—and 30-second political commercials.

Interest groups advocating one position or another—health care reform, trade agreements, affirmative action—also use paid advertising on television and radio to influence voters' choices on election day. These so-called **issue ads** permit groups to spend unlimited and undisclosed amounts of money so long as they do not explicitly call for the election or defeat of a candidate. Interest groups have mounted expensive advertising campaigns on health care reform and gun legislation in an

issue ad
Commercial advertising on radio and television advocating a particular position on an issue, paid for by interest groups and often designed to influence voters' choices on election day.

effort to sway votes in Congress, and in the weeks before recent general elections they have spent millions to influence votes. In referendum elections, advertising is the most important source of information in voter decision making.[12]

For several decades the network evening news programs on CBS, NBC, and ABC captured more than 90 percent of the audience for television news at set times in the morning and early evening hours. Over the last 15 years, with the rise of cable television and the advent of the Internet, prime-time viewership on the broadcast networks has declined to about 50 percent. The growth of around-the-clock cable news and information shows is one of the most important developments in recent years. More than half of the public are regular viewers of CNN, CNBC, MSNBC, or Fox News; and more than three in four regularly watch network prime-time news shows.[13]

Recent technological advances have created intense competition for advertising revenues and contributed to sweeping changes in the manner in which news is transmitted and received. Satellites, cable television, computers, and videocassette recorders (VCRs) make vast amounts of political information available 24 hours a day. These technologies eliminate the obstacles of time and distance and increase the volume of information that can be stored, retrieved, and viewed.

The Persistence of Radio

Television and the newer media have not displaced radio. On the contrary, radio continues to reach more American households than does television. Only one household in a hundred does not have a radio, compared with four in a hundred without a TV. Nine out of ten Americans listen to the radio every day.[14] Cars and radios seem to go together.

Americans get more than "the facts" from radio. They also get analysis and opinion from their favorite commentators and talk show hosts like conservatives Rush Limbaugh, Alan Keyes, Michael Reagan, and G. Gordon Liddy, or liberals like Mary Mason, Tom Leykis, or Mario Cuomo. These hosts have their own home pages on the World Wide Web and provide around-the-clock opinion on politics. Talk radio has been more closely identified with conservatives. Former House Speaker Newt Gingrich and other Republicans in the U.S. House of Representatives made widespread use of it. The popularity of the talk-show format has been applied as well to television. John McCain was a constant guest on many talk shows, as were Al Gore and George W. Bush during the election campaigns.

The Continuing Importance of Newspapers

Despite vigorous competition from the broadcast media, Americans still read newspapers. Daily newspaper circulation been declining to about 56 million nationwide—or about one copy for every four people—for the past 20 years.[15] Another indication of the print media's pervasiveness is the rise of nationwide newspapers. *The Wall Street Journal*, with a circulation of more than 1.7 million, has long acted as a national newspaper specializing in business and finance. *The Wall Street Journal* also boasts more than 400,000 subscribers to its online newspaper.[16] Other national newspapers with more general interests have also emerged. *USA Today*, created in 1982 by the Gannett Corporation, now has a circulation of more than 1.6 million. In addition, *The New York Times* has a national edition that is read by more than 1 million people. The circulation figures for newspapers mask a troubling decline in readership among younger persons. There is about a 30 percentage point differential in readership between the young and the old, with younger persons much less likely to

read newspapers.[17] Unless this difference can be reversed or newspapers find a way to reinvent themselves through something like the Internet, they will decline in importance as their readers die off.

The World Wide Web

We have only begun to see the potential effect of the Internet on American politics. From its humble beginnings as a Pentagon research project in the 1970s, the Web has blossomed into an international phenomenon. There are now more than 1 billion documents on the Web,[18] and more than 15 million unique domains registered worldwide, including one for this book (**http://www.prenhall.com/burns**). The Web opens up resources for citizens in dramatic ways. One study found that nearly half of Americans go online to search for news on a particular topic; somewhat smaller proportions go online for updates on stock quotes and sports scores. Fewer people use the Internet as their primary source of news—29 percent.[19]

Extensive use of computers by young children has left them vulnerable to sexual predators and commercial frauds, opening the issue of whether government regulation is needed. Parental supervision remains the best protection.

One application in electoral politics is candidate home pages where voters can learn about those seeking office or about ballot referenda. A second application of the Web is to mobilize citizens behind a candidate or cause. Minnesota Governor Jesse Ventura and presidential primary contender John McCain effectively used the Internet to get the word out to supporters about campaign events. The Internet is an inexpensive and efficient way to communicate with volunteers and will become an even larger component of campaigns in the future. Users of the Internet can also interact with other people or politicians about politics through electronic mail and chat rooms.

A third way the Internet is changing American politics is in fund raising. McCain's primary campaign demonstrated the usefulness of the Internet to raise contributions, collecting twice as much money over the Internet as Gore and Bush.[20] Once a candidate gains public recognition, as McCain did after his victory in the New Hampshire primary, it is possible to raise money quickly and inexpensively via the Internet.

THE CHANGING ROLE OF AMERICAN NEWS MEDIA

Political Mouthpiece

At the time of the ratification of the Constitution, newspapers consisted of a single sheet, often printed irregularly by store owners to hawk their services or goods. Newspapers rarely lasted more than a year, due to delinquent subscribers and high costs.[21] But the framers understood the important role the press should play as a watchdog of politicians and government, and they included freedom of the press in the Bill of Rights.

The new nation's political leaders, such as Alexander Hamilton and Thomas Jefferson, recognized the need to keep voters informed. Political party organizations as we know them did not exist, but the active role of the press in supporting the Revolution had fostered a growing awareness of the political potential of newspapers. Hamilton recruited staunch Federalist John Fenno to edit and publish a newspaper in the new national capital of Philadelphia. Jefferson responded by attracting Philip Freneau, a talented writer and editor and a loyal Republican, to do the same for the Republicans. (Jefferson's Republicans later became the Democratic party.) The two papers became the nucleus of competing partisan newspaper networks throughout the nation.

Although the two newspapers competed in Philadelphia only several years, their lasting significance was as a model for future partisan newspapers. Federalist and Republican editors relied on each other for government news and editorials. The free mailing of newspapers granted by the U.S. Post Office allowed broader coverage.

The early American press served as a mouthpiece for political leaders. Its close connection with politicians and political parties offered the opportunity for financial stability, but at the cost of journalistic independence.

MEDIA IN JAPAN AND THE UNITED STATES: WATCHDOG OR LAPDOG?

A comparison of the media in Japan and the United States illustrates the strengths and weaknesses of both. In Japan the media are independently owned but work closely with one another in alliances, whereas in the United States media con-glomerates include diverse businesses like General Electric or Disney. Compare this list of the six largest media outlets in Japan and the United States; for U.S. firms we also provide the business that owns the media outlet.

Japan*	United States
Asahi (newspaper)	General Electric (owns NBC and CNBC and, in partnership with Microsoft, MSNBC)
Yomiuri (newspaper)	
Tokyo Broadcasting	Dun and Bradstreet (owns *The Wall Street Journal*)
Shueisha (publishing house)	Westinghouse (owns CBS)
Nihon Television Broadcasting	Gannett (owns *USA Today*)
Nihon Keizai Newspaper	Walt Disney (owns ABC)
	Time Warner (owns TBS, CNN, TNT)

Although media firms are owned separately in Japan, this arrangement does not foster greater media independence, nor are the media in Japan more challenging and investigative than U.S. media. Rather, Japanese reporters are organized into reporter clubs that are affiliated with a specific government news source, and they gain all their information through that source. Japanese reporters know more about the inner workings of politics in their country than most investigative reporters in the United States know about the inner workings of our government. Yet Japanese reporters rarely print what they know, often reporting only the official government line. As a result, whatever stories are printed are the same in each of Japan's newspapers. For these reasons, the Japanese media have earned a reputation for being a lapdog of the government rather than a watchdog. Despite the trend toward large corporations owning the major news providers in the United States, strong support for journalistic independence remains, and news reporting is driven by competition among news media to get the story.

*D. Eleanor Westney, "Mass Media as Business Organizations: A U.S.–Japanese Comparison," in *Media and Politics in Japan*, ed. Susan J. Pharr and Ellis S. Krauss (University of Hawaii Press, 1996), pp. 47–88.

Financial Independence

The Jacksonian era of the 1820s and 1830s was characterized by expansion of the right to vote to all white adult males through the elimination of property qualifications for voting. The press began to shift its appeal away from elite readers and toward large masses of less well educated and less politically interested readers. This popularization of the newspapers was reinforced by rising literacy rates that supported greater circulation for them. These two forces—increased political participation by the common people and the rise of literacy among Americans—began to alter the relationship between politicians and the press.

Some newspaper publishers began to experiment with a new way to finance their newspapers. They charged a penny a paper, paid on delivery, instead of the traditional annual subscription fee of $8 to $10, which was beyond the ability of most readers to pay. The "penny press," as it was called, expanded circulation and put more emphasis on advertising, enabling newspapers to become financially independent of the political parties.

The changing finances of newspapers also affected the definition of news. Before the penny press, all news was political—speeches, documents, editorials—directed at politically interested readers. The penny press reshaped the definition of news as it sought to appeal to less politically aware readers with human interest stories and reports on sports, crime, public trials, and social activities.

"Objective Journalism"

By the early decades of the twentieth century, many journalists began to argue that the press should be independent of the political parties. *New York Tribune* editor Whitelaw Reid eloquently expressed this sentiment: "Independent journalism! That is the watchword of the future in the profession. An end of concealments because it would hurt the party; an end of one-sided expositions . . . an end of assaults that are not believed fully just but must be made because the exigency of party warfare demands them."[22]

Journalists began to view their work as a profession and established professional associations with journals and codes of ethics. This professionalization of journalism reinforced the notion that journalists should be independent of partisan politics. Further strengthening the trend toward objectivity was the rise of the wire services, which were deliberately politically neutral to attract more customers.

The Impact of Broadcasting

Radio and television changed the media's role in politics by nationalizing and personalizing the news. Radio networks were created in the 1920s. Radio carried political speeches, campaign advertising, and coverage of political events such as national

party conventions.[23] Radio provided a means to bypass the screening of editors and reporters, since politicians could speak directly to listeners. It also contributed to increased interest in national and international news, since activities outside a listener's local area could be heard as if one were actually there.

President Franklin Roosevelt used radio with a new effectiveness. Before 1933 most radio addresses were formal orations, but Roosevelt spoke to his audience on a personal level that showed how radio could be used as a one-to-one conversation. Roosevelt's "fireside chats" established a standard for presidential use of the broadcast media still followed today. When Roosevelt began speaking over the microphone, he would visualize the average citizen in front of him. "His face would smile and light up as though he were actually sitting on the front porch or in the parlor with them."[24]

Franklin D. Roosevelt was the first president to recognize the effectiveness of radio to reach the public. His fireside chats were the model for later presidents.

Television added a visual dimension, which contributed to rising audience interest in national events. By 1963 the then two largest networks expanded their evening news programs from 15 to 30 minutes. Today news broadcasting has expanded to the point where many local stations provide 90 minutes of local news every evening as well as a half-hour in the morning and at noon. Programs such as *60 Minutes*, *20/20*, and other news magazine shows are among the most popular in the prime-time evening hours.

The rise of cable television brought 24-hour news coverage. During the Clinton impeachment hearings and the 2000 Florida ballot-counting controversy, American cable news was watched at home and around the world for its instantaneous coverage. Other stations now provide coverage of Congress, the courts, and state and local governments.

Investigatory Journalism

Today news reporters do more than convey the news. They investigate it, and their investigations often have political consequences. Notable examples of influential investigatory reporters include Seymour Hersh of *The New York Times*, who exposed *The Pentagon Papers* on how the United States became involved in the Vietnam War; Robert Woodward and Carl Bernstein of *The Washington Post*, who played an important role in uncovering the Watergate conspiracy; Nina Totenberg of National Public Radio, whose reporting on sexual harassment charges against Clarence Thomas helped force the Senate Judiciary Committee to extend the hearings on his confirmation to the U.S. Supreme Court; and Michael Isikoff of *Newsweek*, who broke the story of Bill Clinton's alleged perjury involving sexual relations with Monica Lewinsky.

Media Conglomerates

Newspapers and television are big business. What happens if a few people corner the market on newspapers and television stations? Is the free flow of information to the public endangered? Is too much power to influence public opinion in the hands of too few people?

As in other sectors of the economy, media companies have merged with others and created large conglomerates. Radio networks and newspapers were among the first to purchase television stations when television was in its infancy. These mergers established cross-ownership patterns that persist in media ownership today. The Gannett Corporation, for example, owns 87 daily newspapers and 21 television stations and cable television systems—assets that provide news coverage to nearly 17 percent of the United States.[25] *The Chicago Tribune* substantially expanded its reach of newspapers and television stations in 2000 when it paid $6 billion for *Times/Mirror*, publisher of the *Los Angeles Times* and 10 other newspapers, 22 TV stations, 4 radio stations, and a growing online business.[26] The Federal Communications Commission (FCC) reinforced the trend toward media conglomeration by permitting one owner to control up to 30 AM and 30 FM radio stations. Previously, ownership was less concentrated, in part because the government was granting licenses to a finite number of stations.

Australian-born Rupert Murdoch owns dozens of U.S. television stations, magazines, publishing organizations, and movie studios.

Another concern has been the gobbling up of American communication assets by large corporations and foreign interests. Local firms used to own the local newspapers, radio, and television stations. Today large conglomerates, many of them foreign, have acquired ownership of many newspapers and broadcasting stations. The merger of the Disney organization with ABC/Capital Cities, approved early in 1996, cost Disney $19 billion but gave it control not only of the ABC television network but also ESPN, the cable sports station. Months later, the Westinghouse Company bought the CBS television network for $7.5 billion,[27] and CBS merged with Viacom in May 2000 at a cost estimated at $50 billion. Time Warner purchased Turner Broadcasting System in late 1996 for reportedly just under $7 billion,[28] and it, in turn, was purchased by America-OnLine (AOL) for $165 billion.[29] The foremost example of foreign involvement in our news media is Australian Rupert Murdoch, founder of the Fox network, who owns 22 television stations in the United States, the Family Channel, and 20th-Century Fox. Murdoch also owns HarperCollins and *TV Guide* magazine, which has the largest magazine circulation in America.

Media conglomerates with large financial resources now dominate the media business and have contributed to the control of news. Are a few media conglomerates likely to provide sufficient competition of ideas to support a democratic system?[30] And without them, can local populations scattered around the country, depending only on local media, find out what is happening in the nation's capital? Why not have government-owned media carry out educational and information functions, as they do in Great Britain and France?[31] The answer is that Americans continue to put great stock in the independence of the press and the news media and find centralized, government-owned media unacceptable.

When reporting national news, local outlets depend heavily on news that is gathered, edited, and distributed by national organizations like United Press International and Associated Press. As a result, some people contend that information these days is more diluted, homogenized, and moderated than it would be if the newspapers and broadcast stations were locally owned and the news was gathered and edited locally.[32]

Regulation of the Media

Regulation of the broadcast media has existed in some form since its inception. Because of the limited number of television and radio frequencies, government has overseen matters like licensing, financing, and even content. One such regulation required "fairness" in news programming.[33] As written into law and interpreted by the Federal Communications Commission, the **fairness doctrine** imposed an obligation on radio and television license holders to ensure that differing viewpoints were presented about controversial issues or persons. With the advent of cable television and the Reagan administration's antiregulatory campaign, much of the fairness doctrine was repealed in 1987 and the final remnants of it were repealed in 2000. Will broadcasters provide fair and balanced news coverage in the absence of regulation? Those who pushed for repeal think so.[34]

THE NEW MEDIATOR IN AMERICAN POLITICS

The pervasiveness of newspapers, magazines, radio, television, and the Web does not prove their political influence. But it does place those who determine what we read, hear, and see in a position to be influential because they can reach so much of the American public so quickly. With a large population scattered over a continent, both the reach and the speed of the modern media elevate the importance of those in charge of it.

Political parties and interest groups have long been political mediators that help organize the world of politics for the average citizen. Their role is less important today because the media now serve that function and political parties have largely lost control over the nominating process (see Chapters 7 and 9). Greater attention is

fairness doctrine
Doctrine interpreted by the Federal Communications Commission that imposed on radio and television licensees an obligation to ensure that different viewpoints were presented about controversial issues or persons; repealed in 1987.

now given to judging candidates not so much in terms of party affiliation and platform but in terms of character and competence. The press, not the parties, perform this evaluative function.

The news media have also taken over the role of "speaking for the people." Journalists report what "the people" want and think, and then they tell the people what politicians and policy makers are doing about it. Politicians realize how dependent they are on the media for getting their message out to voters, and they also know a hostile press can hurt them. Clearly, today's politicians have to spend much of their time cultivating the press.

The amount of television news devoted to politics has been declining and now constitutes less than one minute per thirty-minute broadcast. A major effort to get local television stations to devote a few minutes to candidate debate in their nightly local news ended up with stations averaging 45 seconds a night, or as one observer put it, just enough time for to "let candidates clear their throats."[35] In large urban areas it is rare for viewers to see stories about their member of Congress, in part because there are several congressional districts in that media market. Newspapers do a better job of covering politics, in part because they devote more attention to it. More broadly, the mediating role played by the media is limited by the declining political news content of broadcast media.

The Media and Public Opinion

Scholars, journalists, politicians, and political pundits have long debated the power of the media over public opinion. Do journalists and editors really shape opinions? Do they alter people's behavior? Can they even affect our core values? For a long time, analysts tended to play down the influence wielded by the media in American politics as compared with the influence wielded by political leaders. The impact of Franklin D. Roosevelt's fireside chats came to symbolize the power of the politician against that of the news editor. Roosevelt spoke directly to his listeners over the radio in a way and at a time of his own choosing, and no network official was able to block or influence that direct connection. President John Kennedy's use of the televised press conference represented a similar direct contact with the public. President Ronald Reagan was nicknamed the "Great Communicator" because of his ability to talk persuasively and often passionately about public policy issues with the people through television.

Broadcasters and journalists are now so important to the political process that elected officials and politicians spend considerable time trying to learn how to use them. Presidential events and "photo opportunities" are planned with the evening news and its format in mind.[36] Members of Congress use Capitol Hill recording studios to tape messages for local television and radio stations. White House press briefings are frequently included in the evening news. How government officials use the press, how the press uses government officials, and to what extent the press and television can and should be regulated are critical questions.

Factors That Limit Media Influence on Public Opinion

People are not just empty vessels into which politicians and journalists pour information and ideas. How people interpret political messages depends on a variety of factors: political socialization, selectivity, needs, and the individual's ability to recall and comprehend the message.

POLITICAL SOCIALIZATION   Although we would like to believe we consume the news with an open mind, the reality is that we employ a set of *filters*, screens that help us interpret and integrate information. When we watch television or read newspapers, magazines, and books, we bring with us values and attitudes that have been shaped by family, peers, school, and the groups to which we belong.[37] We develop our political attitudes, values, and beliefs through an education process that social scientists call **political socialization**. (See Chapters 4 and 8 for more detail on this

"Hey, do you want to be on the news tonight or not? This is a sound bite, not the Gettysburgh Address. Just say what you have to say, Senator, and get the hell off."

political socialization
The process by which we develop our political attitudes, values, and beliefs.

You Decide . . .

Should the government protect children from excessive violence and sex on TV?

The media are a powerful socializing agent. Many agree that there is too much violence and sex on television. Both candidates in the 2000 presidential race stressed the importance of taking action against the entertainment industry if it persists in marketing adult materials to children. The candidates did not specify what actions they would take, but presumably they would include legislation and prosecution.

The V-chip is a computer chip that can be installed in a television set to permit parents to restrict access to certain television programs. Some favor this type of system as a means of informing parents of the content of programs and permitting them to limit access to inappropriate programs. Others oppose such ratings systems and say the V-chip is a form of censorship. Shouldn't parents enforce their own standards by monitoring what their children watch? Will the V-chip exert any pressure on the television industry to clean up its act?

selective exposure

The process by which individuals screen out those messages that do not conform to their own biases.

selective perception

The process by which individuals perceive what they want to in media messages and disregard the rest.

process.) The media, particularly television, may influence our values and attitudes, but they are not as important as family in the formation of our political attitudes.[38] Moreover, face-to-face contacts with friends and business associates (*peer pressure*) often have far more impact than the impersonal television or newspaper. Strong identification with a party also acts as a powerful filter.[39] A conservative Republican from Arizona might watch the "liberal Eastern networks" night after night and year after year and complain about their biased news coverage while sticking to her own opinions. A liberal from New York will often complain about right-wing talk radio, even if he listens to it every night on the way home from work.

SELECTIVITY   People practice **selective exposure**—screening out those messages that do not conform to their own biases. They subscribe to newspapers or magazines that support their views. People also practice **selective perception**—perceiving what they want to in media messages and disregarding the rest.[40] One dramatic example was the differing reactions of Democrats and Republicans to reports of President Clinton's sexual relationship with Monica Lewinsky, a former White House intern, and the possibility that he encouraged her to lie under oath. In the first weeks after the story broke, Republicans were four times more likely than Democrats to believe that Clinton had been sexually involved with Lewinsky.[41] More than two-thirds of Republicans and Democrats agreed that Clinton committed perjury before the grand jury, but they had dramatically different opinions on whether Clinton should remain in office. Just over one-third of Republicans wanted Clinton to remain in office, while 63 percent of Independents and 87 percent of Democrats felt that Clinton should continue as president.[42] When Attorney General Janet Reno directed federal marshals and immigration authorities to use force to take Elian Gonzalez from his Miami relatives and turn him over to his father, Republicans talked about storm trooper tactics while Democrats talked about reuniting a child with his father.

NEEDS   People read newspapers, listen to the radio, or watch television for very different reasons—sometimes because they are bored, tired, or have nothing better to do, sometimes because they want information.[43] People who seek information and cultivate an interest in politics are affected by what they read and see differently from those who use media primarily for entertainment.[44] For those seeking entertainment, gossip about politicians' peccadilloes is more important than those politicians' opinions or votes. Members of the broader audience are also more likely to follow news that directly affects their lives, such as interest rate changes or the price of gasoline.[45]

RECALL AND COMPREHENSION   Still another limitation of media influence on public opinion is the extent to which the audience can recall the stories or comprehend their importance. Candidates and officials send out vast amounts of information designed to influence what people think and do, especially how they vote, but people forget or fail to comprehend much of it.[46] The fragmentary and rapid mode of presentation of television news contributes to the problem.

Given the abundance of information available about politics and government, it is not surprising that most people pick and choose which media source—television, radio, newspapers, cable, the Internet—they pay attention to and which news stories they consider important.[47] The best predictor of retention of news stories is political interest. People tend to fit today's news stories into their general assumptions or beliefs about government, politicians, or the media itself.

AUDIENCE FRAGMENTATION   With the growth of cable television and new media like the Internet, the influence of any one media source is weakened. Because people are scattered across a larger number of press outlets, and these outlets cover politics in varied ways, the impact of the press will be more disparate.

Are the Media Biased?

Americans tend to blame the media for lots of things. Conservatives complain "the media are too liberal." Speaking of the media, radio talk show host Rush Limbaugh argues, "They all just happen to believe the same way. . . . They are part of the same culture as Bill Clinton."[48] Liberals contend the mainstream press is controlled by the ruling class, and they charge that government propaganda distorts the facts. Conservatives say the press is too liberal in its selection of news covered and the interpretation of events. Liberals point to newspaper endorsements of Republican presidential candidates to support their claim that newspapers are biased toward conservative policies and candidates.

Newspapers, magazines, and television stations are business corporations concerned about profits. This means they work to boost circulation and ratings and must please their advertisers, sponsors, and stockholders. Do the preferences of advertisers or corporate owners show up in news reporting? Reporters and editors pride themselves on impartial reporting of the facts.[49] Yet some liberal critics contend that the media reflect a conservative bias not only in what they report but also in what they choose to ignore. Political scientist Michael Parenti states that journalists "rarely doubt their own objectivity even as they faithfully echo the established political vocabularies and the prevailing politico-economic orthodoxy."[50]

Newspapers and television management go to some lengths to insulate reporters from their advertising and business operations, in part to reduce criticism about favorable treatment of large advertisers or the corporate owners. When the management of *The Los Angeles Times* attempted to foster closer relations between the business and news divisions, it was criticized for insensitivity to this concern.[51] Another internal check on media bias is the fact that news coverage involves many reporters and a host of editors, all of whom have input into what is covered and how it is presented.

Some commentators have suggested that a possible bias flows from the fact that reporters and editors become too friendly with those they write about. David Broder of *The Washington Post* voices his concern about the confusion of roles by journalists who have served in government. According to Broder, a line should divide objective journalism from partisan politics, but many in the print and television media have crossed this line. Broder opposes the idea of journalists' becoming government officials and vice versa.[52] Others argue that journalists with previous government service have close working relationships with politicians and can give us a valuable perspective on government without losing their professional neutrality.

A frequent criticism is the media's alleged political bias, whether liberal or conservative. But to whom are these critics referring? To reporters, writers, editors, producers, or owners of TV and newspapers? Do they assume a journalist's personal politics will be translated into biased reporting? And does the public think so? Journalists are usually more liberal than the population as a whole; editors tend to be a bit more conservative than their reporters are; and media owners are more conservative still. Polling data demonstrate that slightly more than half the journalists classify themselves as liberals, compared with only about one-fourth of the general public (Table 10–1).[53] Elite journalists—those who work for national news media organizations—tend to share a similar culture: cosmopolitan, urban, upper class. Their approach to the events and issues they cover is governed by their common worldview, which may be derived from their professional training.[54] The result, some contend, is that elite journalists give greater weight to the side of issues that corresponds to their own version of reality.[55]

One bias of the media that does not have a particular partisan or ideological slant is the bias toward sensationalism. Scandals of all types happen to liberals and conservatives, Republicans and Democrats. Once the province of tabloids like *National Enquirer*, stories about scandal have become commonplace in mainstream media in recent years.

Thinking It Through . . .

The movement to have a ratings system for television programs gained enough support that all major television networks except NBC proposed their own rating system similar to that used for movies, in part to avoid one legislated by Congress. The ratings indicate if the program contains violence, sex, or language that might be objectionable.

Jack Valenti, president of the Motion Picture Association of America, argues that these ratings help parents make decisions. Valenti and others in the television industry say that to go further than their proposal would violate First Amendment rights.

The opposition says these ratings are insufficient because they do not give enough information about the programs, such as the degree of violence or the type of sexual material. Most parent and family groups want a more detailed system of ratings and description of program content.

Those who oppose such ratings systems contend that, once started, they can become a form of censorship. Moreover, they assert there is a lot of subjectivity in evaluating programs. What some may see as too violent or sexually explicit, others may not find objectionable. Then there is the added cost to equip televisions with V-chips and to employ people to rate the programs. Ultimately it will be advertisers who pay the costs of the ratings and consumers who pay for the V-chip.

The counterargument is that children learn what is acceptable behavior from the media, especially television. Critics point to an increasing incidence of violent and sexually explicit actions and language on TV. They contend the industry will not regulate itself. The V-chip, when combined with content disclosure and a detailed ratings system, would give parents control over this powerful socializing force.

Early in the 1992 presidential campaign, Bill Clinton's press coverage turned negative as reports circulated in the *Star*, a supermarket tabloid, that he and Gennifer Flowers, a former Arkansas state employee, had had a twelve-year-long extramarital affair. Clinton, with Mrs. Clinton by his side, denied the Flowers account in an interview on *60 Minutes*, a CBS-TV news program, on Superbowl Sunday. Because Flowers had been paid for her story by the *Star*, some people discounted the story. Others were doubtful that tabloid papers like the *Star* ever print anything close to the truth. Despite the existence of tapes that appeared to confirm the Flowers account, the press essentially dropped the story.

After winning the presidency, Clinton was dogged by a series of accusations of unwanted sexual advances toward Paula Jones and Kathleen Willey and of a consensual affair with Monica Lewinsky. In a transcript of his deposition in the Jones sexual harassment suit, Clinton admitted having an affair with Gennifer Flowers. This raised anew questions of how the media had reported the original accusations. Did the press handle those stories properly?

TABLE 10–1 The Politics of Journalists and the Public			
	Washington-Based Reporters	Newspaper Editors (National)	Public
Party Identification			
Democrat	50%	31%	34%
Republican	4	14	28
Independent	37	39	25
Other	9	7	8
Self-Described Ideology			
Liberal	61	32	20
Moderate	30	35	34
Conservative	9	25	27

SOURCE: The Roper Center, *The Public Perspective*, October/November 1996, p. 8, based on a Media Studies Center/Roper Center survey of 1,200 persons conducted in September 1995.

Newspapers and television news often set a tone of dissatisfaction with the performance of the national government and cynicism about politics and politicians. A critical tone may be an inevitable element of the mindset of the press, but to whose benefit does that critical tone work? The media are accused of having an anti-incumbent bias, a generational bias, and a bias fostering continuing crises.[56] The question is not whether the press is biased, but whether a press bias—whatever the direction—seeps into the content of the news. The answer to that question is still not settled.

Public Opinion

The media shape public perceptions and knowledge. Television, with all its concreteness and drama, has an emotional impact that print cannot hope to match.[57] Television cuts across age groups, educational levels, social classes, and races. Newspapers provide more detail about the news and often contain contrasting points of view, at least on the editorial pages, that help inform the public. Two important influences of print and broadcast media are *agenda setting* and *issue framing*.

AGENDA SETTING   By calling public attention to certain issues, the media help to determine what topics will become the subject of public debate and legislation.[58] However, the agenda-setting function of the media is not uniformly pervasive. The audience and the nature of the issue limit it.[59]

According to former Vice-President Walter Mondale, "If I had to give up . . . the opportunity to get on the evening news or the veto power, . . . I'd throw the veto power away. [Television news] is the President's most indispensable power."[60] Ronald Reagan, more than any president before him, effectively used the media to set the nation's agenda. Reagan and his advisers carefully crafted the images and scenes of his presidency to fit television. Thus television became an "electronic throne."

ISSUE FRAMING   Politicians, like everybody else, try to frame issues to win arguments, and they try to influence the "spin" the media will give to their actions or issues. Examples abound. Those who opposed U.S. intervention in Bosnia tried to portray such action as another Vietnam. Opponents of permanent normal trade relations with China framed it as a human rights travesty. When Bill Clinton wanted to forestall a Republican tax cut, he framed the use of the budget surplus to rescue Social Security. Those who favor abortion define the issue as one of freedom of choice; those who oppose it define it as murder. In referendum campaigns, the side that wins the battle of interpreting what the referendum is about wins the election.[61]

THE MEDIA AND ELECTIONS

News coverage of campaigns and elections is greatest in presidential contests, decreases in statewide races for governor or senator, and decreases still further for other races. Generally, the more news attention given the campaign, the less likely voters are to be swayed by any one source. Hence, news coverage is likely to be more important in a city council contest than in an election for president or the Senate. In most city elections there are only one or two sources of information about what candidates say and stand for; for statewide and national contests, there are multiple sources.

Diversification of the news media also lessens the ability of any one medium to dominate politics. Newspaper publishers who were once seen as very important in state and local politics know that today politicians and their media advisers can communicate their message through television, radio, direct mail, videocassettes, the Internet, and cable television. Hence, there is now more competition among the various media, and politicians and candidates can get their message out regardless of what the editor of the state's largest newspaper may think.

"I'm still undecided—I like Leno's foreign policy, but Letterman makes a lot of sense on domestic issues."

How the Media Affect Elections

Candidates see the media as the means to communicate their message and win votes. The extensive use of television has made being "good on television" much more important, fostered a growth industry in political consulting, and made visibility the watchword in politics.

CHOICE OF CANDIDATES   Television greatly affects the public's idea of what traits are important in a candidate. A hundred years ago, successful candidates needed a strong pair of lungs; today it is a telegenic appearance, a pleasing voice, and no obvious physical impairments. Back in the 1930s, the press chose not to show Franklin Roosevelt in his wheelchair or using braces, whereas today the country knows every intimate detail of the president's health. The importance of the public's perception of these traits is evident in the ridicule often directed at candidates. In 2000, George W. Bush was lampooned for his inability to answer reporters' questions on foreign affairs, and Al Gore was the subject of jokes for following a consultant's advice to bring out the Alpha male side of his personality.

Although the media insist they pay attention to all candidates who have a chance to win, they also influence who gets such a chance. Consequently, candidates have to come up with creative ways to attract media attention. Paul Wellstone in his first Minnesota Senate campaign said in his advertisements that he did not have much money to pay for ads, so he would have to talk fast to cram what he had to say into fewer commercials. His witty commercial became a news event itself—it got Wellstone additional coverage, and Wellstone won.

In the 2000 elections, three U.S. Senate candidates in states bordering Canada organized bus trips to Canada for people to purchase prescription drugs at Canadian prices, which were sharply lower than in the United States. Montana Senate candidate Byron Schweitzer called his excursions "The Run for the Border" and generated substantial positive media coverage for his campaign through the tactic.[62]

CAMPAIGN EVENTS   Candidates schedule events—press conferences, interviews, "photo ops"—in settings that reinforce their verbal messages. Many events organized by campaigns fail to receive attention from reporters because of competing news stories and a sense that the events were staged primarily to generate news coverage. The absence of suspense or real news at the party presidential nominating conventions is one reason why the networks have dramatically cut back their coverage. In 1952 the average television set was tuned to the political conventions for 26 hours, or an average of more than three hours a night for the eight nights of convention coverage.[63] In 2000, in contrast, the major networks provided only one or two hours of prime-time coverage each evening. Political parties have sought, in vain, to regain audience interest by

Thinking It Through . . .

Some people dismiss reporting on sex scandals as prudish and unrelated to governing. Others, like Larry Sabato, a political scientist who has written on the media, disagree. Sabato says the press "didn't reveal what most of them knew then about Clinton and all the other women. If the press had done its job in '92, the country would not be facing this horrible dilemma in '98."[*]

The question of how to report sexual misbehavior by political candidates is unresolved. It is debatable whether such matters ought to be reported at all. Reporters appear to be looking for ways to avoid such stories. The public wants to know whether candidates meet high standards of personal conduct, but they react negatively to coverage that is too aggressive. Public reaction to the explicit details of the Starr report is instructive: 84 percent of the public wanted to know the conclusions of the investigation, but 70 percent felt that Congress should have omitted the details of the sexual encounters.[**]

[*] Larry J. Sabato, quoted in William Power, "News at Warp Speed," *National Journal*, January 31, 1998, p. 220.

[**] Frank Newport, "Initial Reaction Mixed on Delivery of Starr Report to Congress," Gallup Organization, September 12, 1998. See also www.gallup.com/poll_archives/980912.htm.

With the Internet, citizens now have the opportunity to interact with each other on a wide range of political topics. In this sense, the Internet is something like a town meeting, but without people leaving their homes or offices. In chat rooms on the World Wide Web, people express ideas and respond to each other's opinions. Examples of chat rooms include Abortion Chat, Democrat Chat, Environment Chat, Republican Chat, and Congress Chat. Most chat rooms offer group discussions in which anyone in the group can read and send messages, but some chat rooms also permit private messages to be sent.

As with town meetings, politicians can learn about public sentiment via the Web. They can participate in a chat room or read postings on the Internet in what is called Usenet. Reading messages posted on Usenet permits politicians to gauge public opinion and tap into particular segments of the population. But because those who use the Internet are not a representative sample of the general public, politicians should be wary not to generalize from the opinions expressed through this medium.

relying on "movie stars, entertainment routines, and professionally produced documentaries to spice up their conventions."[64]

TECHNOLOGY   Although the expense associated with media technology has contributed to the skyrocketing costs of campaigning, it also has made politics more accessible to more people. Thanks to satellites, candidates can conduct local television interviews without actually traveling to local studios. Specific voter groups can be targeted through cable television or low-power television stations that reach homogeneous neighborhoods and small towns. Videocassettes with messages from the candidates further extend the campaign's reach.[65] All serious candidates for Congress and governor in 2000 made themselves and their positions available through a home page on the World Wide Web.

Image Making

Attempts to spin the news and to portray candidates in the best possible light are not new. Presidential campaign sloganeering such as "Tippecanoe and Tyler Too" in 1840 and "Abe the Rail Splitter" in 1860 were used to convey the candidate's image. Radio, television, and the Web have expanded the ability to project images, and that expansion has in turn affected candidates' vote-getting strategies and their manner of communicating messages. Television is especially important because of the power of the visual image. But candidates recognize that their messages about issues are often ignored. The press tends to emphasize goofs and gossip or tensions among party leaders.

Media Consultants

Television has contributed to the rise of new players in campaign politics—*media consultants*, campaign professionals who provide candidates with advice and services on media relations, advertising strategy, and opinion polling.[66] For instance, a media consultant advised Al Gore on the colors and style of clothing he should wear, emphasizing earth tones and finding ways to convey his masculinity.[67]

A primary responsibility of a campaign media consultant is to present a positive image of the candidate and to reinforce negative images of the opponent. Some media consultants have been credited with propelling candidates to success. Dick Morris was seen as important to Clinton's resurgence after the 1994 congressional election defeats, until he had to resign from the campaign following a personal scandal. Republican consultants Mike Murphy and Stuart Stevens and Democratic consultants Rob Klain and Carter Eskew have acquired powerful reputations. But media consultants have also been blamed for the negativity of recent presidential campaigns.

Media consultants have taken over the role formerly played by party politicians. Before World War II, party professionals groomed candidates for office at all levels. Such leaders made their judgments about possible candidates on the basis of their chances of victory and observation of the candidates' performance under fire, decisiveness, conviction, political skill, and other leadership qualities. Party professionals advised candidates which party and interest group leaders to placate, which issues to stress, and which topics to avoid.

Today consultants coach candidates about television technique, appearance, and subject matter. Consultants report the results of *focus groups* (small sample groups of people who are asked questions about candidates and issues in a discussion setting) and *public opinion polls*, which in turn determine what the candidate says and does. Some critics allege that political consultants have become a new "political elite" who can virtually choose candidates by determining in advance which men and women have the right images, or at least images that can be restyled for the widest popularity.[68] But political consultants who specialize in media advertising and image making realize

their own limitations in packaging candidates. As one media consultant put it, "It is a very hard job to turn a turkey into a movie star; you try instead to make people like the turkey."[69]

The Media and Voter Choice

As television has become increasingly important to politics, and as the political parties have been weakened with such reforms as primary elections, news coverage of candidates has taken on added significance. Although some critics think reporters pay too much attention to candidates' personality and background, others say character and personality are among the most important characteristics for readers and viewers to know about. What is not in dispute is the central role the news media play in our democratic process.

THE HORSE RACE   What voters know about candidates is based largely on what they see on television, read in newspapers, and hear on the radio. One criticism often heard is that voters do not get the kind of information about candidates and issues that would enable them to make an informed choice. Journalists are more likely to comment on a candidate's standing in the polls compared to other candidates—what is sometimes called the "horse race."[70] "Many stories focus on who is ahead, who is behind, who is going to win, and who is going to lose, rather than examining how and why the race is as it is."[71] Reporters focus on the tactics and strategy of campaigns because they perceive that the public is interested and influenced by such coverage.[72] The media's propensity to focus on the "game" of campaigns displaces coverage of issues.

NEGATIVE ADVERTISING   Political advertising has become increasingly negative in tone. A rule of thumb in the old politics was to ignore the charges of the opposition, thus according one's rival no importance or standing. That practice has changed as candidates today trade charges and countercharges.

Voters say they are turned off by the attack style of politics, but the widespread perception among campaign consultants is that negative campaigning works. This seeming inconsistency may be explained by some evidence suggesting campaigns that foster negative impressions of the candidates contribute to lower turnout.[73] Negative advertising may thus discourage some voters who would be inclined to support a candidate (called *vote suppression*), while reinforcing the inclination of committed supporters to come out to vote.

WE THE PEOPLE

Profile of a Media Consultant

Dawn Laguens is a partner in the political consulting firm of Laguens Hamburger Stone. Dawn says her family believes she was destined for politics because the day she was christened in Arlington, Virginia, President Lyndon Johnson was attending church service there, and reporters captured a photo of the president with the new baby. Born in Washington, D.C., where her father was comptroller for the Department of Defense, she first became involved in politics in the fourth grade, where she started a student council in part to be sure playground rules were more fair to girls. She went on to be elected high school student body president and president of the student union at Louisiana State University. She later transferred to New Orleans University, where she ran a charitable foundation—the Vincent Memorial Legacy—which conducted outreach activities in the community and provided advocates for people with housing problems. Through her extracurricular activities, Dawn learned she preferred activism to academics, and she has not returned to college to complete her undergraduate degree.

One lesson she learned from her experience advocating for charity was that if you really want to make a difference, you need to be involved in politics. Her first work on a campaign was as deputy director of an unsuccessful mayoral candidacy in New Orleans. She went from there to a position as political director of the Coalition Against Racism and Nazism. David Duke, a white supremacist from Louisiana, was running for the U.S. Senate in 1990, and Laguens and the Coalition worked to defeat him. As part of that effort, she helped produce a commercial that won the Cleo award for best political ad in the nation that year.

Media consulting and campaign strategy became her passion. She is involved in all aspects of political communication, including message development, advertising production, and strategy. She has a wide range of clients and has developed a specialization in ballot initiative campaigns. In 2000 she managed media for Debbie Stabenow's successful bid for the U.S. Senate from Michigan. Other clients in recent years have included Planned Parenthood, organized labor, the gay community, the Nature Conservancy, and U.S. House candidates Dennis Moore and Tom Udall.

Laguens loves her work because it is always different, creative, and she can test her mettle against the bright minds working on the other side. In her spare time she and her partner are raising triplets.

INFORMATION ABOUT ISSUES   In recent elections the media have experimented with a more issues-centered focus through what has been called *civic journalism*. With funding from charitable foundations, some newspapers have been identifying the concerns of community leaders and talking to ordinary voters, and then writing campaign stories from their point of view.[74] Some newspaper editors and reporters disagree with this approach; rather, they believe the media should respond to newsworthy events. Advocates of civic journalism counter that important concerns of the community are often overshadowed by news events like murders and violence.

MAKING A DECISION   Newspapers and television seem to have more influence in determining the outcome of primaries than of general elections,[75] probably because voters are less likely to know about the candidates and have fewer clues about how they stand in a primary. By the time of the November general election, however, party affiliation, incumbency, and other factors moderate the impact of media messages. The mass media are more likely to influence undecided voters who, in a close election, can determine who wins and who loses.

ELECTION NIGHT REPORTING   Does TV coverage on election night affect the outcome of elections? Election returns from the East come in three hours before the polls close on the West Coast. Because major networks often project the presidential winner well ahead of poll closings in western states, some western voters have been discouraged from voting. As a result, voter turnout in congressional and local elections has been affected. In a close presidential election, however, such early reporting may well stimulate turnout because voters know their vote could determine the outcome. In short, it is only in elections in which one candidate appears to be winning by a large margin that television reporting makes voters believe their vote is meaningless.[76]

THE MEDIA AND GOVERNANCE

The press rarely follows the policy process to its conclusion. Rather, it leaves the issue at the doorstep of public officials. By the time a political issue reaches the stages of policy formulation and implementation, the press has moved on to another issue. When policies are being formulated and implemented, decision makers are at their most impressionable, yet the press has little impact at this stage.[77]

Lack of press attention to how policies are implemented explains in part why we know less about how bureaucrats go about their business than we do about heated legislative debates or presidential scandals. Only in the case of a policy scandal, such as the lax security of nuclear secrets at Los Alamos, does the press take notice. "Most executives would be satisfied with a press strategy of no surprises. All their press officers need do to be doing their job is provide a rudimentary early warning system [for crises] and issue routine announcements."[78] But the assumption of most policy makers, even those handling classified national security information, is that their actions will leak out to the media sooner or later.

Some media critics contend a negative consequence of the media's approach to policy coverage is pressure on policy makers to resolve a problem immediately once it receives media focus. Foreign policy may be in particular danger from such quick responses:

> If an ominous foreign event is featured on TV news, the president and his advisers feel bound to make a response in time for the next evening news broadcast. . . . If he does not have a response ready by the late afternoon deadline, the evening news may report that the president's advisers are divided, that the president cannot make up his mind, or that while the president hesitates, his political opponents know exactly what to do.[79]

Political Institutions and the News Media

Presidents have become the stars of the media, particularly television, and have made the media their forum for setting the public agenda and achieving their legislative aims. Presidential news conferences command attention (see Table 10–2). Every public activity, both professional and personal, is potentially newsworthy; a presidential illness can become front-page news, as can presidential vacations and family pets. A president attempts to manipulate news coverage to his benefit. Speeches are used to set the national agenda or spur congressional action. Travel to foreign countries usually boosts popular support at home, thanks to the largely favorable news coverage. Better yet for the president, most coverage of the president—either at home or abroad—is favorable or at worst neutral.[80] President Clinton's trip to Israel during the height of the impeachment furor may have helped distract attention from his domestic problems, in both senses of that word.

Congress is more likely to get negative coverage than either the White House or Supreme Court. Congress is a fragmented body unable to act quickly.[81] Unlike the presidency, it lacks an ultimate spokesperson—a single individual who can speak for the whole institution.[82] Congress does not make it easy for the press to cover it. While the White House engages in the "care and feeding" of the press corps, Congress does not arrange its schedule to suit the media; floor debates, for example, often compete with committee hearings and press conferences.[83] Singularly dramatic actions rarely occur in Congress; the press, therefore, turns to the president to describe federal government activity on a day-to-day basis and treats Congress largely as a foil to the president. Most coverage of Congress is of its reaction to the initiatives of the president.[84]

The federal institution least dependent on the press is the Supreme Court, which does not rely on public communication for political support. Rather, it relies indirectly on public opinion for continued deference to and compliance with its decisions.[85] The Court has strong incentives to avoid the perception of manipulating the press, so it retains an image of aloofness from politics and public opinion. The justices' manipulation of press coverage of the Court is far more subtle and complex than that of the other two institutions.[86] For example, the complexity of the Supreme Court's decision in the Florida vote recounting case with multiple dissents and concurrences and with no press release or executive summary made broadcast reporting on the decision difficult.

The news media's greatest role may be at the local level. Most of us have multiple sources for finding out what is happening in Washington that act as a check on

TABLE 10–2 Presidential News Conferences with White House Correspondents

President	Average per Month	Total Number
Herbert Hoover (1929–33)	5.6	268
Franklin D. Roosevelt (1933–45)	6.9	998
Harry Truman (1945–53)	3.4	334
Dwight Eisenhower (1953–61)	2.0	193
John Kennedy (1961–63)	1.9	64
Lyndon Johnson (1963–69)	2.2	135
Richard Nixon (1969–74)	0.5	37
Gerald Ford (1974–77)	1.3	39
Jimmy Carter (1977–81)	0.8	59
Ronald Reagan (1981–89)	0.5	44
George Bush (1989–93)	3.0	142
Bill Clinton (1993–99)	2.0	192

SOURCE: *Weekly Compilation of Presidential Documents*, vol. 31, *Annual Index* (p. C12); Interview, White House Press Office, December 27, 2000.

the biases and limitations of reporters who cover national government and policy. But when it comes to finding out about the city council, the school board, or the local water district, most of us are dependent on the work of a single reporter. Consequently, the media's influence is much greater when there are fewer news sources.

Not all who think the media are powerful agree that their power is harmful. After all, they argue, the media perform a vital educational function. Almost 70 percent of the public think the press is a watchdog that keeps government leaders from doing bad things.[87] At the very least, the media have the power to mold the agenda of the day; at most, in the words of the late Theodore White, they have the power to "determine what people will talk and think about—an authority that in other nations is reserved for tyrants, priests, parties, and mandarins."[88]

POLITICS ONLINE

How To Be Your Own News Filter

We live in a time with more and more ways to learn what is happening around the world and in our community. Baseball fans used to turn to the sports pages of newspapers to get the box scores on games around the country; or people would turn to the weather page to learn what the forecast was for a city they were traveling to later in the week. Now there is no reason to wait until the newspaper arrives. You can learn the box scores on the Internet soon after the game ends, and the weather forecasts as rapidly.

The same principle applies to virtually all categories of news. Imagine getting only the news that interests you delivered every morning to your personal e-mail account. You can sign up for exactly that with most major newspaper websites, usually at no charge. Just look for the place to sign up for the e-mail newsletter. E-mail newsletters will be sent daily containing just the topics you like: entertainment, sports, business, lifestyles, and American politics. *USA Today* at: www.usatoday.com, *The New York Times* at: www.nytimes.com, *The Washington Post* at: www.washingtonpost.com, and *The Wall Street Journal* at: www.wsj.com all provide a form of e-mail headlines.

Not only in the print media can you act as your own gatekeeper, but you can also see or listen to only those reports that interest you in the broadcast media. Try going to major television media websites such as: www.msnbc.com, www.cbsnews.com, www.abcnews.com, www.cnn.com, and www.foxnews.com, or to radio websites like: www.npr.org. On these websites you can select which news reports you want to see or listen to, or even read them as text articles. Much like the newspaper sites, most of these sites also offer free headlines that can be e-mailed to your account. This is especially handy if you want to monitor a particular issue and cannot listen or watch the program in real time.

You can also make sure that your Web browser's home page shows only those topics, stories, articles, and headlines that interest you most—even your local weather. One place to do this is at: www.msn.com. You'll first need to create a free Passport account; then locate the places where you can click to change the content, layout, and even colors of your home page.

SUMMARY

1. The news media include newspapers, magazines, radio, television, films, recordings, books, and electronic communications, in all their forms. These means of communication have been called "the other government" and "the fourth branch of government."

2. The news media are a pervasive feature of American politics and generally help to define our culture. The rise of new communications technologies has made the media more influential throughout American society. The news media provide a "linking" function between politicians and government officials and the public.

3. Our modern news media emerged from a more partisan and less professional past. The autonomy of the media from political parties is one of the important changes. Now journalists strive for

objectivity and see themselves as important to the political process. They also engage in investigative journalism.

4. Broadcasting on radio and television has changed the news media, and most Americans use television and radio as primary news sources. The role of corporate ownership of media outlets, especially media conglomerates, raises questions about media competition and orientation.

5. The influence of the mass media over public opinion is significant yet not overwhelming. People may not pay much attention to the media or believe all they read or see or hear. They may be critical or suspicious of the media and

hence resistant to it. People tend to "filter" the news in part through their political socialization, selectivity, needs, and ability to recall or comprehend the content of the news.

6. The media are criticized as biased both by conservatives (who charge that the media are too liberal) and by liberals (who claim that the media are captive of corporate interests and major advertisers). Little evidence exists of actual, deliberate bias in news reporting.

7. A major effect of mass media news is agenda setting—that is, determining what problems will become salient issues for people to form opinions about and to discuss. The media are also

influential in defining issues for the general public.

8. Presidential campaigns are dominated by media coverage during both the pre- and post-convention stages. One effect of media influence is that most people seem more interested in the contest as a "game" or "horse race" than as an occasion for serious discussion of issues and candidates. Another effect has been the rise of image making and the media consultant.

9. The press serves as observer of and participant in politics as watchdog, agenda setter, and check on the abuse of power, but it rarely follows the policy process to its conclusion.

KEY TERMS

mass media 224
news media 224

issue ad 225
fairness doctrine 230

political socialization 231
selective exposure 232

selective perception 232

FURTHER READING

STEPHEN ANSOLABEHERE AND SHANTO IYENGAR, *Going Negative: How Attack Ads Shrink and Polarize the Electorate* (Free Press, 1996).

TIMOTHY COOK, *Governing with the News: The News Media as a Political Institution* (University of Chicago Press, 1998).

TIMOTHY E. COOK, *Making Laws and Making News: Press Strategies in the U.S. House of Representatives* (Brookings Institution, 1990).

TIMOTHY E. COOK, *Governing with the News: The News Media as a Political Institution* (University of Chicago Press, 1998).

RICHARD DAVIS, *The Web of Politics: The Internet's Impact on the American Political System* (Oxford University Press, 1999).

RICHARD DAVIS AND DIANA MARIE OWEN, *New Media and American Politics* (Oxford University Press, 1998).

JAMES FALLOWS, *Breaking the News: How the Media Undermine American Democracy* (Pantheon Books, 1996).

SUZANNE GARMENT, *Scandal: The Culture of Mistrust in American Politics* (Times Books, 1991).

DORIS A. GRABER, *Mass Media and American Politics*, 5th ed. (Congressional Quarterly Press, 1997).

DORIS A. GRABER, *Media Power in Politics*, 4th ed. (Congressional Quarterly Press, 2000).

LAWRENCE K. GROSSMAN, *The Electronic Republic: Reshaping Democracy in the Information Age* (Viking, 1995).

RODERICK P. HART, *Campaign Talk: Why Elections Are Good for Us* (Princeton University Press, 2000).

STEPHEN HESS, *Live from Capitol Hill: Studies of Congress and the Media* (Brookings Institution, 1991).

KATHLEEN HALL JAMIESON AND JOSEPH N. CAPPELLA, *Spiral of Cynicism: The Press and the Public Good* (Oxford University Press, 1997).

PHYLISS KANISS, *Making Local News* (University of Chicago Press, 1991).

HOWARD KURTZ, *Spin Cycle: Inside the Clinton Propaganda Machine* (Free Press, 1998).

PAUL J. LAVRAKAS AND MICHAEL W. TRAUGOTT, *Election Polls, The News Media and Democracy* (Chatham House, 2000).

PAUL J. LAVRAKAS AND MICHAEL W. TRAUGOTT, EDS., *Election Polls, The News Media and Democracy* (Chatham House, 2000).

S. ROBERT LICHTER, STANLEY ROTHMAN, AND LINDA S. LICHTER, *The Media Elite* (Adler and Adler, 1986).

JOHN ANTHONY MALTESE, *Spin Control: The White House Office of Communications and the Management of Presidential News* (University of North Carolina Press, 1992).

THOMAS E. PATTERSON, *OUT OF ORDER* (KNOPF, 1993).

MARTIN PLISSNER, *The Control Room: How Television Calls the Shots in Presidential Elections* (Free Press, 1999).

TOM ROSENSTEIL, *Strange Bedfellows: How Television and the Presidential Candidates Changed American Politics, 1992* (Hyperion, 1993).

LARRY J. SABATO AND S. ROBERT LICHTER, *Peepshow: Media and Politics in an Age of Scandal* (Rowman & Littlefield, 2000).

SIMON SERFATY, *The Media and Foreign Policy* (St. Martin's Press, 1990).

JAMES A. THURBER, CANDICE J. NELSON, AND DAVID A. DULIO, EDS., *Crowded Airwaves: Campaign Advertising in Elections* (Brookings Institution Press, 2000).

DARRELL M. WEST, *Air Wars: Television Advertising in Election Campaigns, 1952–1992* (Congressional Quarterly Press, 1993).

11

CONGRESS: THE PEOPLE'S BRANCH

T

HE UNITED STATES CONGRESS IS ONE OF THE

MOST PRAISED YET MOST CRITICIZED POLITICAL INSTITUTIONS

IN THE WORLD. IT IS PRAISED BECAUSE IT IS A REPRESENTATIVE
and democratic institution. It is praised, too, because it is deliberative and open. And it
is revered because many outstanding legislators have served in Congress and contributed greatly to the success of the American political experiment.

Yet Americans relentlessly criticize both Congress and its members. Citizens think
members of Congress don't understand their needs and put the concerns of special
interests ahead of those of their regular constituents. Sixty-two percent of participants
in one national survey complained that "Congress creates more problems than it
solves."[1] Congress is also criticized for being irrelevant, slow, and overly partisan.

Although most Americans profess a devotion to democracy, many have little or
no appreciation of what it takes to make democracy work. "People do not wish to see
uncertainty, conflicting options, long debate, competing interests, confusion, bargaining, and compromised, imperfect solutions," write political scientists John Hibbing
and Elizabeth Theiss-Morse. Instead, they would like their government to perform its
job quietly, efficiently, and without public bickering and gridlock. "In short," Hibbing
and Theiss-Morse conclude, the American people "often seek a patently unrealistic
form of democracy."[2]

Congress may be criticized, but it plays a key role in the American political system. Presidents cannot lead if they do not have a working relationship with both chambers of Congress. Congress controls decisions on budgets, taxes, trade policy, the shape
of the federal bureaucracy, and appointments to the cabinet, the embassies, and the
courts. A president has a certain amount of freedom in foreign policy, yet even here a
president's policies will rarely be successful or properly implemented without support
from Congress. For this reason President George Bush sought congressional support
before the Persian Gulf War.

Because ours is a system of shared powers, Congress and the president are
forced to work together while protecting their often-different policy positions. The
pressure to compromise and consequently to appear inconsistent is often seen by the
public and the media as a negative, when in fact it is a necessary result of divided
public opinion.

In this chapter we examine the politics of representation and how Congress orga-
nizes itself to do its work of making laws and representing the people. We also look at

CHAPTER MEDIA

POLITICS ONLINE
*What's Happening in
Congress Today?*
www.prenhall.com/burns

how this highly public, open, and political institution cannot avoid provoking conflicts that lead to sometimes bitter clashes with the White House and other rivals for influence in the shaping of American public policies.

CONGRESSIONAL ELECTIONS

The entire membership of the House of Representatives (435) is elected to two-year terms in even-numbered years. Elections for the six-year Senate terms are staggered, so that one-third of the Senate's 100 members are chosen every two years. Members of the House of Representatives must be 25 years old and have been citizens for seven years. Senators must be at least 30 years old and have been citizens for nine years. House and Senate candidates must live in the states in which they are elected.

Members of Congress are politicians who get their jobs by winning an election. Ironically, it is often good politics for them to deny they are politicians and to lead the charge against the institution they serve in. The willingness of "House members to stand and defend their own votes or voting record contrasts sharply with their disposition to run and hide when a defense of Congress might be called for," writes political scientist Richard F. Fenno, Jr. "Members of Congress run *for* Congress by running *against* Congress. The strategy is ubiquitous, addictive, cost-free, and foolproof. . . . In the short run, everybody plays and nearly everybody wins. Yet the institution bleeds from 435 separate cuts."[3]

The outcome of any congressional election depends on many factors. By far the most important is the nature of the state or district in which the candidate runs. The most common is a **safe seat**—one that is predictably won by one party or the other. Or it could be a competitive one, sometimes called a "swing district" in House races. Other factors affecting winning elections are personal appeal of the candidate, whether the opponent is an incumbent or a newcomer, local issues, campaign strategies, the fund-raising abilities of the candidate, and,

Freshmen House of Representatives of the 107th Congress, who took office in January 2001, on the steps of the U.S. Capitol for their "class" picture.

safe seat

An elected office that is predictably won by one party or the other, so reelection is almost taken for granted.

occasionally, national political tides, such as in the 1964, 1974, and 1994 elections.

Incumbents have traditionally enjoyed a great advantage over challengers, but incumbency isn't always an advantage. "Outsiders" like Ross Perot, Ralph Nader, Steve Forbes, and Rush Limbaugh have targeted "Washington insiders" and helped create a climate of antagonism toward Congress as an institution. Because of this climate, there have been repeated yet unsuccessful efforts in Congress to pass constitutional limits on congressional terms. But more than 90 percent of incumbents who run for reelection to Congress beat their challengers; more than 98 percent of House members were reelected in 2000, and 23 of 29 U.S. senators won reelection, for a success rate of almost 80 percent.

The Politics of Drawing House District Lines

Every state, according to the Constitution, has two U.S. senators; each senator represents his or her entire state. House of Representatives seats are distributed or apportioned among the states according to population. House districts have about 650,000 people in them.

The Constitution requires a national census every ten years. As a result of the 2000 census, Congress had to reallocate seats based on population shifts. New York and Pennsylvania lost two House seats, Ohio, Indiana, Illinois, Wisconsin, and Michigan all lost one seat. Florida, Georgia, Texas, and Arizona gained two seats. Colorado, Nevada, North Carolina and California gained one seat each.

Congress must provide for **reapportionment** of congressional seats among the states. Each state has the right to at least one seat; smaller population states such as Alaska, Wyoming, and Vermont have House seats with as many as 100,000 citizens less than a normal House seat elsewhere.

State legislators, or in some states **redistricting** commissions, draw the district lines for these House seats, although their proposals are subject to the approval or veto of the state's governor. In practice, in most states the party in control of the state legislature traditionally draws the district boundaries to enhance its own political fortunes.[4] This process is known as **gerrymandering**, after Governor Elbridge Gerry of Massachusetts, who, in 1811, reluctantly signed a redistricting bill that created a distinctly partisan district shaped like a salamander. Party-controlled gerrymandering explains why so many districts are "safe" for one party. However, if the partisanship is so biased that it makes it impossible for the other party to win, the legislature risks federal judicial objections. The U.S. Supreme Court has held that under certain circumstances, which it has never specified, excessive partisan gerrymandering might be unconstitutional.[5]

Indeed, the federal courts have insisted for years that state legislatures have to draw state and national legislative districts subject to both constitutional specifications and requirements of national laws. In *Baker v Carr* (1962), the U.S. Supreme Court held that voters do have *standing* (the right) to challenge how state legislatures allocate legislative seats, and that such questions should be considered by the federal courts.[6] Soon after the *Baker v. Carr* ruling, the Court announced that as far as U.S. House of Representatives seats are concerned, "As nearly as practicable one man's vote in congressional elections is to be worth as much as another's."[7]

Finally, although a state legislature can design its U.S. House of Representative districts to virtually guarantee the election of a member of a particular minority, it must be careful not to do so in a fashion that focuses *only* on racial considerations and ignores such matters as county lines and city boundaries.[8] Indeed, the Supreme

Why Do Incumbent Members of Congress Usually Win?

- They enjoy better name recognition, and to be known at all is generally to be known favorably. Challengers are almost always less well known.

- They enjoy free mailings (called the franking privilege) to every household in the state or district. These mailings—which often resemble campaign brochures—portray members as hardworking and influential.

- They have greater access to the media.

- They raise campaign money more easily than challengers, because lobbyists and political action committees (PACs) seek their ears and their favors. Also, many campaign contributors know that incumbents are more likely than challengers to get reelected, so they give to those they know will win. (PACs in recent elections have given as much as $8 out of every $10 to incumbents.)

- They usually have had more campaign experience, and they can claim to have had more experience in Congress and in Washington. And they usually are better campaigners.

- They have staffs to help with casework and constituency services for the folks back home.

- They take credit for federal money that gets allocated to their region.

- They are in a better position than challengers to take advantage of government research staffs, new government studies, and even classified information.

No one of these factors can guarantee a member's reelection, yet skillful use of them makes it difficult to unseat a healthy incumbent.

reapportionment
The assigning by Congress of congressional seats after each census. State legislatures reapportion state legislative districts.

redistricting
The redrawing of congressional and other legislative district lines following the census, to accommodate population shifts and keep districts as equal as possible in population.

gerrymandering
The drawing of election district boundaries to benefit a party, group, or incumbent.

The word "gerrymander" comes from the name of a governor of Massachusetts, Elbridge Gerry, and the salamander-shaped district that was created to favor his party in 1811.

Court has ruled that making race "the predominant factor," while ignoring traditional redistricting principles such as compactness, is unconstitutional.[9]

THE STRUCTURE AND POWERS OF CONGRESS

The most important feature of Congress is its **bicameralism**—that is, it is made up of two houses. Few other national legislatures are genuinely bicameral. Many have two houses, but one is usually ceremonial in practice. In the United States, the Senate and the House each have an absolute veto over the other's law making. Each chamber runs its own affairs, sets its own rules, and conducts its own investigations. The law-making role, however, is shared. Each must be seen as a separate institution, even though both houses reflect similar political forces and share common organizational patterns.

In other countries the "upper" house often has significantly fewer powers than the supposed "people's" house. For example, the French Senate (indirectly elected by local and regional officeholders) has full powers of debate and amendment, but the government can push through legislation blocked or amended in the Senate by obtaining a favorable vote in the lower house (the National Assembly).

In Germany, the upper house (Bundesrat) is composed of delegates named by the state governments. The size of the delegation is based on population, but each state's delegation casts its votes as a bloc in Bundesrat votes. The Bundesrat lacks the legislative powers of the lower house (Bundestag), but it does allow for the involvement of the states in legislation that affects them and their relationship to the federal government. The Bundesrat often plays a key political role, especially when its majority differs from the majority in the Bundestag.

The Consequences of Bicameralism

As James Madison explained in *The Federalist*, No. 51, the protection against giving too much power to the legislature "is to divide the legislature into different branches; and to render them, by different modes of election and different principles of action, as little connected with each other as the nature of their common functions, and their common dependence on the society will admit." (*The Federalist*, No. 51, is reprinted in the Appendix.)

The House of Representatives was expected to reflect the popular will of the average citizen, whereas the Senate was to provide for stability, continuity, and deliberation. The framers hoped the Senate would stem any rash populist impulses of the other chamber. Although the Seventeenth Amendment to the Constitution (1913), which provides for direct election of U.S. senators, altered the character of the Senate's membership, the two chambers still have differences (see Table 11–1). However, the two houses are more similar today in their membership and operations than they were two hundred or even one hundred years ago.

Defenders of bicameralism say it serves as a moderating influence on the partisanship or possible errors of either of the chambers. This constitutionally mandated structure also guarantees that many votes will be taken before a policy is finally approved. It provides more opportunities, too, for bargaining and allows legislators with different policy goals a role in the shaping of national laws.

The Senate is the only legislature in the United States where the principle of equal representation does not apply. As noted earlier, the number of senators from each state is not based on population. Because each state has two senators regardless of population, the Senate represents constituencies that are more rural, white, and conservative than would be the case if the one-person, one-vote norm applied to Senate elections.

Does it matter that California's 35 million (and growing!) people have the same two Senate votes as Wyoming's less than 500,000? Such disparities make the Senate the most malapportioned elected legislature in the democratic world, giving the advantage to citizens in the smaller as opposed to larger states. Frances Lee and

bicameralism
The principle of a two-house legislature.

TABLE 11–1 Differences Between the House of Representatives and the Senate

House of Representatives	Senate
Two-year term	Six-year term
435 members	100 members
Smaller constituencies	Larger constituencies
Fewer personal staff	More personal staff
Equal populations represented	States represented
Less flexible rules	More flexible rules
Limited debate	Extended debate
More policy specialists	Policy generalists
Less media coverage	More media coverage
Less prestige	More prestige
Less reliance on staff	More reliance on staff
More powerful committee leaders	More equal distribution of power
Very important committees	Less important committees
20 major committees	20 major committees
Nongermane amendments (riders) not allowed	Nongermane amendments (riders) allowed
Important Rules Committee	Special treaty ratification power
Some bills permit no floor amendments (closed rule)	Special "advice and consent" confirmation power
	Filibuster allowed

Bruce Oppenheimer conclude that the size of a state's population affects senator-constituent relationships, fund raising and elections, strategic behavior within the Senate, and ultimately policy decisions.[10] Retired U.S. Senator Daniel Patrick Moynihan (D.-N.Y.), who knew firsthand how citizens of larger states fared less well in U.S. Senate policy battles, predicted that "some time in the next century the United States is going to have to address the question of apportionment in the Senate."[11] That may be so, but the prospects for changing the one state/two U.S. senators constitutional rule are highly unlikely in the near future.

The Constitutional Separation of Powers

In Article I, the Constitution outlines the structure, powers, and responsibilities of Congress, giving it "All legislative Powers herein granted": the power to spend and tax in order to "provide for the common Defense and general Welfare of the United States"; the power to borrow money; the power to regulate commerce with foreign nations and among the states; the power to declare war, raise and support armies, and provide and maintain a navy; the power to establish post offices; and the power to set up the federal courts under the Supreme Court. As a final catchall, the Constitution gave Congress the right "to make all Laws which shall be necessary and proper for carrying into Execution" the powers set out. Several nonlegislative functions were also granted, such as participating in the process of constitutional amendment and impeachment (given to the House) and trying an impeached federal officer (given to the Senate).

The Constitution stipulates the grounds for impeachment that can lead to the removal from office of a president or vice president or other federal officers, including federal judges, are the commission of "High Crimes and Misdemeanors" (never clearly defined). The House sits to determine whether or not an official's actions reach the level of impeachable offenses, and if so, it can impeach by a majority vote. The Senate sits as a court to decide if the impeached official should be convicted, and whether the nature of the offense warrants removal from office. A two-thirds vote is

needed to convict; thus a minority of just 34 senators can reject a conviction or removal of an impeached official.

The Constitution confers additional responsibilities on the Senate. The Senate has the power to confirm many presidential nominations—sometimes as many as 500 key executive and judicial nominees a year. In a two-year session of Congress there may be more than 4,000 civilian nominations and 70,000 military nominations needing senatorial approval. Many of these nominations are approved in large blocks. The Senate must also play a crucial "advice and consent" role in treaty making—formal agreements between the United States and one or more countries. All treaties must be approved by a two-thirds vote in the Senate before they can be ratified by a U.S. president.

The House has some distinctive responsibilities, but they are not as important as those given to the Senate. For example, although all revenue bills must originate in the House, this practice does not give the House much advantage, because the Senate can freely amend spending bills, sometimes changing everything except the title.

The framers did not intend Congress to be all-powerful. They reserved certain authority for the states and for the people and gave other powers to the executive and judicial branches of the national government. As time passed, Congress has gained power in some respects and lost it in others. The power of Congress also changed with the president and the times.

As the role and authority of the national government have expanded, so have the policy-making and oversight responsibilities of Congress. Still, Congress has difficulty keeping pace with its great rival, the president. The president's national security responsibilities, preparation of the budget, media visibility, and agenda-setting influence have all enhanced the position of the presidency. The growth of executive authority may be part of a worldwide trend. Legislative bodies almost everywhere have become subordinate to the executive at all levels of government.

The House of Representatives

The organization and procedures in the House are different from those in the Senate, if only because the House is more than four times as large as the Senate. *How* things are done affects *what* is done. The House assigns different types of bills to different calendars. For instance, financial measures—tax or appropriations bills—are put on a special calendar for quicker action.

The House has other ways to speed up law making, including electronic voting. Ordinary rules may be suspended by a two-thirds vote, or immediate action may be taken by *unanimous consent* of the members on the floor. By sitting as the *committee of the whole*, the House is able to operate more informally and more quickly than under its regular rules. A *quorum* in the committee of the whole requires only 100 members, rather than a majority of the whole chamber, and voting is quicker and simpler. Members are limited in how long they can speak, and debate may be cut off simply by majority vote.

THE SPEAKER   The **Speaker** is the presiding officer in the House of Representatives.[12] The Constitution mandates that the House of Representatives shall choose its Speaker, yet it does not say anything about the duties or powers of the office. This officer is formally elected by the entire House yet is actually selected by the majority party. As the highest-ranking officer in Congress, the Speaker represents it on ceremonial occasions. Third in line of succession to the presidency (in case of death, resignation, or impeachment), the Speaker must keep the White House informed about his whereabouts.

The routine powers of the Speaker include recognizing members who wish to speak, ruling on questions of parliamentary procedure, and appointing members to

Speaker

The presiding officer in the House of Representatives, formally elected by the House but actually selected by the majority party.

temporary committees, not the major standing or regular committees. Revolts in 1910 by rank-and-file Progressives stripped Speakers of much of their previous power, including control over who served on which congressional committees. In general, the Speaker today directs business on the floor of the House. More significant, of course, is a Speaker's political and behind-the-scenes influence.

When the Republicans won control of the House in 1994, they elected representative Newt Gingrich (R.-Georgia) as Speaker. As the first Republican Speaker in 40 years, he was a novelty in Washington. "I had set out to do a very unusual job," said Gingrich, "which was part revolutionary, part national political figure, part Speaker, part intellectual."[13]

Gingrich established his authority—naming committee chairs, bypassing the seniority rule, reorganizing House committees, and reducing perks and committee staffs. He pushed through some of the legislation outlined in the Republican Contract with America. He delegated considerable power to fellow Republican leaders, yet claimed for himself the main role as spokesperson for major policy initiatives. He published books detailing his ideas about government and his party, and he cheerfully took on the White House and the national press.[14]

Following a volatile tenure and a two-year investigation, the House Ethics Committee found Gingrich had disregarded standards of conduct that applied to the use of tax-exempt funds. He had insisted there was little overlap between his partisan political activities and his supposedly nonpartisan educational endeavors. But the committee recommended, and the House of Representatives quickly passed, a reprimand of Gingrich and imposed a fine of $300,000 for misusing charitable deductions for political purposes and for misleading the House Ethics Committee. This was an unprecedented rebuke for a Speaker.

Gingrich retired both as Speaker and as a member of Congress following his party's poor showing in the midterm election of 1998. Republicans soon selected Illinois Representative J. Dennis Hastert as Speaker. Hastert, a former high school teacher and wrestling coach, had served for 6 years in the Illinois state legislature and 12 in the U.S. House of Representatives before becoming Speaker of the House. "It's a calling that I have not sought," said Hastert about the Speakership. "However, it is a duty that I cannot ignore."[15] Hastert displays a low-key, quiet self-confidence that has pleased most Republican House members. He concentrates on central issues on which Republicans can agree, aware that he is trying to lead a House with only a slender margin of majority control.[16] Speaker Hastert was reelected Speaker for the 107th House of Representatives; he even picked up a vote from a Democrat!

OTHER HOUSE OFFICERS   The Speaker is assisted by a **majority leader**, who helps plan party strategy, confers with other party leaders, and tries to keep members of the party in line. The minority party elects a **minority leader**, who usually steps into the Speakership when his or her party gains a majority in the House. (These positions are also sometimes called majority and minority floor leaders.) Assisting each floor leader are the party **whips**. (The term comes from the "whipper-in," who in fox hunts keeps the hounds bunched in a pack.) The whips serve as liaisons between the House leadership of each party and the rank-and-file. They inform members when important bills will come up for a vote, prepare summaries of the bills, do nose counts for the leadership, exert pressure (sometimes mild and sometimes heavy) on members to support the leadership, and try to ensure maximum attendance on the floor for critical votes.

At the beginning of the session and occasionally afterward, each party holds a **party caucus** of all its members (called a *conference* by Republicans) to elect party officers, approve committee assignments, elect committee leaders, discuss important legislation, and perhaps try to agree on party policy.

Republican Dennis Hastert, Speaker of the House of Representatives.

majority leader
The legislative leader selected by the majority party, who helps plan party strategy, confers with other party leaders, and tries to keep members of the party in line.

minority leader
The legislative leader selected by the minority party as spokesperson for the opposition.

whip
Party leader who is the liaison between the leadership and the rank-and-file in the legislature.

party caucus
Meeting of party members in a chamber of the legislature to select the party leadership in that chamber and to develop party policy. Called a *conference* by Republicans.

"Listen, pal! I didn't spend seen million bucks to get here so I could yield the floor to you."

closed rule
A procedural rule in the House of Representatives that prohibits any amendments to bills or provides that only members of the committee reporting the bill may offer amendments.

open rule
A procedural rule in the House of Representatives that permits floor amendments within the overall time allocated to the bill.

hold
A practice in the Senate whereby a senator temporarily blocks the consideration of a bill or nomination.

president pro tempore
Officer of the Senate selected by the majority party to act as chair in the absence of the vice-president.

filibuster
A practice in the Senate whereby a senator holds the floor and thereby delays proceedings and prevents a vote on a controversial issue.

cloture
Procedure for terminating debate, especially filibusters, in the Senate.

THE HOUSE RULES COMMITTEE   The House, unlike the Senate, has a Rules Committee that regulates the time of floor debate for each bill and sets limitations on floor amendments. By refusing to grant a *rule*, the committee can delay consideration of a bill. A **closed rule** prohibits amendments altogether or provides that only members of the committee reporting the bill may offer amendments; closed rules are usually reserved for tax and spending bills. An **open rule** permits debate within the overall time allocated to the bill.

From the New Deal era in the mid-1930s until the mid-1960s, the Rules Committee was dominated by a coalition of Republicans and conservative Democrats. Liberals denounced it as unrepresentative, unfair, and dictatorial. More recently, the Rules Committee membership has come to reflect the views of the general makeup of the majority party. The Rules Committee today is an arm of the leadership, and rather than block legislation, it offers a "dress rehearsal" on procedural issues, like time allotted for debate to those trying to press for new measures.

The Senate

The Senate has the same basic committee structure, elected party leadership, and decentralized power as the House, but because the Senate is a smaller body, its procedures are more informal, and it permits more time for debate. It is a more open, fluid, and decentralized body now than it was a generation or two ago. Indeed, it is often said that the Senate has one hundred separate power centers and is so splintered that the party leaders have difficulty arranging the day-to-day schedule.[17]

The Senate is individualistic. It has always operated under rules that vest great power in the individual senator. Extended debate allows senators to hold the floor as long as they wish unless a supermajority of 60 colleagues votes to end debate. "And, the Senate's permissive amending rules enable any senator to offer any and as many amendments as she pleases to almost any bill and those amendments need not even be germane [related to the measure]."[18]

In recent years, senators have used a practice called the **hold**. A hold is a procedure allowing any senator to block temporarily the consideration of either a legislative bill or a presidential nomination. Found nowhere in the Constitution or in Senate rules, the hold has "evolved as a courtesy for senators who could not be present when a vote was scheduled or who needed time to bone up on a subject before the floor debate began."[19] But over the past decade the hold has been expanded beyond its past purposes and is now often a tactic to kill a bill or nomination.

The president of the Senate (the vice-president of the United States) has little influence over Senate proceedings. A vice-president can vote only in case of a tie. The Senate elects a **president pro tempore**, usually the most senior member from the majority party, who acts as chair in the absence of the vice-president. Presiding over the Senate on most occasions is a thankless chore, so the president pro tempore regularly delegates this responsibility to junior members of the chamber's majority party.

The *Senate majority leader*—the elected leader of the majority party in the Senate—is an influential person within the Senate and sometimes nationally. The current majority leader, Senator Tom Daschle (D.-South Dakota), for example, has become a spokesperson for the Democratic party. As the Senate's power broker, the majority leader has the right to be the first senator heard on the floor. In consultation with the *Senate minority leader*, the majority leader determines the Senate's agenda and has much to say about committee assignments for members of the majority party. But the position confers less authority than the Speakership in the House, and its influence depends on the person's political and parliamentary skills and on the national political situation.[20] Senate majority leaders have to be persuaders and negotiators, not only working closely with the minority leader but also working with a number of powerful majority and minority senators as well as with the White House.

Party machinery in the Senate is somewhat similar to that of the House. There are party caucuses (conferences), majority and minority floor leaders, and party

whips. Each party has a *policy committee*, composed of the leaders of the party, which is theoretically responsible for the party's overall legislative program. In the Senate the party policy committees assist the leadership in monitoring legislation and provide policy expertise. Unlike the House party committees, the Senate's party policy committees are formally provided for by law, and each has a regular staff and a budget. Although the Senate party policy committees have some influence on legislation, they have not asserted strong legislative leadership or managed to coordinate policy.

During the past 20 years the U.S. Senate has become more partisan than it had been previously. "Senators known for compromise, moderation and institutional loyalty," write political scientists Nicol Rae and Colton Campbell, "have been replaced with more ideological and partisan members who see the chamber as a place to enhance their party fortunes."[21] Partisanship in the Senate was vehement during the Bill Clinton impeachment proceedings and to a lesser extent in the confirmation battle of George W. Bush's nominee John Ashcroft as his attorney general.

Senator Trent Lott of Mississippi, Republican minority leader.

THE FILIBUSTER A major difference between the Senate and the House is that debate is less limited in the Senate. A senator who gains the floor may go on talking until he or she relinquishes the right to talk voluntarily or through exhaustion. This right to unlimited debate may be used by a small group of senators to **filibuster**—that is, delay Senate proceedings by talking continually to postpone or prevent a vote.

At one time the filibuster was a favorite weapon of southern senators intent on blocking civil rights legislation. More recently the filibuster has been used for a wider range of issues. In 1993, Republicans used a filibuster to kill President Clinton's economic stimulus package and Democrats considered filibusters to derail the Ashcroft confirmation and parts of the Bush tax plan.

A filibuster, or the threat of a filibuster, is typically most potent at the end of a congressional session, when there is a fixed date for adjournment, because it could mean that many bills that have otherwise made it through the legislative process will die for lack of a floor vote. The knowledge that a bill might be subject to a filibuster is often enough to force a compromise satisfactory to its opponents. Sometimes the leaders, knowing that a filibuster will tie up the Senate and keep it from enacting other needed legislation, do not bring a controversial bill to the floor.

A filibuster can be defeated. Until 1917 the Senate could terminate a filibuster only if every member agreed. That year, however, the Senate adopted its first debate-ending rule, or **cloture**. Now, as long as the senators who are doing the talking stay on their feet, debate can be stopped only by a cloture vote. The rule of cloture specifies that two days after 16 members sign a petition, the question of curtailing debate must be put to a vote. If three-fifths of the total number of senators (60 of the 100 members) vote for cloture, no senator may speak on the measure under consideration for more than one hour. Then a final vote must be taken after no more than 30 hours of debate, including all delaying tactics, such as quorum calls and roll call votes on procedure.

There has been an increase in the use and threat of filibusters in recent years, and these tactics have often been used for partisan and parochial purposes. Indeed, senators usually anticipate a filibuster on controversial measures, and the threat is often sufficient to force the majority to compromise and modify its position.[22] Both parties have learned to use the filibuster when they are in the minority. The Senate has averaged a few dozen filibusters in recent years; nearly 50 cloture votes were held in 1999–2000.[23]

Tom Daschle from South Dakota, majority leader of the Senate, is the official spokesperson for the Democrats in the Senate.

THE POWER TO CONFIRM The Constitution leaves the precise practices of the confirmation process somewhat ambiguous: "The President . . . shall nominate, and by and with the Advice and Consent of the Senate, shall appoint Ambassadors, other public Ministers and Consuls, Judges of the Supreme Court, all other officers of the United States."

The framers of the Constitution regarded the confirmation process—the Senate's "advice and consent" power—as an important check on executive power. Alexander Hamilton viewed it as a way for the Senate to prevent the appointment of "unfit characters."

As with other legislative business, the confirmation process starts in committees, with the relevant standing committee having jurisdiction. For example, the Judiciary Committee considers federal judges and Supreme Court nominees; the Foreign Relations Committee considers ambassadorial appointments. Nominees appear before the committee to answer questions, and they typically meet individually with key senators before the hearing.

Presidents have never enjoyed exclusive control over hiring and firing in the executive branch. The Senate jealously guards its right to confirm or reject or even delay major appointments; during the period of strong Congresses after the Civil War, presidents had to struggle to keep their power to appoint and dismiss. But for most of the past hundred years, presidents gained a reasonable amount of control over top appointments, in part because a growing number of people in and out of Congress believe that chief executives without compatible cabinet-level appointees of their choice cannot be held accountable. The Senate's advise and consent powers sometimes force presidents to make compromises, plainly constraining their ability to use the presidential appointment power.

The Senate's role in the confirmation process was never intended to prevent a president from taking political considerations into account when appointments are made, but rather to use the political judgment of senators as a safeguard against weak or ill-advised nominees. When the Senate was Democratic and the White House Republican, conservatives complained that the Senate was interfering with the executive power of the president by rejecting nominees because of their political beliefs. Yet when the Republicans controlled the Senate and the Democrats the White House, it was the liberals who made the same complaint.

In recent years the Senate has taken a tough stand on some presidential appointments and spent more time evaluating and screening presidential nominations. The Senate rejected several nominees of Presidents Ronald Reagan and George Bush, and Presidents Bill Clinton and George W. Bush had to withdraw nominees for attorney general, secretary of labor, and several other posts, including federal judgeships because of Senate opposition.

By a tradition called **senatorial courtesy**, a president confers with the senator or senators in his own political party from the state where an appointee is to work. Occasionally, too, a president has to take into account the views of a politically powerful senator in the opposition party. A nomination is less likely to secure Senate approval against the objection of these senators, especially if these senators are members of the president's party. Thus, for nearly all district court judgeships and a variety of other positions, senators can exercise what is, in fact, a veto that can be overridden only with difficulty. Further, it is usually exercised in secret and subject to little accountability. Since this form of patronage or influence is sufficiently important to senators it is likely to continue.

As noted earlier, a controversial practice has emerged in recent years that allows an individual senator to request of the Senate leadership that a hold be placed on a nomination. The hold is requested to permit that senator to meet with the nominee, to gain more information about the nominee, or similar purposes. Such holds have become more frequent and are used to delay an appointment, to extract concessions from the president or other senators, or sometimes even to kill a nomination. Presidents have protested this recent practice.

It is useful to note a distinction between *judicial* appointments, especially those to the Supreme Court, and *administration* appointments. The Senate plays a greater role in judicial appointments because federal judges serve for life and constitute an independent and vital branch of the government.[24] When it comes to cabinet-level

senatorial courtesy
Presidential custom of submitting the names of prospective appointees for approval to senators from the states in which the appointees are to work.

WOMEN IN THE U.S. SENATE SPEAK UP

The nine women members of the U.S. Senate in 2000 collaborated on a book about their experiences in the Senate. The six Democrats and three Republicans met for dinner every few weeks over a two-year period not to make deals but to lend support to one another by sharing experiences and discussing issues that mattered to them. They had to excel in what until very recently was considered an exclusive men's club.

They were nine individuals out of a group of one hundred making up the Senate. In the ordinary work of each day, they did not consider themselves "women senators," yet each of them appreciated that they bring a different perspective to issues facing the Senate.

Here are a few of their stories:

Women senators pose before a book-signing for their book Nine and Counting: The Women of the Senate.

U.S. Senator Patty Murray (D.-Wash.)

I was told that I hadn't been in line long enough, that I didn't have the history, that I couldn't raise the money. Believe it or not, I was told many times that I was too short. I was actually advised to run as <u>Pat</u> *Murray, so that people might think I was a man. And I said, "Wait a minute—I'm running* <u>because</u> *I'm a woman. I'm running because we* <u>need</u> *women." And they didn't want people to know I had young kids because their reaction, of course, would be "Oh, my God, how are you going to take care of your kids?" I said, "I'm running* <u>because</u> *I have young kids. We need policy makers who understand what women are going through so these policies work for women." I was angry. Imagine! They wanted me to trick voters into thinking I was a man. I said, "No way. If I get this job it's because I am a woman and I want people to know I'm a woman."*

U.S. Senator Olympia Snowe (R.-Maine)

We certainly don't want to communicate that all of the women in the Senate are homogeneous, with the women sitting on one side and the men sitting on the other. That would be a pretty antiquated point of view, and that's not the case at all. Every one of us is different—in our political positions, our styles, our life experiences. However, women just come from a different place than men do in

terms of being more relationship-oriented and more collaborative. In fact, many of the skills women develop in life actually work pretty well in this institution. When you think about it, maybe women are particularly well suited to the Senate, where collaboration is an essential ingredient in getting things done.

U.S. Senator Blanche Lincoln (D.-Ark.)

When Blanche Lincoln was first elected to Congress at the age of thirty-three,

she recalls, several older congressmen just couldn't get over it. "Why, I have granddaughters who are your age!" one of them exclaimed. Lincoln flashed a big smile, and replied, "I'll bet your granddaughters are glad I'm here."

SOURCE: *Nine and Counting: The Women of the Senate* (Morrow, 2000), pp. 45, 130, 191. © 2000 by Barbara Mikulski, Kay Bailey Hutchison, Dianne Feinstein, Barbara Boxer, Patty Murray, Olympia Snowe, Susan Collins, Mary Landrieu, Blanche L. Lincoln, with Catherine Whitney. Reprinted by permission of Harper Collins, Publishers, Inc.

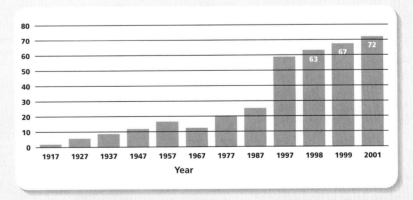

Number of Women in U.S. Congress

SOURCE: Rutgers University Center for the American Woman and Politics. Reprinted from *The Washington Post*, October 12, 1998, p. 10. Updated by the authors.

positions in the executive branch, it is assumed that a president ought to be able to choose those who will carry out the general views of the White House; in contrast, a president is not expected to enjoy partisan loyalty from those nominated to the bench.

THE JOB OF THE LEGISLATOR

The elegant U.S. Capitol building is the working center of our nation's legislative process. It is flanked by half a dozen House and Senate office buildings, the sprawling Library of Congress, and a number of other office buildings that help Congress do its work (Figure 11–1). Although staff size has been cut in recent years, members of Congress still employ about 16,000 staff aides who work in Washington, D.C., or in local district offices. Another 4,300 work for the General Accounting Office, the Congressional Research Service, the Congressional Budget Office, and other agencies under the direct control of Congress.[25] (We exclude for this count the Library of Congress and the U.S. Government Printing Office, which technically report to Congress, yet in fact serve the entire government as well as the general public.)

Congressional staffs grew enormously in the 1960s and 1970s. But in more recent years, critics and some elected officials called for major reductions in the number of both staffs and committees. As a result of cutbacks and certain reorganizations during the 1990s, staffs are about 10 percent smaller now than they were a decade ago.

Legislators as Representatives

Congress has a split personality. On the one hand, it is a *law-making institution* that writes laws and makes policy for the entire nation. In this capacity, all the members are expected to set aside their personal ambitions and perhaps even the concerns of their own constituencies. Yet Congress is also a *representative assembly*, made up of 535 elected officials who serve as links between their constituents and the national government. The dual roles of making laws and responding to constituents' demands force members to balance national concerns against the specific interests of their states or districts.

Members of Congress perceive their roles differently. Some believe they should serve as **delegates** from their districts. These legislators believe it is their duty to find out what "the folks back home" want and act accordingly. Other members see their role as that of **trustee**. Their constituents, they contend, did not send them to Congress to serve as mere robots or "errand-runners." They act and vote according to

HOUSE OF REPRESENTATIVES   **SENATE**

House Chamber · Old House Chamber · Rotunda · Old Senate Chamber · President's Room · Vice-President's Room · Senate Chamber

FIGURE 11–1 The Capitol Building

their own view of what is best for their district or state as well as the nation. As one member explained, "I have a responsibility not only to follow [my constituents], but to inform them and lead them. I'm not going to betray my responsibility to my constituents. I owe them not only my industry but my judgment. That's why they sent me here."[26] In this view a legislature is a place for deliberation and learning, not a mere gathering of ambassadors from localities.

Most legislators shift back and forth between the delegate and trustee roles, depending on their perception of the public interest, their standing in the last and next elections, and the pressures of the moment. Most also view themselves more as free agents than as instructed delegates for their districts. And recent research suggests that they often are free, since about 50 percent of citizens are unaware of how their representatives voted on major legislation and often believe their representative voted in accord with constituent policy views. Still, nearly everyone in Congress spends a lot of time building constituency connections, mending political fences, reaching out to swing voters, and worrying about how a vote on a controversial issue will "play" back home.[27]

Legislators as Lawmakers

About 5,000 bills are introduced in the House every two years and sometimes as many as 3,000 in the Senate. Members of Congress cast as many as a thousand votes each year.[28] When they vote, members of Congress are influenced by their own philosophy and values, their perceptions of their constituents' interests, the views of their trusted colleagues and staff, their partisan ties, and party leaders, lobbyists, and the president.

POLICY AND PHILOSOPHICAL CONVICTIONS   Members are influenced by their ideological beliefs most of the time. Their experiences and their attitudes about the role of government shape their convictions and help explain a lot of the differences in voting patterns.[29] A liberal on social issues is also likely to be a liberal on tax and national security issues. On controversial issues such as Social Security reform, tax cuts, or defense spending, knowing the general philosophical leanings of individual members provides a helpful guide both to how they make up their minds and how they will vote.

VOTERS   Rarely does a legislator consistently and deliberately vote against the wishes of the people back home, but a paradox is evident here. Members of Congress sometimes think what they do and how they vote makes a lot of difference to voters back home. Yet the fact is most voters most of the time don't know how their member of Congress votes. In practice, most voters don't follow most issues that come before Congress. Most citizens don't even know the names of their senators and representative.[30] Aside from periodic polls, members hear most often from the **attentive public**—those who follow public affairs carefully—rather than the general public. Nearly 70 percent of constituents say they have not visited, faxed, phoned, e-mailed, or even written their members of Congress in the past four years.[31] Still, members of Congress are generally concerned about how they will explain their votes, especially around election day. Even if only a few voters are aware of their stand on a given issue, this group might make the difference between victory and defeat.

COLLEAGUES   Legislators are often influenced by the advice of their close friends in Congress. Their busy schedules and the great number of votes force them to depend on the advice of like-minded colleagues. In particular, they look to respected members of the committee who worked on a bill.[32] Legislators find out how their friends stand on an issue, listen to the party leadership's advice, and take into account the various committee reports. Sometimes, members are influenced to vote one way merely because they know a colleague is on the other side of the issue. For

delegate
A view of the role of legislators that holds that they should represent the views of their constituents even when personally holding different views.

trustee
A view of the role of legislators that holds that they should vote independently based on their judgment of the facts.

attentive public
Those who follow public affairs carefully.

some legislators, the state delegation (senators and representatives from their home state) reinforces a common identity. Texas Democrats have long been a strong and cohesive delegation; other states, like California, have less cohesive state delegations.

A member may also vote with a colleague in the expectation that the colleague will later vote for a measure about which the member is concerned—called **log rolling**. Some vote trading takes place to build coalitions so that members can "bring home the bacon" to their constituents. Other vote trading reflects reciprocity in congressional relations or deference to colleagues' superior information or expertise.

CONGRESSIONAL STAFF   Representatives and senators used to be at a distinct disadvantage in dealing with the executive branch because they were overly dependent on information supplied by the White House or lobbyists. The complexity of the issues and increasingly demanding schedules created pressures for additional staff. Congress responded and gradually expanded its staffs, and this expansion has strengthened the role of Congress in the public policy process.

All members of Congress have personal staff members working for them both in their Washington and home-district offices. About one-third of the House of Representatives staff and one-fourth of the Senate staff are based back home. Local staff members help members of Congress communicate with the voters and provide constituency services and casework. (Helping people with a misplaced Social Security check or helping them qualify for veteran's benefits are examples of casework provided by congressional offices.) Much of the work done in district offices is akin to a continuous campaign effort: generating favorable publicity, arranging for local appearances and newspaper interviews, scheduling, and contacting important civic and business leaders in the region.

Members rely heavily on the advice of congressional staffers. Staff draft bills, do research, and are often involved in negotiating and coalition building. Staff specialists in policy areas sometimes deal on a day-to-day basis with their counterparts in the executive branch departments and with interest groups. With their direct access to the members of Congress they serve, these staff aides are often among the most influential people in Washington.

But we should not exaggerate the independent power base of staffers. They can be summarily fired at the whim of those they serve. Although they cannot be dismissed because of their race, sex, or national origin, they know that if they wander too far from the views of the one person who can fire them, they will quickly be called back into line. They are, however, asked to help raise money for their bosses.[33]

PARTY   Members generally vote with their party. Whether as a result of party pressure or natural affinity, on major bills there is a tendency for most Democrats to be arrayed against most Republicans. Partisan voting has been increasing in the House since the early 1970s and has intensified since the 1994 elections. Indeed, party-line voting has been greater in recent years than at any time in recent decades. Party differences are stronger over domestic, regulatory, and welfare reform measures than over foreign policy or civil liberty issues. Ninety-eight percent of House Republicans, for example, voted to impeach Bill Clinton in a historic vote in late 1998; 98 percent of House Democrats voted against impeachment.

Congressional redistricting has helped increase partisanship in congressional voting. "Advances in computer-driven mapping capabilities have made an art form of the old-fashioned gerrymandering that occurs where congressional districts are redrawn after each decennial census." Party operatives in the states can with great precision draw district lines to create relatively safe Democratic or Republican districts, "increasing the number of secure members answerable to only their own party's primary votes."[34]

log rolling
Mutual aid and vote trading among legislators.

As redistricting efforts in many states have ensured more safe seats, the House of Representatives has more members who are not inclined to compromise or be moderate. Consequently, House Republicans have become more politically conservative and House Democrats more confirmed liberals. The House is more politically partisan than the Senate not because of personalities but more due to these constitutional-political procedures.

Party leaders in both chambers do their best to get their members to vote together. Republican leaders claim cohesive voting is the only way Republicans can implement their party platform and satisfy the majorities who elected them in recent years. Senators are usually more independent, so party leaders in the Senate have a harder time encouraging party discipline than do leaders in the House.

The regional realignment in the American South has had the effect of diminishing the number of Democratic conservatives and strengthening Republican conservatives. There has been a similar decline of Republican moderates and a rise in more uniformly liberal Democratic districts.

In 2000, for example, on important party-unity legislation, that is, where the party leadership tried to rally its forces to vote with it, Republicans succeeded in holding an average of 88 percent of their conference in line in the House and 89 percent in the Senate. Democrats won party support in the House 82 percent of the time and in the Senate 88 percent of the time.[35] Republican moderates from the Northeast were most likely to split from their party ranks, while the few remaining conservative Democrats from the South are generally the most willing to side with the GOP when the parties lock horns.

Many forces—regional, local, ties of friendship—can override party influence. Members are sometimes influenced by ideological groups, ethnic caucuses, regional groupings, and even the class of colleagues with whom they were elected—for example, "the class of 1994." Ideological groups in Congress ranging from the Congressional Black Caucus to the more conservative Blue Dog Coalition of conservative Democrats or the even more conservative Family Concerns and New Federalists groups can also provide voting cues.[36]

INTEREST GROUPS   Interest groups, acting through their lobbyists and political action committees (PACs), make substantial contributions to congressional elections. These PACs give disproportionately to incumbents; at least 70 percent of PAC contributions went to incumbents in recent years.[37] In addition to their role as financiers of elections, interest groups are important participants in the legislative process because they provide information.

Interest groups not only watch and try to influence national legislators, but they also carefully watch one another. If a member of Congress tries to insert a "special interest" measure into an appropriations bill that is especially favorable to oil or education interests, for example, the odds are excellent that opposing interest groups are going to see this and exert their lobbying pressure to campaign for this measure's defeat. "The result is," says Senator Joe Lieberman of Connecticut, "that everyone on Capitol Hill is keeping a close eye on everyone else, creating a self-adjusting system of checks and balances."[38]

Interest groups can also be effective when they mobilize grass-roots activists and rally various constituencies to lobby their home state members of Congress. For example, higher education lobbying groups have effectively mobilized students and educators to write and call members of Congress on behalf of student aid and related provisions in various measures before the Congress.[39] And tobacco companies spent huge sums to fight taxes on cigarettes.

Most members of Congress deny the popular perception that interest groups "buy" their votes, yet political contributions certainly do influence the parties and help provide access to members of Congress. This is the way one prominent senator sees it:

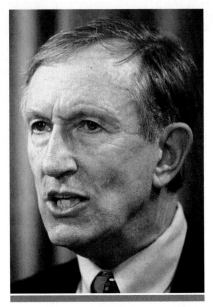

In May of 2001 U.S. Senator Jim Jeffords of Vermont, a long term Republican in state and national political office, switched party affiliation and became an Independent. He did so because he believed the Republican Party had grown too conservative and was putting undo pressure on him to vote the party line. His critical shift out of the Republican Party turned control of the Senate over to the Democratic Party.

In my experience I have found it to be not so much individual senators as the national parties and their congressional caucuses that become most dependent on special interest groups for money and grassroots support. They therefore advance the legislative priorities of some of the most ideological of those groups higher on their congressional agenda, which, in turn, further separates the parties and intensifies partisanship.[40]

THE PRESIDENT   Through effective use of their constitutional and political powers, presidents are usually partners with Congress in the legislative process. Members of Congress are invariably reluctant to admit that they are influenced by pressure from the White House. On domestic issues, legislators generally say they are more likely to be influenced by their own convictions or by their constituents than by what the White House wants. But presidents and their aides work hard to influence public opinion and to win members over to the president's point of view.

On key votes, presidents win needed majority support less than half the time. In his first term, Bill Clinton won an impressive 64 percent support from Congress on roll call votes on which he had taken a clear position.[41] However, he enjoyed much less success in his second term.

For a variety of reasons, especially because of the tendency of the nation to rally around the president in time of foreign crisis, presidents have more influence on how members of Congress vote on foreign policy or national security issues than on domestic policy.[42] Former president George Bush benefited from a bipartisan coalition that passed the resolution authorizing the use of military force in the Persian Gulf. President Clinton benefited from strong Republican support in Congress to help win approval for the various free trade agreements, even when large numbers in his own party opposed these measures.

THE LEGISLATIVE OBSTACLE COURSE

Congress operates under a system of multiple vetoes. The framers intentionally dispersed powers so they could not be accumulated by any would-be tyrant. Follow a bill through the legislative process, and you clearly see this dispersion of power (see Figure 11–2). The procedures and rules of the Senate differ somewhat from those of the House, but in each chamber power is fragmented and decentralized.

Every bill, including those drawn up in the executive branch, must be *introduced* in the House and the Senate by a member of that body. Bills are then *referred* by the leadership to the appropriate **standing committee**. A standing committee is one of the permanent working units established in the rules of the House and the Senate. Standing committees continue from one session to the next and are generally organized along policy lines (foreign policy, agriculture, and so forth). Their importance arises from the fact that most legislative measures are first considered in the appropriate standing committee or one of its relevant subcommittees. (See Table 11–2 for a list of both standing and select committees.)

Roughly 85 percent of the bills introduced in every two-year session of Congress die in committees for lack of support.[43] When bills have significant backing, a committee or subcommittee holds *hearings* to receive opinions. It then meets to *mark up* (discuss and amend) and vote on the bill. If the subcommittee and then the parent committee vote in favor of the bill, it is *reported*—that is, sent to the full chamber—where it is *debated* and *voted* on. In the House the bill must go first to the Rules Committee for a *rule* (specifying the length of debate and whether the bill may be amended).

In the Senate, it is not uncommon for legislators to attach **riders**—provisions that may have little relationship to the bill they are riding on. For

standing committee

A permanent committee established in a legislature, usually focusing on a policy area.

rider

A provision that may have little relationship to the bill it is attached to in order to secure its passage.

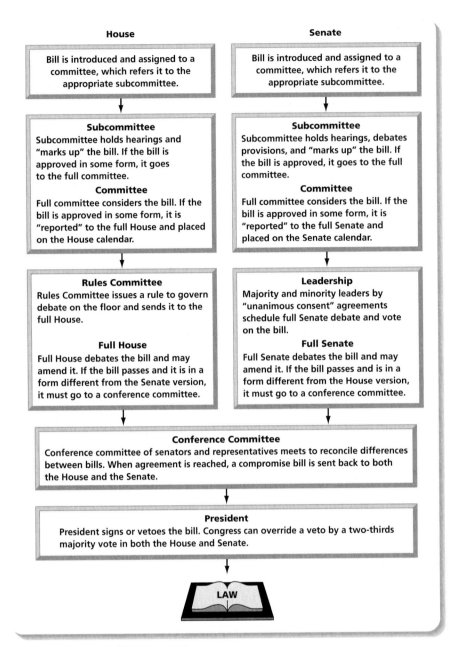

House

Bill is introduced and assigned to a committee, which refers it to the appropriate subcommittee.

Subcommittee
Subcommittee holds hearings and "marks up" the bill. If the bill is approved in some form, it goes to the full committee.

Committee
Full committee considers the bill. If the bill is approved in some form, it is "reported" to the full House and placed on the House calendar.

Rules Committee
Rules Committee issues a rule to govern debate on the floor and sends it to the full House.

Full House
Full House debates the bill and may amend it. If the bill passes and it is in a form different from the Senate version, it must go to a conference committee.

Senate

Bill is introduced and assigned to a committee, which refers it to the appropriate subcommittee.

Subcommittee
Subcommittee holds hearings, debates provisions, and "marks up" the bill. If the bill is approved, it goes to the full committee.

Committee
Full committee considers the bill. If the bill is approved in some form, it is "reported" to the full Senate and placed on the Senate calendar.

Leadership
Majority and minority leaders by "unanimous consent" agreements schedule full Senate debate and vote on the bill.

Full Senate
Full Senate debates the bill and may amend it. If the bill passes and is in a form different from the House version, it must go to a conference committee.

Conference Committee
Conference committee of senators and representatives meets to reconcile differences between bills. When agreement is reached, a compromise bill is sent back to both the House and the Senate.

President
President signs or vetoes the bill. Congress can override a veto by a two-thirds majority vote in both the House and Senate.

LAW

FIGURE 11–2 How a Bill Becomes a Law

example, riders that have little to do with spending money can be attached to appropriations bills. "In recent years, members of Congress have found the 'rider' to be a particularly helpful way of stripping from law various provisions that protect the environment."[44] The House of Representatives has stricter rules that require amendments to be relevant to the bill if they are allowed at all, but no such rule is enforced in the Senate. Senators use riders to force the president to accept legislation attached to a bill that was otherwise popular, because the president has either to accept the *entire* bill or to veto it. There has been an increase in the number of riders to appropriations bills in recent years. Republicans in both the House and Senate skirmished with President Clinton by adding riders concerning restrictions on abortion, on enforcement of environmental laws, and the right of nonprofit groups that receive federal grants to lobby.[45]

Except for tax bills, the House and Senate discuss bills simultaneously rather than waiting for one to act first. If only one chamber passes a bill at the end of that

TABLE 11-2 Congressional Standing and Select Committees

House	Senate	Joint Committees
Agriculture	Agriculture, Nutrition, and Forestry	Economics
Appropriations	Appropriations	Printing
Armed Services	Armed Services	Taxation
Budget	Banking, Housing, and Urban Affairs	On the Library
Education and the Workforce	Budget	
Energy and Commerce	Commerce, Science, and Transportation	
Financial Services	Energy and Natural Resources	
Government Reform	Environment and Public Works	
House Administration	Finance	
International Relations	Foreign Relations	
Judiciary	Governmental Affairs	
Resources	Health, Education, Labor, and Pensions	
Rules	Indian Affairs	
Science	Judiciary	
Select Intelligence	Rules and Administration	
Small Business	Select Ethics	
Standards of Official Conduct	Select Intelligence	
Transportation and Infrastructure	Small Business	
Veterans' Affairs	Special Aging	
Ways and Means	Veterans' Affairs	

congressional term, it dies. If both houses pass bills on the same subject but there are differences between the bills—and there often are—the two versions must go to a *conference committee* for *reconciliation*. If a bill does not make it through both chambers in identical form in the same Congress (two-year term), it must begin the entire process again in the next Congress.

When a bill has passed both houses in identical form, it then goes to the president, who may *sign* it into law or *veto* it. If Congress is in session and the president waits ten days (excluding Sundays), then the bill becomes law *without* his signature. If Congress has adjourned and the president waits ten days without signing the bill, it is then defeated by a **pocket veto**. Except for the pocket veto, when a bill is vetoed it is returned to the chamber of its origin by the president with a message explaining the reasons for the veto. Congress can vote to **override** the veto with a two-thirds vote in each chamber, but assembling such an extraordinary majority is often difficult.

Authorization and Appropriation

Congress legislates by a two-step process: first it *authorizes*; then it *appropriates*. After Congress and the president authorize a program by passing a law, Congress, with the president's concurrence, has to appropriate the funds by yet another measure to implement it. Appropriations are processed by the House and Senate Appropriations Committees and their subcommittees. For example, the 1998 Higher Education Act and its several titles reauthorized a variety of programs for a five-year period, including those for federal loans and grants for college students. The authorization act set the limits on the amount that students may borrow and the conditions under which they must pay back the loan. But the authorization is useless until Congress appropriates funds and the president signs the appropriations bill into law each year. Congress often appropriates less money than it has authorized.

pocket veto

A veto exercised by the president after Congress has adjourned; if the president takes no action for ten days, the bill does not become law and is not returned to Congress for a possible override.

override

An action taken by Congress to reverse a presidential veto that requires a two-thirds majority in each chamber.

The Importance of Compromise

Since it takes a majority vote in two chambers of Congress and the signature of the president before a bill becomes a law, sponsors of new legislation have to be willing to compromise. One tactical decision at the start is whether to push for action in the Senate first, in the House first, or in both simultaneously. For example, if it appears that the Senate is not likely to approve a bill, its sponsors may seek passage in the House and hope that a sizable victory there will spur the Senate into action. Another tactic concerns the committee that will consider a bill. Normally, referral to a committee is automatic, but sometimes sponsors have discretion. A bill that involves more than one jurisdiction can be written in such a way that it may go to a committee that will look more kindly on it.

Getting a bill through Congress requires that majorities and sometimes super-majorities be mobilized over and over again—in subcommittee, in committee, in chamber, and possibly again in chamber to override a presidential veto. These majorities shift and change, and they involve different legislators in different situations at different points in time. Thus coalitions must be built again and again.[46]

COMMITTEES: THE LITTLE LEGISLATURES

It is sometimes said Congress is a collection of committees that come together in a chamber every once in a while to approve one another's actions. There is much truth in this. Congress has long relied on committees to get its work done. Woodrow Wilson, a political scientist before he became president, expressed a similar thought: "Congress in session is Congress on display. Congress in committee is Congress at work."[47] More precisely, Congress in sub-committee is Congress at work, because the initial struggle over legislation takes place in subcommittees.[48]

Congress utilizes **joint committees** whose members are selected from both houses to oversee such institutions as the Library of Congress or to investigate issues

BELOW THE BELTWAY

Toles. © 1999. *Universal Press Syndicate.*

joint committee
Committee composed of members of both the House of Representatives and the Senate; such committees oversee the Library of Congress and conduct investigations.

like campaign finance reform. Committees organized to conduct investigations are called **select or special committees**.

The House of Representatives divides standing committees into three categories:

1. *Exclusive committees* include Appropriations, Ways and Means, and Rules; members who serve on one of these committees may not serve on any other standing committee.

2. *Major committees* include committees like Armed Services; members can serve on only one of these committees, but can add assignments to two nonmajor committees.

3. *Nonmajor committees*, such as Small Business, permit membership in two or three of these. House members rarely serve on more than three standing committees.

Occasionally a bill flies through a committee. More typically, however, it is kept in committee for a long while, and if and when it is reported back to the chamber, more often than not it has been amended considerably, sometimes beyond recognition. A committee reports out favorably only a small fraction of all the bills that come to it.

Although a bill can be forced to the floor of the House of Representatives through a **discharge petition** signed by a majority of the membership, legislators are reluctant to bypass committees. They regard committee members as experts in their fields. Sometimes, too, they are reluctant to risk the anger of committee leaders. And there is a strong sense of *reciprocity*: "You respect my committee's jurisdiction, and I will respect yours." Not surprisingly, few discharge petitions gain the necessary number of signatures.

While members of the House hold relatively few committee assignments, each senator normally serves on three standing committees and at least seven subcommittees. Among the most important Senate committees are Appropriations, Budget, Finance, and Foreign Relations.

Committees are not all alike. Some are powerful; others are less important. Because of the Senate's special role in foreign policy, for example, the Senate Foreign Relations Committee is usually more influential than the House Committee on International Relations. For the two Appropriations Committees, however, the reverse is true; the House Appropriations Committee plays a more significant role than the Senate Appropriations Committee, although these differences are less than they used to be.

Choosing Committee Members

Control and staffing of standing committees are partisan matters. The chair and a majority of each standing committee come from the majority party. The minority party is represented on each committee roughly in proportion to its membership in the entire chamber, except on some powerful committees on which the majority may want to enhance its position. Because Republicans and Democrats were evenly divided in the Senate after the 2000 elections 50 to 50, party leaders negotiated an equal split of membership on Senate committees. However, Republicans retained the committee chairmanships in recognition of Vice-President Dick Cheney providing the fifty-first vote in tie-breaking situations.

Getting on a politically advantageous committee is important to members of Congress. A representative from Kansas, for example, would rather serve on the Agriculture Committee than on the Banking and Financial Services Committee. Members usually stay on the same committees from one Congress to the next, although less senior members who have had less desirable assignments often seek better committees when places become available.

select or special committee
A congressional committee created for a specific purpose, sometimes to conduct an investigation.

discharge petition
Petition that, if signed by a majority of the members of the House of Representatives, will pry a bill from committee and bring it to the floor for consideration.

How are committee members chosen? In the House of Representatives, a Committee on Committees of the Republican membership allots places to Republican members. This committee is composed of one member from each state having Republican representation in the House; the member is generally the senior member of the state's delegation. Because each member has as many votes in the committee as there are Republicans in the delegation, the group is dominated by senior members from the large state delegations. On the Democratic side, assignment to committees is handled by the Steering and Policy Committee of the Democratic caucus in negotiation with senior Democrats from the state delegations.

In the Senate, veteran members also dominate the assignment process. Each party has a small Steering Committee that makes committee assignments. In making assignments, leaders are guided by various considerations: how talented and cooperative a member is, whether his or her region is already well represented on a committee, and whether the assignment will aid in reelecting the member. There sometimes are fierce battles within these committees, battles about liberal/conservative, rural/urban, environment/industry, and other differences.

One way Congress copes with its huge workload is that its committees and subcommittees are organized around subject matter specialties. This specialization allows members to develop technical expertise in specific areas and to recruit skilled staffs. Thus Congress is often able to challenge experts from the bureaucracy. Interest groups and lobbyists realize the great power a specific committee has in certain areas and focus their attention on its members. Similarly, members of executive departments are careful to cultivate the committee and subcommittee chairs and members of "their" committees.

How each chamber in Congress uses committees is critical in its role as a partner in policy making, both with the other house in Congress and with the executive branch. In recent years progress has been made in opening hearings to the public and improving the quality of committee staffs, but it is difficult to restructure committee jurisdictions so they do not overlap. Thus, a dozen different committees deal with energy, education, and the war on drugs. Efforts to make the committee system more efficient are often considered threats to the delicate balance of power within the chamber.

A 50/50 Split

Following the extraordinarily close outcome of the 2000 election, the Senate voted to grant Democrats and Republicans an equal number of seats on committees and an even share of the money to run the panels. . . .

Senator Trent Lott, the Republican leader, and Senator Tom Daschle, the Democratic leader, negotiated the proposal over several weeks and presented it to their respective parties, hailing it as a formula for bipartisanship.

A reluctant Republican conference signed off on the proposal after two days of discussion, realizing it was the best deal they could secure under the circumstances, Mr. Lott said.

"It's going to force us to work together more than we have in the past," Mr. Lott said. "No doubt. I don't think that's bad. I think this is a framework for bipartisanship."

. . . Neither party got everything it wanted, although Republicans were forced to bend the most. While Republicans retained control of the Senate because the Constitution gave the vice-president the right to break the votes, they were forced to share control of their committees, though they kept the chairmanships.

The resolution called for an equal division of committee assignments and an equal share of money between the two parties to run the committees, which meant Democrats could hire more policy experts and buy more computers. In the past, Republicans held a one-third advantage in staff, office space, and money.

SOURCE: Lizette Alvarez, "Senate to Divide Power and Money Equally in Panels," *The New York Times*, January 6, 2001, p. 1.

Seniority Rule

Forty years ago committee chairs determined the workload of committees, hired and fired staff, formed subcommittees, and assigned them jurisdictions, members, and aides. Chairs also managed the most important bills assigned to their committees. Since the mid-1970s, however, junior members have insisted they be given more authority. Subcommittee chairs also became more independent. In recent years there have also been moves to strengthen the powers of the party leaders and caucuses at the expense of the committee chairs.

Most chairs are selected on the basis of the **seniority rule**; the member of the majority party with the longest continuous service on the committee becomes chair upon the retirement of the current chair or a change in the party in control of Congress. The seniority rule gives power to representatives who come from safe districts where one party is dominant and a member can build up years of continuous service. Conversely, the seniority rule lessens the influence of states or districts where the two parties are more evenly matched and where there is more turnover.

Both Democrats and Republicans have occasionally passed over the most senior committee member in order to place someone with more energy or with

seniority rule

A legislative practice that assigns the chair of a committee or subcommittee to the member of the majority party with the longest continuous service on the committee.

How would you "reform" Congress?

Which of these proposed reforms do you think should be adopted to improve Congress?

Move to a European-style parliamentary system

Extend House terms to four years

Limit House and Senate tenure to 12 years

Provide for public financing of campaigns and ban campaign contributions

Permit only people who live in a district or state to contribute to candidates for Congress

Radically reduce the number of committees and subcommittees

Strengthen the power and resources of the party leaders

Reduce the size of congressional staffs

Abide by an agenda agreed to at the beginning of each session

Have shorter sessions for Congress so members can spend more time in their districts

a more compatible policy perspective in a committee chair position. Under Newt Gingrich's term as Speaker, a few aging committee chairs were replaced with members more allied with the Republican policy positions. It is not uncommon these days for a member of Congress to become chair of an important subcommittee after only one or two terms, and indeed such placement is the tradition in the Senate.

Still, the practice of elevating the senior member of a committee to serve as committee chair remains a general rule. It has long been respected in Congress for several reasons: it encourages members to stay on a committee; it encourages specialization and expertise; it also reduces the interpersonal politics that would arise if several members of a committee "ran" for election to become chair. However, one legacy from the Speaker Newt Gingrich era of the mid-1990s that remains is a Republican House rule that limits committee chairs to just three terms.[49] This limit brought about a lot of turnover and a fair amount of intraparty squabbles to decide who would become chair of certain key committees. Republicans departed from the seniority rule in several cases when they picked new committee chairs as the 107th Congress began in 2001.

Investigations and Oversight

The power to *investigate* is one of Congress's most important functions. Congress conducts investigations to determine if legislation is needed, to gather facts relevant to legislation, to assess the efficiency of executive agencies, to build public support, to expose corruption, and to enhance the image or reputation of its members.[50] Hearings by standing committees, their subcommittees, or special select committees are an important source of information and opinion. They provide an arena in which experts can submit their views.

Another important function of congressional hearings is the *oversight* function—the responsibility to question executive branch officials to see whether their agencies are complying with the wishes of the Congress and conducting their programs efficiently. Authorization committees regularly hold oversight hearings, and appropriations committees, exercising "the congressional power of the purse," often use appropriations hearings to communicate committee members' views about how agency officials should conduct their business. Cabinet members and agency heads have been known to dread the loaded questions of hostile members of Congress and to hate having to watch themselves on the evening news trying to explain why their agency made some mistakes.

Conference Committees

When the framers created a two-house national legislature, they anticipated the two chambers would represent sharply different interests. The Senate was to be a small chamber of persons elected indirectly by the state legislatures to hold long, overlapping terms. It was to be a chamber of deliberation, a gathering of wise leaders who would counsel and sanction a president. The House of Representatives, elected anew every two years, was to be a more direct reflection of the people.

The Senate did serve as a check on the House, especially in the late nineteenth and early twentieth centuries, when it was extremely conservative and something of a rich man's club. But today the House tends to be more conservative than the Senate. Executive departments and agencies, for instance, occasionally consider the Senate to be a court of appeals for appropriations that have been shot down by the House.

Given the differences between the House and the Senate, it is not surprising that the version of a bill passed by one chamber may differ substantially from the version passed by the other. Only if both houses pass an absolutely identical measure can

conference committee
Committee appointed by the presiding officers of each chamber to adjust differences on a particular bill passed by each but in different forms.

it become law. Most of the time one house accepts the language of the other, but about 10 to 12 percent of all bills passed, usually major ones, must be referred to a **conference committee**—a special committee of members from each chamber—that settles the differences between versions.[51] Both parties are represented, but the majority party has more members.

The proceedings of a conference committee are usually an elaborate bargaining process. When the revised bill is brought back to the two chambers, the conference report can be accepted or rejected (often with further negotiations ordered), but it cannot be amended. Conference members of each chamber must convince their colleagues that any concessions made to the other chamber were on unimportant points and that nothing basic to the original version of the bill was surrendered.

How much leeway does a conference committee have? Ordinarily members are expected to end up somewhere between the different versions. On matters for which there is no clear middle ground, members are sometimes accused of exceeding their instructions and producing an entirely new bill. For this reason, the conference committee has been called a "third house" of Congress and one of the most significant institutions within the Congress.[52]

Which chamber, House or Senate, wins more often in conference committees? On the surface it appears that the Senate's version wins more often, but this is partly because the Senate often acts on its legislation after the House. But by approving the initial bill first and thereby setting the agenda on an issue, the House often has more of an impact on the final outcome than the Senate.

CONGRESS: AN ASSESSMENT AND A VIEW ON REFORMS

Two hundred and fifteen years after its creation, Congress is a larger, more vital, and very different kind of institution from the one the framers envisioned. Yet most of its major functions remain the same, and their effective exercise is crucial to the health of our constitutional democracy. Even in the twenty-first century, we still look to Congress to make laws, raise revenues, represent citizens, investigate abuses of power, and oversee the executive branch.

Today most members must engage in continual electioneering to stay in office. Members appear driven by their desire to win reelection, so that much of what takes place in Congress seems mainly designed to promote reelection. These efforts usually pay off for members of Congress: most who want to get reelected do. At the same time, these efforts also pay off for our democracy. The concern of members with reelection fosters *accountability* and the desire to please the voters.

William Cohen, a popular Republican senator from Maine (and later secretary of defense in the Clinton administration), observed when he retired from the Senate that he admired Congress's deliberative process, yet he worried that too many checks and too much partisanship made it hard for Congress to get needed results:

> Our republic, we know, was designed to be slow-moving and deliberative. Our founding fathers were convinced that power had to be entrusted to someone, but that no one could be entirely trusted with power. They devised a brilliant system of checks and balances to prevent the tyranny of the many by the few. They constructed a perfect triangle of allocated and checked power. . . . There could be no rash action, no rush to judgment, no legislative mob rule, no unrestrained chief executive.
>
> The difficulty with this diffusion of power in today's cyberspace age is that everyone is in check, but no one is in charge. . . .
>
> But more than the constitutional separation of powers is leading to the unprecedented stalemate that exists today. There has been a breakdown in

Thinking It Through . . .

No reform is neutral in terms of effects. Some groups will benefit more than others from the passage of each reform proposal. Most reforms also have unanticipated consequences that may create more problems than they solve. Some would require amendments to our Constitution. Still, the search goes on for practical ways to improve Congress's ability to do the people's work.

Congress spent a lot of time in the 1990s trying to come up with procedural and fund-raising reforms, yet despite great public pressure to reform, Congress did little to alter its traditional ways.

civil debates and discourse. Enmity at times has become so intense that members of Congress have resorted to shoving matches outside the legislative chambers.[53]

How does such a Congress make any progress? In an institution where most members act as individual entrepreneurs and consider themselves leaders, the task of providing institutional leadership is increasingly difficult. With limited resources, and only sometimes aided by the president, congressional leaders are asked to bring together a diverse, fragmented, and independent institution. The congressional system acts only when majorities can be achieved. That the framers accomplished their original objective—creating a Congress that would not move with imprudent haste—has been generally well realized.

Americans often characterize Congress as a bickering, timid, ignorant, selfish, or narrow-minded body. Yet they also admire the stamina and civic responsibility of their own member of Congress. Individual members of Congress are almost always more popular than the institution. Typically, an individual member of Congress enjoys a 60–65 percent approval rating, whereas Congress as an institution fluctuates between a 35–50 percent approval rating by the general public, perhaps because people judge individual members primarily on how well they serve the interests of their states and districts and on their personal appeal.

Some of the criticism of Congress is justified. However, critics usually forget that our national legislature is particularly exposed, and some of our expectations of it are unrealistic. First, Congress does nearly all its work directly in the public eye, even more public now that it is televised live on C-SPAN. Unfortunate incidents—quarrels, name-calling, evasive actions, inaccurate statements, and ethical lapses—that might be hushed up in the executive or judicial branches are observed and duly reported by the media.

Second, Congress by its nature is controversial and argumentative. Its 535 members are found on both sides, sometimes on half a dozen sides, of every important question. Moreover, during the 1990s Congress raised taxes and cut services, closed military bases, reduced spending for welfare, the arts, and many research programs, shut down the government, and impeached a highly approved president—not a recipe for popularity!

Criticisms of Congress

CONGRESS IS INEFFICIENT   House and Senate procedures are, some charge, simply not suited to the needs of a modern information-age nation. Some of this criticism is exaggerated. Evaluating procedure and structure is difficult to separate from evaluating policy, about which everyone has an individual preference. Congress deals with an enormous number of complex measures. Many procedures expedite handling of bills, and the committee and subcommittee system is a reasonable device for hearing arguments and compiling information.

Still, the question of efficiency remains. Study groups inside and outside Congress have urged the chambers to reduce the number of committee assignments, establish better information systems, centralize more power in their leadership positions, and strengthen majority rule. Congress has done many of these things recently, yet the pace of legislation has not improved.

CONGRESS IS UNREPRESENTATIVE   The complaint is often made that Congress represents constituents' interests over the national interest. Defenders of Congress respond that representing their districts is precisely what Congress was designed to do. Legislators are described as being obsessed with staying in office—indeed, as concentrating solely on winning reelection—often at the expense of criti-

cal national issues such as Social Security, drug abuse, foreign policy, and trade.

Congress is supposed to reflect geographical and narrow interests, to register the diversity of the United States. In *The Federalist*, No. 57, James Madison wrote: "Who are to be the electors of the Federal Representatives? Not the rich more than the poor; not the learned more than the ignorant; not the haughty heirs of distinguished names more than the humble sons of obscure and unpropitious fortune."[54] Yet as the costs of campaigning increase, and as the majority of elected officials continue to come from the upper and upper-middle classes, we do have to ask whether ours is the open, representative, responsive, and responsible legislative system we can point to with pride as a model for those in other parts of the world who yearn for constitutional democracy. Can a Congress that has only 14 percent women and 7 percent African American membership truly represent our 51 percent female and 13 percent black populations?[55] That most members are the products of middle- and upper-middle-class families does not necessarily mean they are interested only in improving the position of that portion of the population. Affluent white males like Senators Edward Kennedy (D.-Mass.) and Jay Rockefeller (D.-W.Va.), for instance, are strong advocates of legislation to protect women, minorities, and the poor.[56]

WE THE PEOPLE

Profile of the 107th Congress, 2001–2003

	U.S. Senate (100)	U.S. House (435)
Republicans	49	221
Democrats	50	212
Independents	1	2
Sex		
Men	87	376
Women	13	59
Religion		
Catholic	24	125
Jewish	10	27
Protestant	53	251
Other	11	35
Average Age	60	54
Racial/Ethnic Minorities	3	63
Occupation		
Lawyers	53	156
Education	16	92
Business/Banking	24	159
Agriculture	6	25
Journalism	7	9
Engineering	0	9
Real Estate	4	24

SOURCE: *Congressional Quarterly Weekly*, January 20, 2001, pp. 180–181 (updated by authors May 29, 2001).

CONGRESS IS UNETHICAL Some critics claim we have "the best Congress money can buy."[57] Many people—including U.S. Senator John McCain, who made this charge a central theme in his bid for the 2000 presidential nomination—allege that special interests and single-issue groups are stronger than ever, and that they are able to delay or block proceedings in Congress. The current system of financing congressional elections has been called a scandal because it forces members of Congress to beg for money from wealthy individuals and political action committees representing interest groups whose primary purpose is to seek support for pet legislation.

In response to occasional scandals, both houses passed ethics codes and created ethics subcommittees. These codes require public disclosure of income and property holdings by legislators, key aides, and spouses. They also ban most gifts of over $100 to a legislator, a staff member, or a legislator's family from a registered lobbyist, an organization with a political action committee, a foreign

government, or a business with an interest in legislation before Congress. But valuable as these changes have been, they have apparently failed to improve the image of Congress.[58]

Defenders of Congress insist these charges are overstated. They say money would hardly influence the three dozen or more millionaires who are members of the Senate and the one hundred or so members of the House who are well-off financially. Defenders of Congress also point out that some members of Congress regularly turn down certain types of campaign contributions.

CONGRESS LACKS COLLECTIVE RESPONSIBILITY   Some critics see the main problem in Congress as the dispersion of power among committee and sub-committee leaders, elected party officials, factional leaders, informal caucus leaders, and other legislators. It is a "nobody's-in-charge" system. This dispersion of power means that to get things done, congressional leaders must bargain and negotiate. The result of this "brokering" system is that laws may be watered down, defeated, delayed, or written in vague language. According to some critics, too much leeway is given to unelected bureaucrats to develop the regulations that will implement the legislation. Accountability is confused, responsibility is eroded, and well-organized special interests that know how to work the system have an unfair advantage.

A Defense of Congress

Poking fun at Congress has been a national pastime for generations. Will Rogers told some of his best jokes at the expense of Congress, as Jay Leno and David Letterman do today. Cartoonists love Congress for its unfailing ability to put its worst foot forward. Even members of Congress, as noted earlier, often run against Congress when they are at home in their districts.

The challenge that confronted the framers—how to reconcile the need for executive energy with republican liberty—is still with us. The history of constitutional democracy has always been the search for limitations on absolute power and for techniques of sharing power. Our American style of constitutionalism and separation of powers often means a slow-moving and sometimes inefficient decision-making system. It means a system that often hinders rather than facilitates leadership, a system that invites contention, division, debate, delay, and political conflict. Critics call this gridlock or deadlock or even paralysis. Defenders of Congress prefer to call it the world's greatest deliberative body. They point out that the framers of the U.S. Constitution took great efforts to insulate policy-making processes from the momentary fancies of the people.

Newly elected presidents and members of Congress always arrive in Washington enthusiastically ready to enact the people's wishes. But they find that governing is invariably tougher and slower than they expected because government deals with complex issues about which there often is little consensus. Building policy majorities is hard because complex problems generate complex solutions, and the structure of Congress requires supermajorities to agree to serious changes. Thus the president's veto, the filibuster, the use of holds and legislative riders all make it harder to build a consensus for change. Not only is there often a lack of consensus in Congress, "there is a lack of consensus [on most major issues] among the public about what should be done."[59] And this makes it hard for legislators who are, after all, eager to please voters and remain in office.

Criticism of Congress—its alleged incompetence, its overresponsiveness to organized interests, its inefficiencies, its partisan character—are difficult to separate from the context of policy preferences and democratic procedures. Sometimes criticism tells us more about the critic than it does about the effec-

tiveness of Congress. Constitutional democracy is not the most efficient form of government. Congress was never intended to act swiftly; it was not created to be a rubber stamp or even a cooperative partner for presidents. Its greatest strengths—its diversity and deliberative character—also weaken its position in dealing with the more centralized executive branch. Its members will rarely be fast on their feet. Not surprisingly, the 535 members, divided into two houses, two parties, dozens of committees, and nearly two hundred subcommittees, often have a difficult time arriving at a common strategy to collaborate with or to resist whoever is president.

POLITICS ONLINE

What's Happening in Congress Today?

When you visit Washington, D.C., be sure to visit the Capitol. The tour will give you a sense of the history of the building, and you will see and feel the bustle of lawmaking if Congress is in session. Also be sure to visit one of the office buildings to see committee rooms and an office of a representative or senator. If you do not have a chance to visit the Capitol, you can take a virtual tour of the building by going to the website for this book and Chapter 11 at: www.prenhall.com/burns.

One reason not to limit your tour of the Capitol to the two legislative chambers is that a lot of what happens in Congress happens in committees and subcommittees, and much of a legislator's time is spent meeting with constituents and supervising staff. To get a sample of what is going on in Congress at any given moment, you can check out any of three channels of C-SPAN, either on television or through the Internet at: www.cspan.org. If you miss an important hearing or floor speech, C-SPAN often replays the day's proceedings in the evening or on the weekend. The C-SPAN home page also provides an updated schedule of events.

You can also check on upcoming House and Senate schedules and find a vast amount on information on legislation and committees at the Thomas site: Thomas.loc.gov, maintained by the Library of Congress. The U.S. House of Representatives official home page: www.house.gov, and the U.S. Senate official home page: www.senate.gov, also offer a wide array of information and educational services, including schedules, votes, legislation, histories, and even ways to e-mail your own representative or senator.

SUMMARY

1. Congress plays a crucial role in our system of shared powers, controlling key decisions and constraining presidents. Yet, over time, Congress has lost some influence as the presidency has gained influence. In the last two decades, however, Congress has become more capable as a policy-making competitor for presidents. Redistricting and reapportionment have shaped a Congress that somewhat more accurately reflects the population.

2. The most distinctive feature of Congress is its bicameralism, which the framers intended as a moderating influence on partisanship and possible error. Each chamber has a few distinctive functions. Their organizations and procedures also differ slightly, as do their political environments.

3. Congress performs these functions: representation, law making, consensus building, overseeing the bureaucracy, policy clarification, and investigating. The Senate also confirms or denies presidential appointments and participates in the ratification of treaties.

4. As a collective body, Congress must attempt to accomplish its tasks even as most of its members serve as delegates or trustees for their constituents. When they vote, members are influenced by their philosophy and values, their perceptions of constituents' interests, and the views of trusted colleagues and staff, partisan ties and party leaders, lobbyists, and the president.

5. Congress does an excellent job of representing the values and views of most of their constituents. But they are cautious about enacting proposed measures by their own colleagues or the legislative agenda put forward by presidents. Most legislation dies for lack of majority support. In addition the legislative obstacle course sometimes involves filibusters, riders, holds, and an occasional override of a presidential veto.

6. Most of the work in Congress is done in committees and subcommittees. Congress has attempted in recent years to streamline its committee system and modify its methods of selecting committee chairs. Seniority practices are still generally followed, yet the threat of removal forces committee chairs to consult with younger members of the majority party. Subcommittees are important. They can prevent or delay legislation from being enacted. But there are numerous other stages where bills can be killed, making it easier to stop legislation than to enact it.

7. Members of Congress are motivated by the desire to win reelection, and much of what Congress does is in response to this motive. Members work hard to get favors for their districts, to serve the needs of constituents, and to maintain a high visibility in their districts or states. Incumbents have advantages that help explain their success at reelection: they have greater name recognition; they have large staffs; they are much better able to raise campaign money; and they have greater access to the media.

8. Individual members of Congress are more popular than the institution. Congress is criticized for being inefficient, unrepresentative, unethical, and lacking in collective responsibility. Yet criticisms of Congress are difficult to separate from the context of policy preference and democratic procedures. Congress's greatest strengths—its diversity and deliberative character—also contribute to its weaknesses.

KEY TERMS

safe seat 244
reapportionment 245
redistricting 245
gerrymandering 245
bicameralism 246
Speaker 248
majority leader 249
minority leader 249

whip 249
party caucus 249
closed rule 250
open rule 250
hold 250
president pro tempore 250
filibuster 250
cloture 250

senatorial courtesy 252
delegate 255
trustee 255
attentive public 255
log rolling 256
standing committee 258
rider 258
pocket veto 260

override 260
joint committee 261
select or special committee 262
discharge petition 262
seniority rule 263
conference committee 264

FURTHER READING

JOEL D. ABERBACH, *Keeping a Watchful Eye: The Politics of Congressional Oversight* (Brookings Institution, 1990).

SARAH A. BINDER AND STEVEN S. SMITH, *Politics or Principles? Filibustering in the United States Senate* (Brookings Institution, 1997).

BILL BRADLEY, *Time Present, Time Past: A Memoir* (Knopf, 1996).

DAVID W. BRADY AND CRAIG VOLDEN, *Revolving Gridlock: Politics and Policy from Carter to Clinton* (Westview Press, 1998).

ADAM CLYMER, *Edward M. Kennedy: A Biography* (William Morrow, 1999).

ROGER H. DAVIDSON AND WALTER J. OLESZEK, *Congress and Its Members*, 5th ed. (Congressional Quarterly Press, 1996).

CHRISTOPHER J. DEERING AND STEVEN S. SMITH, *Committees in Congress*, 3d ed. (Congressional Quarterly Press, 1997).

LAWRENCE C. DODD AND BRUCE J. OPPENHEIMER, EDS., *Congress Reconsidered*, 5th ed. (Congressional Quarterly Press, 1993).

RICHARD F. FENNO, JR., *Home Style: House Members in Their Districts* (Little, Brown, 1978).

RICHARD F. FENNO, JR., *Learning to Govern: An Institutional View of the 104th Congress* (Brookings Institution, 1997).

RICHARD F. FENNO, JR., *Senators on the Campaign Trail: The Politics of Representation* (University of Oklahoma Press, 1996).

MORRIS FIORINA, *Congress: Keystone of the Washington Establishment*, 2d ed. (Yale University Press, 1989).

PAUL HERRNSON, *Congressional Elections*, 3d ed. (Congressional Quarterly Press, 2000).

JOHN R. HIBBING AND ELIZABETH THEISS-MORSE, *Congress as Public Enemy: Public Attitudes Toward American Political Institutions* (Cambridge University Press, 1995).

GODFREY HODGSON, *The Gentleman from New York: Daniel Patrick Moynihan* (Houghton Mifflin, 2000).

LINDA KILLIAN, *The Freshmen: What Happened to the Republican Revolution?* (Westview Press, 1998).

FRANCES E. LEE AND BRUCE I. OPPENHEIMER, *Sizing Up the Senate: The Unequal Consequences of Equal Representation* (University of Chicago Press, 1999).

JOSEPH I. LIEBERMAN, *In Praise of Public Life* (Simon & Schuster, 2000).

TOM LOFTUS, *The Art of Legislative Politics* (Congressional Quarterly Press, 1994).

JANET M. MARTIN, *Lessons from the Hill: The Legislative Journey of an Education Program* (St. Martin's Press, 1993).

DAVID R. MAYHEW, *America's Congress: Actions in the Public Sphere, James Madison Through Newt Gingrich* (Yale University Press, 2000).

BARBARA MIKULSKI, KAY BAILEY HUTCHISON, ET AL., *Nine and Counting: The Women of the Senate* (William Morrow, 2000).

WALTER J. OLESZEK, *Congressional Procedures and the Policy Process*, 4th ed. (Congressional Quarterly Press, 1995).

Norman Ornstein, Thomas Mann, and Michael Malbin, *Vital Statistics on Congress, 1999–2000* (AEI Press, 2000).

Ronald M. Peters, Jr., ed., *The Speaker: Leadership in the U.S. House of Representatives* (Congressional Quarterly Press, 1995).

David E. Price, *The Congressional Experience: A View from the Hill* (Westview Press, 1993).

Nicole Rae and Colton Campbell, eds., *New Majority or Old Majority: The Impact of Republicans on Congress* (Rowman and Littlefield, 1999).

Warren B. Rudman, *Combat: Twelve Years in the U.S. Senate* (Random House, 1996).

Barbara Sinclair, *Unorthodox Lawmaking: New Legislative Processes in the U.S. Congress, 2nd ed.* (Congressional Quarterly Press, 2000).

Darvell M. West, *Patrick Kennedy: The Rise to Power* (Prentice Hall, 2001).

Students of Congress also should consult *Congressional Quarterly Weekly, National Journal, Roll Call,* and *The Hill.*

12

THE PRESIDENCY: THE LEADERSHIP BRANCH

A S HE TRAVELED SLOWLY UP THE EAST COAST FROM MOUNT VERNON TO NEW YORK (THE TEMPORARY SEAT OF GOVERNMENT) IN 1789, NEWLY ELECTED PRESIDENT George Washington was saluted with parades and fireworks. His whole trip was one long ovation, a celebration of the people's yearning for a strong individual who could provide continuity and leadership for the nation.

Yet Washington and his compatriots were of two minds about the power of the presidency. The framers both admired and feared centralized leadership. They realized the country needed a more effective national government, yet they were suspicious of the potential abuses of power, especially power vested in a single individual. Given what they had lived through in preceding decades, they had every right to these fears. Moreover, they hardly wanted to jeopardize the rights and liberties they had fought so hard to win in the Revolution.

Today, in the twenty-first century, we still have not resolved our ambivalence toward the presidency. Should a president be "above politics" and wait for a consensus to emerge from the people and Congress? Or should presidents be clearly political, leading the people and leading Congress? Should presidential powers be narrowly defined? Or should the presidency be granted broad authority to respond to national and international emergencies? Does the enlarged role of the presidency under today's circumstances undermine some of the fundamental checks and balances in our constitutional democracy? Should we be willing to overlook a president's personal failings if his performance of official duties meets with public approval? In this chapter we explore these questions as we look at the jobs we ask presidents to perform.

THE POLITICS OF SHARED POWERS

Original Intent

T he framers of the Constitution created a presidency of limited powers. They wanted a presidential office that would steer clear of parties and factions, enforce the laws passed by Congress, handle communications with foreign governments, and help states put down disorders. They wanted a presidency strong enough to match Congress, yet not so strong it would overpower Congress.

CHAPTERMEDIA

 POLITICS ONLINE
Want to Visit the West Wing?
www.prenhall.com/burns

PRESIDENTIALISM IN OTHER DEMOCRACIES

The United States is among a very few democracies in which a strong presidential system has coincided with democratic rule. Elsewhere, democratic presidential regimes have often given way to authoritarian presidential rule.

Most democracies are based on the parliamentary system of government (as in Australia, Britain, and Israel) that confers full powers on a parliament, which then delegates executive powers to a handful of its members. These officials, the head of government (a prime minister or premier or chancellor), and cabinet ministers, make up what is known as "the Government." The Government serves only so long as it *maintains the confidence of a majority* in the lower house of parliament. If the parliament indicates its loss of support for the Government by a vote of censure, or a vote of no-confidence, or even by defeating a major piece of Government-sponsored legislation, the Government resigns, either to allow a new Government to be formed or to call for new parliamentary elections. In parliamentary systems, the head of state (usually a president elected by parliament but sometimes, as in Britain, a hereditary monarch) has only ceremonial responsibilities.

In the recent wave of democratizations, a number of countries have experimented with a mixed presidential-parliamentary system. Based on the French Fifth Republic (1958–present), the mixed system includes a popularly elected presidency that has extensive powers of its own, notably in foreign and defense matters, *and* a prime minister and cabinet accountable to the parliament. This mixed presidential-parliamentary system has been adopted in Russia, Poland, the Czech Republic, and several other new democracies.

There is a lively debate on which pattern of government—presidential, parliamentary, or the mixed presidential-parliamentary system—is most conducive to democracy. Some fear that powerful presidents are a source of authoritarianism. Others claim that a strong president is needed to give leadership and coherence to the often fragmented parliaments in newer democracies. Still others see the solution in some kind of hybrid.

It is true that historically most presidential regimes have given way to dictatorships. But in many of these cases, the causes for the failure of democracy were less with the specific institutions than with the attitudes and commitments of the people and their leaders. It is unlikely that any single set of institutions can create or perpetuate democratic government. The presence of democratic values is more important in building and maintaining democracy than the existence of a particular institutional arrangement.

They combined the ceremonial head of the nation with the chief executive of government. The term of office would be four years, and presidents would be indefinitely eligible to succeed themselves. (The two-term limit was added as the Twenty-second Amendment to the Constitution in 1951.)

Although independent from the legislature, presidents would still share considerable power with Congress. To enact government business, the separate branches would have to cooperate and consult with one another. A president's major appointments would have to be approved by the Senate; Congress could override the chief executive's veto by a two-thirds vote of each chamber, and the president could ratify treaties only with the advice and consent of two-thirds of the Senate. Appropriations would be initiated by Congress, not the president.

But even a president whose power was limited by a system of checks and balances worried many Americans in 1787. The framers deliberately outlined the powers of the president broadly. The president, they thought, should have discretionary power to act when other governmental branches failed to meet their responsibilities or to respond to the urgencies of the day. But Congress retained the right to impeach and remove a president if members of Congress believed a president had failed to abide by the Constitution.

Divided Powers

Our constitutional democracy was designed to be one of both shared powers and divided powers. The framers wanted disagreement as well as cooperation because they assumed that the checks and balances within the government would prevent the president and Congress from "ganging up" against the people's liberties. The framers actually made disagreement inevitable by providing that the president, Senate, and House of Representatives would be elected by different constituencies and for different lengths of service.

The United States is rare among major world powers because it is neither a parliamentary democracy nor a wholly executive-dominated government. Our Constitution plainly invites both Congress and president to set policy and govern the nation. Leadership and policy change are encouraged only when Congress and president, and sometimes these two and the courts, concur on the desirability of new directions.

A president and members of Congress are legitimate participants in a whole range of policy activities. Triumphs for a president acting alone in a system of separated powers are rare. "Whenever powers are shared, attention must be devoted to the other decision makers," writes political scientist Charles O. Jones. "How do they view the problem? What are their present commitments? On what basis will they

compromise? The test in a separated system is not simply one of presidential success. It is rather one of achievement by the system, with presidents and members of Congress inextricably bonded and similarly judged."[1]

The politics of shared power has often been stormy, a subject we treat in detail in the next chapter. Making a separation of powers system work is never easy. A president is usually helped when majorities of his party are in control of Congress, which can join together what the framers separated. In recent decades, however, **divided government**, in which one party controls the executive branch and the other the legislative branch, has been the norm.

Democrat Bill Clinton served his last six years with a Congress controlled by Republicans. Republican George W. Bush won election in 2000 with a slim majority of Republicans in the House of Representatives and a U.S. Senate initially divided and soon controlled by a razor-thin Democratic majority. Thus, for all practical purposes, divided government endures, forcing presidents to govern from the center. President George W. Bush, like others before him, reached out to moderates in the other party for support, yet he, too, found that divided government inevitably encourages compromises and a certain amount of gridlock. More on this in the next chapter.

The Evolution of Presidential Influence

The formal powers the U.S. Constitution vests in a president have not been changed over the last two hundred years. But the influence of modern presidents is considerably greater today than it was two hundred years ago. The power and influence of any given president are partly the consequences of the incumbent's character and energy, combined with the needs of the time, the party balance in Congress, the values of the citizenry, and the challenges to our nation's survival. By and large, the history of presidential power is one of steady, if uneven, growth. Of the individuals who have filled the office, about one-third have enlarged its powers. Andrew Jackson, Abraham Lincoln, and both Roosevelts, for example, redefined both the institution and many of its powers by the way they set priorities and responded to crises.

In the evolution of executive power, Congress and the courts have sometimes been willing partners. In emergencies Congress often delegates discretion to the executive branch. In resolving complex problems, the legislature sometimes seems incapable of dealing with matters that are highly technical or that require immediate response and constant management. This weakness of Congress is not unique among legislative bodies. During the last two centuries, in all democracies and at all levels, power has drifted from legislators to executives. The English prime minister, the French president, governors of our states, and mayors of our cities all play more dominant roles than they did, generally speaking, a hundred years ago. This has been so in large part because people turn to executives to encourage a growing economy and press national interests in the international system.

Two centuries of national expansion and crises have increased the influence of the president beyond that specified by the Constitution. As we saw in Chapter 11, the complexity of Congress's decision-making procedures, its unwieldy numbers, and its constitutional responsibilities make it a more public, deliberative, and divided institution than the presidency. When crises occur, Congress traditionally holds debates and, almost as predictably, delegates authority to the president, charging the executive branch to take whatever actions are deemed necessary. Or Congress has allowed presidents to take charge, as was essentially what it did in the 1990s in response to presidential calls for U.S. involvement in Kuwait, Somalia, Haiti, Iraq, and Yugoslavia.

In the history of presidential–Supreme Court relations, the nation's highest court has generally favored an expansive interpretation of presidential power. The Court has on occasion halted a presidential action or ruled a presidential decision unconstitutional, but it has more frequently given legitimacy to the growth of presidential power.

divided government
Governance divided between the parties, especially when one holds the presidency and the other controls Congress.

Who Were the Best and Worst Presidents?

Several news organizations have published rankings of presidents by political historians and biographers. These lists often reveal as much about the professors and writers or the sponsoring organizations as the presidents, yet there is widespread agreement about the top five best and worst presidents. *The New York Times* and *Chicago Sun Times* published surveys that were almost identical in the mid-1990s. *The Wall Street Journal* published a ranking that relied on what it considered more balanced (that is, a survey with approximately equal number of experts on the left and right) than earlier surveys of presidential greatness. As a result Ronald Reagan and Dwight Eisenhower rose in their ranking, and Herbert Hoover and Calvin Coolidge escaped the bottom ten on its list.

New York Times/Chicago Sun Times Rankings (1996)

The Ten Best	The Ten Worst
1. Abraham Lincoln	1. Warren Harding
2. George Washington	2. James Buchanan
3. Franklin Roosevelt	3. Franklin Pierce
4. Thomas Jefferson	4. Ulysses Grant
5. Theodore Roosevelt	5. Andrew Johnson
6. Woodrow Wilson	6. Millard Fillmore
7. Harry Truman	7. Richard Nixon
8. Andrew Jackson	8. John Tyler
9. James Polk	9. Calvin Coolidge
10. Dwight Eisenhower	10. Herbert Hoover

Sources: Steve Neal, "Putting Presidents in Their Place," *Chicago Sun-Times*, November 19, 1995, pp. 30–31; Arthur M. Schlesinger, Jr., "The Ultimate Approval Rating," *The New York Times Magazine*, December 15, 1996, pp. 46–51.

The Wall Street Journal/Federalist Society Rankings (2000)

The Ten Best	The Ten Worst
1. George Washington	1. James Buchanan
2. Abraham Lincoln	2. Warren Harding
3. Franklin Roosevelt	3. Franklin Pierce
4. Thomas Jefferson	4. Andrew Johnson
5. Theodore Roosevelt	5. Millard Fillmore
6. Andrew Jackson	6. John Tyler
7. Harry Truman	7. Richard Nixon
8. Ronald Reagan	8. Ulysses Grant
9. Dwight Eisenhower	9. Zachary Taylor
10. James Polk	10. Jimmy Carter

Source: James Lindgren and Steven Calabresi, "Ranking the Presidents," *The Wall Street Journal*, November 16, 2000, editorial page.

Several factors have strengthened the presidency in recent decades. The danger of war and the destructive potential of new weaponry plainly increased the president's influence. The cold war—with its enormous standing armies, nuclear weapons, and widespread intelligence and alliance operations—invited presidential leadership in national security matters. The post–cold war period has not reduced the need for presidential leadership, for the United States finds it still has extensive peace-making, peacekeeping, and global economic leadership responsibilities.

Television has contributed to the growth of presidential influence. Previously, presidents had to rely on the press and party leaders in and out of Congress to get their message to the American people. With immediate access to vast television audiences, presidents can take their case directly to the people.

The growth of federal involvement in economic and social issues and the increasing complexity of public policies have increased presidential responsibility and contributed to the growth of agencies reporting directly to the White House. Problems not easily delegated to any one department often get pulled into the White House. When new programs involve several federal agencies, someone near the president is often asked to reconcile conflicts and set a consistent policy. White House aides, with some justification, claim the presidency is the only place in government where it is possible to establish and coordinate national priorities. Presidents set up central review and coordination units that help formulate new policies, settle jurisdictional disputes among departments, and provide access for the well-organized interest groups that want their views to be given weight in decision making.

Has there been a decline in the influence of presidents in recent years? Some people think so, pointing to diminished support for certain presidents in the wake of scandals, such as Watergate (Nixon), Iran-Contra (Reagan), and ethical problems in the Clinton presidency. The near impeachment of Richard Nixon and the impeachment of Bill Clinton are cited as decreasing respect for the presidency. The closeness of the 2000 presidential election and the sharp partisan divisions surrounding the Florida recount, plus the various court decisions in the 2000 presidential election, may also have limited the influence of George W. Bush. It is hard enough for a president to lead the nation, but it is harder still when he comes to the White House not having won the popular vote and after bitter disputes about voting irregularities and uncounted votes.

Still, it is generally agreed that events and forceful presidents over the last century have had the effect of magnifying the office and its potential influence. Presidential leadership in the cold war, in the Middle East, in the Balkans, and in international trade matters are all examples where presidents have played very significant policymaking roles.

The United States continues to struggle with the challenging paradox posed by some of the constitutional framers: If presidents have too much power, they could become arbitrary rulers and even tyrants; on the other hand, if presidents have too little power, they may be enfeebled and ineffective leaders.

There is little reason today to assume the role and impact of the American presidency will diminish in importance in coming decades. Not only does the president continue to be the primary focus of the nation's dreams and political aspirations; the nation's chief executive plays a central role as the nation's policy maker, party leader, chief administrator, and morale builder.[2]

Although we may dislike and even condemn individual presidents, public attitudes toward the institution of the presidency remain positive. We want to believe in our presidents; we want them to provide unifying leadership. Perhaps this is peculiarly the case in America, where we have no royal family, no established church, and no other common source of ceremonial leadership.

IN SEARCH OF THE PERFECT PRESIDENT

The framers conceived their president in the image of George Washington, the man they expected would first occupy the office. Like Washington, the American chief executive is expected to be a wise, moderate, dignified, unifying leader of all the people. No one commanded the trust and respect that Washington did, and he was unanimously elected as the first president of the new Republic in 1789. George Washington knew the people needed to have confidence in their fledgling government, a sense of continuity with the past, and a time of calmness and stability free of emergencies and crises. He knew, too, that the new nation faced foreign dangers.

Today, if presidents take charge and try to run the country, they are often accused of being dictatorial and trying to impose their will on the nation. If they are not activist leaders, however, they are criticized for being weak or passive, and, even more likely, they are blamed for whatever happens to be wrong with the country. People who like what a president is doing are champions of presidential leadership; people who disapprove of what a president is doing point to the dangers of dictatorship.

Article II of the Constitution outlines the nature and scope of presidential power (see page 45 of this text). It responded to George Washington's calls for executive leadership. He was sensitive to the fine line between providing strong leadership and infringing on individual rights and liberties. He knew then—as every president after him has either known or learned—that Americans have a strong streak of antigovernment and even anti-authority sentiment.[3]

What kind of person does it take to perform this delicate balancing act? Our Constitution establishes only three qualifications for the office: a president must be at least 35 years of age, have lived in the United States for 14 years, and be a natural-born citizen. Yet the "unwritten presidential job description"—the one we carry around in our heads—says a president has to be many things to many people.

CHARACTER AND HONESTY   Voters often place as much emphasis on a presidential candidate's character and integrity as they do on a candidate's political philosophy and past experience. Such emphasis is not misguided. Presidents have enormous influence, especially in times of crisis. They recruit the people who run the executive departments and serve on our courts, and thus they have much to do with governmental performance and ethics. Hence it is important to weigh their character, allegiance to constitutional and democratic values, and ability to manage their emotions and turn them to constructive purposes.[4]

Concerns about presidential character are as old as the presidency itself. In 1800, for example, religious leaders denounced Thomas Jefferson from their pulpits as "godless," and in the 1820s Andrew Jackson was pilloried as a barbarian and adulterer.

The election of 1884 provides a fascinating case study of character in politics. In that election, Democratic candidate Grover Cleveland was charged with fathering a child out of wedlock. Cleveland took responsibility and agreed to pay for the child's upbringing. Not surprisingly, this became a hot issue for his opponent, James G. Blaine. The dilemma was that while Cleveland's private life raised doubts, he was responsible in his political and professional life. Blaine, on the other hand, had an "upright" private life yet was less well regarded for his political integrity. Voters elected Cleveland.

Bill Clinton had major character flaws, yet his political supporters hoped, sometimes in vain, that he would avoid reckless behavior and concentrate on the policy initiatives they favored. Clinton was impeached by the House of Representatives and

nearly removed from office by the Senate for his moral weakness. What was remarkable was that an unusually large number of Americans (often 60 percent or more) continued to approve of Clinton's handling of the job of the presidency while decidedly disapproving of his personal behavior. Most people apparently judged Clinton on how well the economy did, on traditional "peace and prosperity" measures, and on his adroit political and communication skills rather than on his personal morals.

Still, Americans want presidents they can trust, individuals who have a basic respect for others as well as a commitment to serve the public interest. A sense of decency, integrity, and fair play will always be part of what is wanted in a president. Here, briefly, are some additional qualities Americans yearn for in an ideal president.

- *Courage:* Americans want a leader who takes firm stands on issues, is concerned about the average citizen, and places the country's interests ahead of politics. A president should have the intellectual courage to take risks and do what is right, even when it is not popular or easy; the willingness to serve all the people, not just those who bankrolled his candidacy; and the perseverance not to give up after initial legislative or political defeats.

- *Experience:* Americans want presidents who have proven competence in understanding complex policy issues. Presidents need to be skilled at bringing people together to solve intricate policy problems.

- *Political Savvy:* Presidents need an understanding of the role of politics in governing and the ability to be an effective politician working with people of all political viewpoints. The job requires recognition that coalition building is a central and constant part of the job.

- *A Sense of History and Constitutionalism:* Americans want a president to have a great respect for the U.S. Constitution and American values, exhibiting a solid grasp of how governments and markets work and how diplomacy and U.S. trade work.

- *Vision:* The ideal president should have ideas and programmatic plans to make the country stronger. We ask presidents to clarify options and help set the nation's policy agenda. A president must take positions on the compelling issues of the day—economic opportunity, civil rights, education, trade, nuclear proliferation, terrorism, equality, and so on. The president has to be a forest person, not one overwhelmed by the trees or leaves.

- *Listening and Teaching Skills:* Our best presidents both listen to us and lead us. They know that while a clear vision can excite us, it does not necessarily teach or rally us. We want presidents who give us a sense not only of who they are, but, more important, of who we are and what kind of nation we might become.

- *Communication Skills:* Ideas and wisdom are of little use if a president cannot motivate and rally the public and empower constituencies to act. Presidents have to develop impressive speaking and media management skills.

- *Morale-Building Skills:* The presidency is more than just a constitutional or political office; it has to help us navigate through crises and transitions and unify us when we experience national setbacks and tragedy. At their best, presidents remind us of our mutual obligations, shared beliefs, and the trust and caring that bind us together. Americans understandably yearn for presidents like George Washington and Abraham Lincoln, who can bring us together and challenge us to be better.

History conditions different cultures to expect different things of their national leaders. Doubtless in the United States we exaggerate the capacity for what even heroic presidents have done and can do to change the course of events.[5] Do we ask too much of our presidents? Sure we do. We want vision, character, competence,

intelligence, honesty, stamina, inspiration, sound judgment, wisdom—and of course—someone who shares our political beliefs.

THE CHALLENGING JOB OF BEING PRESIDENT

The president has many responsibilities:

- To serve as chief executive of the federal bureaucracy
- To nominate and appoint key officials
- To implement and enforce laws
- To veto unwise bills
- To negotiate treaties
- To recognize foreign nations
- To serve as commander in chief
- To serve as chief of state
- To pardon or grant clemency
- To propose an annual budget
- To develop policies that promote peace and prosperity

All but the last two of these responsibilities are spelled out in the Constitution. Others are designated by laws enacted by Congress. But today a president is asked to perform additional roles not spelled out in the Constitution. We want the chief executive to be an international peacemaker as well as a national morale builder, a politician in chief as well as a commander in chief. We want the president to be the architect of a new world order, or at least a peaceful world order, who negotiates favorable trade pacts with major trading partners. In addition to the obvious leadership responsibilities a president has in foreign policy, economics, and domestic policy, a variety of broad functional kinds of leadership are expected of a president. These policy areas and functions permit us to develop a presidential job profile (see Table 12–1).

Presidents as Crisis Managers

"The President shall be Commander in Chief of the Army and Navy of the United States," reads Section 2 of Article II of the Constitution. Even though this is the first of the president's powers listed in the Constitution, the framers intended the military role to be a limited one—far less than a king's. Congress would declare war, making the rules for the army and navy, and control the funding of wars, yet it was

The One Quality Voters Say They Want Most in a President

Honesty/integrity	43%
Leadership/ability to make decisions	11
Sense of responsibility to people	6
Believes United States rates first	5
Understanding of the poor	4
Sound economic program	4
Intelligence	2
Good judgment	2
Self-confidence	2
Experience	2
High moral standards	2
Accessibility	1
Other	3
No answer/don't know	12

SOURCE: CBS News/New York Times Poll, April, 1996.

TABLE 12–1 A Presidential Job Description

	Examples of Policy Responsibilities		
	Foreign Policy	**Economic Policy**	**Domestic Policy**
Crisis management	Clinton's authorizing bombing of Iraq	FDR's handling of the Depression, 1930s	Initiating federal disaster relief
Symbolic and morale-building leadership	G.W. Bush's visit to Mexico to celebrate trade and friendship	Granting most-favored-nation status to China	Visiting flood and disaster victims
Recruitment of top officials	Selecting Joint Chiefs of Staff chair	Reappointing Alan Greenspan to head the Fed	Nominating Supreme Court justices
Priority setting and problem clarification	Working with United Nations on peacekeeping priorities	Outlining tax-cut or revenue-producing programs	Setting priorities in environmental protection and health care
Legislative and political coalition building	Negotiating with Congress on new members of NATO	Working out a tax cut with Congress	Clinton's efforts to pass health care reform
Program implementation, administration, and oversight	Hosting Middle East peace talks	Monitoring Internal Revenue Service performance	Appraising the impact of federal social programs

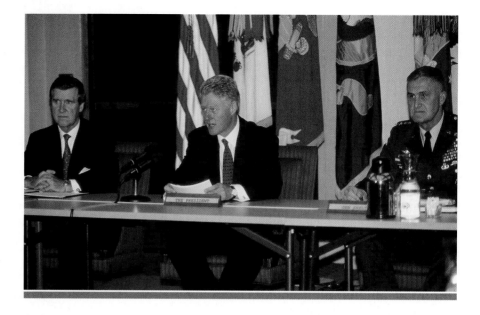

President Bill Clinton with Defense Secretary William Cohen and General Henry Shelton, chair of the Joint Chiefs of Staff.

important, the framers insisted, that the people's elected representative—the president—be in charge of the military.

This principle of *civilian control over the military* is a central element in our constitutional democracy.[6] It means all soldiers and sailors, from the newest recruit to every general and admiral, take their orders from and owe their allegiance to the one person elected by all the people. The professional military, no matter what their own personal political views and values, take their military orders from the president and his chief civilian agent, the secretary of defense.

When crises and national emergencies occur, Americans instinctively turn to the chief executive, who is expected to provide the appearance of a confident, "take-charge" executive with a steady hand at the helm. Public necessity forces presidents to do what Lincoln and Franklin Roosevelt did during the national emergencies of their day: provide the stability and continuity needed to protect the union and safeguard vital American interests.

The primary factor underlying this transformation in the president's function as commander in chief has been the changed role of the United States in the world, especially since World War II. In recent decades every president has argued for and won support for the use of U.S. troops overseas as part of the North Atlantic Treaty Organization (NATO) or the various United Nations peacekeeping forces. Nations grew dependent on our assistance, which often was spelled out in treaties, pacts, and diplomatic agreements. These commitments, plus the fear of nuclear war and the importance of deterrence, prompted Congress to give presidents great flexibility in making foreign policy.

Presidents are expected to be crisis managers in the domestic sphere as well. Whenever things go wrong, we demand presidential-level planning and problem solving. When terrorists attack U.S. citizens or U.S. naval vessels, people assume their president will retaliate or at least track down the terrorists. When a disastrous oil spill occurs, or a natural disaster happens, people expect the president to step in and assist. Even when there is little a president can do, the involvement by the chief executive signals that the government will do what it can and conveys empathy on the part of the president.

The Constitution delegates to Congress the authority to declare the legal state of war (with the consent of the president), but as commander in chief, the president often starts the actual fighting or initiates actions that lead to war. From George Washington's time until today, a president, by ordering troops into hostile areas, has often decided when and where Americans will fight and when they will not. When the

president has political support for such actions, Congress has gone along. But, as we shall discuss in the next chapter, some members of Congress believe this power of the president to begin armed conflicts without prior congressional approval has been abused by recent presidents.

Presidents as Morale Builders

As chiefs of state, presidents are the symbolic equivalent of the British monarch—projecting a sense of national unity and serving as the country's chief ceremonial leader. The framers of the Constitution did not fully anticipate the symbolic and morale-building functions a president must perform. Certain magisterial functions, such as receiving ambassadors and granting pardons, were conferred. But over time the presidency has acquired enormous symbolic significance.

Presidents are the nation's number-one celebrities; almost anything they do is news. Presidents command attention merely by jogging, fishing, golfing, or going to church. By their actions they can arouse a sense of hope or despair, honor or dishonor.

The morale-building job of the president involves much more than just ceremonial cheerleading or quasi-chaplain duties. Presidential leadership, at its finest, radiates national self-confidence and helps unlock the possibility for good that exists in the nation. Our best leaders have been able to provide this special and often intangible element.

Presidents as Recruiters

Presidents make more than 4,000 appointments, including hundreds of federal judgeships and top positions in the military and diplomatic service. Recall, however, that many appointments require the approval of the Senate. Effective presidents shrewdly use their appointment powers not only to reward campaign supporters and enhance ties to Congress, but also to communicate priorities and policy directions. Moreover, the White House in recent decades has often placed campaign aides in key deputy positions to ensure loyalty to the White House.[7]

Besides identifying and recruiting them, the president must also try to keep the most talented of these officials in government as long as possible. Many able people come to top positions in the cabinet or subcabinet and stay for just two or three years. Among the reasons for these short terms is that top federal posts do not pay as much as similar positions in the private sector, and living in Washington is expensive.

Presidents have a lasting impact beyond their terms of office by their power to nominate federal judges. For example, President Dwight Eisenhower's nomination of Earl Warren to be chief justice of the United States was one of his most significant decisions in the area of domestic policy. Warren served for more than 15 years and presided over vast changes in civil rights and civil liberties. President Clinton nominated hundreds of federal judges, including Supreme Court justices Ruth Bader Ginsburg and Stephen Breyer, who are likely to have long-term effects. In a similar way, the selection of a secretary of state, a top economic adviser, a secretary of the treasury, a Federal Reserve Board member, or a top White House aide can have a substantial impact on long-term national policy. But Supreme Court appointments, because they are lifetime positions, overshadow almost all the others.

Various financial disclosure and conflict-of-interest requirements, imposed on presidential appointees as a result of the Ethics in Government Act of 1978, discourage some potential appointees from accepting government jobs. They must fill out many forms, and they must testify at sometimes complicated, time-consuming, confusing, and embarrassing congressional hearings. Media scrutiny of citizen-leaders called to government service has also become more intensive. Recruiters for recent presidents report they often have to go to their second or third choice before they find someone willing to accept an appointment.[8] A president must strengthen the

What Is the Pardon Power?

Article II, Section 2, of the U.S. Constitution provides that the president shall have the power to grant "Reprieves" and "Pardons" for offenses against the United States, except in cases of impeachment. This authority, the roots of which can be traced directly to the royal authority of the king of England, is probably the most imperial and often the most delicate power a president exercises. The pardon power is generally a tool of mercy, an instrument to correct miscarriages of justice and to restore full civil rights to those who have served their sentences and are expected to be law abiding.

The pardon power permits a president to be merciful, but it can also be used strategically when a pardon can restore peace and stability. George Washington used this power to help end the Whiskey Rebellion. Presidents Abraham Lincoln and Andrew Johnson used it to provide amnesty to Confederate leaders and soldiers. Presidents Gerald Ford and Jimmy Carter used it for Vietnam War draft evaders. President Ford also used it to pardon Richard Nixon, one of the most controversial exercises of the pardon power. Clinton, on his final day in office, pardoned his half-brother, one of his former business partners, one of his former cabinet members, and a fugitive commodities trader, Marc Rich, whose former wife was a big contributor to Clinton's campaigns and presidential library.

Line of Succession to the Presidency

The Constitution leaves succession after the vice-president up to Congress. Thus this is the line of succession according to a law passed by Congress in 1947 and by the Twenty-fifth Amendment. However, the constitutional qualifications still apply. For example, if the secretary of state was born in a foreign country of parents who were not U.S. citizens, he or she would be bypassed in this line.

1. Vice-President
2. Speaker of the House of Representatives
3. Senate President Pro Tempore
4. Secretary of State
5. Secretary of the Treasury
6. Secretary of Defense
7. Attorney General
8. Secretary of the Interior
9. Secretary of Agriculture
10. Secretary of Commerce
11. Secretary of Labor
12. Secretary of Health and Human Services
13. Secretary of Housing and Urban Development
14. Secretary of Transportation
15. Secretary of Energy
16. Secretary of Education
17. Secretary of Veterans Affairs

hand of the ablest people working in the bureaucracy and promote them to higher positions at the senior reaches of the executive branch.[9]

Presidents as Priority and Agenda Setters

Presidents, by custom, have become responsible for proposing initiatives in foreign policy and economic growth and stability. This was not always the case. But beginning with Woodrow Wilson, and especially since the New Deal, a president has been expected to propose reforms to ensure domestic progress. New ideas are seized upon by a presidential candidate searching for campaign issues, and they are later refined and implemented by the executive office staff, by special presidential task forces, and by Congress.

NATIONAL SECURITY POLICY   The framers foresaw a special need for speed and unity in dealing with other nations. As a result, presidents generally have more leeway in foreign policy and military affairs than they have in domestic matters. The Constitution vests in a president command of the two major instruments of foreign policy—the diplomatic corps and the armed services. It also gives the chief executive responsibility for negotiating treaties and commitments with other nations, although the Senate must consent to treaty ratifications, and almost all international agreements require congressional action for their implementation.

Congress has granted presidents discretion in initiating foreign policies, for diplomacy frequently requires quick action. The Supreme Court has upheld strong presidential authority in this area. In *United States v Curtiss-Wright* (1936), the Court referred to the "exclusive power of the president as the sole organ of the federal government in the field of international relations—a power which does not require as a basis for its exercise an act of Congress, but which, of course, like every other governmental power, must be exercised in subordination to the applicable provisions of the Constitution."[10] These are sweeping and much-debated words.[11] Still, a determined Congress that knows what it wants does not lack power in foreign relations. Congress must authorize and appropriate the funds that back up the president's policies abroad.

President Clinton and Russian President Vladamir Putin sign the strategic Cooperation Initiative while attending the United Nations Millennium Summit on September 6, 2000.

ECONOMIC POLICY   Ever since the New Deal, presidents have been expected to promote policies to keep unemployment low, fight inflation, keep taxes down, and promote economic growth and prosperity. The Constitution did not specify these duties for the executive, yet presidents know that when the nation is not prosperous and jobs are scarce, they may suffer the fate of Herbert Hoover, who was denounced for his alleged inaction at the beginning of the Great Depression. The growth and complexity of economic problems since the Depression of the 1930s have placed more economic responsibility in the president's hands. The delicate balancing required to keep a modern economy operating means presidents must make key fiscal and budgetary policy decisions.[12] The presidential elections in 1980, 1992, and 1996 turned largely on the economy.

Although presidents sometimes get their economic advice elsewhere, their chief advisers on economic policy are the secretary of the treasury, the three members of the Council of Economic Advisers, and the director of the Office of Management and Budget. The chair of the Federal Reserve Board of Governors is also an influential, if independent, adviser on the economy.

DOMESTIC POLICY   A leader is one who knows where the followers are. Abraham Lincoln did not invent the antislavery movement. John Kennedy and Lyndon Johnson did not begin the civil rights movement. Bill Clinton was not the first leader to notice the unfairness of health care and welfare policies. Similarly, George W. Bush's campaign promises were shaped by public concern about prescription drug costs more than by him. But they all, in their respective times, became embroiled in these controversies, for a president cannot long ignore what divides or inspires a nation.

Presidents as Legislative and Political Coalition Builders

The Constitution provides that the president "shall from time to time give to the Congress information on the State of the Union, and recommend to their Consideration such Measures as he shall judge necessary and expedient." From the start, strong presidents have exploited this power. George Washington and John Adams went in person to Congress to deliver information and recommendations. Thomas Jefferson and many presidents after him sent written messages, but Woodrow Wilson restored the practice of delivering a personal, and often dramatic, message. (For these and related messages, see **www.whitehouse.gov**)

Less public, yet equally important, are the frequent written policy messages dispatched from the White House to the members of Congress on a range of public problems. These messages are important in defining the administration's position and in giving assistance to friendly legislators. Moreover, these messages are often accompanied by detailed drafts of legislation, which members of Congress sponsor with little or no change. These White House proposals, the products of bill-drafting experts on the president's staff or in the executive departments and agencies, may be strengthened or diluted by Congress, but many of the original provisions survive.

Presidents cannot escape political coalition building. As candidates, they made promises to the people and assembled an electoral coalition of supporters. To get things done and to get reelected, however, they must work with interest groups and people who have differing loyalties and responsibilities. Inevitably, presidents become embroiled in legislative, bureaucratic, and lobbying politics, and their approval ratings often suffer as a consequence.

Despite their formal powers, presidents can rarely command; they spend most of their time *persuading* people. The power to persuade is the president's chief resource, and that power comes through bargaining. Bargaining, in turn, comes primarily through getting others to believe it is in their self-interest to cooperate. Presidents and their aides spend a lot of time dispensing favors to various members of Congress from whom they are seeking votes and political support. Hence the skill of

a president in communicating and winning others over is the necessary energizing factor in moving the institutions of the national government to action.

Presidents often clash with Congress, as we shall discuss in the next chapter, yet they cooperate and collaborate just as often, if not more so. Plainly, working with the Congress is a major part of the job of being president.

Presidents as Molders of Public Opinion

The press conference is an example of how a president can employ the machinery of communication to build legislative and political coalitions. Years ago press conferences were rather casual affairs. Franklin Roosevelt ran his get-togethers informally and was a master at withholding information as well as giving it. Under Harry Truman the conference became an institutionalized part of the presidential communications apparatus. John Kennedy authorized live telecasts of press conferences and used them frequently for direct communication with the people. Ronald Reagan and Bill Clinton effectively used five-minute Saturday afternoon radio chats to communicate their views, ask for support, and win Sunday morning media coverage.

Presidents regularly commission polls to find out how they are doing. They want to learn about the public's views, estimate the strength and direction of its thinking, and respond to it. Public opinion can be unstable and unpredictable. Richard Nixon's dramatic drop of nearly 40 percentage points in public opinion polls as a result of the Watergate scandal helped force his resignation. George Bush won solid public approval during and after the successful military efforts in the Persian Gulf in early 1991, yet his popular approval diminished sharply during the economic downturn that followed. Most presidents lose support the longer they are in office. Dissatisfaction sets in; interest groups grow impatient; unkept promises must be accounted for; and the president gets blamed for things that go wrong.

Bill Clinton surprisingly retained and even gained popularity the longer he was in office. Indeed, the more personal trouble Clinton got into, the more his public approval ratings went up—even after he was impeached by the U.S. House of Representatives. The Clinton years of "peace, prosperity, and moderation" kept his approval ratings high.[13] He also reinvented himself as a warrior against the Newt Gingrich–led Congress, yet he prudently collaborated, when necessary, on a number of Republican initiatives, such as welfare reform, balancing the budget, and crime prevention.

Bill Clinton had especially testy relations with the press and complained a lot about the media.[14] He used every available means to get his message out to the Amer-

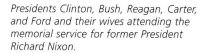

Presidents Clinton, Bush, Reagan, Carter, and Ford and their wives attending the memorial service for former President Richard Nixon.

EVALUATING BILL CLINTON'S PRESIDENCY

An impressive 66 percent of the American people approved of the job Bill Clinton did at the end of his two terms. That was higher than Ronald Reagan's 63 percent or Dwight Eisenhower's 60 percent at the end of their two terms. Yet if Clinton won exceptionally high marks for his job as president, he won uncommonly low marks as a person or moral exemplar.[*]

Clinton's greatest successes were sustaining economic growth and job development, reducing the debt and creating a budget surplus, reforming the welfare system, keeping America out of war, and encouraging international trade through the North American Free Trade Agreement and other trade agreements. Polls of the American public concluded that his worst failings were his affair with Monica Lewinsky and the ensuing impeachment, setting the wrong moral tone for the country, his inability to win congressional approval for his health care reform package, and some unfortunate pardons at the end of his term.

In short, Bill Clinton, like FDR and Ronald Reagan before him, stirred

Bill Clinton expended considerable effort to bring about peace in the Middle East during his presidency, holding numerous summits and traveling to the area frequently. Here he meets with Israeli Prime Minister Ehud Barak and Palestinian leader Yasser Arafat, as well as UN Secretary General Kofi Annan and Egyptian President Hosni Mubarak, in October 2000, in an ultimately unsuccessful effort to end the bloodshed.

great passions, affirmatively and negatively. His place in history is hard to predict, but it is unlikely he will be judged either among the great or the worst presidents. Part of the verdict on his presidency will depend on what happens to our peace and prosperity in the next decade.

[*]Albert R. Hunt, "Clinton Ends His Tenure on High Note," *The Wall Street Journal*, December 14, 2000, p. A9.

---

ican public.[15] He was the first president to appear on MTV and, at least in his early years, he regularly turned up at town meetings and talk shows. He had to deal with the press in an era of "in your face journalism," where many of the old rules and courtesies about the separation of public and private life had disappeared, especially those having to do with marital and extramarital relations. We have to remember, however, that Thomas Jefferson, Abraham Lincoln, and Franklin Roosevelt were all vilified by the press and rarely shown much reverence in their lifetimes. Presidents, along with members of Congress, are always fair game for media critics.[16]

Presidents as Party Leaders

As chief of government, each president is called on to act as partisan political leader. Most presidents since Thomas Jefferson have been party leaders, and generally the more effective the president, the more use he has made of party support. Woodrow Wilson, the two Roosevelts, and Ronald Reagan fortified their executive and legislative influence by mobilizing support within their party. Reagan and Clinton were uncommonly effective fund raisers for their political parties.

Someone or something is needed to grease the wheels of government, which, if left to their own devices, grind slowly. A president who can use help from his party

and galvanize a relatively cohesive party sometimes supplies the needed push to overcome gridlock. Yet presidents are often led by their party, or at least constrained by it, as much as they lead it; no president has ever wholly dominated his party.[17]

Presidents as Administrators

The Constitution charges the president to "take Care that the Laws be faithfully executed." Presidents, however, must delegate much of their administrative authority. Because their other responsibilities demand most of their attention, presidents are dependent on their subordinates. Theoretically, at least, orders flow down an administrative line: from president, to cabinet members, to bureau chiefs, to smaller offices. Like all top executives, a president is assisted by a staff who advise the chief executive. This *line and staff organization* is typical of every bureaucratic entity, whether it be the army, General Motors, or the United Nations.

THE WHITE HOUSE STAFF   Presidents have come to rely heavily on their personal staffs. Nowhere else—not in Congress, not in the cabinet, not in the party—can presidents find the loyalty and single-mindedness that often develops among their closest White House aides.[18] Cabinet heads, on the other hand, are often perceived as staunch advocates of their departments and the constituencies their departments serve. Presidents assume, however, that their aides will provide them with sound policy advice, but there are sometimes substantial costs to listening only to one's closest associates. The White House can usually be thought of as a palace court in which strong presidents create an environment that weeds out any assistant who persists in presenting irritating or opposing views.

The number of employees in the presidential entourage grew steadily from the early 1900s through the early 1990s. Today a White House staff of about 400 operates at a slight reduction from previous years. This staff makes up just one part of the Executive Office of the President.

The staff of the White House office can be categorized by their primary functions: (1) domestic policy; (2) economic policy; (3) national security or foreign policy; (4) administration and personnel matters (as well as personal paperwork and scheduling for the president); (5) congressional relations; and (6) public relations.

Presidential aides sometimes insist they are simply the eyes and ears of the president, that they make few important decisions, and that they never intrude between the chief executive and the heads of departments. But the inevitable emergence of a few strong White House advisers makes this traditional picture inaccurate.[19] Some White House aides, impatient with bureaucratic and congressional bottlenecks or even political sabotage, come to view the presidency as if it alone were the whole government.

THE INSTITUTIONALIZED EXECUTIVE OFFICE   Approved by Congress in 1939, the **Executive Office of the President** was the recommendation of Franklin Roosevelt's Committee on Administrative Management. The intention was to provide presidents with the help they obviously needed to carry out the growing responsibilities imposed by the Great Depression and by the enlarged role of government. The Executive Office of the President consists of the Office of Management and Budget, the Council of Economic Advisers, and several other staff units (see Figure 12–1).

The **Office of Management and Budget (OMB)** is the central presidential staff agency. Its director advises the president in detail about the hundreds of government agencies—how much money they should be allotted in the budget and what kind of job they are doing. OMB seeks to improve the planning, management, and statistical work of the agencies. It makes a special effort to see that each agency conforms to presidential policies in its dealings with Congress; each agency has to clear its policy recommendations to Congress through OMB first.[20]

Through the long budget preparation process, presidents use OMB as a way of conserving and centralizing their own influence. A budget is more than just a finan-

Executive Office of the President
The cluster of presidential staff agencies that help the president carry out his responsibilities. Currently the office includes the Office of Management and Budget, the Council of Economic Advisers, and several other units.

Office of Management and Budget
Presidential staff agency that serves as a clearinghouse for budgetary requests and management improvements.

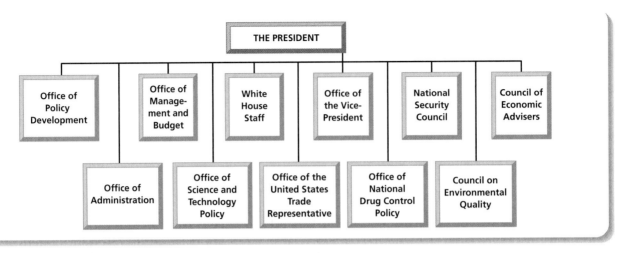

FIGURE 12–1 Executive Office of the President

Source: *United States Government Manual, 2000/2001* (Government Printing Office, 2000), p.87.

cial plan, because it reflects power struggles and indicates national priorities (and wishful thinking). To the president, the budget is a means of control over administrators who may be trying to join ranks with other politicians or interest groups to thwart presidential priorities.

THE CABINET   It is hard to find a more unusual institution than the president's **cabinet**. The cabinet is not specifically mentioned by name in the Constitution, yet since George Washington's administration, every president has had one. Washington's consisted of his secretaries of state, treasury, and war, plus his attorney general.

Today the selection of cabinet members is the first major job for the president-elect. The cabinet consists of the president, the vice-president, the heads of the 14 executive departments, and a few others a president considers cabinet-level officials. The cabinet has always been a loosely designated body, and it is not always clear who belongs in it. In recent years, certain executive branch administrators and White House counselors have been accorded cabinet rank.

George W. Bush recruited a notably diverse cabinet that included several women, two African Americans, two Asian Americans, and other minorities. His key appointments at Defense, State, and Treasury had all served extensively in previous Republican administrations. One of his nominees, Linda Chavez, had to withdraw when a controversy developed over her having housed and employed an undocumented alien. Bush's attorney general appointment, former Missouri governor and U.S. senator John Ashcroft, won confirmation by a 58 to 42 vote after heated hearings and debates over some of his political beliefs and past votes.

Cabinet government as practiced in parliamentary systems—where the voice and the vote of the cabinet members count for a lot—simply does not exist in the United States.[21] In fact, an American president is not required by the Constitution to form a cabinet or to hold regular meetings. Presidents John Kennedy, Lyndon Johnson, and Richard Nixon all preferred small conferences with individuals specifically involved in a problem. Kennedy saw no reason to discuss defense department matters with his secretaries of agriculture and labor, and he thought cabinet meetings wasted valuable time. Both Jimmy Carter and Ronald Reagan tried to revive the cabinet, and both met often with their cabinets during their first two years. But the longer they remained in office, the less frequently they met with their cabinets as a whole. Bill Clinton, like those he followed, seldom called for full cabinet meetings, holding just 18 full cabinet meetings in his first term and even fewer during his second.[22]

Presidential advisers and the heads of various White House–based cabinet-level councils, such as the National Security Council and the Office of Management

cabinet

Advisory council for a president, consisting of the heads of the executive departments, the vice-president, and a few others the president considers cabinet-level officials.

and Budget, have gained equal or even superior status to many cabinet secretaries. This shift occurred in part because these advisers are physically located in or next door to the White House (see Figure 12–2). Further, presidents are aware that some cabinet members adopt narrow "advocate" views: the Agriculture Department secretary is a strong advocate for the farmers; the Housing and Urban Development Department secretary is an ambassador for the housing industry and, to some extent, also for big city mayors; and so on through much of the cabinet, especially those preoccupied with domestic policy matters.

THE VICE-PRESIDENCY

Although the vice-presidency is now very much a part of the presidential establishment, it has been so for only a couple of generations. Until the 1950s, most vice-presidents served mainly as president of the Senate. Up to that time, the vice-president was at best a "fifth wheel" and at worst a political rival who sometimes connived against the president. The office was often dismissed as a joke. One reason for the vice-president's posture as an outsider was that presidential nominees usually chose running mates who were geographically, ideologically, demographically, and in other ways likely to "balance the ticket."

Ideally, a vice-president performs several tasks in addition to the ceremonial function of acting as president of the Senate. A vice-president gets to cast the tie-breaking vote if the Senate has a tie vote. The vice-president is also a member of the National Security Council.

The real test of the role of vice-president is whether he or she is fully integrated into the decision-making process in the White House. Inevitably all vice-presidents are "back-up equipment" in case something happens to the president. They can head up any number of councils, visit any number of countries, and still not be much involved in the day-to-day operations of the presidency. President Jimmy Carter included Walter Mondale in the daily processes of decision making in the White House; President Ronald Reagan sometimes included George Bush in a similar way; President Clinton used Al Gore as an important adviser and confidant on domestic as well as foreign policy matters and key appointments.

West Wing

Vice-President's Office

Cabinet Room

East Wing

Presidential Briefing Room

Oval Office

FIGURE 12–2 The White House

Source: Adapted from *The Washington Post,* February 5, 1993, p. A23.

George W. Bush selected Dick Cheney for his vice-president in large part because Cheney's prior experience in Congress, in the White House, and in the cabinet brought credibility to the Bush campaign. His previous government positions would strengthen Bush's governing ability if the ticket won the White House. After the election Cheney headed up the presidential transition team, recruiting senior administrators and shaping the legislative agenda. Cheney became as important, if not more important, than any previous vice-president.

The vice-presidency has been significantly affected by two constitutional amendments. The Twenty-second Amendment, ratified in 1951, imposes a two-term limit on presidents; consequently, vice-presidents have a better chance of moving up to the Oval Office. The Twenty-fifth Amendment, ratified in 1967, confirms the practice of making the vice-president not an acting president, but president, in the event of the death of a president. Also of significance, this amendment outlines a procedure to determine whether an incumbent president is unable to discharge the powers and duties of the office and establishes procedures to fill a vacancy in the vice-presidency.[23] For a few hours in 1985, George Bush became the first "acting president" when President Reagan underwent a minor cancer operation.

The amendment also provides that in the event of a vacancy in the office of vice-president, the president nominates a vice-president, who takes office upon confirmation by a majority vote of both houses of Congress. This procedure generally ensures the appointment of a vice-president in whom the president has confidence. Thus vice-presidents who have to take over the presidency can be expected to reflect most of their predecessor's policies.

Although the sort of tensions between president and vice-president that existed in the past rarely affected Clinton and Gore or Bush and Cheney, tension between a president and a vice-president is natural. After all, except for the vice-president, everybody who works closely with a president can be fired. It is almost certain that vice-presidents will continue to have an undefined ad hoc set of assignments, subject more to the goodwill and mood of the president than to any fixed description.[24]

Vice-President Dick Cheney.

KEEPING PRESIDENTS ACCOUNTABLE

This nation has had great presidents, yet we have also had ineffective and flawed presidents. We have no foolproof way to guarantee that our presidents will possess the leadership skills and moral character the job requires.

Accountability refers to a president's responsiveness to the will of the majority and taking responsibility for one's actions. Accountability implies as well that important presidential decisions will be explained to the public to allow citizens to evaluate how well a president is handling the assignments of the office. Here are some of the ways presidents are constrained and held to account:

Reelection and Legacy

Presidents want to win reelection because reelection is a validation of their first term as well as an opportunity for them to continue to implement their agenda. To win reelection, a president has to win the approval of large numbers of attentive citizens. It is in this sense that elections hold a president to account after four years in office.

But even midterm congressional elections also serve as a check on presidents. For example, Lyndon Johnson, Gerald Ford, and Bill Clinton all suffered major losses in their party's ranks in the Congress in 1966, 1974, and 1994. These losses sent a stark message to the White House and affected how these presidents behaved. In Clinton's case, it had the effect of influencing him to move to the political center.

Every president also wants to leave a legacy that will be viewed positively by historians and later generations. Thus presidents usually are inclined to do what is right in hopes of being judged successful and effective.

Should presidents be limited to two terms in office?

Before he left office, former President Ronald Reagan called for the repeal of the Twenty-second Amendment to the Constitution, the one that limits a president to two terms. Why do you think he opposed the amendment? What additional reasons could be put forth to persuade people to repeal this relatively new (1951) provision in the Constitution? What are the best reasons for retaining the Twenty-second Amendment?

Congress and the President

The framers of the Constitution deliberately designed Congress as a formal check on the presidential exercise of power. Congress would be the primary lawmaker and even have the right to override a presidential veto. Congress could refuse to approve presidential nominees to the executive departments, to the courts, and to diplomatic posts. And Congress also was given that ultimate weapon—impeachment and conviction—to remove a president from office.

The Supreme Court and the President

The framers of the Constitution intended the Supreme Court to serve as a check on the potential abuses of power by presidents. The Court, they hoped, would comprise wise and well-educated statesmen who would strive to preserve the Constitution, especially from legislative and executive wrongdoing. Most of the framers believed the Supreme Court would work hand-in-hand with the executive. Some even viewed the courts as an executive department, involved in executing, interpreting, and applying the laws.

But presidents and the courts have had their share of clashes. In a good many instances, presidents have won these differences of opinion, yet the exceptions are notable:

> Thomas Jefferson was told by the Supreme Court that he had acted wrongly in one of his military initiatives.

> Abraham Lincoln was rebuffed for using military courts in areas outside the war zone where the Court said they were not justified.

> Franklin Roosevelt saw several of his early New Deal initiatives struck down by the Court as unconstitutional.

> Harry Truman was ordered by the Court to release steel mills from federal control.

> Richard Nixon's policies were overturned by the Supreme Court or lower federal courts on dozens of occasions, most notably, of course, in the summer of 1974, when the Supreme Court directed him to release certain White House tape recordings for use in a criminal investigation.

> The Court upheld Paula Jones's right to file a civil suit involving Bill Clinton's private behavior while he was still serving as president.

A Watchdog Media and the President

Ronald Reagan once walked away from one of his news conferences and, turning to an aide, blasted reporters, not realizing a microphone was picking up every word. John F. Kennedy canceled more than 50 White House subscriptions to the *New York Herald Tribune* because he was furious about the way the paper treated his administration. Bill Clinton complained about "gotcha journalism." George W. Bush, when running for the White House, referred over a live microphone to a prominent *New York Times* reporter as a "major league [epithet]." All recent presidents complain that the media misrepresent them and disproportionately report bad news.

Enjoying First Amendment rights in this country, reporters usually go about their business of analyzing and criticizing presidents with gusto. Scores of media representatives are stationed at the White House, and they travel everywhere the president goes, reporting on every move.

Presidents, of course, want their initiatives publicized and praised. But journalists and commentators believe they should provide a context in which presidential statements can be understood; hence they not only tell people what a president says, but often try to explain what the statement means. A free press is a basic check on presidents.

Most presidents have been patient and respected criticism as essential in a democracy. However, presidents and their aides engage in extensive public rela-

tions efforts aimed at winning admiration and support for the president and White House policies.[25] Out-of-town editors are invited in for special briefings, and extra effort is made to get the president out of Washington for meetings with local and regional media representatives, who are generally viewed as less critical than Washington-based media. White House media experts devise ways to get the president's point of view out to the public, to get the president on prime-time television, or to arrange for flattering photo opportunities.

No matter who is in the White House, presidents and the media will be in conflict. This ongoing struggle is inherent in a constitutional democracy. Exposés of campaign-contribution scandals and the Monica Lewinsky affair in the 1990s fortified the media's role in bringing these events to public attention. Further, because the media—especially television—are viewed as more trustworthy and believable than some other national institutions, most Americans, most of the time, believe what they hear and see on television. But the resources of the White House and the amount of free media coverage given presidents—especially communicators like Franklin Roosevelt, John Kennedy, and Ronald Reagan—provide an effective counterpoint to the media.

Public Opinion and Presidential Accountability

Presidents, in practice, are influenced by their anticipation not only of the next election but also of tomorrow's headlines and editorials, next week's public opinion polls, and next month's congressional hearings.

Presidents are subjected to a barrage of polls that judge their day-to-day or even minute-to-minute actions. In many ways, the time frame for presidential decision making and problem solving has been dramatically shortened. Issues cannot ripen, problems cannot be debated, discussed, and analyzed over several days. CNN-MSNBC-Fox television and website instant news analysis may indeed be holding presidents to instant accountability.

Although presidents on occasion have tried to govern without the benefit of public support, they have seldom succeeded. However, one of the more confusing aspects of presidential accountability is the way Americans find it convenient to blame the president for a whole range of problems, regardless of whether the problems were subject to presidential control. We generally withhold applause when a president's work is good, but we seldom fail to fault presidents when there are blunders.

As noted, most presidents lose public support over time. The decline in approval is in good measure a function of the understandable inability of a president to live up to the exaggerated buildup almost every president receives during the presidential honeymoon period (see Figure 12–3).

Political scientists are not exactly sure what people mean when they say they "approve" of a president's job performance. People respond to presidents at least as much through emotions as they do a rational understanding of the government's performance or a president's precise position on issues. But we do know that positive economic success helps a president's standing in the polls. Major nationally televised addresses also give a president a boost in public approval. Similarly, short successful wars and diplomatic breakthroughs at least temporarily improve a president's public approval. A president's favorable standing in the polls may help win congressional backing of White House policy measures; legislative victories, in turn, probably help enhance a president's standing in the polls.[26]

With the cold war era long over, a president's primary responsibility in the twenty-first century is to promote a successful domestic economy and productive trade relations. There will be occasional foreign policy tests, such as the U. S. intelligence-gathering plane that was forced down in China early in the Bush

Why Presidential Approval (in Polls) Usually Declines the Longer Presidents Are in Office

- Expectations that are raised in campaigns are dashed as time forecloses resources and options.

- Things that go wrong get blamed, rightly or wrongly, on presidents, whether or not presidents have the power to deal with these matters.

- Rising disapproval of incumbent presidents is often influenced by inflation and unemployment.

- Major negative events, such as the Vietnam War, Watergate scandal, or stock market declines, influence how people evaluate presidents.

- Press and media criticism accumulates over time and sharpens the public's dissatisfaction with a president. Perhaps, too, time in office simply wears out our welcome for a president.

Thinking It Through...

Reagan said the people should be able to reelect a president as many times as they want, just as they now reelect House and Senate members. He also hinted that the Twenty-second Amendment might weaken a president late in his second term by making him a lame duck, less powerful because everyone knows he will not be around in a year or so. Advocates of repeal also say we may sometimes need to keep a veteran president in office during a crisis period, much as we retained Franklin Roosevelt in 1940. Others say eight years may not be enough time to resolve certain major problems.

The Twenty-second Amendment is not only a limit on the incumbent but also on the electorate, the first since the ratification of the Constitution to restrict the power of the electorate rather than expand it. It is based, advocates of repeal suggest, on the assumption that the voters cannot be trusted.

Those who favor keeping the Twenty-second Amendment cite these reasons: First, the presidency is so powerful today that we need the Twenty-second Amendment as an additional check and balance against abuse of this power. Second, the amendment encourages both parties to seek out effective candidates to succeed to office and discourages dependence on a single ruler. Third, few leaders are likely to have the health, the intellectual energy, and the new ideas needed to perform the demanding responsibilities of the presidency beyond eight years in office. Finally, Americans have always believed in citizen-leaders rather than career politicians, and this amendment encourages this ideal.

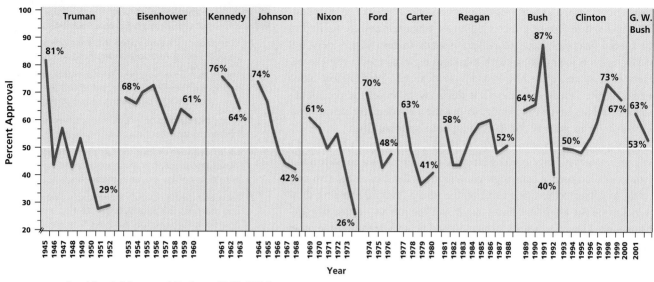

FIGURE 12–3 Presidential Approval Ratings, 1945–2001

SOURCE: The Gallup Organization, www.gallup.org.

administration, but every recent president has found it imperative to create the impression that he has a plan for improving the economy. George W. Bush's father failed to do so, but the younger Bush's success or failure will likely be determined by his domestic rather than his foreign policies.

Ultimately no safeguard can hold a wayward president or a corrupt White House aide completely accountable. Our framers designed a constitutional system that does not depend on our finding angels to run the government. It assumes presidents, even good ones, need checks on their powers. James Madison's advice remains crucial: "A dependence on the people is, no doubt, the primary control of the government, but experience has taught mankind the necessity of auxiliary precautions" (see *The Federalist*, No. 51, in the Appendix of this book). Americans must vigilantly maintain the effectiveness of these "auxiliary precautions"—Congress, political parties, the courts, the press, the Bill of Rights, and concerned citizens' groups—to ensure a properly balanced and constitutional presidency.

PRESIDENTIAL GREATNESS? HOW WE JUDGE THEM

Most Americans judge contemporary presidents against the standard of the Mount Rushmore presidents. We want presidents who can summon us to live up to our shared ideals about liberty and freedom and who will pay close attention to our immediate needs.[27]

In sum, we use varying and sometimes unfair standards when we judge presidents. We expect a lot and leave little room for error. The opinions of historians differ from what the general public believes.

Historians and political scientists occasionally publish rankings of presidents. They rate presidents as outstanding, great, or near great on the basis of whether they brought about desirable changes and acted wisely to guide the nation through turbulent times. "We honor the great presidents of the past" wrote presidential historian Clinton Rossiter, "not for their strength but for the fact that they used it wisely to build a better America."[28]

One of the paradoxes of presidential greatness is that we yearn for the democratic "common person" and simultaneously for a leader who is uncommon, charismatic, visionary, and heroic. Political scientist Harold J. Laski once suggested, "He must have 'common opinions.' But it is equally important that he be an 'uncommon

man.' The public must see themselves in him, but they must, at the same time, be confident that he is something bigger than themselves."[29]

The great presidents, often to the consternation of legal scholars and Congress, stretched the Constitution and *strengthened the presidency* to bring about change. Sometimes this is called the "doctrine of necessity"—doing what needs to be done. Thus those presidents considered "great" often were those who gave Congress the hardest time. They sometimes exercised powers that were thought to be solely or primarily congressional. Some of the presidents regularly challenged Congress and the Supreme Court as well.

What did the great presidents do? President Washington, more than any other person, converted the paper notions outlined in the Constitution into an enduring, practical governing process. With extraordinary character he set the precedents that balanced self-government and leadership, chief of state and chief executive, constitutionalism and statesmanship.

Thomas Jefferson, a genius in his generation, was a skilled organizer and a resourceful party leader and chief executive. He made mistakes, yet he adapted the presidency to the new realities of his day. His expansions of territory with the Louisiana Purchase, his sponsorship of the Lewis and Clark expedition, and similar bold ventures assures him a revered status among presidents.

President Lincoln is remembered for saving the union and is revered as the nation's foremost symbol of democracy and tenacious leadership in the nation's ultimate crisis. President Franklin Delano Roosevelt is viewed as guiding the nation through its worst economic crisis and for rallying the nation and the world to defeat Hitler's nazism.

These presidential accomplishments are part of the legend of America. Yet this heroic view of presidents raises a good many questions. If presidents alone were responsible for these and similar feats, it is little wonder that our expectations are so high concerning what current and future presidents should accomplish.

In fact, of course, a variety of people and institutions contributed to the achievements credited to past presidents. History seldom adequately honors the reformers and leaders who provided behind-the-scenes leadership. The best presidents surround themselves with talented advisers and administrators. Great leadership depends on situation, resources, opportunity, and on teams of leaders. Being at the right place at the right time also helps.

Many of the great presidents made mistakes, sometimes great mistakes. And the great presidents typically look better a few years later than they did while they were among the living. Harry Truman is a prime example of a presidential leader who was viewed as a lesser light while in office but was later recognized as great.

We learn a lot by those presidents we judge as failures. President Warren G. Harding was ranked near or at the bottom by experts because his administration was so corrupt; his loyalty to his friends was fatal. Others rank near the bottom because they lacked a compelling program, vision, political skill, or integrity. While Richard Nixon was respected for his foreign policy initiatives, especially for his recognition of the People's Republic of China, he is nonetheless viewed as one of the lesser presidents because he lied to the American public, plotted a cover-up of illegal and unconstitutional activities, resigned in disgrace, and, in the eyes of many, disgraced the dignity of the Oval Office. Bill Clinton will doubtless be judged a good political leader yet flawed in character.

First Lady: A Search for the Appropriate Role

Political spouses have often influenced their husbands or wives. Earlier presidential spouses—including Dolley Madison, Edith Wilson, and Eleanor Roosevelt—counseled and lobbied their presidential husbands. Every "first spouse" defines her responsibilities differently. Bess Truman and Pat Nixon chose to remain in the background. Lady Bird Johnson, Betty Ford, and Rosalynn Carter undertook projects of special interest to them. Hillary Rodham Clinton became an influential and important adviser to President Bill Clinton.

Hillary Clinton was as controversial as she was influential. Her role as an advocate of health care initiatives and women's rights attracted criticism as well as praise. Her role in the Whitewater real estate development and her alleged failure to answer specific questions about it caused additional concerns. She became the first First Lady to be subpoenaed to testify before a grand jury, and she, along with her husband, was questioned by a federal independent counsel.

Hillary Clinton was hailed as a first lady for our times and a model for contemporary women who choose to have both a career and a family. She was criticized in the press, satirized in the novel *Primary Colors*, and ridiculed by opposition politicians and pundits. She stood by her husband throughout the Monica Lewinsky scandal and energized Democratic opposition to her husband's impeachment. In 2000 she won election as a U.S. senator from New York.

The high-profile Hillary Clinton model of service as First Lady is unlikely to become the standard model. Laura Bush a former school librarian, prefers playing a lower profile role. One of her keen interests is promoting reading and celebrating books and authors. In Texas she founded an annual book festival for Texas public libraries. She is likely to sponsor similar programs as First Lady. And she has made it clear that she will not be involved in policy development. Unlike Hillary Clinton, she has an office in the east wing rather than the high-status west wing of the White House.

POLITICS ONLINE

Want to Visit the West Wing?

Anyone who thinks politics is not interesting to television viewers has not looked at the ratings for *West Wing*. The consistently popular weekly television show is a fictional version of the activities that take place in the West Wing of the White House. Americans find the exercise of power fascinating, and the interpersonal tensions and different motivations make for good television.

A real visit to the West Wing of the White House is difficult to arrange because it is the working space of the president of the United States. In addition to security concerns, there is the reality of limited space and the pressures of governing. To get a sense of the space, however, you can take a virtual tour by going to:
www.whitehouse.gov/history/whtour.

One quick way to get a sense of recent presidents and how the West Wing really works is to go to their respective presidential library home pages and search on a topic of interest to you. Some libraries have documents online; others provide sound files from presidential speeches, online slide shows; and still others have links to books and documents on the president. For an overview of the presidential library system with links to each presidential library go to:
www.nara.gov/nara/president/address.html.

SUMMARY

1. The framers created a presidency with limited powers. To enact government business, the president must cooperate with Congress, but powers are divided among the branches, and the politics of shared power has often been stormy. In general, however, the role and influence of presidents have increased in the course of the nation's history.

2. The expansion of presidential influence has been a continual development during the past several decades. Crises, both foreign and economic, have enlarged these powers. When there is a need for decisive action, presidents are asked to supply it. Congress, of course, is traditionally expected to share in the formulation of national policy. Every president must

learn anew the need to work closely with the members of Congress.

3. Every four years Americans search for a new president. We yearn for honest, experienced, effective presidents who will propose solutions to the nation's toughest problems. Doubtless we expect far more than is reasonable, but we inevitably want someone as good as Washington, Lincoln, and FDR.

4. Presidents must act as crisis-managing, morale-building, personnel-recruiting, priority-setting, coalition-building, public opinion-molding, party, and managerial leaders. No president can divide the job into tidy compartments. Ultimately, these responsibilities overlap.

5. The vice-presidency is now a part of the presidential establishment, and recent

vice-presidents have been increasingly integrated into the White House decision-making process.

6. Presidential power is usually exercised for important and noble ends, yet it can also on occasion be abused. Presidents, however, are held to account by a variety of checks and balances, including elections and legacy, Congress, the court, the media, and public opinion.

7. Presidential greatness is something often talked about yet harder to define. But nearly everyone considers Lincoln, Washington, and Franklin Roosevelt as outstanding presidents. Presidents are viewed as great when they brought about desirable progress and guided the nation through crises.

KEY TERMS

divided government 275

Executive Office of the
President 282

Office of Management and
Budget 282

cabinet 287

FURTHER READING

DAVID GRAY ADLER AND LARRY N. GEORGE, EDS., *The Constitution and the Conduct of American Foreign Policy: Essays on Law and History* (University Press of Kansas, 1996).

PAUL BRACE AND BARBARA HINCKLEY, *Follow the Leader: Opinion Polls and the Modern Presidents* (Basic Books, 1992).

THOMAS E. CRONIN, ED., *Inventing the American Presidency* (University Press of Kansas, 1989).

THOMAS E. CRONIN AND MICHAEL A. GENOVESE, *The Paradoxes of the American Presidency* (Oxford University Press, 1998).

TERRY EASTLAND, *Energy in the Executive* (Free Press, 1992).

MICHAEL A. GENOVESE, *The Power of the American Presidency, 1989–2000* (Oxford University Press, 2000).

DAVID GERGEN, *Eyewitness to Power: The Essence of Leadership—Nixon to Clinton* (Simon & Schuster, 2000).

FRED GREENSTEIN, *The Presidential Difference* (Free Press, 2000).

ERWIN C. HARGROVE, *The President as Leader: Appealing to the Better Angels of Our Nature* (University Press of Kansas, 1998).

CHARLES O. JONES, *Passages to the Presidency, From Campaigning to Governing* (Brookings Institution, 1998).

MARK LANDY AND SIDNEY M. MILKIS, *Presidential Greatness* (University Press of Kansas, 2000).

LEONARD W. LEVY AND LOUIS FISHER, EDS., *Encyclopedia of the American Presidency* (Simon & Schuster, 1994).

JOHN A. MALTESE, *Spin Control: The White House Office of Communications and the Management of the Presidential News* (University of North Carolina Press, 1992).

SIDNEY M. MILKIS, *The President and the Parties: The Transformation of the American Party System Since the New Deal* (Oxford University Press, 1993).

SIDNEY M. MILKIS AND MICHAEL NELSON, *The American Presidency: Origins and Development, 1976–1998*, 3d ed. (Congressional Quarterly Books, 1999).

MICHAEL NELSON, ED., *The Presidency and the Political System*, 6th ed. (Congressional Quarterly Press, 2000).

RICHARD E. NEUSTADT, *Presidential Power and the Modern Presidents* (Free Press, 1991).

HUBERT S. PARMET, *George Bush: The Life of a Lone Star Yankee* (Scribner's, 1998).

BRADLEY H. PATTERSON, JR., *The White House Staff: Inside the West Wing and Beyond* (Brookings Institution, 2000).

JAMES P. PFIFFNER, *The Strategic Presidency: Hitting the Ground Running*, 2d ed. (University Press of Kansas, 1996).

GLENN A. PHELPS, *George Washington and American Constitutionalism* (University Press of Kansas, 1993).

LYN RAGSDALE, *Vital Statistics on the Presidency*, rev. ed. (Congressional Quarterly Press, 1998).

SHELLEY LYNNE TOMKINS, *Inside OMB: Politics and Process in the President's Budget Office* (M. E. Sharpe, 1998).

KENNETH T. WALSH, *Feeding the Beast: The White House Versus the Press* (Random House, 1996).

SHIRLEY ANNE WARSHAW, *Powersharing: White House–Cabinet Relations in the Modern Presidency* (State University of New York Press, 1996).

13

CONGRESSIONAL-PRESIDENTIAL RELATIONS

EWLY ELECTED PRESIDENT GEORGE W. BUSH
CAME TO THE WHITE HOUSE IN 2001 WITH DAUNTING
CHALLENGES AND A "WEAK HAND." AS VETERAN *WASHINGTON*
Post reporter David Broder noted, Bush enjoyed "No majority. No mandate. Not even broad agreement that he deserved the prize that fell into his hands when the Supreme Court, itself deeply divided, ordered the ballot recounts in Florida must halt."[1] This is hardly the way a president wants to launch a presidency.

Still, George W. Bush immediately set in motion legislative initiatives for a major tax cut, for increased spending on education and military pay, and for prescription drug coverage for Medicare recipients, among other things. He had campaigned on these issues, even though he understood that he might have to scale back some of his plans in order to win bipartisan support. But he understood, too, that the American people expect presidents to set the nation's policy agenda and that elections, even with unclear mandates, are part of the process of bringing about changes in public policy.

As soon as an election concludes, a president inevitably must try to win congressional support for his policies. This is never easy, even for presidents who have won decisive election victories. Members of the opposing party in Congress have their own agendas, and even members of the president's own party in Congress can pose a challenge to presidential plans. Such was the case in George W. Bush's first months in the White House, when Senator John McCain (R.-Ariz.) fought for campaign finance reform as a top priority—an issue the president did not especially support.

Tensions between Congress and presidents go back to the origins of American government. Alexander Hamilton, General George Washington's chief aide, complained about the deadlock rooted in the design of the Continental Congress more than 200 years ago. Yet it was the intention of the framers of the U.S. Constitution to create a government of sharply limited powers and separated institutions that would both share and compete for power. The framers saw the separation of powers not necessarily as a weakness but as a source of strength, and especially as a way to ensure deliberation and to prevent tyranny.

The popular assumption is that a president—as chief executive and commander in chief—essentially guides Congress in most of its law-making activity. But the reality is often different. The decentralized nature of Congress, the independent and entrepreneurial mode of legislators, and the institutional responsibilities and pride of Congress all conspire against presidential policy leadership.

CHAPTERMEDIA

 POLITICS ONLINE

*Are Limitations on
  Presidential War Powers
  Outdated?*
www.prenhall.com/burns

 POLISIM
Who's Got the Power?
www.prenhall.com/burns

Presidents are sometimes opposed by members of their own party, as George W. Bush was by Senator John McCain, his former opponent in the presidential campaign, on the matter of campaign finance reform.

Soon after a new president takes office—as both Bill Clinton and George W. Bush found out—members of Congress take the measure of the new White House occupant. Will the president reach out and try to cooperate with Congress? Will the president overreach and push too fast—as Clinton did with his health care proposal? Will the president be highly partisan or bipartisan? Will the president try to intimidate and coerce reluctant legislators? And how much can Congress exert its leadership?

Who should be in charge? The fact that responsibility and power are fragmented in our federal government often creates a fascinating blame game, with the president blaming Congress and Congress blaming the president. This happened between President Ronald Reagan and the Democrats in Congress in the 1980s and between Clinton and the Newt Gingrich–led Congress of the mid-1990s.

The success of Congress or the president is influenced by the partisan and ideological makeup of Congress, the popularity and skills of the president, the strength of the political parties, and the nature of various events that shape the politics of the times.

In this chapter we begin by looking at our complicated system of separate branches, which of necessity must find ways to work together. What did the framers intend? What has evolved over the years? Why do members of Congress often see things differently from the way presidents do? What are some of the ongoing controversies between the two branches? And what are some of the ways presidents try to win congressional support?

SEPARATE BUT EQUAL BRANCHES

The Constitution's writers saw Congress as the central, if not dominant, branch of government. Congress would have the power of the purse, in addition to extensive supervision of interstate and foreign commerce and the currency. Congress would also play a crucial role in military and foreign policy matters since only Congress could declare war and only the Senate could approve treaties. And Congress was granted the all-important power to make laws "which shall be necessary and proper" for carrying out its specified powers.

Presidents do not personally introduce legislation, but they are invited to give Congress information on the State of the Union and recommend measures they deem necessary for the good of the nation. Thus, in practice, presidents are invited to shape the nation's legislative agenda; it would be unthinkable for a president today not to submit an extensive legislative program to the Congress.

America's first presidents deferred to Congress on many issues, but gradually presidents began to play a more assertive role in the legislative process. A stronger executive gradually evolved to provide balance and leadership.

Congress was sometimes a willing participant in giving additional power to presidents. The rise in importance of the presidency in legislating did not, however, follow a clear linear path. Some of the more ambitious chief executives, such as Thomas Jefferson, used the newly formed political parties to exert influence in Congress. Others, such as Andrew Jackson, marshaled public opinion to gain influence with the Congress. Still others, such as Abraham Lincoln and Franklin Roosevelt, gained additional powers during national crises. In between these influence-aggrandizing presidents were less assertive or weaker chief executives. Thus, an institutional ebb and flow characterized the relationship between Congress and presidents. What was designed in many ways as a congressionally centered system evolved by the early twenty-first century into a system centered around the presidency.

But Congress can impose its will on presidents, as Ronald Reagan found out when Congress rejected his strongly argued plea for millions in military aid to Nicaragua rebels, and Bill Clinton discovered when Congress refused to enact his health care reform measures and when the Senate failed to ratify a Comprehensive Test Ban Treaty. Virtually every president has also faced setbacks in dealing with Congress on confirmation of nominees to the cabinet or the courts.

The separation of powers and divided government can be obstacles, yet they are not barriers to good public policy making. Indeed, a certain amount of delay and the need for compromise often make for better public policy. Presidents and Congress can legislate when the leaders of both institutions bargain and compromise. Although the Constitution distributes power and invites a continuous struggle between these rival branches, it also requires them to collaborate. And despite all the media attention highlighting their disagreements, these institutions usually do cooperate. Even when the relationship is highly partisan and hostile, bills get passed and become law, appointments are confirmed, budgets are enacted, and the government receives both the funding and the general direction it needs to get work done. This necessary cooperation generally takes place even when the White House and Congress are divided between the two major parties. And it is not a matter of one side winning and the other losing so much as a series of compromises between the two branches.

Most presidential budget requests eventually win approval, although Congress jealously guards its right to modify them, especially in certain areas such as defense and agriculture. Presidents, regardless of party, have about a fifty-fifty chance of getting their legislative proposals adopted by Congress. Whether this is a good thing or a bad thing depends on one's policy perspectives and partisan affiliation. Presidential scholar George Edwards, who carefully examined *major* legislative measures proposed by recent presidents, finds that less than 50 percent of these measures become law (see Figure 13–1). Thus, at least some of the time, presidents fail to win congressional backing even on their most cherished measures.[2]

"You've been around here longer than I have. What *are* 'congressional ethics'?"

WHY CONGRESS OFTEN VIEWS THINGS DIFFERENTLY

The framers divided legislative powers by creating two co-equal houses, which further magnified potential checks on a president's ability to lead. But the framers were worried, almost in equal measure, about ineffective government and the abuse of executive authority. Some additional factors encourage members of Congress to look at policy making and political decisions through lenses different from those of their counterparts down Pennsylvania Avenue at the White House.

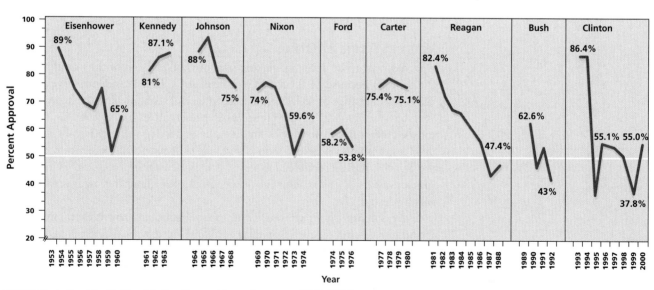

FIGURE 13–1 Presidential Legislative Support from Congress, 1953–2000

SOURCE: *Congressional Quarterly*, January 6, 2001, p. 52.

Note: Percentages represent average scores for both chambers of Congress.

Constitutional Ambiguities

Article I of the Constitution grants Congress "all legislative Powers" but limits those powers to those "herein granted." It then sets forth in some detail the powers vested in Congress. In contrast, Article II vests in the president "the executive Power" without limiting it to such powers as are "herein granted" and then proceeds to describe those powers in very general terms.

Is this difference in language between Articles I and II significant? Some scholars and most presidents have argued that a president is granted by Article II a general and undefined power to act to promote the well-being of the United States, subject only to precise constitutional limits. Therefore, they contend, a president is *not* limited to the specific powers spelled out in the Constitution, as is Congress, but has all the executive powers of the United States. Other scholars and many members of Congress say the president either has no such inherent power or has it only in extraordinary circumstances.[3]

Whatever the intent of the Constitution, the president has often exercised powers not expressly granted by it. These powers have been given a variety of names: *implied*, *inherent*, or *emergency powers*. For example, Bill Clinton ordered retaliatory bombings in Sudan and Afghanistan after U.S. embassies in Africa were bombed, and he did so without asking for congressional approval. Clinton also worked out a way to lend Mexico billions of dollars to stabilize its currency, even though Congress had essentially refused to do so. Actions like these prompt many in Congress to criticize presidents, even if they believe that in certain emergencies a president must act promptly without clear constitutional or statutory support.

Different Constituencies

Members of Congress represent state and local districts, and hence they reflect specific geographic, ethnic, and economic interests. James Madison and other framers of the Constitution anticipated that legislators would often be pressured by local and state interests to adopt a narrow or parochial view, as opposed to a national view, on certain policy issues, and presidents and their aides often think Madison was right. Members of Congress, of course, see sensitivity to state and local concerns as essential to their job as representatives and to their prospects for reelection. As a result, members of Congress—even those from a president's own party and own region—may look at problems and solutions somewhat differently from the way a president does, as a president represents, or at least is expected to represent, a national perspective.

Varying Terms of Office

Another reason the decision-making pace of Congress and of the president is not the same is because of their different terms of office. Presidents serve for four years with a chance of reelection to a second term; senators have the luxury of six-year terms; members of the House of Representatives are elected for two-year terms. Different constituencies and lengths of service make these national officials responsive to different moods and points of view. Different electoral forces are at work in different election years. A majority of the voters can win control over only part of the national government at a time, and this arrangement, too, was by design.

Presidents often act quickly to shape national priorities in their first months following the flush of their electoral victory, to win support for their agendas before a possible decline in public approval. Congress, on the other hand, usually moves more slowly "because it represents a vast array of local interests."[4] Another obvious difference in the speed of their two branches has to do with numbers: there is one president, but there are 435 members of the House and 100 senators.

Divided Government

Since 1952 there has been a split in partisan control of the presidency and Congress for most of the time. Republican Presidents Dwight Eisenhower, Ronald Reagan, George Bush, Gerald Ford, and Richard Nixon had to deal with Congresses that were most of the time under the control of Democrats. Only John Kennedy, Lyndon Johnson, and Jimmy Carter enjoyed majority control by their own party in Congress, and even they had considerable trouble getting support for their legislative programs.

Many people believe that presidents will generally enjoy more success in Congress when their party has clear control of both houses in Congress. "Unified party control is necessary, the argument goes, for ensuring that the two branches share common policy and electoral motivations," writes political scientist Sarah Blinder. "Under divided government, competing policy views and electoral incentives are sure to make legislative compromise unlikely."[5] Both parties seek a record that will enhance their election chances. This has been the case in recent decades, yet divided government is only one of many reasons that presidents fail to win the cooperation they would like to get from Congress.

Role of Political Parties

Most members of Congress finance their election campaigns with only minimal assistance from their national political party. They customarily respond to local conditions and run their campaigns independently of their party's presidential candidate or national platform. And changes in the electorate in recent years that enhance an incumbent's chances of reelection weaken the connection between the president and fellow partisans in Congress. Members of the president's party have typically run well ahead of their president in elections in their home districts, and thus they are less fearful of punishment for ignoring occasional party appeals for loyalty. They are more likely to go along with the president when a measure converges with their own political philosophy and is in the interest of their home district or state. And although parties have become vigorously partisan within Congress, especially in the House of Representatives, there are always several independent thinkers who will at times—sometimes crucial times for the White House—go their own way rather than cooperate with the White House, even when the president is a member of the same party.[6]

On the other hand, partisan affiliation is the most important predictor of how members of Congress vote. Congressional partisanship has been consistently strong on matters such as the Clinton impeachment and the John Ashcroft confirmation. Indeed, Clinton's problems with Congress often came about because the Republican party was so strong in his last several years that he had trouble winning support from them unless he proposed things the congressional Republicans wanted.

Fluctuating Public Support

In recent years Americans have generally held presidents in higher esteem than Congress as an institution—even after Bill Clinton was impeached—and this difference has consequences (see Figure 13–2). Greater prestige for the presidency can give the president a slight edge in battles with Congress.

Congress may be viewed by many people as slow or inefficient, in part because it has to represent local interests and respond to particular constituencies.[7] Yet when presidents decline in popularity, such as Nixon did after the Watergate scandal, or when a president loses moral authority, as Clinton did after the Lewinsky affair, Americans turn to Congress to hold the president and the presidency accountable.

The Need for Supermajorities

Although we have been taught that American government operates on the principle of majority rule, the reality is that the Senate's filibuster power, a president's veto authority, and the Senate's treaty approval responsibilities

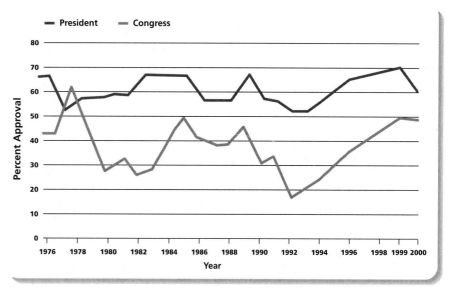

FIGURE 13–2 Presidential and Congressional Approval Ratings, 1976–2000

SOURCES: The Gallup Poll, CBS News/New York Times Poll, NBC News/Wall Street Journal Poll. Updated by the authors.

sometimes make *supermajorities* necessary. (At least 60 votes in the Senate are needed to end a filibuster; at least two-thirds of the senators present must concur on a proposed treaty; and a two-thirds supermajority vote in both the Senate and the House are needed to override a presidential veto of a proposed law.) The filibuster in the Senate has become more common in recent years. The filibuster effectively gives a veto to any 40 senators whose states may represent as little as 10 percent of the population, and whose views might not be especially centrist. Similarly, these realities make it harder for presidents to gain acceptance for their programs. They also cause members of Congress to be frustrated: "The harsh reality that new members discover is that developing supermajority coalitions around complex issues is difficult," write political scientists David W. Brady and Craig Volden. "Policy gridlock is the result of not being able to build such coalitions without violating the trust of the folks back home."[8]

In short, different constituencies, different powers, different time perspectives, and sometimes different parties help explain why members of Congress view their responsibilities and their political needs differently from the way presidents view theirs. The wonder sometimes is how they get along at all.

CONTROVERSY BETWEEN THE BRANCHES

The past few decades have been packed with political and legal controversies, ranging from the proper use of the war-making power to the intensely partisan politics when Bill Clinton was impeached. Some of these disputes were resolved in the courts, some were worked out between Congress and the administration, and others persist as disputes between the branches.

The War Power

Disputes have arisen over war powers because of seemingly contradictory passages in the Constitution, which states that Congress has the power to declare war, but it gives the president the ability to make war. Executive power is vested in the president, who shall be commander in chief of the army and navy.

James Madison and his colleagues recognized that the starting of a war or military hostility were the powers of a government most susceptible to abuse and the most dangerous. Abraham Lincoln, when he served in the U.S. Congress, aptly expressed the founders' intent when he wrote:

> The provision of the Constitution giving the war-making power to Congress was dictated, as I understand it, by the following reasons. Kings had always been involving and impoverishing their people in wars, pretending generally, if not always, that the good of the people was the object. This our convention understood to be the most oppressive of all kingly oppressions, and they resolved to so frame the Constitution that no one man should hold the power of bringing this oppression upon us.[9]

The Constitution gives Congress, not the president, the authority to declare war. Yet in the last few decades, our presidents have sent troops or bombing missions into many nations, including Korea, Vietnam, Grenada, Panama, the Persian Gulf, and Yugoslavia, without asking Congress to declare war.

Presidents and other officials contend that presidents are better informed than Congress. Modern presidents need the flexibility and secrecy to respond quickly to military threats to the nation's security interests. One State Department official, in what many might call constitutional revisionism, described the president's war-making authority as: "The Constitution leaves to the President the judgment to determine whether the circumstances of a particular armed attack are so urgent and the potential consequences so threatening to the security of the U.S. that he should act without formally consulting the Congress."[10] And Madeleine Albright, Clinton's secretary of state, told members of Congress that the constitutional authority as commander in chief allows presidents "to use armed forces to protect our national interests."[11]

Some members of Congress and several scholars believe the actions of recent presidents in unilateral acts of executive war-making are in direct defiance of the war clause of the Constitution. They blame impatient and "imperial" presidents. "The absolutist pretensions of Bill Clinton which hearken to the swollen claims of the Stuart kings, have eviscerated the war power clause," writes political scientist David Gray Adler. "He has asserted the executive power to commence war at his pleasure, to determine its course and direction, and its intensity and duration."[12]

Others blame Congress for being passive and abdicating its constitutional authority to the presidency. Constitutional scholar Louis Fisher holds that Congress has repeatedly abdicated its fundamental war powers to the president. The framers knew what monarchy looked like and rejected it, writes Fisher. "Yet especially in matters of the war power, the United States is recreating a system of monarchy while it professes to champion democracy and the role of law abroad."[13] Fisher calls on members of Congress to reeducate themselves on their constitutional prerogatives.

In the aftermath of the Vietnam War, Congress tried to reassert its role and authority in the use of military force. In 1973 Congress enacted the War Power Resolution over Richard Nixon's veto. It declared that henceforth a president can commit the armed forces of the United States only: (1) after a declaration of war by Congress; (2) by specific statutory authorization; or (3) in a national emergency created by an attack on the United States or its armed forces. After committing the armed forces under the third circumstance, the president is required to report to

President Franklin D. Roosevelt signed the declaration of war against Japan on December 8, 1941, as leaders of Congress looked on. It was the last time a president of the United States signed a formal declaration of war.

Congress within 48 hours. Unless Congress declares war, the troop commitment must be ended within 60 days.

This resolution signaled a new determination by Congress to take its prerogatives seriously, yet presidents have generally ignored it. And many leading scholars now believe this earnest and well-intentioned effort by Congress to reclaim its proper role actually gave away more authority than previous practices had already done. They say it was ill conceived and badly written, full of tortured ambiguity and self-contradiction. "The statute further subordinates Congress to presidential war initiatives and should be repealed in its entirety."[14]

Most observers believe the United States is best served when both president and Congress are fully engaged partners in foreign and defense policy making. Congressman Lee Hamilton sums up the virtues of joint action by these rival branches: "I believe that a partnership, characterized by creative tension between the president and the Congress, produces a foreign policy that better serves the American national interest—and better reflects the values of the American people—than policy produced by the President alone."[15]

Confirmation Politics

As noted in Chapter 11, the Constitution gives the Senate a crucial role in approving key presidential nominees, including members of his cabinet, senior military officials, and ambassadors. Senators normally defer to presidents, especially newly elected ones, on their choice for members in their cabinet. Standard differences in party ideology are not adequate reasons for blocking an appointment.

The Senate has rejected only nine proposed cabinet members (see Table 13–1) yet forced the withdrawal of others. Clinton saw three of his cabinet nominees withdraw because of Senate opposition. George W. Bush's first nominee for secretary of labor withdrew from the confirmation process even before Bush was sworn into office. The Senate has also rejected 28 of 145 nominees for the U.S. Supreme Court, and many more for the other courts.[16]

Bill Clinton faced a Republican-controlled Senate that used its "advice and consent" authority to deny or delay many of his nominations. Some senators insisted on an ideological veto over Clinton nominees, while others merely demanded a share of judicial patronage. Senator Orrin Hatch (R.-Utah) wrote that several of Clinton's

TABLE 13–1 Cabinet Nominees Rejected by the Senate

Nominee	Position	President	Date	Vote
Roger B. Taney	secretary of treasury	Jackson	1834	18–28
Caleb Cushing	secretary of treasury	Tyler	1843	19–27
Caleb Cushing	secretary of treasury	Tyler	1843	10–27
Caleb Cushing	secretary of treasury	Tyler	1843	2–29
David Henshaw	secretary of navy	Tyler	1844	6–34
James M. Porter	secretary of war	Tyler	1844	3–38
James S. Green	secretary of treasury	Tyler	1844	*
Henry Stanbery	attorney general	A. Johnson	1868	11–29
Charles B. Warren	attorney general	Coolidge	1925	39–41
Charles B. Warren	attorney general	Coolidge	1925	39–46
Lewis L. Strauss	secretary of commerce	Eisenhower	1959	46–49
John Tower	secretary of defense	Bush	1989	47–53

SOURCE: Senate Historical Office.

aNot recorded

nominees for federal court posts were not confirmed because Clinton failed to consult with the senators from states where the judgeships were located. "Senators from the states where the judgeship is located are the ones who usually exercise the power to oppose nominees, since they represent the citizens who will be subject to the decisions of that nominee."[17]

Some critics say the Senate has turned the process of confirming judges into a political sideshow for the political parties to curry favor with their more ideological supporters. Many Republicans trace this trend to the demonization of Judge Robert H. Bork by Senate Democrats in 1987, when they defeated his nomination (by Ronald Reagan) to the Supreme Court.

One former Reagan administration official says the confirmation process has become highly destructive because legislators are often guided more by what their campaign contributors want rather than by what they believe is right. "The confirmation process . . . is no longer controlled by the senators," says William Bradford Reynolds. "It is, for the most part, controlled by well-endowed constituency groups with their own special-interest agendas. Thus, the process has deteriorated into personal attacks, largely uncivil and underserved."[18]

While the Senate confirms the vast majority of presidential nominees for judicial or executive branch positions, there is considerable political bargaining and behind-the-scenes testiness. Political clashes induced by party polarization and divided government have led to a drawn-out confirmation process. Some of Clinton's federal court nominees had to wait three to four years before confirmation. And Clinton appointed judges who were more conservative than he might otherwise have appointed. He also had to trade appointments with prominent Republican senators to get their cooperation for some of his nominees.

Most people respect the notion that presidents elected by the entire nation deserve to have members of their cabinet who generally agree with them. Thus senators do not ordinarily object to nominees because of differences in party ideology. Yet a president's discretion is not unlimited. When George W. Bush nominated former U.S. Senator John Ashcroft to be attorney general, even though few people questioned his integrity and experience, there was strong opposition to him because of his positions on abortion and civil rights matters. Democrats sharply criticized his nomination and questioned him and other witnesses at length in the Ashcroft confirmation hearings. Nonetheless, he was confirmed by a vote of 58 to 42.

The confirmation provision in the Constitution has fulfilled most of the intentions of the framers. Unqualified nominees are usually, though not always, rejected. The process has sometimes deterred appointments of people who hold especially strident political views. The Senate's role in the confirmation process was never intended to eliminate politics but rather to use politics as a safeguard. Senators plainly, perhaps in recent years more than ever, use this process to make their political and policy views known to prospective confirmees as well as to the White House. And this is equally true for liberal senators such as Ted Kennedy or Joe Biden as it is for conservatives like Jesse Helms and Orrin Hatch.

On balance, the very existence of this sometimes contentious process deters presidents from appointing weak, questionable, radical, or "unfit characters." On the other hand, presidents who prepare and bargain well are still able to appoint talented people they want in important public service positions.

Executive Privilege

The presidential claim of **executive privilege** is yet another area of controversy between presidents and Congress. The Constitution does not authorize presidents to withhold information because Congress and the public need information to do their

A president's choices of cabinet members are usually approved without much difficulty, but George W. Bush's nomination of former Senator John Ashcroft for attorney general ran into considerable controversy because of some of Ashcroft's positions on racial matters and his vehement opposition to abortion. However, strong Republican support carried the confirmation by a vote of 58 to 42.

executive privilege
The right under certain conditions for a president to withhold or protect information related to national security.

President Richard Nixon held out vigorously against turning over tapes he had recorded of conversations in the Oval Office relating to Watergate. He claimed they were covered by executive privileges.

jobs. However, courts have recognized that presidents can keep secret some limited and narrowly defined kinds of information, especially information, which if released, would jeopardize national security.

One constitutional historian argues that executive privilege is a myth, without constitutional basis.[19] But presidents have in fact been withholding documents from Congress at least as far back as when President George Washington refused to share sensitive documents with a House committee studying an Indian massacre of federal troops. In this 1792 incident, Washington had the full support of his cabinet. Later he did share the information with Congress. But both then and later in his administration he set the precedent for the use of executive privilege to protect the public interest. Thomas Jefferson and the primary author of the Constitution, James Madison, also withheld information during their presidencies.

Most scholars, the courts, and even most members of Congress have long agreed that a president does have the implicit, if not constitutionally explicit, right to withhold information that could truly harm the nation's security. It was through the use of executive privilege, for example, that during World War II, the time and place of the Normandy Beach D-Day invasion were properly kept secret.

It was only in the Eisenhower administration of the 1950s that the term "executive privilege" began to be used, but it was the much more aggressive use of this claim by Richard Nixon that gave executive privilege its bad name.[20] In the Watergate scandal, President Nixon hid information to protect his administration from congressional and public scrutiny. He and his lawyers went so far as to claim that the decision to invoke executive privilege was not subject to review by Congress or the courts. And, in the famous Nixon tapes case of 1974, Nixon refused to turn over documents to congressional committees and to the judiciary.

The Supreme Court, speaking through Chief Justice Warren Burger, held Nixon's claims erroneous. The Court, in effect, said vital national security considerations could on occasion permit presidents to exercise executive privilege because the release of certain information would be damaging to the nation's security interests. But the court also ruled that national security was not being threatened, that this was a criminal case, and hence President Nixon had to yield his tapes (which helped doom his presidency). In this complicated decision, although the Supreme Court ruled against Nixon's claim, it did acknowledge for the first time the constitutionality of the executive privilege.[21] Yet it held that there is no absolute unreviewable executive privilege.

During the Clinton presidency, Congress requested a number of documents concerning U.S. foreign policy toward Haiti. The White House refused, claiming these documents contained sensitive national security information. Congress backed off, but was unhappy about the lack of cooperation in this and related incidents. The Clinton administration claimed executive privilege on at least a dozen occasions, often in cases related to various independent counsel investigations of Clinton or cabinet members.[22] Evidence plainly suggests that Clinton and his attorneys misused the claim of executive privilege, especially in their efforts to delay or undermine congressional and independent counsel investigations of the Monica Lewinsky affair.[23] Executive privilege cannot be asserted in either congressional or judicial proceedings when the issue is basically one of refusing to cooperate in investigations of personal wrongdoing.

Presidents and members of Congress will continue to differ over the way executive privilege is exercised. There is no way this matter can be settled once and for all. It is a matter that will be revisited in each administration, and invariably it will be tested by presidents and by the legislative branch. On occasion,

courts will try to settle this ongoing dispute about the limits and conditions under which a president can invoke this well-established, if sometimes abused, presidential practice.

Executive Orders

Executive orders, though not provided for in the Constitution, have become a generally accepted presidential practice. Beginning with George Washington, presidents have issued more than 13,000 executive orders. These orders have been used to declare American neutrality in the war between France and England (1793), the internment of Japanese-Americans during World War II, and Bill Clinton's protection of large tracts of federal land as "national monuments" in Arizona, Colorado, Oregon, Utah, and Washington.

An **executive order** is a presidential directive that has the force of law. It can be challenged in the courts, and it can be overturned by subsequent presidents. Most executive orders are reasonable modifications or specific implementations of past legislation. But some presidential executive orders have antagonized members of Congress and led to charges that presidents were usurping the law-making functions assigned to Congress.

President Clinton, like presidents before him, made bold use of executive orders as a way to circumvent a Congress that often was unfriendly to certain of his initiatives. Reliance on executive orders is a strategy a president uses when traditional avenues are denied to the White House. Clinton used this power extensively (on more than 350 occasions),[24] strategically, and across many types of policy. He set a standard that George W. Bush and other successors will follow, especially when Congress is controlled by the opposition party.[25]

The president's power to shape public policy through executive orders has grown along with the expansion of other executive branch responsibilities. While some of these responsibilities have been delegated to presidents by Congress, presidents have also assertively assumed additional authority on their own. Courts can, but seldom do, strike down executive orders.

Members of Congress, especially in the opposition party, look suspiciously on presidents making policy decisions they think belong in the legislative process. The dispute is not resolved by the Constitution, which "avoids specifying precisely what decisions must be made under all current and future contingencies."[26]

Presidents, especially in modern times, rarely view their job as merely implementing laws as Congress passed them. Because the laws passed by Congress usually have not been written with all the details specified, considerable discretion is left to presidents and the agencies of the executive branch. And most presidents view themselves as an authority in their own right, not subordinates to Congress but co-equal with it.

Presidents have to exercise this power responsibly. "Should they go too far or fast, or move into the wrong areas at the wrong time, they would find that there are heavy political costs to be paid. . . . It is a matter of strategy. Presidents have to calculate . . . the costs as well as the benefits. . . . They have to pick their spots. But they will constantly be on the lookout, ready to move, and quite capable of moving if that is what they decide to do.[27]

Veto Politics

The Constitution provides that bills passed by the U.S. House of Representatives and Senate "shall be presented to the President of the United States," and the president can then approve the measure or **veto** it. If a bill is vetoed by a president, it can be enacted only if the veto is overridden, which requires a two-thirds vote in each chamber of Congress.

executive order
An order issued by a president or governor that has the force of law.

veto
Rejection of legislation by a president or governor .

Another variation of the veto is called the **pocket veto**. In the ordinary course of events, if a president does not sign or veto a bill within ten weekdays after receiving it, the bill becomes law without the president's signature. But if Congress adjourns within the ten days, the president—by taking no action—can kill the bill.

The crucial importance of the veto power lies in the difficulty of getting the required two-thirds majority to override the veto in both houses. Historically Congress has overridden less than 10 percent of presidents' regular vetoes (see Table 13–2). This obstacle means that presidents have a vital bargaining chip in the last stages of the legislating and the appropriating processes. Even the threat of a veto can frequently strengthen a president's hand in persuading and negotiating. Presidents merely indicate, either publicly or through their legislative aides, that bills under consideration by Congress will be turned back unless certain changes are made. More broadly, a president can use the threat of a veto against a bill Congress wants in exchange for other bills the president wants. Still, most of the time, the veto is essentially a negative weapon, more useful to presidents who want to block legislation than for a president who is pressing for programmatic changes.

Of course, a unified Congress that could repeatedly mobilize a two-thirds majority against a president could virtually take control of the law-making process. This has rarely been done in U.S. history, but such was the fate of President Andrew Johnson in the 1860s.[28]

Because the Constitution is fairly clear about the veto power, the regular use of it by presidents stirs little controversy. Franklin Roosevelt holds the record with 635 vetoes; Ronald Reagan vetoed 78 in his two terms; and Bill Clinton vetoed only 37 times in his eight years. In late 1999 President Clinton vetoed a Republican-backed appropriation bill and threatened to veto it again and again until Congress made major compromises with him. His use of the veto worked; Congress eventually went along on about two-thirds of the spending items that Clinton wanted. How often a president uses the veto power depends on factors like the composition of Congress and the extent to which the branches agree on policy.

The Item Veto

What did become controversial was the short life of the **item veto**. Ronald Reagan and other presidents had long sought to give the president the authority to strike specific items from the budget passed each year by Congress without having to veto the entire bill. Congress, in a surprising move that in effect delegated some of its power to the presidency, enacted the Line Item Veto Act, which President Clinton signed into law in 1996. Advocates of the item veto believed it would enable presidents to cut wasteful and ill-advised spending projects whose main purpose was to help an individual member of Congress win reelection. What was notable about the enactment of the item veto legislation was that a Congress controlled by Republicans actually voted to strengthen a Democratic president, Bill Clinton.

President Clinton exercised the item veto on ten occasions. But in mid-1998, the Supreme Court ruled, in a 6–3 decision, that Congress had improperly ceded to the president the power to rewrite legislation when it had passed the Line Item Veto Act. Supreme Court Justice Anthony Kennedy aptly summarized why the Court ruled as it did: "By increasing the power of the President beyond what the framers envisioned, the statue compromises the political liberty of our citizens, liberty which the separation of powers seeks to secure."[29]

Budget and Spending Politics

Battles over budgets and spending have been at the heart of national politics since the beginning of the Republic. The Constitution explicitly gives Congress the power to appropriate money; presidents are charged with implementing and administering the spending.

pocket veto
A veto exercised by the president after Congress has adjourned; if the president takes no action for ten weekdays, the bill does not become law and is not returned to Congress for a possible override.

item veto
Power of an executive to veto parts of legislation approved by a legislature. Most state governors have this power. It was granted by Congress to the president in 1996 but declared unconstitutional the next year by the U. S. Supreme Court.

TABLE 13–2 Presidential Vetoes, 1789–2001

President	Regular Vetoes	Pocket Vetoes	Total Vetoes	Overridden
Washington	2	0	2	0
J. Adams	0	0	0	0
Jefferson	0	0	0	0
Madison	5	2	7	0
Monroe	1	0	1	0
J. Q. Adams	0	0	0	0
Jackson	5	7	12	0
Van Buren	0	1	1	0
W. Harrison	0	0	0	0
Tyler	6	4	10	1
Polk	2	1	3	0
Taylor	0	0	0	0
Fillmore	0	0	0	0
Pierce	9	0	9	5
Buchanan	4	3	7	0
Lincoln	2	5	7	0
A. Johnson	21	8	29	15
Grant	45	*49	*94	4
Hayes	12	1	13	1
Garfield	0	0	0	0
Arthur	4	8	12	1
Cleveland (both terms)	346	238	584	7
B. Harrison	19	25	44	1
McKinley	6	36	42	0
T. Roosevelt	42	40	82	1
Taft	30	9	39	1
Wilson	33	11	44	6
Harding	5	1	6	0
Coolidge	20	30	50	4
Hoover	21	16	37	3
F. Roosevelt	372	263	635	9
Truman	180	70	250	12
Eisenhower	73	108	181	2
Kennedy	12	9	21	0
L. Johnson	16	14	30	0
Nixon	26	17	43	7
Ford	48	18	66	12
Carter	13	18	31	2
Reagan	39	39	78	9
Bush	29	17	44	1
Clinton	36	1	37	2
Total	1,484	1,069	2,551	106

SOURCE: U.S. Senate Historical Office, Senate Library, January 2001.

*Includes one pocket veto in which the bill was not placed before the president for signature.

Congress dominated the budget-making process until 1921, when it approved the Budget and Accounting Act of 1921. That act mandated that the president submit annual budgets to Congress, and it established a Bureau of the Budget that in 1970 became the Office of Management and Budget. Presidents have played an increasingly powerful role in shaping the federal budget.

President Nixon, however, overplayed his role when his White House developed legal theories that justified **impoundment**—not spending funds for purposes Congress had authorized—as an inherent constitutional power of the president. Impoundment had been used by presidents going back to George Washington. Actually, some impoundment can be justified to accommodate a change in events (if a war ends, for example), or to alter a managerial approach (for efficiency).

Nixon stretched the use of impoundment to new lengths. He claimed the Democratic Congress was authorizing too much spending that caused rising budget deficits. Congress responded that Nixon was using impoundment to set policy in explicit violation of the Constitution. Congress not only complained, it approved the 1974 Congressional Budget and Impoundment Control Act.

This act specified how a president could spend or refuse to spend monies approved by Congress. But it also set in motion years of wrangling between Congress and the White House about how best to estimate revenues and move toward balanced budgets.

In the Budget Act of 1974, Congress, among other things, restored greater budget authority. The act called for both the president and Congress to make budget forecasts with an eye toward achieving balanced budgets. But this proved a major challenge for Congress, where there is no chief executive like the president, so there could be no comparable (to the executive) powers for a congressional budget office. "Congress is inherently decentralized between two chambers, two parties, and various appropriation, authorization, and tax committees," writes Louis Fisher. "No amount of procedure tinkering can hide that reality."[30]

Congress tried again in 1985 to restructure the budget-making process by passing the Balanced Budget and Emergency Deficit Control Act. That legislation set a schedule for reducing the budget deficit to zero by 1991 and stipulated that both Congress and the White House had either to agree on a plan to meet each year's budget targets, or accept automatic budget cuts. In practice, however, Congress and presidents found ways to evade deficit targets.

Every budget cycle witnesses a new round of clashes between the branches. In recent years Congress has almost always failed to pass all of the appropriations bills by the beginning fo the fiscal year. Instead, the two branches have had to rely on *continuing resolutions*, extending the authority for government spending to a few days or months. This often led to confusion, constant bickering, and in 1995 to an especially bruising showdown between the Newt Gingrich-led Republican Congress and the Clinton Democratic White House. It resulted in two shutdowns of the federal government. "Having failed to agree on a new budget or on continuing resolutions to keep the government going in the meantime, the government ran out of money and federal workers locked the door of government offices around the country," writes Donald Kettl. "Even national parks, the Smithsonian Institution, and the Washington Monument were shuttered."[31] Despite these clashes, Congress voted to give the president greater budget power through the item veto.

George W. Bush came to the presidency when budgets were in balance and the country was enjoying impressive surpluses and thus should have a somewhat easier time working on budget matters with Congress. Yet the hard-to-control parts of the national budget continue to grow, and the two parties have strongly competing views about the size of tax cuts, whether defense spending should be increased, the role of the surplus to help finance Social Security and Medicare, and the timetable for paying down the national debt. Executive-legislative struggles over budget policy remain as a constant in the nation's capital.

THE IMPEACHMENT OF BILL CLINTON

In all of our history only two presidents have been impeached— Andrew Johnson in 1868 and Bill Clinton in 1998. Richard Nixon was about to be impeached in 1974 when he abruptly resigned from office.

The Clinton impeachment hearings dramatized the House Judiciary Committee and its role in establishing whether an impeachment is justified. Nationally televised debates by the full House of Representatives were heated and partisan. Opinion polls showed the public solidly opposed to impeachment and removal from office, yet House Republicans remained unified in the effort to impeach. Two articles of impeachment were passed by the House of Representatives: for perjury before a federal grand jury (228 to 206) and for obstruction of justice (221 to 212). Most House Republicans voted for impeachment, and most House Democrats voted against the articles of impeachment. The matter was then turned over to the Senate.

The proceedings in the Senate were in marked contrast to the House deliberations. They were more formal, less heated, and in the end less partisan. Representatives from the House Judiciary Committee acted as the prosecutors, while lawyers for the president defended Bill Clinton. It would have taken a two-thirds majority, or 67 votes in the Senate, to convict Clinton, but only 45 senators voted to convict him on perjury charges; 10 Republicans defected to join 45 Democrats in

The House Judiciary Committee investigated charges that President Clinton had lied about his relationship to Monica Lewinsky to determine if they warranted impeachment. After long and angry argument between Republican and Democratic members, two articles of impeachment were passed by the House of Representatives, and the matter was turned over to the Senate for trial.

voting "not guilty." Fifty senators (all Republicans) voted to convict Clinton on the obstruction of justice charges, while 5 Republicans joined all 45 Democrats in voting "not guilty."

In the end it was the office of the presidency that saved the president. Republicans argued that when Clinton chose not to tell the truth, he put himself above the law and his oath of office. Democrats agreed that the president's conduct was wrong, boorish, indefensible, and even reprehensible, but they did not believe what Clinton did threatened the Republic. The president's legal team argued convincingly that Clinton's wrongdoings in the Monica Lewinsky affair were simply not fit subjects for impeachment. To remove a president on this basis, they

contended, would lower the impeachment bar too far and create an unhealthy precedent.

Some scholars believe this whole process was very damaging for the presidency and perhaps, too, for Congress. But most observers realized national institutions are resilient and fulfill their assigned responsibilities. Most people also believe that the Constitution prevailed.

One lesson of the Clinton impeachment process is that an impeachment conducted primarily along partisan lines is unlikely to succeed under our constitutional system of checks and balances. A second lesson is that impeachment was designed primarily for crimes against the state, against the system of government itself.

COALITION BUILDING

Our system of separation of powers and the nature of our party system ordinarily requires that presidents find common ground and build bipartisan coalitions if they want to get legislation approved by Congress. This is not an easy task in a country so large and divided and in a Congress that, as we have noted, is highly decentralized and designed more for deliberation than collaboration.

Lessons from recent presidencies have led scholars to agree that presidents have to win the support of the American people in order to win the support of Congress. Political scientist George Edwards summarizes the realities:

1. Members of Congress are responsive to public opinion.

2. Public support is crucial to the president's success.

3. Presidents must not only earn public support with their performance in office but also must actively take their case to the people. Moreover, they must not only do it at reelection time but all the time.

4. Through the permanent campaign, the White House can persuade or even mobilize the public.32

Presidents use state of the union addresses, news conferences, and travel around the country in an effort to win political support for their programs. Presidents also spend considerable time meeting with reporters, editors, and publishers—both individually and in groups—trying to make the case for their legislative priorities. John Kennedy, Ronald Reagan, and Bill Clinton are considered to have been effective communicators. But careful analysis of their ability to sway the public suggests they were able to influence the public for only brief periods and usually on foreign policy matters or during short-term crises.[33]

All presidents face the challenge that it is hard to win the public's attention, and the public's attention span is generally short. While it is true that television has made presidents more important in terms of national visibility, it has not necessarily made them more popular or persuasive. Indeed, several retired presidents say one of their chief difficulties was trying to rouse the public's concern about major national issues.

Presidential efforts to rally public support for White House initiatives are inevitably aimed at building coalitions in Congress. A president's efforts at public relations are greatly helped, of course, if the president's party controls Congress. A president has almost twice as much likelihood of success of winning approval of significant White House–endorsed legislation with a like-minded partisan Congress than with the opposition party in control of Congress.[34]

But presidents must deal with the Congress they inherit. Presidents go to considerable lengths to reward their allies and to entice potential supporters to cross over and support at least some of the their legislative proposals. Sometimes this reaching out involves incorporating opponents' policy suggestions into the president's larger program. Sometimes a president will meet one-on-one with a key member and personally lobby the legislator.

White House aides are specifically assigned to build coalitions in both chambers of Congress. These aides spend a lot of time on Capitol Hill, talking with party and committee leaders and serving as ambassadors from the White House to various supporters and would-be supporters who could make the difference in whether a president's legislative program succeeds or fails.[35]

An ambitious agenda is difficult to pass in good times, but in a divided government, legislative victories are much harder to achieve. Clinton co-opted several Republican issues, such as welfare reform, crime measures, and deficit-reduction initiatives, and enjoyed success on these issues.

George W. Bush, who was narrowly elected and inherited a divided Congress, faced a challenge as he set about to build political coalitions in Congress. He had enjoyed success in his bipartisan efforts in Texas, where he had served as a popular

governor for six years. During the election campaign he emphasized his abilities as a bipartisan uniter. But some of his campaign promises, like school vouchers and his opposition to abortion, invited partisan opposition.

THE CAPACITY TO LEAD

Writing about Franklin D. Roosevelt's relations with Congress in the 1930s, James MacGregor Burns wrote the following in his prize-winning political biography, *Roosevelt: The Lion and the Fox.* Nearly 50 years later, these observations are still true:

> The classic test of greatness in the White House has been the Chief Executive's capacity to lead Congress. Weak presidents have been those who had no program to offer, or whose proposals have been bled away in the endless twistings and windings of the legislative process. Strong presidents have been those who finessed or bulldozed their programs through Congress. . . .
>
> If Roosevelt had even stopped during these turbulent days [of his first term] to list his methods of dealing with Congress, the result might have looked something like this:

> 1. Full use of constitutional powers, such as the veto
>
> 2. Good timing
>
> 3. Drafting of measures in the executive branch
>
> 4. Almost constant pressure, adroitly applied
>
> 5. Careful handling of patronage
>
> 6. Face-to-face persuasiveness with legislative leaders
>
> 7. Appeal to the people.[36]

Congress can, of course, play a decisive role in setting and sometimes shaping the national policy agenda. It is difficult for an unwieldy plural institution to lead, yet Congress sometimes acts as a leadership institution as well as a representative institution. This happens when a party enjoys strong majorities in both chambers, when a president is vulnerable or is politically wounded (as Nixon was in 1973 and 1974), and when Congress has strong leaders, as when Lyndon Johnson served as Senate majority leader in the late Eisenhower years.

The discussions in the past few pages highlight most of the prominent areas where presidents and Congress regularly contest each other's authority. Does all this suggest that there is too much deadlock? Some reformers think so and call for major restructuring of the U.S. political system along parliamentary lines. But most political scientists defend the American system of congressional-presidential relations, saying despite the clashes and conflict, it generally reflects the cautious temperament of the American people. The system, these defenders say, was intended to have checks and balances—and tension in it. It is, moreover, especially well designed to protect the liberties of individuals and minorities, and it has succeeded in preventing authoritarianism. Most Americans, prize a certain amount of delay on presidential initiatives. The genius of the Congress, they add, is its continuing capacity for deliberation, debate, and reflection. What might appear as harmful delay to one person is an act of deliberation or conscientious review to another person. So it is with congressional-presidential relations. Which branch you want strengthened varies from time to time, often in direct relation to your partisan and policy values.

SUMMARY

1. The framers of the U.S. Constitution created a presidency that must win cooperation from Congress to get the work of government done. Law-making and policy-making powers are divided, and the politics of shared power has often been stormy. In general, however, Congress and presidents somehow find ways to collaborate and solve problems.

2. The relationship between a president and Congress is the most important one in the American political system, and while presidents spend great energy courting the media and appealing to the public, they do so in large part to gain support in the Congress. A president may not like it, but sustained cooperation from majorities in Congress is a necessity.

3. Several factors can cause conflict in our system of separated institutions sharing power. Among them are constitutional ambiguities, different constituencies,

varying terms of office, divided party control of the different branches, and fluctuating support of a president or the Congress.

4. The media has a way of exaggerating presidential tensions or disputes with Congress, yet there are clashes between the branches over presidential nominations, vetoes, budget proposals, military actions, or over the exercise of executive privilege and executive orders. These and other political realities are part of the continuing struggle that shapes presidential-congressional relations.

5. Presidential powers have increased over the past 60 years in good part because of grants of power by Congress to the presidency. Not surprisingly, many of these delegated powers have come in military and foreign policy areas and are due to the increased role of the U.S. in global affairs.

6. The framers created a presidency of limited powers, yet the role and lead-

ership responsibilities of presidents increased as a result of national security and economic emergencies throughout the past several generations and because of the nation's world leadership responsibilities in this era. Congress usually tries to assert itself and serve as a reasonable and responsible check on the exercise of presidential power. It is sometimes effective and sometimes less effective in this role; yet no president can ever take congressional support for granted, and presidents can always expect at least suspicion if not hostile actions from the opposition party in Congress.

7. Presidents spend considerable time trying to win both public and congressional support for their policy agenda. They hold press conferences, travel to key states, and engage in one-on-one lobbying as part of an overall effort to pass their priorities.

KEY TERMS

executive privilege 305   veto 307   pocket veto 308   item veto 308
executive order 307

FURTHER READING

DAVID GRAY ADLER AND MICHAEL A. GENOVESE, EDS., *The Presidency and the Law: The Clinton Legacy* (University Press of Kansas, 2002).

JON BOND AND RICHARD FLEISHER, EDS., *Polarized Politics: Congress and the President in a Partisan Era* (Congressional Quarterly Press, 2000).

DAVID BRADY AND CRAIG VOLDEN, *Revolving Gridlock: Politics and Policy from Carter to Clinton* (Westview Press, 1998).

JAMES MACGREGOR BURNS AND GEORGIA SORENSON, *Dead Center: Clinton-Gore Leadership and the Perils of Moderation* (Scribner's, 1999).

CHARLES M. CAMERON, *Veto Bargaining: Presidents and the Politics of Negative Power* (Cambridge University Press, 1999).

STEPHEN CARTER, *The Confirmation Mess: Cleaning Up the Federal Appointment Process* (Basic Books, 1994).

MORRIS FIORINA, *Divided Government*, 2d ed. (Allyn and Bacon, 1996).

LOUIS FISHER, *Congressional Abdication on War and Spending* (Texas A & M Press, 2000).

LOUIS FISHER, *The Politics of Shared Power: Congress and the Executive*, 4th ed. (Texas A & M Press, 1998).

CHARLES O. JONES, *The Presidency in a Separated System* (Brookings Institution, 1994).

DAVID MAYHEW, *Divided We Govern* (Yale University Press, 1991).

MARK PETERSON, *Legislating Together* (Harvard University Press, 1994).

RICHARD A. POSNER, *An Affair of State: The Investigation, Impeachment and Trial of President Clinton* (Harvard University Press, 1999).

MARK ROZELL, *Executive Privilege: The Dilemma of Secrecy and Democratic Accountability*, 2d ed. (University Press of Kansas, 2000).

ARTHUR M. SCHLESINGER, JR., *The Imperial Presidency* (Houghton Mifflin, 1972).

ROBERT J. SPITZER, *The Presidential Veto: Touchstone of the American Presidency* (State University of New York Press, 1988).

JAMES A. THURBER, ED., *Rivals for Power: Presidential-Congressional Relations* (Congressional Quarterly Press, 1996).

EMILY FIELD VAN TASSEL AND PAUL FINKELMAN, EDS., *Impeachable Offenses: A Documentary History from 1787 to the Present* (Congressional Quarterly Press, 1999).

See also *Legislative Studies Quarterly* and *Presidential Studies Quarterly*.

14

THE JUDICIARY: THE BALANCING BRANCH

F OREIGN VISITORS ARE OFTEN AMAZED AT THE POWER OF AMERICAN JUDGES. IN 1834, AFTER HIS VISIT TO THE UNITED STATES, FRENCH ARISTOCRAT ALEXIS DE TOCQUEVILLE wrote: "If I were asked where I place the American aristocracy, I should reply without hesitation . . . that it occupies the judicial bench and bar. . . . Scarcely any political question arises in the United States that is not resolved, sooner or later, into a judicial question."[1] A century later British political scientist Harold J. Laski observed, "The respect in which federal courts and, above all, the Supreme Court are held is hardly surpassed by the influence they exert on the life of the United States."[2]

Why do judges play such a central role in our political life? In 1803 Chief Justice John Marshall successfully claimed for judges the power of **judicial review**, that is, the power to authoritatively interpret the Constitution. Only a constitutional amendment or a later Supreme Court can modify the Court's doctrine. Justice Felix Frankfurter suggested tersely: "The Supreme Court is the Constitution."

Judges—and not just those on the Supreme Court—resolve disputes involving millions of dollars, decide conflicts among interests, supervise the criminal justice system, and make rules affecting the lives of millions of people. They not only settle legal conflicts, but they have, in some cases, become managers of schools, prisons, mental hospitals, and complex businesses. Sometimes they decide the details of how these institutions should be run. Still, the scope and nature of judicial power limit the role of judges.

THE SCOPE OF JUDICIAL POWER

T he American judicial process rests on an **adversary system**. A court of law is a neutral arena in which two parties argue their differences and present their points of view before an impartial arbiter. The adversary system is based on the *fight theory*; that is, arguments over law and evidence, which may or may not arrive at the truth, aim at fairness in the judicial system.[3] The logic of the adversary system imposes formal restraints on the scope of judicial power.

Judicial power is essentially *passive*. Judges cannot instigate a case. Moreover, not all disputes are within the scope of judicial power. Judges decide only **justiciable disputes**—those that grow out of actual cases and are capable of settlement by legal methods. Judges do not use their power unless there is a real case or controversy. "It was never thought that . . . a party beaten in the legislature could transfer to the courts an inquiry

CHAPTER MEDIA

 POLITICS ONLINE
Oral Argument: How Good Are You at Thinking on Your Feet?
www.prenhall.com/burns

Statutory Law

Law that comes from authoritative and specific law-making sources, primarily legislatures but also including treaties and executive orders.

Common Law

Judge-made law that originated in England in the twelfth century, when royal judges traveled around the country settling disputes in each locality according to prevailing custom. The common law continues to develop according to the rule of *stare decisis*, which means "let the decision stand." This is the rule of precedent, which implies that a rule established by a court is to be followed in all similar cases.

Equity Law

Law used whenever common law remedies are inadequate. For example, if an injury done to property may do irreparable harm for which money damages cannot provide compensation, under equity a person may ask the judge to issue an injunction ordering the offending person not to take the threatened action. If the wrongdoer persists, he or she may be punished for contempt of court.

Constitutional Law

Statements interpreting the United States Constitution that have been given Supreme Court approval.

Admiralty and Maritime Law

Law applicable to cases concerning shipping and waterway commerce on the high seas and on the navigable waters of the United States.

Administrative Law

Law relating to the authority and procedures of administrative agencies as well as to the rules and regulations issued by those agencies.

Criminal Law

Law that defines crimes against the public order and provides for punishment. Government is responsible for enforcing criminal law, the great body of which is enacted by states and enforced by state officials in state courts. The criminal caseload of federal judges is growing.

Civil Law

Law that governs the relations between individuals and defines their legal rights. However, the government can also be a party to a civil action. Under the Sherman Antitrust Act, for example, the federal government may initiate civil as well as criminal action to prevent violations of the law.

as to the constitutionality of a legislative act."[4] In addition, litigants must have *standing to sue*; that is, they must have sustained or be in immediate danger of sustaining a direct and substantial injury. It is not enough merely for people to have a general interest in a subject or to believe that a law is unconstitutional.

Of increasing importance in recent years are **class action suits**, in which a small number of persons represent all other people similarly situated—a suit on behalf of all students in a university, for example, or all hospital patients, or all persons who smoke a particular brand of cigarettes. "Would-be class action litigants must show that they are proper representatives for the class of persons they seek to champion, that the types of issues they wish to raise are common to the class, and they must be able to demonstrate how a remedy can be formed that will meet the needs of the class."[5]

Courts cannot resolve all constitutional disputes. Some raise **political questions** that would require the use of methods and remedies not suitable for a court, and are better left to the other branches, or which are explicitly assigned by the Constitution to Congress or the president. Which of two competing state governments is the proper one? Which group of officials of a foreign nation should the United States recognize as the government of that nation?[6] These are political questions.

Do Judges Make Law?

"Do judges make law? 'Course they do. Made some myself," remarked Jeremiah Smith, judge of the New Hampshire Supreme Court.[7] Most judges are less candid. Judges obviously make law, but to admit it is somehow disturbing. Such statements do not conform to our notions of what judges should do.

Why do we think judges should not make law? Many people equate a judge's role with that of a referee in a prizefight. We expect referees to be impartial and disinterested, treating both parties as equals. We expect them to apply rules, not make them. Laws are not made, however, in the same way as the rules of a sport, and herein lies the answer to our question. Not only do judges make law, but they must. Legislatures make law by enacting statutes, but judges apply the statutes to concrete situations. Statutes are drawn in broad terms: drivers shall act with "reasonable care"; no one may make "excessive noise" in the vicinity of a hospital; employers must maintain "safe working conditions." Such broad terms must be used because legislators cannot know exactly what will happen in the future. Courts must judge their application in concrete cases.

These problems are intensified when judges are asked—as American judges are—to apply our more than 200-year-old Constitution. The Constitution is full of generalizations: "due process of law," "equal protection of the laws," "unreasonable searches and seizures," "Commerce . . . among the several States." Recourse to the intent of the framers or to the words of the Constitution may not help judges faced with cases involving electronic wiretaps, multinational corporations, the Web, or birth control.

Adherence to Precedent

Just because judges make policy, however, they are not free to do whatever they wish. They are subject to a variety of limits on what they decide—some imposed by the political system of which they are a part and some imposed by the legal profession. Among these constraints is the rule of *stare decisis*, the rule of precedent.

Stare decisis pervades our judicial system. Judges are expected to abide by previous decisions of their own courts and by rulings of superior courts. Although adherence to precedent is normal, the doctrine of *stare decisis* is not very restrictive.[8] Judges may distinguish between precedents because of differences in the context of cases, and many questions of law have conflicting precedents that can be used to support a decision for either party.

The doctrine of *stare decisis* is even less controlling in the field of constitutional law. Because the Constitution itself, rather than any one interpretation of it, is binding, the Court can *reverse* a previous decision it no longer wishes to follow, as it has done hundreds of times. Supreme Court justices are, therefore, not seriously restricted by *stare decisis*. As the first Justice John Marshall Harlan told a group of law students, "I want to say to you young gentlemen that if we don't like an act of Congress, we don't have too much trouble to find grounds for declaring it unconstitutional."[9] Since 1789 the Supreme Court has reversed 219 of its own decisions as well as overturned more than 159 acts of Congress, more than 956 pieces of state legislation and state constitutional provisions, and more than 112 city ordinances.[10]

FEDERAL JUSTICE

"The judicial Power of the United States," says Article III of the Constitution, "shall be vested in one supreme Court, and in such inferior Courts as the Congress may from time to time ordain and establish." Courts created to carry out this judicial power are called *Article III* or *constitutional courts.* Congress may also establish *Article I* or *legislative courts*—courts, for instance, to handle bankruptcies and veterans' appeals—to carry out the legislative powers the Constitution has granted to it. The main difference between a legislative and a constitutional court is that the judges of a legislative court need not be appointed to "hold their Offices during good Behavior" and may be assigned other than purely judicial duties, such as supervising tax collections.

The Constitution requires a Supreme Court. It is a necessity if the national government is to have the power to make and enforce laws that take precedence over those of the states. The lack of such a court to maintain national supremacy, ensure uniform interpretation of national legislation, and resolve conflicts among the states was one of the glaring defects of government under the Articles of Confederation.

Congress decides whether there will be other courts in addition to the Supreme Court. The First Congress divided the nation into circuits and created lower courts for each. That decision, though often supplemented, has never been seriously questioned. The Constitution also allows Congress to determine the size of the Supreme Court.

Federal Courts of General Jurisdiction

Today the hierarchy of federal courts of general jurisdiction consists of district courts, courts of appeals, and one Supreme Court (see Figure 14–1). In cases affecting ambassadors, other public ministers, and consuls, and in cases in which a state is a party, the Supreme Court has **original jurisdiction**, the authority of a court to hear a case "in the first instance." In all other cases, the Supreme Court has **appellate jurisdiction**—power to review decisions of other courts and agencies—except when Congress determines otherwise.

Although the Supreme Court and its justices receive most of the attention, the workhorses of the federal judiciary are the district courts within the states, in the District of Columbia, and in U.S. territories. Each state has at least one district court. Larger states have as many as the demands of judicial business and the pressure of politics require, although no state has more than four. There are 94 district courts in the 50 states, the District of Columbia, and the Commonwealth of Puerto Rico. Each has at least 2 judges but may have as many as 28. District judges normally sit separately and hold court by themselves, and hold office for life. District judges appoint

judicial review
The power to authoritatively interpret the Constitution.

adversary system
A judicial system in which a court of law is a neutral arena where two parties argue their differences.

justiciable dispute
A dispute growing out of an actual case or controversy and that is capable of settlement by legal methods.

class action suit
Lawsuit brought by an individual or a group of people on behalf of all those similarly situated.

political question
A dispute that requires knowledge of a nonlegal character, or the use of techniques not suitable for a court, or explicitly assigned by the Constitution to Congress or the president; judges refuse to answer constitutional questions that they declare are political.

stare decisis
The rule of precedent, whereby a rule or law contained in a judicial decision is commonly viewed as binding on judges whenever the same question is presented.

appellate jurisdiction
The authority of a court to review appeals of the decisions made by lower courts.

original jurisdiction
The authority of a court to hear a case "in the first instance."

Whether the Ninth Circuit should be split in two has been debated for years. It is the largest federal appellate court, with 28 circuit judges and 99 district judges. Geographically it is the size of Western Europe and contains 20 percent of the U.S. population. It reaches from Arizona, California, and Nevada to Idaho, Oregon, Montana, and Washington, and up to Alaska, as well as over to Hawaii and the Pacific territories. In addition, the Ninth Circuit has some of the most liberal judges, who often rule in conflict with the more conservative U.S. and California Supreme Courts. Is it too big to function properly?

THE SUPREME COURT
(original and appellate jurisdictions)

Court of Appeals for the Armed Forces
and other Legislative Courts

12 Courts of Appeals
(general appellate jurisdiction)

Court of Appeals for the Federal Circuit
(specialized appellate jurisdiction)

State Courts of Last Appeal

Independent Regulatory Agencies
For example,
National Labor Relations Board
Federal Communications Commission

94 U.S. District Courts
(original jurisdictions)

FIGURE 14–1 **The Structure of the Federal Courts**

and are assisted by clerks, bailiffs, stenographers, law clerks, court reporters, probation officers, and magistrates.

District courts are the trial courts of original jurisdiction. They are the only federal courts that regularly employ **grand juries** (indicting) and **petit juries** (trial). When cases tried before district judges involve citizens of different states, judges apply the appropriate state laws. Otherwise, district judges are concerned with federal laws. For example, they decide cases involving crimes against the United States—suits under the national revenue, postal, patent, copyright, trademark, bankruptcy, and civil rights laws.[11]

Magistrate judges are increasingly important. After being screened by panels composed of residents of the judicial districts, full-time magistrates are appointed by the judges of the district court for eight-year renewable terms, part-time magistrates for four-year renewable terms. There are 429 full-time and 76 part-time federal magistrate judges.

Magistrates "look like a judge, act like a judge, and speak like a judge."[12] Most wear robes and since 1990 are called "Judge." They issue arrest warrants, hold hearings to determine whether arrested persons should be held for action by the grand jury, and, if so, set bail. They hear motions subject to varying kinds of review by their district judges. They preside over civil trials—jury and nonjury—with the consent of both parties, and over nonjury trials for petty offenses with the consent of the defendants. Under the supervision of the district judge, and with the consent of the accused, magistrates may preside over the selection of a jury for a felony trial.[13]

District judges are bound by the precedents of higher courts, but they have considerable discretion in applying them. Except for the few cases that may be taken directly to the Supreme Court, decisions of district courts are reviewable by a **court of appeals**. Courts of appeals are located geographically in 12 *judicial circuits*, (see Figure 14–2). A thirteenth appellate court is the Court of Appeals for the Federal Circuit, which is located in the District of Columbia and has national jurisdiction, though it deals primarily with appeals in patent, copyright, and international trade cases. Each circuit court of appeals consists of 6 to 28 permanent judgeships (179 in all). They normally hear cases in panels of three judges, but for especially important and controversial cases, all judges may be present; that is, they sit *en banc*. Although courts of appeals have only appellate jurisdiction, they are powerful policy makers. Less than 1 percent of their decisions are appealed to the Supreme Court. As the pol-

grand jury

A jury of 12 to 23 persons who, in private, hear evidence presented by the government to determine whether persons shall be required to stand trial. If the jury believes there is sufficient evidence that a crime was committed, it issues an indictment.

petit jury

A jury of 6 to 12 persons who determine guilt or innocence in a civil or criminal action.

magistrate judge

An official who performs a variety of limited judicial duties.

court of appeals

A court with appellate jurisdiction that hears appeals from the decisions of lower courts.

habeas corpus

A court order requiring explanation to a judge why a prisoner is held in custody.

icy role of federal courts has become a prominent political issue, more attention has focused on these courts and the judges who serve on them.[14]

Some members of Congress have called for a term limit for members of the federal judiciary, perhaps for a nonrenewable term of 18 years. If such a limit were adopted, presidents could appoint one justice about every two years, but presidents, including one who served for two terms, could still not appoint a majority of the Supreme Court.[15] For more information about the federal judiciary, go to our website for a link (www.prenhall.com/burns), or go directly to the site for the Administrative Office of the U.S. Courts at www.uscourts.gov.

State and Federal Courts

In addition to federal courts, each state maintains a judiciary of its own, and many large municipalities have judicial systems as complex as those of the states. State courts primarily interpret and apply their state constitutions and law. Most litigation occurs in these courts. For more information on state courts as well as links to state court websites, go to our home page (www.prenhall.com/burns) or go directly to the National Council of State Courts at www.ncsc.us/.

The federal and state court systems are related, but they do not exist in a superior-inferior relationship. Except for the limited **habeas corpus** jurisdiction of the district courts (the power to release persons from custody if the judge is not satisfied that the person is being detained constitutionally), the Supreme Court is the only federal court that may review state court decisions, and only when there is a conflict with federal law.

Other than the original jurisdiction the Constitution vests directly in the Supreme Court, no federal court has any jurisdiction except that granted to it by an act of Congress. Congress also determines whether the judicial power of the United States will be exercised exclusively by federal courts or concurrently by both federal and state courts.

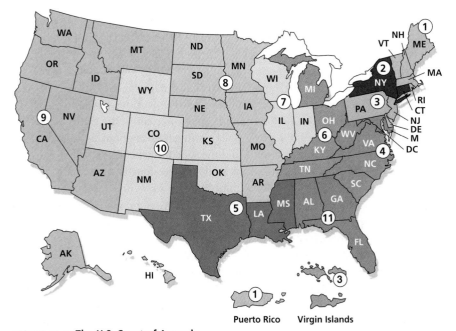

FIGURE 14–1 The U.S. Court of Appeals

SOURCE: *The Federal Register.*

Thinking It Through...

Republicans have tried to split the Ninth Circuit, isolating California and Nevada in one circuit and creating a new one for the other states. Logging, mining, and oil interests in the Pacific Northwest support the split because they view judges in California as too liberal and pro-environment.

The Senate voted to approve the split in 1997, but the House of Representatives did not. A commission selected by Chief Justice William H. Rehnquist studied the matter and recommended that the Ninth Circuit remain intact but divided into three geographic divisions. Although Chief Justice Rehnquist endorsed the report, there is still no consensus in Congress about what should be done.

Types of Courts

Examples of Special Article III (Constitutional) Courts

In addition to courts of general jurisdiction, Congress has created constitutional courts with special jurisdiction:

United States Court of International Trade (formerly U.S. Customs Court)

Consists of nine judges who review rulings of customs collectors and conflicts arising under various tariff and trade laws.

Foreign Intelligence Surveillance Court

Composed of seven district court judges appointed by the chief justice. They serve on a regular rotation and meet in secret to hear requests from the Department of Justice acting on behalf of the National Security Agency, the Federal Bureau of Investigation, and other intelligence agencies that engage in electronic surveillance and physical searches of the homes and offices of foreign agents.

Examples of Article I (Legislative) Courts

United States Court of Claims

Consists of 16 judges appointed for 15-year terms who have jurisdiction over all property and contract damage suits against the United States.

United States Court of Appeals for the Armed Forces

Consists of five civilian judges appointed for 15 years each by the president with the consent of the Senate. This court, created by Congress under its grant of authority to make the rules and regulations for "land and naval forces," applies military law, which is separate from the body of law that governs the rest of the federal court system.

Bankruptcy Judges

Almost 300 judges appointed by the courts of appeals to serve as adjuncts to the federal district courts for terms of 14 years each. These judges handle bankruptcy matters subject to review by federal district judges.

United States Court of Veteran Appeals

Consists of two to six judges who hear appeals from certain administrative decisions of the Veterans Administration.

defendant
In a criminal action, the person or party accused of an offense.

plea bargain
Negotiations between a prosecutor and defendant aimed at getting the defendant to plead guilty for a lesser offense to avoid having to stand trial for a more serious offense.

PROSECUTION AND DEFENSE

Federal Lawyers

Judges decide cases; they do not prosecute persons. On the federal level, the job of prosecution falls to the Department of Justice: the attorney general, the solicitor general, the 94 U.S. attorneys, and some 1,200 assistant attorneys. The president, with the consent of the Senate, appoints a U.S. attorney for each district court. U.S. attorneys serve four-year terms but may be dismissed by the president at any time. These appointments are of great interest to senators, who exercise significant influence over the selection process. Because U.S. attorneys are almost always members of the president's political party, it is customary for them to resign if the opposition party wins the White House.

The attorney general, in consultation with the U.S. attorney in each district, appoints assistant attorneys. Some districts have only one; the largest, the Southern District of New York, has more than 65. These attorneys, working with the U.S. attorney and assisted by the Federal Bureau of Investigation and other federal law-enforcement agencies, begin proceedings against those alleged to have broken federal laws. They also represent the United States in civil suits.

Prosecutors and the Solicitor General

Prosecutors decide whether to charge an offense and which offense to charge. They have largely unreviewable discretion. "So long as the prosecutor has probable cause to believe that the accused committed an offense defined by statute, the decision whether or not to prosecute, and what charge to file or bring before a grand jury, generally rests entirely in his [or her] discretion."[16]

Prosecutors negotiate with the lawyers for **defendants** (those accused of an offense) and often work out a **plea bargain**, whereby defendants agree to plead guilty to a lesser offense to avoid having to stand trial and face a sentence for a more serious offense. Prosecutors make recommendations to judges about what sentences to impose.

Attorneys from the Department of Justice and from other federal agencies participate in more than half the cases on the Supreme Court's docket. Of special importance is the *solicitor general* (SG), who represents the federal government before the Supreme Court. (The SG appears before the Supreme Court in formal attire—dark vest, tails, and striped pants.) When the solicitor general petitions the Supreme Court and asks it to review an opinion of a lower court, the Court is likely to do so. "Overall, the government is involved in about two-thirds of all cases heard during a term, and the solicitor general's record of wins has been fairly consistent," winning about three-fourths of the time until the Clinton years, when the administration's views on constitutional interpretation clashed with those of the more conservative Supreme Court majority.[17] Moreover, no appeal may be taken on behalf of the United States to any appellate court without the approval of the solicitor general.

The solicitor general (sometimes called the "Tenth Justice") has traditionally been given considerable independence from the White House. But in recent decades that independence has been reduced. The Reagan and Bush administrations used the SG to try to persuade the justices to limit affirmative action and to restrict the right of women to have abortions.[18] The Clinton administration continued in the activist manner, although on the opposite side on many issues. (Briefs filed by the solicitor general may be found on the Web at www.usdoj.gov/osg/briefs/search.html.)

Federal Defense Lawyers

The federal government provides lawyers for poor defendants in criminal trials. District courts have some discretion in how they provide this assistance. Most districts use the traditional system of assigning a private attorney. About half the judicial districts, however, have opted to use the **public defender system**. Salaried public defenders operate under the general supervision of the Administrative Office of the United States Courts. The Judicial Conference of the United States has said the most important problem confronting the public defender program is lack of money.

The Legal Services Corporation (LSC) provides financial assistance to 323 organizations that furnish legal help to the poor in noncriminal legal matters. It is governed by an 11-member board of directors appointed by the president with the advice and consent of the senate. The corporation is the center of controversy. There are those (primarily Republicans) who would like to abolish it. They have barred it from filing class action suits; from representing prisoners, illegal aliens, and people being evicted from public housing for alleged drug activity; from litigating abortion or redistricting issues; and from challenging the legality of state or federal welfare laws. These restrictions extend not just to the use of federal funds but to the Legal Services Corporation's use of nonfederal money raised from private or state sources. The Legal Services Corporation is thus restricted to suing landlords, employers, husbands, or wives in traditional legal battles.

On the other side are those (primarily Democrats) who would fund the Legal Services Corporation more fully and would allow it to use class action suits to challenge the status quo. Some legal aid lawyers and organizations have challenged the restrictions on what it may do as unconstitutional.[19]

THE POLITICS OF JUDICIAL SELECTION

The selection of federal judges has always been a significant part of the political process. It makes a difference who serves on the federal courts. As the courts play an even more important role in the political process, and as more and more interests—African Americans and women, for example—participate in that process, judicial selection politics has come front and center on the political stage.

The president selects federal judges with the advice and consent of the Senate. Political reality imposes constraints on the president's discretion, so the selection of a federal judge is actually a complex bargaining process. The principal figures involved are the candidates, the president, and the "subpresidency for judicial selection"[20] consisting of key members of the Department of Justice, United States senators, the American Bar Association, party leaders, and, increasingly, interest groups. In addition, recent presidents have inserted the White House much more directly into the process than their predecessors did.

Department of Justice officials and key White House staff meet often to review proposed names. Before the White House submits names of nominees for the federal district courts to the Senate, the president observes the practice of **senatorial courtesy**—the presidential custom of submitting the names of prospective appointees for approval to senators from the states in which the appointees are to work. Even a senator from the opposition party is usually consulted. If negotiations are deadlocked between the senators or between the senators and the Department of Justice, a seat may stay vacant for years.[21] The custom of senatorial courtesy does not apply to Supreme Court appointments and is generally not observed in the selection of judges for the courts of appeals because these judges do not serve in any one senator's domain. This difference in selection politics means that district court judges often reflect values different from those of judges appointed to the courts of appeal or the Supreme Court.[22]

Factors Constraining Federal Judges

- The Constitution
- Precedent (*stare decisis*)
- Statutory law
- Legal thought as found in books and law reviews
- Opinions of other courts
- Interest groups
- Public opinion
- Media opinion
- Views of colleagues
- Views of law clerks
- Contemporary events and general social environment
- Traditions of the law
- Actions of the legislature, past and future
- Actions of executives, past and future
- Limitations of time and staffing

---

public defender system
Arrangement whereby public officials are hired to provide legal assistance to people accused of crimes who are unable to hire their own attorneys.

senatorial courtesy
The presidential custom of submitting the names of prospective appointees for approval to senators from the states in which the appointees are to work.

CONFIRMATION POLITICS

An examination of recent nomination battles highlights the interplay of party, race, gender, ideology, and judicial philosophy in the process of selecting and confirming a Supreme Court justice.

Robert Bork.

The Bork Battle

When Justice Lewis F. Powell, Jr., who cast the pivotal vote on such critical issues as affirmative action and abortion, announced his retirement as he neared 80 years of age at the end of the term in July 1987, President Reagan quickly nominated Judge Robert Bork, a member of the Court of Appeals for the District of Columbia and a noted jurist and legal scholar. Despite Bork's controversial writings on many current constitutional issues, his scholarly and legal qualifications made it appear initially that he would be confirmed. However, his nomination so offended women's and black organizations that they organized a campaign to block Bork's confirmation. After almost four months of national debate, 12 days of acrimonious questioning by the members of the Senate Judiciary Committee, and 23 hours of debate on the Senate floor, the Senate voted 58 to 42 against Bork's confirmation.

David Souter.

The Souter Solution

The political bruises resulting from the Bork confirmation proceedings were traumatic. Political pundits speculated that in the future, presidents would seek noncontroversial candidates for the Supreme Court. This prediction came true in 1990 with George Bush's nominee to replace William J. Brennan, Jr., leader of the liberal bloc on the Supreme Court. President Bush chose David Souter, a member of the New Hampshire Supreme Court. Educated at Harvard and Oxford, he had written no law articles, made practically no speeches, and lived the secluded life of a sitting judge. When he appeared before the Judiciary Committee, Souter steadfastly refused to answer any questions that might reveal his orientation on abortion and privacy issues, to the frustration of the Senate Democrats. He was confirmed by an overwhelming vote. He became one of the more liberal judges.

Clarence Thomas.

The Thomas Tangle

When Justice Thurgood Marshall retired in 1991, President Bush sent to the Senate the name of a controversial jurist,

Liberal interest groups, such as People for the American Way and Alliance for Justice, as well as conservative groups, such as the Heritage Foundation and a coalition of 260 conservative organizations and 35 talk show hosts called the Judicial Selection Monitoring Project, monitor potential judicial candidates. These organizations used to wait until after the president sent the name of a nominee to the Senate, but now they are active in the preliminaries, making known their views even before the names of nominees are released to the public or sent to the Senate Judiciary Committee.

The American Bar Association's Standing Committee on the Federal Judiciary once played a special role in evaluating candidates. Presidents were hesitant to sub-

Judge Clarence Thomas, then sitting on the Court of Appeals for the District of Columbia. Thomas is a conservative African American. Prior to his brief service on the Court of Appeals, he had served as chair of the Equal Employment Opportunity Commission (EEOC) and in the Office of Civil Rights. During five days of grueling questions about his constitutional views, Judge Thomas, as had his predecessor, refused to respond. The Senate Judiciary Committee narrowly recommended his confirmation.

Two days before the Senate was due to vote on his confirmation, documents leaked to the press revealed that a former associate of Judge Thomas, Anita Hill, had accused him of sexually harassing her when she worked for him

in the Department of Education and the EEOC. Women's and liberal groups exploded in outrage. There followed three days of dramatic and emotion-charged hearings telecast to the nation in which Judge Thomas categorically denied the charges presented persuasively by his accuser. Panels of witnesses pro and con came forward to testify. Thomas was confirmed by the Senate 52 to 48, one of the closest confirmation votes for a Supreme Court justice.

The Clinton Choices

Almost as soon as President Bill Clinton took office, Justice Byron White announced he would leave the Court at the end of its 1992–93 term. It was clear that with this appointment, Clinton could arrest the Court's conservative drift and fulfill his campaign pledge to appoint justices committed to protect the right of privacy—that is, to preserve a woman's freedom to choose an abortion.

After several months of deliberation, including the embarrassingly public consideration of other candidates, President Clinton nominated Ruth Bader Ginsburg. Judge Ginsburg was a 13-year veteran of the Court of Appeals for the District of Columbia, to which President Carter had appointed her. On the Court of Appeals she had earned a reputation for fairness and moderation. She was readily confirmed by the Senate and took her seat for the opening of the 1993–94 term.

Clinton had a second opportunity when Harry A. Blackmun, at age 85,

announced his intention to leave the Court during the spring of 1994. Blackmun, best known for writing the opinion in *Roe v Wade*, was thought at first to be a judicial conservative, but by the time of his retirement, he had become the most liberal member of the Court. President Clinton nominated Stephen G. Breyer, chief judge of the First Circuit, a noncontroversial judicial moderate. Justice Breyer, a graduate of Stanford University, Oxford, and Harvard Law School, served as Supreme Court law clerk for Justice Arthur Goldberg and was a member of the faculty at Harvard Law School before being appointed by President Carter as a federal appeals court judge. After a cordial hearing before the Senate Judiciary Committee in July 1994, Breyer was easily confirmed by the Senate.

Ruth Bader Ginsburg.

Stephen G. Breyer.

mit for Senate confirmation a candidate rated "not qualified" by the ABA. In recent years, conservative groups mounted an attack on the ABA's role, contending it reflects a liberal bias and gave low ratings to conservative nominees. In response to this criticism, Senator Orrin Hatch, current chair of the Judiciary Committee, announced that the ABA committee no longer has any special status and no longer is part of the official process. In March 2001, President George Bush announced that the ABA would no longer be asked to evaluate judicial candidates before nomination, but some Democratic senators said they could not vote on judicial nominees without first considering the ABA's views.[23]

TABLE 14–1 Party Affiliation of District Judges and Court of Appeals Judges Appointed by Presidents

President	Party	Appointees from Same Party
Roosevelt	Democrat	97%
Truman	Democrat	92
Eisenhower	Republican	95
Kennedy	Democrat	92
Johnson	Democrat	96
Nixon	Republican	93
Ford	Republican	81
Carter	Democrat	90
Reagan	Republican	94
Bush	Republican	89
Clinton	Democrat	88

SOURCES: Sheldon Goldman, "Judicial Selection Under Clinton: A Midterm Examination," *Judicature*, May/June 1995, p. 280; Sheldon Goldman and Elliot Slotnick, "Clinton's Second Term Judiciary: Selection Under Fire," *Judicature*, May/June 1999. See also the Alliance for Justice, Judicial Selection Project, at www.afj.org/jsp/home.html.

Senate: Advice and Consent

The normal presumption is that the president should be allowed considerable discretion in the selection of federal judges. Despite this presumption, the Senate takes seriously its responsibility in confirming judicial nominations, especially when the party controlling the Senate is different from that of the president, as has often been the case in recent years.

Until recently, most judicial appointments, especially those for the lower federal courts, were processed without much controversy. However, "now that lower court judges are more commonly viewed as political actors, there is increasing Senate scrutiny of these nominees."[24] The battle over judicial confirmations ordinarily takes place before the Senate Judiciary Committee. The Senate usually goes along with the recommendations of its Judiciary Committee without much debate, yet floor debates are not all that rare. Overall, the Senate has refused to confirm 29 of the 138 presidential nominations for Supreme Court justices.[25]

Prior to 1955, the common practice was for the Senate to look into candidates' qualifications and background but not to interview them in person. But in the last two decades, the committee has felt free to ask judicial nominees a wide range of questions, since their political orientation is a major factor in determining how they might vote on particular cases and controversies. Except for Robert Bork, nominated by President Ronald Reagan in 1987, most judicial nominees have steadfastly refused to answer questions that might reveal how they would decide a case. But Judge Bork had written so many articles, made so many speeches, and decided so many cases that he thought he had to clarify his constitutional views. His candor may well have contributed to the Senate's rejection of him and has scared off subsequent nominees from responding to similar questions.

The Role of Party, Race, and Gender

Presidents so seldom nominate judges from the opposing party (around 90 percent of judicial appointments since the time of Franklin Roosevelt have gone to candidates from the president's party) that partisan considerations are taken for granted, and partisan affiliation is rarely mentioned (see Table 14–1). Today more attention is paid to other characteristics, such as race and gender.[26]

President Jimmy Carter, who had no opportunity to make an appointment to the Supreme Court, selected more African Americans, Hispanics, and women for the lower federal courts than all other prior presidents combined—40 women, 37 African Americans, and 16 Hispanics. President Ronald Reagan, although the first to appoint a woman to the Supreme Court, appointed fewer minority members or women than did Carter, perhaps in part because fewer minorities and women could pass the Reagan administration's ideological screening.[27] Twenty percent of George Bush's appointees were women, 7 percent African Americans, and 4 percent Hispanics.[28]

Bill Clinton promised to appoint federal judges who would be more representative of the ethnic makeup of the United States. "There will not be an ideological blood test, like there was during the Reagan and Bush years, to see if the candidate is a moderate or liberal," said a prominent Democratic member of the Senate Judiciary Committee, "but there will be an insistence upon diversity." Clinton lived up to his pledge; he named more women and minorities to the bench than his predecessors had (Figure 14–3).

The Role of Ideology

Finding a party member is not enough; presidents want to pick the "right" kind of Republican or "our" kind of Democrat to serve as judges. By and large they have been able to achieve this goal. Judges picked by Republican presidents tend to be judicial conservatives (with the notable exception of President Dwight Eisenhower's appointments of Chief Justice Earl Warren and Justice William J. Brennan, Jr.). Judges picked by Demo-

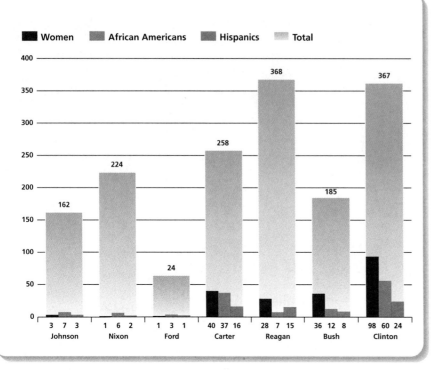

	Women	African Americans	Hispanics	Total

FIGURE 14–3 Female and Minority Appointments to Federal Judgeships.

SOURCE: Sheldon Goldman and Elliot Slotnick, "Clinton's Second Term Judiciary: Selection Under Fire," *Judicature*, May/June 1999; updated from the Alliance for Justice, Judicial Selection Project (www.afg.org/jsp).

cratic presidents are more likely to be liberals. Both of these orientations are tempered by the fact that judges must go through a senatorial confirmation process that, during recent administrations, has been rigorous and driven by opposition to the White House.[29]

President Ronald Reagan's two terms made it possible for him to join Presidents Franklin D. Roosevelt and Dwight D. Eisenhower as the only presidents in the last century to appoint a majority of the federal bench. All told, Reagan appointed 368 lifetime judges. His administration acted carefully to nominate only those whose views about the role of the courts and constitutional issues were consistent with Reagan's own.[30] Not only were a large number of judicial conservatives appointed, but many of them—because they were comparatively young—will continue to have an effect on judicial policy well into the twenty-first century. But despite the care given to their selection, there is some evidence that the Reagan judges may not be that much more conservative than judges appointed by other Republican presidents.[31]

Because President Bush was less committed to conservatism than Reagan, conservative organizations—the Heritage Foundation, the Pacific Legal Foundation, and the Federalist Society—focused more attention on his judicial nominees. Bush appointed 148 district judges, 37 appellate judges, and 2 Supreme Court justices— David Souter and Clarence Thomas. It turned out that his appointees, with the exception of Justice Souter, were among the most conservative in recent history[32] and helped consolidate the Court's "turn to the right."

President Clinton gave Democratic senators "clear guidelines about the kind of judges he wants,"[33]—competent professionals who would bring diversity to the bench. But after the Republicans took control of the Senate in 1994, President Clinton instructed his advisers to consult closely with Republican Senator Orrin Hatch, chair of the Senate Judiciary Committee. Clinton abandoned or declined to nominate several judicial nominees opposed by conservative interest groups and had to reach compromises with Republican senators.

PEOPLE

Departing from the original intent of the Constitution undermines the legitimacy of the Court and leads to judicial legislation.

INTERPRETING THE CONSTITUTION: ORIGINAL INTENT

Justice Antonin Scalia

Justice Antonin Scalia, a staunch conservative, contends that departing from the original intent of the Constitution undermines the legitimacy of the Court and leads to judicial legislation.

The principal theoretical defect of non-originalism, in my view, is its incompatibility with the very principle that legitimizes judicial review of constitutionality. Nothing in the text of the Constitution confers upon the courts the power to inquire into, rather than passively assume, the constitutionality of federal statutes.

Justice Scalia maintains that originalism—holding to the original intent of the framers of the Constitution—is more compatible with the purpose of a constitution in a democracy:

A democratic society does not, by and large, need constitutional guarantees to insure that its laws will reflect "current values." Elections take care of that quite well. The purpose of constitutional guarantees—and in particular those constitutional guarantees of individual rights that are at the center of this controversy—is precisely to prevent the law from reflecting certain changes in original values that the society adopt-

ing the Constitution thinks fundamentally undesirable. Or, more precisely, to require the society to devote to the subject the long and hard consideration required for a constitutional amendment before those particular values can be cast aside.

Originalism, according to Justice Scalia,

establishes a historical criterion that is conceptually quite separate from the preferences of the judge himself. And the principal defect of that approach—that historical research is always difficult and sometimes inconclusive—will, unlike nonoriginalism, lead to a more moderate rather than a more extreme result. The inevitable tendency of judges to think that the law is what they would like it to be will, I have no doubt, cause most errors in judicial historiography to be made in the direction of projecting upon the age of 1789 current, modern values—so that as applied, even as applied in the best of faith, originalism will (as the historical record shows) end up as something of a compromise. ★

SOURCE: Justice Antonin Scalia, "Originalism: The Lesser Evil," *University of Cincinnati Law Review* 55 (1989), p. 894.

DEBATE

A CONTEMPORARY RATIFICATION

Justice William Brennan, Jr.

Justice William J. Brennan, Jr., a leading liberal on the Court from 1956 to 1990, points out the problems with appealing to original intent:

> It is arrogant to pretend that from our vantage we can gauge accurately the intent of the Framers on application of principle to specific, contemporary questions. All too often, sources of potential enlightenment such as records of the ratification debates provide sparse or ambiguous evidence of the original intention. Typically, all that can be gleaned is that the Framers themselves did not agree about the application or meaning of particular constitutional provisions, and hid their differences in cloaks of generality. Indeed, it is far from clear whose intention is relevant—that of the drafters, the congressional disputants, or the ratifiers in the states?—or even whether the idea of original intention is a coherent way of thinking about a jointly drafted document drawing its authority from a general assent of the states. And apart from the problematic nature of the sources, our distance of two centuries cannot but work as a prism refracting all we perceive.

Justice Brennan maintains that constitutional interpretation is compatible with democratic governance:

> The view that all matters of substantive policy should be resolved through the majoritarian process has appeal under some circumstances, but I think it ultimately will not do. . . . Faith in democracy is one thing, blind faith quite another. Those who drafted the Constitution understood the difference. One cannot read the text without admitting that it embodies substantive value choices, it places certain values beyond the power of any legislature.
>
> We current Justices read the Constitution in the only way that we can: as twentieth-first century Americans. We look to the history of the time of framing and to the intervening history of interpretation. But the ultimate question must be: what do the words of the text mean in our time? For the genius of the Constitution rests not in any static meaning it might have had in a world that is dead and gone, but in the adaptability of its great principles to cope with current problems and current needs. ★

SOURCE: Justice William J. Brennan, Jr., "The Constitution of the United States: Contemporary Ratification." Lecture delivered at Georgetown University, October 12, 1985.

The ultimate question must be: what do the words of the text mean in our time?

For further information about this debate, go to **www.prenhall.com/burns** *and click on the Debate Icon in Chapter 14.*

By the end of his first term, Clinton had nominated and the Senate had confirmed 198 judges and 2 justices of the Supreme Court.[34] In his second term, Clinton faced increasing opposition from the Republican-controlled Senate, which slowed down confirmations to such an extent that Chief Justice Rehnquist, in his annual reports on the federal judiciary, scolded the Senate for jeopardizing the ability of the federal courts to do their work. Despite the slowdown in Senate confirmations, by the time Clinton left office he had named 367 of the approximate total of 800 federal judges, and appointed a large number of women and minorities.[35]

The Role of Judicial Philosophy

What about a candidate's judicial philosophy? Does a candidate believe that judges should interpret the Constitution to reflect what the framers intended and what its words literally say; that is, does the candidate believe in **judicial restraint**? Or does the candidate believe the Constitution should be adapted to reflect current conditions and philosophies; that is, does the candidate believe in **judicial activism**?

Throughout most of our history, federal courts have been more conservative than Congress, the White House, or state legislatures. Prior to 1937, judicial self-restraint was the battle cry of liberals who objected to judges interpreting the due process clauses of the Fifth and Fourteenth Amendments to strike down many laws passed to protect labor and women and to keep the national and state governments from regulating the economy. These judges broadly construed the words of the Constitution to prevent what they thought to be unreasonable regulations of property.

By the time of Richard Nixon, Ronald Reagan, and George Bush, however, the judicial shoe was on the other foot, and it was conservatives who were advocates of judicial self-restraint. What is needed, they argued, are judges who will let Congress, the president, and the state legislatures regulate or forbid abortions, adopt prayers for public schools, impose capital punishment, and not hinder law enforcement.

Still, it would be wrong to assume that judicial philosophy is nothing more than another way to argue about political ideology. Some conservatives, for example, favor judicial activism because they want current judges to reverse the last half-century of precedents on civil rights and to protect property rights from government regulation. Some liberals favor judicial restraint because they believe democratic self-governance will flourish when judges stay out of policy debates. Hence, the debate over the Supreme Court's role today is less about activism and restraint than it is about competing conceptions of the proper balance between government authority and individual rights, between the power of legislatures and that of courts.

Judicial Longevity and Presidential Tenure

Ideology and judicial philosophy affect not only presidents' nominations for the federal courts but also when sitting judges choose to retire. Because federal judges serve for life, they may be able to schedule their retirement to allow a president whose views they approve to nominate their successors. Chief Justice Roger B. Taney stayed on the bench long after his health began to fail to prevent President Abraham Lincoln from nominating a Republican. In 1929 Chief Justice William Howard Taft wrote: "I am older and slower and less acute and more confused. However, as long as things continue as they are, and I am able to answer in my place, I must stay on the court in order to prevent the Bolsheviki [Herbert Hoover, a conservative Republican, was in the White House] from getting control."[36]

Although Chief Justice Warren Burger denied that he retired in 1986 in order to permit President Ronald Reagan to replace him with a constitutional conservative, his retirement gave Reagan an opportunity to rejuvenate the conservative wing of the Court by promoting William H. Rehnquist to the chief justiceship. Reagan then picked another constitutional conservative, Antonin Scalia, to take the seat vacated by Rehnquist.[37] Liberal Supreme Court Justices William J. Brennan, Jr., and Thurgood Marshall held onto their seats well into their 80s, and many assumed

judicial restraint
Judicial philosophy proposing that judges should interpret the Constitution to reflect what the framers intended and what its words literally say.

judicial activism
Judicial philosophy proposing that judges should interpret the Constitution to reflect current conditions and values.

that they were doing so in the hope that they might be able to stay on the Court until a president more congenial to their views might be in the White House. They did not make it. Republican President Bush, rather than a Democrat, appointed their successors. It should be noted, however, that personal and institutional factors other than partisan concerns are the main reason justices retire.

Reforming the Selection Process?

The televised Bork and Thomas confirmation hearings aroused considerable criticism from both liberals and conservatives and created widespread complaints that "something is wrong with the process." Subsequently, a group of experts recommended that an attempt be made to constrain the partisan politics surrounding the confirmation process for Supreme Court justices. They proposed that "Supreme Court nominees should no longer be expected to appear as witnesses during the Senate Judiciary Committee's hearings on their confirmation" and that the Senate should return to the practice of judging nominees on their written record and on the testimony of legal experts.[38] A bipartisan commission on judicial selection from the Miller Center of Public Affairs at the University of Virginia recommended that the time between nominations and Senate confirmation be shortened.[39]

The politics of judicial selection may shock those who like to think judges are picked strictly on the basis of legal merit and without regard for ideology, party, gender, or race. But as a former Justice Department official observed, "When courts cease being an instrument for political change, then maybe the judges will stop being politically selected."[40] Moreover, as another scholar put it, "Supreme Court Justices have always been appointed for political reasons by politicians, and their confirmation process has always been dictated by politicians for political purposes." "In fact," he concluded, "not despite the politicization of the appointment and confirmation process, but because of it, the Supreme Court has endured as a flexible, viable force in the American democracy for over 200 years."[41]

CHANGING THE NUMBERS   One of the first actions of a political party after gaining control of the White House and Congress is often to increase the number of federal judgeships. With divided government, however, when one party controls Congress and the other holds the White House, a stalemate is likely to occur, and relatively few new judicial positions will be created. During Andrew Johnson's administration, Congress went so far as to reduce the size of the Supreme Court to prevent the president from filling two vacancies. After Johnson left the White House, Congress returned the Court to its former size to permit Ulysses S. Grant to fill the vacancies.

In 1937, President Franklin Roosevelt proposed an increase in the size of the Supreme Court by one additional justice for every member of the Court over the age of 70, up to a total of 15 members. Ostensibly, the proposal was aimed at making the Court more efficient. In fact, Roosevelt and his advisers were frustrated because the Court had declared much of the early New Deal legislation unconstitutional. Despite Roosevelt's popularity, his "court-packing scheme" aroused intense opposition. Roosevelt's proposals to change the Court's size failed. He lost the battle but won the war, as the Court began to sustain some important New Deal legislation.

CHANGING THE JURISDICTION   Congressional control over the structure and jurisdiction of federal courts has been used to influence the course of judicial policy making. Although unable to get rid of Federalist judges by impeachment, the Jeffersonians abolished the circuit courts created by the Federalist Congress just before they lost control. In 1869 radical Republicans in Congress altered the Supreme Court's appellate jurisdiction in order to snatch from the Court a case it was about to review involving the constitutionality of some Reconstruction legislation.[42]

Each year a number of bills are introduced in Congress to eliminate the jurisdiction of federal courts over cases relating to abortion, school prayer, and school busing, or to eliminate the appellate jurisdiction of the Supreme Court over such matters. These attacks on federal court jurisdiction spark debate about whether the Constitution gives Congress authority to take such actions. And Congress has not yet decided to do so, because it would amount to a fundamental shift in the relationship between Congress and the Supreme Court. As one scholar concluded: "History suggests the public has seen such attempts for precisely what they are, as attacks on judicial independence, and such attacks have been resisted."[43]

HOW THE SUPREME COURT OPERATES

The Supreme Court's term runs from the first Monday in October through the end of June. The justices listen to oral arguments for two weeks each month from October to April, and then adjourn for two weeks to consider the cases and to write opinions. By agreement, six justices must participate in each decision. Cases are decided by a majority vote. In the event of a tie vote, the decision of the lower court is sustained, although on rare occasions it may be reargued.

At 10:00 a.m. on the days when the Supreme Court sits, the eight associate justices and the chief justice, dressed in their robes (Chief Justice Rehnquist has four gold stripes on each sleeve of his robe),[44] file into the courtroom. As they take their seats—arranged according to seniority, with the chief justice in the center—the clerk of the Court introduces them as the "Honorable Chief Justice and Associate Justices of the Supreme Court of the United States." Those present in the courtroom, asked to stand when the justices enter, are seated, and counsel take their places along tables in front of the bench. The attorneys for the Department of Justice are at the right. The other attorneys are dressed conservatively; sport coats are not considered proper. Dress and ceremony are all part of the high ritual of the Court (see Figure 14–4).

1. Courtyards
2. Solicitor General's Office
3. Lawyers' Lounge
4. Marshall's Office
5. Main Hall
6. Court Room
7. Conference and Reception Rooms
8. Justices' Conference Room
9. Chief Justice's Chambers
10. Justices' Chambers

writ of *certiorari*
A formal writ used to bring a case before the Supreme Court.

FIGURE 14–4 **The Supreme Court Building**

Which Cases Reach the Supreme Court?

When citizens vow to take their cases to the highest court of the land even if it costs their last penny, they underestimate the difficulty of securing Supreme Court review and misunderstand the Court's role. The rules for appealing a case are established by the Supreme Court and Congress. Until 1988, the Supreme Court was obliged by law to review a large number of appeals. Today, however, almost all appeals come to the Court by means of a discretionary **writ of *certiorari***, a formal writ used to bring a case before the Court but which may simply be denied. Since the Supreme Court's docket is now largely discretionary, it has the power to set its own agenda and to decide which cases to decide. As a result, the justices decide fewer than 100 of the more than 8,000 cases appealed to them annually.[45] That is half the number of cases decided annually two decades ago.[46]

The crucial factor in determining whether the Supreme Court reviews a case is its importance to the operation of the governmental system as a whole. The Supreme Court will review a case only if the claim has broad public significance. For instance, the rulings among the courts of appeals may conflict; by deciding a case, the Supreme Court establishes which ruling is to be followed. Or a case may raise a constitutional issue on which a state supreme court has presented an interpretation with which the Court disagrees.

WE THE PEOPLE

Needed: Minority Clerks at the Court

A congressional hearing in 1999 on the Supreme Court's annual budget took a valuable detour as Justices Clarence Thomas and David Souter engaged in a lengthy colloquy with lawmakers about the Court's dismal record in recruiting and hiring minority law clerks.

Each of the nine justices personally selects up to four law clerks each term to help with screening appeals and drafting opinions. The 1999 crop of 34 clerks included only one minority member—a Hispanic woman—and for the second year running, the Court hired no African-American clerks. Of the 428 clerks hired over the years by the current justices, only 7 have been black, according to figures compiled by *USA Today*.

Chief Justice William Rehnquist has not hired even one African-American clerk in 27 years on the Court.

"There is not a person at the Court who would not want to change this," said Justice Thomas, the second African American to sit on the Court, responding to questioning by Democratic lawmakers. Justice Souter also expressed displeasure with the lopsided numbers and the perception they create. But other comments by the two justices suggested a reluctance to alter the clubby "feeder system" from top-tier law schools and judges that produces a nearly all-white coterie of high-caliber clerks.

SOURCE: Editorial, *The New York Times*, March 18, 1999, p. A24.

The Court grants cases based on the *rule of four*. If four justices are sufficiently interested in a petition for a writ of *certiorari*, it will be granted and the case brought forward for review. The justices' law clerks read the petitions and write a memorandum on each, recommending whether a review should be granted, and circulate it to all the justices except Justice John Paul Stevens, whose law clerks review the petitions for him, and he reads a few of them himself.[47]

Denial of a writ of *certiorari* does not mean that the justices agree with the decision of the lower court, nor does it establish precedent. Refusal to grant a review may indicate all kinds of possibilities. The justices may wish to avoid a political "hot potato," or the Court may be so divided on an issue that it is not yet prepared to take a stand.[48]

The Powers of the Chief Justice

The chief justice of the United States is appointed by the president upon confirmation by the Senate and holds tenure for life. This method of selecting the chief justice gives him (in our entire history they have all been men) greater visibility than if selected by rotation of fellow justices, as is the practice in the state supreme courts, or by seniority, as is the practice in the federal courts of appeals. But as Chief Justice Rehnquist said when he was still an associate justice, the chief deals not with "eight subordinates whom he may direct or instruct, but eight associates who, like him, have tenure during good behavior, and who are as independent as hogs on ice."[49]

The ability of the chief justice to influence the Court has varied considerably.[50] Chief Justice Charles Evans Hughes ran the conferences like a stern schoolmaster, keeping

Chief Justice William Hubbs Rehnquist presided at the Senate hearing on the impeachment of President Clinton.

The Committee on Long Range Planning of the Judicial Conference of the United States has studied the increasing caseload of federal courts and projects a continued growth in cases and a need for more judges:

Year	District Court Caseloads	Judges	Circuit Court Caseloads	Judges
1950	91,005	224	2,830	65
1960	87,421	245	3,899	68
1970	125,423	401	11,662	97
1980	196,757	516	23,200	132
1990	264,409	575	40,898	156
2000	386,200	940	84,800	430
2010	642,500	1,510	171,600	840
2020	1,109,000	2,530	325,100	1,580

SOURCE: Committee on Long Range Planning, Judicial Conference of the United States, *Proposed Long Range Plan for the Federal Courts* (Judicial Conference of the United States, 1995), pp. 14–15.

amicus curiae

Literally, "friend of the court" brief, filed by an individual or organization to present arguments in addition to those presented by the immediate party to the case.

the justices on the point, moving the discussion along, and doing his best to work out compromises in order to achieve unanimous decisions, which carry greater weight. Chief Justice Harlan F. Stone, on the other hand, encouraged justices to state their own points of view and let the discussions wander. Chief Justice Warren Burger was not very successful in leading conferences. He devoted much of his time to judicial reform, speaking to bar associations and trying to build political support for modernizing the judicial process.

William H. Rehnquist had 15 years of Court experience prior to his elevation to chief justice. He "has not utilized his position as Chief Justice to shape the decisions of the Court."[51] But as the Reagan-Bush justices are still a majority, his constitutional views on federalism and affirmative action, formerly expressed in his dissenting opinions, are now becoming the opinions of the Court.[52]

"The Chief Justiceship does not guarantee leadership. It only offers its incumbent an opportunity to lead."[53] Yet the chief justice "sets the tone, controls the conference, assigns the most opinions, and usually, takes the most important, nation-changing decisions for himself. . . . The Chief Justice remains first among equals." Periods in Court history are often named after the chief justice, who is responsible for the institution's character."[54]

The Role of the Law Clerks

Beginning in the 1920s and 1930s, federal judges began hiring the best recent graduates of law schools to serve as clerks for a year or two. As the judicial work load increased, more law clerks have been appointed. Today each Supreme Court justice is entitled to four clerks. Clerks screen writs of *certiorari* and draft opinions for the justices. As the number of law clerks and computers has increased, so has the number of concurring and dissenting opinions. As a result, today's opinions are longer and have more footnotes and elaborate citations of cases and law review articles.

Amicus Curiae Briefs

Before a case is heard in open court, the justices receive printed *briefs* from each side, presenting legal arguments, historical background, and relevant precedents. In addition, the Supreme Court may receive briefs from *amici curiae* (literally, "friends of the court"), filed by individuals, organizations, or government agencies that have an interest in the case and claim they have information of value to the Court.

Often organizations file *amicus curiae* briefs before the Supreme Court grants a writ of *certiorari* in order to encourage the Supreme Court to review the case. Their doing so enhances the probability that the Court will take the case for review but has almost no influence on how the case is decided.[55] An *amicus* brief may help the justices by presenting arguments or facts that the parties to the case have not raised.

These briefs usually urge the Court to reach a particular decision. In *Webster v Reproductive Health Services*, dealing with a Missouri law regulating abortions and asking the Court to reverse *Roe v Wade*, 78 *amicus* briefs were filed.[56] In *United States v Lopez*, which challenged congressional authority to ban guns in and around schools, more than 40 parties filed a dozen *amicus* briefs. Ohio, New York, and the District of Columbia argued in favor of federal power, as did associations of police and school officials. On the other side were some conservative public interest firms, the National Governors Association, and the National League of Cities.[57]

The practice of filing *amicus curiae* briefs also guarantees that the Department of Justice is represented if a suit questions the constitutionality of an act of Congress or the executive branch. The solicitor general uses these briefs to bring to the Court's attention the views of the current administration.[58]

Oral Arguments

Formal oratory before the Supreme Court, once lasting for several days, is a thing of the past. As a rule, counsel for each side is now allowed only 30 minutes. Lawyers use a lectern with two lights: a white light flashes five minutes before time is up; when the red light goes on, the lawyer must stop, even in the middle of an "if."

The entire procedure is informally formal. Sometimes, to the annoyance of attorneys, justices talk among themselves or consult briefs or books during oral arguments. Other times, if justices find a presentation particularly bad, they will tell the attorneys so. Justices freely interrupt the lawyers to ask questions and request additional information. In recent years, "the justices seem barely able to contain themselves, often interrupting the answer to one question with another query."[59] Hence, the 30-minute limit is problematic, especially when the solicitor general participates, since his 10 minutes come out of the time of the two parties before the Court.

If a lawyer is having a difficult time, the justices may try to help him or her out with a question. Occasionally, justices bounce arguments off a hapless attorney and at one another. Justice Antonin Scalia is a harsh questioner. "When Scalia prepares to ask a question, he doesn't just adjust himself in his chair to get closer to the microphone like the others; he looks like a vulture, zooming in for the kill. He strains way forward, pinches his eyebrows, and poses the question, like '. . . do you want us to believe?'"[60] Justice Ruth Bader Ginsburg is a particularly persistent questioner, frequently rivaling Justice Scalia in asking the most questions.[61] Justice Clarence Thomas almost never asks a question. Justice David Souter has a thick New England accent. He once asked an attorney during oral arguments in an affirmative action case, "What's the floor?" The attorney hemmed and hawed until, with a smile, Souter explained he meant, "What's the flaw?"[62] Oral arguments in landmark cases may be listened to on the Web by going to **www.oyez.nwu.edu.**

Behind the Curtains: The Conference

On Wednesday afternoons and Fridays the justices meet in private conference. They have heard the oral arguments and studied the briefs. Each brings to the meeting a red leather book in which the cases and the votes of the justices are recorded. These conferences are held in secret. They are usually a collegial but vigorous give-and-take.

The chief justice presides, usually opening the discussion by stating the facts, summarizing the questions of law, and suggesting how to dispose of each case. Each justice, in order of seniority, then gives his or her views and conclusions. Chief Justice Rehnquist tries to see to it that "everybody [speaks] once before the vote is taken."[63] Recently the justices have not bothered with formal votes because their votes are clear from their discussion of the case.[64]

Patrick Oliphant, Universal Press Syndicate.

Thinking It Through . . .

Politicians and judges disagree over whether the number of judges should be increased. Some warn of the bureaucratization of the judiciary and the fragmentation of federal law. Others argue that if the number is not increased, citizens will confront lengthy delays and a denial of access to justice.

Second Circuit Judge Jon O. Newman argues that the number of judges should not rise above one thousand because there would be a drop in the quality of judges, increased bureaucracy, inefficiency in large appellate courts, and a fragmentation of federal law. He and others recommend shifting to state courts cases involving routine traffic accidents, drug possession, tax, and other civil litigation.*

By contrast, Ninth Circuit Judge Stephen Reinhardt contends that freezing the size of the bench would be elitist. An increase in the number of judges would ensure access to justice for the poor, minorities, and other disadvantaged people. He maintains that large federal courts can and do work well.**

*Jon O. Newman, "1,000 Judges—The Limit for an Effective Judiciary," *Judicature* 76 (1993), p. 187.

**Stephen Reinhardt, "Whose Federal Judiciary Is It Anyway?" *Loyola of Los Angeles Law Review* 27 (1993), p. 1.

Opinions

As a general rule, Supreme Court opinions state the facts, present the issues, announce the decision, and, most important, explain the reasoning of the Court. These opinions are the Court's principal method of expressing its views to the world. Their primary function is to instruct judges of state and federal courts how to decide similar cases in the future.

Judicial opinions may also be directed at Congress or at the president. If the Court regrets that "in the absence of action by Congress, we have no choice but to . . ." or insists that "relief of the sort that petitioner demands can only come from the political branches of government," it is asking Congress to act.[65] Justices also use opinions to communicate with the public. A well-crafted opinion may increase support for a policy the Court favors.

ASSIGNING OPINIONS   When voting with the majority, the chief justice decides who will draft the **opinion of the Court**. When the chief justice is in the minority, the senior justice among the majority makes the assignment. The justice assigned to write the opinion must give persuasive reasons for the outcome, for no vote in conference is final until the opinion of the Court has been agreed to. Justices are free to change their minds if not persuaded by draft opinions.

Justices are free to write a **dissenting opinion** if they wish. Dissenting opinions are, in Chief Justice Charles Evans Hughes's words, "an appeal to the brooding spirit of the law, to the intelligence of a later day."[66] Dissenting opinions are quite common, as justices hope that some day these dissenting opinions will command a majority of the Court. If a justice agrees with the majority on how the case should be decided but differs on the reasoning, that justice may write a **concurring opinion**.

CIRCULATING DRAFTS   Writing the opinion of the Court is an exacting task. The document must win the support of at least four—even more, if possible—intelligent, strong-willed persons. Assisted by the law clerks, the assigned justice writes a draft and sends it to colleagues for comments. If the justice is lucky, the majority will accept the draft, perhaps with only minor changes. If the draft is not satisfactory to the other justices, it must be redrafted and recirculated until a majority reaches agreement.

The two weapons justices can use against their colleagues are their votes and the threat of writing dissenting opinions attacking the majority's opinion. Especially if the Court is closely divided, one justice may be in a position to demand that a certain point or argument be included in, or removed from, the opinion of the Court as the price of his or her vote. Sometimes such bargaining occurs even though the Court is not closely divided. An opinion writer who anticipates that a decision will invite critical public reaction may want a unanimous Court and therefore will compromise to achieve unanimity. For this reason, the Court delayed declaring school segregation unconstitutional, in *Brown v Board of Education*,[67] until unanimity was secured. The justices understood that any sign of dissension on the bench on this major social issue would be an invitation to evade the Court's ruling.

RELEASING OPINIONS TO THE PUBLIC   In the past, justices read their entire opinions from the bench on "Opinion Days." Now, they give only brief summaries of the decision and their opinions. Copies are immediately made available to reporters and the public and published in the official *United States Supreme Court*

opinion of the court

An opinion explaining the decision of the Supreme Court or any other appellate court.

dissenting opinion

An opinion disagreeing with the decision of the Court.

concurring opinion

An opinion that agrees with the decision of the Court but differs on the reasoning.

Reports. Since April 2000, the Court makes its opinions available on its website: www.supremecourtus.gov.

After the Court Decides

Victory in the Supreme Court does not necessarily mean that winning parties get what they want. The Court does not implement its own decision but *remands*, that is, sends the case back to the lower court with instructions to act in accordance with its opinion. The lower court often has considerable leeway in interpreting the Court's mandate as it disposes of the case.

Decisions whose enforcement requires only the action of a federal agency usually become effective immediately. Thus, when the Supreme Court held that President Richard M. Nixon had to turn over confidential White House materials,[68] the president promptly complied.

The impact of a particular Supreme Court ruling on the behavior of those who are not immediate parties to a lawsuit is more uncertain. The most important rulings require a change in the behavior of thousands of administrative and elected officials. Sometimes Supreme Court pronouncements are simply ignored. For example, despite the Court's holding that it is unconstitutional for school boards to require students to pray within a school, some schools continue this practice.[69] And for years after the Supreme Court held public school segregation unconstitutional, many school districts remained segregated.[70]

The most difficult Supreme Court decisions to implement are those that require the cooperation of large numbers of officials. For example, a Supreme Court decision announcing a new standard for warrantless searches is not likely to have an impact on the way police make arrests for some time, since not many police officers subscribe to the *United States Supreme Court Reports.* The process is more complex. Local prosecutors, state attorneys general, chiefs of police, and state and federal trial court judges must all participate to give meaning to Supreme Court decisions. The Constitution may be what the Supreme Court says it is, but a Supreme Court opinion, for the moment at least, is what a trial judge or police officer or a prosecutor or a school board or a city council says it is.

"Do you ever have one of those days when *nothing* seems constitutional?"

The Wall Street Journal, August 3, 1998. By permission of Cartoon Features Syndicate.

JUDICIAL POWER IN A CONSTITUTIONAL DEMOCRACY

An independent judiciary is one of the hallmarks of a free society. As impartial dispensers of equal justice under the law, judges should not be dependent on the executive, the legislature, parties to a case, or the electorate. But judicial independence, essential to protect judges in their role as legal umpire, raises basic problems when a democratic society decides—as ours has—also to allow these same judges to make policy. Perhaps in no other society do the people resort to litigation as a means of making public policy as much as they do in the United States. For example, African American organizations turned to litigation to get relief from segregation practices in the 1930s and 1940s.

The involvement of courts in politics exposes the judiciary to political criticism. Throughout our history, the Supreme Court has been attacked for engaging in "judicial legislation." This is nothing new. Yet the active role of the federal courts on behalf of liberal causes since 1937 and Republican attacks on that role have returned these issues to the forefront of public debate.

Whereas in earlier times judges occasionally told public officials what they could *not* do, today they often tell them what they *must* do. For example, federal judges, responding to class action complaints, have told Congress, state legislatures, and local officials that they must provide attorneys for the poor, ensure adequate care

Who Were the Great Chief Justices?

Although this question is asked often, the answers tell you as much about the values of the evaluators as they do about the merits of the justices. Nonetheless, a survey asked law school deans and professors of law and political science to evaluate the performance of those who served on the Supreme Court from 1789 to 1970.

The chief justices rated "great" were:

John Marshall (1801–35)

Roger B. Taney (1836–64)

Charles Evans Hughes* (1910–16, 1930–41)

Harlan F. Stone* (1925–46)

Earl Warren (1953–69)

Those ranked "near great" were:

Morrison R. Waite (1874–88)

Edward D. White (1910–21)

William H. Taft (1921–30)

One was ranked "average":

Melville Fuller (1888–1910)

*Served as both an associate and chief justice.

Source: Henry J. Abraham, *Justices, Presidents, and Senators: A History of U.S. Supreme Court Appointments from Washington to Clinton* (Rowman & Littlefield, 1999), pp. 369–72.

---

for mental patients, modernize prisons, and even break up the telephone system. Often judges retain jurisdiction for years as they preside over the implementation of the decrees they have issued.[71] Judges have always been policy makers; that role is not a matter of choice but flows from the roles they play in deciding cases.

The Great Debate over the Proper Role of the Courts

Some people contend that the courts have a duty to protect the interests of the public. Defenders of this *activist* judicial role argue that if Congress, the White House, and the state legislatures are unwilling or unable to resolve pressing problems when people are denied justice and their constitutional rights, then the courts must address those problems. The Supreme Court, they say, should be "a leader in a vital national seminar that leads to the formulation of values for the American people."[72]

Critics of judicial activism contend that for the last half century the federal courts, in their zeal to protect people, became unhinged from their political moorings in the political and constitutional system. Even if courts make the "right" decisions, these critics argue, it is still not right for them to take over the legislative function of elected representatives. Courts should exercise self-restraint.

Others claim the debate between those who favor judicial activism and those who favor judicial restraint oversimplifies the choices. Judges, they argue, should take a leadership role in some areas but a restrained role in others. They stand with Chief Justice Harlan F. Stone, who argued that courts have a special duty to intervene: (1) whenever legislation restricts the political process by which decisions are made, or (2) whenever legislation restricts the rights of "discrete and insular minorities," and (3) when guarantees of the Bill of Rights are violated. In all other areas, the political process should be allowed to work, and judges should not set aside legislation or interfere with administrative agencies merely because they would prefer some other policy or even some other interpretation of the Constitution.[73]

The People and the Court

Whether judges are liberal or conservative, defer to legislatures or not, try to apply the Constitution as they think the framers intended or interpret it to conform to current values, there are linkages between what judges do and what the people want done. The linkages are not direct, and the people never speak with one mind, but these linkages are the heart of the matter.[74] In the first place, the president and the Senate are likely to appoint justices whose decisions reflect their values. Therefore, elections matter, because the perspectives of those who nominate and confirm the judges are reflected in the composition of courts. For instance, in 1992 the Supreme Court, by a 5 to 4 vote in *Planned Parenthood v Casey*, refused to overturn *Roe v Wade* and upheld its core holding—that the Constitution protects the right of a woman to an abortion—although upholding state regulations that do not "unduly burden" that right.[75] This close vote on abortion made it clear that the 2000 presidential election could determine whether that right would continue to be protected, depending on retirements from the bench and new appointments to the Court.

Scholars debate how public opinion influences what judges decide, whether it is direct or indirect through presidential selection and Senate confirmation of judges, but there is little question that there is a correlation between public opinion and judicial decisions.[76] Judicial opinions that reflect what the people want have the greatest survival value. When a new political

coalition takes over the White House or Congress, the old regime may stay on in the federal courts. New electoral coalitions eventually take over the federal courts, and before long, new interpretations of the Constitution reflect the dominant political ideology.

Judges have neither armies nor police to execute their rulings. Although Congress cannot reverse Supreme Court decisions that relate to constitutional interpretations, and only six Supreme Court decisions have been reversed by formal constitutional amendment, the political system alters judicial policy in more subtle ways. Decisions are binding on the parties to a particular case, but the policies that result from judicial decisions are effective and durable only if they are supported by the electorate. To win a favorable Supreme Court decision is to win something of considerable political value.

"American courts are not all-powerful institutions."[77] If the Court's policies are too far out of step with the values of the country, the Court is likely to be reversed. In Chief Justice William H. Rehnquist's words, "No judge worthy of his salt would ever cast his vote in a particular case simply because he thought the majority of the public wanted him to vote that way, but that is quite a different thing from saying that no judge is ever influenced by the great tides of public opinion that run a country such as ours."[78]

"The people" speak in many ways and with many voices. The Supreme Court—and the other courts—represent and reflect the values of some of these people. Although the Court is not the defenseless institution portrayed by some commentators, and its decisions are as much shapers of public opinion as reflections of it, ultimately the power of the Court in a constitutional democracy rests on retaining the support of most of the people most of the time. The Court's power rests, as Chief Justice Edward White observed, "solely upon the approval of a free people,"[79] No better standard for determining the legitimacy of a governmental institution has been discovered.

POLITICS ONLINE

Oral Argument: How Good Are You at Thinking on Your Feet?

Not long after the Supreme Court heard oral arguments in the *Bush v. Gore* decision about the Florida vote count, the Court made available audiotapes of the proceedings. For many Americans, listening to the oral argument was a new experience. The Court had always been resistant to televising oral arguments, and releasing audio tapes so soon after an oral argument was unique. Television viewers who heard the oral argument while watching TV were able to see drawings of the participants and were told (in text) who was speaking.

For most viewers, the process of Supreme Court oral arguments was probably surprising. Unlike trial courts, there are no witnesses, only attorneys answering questions from the justices. Often the attorney is in mid-sentence when he is asked another question. Attorneys who argue before the Supreme Court clearly must be quick on their feet. They must try to answer questions directly because they do not know if they will get to say all they have prepared on any given question. They must also be respectful, even though they are frequently interrupted and challenged. Sometimes justices ask what appear to be friendly questions in an effort to structure the discussion and perhaps influence the later deliberations of the justices. Other times, the questions seem much more pointed.

To listen to the tape of the *Bush v. Gore* oral argument or many other oral argments, you can go to: http://oyez.nwu.edu. This site has abstracts and opinions from major court cases, plus oral arguments from selected cases. The site also has a virtual tour of the U.S. Supreme Court building and biographies of the current justices.

SUMMARY

1. The American judicial process is based on the adversary system. Judges in the United States play a more active role in the political process than they do in most other democracies. Federal courts are established by and receive their jurisdiction directly from Congress, which must decide the constitutional division of responsibilities among federal and state courts.

2. Federal judges apply federal, criminal, and civil law. Although bound by procedural requirements, including *stare decisis*, they can exercise discretion.

3. The Supreme Court has almost complete control over the cases it chooses to review as they come up from the state courts, the courts of appeals, and district courts. Its nine justices dispose of thousands of cases, but most of their time is concentrated on the fewer than 100 cases per year that establish guidelines for lower courts and the country.

4. A continuing concern of major importance is the reconciliation of the role of judges—especially those on the Supreme Court—as independent and fair dispensers of justice with their vital role as interpreters of the Constitution. This is an especially complex problem in our democracy because of the power of judicial review and the significant role courts play in making public policy.

5. The debate about how judges should interpret the Constitution is almost as old as the Republic. More than two hundred years after the Constitution was adopted, the argument between those who contend judges should interpret the document literally and those who believe they cannot, and should not, remains in the headlines.

6. Partisanship and ideology are important factors in the selection of federal judges, and these factors ensure a linkage between the courts and the rest of the political system, so that the views of the people are reflected, even if indirectly, in the work of the courts. In recent decades candidates for the presidency and the Senate have made judicial appointments an issue in their election campaigns.

KEY TERMS

judicial review 319
adversary system 319
justiciable dispute 319
class action suit 319
political question 319
stare decisis 319

appellate jurisdiction 319
original jurisdiction 319
grand jury 320
petit jury 320
magistrate judge 320
court of appeals 320

habeas corpus 320
defendant 322
plea bargain 322
public defender system 323
senatorial courtesy 323
judicial restraint 330

judicial activism 330
writ of *certiorari* 332
amicus curiae 334
opinion of the court 336
dissenting opinion 336
concurring opinion 336

FURTHER READING

HENRY J. AARON AND ROBERT D. REISCHAUER, EDS., *The Judiciary: Setting National Priorities: The 2000 Election and Beyond*, (Brookings Institution Press, 1999).

HENRY J. ABRAHAM, *The Judiciary: The Supreme Court in the Governmental Process*, 10th ed. (New York University Press, 1996).

HENRY J. ABRAHAM, *Justices, Presidents, and Senators: A History of U.S. Supreme Court Appointments from Washington to Clinton* (Rowman & Littlefield, 1999).

CORNELL CLAYTON AND HOWARD GILMAN, EDS. *Supreme Court Decision-Making: New Institutionalist Approaches* (University of Chicago Press, 1999).

CLARE CUSHMAN, *The Supreme Court Justices: Illustrated Biographies, 1789–1995*, 2d ed. (Congressional Quarterly Press, 1996).

LEE EPSTEIN AND JACK KNIGHT, *The Choices Justices Make* (C.Q. Press, 1998).

JERRY GOLDMAN, *The Supreme Court's Greatest Hits (A CD of 70 Hours of Oral Arguments)* (Northwestern University Press, 1999).

SHELDON GOLDMAN, *Picking Federal Judges: Lower Court Selection from Roosevelt Through Reagan* (Yale University Press, 1997).

KERMIT L. HALL, ED., *The Oxford Companion to the Supreme Court of the United States* (Oxford University Press, 1992).

PETER IRONS, *A People's History of the Supreme Court* (Viking, 1999).

EDWARD LAZARUS, *Closed Chambers: The First Eyewitness Account of the Epic Struggles Inside the Supreme Court* (Times Books, Random House, 1998).

PAUL C. LIGHT, *The New Public Service* (Brookings Institution Press, 1999).

CHARLES LOPEMAN, *The Activist Advocate: Policymaking in State Supreme Courts* (Praeger, 2000).

DAVID M. O'BRIEN, ED., *Judges on Judging: Views from the Bench* (Chatham House, 1997).

DAVID M. O'BRIEN, *Storm Center: The Supreme Court in American Politics*, 5th ed. (W. W. Norton, 2000).

J. W. PELTASON, *Federal Courts in the Political Process* (Doubleday, 1955).

TERRI JENNINGS PERETTI, *In Defense of a Political Court* (Princeton University Press, 1999).

GERALD N. ROSENBERG, *The Hollow Hope: Can Courts Bring About Social Change?* (University of Chicago Press, 1991).

C. K. ROWLAND AND ROBERT A. CARP, *Politics and Judgment in Federal District Courts* (University Press of Kansas, 1996).

PETER RUSSELL AND DAVID M. O'BRIEN, EDS., *Judicial Independence in the Age of Democracy: Critical Perspectives from Around the World* (University Press of Virginia, 2001).

ELLIOT E. SLOTNICK, Judicial Politics: *Readings from "Judicature,"* 2d ed. (American Judicature Society, 1999).

HARRY P. STUMPF, *American Judicial Politics*, 2d ed. (Prentice Hall, 1998).

DAVID ALISTAR YALOF, *Pursuit of Justices: Presidential Politics and the Selection of Supreme Court Nominees* (University of Chicago Press, 1999).

15

THE BUREAUCRACY: THE REAL POWER?

T HE FEDERAL GOVERNMENT IS BIG. EVEN AFTER
MAJOR EFFORTS IN THE 1990S TO DOWNSIZE AND "REINVENT"
THE FEDERAL BUREAUCRACY, IT EMPLOYS NEARLY 2.7 MILLION
civilian federal workers and 1.4 million uniformed military personnel. The federal government will spend over $2 trillion in fiscal year 2002.[1] When Thomas Jefferson became president in 1801, the federal government employed just over 2,000 individuals, mostly postmasters, Indian commissioners, tax collectors, lighthouse keepers, and clerks. Our bureaucratic agencies, then and now, reflect how our political system has tried to identify our most important national goals and how policies are implemented.

Big bureaucracy today is a fact of life. But Americans have decidedly contradictory attitudes about the role of government. We like, even if we usually take for granted, the countless services government provides, such as postal delivery, national parks, food and drug inspections, federal emergency relief, and so on. Yet we dislike the idea of big government and wasteful bureaucracies. "Bureaucracy is inherently controlling. . . . Most of us do not like being controlled, even for the collective good. Even worse, bureaucracy strives. . . . to deliver even-handed treatment and to administer policies in a disinterested manner, showing no favoritism. But, of course, most of us think of other people as 'the rule' and ourselves as the exception."[2]

Some critics believe the federal bureaucracy is an overzealous guardian of the status quo and is too lazy or unimaginative to innovate or experiment. Others fear that a powerful national bureaucracy encourages a wasteful welfare state. Many people also think the federal bureaucracy is too large, too powerful, too unaccountable; 64 percent of respondents in a national survey complained that the federal government controls too much of our daily lives.[3]

Bureaucracy's chief characteristics are continuity, predictability, impartiality, standard operating procedures, and the inevitable "red tape." Large government bureaucracies are not characterized by flexibility, creativity, boldness, and innovation. Even when government agencies work well, and even when they are reasonably creative, we usually take them for granted rather than celebrate them.[4] It is as natural to rail against red tape as it is to complain about taxes and regulations.

In this chapter we explain who the bureaucrats are, examine the origins, functions, and realities of our national public bureaucracy, and explore how elected officials are trying to make the bureaucracy leaner, more responsive, and more accountable to the American people. It is important to ask whether our

CHAPTERMEDIA

 POLITICS ONLINE
Want To Be a Bureaucrat?
www.prenhall.com/burns

POLISIM
*Balancing the Nation's
Checkbook*
www.prenhall.com/burns

Red Tape

The term "red tape" comes from the ribbon English civil servants once used to tie up and bind legal documents. Today, along with death and taxes, we think of red tape as inevitable. We are annoyed when we have to wait in lines while officials check files or consult with their supervisors. We are furious when officials lose important documents. Red tape often takes the form of an official's punctilious adherence to rigid procedures. We may view it as a hopeless tangle of rules and regulations that keep public servants from doing anything but stamping and shuffling papers.

But these same rules and regulations help ensure that public servants act impartially. In other words, red tape stems from our desire not to give public servants too much discretion and to hold them accountable. After all, they are spending our money. Remember, too, that one person's red tape is another person's prudent system or proper cautiousness.

bureaucracy and its methods are stifling innovation, productivity, and common sense.

BUREAUCRACY: A PERENNIAL POLITICAL ISSUE

Democrats and Republicans have been arguing over the proper role of government for more than a century, and especially since the New Deal programs of the 1930s. Bashing federal bureaucracies, especially the always unpopular Internal Revenue Service, is a great American pastime. Few of us have not been offended, irritated, or frustrated at one time or another in dealing with the Internal Revenue Service (IRS), the Immigration and Naturalization Service (INS), U.S. Custom agents, the Food and Drug Administration, or similar federal bureaucracies. No matter that these same agencies can also be a big help to us or serve the country well; we mainly remember the mistakes, delays, and hassles. As many as 2 million people, for example, are audited each year by the IRS. And despite the fact that most IRS agents do their job well and are fairminded as they go after tax cheaters and tax evaders, there are well-documented instances of IRS intimidation and abuse.[5]

People believe that their lives are overregulated and the rules are numerous and unflexible. One critic writes that government "acts like some extraterrestrial power, not an institution that exists to serve us. Its actions have an arbitrary quality. It almost never deals with real-life problems in a way that reflects understanding of the situation."[6]

Democrats bragged at the end of the Clinton-Gore administration that they had reduced the number of federal workers by more than 300,000 and shrunk federal spending from 22 to 19 percent of the gross domestic product. Al Gore led bureaucracy reform efforts that were aimed at putting customers first, empowering federal workers to get more effective results, cutting red tape, and, in general, borrowing entrepreneurial ideas from the private sector about competition, choice, and reliance on the market.[7]

George W. Bush campaigned for the White House by charging that the federal bureaucracy was far too large, and that much of what the federal government was

bureaucrat

Career government employee.

bureaucracy

A professional corps of officials organized in a pyramidal hierarchy and functioning under impersonal, uniform rules and procedures.

spoils system

System of public employment based on rewarding party loyalists and friends.

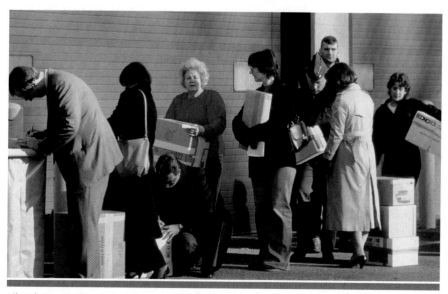

Like these people waiting in line to mail packages, the public is often annoyed by bureaucratic rules.

doing should be done either by the private sector or local government. Bush promised to contract out to private companies or "faith-based" institutions—churches, synagogues, and charities—a lot of what federal bureaucrats did. He pledged also not to replace thousands of federal managers scheduled to retire during his presidency.[8]

Public opinion surveys regularly find that no matter who is president, most Americans are skeptical about whether they can trust the federal government to do what is right (see Table 15–1). With public moods like this, it is not surprising that candidates for office criticize federal bureaucrats.

THE FEDERAL BUREAUCRACY

Bureaucrats, or career government employees, work in the executive branch, in the 14 cabinet-level departments, and in the more than 50 independent agencies embracing about 2,000 bureaus, divisions, branches, offices, services, and other subunits of government. Five big agencies—the Departments of the Army, the Navy, and the Air Force (all three in the Department of Defense), the Department of Veterans Affairs, and the U.S. Postal Service—tower over the others in size. Most agencies are directly responsible to the president, yet some, like the Postal Service, are partly independent. Agencies exist by act of Congress; legislators can abolish them either by passing a new law or by withholding funds.

The terms "bureaucrat" and "bureaucracy" date from the early nineteenth century. Initially referring to a cloth covering the desks of French government officials in the eighteenth century, the term "bureau" came to be linked with the suffix "ocracy" signifying rule of government (as in "democracy" or "aristocracy"). **Bureaucracy**, as the term came to be used a century ago, referred to a rational, efficient method of organization. The term typically refers to the whole body of non-elected and nonappointed government officials in the executive branch who work for presidents and their political appointees. In this chapter we use the terms "bureaucracy" and "bureaucrat" in their neutral sense, although popular usage of these terms is typically negative.

Bureaucracies are public or private organizations that are large and hierarchical in structure, with each employee accountable to a superior through a chain of command. They provide each employee with a defined role or responsibility, base their decisions on impersonal rules, and hire and promote employees according to skills related to their jobs.[9] Bureaucracies in the modern sense came into being in government to provide predictability and efficiency and to minimize the arbitrary practices that so often characterized rule under dictatorial monarchs.

Bureaucracy in a large, complex society is virtually inevitable. Most of us will work in some public or private bureaucracy for part, if not most, of our careers. Public bureaucracies pose special challenges because they report to competing political institutions and must function within our constitutional democracy of shared powers and multiple checks and balances.

How Did the Bureaucracy Evolve?

From 1789 until about 1829, the federal service in this country was drawn from an upper-class, white male elite. In 1829 President Andrew Jackson called for greater participation by the middle and lower classes. He introduced what was labeled a **spoils system**, which his successors in office followed until well into the 1890s. This system, epitomized by the

Executive Branch Departments

- Department of State (1789)
- Department of the Treasury (1789)
- Department of Defense (1947, originally War, 1789)
- Department of Justice (1789)
- Department of the Interior (1849)
- Department of Agriculture (1862)
- Department of Commerce (1913, originally Commerce and Labor, 1903)
- Department of Labor (1913, originally Commerce and Labor, 1903)
- Department of Health and Human Services (1979, originally Health, Education and Welfare, 1953)
- Department of Housing and Urban Development (1965)
- Department of Transportation (1966)
- Department of Energy (1977)
- Department of Education (1979)
- Department of Veterans Affairs (1989)

Dates indicate when the department was established.

TABLE 15–1 Citizen Confidence in Federal Government

Q: "How much of the time do you think you can trust the government in Washington to do what is right: just about always, most of the time, or only some of the time?"

Just about always	4%
Most of the time	25
Only some of the time	63
Never	6
Not sure	2

SOURCE: Council for Excellence in Government, poll conducted by Peter Hart and Robert Teeter, May–June 1999. N=1214.

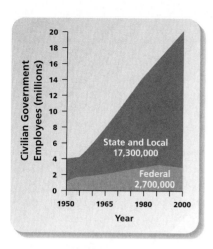

FIGURE 15–1 Civilian Government Employees, 1950–2000

SOURCE: Bureau of Labor Statistics, U.S. Department of Labor.

phrase "to the victor belong the spoils," operated on the theory that party loyalists should be rewarded and that government would be effective and responsive only if supporters of the president held most key federal posts. Besides, it was assumed that government should not be complicated; anybody should be able to do the job. With each new president came a full turnover in the federal service.

Later in the nineteenth century, however, a sharp reaction set in against the spoils system. In response to abuses such as bribery and poor performance, and most immediately to the assassination of President James Garfield in 1881 by a disappointed office seeker, Congress passed the Pendleton Act. It set up a limited **merit system** based on a testing program for evaluating candidates. Federal employees were to be selected and retained according to their "merit," not their party connections or loyalty. Federal service was placed under the control of a three-person bipartisan board called the Civil Service Commission, which functioned from 1883 to 1978.[10]

By the 1950s coverage under the merit system had grown from 10 percent of all federal employees, when it was first established, to about 90 percent. In 1978 the Civil Service Reform Act abolished the Civil Service Commission and split its functions between two new agencies. This split was made to eliminate the possible conflict of interest in an agency that recruits, hires, and promotes employees also being the same agency that passes judgment on employee grievances about fairness and discrimination.

Today the **Office of Personnel Management (OPM)** administers civil service laws, rules, and regulations (**www.opm.gov**). An independent Merit Systems Protection Board is charged with protecting the integrity of the federal merit system and the rights of federal employees. It conducts studies of the merit system, hears and decides charges of wrongdoing, considers employee appeals against adverse agency actions, and orders corrective and disciplinary actions against an agency executive or employee when appropriate (**www.mspg.gov**).

Who Are the Bureaucrats?

We are mainly interested here in the approximately 2.7 million civilians—including postal workers and excluding about 1.4 million in the military services—who make up the executive branch of the federal government (Figure 15–1). Certain facts about these people need to be emphasized:

1. Only about 15 percent of the career civilian employees work in the Washington area. The vast majority are scattered throughout the country and around the world.

2. More than 25 percent of the civilian employees work for the army, the navy, the air force, or some other defense agency; another 30 percent work for the U.S. Postal Service.

3. Welfare may consume a sizable portion of the U.S. budget, yet the federal bureaucracy that administers it is relatively small. Less than 10 percent of the bureaucrats work for welfare agencies such as the Social Security Administration or the Department of Veterans Affairs.

4. Bureaucrats are more broadly representative of the nation than are legislators or politically appointed executives in terms of social origin, education, religion, and other background factors.

5. Thousands of different personnel skills are represented in the federal government; however, most federal employees are white-collar workers: secretaries, clerks, lawyers, inspectors, engineers.

Most bureaucrats are honest professionals and experts at their business. Presidents, Congress, and other elected officials sometimes ignore the bureaucracy's advice at their peril. One example was provided by the Central Intelligence Agency's perceptive memoranda (many of them later published in the celebrated *Pentagon Papers*) warning that the Vietnam War as President Lyndon Johnson wanted to con-

merit system

A system in which selection and employment depend on demonstrated performance rather than political patronage.

Office of Personnel Management (OPM)

Agency that administers civil service laws, rules, and regulations.

duct it would be a failure. This was good advice. Yet the bureaucracy is not always right. John F. Kennedy may have been misled by government intelligence officials in the Bay of Pigs episode.

What Do Bureaucrats Do?

After Congress has passed and the president has signed a bill into law, it must be implemented. Implementation of legislation is the function of the executive branch, its bureaucracy, and, in some instances, state, county, and local governments.

More is involved in policy implementation than the mechanical translation of laws into practice. Indeed, it is during this stage that many key decisions are made. Legislation is often deliberately vague to conceal serious policy differences among supporters of a bill. Legislators frequently are more concerned with the symbolic potency of legislation than with its content. Thus Congress often sets general goals and passes the responsibility for interpretation on to the bureaucrats, who then have considerable latitude to translate general guidelines into specific directives. Bureaucrats are sometimes blamed for the confusion, yet they are merely trying to carry out ambiguous policies in a political atmosphere characterized by conflict and competition.

Consider the example of civil rights legislation. Often differences among women's groups, African American groups, Latino groups, employer groups, and trade unions are momentarily resolved and a bill becomes law. But after the bill has been enacted, the coalition that supported the bill falls apart, and conflicting pressures are felt by the agencies trying to implement the policies. Employers claim that the regulations are unrealistic and interfere with their rights; women's groups contend the agencies are failing to enforce the law vigorously enough; African American groups claim the agencies favor the women's groups but ignore African Americans. The more controversial the issue, the greater the chance of disputes, as powerful interest groups clash over a program and force bureaucrats to move cautiously.

The implementation process involves a long chain of decision points. At each point a public official or community leader can advance or delay the program. The more decision points a program needs to clear, the greater the chance of failure or delay. Special problems result if the successful implementation of a national program depends on the cooperation of state and local officials. One state or community may be eager to help; another may be opposed to a program and try to stop it.

A number of federal programs have failed to accomplish their desired goals because of problems in implementation. Sometimes these difficulties lead to the outright failure of a program, but more often they mean excessive delay, watered-down goals, or cost overruns. John Kennedy's economic reform programs in Latin America, Lyndon Johnson's Model Cities program, Richard Nixon's and Gerald Ford's crime control programs, the Reagan-Bush anti-drug crusade, and Bill Clinton's national service program all faced problems of implementation.

Like so much of politics, successful policy implementation cannot be guaranteed. It depends on the creation of effective routines, the ability to adjust to changing circumstances, the quality of the working relationship between agencies at various levels, the degree of conflict invoked by the policy, and its general level of public support.

How Is the Bureaucracy Organized?

FORMAL ORGANIZATION   The executive branch departments are headed by cabinet members called *secretaries* (except Justice, which is headed by the attorney general). Cabinet secretaries are directly responsible to the president. Although departments vary greatly in size, they have certain features in common. A *deputy* or an *undersecretary* takes part of the administrative load off the secretary's shoulders, and several assistant secretaries direct major programs. The secretaries have assistants who help them in planning, budget, personnel, legal services, public relations, and other staff functions.

The standard name for the largest subunit of a department is the **bureau**, sometimes called an office, administration, or service. Bureaus are the working units of the federal government. In contrast to the big departments, which often consist of a variety of agencies, bureaus usually have fairly definite and clear-cut duties, as their names show: the Bureau of the Census in the Commerce Department, the Forest Service in the Agriculture Department, the Social Security Administration in the Department of Health and Human Services, the United States Mint in the Treasury Department, the Bureau of Indian Affairs and the National Park Service in the Interior Department, and the Bureau of Prisons, Federal Bureau of Investigation, and Drug Enforcement Administration in the Justice Department.

Government corporations, such as the Corporation for Public Broadcasting and the Federal Deposit Insurance Corporation, are a cross between business corporations and regular government agencies. Government corporations were designed to make possible a freedom of action and flexibility not always found in the regular agencies. These corporations have been freed from certain regulations of the Office of Management and Budget and the comptroller general. They also have more leeway in using their own earnings. Still, because these corporations are a part of the government, the government retains some control over their activities.

Independent agencies are government entities that are not corporations and do not fall within cabinet departments. They consist of many types of organizations with differing degrees of independence. Many, however, are no more independent of the president and Congress than the cabinet departments. The huge General Services Administration (GSA), for example, which operates and maintains federal properties, is not represented in the cabinet, but its director is responsible to the White House and its actions are closely watched by Congress.

Another type of agency is the **independent regulatory board** or commission. Examples are the Securities and Exchange Commission and the Federal Reserve Board. Congress deliberately set up these boards to keep them somewhat free from White House influence; the president nominates their members and the Senate confirms them, but the president cannot fire them. Congress has protected their independence in several ways: the boards are headed by three or more commissioners with overlapping terms; they often have to be bipartisan in membership (that is, they must have some Democrats as well as some Republicans); and members are appointed for fixed terms in office, some for only 3 years but others for up to 14 years.

By assigning specific functions to each unit, placing an official at the head, and holding that official responsible for performance, formal bureaucracy allows for both specialization and coordination, permits ready communication, and in general makes a large and complex organization more manageable.

ASSISTANT SECRETARIES: A WEAK LINK   Although presidents can usually recruit people of prominence and influence as cabinet secretaries, they find it harder to hire outstanding people at the assistant secretary level. Assistant secretaries are supposed to infuse the views and values of the White House into the federal bureaucracy. These citizen policy makers serve as links between the people who elect the presidents and the civil servants.

Many people, however, are not willing to interrupt their professional or business careers to become assistant secretaries. Over the last three decades the position has become one of relatively low pay, little prestige in Washington, short tenure (people stay, on average, about two years in these posts), and high cost to one's family. As a result, presidents often fill these slots with relatively young people who, from the day they arrive in Washington, are looking for their next job. Assistant secretaries are forced to wear "kid gloves" with those they are supposed to regulate because it is from them that their next job is often likely to come. Others have strong ideological convictions but little experience in administration and congressional politics. Still others use the position as a transition to retirement.

bureau
The largest subunit of a government department or agency.

government corporation
Cross between a business corporation and a government agency, created to secure greater freedom of action and flexibility for a particular program.

independent agency
A government entity that is independent of the legislative, executive, and judicial branch.

independent regulatory board
An independent agency or commission with regulatory power whose independence is protected by Congress.

Most civil servants have virtually secure jobs. All they have to do to ignore assistant secretaries is to wait them out for a year or two. Moreover, in and around Washington, government workers constitute a powerful political group. Assistant secretaries who try to significantly alter the policy directions of those who are supposedly under their supervision rarely succeed.

THE SENIOR EXECUTIVE SERVICE   The Civil Service Reform Act of 1978 created the Senior Executive Service. This pool of about 8,000 career officials (which can include up to 10 percent political appointees by an administration) can be filled without senatorial confirmation. The service was created to make senior career bureaucrats more responsive to the goals and policy preferences of the White House. This new service gave presidents greater flexibility in selecting, promoting, and rewarding with financial bonuses those in the top career service who are productive and responsive.

The Senior Executive Service has had mixed success. Government salaries haven't been competitive enough to attract or retain some people who would have been outstanding public servants. Yet recent presidents have shrewdly used this flexibility to their advantage to discipline the upper reaches of the executive branch. (For the website of the Senior Executive Service, see **www.gov/ses/**.)

THE OFFICE OF MANAGEMENT AND BUDGET   Ever since Franklin Roosevelt strengthened the presidential staff, the budget bureau (currently called the **Office of Management and Budget**) has been a key resource. OMB's primary task is to prepare the president's annual budget. The budget is a major vehicle for shaping a president's policy priorities. It is the place and the process that determines which programs will get more funds, which will be cut, and which will remain the same. Departments and agencies fight to win larger chunks of the president's budget projections. OMB supervises the preparation of the budget and hence assists very directly in the formulation of policy. It evaluates the merits of the countless proposals and pleas that constantly pour into the White House.

OMB's staffers are career officials trained to evaluate ongoing projects and new spending requests. Its top officials are presidential appointees, and they are often among a president's most important advisers. They help make critical decisions not only about the budget but also about management practices, collaboration among government agencies, and legislative planning. OMB makes sure that both the departments and Congress are informed of the president's legislative preferences, and it plays an important role in expanding the policy and administrative options open to a president.

INFORMAL ORGANIZATION   To study a formal organization is only to begin to understand how bureaucracy works, for we also need to understand the informal organization (see Figure 15–2). Bureaucrats differ in attitudes, motives, abilities, experiences, and political clout, and these differences matter. Leadership in an organization is exercised in a variety of places; some officials may have considerably more influence than others with the same formal status. Further, loyalties of officials cut across the formal aims of the agency.

Informal organization can have a significant effect on administration. A subordinate official in an agency may be especially close to the chief because they went to the same college, or because they play racquetball together, or because the subordinate knows how to ingratiate himself with the chief. A staff official may have tremendous influence not because of formal authority but because of experience, fairness, common sense, and personality. If an agency is headed by a chief who is weak or unimaginative, a vacuum may develop that encourages others to take over. Such informal organization and communication, cutting across regular channels, are inevitable in any organization—public or private, civilian or military.

Office of Management and Budget
Presidential staff agency that serves as a clearinghouse for budgetary requests and management improvements.

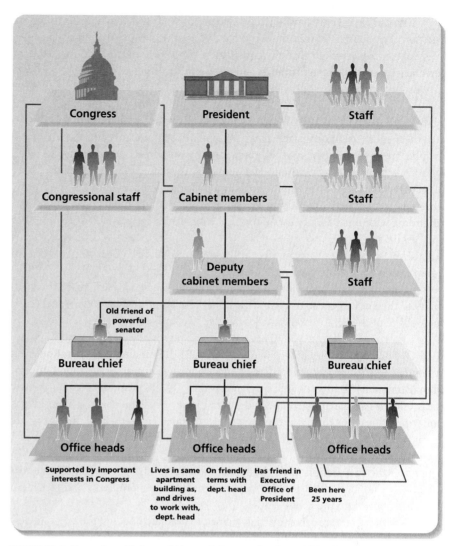

Congress

Congressional staff

President

Cabinet members

Staff

Staff

Deputy cabinet members

Staff

Old friend of powerful senator

Bureau chief

Bureau chief

Bureau chief

Office heads

Office heads

Office heads

Supported by important interests in Congress

Lives in same apartment building as, and drives to work with, dept. head

On friendly terms with dept. head

Has friend in Executive Office of President

Been here 25 years

FIGURE 15–2 Formal and Informal Lines of Communication within the Executive Branch

THE BUREAUCRACY IN ACTION

Hiring Practices and Employee Regulations

Senior government administrators work with the Office of Personnel Management in staffing their agencies. The OPM acts as a policy maker for recruiting, examining, and appointing government workers. It advertises for new employees, prepares and administers oral and written examinations throughout the country, and compiles a roster of names of those who pass the tests. The OPM delegates to the individual agencies the responsibility for hiring new personnel, subject to its standards. Individual agencies may promote people from within or transfer a civil servant from another agency in the government. If, however, they wish to consider an "outsider," they request the OPM to certify possible candidates from its roster of applicants. The OPM typically certifies the top three applicants who have applied for the opening, and the agency normally selects one of these. However, the agency can decide to make no appointment or to request other applicants if it thinks none of the three is qualified.

These procedures are intended to protect the merit principle and to meet agencies' needs for qualified personnel. In practice, the two objectives sometimes come into conflict. Trade-offs have to be made, particularly between central control by OPM and delegation of discretionary authority to the agencies. And sometimes the pursuit of both objectives is enfeebled by the introduction of additional and often incompatible objectives—the veteran preference system, for example.

THE HATCH ACT, OLD AND NEW   In 1939 Congress passed an Act to Prevent Pernicious Political Activities, usually called the **Hatch Act** after its chief sponsor, Senator Carl Hatch of New Mexico. The act was designed to neutralize the danger of a federal civil service being able to shape, if not dictate, the election of presidents and members of Congress. In essence, the Hatch Act permitted federal employees to vote in government elections, but not to take an active part in partisan politics. The Hatch Act also made it illegal to dismiss federal officials below cabinet and subcabinet rank for partisan reasons.[11]

In 1993 Congress, with the encouragement of the Clinton administration, overhauled the Hatch Act and made many forms of participation in partisan politics permissible. The revised Hatch Act still bars federal officials from running as candidates in partisan elections, but it does permit most federal civil servants to hold party positions and involve themselves in party fund raising and campaigning. This new law was welcomed by those who believed the old Hatch Act discouraged political participation by more than 2 million individuals who might otherwise be vigorous political activists.[12]

The new Hatch Act spells out many restrictions on federal bureaucrats; they cannot raise campaign funds in their agencies, and those who work in such highly sensitive federal agencies as the CIA, FBI, Secret Service, and certain divisions of the IRS are specifically barred from nearly all partisan activity. Those who work in the U.S. military have stricter rules regulating their political involvement. The rules for federal civilian employees specify that they:

May register and vote as they choose

May assist in voter registration

May express opinions about candidates and issues

May participate in campaigns as off-duty activities

May contribute money to political organizations or attend political fund-raising functions

May wear or display political badges, buttons, or stickers

May attend political rallies and meetings

May join political clubs or parties

May seek and hold positions in political parties

May campaign for or against referendum questions, constitutional amendments, and municipal ordinances

May not be candidates for public office in partisan elections

May not use official authority to interfere with or affect the results of an election

May not collect contributions or sell tickets to political fund-raising functions from subordinate employees

May not solicit funds or discourage the political activity of any person who has business before the employee's office

May not solicit funds or discourage political activity by any person who is the subject of an ongoing audit, investigation, or enforcement action.

GOVERNMENT EMPLOYEE UNIONS   Since 1962, federal civilian employees have had the right to form unions or associations that represent them in seeking to improve government personnel policies, and about one-third of them have joined such unions. Some of the more important unions representing federal employees

Principles of Bureaucratic Management

Followers of the noted German sociologist Max Weber contended that a properly run bureaucracy could be a model of efficiency based on rational and impartial management.* President Woodrow Wilson, when he was a Princeton University professor, adopted many of these views in his writings. Politics and public administration, he said, should be carefully separated. Leave politics to Congress and management to administrators who adhere to the laws passed by Congress.

According to the textbook model, bureaucrats should be closely controlled by established rules and regulations. Although this is not always true in practice, it is generally the case. Administrators are not free to make any rules they wish or to decide disputes any way they please. Several kinds of limitations exist:

1. The legislative power of Congress compels agencies to interpret and apply laws as Congress would wish. Congress can amend a law to make its intent clearer, conduct oversight hearings and investigations, or restrict appropriations.

2. Congress has closely regulated the procedures to be followed by regulatory agencies. Under the Administrative Procedures Act of 1946, agencies must publicize their procedures and organization, give advance information of proposed rules to interested persons, allow such persons to present written information and arguments, and allow parties appearing before the agency to be accompanied by counsel and to cross-examine witnesses.

3. Under certain conditions, final actions of agencies may be appealed to the courts.

4. Some federal agencies are created for the specific purpose of overseeing and limiting their fellow agencies. Examples are the Office of Management and Budget (OMB), which is supervised by the White House, and the General Accounting Office (GAO), which is supervised by Congress.

5. Administrators must keep in mind the demands of professional ethics, the advice and criticism of experts, and the attitudes of Congress, the president, interest groups, political parties, and citizens. In the long run, these informal safeguards may be the most important of all.

This textbook model remains influential because it reflects reality. Laws of Congress, although not the whole story, are an important part of the story. Federal agencies and career servants are creatures of the enabling laws under which they work.

*For an examination of Max Weber's ideas on bureaucracy, see Brian Fry, *Mastering Public Administration: From Max Weber to Dwight Waldo* (Chatham House, 1989).

Hatch Act
Federal statute barring federal employees from active participation in certain kinds of politics and protecting them from being fired on partisan grounds.

ome 50 million Americans have tried marijuana, and 20 million are reputed to use it regularly. About 6 million use cocaine, and about 500,000 are heroin addicts. The rise of "crack" is rapidly destroying lives and neighborhoods. Drug use and abuse cost the economy tens of billions in health and criminal justice expenses and lost productivity. The trade puts everyone at risk, not just those who use drugs. Drug use by federal employees can be particularly hazardous, especially by air traffic controllers and top governmental policy makers.

Do the consequences of drug use justify across-the-board, random, unannounced drug and urinalysis tests for policy makers, senior civil servants, and other civil servants as a condition of employment?

today are the American Federation of Government Employees, the National Treasury Employees Union, the National Association of Government Employees, and the National Federation of Federal Employees.

Unlike unions in the private sector, these groups lack the right to strike and are not able to bargain over pay and benefits. What can they do? They can attempt to negotiate better personnel policies and practices for federal workers; they can represent federal bureaucrats at grievance and disciplinary proceedings; and they can also lobby Congress on measures affecting personnel changes.

Challenges in Hiring and Retaining Civil Servants

As the twenty-first century began, it became increasingly clear that federal departments and agencies were having a hard time recruiting talented individuals, partly because of lower wages paid by government, as opposed to the private sector. There is a pay gap of 20–25 percent between comparable federal and private jobs.[13] Moreover, unlike the private sector, federal work rules provide few rewards for performance. And, of course, stock options are nonexistent in the federal government.

Political scientist Paul Light warns that the attractiveness of a federal job has lost some, if not much, of its past luster: "Sad to say, when young Americans are asked to picture themselves in public service careers, particularly at the federal level, they picture themselves in dreaded jobs, where seniority, not performance rules."[14]

Many federal civil servants consider leaving the government because of low pay. Some also find it hard to work for the government when politicians and the media are regularly criticizing their agencies. Another factor that may contribute to lowered morale in the bureaucracy is that innovative performance is more difficult because the federal government, as noted earlier, has an institutional bias in favor of continuity rather than change. Job security and caution are far more the hallmarks of federal bureaucracies than risk-taking and entrepreneurship. Still, talented career and appointed executives in the federal government have transformed programs such as the Federal Emergency Management Agency and the Department of Housing and Urban Development's Office of Community Planning.[15]

Efforts at Reform

A task force on reinventing government in the mid-1990s greatly trimmed the 10,000-page *Federal Personnel Manual*, which had specified everything down to the color of personnel folders. "We actually hauled it out to a dumpster in a wheelbarrow. The death of the manual gave agencies more freedom to tailor things to fit their own operations."[16]

Many federal agencies are changing how they hire people and go about their work. Innovation and customer service have become government priorities. Hierarchical organizations have become structurally somewhat flatter. Applicants can now use regular résumés instead of federal forms in applying for government jobs. A website (**www.opm.gov**) lets people find out what jobs are available, and applicants can apply by phone or fax for many jobs. And workers are being evaluated and rewarded with bonuses for how well their teams achieve measurable results.

The government has also tried to make the federal bureaucracy a more family-friendly workplace. The Family Leave Act passed in 1993 and other measures or experiments have encouraged job sharing, part-time work, alternative work schedules, telecommuting from home, and child and elder services.

Bureaucratic Realities

Career administrators are in a good position to know when a program is not operating properly and what action is needed. But one of the major complaints about bureaucrats is that they do not go out of their way to make things better. The problem is that many bureaucrats often learn by hard experience that they are more likely to get into trouble by attempting to improve or change programs than if they just do

iron triangle

A mutually supporting relationship among interest groups, congressional committees and subcommittees, and government agencies that share a common policy concern.

nothing. Hardening of administrative arteries is more likely, some critics say, than administrative aggressiveness.

Often the fiercest battles in Washington are not over principles or programs but over jurisdictional boundaries, personnel cuts, and fringe benefits. Career employees come to believe the expansion of their organization is vital to the public interest. They sometimes become more skillful at building political alliances to protect their own organization than at building political alliances to ensure their programs' effectiveness.

Career administrators usually try hard to be nonpartisan, yet they are inevitably involved in politics. Some of them have more bargaining and alliance-building skills than the elected and appointed officials to whom they report. In one sense, agency leaders are at the center of action in Washington. Over time, administrative agencies may come to resemble entrenched pressure groups in that they operate to advance their own interests. The FBI is a good example; it is always seeking more funds, new projects, and as much independence as possible from the Justice Department in which it is located.

The growth of federal programs from the 1930s through the 1970s brought an increase in the number of policy aides on Capitol Hill, of Washington law firms that specialize in assisting clients who are interested in policy development, and of lobbyists (some say at least 40,000) who work with Congress and the federal bureaucracy to advance various economic and professional interests.

Special interest groups that perceive real or potential harm to their interests cultivate the bureau chiefs and agency staffs who have jurisdiction over their programs. They also work closely with the committees and subcommittees of Congress that authorize, appropriate, and oversee programs run by these key bureaucracies. Recognizing the power of interest groups, bureau chiefs frequently recruit them as allies in pursuing common goals. What these bureau officials have in common with interest groups and their allies in Congress is a shared view that more money should be spent on federal programs run by the bureau in question. These alliances among bureaucrats, interest groups, and subcommittee members and their staffs on Capitol Hill are sometimes described as **iron triangles**.

The executive branch is not necessarily the smooth operating hierarchy it is made to appear on an organization chart. The president, cabinet members, and their politically appointed undersecretaries and assistant secretaries have their work cut out for them as they try to impose their will on the permanent civil service. Bureaucrats, with their strong allies in Congress and the interest groups, often resist change and direction from their appointed or elected political "superiors."[17] Some view these external relations as "administrative guerrilla warfare" and a serious roadblock to holding elected leaders accountable. Others view the clash over values as inevitable in a system that provides ample opportunities for such clashes. After all, the bureaucracy is merely one more forum for registering the many demands that people make upon government.

THE CASE OF BUREAU CHIEF GEORGE BROWN

The following case is fictional, yet based on actual experiences of typical bureaucrats. (Note that not only is our main character, George Brown, fictitious, but so are the Bureau of Erosion and the Department of Conservation. Other agencies mentioned do exist. This case illustrates some of the painful choices bureaucrats have to make.)

George Brown, age 47, is chief of the Bureau of Erosion in the Department of Conservation. A graduate of North Dakota State University, Brown is a career official in the federal service and a member of the Senior Executive Service. His appointment to the post was a result of both ability and luck. When his old bureau chief retired, the president wanted to bring in an erosion expert from Illinois, but influential members of Congress pressed for the selection of a recently "retired" (actually he was defeated

Thinking It Through...

Unannounced drug testing raises serious Fourth Amendment questions. The idea that a group of people should be subjected to random searches without reasonable individual cause has been resisted since the outset of our life as a nation. When Congress, or the president, or the head of a federal agency requires testing as a condition of employment, even if evidence of drug use would not be used to dismiss employees, skeptical judges must be persuaded that the testing is not an "unreasonable" search and seizure.

The Supreme Court ruled in two 1989 decisions involving railway workers and U.S. Customs Service employees that mandatory blood and urine tests may be required for certain workers without a showing of "individualized suspicion." Writing for the Court in the railway workers' case, Justice Anthony Kennedy said the government's interest in testing even without a showing of individual suspicion is compelling. Employees subject to the tests discharge duties fraught with such risks of injury to others that even a momentary lapse of attention can have disastrous results.

The two cases dealt with post-accident testing of railway personnel on duty at the time of a major accident and with customs officials who carry firearms, handle classified information, or intercept drugs.

Drug testing of all federal employees, or even only those in policy-making positions, presents difficult constitutional issues. Supporters of privacy rights and civil liberties are uncomfortable with carrying this policy too far. Drug testing, some concede, may be necessary for certain individuals where public safety is genuinely involved, but it is not needed and would be an unconstitutional deprivation of privacy rights under the Fourth Amendment as a general policy.

THE JAPANESE BUREAUCRACY

In Japan the most prestigious job a college student can aspire to is not a doctor, lawyer, corporate executive, or even a politician. It is to become a top-level member of the national bureaucracy. One recent college graduate who passed the entrance exam for Japan's Ministry of Foreign Affairs (the equivalent of the U.S. State Department) was featured in his local newspaper and received congratulatory messages from his governor and national politicians from his home province.

A comparison of television news programs in Japan and the United States found that 26 percent of the news stories in Japan were about the bureaucracy, whereas only 2 percent in the United States were about the bureaucracy. The most news stories in the United States were about the president (25 percent); in

Japan the prime minister was the subject of only 7 percent of news stories.

The popularity of a top-level bureaucratic job is also shown by the recruitment patterns of bureaucrats. More than 50 percent of all of Japan's top bureaucrats graduated from Japan's best university, Tokyo University, with the most difficult major, an undergraduate degree in law. When Japan's second-best university, Kyoto University, is included, fully three-fourths of all Japan's high-level bureaucrats came from these two universities. In Japan, only the best and brightest students go on to elite careers in the national bureaucracy.

SOURCE: Ellis S. Krauss, "Portraying the State: NHK Television News and Politics," in *Media and Politics in Japan*, ed. Susan J. Pharr and Ellis S. Krauss (University of Hawaii Press, 1996).

in the last election!) member of the House of Representatives from a farm state. After deadlock and delay, Brown, then a division head in the Bureau of Erosion, was promoted to bureau chief as a compromise.

Early in March of Brown's second year in his new post, his boss, the secretary of conservation, summoned him and the other bureau heads to an important conference and informed them that he had just attended a cabinet meeting in which the president had called on each department to make at least a 10 percent cut in spending in the coming fiscal year. The president, the secretary reported, was responding to popular demands for federal fiscal restraint.

Brown quickly calculated what this cutback would mean for his agency. For several years the Bureau of Erosion had been spending about $1.7 billion a year to help farmers protect their farmland. Could it get along on about $1.53 billion, and where could savings be made? Returning to his office, Brown called a meeting of his personnel, budget, and management officials. After hours of discussion, it was agreed that savings could be effected only by decreasing the scope of the program, a step that would involve terminating about 400 of the bureau's employees. Brown asked his subordinates to prepare a list of employees who were the least useful to the bureau. He would decide which to drop after checking with the affected members of Congress.

A few weeks later Brown presented a $1.6 billion budget to Conservation Secretary Jones, who approved it and passed it along to the White House. The president then went over the figures with the director of the Office of Management and Budget, and a few weeks later the White House submitted the budget for the whole executive department to Congress.

Meanwhile Brown was running into trouble. News of the proposed budget cut had leaked to the bureau's personnel in the field. Nobody knew who would be dropped, and some employees were already looking around for other positions. Morale fell. Hearing of the cut, farmers' representatives in Washington notified local farm organizations throughout the country. Soon Brown began to receive letters demanding certain services be maintained. Members of the farm bloc in Congress were also becoming restless.

Shortly after the president's budget went to Congress, Representative Jim Smith of Kansas asked Brown to meet with him. Smith was chair of the Subcommittee on Agriculture of the influential House Appropriations Committee. Smith said his fellow subcommittee members, both Democratic and Republican, all agreed the Erosion Bureau's budget must not be cut. The farmers needed even more than the usual $1.7 billion because of severe flood conditions in some sections of the country. He warned that farmers would really be outraged if the program was reduced. Members of Congress from agricultural states, Smith went on, were under tremendous pressure. Leaders of farm groups in Washington were mobilizing farmers everywhere. Besides, Smith said, the president was unfair in cutting down on the farm program; he did not understand agricultural problems, and he failed to recognize that programs designed to increase agricultural

output were the best way to reduce the trade imbalance. Let the cuts in federal programs be made elsewhere.

Smith then came to the point. Brown, he said, must vigorously oppose the budget cut. Hearings on appropriations would begin in a few days, and Brown as bureau chief would, of course, testify. At that time he must insist that the cuts would hurt the bureau and undermine its whole program. Brown would not have to volunteer this statement, Smith said. He could just respond to leading questions put by committee members. Brown's testimony, Smith thought, would help clinch the argument against the cut because the committee would respect the judgment of the administrator closest to the problem. Other bureaucrats were fighting to save their appropriations. Obviously, said Smith, they are counting on public reaction to get them exemptions from the 10 percent cutback, and Brown would be foolish not to do the same.

Brown was in an embarrassing position. He had submitted his estimates to the secretary of conservation and to the president, and it was his duty to back them up. The rules of the game demanded, moreover, that agency heads defend budget estimates submitted to Congress, whatever their personal feelings might be. The president had appointed Brown to his position and had a right to expect loyalty. On the other hand, Brown was on the spot with his own agency. His employees all expected their chief to look out for them. Brown had developed cordial relations with his staff, and he squirmed at the thought of having to let more than a thousand employees go. What would they think when they heard him defend the cut? More important, he needed to maintain friendly relations with the farmers, the farm organizations, and the farm bloc in Congress. Finally, Brown was committed to the work of his department. He grasped its true importance, whereas the president's budget advisers did not. And he knew that his pet project—aid to poverty-stricken areas in Appalachia—would probably be sacrificed because it was not supported by a powerful constituency.

Brown turned for advice to an old friend in the Office of Management and Budget. This friend urged him to defend the president's budget. He appealed to Brown's professional pride as an administrator and career public servant. He reminded him that the chief executive must have control of the budget and that agency heads must subordinate their interests to the executive program. He said the only way to balance the budget would be for all agencies to make program cuts. As for the employees to be dropped—well, that was part of the game. Some of them might be able to get jobs in other government agencies; civil service would protect their status. Anyway, they would understand Brown's position. In a parting shot he mentioned that the president had Brown in mind for bigger things.

The next day Brown had lunch with a North Dakota senator, wise and experienced in Washington ways, who had helped him get his start in government. The senator was sympathetic. But there was no doubt about what Brown should do, the senator said. He should follow Representative Smith's plan, of course, being as diplomatic as possible about it. That way he would protect his position with those who would be most important in the long run.

"After all," the senator said, "presidents come and go, parties rise and fall, but Smith and the other members of Congress will be here a long time, and so will the farm organizations. They can do a lot for you in future years. And remember one other thing," the senator concluded. "These people are the elected representatives of the people. Constitutionally, Congress has the power to spend money as it sees fit. Why should you object if they want to spend an extra $78 or $80 million?"

Brown realized his dilemma was worse than ever. The arguments on both sides were persuasive. He felt hopelessly divided in his loyalties and responsibilities. The president expected one thing of him; Congress expected another. As a professional administrator, he felt obliged to side with the president. As head of a bureau, however, he wanted to protect his team and his programs. His future? Whatever decision he made, he was bound to antagonize important people and interests.

Can certain problems be better handled by private industry than by government bureaucracies?

Privatization is the process of contracting public services to private organizations. Examples of privatization include the contracting out by the Air Force of the building of fighter planes and the contracting out by several state governments of the construction and operation of prisons. The National Aeronautics and Space Administration contracts out most of the manufacturing of its space vehicles.

Private or nonprofit firms handle a vast array of services, from repairing ships to delivering meals-on-wheels to the home-bound elderly. Some people contend that our public schools might be more effectively operated by private firms. Advocates of privatization claim it would reduce costs and provide better service than reliance on the federal and state bureaucracies.

"Think of it. Presidents come and go, but WE go on forever!"

Berry's World. Reproduced by permission of Newspaper Enterprise Association, Inc.

After much soul searching, Brown decided the issue involved more than loyalties, ambitions, and programs. Ultimately it boiled down to two questions: First, to whom was he, Brown, legally and administratively responsible? Formally, of course, he was responsible to the chief executive who appointed him, who was accountable to the people. Brown knew, too, that he was accountable to Congress, which after all has the power over all fiscal matters. Second, which course of action did he think was better for the welfare of all the people? Looking at the question this way, he believed the president was right in asking for fiscal restraint. As a taxpayer and consumer himself, Brown recognized the need to balance the budget and reduce the national debt. To be sure, Congress must make the final decision. Yet to make the decision, Congress had to act on the advice of the administration, and the administration should speak with one voice for the majority of the people, or it should not be speaking out at all.

With mixed feelings, Brown decided to support the president. Being a seasoned alliance builder, however, he hedged his bets. He came out strongly for the president's budget, yet at the same time he sent friendly members of Congress some questions to be asked of him in congressional hearings so he could explain the impact of the cutbacks. He also circulated to some of these same members of Congress an analysis of the impact of personnel and funding cuts in their states and districts.

BUREAUCRATIC ACCOUNTABILITY

Should bureaucrats be accountable to the president, the cabinet, the majority in Congress, or the people who elected the president? Plainly, most Americans would like the bureaucracy to be responsive to them as taxpaying customers. In general terms, they would say the bureaucracy should be responsive to the public interest. But defining the public interest is the crucial problem. The president and the House and the Senate and the committees of Congress all claim to speak on behalf of the public interest.

To whom bureaucrats should be accountable is an inherently political question. Accountability to the White House, for example, depends in large measure on the supporters' partisanship toward the president. Republicans, not surprisingly, favor strong presidential control over the bureaucracy when Republicans occupy the White House, as do Democrats when their party wins the White House.

To the President

Modern presidents invariably contend the president should be in charge, for the chief executive is responsive to the broadest constituency. A president, it is argued, must see that popular needs and expectations are converted into administrative action. When the nation elects a conservative president who favors cutbacks in federal programs and less governmental intervention in the economy, his policies must be carried out by the bureaucracy. The voters' wishes can be translated into action only if the bureaucrats support presidential policies.

Yet, as we have seen, under the American system of checks and balances the party winning a presidential election does not acquire total control of the national government. Under our Constitution, the president is not even the undisputed master of the executive structure. Presidents come into an ongoing system over which they have little control and within which they have little leeway to make the bureaucracy responsive. Still, some presidential control over the bureaucracy may be exercised through the president's powers of appointment, reorganization, and budgeting. More specifically, a president can attempt to control the bureaucracy by appointing or promoting sympathetic personnel, mobilizing public opinion and congressional pressure, changing the administrative apparatus, influencing budget decisions, using extensive personal persuasion, and if all else fails, shifting a bureaucracy's assignment to another department or agency (although this shift requires tacit if not explicit congressional approval).[18]

Presidents appoint about 4,000 people to top positions within the executive branch; however, many of these are confidential assistants or special aides to cabinet officers who require Senate confirmation and are not exclusively a president's choice. Some critics suggest that a president's hand could be strengthened if the chief executive were able to make two or three times as many political appointments.

To Congress

Congress has a number of ways to exercise control over the bureaucracy: by establishing agencies, formulating budgets, appropriating funds, confirming personnel, authorizing new programs or new shifts in direction, conducting investigations and hearings, reorganizing authority, and rebuking officials.

The foundation of this bureaucratic power is legal authority. A bureaucrat's information and expertise augment this legal authority. Ordinarily, bureaucrats know more than anyone else about their programs and the consequences of what they are doing. Recognizing this, Congress often requests agency heads to frame policy proposals and to provide estimates for the costs of what they propose. Agency heads respond because they know if they fail to provide accurate information, Congress has ways of reducing agency funds.

Most constituents, especially businesspeople, turn to their members of Congress for help as they battle federal red tape. Members of Congress earn political credit by interceding in federal agencies on behalf of their constituents. Still, Congress is under fire, at least in some quarters, for encouraging the growth of federal spending and allowing the bureaucracy to become too independent. Members of Congress, so this reasoning goes, profit from the growth and complexity of the federal government.

The brutal fact is that only a small minority of our 535 members of Congress would trade the present bureaucratic structure for one which was an efficient, effective agent of the general interest—the political payoffs of the latter are lower than those of the former. Congressional talk of inefficient, irresponsible, out-of-control bureaucracy is typically just that—talk—and when it is not, it usually refers to agencies under the jurisdiction of other legislators' committees. Congress can abolish or reorganize an agency. Congress can limit or expand an agency's jurisdiction, or allow its authority to lapse entirely. Congress can slash an agency's appropriations.

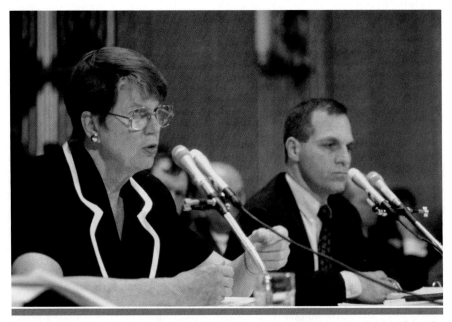

Congress called upon Attorney General Janet Reno and FBI Director Louis Freeh to explain why the Justice Department had not investigated fund-raising irregularities by President Clinton and the Democrats in the 1996 presidential campaign.

Thinking It Through...

Critics of privatization point to the cost overruns and waste in the procurement of weapons systems as failures of privatization. According to David Osborne and Ted Gaebler, privatization is one answer, but not the answer:

Services can be contracted out or turned over to the private sector. But governance cannot. We can privatize discrete [governmental programs], but not the overall process of governance. If we did, we would have no mechanism by which to make collective decisions, no way to set the rules of the marketplace, no means to enforce rules of behavior. We would lose all sense of equity and altruism: services that could not generate a profit, whether housing for the homeless or health care for the poor, would barely exist. . . .

Business does some things better than government, but government does some things better than business. The public sector tends to be better, for instance, at policy management, regulation, ensuring equity, preventing discrimination or exploitation, ensuring continuity and stability of services, and ensuring social cohesion. . . . Business tends to do better at performing economic tasks, innovating, replicating successful experiments, adapting to rapid change, abandoning unsuccessful or obsolete activities, and performing complex or technical tasks.[*]

Would we be better off if the U.S. Postal Service were turned over to private firms? A business executive who served as postmaster general, Anthony Frank, says no. He praises the Postal Service for its high on-time delivery and points out that all Americans, no matter where they live, get essentially the same service at the same price. "If you privatize it," Frank pointed out, "the cost would go up for a lot of Americans." Frank added that it is anywhere from 10 to 100 percent more expensive in most industrial nations, and they seldom have overnight service.[**]

*David Osborne and Ted Gaebler, *Reinventing Government: How the Entrepreneurial Spirit Is Transforming the Public Sector* (Addison-Wesley, 1992), pp. 45–46. See also Charles Haddad, "Private Prisons Don't Work," *Business Week*, September 11, 2000, pp. 95–98.

**Anthony Frank, quoted in an interview in *USA Today*, January 8, 1992, p. 7A.

Why Presidents Like to Reorganize the Bureaucracy

- Shake up an organization to increase managerial control
- Simplify or streamline the bureaucracy or a specific agency
- Reduce costs by lessening overlap, duplication, inefficiencies
- Symbolize priorities by signaling new responsibilities in new agencies
- Improve program effectiveness by bringing separate but logically related programs to the same agency
- Improve policy integration by placing competitive or conflicting interests within a single organization
- Downgrade the importance of a program to weaken it
- Increase power over an unresponsive agency by installing their own people.

Congress can investigate. Congress can do all these things, but individual congressmen generally find reasons not to do so.[19]

Congress, it is charged, anxious whenever possible to avoid conflict, adopts such sweeping legislation and delegates so much authority to the bureaucracy that bureaucrats, in effect, have become the nation's lawmakers. Congress could pass laws with precise wording, but it would get too bogged down in details to complete its work.

It is not Congress as a whole that shares direction over the bureaucracy with the president. More accurately, individual members and committees specialize in the appropriations and oversight processes. They oversee policies of a particular cluster of agencies—often the agencies serving constituents in their own districts. Some legislators stake out a claim over specific areas. Members of Congress, who see presidents come and go, come to think they know more about particular agencies than the president does (and often they do). Some congressional leaders prefer to seal off "their" agencies from presidential direction and maintain their influence over public policy. Sometimes their power is institutionalized; the Army Corps of Engineers, for example, is given authority by law to plan public works and report to Congress without going through the president.

Whose Bureaucracy Is This, Anyway?

Both presidents and members of Congress strive to exercise control over the bureaucracy, and interest groups and court rulings also influence the way the bureaucracy operates. For their part, career bureaucrats say they are responsive to the laws and statutes they work under and to their own standards of professionalism and responsibility. The search for improved means of ensuring bureaucratic accountability is never ending. Experiments with countless reforms—reorganization, deregulating the public service, sunset practices, selective privatization, budgetary planning, and oversight hearings—also continue.

It is increasingly clear, moreover, that virtually all national bureaucracies are more responsive today than once was the case. Even organizations such as the FBI or the Corps of Engineers are now more accountable to Congress and the White House, and ultimately to the American people. "Thanks to Freedom of Information statutes and other 'sunshine' legislation, [the bureaucracy] has become less selective, and the weakening of iron triangles has made it much more responsive to broad constituencies and much less the creature of its own clients."[20]

WHAT THE PUBLIC THINKS OF BUREAUCRATS AND THE BUREAUCRACY

Big bureaucracy in the abstract is unpopular. It engages in many activities that most people find offensive, like taxing, inspecting, or regulating. Big bureaucracy is sometimes defined as that part of the government people dislike.

As individuals, civil servants are appreciated, but as a class they are not. Citizens who have dealings with federal employees on a face-to-face basis say they are pleased by employees' performance. Three-quarters of the public who have dealings with federal bureaucrats find them "helpful" and say bureaucrats treated them "fairly."[21] In contrast to scorn for bureaucrats and bureaucracy in general, Americans seem to approve the conduct of individual federal employees—Postal Service delivery persons, forest rangers, Veterans Affairs Department officials, or county field agents who help with the local 4-H programs. They also admire astronauts, marines, FBI agents, and Coast Guard officers, all of whom are also federal employees.

Red Tape and Waste

Americans are skeptical of, if not cynical about, big government. They equate bigness with remoteness, incompetence, and unresponsiveness. They also assume that the bigger government gets, the less efficient it is, and the more it wastes. Perhaps the most criticized aspect of the federal bureaucracy is that career public employees seem to enjoy the closest thing to job security; they are almost as secure in their jobs as if they were confirmed for life as members of the Supreme Court.

A central problem with the bureaucracy, critics say, is that we have failed to subject it to the control and discipline alleged to operate in the private sector. Despite the talk about numerous federal programs being eliminated or down-sized, most federal agencies survive. The tests of efficiency and cost effectiveness that are the basic standards of business are much less important in decisions about which federal programs will survive. Outdated and ineffective programs endure because both Republicans and Democrats have forged coalitions of convenience based on a desire to deliver favors and protect programs located in their particular districts.

Congress throughout the 1990s took steps to downsize federal agencies. It abolished the Interstate Commerce Commission; it called for the gradual privatization of Amtrak; and it scaled back the Environmental Protection Agency, the Bureau of Mines, the Bureau of Indian Affairs, and several scientific advisory boards and projects. Many Republicans in Congress wanted to end support for public broadcasting, saying that *Sesame Street*, *Car Talk*, and *Wall Street Week* would all be picked up by the networks and that today's abundance of cable television channels makes publicly subsidized broadcasting no longer necessary.[22]

A few years ago there was a Republican crusade to dismantle the Departments of Energy, Commerce, Housing and Urban Development, and Education. "But even as they claimed a mandate to end 'big government,' these Republicans discovered that voter sentiment about closing down agencies typically ranged from apathy to uneasiness to outright opposition."[23] Moreover, various interest groups came to the defense of these departments. For example, a coalition of major corporations—including AT&T, IBM, Boeing, General Electric, and Motorola—supported the Commerce Department and its trade promotion and industrial research operations.[24]

In the 2000 election, Republicans avoided the issue of closing down federal departments and stressed instead that we should rely less on the federal government and more on the private sector and "faith-based" institutions such as churches.

Two Cheers for Bureaucracy

Recent efforts by some state and local government levels have made their bureaucracies more entrepreneurial. The cities of St. Paul, Minnesota, and Indianapolis, Indiana, and the states of Florida and Massachusetts have introduced various market incentives, rewards, and public-private partnerships that encourage efficiency and responsiveness.[25] They have shown that competition and incentives can prudently be built into various government monopolies so that bureaucracies become more responsive to their customers.

In the private sector, if you are displeased with the service provided by a company such as AT&T, you can switch to MCI or Sprint, and this is now happening to some government services. It used to be that you could use only the U.S. Postal Service to deliver your messages, whether you liked the service or not. Now numerous delivery services compete with the postal service; fax and e-mail have become popular means of communication. (It should be noted that the postal service is getting better—credit this to the competition.)

A comparison of the performance of the U.S. bureaucracy with most bureaucracies in the world suggests we should be grateful for the service we get from our

Among its proposed reforms of the bureaucracy, Congress wanted to end support of public broadcasting, claiming that programs like Sesame Street *could support themselves on commercial television. The public, however, disagreed, and Big Bird, the Grouch, and other childhood favorites still receive government subsidies.*

public employees. The U.S. Postal Service provides a good example. Although it is sometimes criticized as being a dinosaur, it is more efficient and less costly than comparable services around the world. Another example is the United States tax system; although it is constantly cursed and has been properly chided for its abuses of power, it is the most effective and efficient such system in the world.

POLITICS ONLINE

Want To Be a Bureaucrat?

Close to 90,000 different agencies exist in federal, state, and local government. You may wonder what all these agencies do and why they employ so many people. The Internet provides excellent resources for understanding these questions. The website for this text has prepared an Interactive graphic that will allow you to match some government agencies with what they do. This graphic is located at: www.amgovtplace.com/interactivegraphics/bureaucracy.html.

In addition, each agency or department usually has its own website. A complete listing of federal agencies can be found at:
www.lib.lsu.edu/gov/fedgovall.html. The site contains links to each agencies' home page.

Most of these agencies are constantly looking for interns and full-time employees. It is estimated that over 25,000 government positions are open on any given day. From research to law enforcement, the government employs people in virtually every field. For detailed information on federal employment opportunities, go to the Office of Personnel Management site at:
www.opm.gov or to the federal employment search engine at:
www.fedworld.gov/jobs/jobsearch.html.

State and local jobs are also available and information about them can be found at city and state home pages. Information on accessing these sites will be available in later chapters.

SUMMARY

1. Bureaucracy's chief characteristics are continuity, predictability, impartiality, standard operating procedures, and the inevitable "red tape." Our bureaucratic agencies reflect how our political system has tried to identify our most important national goals and how policies are implemented.

2. We often condemn bureaucracy and bureaucrats, yet we continue to turn to them to solve our toughest problems and to render more and better services. In the last decade there have been major efforts to overhaul and improve the workings of the federal bureaucracy. Despite numerous initiatives to streamline the government, eliminate waste, and make government more like an effective business, critics continue to call for less bureaucracy and more reforms.

3. Most of the 2.8 million civilian employees of the federal government serve under a merit system that protects their independence of politics. They work in one of the 14 cabinet departments as well as government corporations, independent agencies, and independent regulatory boards or commissions. A major responsibility is policy implementation.

4. The federal government's Office of Personnel Management sets policy for recruiting and evaluating federal workers. Various restrictions exist on federal workers that prevent them from running for political office or political party fund-raising activities. The federal bureaucracy general prizes continuity, stability, and following the rules more than risk-taking or innovation.

5. The American bureaucracy has at least two immediate bosses: Congress and the president. It must pay considerable attention as well to the courts and their rulings and, of course, to well-organized interest groups and public opinion. In many ways the bureaucracy is a semi-independent force—a fourth branch of government—in American politics.

6. Debates and controversy over big government and big bureaucracy, and over how to reorganize and eliminate waste in them, continue. Compared with many other nations and their centralized bureaucracies, the hand of bureaucracy rests more gently and less oppressively on Americans than on citizens elsewhere. Efforts to make the bureaucracy more responsive are enduring struggles in a constitutional democracy.

KEY TERMS

bureaucrat 344
bureaucracy 344
spoils system 344
merit system 346

Office of Personnel Management (OPM) 346
bureau 348
government corporation 348

independent agency 348
independent regulatory board 348

Office of Management and Budget 349
Hatch Act 351
iron triangle 352

FURTHER READING

JOEL D. ABERBACH, *Keeping a Watchful Eye: The Politics of Congressional Oversight* (Brookings Institution, 1990).

DAN BAUM, *Smoke and Mirrors: The War on Drugs and the Politics of Failure* (Little, Brown, 1996).

BARRY BOZEMAN, *Bureaucracy and Red Tape* (Prentice Hall, 2000).

SHELLEY L. DAVIS, *Unbridled Power: Inside the Secret Culture of the IRS* (Harper Business, 1997).

JOHN J. DIIULIO, JR., ED., *Deregulating the Public Service: Can Government Be Improved?* (Brookings Institution, 1994).

JOHN J. DIIULIO, JR., GERALD GARVEY, AND DONALD F. KETTL, *Improving Government Performance: An Owner's Manual* (Brookings Institution, 1993).

JOHN D. DONAHUE, ED., *Making Washington Work: Tales of Innovation in the Federal Government* (Brookings Institution, 1999).

JAMES W. FESLER AND DONALD F. KETTL, *The Politics of the Administrative Process* (Chatham House, 1991).

CHARLES T. GOODSELL, *The Case for Bureaucracy*, 3d ed. (Chatham House, 1994).

AL GORE, *The Best Kept Secrets in Government: How the Clinton Administration Is Reinventing the Way Washington Works* (Random House, 1996).

AL GORE, *Creating a Government That Works Better and Costs Less: The Report of the National Performance Review* (Plume-Penguin, 1993).

PHILIP K. HOWARD, *The Death of Common Sense: How Law Is Suffocating America* (Random House, 1994).

RONALD N. JOHNSON AND GARY D. LIBECAP, *The Federal Civil Service System and the Problem of Bureaucracy* (University of Chicago Press, 1994).

HERBERT KAUFMAN, *The Administrative Behavior of Federal Bureau Chiefs* (Brookings Institution, 1981).

DONALD F. KETTL, *Reinventing Government: A Fifth Year Report Card* (Brookings Institution, 1998).

ANDREW KOHUT, ED., *Deconstructing Distrust: How Americans View Government* (Pew Research Center for the People and the Press, 1998).

PAUL C. LIGHT, *The New Public Service* (Brookings Institution, 1999).

PAUL C. LIGHT, *Thickening Government: Federal Hierarchy and the Diffusion of Accountability* (Brookings Institution, 1995).

PAUL C. LIGHT, *The Tides of Reform: Making Government Work, 1945–1995* (Yale University Press, 1997).

DAVID OSBORNE AND TED GAEBLER, *Reinventing Government: How the Entrepreneurial Spirit Is Transforming the Public Sector* (Addison-Wesley, 1992).

DAVID OSBORNE AND PETER PLASTRIK, *Banishing Bureaucracy: The Five Strategies for Reinventing Government* (Addison-Wesley, 1997).

JAMES Q. WILSON, *Bureaucracy: What Government Agencies Do and Why They Do It* (Basic Books, 1989).

Four useful journals are *Journal of Policy Analysis and Management, National Journal, Public Administration Review,* and *Government Executive.*

16

FIRST AMENDMENT FREEDOMS

CHAPTER MEDIA

 POLITICS ONLINE

Surf Watch: Pornography on the Internet
www.prenhall.com/burns

"ONGRESS SHALL MAKE NO LAW," DECLARES THE FIRST AMENDMENT, "RESPECTING AN ESTABLISHMENT OF RELIGION, OR PROHIBITING THE FREE EXERCISE THEREOF, or abridging the freedom of speech, or of the press, or the right of the people peaceably to assemble, and to petition the Government for a redress of grievances." In this one sentence our Constitution lays down the fundamental principles of a free society: freedom of conscience and freedom of expression. These freedoms are essential to our individual self-determination and to our collective self-governance—to government by the people.

Yet these freedoms were not constitutionally guaranteed until the addition in 1791 of the first ten amendments, the Bill of Rights. For that reason, we begin this chapter by discussing the rights in the original Constitution and in the Bill of Rights as applied to both the national and state governments before turning to the "first freedoms" of religion, speech, press, and assembly.

RIGHTS IN THE ORIGINAL CONSTITUTION

Even though most of the framers did not think a Bill of Rights was necessary, they considered certain rights important enough to be spelled out in the Constitution. These rights included the writ of *habeas corpus* and protection against *ex post facto* laws and bills of attainder.

Foremost among constitutional rights is the **writ of *habeas corpus*.** Literally meaning "produce the body," this writ is a court order directing any official having a person in custody to produce the prisoner in court and explain why the prisoner is being held. As originally used, the writ was merely a judicial inquiry to determine whether a person in custody was being held as the result of the action of a court with proper jurisdiction. But over the years it developed into a remedy for any illegal confinement. People being held can appeal to a judge, usually through an attorney, stating why they believe they are held unlawfully and should be released. The judge then orders the jailer or a lower court to show cause why the writ should not be issued. If a judge finds a petitioner is detained unlawfully, the judge may order the prisoner's immediate release. Although state judges lack jurisdiction to issue writs of *habeas corpus* to find out why federal authorities are holding persons, federal district judges may do so to find out if state and local officials are holding people in violation of the Constitution or national laws.

At the outset it is helpful to clarify certain terms—liberties, rights, freedoms, and privileges—that are often used interchangeably in discussions of rights and freedoms. We offer these definitions:

Civil liberties: The freedoms of all persons that are constitutionally protected against governmental restraint; the freedoms of conscience, religion, and expression, for example, which are secured by the First Amendment. These civil liberties are also protected by the due process and equal protection clauses of the Fifth and Fourteenth Amendments.

Civil rights: The constitutional rights of all persons, not just citizens, to due process and the equal protection of the laws; the constitutional right not to be discriminated against by governments because of race, ethnic background, religion, or gender. These civil rights are protected by the due process and equal protection clauses of the Fifth and Fourteenth Amendments and by the civil rights laws of national and state governments.

Rights of persons accused of crimes: The rights of all persons, guilty as well as innocent, to protection from abusive use by the government of the power to prosecute and punish persons accused of violating criminal laws. These rights are secured by the Fourth, Fifth, Sixth, Eighth, and Fourteenth Amendments.

Political rights: The rights of citizens to participate in the process of governance flowing from the right to vote. These rights are secured by the Fourteenth, Fifteenth, Nineteenth, and Twenty-third Amendments.

Legal privileges: Privileges granted by governments to which we have no constitutional right and which may be subject to conditions or restrictions; for example, the right to welfare benefits or to a driver's license. But once such privileges are granted, we may have a legal right to them, and they cannot be denied except for "reasonable reasons" and by appropriate procedures.

Common law: Judge-made law based on the interpretation and application of legal principles—the principle of freedom of speech, for example. Australia, England, and the United States are *common law* countries, in contrast with *civil law* countries on the European Continent.

Civil law: It evolved from Roman law and is based on codes that are strictly applied by judges. The term *civil law* also refers to law that applies to disputes between individuals and the government that carry no criminal penalties.

writ of *habeas corpus*

A court order requiring explanation to a judge why a prisoner is held in custody.

ex post facto law

Retroactive criminal law that works to the disadvantage of an individual; forbidden in the Constitution.

In recent years, the use of the writ of *habeas corpus* by federal courts to review convictions by state courts has been widely criticized. Some people believe the writ has been abused by state prisoners to get an endless and expensive round of reviews, which sometimes lead to convictions being set aside by a federal judge after the matter has been reviewed by two or more state courts. Partly because of concerns about maintaining the principles of federalism, and partly because of the growing caseloads of federal courts, the Supreme Court and Congress have severely restricted the *habeas corpus* discretion of federal judges. The Antiterrorism and Effective Death Penalty Act of 1996, for example, restricts the number of times a person may be granted a *habeas corpus* review, stops appeals for most *habeas* petitions at the level of the U.S. Court of Appeals, and calls for deference by federal judges to the decisions of state judges unless they are clearly "unreasonable."[1]

An ***ex post facto* law** is a retroactive criminal law making a particular act a crime that was not a crime when an individual committed it, or increasing punishment for a crime after the crime was committed, or lessening the proof necessary to convict for a crime after it was committed. This constitutional prohibition does not prevent the retroactive application of laws that work to the benefit of an accused person—a law decreasing punishment, for example—or prevent the retroactive application of civil law, such as an increase in income tax rates applied to income already earned.

Bills of attainder are legislative acts inflicting punishment, including deprivation of property, without a trial on named individuals or members of a specified group. For example, Congress enacted a bill of attainder when it accused three federal employees of being disloyal in an appropriations bill and fired them.

THE BILL OF RIGHTS AND THE STATES

Although it was the framers who wrote the Constitution, in a sense it was the American people who drafted our basic charter of rights. As we saw in Chapter 1, the Constitution drawn up in Philadelphia included guarantees of a few basic rights, but it lacked a specific bill of rights similar to those in most state constitutions. The Federalists argued that the Constitution established a limited government that would not threaten individual freedoms, and therefore a bill of rights was unnecessary. The Anti-Federalists were not persuaded, and the omission aroused widespread suspicion. As a result, in order to persuade delegates to the state ratification conventions to vote for the Constitution, the Federalists promised to correct this deficiency. In its first session, the new Congress made good on that promise by proposing 12 amendments, 10 of which were ratified and became part of the Constitution.[2]

Note that the Bill of Rights literally *applies only to the national government*, not state governments.[3] Why not the states? The framers were confident that states could control their own state officials, and most state constitutions already had bills of rights. It was the new and distant central government the people feared. As it turned out, those fears were largely misdirected. The national government has generally shown less tendency to curtail civil liberties than have state and local governments.

When the Fourteenth Amendment, which does apply to the states, was adopted in 1868, supporters contended that its **due process clause**—which states that no person shall be deprived of life, liberty, or property without due process of law—limits states in precisely the same way the Bill of Rights limits the national government. At least, they argued, freedom of speech is protected by the Fourteenth Amendment. But for decades

the Supreme Court refused to interpret the Fourteenth Amendment in
this way. Then in *Gitlow v New York*
(1925), the Court announced that it
assumed "that freedom of speech and
of the press—which are protected by
the First Amendment from abridgment by Congress—are among the
fundamental personal rights and 'liberties' protected by the due process
clause of the Fourteenth Amendment
from impairment by the States."[4]

    Gitlow v New York was a revo-
lutionary decision. For the first time,
the U.S. Constitution protected free-

BRITAIN ACQUIRES PROTECTION FOR FREEDOM OF EXPRESSION

After hundreds of years without constitutional guarantees for freedom of
expression, the European Convention of
Human Rights became the law of the
land for Great Britain on October 2, 2000.
The convention defines and puts on
paper certain human rights—freedom of
expression, the right to a fair trial, privacy, among other rights—for the first
time in Britain. British courts now increasingly look to the European Convention
and how it has been interpreted and
applied by courts on the continent.

For further discussion, see Donald W. Jackson, *The
United Kingdom Confronts the European Conven-
tion on Human Rights* (University of Florida Press,
1997); also Alec Stone Sweet, *Governing with
Judges: Constitutional Politics in Europe* (Oxford
University Press, 2000).

dom of speech from abridgment by state and local governments. In the 1930s and
continuing at an accelerated pace during the 1960s, through the **selective incorporation** of provision after provision of the Bill of Rights into the due process clause,
the Supreme Court applied various rights to the states.[5] Today the Fourteenth
Amendment imposes on the states all the provisions of the Bill of Rights except those
of the Second and Third Amendments, the Fifth Amendment provision for indictment by a grand jury, the Seventh Amendment right to a jury trial in civil cases, and
the Ninth and Tenth Amendments (see Table 16–1).

TABLE 16–1 Selective Incorporation and the Application of the Bill of Rights to the States

Right	Amendment	Year
Public use and just compensation for the taking of private property by the government	5	1897
Freedom of speech	1	1925
Freedom of the press	1	1931
Fair trial	6	1932
Freedom of religion	1	1934
Freedom of assembly	1	1937
Free exercise of religion	1	1940
Separation of religion and government	1	1947
Right to a public trial	6	1948
Right against unreasonable searches and seizures	4	1949
Freedom of association	1	1958
Exclusionary rule	4	1961
Ban against cruel and unusual punishment	8	1962
Right to counsel in felony cases	6	1963
Right against self-incrimination	5	1964
Right to confront witness	6	1965
Right of privacy	1,3,4,5,9	1965
Right to impartial jury	6	1966
Right to a speedy trial and to compulsory process for obtaining witnesses	6	1967
Right to jury trial in nonpetty cases	6	1968
Right against double jeopardy	5	1969

bill of attainder
Legislative act inflicting punishment,
including deprivation of property, without a trial, on named individuals or
members of a specific group.

due process clause
Clause in the Fifth Amendment limiting
the power of the national government;
similar to clause in the Fourteenth
Amendment prohibiting state governments from depriving any person of
life, liberty, or property without due
process of law.

selective incorporation
The process by which provisions of the Bill
of Rights are brought within the scope of
the Fourteenth Amendment and so
applied to state and local governments.

Selective incorporation of most provisions of the Bill of Rights into the Fourteenth Amendment is probably the most important constitutional development since the writing of the Constitution. It has profoundly altered the relationship between the national government and the states. It made the federal courts, under the guidance of the Supreme Court of the United States, the most important protectors of our liberties.

Recently, however, there has been a renewal of interest in state constitutions as independent sources of additional protection for civil liberties and civil rights.[6] Advocates of what has come to be called *new judicial federalism* contend that the U.S. Constitution should set minimum but not maximum standards to protect our rights. State bills of rights sometimes provide more protection of rights—the rights to equal education and personal privacy, for instance—than does the national Bill of Rights or the Supreme Court's rulings on its guarantees. Despite the revival of interest in state bills of rights, the U.S. Supreme Court and the national Bill of Rights remain the dominant protectors of civil liberties and civil rights.

FREEDOM OF RELIGION

The first words of the First Amendment are emphatic and brief: "Congress shall make no law respecting an *establishment* of religion, or prohibiting the *free exercise* thereof." Note there are *two* religion clauses: the establishment clause and the exercise clause. The Supreme Court has struggled to reconcile these two clauses, both of which are cast in absolute terms, and either of which, if expanded to a logical extreme, would clash with the other. Does a state scholarship for blind students given to a college student who decides to attend a college to become a minister violate the establishment clause by indirectly aiding religion? Or would denying the scholarship violate the student's free exercise of religion? The Supreme Court has held that giving such benefits does not violate the establishment clause.[7]

The Establishment Clause

In writing what has come to be called the **establishment clause**, the framers were reacting to the English system, wherein the Crown was the head not only of the government but also of the established church—the Church of England—and public officials were required to take an oath to support the established church as a condition of holding office. The establishment clause goes beyond merely separating government from religion by forbidding the establishment of a religion. It is designed to prevent three evils: government sponsorship of religion, government financial support of religion, and government involvement in religious matters. However, the clause does not prevent governments from "accommodating" religious needs. To what extent and under which conditions governments may accommodate these needs are at the heart of much of the debate in the Supreme Court and the country over interpreting the clause.

Controversies over the establishment clause are not easy to resolve. They stir deep feelings and frequently divide the justices among themselves. The prevailing interpretation stems from the decision in *Everson v Board of Education* (1947) that the establishment clause creates a "wall of separation" between church and state and prohibits any law or governmental action designed to specifically benefit any religion, even if all religions are treated the same.[8] That decision, though, was decided by a bare majority and upheld state support for transportation of children to private religious schools as a "child benefit."

The separation of church and state was further elaborated in *Lemon v Kurtzman* (1971), which laid down a three-part test: (1) a law must have a secular legislative purpose; (2) it must neither advance nor inhibit religion; and (3) it

establishment clause

Clause in the First Amendment that states that Congress shall make no law respecting an establishment of religion. It has been interpreted by the Supreme Court to forbid governmental support of any or all religions.

must avoid "excessive government entanglement with religion."[9] This so-called *Lemon* test is often, but not always, used because the justices remain divided over how much separation between government and religion is required by the First Amendment.

Another test, championed by Justice Sandra Day O'Connor, is the *endorsement test.* Justice O'Connor believes that the establishment clause forbids governmental practices that a reasonable observer would view as endorsing religion, even if there is no coercion.[10] The endorsement test has been honed in a series of decisions as the Court struggled with the question of whether governments may allow religious symbols to be displayed on, in, or near public properties and in public places. For example, the Court concluded that when a nativity scene was displayed in a shopping district together with Santa's house and other secular and religious symbols of the Christmas season, there was little danger that a reasonable person would conclude that the city was endorsing religion.[11] But the Constitution does not permit a city government to display the nativity scene on the steps of the city hall, because, in this context, the city gives the impression that it is endorsing the display's religious message.[12]

The Court's three most conservative justices—Chief Justice William Rehnquist and Justices Antonin Scalia and Clarence Thomas—support a *nonpreferentialist test.*[13] They believe the Constitution prohibits favoritism toward any particular religion but does not prohibit government aid to *all* religions. In their view, government may accommodate religious activities and even give nonpreferential support to religious organizations, so long as individuals are not legally coerced into participating in religious activities, and religious activities are not singled out for favorable treatment.

By contrast, the more liberal justices—Justices David H. Souter, John Paul Stevens, Ruth Bader Ginsburg, and Stephen Breyer—usually maintain that there should be *strict separation* between religion and the state.[14] They generally hold that even indirect aid for religion, such as scholarships or teaching materials and aids for students attending private religious schools, crosses the line separating the government from religion.

Applying these generalizations, we find that the establishment clause forbids states—including state universities, colleges, and school districts—from introducing

Prayer Before School Football Games

The school prayer issue occasioned a spirited argument at the Supreme Court during which a majority of the justices expressed reluctance to permit organized prayer at public high school football games. Such prayers almost inevitably give official endorsement to religious beliefs that may offend some students and parents.

The case started when a Mormon family and a Roman Catholic family sued a small school district in Texas, objecting to the Christian prayers offered by chaplains at school events. Since then, the district has modified its policies to have a student chosen in a schoolwide election offer a pregame invocation or message of his or her own choosing. The district is trying to persuade the court that prayer led by such an "independent speaker" creates no constitutional problem—unlike clergy-led prayer at graduation, which the court outlawed in a decision eight years ago.

It proved a difficult sell. Six justices suggested that using an elected student surrogate to deliver the prayer could not mask the school's role in organizing the religious worship or overcome the risk of indirect coercion inherent in prayer exercises in elementary and secondary schools.

SOURCE: *Santa Fe Independent School District v Doe*, 120 S. Ct. 2266 (2000).

Court cases have sought to prohibit prayers before football games because they coerce students of all faiths to participate in a school-sponsored religious ceremony.

AID FOR CHILDREN ATTENDING PAROCHIAL SCHOOLS

A troublesome area concerning the separation of church and state involves attempts by many states to provide financial assistance to students who attend parochial schools. The Supreme Court has tried to draw a line between permissible tax-provided aid to schoolchildren and impermissible aid to religion.

At the college level the problems are relatively simple. Tax funds may be used to construct buildings and operate educational programs at church-related schools, as long as the money is not spent directly on buildings used for religious purposes or on teaching religious subjects. Even if students choose to attend religious schools and become ministers, government aid to these students is permissible, because such aid has a secular purpose. Its effect on religion is the result of individual choice "and it does not confer any message of state endorsement of religion."*

At the elementary and secondary levels, however, the constitutional problems become more complicated. Here the secular and religious parts of institutions and instruction are much more closely interwoven. Also, students are younger and more susceptible to indoctrination, so the chances are greater that aid to church-operated schools might become aid to religion.

Despite the constitutional obstacles, some states have provided tax credits or deductions for those who send their children to private, largely church-affiliated schools. Such deductions or credits available *only* to parents of children attending nonpublic schools are unconstitutional, but allowing taxpaying parents to deduct or take a credit from their state income taxes for what they paid for tuition and other costs to send their children to school— public or private—is constitutional, even if most of the benefit goes to those who send their children to private religious schools.**

The Supreme Court has also approved using tax funds to provide students who attend primary and secondary church-operated schools (except those that deny admission because of race or religion) with textbooks, standardized tests, lunches, transportation to and from school, and diagnostic services for speech and hearing problems. For example, the Court upheld the assignment of a sign-language interpreter, paid for by public funds, to accompany a deaf child to a parochial school on the ground that this is aid to the student, not to a religion.*** And the Court recently upheld programs that provide tax-supported teachers to teach remedial and enrichment classes to dis-advantaged students, as well as programs providing computers in both public and parochial schools.****

Tax funds may *not* be used in religious schools to pay teachers' salaries, purchase equipment, produce teacher-prepared tests, repair facilities, or transport students on field trips. School authorities may not permit religious instructors to come into public school buildings during the school day to provide *religious* instruction, even on a voluntary basis.

A hot controversy remains whether states may use tax money to give parents vouchers for the tuition of children to attend schools of their choice, including religious schools. Cleveland, Milwaukee, and Florida have experimented with vouchers, but their programs have been challenged in the courts. Opponents argue that such voucher programs violate the establishment clause, while supporters counter that they do not, and to deny the use of vouchers for attending religious schools violates the free exercise clause. The Supreme Court has yet to rule on the matter.

*Witters v Washington Department of Services for the Blind, 474 US 481 (1986).

**Mueller v Allen, 463 US 388 (1983).

***Zobrest v Catalina Foothills School District, 515 US 1 (1993).

****Agostini v Felton, 521 US 74 (1997); Mitchell v Helms, 120 S.Ct. 2530 (2000).

devotional exercises into the public school curriculum, including school graduations and pre–football game events.[15] However, the Supreme Court has not, as some people assume, entirely prohibited prayer in public schools. It is not unconstitutional for students to pray in a school building. What is unconstitutional is sponsorship or encouragement of prayer *by public school authorities*.[16] Devotional reading of the Bible, recitation of the Lord's Prayer, and posting of the Ten Commandments on the walls of classrooms in public schools are also prohibited by the Constitution. A state may not forbid the teaching of evolution or require the teaching of "creation science"—the belief that human life did not evolve but rather was created by a single act of God.[17]

Tax exemptions for church properties, similar to those granted other nonprofit institutions, are constitutional. State legislatures and Congress may also hire chap-

lains to open each day's legislative session—a practice that has continued without interruption since the first session of Congress. But if done in a public school, this practice would be unconstitutional. Apparently, the difference is that legislators, as adults, are not "susceptible to religious indoctrination or peer pressure."[18] Also, as the joke goes, legislators need the prayer more.

The Free Exercise Clause

The right to hold any or no religious belief is one of our few absolute rights. The **free exercise clause** affirms that no government has authority to compel us to accept any creed or to deny us any right because of our beliefs or lack of them. Requiring religious oaths as a condition of public employment or as a prerequisite to running for public office is unconstitutional. In fact, the original Constitution states: "No religious Test shall ever be required as a Qualification to any Office or public Trust under the United States" (Article VI).

Although carefully protected, the right to practice a religion has had less protection than the right to hold particular beliefs. Prior to 1990 the Supreme Court carefully scrutinized laws allegedly infringing on religious practices and insisted that the government provide some compelling governmental interest to justify actions that might infringe upon somebody's religion: In other words, the First Amendment was thought to throw "a mantle of protection" around religious practices, and the burden was on the government to justify interfering with them in the least restrictive way.

Then, in *Employment Division v Smith* (1990), the Rehnquist Court significantly altered the interpretation of the free exercise clause by discarding the compelling governmental interest test for overriding the interests of religious minorities.[19] As long as a law is generally applicable and does not single out and ban religious practices, the law may be applied to conduct even if it burdens a particular religious practice.

The ruling in *Employment Division v Smith* was controversial and led Congress to enact the Religious Freedom Restoration Act of 1993 (RFRA), which aimed to override the *Smith* decision and to restore the earlier test prohibiting the government—federal, state, or local—from limiting a person's exercise of religion unless the government demonstrates a compelling interest that is advanced by the least restrictive means. Congress asserted its power to pass RFRA because the Fourteenth Amendment gives it the authority to enforce rights secured by that amendment, including the right to free exercise of religion.

However, when the Catholic archbishop of San Antonio was denied a building permit in 1997 to enlarge a church in Boerne, Texas, because the remodeling did not comply with the city's historical preservation plan, he claimed that the city's denial of a building permit interfered with religious freedom as protected by the Religious Freedom Restoration Act. The Supreme Court then ruled RFRA to be unconstitutional because Congress was attempting to define—rather than enforce or remedy—constitutional rights and thereby was assuming the role of the courts, which contradicted "vital principles necessary to maintain separation of powers and the federal balance."[20]

Tensions between the establishment and free exercise clauses have recently become more prominent. On the one hand, the University of Virginia denied a Christian student group funds to pay for the printing of its newspaper, *Wide Awake*, because it interpreted the establishment clause to forbid allocating student fee money to a newspaper that "primarily promotes a belief in or about a deity." The students argued that the university deprived them of their freedom of speech, including religious speech, and the Supreme Court agreed with the students.[21] On the other hand, some Christian students at the University of Wisconsin objected to the use of mandatory student activity fees for funding groups they deemed offensive and contrary to their religious beliefs. They argued that they should be exempt from paying that portion of their fees, but the Supreme Court rejected their claim.[22]

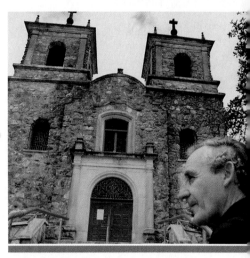

Reverend Anthony Cummins, pastor of St. Peter the Apostle Church, in front of his church in Boerne, Texas, after a battle with city officials who denied the church permission to build an addition to the historic structure.

free exercise clause
Clause in the First Amendment that states that Congress shall make no law prohibiting the free exercise of religion. Children may pray in public schools, provided that the prayer is not authorized, organized, or endorsed by the school authorities.

You Decide...

Should the Bill of Rights be amended to prohibit flag burning?

The American flag arouses patriotic emotions in Americans, many of whom fought and saw friends die under that banner. It is understandable that they would be angry to see that flag burned by protesters. Do you think the Constitution should be amended to give Congress the right to prohibit desecration of the American flag? Or would a constitutional amendment to prohibit flag burning be an unconstitutional violation of free speech?

bad tendency test
Interpretation of the First Amendment that would permit legislatures to forbid speech that has a tendency to cause people to engage in illegal action.

clear and present danger test
Interpretation of the First Amendment that holds government cannot punish a person for speech unless the speech presents a clear and present danger that it will lead to illegal acts. To shout "Fire!" falsely in a crowded theater is Justice Oliver Wendell Holmes's famous example.

preferred position doctrine
Interpretation of the First Amendment that holds that freedom of expression is so essential to the operation of a democracy that judges should give it special protection and should almost never allow governments to punish persons for what they say, only for what they do.

nonprotected speech
Libel, obscenity, fighting words, and commercial speech, which are not entitled in all circumstances to constitutional protection.

FREE SPEECH AND FREE PEOPLE

Government by the people is based on every person's right to speak freely, to organize in groups, to question the decisions of the government, and to campaign openly against them. Only through free and uncensored expression of opinion can government be kept responsive to the electorate and political power transferred peacefully. Elections, separation of powers, and constitutional guarantees are meaningless unless all persons have the right to speak frankly and to hear and judge for themselves the worth of what others have to say. As Justice Oliver Wendell Holmes observed, "The best test of truth is the power of the thought to get itself accepted in the competition of the market. . . . That at any rate is the theory of our Constitution. It is an experiment, as all life is an experiment."[23]

Free speech is not simply the personal right of individuals to have their say; it is also the right of the rest of us to hear them. John Stuart Mill, whose *Essay on Liberty* (1859) is the classic defense of free speech, put it this way:

> The peculiar evil of silencing the expression of opinion, is that it is robbing the human race. . . . If the opinion is right, they are deprived of the opportunity of exchanging error for truth; if wrong, they lose what is almost as great a benefit, the clearer perception and livelier impression of truth, produced by its collision with error.[24]

Americans overwhelming support the principle of freedom of expression in general. Yet some who say they believe in free speech draw the line at ideas they consider dangerous, or when speech is directed at them or is critical of their race, religion, or ethnic origin. But what is a dangerous idea? Who decides? In the realm of political ideas, who can find an objective, eternally valid standard of right? The search for truth involves the possibility—even the inevitability—of error. The search cannot go on unless it proceeds freely in the minds and speech of all. This means, in the words of Justice Robert Jackson, "Freedom to differ is not limited to things that do not matter much. That would be a mere shadow of freedom. The test of its substance is the right to differ as to things that touch the heart of the existing order."[25]

Even though the First Amendment explicitly denies Congress the power to pass any law abridging freedom of speech, the amendment has never been interpreted in absolute terms. Like almost all rights, the freedoms of speech and of the press are limited. In discussing the constitutional power of government to regulate speech, it is useful to distinguish among *belief*, *speech*, and *action*.

At one extreme is the right to *believe* as we wish. Despite occasional deviations in practice, the traditional American view is that government should not punish a person for beliefs or interfere in any way with the freedom of conscience. At the other extreme is *action*, which is usually subject to governmental restraint. As has been said, "The right to swing your arm ends where the other person's nose begins."

Speech stands somewhere between belief and action. It is not an absolute right, as is belief, but neither is it as exposed to governmental restraint, as is action. Some kinds of speech—libel, obscenity, fighting words, and commercial speech—are not entitled in all circumstances to constitutional protection. Many problems arise in distinguishing between what does and does not fit into the categories of nonprotected speech. People disagree, and it usually falls upon the courts to decide and to defend the free speech of individual and minority dissenters.

The Act of Judging: Line-Drawing

Plainly, questions of free speech require that judges weigh a variety of factors: What was said? Where was it said? How was it said? Which level of government is attempting to regulate the speech—a city council speaking for a few people, or the Congress speaking for many? (The Supreme Court is much more deferential to acts of Congress than to those of a city council or state legislature.) How is the government attempting to regulate the speech—by prior restraint (censorship) or by punishment

after the speech? Why is the government doing so—to preserve the public peace or to prevent criticism of those in power? These and scores of other considerations are involved in the never-ending process of determining what the First Amendment permits and what it forbids.

Historic Constitutional Tests

It is useful to start with the three constitutional tests developed in the first part of the twentieth century: the bad tendency test, the clear and present danger test, and the preferred position doctrine. Although they are no longer applied, they provide a background for the current judicial approach to governmental regulation of speech and to the courts' expanding protection for free speech.

THE BAD TENDENCY TEST   This test was rooted in the English common law. According to the **bad tendency test**, judges presumed it was reasonable to forbid speech that has a tendency to corrupt society or cause people to engage in illegal action. The test was abandoned because it swept too broadly and ran "contrary to the fundamental premises underlying the First Amendment as the guardian of our democracy."[26] Some legislators still appear to hold this position today, and it also seems to be the view of some college students, who want to see their institution punish student colleagues or faculty who express "hateful" or "offensive" ideas.

THE CLEAR AND PRESENT DANGER TEST   This is perhaps the most famous test. The **clear and present danger test** was formulated by Justice Oliver Wendell Holmes, Jr., in *Schenck v United States* (1919), as an alternative to the bad tendency test. In the words of Justice Holmes: "The question in every case is whether the words are used in circumstances and are of such a nature as to create a clear and present danger that they will bring about substantive evils that Congress has a right to prevent."[27] A government should not be allowed to interfere with speech unless it can prove, ultimately to a skeptical judiciary, that the particular speech in question presents an immediate danger—for example, speech leading to a riot, the destruction of property, or the corruption of an election.

Supporters of the clear and present danger test concede speech is not an absolute right. Yet they believe free speech to be so fundamental to the operations of a constitutional democracy that no government should be allowed to restrict speech unless it can demonstrate a close connection between the speech and an imminent lawless action. To shout "Fire!" falsely in a crowded theater is the most famous example of unprotected speech.

THE PREFERRED POSITION DOCTRINE   This was advanced in the 1940s when the Court applied all of the guarantees of the First Amendment to the states. The **preferred position doctrine** came close to the position that freedom of expression—that is, the use of words and pictures—should rarely, if ever, be curtailed. This interpretation of the First Amendment gives these freedoms, especially freedom of speech and of conscience, a preferred position in our constitutional hierarchy. Judges have a special duty to protect these freedoms and should be most skeptical about laws trespassing on them. Once that judicial responsibility was established, judges had to draw lines between nonprotected and protected speech, as well as between speech and nonspeech.

NONPROTECTED AND PROTECTED SPEECH

Today, the Supreme Court holds that only four narrow categories of speech—*libel, obscenity, fighting words,* and *commercial speech*—are **nonprotected speech** because they lack social redeeming value and are not essential to democratic deliberations and self-governance.

The fact that nonprotected speech does not receive First Amendment protection does not mean that the constitutional issues relating to these kinds of speech are

Police arrest Scott Tyler of Chicago after he set fire to an American flag on the steps of the Capitol building in Washington. The Supreme Court ruled that freedom of speech even covers "symbolic speech" like burning the U.S. flag.

Thinking It Through...

On June 21, 1989 the Supreme Court, in *Texas v Johnson*, decided by a 5 to 4 vote that the First Amendment protects the act of burning the flag as freedom of expression. President George Bush denounced the decision and called for a constitutional amendment that would nullify it. Congress responded by passing a federal law that would make it a crime to burn or to deface the flag—whatever one's purposes or intent. In June 1990 the Supreme Court declared that law unconstitutional in *United States v Eichman*.

A Flag Amendment to the Constitution would give Congress the power to prohibit flag desecration. Public opinion polls show strong support for it. Forty-nine state legislatures have already indicated they would ratify such an amendment, far more than the 36 needed. A Senate majority has several times voted in favor of such an amendment, but has fallen short of the two-thirds majority needed to pass a constitutional amendment.

Before you decide, you might want to read the opinions of the Supreme Court justices in *Texas v Johnson*, 491 US 397 (1989) and *United States v Eichman*, 496 US 310 (1990). You may listen to the oral arguments in these cases by going to the Oyez website at www.oyez.nwu.edu.

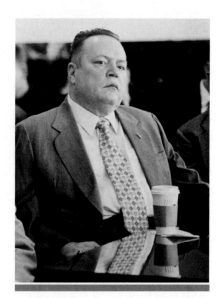

Hustler *publisher Larry Flynt agrees to a plea bargain in which obscenity charges were dropped and a fine imposed if Flynt removed X-rated videos from a downtown store.*

simple. How we prove *libel*, how we define *obscenity*, how we determine which words are *fighting words*, and how much *commercial* speech may be regulated remain hotly contested issues.

Libel

At one time newspaper publishers and editors had to take considerable care about what they wrote for fear they might be prosecuted for **libel**—written defamation or false statements—by the government or sued by individuals. Today, through a progressive elevation of constitutional standards, it has become more difficult to win a libel suit against a newspaper or magazine.

Seditious libel—defaming, criticizing, and advocating the overthrow of government—was once subject to criminal penalties but no longer is. Seditious libel was rooted in the common law of England, which has no First Amendment. In 1798, only seven years after the First Amendment had been ratified, Congress enacted the first national law aimed against **sedition**, the Sedition Act of 1798. Those were perilous times for the young Republic, for war with France seemed imminent. The Federalists, in control of both Congress and the presidency, persuaded themselves that national safety required some suppression of speech. But popular reaction to the Sedition Act helped defeat the Federalists in the elections of 1800, and the Sedition Act expired in 1801. The Federalists had failed to grasp the democratic idea that a person may criticize the government, oppose its policies, and work for the removal of those in power, but still be loyal to the nation. They also failed to grasp the distinction between *seditious speech* and *seditious action*—conspiring to commit and engaging in violence against the government, which can be prosecuted and punished.

Another attempt to limit political criticism of the government was the Smith Act of 1940. That law forbid advocating the overthrow of the government, distributing material advocating the overthrow of government by violence, and organizing any group having such purposes. In 1951, during the cold war, the Supreme Court agreed that the Smith Act could be applied to the leaders of the Communist party who had been charged with conspiring to advocate the violent overthrow of the government.[28]

Since then, however, the Court has substantially modified constitutional doctrine, giving all political speech First Amendment protection. In *The New York Times v Sullivan* (1964), seditious libel was declared unconstitutional.[29] Now, neither Congress nor any government may outlaw mere advocacy of the abstract doctrine of violent overthrow of government: "The essential distinction is that those to whom the advocacy is addressed must be urged to do something now or in the future, rather than merely to believe in something."[30] Moreover, advocacy of the use of force may not be forbidden "except where such advocacy is directed to inciting or producing imminent lawless action and is likely to incite or produce such action."[31]

In the landmark ruling in *The New York Times v Sullivan* and subsequent cases, the Supreme Court established guidelines for libel cases and severely limited state power to award monetary damages in libel suits brought by public officials against critics of official conduct. Neither public officials nor public figures can collect damages for comments made about them unless they can prove with "convincing clarity" the comments were made with "actual malice." *Actual malice* means not merely that the defendant made false statements but that the "statements were made with a knowing or reckless disregard for the truth."[32]

Public figures cannot collect damages even when subject to outrageous, clearly inaccurate parodies and cartoons. Such was the case when *Hustler* magazine printed a parody of the Reverend Jerry Falwell; the Court held parodies and cartoons cannot reasonably be understood as describing actual facts or actual events.[33] Nor does the mere fact that a public figure is quoted as saying something that he or she did *not* say amount to a libel, unless the alteration in what the person said was made deliberately, with knowledge of its falsity, and "results in material change."[34]

libel

Written defamation of another person. Especially in the case of public officials and public figures, the constitutional tests designed to restrict libel actions are very rigid.

sedition

Attempting to overthrow the government by force or to interrupt its activities by violence.

Constitutional standards for libel charges brought by private persons are not as rigid as those for public officials and figures. State laws may permit private persons to collect damages without having to prove actual malice if they can prove the statements made about them are false and were negligently published.[35]

Obscenity and Pornography

Obscene publications are not entitled to constitutional protection, but members of the Supreme Court, like everybody else, have great difficulty in defining obscenity. As Justice Potter Stewart put it, "I know it when I see it."[36] Or, as the second Justice John Marshall Harlan explained, "One man's vulgarity is another man's lyric."[37]

In *Miller v California* (1973), the Court finally agreed on a constitutional definition of **obscenity**. A work may be considered legally obscene provided: (1) the average person, applying contemporary standards of the particular community, would find that the work, taken as a whole, appeals to a prurient interest in sex; (2) the work depicts or describes in a patently offensive way sexual conduct specifically defined by the applicable law or authoritatively construed; and (3) the work, taken as a whole, lacks serious literary, artistic, political, or scientific value.[38]

Pornography used to be merely a synonym for obscenity. The *Miller* standard has meant that only hard-core pornography is constitutionally unprotected. X-rated movies and adult theaters that fall short of the constitutional definition of obscenity are entitled to some constitutional protection, but less protection than political speech, and they are subject to greater government regulation. Cities may, as New York City has done, also regulate where adult theaters may be located by zoning laws,[39] and they may ban totally nude dancing in adult nightclubs.[40] Under narrowly drawn statutes, state and local governments can also ban the sale of "adult" magazines to minors, even if such materials would not be considered legally obscene if sold to adults.

The Court has also held that *child pornography*—sexually explicit materials either about minors or aimed at them—is not protected by the First Amendment.[41] Just as the government may protect minors, so apparently may it protect members of the armed forces. The Supreme Court left standing a ruling of a lower court upholding an act of Congress forbidding the sale or rental on military property of magazines or videos whose "dominant theme" is to portray nudity "in a lascivious way."[42]

Pressure for regulating pornography came primarily from political conservatives and religious fundamentalists concerned that it undermines moral standards. More recently, some feminists have joined them, arguing that pornography is degrading and perpetuates sexual discrimination and violence. They argue that just as sexually explicit materials about minors are not entitled to First Amendment protection, so should there be no protection for pornographic materials. They contend that pornography promotes sexual abuse of individual women and maintains the social subordination of women as a class. Some feminists define pornographic materials more broadly than the Court has and would include sexually explicit pictures or words that depict women as sexual objects enjoying pain and humiliation or that present abuse of women as a sexual stimulus for men.[43]

Not all feminists favor antipornography ordinances, yet those who do have been joined by social conservatives, and thus a new battle over pornography continues to be fought. For this new antipornography coalition to be successful, a substantial alteration in constitutional doctrine will be required. Unlike the Canadian Supreme Court, which redefined obscenity to include materials that degrade women,[44] the U.S. Supreme Court does not appear willing to substantially change current doctrine.

The Communications Decency Act of 1996

The Communications Decency Act of 1996 made it a federal crime to use the Internet to knowingly transmit obscene or indecent and "patently offensive" words or pictures to minors. Indecency is defined as communication that depicts patently offensive materials about sexual or excretory activities, as measured by contemporary community standards.

In defending the act before the Supreme Court, the Justice Department contended: "The Internet threatens to give every child a free pass into the equivalent of every adult bookstore and every adult video store in the country." The American Civil Liberties Union countered, "The government cannot reduce the adult population to reading or viewing only what is appropriate for children."

The Supreme Court struck down the provisions against transmission of indecent communication and agreed with the district judge that the Internet "as the most participatory form of mass speech yet developed, deserves the highest protection from governmental intrusion." Cyberspace, the Supreme Court concluded, should be treated like books and magazines and thus subject to their broad constitutional protection. The Internet, unlike broadcasting, is not a scarce commodity and should not be subject to the same kind of regulation as the broadcast industry. Moreover, the Internet is not as invasive as radio or television and should be given the same constitutional protection as the print media.

Congress followed with the Child Online Protection Act of 1998, which its supporters contend is narrower than the Communications Decency Act. The new law makes it a crime for the operator of a commercial website to knowingly make available to those under age 17 sexually explicit material considered "harmful to minors."

The decision in *Reno v ACLU* (1997) merits your close attention. Appropriately, the decision and the oral argument can be found on the Web, at www.findlaw.com. You can also learn more about this case and other controversies over First Amendment freedoms at the Freedom Forum's home page: www.freedomforum.org.

obscenity
Quality or state of a work that, taken as a whole, appeals to a prurient interest in sex by depicting sexual conduct in a patently offensive way and that lacks serious literary, artistic, political, or scientific value.

You Decide . . .

Hate speech on campus

Recent incidents of blatantly offensive signs and comments on college campuses have led to cases challenging so-called "hate codes." That speech may be insulting or racially offensive or sexist does not mean that it lacks constitutional protection. As the Supreme Court has repeatedly said, "If there is a bedrock principle underlying the First Amendment, it is that the Government may not prohibit the expression of an idea simply because society finds the idea offensive or disagreeable."* Do you think students should be punished for insulting or vicious remarks about minorities on campus?

*United States v Eichman, 496 US 310 (1990).

fighting words
Words that by their very nature inflict injury upon those to whom they are addressed or cause acts of violence by them.

commercial speech
Advertisements and commercials for products and services that receive less First Amendment protection, primarily false and misleading ads.

prior restraint
Restraint or censorship imposed before a speech is made or a newspaper published, usually presumed to be unconstitutional.

Fighting Words

Fighting words were held to be constitutionally unprotected because "their very utterance may inflict injury or tend to incite an immediate breach of peace."[45] That the words are abusive, offensive, and insulting, or that they create anger, alarm, or resentment is not sufficient. Thus, a four-letter word worn on a sweatshirt was not judged to be a fighting word in the constitutional sense, even though it was offensive and angered some people.[46] In recent years, the Court has overturned convictions for uttering fighting words and struck down laws that criminalized "hate speech"—insulting racial, ethnic, and gender slurs.[47]

Commercial Speech

Commercial speech—such as advertisements and commercials—was held to be unprotected because it was deemed to have lesser value than political speech. But in recent years the Court has reconsidered and extended more protection to commercial speech, as it has to fighting words. In *44 Liquormart, Inc. v Rhode* Island (1996), for instance, the Court struck down a law forbidding the advertising of the price of alcoholic drinks.[48] It now appears that states may only forbid and punish false and misleading advertising, along with advertising the sale of anything illegal—for example, narcotics. Although the Supreme Court has not specifically removed it from the nonprotected category, the Court has so interpreted the First, Fifth, and Fourteenth Amendments to provide considerable constitutional protection for commercial speech.

Protected Speech

Apart from these four categories of nonprotected speech, all other expression is constitutionally protected, and courts strictly scrutinize government regulation of such speech. The Supreme Court uses the following doctrines to measure the limits of governmental power to regulate speech.

PRIOR RESTRAINT   Of all the forms of governmental interference with expression, judges are most suspicious of those that impose **prior restraint**—censorship before publication. Prior restraints include governmental review and approval before a speech can be made, before a motion picture can be shown, or before a newspaper can be published. Most prior restraints are unconstitutional, as the Court has said: "Any system of prior restraints of expression comes to this Court bearing a heavy presumption against its constitutional validity."[49] About the only prior restraints approved by the Court relate to military and security matters, but also to high school authorities' control over the style and content of student newspapers.[50] Student newspapers at colleges and universities receive the same protections as other newspapers, because they are independent and financially separate from the college or university.

VOID FOR VAGUENESS   Laws must not be so vague that people do not know whether their speech would violate the law and, thus, are afraid to exercise protected freedoms. Laws must not allow those who administer them so much discretion that they may discriminate against those whose views they dislike. For these reasons, the Court strikes down laws under the void for vagueness doctrine.

LEAST DRASTIC MEANS   Even for an important purpose, a legislature may not pass a law that impinges on First Amendment freedoms if other, least drastic means are available. To illustrate, a state may protect the public from unscrupulous lawyers, but it may not do so by forbidding attorneys from advertising their fees for simple services. The state could adopt other ways to protect the public from such lawyers that do not impinge on their freedom of speech; it could, for example, provide for the disbarment of lawyers who mislead their clients.

CONTENT AND VIEWPOINT NEUTRALITY   Laws concerning the time, place, or manner of speech that regulate some kinds of speech but not others, or that regulate speech expressing some views but not others, are much more likely to be struck down than those that are content-neutral or viewpoint-neutral; that is, laws that apply to *all* kinds of speech and to *all* views. For example, the Constitution does not prohibit laws forbidding the posting of handbills on telephone poles. Yet laws prohibiting only religious handbills or handbills advocating racism or sexism would, in all probability, be declared unconstitutional because they would relate to the kind of handbills or what is being said, rather than applying to all handbills regardless of what they say.

The lack of viewpoint neutrality was the grounds for the Court striking down a St. Paul, Minnesota, ordinance that prohibited the display of a symbol that would arouse anger on the basis of race, color, creed, religion, or gender. The ordinance was not considered viewpoint-neutral because it did not forbid displays that might arouse anger for other reasons, for example, because of political affiliation.[51]

FREEDOM OF THE PRESS

Courts have carefully protected the press's right to publish information, no matter how journalists get it. But some reporters, editors, and others argue that this is not enough. They insist that the First Amendment gives them the right to ignore legal requests and to withhold information. They also contend that the First Amendment gives them a *right of access*, a right to go wherever they need to go to get information.

Does the Press Have the Right to Withhold Information?

Although most reporters have challenged the right of public officials to withhold information, they claim the right to do so themselves, including the right to keep information from grand juries and legislative investigating committees. Without this right to withhold information, reporters insist they cannot assure their sources of confidentiality, and they will not be able to get the information they need to keep the public informed.

The Supreme Court has, however, refused to acknowledge that reporters, and presumably scholars, have a constitutional right to ignore legal requests such as subpoenas and withhold information from governmental bodies.[52] It is up to Congress and the states to provide such privileges for news reporters, and many states have passed so-called *press shield laws* providing some protection for reporters from state court subpoenas.

Does the Press Have the Right to Know?

The press has argued that if reporters are excluded from places where public business is conducted or are denied access to information in government files, they are not able to perform their historic function of keeping the public informed. In similar fashion, some reporters argue that they may enter facilities such as food markets, child care centers, and homes for the mentally ill, even using false identities, to expose racial discrimination, employment discrimination, and financial frauds. The Supreme Court, however, has refused to acknowledge a *constitutional right of the press to know*, although it did concede that there is a First Amendment right for the press, along with the public, to be present at criminal trials.[53]

Although they have no constitutional obligation to do so, many states have adopted *sunshine laws* requiring government agencies to open their meetings to the public and the press. Congress requires most federal executive agencies to open hearings and meetings of advisory groups to the public, and most congressional committee meetings are open to the public. Federal and state courtroom trials are

Thinking It Through...

The speech of faculty and staff at universities and colleges, public or private, is protected by the Constitution from regulation by the government. As state agencies, public universities and colleges are subject to the restrictions of the Constitution. Nonetheless, as an employer a public university has some leeway in regulating the speech of its employees, more leeway than it has in regulating the speech of its students—especially student speech outside of the classroom or away from residence halls. The administration has some discretion—in fact, under federal laws, some obligation—to control racially or sexually harassing speech by faculty and staff. In its role of landlord for residence halls, universities and colleges have the authority to impose reasonable time, place, and manner regulations. As institutions of higher learning, they have the responsibility to overcome bigotry and stereotyping.

Private universities and colleges are not subject to constitutional limitations on how they may regulate the speech of their students. However, private universities that receive federal funds may find that their freedom to punish the use of offensive speech by students is limited by federal laws and regulations. Federal and state laws regulating the responsibilities of employers to provide a workplace free from sexual harassment also apply to universities, both private and public.

also open, but judicial conferences, in which the judges discuss how to decide the cases, are not.

Congress has authorized the president to establish a classification system to keep some public documents and governmental files secret, and it is a crime for any person to divulge such classified information. So far, however, although they have been threatened, no newspapers have been prosecuted for doing so.

The Freedom of Information Act (FOIA) of 1966 as amended liberalized access to nonclassified federal government records. This act makes the records of federal executive agencies available subject to certain exceptions, such as private financial transactions, personnel records, criminal investigation files, interoffice memoranda, and letters used in internal decision making. If federal agencies fail to move promptly on requests for information, applicants are entitled to speedy judicial hearings. The burden is on an agency to explain its refusal to supply material, and if the judge decides the government has improperly withheld information, the government has to pay the legal fees. Since the inception of FOIA, more than 250,000 people have requested information, and more than 90 percent of these requests have been granted.

President Bill Clinton issued an executive order calling for automatic declassification of almost all government documents after 25 years. Any person who wants access to documents that are not declassified can appeal to an Interagency Security Classification Appeals panel, which has a record of ruling in favor of releasing documents. The Electronic Freedom of Information Act of 1996 requires most federal agencies to put their files online and to establish an index of all their records. The National Aeronautics and Space Administration (NASA) has done the most of the federal agencies (see www.firstgov.com). One of the most frequent requests to NASA's Electronic Reading Room is for documents relating to unidentified flying objects (UFOs).

Free Press versus Fair Trials

When newspapers and television report in vivid detail the facts of a crime, interview prosecutors and police, question witnesses, and hold press conferences for defendants and their attorneys—as in the O. J. Simpson murder and Oklahoma City bombing cases—they may so inflame the public that finding a panel of impartial jurors and conducting a fair trial is difficult. In England, strict rules determine what the media may report, and judges do not hesitate to punish newspapers that comment on pending criminal proceedings. In the United States, in contrast, free comment is protected. Yet the Supreme Court has not been indifferent to protecting persons on trial from inflammatory publicity. Its remedies have been to order new trials or to instruct judges to impose sanctions on prosecutors and police, not on reporters.

Federal rules of criminal procedure forbid radio or photographic coverage of criminal cases in federal courts, but most states permit televising courtroom proceedings, and court TV programs have become very popular.

OTHER MEDIA AND COMMUNICATIONS

When the First Amendment was written, freedom of "the press" referred to leaflets, newspapers, and books. Today the amendment protects other media as well—the mails, motion pictures, billboards, radio, television, cable, telephones, fax machines, and the Internet. Because each form of communication entails special problems, each needs a different degree of protection.

The Mails

More than 80 years ago, Justice Oliver Wendell Holmes, Jr., wrote in dissent: "The United States may give up the Post Office when it sees fit, but while it carries it on, the use of the mails is almost as much a part of free speech as is the right to use our

tongues."[54] In 1965 the Court adopted Holmes's view by striking down an act that had directed the postmaster general to detain foreign mailings of "communist political propaganda" and to deliver these materials only upon the addressee's request.[55] The Court has also set aside federal laws authorizing postal authorities to exclude from the mails materials they consider obscene.

Although government censorship of mail is unconstitutional, household censorship is not. The Court has sustained a law giving householders the right to ask the postmaster to order mailers to delete their names from certain mailing lists and to refrain from sending any advertisements that they believe to be "erotically arousing or sexually provocative."[56] Moreover, Congress may forbid—and has forbidden—the use of mailboxes for any materials except those sent through the United States mails.

Handbills, Sound Trucks, and Billboards

Religious and political pamphlets, leaflets, and handbills have been historic weapons in the defense of liberty, and their distribution is constitutionally protected. So, too, is the use of their contemporary counterparts—sound trucks and billboards. A state cannot restrain the distribution of leaflets merely to keep its streets clean,[57] but it may impose reasonable restrictions on their distribution so long as they are neutrally enforced, without regard to the content of the expression.

Motion Pictures and Plays

Prior censorship of films to prevent the showing of obscenity is not necessarily unconstitutional; however, laws calling for submission of films to a government review board are constitutional only if there is a prompt judicial hearing. The burden is on the government to prove to the court that the particular film in question is obscene. Prior censorship of films by review boards used to be common in some places. Live performances, such as plays and revues, are also entitled to constitutional protection.[58]

Broadcast and Cable Communications

Television remains an important means of distributing news and appealing for votes, though the Web has been gaining in popularity. Yet of all the mass media, broadcasting receives the least First Amendment protection. Congress has established a system of commercial broadcasting, supplemented by the Corporation for Public Broadcasting, which provides funds for public radio and television. The Federal Communications Commission (FCC) regulates the entire system by granting licenses and making regulations for their use.

The First Amendment would prevent censorship if the FCC tried to impose it. The First Amendment does not, however, prevent the FCC from imposing sanctions on stations that broadcast filthy words, even though such indecencies are not legally obscene.[59] The FCC did precisely that when it fined Infinity Broadcasting for indecent remarks by "shock jock" Howard Stern. Nor does the First Amendment prevent the FCC from refusing to renew a license if, in its opinion, a broadcaster does not serve the public interest.

The Supreme Court allowed more governmental regulation of broadcasters than of newspaper and magazine publishers because there were a limited number of airwaves. However, technological changes such as cable television, videotapes, and satellite broadcasting have opened up new means of communication and brought competition to the electronic media. Recognizing these changes, Congress passed the Telecommunications Act of 1996, allowing telephone companies, broadcasters, and cable TV stations to compete with one another. In adopting the act, Congress did not abandon all government regulation of the airways. On the contrary, the act calls for many new regulations, for example requiring that all new television sets sold in the United States be equipped with V-chips that allow viewers to block programs containing violent or sexual material.

At a press conference, Howard Stern defends his use of raunchy language and subject matter that led to the FCC fining the Infinity Broadcasting network.

The Court has upheld a congressional requirement that cable television stations must carry the signals of local broadcast television stations.[60] The Court has also held that Congress may authorize cable operators to refuse access to leased channels for "patently offensive" programs. The Court, however, struck down congressional requirements that if a cable operator allows such offensive programming, it must be blocked and unscrambled through special devices. In *United States v Playboy Entertainment Group* (2000), the Court underscored the greater protection for cable than for broadcast television. Whereas broadcast television may be required to provide programming for children and not air violence at certain times, the Court held that such rules do not apply to cable television because unwanted programming can be blocked at the household.[61]

Telecommunications and the Internet

More than 30 million Americans log on to the Internet to buy books, clothing, jewelry, airplane tickets, stocks, and bonds. Because the Internet has become a commercial marketplace and a major channel for communication, Congress is struggling with issues raised by cyberspace communication: Should the national government preempt state taxation? Do existing laws against copyright piracy apply to the Web? Should there be national regulation of junk e-mail, or can state laws take care of the problem? Should Congress try to protect the privacy of those who use the Web? (For more information about privacy and developments on the Web, go to the Electronic Privacy Information Center at **www.epic.org**.)

As Congress and the state legislatures begin to deal with these and other new problems, legislators and judges will have to apply traditional constitutional principles to new technologies and means of communication. The Court distinguishes between a limited ban on indecent messages on radio and broadcast television and those on telephones, cable television, and the Internet. Radio and broadcast messages are readily available to children and can intrude into the privacy of the home without prior warning. By contrast, telephone messages may be blocked, and access by minors is more readily restricted.[62] In its first ruling on First Amendment protection for the Internet, *Reno v American Civil Liberties Union* (1997), the Court struck down provisions of the Communications Decency Act of 1996 that had made it a crime to send obscene or indecent messages to anyone under 18 years of age. The Court emphasized the unique character of the Internet, holding that it is less intrusive than radio and broadcast television.[63]

FREEDOM OF ASSEMBLY

In the fall of 1998, Khallid Abdul Muhammad, a known racist and anti-Semite, organized a "Million Youth March" in New York City. Mayor Rudolph Giuliani denied a permit for the march on grounds that it would be a "hate march." A federal appeals court upheld a lower court ruling that denial of the permit was unconstitutional; however, the three-judge panel placed restrictions on the event, limiting its duration to four hours and scaling it back to a six-block area. The march proceeded, surrounded by police in riot gear who broke up the demonstration after Muhammad delivered a vitriolic speech against police, Jews, and city officials.[64]

It took judicial authorities to defend the rights of these unpopular speakers and marchers, but it is not always the "bad guys" whose rights have to be protected by the courts. It also took judicial intervention in the 1960s to preserve for Martin Luther King, Jr., and for those who marched with him, the right to demonstrate in the streets of southern cities on behalf of civil rights for African Americans.

Such incidents present a classic free speech problem. It is almost always easier, and certainly politically more prudent, to maintain order by curbing public demonstrations of unpopular groups. On the other hand, if police did not have the right to order groups to disperse, public order would be at the mercy of those who resort to street demonstrations to create tensions and provoke street battles.

New York City police in riot gear formed a human wall in front of the Million Youth March and charged the stage after Khallid Abdul Muhammad, organizer of the rally, urged the audience to riot and kill.

Public Forums and Time, Place, and Manner Regulations

The Constitution protects the right to speak, but it does not give people the right to communicate their views to everyone, every place, at every time they wish. No one has the right to block traffic or to hold parades or make speeches in public streets or on public sidewalks whenever he or she wishes. Governments may not censor what can be said, but they can make *reasonable time, place,* and *manner* regulations for protests or parades. The Supreme Court has divided public property into three categories: public forums, limited public forums, and nonpublic forums. The extent to which governments may limit access depends on the kind of forum involved.

Public forums are public places historically associated with the free exercise of expressive activities, such as streets, sidewalks, and parks. Courts look closely at time, place, and manner regulations that apply to these traditional public forums to ensure that they are being applied evenhandedly and that action is not taken because of what is being said rather than how and where or by whom it is being said.[65]

Other kinds of public property, such as rooms in a city hall or after-hour use of school buildings, may be designated as *limited public forums*, available for assembly and speech for limited purposes, a limited amount of time, and even for a limited class of speakers (such as only students, only teachers, or only employees), provided the distinctions between those allowed access and those not allowed access are not biased.

Nonpublic forums include public facilities such as libraries, courthouses, prisons, schools, swimming pools, and government offices that are open to the public but are not public forums. As long as people use such facilities within the normal bounds of conduct, they may not be constitutionally restrained from doing so. However, people may be excluded from such places as a government office or a school if they engage in activities for which the facilities were not created. They have no right to interfere with programs or try to take over a building—especially facilities such as a university president's office—in order to stage a political protest.

Does the right of peaceful assembly include the right to violate a law nonviolently but deliberately? We have no precise answer, but in general, **civil disobedience**, even if peaceful, is not a protected right. When Dr. Martin Luther King, Jr., and his followers refused to comply with a state court's injunction forbidding them to parade in Birmingham without first securing a permit, the Supreme Court sustained their conviction, even though there was serious doubt about the constitutionality of the injunction and the ordinance on which it was based.[66]

More recently, the First Amendment right of anti-abortion protesters to picket in front of abortion clinics has come into conflict with a woman's right to go to an abortion clinic. Protesters have often massed in front of clinics, shouting at employ-

civil disobedience
Action in which people refuse to obey the law or comply with the orders of public officials as a means of expressing their opposition to the government or some of its laws.

ees and patrons and blocking entrances to the clinic. The Supreme Court has struck down provisions that prohibit protesters from peacefully, even if assertively, expressing their views. But the Court has upheld injunctions that keep anti-abortion protesters outside of a reasonable buffer zone around abortion clinics and also upheld injunctions that were issued because of prior unlawful conduct by the protesters. The proper constitutional test for such injunctions is "whether the challenged provisions . . . burden no more speech than necessary to serve a significant government interest," such as public safety or the right of women to go into such a clinic.[67]

The combination of written guarantees for rights and freedoms and their judicial enforcement is one of the basic features of our government and political system. As Supreme Court Justice Robert H. Jackson wrote:

> The very purpose of a Bill of Rights was to withdraw certain subjects from the vicissitudes of political controversy, to place them beyond the reach of majorities and officials and to establish them as legal principles to be applied by the courts. One's right to life, liberty, and property, to free speech, a free press, freedom of worship and assembly, and other fundamental rights may not be submitted to vote: they depend on the outcome of no elections.[68]

The connection between constitutional limitations and judicial enforcement is an example of the "auxiliary precautions" James Madison believed were necessary to prevent arbitrary governmental action. Citizens in other free nations rely on elections and political checks to protect their rights; in the United States we also appeal to judges when we fear our freedoms are in danger.

POLITICS ONLINE

Surf Watch: Pornography on the Internet

Should government regulate the content of Internet communications that include indecent words or pictures that children can access with the click of a mouse? In 1996 Congress passed the Communications Decency Act, which made it illegal to send "indecent" or "patently offensive" words or pictures online where they can be found by children. In defending the act before the Supreme Court, the Justice Department contended: "The Internet threatens to give every child a free pass to the equivalent of every adult bookstore and every adult video store in the country." But the American Civil Liberties Union countered that "the government cannot reduce the adult population to reading or viewing only what is appropriate for children."

During oral arguments, it appeared that the justices were uncertain whether Internet speech is most like speech on a street corner or in a park, communication over the telephone, or some type of publication. To read how the Court resolved this contentious issue, log onto www.prenhall.com/burns and view the case of *Reno v American Civil Liberties Union*, and also access the Communications Decency Act of 1996.

More recently, in an effort to keep pornography out of public schools, Congress passed the "Children's Internet Protection Act." This legislation mandates that schools using federal money for computer services must make use of a government-created filter device designed to block pornographic material. For more information log onto: www.cybertelecom.org/cda/cipatext.htm

For different perspectives on these issues, check out the American Civil Liberties Union at: www.aclu.org and the American Center for Law and Justice at: www.aclj.org.

SUMMARY

1. The Constitution protects our right to seek a writ of *habeas corpus* and forbids *ex post facto* laws and bills of attainder.

2. First Amendment freedoms—freedom of religion, freedom from the establishment of religion, freedom of speech, freedom of the press, freedom of assembly and association—are at the heart of a healthy constitutional democracy.

3. Since World War I, the Supreme Court has become the primary branch of government for giving meaning to these constitutional restraints. And since 1925 these constitutional limits have been applied not only to Congress but to all governmental agencies—national, state, and local.

4. The First Amendment forbids the establishment of religion and also guarantees the free exercise of religion. These two freedoms, however, are often in conflict with each other and represent conflicting notions of what is in the public interest.

5. The Supreme Court holds that there are four categories of nonprotected speech—libel, obscenity, fighting words, and commercial speech. All other speech is protected under the First Amendment, and government may regulate that speech only when it has a compelling reason and does so in a content-neutral way.

6. Over the years, the Supreme Court has taken a practical approach to First Amendment freedoms. It has refused to make them absolute rights above any kind of governmental regulation, direct or indirect, or to say that they must be preserved at whatever price. But the justices have recognized that a constitutional democracy tampers with these freedoms at great peril. They have insisted upon compelling justification before permitting these rights to be limited. How compelling the justification is, in a free society, will always remain an open question.

KEY TERMS

writ of *habeas corpus* 364
ex post facto law 364
bill of attainder 365
due process clause 365
selective incorporation 365

establishment clause 366
free exercise clause 369
bad tendency test 370
clear and present danger
    test 370

preferred position doctrine 370
nonprotected speech 370
libel 372
sedition 372
obscenity 372

fighting words 374
commercial speech 374
prior restraint 374
civil disobedience 379

FURTHER READING

JAMES MACGREGOR BURNS AND STEWART BURNS, *A People's Charter: The Pursuit of Rights in America* (Knopf, 1991).

T. BARTON CARTER, *The First Amendment and the Fifth Estate: Regulation of Electronic Mass Media*, 4th ed. (Foundation Press, 1996).

JESSE CHOPER, *Securing Religious Liberty: Principles for Judicial Interpretation of Religion Clauses* (University of Chicago Press, 1995).

EDWARD J. CLEARY, *Beyond the Burning Cross: A Landmark Case of Race, Censorship, and the First Amendment* (Random House, 1995).

STEPHEN M. FELDMAN, ED., *Law and Religion: A Critical Anthology* (New York University Press, 2000).

MIKE GODWIN, *Cyber Rights: Defending Free Speech in the Digital Age* (Times Books, 1998).

KENT GREENAWALT, *Fighting Words: Individuals, Communities, and Liberties of Speech* (Princeton University Press, 1995).

NAT HENTOFF, *Living the Bill of Rights: How to Be an Authentic American* (Harper-Collins, 1998).

LEONARD W. LEVY, *Emergence of a Free Press* (Oxford University Press, 1985).

LEONARD W. LEVY, *The Establishment Clause: Religion and the First Amendment* (Macmillan, 1986).

ANTHONY LEWIS, *Make No Law: The Sullivan Case and the First Amendment* (Random House, 1991).

CATHARINE A. MACKINNON, *Only Words* (Harvard University Press, 1993).

ALEXANDER MEIKLEJOHN, *Political Freedom: The Constitutional Powers of the People* (Harper & Row, 1965).

JOHN STUART MILL, *Essay on Liberty* (1859), in *The English Philosophers from Bacon to Mill*, ed. Arthur Burtt (Random House, 1939), pp. 949–1041.

JOHN T. NOONAN, JR., *The Lustre of Our Country: The American Experience of Religious Freedom* (University of California Press, 1998).

J. W. PELTASON AND SUE DAVIS, *Understanding the Constitution*, 15th ed. (Harcourt College Division, 2000).

FRANK S. RAVITCH, *School Prayer and Discrimination: The Civil Rights of Religious Minorities and Dissenters* (Northwestern University Press, 1999).

NADINE STROSSEN, *Defending Pornography: Free Speech, Sex, and the Fight for Women's Rights* (Scribner's, 1995).

17

RIGHTS TO LIFE, LIBERTY, AND PROPERTY

CHAPTER MEDIA

 POLITICS ONLINE
*Are Your E-Mail Messages
Private?*
www.prenhall.com/burns

IN COUNTRIES AROUND THE WORLD, MEN AND WOMEN ARE REBELLING AGAINST THE POLICE STATES UNDER WHICH THEY LIVE, AGAINST GOVERNMENTS IN WHICH the police are unrestrained in how they go about finding and punishing so-called "enemies of the people." In the United States we sometimes get impatient about the time-consuming steps that must be followed before criminals are taken off the streets, and about the endless rounds of appeals and reviews available to those charged with crimes. But we need to remember how fortunate we are to live in a society that values *due process*—established rules and regulations that restrain those in government who exercise power. Such procedures are not available to citizens in Iraq, China, and much of Africa and South America, as well as elsewhere in the world.

Public officials in the United States do have great power. Under certain conditions they can seize our property, put us in jail, and—in extreme circumstances—even take our lives. The framers of our Constitution recognized that it is necessary—but dangerous—to give power to those who govern. It is so dangerous that to keep our officials from becoming tyrants, we do not depend on the ballot box alone. Because political power can threaten our liberty, we parcel it out in small chunks and surround it with restraints. No single official can decide to take our lives, liberty, or property. Officials must act according to the rules. If they act outside the scope of their authority or contrary to the law, they can be restrained, dismissed, or punished. These rights to due process are the precious rights of all who live under the American flag—rich or poor, young or old, black or white, man or woman, alien or citizen.

In this chapter we look at the rights of all persons to due process, but before we do, let us look at the rights that flow from citizenship.

CITIZENSHIP RIGHTS

Every nation has rules that determine nationality and define who is a member of, owes allegiance to, and is a subject of the nation. But in a constitutional democracy, citizenship is an *office* and, like other offices, it carries with it certain powers and responsibilities. How citizenship is acquired and retained is therefore a matter of considerable importance.

How Citizenship Is Acquired and Lost

The basic right of citizenship was not given constitutional protection until 1868, when the Fourteenth Amendment was adopted; prior to that, each state determined citizenship. The Fourteenth Amendment states: "All persons born or naturalized in the United States, and subject to the jurisdiction thereof, are citizens of the United States and of the State wherein they reside." This means that all persons born in the United States, except children born to foreign ambassadors and ministers, are citizens of this country regardless of the citizenship of their parents. (Congress has defined the United States for this purpose to include Puerto Rico, Guam, the Northern Marianas, and the Virgin Islands.) A child born to an American citizen living abroad or who has an American citizen as a grandparent is an American citizen if either the parent or grandparent has lived in the United States for at least five years, including two of which were after age 14. Although the Fourteenth Amendment does not make Native Americans citizens of the United States and of the states in which they live, Congress did so in 1924.

NATURALIZATION   Citizenship may also be acquired by **naturalization**, a legal action conferring citizenship upon an alien. Congress determines naturalization requirements. Today, with minor exceptions, nonenemy aliens over age 18 who have been lawfully admitted for permanent residence and who have resided in the United States for at least five years and in the state for at least six months are eligible for naturalization. Any state or federal court in the United States or the Immigration and Naturalization Service (INS) can grant citizenship. The INS, with the help of the Federal Bureau of Investigation (FBI), makes the necessary investigations.

Any person denied citizenship after a hearing before an immigration officer may appeal to a federal district judge. Citizenship is granted if the judge is satisfied that the applicant has met all the requirements after reviewing the FBI check that no disqualifying felony conviction has been found. The applicant

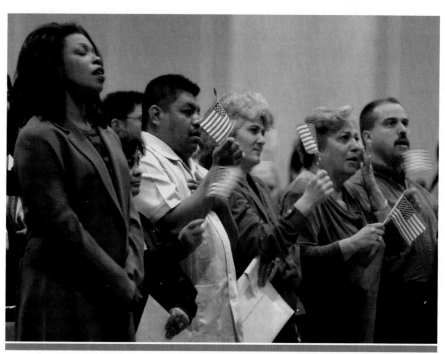

Proud naturalized citizens are sworn in at an emotional ceremony.

naturalization

A legal action conferring citizenship upon an alien.

renounces allegiance to his or her former country, swears to support and defend the Constitution and laws of the United States against all enemies, and promises to bear arms on behalf of the United States when required to do so by law. Those whose religious beliefs prevent them from bearing arms are allowed to take an oath swearing that, if called to duty, they will serve in the armed forces as noncombatants or will perform work of national importance under civilian direction. The court or INS then grants a certificate of naturalization.

Naturalized citizenship may be revoked by court order if the government can prove citizenship was secured by deception. But citizenship cannot be taken from people because of what they have done—for example, for committing certain crimes, voting in foreign elections, or serving in foreign armies. In addition, citizenship, however acquired, may be renounced voluntarily. Even so, the government must prove that the citizen "not only voluntarily committed the expatriating act prescribed in the statute, but also intended to relinquish his citizenship."[1]

DUAL CITIZENSHIP   Because each nation has complete authority to decide for itself the definition of nationality, it is possible for a person to be considered a citizen by two or more nations. **Dual citizenship** is not unusual, especially for people from nations that do not recognize the right of individuals to renounce their citizenship, called the **right of expatriation**. (One of the issues of the War of 1812 was that England did not recognize sailors born in England as having abandoned their English citizenship on becoming naturalized American citizens.) Children born abroad to American citizens may also be citizens of the nation in which they were born. Children born in the United States of parents from a foreign nation may also be citizens of their parents' country.

Among the nations that allow dual citizenship are Canada, Mexico, France, and the United Kingdom. One expert estimates that, based on the number of American children born to foreign-born parents, the number of Americans eligible to hold citizenship in another country grows by at least 500,000 a year.[2] Moreover, with more than 7 million Mexican-born immigrants in the United States and their American-born children now becoming eligible to apply for Mexican citizenship, the number of dual citizens in the United States is on the rise. Dual citizenship carries negative as well as positive consequences; for example, a person with dual citizenship may be subject to national service obligations and taxes in both countries.

Rights of American Citizens

An American becomes a citizen of one of our states merely by residing in that state. *Residence* as understood in the Fourteenth Amendment means the place one calls home. The legal status of residence should not be confused with the fact of physical presence. A person may be living in Washington, D.C., but be a citizen of California—that is, consider California home and vote in that state.

Most of our most important rights flow from *state* citizenship. In the *Slaughter-House Cases* (1873), the Supreme Court carefully distinguished between the privileges of United States citizens and those of state citizens. It held that the only privileges of national citizenship are those that "owe their existence to the Federal Government, its National Character, its Constitution, or its laws." These privileges have never been completely specified, but they include the right to use the navigable waters of the United States and to protection on the high seas, to assemble peacefully and petition for redress of grievances, to vote if qualified to do so under state laws and have one's vote counted properly, as well as to travel throughout the United States.

THE RIGHT TO LIVE AND TRAVEL IN THE UNITED STATES   This right, which is not subject to any congressional limitation, is perhaps the most precious aspect of American citizenship. Aliens have no such right. They may be stopped on the high seas or at the borders and turned away if they fail to meet the terms and conditions

dual citizenship
Citizenship in two or more nations.

right of expatriation
Right of individuals to renounce their citizenship.

An estimated 2.3 to 2.4 million undocumented aliens—mostly from Mexico and other nations in Central and South America and a few from Canada and Poland—illegally cross our borders, not because they fear political persecution but because they see greater economic opportunity in the United States. Even though most undocumented immigrants from Mexico return to Mexico after only two years and well over half return within 10 years, undocumented aliens present a big political problem.

stipulated by the Congress for admission. Today millions of people around the world yearn to come and live in the United States, but only American citizens have a constitutionally guaranteed right to do so.

THE RIGHT TO TRAVEL ABROAD   The right to international travel can be regulated within the bounds of due process. Under current law it is unlawful for citizens to leave or enter the United States without a valid passport (except as otherwise provided by the president, as has been done for travel to Mexico, Canada, and parts of the Caribbean).

Rights of Aliens

During periods of hostility toward aliens, the protections of citizenship are even more precious. True, the Constitution protects many rights of *all persons*, not just of American citizens; for example, neither Congress nor the states can deny to aliens the right of freedom of religion or the right of freedom of speech. Nor can any government deprive any person, alien or citizen, of the due process of the law or equal protection under the laws.

However, Congress may deny or limit welfare and many other kinds of benefits to aliens. Congress has denied most federally assisted benefits to illegal immigrants and has permitted states to deny them many other benefits, making an exception only for emergency medical care, disaster relief, and some nutrition programs. While states have considerable discretion over what benefits they give to aliens, the Supreme Court has held that states cannot constitutionally exclude children of undocumented aliens from the public schools or charge their parents tuition.[3]

Admission to the United States

President Franklin Roosevelt, reminding us of our heritage as a haven for people fleeing religious and political persecution, opened his address to a convention of the Daughters of the American Revolution with the salutation, "Fellow immigrants and revolutionaries." Some Americans, however, are concerned that admitting so many people from abroad will dilute American traditions and values. Throughout our history debates have flared among those wishing to open our borders and those wishing to close them.

property rights
The rights of an individual to own, use, rent, invest in, buy, and sell property.

Immigrants arriving at Ellis Island in 1900 came with high hopes but few material possessions.

Aliens do not have a constitutional right to enter the United States. Congress has wide discretion in setting the numbers, terms, and conditions under which aliens can enter and stay in the United States. The Immigration Act of 1965, as amended in 1990 and 1996, sets an annual ceiling of 675,000 for nonrefugee aliens allowed to come here as permanent residents, but when refugees and other exempt categories are added, more than 800,000 people enter the United States each year. The law also sets an annual limit on immigrants from any single country. Preference is given for family reunification and to people who have special skills or who are needed to fill jobs for which U.S. workers are not available. Another provision allows for the admission of "millionaire immigrants" who are willing and able to invest a substantial sum to create or support a business in the United States that will provide jobs for Americans. There have been few takers for admission under this provision. There is also a "diversity" category to provide visas for 55,000 immigrants from 34 countries, whether or not they have relatives living in the United States. These visas are drawn annually by lottery from a pool of qualified applicants.

In addition to regularly admitted aliens, in recent years more than 100,000 political refugees have been admitted. *Political refugees* are people who have well-founded fears of persecution in their own countries based on their race, religion, nationality, social class, or political opinion. People admitted as political refugees can apply to become permanent residents after one year. The attorney general, acting through the Immigration and Naturalization Service, may also grant *asylum* to applicants who have well-founded fears of persecution in the country to which they would be returned, based on their race, religion, nationality, membership in a particular social group, or political opinion. It is not enough, however, that applicants face the same terrible conditions that all other citizens of their country face, or that they wish to escape bad economic conditions. They must show specific danger of persecution.

The Immigration and Naturalization Service may turn back at the border persons seeking asylum when it considers their requests insubstantial, or even hold them in detention camps. The president may order the Coast Guard—as both former President George Bush and Bill Clinton did with respect to Haitian and Cuban refugees—to stop people on the high seas before they enter the territorial waters of the United States and return them to the country from which they have fled without determining whether they qualify as refugees.[4] Nonetheless, many people are still willing to risk great danger to get here and suffer detention once they arrive, just for the chance of being granted asylum.

Once in the United States, aliens are subject to the full range of obligations, including the payment of taxes. Aliens are counted in the census for the purpose of apportioning seats in the U.S. House of Representatives. Legally admitted aliens may be deported for a variety of reasons—for example, conviction of crimes involving immoral acts, turpitude, incitement of terrorist activity, illegal voting in elections, and conviction of domestic violence.

PROPERTY RIGHTS

Constitutional Protection of Property

Property does not have rights. People do. People have the right to own, use, rent, invest in, buy, and sell property. Historically, the close connection between liberty and ownership of property, between property and power, has been emphasized in American political thinking and American political institutions. A major purpose of the framers of the Constitution was to establish a government strong enough to protect people's rights to use and enjoy their property. At the same time, the framers wanted to limit government so it could not endanger that right. As a result, the framers included in the Constitution a variety of clauses protecting **property rights**.

Thinking It Through . . .

The inability to keep illegal aliens out of the country is not a question of constitutional power, for Congress has complete power over the admission of aliens. Rather, the problems are political and practical. Although Congress has authorized an increase in the number of border patrol guards and funded additional fencing of the California-Mexican border, there are thousands of miles of borders. Moreover, it is difficult to track down undocumented aliens once inside the United States and then expel them in a fashion consistent with the practices and policies of a free society.

Congress faces conflicting pressures: from Hispanic groups concerned that making it illegal to hire undocumented workers will make employers hesitate to hire any Hispanics; from employers who do not want to keep costly records and investigate the legal status of everybody they hire; from employers of farm workers who want to be sure they will have enough laborers to pick seasonal crops; from American workers who do not want undocumented workers being used to keep wages low; and from city and local governmental officials who have to find the funds to provide social services for undocumented aliens.

The United States government tends to consider immigration policy a purely internal matter. In California and some other states there are strong anti-immigration pressures. Immigration policy clearly affects our relations with other nations, most especially with Mexico, as the lengthy negotiations over the North American Free Trade Agreement (NAFTA) demonstrated. Although we view immigration policy as a matter of national sovereignty, Mexicans see it as a matter that directly affects them and have advocated "open borders."

Of special concern to the framers were the efforts of some state legislatures to protect debtors at the expense of their creditors by issuing paper currency and setting aside private contracts. To prevent these practices, the legal tender and contract clauses in the Constitution forbid states from making anything except gold or silver legal tender for the payment of debts and from passing any "Law impairing the Obligation of Contracts."

The **contract clause** (Article I, Section 10) was designed to prevent states from extending the period during which debtors could meet their payments or otherwise get out of contractual obligations. The framers had in mind an ordinary contract between private persons. However, beginning with Chief Justice John Marshall (1801–35), the Supreme Court expanded the coverage of the clause to prevent states from taking away privileges previously conferred on corporations. In effect, the contract clause was used to protect property and to maintain the status quo at the expense of a state's power.

In the late nineteenth century, however, the Supreme Court gradually began to restrict the coverage of the contract clause and to subject contracts to what in constitutional law are known as **police powers**—the powers of states to protect the public health, safety, welfare, and morals of their residents. By 1934 the Supreme Court actually held that even contracts between individuals—the very ones the contract clause was intended to protect—could be modified by state law to avert social and economic catastrophe.[5] Although the contract clause is still invoked occasionally to challenge state regulation of property, it is no longer a significant limitation on governmental power.

What Happens When the Government Takes Our Property?

Both the national and state governments have the power of **eminent domain**—the power to take private property for public use—but the owner must be fairly compensated. This limitation, contained in the Fifth Amendment, was the first provision of the Bill of Rights to be enforced as a limitation on state governments as well as on the national government.[6]

What constitutes a "taking" for purposes of eminent domain? Ordinarily, but not always, the taking must be direct, and a person must lose title and control over the property. Sometimes, especially in recent years, the courts have found that a governmental taking has gone "too far," and the government must pay compensation to its owners, even when title is left in the hands of the owners.[7] These are called **regulatory takings**. Thus, if a government creates landing and takeoff paths for airplanes over property adjacent to an airport, making the land no longer suitable for its prior use (say, raising chickens), compensation is warranted.

"Just compensation" is not always easy to define. When there is a dispute over compensation, the courts make the final resolution based on the rule that "the owner is entitled to receive what a willing buyer would pay in cash to a willing seller at the time of the taking."[8] An owner is not entitled to compensation for the personal value of an old, broken-down house that is loved dearly—just the value of the old, broken-down house.

DUE PROCESS RIGHTS

Perhaps the most difficult parts of the Constitution to understand are the clauses in the Fifth and Fourteenth Amendments forbidding the national and state governments to deny any person life, liberty, or property without due process of law. Cases involving these clauses have resulted in hundreds of Supreme Court decisions. Even so, it is impossible to explain *due process* precisely. In fact, the Supreme Court has refused to give due process a precise definition and has emphasized that "due process, unlike some legal rules, is not a technical conception with a fixed content unrelated to time, place and circumstances."[9] We define **due process** as rules and regulations that restrain those in government who exercise power. There are, however, basically two kinds of due process: procedural and substantive.

---

contract clause

Clause of the Constitution that was originally intended to forbid state governments to modify contracts made between individuals; for a while interpreted to forbid state governments from adversely affecting property rights; no longer interpreted so broadly and no longer constrains state governments from exercising their police powers.

police powers

Inherent powers of state governments to pass laws to protect the public health, safety, and welfare; the national government has no directly granted police powers, but through other delegated powers accomplishes the same goals.

eminent domain

Power of a government to take private property for public use; the U.S. Constitution gives national and state governments this power and requires them to provide just compensation for property so taken.

regulatory taking

Government regulation of property so extensive that government is deemed to have taken the property by the power of eminent domain, for which it must compensate the property owners.

due process

Established rules and regulations that restrain those in government who exercise power.

Procedural Due Process

Traditionally, **procedural due process** refers not to the law itself but to the *way in which a law is applied.* To paraphrase Daniel Webster's famous definition, the due process of law requires a procedure that hears before it condemns, proceeds upon inquiry, and renders judgment only after a trial or some kind of hearing. Originally, procedural due process was limited to criminal prosecutions, but it now applies to most kinds of governmental proceedings. It is required, for instance, in juvenile hearings, disbarment proceedings, proceedings to determine eligibility for welfare payments, revocation of drivers' licenses, and disciplinary proceedings in state universities and public schools.

A law may also violate the procedural due process requirement if it is too vague or if it creates an improper presumption of guilt. A vague statute fails to provide adequate warning and does not contain sufficient guidelines for law enforcement officials, juries, and courts.

The liberty that is protected by due process includes "the right of the individual to contract, to engage in any of the common occupations of life, to acquire useful knowledge, to marry, to establish a home and bring up children, to worship God according to the dictates of his own conscience, and generally to enjoy those common law privileges long recognized as essential to the orderly pursuit of happiness by free men."[10] The property protected by due process includes a variety of rights that may be conferred by state law, such as certain kinds of licenses, protection from being fired from some jobs except for just cause (for example, incompetence) and according to certain procedures, as well as protection from deprivation of certain pension rights.

Substantive Due Process

Procedural due process places limits on *how* governmental power may be exercised; **substantive due process** places limits on *what* a government may do. Procedural due process mainly limits the executive and judicial branches because they apply the law and review its application; substantive due process mainly limits the legislative branch because it enacts laws. Substantive due process means that an "unreasonable" law, even if properly passed and properly applied, is unconstitutional. It means that there are certain things governments *should not be allowed to do.*

Before 1937, substantive due process was used primarily to protect the right of employers to make contracts with employees freely, without government interference. During this period the Supreme Court was dominated by conservative jurists who considered almost all social welfare legislation unreasonable. They used the due process clause to strike down laws setting maximum hours of labor, establishing minimum wages, regulating prices, and forbidding employers to fire workers because they joined a union.

Since 1937 the Supreme Court has largely refused to apply the doctrine of substantive due process in reviewing laws regulating business enterprises and economic interests. The Court now believes that deciding what constitutes reasonable regulation of business and commercial life is a legislative, not a judicial, responsibility. As long as the justices find a conceivable connection between a law regulating business and the promotion of the public welfare, the Supreme Court will not interfere with laws passed by Congress or state legislatures.

This does not mean, however, that the Court has abandoned substantive due process. On the contrary, substantive due process has taken on new life as a protector of civil liberties, most especially the right of privacy. Substantive due process has deep roots in concepts of natural law and a long history in the American constitutional tradition. For most Americans most of the time, it is not enough merely to say that a law reflects the wishes of the popular or legislative majority. We also want our laws to be just, and we continue to rely heavily on judges to decide what is just.

procedural due process
Constitutional requirement that governments proceed by proper methods; places limits on how governmental power may be exercised.

substantive due process
Constitutional requirement that governments act reasonably and that the substance of the laws themselves be fair and reasonable; places limits on what a government may do.

PRIVACY RIGHTS

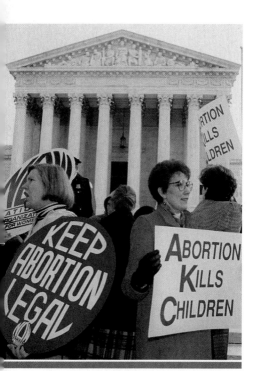

The battle over abortion has been fought in the courts and on the streets, and has been a key issue in recent presidential elections. Republicans anticipate that George W. Bush will appoint justices to the Supreme Court who will reverse Roe v Wade.

The most important extension of substantive due process in recent decades has been its expansion to protect the right of privacy, especially marital privacy. Although there is no mention of the right of privacy in the Constitution, in *Griswold v Connecticut* (1965) the Supreme Court pulled together elements of the First, Third, Fourth, Fifth, Ninth, and Fourteenth Amendments to recognize that personal privacy is one of the rights protected by the Constitution.[11]

There are three aspects of this right: (1) the right to be free from governmental surveillance and intrusion, especially in marital matters; (2) the right not to have private affairs made public by the government; and (3) the right to be free in thought and belief from governmental regulations.[12]

Abortion Rights

The most controversial aspect of constitutional protection of privacy relates to the extent of state power to regulate abortions. In *Roe v Wade* (1973) the Supreme Court ruled: (1) during the first trimester of a woman's pregnancy, it is an unreasonable and therefore unconstitutional interference with her liberty and privacy rights for a state to set any limits on her choice to have an abortion or on her doctor's medical judgments about how to carry it out; (2) during the second trimester, the state's interest in protecting the health of women becomes compelling, and a state may make a reasonable regulation about how, where, and when abortions may be performed; and (3) during the third trimester, when the life of the fetus outside the womb becomes viable, the state's interest in protecting the unborn child is so important that the state can prohibit abortions altogether, except when necessary to preserve the life or health of the mother.[13]

The *Roe* decision led to decades of heated public debate and attempts by Presidents Ronald Reagan and George Bush to select Supreme Court justices who might be expected to reverse it. Nonetheless, *Roe v Wade* was reaffirmed in *Planned Parenthood v. Casey* (1992). A bitterly divided Rehnquist Court, by a five-person majority (O'Connor, Kennedy, Souter, Blackmun, and Stevens), upheld the view that the due process clauses of the Constitution protect a woman's liberty to choose an abortion prior to viability. The Court, however, held that the right to have an abortion prior to viability may be subject to state regulation that does not "unduly burden" it. In other words, states may make "reasonable regulations" on how a woman exercises her right to an abortion so long as they do not prohibit any woman from making the ultimate decision on whether to terminate a pregnancy before viability.[14]

Applying the *undue burden* test, the Court has held, on the one hand, that states can prohibit the use of state funds and facilities for performing abortions; states may make a minor's right to an abortion conditional on her first notifying at least one parent or a judge; and states may require women to sign an informed consent form and to wait 24 hours before having an abortion. On the other hand, a state may not condition a woman's right to an abortion on her first notifying her husband. The Court also struck down Nebraska's ban on "partial birth" abortions in *Stenberg v Carhart* (2000), because it completely forbid one kind of medical procedure and provided no exception for when a woman's life is at stake and thus imposed an "undue burden" on women.[15]

Sexual Orientation Rights

Although there is general agreement on how much constitutional protection is provided for marital privacy, in *Bowers v Hardwick* (1986) the Supreme Court refused to extend such protection to relations between homosexuals.[16] By a 5 to 4 vote, the Court refused to declare unconstitutional a Georgia law that made consensual sodomy a crime. That homosexual sodomy occurs in the privacy of the home, said the majority, does not matter. But a number of state supreme courts, including that in Georgia, found greater privacy protection in their state constitutions than the U.S.

Supreme Court found in the U.S. Constitution. In 1999 the Vermont state supreme court held that same-sex couples must be given the same benefits and protections as married couples.[17]

In *Boy Scouts of America v Dale* (2000), again by a 5 to 6 vote, the Supreme Court held that a New Jersey public accommodations law could not be applied to keep the Boy Scouts from excluding gays from being Scout leaders.[18] The Court majority concluded that the Boy Scouts are a private association, and as such they have a right to exclude people whose beliefs and conduct are inconsistent with the Scouts' views and mission.

The U.S. Supreme Court, in *Romer v Evans* (1996), struck down an initiative amending the Colorado constitution that prohibited all legislative, executive, or judicial action designed to protect homosexuals at any level of state or local government. This provision violated the equal protection clause because it lacked a rational basis and simply represented a prejudice toward a particular group of people. Justice Antonin Scalia in dissent accused the Court of taking sides in "the cultural wars through an act not of judicial judgment but of political will."[19]

Because of the strong emotions on both sides of this issue, the right of privacy as an element of substantive due process is one of the developing edges of constitutional law, one about which people both on and off the Court have strong disagreements. How the Supreme Court handles privacy issues has become front-page news.

RIGHTS OF PERSONS ACCUSED OF CRIMES

Despite what you sometimes see in television police dramas, law enforcement officers have no general right to break down doors and invade homes. They are not supposed to search people except under certain conditions, and they have no right to arrest them except under certain circumstances. They also may not compel confessions, and they must respect other procedural guarantees aimed at ensuring fairness and the rights of the accused. Persons accused of crimes are guaranteed these and other rights under the Fourth, Fifth, Sixth, Eighth, and Fourteenth Amendments.

Freedom from Unreasonable Searches and Seizures

According to the Fourth Amendment, "The right of the people to be secure in their persons, houses, papers, and effects, against unreasonable searches and seizures, shall not be violated, and no Warrants shall issue, but upon probable cause, supported by Oath or affirmation, and particularly describing the place to be searched, and the persons or things to be seized."

Protection from unreasonable searches and seizures requires police, if they have time, to obtain a valid **search warrant**, issued by a magistrate after the police indicate under oath that they have *probable cause* to justify its issuance. Magistrates must perform this function in a neutral and detached manner and not serve merely as rubber stamps for the police. The warrant must specifically describe: (1) what place is to be searched, and (2) what things are to be seized. *General search warrants*—warrants that authorize police to search a particular place or person without limitation—are unconstitutional. A search warrant is usually needed to search a person in any place he or she has an "expectation of privacy that society is prepared to recognize as reasonable," for example, in a hotel room, in a rented home, in a friend's apartment.[20] In short, the Fourth Amendment protects people, not places, from unreasonable governmental intrusions.[21]

Police may make reasonable *warrantless searches* in *public places* if and the officers have probable cause, or at least a reasonable suspicion, that the persons in question have committed or are about to commit crimes. No later than two days after

The Crime Control and Safe Streets Act of 1968

1. Makes it a crime for any unauthorized person to tap telephone wires or to use or sell, in interstate commerce, electronic bugging devices.

2. Empowers the United States attorney general to secure a warrant from a federal judge authorizing federal agents to engage in bugging to track down persons suspected of certain federal crimes.

3. Permits wiretaps without prior court approval for 48 hours in emergency situations involving certain crimes, such as child pornography, illegal currency transactions, offenses against witnesses of crimes, or immediate danger of death or serious injury.

4. Authorizes the principal prosecuting attorney of any state or political subdivision to apply to a state judge for a warrant approving wiretapping or other intercepts for felonies. (Most state and local jurisdictions allow such intercepts.)

5. Permits judges to issue warrants only if they decide probable cause exists that a crime is being, has been, or is about to be committed, and that information relating to that crime may be obtained only by wiretapping.

6. Allows the use in federal courts of an accused person's confession to police if "the totality of the circumstances" establish that it was not coerced by police, rather than requiring officers to inform the accused of their *Miranda* rights.

search warrant
A warrant issued by a magistrate that authorizes the police to search a particular place or person, specifying the place to be searched and the objects to be seized.

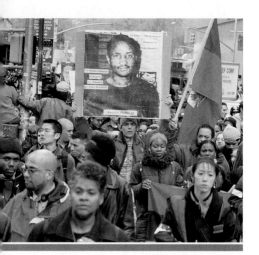

When police fired 41 bullets into an unarmed black man, protests erupted in the Bronx, New York neighborhood.

making such an arrest, the police must take the arrested person to a magistrate so that the magistrate—not just the police—can decide whether probable cause existed to justify the warrantless arrest.[22] Probable cause, however, does not, except in extreme emergencies, justify a warrantless arrest of people in their own homes.

Under the common law, police officers apprehending a fleeing suspected felon can use weapons that might result in the felon's serious injury, even death. But the Fourth Amendment places substantial limits on the use of what is called *deadly force*. It is unconstitutional to shoot at an apparently unarmed, fleeing, suspected felon unless the officer has probable cause to believe that the suspect poses a significant threat of death or serious injury to the officer or others. Also, when feasible, the officer must first warn the suspect: "Halt or I'll shoot."

Not every time the police stop a person to ask questions or to seek that person's consent to a search is there a seizure or detention requiring probable cause or a warrant. If the police just ask questions or even seek consent to search an individual's person or possessions in a noncoercive atmosphere, there is no detention. "So long as a reasonable person would feel free 'to disregard the police and go about his business,' the encounter is consensual and no reasonable suspicion is required." But if the person refuses to answer questions or consent to a search, and the police, by either physical force or a show of authority, restrain the movement of the person, even though there is no arrest, the Fourth Amendment comes into play.[23] For example, if police approach people in airports and request identification, this act by itself does not constitute a detention. The same is true if police ask bus passengers for consent to search their luggage for drugs. But if the police do more, especially after consent is refused, then their actions require them to have some objective justification for the search beyond mere suspicion.

The Supreme Court also upheld, in *Terry v Ohio* (1968), a *stop and frisk* exception to searches of individuals, when officers have reason to believe they are armed and dangerous, or have committed or are about to commit a criminal offense. The so-called *Terry* search is limited to a quick pat-down to check for weapons that might be used to assault the arresting officer, to check for contraband, to determine identity, or to maintain briefly the status quo while obtaining more information.[24] If an officer stops and frisks a suspect to look for weapons and finds criminal evidence that might justify an arrest, then the officer can make a full search.[25] Police and border guards may also conduct *border* searches—searches of persons and the goods they bring with them at border crossings.[26] The border search exception also permits officials to open mail entering the country if they have "reasonable cause" to suspect it contains merchandise imported in violation of the law.[27]

There are several other exceptions to the general rule against warrantless searches and seizures of what is found by police and customs officials. The most important are:

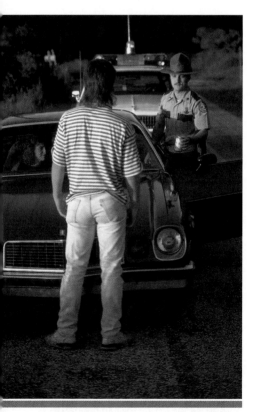

Police may detain and search cars and their passengers if they have probable cause to believe the passengers may be involved in criminal activity.

The Plain-View Exception: The plain-view exception permits officers to seize evidence without a warrant if: (1) they are lawfully in a position from which the evidence can be viewed; (2) it is immediately apparent to them that the items they observe are evidence of a crime or are contraband; and (3) they have probable cause to believe—a reasonable suspicion will not do—that the evidence uncovered is contraband or evidence of a crime.[28]

Exigent Circumstances: Searches are permissible when officers do not have time to secure a warrant before evidence is destroyed, or a criminal escapes capture, or when there is need "to protect or preserve life or avoid serious injury." An example is that fire fighters and police may enter a burning building without a warrant and may remain there for a reasonable time to investigate the cause of the blaze after the fire has been extinguished. However, after the fire has been put out, the emergency is not to be used as an excuse to make an exhaustive, warrantless search for evidence.

The Automobile Exception: If officers have probable cause to believe that an automobile is being used to commit a crime, even a traffic offense, or that it contains persons who have committed crimes, or that it contains evidence of crimes, they may stop the automobile, detain the persons found therein, and search them and any containers or packages found inside the car.[29] Once an automobile has been lawfully detained, the police officers may order the driver and passengers to get out of the car without violating the Fourth Amendment.[30]

Foreign Agents: Although never directly sustained by the Supreme Court, Congress has endorsed the presidential claim that a president can authorize warrantless wiretaps and physical searches of agents of foreign countries. Congress created a special Foreign Intelligence Surveillance Court to approve such requests; this court, consisting of seven federal district judges, meets in secret.[31]

In addition, various administrative searches by nonpolice government agents, such as teachers and health officials, do not require search warrants. Rules governing the conduct of such administrative searches are more lenient than are those for searches by police investigating crimes. Administrative searches conducted without grounds for suspicion of particular individuals have been upheld in certain limited circumstances.[32]

One recent troublesome area relates to compulsory, random drug testing. The Supreme Court has upheld the constitutionality of blood and urine tests of rail employees involved in train accidents, of federal employees, and of high school students engaged in interscholastic athletic competitions. But it struck down a Georgia law requiring candidates for designated state offices to certify that they had taken a drug test and that the test result was negative, because Georgia failed to show why this invasion of personal privacy was necessary.[33]

THE EXCLUSIONARY RULE   In *Mapp v Ohio* (1961), the Supreme Court adopted a rule excluding from a criminal trial evidence that the police obtained unconstitutionally or illegally.[34] This **exclusionary rule** was adopted to prevent police misconduct. Critics of the exclusionary rule question why criminals should go free just because of police misconduct or ineptness,[35] but the Supreme Court has refused to abandon the rule. It has made some exceptions to it, however, such as cases in which police relied in "good faith" on a search warrant that subsequently turned out to be defective or granted improperly.[36]

THE RIGHT TO REMAIN SILENT   During the seventeenth century, certain special courts in England forced confessions from religious dissenters. The British privilege against self-incrimination developed in response to these practices. Because they were familiar with this history, the framers of our Bill of Rights included in the Fifth Amendment the provision that persons shall not be compelled to testify against themselves in criminal prosecutions. This protection against self-incrimination is designed to strengthen the fundamental principle that no person has an obligation to prove innocence. Rather, the burden is on the government to prove guilt.

The privilege against self-incrimination applies literally only in criminal prosecutions. But it has always been interpreted to protect any person subject to questioning by any agency of government, such as a congressional committee. It is not enough, however, to contend that answers might be embarrassing or might lead to loss of a job or even to civil suits; persons must have a reasonable fear that their answers might support a criminal prosecution against them.

Sometimes authorities would rather have information from witnesses than prosecute them. Congress has established procedures so that prosecutors and congressional committees may secure a grant of **immunity** for such a witness. When immunity has been granted, a witness no longer has a constitutional right to refuse to testify, and the government cannot use the information derived directly from the

Use of metal detectors and locker searches at schools does not require search warrants and other protections applied to police searches.

exclusionary rule
Requirement that evidence unconstitutionally or illegally obtained be excluded from a criminal trial.

immunity
Protection granted by prosecutors to witnesses in exchange for giving up their constitutional right not to testify against themselves.

"The court finds itself on the horns of a dilemma. On the one hand, wiretap evidence is inadmissable, and on the other hand, I'm dying to hear it."

compelled testimony in any subsequent prosecution, though the witness may still be prosecuted for crimes on the basis of other evidence.

THE MIRANDA WARNING   Police questioning of suspects is a key procedure in solving crimes. Roughly 90 percent of all criminal convictions result from guilty pleas and never reach a full trial. Police questioning, however, can easily be abused. Police officers sometimes forget or ignore the constitutional rights of suspects, especially those who are frightened and ignorant. Unauthorized detention and lengthy interrogation to wring confessions from suspects, common practice in police states, were not unknown in the United States.

Federal and state laws require police officers to take people they have arrested before a magistrate promptly so that the magistrate may inform them of their constitutional rights and allow them to get in touch with friends and seek legal advice. Despite these requirements, police were often tempted to quiz suspects first, trying to get them to confess before a magistrate informed them of their constitutional right to remain silent.

To put an end to such practices, the Supreme Court, in *Miranda v Arizona* (1966), announced that no conviction could stand if evidence introduced at the trial had been obtained by the police during "custodial interrogation" unless suspects were notified that they have a right to remain silent and to have an attorney present during questioning by police, as well as have a lawyer appointed to represent them if they cannot afford to hire their own attorney.[37] If suspects answer questions in the absence of an attorney, the burden is on prosecutors to demonstrate that suspects knowingly and intelligently gave up their rights to remain silent. Failure to comply with these requirements leads to reversal of a conviction, even if other evidence is sufficient to establish guilt.

Critics of the *Miranda* decision believe the Supreme Court severely limited the ability of the police to bring criminals to justice. Over the years, the Court has modified the original ruling by allowing evidence obtained contrary to the *Miranda* guidelines to be used to attack the credibility of defendants who offer testimony at their trial that conflicts with their statements to the police. Congress tried to get around *Miranda* in the Crime Control and Safe Streets Act of 1968 by allowing confessions made in violation of *Miranda* to be used as evidence in federal courts. But in a decision handed down in June 2000, the Court reaffirmed the constitutionality of the *Miranda* doctrine. In an opinion by Chief Justice William H. Rehnquist, the Court held that the *Miranda* warning is not merely a rule of evidence to enforce the constitutional guarantee, but is itself constitutionally required and applies in both state and federal courts.[38]

Fair Trial Procedures

Many people consider the rights of persons accused of a crime to be less important than other rights. But, as Justice Felix Frankfurter observed, "The history of liberty has largely been the history of observance of procedural safeguards." Further, these safeguards have frequently "been forged in controversies involving not very nice people."[39] Nonetheless, they guarantee that all persons accused of crimes will have the right to representation by counsel and to a fair trial by an impartial jury.

THE RIGHT TO COUNSEL   If after questioning by police the suspect is arrested and charged with a crime, the Supreme Court has ruled that the accused has a constitutional right to counsel at every stage of the criminal proceedings—preliminary hearings, bail hearings, trial, sentencing, and first appeal.

INDICTMENT   Except for members of the armed forces, the national government cannot require anyone to stand trial for a serious crime except on the basis of a grand jury indictment; states are not required to use grand juries, and those that do not, vest

The Miranda warning is read to a suspect by a police officer to inform him of his rights, such as the right to remain silent and the right to have an attorney present.

prosecutors with the power to seek indictments. A **grand jury** is concerned not with a person's guilt or innocence but merely with whether there is enough evidence to warrant a trial. The grand jury has wide-ranging investigatory powers and "is to inquire into all information that might bear on its investigations until it is satisfied that it has identified an offense or satisfied itself that none has occurred."[40] The strict rules that govern jury proceedings do not apply. The grand jury may admit hearsay evidence, and the exclusionary rule to enforce the Fourth Amendment does not apply. If a majority of the grand jurors agree that a trial is justified, they return what is known as a true bill, or **indictment**.

The Constitution guarantees the accused *the right to be informed of the nature and cause of the accusation* so that he or she can prepare a defense. After indictment for an offense, prosecutors and the attorney for the accused usually discuss the possibility of a **plea bargain**—that is, the defendant pleads guilty to a lesser offense that carries a shorter prison sentence. Prosecutors, faced with more cases than they can handle, like plea bargains because they save the expense and time of going to trial. Likewise, defendants are often willing to "cop a plea" for a lesser offense to avoid the risk of more serious punishment.

When defendants plead guilty, they are usually forever prevented from raising objections to their conviction. That is why, before accepting guilty pleas, the judge questions defendants to be sure their attorneys have explained the alternatives and they know what they are doing.

THE TRIAL   After indictment and preliminary hearings that determine bail and what evidence will be used as evidence against the accused, the Constitution guarantees a *speedy and public trial*. Do not, however, take the word "speedy" too literally. Defendants are given time to prepare their defense and, in fact, often ask for delays, because delay often works to their advantage. In contrast, if the government denies the accused a speedy trial, not only is the conviction reversed but the case must also be dismissed outright.

Under the Sixth Amendment, the accused has a right to trial before a **petit jury** selected from the state and district in which the alleged crime was committed. Although federal law requires juries of 12 members, the Supreme Court has held that states may try defendants before juries consisting of at least 6 persons. Conviction in federal courts must be by unanimous vote, but the Court has ruled that state courts may render guilty verdicts by nonunanimous juries, provided such juries consist of 6 or more persons.[41]

An *impartial jury*, one that meets the requirements of due process and equal protection, consists of persons who represent a fair cross-section of the community. Although defendants are not entitled to juries on which there must be members of their own race, sex, religion, or national origin, government prosecutors cannot strike people from juries because of race or gender, and neither can defense attorneys use what are called *peremptory challenges* to keep people off juries because of race, ethnic origin, or sex.[42]

During the trial, the defendant has a right to obtain witnesses in his favor and to have the judge subpoena witnesses to appear at the trial and testify. Both the accused and witnesses may refuse to testify on the grounds that their testimony would tend to incriminate them. If they testify, the prosecution has the right to cross-examine them, just as the accused has the right to confront and to cross-examine witnesses.

Sentencing and Punishment

At the conclusion of the trial, the jury recommends a verdict of guilty or not guilty. If the accused is found guilty, the judge then hands down the sentence. The Eighth Amendment forbids the levying of excessive fines and the inflicting of cruel and unusual punishment.

The Miranda Warning

In *Miranda v Arizona* (1966), the Supreme Court held that before questioning criminal suspects, the police must warn them that:

1. They have a right to remain silent.

2. Anything they say may and will be used against them in a court of law.

3. They have the right to presence of a lawyer during police questioning.

4. If they cannot afford an attorney, one will be appointed for them.

5. They have a right to terminate police questioning at any point.

grand jury
A jury of 12 to 23 persons who, in private, hear evidence presented by the government to determine whether persons shall be required to stand trial; if the jury believes there is sufficient evidence that a crime was committed, it issues an indictment.

indictment
A formal charge issued by a grand jury against an individual for a specified crime; also called a *true bill*.

plea bargain
Negotiations between prosecutor and defendant aimed at getting the defendant to plead guilty in return for the prosecutor's agreeing to reduce the seriousness of the crime for which the defendant will be charged.

petit jury
A jury of 6 to 12 persons that determines guilt or innocence in a civil or criminal action.

Cruel and Unusual Punishment

The Eighth Amendment ban against cruel and unusual punishment limits government in three ways:

1. It limits the kinds and methods of punishment that may be imposed, prohibiting, for example, torture, intentional denial of medical care, inhumane conditions, unnecessary or wanton inflicting of pain, and deliberate indifference to medical and other needs of prisoners.[*]

2. It prohibits punishments grossly disproportionate to the severity of the crime. However, the Supreme Court has been reluctant to review legislative prescriptions of terms of punishment, and successful challenges to the severity of punishments have been extremely rare.[**]

3. It limits the power of the government to decide what can be made a criminal offense. For example, the mere act of being a chronic alcoholic may not be made a crime because alcoholism is an illness. However, being drunk in public may be a criminal offense.

[*]*Hudson v McMillian*, 503 US 1 (1992); *Farmer v Brennan*, 511 US 825 (1994).

[**]*Hutto v Davis*, 454 US 370 (1982); *Solem v Helm*, 463 US 277 (1983).

In federal courts, judges follow the sentencing guidelines set down by the United States Sentencing Commission. Such sentences are not considered cruel and unusual. Many states have also established guidelines for sentencing by state courts.

THREE STRIKES AND YOU'RE OUT   Although the crime rate has actually been going down in the past few years, public concern about crime still remains high. At the national and state level, presidents, governors, and legislators vie with one another to show their toughness on crime. Virginia, Washington, and a number of other states have *three strikes and you're out* laws, requiring lifetime sentences without the possibility of parole for those convicted of three felonies. In some states, the felonies have to be for violent crimes; in others any three felonies will do. Scholars are skeptical that "three strikes and you're out" laws will reduce the crime rate. Moreover, constructing more jails to take care of aging felons will certainly require great expenditures of public funds.

APPEALS AND DOUBLE JEOPARDY   After trial, conviction, and sentencing, defendants may appeal their convictions if they claim they have been denied some constitutional right or denied the due process and equal protection of the law. The Fifth Amendment also provides that no person shall be "subject for the same offense to be twice put in jeopardy of life or limb." **Double jeopardy** does not prevent punishment by the national and the state governments for the same offense or for successive prosecutions for the same crime by two states. Nor does the double jeopardy clause forbid civil prosecutions, even after acquittal in a criminal trial for the same conduct.[43]

THE DEATH PENALTY   Capital punishment remains controversial. Japan and the United States are the only two industrialized countries to retain the death penalty. The 15 members of the European Union outlawed capital punishment, and courts in South Africa, Hungary, and other Central and East European countries have declared it unconstitutional and a denial of human dignity.

After a ten-year moratorium on executions in the late 1960s and early 1970s, the U.S. Supreme Court ruled the death penalty is not necessarily cruel and unusual punishment if it is imposed for conviction of crimes that resulted in a victim's death, if the procedures used by the courts "ensure that death sentences are not meted out wantonly or freakishly," and if these processes "confer on the sentencer sufficient discretion to take account of the character and record of the individual offender and the circumstances of the particular offense to ensure that death is the appropriate punishment in a specific case."[44]

In the 1990s, the Rehnquist Court made it easier to impose death sentences, cut back on appeals, and carry out executions. More states also added the death penalty (there are now 38), and the national government increased the number of crimes for which the death penalty may be imposed. As a result, the number of persons on death row increased dramatically. Since capital punishment was reinstated in 1976, more than 600 people have been executed nationwide, and more than 3,600 are on death row. As the number of executions has increased, however, concerns have also grown about the fairness of how capital punishment is imposed.

HOW JUST IS OUR SYSTEM OF JUSTICE?

What are the major criticisms of the American system of justice? How have they been answered? How accurate are TV shows and movies that highlight criminals going free and innocent people being imprisoned? Do they accurately reflect how our system of justice works?

double jeopardy
Trial or punishment for the same crime by the same government; forbidden by the Constitution.

Too Many Loopholes?

Some observers argue that by overprotecting criminals and placing too much of a burden on the criminal justice system not to make any mistakes, we delay justice, encourage disrespect for the law, and allow guilty persons to go unpunished. Justice should be swift and certain without being arbitrary. But under our procedures, criminals may go unpunished because: (1) the police decide not to arrest them; (2) the prosecutor decides not to prosecute them; (3) the grand jury decides not to indict them; (4) the judge decides not to hold them for trial; (5) the jury decides not to convict them; (6) the appeals court decides to reverse the conviction; (7) the judge decides to release them on a *habeas corpus* writ; or (8) the president or governor decides to pardon, reprieve, or parole them if convicted. As a result, the public never knows whom to hold responsible when laws are not enforced. The police blame prosecutors, prosecutors blame the police, and they all blame the juries and judges.

Others take a different view and point out that there is more to justice than simply securing convictions. All the steps in the administration of criminal laws have been developed over centuries of trial and error, and each step has been constructed to protect ordinary persons from particular abuses by those in power. History warns against entrusting the instruments of criminal law enforcement to a single officer. For this reason, responsibility is vested in many officials.

Too Unreliable?

Critics who say that our system of justice is unreliable often point to trial by jury as the chief source of trouble. No other country relies as heavily on trial by jury as does the United States. Jury trials are also time-consuming and costly. Trial by jury, critics argue, leads to a theatrical combat between lawyers who base their appeals on the prejudices and sentiments of the jurors. "Mr. Prejudice and Miss Sympathy are the names of witnesses whose testimony is never recorded, but must nevertheless be reckoned with in trials by jury."[45]

The jury system allows for what is called *jury nullification*, in which jurors ignore their instructions to consider only the evidence presented in court, and, by voting for acquittal, express their displeasure with the law or the actions of prosecutors or police. Jury nullification has a long history. In colonial times juries refused to convict colonists of political crimes against the king as a way to protest British rule. Before the Civil War, northern juries refused to convict people for helping runaway slaves. Before the 1970s, white southern juries sometimes refused to convict police for brutality against blacks.

Responding to growing public disenchantment with juries after a raft of unpopular verdicts, states have been rewriting the rules for the jury system. These changes include making it more difficult for people to be excused from jury service, allowing for nonunanimous decisions, limiting how long jurors can be sequestered, and exerting more control by judges over lawyer's statements to jurors in order to prevent appeals to jurors' emotions.

Defenders of the jury system reply that trial by jury provides a check by non-professionals on the actions of judges and prosecutors. There is no evidence that juries are unreliable; on the contrary, decisions of juries do not significantly differ from those of judges.[46] Moreover, the jury system helps to educate citizens and enables them to participate in the application of their country's laws.

Too Discriminatory?

During the last several decades, the Supreme Court has worked particularly hard to enforce the ideal of equal justice under the law. Persons accused of a crime who cannot afford attorneys must be furnished them at government expense. If transcripts are required for appeals, such transcripts must be made available to those who cannot afford to purchase them. If appeals are permitted, the government must provide attorneys for at least one appeal of the decision of the trial court. Poor people cannot be

THE DEATH PENALTY ON TRIAL

As the number of death row inmates and executions has grown, debate over the fairness and permissibility of capital punishment has become widespread. The American Bar Association called for a halt to executions because the death penalty is administered in ways that deny fundamental due process and the equal protection of law. Christian televangelist Pat Robinson joined the ABA and Catholic bishops in calling for a moratorium on executions. Illinois Republican Governor George Ryan declared a moratorium on executions in his state because more death row inmates were released from prison in recent years who had been wrongly convicted than were executed. Other prominent Republicans and Democrats also began questioning the system of imposing the death penalty.

The debate about the fairness of capital punishment was sparked by the increasing number of inmates who have been released because new DNA evidence proved their innocence—often after spending a decade or more on death row. DNA evidence is useful, however, only in cases of rape or murder when blood or tissue samples remain. A recent poll found that 92 percent of Americans say prison inmates convicted before the technology was available should be given the opportunity to submit to DNA tests now. For more information, go to Gallup's website: www.gallup.com/index.html.

This debate has refocused the controversy by drawing into question the fairness of the entire process of capital punishment. Critics point out the seemingly randomness in imposing capital punishment. Public prosecutors seek the death penalty in less than 5 percent of all murder cases. Defendants often agree to plea bargains in return for life sentences. When murder trials are held, some juries refuse to impose death sentences. And of those sentenced to death, some receive clemency or are pardoned.

A study of more than 4,500 capital cases released in June 2000 found that more than two-thirds of all death sentences are overturned. Why? The primary reasons are that defense lawyers were incompetent,

Illinois governor George Ryan called a halt to executions in his state because of mishandling and inadequate defense of accused individuals who were later discovered to be innocent.

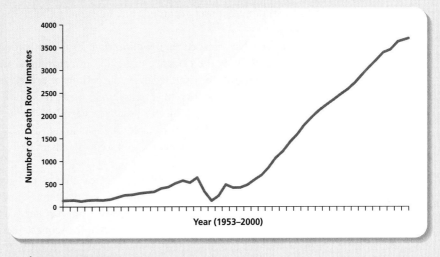

Death Row Inmates

imprisoned because of inability to pay a fine. Nor, once sentenced, can poor people be kept in jail beyond the term of the sentence because they cannot afford to pay a fine. Even for civil proceedings—divorce proceedings, for example—fees cannot be imposed that deny poor people their fundamental rights, such as the right to obtain a divorce.

Unfair to Minorities?

One of the more acute problems of our society is the tension between the police and the African American and Hispanic communities congregated in the ghettos and barrios of our large cities. Many members of minorities do not believe they have

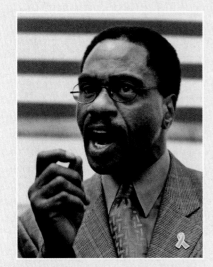

Rubin "Hurricane" Carter was a boxer who was wrongly convicted of a murder in 1967 and spent 21 years on death row before he was exonerated and released.

important evidence was overlooked by police, witnesses lied, and prosecutors sometimes withheld evidence from the defense.

Besides the apparent randomness in who is sentenced to death and later executed, racial discrimination in the imposition of capital punishment is a major concern. Blacks who murder whites are much more likely to receive death sentences than whites who murder blacks or blacks who kill blacks. The American public generally supports the death penalty, though support slipped in 2000 to 66 percent, the lowest point since 1978. Some people are morally opposed to capital punishment because of its finality; others maintain that it should be inflicted on those who commit heinous murders,

and still others insist that it is too arbitrary and randomly imposed—or as Justice Potter Stewart put it, "Death sentences are cruel and unusual in the same way that being struck by lightening is cruel and unusual."

Sources: "A Life or Death Gamble," *Newsweek,* May 29, 2000, pp. 22–27; Barry Scheck, Peter Neufeld, and Jim Dwyer, *Actual Innocence: Five Days to Execution, and Other Dispatches from the Wrongly Convicted* (Doubleday, 2000); Harry Weinstein, "Death Penalty Is Overturned in Most Cases," *The Los Angeles Times,* June 20, 2000, p. A1; reporting James S. Liebman, "A Broken System: Error Rates in Capital Cases, 1973–1995." See *McCleskey v Kemp,* 481 US 279 (1987); Walter Berns, *For Capital Punishment: Crime and Morality of the Death Penalty* (Basic Books, 1979); Justice Potter Stewart, concurring in *Furman v Georgia,* 408 US 238 (1972); Charles L. Black, Jr., *Capital Punishment: The Inevitability of Caprice and Mistake* (W.W. Norton, 1974).

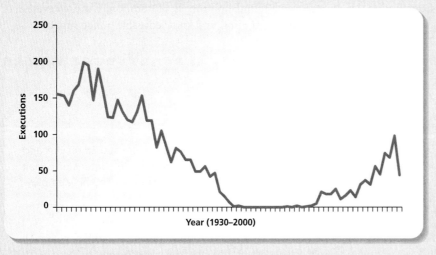

Year (1930–2000)

Executions in the United States

Source: U.S. Department of Justice, Bureau of Criminal Justice Statistics and the Death Penalty Information Center. For more information go to Death Penalty Information Center at www.deathpenaltyinfo.org.

equal protection under the law. "Whether the stated belief is well founded or not is," as one political scientist observed, "at least partly beside the point. The existence of the belief is damaging enough."[47]

Some blacks consider the police to be enforcers of white law. Studies proving prejudice on the part of some white police officers and examples of rough, if not brutal, police treatment of blacks are ample evidence to support this viewpoint. One study in California found that "the rate of unfounded arrest was four times higher for African Americans than Anglos. Latino rates were double those of Anglos."[48] Police use of **racial profiling** also concerns blacks, Hispanics, and whites.[49]

racial profiling
Police target racial minorities as potential suspects of criminal activities.

In recent decades action has been taken to recruit more African Americans, Hispanics, and women as police officers, including appointment to command posts. In larger cities there are now oversight boards including civilians to which complaints about police misconduct can be brought. **Community policing** is also being substituted in some cities for the traditional police procedures. Police departments work with churches and other local community groups and take police out of patrol cars to walk the beat and work in neighborhoods. Community policing, when combined with working with community organizations to sponsor crime-prevention programs, appears not only to reduce crime but to improve minorities' confidence in the police.[50]

THE SUPREME COURT AND CIVIL LIBERTIES

Clearly, judges play a major role in enforcing constitutional guarantees. Such reliance on judicial protection of our civil liberties focuses public attention on the Supreme Court. Yet only a small number of controversies are actually carried to the Supreme Court, and a Supreme Court decision is not the end of the judicial process. Lower-court judges as well as police, superintendents of schools, local prosecutors, school boards, state legislatures, and thousands of others clarify the Court's doctrines.

Moreover, the Supreme Court can do little unless its decisions over time reflect a national consensus. As Supreme Court Justice Robert H. Jackson (on the Court 1941–54) observed:

> It is my belief that the attitude of a society and of its organized political forces, rather than its legal machinery, is the controlling force in the character of free institutions. Any court that undertakes by its legal processes to enforce civil liberties needs the support of an enlightened and vigorous public opinion.[51]

Thus, the Bill of Rights—and the other procedural and substantive liberties of our Constitution—cannot rest on a foundation merely of tradition. The preservation of these rights depends on wide, continuing, and knowledgeable public support.

community policing
Recent programs to move police from patrol cars into neighborhoods, where they walk the beat and work with churches and other community groups to reduce crime and improve relations with minorities.

POLITICS ONLINE

Are Your E-mail Messages Private?

The e-mail message you send or receive at work or at school may not be private. Employers and some educational institutions assert their right to periodically monitor the content of e-mail run through their servers or addresses. For information on the current e-mail privacy policy and how employers and universities can monitor your e-mail go to:
www.nolo.com/encyclopedia/articles/ilaw/email_privacy.html.

You should not assume that because you have deleted e-mail messages from your computer at work or at school, that these messages cannot be read by others; these messages are probably backed up on the institutional mainframe computer. One alternative to ensure your e-mail is private is to send personal messages on your own account.

You may have received unsolicited messages from business, travel, or other websites. Most likely these companies bought your address from a company you patronized. Businesses are free to buy and sell your address unless you indicate that you do not want your address shared. In this sense, the sale and resale of e-mail lists is like the sale of conventional mailing lists. For many e-mail users, unsolicited use of their e-mail address is annoying. To limit this annoyance, be sure to check the box that specified that you do not want to give your address out (if such an option exists). Many e-mail servers like Yahoo and Hotmail offer a "block sender" option. Check this option on your next junk mail message, and the server will block that company from sending you mail in the future.

For an interesting example of an internet privacy case, read: www.prenticehall.burns/com for this chapter, or check the websites of groups concerned about Internet privacy like: www.eff.org/CAF, and go to their academic freedom home page.

SUMMARY

1. One of the basic distinctions between a free society and a police state is that in a free society there are effective restraints on the way public officials, especially law enforcement officials, perform their duties. In the United States the courts enforce these constitutional restraints.

2. The Constitution protects the acquisition and retention of citizenship. It protects the basic liberties of citizens as well as aliens.

3. The Constitution protects our property from arbitrary governmental interference, although debates about which interferences are reasonable and which are arbitrary are not easily settled.

4. The Constitution imposes limits not only on the procedures government must follow but also on the ends it may pursue. Some actions are out of bounds no matter what procedures are followed. Legislatures have the primary role in determining what is reasonable and what is unreasonable. However, the Supreme Court continues to exercise its own independent and final review of legislative determinations of reasonableness, especially on matters affecting civil liberties and civil rights.

5. The Supreme Court has pulled together elements from the First, Fourth, Fifth, Ninth, and Fourteenth Amendments to recognize a constitutionally protected right to personal privacy, especially with regard to marital privacy, including the right of a woman to choose an abortion.

6. The framers knew from their own experiences that in their zeal to maintain power and to enforce the laws, public officials are often tempted to infringe on the rights of those accused of crimes. To prevent such abuse, the Bill of Rights requires federal officials to follow detailed procedures in making searches and arrests and in bringing people to trial.

7. The Supreme Court continues to play a prominent role in developing public policy to protect the rights of the accused, to ensure that the innocent are not punished, and to guarantee that the public is protected against those who break the laws. The Court's decisions influence what the public believes and how police officers and others involved in the administration of justice behave. But the Court alone cannot guarantee fairness in the administration of justice.

KEY TERMS

naturalization 384
dual citizenship 385
right of expatriation 385
property rights 386
contract clause 388
police powers 388

eminent domain 388
regulatory taking 388
due process 388
procedural due process 389
substantive due process 389

search warrant 391
exclusionary rule 393
immunity 393
grand jury 395
indictment 395

plea bargain 395
petit jury 395
double jeopardy 396
racial profiling 399
community policing 400

FURTHER READING

JEFFREY ABRAMSON, *We, The Jury: The Jury System and the Ideal of Democracy* (Basic Books, 1994).

LIVA BAKER, *Miranda: Crime, Law and Politics* (Atheneum, 1983).

DAVID COLE, *No Equal Justice: Race and Class in the American Criminal Justice System* (New Press, 1999).

GEORGE P. FLETHER, *Basic Concepts of Criminal Law* (Oxford University Press, 1998).

DAVID J. GARROW, *Liberty and Sexuality: The Right to Privacy and the Making of Roe v. Wade* (Macmillan Publishing Co., 1994).

KENNETH KARST, *Law's Promise, Law's Expression: Visions of Power in the Politics of Race, Gender, and Religion* (Yale University Press, 1993).

RANDALL KENNEDY, *Race, Crime, and the Law* (Pantheon, 1997).

ANTHONY LEWIS, *Gideon's Trumpet* (Random House, 1964).

JOHN R. LOTT, JR., *More Guns, Less Crime: Understanding Crime and Gun Control Laws* (University of Chicago Press, 2000).

DAVID M. O'BRIEN, *Constitutional Law and Politics*, Vol. 2, *Civil Rights and Civil Liberties*, 4th ed. (W.W. Norton, 2000).

J. W. PELTASON AND SUE DAVIS, *Understanding the Constitution*, 15th ed. (Harcourt College Division, 2000).

BARRY SCHECK, PETER NEUFELD, AND JIM DWYER, *Actual Innocence: Five Days to Execution, and Other Dispatches from the Wrongly Convicted* (Doubleday, 2000).

JUDITH N. SHKLAR, *American Citizenship: The Quest for Inclusion* (Harvard University Press, 1991).

MELVIN UROFSKY, *Lethal Judgments: Assisted Suicide and American Law* (University Press of Kentucky, 2000).

U.S. COMMISSION ON IMMIGRATION REFORM, *Report to Congress: Executive Summary: Becoming an American, Immigration and Immigrant Policy* (U.S. Commission on Immigration Reform, 1997).

WELSH S. WHITE, *The Death Penalty in the Nineties* (University of Michigan Press, 1991).

ROBERT V. WOLF and AUSTIN SARAT, EDS., *The Jury System* (Chelsea House, 1998).

18

EQUAL RIGHTS UNDER THE LAW

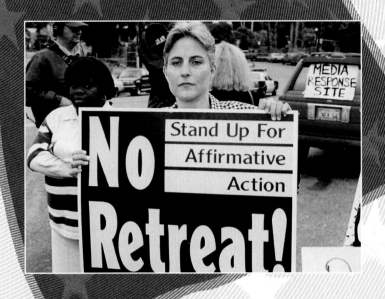

C ONSIDER AGAIN THE RINGING WORDS OF THE
DECLARATION OF INDEPENDENCE: "WE HOLD THESE
TRUTHS TO BE SELF-EVIDENT, THAT ALL MEN ARE CREATED
equal, that they are endowed by their Creator with certain unalienable Rights, that
among these are Life, Liberty, and the pursuit of Happiness." In this one sentence the
Declaration affirmed the precious rights of *equality* and *liberty* and appeared to rate
equality at least on a par with liberty. Although the Declaration does not specify equality of white, Christian, or Anglo-Saxon men (at that time "all men" meant white, property-owning Anglo-Saxon men), it has taken more than two hundred years for that definition to be expanded to include all races, all religions, and all women. This creed of
individual dignity and equality is older than our Declaration of Independence; its roots
go back into the teachings of Judaism and Christianity.

What about the Constitution? What does that historic document say about the
framers' attitude toward liberty and equality? Although you will not find any reference
to equality (the word never appears in the Constitution or in the Bill of Rights), we
know the framers believed that all men—at least all white men—were equally entitled
to life, liberty, and the pursuit of happiness. But like the Declaration, the Constitution
referred only to "men" or "him," not to women, and none of its lofty sentiments applied
to slaves, who enjoyed neither liberty nor equality.

The framers resolved their ambiguity about what kind of equality and for whom
by creating a system of government designed to protect what they called *natural rights*.
(Today we speak of *human rights*, but the idea is the same.) By **natural rights** the
framers meant that every person has an equal right to protection against arbitrary
treatment, an equal right to the liberties guaranteed by the Bill of Rights. These rights
do not depend on citizenship; they are not granted by governments. They are the rights
of *all people*.

The terms *civil liberties* and *civil rights* are often used interchangeably to refer to
rights that are protected by the constitutional systems of constitutional democracies.
Civil liberties is sometimes used more narrowly to refer to freedom of conscience, religion, and expression. *Civil rights* is used to refer to the right not to be discriminated
against because of race, religion, gender, ethnic origin, or sexual orientation. Our Constitution provides two ways of protecting civil rights: first, it ensures that *government
officials do not discriminate* against us; second, it grants national and state governments
the power to *protect* these civil rights against interference *by private individuals*.

CHAPTERMEDIA

 POLITICS ONLINE
Reparations for Slaves?
www.prenhall.com/burns

 POLISIM
*Travel the Civil Rights
  Timeline*
www.prenhall.com/burns

This chapter is concerned with both the protection of our rights from abuse *by government* and the protection *through government* of our right to be free from abuse by our *fellow citizens*. In this chapter we focus on the struggles of African Americans, women, Hispanics, Asian Americans, and Native Americans to secure the basic civil rights to the vote, to an education, to a job, and to a place to live on equal terms with their fellow citizens.

EQUALITY AND EQUAL RIGHTS

Americans are committed to equality. *Equality*, however, is an elusive term. The concept for which there is the greatest consensus and is most clearly written into the Constitution is that everybody should have *equality of opportunity* regardless of race, ethnic origin, religion, and, in recent years, gender and sexual orientation. Ensuring this equality of opportunity has led to the historic struggle for civil rights in this country.

A variation of the concept of equal opportunity is *equality of starting conditions*. There is not much equal opportunity if one person is born into a well-to-do family, lives in a safe suburb, is well fed, and receives a good education, while another is born into a poor, broken family, lives in an inner-city neighborhood, and attends inferior schools. Thus, it is argued, if we are to have equality of opportunity in a meaningful sense, we must provide opportunities for the disadvantaged through federal programs such as Head Start, which provides children from poor families with preschool experiences that prepare them for elementary school.

Empowering people so they share equal starting conditions can be accomplished by ensuring that individuals are not placed at a disadvantage because of prejudice or poverty. Traditional emphasis has been upon *individual* achievement, but such action sometimes shades into a concept of *equality between groups*. When large disparities in wealth and advantage exist between groups—as between blacks and whites or between women and men—equality becomes a highly divisive political issue. The disadvantaged tend to emphasize economic and social factors that exclude them from the mainstream. They champion programs like **affirmative action**, which are designed to provide special help to people based upon their group memberships. Those who are advantaged, however, often act to maintain the status quo and downplay socioeconomic disparities. As a result, whether such programs promote or deny equality remains one of the most controversial current debates.

Finally, equality can also mean *equality of results*. One perennial debate, especially among college students, is whether social justice and genuine equality can exist in a nation in which some people have so much and others have so little, and where the gap between them grows ever wider. Socialists and others call for a more equal distribution of wealth, yet such a view has had little support in the United States. There is considerable support for guaranteeing a minimum floor—a "safety net"—below which no one should be allowed to fall, but many people fear that insistence on equality of results would undermine equality of opportunity. The American view is not that everybody should have the same amount of material goods, but that, whatever a person's economic status for the moment, he or she should be able to expect that things will get better, and that hard work and risk-taking will be rewarded.

THE QUEST FOR EQUAL JUSTICE

To put into perspective the court decisions, laws, and other governmental actions relating to civil rights for women and minorities, we review here the political history and social contexts in which these constitutional issues were raised. Constitutional questions do not involve only court decisions, laws, and constitutional amendments; they encompass the entire social, economic, and political system.

natural rights
Rights of all people to dignity and worth.

affirmative action
Remedial action designed to overcome the effects of past discrimination against minorities and women.

Although the struggles of all groups are interwoven, they are not identical, so we deal briefly and separately with each.

White versus Black

Americans had a painful confrontation with the problem of race before, during, and after the Civil War. As a result of the northern victory, the Thirteenth, Fourteenth, and Fifteenth Amendments became part of the Constitution. During Reconstruction, Congress passed a series of civil rights laws to implement these amendments and established programs to provide educational and social services for the freed slaves. But the Supreme Court struck down many of these laws, and it was not until the 1960s that progress was again made toward ensuring African Americans their civil rights.

SEGREGATION AND WHITE SUPREMACY   Before Reconstruction programs had any significant effect, however, the white southern political leadership was restored to power, and by 1877 Reconstruction was ended. Northern political leaders abandoned African Americans to their fate at the hands of their former white masters; presidents no longer concerned themselves with the enforcement of civil rights laws; and Congress enacted no new ones. The Supreme Court either declared old laws unconstitutional or interpreted them so narrowly that they were ineffective. The Court also gave such a limited construction to the Thirteenth, Fourteenth, and Fifteenth Amendments that they failed to accomplish their intended purpose of protecting the rights of African Americans.

White supremacy was unchallenged in the South, where most African Americans lived. They were kept from voting; they were forced to accept menial jobs; and they were denied educational opportunities. African Americans were being lynched on an average of one every four days, and few whites raised a voice in protest.

During World War I, African Americans began to migrate to northern cities to seek jobs in war factories. Their relocation was accelerated in the 1930s by the depression and in the 1940s by World War II. Although discrimination continued, there were more jobs and more social gains. As migration of African Americans out of the rural South into southern and northern cities shifted the racial composition of cities, the African American vote became important in national elections. These changes created an African American middle class opposed to segregation as a symbol of servitude and a cause of inequality. By the middle of the twentieth century, urban African Americans were active and politically powerful citizens. There was a growing demand for the abolition of color barriers.

THE NATIONAL GOVERNMENT RESPONDS   In the 1930s, African Americans began resorting to lawsuits to challenge the doctrine of segregation. After World War II, this civil rights litigation began to have an impact. In the years that followed, the Supreme Court, beginning with *Brown v Board of Education* (1954), outlawed all forms of government-imposed segregation and struck down most of the devices that had been used by state and local authorities to keep African Americans from voting.

Presidents Harry S. Truman and Dwight D. Eisenhower used their executive authority to fight segregation in the armed services and the federal bureaucracy. They directed the Department of Justice to enforce whatever civil rights laws were available, but Congress still held back. In the late 1950s, an emerging national consensus in favor of governmental action to protect civil rights plus the political clout of African Americans in the northern states began to have some influence on Congress. In 1957 Congress overrode a southern filibuster in the Senate and enacted the first federal civil rights laws since Reconstruction.

A TURNING POINT   Even after the Supreme Court declared government-imposed racial segregation unconstitutional, most African Americans were still kept from voting. Many legal barriers in the path of equal rights had fallen, yet most African Americans

Martin Luther King, Jr.

"Five score years ago, a great American in whose symbolic shadow we stand signed the Emancipation Proclamation. This momentous decree came as a great beacon light of hope to millions of Negro slaves who had been seared in the flames of withering injustice. It came as a joyous daybreak to end the long night of captivity. But one hundred years later, we must face the tragic fact that the Negro is still not free. One hundred years later, the life of the Negro is still sadly crippled by the manacles of segregation and the chains of discrimination. One hundred years later, the Negro lives on a lonely island of poverty in the midst of a vast ocean of material prosperity. One hundred years later, the Negro is still languishing in the corners of American society and finds himself an exile in his own land. So we have come here today to dramatize an appalling condition. . . .

I have a dream that one day this nation will rise up and live out the true meaning of its creed: 'We hold these truths to be self-evident, that all men are created equal.'

I have a dream that one day on the red hills of Georgia the sons of former slaves and the sons of former slave owners will be able to sit down together at the table of brotherhood.

I have a dream that one day even the state of Mississippi, a desert state sweltering with the heat of injustice and oppression, will be transformed into an oasis of freedom and justice.

I have a dream that my four little children will one day live in a nation where they will not be judged by the color of their skin but by the content of their character."

SOURCE: Martin Luther King, Jr., address at the Lincoln Memorial, August 28, 1963. To listen to the speech, go to our website (www.prenhall.com/burns) or to the History and Politics Out Loud website at www.hpol.org, or go directly to database.library.nwu.edu/scripts/webobjects.exe/hpol.woa/wa/displayclip?wosid=v3600pn400fa200p7clipid=72.

still could not buy houses where they wanted, secure the jobs they needed, find educational opportunities for their children, or eat in a restaurant or walk freely on the streets of "white neighborhoods."

But times were changing. What had once been thought of as a "southern problem" was finally being recognized as a national challenge. A massive social, economic, and political movement began to supplement the struggles in the courtrooms. It began in Montgomery, Alabama, on December 1, 1955, when Rosa Parks refused to give up a seat in the front of a bus and was removed from the bus. The black community responded by boycotting city buses.

The boycott worked. It also produced a charismatic national civil rights leader, the Reverend Martin Luther King, Jr. Through his doctrine of nonviolent resistance, Dr. King gave a new dimension to the struggle. By the early 1960s, new organizational resources came into existence in almost every city to support and sponsor sit-ins, freedom rides, live-ins, and other nonviolent demonstrations. These measures were often met with violence, and some state and local governments failed to protect the victims or to prosecute those responsible for the violence.[1]

The forces of social discontent exploded in the summer of 1963. The explosion started with a demonstration in Birmingham, Alabama, which was countered with fire hoses, police dogs, and mass arrests. It ended in a march in Washington, D.C., where at least 250,000 people heard Dr. King and other civil rights leaders speak, and countless millions watched them on television. By the time the summer was over, there was hardly a city, North or South, that had not had demonstrations, protests, or sit-ins. Some also had violence.

This direct action had some effect. Many cities enacted civil rights ordinances, more schools were desegregated, and President John Kennedy urged Congress to enact a comprehensive civil rights bill. Late in 1963, the nation's grief over the assassination of President Kennedy, who had become identified with civil rights goals, added political fuel to the drive for decisive federal action to protect civil rights.[2] President Lyndon Johnson made civil rights legislation his highest priority, and on July 2, 1964, after months of debate, he signed into law the Civil Rights Act of 1964.[3]

TWO SOCIETIES? By the early 1970s the legal phase of the civil rights movement had come to a close, but as things got better, discontent grew. Millions of impoverished African Americans demonstrated growing impatience with the discrimination that remained. This volatile situation gave way to racial violence and disorders. In 1965 a brutal riot took place in Watts, a section of Los Angeles. In 1966 and 1967 the disorders increased in scope and intensity. The Detroit riot in July 1967, the worst such disturbance up to that time in modern American history, made clear the deep divisions between the races and the urgency of taking corrective action.[4]

THE KERNER COMMISSION President Johnson appointed a special Advisory Commission on Civil Disorders to investigate the origins of the riots and to recommend measures to prevent such disasters in the future. When the commission (called the Kerner Commission after its chair, Illinois Governor Otto Kerner) issued its report, it said in stark, clear language: "What white Americans have never fully understood— but what the Negro can never forget—is that white society is deeply implicated in the ghetto. White institutions created it, white institutions

maintain it, and white society condones it." The basic conclusion of the commission was: "Our nation is moving toward two societies, one black, one white—separate and unequal" and that "only a commitment to national action on an unprecedented scale" could change this trend.[5]

The commission made sweeping recommendations on jobs, education, housing, and the welfare system. But other events diverted attention from these recommendations: the Vietnam War; Watergate; the elections of Ronald Reagan and George Bush, who were reluctant to take governmental actions to enforce civil rights; and a growing skepticism about the effectiveness of governmental action generally.

The Clinton administration was more sympathetic toward the use of governmental power to deal with issues of inequality than its immediate predecessors, but because of budgetary constraints and Republican opposition to "big government" programs, it was largely unable to promote any major initiatives directly aimed at the problems of the inner cities.

Women's Rights

The struggle for equal rights for women was intertwined with the battle to secure equal rights for African Americans. The Seneca Falls Women's Rights Convention (1848), which launched the women's movement, involved men and women who actively campaigned to abolish slavery. But as the Civil War approached, women were urged to abandon their cause and devote their energies to getting rid of slavery.[6] The Civil War brought the women's movement to a halt, and the temperance movement to prohibit the sale of liquor diverted attention away from women's rights as well. The Fourteenth and Fifteenth Amendments did not advance voting rights for women, even as they guaranteed that right to freed male slaves.

By the turn of the century, however, a vigorous campaign was under way for **women's suffrage**—the right to vote. The first victories came in western states, where Wyoming led the way. As a territory, Wyoming had given women the right to vote. When members of Congress in Washington grumbled about this "petticoat provision," the Wyoming legislators replied they would stay out of the Union one hundred years rather than come in without women's suffrage. Congress gave in and admitted

Fire fighters in Birmingham, Alabama, turned their hoses full blast on civil rights demonstrators in the 1960s. At times the water came with such force, even on children, that it literally tore the bark off fully grown trees.

Rosa Parks's decision not to give up her seat on the bus in Montgomery, Alabama, sparked a boycott by African Americans who, for more than a year, refused to ride the segregated city buses.

women's suffrage
The right of women to vote.

What Is Sexual Harassment?

The Supreme Court has interpreted Title VII of the Civil Rights Act of 1964 to impose on employers an obligation to provide a workplace environment that does not subject any employee to sexual harassment. Sexual harassment comes in two forms: (1) "quid pro quo," in which an employer makes it a condition of employment (hiring, promotion, etc.) that a person provide sexual favors; and (2) situations in which an employee experiences discrimination because of being forced to work in a "hostile environment." A hostile environment is defined as a workplace "permeated" with intimidation, ridicule, and insult that is severe or pervasive.

Sexual harassment was brought to national attention by accusations made against Justice Clarence Thomas by Anita Hill at the time of his Senate confirmation, by the lawsuit brought by Paula Jones against President Bill Clinton for allegedly seeking sexual favors when he was governor of Arkansas and she was an employee, and by Kathleen Willey, who contended that President Clinton groped her.

In the Paula Jones case, the judge dismissed the charge on the grounds that, even if what Ms. Jones said was true, there was no evidence that she had been deprived of her constitutional or legal rights, nor had she suffered any job discrimination. However, this was a case that would not die, and Ms. Jones and her lawyers appealed the decision. After prolonged negotiations over money, in November 1998 President Clinton agreed to pay $850,000 to settle the claim of sexual harassment, and Ms. Jones dropped her demand that he apologize.

Susan B. Anthony and Elizabeth Cady Stanton were the two most influential leaders of the women's suffrage movement in the nineteenth century.

Wyoming to the Union. By the end of World War I, more than half the states had granted women the right to vote in some or all elections.

To many suffragists this state-by-state approach seemed slow and uncertain. They wanted a decisive victory—a constitutional amendment that would force all states to allow qualified women to vote. Finally, in 1919, Congress proposed the Nineteenth Amendment. Opposition to granting voting rights to women was intertwined with opposition to granting voting rights to African Americans. Many southerners opposed the amendment because it gave Congress enforcement power, which might bring federal officials to investigate elections to ensure that the amendment was being obeyed—an interference that might call attention to how blacks were being kept from voting.

With the ratification of the Nineteenth Amendment in 1920, women won the right to vote, but they were still denied equal pay and equal rights, and they suffered numerous legal disabilities imposed by both national and state laws. In the 1970s and 1980s the unsuccessful struggle to secure the adoption of the Equal Rights Amendment occupied much of the attention of the women's movement, but there are now other goals, and the political clout of women is mobilized behind issues that range from equal pay to world peace, sexual harassment, abortion rights, and election to office.[7]

Hispanics

The struggle for civil rights has not been limited to women and African Americans. Each new wave of immigrants has been considered suspect by those who arrived earlier—all the more so if its members were not white or English speaking. Formal barriers of law and informal barriers of custom combined to deny equal rights. But as groups established themselves—first economically, then politically—most of these barriers were swept away, and constitutionally guaranteed rights were asserted.

As we discussed in Chapter 5, most Hispanics—many of whose ancestors have been Americans for generations—are bilingual, speaking English as well as Spanish. However, because English may not be their first language, it has been difficult for some Hispanics to establish themselves educationally or to advance into the ranks of executives and professionals. Although not as visible as African Americans, Hispanics have suffered the same kinds of discrimination in employment, education, and accommodations.

Hispanic political clout has been unrealized because of internal political differences and because many Hispanics are not citizens or registered to vote. However, after California adopted Proposition 187 in 1994, which denied medical, educational, and social services to illegal immigrants, and Congress amended the federal welfare laws to curtail benefits to noncitizens, many immigrants rushed to become naturalized. In the 2000 election both George W. Bush and Al Gore campaigned vigorously among Hispanics, and more voted in 2000 than in 1996, with big increases in California and Texas.

Asian Americans

The term "Asian American" describes approximately 10 million individuals from many different countries and many different ethnic backgrounds. Most do not think of themselves as "Asians" but as Americans of Chinese, Japanese, Vietnamese, Cambodian, Korean, or other specific ancestry. They live chiefly in the western states, but there has been a rapid increase in Asian Americans in New York and Texas.

Although Asian Americans are often considered a "model minority" because of their general success in education and business, the U.S. Civil Rights

Commission found that "Asian-Americans do face widespread prejudice, discrimination and barriers to equal opportunity" and that racially motivated violence against them "occurs with disturbing frequency."[8]

CHINESE AMERICANS   The Chinese were the first Asians to come to the United States. Beginning in 1847, when young male peasants came here to get away from poverty and to work in mines, on railroads, and on farms, the Chinese encountered economic and cultural fears of the white majority, who did not understand them or their culture. In response, the Chinese seldom tried to assimilate but instead gravitated to "Chinatowns." Discriminatory immigration and naturalization restrictions, imposed beginning in 1882, were strengthened in later years and were not removed until the end of World War II.

Since that time, the Chinese have moved into the mainstream of American society, and they are beginning to run for and win local political offices. In 1996 Gary Locke, a Democrat and a graduate of Yale and Boston University Law School, was elected governor of Washington, the first Chinese American to become governor of a continental state.

In the war hysteria following the outbreak of World War II, Japanese Americans were rounded up and transported to internment camps.

JAPANESE AMERICANS   The Japanese first migrated to Hawaii in the 1860s and then to California in the 1880s. Most Japanese immigrants remained in the West Coast states. By the beginning of the twentieth century, they faced overt hostility. In 1905 labor leaders organized the Japanese and Korean Exclusion League, and in 1906 the San Francisco Board of Education excluded all Chinese, Japanese, and Korean children from neighborhood schools. Some western states passed laws denying the right to own land to aliens who were ineligible to become citizens—meaning aliens of Asian ancestry.

During World War II, anti-Japanese hysteria provoked the internment of West Coast Japanese—most of whom were loyal American citizens guilty of no crimes—in prison camps in California, Colorado, and some other states. During this time the property of Japanese Americans was often sold at confiscatory rates, and many lost their businesses, jobs, and incomes. Following the war, the exclusionary acts were repealed. In 1988 President Ronald Reagan signed a law providing $20,000 restitution to each of the approximately 60,000 surviving World War II internees.

OTHER ASIAN AMERICANS   Like other Asian Americans, Koreans faced overt discrimination in jobs and housing, but a Korean middle class has been growing, with many becoming teachers, doctors, and lawyers. Many others operate small family businesses such as dry cleaners, florist shops, service stations, and small grocery stores, often in inner cities.[9] As prosperous small businesspeople, they are often the target of the anger of the poor people whose neighborhoods they serve. Many Korean stores in African American neighborhoods were destroyed in the 1992 Los Angeles riots.

When Filipinos first came to the United States in the early part of this century, they were considered American nationals because the United States owned the Philippine Islands, their native country. Nonetheless, they were denied their rights to full citizenship and faced discrimination and even violence, including anti-Filipino riots in the state of Washington in 1928 and later in California, where nearly one-third of the approximately 1.5 million Filipinos live.[10] Their economic status has improved, but their influence in politics remains as small as their numbers.

The newest Asian arrivals consist of more than a million refugees from Vietnam, Laos, and Cambodia, who first came to the United States in 1975 and settled mostly in California. Although this group included middle-class people who left during the fall of Saigon following the end of the Vietnam War, it also consisted of large numbers of "boat people" who came to our shores without any financial resources. In a relatively short time, most established themselves economically. Although they are starting to have political influence, some remain socially and economically segregated.

Native Americans

Almost half of the more than 2 million Native Americans live on or near a *reservation*—a tract of land given to the tribal nations by treaty—and are enrolled as members of one of the 550 federally recognized tribes, including 226 groups in Alaska.[11] About 200 different Native American languages are spoken.

Native Americans speak of their tribes as "nations," yet they are not possessed of the full attributes of sovereignty. Rather, they are a separate people with power to regulate their own internal affairs, subject to congressional supervision. States are precluded from regulating or taxing the tribes or extending the jurisdiction of their courts over the tribes unless authorized to do so by Congress.[12] In recent years Congress has stepped in to mediate growing tensions between Indian tribes who used their sovereignty over reservations to operate gambling casinos and the states in which these reservations are located.

By acts of Congress, Native Americans are citizens of the United States and of the states in which they live. They have the right to vote. Native Americans living off reservations and working in the general community pay taxes just as everybody else; off reservations they have the same rights as any other Americans. If they are enrolled members of a recognized tribe, they are entitled to certain benefits created by law and by treaty. The Bureau of Indian Affairs of the Department of the Interior administers these benefits.

During the period of assimilation that began in 1887 and lasted until 1934, tribal governments were weak, some reservations were dissolved, and more than 100 tribes had their relationship with the federal government severed.[13] The civil rights movement of the 1960s created a more favorable climate for the concerns of Native Americans. Their goals were to reassert treaty rights and secure greater autonomy for the tribes. Under the leadership of the Native American Rights Fund (NARF), more Indian law cases were brought in the last several decades than at any time in our history.[14]

As a result of the militancy of Native American leaders and a greater national consciousness of the concerns of minorities, most Americans are now aware that many Native Americans live in poverty. Native Americans "are in far worse health than the rest of the population, dying earlier and suffering disproportionately from alcoholism, accidents, diabetes, and pneumonia."[15] Although in recent years the rest of the United States has enjoyed less than 4 percent unemployment, many reservations continue to experience 50–60 percent unemployment. Some reservations lack adequate health care facilities, educational opportunities, decent hous-

Sioux Indians took part in a 220-mile March of Memory to mark the 100th anniversary of the Battle of Wounded Knee, when U.S. troops opened fire and killed 200 men, women, and children.

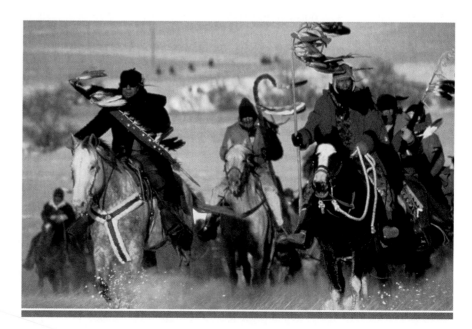

ing, and jobs. Congress has started to compensate Native Americans for past injustices and to provide more opportunities for the development of tribal economic independence, and judges are showing greater vigilance in the enforcement of Indian treaty rights.

In 1986 Ben Nighthorse Campbell became the first Native American to be elected to Congress. He was elected as a Democrat from Colorado but became a Republican after being elected to the Senate in 1992.

EQUAL PROTECTION OF THE LAWS: WHAT DOES IT MEAN?

The **equal protection clause** of the Fourteenth Amendment declares that no state (including any subdivision thereof) shall "deny to any person within its jurisdiction the equal protection of the laws." Although there is no parallel clause explicitly limiting the national government, the Fifth Amendment's **due process clause**, which states that no person shall "be deprived of life, liberty, or property, without due process of law," has been interpreted to impose the same restraints on the national government as the equal protection clause imposes on the states.

The equal protection clause applies only to the *actions of governments*, not to those of private individuals. If a discriminatory action is performed by a private person, it does not violate the Constitution, although it may violate federal and state laws. The equal protection clause does not, however, prevent governments from creating various classifications of people in its laws. What the Constitution forbids is *unreasonable* classifications. In general, a classification is unreasonable when there is no relation between the classes it creates and permissible governmental goals. A law prohibiting redheads from voting, for example, would be unreasonable. On the other hand, laws denying persons under 18 the right to vote, to marry without the permission of their parents, or to apply for a license to drive a car appear to be reasonable (at least to most persons over 18).

Constitutional Classifications and Tests

One of the most troublesome constitutional questions is how to distinguish between constitutional and unconstitutional classifications. The Supreme Court uses three tests for this purpose: (1) the *rational basis* test, (2) the *strict scrutiny* test, and (3) the *heightened scrutiny* test.

THE RATIONAL BASIS TEST   The traditional test to determine whether a law complies with the equal protection requirement places the burden of proof on those attacking the law. They must show that the law has no rational or legitimate governmental goals. For example, the Supreme Court has held that a state might deny unemployment benefits to those who attend day school but make them available to those who attend night school. This classification of schools meets the rational basis test since it is reasonable to assume that students who go to school during the day are less likely to be available for employment than are those who go to school after work.[16]

SUSPECT CLASSIFICATIONS AND STRICT SCRUTINY   When a law is subject to strict scrutiny, the courts must be persuaded that there is both a "compelling public interest" to justify such a classification and no less restrictive way to accomplish this compelling purpose. The Court applies the strict scrutiny test to suspect classifications. A *suspect classification* is a class of people deliberately subjected to such unequal treatment in the past, or relegated by society to a position of such political powerlessness as to require extraordinary judicial protection.[17]

Classifications based on race or national origin are always suspect. It does not make any difference if the laws are designed for supposedly benign purposes—that

equal protection clause
Clause in the Constitution that forbids any state to deny to any person within its jurisdiction the equal protection of the laws. By interpretation, the Fifth Amendment imposes the same Limitation on the national government. This clause is the major constitutional restraint on the power of governments to discriminate against persons because of race, national origin, or sex.

due process clause
Clauses in the Fifth and Fourteenth Amendments stating that the national (Fifth) and state (Fourteenth) governments shall not deprive any person of life, liberty, or property without due process of law.

is, to help persons of a particular race or national origin. For example, the Supreme Court has held that laws that give preference for public employment based on race are subject to strict scrutiny.

QUASI-SUSPECT CLASSIFICATIONS AND HEIGHTENED SCRUTINY   To sustain a law under this test, the burden is on the government to show that its classification serves "important governmental objectives." Classifications based on gender are subject to heightened scrutiny. Not until 1971 was any classification based on gender declared unconstitutional. Before that time, many laws provided special protection for women—such as a Michigan law forbidding any woman other than the wife or daughter of a tavern owner to serve as barmaid. As Justice William J. Brennan, Jr., wrote for the Court : "There can be no doubt that our nation has had a long and unfortunate history of sex discrimination. Traditionally such discrimination was rationalized by an attitude of 'romantic paternalism' which in practical effect put women, not on a pedestal, but in a cage."[18]

Today the Court's view is that treating women differently from men (or vice versa) is forbidden when supported by no more substantial justification than "the role-typing society has long imposed upon women."[19] If the government's objective is "to protect members of one sex because they are presumed to suffer from an inherent handicap or to be innately inferior," that objective is illegitimate.[20] The Supreme Court has struck down most laws brought before it that were alleged to discriminate against women.

POVERTY AND AGE   Just as racial minorities and women are entitled to special constitutional protection, it is argued, so too should the poor and the elderly be. But the Supreme Court rejected the argument "that financial need alone identifies a suspect class for purposes of equal protection analysis."[21] However, state supreme courts in Texas, Ohio, and elsewhere have ruled that unequal funding for public schools as a result of "rich" districts spending more per pupil than "poor" districts violates their state constitutional provisions for free and equal education.

Age is not a suspect class. Many laws commonly make distinctions based on age: to obtain a driver's license, to marry without parental consent, to attend schools, to buy alcohol, and so on. Many governmental institutions have age-specific programs: for senior citizens, for adult students, for midcareer persons. The Supreme Court has repeatedly refused to make age a suspect classification requiring extra judicial protection. "States may discriminate," as Justice Sandra Day O'Connor observed, "on the basis of age without offending the Fourteenth Amendment if the age classification in question is rationally related to a legitimate state interest."[22]

Congress, however, responding to "gray power," frequently treats age as a protected category. Congress has made it illegal for most employers to discriminate on the basis of old age. Except for a few exempt occupations, employers may not impose mandatory retirement requirements. Congress also attempted to extend the protections against age discrimination to cover state employees, but the Supreme Court ruled that Congress lacks the constitutional authority to open the federal courts to suits by state employees for alleged age discrimination. State employees are limited to recovering monetary damages under state laws in state courts.[23]

FUNDAMENTAL RIGHTS AND STRICT SCRUTINY   The Court also strictly scrutinizes laws impinging on *fundamental rights*. What makes a right fundamental in the constitutional sense? It is not the importance or the significance of the right that makes it fundamental, but whether it is explicitly or implicitly *guaranteed by the Constitution*. Under this test, the rights to travel and to vote have been held to be fundamental, as well as First Amendment rights such as the right to associate for the advancement of political beliefs. Rights to an education, to housing, or to welfare benefits have not been held fundamental. Important as these

rights may be, there are no constitutional provisions specifically protecting them from governmental regulation.

Proving Discrimination

Does the fact that a law or a regulation has a differential effect—what has come to be known as *disparate impact*—on persons of a different race or sex by itself establish that the law is unconstitutional? In one of its most important decisions, *Washington v Davis* (1976), the Supreme Court said no.[24] "An unwavering line of cases" from the Supreme Court "hold that a violation of the Equal Protection Clause requires state action motivated by discriminatory intent; the disproportionate effects of state action are not sufficient to establish such a violation."[25] Or, as the Court said in another case: "The Fourteenth Amendment guarantees equal laws, not equal results."[26]

What do these rulings on disparate impact mean in practical terms? They mean, for example, that even when city ordinances permit only single-family residences and thus make low-cost housing projects impossible, they are not unconstitutional—even if their effect is to keep minorities from moving into the city—unless it can be shown that they were adopted with the *intent* to discriminate against minorities. Another example: preference for veterans in public employment does not violate the equal protection clause, even though its effect is to keep many women from getting jobs; the distinction between veterans and nonveterans was not adopted deliberately to create a sex barrier.

What is constitutional can nonetheless be illegal. For example, state laws creating legislative districts with no intent to discriminate against African Americans, but which in effect dilute their voting power, are not unconstitutional. But in the Voting Rights Act of 1965, Congress made voting requirements illegal if they do, in fact, dilute the voting power of African Americans, even if they were adopted with no such intention. The Voting Rights Act of 1965 tests the legality of state voting laws and practices by their *effects* rather than by the *intentions* of those who passed them.

VOTING RIGHTS

Under our Constitution, it is the states, not the federal government, that regulate elections and voting qualifications. However, Article I, Section 4, gives Congress the power to supersede state regulations as to the "Times, Places and Manner" of elections for representatives and senators. Congress has used this authority, along with its authority under Article II, Section 2, to set the date for selection of electors, to set age qualifications and residency requirements to vote in national elections, to establish a uniform day for all states to hold elections for members of Congress and presidential electors, and to give American citizens who reside outside the United States the right to vote for members of Congress and presidential electors in the states in which they previously lived.

Limitations on the states' power to set voting qualifications are contained in the Fourteenth Amendment (forbidding qualifications that have no reasonable relation to the ability to vote), the Fifteenth Amendment (forbidding qualifications based on race), the Nineteenth Amendment (forbidding qualifications based on sex), and the Twenty-sixth Amendment (forbidding states to deny citizens 18 years of age or older the right to vote on account of age). These amendments also empower Congress to enact the laws necessary to enforce their provisions.

Protecting Voting Rights

In the 1940s the Supreme Court began to strike down one after another of the devices that had been used to keep African Americans from voting. In *Smith v Allwright* (1944) the Court declared the **white primary** (a primary operated by the Democratic party that, in the then one-party South, was where public officials were actually chosen) unconstitutional.[27] In 1960 it held that **racial gerrymandering**—the drawing of election districts to ensure that African Americans would be a minority in all districts—was contrary to

white primary
Primary operated by the Democratic party in southern states that, before Republicans gained strength in the "one-party South," essentially constituted an election; ruled unconstitutional in *Smith v Allwright* (1944).

racial gerrymandering
The drawing of election districts so as to ensure that members of a certain race are always a minority in the district; ruled unconstitutional in *Gomillion v Lightfoot* (1960).

poll tax

Payment required as a condition for voting; prohibited for national elections by the Twenty-fourth Amendment (1964) and ruled unconstitutional for all elections in *Harper v Virginia Board of Election* (1966).

literacy test

Literacy requirement imposed by some states as a condition of voting, generally used to disqualify blacks from voting in the South; now illegal.

the Fifteenth Amendment.[28] In 1964 the Twenty-fourth Amendment eliminated the **poll tax**—payment required as a condition for voting—in presidential and congressional elections. In 1966 the Court held that the Fourteenth Amendment forbade the poll tax as a condition in any election.[29]

In many southern areas, **literacy tests** were used to discriminate against African Americans. Some states required applicants to demonstrate that they understood the national and state constitutions and, furthermore, that they were persons of good character. Although poor whites often avoided registering out of fear of embarrassment from failing a literacy test, the tests were more often used to discriminate against African Americans.[30] Whites were often asked simple questions; blacks were asked questions that would baffle a Supreme Court justice. "In the 1960s southern registrars were observed testing black applicants on such matters as the number of bubbles in a soap bar, the news contained in a copy of the Peking Daily, the meaning of obscure passages in state constitutions, and the definition of terms such as *habeas corpus*."[31] In Louisiana, 49,603 illiterate white voters were able to persuade election officials they could understand the Constitution, but only two illiterate black voters were able to do so.

Those wishing to deny African Americans the right to vote were forced to rely on registration requirements. On the surface such requirements appeared to be perfectly proper, but it was the way they were administered that kept African Americans from the polls. White election officers confronted African Americans trying to register while white police stood guard; white judges heard appeals of decisions made by registration officials. Officials often seized on the smallest error in an application form as an excuse to disqualify a black voter. In one parish in Louisiana, after four white voters challenged the registration of some black voters on the grounds that those voters had made an "error in spilling" (*sic*) in their applications, registration officials struck 1,300 out of approximately 1,500 black voters from the rolls.[32]

The Voting Rights Act of 1965

For two decades after World War II, under the leadership of the Supreme Court, many limitations on voting were declared unconstitutional, but this approach still did not open the voting booth to African Americans. Finally Congress acted. The Civil Rights Act of 1964 had hardly been enacted when events in Selma Alabama, dramatized the inadequacy of depending on the courts to prevent racial barriers in polling places. Led by Martin Luther King, Jr., a voter registration drive in Selma, produced arrests, marches on the state capital, and the murder of two civil rights workers. Still there was no dent in the color bar at the polls. Responding to events in Selma, President Lyndon Johnson made a dramatic address to Congress and the nation calling for federal action to ensure that no person would be deprived of the right to vote in any election for any office because of color or race. Congress responded with the Voting Rights Act of 1965.

Section 2 of the Voting Rights Act prohibits voting qualifications or standards that result in a denial of the right of any citizen to vote on account of race and color. Section 5 requires that states that had a history of denying African Americans or Hispanic citizens the right to vote must clear with the Department of Justice changes in voting practice or laws that might dilute the voting power of these groups.[33] What precisely constitutes "dilution" and how it is to be measured are the subject of much litigation. Examples include changes in the location of polling places; changes in candidacy requirements and qualifications; changes in filing deadlines; changes from ward to at-large elections; changes in boundary lines of voting districts; and changes that affect the creation or abolition of an elective office and imposition by state political parties of fees for delegates to nominating conventions.[34]

Following the 1990 census, the Department of Justice pressured southern state legislatures to draw as many districts as possible in which minorities would constitute a majority of the electorate. Most of these districts tended to be Democratic, leaving the other congressional districts in these states heavily white and Republican. The lower federal courts sustained the Department of Justice's interpretation. As a result, there was a considerable increase in the number of congressional districts represented by minorities and Republicans.

The Supreme Court, however, in a series of cases beginning with *Shaw v Reno* (1993), announced that although it was a legitimate goal for state legislatures to take race into account when they drew electoral districts in order to increase the voting strength of minorities, they could not make race the sole or predominant reason for drawing district lines. The Department of Justice, said the Supreme Court, was wrong in forcing states to create as many **majority-minority districts** as possible. A test case involved the North Carolina legislature's creation of a majority-minority district 160 miles long and in some places only an interstate highway wide. "If you drove down the interstate," said one legislator about this district, "with both car doors open, you'd kill most of the people in the district." North Carolina's reapportionment scheme, the Supreme Court declared, was so "irrational on its face that it can be understood only as an effort to segregate voters into separate voting districts because of their race." To comply with the Voting Rights Act, the Supreme Court explained, states must provide for districts roughly proportional to the minority voters' respective shares in the voting-age population.[35]

Since then the Court has expanded *Shaw* by clarifying that it was not meant to suggest that a "district must be bizarre on its face before there is a constitutional violation." Legislatures may be aware of racial considerations when they draw district lines, but when race becomes the overriding motive, the state violates the equal protection clause.[36] As a result, many southern states have had to redraw legislative districts. However, even when African-American incumbents ran in these newly drawn districts with majority white electors, they were reelected.[37]

Thurgood Marshall (center), George C. E. Hayes (left), and James Nabrit, Jr., (right) argued and won Brown v Board of Education of Topeka *before the Supreme Court in 1954.*

EDUCATION RIGHTS

Until the Supreme Court struck down such laws in the 1950s, southern states had made it illegal for whites and blacks to ride in the same train cars, attend the same theaters, go to the same schools, be born in the same hospitals, or be buried in the same cemeteries. **Jim Crow laws**, as they came to be called, blanketed southern life. How could these laws stand in the face of the equal protection clause? This was the question raised in *Plessy v Ferguson* (1896).

In the *Plessy* decision, the Supreme Court endorsed the view that governmentally imposed racial segregation in public transportation, and presumably in public education, did not necessarily constitute discrimination if "equal" accommodations were provided for the members of both races[38]—but the "equal" part of the formula was meaningless. African Americans were segregated in unequal facilities and lacked the political power to protest effectively. The passage of time did not lessen the inequalities. Beginning in the late 1930s, African Americans started to file lawsuits challenging the doctrine. They cited facts to show that in practice, separate but equal always resulted in discrimination against African Americans.

The End of Separate but Equal: *Brown v Board of Education*

At first the Supreme Court was not willing to upset the separate but equal doctrine, but in *Brown v Board of Education of Topeka* (1954), the Court finally reversed the *Plessy* doctrine as it applied to public schools by holding that "separate but equal" is a contradiction in terms. *Segregation is itself discrimination.*[39] A year later the Court ordered school boards to proceed with "all deliberate speed to desegregate public schools at the earliest practical date."[40]

majority-minority district
A congressional district created to include a majority of minority voters; ruled constitutional so long as race is not the main factor in redistricting.

Jim Crow laws
State laws formerly pervasive throughout the South requiring public facilities and accommodations to be segregated by race; ruled unconstitutional.

Residents of the Charlestown section of Boston took part in a "March Against Forced Busing" in May 1976.

But many school districts moved very slowly, and in the 1960s Congress and the president joined even more directly in the battle against school segregation. Title VI of the Civil Rights Act of 1964, as subsequently amended, stipulated that federal dollars under any grant program or project must be withdrawn from an entire school or institution of higher education that discriminates "on the ground of race, color, or national origin" gender, age, or disability in "any program or activity receiving federal financial assistance."

From Segregation to Desegregation—But Not Yet to Integration

School districts that had operated two kinds of schools, one for whites and one for African Americans, now had an obligation to develop plans and programs to move from segregation to integration. For such school districts, desegregation would not be enough; they would have a duty to bring about integration. If they failed to do so on their own initiative, federal judges would supervise the school districts to ensure that they were doing what was necessary and proper to overcome the evils of segregation.

But since most whites and most African Americans continued to live in separate neighborhoods, merely removing legal barriers to school integration did not by itself integrate the schools. To overcome this residential clustering by race, some federal courts mandated busing across neighborhoods, moving white students to once predominantly black schools and vice versa. Busing students was not popular and fostered widespread protest in many cities.

The Supreme Court sustained busing only if it was to remedy the consequences of *officially* sanctioned, that is, **de jure segregation**. The Court refused to permit federal judges to order busing to overcome the effects of **de facto segregation**, segregation that arises as a result of social and economic conditions such as housing patterns.

Since *Brown v Board of Education*, the federal government has intervened in more than 500 school desegregation cases. However, there has been no such judicial action for northern schools that have de facto segregation. As a result, many southern cities now have more integrated schools than do large northern cities. Both in the North and South, many school districts in central cities today are predominantly African American or Hispanic. This segregated pattern of schools is partly the result of "white flight" to the suburbs in the 1970s and 1980s and the transfer of white students to private schools to escape court-ordered busing. In more recent years it is also due to higher birth rates and immigration among African Americans and Hispanics.[41]

After a period of vigorous federal court supervision of school desegregation programs, the Supreme Court has started to restrict the role of federal judges.[42] It has instructed some of them to restore control of a school system to the state and local authorities and to release districts from any busing obligations once a judge concludes that the authorities "have done everything practicable to overcome the past consequences of segregation."[43]

Political support for busing and for other efforts to integrate the schools is fading.[44] Many school districts have eliminated mandatory busing, with the result, according to one expert, that we may get "to a level of segregation we haven't seen since before the civil rights movement."[45] Some African American leaders, while still supporting desegregation efforts, are now more concerned about improving the quality of inner-city schools than desegregating them.

RIGHTS OF ASSOCIATION, ACCOMMODATIONS, JOBS, AND HOMES

Association

As we have noted, the Fifth and Fourteenth Amendments apply only to governmental action, not to private discriminatory conduct. As Justice William O. Douglas said, our Constitution creates "a zone of privacy which precludes govern-

de jure segregation
Laws that made it a crime for black or white people to go to school together, or to be served together in public places, or to sit together in public transportation.

de facto segregation
Segregation that comes about because of economic or social conditions or results from individual choices.

commerce clause
The clause (Article I) in the Constitution that gives Congress the power to regulate commerce among the states, with other nations, and with the Indian tribes. This clause provides the constitutional basis for most national regulations of our economy, as well as for much civil rights legislation.

ment from interfering with private clubs or groups. The associational rights which our system honors permit all-white, all-black, all-brown, and all-yellow clubs to be established. They also permit all-Catholic, all-Jewish, or all-agnostic clubs. . . . Government may not tell a man or a woman who his or her associates must be. The individual may be as selective as he desires."[46]

Families, churches, or private groups organized for political, religious, cultural, or social purposes are constitutionally different from large associations organized along other lines. The Supreme Court, for example, has upheld the application of laws forbidding sex or racial discrimination by organizations such as the Jaycees, the Rotary Club, and large (in this case more than 400 members) private eating clubs. Such associations and clubs are not small intimate groups. Nor were they able to demonstrate that allowing women or minorities to become members would change the content or impact of their purposes.[47] In *Boy Scouts of America v Dale* (2000), however, the Court held that the Boy Scouts may exclude homosexuals because of the association's overall mission.[48]

Accommodations

In 1883 the Supreme Court had declared unconstitutional an act of Congress that made it a federal offense for any operator of a public conveyance, hotel, or theater to deny accommodations to any person because of race or color on the grounds that the Fourteenth Amendment does not give Congress such authority.[49] Since the 1960s, however, the constitutional authority of Congress to legislate against discrimination by private individuals is no longer an issue because the Court has broadly construed the **commerce clause**—which gives Congress the power to regulate interstate and foreign commerce—to justify action against discriminatory conduct by individuals. Congress has also used its power to tax and spend to prevent not only racial discrimination but also discrimination based on ethnic origin, sex, disability, and age.

WE THE PEOPLE

Native Americans and Welfare Reform

"The 1996 welfare reform legislation, with its stricter work and job training requirements, is affecting Native American college enrollment, curriculum, and student services, according to a recent survey. The reservations on which most of the colleges are located have relatively high numbers of welfare recipients. . . . Given these needs, many states and tribes are turning to the colleges to provide remedial education and job training to reservation residents.

To examine the changes that have occurred since the welfare reform legislation was passed, the American Indian Higher Education Consortium (AIHEC) surveyed all 30 tribal colleges in the United States in spring 1998. . . .

The most obvious effects of the welfare reform provisions are on college enrollments. On the one hand, welfare recipients may get pushed out of higher education and into jobs; on the other, the new requirements may drive recipients who lack basic skills into basic adult education, GED, and vocational training programs.

Of the 18 colleges that responded, 11 colleges (61 percent) have seen enrollment changes that they believe are attributable to welfare reform. The reported shifts are varied: four of the colleges mentioned increases in enrollment: three felt the enrollment changes have been mixed; one college said enrollment has declined; one college believed the students were getting younger; and two did not mention the direction of the enrollment changes. . . .

In addition to educating welfare recipients, the colleges are actively involved in helping them complete their transition into the labor force. For example, virtually all of the responding colleges (16, or 89 percent) work with local welfare agencies to coordinate their activities. Furthermore, seven of the colleges currently offer placement services for their students and graduates; two are planning to do so in the future; and two assist their students informally. These efforts continue despite an acute lack of available jobs.

According to recent Department of Commerce data, the average unemployment rate on reservations with tribal colleges is 28 percent and may be higher than 40 percent on some reservations. Some of the tribal colleges are following the paths of their students after graduation; 13 of the colleges said they currently track the employment or enrollment status of their graduates."

SOURCE: Alisa F. Cunningham, "Survey Reports Tribal Colleges' Response to Welfare Reform," *Tribal College Journal: Journal of American Indian Higher Education* (Winter 1998–99), p. 36.

TITLE II: PLACES OF PUBLIC ACCOMMODATION   For the first time since Reconstruction, the Civil Rights Act of 1964 authorized the massive use of federal authority to combat privately imposed racial discrimination. Title II makes it a federal offense to discriminate against any customer or patron in a place of public accommodation because of race, color, religion, or national origin. It applies to any

inn, hotel, motel, or lodging establishment (except establishments with fewer than five rooms and occupied by the proprietor—in other words, small boardinghouses); to any restaurant or gasoline station that serves interstate travelers or serves food or products that have moved in interstate commerce; and to any movie house, theater, concert hall, sports arena, or other place of entertainment that customarily presents films, performances, athletic teams, or other sources of entertainment that are moved in interstate commerce. Within a few months after its adoption, the Supreme Court sustained the constitutionality of Title II.[50] As a result, public establishments, including those in the South, opened their doors to all customers.

TITLE VII: EMPLOYMENT   Title VII of the 1964 Civil Rights Act made it illegal for any employer or trade union in any industry affecting interstate commerce and employing 15 or more people (and, since 1972, any state or local agency such as a school or university) to discriminate in employment practices against any person because of race, color, national origin, religion, or sex. Employers have an obligation to create workplaces that avoid abusive environments. Related legislation made it illegal to discriminate against those with physical handicaps, veterans, or persons over 40.

There are a few exceptions. Religious institutions such as parochial schools may use religious standards. Age, sex, or handicap may be considered where occupational qualifications are absolutely necessary to the normal operation of a particular business or enterprise—for example, hiring only women to work in women's locker rooms.

The Equal Employment Opportunity Commission (EEOC) was created to enforce Title VII. The commission works together with state authorities to try to bring about compliance with the act and may seek judicial enforcement of complaints against private employers. The attorney general prosecutes Title VII violations by public agencies. Not only do aggrieved persons have a right to sue for damages for themselves, but also they can do so for other persons similarly situated in a **class action suit**. The vigor with which the EEOC and the attorney general have acted has varied over the years, depending on the commitment of the president in office and the willingness of Congress to provide an adequate budget for the EEOC.[51]

Title VII was supplemented by a 1965 presidential executive order requiring all contractors doing work for the federal government, including universities, to adopt and implement affirmative action programs to correct "underutilization" of women and minorities. Such programs may not establish racial or ethnic quotas for minorities or women, but they may require contractors to establish timetables and goals; to follow open recruitment procedures; to keep records of applicants by race, sex, and national origin; and to explain why their labor force does not reflect the same proportion of persons within the appropriate labor market pools. Failure of contractors to file and implement an approved affirmative action plan may lead to loss of federal contracts or grants.

THE FAIR HOUSING ACT AND AMENDMENTS, 1968 AND 1988   Housing is the last frontier of the civil rights crusade, the area in which progress is slowest and genuine change most remote.

> Segregated housing contributes mightily to a vicious circle that also includes educational and employment discrimination.... Because of poor schools for many minorities, they cannot find well-paying jobs. Without such jobs they often cannot afford to live in nicer neighborhoods with decent housing. And because of their location in less desirable communities, good educational systems are less likely to be available.[52]

In 1948 the Supreme Court made **racial or religious restrictive covenants** (a provision in a deed to real property restricting its sale) legally unenforceable.[53] The 1968 Fair Housing Act forbids discrimination in housing, excluding from its protection so-called "Mrs. Murphy boarding houses," housing owned by private individuals who own no more than three houses; dwellings that have no more than four

class action suit
Lawsuit brought by an individual or a group of people on behalf of all those similarly situated.

racial or religious restrictive covenants
A provision in a deed to real property excluding its sale to persons of a particular race or religion. Judicial enforcement of such deeds is unconstitutional.

separate living units in which the owner maintains a residence; and religious organizations and private clubs housing their own members on a noncommercial basis. For all other housing, the act forbids owners to refuse to sell or rent to any person because of race, color, religion, national origin, sex, or physical handicap or because a person has children. Discrimination in housing also covers efforts to deny loans to minorities.

The Department of Justice has filed hundreds of cases, especially those involving large apartment complexes, yet African Americans and Hispanics continue to face discrimination in housing. Realtors continue to steer African Americans and Hispanics toward neighborhoods that are not predominantly white, to require larger rental deposits from minorities than from whites, and to even refuse outright to sell or rent to minorities.[54] Yet less than 1 percent of these discriminatory actions are complained about because they are so subtle that victims are often unaware that they are being discriminated against. However, the number of discrimination complaints received by the Department of Housing and Urban Development and local and state agencies has been increasing as the result of more aggressive enforcement.

Voluntary segregation obviously exists. "It's a fact of life that blacks like to live in black neighborhoods and whites like to live in white neighborhoods," according to Daniel Mitchell, who added, "Real estate agents generally like to bring customers to places they will like and where the agent can make a sale."[55] Whatever the reasons, housing segregation persists.

Allan Bakke, who challenged the constitutionality of the University of California's affirmative action program.

AFFIRMATIVE ACTION: IS IT CONSTITUTIONAL?

When white majorities were using governmental power to discriminate against African Americans, civil rights advocates cited with approval the famous words of the first Justice John Marshall Harlan: "Our Constitution is color-blind and neither knows nor tolerates class among citizens."[56] But by the 1960s there was a new set of constitutional and national policy debates. Many people began to assert that government neutrality is not enough. If governments and universities and employers stopped discriminating yet changed nothing else, those previously discriminated against would still be kept from equal participation in American life. Because they had been so disadvantaged by past discrimination, they suffered disabilities not shared by white males in the competition for openings in medical schools, for skilled jobs, or for their share of government grants and contracts.

Remedies to overcome the consequences of past discrimination against African Americans, Hispanics, Native Americans, and women are known as *affirmative action* by those who support them, but they are regarded as *reverse discrimination* by those who oppose them. The Supreme Court's first major statement on the constitutionality of affirmative action programs came in a celebrated case relating to university admissions. Allan Bakke—a white male and a top student at Minnesota and Stanford Universities, as well as a Vietnam War veteran—applied both in 1973 and 1974 to the medical school of the University of California at Davis. In each of those years the school admitted 100 new students, 84 in a general admissions program and 16 in a special admissions program created for minorities who had previously been underrepresented. Bakke's application was rejected each year while students with lower grade-point averages, test scores, and interview ratings were admitted under the special admissions program. After his second rejection, Bakke brought suit in federal court claiming he had been excluded because of his race, contrary to requirements of the Constitution and Title VI of the Civil Rights Act of 1964.

In *University of California Regents v Bakke* (1978), the Supreme Court ruled the California plan unconstitutional.[57] But the Court also declared that affirmative action programs are not necessarily unconstitutional. In order to achieve a diversified student body, a state university may properly take race and ethnic background into account as one of several factors in choosing students. The problem with the

PEOPLE

Affirmative action does not mean admitting or hiring unqualified or less meritorious candidates.

IN DEFENSE OF AFFIRMATIVE ACTION

Theodore M. Shaw[*]

The goal of affirmative action is to break the cycle of discrimination and to enlarge opportunity for everyone. It is a moderate, effective remedy for exclusion, to achieve equality which is real and not illusory. As Justice Harry Blackmun has eloquently stated, "In order to get beyond racism, we must first take racism (and sexism) into account."

Affirmative action is not a single, rigid concept, but rather a mosaic of actions designed to eliminate artificial barriers and to allow merit to shine through. The particular affirmative measures utilized will vary in different circumstances, flexibly addressing the problem at hand.

Affirmative action does not mean admitting or hiring unqualified or less meritorious candidates. However, it may mean refining our definitions of merit. Affirmative action recognizes that we have not achieved the ideal of either merit selection or a colorblind and genderblind society. In addition to invidious discrimination based on race, ethnicity, and gender, our employment and contracting systems have always relied upon such non-merit-related criteria as nepotism, cronyism, and the "old boy network."

Affirmative action produces benefits for the entire community and nation.

For example, as women have entered the medical profession and the United States Congress, more attention has been focused on crucial health needs of all women, such as breast cancer research.

Businesses have found that affirmative action is good for the bottom line. Productivity is improved in many instances, and a work force that reflects the diversity of the markets they serve allows businesses to compete more effectively. The Business Roundtable and the National Association of Manufacturers have repeatedly endorsed affirmative action.

We believe that there ought to be more opportunity for all poor and working-class people, who have been hurt by structural changes in our economy even while governmental and social policies much of the last 15 years have been tilted in favor of the rich, with the result that the wealthiest of Americans have become richer while the middle class has shrunk, and millions of people joined the ranks of the impoverished. ★

SOURCE: U.S. Congress, House of Representatives, Subcommittee on Employer-Employee Relations of the Committee on Economic and Educational Opportunities, 104th Cong., 1st Sess., *Hearings on Affirmative Action in Employment* (Government Printing Office, 1995), pp. 167–86.

DEBATE

TOWARD ENDING PREFERENCES IN EDUCATION AND EMPLOYMENT

Brian W. Jones[*]

I maintain that government-imposed preferential policies based upon race and gender, whether in the employment or education context, have outlived their usefulness, so to speak, and presently do a great deal more social harm than good. While 30 years ago such policies may have been an important tool for breaking down the systemic barriers to black entry into the economic mainstream, they have today, I think, reached the point of diminishing returns. . . .

The cost of preference policies can be measured in terms of: (1) the social discord created between preferred and nonpreferred groups, and among the preferred groups; (2) the opportunity cost of mismatched minority talent and capital; (3) the economic cost to employers of complying with affirmative action mandates; (4) the injury done to innocents; and (5) the damage done to the constitutional ideal of equality.

Despite their significant social and economic cost, race and gender preferences in America are today justified essentially on two grounds: (1) the remediation of disadvantage caused by past discrimination; and (2) the desire to promote diversity.

Remediation of disadvantage was in fact the original moral claim of the proponents of affirmative action. . . . However, that justification today contains insuperable flaws. First, preferen-

tial policies today tend to benefit the least disadvantaged among and within preferred groups. Middle-class white women are now the primary beneficiaries of preferences, largely due to their relatively high level of education and cultural advantage.

The second justification for preferential policies is the notion of diversity. By diversifying the ranks of our employees, the theory goes, we will breed transracial familiarity and, consequently, harmoniously dynamic workplaces.

The anecdotal evidence suggests that both of these theories have been woefully inaccurate. Race relations in contexts where preference is writ large—college campuses and municipal employment, for example—have often become toxic as a result of increasing racial antagonism.

A truly constructive civil rights policy in America should focus on constructive efforts to confront the real underlying problems of performance in some of America's most distressed communities. A truly affirmative civil rights policy must concern itself with the hard work of improving the performance of disadvantaged individuals. ★

> I maintain that government-imposed preferential policies based upon race and gender, whether in the employment or education context, have outlived their usefulness.

SOURCE: U.S. Congress, Senate, Committee on Labor and Human Resources, 104th Cong., 1st Sess., *Hearings on Affirmative Action and the Office of Federal Contract Compliance* (Government Printing Office, 1995), pp. 77–82.

For further information about this debate, go to **www.prenhall.com/burns** *and click on the Debate Icon in Chapter 18.*

California plan was it created a quota—a category of admissions from which whites were excluded solely because of race.

After *Bakke*: Refinements and Uncertainty

Following *Bakke* in the 1980s, the Court dealt with a variety of affirmative action programs, sustaining most but not all of them. As the justices continued to disagree on the application of the equal protection clause, opposition to such programs became more heated.

In *Richmond v Croson* (1989) the Rehnquist Court struck down a regulation by the city of Richmond requiring nonminority city contractors to subcontract at least 30 percent of the dollar amount of their contracts to one or more minority business enterprises. Writing for the Court, Justice Sandra Day O'Connor called into question the validity of most government affirmative action plans and stated, "Race-sensitive remedial measures are to be justified only after a strong basis in evidence has established that remedial action is necessary to overcome the consequences of past discriminatory action."[58]

Since *Croson*, a bare majority of the Court has rejected the view that racial classifications, whether benign or hostile, should ever be subject to less than strict scrutiny by either the national or state and local governments.[59] And as we have noted, the Rehnquist Court is similarly opposed to the use of race as the sole criterion in the drawing of electoral district lines.[60]

The Court declined to review a decision by the Court of Appeals for the Fifth Circuit in *Hopwood v Texas* (1996), striking down the University of Texas law school's affirmative action plan for admission of students.[61] That decision, along with some other lower court rulings, called into question the holding in *Bakke* that race may be used as one factor in university admissions in order to achieve a diverse student body.

Thus, until matters are clarified by the Supreme Court, as far as the United States Constitution is concerned, race—and presumably gender—may no longer be considered as a factor for admission to public universities and colleges in the Fifth Circuit (Texas, Louisiana, and Mississippi), but may be considered in the rest of the nation. It is nonetheless clear that the Supreme Court is closely scrutinizing programs that provide a preference based on race or ethnic origin or gender.

California's Proposition 209 and Other Plans

In July 1995, the Regents of the University of California voted to eliminate race or gender as factors in employment, purchasing, contracting, or admissions at the University of California. Then in November 1996, Californians voted overwhelmingly for Proposition 209 to amend the state constitution to forbid state agencies—including schools, colleges, and universities—to discriminate against or grant preferential treatment to any individual or group on the basis of race, sex, color, ethnicity, or national origin in public employment, public education, or public contracting, except where necessary to comply with a federal requirement.

Although Proposition 209 clearly forbids universities and other state agencies to take race and gender into account, it does not appear to make unconstitutional state-supported outreach programs designed to recruit more women and minorities to become scientists and engineers, nor does it prevent state universities from continuing outreach programs aimed at schools with large minority enrollments. In fact, due to such outreach programs, 17.6 percent of the students admitted in the 2000–2001 academic year into the University of California came from "underrepresented groups"—African Americans, Native Americans, and Hispanics. Although that was a drop from the 18.8 percent admitted in the last year before racial preferences were eliminated, it was less than predicted.[62]

Opponents of affirmative action had hoped that the adoption of Proposition 209 in California would start a national movement to restrict or eliminate affirmative action programs, and some federal programs designed to give women- and

minority-owned businesses greater access to federal contracts were cut back. Under pressure from the Office of Civil Rights, some universities stopped offering scholarships based solely on race or ethnicity.[63] But Congress has not moved to limit other federal affirmative action programs.

In the state of Washington, Initiative 200, almost identical to California's Proposition 209, called for abolishing preferential treatment in hiring and contracting. It received 58 percent of the popular vote, despite the fact that Governor Gary Locke and leading businesses outspent their opponents 3 to 1. Heartened by that victory, opponents of affirmative action moved toward putting the question before voters in other states, including Nebraska and Michigan.

California, Washington, Texas, Florida, and some other states have abandoned affirmative action programs and adopted the strategy of automatic admissions for a certain percentage of all high school graduates as a means of maintaining diversity in colleges and expanding educational opportunities for minorities. California offers admission to the top 4 percent of high school graduates, Texas offers admission to the top 10 percent, and Florida to the top 20 percent of every high school graduating class.

Public support for affirmative action as measured in public opinion polls varies by race, social class, education, and life experience, but close inspection suggests that "whites and blacks are not separated by unbridgeable gaps on affirmative action issues, at least not insofar as college admissions decisions are concerned."[64] People's responses seem to depend to a significant degree on how the survey question is put. If the question asked is something like, "Are you in favor of abolishing preferences in hiring or college admissions based on race or gender?" most people say yes. But if the question is something like, "Do you favor affirmative action programs to increase the number of minorities in colleges or in jobs?" there is general support for such programs.

Clearly the debate over the merits and constitutionality of affirmative action is not over. There are more decisions to come as the courts—and the nation—debate whether affirmative action is a vital tool to overcome decades of discrimination that needs to be "amended not ended." Or, as the proponents of Proposition 209 contend, has affirmative action served its purpose, so that government-mandated preference for any person based on race or gender is always unfair and unjust to those not given the preference and demeaning to those to whom it is offered?

EQUAL RIGHTS TODAY

Today legal barriers have been lowered, if not removed, by civil rights legislation, executive orders, and judicial decisions. Important as these victories are, "They were victories largely for the middle class—those who could travel, entertain in restaurants, and stay in hotels. Those victories did not change life conditions for the mass of blacks who are still poor."[65]

More than a generation after the Kerner Commission issued its report, life for inner-city minorities is worse. As prosperous middle-class African Americans have moved out of the inner city, the remaining *underclass*, as they are coming to be called, has become even more isolated from the rest of the nation.[66] Children are growing up on streets where drug abuse and crime are everyday events. They live in "separate and deteriorating societies, with separate economies, diverging family structures and basic institutions, and even growing linguistic separation within the core ghettos. The scale of their isolation by race, class, and economic situation is much greater than it was in the 1960s, impoverishment, joblessness, educational inequality, and housing insufficiency even more severe."[67]

One of the difficulties is that, as conditions have become better for many African Americans and Hispanics, the less fortunate see them as getting worse; however, most Americans see conditions for minorities as improving. "Both perceptions will be correct.

And the fact that both are correct in arriving at opposite perceptions of what is going on will itself lead to further misunderstanding."[68]

Despite the lack of improvement in social conditions, the push for integration has lessened:

> In fact, power on both sides of the color line is based to some extent on acceptance of segregation. On the black side of the color line, it is advantageous to keep African Americans within black electoral areas and keep black-controlled resources within black institutions; integrationist policies are often viewed as posing larger threats than they actually do. On the white side of the line . . . some residents in outlying suburbs see critical advantages in their almost all-white and all middle-class status.[69]

Some contend that attention should be paid to the plight of the underclass and that, instead of focusing on issues of race, what is needed is a policy of providing jobs and improving education.[70] Others say there has to be a revival of the civil rights crusade, a restoration of vigorous civil rights enforcement, job training, and, above all, an attack on residential segregation.[71]

POLITICS ONLINE

Reparations for Slaves?

Whether or not the U.S. government should pay reparations to the descendants of slaves is a new and controversial issue in race relations. Civil rights and class action lawyers, including Harvard Law School Professor Charles J. Ogletree, are preparing this case. Reparations considered in the past included victims of nuclear fallout in the Mountain West, and Japanese-Americans who were interred during World War II.

The scope of a reparations program for U.S. slavery would be large and costly. Arguments for the reparations include an admission by the government that it was wrong to tolerate slavery, and restitution for the economic losses incurred by the slaves and their descendants. Arguments against reparations include the cost of the program and the reinforcement of racial classifications and thinking. For views both in favor and against reparation, visit: **www.true-blue.org/page8.html.**

The reparations issue became more controversial when David Horowitz, a conservative journalist, attempted to place an ad in college newspapers around the country titled "10 Reasons Why Reparations for Blacks Is a Bad Idea for Blacks—and Racist Too." To read the ad, go to: **www.frontpagemag.com/horowitznotepad/2001/hn01-02.htm.** Some school newspapers, like the *Harvard Crimson,* refused to run the ad. At colleges where the ad was run, protesters destroyed copies of the newspaper and demanded apologies. To read more about this controversy, go to: **www.newsmax.com/archives/articles/2001/3/7/221937.shtml.**

The reparations issue taps into strongly held views about race, slavery, and equal opportunity. As this episode illustrates, the feelings about this issue are so intense that it is even difficult to debate.

SUMMARY

1. Americans are committed to equality, an elusive term, with most support for equality of opportunity, some for equality of starting conditions, and some for equality of results.

2. Progress in securing civil rights for African Americans was a long time in coming. After the Civil War the national government briefly tried to secure some measure of protection for the freed slaves and to enforce the Thirteenth, Fourteenth, and Fifteenth Amendments and the civil rights laws passed to implement them. But when federal troops withdrew from the South in 1877, the national government withdrew from the field and blacks were left to their own resources. Not for nearly a century did the national government take action to prevent racial segregation and discrimination against blacks.

3. The crusade for women's rights was born partly out of the struggle to abolish slavery. Similarly, the modern women's movement learned and gained power from the civil rights movements of the 1950s and early 1960s. The fate of these two social movements has long been intertwined.

Women secured the right to vote in the Nineteenth Amendment.

4. Concern for equal rights under the law continues today for African Americans and women. Hispanics, Asian Americans, and Native Americans have also experienced discrimination.

5. The Supreme Court uses a three-tiered approach to evaluate the constitutionality of laws challenged as violating the equal protection clause. Laws touching economic concerns are sustained if they are rationally related to the accomplishment of a legitimate government goal. Laws that classify people because of sex or illegitimacy are subject by the courts to heightened scrutiny and are sustained only if they serve important governmental objectives. Strict scrutiny is used to review laws that touch fundamental rights or classify people because of race or ethnic origin. Such laws will be sus-

tained only if the government can show a compelling public purpose.

6. A series of constitutional amendments, Supreme Court decisions, and laws passed by Congress have now secured the right to vote to all Americans, age 18 and over. Following the Voting Rights Act of 1965, the Justice Department can oversee practices in locales with a history of discrimination. Recent Supreme Court decisions have refined the lengths to which legislatures can go, or are obliged to go, in creating minority-majority districts.

7. *Brown v Board of Education of Topeka* (1954) struck down the "separate but equal" doctrine that had justified segregated schools in the South, but school districts responded slowly. The Supreme Court demanded compliance, and some federal courts mandated busing children across neighborhoods to comply. Still, full integration has proved elusive,

as "white flight" has made many inner cities, and their schools, predominantly black or Hispanic.

8. Discrimination in public accommodations was outlawed by the Civil Rights Act of 1964. This act also provided for equal employment opportunity. The Fair Housing Act of 1968 and its 1988 amendments forbid discrimination in housing.

9. The desirability and constitutionality of affirmative action programs that provide special benefits to those members of groups subjected to past discrimination divide the nation and the Supreme Court. Remedial programs tailored to overcome specific instances of past discrimination are likely to pass the Supreme Court's suspicion of race, national origin, and sex classifications. However, the courts must still clarify constitutional issues concerning preferential treatment in school admissions and hiring practices.

KEY TERMS

natural rights 404
affirmative action 404
women's suffrage 407
equal protection clause 411
due process clause 411

white primary 413
racial gerrymandering 413
poll tax 414
literacy test 414
majority-minority district 415

Jim Crow laws 415
de jure segregation 416
de facto segregation 416
commerce clause 416
class action suit 418

racial or religious restrictive covenants 418

FURTHER READING

Barbara R. Bergman, *In Defense of Affirmative Action* (Basic Books, 1996).

William G. Bowen and Derek Bok, *The Shape of the River: Long-Term Consequences of Considering Race in College and University Admissions* (Princeton University Press, 1998).

Taylor Branch, *Parting the Waters: America in the King Years, 1954–1963* (Simon & Schuster, 1988).

Taylor Branch, *Pillar of Fire: America in the King Years, 1963–65* (Simon & Schuster, 1998).

Keith J. Bybell, *Mistaken Identity: The Supreme Court and the Politics of Minority Representation* (Princeton University Press, 1998).

David Dent, *In Search of Black America: Discovering the African-American Dream* (Simon & Schuster, 2000).

Janet Dewart, ed., *The State of Black America* (National Urban League, published annually).

William N. Eskridge, Jr., *Gaylaw: Challenging the Apartheid of the Closet* (Harvard University Press, 2000).

Bernard Grofman, ed., *Legacies of the 1964 Civil Rights Act* (University Press of Virginia, 2000).

Andrew Hacker, *Two Nations: Black and White, Separate, Hostile, Unequal* (Charles Scribner's Sons, 1992).

Randall Kennedy, *Race, Crime, and the Law* (Pantheon, 1997).

Philip A. Klinker and Rogers M. Smith, *The Unsteady March: The Rise and Decline of Racial Equality in America* (University of Chicago Press, 2000).

Richard Kluger, *Simple Justice: The History of Brown v Board of Education* (Knopf, 1976).

Gary Orfield, Susan E. Eaton, and the Harvard Project on School Desegregation, *Dismantling Desegregation: The Quiet Reversal of Brown v Board of Education* (New Press, 1996).

J. W. Peltason, *Fifty-eight Lonely Men: Southern Federal Judges and School Desegregation* (University of Illinois Press, 1971).

Michael J. Perry, *We the People: The Fourteenth Amendment and the Supreme Court* (Oxford University Press, 1999).

Ruth Rosen, *The World Split Open: How the Modern Women's Movement Changed America* (Viking, 2000).

Girardeau A. Spann, *The Law of Affirmative Action: Twenty-five Years of Supreme Court Decisions on Race and Remedies* (New York University Press, 1999).

Roberto Suro, *Strangers Among Us: How Latino Immigration Is Transforming America* (Knopf, 1998).

Stephen Thernstrom and Abigail Thernstrom, *America in Black and White* (Simon & Schuster, 1997).

19

MAKING ECONOMIC AND REGULATORY POLICY

E CONOMIC FREEDOM AND POLITICAL FREEDOM GO

HAND IN HAND. YET THE CLOSE AND FAVORABLE ASSOCIATION

BETWEEN DEMOCRACY AND FREE MARKET CAPITALISM CONCEALS
a paradox. "A market-capitalist economy inevitably generates inequalities in the political resources to which different citizens have access," writes political scientist Robert Dahl. "Thus a market-capitalist economy seriously impairs political equality."[1] No matter how much a society may strive to be democratic, if its citizens are economically unequal, they are unlikely to be politically equal. Consequently, there is always a tension between democracy and a capitalist economy.

Plainly, economics matters. And so does the way in which a nation makes its economic, social, and foreign policies.

The preceding chapters concentrated on the structure of our federal system and how government institutions are organized and operate. In this chapter and the two chapters that follow, we focus on what the national government *does*—how voters, interest groups, and institutions (Congress, the White House, the executive branch, the courts) interact to promote the general welfare and provide for the common defense. We will be talking about making and implementing *public policy*.

PUBLIC POLICY

T housands of individuals work in Washington in the policy-making process. One of the most fascinating aspects of Washington politics is the way policy activists in government and nongovernmental organizations (research institutes, foundations, the media) join forces. These policy subsystems grow up around interrelated issues. Formal titles are less important for participation in the group than information, imagination, energy, and persistence. Important players include White House staff and executive branch officials, senior congressional committee staff, lobbyists, professional political consultants, and unelected policy specialists. Also influential are journalists and media pundits and nongovernmental research organizations—"think tanks" such as the Brookings Institution, American Enterprise Institute, and Heritage Foundation. Policy activists help clarify issues, resolve conflicts, and facilitate cooperation across institutions.

But some matters of great importance never get on the public agenda. Matters like the growing disparity in income between the very rich and the poor, as well as the problems of our cities fail to get the attention that some people think they deserve. Indeed,

CHAPTERMEDIA

POLITICS ONLINE
How Large a Deficit?
www.prenhall.com/burns

POLISIM
What Can You Get for $4 Trillion?
www.prenhall.com/burns

There are numerous approaches to the study of public policy making. The choice of which approach is most appropriate depends on what policies are being considered, the particular stage of the process selected for analysis, and the analyst's assumptions and political values. Nevertheless, the following distinct stages in the policy-making process can be identified.

- *Problem Identification:* What is the problem? How and by whom is the problem defined? How does the problem fit with existing policy categories and priorities? Does the government need to help out, intervene, regulate, or make some kind of decision? Should the issue or problem even be placed on the government's agenda? What forces determine whether the problem will reach the attention of government officials? A variety of factors and people are involved in problem identification: events, crises, changes in expert opinion, changes in mass opinion, interest-group agitation, and involvement by elected officials and their staffs.

- *Policy Formulation:* What should be done? What alternatives should analysts consider? How should the alternatives be assessed? Who should be involved in the planning and design of the policy?

- *Policy Adoption:* Who needs to act? What branch of government should get involved? What constitutional, legal, or political requirements must be met? How specific or how general must the decision be? Should Congress or some regulatory body be asked to hold hearings on the matter and come up with recommendations? Or should the matter be turned over to the president, who can issue executive orders and deliver major addresses urging the public to comply?

- *Policy Implementation:* Once adopted, how should the policy be carried out? At what level of government—federal, state, local, or all three—will the policy be most effectively implemented? How much money should be spent, where, and how? How can the policy be administered effectively? How and by whom will the implementation of the policy be defined? During this stage policy is translated into practice.

- *Policy Evaluation:* Is the policy working? How is the effectiveness of the policy measured? Who evaluates the policy? What are the consequences of policy evaluation and congressional oversight? Program supporters and administrators tend to exaggerate the success of their favorite programs to justify the funds allocated to them. On the other hand, an agency may build in delays and deficiencies during evaluation to hide the real cost of its operations. Evaluation is never entirely nonpolitical; it is sometimes used by one party, branch of government, department, or agency against another.

fiscal policy

Government policy that attempts to manage the economy by controlling taxing and spending.

there are many ways in which issues fail to reach the national political agenda, and one of the advantages of our federal system is that some issues are dealt with at the state and local level. However, "nondecisions" can occur at any level of government. The absence of government activity does not necessarily mean government is without a policy in that area, for *inaction is itself a policy*. Inattention to an issue can be as important as decisive action.

ECONOMIC POLICY

Our national government has tremendous economic power. Through two types of economic policy—**fiscal policy** (taxing and spending) and **monetary policy** (control of the money supply and interest rates)—the government attempts to manage the economy's ups and downs, moderating both while encouraging steady economic growth. The goal is to smooth out the booms and busts of the business cycle so that unemployment and inflation are kept at a minimum and to allow real income to rise. This management power emerged in the twentieth century through such developments as the Federal Reserve System, the income tax, deficit spending, and the growth of government spending.

Does the government have the same direct control over the national economy that it has, say, over the military or national parks? No. Only if we had a socialized economy administered from Washington would we have a *managed economy* in that sense. In our capitalist economy, a great deal of power is left to private individuals and enterprises. Yet the government keeps a firm hand on many of the gears and levers that guide not only the economy's general direction but the rate at which it moves. These controls are taxes, spending, and borrowing.

Fiscal Policy

Of the two great instruments used to manage the economy we begin with fiscal policy—federal taxing and spending. Nothing reflects the growth of federal programs and the rise of big government more clearly than the increased spending by the national government. In 1933 the national government spent only $4 billion, about $30 per capita. In 2001 the respective figures were 1.8 trillion, about $6,500 per capita.

Today, federal, state, and local governments spend sums of money equal to about one-third of the income of all Americans. The national government is the biggest spender of all—more than all state and local governments combined. Our national government annually spends about 23 percent of the gross domestic product (GDP), or nearly one dollar out of every four. The national debt is about $3.6 trillion, and we pay $240 billion each year in interest payments on that debt (see Table 19–1).

Where the Money Comes From

"In this world," Benjamin Franklin once said, "nothing is certain but death and taxes." Tax collecting is one of the oldest activities of government. Today the federal government gets most of its funds from personal and corporate income taxes. Other moneys come from borrowing, special fees and fines, grants and gifts, and administrative and commercial revenues. Putting power over taxation into the hands of the people was a major achievement in the development of self-government. "No taxation without representation" has been a battle cry the world over. The Constitution clearly provided that Congress "shall have Power To lay and collect Taxes, Duties, Imposts, and Excises." **Tariffs** (import duties) and **excise taxes** (consumer taxes on a specific kind of merchandise)

have to be levied uniformly throughout the United States; direct taxes other than income taxes have to be apportioned among the states according to population.

Raising money is only one objective of taxation. Regulation and, more recently, promoting economic growth are other objectives. In a broad sense all taxation regulates human behavior. For example, a **progressive tax**—by which people with high incomes pay larger fractions of their incomes than people with low incomes—has a leveling tendency on people's wealth.

In the federal budget for Fiscal Year 2001 (see Figure 19–1 on page 430), federal receipts include the following:

1. *Individual income taxes.* Taxes on individuals' incomes account for about forty-eight percent of the federal government's tax revenue. Over the years, the income tax has grown increasingly complex as Congress responded to claims for differing kinds of exemptions and rates. Some members of Congress have advocated simplification or even elimination of the income tax in favor of a national sales tax.

2. *Corporate income taxes.* These taxes account for just under 10 percent of the national government's tax revenues. As late as 1942, revenue from corporate income taxes exceeded that from individual income taxes.

3. *Payroll receipts.* These payroll taxes are the second largest and most rapidly rising source of federal revenue, accounting for 33.2 percent of all federal revenue, not including borrowing. Most people pay more in Social Security taxes than in federal income taxes. These are highly **regressive taxes**, meaning that low-income people generally pay larger fractions of their income than do high-income people.

4. *Excise taxes.* These taxes on liquor, tobacco, gasoline, telephones, air travel, and other so-called "luxury items" account for roughly four percent of federal revenue.

5. *Other* (customs duties and tariffs). Although no longer the main source of federal income, in recent years these taxes provided an annual yield of almost $20 billion.

6. *Borrowing.* Since World War II, the government has regularly resorted to borrowing money to finance itself. Between 1969 and 1998, the government never had a surplus.

When ordinary people are faced with emergency expenses, they borrow money. The same is true of governments. The **deficit** is the difference between the annual revenues raised and the expenditures of government, including the interest on past borrowing. The deficit is not to be confused with the **debt**, which is the total of our deficits, minus our surpluses, over the years.[2] During past military and economic crises, our federal government went heavily into debt; it engaged in deficit spending. But until the late 1990s, we also incurred debts during periods of peace with a relatively healthy economy. The federal government borrowed $23 billion during World War I, about $13 billion during the Great Depression of the 1930s, and $200 billion during World War II. In 2000–2001, the total federal debt was about $3.6 trillion, but the federal budget was estimated to have a surplus of $230 billion.

Borrowing costs money. The federal government borrows from investors who buy treasury notes, treasury bills, and U.S. savings bonds. These investors include individuals (foreign and domestic), U.S. government accounts, banks, and other investors.

The size of the debt and the interest payments alarm many Americans. How was the debt allowed to grow to such an extent? When dealing with this question,

TABLE 19–1 Trends in the Gross Federal Debt

Year	Amount in Billions	Amount as a Percentage of Gross Domestic Product
1950	$256.8	94.2%
1955	274.3	69.4
1960	290.5	56.1
1965	322.3	46.9
1970	380.9	37.7
1975	541.9	34.9
1980	909.0	44.3
1985	1,817.5	33.4
1990	3,206.5	56.4
1995	4,921.0	68.5
2000	5,686.3	59.4
2001*	3,600.0	57.5

SOURCE: U.S. Department of Commerce, *Statistical Abstract of the United States, 2000* (Government Printing Office, 2000), table 7.1.

*Figures are estimates.

monetary policy
Government policy that attempts to manage the economy by controlling the money supply and interest rates.

tariff
Tax levied on imports to help protect a nation's industries, labor, or farmers from foreign competition. It can also be used to raise additional revenue.

excise tax
Consumer tax on a specific kind of merchandise, such as tobacco.

progressive tax
A tax graduated so that people with higher incomes pay a larger fraction of their income than people with lower incomes.

regressive tax
A tax whereby people with lower incomes pay a higher fraction of their income than people with higher incomes.

deficit
The difference between the revenues raised annually from sources of income other than borrowing and the expenditures of government, including paying the interest on past borrowing.

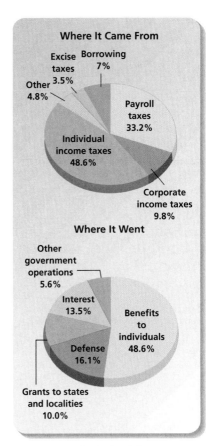

FIGURE 19–1 The Federal Government Dollar

Source: U.S. Department of Commerce, *Statistical Abstract of the United States, 2000* (Government Printing Office, 2000), tables 2.2, 6.1, pp. 30, 109.

debt
The accumulated total of federal deficits, minus surpluses, over the years.

gross domestic product (GDP)
An estimate of the total output of all economic activity in the nation, including goods and services.

entitlement program
Government programs such as Social Security, Medicare, and unemployment insurance to which qualified citizens are "entitled" by national legislation.

Office of Management and Budget (OMB)
Presidential staff agency that serves as a clearinghouse for budgetary requests and management improvements.

keep two considerations in mind. First, the government owes roughly 90 percent of the money to its own citizens rather than to foreign governments or investors, although the amount owed to foreigners is growing. Second, the economic strength and resources of the country are more significant than the size of the debt. Moreover, the recent budget surpluses have shifted the debate to how fast the debt should be paid down while also cutting taxes and increasing spending for vital social programs.

Where the Money Goes

Where does the money go? Much of it, of course, goes for benefit payments and national defense. Specifically, 16 percent goes to national defense; 13 percent to interest on the national debt; 10 percent to grants for states and localities; 48 percent to direct benefit payments for individuals (such as Social Security, Medicare, Medicaid, and other major social programs), and 5.6 percent for all other federal operations (again, see Figure 19–1).

Another way of understanding how the money is spent is to consider federal outlays as a percentage of the nation's **gross domestic product (GDP)**, an estimate of the total output of all U.S. economic activity. The GDP is close to $8 trillion. Spending on domestic **entitlement programs**—programs such as Social Security, Medicare, and unemployment insurance to which qualified citizens are "entitled" by national legislation—runs at about 11 percent of the GDP. Spending for defense is a little more than 3 percent of GDP; payments on the deficit make up another 3 percent of GDP; and nondefense discretionary spending is around 3.3 percent.

Years ago, federal revenues and outlays were so small that national taxing and spending had little impact on the overall economy. Today, the federal government extracts billions of dollars from certain areas of the economy and pumps them back into others, with profound effects on the United States and world economies. Much of the federal budget is "uncontrollable" in the sense that "mandatory growth" (cost of living increases) in many programs is built into the law. These programs do not come up for annual review or decision by either the Congress or the president; they just keep on growing automatically. The most uncontrollable parts of the budget are Social Security, Medicare, unemployment benefits, outstanding contracts, and other fiscal obligations. The most controllable part of the budget is defense spending. Since the collapse of the Soviet Union, real cuts in defense spending have been achieved, dozens of bases closed, and significant reductions made in the size of our military services.

The Budget Process

Before the Budget and Accounting Act of 1921, each executive agency dealt with Congress on its own, requesting that Congress appropriate funds for its activities with little or no presidential coordination. In 1921 the Bureau of the Budget (changed to the Office of Management and Budget in 1970) was created in the Treasury Department, and for the first time, the executive branch presented one budget to Congress.

THE EXECUTIVE BRANCH The federal government's fiscal year begins on October 1. The budget process begins nearly two years in advance, when the various departments and agencies estimate their needs and propose their budgets to the president.[3] While Congress is debating the budget for the coming fiscal year, the agencies are making estimates for the year after that (see Table 19–2). Agency officials take into account not only their needs as they see them but also the overall presidential program and the probable reactions of Congress. Departmental budgets are detailed; they include estimates on expected needs for personnel, supplies, office space, and the like.

The **Office of Management and Budget (OMB)**, a staff agency of the president, handles the next phase. Budget examiners in the OMB review each agency budget and bring it into line with the president's overall plans. Executive branch hearings are

TABLE 19–2 Steps in the Budget Process	
February–December 2001	Executive branch agencies develop requests for funds and submit them to the Office of Management and Budget. The president reviews the requests and makes the fiscal decisions on what goes in his budget.
December 2001	The budget documents are prepared.
January–February 2002	The budget is transmitted to Congress.
March–September 2002	Congress reviews the president's proposed budget, develops its own budget, and approves spending and revenue bills.
October 1, 2002	The fiscal year begins.
October 1, 2002–September 30, 2003	Program managers execute the budget provided in law.
October–November 2003	Data on actual spending and receipts for the completed fiscal year become available.

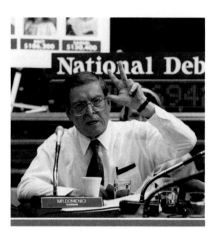

Pete Domenici, Senate Budget Committee Chairman, has a great deal of influence in preparing the budget.

then held to give agencies a chance to clarify and defend their estimates. The OMB director and staff often prune the agencies' requests severely.

Finally, the OMB director goes to the president with a single, consolidated set of estimates of both revenue and expenditures—the product of perhaps a year's work. The president takes several days to review these figures and make adjustments. The budget director also helps the president prepare a budget message that will stress key aspects of the budget and tie it to broad national goals. The president must submit the budget recommendations and accompanying message to Congress between the first Monday in January and the first Monday in February. The president's budget recommendations cover thousands of pages.

THE LEGISLATIVE BRANCH   Presidential submission of a budget proposal is only the beginning. Under our Constitution, Congress must appropriate the funds and raise the taxes. But the president also plays a role, since all appropriation and tax proposals are subject to a presidential veto. Thus the White House is an active participant in the congressional budget battles. When Congress acts on the budget, it does so by first approving the overall budget resolution. Then the actual appropriation of funds is detailed in 13 different bills, each of which is presented to the president for approval.

In 1974 Congress adopted the Budget Reform Act to enhance its role in the budget process. This act specifies that the president must include proposed changes in tax laws, estimates of amounts of revenue lost through existing preferential tax treatments, and five-year estimates of the costs of new and continuing federal programs. The act also calls on the president to seek authorizing legislation for a program a year before asking Congress to fund it.

The 1974 Budget Reform Act also created the **Congressional Budget Office (CBO)**, which gave Congress its own independent agency to prepare budget data and analyze budgetary issues. By February 15 of each year, the CBO furnishes its analysis of the presidential recommendations to the House and Senate Budget Committees. The CBO also provides Congress with biannual forecasts of the economy, analyzes alternative fiscal policies, prepares five-year cost estimates for bills proposed by congressional committees, and undertakes studies requested by committees. The CBO also monitors the results of congressional action on individual appropriations and revenues against the targets or ceilings specified by legislation.

The Gramm-Rudman-Hollings Act (1985), as modified by the 1990 Budget Enforcement Act, called for Congress to adopt a **concurrent resolution** for the next fiscal year by April 15. This resolution set levels of new budget authority and

Congressional Budget Office (CBO)
An agency of Congress that analyzes presidential budget recommendations and estimates the costs of proposed legislation.

concurrent resolution
A resolution passed in the same form by both houses of Congress that expresses the "sense" of Congress on some question. It is not sent to the president and does not have the force of law.

spending, which became the ceiling for the Appropriations Committees. Congress can later adopt a budget resolution that revised or reaffirmed the earlier resolution. In recent years Congress has been resorting to **reconciliation**, in which Congress, by a budget resolution, sets ceilings on what the various Appropriations Subcommittees can appropriate and then leaves the decision of how to achieve the required limits to the committees.

Such budget reform efforts did not by themselves balance the budget, yet they did set in place a discipline and a mind-set that moved toward balancing the budget. Equally, if not more important, was the economic boom of the 1990s that generated huge tax revenues that, together with budget reforms, helped achieve balanced budgets.

Indeed, at the outset of the twenty-first century the U.S. economy was robust enough that the federal budget enjoyed a surplus. This unfamiliar event triggered extensive debates about what should be done with the surplus. Republicans proposed sweeping tax cuts. Democrats favored tax cuts only if Social Security remained properly funded and the cuts would not come at the expense of various social programs.

THE GENERAL ACCOUNTING OFFICE   After Congress appropriates money, it checks on the way that money is being spent by two methods: (1) congressional committees hold *oversight hearings* in which they call on agency heads to explain how they have spent the money; and (2) the **General Accounting Office (GAO)** uses spot-sampling to check vouchers and make audits in the field. The GAO is headed by the **comptroller general**, who is appointed by the president with the approval of the Senate for a 15-year term. Although the comptroller general has the authority to disallow expenditures, approval is no longer needed for the disbursement of funds. In the past 30 years, the GAO has taken on broader responsibilities in investigating and evaluating programs by checking on the adequacy and effectiveness, as well as the honesty, of a program's performance.

The Politics of Taxing and Spending

In addition to raising funds to run the government, taxes also promote economic growth and reward certain types of behavior, such as owning a home, contributing to charities, and investing in high-risk but desirable (from a national standpoint) energy or housing ventures. Cynics suggest, too, that from a member of Congress's point of view, tax legislation has the additional and important function of raising campaign funds. As long as tax legislation is under consideration in Congress, swarms of lobbyists are eager to contribute generously to campaign coffers.[4]

THE TAX BURDEN   No one likes taxes. Most of us complain our tax load is too heavy and that other people are not paying their fair share. People with high incomes who pay a high percentage of their income for federal taxes naturally grumble. People with low incomes complain that even a low tax deprives them of the necessities of life. People with middle incomes consider their situation the worst of all; their incomes are not high, but their taxes are.

What is the best type of tax? Some say a *progressive income tax* (also called a *graduated* income tax) is best because it is relatively easy to collect, hits hardest those who are most able to pay, and hardly touches those at the bottom of the income ladder. Others argue that *excise taxes* are the fairest because they are paid by people who spend money for luxury goods and thus obviously have money to spare. In addition, by discouraging people from buying expensive goods, excise taxes occasionally have a deflationary effect when prices are on the rise. On the other hand, excise taxes are more expensive to collect than income taxes. In some cases, such as the tax on tobacco, they may hit the poor the hardest. Excise taxes also face strong resistance from affected industries: tobacco, liquor, and airlines, for example.

The most controversial tax is a general **sales tax**, which is levied by almost all states on the sale of most goods, sometimes exempting food and drugs. Labor

reconciliation
Process by which Congress sets ceilings on what Appropriations Subcommittees can appropriate.

General Accounting Office (GAO)
An independent investigative arm of Congress established in 1921 to check on receipt and disbursement of public funds and review the performance of government agencies.

comptroller general
Head of the General Accounting Office, appointed by the president with the approval of the Senate for a 15-year term.

sales tax
General tax on sales transactions, sometimes exempting food and drugs.

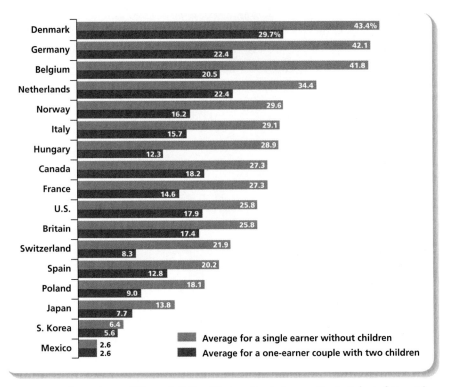

FIGURE 19–2 Percentage of Wages Full-time Workers Pay in Income Tax in Selected Countries.

Source: "Tax Burdens," *The Washington Post*, September 30, 2000, p. A14.

The rates include contributions to social insurance and retirement funds, less cash benefits paid, such as child allowances.

and liberal organizations see sales taxes as *regressive*: because a sales tax is the same for all persons, these taxes are not related to a taxpayer's ability to pay, and poor persons pay a higher percentage of their income in sales taxes for the goods and services they buy than do rich ones. Proponents of a national sales tax stress its potential anti-inflationary effect and point to its successful use in a number of states.

The sales tax is exclusively a state and local tax in the United States, but in Europe a similar tax, a **value-added tax** (**VAT**), is used to raise revenues for national governments (see Figure 19–2). The VAT differs from a sales tax in that it collects a tax on the increased value of a product *at each stage of production and distribution* rather than just at the point of sale, as with a sales tax. A loaf of bread would thus have value added several times: the farmer would pay a value-added tax on the grain before selling to the miller, who would be taxed before selling to the baker, and so forth. The value-added tax is seen by some as a way to infuse a large amount of new revenue into the federal government. Opponents of the tax see it as regressive and increasing the tax burden. States see a federal VAT as invading their turf. Since it taxes consumption and not savings, a VAT could encourage savings and investment, both of which are vital to economic growth.

THE ANTITAX MOVEMENT   California voters set the tax agenda for the entire nation when they passed Proposition 13 in June 1978—a citizen initiative to lower and permanently cap property taxes. Tax limitation measures like Proposition 13 were later approved in scores of states and localities, and the success of the issue at the local level gave antitax activists at the national level renewed energy.

Ronald Reagan in his 1980 presidential campaign promised a 30 percent reduction in income taxes, phased in over a three-year period. Once elected, he made cutting taxes his highest priority. In a stunning victory over the House Democratic leadership, he got most of what he wanted. He had promised that by cutting taxes

value-added tax (VAT)

A tax on increased value of a product at each stage of production and distribution rather than just at the point of sale.

Antitax protests erupted all over the country after Californians passed Proposition 13 in 1978, which placed strict limitations on state government spending.

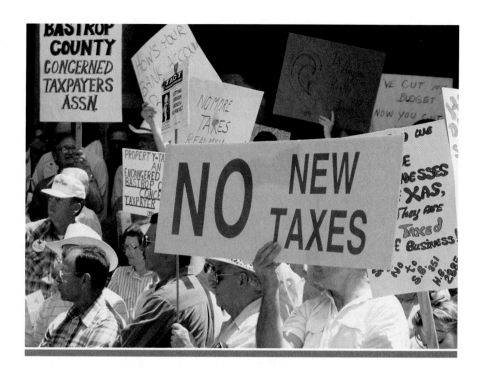

and government spending in nondefense areas, he could stimulate the economy and fund his other priority—national defense. This policy, dubbed "Reaganomics," was based on *supply-side economics*, which holds that economic growth will result from people having more money to spend because of lower taxes, permitting these additional expenditures also to be taxed.

Whether Reaganomics worked is still a partisan issue, because after the Reagan tax cuts, budget deficits grew by leaps and bounds. It certainly did not work as promised, yet few question that it worked politically. After the 1981 tax cut, the agenda of American politics was largely devoted to reducing the high federal budget deficits. Hence the Democrats, who typically would want to propose new or expanded government programs, were put on the defensive. By the end of 1990s, a strong economy and restraint on government spending meant that for the first time in decades there was a budget surplus. How much of these surpluses should be used to pay down the debt, lower taxes, or increase spending for social programs is a subject of intense debate between Democrats and Republicans.

Tax Expenditures

Tax expenditures are government *revenue losses* due to federal tax laws that provide special tax incentives or benefits to individuals and businesses. These benefits, more than $400 billion of them, come from special exclusions, exemptions, or reductions from gross income or from special credits, preferential tax rates, or deferrals of tax liability.

Tax expenditures are one means by which the national government carries out public policy objectives. For example, the government encourages investment in research and development by allowing such costs to be deducted from a company's taxes. Federal grants could also achieve this objective.

Critics assert that the rich get their "welfare" through such loopholes. This form of "welfare" does not require a visible appropriation of money plainly identified in the budget. However meritorious the objectives of tax expenditures are—encouraging home ownership, research and development, retirement savings—these tax benefits do not benefit all levels of society. In many instances, they cause investors to waste their resources on low-yield investments in order to obtain large tax benefits.

tax expenditure
Loss of tax revenue due to federal tax laws that provide special tax incentives or benefits to individuals or businesses.

monetarism
A theory that government should control the money supply to encourage economic growth and restrain inflation.

Federal Reserve Board
The system created by Congress in 1913 to establish banking practices and regulate currency in circulation and the amount of credit available. It is comprised of 12 regional banks, and its major responsibilities are supervised by the Federal Reserve Board of Governors.

MONETARY POLICY

Monetary policy is the second way the national government manages the economy. The core element of **monetarism** is the idea that prices, income, and economic stability are primarily a function of growth in the money supply. Monetarists contend the money supply is the key factor affecting the economy's performance, and restrained yet steady growth in the money supply would encourage solid economic growth but not inflation.

The Federal Reserve System

Monetary policy is not made by either Congress or the president but by the **Federal Reserve Board**, specifically its Federal Open Market Committee. The members of that committee, some of the most powerful people in the United States, have a lot to say about how much interest you pay on the car you are buying and whether you refinance your home because of lower interest rates. They can stimulate the economy so that it could be easier for you to find a job, or slow it down so that it could be harder. Who are these people with so much power, and how do they influence economic policy?

The Board of Governors of the Federal Reserve System ("The Fed") consists of a chair and six other members who are appointed by the president with the consent of the Senate for 14-year terms, with one member's term expiring every two years. These long, staggered terms for members of the board are intended to insulate its members from politics as much as possible. There are 12 Regional Federal Reserve Banks, each headed by a president, with a nine-member board of directors chosen from the private banking business in that district.

The 12 members of the Federal Open Market Committee are all professional economists or bankers. Though their names are unfamiliar to most people, this group, which meets about every six to eight weeks, decides how much money will be allowed to enter the economy, manages foreign currency operations, and regulates banks. It does this by buying and selling government securities, which can encourage either lower or higher interest rates. Other lenders closely watch the decisions of the Fed and typically make their interest rates consistent with Fed decisions. Because lenders make it either more or less expensive to borrow money, they influence a wide range of economic activity.

The chair of the Board of Governors, by tradition an economist, is appointed by the president to a four-year term. The current chair, Alan Greenspan, is one of the most influential national public policy officials. Greenspan was first appointed by President Ronald Reagan in 1987, reappointed by President George Bush, and reappointed by President Clinton. Greenspan's leadership had helped foster economic growth and was widely respected by financial leaders, factors that influenced Clinton's decision to reappoint him. The staff of the Federal Reserve System reports directly to the chair, not to the board, and the chair is the one who appears before Congress and the country to explain the policies of the Federal Reserve System. The chair heads the Federal Open Market Committee and is credited or blamed for the decisions made by the Fed.

At the time the Federal Reserve System was established in 1913, regional banks were located according to the population, economy, and politics of that time. "Today," as John R. Wilke observes, "these locations make little sense. Missouri, once an economic and political power because of its riverboat economy, has two Fed Banks; booming Florida has none. California and its vast economy has only one Fed Bank—which also serves eight other states and covers 20 percent of the population."[5]

The 12 Fed Banks process one-third of the checks written in the United States, and the electronic network dollar volume of transfers is about $200 trillion annually. As its check-clearing business begins to be altered by competition from private

---

Federal Reserve Chair Alan Greenspan.

laissez-faire economics
Economic theory that opposes governmental interference in the economy beyond what is necessary to protect life and property.

Keynesian economics
Economic theory based on the principles of John Maynard Keynes stating that government spending should increase during business slumps and be curbed during booms.

inflation
A rise in the general price level (and decrease in dollar value) owing to an increase in the volume of money and credit in relation to available goods.

clearinghouses, and as new technologies proliferate in the years ahead, Fed operations may come under closer scrutiny. But as one insider commented, "The market has changed, and the technology has changed. . . . [But] do we really want to fool around with the Fed's independence just to save a few hundred million dollars a year?"[6]

Government and Economic Policy

Depression is a hard teacher, and the 1930s had a tremendous impact on American thinking about the role of government in the economy. The Great Depression that began in 1929 brought mass misery. "One vivid, gruesome moment of those dark days we shall never forget," wrote one observer. "We saw a crowd of some fifty men fighting over a barrel of garbage which had been set outside the back door of a restaurant. American citizens fighting for scraps of food like animals!"[7]

Despite the efforts of the Franklin Roosevelt administration to cope with the Depression, it hung on. Faint signs of recovery could be seen in the mid-1930s, but the recession of 1937–38 indicated that the country was by no means out of the woods. Between 8 and 9 million people were jobless in 1939. Then came World War II, and unemployment seemed cured. Millions of people had more income, more security, and higher standards of living. Lord Beveridge in England posed a question that bothered many thoughtful Americans: "Unemployment has been practically abolished twice in the lives of most of us—in the last war and in this war. Why does war solve the problem of unemployment which is so insoluble in peace?"[8]

What can government do to foster jobs and economic growth? Some economists urged the government to reduce spending, lower taxes, curb the power of labor, and generally leave business and the economy alone. This is called **laissez-faire economics**. Another group, deeply influenced by the work of English economist John Maynard Keynes,[9] recommended that when consumer spending and investment decline, government spending and investing should increase. In a recession, government must do the spending and investing if private enterprise will not or can not. Laissez-faire economics is identified with President Herbert Hoover, while Keynesian economics is identified with President Franklin Roosevelt.

Keynesian economics influences government management of the economy. Yet politically, Keynesian economics presents a problem. It is much easier to increase spending and government programs than it is to curb them. As a result, deficit spending became a habit in this country for 50 years. To stimulate demand, the government spent more money than it took in. For many years, this policy was thought to be beneficial to the economy. It was also convenient politically. However, when the national debt soared, both Congress and the president searched for ways to balance the budget.

Economists also found that Keynesian policies, when accompanied by a loose-money policy by the Federal Reserve, resulted in a hidden cost: **inflation**. Because government programs introduced extra money into the economy without a corresponding increase in goods, each dollar became worth less, and prices rose to compensate. Although government spending was not responsible for all inflation, it was viewed as a major contributor; as a result, new economic remedies have been sought.

A BALANCING ACT

Republicans and Democrats alike have concentrated on balancing the federal budget, and they have been successful. But the problem remains that when members of the baby-boom generation start to reach retirement age after 2010, the costs of Medicare, Medicaid, and Social Security will grow dramatically. The Con-

gressional Budget Office has concluded that although the federal surplus will increase over the next decade, it could then decline sharply afterwards. Unless major changes are made, the government may have to fall back on deficit spending to pay for the costs of health and retirement benefits (see Figure 19–3).

Promoting Business and Agriculture

The national government promotes a prosperous economy through its monetary and fiscal policies. It also provides various services to business and industry. The Department of Commerce is sometimes known as the nation's "service center for business." Its cabinet secretary, usually a person with an extensive business background, is a spokesperson for business interests. Historically, the department has been at the center of the government's efforts to promote economic growth and encourage business research and development. Its National Institute of Standards and Technology (NIST) provides highly valued technical assistance that has helped companies study the structures of enzymes, look at submicroscopic flaws in jet-engine turbine blades, and probe the structure and properties of various materials used in biotechnology, electronics, fiber optics, and other fields. The Department of Commerce also undertakes basic research in ocean science and engineering, meteorology, and weather forecasting. Its National Oceanic and Atmospheric Administration is currently performing research on global warming, hurricane predictions, acid rain, marine fisheries, and a wide assortment of undersea research activities.

Also part of the Department of Commerce, the Patent and Trademark Office (PTO) administers the patent system that Congress established "to promote the Progress of Science and useful Arts" under Article I of the Constitution. Each year the United States Patent and Trademark Office issues more than 100,000 patents to cover new and useful inventions that provide their owners certain exclusive rights for 17 years. With the booming e-commerce and knowledge economy, the number of patents issued annually almost doubled in the last decade.[10]

The impressive success and competitiveness of American agriculture owe much to the federal government and its subsidies—almost as much as to fertile soil, hard work, and the technology revolution. Agriculture and food-related businesses are our largest industry—bigger than computers, or automobiles, or the movie and recording industries. Agribusiness generates nearly one out of every five jobs in the private sector and accounts for almost 20 percent of the GDP and 15 percent of our exports. It is also an industry with a high rate of productivity. Thanks in part to federal support for research, agricultural productivity has increased at a rate of about 3 percent a year in the past decades. Farmers in the United States produce about ten times as much per work hour today as they did 50 years ago.

Our great agricultural production reflects one of the most successful partnerships between government and private enterprise. The federal government has invested large sums in basic and applied agricultural research. Much of this work is done at land-grant state universities and colleges. What is learned in the laboratories is tested on experimental farms, and new techniques and products are then made available to farmers through the Agricultural Extension Services of these schools. Local county agents, part of the Agricultural Extension Service, are supported by a combination of national, state, and local funds.

The Great Depression of the 1930s ravaged virtually every farmer. The New Deal helped to get farmers back on their feet by means of credit support, loans, and crop price supports. Federal initiatives in irrigation and rural electrification fostered significant strides in productivity. Loans and credit programs were established to help farmers purchase needed equipment. Some of these programs were eventually self-financing, even though they began with public money. Other federal initiatives stabilized income and output with price supports and acreage controls.

Plainly, the array of subsidies, loans, credits, and related programs of research and investment helped American farmers be successful in the past, but economists

FIGURE 19–3 A Short Lived Federal Budget Surplus?

SOURCE: Congressional Budget Office; "A Short-Lived Surplus," *The New York Times*, October 17, 2000, p. A11.

trade deficit

An imbalance in international trade in which the value of imports exceeds the value of exports.

World Trade Organization (WTO)

Created along with the General Agreement on Tariffs and Trade (GATT) it promotes free trade around the world.

General Agreement on Tariffs and Trade (GATT)

An international trade organization with more than 130 members, including the United States and the People's Republic of China, that seeks to encourage free trade by lowering tariffs and other trade restrictions.

North American Free Trade Agreement (NAFTA)

Agreement signed by the United States, Canada, and Mexico in 1992 to form the largest free-trade zone in the world.

protectionism

Policy of erecting trade barriers to protect domestic industry.

point out that not only do the biggest farmers gain the most from federal programs, but farm subsidies hurt poor people by driving up the price of food. Thus, although helping farmers encourages productivity, it also increases poverty. Political support has recently eroded for the continuation of farm programs costing billions of dollars to subsidize farmers not to grow things.

The 1996 Federal Agriculture Improvement and Reform Act (FAIR) called for an end of subsidies to wheat, corn, feed grain, cotton, and rice farmers over seven years, to be replaced by fixed but declining Freedom to Farm payments. The act continues subsidies at a reduced rate for peanut, sugar, and dairy programs, continues conservation programs that pay farmers to leave idle 36.4 million acres of cropland, provides for crop insurance, and maintains food stamps and other nutrition programs for two years. The assumption behind this act is that the farmers who receive these Freedom to Farm payments, while still being allowed to plant anything they want in any amount they want, will use these cash payments to cushion the loss of subsidies. By 2004 it is hoped that the marketplace will work and farmers will be able to make a living by producing what the nation needs at lower prices for consumers. However, if farm incomes substantially decline or food prices go way up, it is very likely that the Freedom to Farm plan will come under attack and be modified by Congress. And it should be noted that the act only *authorized* this program, which means that each year Congress must *appropriate* the funds to implement it. These yearly battles provide ample opportunities for the many well-organized interests involved in farming to alter how the law is funded.

TRADE POLICY

In 1971 the United States experienced its first **trade deficit**—the value of imports exceeded the value of exports—in more than a century. Since then we have had trade deficits in billions of dollars every year. Congress and the president are under continuing pressure from industry, unions, and regional political leaders to protect American jobs, companies, and communities from foreign competition. These pressures come not only from the textile and auto industries but from glass, steel, shoe, lumber, electronics, book publishing, aluminum, farming, and domestic wine and spirit coalitions, to name just a few. They claim that the trade deficit justifies the imposition of trade sanctions.

The problem is not that we are importing too much but that we are exporting too little. German cars, Japanese radios, and Indonesian textiles are fine products; if other countries produce better cars or shoes at a lower price, then, free traders argue, we should deploy our labor and capital in areas in which we can do better.

The question is also whether our products are given fair treatment by other nations. American agricultural products are denied entry into some countries and are subject to high tariffs in others. American automobile manufacturers complain of unfair restrictions imposed by the Japanese on our cars. Finally, some countries exploit the U.S. advantage in technology by slavishly copying our products and then selling them back to us or to other countries at a profit.

Another unfair trade practice is *dumping*—selling products below the cost of manufacturing or below their domestic price with the intention of driving other producers out of the market and then raising prices to profitable levels. Another practice is government *subsidizing* of certain industries. Some countries, for example, subsidize steel for export. Others require lengthy inspection procedures for imported goods. Japan has protected several of its industries—producers of automobiles and baseball bats, for example—by specifying standards that are virtually impossible for us to meet. The United States, of course, often retaliates by imposing "voluntary" limits on Japanese products.

In 1947 a group of countries formed a trade organization to negotiate free trade by lowering tariffs (taxes on imports that raises their price) and quotas (limits

on the quantity of a particular product that may be imported) and other disadvantages countries face when trading. Today the **World Trade Organization (WTO)**, based on the **General Agreement on Tariffs and Trade (GATT)**, includes more than 130 countries, and its membership accounts for four-fifths of the world's trade. The WTO has negotiated agreements through eight rounds of trade negotiations (the most recent was called the *Uruguay Round*, named after the site of the initial conference). The United States has tried to focus WTO and GATT negotiations on trade in agricultural items, foreign investment, and protection of technological innovations and intellectual property. Although many trade restrictions still face U.S. imports and those of other countries, the WTO and GATT greatly helped to lower tariffs and quotas as well as to increase "fair" trade throughout the world. Many maintain that GATT is one of the most successful innovations in the history of international relations and one of the contributing factors to the post-cold war economic success of the United States.[11]

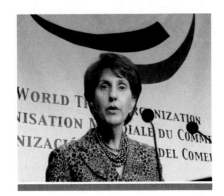

Charlene Barshevsky, United States Trade Representative, addresses a meeting of the World Trade Organization in Seattle in December 1999.

In recent years, however, meetings of the WTO have met with protests, even riots in Seattle and Washington, D.C., because many are concerned that not enough attention is given to the problems of child labor, unequal pay, and pollution around the world.

The North American Free Trade Agreement

In 1992, the United States, Canada, and Mexico signed the **North American Free Trade Agreement (NAFTA)**, which formed the largest free-trade zone in the world, even surpassing the European Community's 15-country conglomerate. Although President George Bush signed NAFTA near the end of his presidency, the agreement could not become law until ratified by Congress. President Bill Clinton promoted NAFTA, even though many members of his own party were its most vigorous opponents. Congress passed NAFTA by a thin margin in a bipartisan vote in which the Democrats were the minority.

Though trade among the United States, Canada, and Mexico is not absolutely "free" or unimpeded, the agreement has had a tremendous impact on the economies of all three countries. Today Mexico is the United States' third most important trading partner, and the United States is Mexico's most important trading partner. Critics of NAFTA remain concerned because Mexican antipollution laws are significantly less stringent than those in the United States, and Mexican workers work for considerably lower wages. Both of these factors make relocation to Mexico attractive to many U.S. companies seeking to lower labor and pollution-control costs.

Barriers to Trade

Protectionism—erecting barriers to protect domestic industry—sounds easy and workable as a solution to trade deficits, but trade deficits are only symptomatic of more profound economic problems. Most economists favor free trade and strongly dislike protectionism because it prevents efficient use of resources and because consumers pay much more for protected products than they would otherwise. Tariffs merely divert attention away from real solutions like increased productivity and capital investments and inevitably invite retaliation from foreign countries.

In the 1930s many nations experienced high unemployment, low production, and general economic misery. The United States was no exception. In an effort to aid ailing American industries, Congress passed the Smoot-Hawley tariff, the highest general tariff the United States had ever had. Supporters hoped high tariffs on imported goods would increase the demand for goods produced in the United States and thus help get the country out of the Great Depression. The exact opposite occurred. Other nations retaliated with high tariffs on American goods. Demand fell, intensifying the Depression.

Later, Congress gave the president power to negotiate mutual tariff reductions with other nations, subject to certain restrictions, and by the early 1970s, tariffs on

Thinking It Through...

What constitutes an "American" car? After finishing this short quiz, you know (if you did not know already) that company name has little relevance. Many foreign companies have plants in the United States that employ American workers and use a high percentage of American parts. General Motors, Ford, and Chrysler all have joint ventures, or have merged, with foreign-owned companies that place some of their models in the "import" category. Is a Toyota Camry an American car if it is built in Mexico in a plant partially owned by Ford? What defines an American product? Ownership of company? Nationality of employees? Location of physical plant? Domestic content of components?

The politics of regulation and new regulatory rules seldom make front page news. Yet every week you read about new regulations or debates about regulatory policy, such as:

"EPA to Require New Pollution Emissions Controls"

"Nutrition Labeling on Products for Kids Proposed"

"FAA Finds Minor Shortcomings at Boeing"

"FAA to Tighten Rule on Takeoffs in Snow and Ice"

"FCC Considers Rules to Spur Economic Growth"

"Meat Inspections Facing Overhaul"

"Bid to Save Fish Puts West on Notice"

"FDA to Set Limits on Breast Implants"

"FDA Approves Laser System for Angioplasty"

"Panel Urges FDA to Approve Female Condom"

"FDA Revises Labeling on Antacids"

"Bank Mergers Pose Challenge to Regulators"

"FAA Plans Close Look at Plane Braking Mechanism"

"FCC Adopts Limits on TV Ads Aimed at Children"

"EPA to Shame Industries into Reducing Pollution"

"FTC Sues Intel"

"President Bans Federal Research on Cloning"

industrial products had been substantially reduced. Trade barriers are less severe today than they were back in the 1930s. But restrictions still exist. Certain tariffs, quotas on imported goods, and import regulations limit American consumption of foreign products. Most exist to protect American farmers, or businesses, or U.S. workers in certain industries. Thus we have restrictions on clothing and textile imports, and these restrictions cost U.S. consumers a lot more than they benefit workers' wages.

The United States has generally backed increased trade and fewer trade barriers, yet many Americans fear *globalization*. Free trade and globalization policies do not confer equal benefits on everyone. Some workers inevitably are worse off as a result of freer international flow of goods and capital. All told, trade barriers cost American consumers approximately $80 billion a year—equal to more than $1,200 per family.[12]

U.S. economic policy in the future will probably be some combination of free trade and selective protectionism. Though protectionism shields highly visible industries from competition at home or abroad, such measures are often another kind of subsidy that protects one industry at the expense of another—and always at high cost to American consumers. Instead, the United States continues, through negotiations with trading partners, to remove unfair trade practices, encourage greater investments in what we have traditionally done well (science, technology, and medical and agricultural research), educate workers with better skills, and encourage labor-management experiments that can maximize productivity with an eye toward higher-quality products that will be highly prized abroad. We also continue our trade adjustment assistance to aid displaced workers and help retrain those who lose their jobs as a direct result of freer trade arrangements.

REGULATORY POLICY

What do lawn mowers, cellular phones, roller blades, Viagra pills, fat substitutes, nicotine patches, pornography, banks, breast implants, cable TV, animal cloning, baby food, and workers' wages have in common? They are all *regulated* in some way by government. Because virtually every activity in the United States is supervised by government in one form or another, regulation is a vast enterprise. Not surprisingly, any activity as pervasive as this generates controversy. From small business owners who have to spend several days each year filling out dozens of forms and complying with federal regulations, to Microsoft's Bill Gates, there is constant criticism of government's regulatory intrusiveness.

The Constitution explicitly authorizes Congress to regulate commerce among the states and with foreign nations. In our earliest years, Congress used this regulatory power to impose or suspend tariffs on imports from other nations. In the nineteenth century, the federal government created a number of agencies to regulate the conduct of citizens and commercial enterprises with an eye toward promoting economic development. Among these were the Army Corps of Engineers (1824), the Patent and Trademark Office (1836), the Steamboat Inspecting Service (1837), and the Copyright Office of the Library of Congress (1870). In 1887, Congress created the Interstate Commerce Commission to deal with the widespread dissatisfaction over the practices of railroads.

Additional regulations came into existence to break up monopolies, to clean up meat-packing conditions such as those exposed in Upton Sinclair's *Jungle* (1906), to prevent the kind of pesticide contamination described in Rachel Carson's *Silent Spring* (1962), to correct the lack of auto safety documented in Ralph Nader's *Unsafe at Any Speed* (1965), and to respond to discrimination in employment on the basis of race, color, national origin, religion, sex, and age. More recently, regulations have been

THE MICROSOFT DEBATE

For years Microsoft has been adding functions to its Windows operating system—Windows 95, 98, and Millennium editions. Critics charge that these functions give a distinct advantage to compatible software produced by Microsoft, enabling it to win a greater share of the market. This tactic may be illegal if it is shown to stifle competition.

The Justice Department's Antitrust Division investigated whether Microsoft was actually stifling competition, and Senate hearings were also held. The Justice Department took Microsoft to court for allegedly violating past agreements in which it pledged not to engage in anticompetitive practices. Microsoft co-founder and chief executive officer, Bill Gates, fumed at the Justice Department's efforts, saying incorporating fewer functions in operating systems would be a major setback not only for Microsoft but for consumers, innovation, and the high-tech industry:

Microsoft President Bill Gates and other software industry executives testify before the Senate Judiciary Committee hearing on anticompetitive practices.

> *The government wants to force us to ship a browser made by a leading competitor, Netscape, with every copy of Windows—a demand that would benefit only Netscape, not consumers. Such a demand is both unprecedented and unreasonable. It's like ordering Ford to sell autos fitted with Chrysler engines. Not only would these proposals undermine our ability to compete, they run counter to the way every industry has evolved over the years—and, more importantly, to what consumers expect when they buy products.[*]*

Is Bill Gates right? Or is Microsoft creating an unfair monopoly? Microsoft's critics argue that if the Justice Department does not restrain Microsoft's expansion into new markets, its monopoly will mow down rivals with market muscle and not necessarily with superior products.[**] Others contend that because of Microsoft's dominance in important computer markets, it deserves close government scrutiny. Yet they point out that "the purpose of antitrust law is to protect consumers, not to help rivals."[***] Federal Reserve Chair Alan Greenspan, though not commenting directly on the Microsoft case, cautioned that what appear to be monopolies very often tend to fade over time with changes in markets and technology. He cited IBM, U.S. Steel, and General Motors as examples. "I would feel uncomfortable if we inhibited various different types of mergers or acquisitions on the basis of some presumed projection as to how the markets would evolve," Greenspan told a congressional panel. "History is strewn with people making projections that have turned out to be grossly inaccurate."[****]

In June 2000, the federal district court ruled that Microsoft had violated antitrust laws. It held that Microsoft should be broken in two, separating its Windows operating system business from the rest of the company. An appeal was made to the Supreme Court, which declined review in order to let the Court of Appeals for the District of Columbia Circuit hear the appeal in 2001. However the appellate court decides, there will undoubtedly be further appeals.

The debate over Microsoft is certain to continue. But, ultimately it could establish for the twenty-first century the rules and limits for the vast computer industry and other high-tech fields.[*****]

[*]Bill Gates, "We're Defending Our Right to Innovate," *The Wall Street Journal*, May 20, 1998, p. A14.

[**]See Robert Bork, "The Most Misunderstood Antitrust Case," *The Wall Street Journal*, May 22, 1998, p. A16. See also Steve Lohr, "Gates on Capital Hill, Presents Case for Microsoft," *The New York Times*, March 4, 1998, pp. A1, C4.

[***]Robert E. Hale, "Antitrust Excess," *The New York Times*, May 20, 1998, p. A23.

[****]Quoted in Jon R. Wilke, "Greenspan Questions Antitrust Efforts," *The Wall Street Journal*, June 17, 1998, p. A2.

[*****]See "Trust and Antitrust," *The Economist*, October 7, 2000; Richard McKenzie, *Trust on Trial: How the Microsoft Case Is Reforming the Rules of Competition* (Perseus, 2000).

enacted to protect us from raw sewage in rivers, lead in paint and gasoline, toxins in the air, radon gas in our homes, and asbestos, cotton dust, and hazardous products in the environment. Expenditures mandated by federal regulations are estimated to cost about $200 billion annually for environmental, health, and safety rules alone.[13]

Presidents and members of Congress are frequently embroiled in the politics of making regulatory policy. There were partisan battles in the 1990s over legislation to enable cable TV, local phone companies, and long-distance carriers to join together; the Brady Bill antagonized many politicians by mandating a waiting period before handguns could be purchased; and battles were waged over air bags and their protection or harm of children. Meat inspections have been overhauled by new government rules. The Food and Drug Administration and the Federal Aviation Administration are continually issuing new guidelines about the foods we eat and the planes we fly. Some members of Congress question whether the health benefits from cleaning up auto emissions are compelling enough to justify the enormous expense of stricter pollution control.[14]

In 1935 there were 4,000 pages of regulations in the *Federal Register* (a daily publication of proposed and existing federal regulations); today there are about 70,000 pages of regulations.[15] Both political parties say regulatory overkill threatens to overwhelm entrepreneurs and divert them from building vital, innovative companies. "Regulations add as much as 33 percent to the cost of building an airplane engine and as much as 95 percent to the price of a new vaccine. Federal regulation also adds about $3,000 to the cost of a new car."[16]

Regulation Defined

In a broad sense, *regulation* is any attempt by the government to control the behavior of corporations, other governments, or citizens. **Regulation**, as we use the term, occurs when the government steps in and alters the natural workings of the open market to achieve some desired goal. Regulation by government interjects political goals and values into the economy in the form of rules that direct behavior in the marketplace. These rules have the force of law and are backed by the government's police power.

All economies follow sets of rules and regulations; there simply are no unregulated economies. The United States operates in a competitive market economy in which wages, prices, the allocation of goods and services, and the employment of resources are generally regulated by the laws of supply and demand. We rely on private enterprise and market incentives to carry out most of our production and distribution.

The presumption in the United States is against government regulation. Most people feel that businesses should be allowed to buy and sell products and produce goods without government regulation. Our government has to justify regulations, and they do so only because people, through the representative process, have come to demand certain protections. Regulation is assumed to be necessary to protect people from undesirable side effects of the market, such as pollution or discrimination or false advertising.

Regulation also compensates for market imperfections. Even those who oppose regulation recognize that the market does not always solve every problem. Consider pollution. For a long time no price was imposed on a business for using air and water to discharge toxic wastes. Therefore, market forces did not consider the social costs of its air and water pollution. When the market fails to set appropriate costs and benefits, pressures develop for the government to step in. The government can, for example, pass regulations imposing penalties for air pollution. Market forces also do not encourage taking a bus instead of a car to work. If government enacted higher taxes on gasoline, our fuel costs would be brought more in line with Europe's. Such a policy would also reduce our dependency on Middle East oil and promote domestic energy production.

regulation

The attempt by government to control the behavior of corporations, other governments, or citizens through altering the natural workings of the open market to achieve some desired goal.

Types of Regulations

It is customary to talk of two general categories of regulation: economic and social regulation. *Economic regulation* generally refers to government controls on the behavior of business in the marketplace: the entry of individual firms into particular lines of business, the prices that firms may charge, the standards of service they must offer. Public utilities, transportation, and television are examples of regulated industries. As already noted, economic regulation began almost as early as the founding of the Republic and expanded in earnest in 1887, when the Interstate Commerce Commission (ICC) was established; it continued in the twentieth century with the Federal Communications Commission (FCC), Commodity Futures Trading Commission (CFTC), and a host of regulatory agencies, boards, or commissions responsible for enforcing statutes in particular industries (see Table 19–3). In the twentieth century, regulatory bodies grew from five to about 80 regulatory organizations that employ about 100,000 people to enforce thousands of federal regulations.

The second type of regulation, *social regulation*, refers to government attempts to correct a wide variety of side effects, usually unintended, brought about by economic activity. Concern for worker health and safety and for environmental hazards has led to social regulation. Social regulation also includes the efforts by government to ensure equal rights in employment, education, and housing. Whereas economic regulation is usually organized along industry lines, social regulation cuts across these lines.

The Environmental Protection Agency (EPA), the Consumer Product Safety Commission (CPSC), and the Occupational Safety and Health Administration (OSHA) are regulatory agencies engaged in social regulation. In economic terms, producers regulated by social regulation must now pay for external costs that once were free, such as using rivers, landfills, or the atmosphere for waste disposal. These costs, however, are then passed along to the consumer, so the true cost of the product is more accurately reflected in its price. Some goods subsequently become too costly, and demand drops. Others become more popular (for instance, safe toys), and demand increases. The final goal of social regulation is the socially beneficial allocation of resources.

TABLE 19–3 Some Regulatory Agencies and Their Missions

	Year Established	Primary Functions
Federal Trade Commission (FTC)	1914	Administers certain antitrust laws concerning advertising, labeling, and packaging to protect consumers from unfair business practices
Food and Drug Administration (FDA)	1931	Establishes regulations concerning purity, safety, and labeling accuracy of certain foods and drugs; issues licenses for manufacturing and distribution.
Federal Communications Commission (FCC)	1934	Licenses civilian radio and television communication; licenses and sets rates for interstate and international communication
Animal and Plant Health Inspection Service	1953	Sets standards; inspects and enforces laws relating to meat, poultry, and plant safety
Environmental Protection Agency (EPA)	1970	Develops environmental quality standards; approves state environmental plans
Occupational Safety and Health Administration (OSHA)	1970	Develops and enforces worker safety and health regulations
Bureau of Alcohol, Tobacco and Firearms	1972	Enforces laws and regulates legal flow of these materials
Consumer Product Safety Commission (CPSC)	1972	Establishes mandatory product safety standards and bans sales of products that do not comply
Nuclear Regulatory Commission (NRC)	1974	Licenses the construction and operation of nuclear reactors and similar facilities and regulates nuclear materials; also licenses the export of nuclear reactors and the export and import of uranium and plutonium

The Occupational Safety and Health Administration, a unit in the Department of Labor, has been one of the most criticized federal regulatory agencies, although that criticism has decreased in recent years. You have no doubt come across reports of its endless rules or warnings to business operators. OSHA has thousands of rules in the Code of Federal Regulations. Despite vigorous efforts by antiregulation groups to slash its budget and cut its staff, OSHA still employs over 2,000 persons, about half of whom are safety and health inspectors.

OSHA was created because interest groups effectively publicized that many people were becoming disabled or were dying from work-related accidents. By 1970, for example, more than 14,000 people were dying each year in industrial accidents, and an estimated 100,000 a year were being permanently disabled in workplace injuries.

The mandate of OSHA is to protect the health and safety of more than 60 million workers in about 5 million workplaces. It is also asked to issue compulsory safety and health standards and to monitor compliance. To achieve these objectives, OSHA is empowered to inspect businesses and to issue notices of violation and fines.

OSHA celebrated its thirtieth anniversary in 2000. It has not been as bad as its critics maintain, but neither has it been as effective as its proponents hoped. OSHA deserves credit for the decrease in work-related injuries and illnesses and for its action against polyvinyl chloride and other serious threats to workers' health. OSHA has tried to concentrate its limited energies on severe health hazards and make more use of its emergency power to restrict dangerous substances. It has dropped many trivial safety rules and focuses on four major industries—construction, heavy manufacturing, transportation, and petrochemicals—that are considered hazardous. It also keeps pressure on a few industries it considers potentially dangerous, such as auto repair, dry cleaning, and building materials.

Congress has created two types of regulatory agencies: those within the executive branch and those that have a degree of independence from Congress and the president. Members of executive branch agencies serve at the pleasure of the president. Executive branch regulatory agencies include the Food and Drug Administration (FDA), the Office of Surface Mining, and the National Highway Traffic Safety Administration. Members of **independent regulatory agencies** are appointed by the president, confirmed by the Senate, and cannot be, except for cause removed by a president as specified by law. Independent agencies, usually headed by a board composed of seven members, include the Federal Communications Commission, the Equal Employment Opportunity Commission, and the Nuclear Regulatory Commission.

The Regulation Debate

The debate about regulation is usually about less versus more, rather than all or nothing. Few Americans call for unlimited government intervention in economic and social activity. And few advocate absolute removal of government participation from the marketplace. Indeed, most people call for more regulation in some areas and less in others. Sometimes those who call for more regulation are surprised by the results, as mandatory air bags in automobiles illustrated.

Automobile air bags have saved thousands of lives since they were made mandatory in the 1980s, but they have also killed dozens of people, including as many as 40 children who were riding in the front passenger seat. Thus a piece of equipment designed as a safety measure turns out to have serious risks to the people it should protect. The federal government issued warnings in 1997 that small children should never sit in the front seat, car manufacturers rushed to redesign their air bags to prevent injury or death to children or small adults, and the government created new regulations for their installation and use.

The deregulation of cable television offers yet another example of unintended results. Soon after the deregulation of television in the mid-1990s, the number of cable subscribers increased. The dramatic growth

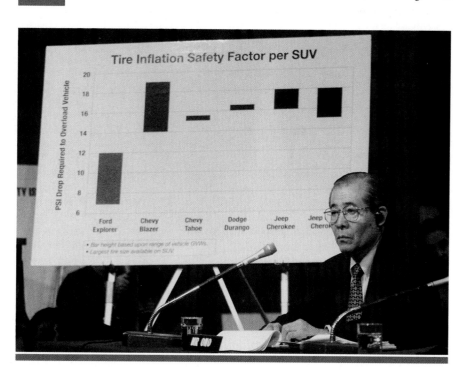

Masatoshi Ono, CEO of the Firestone/Bridgestone Tire Company, responds to questions from the Senate Commerce Committee concerning the numerous fatal accidents attributed to defective tires made by his company.

in access to cable was accompanied by an increase in fees, something the Department of Justice attributed in part to the monopoly held by local cable companies. The Federal Communications Commission and Congress were pressured to address the rapid increases in the cost of cable television, so Congress passed legislation regulating fees. Ironically, rates went up for about half of the country following regulation. Defenders of Congress's law see the fee increases as part of an effort to establish a "benchmark" from which prices will not grow as rapidly in the future. Opponents point not only to the higher costs associated with regulation, but to the fear Congress may seek to regulate subscriber fees as well as the rates the companies pay for programs.

Congress often legislates broad objectives for the regulatory agencies, which then set specific rules for meeting these goals. Agency regulations have been largely in the form of specific rules that a firm may not violate without being punished. Under pressure from businesses and their allies in Congress, recent administrations have cut back some of these regulations. For example, the Occupational Safety and Health Administration trimmed more than a thousand "nitpicking" regulations that governed such things as the shape of toilet seats. Congress also began to acquire better information on the benefits and costs of regulation and increased its oversight of federal regulatory efforts.[17]

Regulating Business

During most of the nineteenth century our national policy was to leave business pretty much alone. However, four major waves of regulatory legislation have occurred: at the turn of the century, in the 1910s, in the 1930s, and in the late 1960s through 1980. In each case, changing circumstances gave rise to the legislation.

Antitrust Policy

Perhaps the number one responsibility of government regulation in our free market system is to maintain competition. Where one company gains a **monopoly**, the market system operates ineffectively. The aim of **antitrust regulations** is to prevent monopolies, break up those that exist, and to restore competition. In the past so-called "natural monopolies," such as electric utilities and telephone companies, were protected by the government because it was assumed that in these fields competition would be grossly inefficient.

In the late nineteenth century, social critics and populist reformers believed consumers were being cheated, especially in the oil, sugar, whiskey, and steel industries, where large monopolies, called **trusts**, worked to reduce competition. People began to have mixed feelings about big business. Americans, who have often been impressed by bigness—the tallest skyscraper, the largest football stadium, the biggest steel mill—and the efficiency that often goes with bigness, became skeptical about giant enterprises.

In 1890, Congress responded by passing the Sherman Antitrust Act, which was designed "to protect trade and commerce against unlawful restraints and monopolies." Henceforth, persons making contracts, combinations, or conspiracies in restraint of trade in interstate and foreign commerce could be sued for damages, required to stop their illegal practices, and subjected to criminal penalties. However, the Sherman Antitrust Act had little immediate impact; presidents made little attempt to enforce it, and the Supreme Court's early interpretation of the act limited its scope.[18]

In 1914, during the administration of Woodrow Wilson, Congress added the Clayton Act to the antitrust arsenal. This act outlawed such specific abuses as charging different prices to different buyers in order to destroy a weaker competitor, granting rebates, making false statements about competitors and their

Regulations that have Improved the Quality of Our Lives

Bans on "quack medicines"

Inspections for livestock diseases

Recalls of defective automobiles

Regulations on industrial pollution

Regulations on lead poisoning

Regulations to encourage clean water

Regulations on asbestos

Regulations on vinyl chloride

Regulations on unsafe toys

Regulations on breast implants

Regulations on fraudulent labeling of children's foods

independent regulatory agency
A government agency that exists outside the three branches of government and is responsible for enforcing particular statutes.

monopoly
Domination of an industry by a single company; also the company that dominates.

antitrust regulation
Federal laws and regulations that try to prevent businesses from dominating a particular market through monopoly or restraint of trade.

trust
A monopoly that controls goods and services, often in combinations that reduce competition.

Merger Mania

During recent years thousands of mergers have taken place, many of them among competing companies: General Motors bought Hughes Aircraft; R.J. Reynolds absorbed Nabisco; GE and RCA merged with General Foods; Warner Communications merged with Time; and McDonnell Douglas became part of Boeing. Airlines have merged. Many banks and financial services companies merged.

With a staff of 350 lawyers, the Antitrust Division of the Department of Justice investigates mergers and acquisitions to determine whether they violate the antitrust laws by unreasonably restraining interstate trade and commerce. If it so determines, it may seek to prevent the merger. The Antitrust Division also has authority to prosecute violators of the laws against price fixing, and it investigates and prepares cases to prevent anticompetitive bid rigging.

The Reagan and Bush administrations generally adopted a permissive policy toward mergers, and few were prevented. These Republican administrations assumed that most mergers were inherently good for the consumer and the economy, not—as the common wisdom had it in the 1960s—that such mergers were suspect. The Clinton administration was more vigorous in enforcing antitrust laws, yet the Justice Department's Antitrust Division and the Federal Trade Commission have generally looked favorably on most mergers. In 2001, approval was given to the largest merger ever, the $111 billion merger of AOL and Time-Warner.

Top Merger and Acquisition Deals of All Time

Acquirer	Acquisition	Year	Value (in billions of dollars)
American On Line (AOL)	Time-Warner	2001	$111.0
Exxon	Mobile	1998	86.4
Travelers Group	Citicorp	1998	72.6
SBC Communications	Ameritech	1998	72.4
AT&T	Tele-Communications	1998	69.9
Vodafone Group	AirTouch Communications	1999	65.9
AT&T	MediaOne	1999	63.1
Qwest Communications	US West	1999	48.5
Viacom	CBS	1999	37.3
BP Amoco	ARCO	1999	33.7

SOURCE: "Paradox of the Internet Era," *The New York Times*, September 12, 1999.

products, buying up supplies to stifle competition, and bribing competitors' employees. In addition, **interlocking directorates** (by which an officer or director in one corporation serves on the board of a competitor) were banned, and corporations were prohibited from acquiring stock in competing concerns if such acquisitions substantially lessened interstate competition. That same year Congress established the Federal Trade Commission (FTC), run by a five-person board, to enforce the Clayton Act and prevent unfair competitive practices. The FTC was to be the "traffic cop" for competition.[19]

REGULATING LABOR AND MANAGEMENT

Government regulation of business is essentially restrictive. Most laws and rules curb business practices and steer private enterprise into socially useful channels. But regulation cuts two ways. In the case of American workers, most laws in recent decades have tended not to restrict labor but to confer rights and opportunities on it. Actually, many labor laws do not touch labor directly; instead they regulate its relations with employers.

Among the more important federal regulations designed to protect workers are:

1. *Public contract.* The Walsh-Healy Act of 1936, as amended, requires that no worker employed under contracts with the national government in excess of $10,000 be paid less than the prevailing wage, and that he or she be paid overtime for all work in excess of 8 hours per day or 40 hours per week.

2. *Wages and hours.* The Fair Labor Standards Act of 1938 set a maximum work week of 40 hours for all employees engaged in interstate commerce or in the production of goods for interstate commerce (with certain exemptions). Work beyond that amount must be paid for at one-and-one-half times the regular rate. Minimum wages, originally set as 25 cents an hour, were progressively increased; the minimum wage was increased to $5.15 an hour as a result of the Minimum Wage Increase Act of 1996.

3. *Child labor.* The Fair Labor Standards Act of 1938 prohibits child labor (under 16 years of age, or under 18 in hazardous occupations) in industries that engage in, or that produce goods for, interstate commerce.

4. *Industrial safety and occupational health.* The Occupational Safety and Health Act of 1970 created the first comprehensive federal industrial safety program. It gave the secretary of labor broad authority to set safety and health standards for companies engaged in interstate commerce.

During the first half of the last century, labor's basic struggle was for the right to organize unions. For decades trade unions had been held lawful by state legislatures, but the courts had chipped away at their status by legalizing anti-union devices. The most notorious was the **yellow-dog contract**, by which employers made new workers, as a condition of employment, promise not to join labor organizations. If labor organizers later tried to unionize the workers, the employers could apply for court orders to stop the organizers. In 1932, the Norris-La Guardia Act made yellow-dog contracts unenforceable and granted labor the right to organize. Under President Franklin D.

Roosevelt, Congress enacted a series of laws to protect workers and their right to form trade unions.

Do unions need federal laws to protect their right to organize? The history of union efforts before 1933 suggests that without federal protection, organizing was extremely difficult. Indeed, union membership and strength were waning fast until New Deal measures granted workers the right to organize and bargain collectively. The 1935 National Labor Relations Act (usually called the Wagner Act) made these guarantees permanent and gave them federal backing. The act makes five types of employer action unfair: (1) interfering with workers in their attempt to organize unions or bargain collectively; (2) supporting company unions (unions set up and dominated by the employer); (3) discriminating against members of unions; (4) firing or otherwise victimizing an employee for having taken action under the act; (5) refusing to bargain with union representatives. The act prevents employers from using violence, espionage, propaganda, and community pressure to resist unionization.

A regulatory commission was established to administer the act. The National Labor Relations Board (NLRB), consisting of five members holding overlapping terms of five years each, operates largely through regional officers, who investigate charges of unfair labor practices and issue formal complaints, and through trial examiners, who hold hearings and submit reports to the board in Washington.

Congress passed a major modification of the labor laws in 1947, the Labor-Management Relations Act, commonly called the Taft-Hartley Act. It remains the most important legislation regulating union activity in the United States.

- It outlaws the **closed shop** (a company that requires an employer to hire and retain only union members in good standing) and permits the **union shop** (a company in which new employees must join the union within a stated period of time).

- It makes it an unfair labor practice for unions to refuse to bargain with employers.

- It allows limited use of the **labor injunction** (a court order forbidding specific individuals or groups to perform acts the court considers harmful to the rights or property of an employer or community).

- It permits states to outlaw union shops. *Right-to-work laws*, which states could now adopt, typically make it illegal for **collective bargaining** agreements (terms and conditions of employment negotiated by representatives of the union and the employer) to contain closed shop, union shop, preferential hiring, or any other clauses calling for compulsory union membership.

The Taft-Hartley Act set up machinery for handling disputes if a work stoppage threatens national health or safety. It has been invoked against strikes in vital sectors of the economy such as atomic energy, coal, shipping, steel, and telephone service. The president or the secretary of labor can attempt to mediate strikes without resorting to the act.

ENVIRONMENTAL PROTECTION

The issue of pollution vividly illustrates the regulatory dilemma. Critics of strict controls on air, water, and noise pollution say the pursuit of a clean environment increases costs of products and causes unemployment. They call attention, for example, to the disastrous economic consequences of the shutdown of companies for pollution violations. Until relatively recently, governments at all levels did little to protect the environment, and what little was done was by state and local governments. In recent decades the national government has taken on new responsibilities, primarily because local governments failed to act.

interlocking directorate
A corporation in which an officer or director sits on the board of a competitor, with the effect of restraining trade.

yellow-dog contract
Contract by an anti-union employer that forces new workers to promise they will not join a union as a condition of employment.

closed shop
A company with a labor agreement whereby union membership is a condition of employment.

union shop
A company in which new employees must join a union within a stated time period.

labor injunction
A court order forbidding specific individuals or groups from performing certain acts (such as striking) that the court considers harmful to the rights and property of an employer or community.

collective bargaining
Method whereby representatives of the union and employer determine wages, hours, and other conditions of employment through direct negotiation.

The primary federal agencies concerned with the environment are the Council on Environmental Quality in the Executive Office of the President, which develops and recommends policy options to the president and Congress, and the Environmental Protection Agency (EPA), which is responsible for enforcing federal environmental laws and regulations. Other federal agencies that regulate the environment include the Interior Department, the Food and Drug Administration, and the Departments of Energy and Transportation.

The National Environmental Policy Act of 1969 set up the controversial requirement of **environmental impact statements** to assess the potential effects of new construction or development on the environment. Most projects utilizing federal funds must file such statements. Since 1970 thousands of statements have been filed. Supporters contend that such statements point out major flaws in projects and can lead to cost saving along with greater environmental awareness. Critics claim environmental impact reviews simply represent more government interference, paperwork, and delays in both the public and private sectors.

A 1970 amendment to the Air Quality Act of 1967 established national standards for states, pollution guidelines for automobiles, and regulations concerning stationary sources of pollution. Yet enforcement of the act greatly disappointed environmentalists, who noted that EPA had brought only about seven of some nearly 300 industrial air toxins under federal regulation. Amendments to the act passed in 1977 extended but did not greatly strengthen the original legislation. Throughout the 1980s the fear of lost jobs and costs for industry and consumers stalled more rigorous enforcement and tighter restrictions.

The 1990 Clean Air Act was designed to remedy the failings and lax enforcement of the 1970 and 1977 acts. It tightened controls on automobiles and the fuel they use. It required automakers to install pollution controls to reduce emissions of hydrocarbons and nitrogen oxides and set stiff standards for the kinds of gas that can be sold. The 1990 act stipulated that plants that emit any of 189 toxic substances have to cut those emissions to the average level of the 12 cleanest similar facilities. Plants posing a 1 in 10,000 risk of cancer to nearby residents by the year 2003 may be shut down. The act also promoted the phasing out of chlorofluorocarbons and other chemicals that harm the earth's protective ozone layer and may contribute to global warming.

The 1990 Clean Air Act has been called the most expensive piece of environmental legislation ever passed, with some estimates saying compliance will cost as much as $25 billion per year. But most people, including leaders in our nation's basic industries, acknowledge we have made a mess of the environment, and the sooner we clean it up the better.

Some economists suggest that the profit motive may be harnessed in the pursuit of pollution control. With this in mind, EPA has pressed for new regulatory strategies that encourage market solutions for ecological problems: "Government sets broad limits on the amount of pollution allowed for a region or industry and allots permits to firms for their share of that total. Polluters can buy or sell these allowances, so that firms that can reduce a pollutant inexpensively will benefit by selling their allowances to dirtier neighbors."[20] Initial efforts along these lines have been successful, saving billions.

THE DEREGULATION DEBATE

One solution to criticism about government regulation has been **deregulation**—cutbacks in the amount of regulation attempted by the federal government, but not dismantling of all regulatory procedures. Deregulation has been tried in the transportation industries, the banking industry, and telecommunications, to name a few. No industry has undergone more extensive deregulation than the transportation

environmental impact statement
A statement required by federal law from all agencies for any project using federal funds to assess the potential effect of the new construction or development on the environment.

deregulation
A policy promoting cutbacks in the amount of federal regulation in specific areas of economic activity.

industry. Over the past generation, airlines, trucking, and railroads have been granted considerable freedom in conducting their operations.

Airline Deregulation

The Civil Aeronautics Board (CAB) was established by the federal government in 1938 to protect airlines from unreasonable competition by controlling rates and fares. Critics charged that airlines competed only in the frequency of flights and in the services they offered. Because there was no competition over price, consumers were forced to pay high rates for services they may not have desired. Others claimed CAB regulation of fares kept them higher than they would have been under competitive conditions. It was also charged that airlines were too slow to open new routes under CAB supervision.

In light of these and other considerations, Congress in 1978 passed the Airline Deregulation Act. The Civil Aeronautics Board was legislated out of existence in 1985, and airlines were free to set whatever fares their markets would bear. Free entry and free exit were allowed in all markets. One of the first results of deregulation was that rural and some medium-sized cities lost service because carriers found it more profitable to use their aircraft in busier markets. Airlines were raising fares on routes over which they had monopolies in order to subsidize lower fares on more competitive routes. Critics charged that safety precautions and maintenance suffered as a result of cutthroat competition and the ease with which new airlines could enter the market.

Although problems have been associated with airline deregulation, it has resulted in generally lower fares, greater choice of routes and fares in most markets, and more efficient use of assets by the industry.[21] Some airlines have been driven into bankruptcy and others have merged, but deregulation of the airlines has been judged a success by the surviving airlines and most observers of the industry. If an airline is overcharging passengers, a competitor will eventually steal those travelers away. Southwest Airlines is an example of a discount airline that took advantage of deregulation to take on larger airlines.[22] Deregulation has strengthened the industry by forcing companies to streamline their operations in order to survive in a competitive market. But, recent mergers of major airlines have worsened the problems caused by deregulation and cancelation of service to rural and medium-sized cities in parts of states in the west.

Telecommunications Reform

After years of debate, President Clinton signed into law the Telecommunications Act of 1996, the most sweeping regulatory reform of telecommunications since the Communications Act of 1934. The act opened up large areas of telecommunications to companies that once were regulated both in the services they could provide and the prices they could charge. The main objective of the new law was to increase competition among phone, cable, and other communications companies. Telephone companies that were once divided into seven local "mini-Bell companies" were allowed to offer services outside their defined regions. Local telephone companies won the freedom to provide long distance service, manufacture communications equipment, and offer video service in competition with cable television. At the same time, local telephone companies opened their networks to competition for local telephone service from cable television and long distance companies. In short, restrictions were removed so that cable television and local and long distance telephone companies could effectively compete with one another.

The Downside of Deregulation: California's Energy Crisis

The deregulation of California's public utilities was intended to encourage competition and to lower prices. But in 2000 and continuing into 2001, the state confronted a severe energy crisis. With major utility companies facing bankruptcy and increasing costs, lighting in public buildings was cut back, rolling blackouts occurred, and the legislature and the governor agreed on a billion dollar bailout.

California's deregulation was unique. Utilities that buy power and deliver it to customers remained under state regulation. They were allowed to sell their generating plants but required to buy power on the daily spot market, while not passing increased costs on to consumers. Companies that bought their power plants were free from state regulation and permitted to sell energy on the open market. Even though energy use grew only modestly, an imbalance between supply and demand resulted in escalating costs that threatened utility companies with bankruptcy.

Other factors also contributed. No new power plants were built in more than a decade, and some energy-producing companies invested in plants in other states and abroad. Unusual weather increased demands for energy, and natural gas prices rose. Environmental restrictions also contributed to the problem.

In response, the legislature passed laws authorizing, among other reforms, the sale of bonds to finance the state's buying of power through long-term contracts, thereby stabilizing prices. Under the plan, California sells the power to consumers, using the utility companies to transmit the electricity and collect the bills. The state will make the money back by selling hydroelectric power at a narrow profit. Governor Gray Davis also announced plans for some of the most aggressive conservation measures in the nation, including curbing retail stores' outdoor lighting. The California energy crisis, however, is a continuing story and may become more acute.

SOURCE: Todd S. Purdum, "California Passes a $10 Billion Plan for Buying Power," *The New York Times*, February 2, 2001, p. A1; and Timothy Egan and Sam Howe Verhovek, "California's Panic Was Moneymaker for Energy Sellers," *The New York Times*, February 11, 2001, p. A1.

Two controversial aspects of the Telecommunications Act of 1996 were regulation of Internet content and the advent of the V-chip to allow parents to block out television shows with objectionable content. However, the Supreme Court struck down the provisions making it a crime for any person knowingly to make indecent material assessable to minors on the Internet. The Court found the provision too vague and held that the Internet receives full protection under the First Amendment.[23] Still, the debate continues on who will decide what is deemed violent or offensive.[24]

EVALUATING REGULATORY POLICY

Although the need for regulation, especially in areas affecting health and safety, is widely accepted, there are concerns about the negative consequences of regulation. A marked decrease in lead paint poisonings, the use of childproof bottle tops, and the banning of many cancer-producing pesticides are all positive outcomes. On the negative side, regulations generally increase the cost of products and may hamper some industries.

- *Regulation distorts and disrupts the operation of the market.* Some governmental intervention upsets the normal adjustment processes of the market and thus encourages higher prices, misallocation of resources, and inefficiency.

- *Regulation may discourage competition.* Some forms of regulation (often the kind desired by industry) actually have the reverse of their desired effect. This is especially true when the government grants operating licenses and charters to maintain a certain level of quality or stability in the market. Regulatory red tape has also been charged with discouraging entry into industries and driving small businesses out.

- *Regulation may discourage technological development.* If the reward for innovation is a new set of rules and a struggle for permission to use a new product, business may not find it worth the effort to innovate.

- *Regulatory agencies are often "captured" by the industries they regulate.* It is suggested that some regulatory bodies are controlled by the businesses they are supposed to be regulating. There is evidence, too, that some bureaucrats consider jobs in regulatory agencies as stepping-stones to lucrative careers in private industry, and the industries encourage this connection.

- *Regulation increases costs to industry and to the consumer.* Some critics estimate that government regulations cost $8,000 to $10,000 annually to every household in the United States. Such figures are disputed by many labor and consumer advocates, who say health and safety standards are the best investment we can make. Every life and every limb we save, and every disease we prevent, represents not only a valuable achievement but also a reduction in the nation's enormous hospital and medical bills.

- *Regulation has often been introduced without cost-benefit analysis.* Critics say too little attention is given to whether the benefits of a particular piece of regulation are great enough to justify its cost. Is it worth it to delay approval of new drugs while some who would benefit may die? Is it worth it to clean up 95 percent of automobile emissions if the cost is many times that of an 85 percent cleanup? Is it worth spending $2 million per cancer case arising from exposure to hazardous waste?

- *Regulatory agencies lack qualified personnel.* Critics of regulation, and some heads of regulatory agencies themselves, say regulators lack expertise. Regulatory agencies complain they need larger budgets to do their job properly and attract more qualified staff. Critics argue, too, that government should not meddle in technological industries about which it knows little.

Deregulation appears to be working better in some areas than in others. In the area of drug deregulation, the results are mixed. The Food and Drug Administration, especially since the early 1980s, relaxed the requirements for introducing new medicines. People in the drug industry applaud these efforts. They argue that as a result of deregulation, the public gets better medicines faster and cheaper. Opponents contend, and with some evidence, that the accelerated approval process is endangering public health by prematurely allowing potentially hazardous drugs on the market. Conversely, many life saving medications are held back until lengthy testing is concluded.

In our federal system the mere fact that the national government stops regulating an industry does not mean the particular industry will be unregulated. On the contrary, sometimes 50 different state regulators take over, making it even more difficult for an industry to operate on a large scale. California, for example, has much tougher automobile emission rules than does the national government. Variations in state regulations are the reason businesspeople themselves sometimes call for more, not less, national regulation; they would prefer one set of national guidelines to 50 different state ones.

In sum, the federal government is heavily involved in making economic and regulatory policies. It collects taxes, regulates the money supply, tries to prevent monopolies that would hurt the consumer, and seeks to promote free trade. It does all this while trying to let the market, not government bureaucrats, shape the demand and price of products and services. Most Americans want their government to play only a limited role in the economy, but competing values such as fairness, equality, protecting the environment, and encouraging healthy competition inevitably encourage elected officials to perform certain balancing or referee responsibilities in order to promote the common good.

POLITICS ONLINE

How Large a Deficit?

Ross Perot, among others, helped make budget deficits a key issue in the 1992 election; since that time, deficit reduction has been a high priority. During the 1980s and early 1990s the national debt had increased dramatically, and as a result, Congress and the White House pushed for balanced budgets. Because the economy has grown, we now have a budget surplus. Indeed, the debate in the 2000 elections was what to do with the budget surplus, how large it will grow, and how long it will last. Some argue that the surpus isn't real, that it is an artifact of how you calculate government revenue and spending. Most observers agree, however, that we have entered a period of budget surpluses, and everyone agrees that we continue to have a substantial national debt.

Some Internet sites report especially on the issue of debt status. The Treasury Department has a Public Debt Awareness Bureau that can be accessed at:
www.publicdebt.treas.gov/.http://www.budget.org.

To see national debt monitioring reports that are frequently updated, go to:
www.toptips.com/debtclock.html or www.brillig.com/debt_clock.

What to do with the surplus is another matter. Republicans want to lower taxes, arguing "Give the money back to the people who earned it." Democrats want to pay down the national debt and maintain current levels of government services. You can obtain detailed budget analysis with interactive features at:
www.federalbudget.com.

Another excellent source for data on the budget is the Office of Management and Budget site at:
www.whitehouse.gov/omb.

SUMMARY

1. The national government influences how wealth is produced and distributed primarily via fiscal policy (taxing and spending), monetary policy (control of the money supply), and regulatory policy.

2. Fiscal policy is implemented by the federal budget, which is annually negotiated between the president and Congress. Monetary policy is primarily under the control of the Federal Reserve System, which has considerable independence from both Congress and the president as it works to supply sufficient amounts of money and credit so that the economy will grow, but not so much that it will lead to inflation.

3. The role of government as promoter of economic growth and jobs is not new. It is as old as the Republic itself. The federal government has long been involved in promoting agriculture and concerned about the health of producers and consumers of these commodities. Working through the Department of Commerce, it also promotes business. The national government is also involved in promoting trade and commerce with other nations. Our ability to buy from other nations and sell them our goods and services has much to do with the health of our economy.

4. Regulation, now a major activity of government, involves altering the natural workings of the open market to achieve some desired goal. Economic regulation aims to control the behavior of business in the marketplace. Social regulation aims to correct the unintended side effects of economic activity and to ensure equal rights in employment, education, and housing.

5. Even though the members of regulatory bodies are nominated by the president, their powers derive from legislative delegation, and their decisions are subject to review by the courts. Independent regulatory agencies have a scope of responsibility in the American economy that sometimes exceeds that of the three regular branches of government.

6. Regulation is a means of eliminating some of the abuses and problems generated by the private economy, while avoiding government ownership and the risks of too much centralization. Regulation is an inevitable by-product of a complex, industrialized, high-technology society.

7. A deregulation movement designed to get the government out of the regulation of certain businesses has taken place during the last 30 years. Liberals sometimes favor deregulation if they believe it will foster more competition. Conservatives generally favor deregulation that will get federal regulators off their backs in areas such as safety, health, and environmental and consumer-protection standards.

KEY TERMS

fiscal policy 428
monetary policy 429
tariff 429
excise tax 429
progressive tax 429
regressive tax 429
deficit 429
debt 430
gross domestic product (GDP) 430
entitlement program 430
Office of Management and Budget (OMB) 430

Congressional Budget Office (CBO) 431
concurrent resolution 431
reconciliation 432
General Accounting Office (GAO) 432
comptroller general 432
sales tax 432
value-added tax (VAT) 433
tax expenditure 434
monetarism 434
Federal Reserve Board 434
laissez-faire economics 436

Keynesian economics 436
inflation 436
trade deficit 438
World Trade Organization (WTO) 438
General Agreement on Tariffs and Trade (GATT) 438
North American Free Trade Agreement (NAFTA) 438
protectionism 438
regulation 442
independent regulatory agency 445

monopoly 445
antitrust regulation 445
trust 445
interlocking directorate 447
yellow-dog contract 447
closed shop 447
union shop 447
labor injunction 447
collective bargaining 447
environmental impact statement 448
deregulation 449

FURTHER READING

JEFFREY H. BIRNBAUM and ALAN S. MURRAY, *Showdown at Gucci Gulch: Lawmakers, Lobbyists, and the Unlikely Triumph of Tax Reform* (Vintage, 1988).

STEPHEN G. BREYER, *Breaking the Vicious Circle: Toward Effective Risk Regulating* (Harvard University Press, 1993).

GARY BRYNER, *Blue Skies, Green Politics: The Clean Air Act of 1990 and Its Interpreta-* tion, 2d ed. (Congressional Quarterly Press, 1995).

GARY BURTLESS, ROBERT J. LAWRENCE, ROBERT E. LITAN, and ROBERT J. SHAPIRO, *Globaphobia: Confronting Fears About Open Trade* (Brookings Institution, 1998).

THOMAS W. CHURCH and ROBERT T. NAKAMURA, *Cleaning Up the Mess:* *Implementation Strategies in Superfund* (Brookings Institution, 1993).

ROBERT W. CRANDALL and HAROLD FURCHTGOTT-ROTH, *Cable TV: Regulation or Competition?* (Brookings Institution, 1996).

ROBERT W. CRANDALL and LEONARD WAVERMAN, *Who Pays for Universal Service? When Telephone Subsides*

Become Transparent (Brookings Institution, 2000).

ROBERT W. CRANDALL et al., *An Agenda for Federal Regulatory Reform* (American Enterprise Institute and Brookings Institution, 1997).

ROBERT M. ENTMAN, *Competition, Innovation and Investment in Telecommunications* (Aspen Institute, 1998).

AL GORE, *Earth in the Balance: Ecology and the Human Spirit* (Houghton Mifflin, 1992).

WILLIAM GREIDER, *Secrets of the Temple: How the Federal Reserve Runs the Country* (Simon & Schuster, 1987).

PHILIP K. HOWARD, *The Death of Common Sense: How Law Is Suffocating America* (Random House, 1994).

ROBERT KUTTNER, *Everything for Sale: The Virtues and Limits of Markets* (Knopf, 1997).

LAWRENCE LESSIG, *Code and Other Laws of Cyberspace* (Basic Books, 2000).

CALVIN MACKENZIE and SARANNA THORTON, *Bucking the Deficit: Economic Policy-Making in America* (Westview Press, 1996).

STEVEN A. MORRISON and CLIFFORD WINSTON, *The Evolution of the Airline Industry* (Brookings Institution, 1995).

PETER G. PETERSON, *Facing Up: Paying Our Nation's Debt and Saving Our Children's Future* (Simon & Schuster, 1994).

ALLEN SCHICK, *The Federal Budget: Politics, Policy, Process*, rev. ed. (Brookings Institution, 2000).

JOHN WARGO, *Our Children's Toxic Legacy: How Science and Law Fail to Protect Us from Pesticides* (Yale University Press, 1997).

BOB WOODWARD, *Maestro: Greenspan's Fed and the American Boom* (Simon & Schuster, 2000).

JEFFREY WORSHAW, *Other People's Money: Policy Changes, Congress and Bank Regulation* (Westview Press, 1997).

DANIEL YERGIN and JOSEPH STANISLAW, *The Commanding Heights: The Battle Between Government and the Marketplace That Is Remaking the Modern World* (Simon & Schuster, 1998).

20

MAKING SOCIAL POLICY

E

VEN THOUGH EDUCATION POLICY IS WIDELY ACKNOWLEDGED TO BE PRIMARILY A LOCAL AFFAIR, BOTH GEORGE W. BUSH AND AL GORE EMPHASIZED THEIR AGENDA for education reform during the 2000 presidential election. The candidates agreed that the federal government needs to significantly increase its funding for education but disagreed on how much to spend and how to spend it. They also agreed on the need to experiment with charter schools.

Republican Bush's education reform proposals included guaranteeing $3 billion in loans to set up 2,000 charter schools, increasing the maximum allowable annual tax-free contributions by parents to savings funds for children tenfold (from $500 to $5,000), and tripling funding for what Bush called "character education."[1] When pressed for details on the scale of his reform agenda, Bush emphasized his support for local control of federal education funds and deemphasized the fact that his proposal involved increased federal funding.

Democrat Gore claimed credit for the Clinton-Gore administration's setting national goals and standards for public education. Gore proposed an increase in federal funding of $115 billion over ten years to create an Education Reform Trust Fund to help schools meet higher standards of smaller classes and better teachers. He also proposed devoting $500 million in federal funds immediately to help substandard public schools and called for monetary incentives for outstanding teachers and principals.[2]

The emphasis given to social policy by both presidential candidates in 2000 illustrates the importance of social policy issues in contemporary American politics. For President George W. Bush, the area of social policy he is most experienced in is education. Not surprisingly, he gave education reform a prominent position in his campaign and in his policy agenda. In education policy—as in welfare reform, crime prevention, and health care—the larger questions are: What is the responsibility of government to assist people who cannot provide for themselves? Where should the line be drawn to exclude certain groups from assistance or to limit their benefits? What is the proper role of the national government in social policy? Finally, given the closeness of the 2000 presidential election and the partisan parity in Congress, will new initiatives in education or social policy generally have much chance of enactment?

The purpose of this chapter is to introduce the basic elements of social policy as an illustration of some broader themes and issues discussed earlier in this book. The making of social policy teaches us a lot about how the separation of powers, the

Orphanages run by religious orders provided for needy children. These orphans attended the Sisters of Charity of the Incarnate World Orphanage in Galveston, Texas, in the late 1890s.

overlapping roles of Congress and the presidency, the implications of federalism, and the role of ideology and public opinion actually work.

THE ROLE OF GOVERNMENT IN SOCIAL POLICY

Debates over private versus public responsibilities in social policy and the role of different levels of government grow out of underlying partisan and ideological divisions in this country that are particularly important now as the nation initiates major changes in social policy. What is the proper role of government in education, welfare, health care, housing, job security, care for the elderly, and public safety? Today these responsibilities are a large part of the agenda of our national government, yet such functions were once thought to be mostly private matters or were left to local government.

Public versus Private

Those who believe that social policy is best left to the private sector do so for a host of reasons, including a belief that individuals need to take responsibility for their own lives rather than relying on the government to take care of them. They doubt the efficiency and effectiveness of public solutions to social problems and are confident the free market will provide opportunities for those with ambition and a willingness to work hard. Opponents of government solutions say public assistance robs people of ambition and defeats the work ethic.

There has long been a difference between Republicans and Democrats over the proper role of national government. Republicans believe that the national government is part of the problem, not the solution, because it is wasteful and inefficient. More effective than government solutions to problems, Republicans believe, is constructing incentives for the private sector to accomplish public purposes. Democrats are more likely to believe that only the national government has the resources and jurisdiction to provide adequate Social Security, help local governments improve the quality of education, and ensure that all Americans, rich and poor, have access to proper medical attention.

Conservatives often point to the long-standing tradition in the United States that private charities, churches, and foundations should raise contributions from individuals and businesses to build hospitals and nursing homes, fund medical research, provide scholarships for students, feed and house the homeless, care for abandoned children, and perform many similar services. The private approach to social policy points to such activities as evidence that people can and will seek to remedy social problems on their own, without the higher taxes, bigger government, and wasteful bureaucracy of public remedies (see Fig. 20–1).

Democrats and liberals believe it is the responsibility of the national government to provide a safety net for individuals, some minimum standard of living—a job, an education, health care, housing, and basic nutrition—for all citizens. They argue that human dignity not only requires this minimum standard of living, but that social policy based on this premise is also pragmatic. Without it, our cities would have far more homeless and hungry people, desperate for survival. Advocates of governmental solutions to social problems point to the inability of charitable giving to meet the needs of poor people, the elderly, and those without health insurance. They contend that the experience of the last half-century in the United States and other advanced industrial democracies has shown that national governmental support for housing, welfare, health care, and education is a necessity.

FIGURE 20–1 Charitable Contributions

SOURCE: U.S. Bureau of the Census, *Statistical Abstract of the United States, 1998* (Washington, D.C.: Government Printing Office, 1998), pp. 396–97; Trust for Philanthropy, at www.aafrc.org/CHAR.HTM.

Note: Amounts are in 1998 dollars adjusted using the CPI. The 2000 figure is a projection based on yearly average increases.

National versus State and Local

The debate about what is the best approach to social policy also involves a debate about which level of government should address social problems—the national government or the state and local governments. Conservatives advocate

leaving the responsibility for dealing with most social policy matters to states and localities, where programs can be adapted to local needs. Liberals counter that history has taught that, on their own, state and local governments are often unable or unwilling to address problems like health care, homelessness, and crime, so the national government has had to play a major role in funding programs and setting standards.

Governors have been increasingly critical of *unfunded mandates*, national programs that the states must administer with little or no federal funding for implementation. The tendency of Congress to impose unfunded mandates forces state governments to raise taxes or reduce funding for other state programs. Governors argue that if Congress inaugurates a new program requiring states to take action, Congress should provide the federal funds to help pay for the state's costs to administer that program.

A BRIEF HISTORY OF SOCIAL POLICY IN THE UNITED STATES

The Preamble to the Constitution lists promoting the general welfare as one of the reasons for the creation of the national government. But the interpretation of "the general welfare" to include national programs dealing with welfare, education, health, and public safety is of relatively recent origin.

Long after other Western democracies had expanded their social services, welfare in the United States was left to private charities and to local governments. Why? Part of the answer is that this nation was seen as the land of opportunity. Our millions of acres of free land, our enormous natural resources, and our technical advances all helped absorb people who otherwise might not have made a go of it. Closely linked with this growth and opportunity was the widely held philosophy of *rugged individualism:* If people did not get ahead, it was their own fault. The idea of equality of opportunity meant that government, state and local as well as national, played only a limited role in people's lives. Rather grudgingly, state governments in the early twentieth century extended relief to needy groups, especially the old, the blind, and the orphaned. But government aid was limited, and much reliance was placed on private charity.[3]

As a result of dramatically changed conditions—the growth of the national and now global economy, world depressions, the mobility of our citizens, and world wars, most Americans today expect governments in general, and the national government in particular, to play a significant role in the delivery of social services. Two social policy reform efforts deserve special attention: the New Deal and the Great Society.

The New Deal

The Great Depression of the 1930s drastically expanded national government social programs. As the economy collapsed after the 1929 stock market crash, and unemployment, homelessness, and poverty rose to unprecedented heights, the inadequacy of state and local government programs and private charities became apparent. In 1933 the federal government began making loans to states and localities for public relief. When state and local funds dried up, the federal government assumed more responsibility. But as the economy recovered, people grew critical of so-called "make-work projects" and the cost and waste of relief programs. They wanted to go back to simple handouts of food or cash by the government. But there was growing support for a well-planned, long-term program that would foster both the security and self-respect of the people needing assistance.

The WPA, part of President Roosevelt's New Deal, created jobs for thousands of workers during the Great Depression of the 1930s.

Old Age, Survivors, and Disability Insurance Trust Fund (OASDI), Established 1940

OASDI provides *retirement* benefits at age 65 (with reduced benefits available as early as 62). This is the largest and best known of the Social Security programs. But OASDI also provides *disability* benefits payable at any age to people who have enough Social Security credits and who have a severe physical or mental impairment that is expected to prevent them from doing "substantial" work for a year or more, or who have a condition that is expected to result in death. Other members of the family of persons eligible for retirement or disability benefits may be entitled to *family* benefits. OASDI also provides *survivors* benefits for certain family members of deceased persons who earned enough Social Security credits while working.

Medicare, Established 1965

Medicare provides hospital insurance (Part A) and medical insurance (Part B). Generally, people who are over age 65 and getting Social Security automatically qualify for Medicare, as do people who have been getting disability benefits for two years. Part A is paid for by a portion of the Social Security tax of people still working. It helps pay for inpatient hospital care, skilled nursing care, and other services. Part B is paid for by monthly premiums by those who are enrolled and from general revenues. It helps pay for doctor's fees, outpatient hospital visits, and other medical services and supplies.

Supplemental Security Income (SSI), Established 1972

Supplemental Security Income makes monthly payments to disabled persons or those over age 65 who have a low income and few assets. Levels of SSI support vary by state based upon cost-of-living differences, and some states add money to that amount. Generally, people who get SSI also qualify for Medicaid, food stamps, and other assistance. SSI benefits are financed by general tax revenues.

SOURCE: Adapted from Social Security Administration home page: www.ssa.gov/pubs/10006.html.

Social Security

A combination of entitlement programs, paid for by employer and employee taxes, that includes retirement benefits, health insurance, and support for disabled workers and the children of deceased or disabled workers.

Social Security

As a part of the New Deal, the United States inaugurated **Social Security** in 1935, perhaps the most significant social legislation in our history. At the time it was controversial; today it is politically untouchable. Social Security is actually many programs, the most important being a retirement program supported by a combination of employee and employer taxes, now covering more than 90 percent of the American work force. Social Security was expanded in 1939 to include financial support for survivors of workers covered by Social Security when the retired worker died, and in 1954 the program was again expanded to include support for disabled workers and for children of deceased or disabled workers.

The Social Security Administration issues checks to more than 48 million Americans every month, and three times as many working people contribute to the fund. The average retired person receives about $780 per month.[4] Reduced benefits are paid to retired persons ages 62–65, and beginning in 2000, full benefits are being paid starting at age 65, even if the person continues to work and regardless of their wage earnings. The universal nature of Social Security is one reason it is politically so popular: everyone benefits, regardless of need.

Social Security is based on the assumption that society must provide a minimal level of financial support for the elderly and the disabled. When large families were common, much of the cost of caring for the elderly was borne by children and grandchildren. Families usually had the resources to provide the necessities of life for Grandma, Aunt Suzie, and Uncle George. But during the 1930s, "taking care of one's own" was no longer a practical solution, given the extensive economic dislocation and fractured families caused by the Depression.

Until the 1970s, growth in Social Security benefits was relatively noncontroversial, largely because "the costs were initially deceptively low," while the benefits increased steadily, making the system politically painless.[5] Since Social Security began, the program has experienced steady growth and is now the world's largest insurance program for retirees, survivors, and people with disabilities. Combined with the cost of Medicare, its expenditures totaled nearly $680 billion by 1999.[6]

Social Security, unlike many welfare programs, is financed not from general taxes but from a trust fund into which taxes on employees and employers are placed—the Federal Insurance Contribution Act, commonly known as FICA. Over the years, Congress added benefits to the Social Security system without adding enough money to the trust fund to cover the added expense. In 1983, Congress was forced to put Social Security on a more sound financial foundation by raising the retirement age at which one qualifies for Social Security benefits, increasing Social Security taxes, and taxing 50 percent of the Social Security payments of upper-income individuals—a percentage that was raised to 85 percent in 1993.

Social Security taxes are now the largest tax paid by roughly two-thirds of all Americans, and for three-quarters of Americans their Social Security tax now exceeds their income tax. Both employers and employees are required to pay 7.65 percent of their earnings, with a total contribution from both sources of under $10,000 per year, into the fund. A single person with no dependents would have to earn $30,000 before paying more federal income tax than Social Security tax; families with two children would have to earn over $40,000 before their income tax would exceed their Social Security tax. Some experts believe that if Social Security expenditures are not controlled, more than half of every paycheck will be used to finance the program by 2040.[7]

Because people are living longer and demanding more benefits, the future financial stability of Social Security has become a major political issue. When the baby boomers retire, the number of people receiving benefits will increase in proportion to those contributing to the system. This increase would not be a problem if the money being contributed to Social Security by today's workers was put away for their eventual retirement. But much of the money taken from today's workers goes to pay for today's retirees. Social Security is thus a transfer program in which today's young workers finance the retirement of today's elderly. At some point, this reality is likely to foster intergenerational tension between workers and retirees.

The Social Security system is now running a surplus, meaning that the amount that is brought in through Social Security taxes is greater than the amount of money going out in benefits. The surpluses are invested in Treasury bonds, with the promise that they will be repaid with interest later. As the baby boomers retire and begin to collect Social Security, these surpluses will likely become deficits. Experts differ on when the next Social Security funding crisis will come, but there is little disagreement that something will have to be done to ensure the viability of Social Security for young people now paying into the system.[8]

Congress has been debating what to do with budget surplus in recent years. Democrats have argued that before enacting tax cuts, the surplus should go to reducing the national debt and strengthening Social Security. Republicans have generally preferred a strategy of tax cuts. The 2000 elections did little to resolve these different approaches.

President Lyndon Johnson's vision of a Great Society relied on the principle of government action to solve economic and social problems.

The Great Society

Another significant expansion of social services came in the 1960s. At a commencement speech at the University of Michigan in May 1964, President Lyndon Johnson described his vision of a Great Society:

> The Great Society rests on abundance and liberty for all. It demands an end to poverty and racial injustice. . . . But that is just the beginning. The Great Society is a place where every child can find knowledge to enrich his mind and to enlarge his talents. . . . It is a challenge constantly renewed, beckoning us toward a destiny where the meaning of our lives matches the marvelous products of our labors.[9]

Johnson's agenda was as broad as his rhetoric, and Congress enacted much of it in a fairly short period of time. Great Society programs dramatically increased the role of the federal government in education, extended voting and civil rights, expanded Social Security to include medical benefits for retired Americans, provided health care to poor Americans, financed housing programs to provide decent housing to the poor, offered job training through the Job Corps, and offered preschool education to poor children in a program called Head Start.[10] The programs of the Great Society were intended to overcome the root causes of poverty. The central article of faith in the Great Society agenda was that social and economic problems could be solved, or at least reduced, by government action.

Since 1968, there has been considerable debate over whether the Great Society was a success or failure.[11] Some Great Society programs were later disbanded during the Reagan and Bush administrations, while spending on other programs was reduced. In 1994, Republicans, controlling the House of Representatives for the first time in 40 years, cut welfare spending.[12]

President Bill Clinton's declaration that "the era of big government is over"[13] and his willingness to "end welfare as we know it"[14] reflected a sense that the national government should do less and that government services should be decentralized as much as possible. Nonetheless, while there has been some modification of the expanded social safety net of the New Deal and Great Society programs, the more important generalization is that these programs continue to shape social policy in enduring ways.

PEOPLE

> I think there is some **good justification for putting some of that money in in accounts of individuals.**

LET THE PEOPLE INVEST

Representative Nick Smith

When the Social Security program was started during the 1930s, Americans debated whether the national government should have a role in providing income insurance and welfare for Americans in their old age. Today, the debate is not whether to keep Social Security, but how it should be funded and whether people should be allowed to invest part of the money themselves. President Bush would allow individuals to invest up to 2 percent of their payroll savings taxes in private accounts of their own choosing. Representative Nick Smith (R-MI) supports the privatization initiative:

Right now Social Security gives a wage earner, on average, a 1.7 percent return on the money they and their employer put in. So in 10 years we are looking at a situation where retirees will be receiving someplace maybe even closer to a 1 percent return because of Social Security taxes continually increasing, and the suggestion of expanding benefits is ever on the minds of this body. So the challenge before us certainly is: How are we going to keep Social Security solvent? What are the changes that can be made? How do we get better than a 1.1 percent return on that particular money?

If we can fix the problem today with a couple trillion dollars of that surplus and start getting a better return on the money that is invested, then we can keep Social Security solvent. . . So I think there

is some good justification for putting some of that money in accounts of individuals, to put it into the safe kind of investments where we can guarantee that it will earn more than what Social Security will pay under the current program, where we can guarantee, if you will, that individuals that decide that they want to stay with the old system will have that option, or they can have the option to. . . choose the different investments that they think will give them the maximum return on their investment. Now is a difficult time to maybe convince some people that they should have part of that investment in equities, in the stock market. Yet, if we just look at last month, last month there was almost a 3.5 percent increase in the money invested in the stock market. Since the 1890s, there has never been a 12-year period where there has been a loss of money invested in equities in the stock market. . .

The real return of Social Security is less than 2 percent for most workers and shows a negative return for some compared to over 7 percent return in the marketplace for any period over a 15-year period. And the private investments are not only a greater return, but it is the security of knowing it is your money, not having politicians in the future reach into that pot and say, well, times are tough in America. We are going to have to reduce benefits or we are going to have to increase taxes on American workers.★

SOURCE: *The Congressional Record*, February 13, 2001.

DEBATE

KEEP THE SECURITY IN SOCIAL SECURITY

Senator Richard Durbin

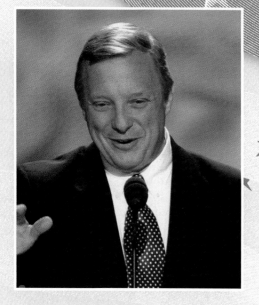

Opponents of privatization do not dispute the relatively low rate of return on current Social Security investments. Rather, they focus on the risks involved in investing in stocks and emphasize the importance of less affluent people having a dependable source of income, even though it may not be sufficient for most people. Finally, they contend that retirees will demand that government make up for any shortfall in the market, worsening the eventual funding problems for Social Security. Senator Richard Durbin opposes privatization:

What would happen if George Bush had his way? If we took 2 percent of the proceeds going into the Social Security trust fund and said they will no longer go into the trust fund but people will be allowed to invest them individually, what impact would that have? Frankly, it could have a very serious and, I think, a very negative impact. Keep in mind that the money being taken out of the payroll taxes each week in America goes to pay the current benefits of Social Security retirees. There is not some huge savings account that is blossoming. But basically we are talking

about a pay-as-you-go system. If you take 2 percent away, you are still going to have the retirees needing their Social Security check. You are going to have to figure out some way to plug this gap. . . .

I readily concede that over the last 8 years. . . the stock market has done very well. . . . It is naive to believe this will go on indefinitely. . . To take your life savings, or take 2 percent of your payroll tax and Social Security, and put it in the stock exchange, you understand there are risks. . . What if George Bush guesses wrong? What if people invest some part of their Social Security into the stock market, and the market goes down and they are losing money? . . . I happen to believe if the Bush privatization scheme goes through and it doesn't work, this Congress will be called on to come up with the money to bail out the families who guessed wrong in the stock market. . . We are literally talking about a Social Security system that benefits tens of millions of Americans today and that many more Americans are counting on for the future. When people start talking about change in Social Security, I am very cautious. ★

SOURCE: *The Congressional Record*, May 23, 2000.

> **What if people invest some part of their Social Security into the stock market, and the market goes down and they are losing money?**

For further information about this debate, go to **www.prenhall.com/burns** *and click on the Debate Icon in Chapter 20.*

1964

- *Civil Rights Act*—the most comprehensive civil rights legislation since Reconstruction

- *Food Stamp Act*—expansion of the New Deal program to improve the nutrition of the poor

- *Economic Opportunity Act*—job training, adult education, and loans to small businesses to attack the roots of unemployment and poverty

- *Nurses Training Act*—grants for training nurses and construction of nursing schools

- *Omnibus Housing Act*—addition of four federal housing programs to existing programs

- *Community Mental Health Centers Act*—federal grants for staffing mental health centers

1965

- *Medicare*—health care benefits for the elderly, linked to Social Security

- *Medicaid*—health care benefits for the poor, linked to Aid to Families with Dependent Children (AFDC)

- *Elementary and Secondary Education Act*—federal funding and programs in public education for disadvantaged children

- *Higher Education Act*—federal funding for colleges and college students

- *Department of Housing and Urban Development*—new department with responsibility for low-rent housing and urban renewal programs

- *Older Americans Act*—Administration on Aging and grants to the states

- *Voting Rights Act*—federal enforcement of right to vote in federal elections within the state voting process

1968

- *Housing and Urban Development Act*—expansion of federal housing and urban development programs

- *Omnibus Crime Control and Safe Streets Act*—federal aid for local law enforcement, crime prevention, and corrections programs

SOURCE: *Congress and the Nation, 1945–1964: A Review of Government and Politics* (Congressional Quarterly Press, 1965); *Congress and the Nation, 1965–1968: A Review of Government and Politics During the Johnson Years* (Congressional Quarterly Press, 1969).

entitlement programs
Programs such as Social Security, Medicare, and unemployment insurance that provide a specified set of benefits as a matter of right to all who meet the criteria established by law.

The Burden of Entitlements and Budget Constraints on Social Policy

The shift from an agenda of expanding the role of national government to contracting that role stems from the Reagan administration's 25 percent reduction in marginal tax rates and a 20 percent increase in defense spending, which resulted in large budget deficits. These deficits left no money for new social programs. Since the Reagan years, the debate shifted from which new national social programs to initiate and fund to how to cut taxes, "save" Social Security from bankruptcy, and keep Medicare expenses under control.

Programs like Social Security are **entitlement programs** because they provide a specified set of benefits as a matter of right to all who meet the criteria established by law. Entitlements constrain any new social policy initiatives because they take up such a large part of the budget. When added up, the portion of the federal budget earmarked for defense spending, entitlements, and interest on the national debt equals 82 percent, with roughly half going to entitlements alone (see Figure 20–2).

The money that the Federal Government uses to pay its bills—its revenues—comes mostly from taxes:

- Individual income taxes will raise an estimated $900 billion in 2000, equal to about 10 percent of GDP.

- Social insurance payroll taxes—the fastest growing category of federal revenues—include Social Security taxes, Medicare taxes, unemployment insurances taxes, and federal employee retirement payments. This category has grown from 2 percent of DPG in 1955 to an estimated 7 percent in 2000.

- Corporate income taxes, which will raise an estimated $189 billion, have shrunk steadily as a percent of GDP, from 4.5 percent in 1955 to an estimated 2.1 percent in 2000.

Except his unsuccessful efforts to expand health care, the Clinton years did not result in a return to a pre-Reagan agenda for social policy. As a "New Democrat," Clinton was willing to support a major reform in welfare programs. He also emphasized economic growth, business and government partnerships, and improved national government efficiency. But the Clinton presidency will be most remembered for its failed effort to enact national health insurance and its success in reforming welfare.

WELFARE

Welfare programs in the United States incorporate job training, transportation subsidies, housing subsidies, free school lunches, food stamps, food for pregnant mothers and babies, and tax credits for low-income people (see Table 20–1). The national government also provides financial assistance to farmers and certain industries and underwrites the cost of such "middle-class welfare" as national parks (supported by taxpayers but rarely used by poor people) and loans to college students. However, when we hear the term "welfare," we tend to think only of public assistance for poor, handicapped, or disadvantaged people.

Public assistance can take many forms:

- Direct payments to single parents with young children, the unemployed, and the disabled

- Vouchers that can be exchanged for food

• Subsidies that reduce the cost of housing or the provision of public housing

• Reduced cost or free access to public transportation, higher education, or job training

• Subsidized medical care.

These programs are targeted to the more than 34.5 million people living under the official poverty line of just under $17,184 for a family of four in 2000, or roughly 13 percent of the population.[15]

Although most poor people are white, the poor tend to be disproportionately African American and Hispanic. Because most poor people also tend to be women and children, scholars refer to the *feminization of poverty*.[16] Women usually get paid less than men for doing the same work and tend to be employed in low-paying jobs. The official government figure is that women make 73 cents for every dollar earned by men.[17] Economists who take into account such characteristics as job experience, education, and other measures of productivity find wage discrimination results in anywhere from 89 cents to 98 cents less for every dollar earned by men in the 27–33 age cohort.[18] Older women do not fare as well as younger women. Divorce adversely affects the living standard of women more than men, and women provide most of the child care.

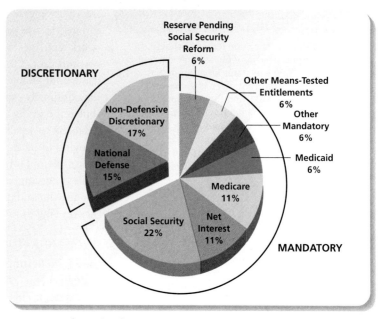

FIGURE 20–2 The Federal Government Dollar—Where It Goes

Means-tested entitlements are those for which eligibility is based on income. The Medicaid program is a means-tested entitlement.

1996 Welfare Legislation

One of the most important policy changes of the past decade occurred in 1996, when Bill Clinton and the Republican-controlled Congress replaced the large welfare program called Aid to Families with Dependent Children (AFDC) with Temporary Assistance for Needy Families (TANF). Dating back to the days of the New Deal, AFDC was federally funded but locally administered. Politicians in both parties had long criticized AFDC as creating a permanent underclass and providing incentives for husbands to abandon their families and for mothers to have illegitimate children. The Personal Responsibility and Work Opportunity Reconciliation Act of 1996 replaced AFDC. Its name captures two themes of the new act—individuals taking more responsibility for themselves and replacing welfare with work.

The burden for administering the new program was shifted entirely to the states. The federal government now gives *block grants* of money to states and generally

TABLE 20–1 Growth in Social Insurance and Benefit Program Payments, 1980–2005 (in billions of 2000 dollars)

Program	1980	1985	1990	1995	2000	2005 (estimated)
Social Security	$248.5	$300.4	$325.7	$377.1	$402.0	$506.0
Medicaid	65.9	103.4	126.6	177.9	218.0	311.0
Medicare	29.7	36.5	54.3	100.8	115.0	175.0
ADFC and TANF	15.5	14.7	16.1	19.4	22.4	25.0
Food Stamps	18.9	19.9	20.8	28.8	28.8	24.0

SOURCE: Office of Management and Budget, *Budget of the United States Government, Fiscal Year 1998* (Government Printing Office, 1997), pp. 118–22; *Budget of the United States Government* (www.access.gpo.gov) and Congressional Budget Office (www.cbo.gov/showdoc.cfm?index=1820$sequence=5).

In December 1996, a commission led by Michael J. Boskin of Stanford University reported that the Consumer Price Index (CPI) overstates inflation by 1.1 percent. The commission went on to recommend that Congress revise the CPI, and that the Bureau of Labor Statistics redesign its methods of calculating it. The Bureau of Labor Statistics revised its CPI formula in 1998, in part in response to the criticisms of the 1996 commission, but its officials admitted that "the CPI cannot be used as a measure of total change in living costs."*

If the CPI were simply one of the many obscure government statistics that is reported almost daily, there would be little to talk about. The CPI, however, is the government's measure of inflation, which is used to adjust government spending on programs such as Social Security, Medicare, and pensions for retired government workers.

While economists may view the CPI as a mere statistic to be examined technically, politicians are surrounded by recipients of entitlements arguing for more relief and by others demanding a balanced budget. The CPI is the political equivalent of a "silver bullet" because much of the entitlement spending in the budget could be reduced if the CPI were adjusted. Politicians in both parties have been reluctant to make this change in the CPI, fearing the wrath of those who benefit from the current CPI formula. But the widespread consensus among economists that the CPI is an overestimate of true inflation persists, as does the temptation not to lower entitlement spending.

SOURCE: Louis Uchitelle, "Measuring Inflation: Can't Do It, Can't Stop Trying," *The New York Times*, March 16, 1997, p. D4.

requires states to match those funds. Federally funded public assistance is limited to five years over a person's lifetime; recipients must engage in work activities within two months of receiving benefits. States can exempt up to 20 percent of cases from the work requirements and lifetime limits—an exemption intended for blind and disabled persons. The law originally excluded legal immigrants from many welfare programs, but at the strong urging of the governors, most welfare benefits were later restored to legal immigrants. To discourage persons on welfare from moving to states with more generous assistance payments, the law gave states the option of limiting welfare to newcomers from another state. This provision was declared unconstitutional by a federal district court judge, who said it "denies 'equal protection of the laws' to indigent families moving from one state to another."[19]

Welfare Reform

Besides reflecting a fundamental American belief in self-help and individualism, the 1996 welfare bill has significant ramifications for our federal system. This *devolution* of power to the states in the area of welfare is seen as a testing ground for the future. Based upon how well states perform their new responsibilities, there may be a resurgence in the role played by the states in setting and implementing social policy. If states are creative and successful in enacting welfare reform, other federal programs and powers may also be handed down to the states.

Since passage of welfare reform in 1996, the number of people on welfare has declined in every state except Hawaii. In fact, during the first three years, the number of families receiving welfare decreased nationally by 1.9 million families, or 43 percent of the total number of families receiving welfare.[20] Governors and reformers are quick to claim credit for this good news, but others point out that the decline in welfare caseloads is due, at least in part, to the robust economy and low unemployment. The real test for welfare reform will come, they say, when the economy hits a downturn.

HEALTH CARE

The federal government is involved with health care in three ways: research, access, and cost control. First, the federal government has a wide range of programs to promote research, target particular diseases, regulate drugs, monitor health care providers, gather and disseminate information, and in general deal with health issues. States receive federal money to construct hospital and research facilities and maintain medical programs, including maternal and child welfare services. The federal government gathers data on infant mortality, life spans, and diseases in an effort to monitor the success of its programs.

The surgeon general of the United States heads the Public Health Service (PHS), the national government's health agency. The service carries out its research through the National Institutes of Health (NIH). Researchers in these institutes, working closely with experts in private laboratories, study causes and seek cures for serious diseases. Fellowships for health research are granted to able scientists and physicians. The NIH grants billions of dollars each year to support the research of university and other scientists and physicians. The Public Health Service also administers grants to states and local communities to help improve public health. Another federal agency promoting health is the Food and Drug Administration (FDA).

Most Americans have private health insurance, usually through their employers, which pays for health care and hospitalization. Private health insurance began

in 1910, when the Montgomery Ward Company started the first health insurance plan for its employees. Limited access to health care and hospitals for those who could not afford private insurance resurfaced during the Great Depression, when large numbers of Americans were unemployed. President Franklin Roosevelt organized a Committee on Economic Security, which recommended compulsory national health insurance, but those recommendations did not go far. However, the committee's recommendations that Social Security provide money for maternal and child health care as well as aid for the disabled were adopted as part of the original Social Security legislation. Harry Truman was reelected in 1948 with universal health care as one of his stated policy goals, but the idea was labeled socialistic and was not seriously pursued.

In 1965, as part of Lyndon Johnson's Great Society legislation, Congress passed Medicare and Medicaid. **Medicare** is the national health insurance program for the elderly and disabled; it provides hospital and medical insurance for people 65 years of age and older. The Medicare program covers most hospital and doctor charges for most acute illnesses, but some catastrophic and long-term conditions result in major costs to patients for which there is no Medicare coverage.

Medicaid provides medical benefits for low-income persons of all ages; it is funded largely by the federal government but also requires state funding and administration. Eligibility for Medicaid is limited to persons who receive welfare cash payments—the visually impaired, the elderly, the disabled, and families with dependent children where one parent is absent, incapacitated, or unemployed.[21] Disabled people are entitled to both Medicare and Medicaid.

The national government is also involved in programs designed to control medical costs. The federal government pays for over 45 percent of health care costs through veterans' hospitals and programs for the poor, elderly, and disabled. Health care costs thus have a profound impact on government budgets. The national government now spends nearly $400 billion on health care,[22] an amount greater than what state and federal governments combined spend on education. If the amount spent on health care were reduced by 2 percent, it would fund the entire Pell Grant program for college students.[23]

A Mostly Private Health Care System

In the United States, when people with some form of health insurance go to a doctor's office or to a hospital, their costs are covered by insurance—the third-party payer—and not by the doctor or the hospital or the patient. These traditional arrangements were called **fee for service**; this meant patients could choose doctors who billed insurance companies for the services they provided. But the traditional ways of paying for health care are rapidly being challenged by other forms of coverage—especially **health maintenance organizations (HMOs)**, in which people or their employers pay a set amount in advance, and the HMO provides health care and covers hospital costs.

Employers have a tax incentive to provide health insurance to employees. The national government treats employers' costs of insurance as a deductible business expense, reducing their corporate tax obligations. These benefits are not counted as taxable income for employees either. In addition, employees may deduct from their federal income taxes any medical expenses that exceed 7.5 percent of their gross adjusted income.

While most Americans have health insurance, approximately 41 million persons are uninsured and are not covered by Medicaid.[24] Many of these people go without any health or dental care.[25] Some rely on public clinics or charity to pay for their medical care. Sensing the need for charity in this area, more than 27 percent of all households in the United States donate an average of $214 a year to volunteer health organizations to help those in need, an amount second only to religious donations.[26]

Medicare
National health insurance program for the elderly and disabled.

Medicaid
Federal program that provides medical benefits for low-income persons.

fee for service
System of health care payment in which patients can choose their own physician, whose bills are then covered by insurance companies.

health maintenance organization (HMO)
Alternative means of health care in which people or their employers are charged a set amount and the HMO provides health care and covers hospital costs.

Problems with Health Care

In recent years more and more Americans have shifted to health care provided by health maintenance organizations or other managed care programs. Responding to perceived public frustration with managed care, Congress is debating a "patient's bill of rights." Not surprisingly, Democrats and Republicans disagree on the particulars, most notably over whether patients should have the right to sue their HMO. But some convergence between the parties has emerged on removing limited access to emergency care and giving people the "right" to choose a specialist. Bipartisan support is also behind some kind of prescription benefit within Medicare.

While it is generally fair to say that Americans have the best health care money can buy, not all Americans have access to this high-quality care. Those without insurance or money either forgo needed services or simply make do with minimum care. Other problems with our health care system include rising costs, allegations that some people are denied treatment while others are subject to unnecessary procedures, high administrative costs because of paperwork, and the high cost of litigation.

RISING COST OF HEALTH CARE   Health care costs in the United States have nearly quadrupled, after controlling for inflation, since 1970[27] (see Table 20–2). Another measure of the rising cost of health care is the percentage of the gross domestic product (GDP) devoted to health care. Even as our economy has grown, the share of it devoted to health care has grown even faster. Pharmaceutical costs have soared, and the costs of children's vaccines have risen 1,000 percent in one decade.[28]

Who pays for the rapid rise in costs? We all do. Employers directly pay a large share of the costs of health insurance; about 6 percent of employee compensation is the cost of health care.[29] Consumers also pay more for health care, and the health care costs paid by the national government have risen 12-fold over the last 20 years. As federal taxpayers we pay through the national government for nearly half of all health expenditures in the United States (Figure 20–3).[30]

One reason costs have risen is people live longer. Life expectancy increased by more than five years between 1970 and 1995, and most experts believe it will rise another year by 2010.[31] As people live longer, they place greater demands on the health care system. New and advanced medical technology—life-support systems, ultrasound, sophisticated x-ray equipment, and genetic counseling—have all increased the costs of health care.

Advances in medications, such as the "cocktail" of drugs for Acquired Immune Deficiency Syndrome (AIDS), are also expensive, as are organ transplants, and these technological marvels have significantly added to the rising costs of health care. Moreover, some of what individuals spend on health care is not essential. Such elective procedures include cosmetic surgery, liposuction, and LASIK surgery for nearsightedness, which are not covered by insurance because they are considered nonessential, but many patients are willing to pay for the procedure.

THE UNINSURED   As noted, roughly 44 million people are not covered by any private health insurance or state or federal Medicaid benefits. The number of people without insurance has been rising.[32] Many of them have jobs but their employers do not provide health insurance, and because their incomes fall above the poverty line, they do not qualify for Medicaid. Uninsured individuals usually seek care in hospital emergency rooms only when their illness has reached a critical stage. Postponing medical care drives up costs because critical care is much more expensive than preventive medicine or early treatment.

But it is not just the poor who are uninsured. People who change jobs may often go without coverage for several months before their new insurance takes effect. And people with serious medical conditions may find the insurance company

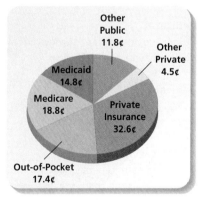

FIGURE 20–3 Who Pays for Health Care?

SOURCE: www.hcfa.gov/stats/nhe-oact/tables/chart.htm.

Note: "Other Public" includes programs such as workers' compensation, public health activity, Department of Defense, Department of Veterans Affairs, Indian health services, and state and local hospital and school health. "Other Private" includes privately funded construction, and non-patient revenues including philanthropy.

unwilling to cover their expenses, claiming that the illness is a "pre-existing condition." Some insurance companies set caps on their coverage, meaning that families faced with very expensive illnesses end up essentially uninsured.

UNNECESSARY PROCEDURES   Some doctors claim that they have to perform procedures that may be unnecessary medically but are needed to reduce the risk of being sued by patients. These procedures are alleged to add up to billions in unnecessary costs, but they do not improve the quality of care provided to patients.[33] To avoid malpractice suits, obstetricians may perform more than 300,000 unnecessary c-sections each year.[34] Critics also accuse hospitals of charging high prices for items that are not used or not needed. Since few patients are knowledgeable enough to audit their hospital bills, insurance companies must monitor these expenses.

There are understandable reasons why people want expensive new tests and procedures. People want to do everything possible to prolong life, and if a test or procedure has a chance, however limited, of doing so, they want it. But the question of who should pay the cost of these expensive new tests is disputed.

ENDLESS PAPERWORK   In medicine as in other activities, paperwork is necessary to document what services were provided and to prevent fraud. But virtually all health care reformers criticize the inefficient and uncoordinated system of paperwork and administration in the present system. The large number of insurance forms combined with abundant government forms costs health care consumers billions.[35] A standardized insurance form, computerized patient records, electronically transmitted prescriptions, and hand-held computers that send doctors' orders and comments to a computer could cut down on paperwork and save time. Some estimate that computerization of the medical industry could save almost 15 percent on overall medical expenditures in the United States.[36]

LITIGATION EXPENSES   Physicians frequently complain about the high cost of malpractice insurance, nine times more costly in the United States than in Canada. Malpractice insurance costs for all physicians have more than doubled in a decade. A physician's insurance coverage routinely costs as much as $60,000 a year.[37] For specialists like obstetricians, premiums are 400 percent higher than for internists.[38]

Trial lawyers who represent people whose health was damaged or families of those whose lives were lost due to medical malpractice defend the huge malpractice awards. They argue that physicians, like all professionals, have a responsibility to exercise sound professional judgment in their jobs, and when they do not, they should provide restitution to victims.

PREVENTION: LIFESTYLE AND ENVIRONMENTAL CAUSES OF ILLNESS   Part of the health care "crisis" in the United States is avoidable. Medicare alone spends billions of dollars each year treating smoking-related diseases, and over the next 20 years the costs to treat such diseases will continue to rise.[39] Other illnesses at least partly related to lifestyle include heart disease, liver disease, and AIDS. In an effort to recover some of the money spent treating illnesses related to cancer, 40 states sued tobacco companies and won a $206 billion dollar settlement in 1998.[40] Much of this settlement money has gone to campaigns discouraging tobacco use, especially among young people.

TABLE 20–2 National Health Expenditures, 1970–1998 (in millions of 1998 dollars)

Year	Total Amount Spent	
	Nominal*	Real
1970	$73.2	$313.9
1975	130.7	401.9
1980	247.3	491.6
1985	428.7	653.1
1990	699.4	876.9
1991	766.8	919.1
1992	836.5	973.9
1993	898.5	1,017.1
1994	947.7	1,043.8
1995	993.3	1,065.8
1996	1,039.4	1,079.1
1997	1,088.2	1,105.2
1998	1,149.1	1,149.1

SOURCE: Health Care Financing Administration, Office of the Actuary, National Health Care Expenditures, June 2, 2000, at www.hcfa.gov/stats/nhe-oact/tables/t1.htm.

*Nominal dollars are the actual dollars spent per year. To compare spending over time, we need to take inflation into account. The Real column accounts for inflation by converting nominal dollars into inflation-adjusted dollars.

Thinking It Through . . .

There is not enough data available yet to assess the impact of medical savings accounts if used on a large scale. So far, only a narrowly defined segment of the population has been able to use them. Most proposals for expanded MSAs would require over $3,000 in deductibles for families and $1,500 for individuals. For many people, such deductibles are prohibitively high.

One of the claims of proponents of MSAs is that their use will drive down costs because consumers will be more conscious of medical costs when it is their own money being spent. This argument presumes that people are willing to challenge the fees health care professionals charge and that there is competition in the medical marketplace. Both assumptions are dubious.

The MSA issue produced heated debates in Congress, in part because Democrats see it as a way to penalize the sick and less affluent. If younger people who are more healthy opt out of conventional insurance in favor of MSAs, their departure would likely drive up the costs for those left behind under conventional insurance coverage.

A Closer Look

HEALTH CARE IN ADVANCED INDUSTRIAL DEMOCRACIES

Advanced industrial democracies like Canada, Germany, Japan, the Netherlands, and the United Kingdom provide health care for their entire population either through national health insurance or a national health service. Although, the United States outspends all these countries in terms of health expenditures as a percent of the gross domestic product. Our high spending on health care does not mean we are a healthier population. Our infant mortality rates, for instance, are among the worst in all industrialized countries, and we rank below average for industrialized nations in male and female life expectancy at birth (see Table).

The United States also differs from other countries in the extent to which health care costs are paid by public funds. Central or local governments fund approximately three-quarters of the cost of health care in most advanced industrial democracies. In 1997, for instance, the government paid 80 percent or more of the costs of health care in Japan, Sweden, and the United Kingdom, 77 percent in Germany, but only 45 percent of the costs in the United States.[*]

In neighboring Canada, about 9 percent of the nation's GDP is devoted to health care spending, and all Canadians are covered by provincial health insurance. Canada's administration of health care is based on a publicly funded system, whereas the program in the United States is divided among public and private insurers. Canada's administrative costs per patient are at least three times lower than ours, and companies in the United States often pay three to five times more than Canadian companies to fund employee health and social benefits, including taxes collected by governments to pay for some of these benefits.

The Canadian health care system is not without its faults. Canadians are taxed at a much higher rate than Americans, in part to pay for the publicly funded system. In addition, patients may face delays in receiving services, espe-

Infant Mortality and Life Expectancy Rates in Ten Industrialized Nations, 1998		
Country	Infant Mortality[*]	Life Expectancy
United States	6.4	76.1
Japan	4.1	80.0
Sweden	3.9	79.2
Netherlands	5.2	78.0
Germany	5.2	77.0
France	5.7	78.5
Canada	5.6	79.2
Australia	5.3	79.9
United Kingdom	5.9	77.2
Italy	6.4	78.4

SOURCE: U.S. Bureau of the Census, *Statistical Abstract of the United States, 1998* (Government Printing Office, 1998), pp. 831–32.

[*]*Note:* Infant mortality rate is the number of deaths of children under one year of age per 1,000 live births in a calendar year. Life Expectancy is the average number of years a person can be expected to live at birth.

cially for routine health problems and elective surgery. Doctors and nurses are also paid less in Canada, and thousands of them have moved to the United States, where salaries are much higher. Costs for health care are also increasing well above the rate of inflation, and the Canadian federal and provincial governments have begun to cut back on funding certain services. Nevertheless, most Canadians express satisfaction with their health care system, and Canada manages to insure all of its people, while spending far less per capita than the United States spends.

[*]Organization for Economic Cooperation and Development, at www.oecd.org/els/health/fad13.htm.

Total Health Care Expenditures as a Share of Gross Domestic Product, 1996

United States 13.6%
Canada 9.5%
France 9.6%
Germany 10.6%
Japan 7.6%
United Kingdom 6.7%

SOURCE: Frequently Asked Data—OECD Health Data 98—National Expenditure on Health (http://cs9-hq.oecd.org/health/fad_l.htm).

Health Care Reform

Although there are many different proposals for health care reform, the essential approaches include single-payer, prepaid health plans, employer-mandated coverage, spending caps, individual responsibility, and medical savings accounts.

SINGLE-PAYER Under a single-payer system the national government, using broad-based taxes, covers the costs of health care and hospitalization and sets the rates. Like the system in Canada, such a plan would provide universal coverage and

benefits to *all* Americans. No longer would people need to worry about the costs of catastrophic illnesses or a change in jobs that would exclude them from coverage. Proponents claim that the single-payer system would save billions of dollars in administrative expenses by reducing the number of insurers from about 1,200 to 1. Opponents of the single-payer system claim it would lead to a bureaucratic mess, with little incentive for innovation, cost control, or diversity of coverage. They further claim that the government would be put in the position of deciding which procedures to pay for and how to ration access to these procedures. As a result, they contend, Americans would lose not only quality in their health care but their freedom of choice.

Business leaders generally oppose single-payer coverage out of concern for costs and what the program would do to taxes and the federal budget. The American Medical Association, U.S. Chamber of Commerce, Health Insurance Association of America, and other interest groups representing health care providers oppose the single-payer system. Labor unions, some senior citizens groups, and most consumer groups advocate this type of plan.

PREPAID HEALTH PLANS   Cost containment has been a frequent refrain of large corporations and consumer groups. In the 1970s and 1980s, business owners reduced benefits, increased payments by employees, and encouraged employees to join managed care plans, especially health maintenance organizations. During the 1980s and 1990s, HMO enrollment increased fourfold, from just under 10 million in 1980 to almost 80 million patients in 1999.[41]

Because there are no national standards of heath care quality, consumer groups are pressing HMOs to improve treatment of specific conditions and are urging Congress and the president to enter the battle.[42] HMOs counter that they provide adequate care at reasonable costs and that national standards would drive up costs. Consumers want the reduced costs associated with HMOs but do not like the limitations on choice of physicians and the right to sue health plans or the lack of coverage for some procedures.[43]

The quality of HMO care and limitations on patient choice became political issues in the 2000 elections. Al Gore called for passage of a "patient's bill of rights," which Bill Clinton had been promoting. A patient's bill of rights would permit a woman to see a gynecologist as her primary care physician; allow for review of the need for medical procedures; leave it to the doctor to determine the length of stay in the hospital; require coverage of emergency care a "prudent layperson" would deem necessary; and remove rules that deny doctors permission to talk to patients. George W. Bush called for granting HMO patients the right to appeal denials of care to an independent review panel; providing report cards on HMOs; giving women direct access to their obstetrician-gynecologist; and in some cases being able to sue HMOs.[44] While both presidential nominees called for expanded rights for HMO consumers, legislation on this matter consistently stalled in both houses, due in part to an aggressive advertising campaign against the reforms that was funded by insurance companies and HMOs.

EMPLOYER-MANDATED COVERAGE   Currently more than 160 million Americans get some form of medical insurance as a benefit that goes with their job.[45] But many small businesses contend that they cannot afford to provide this benefit and stay in business. Some have estimated that the costs of health care for small businesses may be 10–40 percent higher than for large businesses. In businesses with fewer than 25 employees, only about one-third of the workers receive coverage directly from their employer.[46] Mandating coverage does not solve this problem, nor does it take care of those who do not have jobs.

Proponents counter that the negative consequences can be mitigated through tax credits and government subsidies. They also point out that if all small businesses provide health insurance, none of them will be put at a disadvantage compared to

**Do charter schools provide
a better education?**

Communities in various parts of
the United States have been
experimenting with charter
schools in search of a better way to
help failing pupils. These schools are
not subject to many of the rules and
restrictions of public systems, and their
teachers do not require the same sort
of training and credentials. Are charter
schools the answer to our inadequate
public systems?

other small businesses. As noted, the federal government allows businesses to deduct
what they pay in health benefits to employees as a business expense and gives tax
credits to low-income families to purchase coverage for their children.

SPENDING CAPS   Because the cost of providing health care each year consumes a
larger and larger share of our gross domestic product, some have proposed that the
national government impose an overall expenditure cap on health care that applies
not only to public expenditures but to private ones as well. Supporters of a cap
include some prominent Democrats. The American Hospital Association, American
Medical Association, and Pharmaceutical Manufacturers Association vigorously
oppose the idea. They argue that spending caps would limit research and development in medicine and reduce the quality of people entering the medical profession.

INDIVIDUAL RESPONSIBILITY FOR COVERAGE   Another reform proposal is
to apply a free-market approach to health care by abolishing *all* employer-provided
benefits and encouraging individuals to buy health insurance on their own, in much
the same way that individuals are now responsible for purchasing their own automobile insurance. Those with low incomes, including people not now insured, would
have tax credits or vouchers to assist in the purchase of insurance.

   Those who advocate such a market solution say that if individuals purchased their
own insurance, they might pay more attention to costs and more closely monitor doctor and hospital fees. When higher wages are combined with tax credits, some individuals could end up with improved benefits tailored to their individual needs. Such a plan
would also eliminate the need to impose price controls or pay for a large health care
bureaucracy. It is unlikely, however, that employees would recover all they now spend on
health care from their employers, so costs to individual consumers might increase. It is
also unlikely that all uninsured persons who need government assistance could be taken
care of without a tax increase to pay for it. Perhaps most important, such a proposal
would run into so much political opposition that it presents an unlikely alternative.

MEDICAL SAVINGS ACCOUNTS   Congress in 1996 authorized an experiment
with **medical savings accounts**. Medical savings accounts allow individuals to make
tax deductible contributions of $1,462 for an individual or $3,375 for a couple to a
special medical savings account, which can be accumulated from year to year and
used to pay for any medical expenses.[47] Withdrawals for other purposes are taxable
and subject to an early withdrawal penalty.

   Supporters of medical savings accounts say that they will eventually lower
health care costs by giving people the incentive to spend their own money more carefully. They will also allow people to go to a doctor of their own choosing without
prior approval from their insurance company. Opponents of medical savings
accounts say that they amount to nothing more than a tax break for the wealthy and
the healthy. Because of high deductibles, people will be discouraged from getting
needed services and preventive care. Opponents also argue that because healthier
people are more likely to sign up for medical savings accounts, sicker people will pay
higher insurance premiums. Older and less wealthy people will not be able to afford
to invest in medical savings accounts, critics charge, and will be forced to depend on
more expensive insurance.

EDUCATION

medical savings account
Alternative means of health care in
which individuals make tax-deductible
contributions to a special account that
can be saved from year to year and
used to pay for medical expenses.

Americans give a high priority to educating their children. For our nation's
founders, education was closely connected with the survival of democracy
because it provided the citizenry with a moral sense, an ability to reason, and a general knowledge about history and government.[48] Nonetheless, they felt that providing for education should be left to state and local governments and private institu-

tions like churches. Despite an important federal role, today education is one of the areas still solidly under the control of state and local governments.

Most children go to public schools run by local school boards and funded, at least partly, by property taxes. Since local districts vary from areas with expensive homes to very poor neighborhoods, the funds for local schools vary. Children from poor districts are more likely to have lower-quality public schools than those from rich districts. Public schools vary in the uneven quality of teacher preparation, student performance, dropout rates, and in the educational opportunities provided to people of color.

The Federal Role in Education

The federal government's first involvement in education policy was with the Northwest Ordinance of 1785, in which Congress set aside one section in each township for support of public schools. In 1862, the Morrill Land Grant Act provided grants of land to states for universities specializing in the mechanical or agricultural arts. A U.S. Office of Education was established in 1867 to oversee these programs, but the scope of federal involvement was modest by today's standards. In 1944 Congress passed the G.I. Bill, which paid college or university tuition and living expenses for World War II veterans. The G.I. Bill helped provide college education for approximately 20 million veterans.

During the cold war, the view that education, especially in the sciences, is closely linked to national defense became popular. When the Soviet Union launched *Sputnik*— the first satellite to orbit the earth—in 1957, Congress responded in 1958 by passing the National Defense Education Act to upgrade science, language, and mathematics courses.

In 1964 Congress created the Head Start program for preschool children plus college-level work-study programs. Then in 1965 Congress passed the Elementary and Secondary Education Act (ESEA), which supplied educational materials for underprivileged public school students and provided funding for research on how to assist children from underprivileged backgrounds. Yet even with this expanded role, the federal government today funds only one education dollar to every nine provided by state and local governments.[49] Still intact is local control over school construction, curriculum, teacher salaries, teacher standards, and governance.

The federal government has taken a keen interest, however, in dismantling state-imposed racial school segregation. As we have noted, the Supreme Court's landmark 1954 decision in *Brown v Board of Education of Topeka* held that the "separate but equal" public school is unconstitutional. This decision gave the federal government an added incentive to help states improve schools for poor and underprivileged students of all races and put added pressure on local school officials to end segregation.

College and university students also benefit from federal funding. Today more than one-third of all college students receive some federal financial aid.[50] Pell Grants for low-income students and low-interest Guaranteed Student Loans continue to be the most available and most used payment for college expenses.

We ask a lot more of our schools than just to educate students. Schools are now a major means by which basic nutrition is provided to millions of poor children; schools screen at-risk children and attempt to get them medical and psychological assistance; schools provide sex education and sometimes condoms; schools seek to socialize students into acceptable behaviors, often in the face of increasing violence in the surrounding neighborhoods. The presence of police officers in most American high schools is relatively new and speaks to the problems of maintaining some minimal control over violence, drugs, and gangs.

The importance of an educated work force, concerns over equality of educational opportunity, and the increasing mobility of Americans all create pressures for national educational policies and programs. But federal intervention collides with strongly held views that schools are primarily a local matter. Satisfying demands for more effective programs and more accountability to parents may be beyond the reach of the federal government without a dramatic increase in federal funds. As a result, more attention has been directed to innovative efforts by states and local communities to improve their schools.

Thinking It Through . . .

The gospel of privatization holds that charter schools, free of administrative strictures, can be innovative and inherently superior to the traditional management structures they replace. But recent studies from both California and Michigan covering the first decade of the privatization movement show mixed results. This is especially clear in Michigan, where liberal chartering rules have led to explosive growth in the number of charter schools and attracted almost 40 private education companies to the state. About 70 percent of the more than 170 charter schools in Michigan are managed by private, for-profit companies, and the rest by not-for-profit groups. Only about 10 percent of the charter schools in the country as a whole are run by private companies.

A study released last summer by Western Michigan University's Evaluation Center found that competition from charter schools had spurred the surrounding districts to offer new services, including all-day kindergarten and before- and after-school programs. But lax management by local school boards had allowed the privatized charter schools to behave more like private entities than like parts of the public school system, as they are required by law to be. The charter schools boasted of increases in student achievement but often were unwilling to share with the public the test data that would support their claims. They also stand accused of dumping their weaker students into nearby public schools—after being paid to educate them—and screening out disadvantaged and disabled students altogether.

In addition, charter schools had lower pass rates than the overall school districts in which they were located as measured by state-mandated achievement tests. The pass rates at the charter schools tended to remain stable even during years when the pass rates in the surrounding districts rose dramatically.

The Michigan study comports with a 1998 charter school study from the University of California at Los Angeles, which found that California's school boards routinely failed to monitor charter schools, allowing many private companies to do as they wished with public money. Together these studies show that there is nothing magic about privatization and that rebuilding failing schools requires the same intensity, determination and patience no matter who manages the process.

SOURCE: "Charter School Accountability," *The New York Times*, December 28, 2000, p. A22.

You Decide...

Watching President Clinton sign the Brady Bill, which limited access to certain types of guns, are James Brady, Vice-President Gore, Attorney General Reno, and Sarah Brady. Brady was wounded during an assassination attempt on President Reagan.

vouchers

Government program that permits consumers of public services like education to purchase those services on the open market with a voucher.

charter schools

Charter schools receive some public funds but have greater autonomy from government regulation in areas such as teacher certification. Charter schools are part of an effort to provide parents with more choices of where to send their children to school.

Education Reform

Both Republican and Democratic presidential candidates as well as many congressional candidates made education reform and improving public schools the centerpiece of their 2000 campaigns. Neither party wanted the other to be known as the education reform party, and so both stressed their commitment to higher quality, smaller class sizes, and student testing. However, there were differences between the parties in some specific proposals.

Educational Choice

VOUCHERS   One of the more hotly contested education issues is whether states should provide parents with **vouchers**—money toward their child's education. The voucher could be redeemed at a public or private school of the parents' choosing. Vouchers, proponents argue, introduce the element of competition into the educational system. Voucher plans have been tried in a few states and cities with some success. In Milwaukee one of the largest programs has been specifically targeted to help low-income students, covering the full cost of tuition and allowing them to go to private schools.[51]

Republicans proposed vouchers in the 1996 presidential campaign, and in 2000 George W. Bush favored a limited voucher program for parents of students trapped in persistently failing public schools. However, when voucher proposals have been put before the voters, they have been consistently rejected.

CHARTER SCHOOLS   A somewhat less controversial set of proposals has to do with the creation of charter schools. A **charter school** receives public funds but has a contract, or charter, giving it greater autonomy and flexibility than public schools. Proponents of charter schools argue that this autonomy leads to greater accountability. Two-thirds of the states and the District of Columbia permit charter schools, and there are more than 350,000 students attending more than 1,700 charter schools nationwide.[52] The states with the greatest number of charter schools are Arizona, California, and Michigan.[53]

STANDARDIZED TESTS   Another area where the states have been experimenting has been in competency testing for students and teachers. Governors and legislators have pressed for evidence that their investment in education is paying off. Critics of standardized student testing contend that such testing does not take account of the serious deficiencies some students have that cannot be reversed in one school year. Others worry that teachers will tailor their teaching to the tests rather than the broader subject matter.

Much more controversial than student testing is teacher testing. One primary aim of teacher testing is getting rid of incompetent teachers. An outspoken opponent of teacher competency testing is the National Education Association and its state affiliates. The president of the Massachusetts Teachers Association sees teacher testing as "illegal," "unnecessary," and likely "to damage the quality of schools by driving good teachers out of our system."[54] Supporters of teacher testing counter that teachers should be held to minimal standards of knowledge and performance like other professions. Less controversial than teacher testing is the idea of rewarding excellent teachers, something both Al Gore and George W. Bush supported in their 2000 campaigns.

CRIME

In recent years issues about how to control crime, once almost exclusively a state and local responsibility, have been forced onto the national political agenda. The issue of getting tough on crime surfaced in recent presidential campaigns and has been a primary concern of voters in public opinion polls. National politicians in both parties are seeking ways to appear tough on crime and respond to complaints about racial profiling and police brutality.

The fact remains that crime control is primarily a state and local matter. The national government usually acts as a banker, providing grants to states and local governments to hire more police officers, improve the enforcement of drug laws, and deal with organized crime. An exception to this decentralized criminal justice system is the Federal Bureau of Investigation (FBI), created in 1908 and charged with gathering and reporting evidence in matters relating to federal criminal laws. In addition, the FBI provides investigative services on a cooperative basis to local law enforcement in fingerprint identification and laboratory services. Other law enforcement agencies of the federal government include the Drug Enforcement Agency (DEA), which is responsible for preventing the flow of illegal narcotics into the United States, patrols U.S. borders, and conducts joint operations with countries where drugs are produced, and the Bureau of Alcohol, Tobacco and Firearms (ATF), which monitors the sale of destructive weapons and guns inside the United States, regulates alcoholic beverage production, and oversees collection of taxes on alcohol and tobacco.

Legislation has been proposed to require purchasers of guns at gun shows to undergo an identity check on whether they have a record of past criminal activity.

Although the number of violent crimes is decreasing, the widespread perception is that crime and violence are increasing and the federal government needs to step in. As a result, Congress has made more and more crimes federal ones and increased the severity of punishments for them. As more people are put in prisons, the costs for building and running them has increased dramatically.

After years of debate, in 1993 Congress passed and President Clinton signed into law the Brady Bill, which mandates a five-day waiting period and requires background checks by law enforcement officers before a handgun can be purchased. Congress has also banned the sale of some semiautomatic assault weapons.[55] The National Rifle Association (NRA) has been powerful enough to stop most antigun legislation, even though such legislation has had the support of most police chiefs and most of the general public. The debate over gun control at the local, state, and national levels remains intense.

In 1994, Congress passed an omnibus anticrime bill that authorized $30.2 billion in spending on federal crime initiatives. The money funded hiring up to 100,000 new police officers and constructing new prisons and "boot camps" for juvenile offenders. The bill also added new assault rifle restrictions, made a long list of federal offenses punishable by death, imposed federal penalties and programs aimed at curbing domestic violence, and with its "three-strikes-and-you're-out" provision, mandated life imprisonment upon conviction for a third violent felony.

Domestic terrorism, long a worry, became a reality with the bombing of the World Trade Center in New York, the Alfred P. Murah Federal Building in Oklahoma City, and the Olympic Park during the 1996 Atlanta Olympics. Concerns about armed militia movements also became part of the domestic terrorism debate. As with terrorist groups everywhere, domestic terrorism seeks to use fear and violence to achieve political goals. The 1996 Antiterrorism and Effective Death Penalty Act limited federal appeals by inmates sentenced to death, made it easier to deport foreign terrorists, banned fund raising by Americans for foreign terrorist groups, and authorized spending $1 billion to fight terrorism.

Fighting crime remains a major challenge in the next century, but the goal of reducing crime must be balanced by the fact that we do not want to create a police state. We need to combat crime in ways that protect traditional civil liberties. Random drug tests, searches of private automobiles, curfews in urban areas, electronic eavesdropping, sting operations to catch criminals, and other steps law enforcement officials believe are necessary often conflict with the individual liberty and freedom from government restraint that Americans cherish. Must we give up some individual freedoms in order to fight crime? Should we build more prisons and impose harsher sentences on convicted criminals? Or should we focus on remedying the poverty and lack of opportunity that lead to criminal behavior? Like other social policies, policies aimed at fighting crime must ultimately balance competing values, one of the most complex and difficult tasks we delegate to all our governments.

Thinking It Through...

Opponents of any limitations on gun ownership point to the Second Amendment, which protects the right to keep and bear arms—a right valued by more people than just gun owners. But as technology has created more powerful guns, we have had to define what types of arms are protected. The number of guns in the United States has increased dramatically since 1950, up from 54 million to more than 200 million today. Today, one of every three households in this country has a gun. Guns, particularly handguns, are used in violent crimes. Nearly 11,000 murders are committed each year with guns; and 450,000 crimes are committed with guns annually.*

In 1994, Congress voted to ban 19 semiautomatic rifles. This ban left 670 guns other than semiautomatic rifles legal for use in hunting and target practice. Though supporters of this measure say these guns have made killing humans much easier, opponents point out that less than 1 percent of all violent crime is committed by criminals using assault rifles. Though banning only 19 out of nearly 700 assault rifles seems trivial, it could be regarded as a first step toward tight gun control. For two centuries, gun rights advocates have had the power and influence to stop any gun regulation in Congress; today, however, public demands for safe streets and a reduction in crime are pushing Congress to adopt controls.

*Mike Adams, "Gun Fight: Sometimes 911 Just Isn't Quick Enough," *The Arizona Republic,* January 10, 1999. See also U.S. Bureau of the Census, *Statistical Abstract of the United States, 1998* (Government Printing Office, 1998), p. 210.

GUN CONTROL: U.S. AND CANADA

While the homicide rate and use of guns in homicides in the United states has declined in recent years, the average annual homicide rate in the United States has been nearly four times that of Canada. There are 30 times more firearms in the United States than in Canada, even though the U.S. population is only 9 times larger than Canada's. The handgun differential is far greater, with 76 million weapons in the United States as against with 1 million in Canada.*

Possessing weapons in Canada, especially handguns, has traditionally been much more difficult than in the United States, and a law passed by the Canadian parliament in 1995 imposed even more stringent regulations. All weapons, including rifles and shotguns, have to be registered with the police; extensive background searches are required before new weapons can be purchased; and many owners of handguns are required to turn over their weapons to government authorities for safekeeping or disposal.

Some Canadians oppose these tough standards, claiming they lead to growing government interference in the lives of the citizens. They also complain about the high costs of administering the program and the strict limits placed on those who like to hunt. Some argue that criminals will always be able to procure illegal weapons, placing law-abiding citizens at an unfair disadvantage. However, surveys indicate that most Canadians support these gun control measures and perceive that such restrictions help make Canadian society much less violent than its neighbor south of Canada's border.

*http://www.cfc-ccaf.gc.ca/general_public/difference/Default.html

THE POLITICS OF SOCIAL POLICY

Along with how to build a prosperous nation, social issues now dominate the agenda of American politics. Welfare, health care, education, and crime, and their costs are today's political battleground between the parties and between contending interest groups. Both Republicans and Democrats are attempting to address key domestic issues that win broad support. Recent elections demonstrate how unsettled public opinion is on these issues.

The nation long ago answered questions about whether the national government has a role in providing decent housing, adequate health care, and a solid education for all of its citizens. The answer—to use Ronald Reagan's phrase—is that government provides a "safety net" for those who cannot provide for themselves. But how to provide that net is very much debated. And what we can afford and are willing to pay for expanded social services is the problem. The policy battles of recent years have demonstrated that expensive national social policy programs are unlikely to pass. But a party or president who ignores the social policy area is in political peril. Most voters expect public officials to improve education, reduce crime, save Social Security, and expand health care. Such an expansive agenda invites continued political debate and competition.

POLITICS ONLINE

Social Security: What's in it for You?

One of the issues most important to voters and candidates in recent elections has been Social Security. George W. Bush's proposal to permit younger people to invest a portion of their Social Security deductions in higher earning (and higher risk) investments is one notable example. The next time you get a paycheck, look at the FICA deduction. This is the amount going into Social Security. You may be surprised by how much you are investing. To find out how much Social Security benefits you might receive upon retirement go to: www.socialsecurityreform.org.

One concern is that with increasing life expectancy and a shrinking workforce, there may not be enough money in the Social Security trust fund to pay you what you have coming. Another current controversial issue is what, if any, prescription drug benefits senior citizens ought to enjoy as part of their Medicare coverage. Medicare is the health care component of Social Security. This benefit is hotly debated in Congress and was a major topic of concern in some 2000 U.S. Senate races, as candidates in Minnesota and Montana took busloads of people to Canada, where they could buy their prescriptions much more cheaply than in the U. S.

With so much speculation about the future of Social Security and added benefits like prescription drugs, you may want to learn more about these issues. You might start with the official website of the Social Security Administration: www.ssa.gov.

Other websites like www.socialsecurityinfo.com and www.aarp.org/socialsecurity/ provide useful research information, including links to other sites and current news and opinions on Social Security reform.

SUMMARY

1. Conservatives advocate private solutions for most social problems, while liberals argue that it is the responsibility of government to provide a minimum standard of living—including a job, an education, health care, housing, and nutrition—for all citizens. Since the New Deal, some national government involvement in social programs has been widely accepted, although the extent of involvement has waxed and waned. Conservatives generally prefer state and local government action over federal programs.

2. Social Security, inaugurated in 1935 as part of the New Deal, is perhaps the most significant social legislation in U.S. history. Through a system of employee and employer taxes, retired workers and disabled individuals receive monthly payments and health benefits. With the country's changing demographic profile, tensions in the system are likely to increase.

3. Welfare takes many forms, including direct payments to the poor, the unemployed, and the disabled; food stamps; job training; housing subsidies; free school lunches; tax credits; subsidized medical care; and others. Public assistance programs began with the New Deal and have grown ever since.

4. Welfare has long been criticized as creating disincentives to work, and many proposals have been put forward to make programs more effective and efficient. The most recent welfare reform, which became law in August 1996, transferred the administrative burden to the states, including giving them more discretion over recipients and benefits while helping to fund welfare programs through block grants of federal money.

5. The federal government supports medical research and has increased its role in health care cost control and access as the country's mostly private health care system is beset by rising costs, increasing numbers of uninsured Americans, unnecessary procedures, endless paperwork, high litigation costs, avoidable illnesses, and limited access. A variety of proposals for reform are under consideration, including a single-payer system, prepaid health plans, employer-mandated coverage, spending caps, individual responsibility for coverage, and medical savings accounts.

6. Education continues to be primarily a state and local government function in the United States. The federal government plays an important role in helping fund public schools and by pushing national goals for better education.

7. Crime control has been forced onto the national agenda by public perceptions of increases in crime and violence and by politicians eager to accuse opponents of being "soft on crime." Although crime rates since 1991 have actually declined, during the Clinton administration pressures for federal action resulted in passage of the Brady Bill, which imposes a five-day waiting period on the sale of handguns, a ban on some semiautomatic assault weapons, and other proposals that would add to the number of police officers and further restrict gun sales.

KEY TERMS

Social Security 458
entitlement programs 462
Medicare 465

Medicaid 465
fee for service 465

health maintenance
 organization (HMO) 465
medical savings account 470

vouchers 472
charter schools 472

FURTHER READING

ANNE MARIE CAMMISA, *From Rhetoric to Reform? Welfare Policy in American Politics* (Westview, 1998).

FRANK FISCHER, *Evaluating Public Policy* (Nelson-Hall, 1995).

LAURENE A. GRAIG, *Health of Nations: An International Perspective on U.S. Health Care Reform* (Congressional Quarterly Press, 1993).

CHRISTOPHER JENCKS, *The Homeless* (Harvard University Press, 1994).

THOMAS E. MANN AND NORMAN J. ORNSTEIN, eds., *Intensive Care: How Congress Shapes Health Policy* (Brookings Institution, 1995).

DANIEL PATRICK MOYNIHAN, *Miles to Go: A Personal History of Social Policy* (Harvard University Press, 1996).

CHARLES MURRAY, *Losing Ground: American Social Policy, 1950–80* (Basic Books, 1984).

DAVID OSBOURNE AND TED GAEBLER, *Reinventing Government: How the Entrepreneurial Spirit Is Transforming the Public Sector* (Addison-Wesley, 1993).

B. GUY PETERS, *American Public Policy: Promise and Performance*, 4th ed. (Chatham House, 1996).

FRANCES FOX PIVEN AND RICHARD A. CLOWARD, *Regulating the Poor: The Functions of Public Welfare* (Vintage, 1993).

THEDA SKOCPOL, *Social Policy in the United States: Future Possibilities in Historical Perspective* (Princeton University Press, 1995).

BOB WOODWARD, *Agenda: Inside the Clinton White House* (Simon & Schuster, 1994).

2

MAKING FOREIGN AND DEFENSE POLICY

PRESIDENT GEORGE W. BUSH CAMPAIGNED FOR THE WHITE HOUSE VOWING HE WOULD RESTORE AMERICAN "LEADERSHIP" ABROAD. HE ALSO PLEDGED TO RENEW THE bond of trust between the American president and the American military and defend the American people against terrorism and missiles. He came to office when the United States was enormously advantaged by its economic and military strength and by the reality that there are no great-power rivalries threatening the peace of the world. Yet even if the cold war military rivalries are well behind us, this is still an age of dangers and uncertainties.

Several dozen countries suffer from civil unrest, drug wars, and similar internal strife. Democracy is faltering in many of the former Soviet republics as well as in Indonesia, Colombia, Peru, Ecuador, Pakistan, Haiti, Venezuela, and elsewhere. The United Nations World Food Program reports that more than 800 million people around the world suffer from hunger.[1] And intelligence experts claim the risk of a missile attack against the United States involving biological, chemical, or nuclear warheads is greater today than during most of the cold war and "will continue to grow in the coming years."[2] Most Americans recognize that the spread of weapons of mass destruction, terrorism, drugs, poverty, population explosion (the world will grow to 7.2 billion people in the next 15 years), and global environmental problems create a highly unsettled world.

American leaders in recent years have said the United States must remain involved in encouraging democracy and free trade all over the world. Some have called for accelerated campaigns against global poverty and hunger. Still others have called for the United States to intervene in certain countries to advance human rights and reduce the senseless loss of lives.

However, both American public opinion and congressional actions have swung, sometimes unpredictably, between support and opposition to the deployment of U.S. troops in places such as Somalia, Haiti, Bosnia, Kosovo, and Iraq. Our hopes and aspirations are often contradictory. We want to promote democratic values abroad, yet also seek to ensure the security of our energy supply. Energy concerns sometimes force us to support nondemocratic governments, such as the government of Saudi Arabia. We want to protect the environment, yet also support American business overseas; we want to encourage human rights in China, yet want China to buy our airplanes; we want to reprimand India and Pakistan for testing nuclear bombs, but rigorous enforcement of economic sanctions against them would devastate our midwestern and northwestern wheat growers who ship

CHAPTERMEDIA

 POLITICS ONLINE

NAFTA: Does Free Trade Work?
www.prenhall.com/burns

 POLISIM

The Impact of Foreign Aid
www.prenhall.com/burns

What should be our most important foreign and defense policy goals?

This question was asked of a group of leaders that included elected officials, business executives, educators, and journalists, and also a group of ordinary members of the public. The answers showed some interesting variation, but what is of greater concern is how *you* evaluate these goals for our nation. These choices not only involve the U.S. role in international politics but also the shape of our federal budget and the priorities we establish for the nation.

much of their wheat to Asia. We favor progressive free trade and immigration policies, yet worry about job losses that sometimes result from such policies.

Congress and the American people want the United States to remain the premier global power, yet we often balk at the costs. Many people wonder about the need for foreign aid, and a few even question whether a large, well-equipped military is as necessary now as it was during the cold war. Many people also fret about the inefficient United Nations and question whether it is worth supporting at the levels we are contributing to it. We want to maintain instant readiness and superior military strength, yet welcome major tax cuts.

How should we restructure our foreign and defense policies to meet current conditions? Is it possible—or desirable—to fashion a single grand strategy of foreign policy to replace our longtime goal of containing and defeating the Soviet Union? As the once-clear lines between foreign and domestic policy become blurred, how has participation by Congress and the influence of public opinion affected the role of the American president in the politics of foreign policy decision making? And what should our foreign policy be, and who should make it? We explore possible answers to these difficult questions in this chapter.

VITAL INTERESTS IN THE TWENTY-FIRST CENTURY

Our primary foreign policy goal remains, as it has been, to maintain our security and freedom. Over the past several generations, the United States has become involved in world affairs to a degree unprecedented in our history. Much of this activity was due to the cold war, 1945 to 1990. Yet there are other reasons as well. U.S. security and economic interests are inevitably tied to what happens in the rest of the world. Whether we like it or not, events far from home affect our life, liberty, and pursuit of happiness.

Defining Our Vital Interests

Our political values are a critical factor in defining our vital interests. We want peace. We favor human rights. We generally support United Nations peacekeeping missions. We have a commitment to protect weaker nations against aggression. We want to encourage democracy and market-oriented economies. We want, where possible, to improve the standard of living in less-developed nations. We are also committed to improving the global environment. As a global trader, the United States needs markets for its products, imports of raw materials, and adequate supplies of energy. The task of defining our interests requires extensive balancing of sometimes competing goals.

Making foreign and defense policy involves not simply defining our interests, but making tough choices about what to do, especially when resources are limited, risks are high, and our objectives are sometimes in conflict. Policy making invariably involves deciding among options.

George W. Bush's national security advisor, Condoleeza Rice, outlined the key priorities that will best promote America's national interests:

- To ensure that America's military can deter war, project power, and fight in defense of its interests if deterrence fails.

- To promote economic growth and political openness by extending free trade and a stable international monetary system to all nations committed to these principles, including those in the Western Hemisphere, which has too often been neglected as a vital area of U.S. national interest.

- To renew strong and intimate relationships with allies who share American values and can thus share the burden of promoting peace, prosperity, and freedom.

- To focus U.S. energies on comprehensive relationships with the big powers, particularly Russia and China, that can and will mold the character of the international political system.

- To deal decisively with the threat of rogue regimes and hostile powers, which is increasingly taking the form of the potential for terrorism and the development of weapons of mass destruction.[3]

New Foreign Policy Challenges

The United States found it easier to define our national interest when the Soviet Union was the primary rival. But a lot has changed in the past decade. The removal of totalitarian governments has led to the reemergence of ethnic nationalism in some areas of Eastern Europe. Nations such as Yugoslavia and Czechoslovakia broke apart, the former with violence, the later peacefully. The Middle East remains unsettled. In Latin America, although democracies have emerged, there have also been setbacks and economic problems. And China, Burma, Iraq and North Korea remain under totalitarian rule. In Africa, civil and national wars have resulted in the death of millions. The threat of international terrorism is growing.

NUCLEAR AND BIOLOGICAL ARMS CONTROL   Probably the single greatest threat to the security of the United States and the rest of the world is the spread of weapons of mass destruction. At present, only a handful of nations have usable nuclear weapons. What happens if such weapons fall into the hands of so-called "rogue nations" like Libya and Iraq, which have no democratic controls on their governments and whose leaders may have dreams of world conquest, or at least retaliation against the United States?

A few dozen nations, including the United States and Russia, have agreed to curb the sale of materials that could be used in the manufacture of nuclear weapons. This agreement was a direct result of events in early 1990, when Iraq was detected trying to build nuclear weapons. Although the atom accord established limits on the sale of materials or machinery that can be used either for peaceful purposes or for building nuclear bombs, experts still caution that "good intentions on export controls are often undermined by ignorance and greed."[4] Some foreign policy experts suggest that the United States may some day have to resort to "preemptive intervention" in nations like Iran, Iraq, Syria, Libya, or Algeria to keep an outlaw nation from acquiring menacing nuclear weapons.[5] This is hardly a strategy most Americans would like, and no government official has espoused it. Still, modern warfare experts note that "modern missiles and bombs are so powerful that each side will have a strong incentive to strike first and thus stop the enemy from doing anything."[6]

In 1999, Congress rejected the proposed Comprehensive Test Ban Treaty. We can assume there will be renewed efforts to revive it, however. Three former secretaries of defense have advised ratifying the test ban treaty, pointing to its advantages to the United States in international relations. The treaty is an important element of the global nonproliferation regime and crucial to American leadership of those efforts."[7] George W. Bush opposes reviving the test ban treaty, but he has pledged to continue America's decade-old moratorium on nuclear testing that was first instituted by his father.

Some former government officials have suggested that it would be safe now to dispose unilaterally of our entire nuclear arsenal. "In view of the fact that we can achieve our objectives with conventional weapons, there is no purpose to be gained through the use of nuclear weapons," says former arms control negotiator Paul H. Nitze. "To use nuclear weapons would guarantee the annihilation of hundreds of thousands of people."[8]

Thinking It Through...

	Leaders	The Public
Stopping the flow of illegal drugs into the United States	57%	81%
Protecting the jobs of American workers	45	80
Preventing the spread of nuclear weapons	85	82
Controlling and reducing illegal immigration	21	55
Securing adequate supplies of energy	55	64
Reducing U.S. trade deficit with foreign countries	34	56
Improving the global environment	46	53
Combating world hunger	56	62
Strengthening the United Nations	32	45
Maintaining superior military power worldwide	58	59
Defending our allies' security	58	44
Promoting and defending human rights in other countries	41	39
Helping to bring a democratic form of government to other nations	27	29
Protecting weaker nations against foreign aggression	29	32
Helping to improve standards of living in less-developed nations	36	29

SOURCE: John E. Rielly, ed., *American Public Opinion and U.S. Foreign Policy, 1999* (Chicago Council on Foreign Relations, 1999), p. 16.

POPULATION GROWTH AND POVERTY   Most Americans are alarmed at the worldwide population explosion and the resulting poverty. Many of the world's more than 6 billion people are virtually excluded from economic opportunity. In China alone, more than 300 million live below the international poverty level. Moreover, there continues to be a significant transfer of wealth from poor countries to rich, and the information technology revolution accelerates this disparity. Still, our support for population control programs abroad is embroiled in controversy in Congress between anti-abortion and pro-choice interest groups. One of George W. Bush's first acts as president was to restrict funds for advice about family planning abroad.

TRADE WITH JAPAN AND CHINA   A serious trade imbalance exists between the United States and Japan and China. We have tried to force Japan to open its markets to imports of our products and have imposed restrictions on the importing of Japanese products, even though such restrictions made those products cost more. And with the sustained downturn in the Japanese economy, we have tried to be a supportive trade partner.

Trade with China poses other concerns. China has one of the fastest growing economies in the world. Our exports to China have tripled in the last several years, and imports from China have grown rapidly. But human rights advocates believe we should link trade and tariff agreements to China's human rights record. It is well known that China does not regard human rights in the same way that constitutional democracies do. The United States, from time to time, has threatened to withhold normal trade status from China unless there is a marked improvement in China's treatment of dissidents. **Permanent Normal Trade Relations (PNTR) status** is an international trade policy whereby we grant a country the same favorable trade concessions and tariffs that our best trading partners receive.

Loss of trade with China would deal a serious blow to the American economy, especially on the West Coast and to huge companies such as Boeing. In 1998 the United States separated the two issues and extended PNTR status to China.

THE CHEMICAL WEAPONS CONVENTION   The United States has entered into a variety of agreements to restrict the use of biological and chemical materials. President Bill Clinton successfully waged a major legislative battle in 1997 against Senator Jesse Helms and many conservatives over whether the United States should ratify the Chemical Weapons Convention. Treaty supporters, such as Bill Clinton, George Bush, and Senator John McCain (R.-Ariz.), contended that the security of our soldiers and citizens was at stake. They noted we were already destroying our chemical weapons stockpile and argued that other nations must do the same. Routine inspections would take place in all member nations, and this convention (or treaty) would punish nonmembers by restricting their ability to import or export restricted chemicals.

Critics called the Chemical Weapons Convention a dangerous treaty because cheaters could easily evade detection. They also opposed it because Libya, Iraq, Syria, and North Korea are not parties to it. "How can a treaty that professes to address the problem of chemical weapons be credible unless it addresses the threat from the very countries, such as Syria and Iraq, that have actually deployed these weapons?"[9] After heated and prolonged debate, the Senate voted in 1997 for presidential ratification of the treaty calling for our participation in the Chemical Weapons Convention.

THE FORMER SOVIET UNION AND EASTERN EUROPE   Russia and other countries that emerged from the former Soviet Union and its satellites are now torn by economic chaos and shortages. Americans want to be of assistance yet are weary of giving direct aid for fear of it being wasted. Foreign policy experts contend, however, that such investment is essential to help with the transition to a market econ-

permanent normal trade relations status (PNTR)
Trade status granted as part of an international trade policy that gives a nation the same favorable trade concessions and tariffs that the best trading partners receive.

omy and to encourage the gradual development of healthy constitutional democracies in that region.

The transition from communism to capitalism has been a painful one in Russia and elsewhere, so much so that many Russians believe the old system preferable to the new problems and uncertainties. The Communist party still survives.

THE EUROPEAN UNION AND THE FUTURE OF NATO   The European Union has adopted measures that bind European nations together for the purpose of economic growth. They now have a common currency and have eliminated many tariffs and trade restrictions. An economically powerful Europe poses challenges for U.S. companies and trade. With the end of the cold war, the mission, goals, and even membership of the North Atlantic Treaty Organization (NATO) have been redefined. In Bosnia, NATO forces conducted the alliance's first out-of-the-area military operation, and in 1997 NATO was expanded to include the former Warsaw Pact nations of Poland, the Czech Republic, and Hungary.

DRUG TRAFFIC   U.S. relations with Mexico, Colombia, and other Latin American nations are greatly affected by the drug traffic. Drugs smuggled into this country from Western Hemisphere nations feed extensive domestic demand in the United States. Are drugs a domestic problem that needs to be solved at home? Or should American addictions be perceived as a combined domestic, economic, and foreign policy problem? The United States and some of its neighbors have carried out a corporative program of destroying drug crops and interdicting drug imports.

THE GLOBAL ENVIRONMENT   The United States is at the same time one of the world's leading promoters of environmental concerns and because of our size and extensive industrial wealth one of its major polluters. A 1992 U.N. conference in Rio de Janeiro on conserving and improving the world's natural resources pointed the way toward many new environmental policies, but most nations, including the United States, have moved slowly on implementing policies to achieve these goals, despite grim warnings about global warming.

BUDGETING FOR AN EFFECTIVE FOREIGN POLICY   An effective foreign policy is impossible to sustain by rhetoric alone or by noble intentions. "Talk is cheap; leadership is not," said former Secretary of State Warren Christopher. "Leadership in foreign policy requires resources: enough to keep our embassies open and our people trained; enough to maintain constructive relations with the world's great powers; enough to multiply our leverage through international institutions; enough to provide targeted aid to struggling democracies that can one day emerge as allies and export markets; enough to meet threats like terrorism and international crime."[10]

We have closed at least 30 consulates and embassies in recent years. Many embassies operate with obsolete technology and antiquated and unsafe buildings. The United States has more than 14,000 civilian government workers stationed overseas in about 250 diplomatic posts in 160 nations. About 40 percent of these are State Department employees.

The success or failure of U.S. foreign policy may not seem a matter of life and death to many people. Thus we invest relatively fewer resources in foreign policy and in national defense than we did a generation ago. But this approach deserves to be questioned and debated. How much is an effective foreign policy worth? What are the obligations of a foreign policy that seeks to prevent conflicts, promote prosperity, strengthen freedom, block the transfers of destructive arms and technologies, and advocate democratic institutions and practices?

George Marshall (Truman)

John Foster Dulles (Eisenhower)

Dean Rusk (Kennedy and Johnson)

Henry Kissinger (Nixon and Ford)

Cyrus Vance (Carter)

KEY PLAYERS IN FOREIGN POLICY

Although presidents share with Congress the responsibility for making foreign policy, in practice a president has the primary responsibility to shape foreign policy. Presidents can bargain, negotiate, persuade, apply economic pressures, threaten, or even use armed force. In addition, the agencies that carry out foreign policy report directly or indirectly to the president.

In eighteenth-century England, the king controlled foreign policy. The framers of our Constitution tried to redress the balance of power toward Congress. Many of the powers given to Congress by the Constitution reflect the decision to limit the powers of the executive branch. Congress has the power to declare war, to appropriate funds for the armed forces, and to make rules that govern the armed forces. But the president is commander in chief of the armed forces and is authorized to negotiate treaties and receive and send ambassadors—that is, to recognize or refuse to recognize other governments. The Senate confirms ambassadors and gives consent (by a two-thirds vote) to treaty ratification. The courts have the power to interpret treaties, but by and large they have ruled that relations with other nations are matters for the executive to decide. The primacy of the executive in foreign policy is a fact of political life of all nations, including constitutional democracies.

The President's Foreign Policy Advisers

Officially, the president's principal foreign policy adviser is the secretary of state, though other advisers such as national security adviser or vice president are sometimes equally influential. The secretary of state administers the State Department, receives visits from foreign diplomats, attends international conferences, and usually heads our delegation in the General Assembly of the United Nations. The secretary also serves as the administration's chief coordinator of all governmental actions that affect our relations with other nations. In practice, a secretary of state delegates the day-to-day responsibilities for running the State Department and spends most of his or her time negotiating with the leaders of other countries.

Today, because of the interdependence of foreign, economic, and domestic policies, the president calls on a number of civilian and economic advisers in addition to the secretary of state. The conduct of foreign affairs is now the business of several major departments and agencies: State, Defense, Treasury, Agriculture, Commerce, Labor, Energy, the Central Intelligence Agency (CIA), and others. The need for immediate reaction and preparedness has transferred many responsibilities directly to the president, and, to a great extent, to the senior White House aides who assist in coordinating information and advice. Yet no matter what the system for advice and coordination, there are always overlap of responsibilities, redundancy, and competition among agencies.

Secretaries, agency chiefs, and their senior subordinates are chosen by the president and are expected to support and carry out White House decisions. At the same time, they retain a measure of independence; they naturally tend to reflect and defend the views of the departments and agencies they head. As a result, presidents have found a need to appoint White House advisers whose loyalties lie solely with the chief executive.

The National Security Council

The key coordinating agency for the president is the National Security Council (NSC). Created by Congress in 1947, it is intended to help presidents integrate foreign, military, and economic policies that affect national security. The National Security Council serves directly under the president. By law, it consists of the president, vice-president, secretary of state, and secretary of defense. Recent presidents have sometimes included the director of the CIA, the White House chief of staff, and the national security adviser as *ex officio* members of the NSC.

The national security adviser, appointed by the president, has emerged as one of the most influential foreign policy makers, sometimes rivaling in influence the secretary of state. Presidents come to rely on these White House aides both because of their proximity (down the hall in the west wing of the White House) and because they owe their primary loyalties to the president, not to any department or program. Each president has shaped the NSC structure and adapted its staff procedures to suit his personal preferences, but over the years the NSC, as both a committee and a staff, has taken on a major role in making and implementing foreign policy.

The State Department

The primary duty of the State Department is the security of the nation. Among the State Department's main priorities are the following:

1. To promote peace and human rights
2. To negotiate with other nations and international organizations
3. To protect American citizens and interests abroad
4. To promote American commercial interests and enterprises
5. To collect and interpret intelligence
6. To represent an American "presence" abroad.

The State Department's budget of about $6 billion (not counting foreign aid) is the lowest of all the cabinet departments—less than 2 percent of the Department of Defense's more than $315 billion budget (**www.defenselink.mil**; **www.state.gov**). Considering the State Department's role and prestige, its staff of 25,000 worldwide is small, especially compared with the more than 2 million civilian and military personnel in the Department of Defense.

The Foreign Service

The American Foreign Service is the eyes and ears of the United States in other countries. Although part of the State Department, the service represents the entire government and performs jobs for many other agencies. Its main duties are to carry out foreign policy as expressed in the directives of the secretary of state; gather political, economic, and intelligence data for American policy makers; protect Americans and American interests in foreign countries; and cultivate friendly relations with host governments and foreign peoples.

The Foreign Service is composed of officers, reserve officers, and staff officers. At its core are the foreign service officers, comparable to army officers in the military. They are a select, specially trained group expected to take assignments any place in the world on short notice. There are approximately 4,000 such officers; in recent years fewer than 225 junior officers won appointment each year. Approximately two-thirds of our U.S. ambassadors to about 160 nations come from the ranks of the Foreign Service. The others are usually political appointees, large donors or friends of the president.

The Foreign Service is one of the most prestigious yet most criticized career services of the national government. Criticism sometimes comes as much from within as from outside. Critics claim the organizational culture of the Foreign Service stifles creativity; attracts officers who are, or at least become, more concerned about their status than their responsibilities; and requires new recruits to wait 15 years or more before being considered for positions of responsibility. These problems are recognized in Washington, and the task of improving the service continues. Outside critics point to a social homogeneity among the Foreign Service, but that is overstated. Many women and minorities have been recruited in recent years.

Perhaps the greatest challenge for foreign service diplomats is how to function effectively in a high-tech world. Some have even suggested that diplomats posted in foreign countries are no longer needed to gather intelligence or to speak for the

Secretaries of State and the Presidents They Served

George Shultz (Reagan)

James Baker (Bush)

Warren Christopher (Clinton)

Madeleine Albright (Clinton)

Colin Powell (Bush)

United States and that they should be replaced altogether and most of their work be conducted by e-mail, fax, and videoconferencing from Washington. Yet having a diplomat on the scene in Iran or Saudi Arabia who speaks Farsi and Arabic and who knows a country's major leaders personally is often a better method than relying on even the most sophisticated technologies, especially when making subtle judgments about a nation's political, economic, and military policies.[11]

An additional challenge for the Foreign Service is that diplomacy seems to have lost much of its glamour. "College graduates who used to rush to take the Foreign Service Exam no longer bother."[12] Many have opted for careers they believe have more power and prestige in the new global economy.

Intelligence and the CIA

What is the nuclear capability of the North Korean or Iraqi military? What are the internal political struggles in Indonesia or Colombia? How stable is the political situation in Afghanistan, the Congo, or Haiti? Before our foreign policy makers can act on important issues, they have to know as much as possible about other countries: their possible reactions to a particular policy, their strengths and weaknesses, the character of their leaders, and if possible, their strategic plans and intentions. Therefore those who gather and analyze intelligence data are among the most important advisers to policy makers.[13]

The Central Intelligence Agency, an outgrowth of the World War II Office of Strategic Services, was created in 1947 to coordinate the gathering and analysis of information that flows into various parts of the U.S. government from all over the world. In recent years, the CIA has had about 20,000 employees and has helped coordinate and integrate the intelligence products of the State Department's Bureau of Intelligence and Research, the Defense Intelligence Agency (which combines the intelligence operations of the Army, Navy, Air Force, and Marine Corps), the National Security Agency (which specializes in electronic reconnaissance and code breaking), the supersecret National Reconnaissance Office (which runs the U.S. satellite surveillance programs), the National Imagery and Mapping Agency, the Federal Bureau of Investigation (FBI), and a small intelligence operation run by the Departments of Energy and Treasury. These agencies spend about $30 billion a year on intelligence work.[14]

Although most of the information the CIA gathers comes from open sources, the term "intelligence" conjures up visions of spies and undercover agents. Secret intelligence occasionally does supply crucial data. But it is not all glamour; much is routine. Intelligence work involves three basic operations: reporting, research, and dissemination. *Reporting* is based on the close and rigorous observation of developments around the world; *research* is the attempt to detect meaningful patterns out of what was observed in the past and to understand what appears to be going on now; and *dissemination* means getting the right information to the right people at the right time.

CIA analysts detected the military buildup by Iraq's Saddam Hussein in 1990, but their warnings about an invasion of Kuwait were too cautious and too late, according to later analyses. Indeed, President George Bush, himself a former CIA director, is reported to have been led to believe that Iraq had not adequately recovered from its costly war with Iran to mount another military invasion.[15] Other intelligence disappointments include the failure to predict India's nuclear weapons test in 1998 and the faulty guidance that led a U.S. warplane to drop a bomb on the Chinese embassy in Belgrade in 2000.

For 40 years the CIA and other intelligence agencies used their best personnel to understand and help undermine our primary enemy, the Soviet Union. After the Soviet Union crumbled, the CIA had to redefine its role, address new challenges, and curtail its long-term growth pattern. Among its new challenges are gathering intelligence on terrorism, drug trafficking, and the growing number of nations that have ballistic missiles with chemical, biological, and nuclear warheads. Intelligence agencies have also been asked to prevent industrial espionage by other nations.

What about the need for *covert operations*—operations that deliberately try to destabilize governments or insurgent groups in other nations? The CIA has been credited with both successful and failed covert operations abroad. It directed the ill-fated Bay of Pigs invasion of Cuba in 1961. Later the CIA supported the anti-Allende forces in Chile. Yet because of its record and because it must act when our government cannot intervene officially, there is a tendency to credit (or blame) the CIA for many coups, purges, and revolts, whether the agency was involved or not.

The CIA's influence, its information, its secrecy, its speed in communication, its ability to act, and its enormous budget make it controversial. Its relations with Congress have often been tempestuous. Committees now exist in both the Senate and the House of Representatives to hold the CIA accountable to Congress, although earlier efforts by similar committees sometimes failed to do an adequate job.[16]

Congress became outraged at the CIA's leadership in 1994, when it was discovered that a senior CIA agent, Aldrich Ames, had spied for the Soviets and the KGB—the Soviet secret police—for much of the 1980s. Ames confessed to what is considered the worst betrayal of U.S. intelligence in the history of the CIA; it is estimated at least 12 overseas agents or friendly sources were killed because of his deeds.

A few years ago, former Senator Daniel Patrick Moynihan called for dismantling the CIA. He argued it had grown fat and lazy over the years and there was little justification for intelligence agencies to have a budget nearly five times as large as the State Department's. Moynihan agreed that the United States cannot put a complete end to secrecy, which is at times legitimate and necessary. But a widely established culture of secrecy need not remain the tradition in diplomacy and national security operations. "A case can be made . . . that secrecy is for losers. For people who don't know how important information really is. The Soviet Union realized this too late," writes Moynihan. "Openness is now a singular, and singularly American, advantage. . . . It is time to dismantle government secrecy, this most pervasive of Cold War–era regulations. It is time to begin building the supports for the era of openness that is already upon us."[17]

While the U.S. intelligence agencies have made mistakes over the years, most experts believe these agencies are essential. Political scientist Loch Johnson writes, "The likelihood that they contributed significantly to warding off a third world war has been enough to earn their keep."[18] Their analysis of complicated political and military developments in the Middle East, the Balkans and North Korea have also proved strategically important.

An extensive review of the CIA by a bipartisan commission in 1996 recommended strengthening the hand of the director of central intelligence, reducing the work force of the agency, and "refocusing its efforts on global crime such as terrorism, narcotics trafficking, proliferation of weapons of mass destruction, and international organized crime syndicates."[19] The commission recommended the intelligence agencies strengthen their accountability to the executive and legislative branches, yet concluded their missions of information-gathering and analysis remain vital to the security of the United States.[20]

CIA leaders acknowledge they need to collaborate more effectively with the FBI and Defense Department to successfully combat threats from spies, terrorists, cyber sleuths, and criminal groups, who often have few if any ties to foreign governments. The Saudi-born terrorist Osama Bin Laden is a prime example.

THE POLITICS OF MAKING FOREIGN AND DEFENSE POLICY

Foreign policy flows through the same institutional and constitutional structures as domestic policy. Together public opinion, interest groups, foreign countries, political parties, and Congress affect the politics of making foreign policy. Yet these structures operate somewhat differently from the way they do in domestic affairs.

Public Opinion

In crisis situations—such as the bombing of Iraq in 1998 and 2001, the president together with military and intelligence advisers make decisions. Yet even in these situations, presidents and their advisers know their decisions will ultimately require support from the public and from Congress.

In normal situations, the public appears to consist of three subcategories. The largest, constituting perhaps as much as 75 percent of the adult population, is the *mass public.* This group knows little about the details of foreign affairs, despite the subject's importance. The mass public concerns itself with foreign affairs mainly in conflict situations, especially those involving the use of American troops abroad. The second group is the *attentive public,* constituting perhaps 15–20 percent of the population. It maintains an active interest in foreign policy. The *opinion makers* are the third and smallest public; as editors, teachers, writers, and political and business leaders, they transmit information and judgments on foreign affairs and mobilize the support of the other two publics.

Still, many people in this country are indifferent or uninformed about foreign and defense policy. Foreign affairs issues are more remote than domestic issues. People have more firsthand information about unemployment, inflation, crime, and health care costs than about Japanese economic reform or Indonesian political problems. Most Americans have a poor sense of world geography and an even weaker grasp of geopolitics. Sometimes it seems that only when American soldiers or civilians overseas are killed does the mass public become directly concerned with foreign affairs.

Most Americans do recognize that their lives, jobs, and security inevitably reflect international developments. "Contrary to a widely held assumption, their concern does not stop at the water's edge," writes Steven Kull.[21] A survey of American views on foreign and defense policy concludes that most Americans accept the United States has serious obligations:

> Relief from the long competition with the Soviet Union and the lack of a clear external threat have made Americans more reluctant to use force abroad and

The American public is especially concerned when our troops are under attack, as was the case when terrorists bombed the USS Cole or when a Chinese pilot rammed a U. S. reconnaissance plane near the coast of China in 2001.

become involved in the affairs of other countries. But they want to maintain current levels of defense in an uncertain world and are committed to diplomatic engagement through alliances and multilateral organizations.[22]

The State and Defense Departments generally make an effort to keep people informed about those areas of policy they think should be discussed publicly and to keep themselves informed about public opinion. Yet despite occasional talk about open and democratic policymaking, most foreign policy negotiations are conducted in secret. Even Congress is sometimes kept at a distance, as was the case when the Iranians were encouraged to send arms to Bosnia while President Clinton was assuring Congress that the United States was complying with the arms embargo.

Special Interests

It is difficult to generalize about the impact of interest groups on American foreign policies. At moments of international crisis, a president is usually able to mobilize public support so that interest groups find it difficult to exert much influence. As a general rule, special interest groups other than major economic interests rarely have a decisive role in the formulation of foreign policy.

Ethnic interest groups, however, sometimes play an important role in foreign policy decisions. As a nation of immigrants and the children and grandchildren of immigrants, our citizens often retain a special bond with their country of origin. Thus Irish Americans, Jewish Americans, Cuban Americans, African Americans, Asian Americans, Polish Americans, Greek Americans, Arab Americans, and Mexican Americans take a keen interest in decisions affecting Ireland, Israel, Cuba, South Africa, China, Poland, Greece, the Middle East, and Mexico. Such groups sometimes exert great pressures on policy makers to support (or contest in the case of Cuba) the country to which they are emotionally linked. Congress listens.

Governmental entities can also be a special interest. Thus the air force may be as influential in determining the size and shape of the U.S. strategic bomber force as any contractor, or party, or interest group.

Foreign Countries

Most countries have embassies that lobby for their interests in Washington. In addition, some countries like Japan have built up a powerful network of lawyers, lobbyists, and Washington-based publicists who are retained by Japanese companies and trade associations, as well as by the Japanese government, to defend their extensive economic interests in the United States.[23] Lobbyists representing industrialized countries like South Korea, Taiwan, Singapore, Brazil, and Mexico have also expanded their Washington lobbying efforts to fight U.S. protectionism and import quotas on textiles, shoes, and other products.

Whether or not foreign governments and business interests influence our foreign policy became an issue after large Chinese and Indonesian contributions to Bill Clinton's 1996 reelection campaign came to light. The president vigorously denied that contributions bought influence, and the Democratic National Committee returned the money. But foreign contributions were an issue that plagued Al Gore's presidential campaign in 2000. George W. Bush's Inaugural Committee returned a $100,000 gift in early 2001 to a donor who had questionable ties with foreign leaders.[24]

Political Parties

Political parties do not usually play a major role in shaping foreign and defense policy for two reasons: (1) many Americans still prefer to keep partisan politics out of foreign policy; (2) parties usually take less clear and candid stands on foreign policy than they do on domestic policy. Party platforms often obscure the issues instead of highlighting them, and many members of Congress fail to follow any strict party line when it comes to foreign policy.

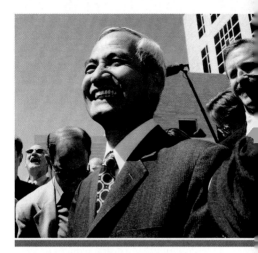

Suspicion of espionage was directed at Wen Ho Lee, a scientist at Los Alamos laboratory. Lee later was released from jail after pleading guilty to one of 59 charges for downloading secret nuclear weapons information.

The World Trade Organization (WTO)

The World Trade Organization (WTO) is a global international organization that deals with the rules of trade between nations. With 500 staff members based in Geneva, Switzerland, the organization is responsible for facilitating trade deals, overseeing negotiations, and managing disputes among its 140 member countries. The United States and China rank among the largest and most influential members, but developing or less developed countries have a strong presence as well.

The original vision for the WTO came out of the Bretton Woods Conference in 1944. It was at this meeting that the plans for the International Monetary Fund, the World Bank, and the International Trade Organization (ITO) were first presented. But the charter for the ITO faced strong opposition in the U.S. Congress and was eventually abandoned. Still, there was a need for an international trade organization, and in 1947 the United States signed on to the General Agreement on Tariffs and Trade (GATT) along with seven other countries. By 1994 the GATT had 128 members but was in need of structural revision. That revision came on January 1, 1995 when the larger World Trade Organization subsumed the GATT.

The basic operating philosophy of the WTO is that increased world trade means increased economic growth. The WTO facilitates international trade by insisting on low tariffs for imported goods, requiring all of its members to refrain from giving preferential treatment to their own products over imports and penalizing countries for discriminating in favor of imports from one country over another.

The WTO became the center of intense debates about globalization and its consequences during a WTO Seattle meeting in late 1999. The Seattle meeting prompted a coordinated mass revolt in the United States against global capitalism. Up to fifty thousand people protested in the streets before and during the meeting, representing a wide-ranging coalition of unionists, environmentalists, consumer advocates, human-rights advocates, farmers, organic food lovers, AIDS activists and others.

The issues that inspired the mass protest range from concerns over environmental, labor and agricultural standards to human rights and cultural imperialism. One of the most common critiques of the WTO concerns the organization's ability to override progressive environmental and social legislation within member states. For example, in recent years the WTO has prohibited South African companies from producing life-saving AIDS medication and forced the United States to buy shrimp caught in nets known to kill thousands of endangered sea turtles. If a member state fails to comply with a WTO ruling, they face strict fines and trade sanctions that can cost hundreds of millions of dollars.

bipartisanship

A policy that emphasizes a united front and cooperation between the major political parties, especially on sensitive foreign policy issues.

Should parties be concerned with foreign policy? At the end of World War II, sentiment grew strong for a bipartisan approach to foreign policy. An ambiguous term, **bipartisanship** in foreign affairs generally means: (1) collaboration between the executive and the congressional leaders of both parties; (2) support of presidential foreign policies by both parties in Congress; and (3) downplaying major foreign policy differences in national elections and especially in presidential debates. Overall, bipartisanship is an attempt to remove the issues of foreign policy from partisan politics.

But not everybody agrees that bipartisanship is desirable. There is virtue, critics say, in debating contending ideas—such as foreign aid or the missile defense shield. The bipartisan consensus that encouraged the escalation of the Vietnam War may well have led to miscalculations in our policy making in the mid-1960s.

The Role of Congress

Despite the importance of foreign and defense policy, and even though Congress can block the president's policy and undermine the chief executive's decisions, Congress as an institution seldom makes foreign policy directly. The power of Congress is mainly consultative, although the legislature has taken the initiative in some trade and foreign economic and military assistance questions. In addition, Congress is authorized to define the limits of presidential war-making powers.[25] And, of course, Congress, through its budget-making powers, can encourage or discourage foreign policy initiatives. Individual members of Congress, however, are sometimes included within the circle of those who make foreign and defense policy decisions. Senator Jesse Helms's personal involvement (some would say vendetta) against foreign aid programs and paying United Nations dues is a good example of how one member of Congress can play a significant role in influencing foreign policy.

Congress is a crucial link between policy makers and the public. Congress wants a voice—especially "meaningful consultation" with the president in matters of foreign relations. Some members of Congress, for example, asked for a full-scale debate before commitment of U.S. troops to bombing Iraq in 1998 but were not given that opportunity. Congress is often divided on issues of foreign and defense policy—as it has been, for example, on the Chemical Weapons Convention and foreign aid.

Foreign Policy in a Democracy

A democratic foreign policy is presumably one in which policy makers are known and are held accountable to the people. That is a tough test for any policy, yet it is especially tough for foreign policy because of the frequent need to act with speed and sometimes with secrecy, the generally low level of information among the general public, the anonymity of most foreign policy leaders, and, of course, the complexity of most international issues and strategic policy options. Still, the American public wants to be consulted and informed, and it wants its leaders accountable.[26]

In Vietnam, American policy makers miscalculated the character of the war as well as the commitment of the Vietnamese who opposed the Saigon government. And because these policy makers knew to some extent that they had made mistakes and believed the American people and Congress might not support them in what they thought necessary, they tried to conceal these difficulties.[27]

A constitutional democracy may not be able to keep leaders from making mistakes, but in a policy area in which big mistakes can be made, mistakes even-

tually become public. It is then that the safeguarding agencies of democracy—the opposition party, the press, and public opinion—go to work. Changes are demanded, and policies are changed. In the case of Vietnam, public resistance to the war eventually forced the United States to get out. The way in which these agencies of democracy worked in the United States doubtless encouraged the United States to withdraw from both the Vietnam and Somalia conflicts faster than might otherwise have been the case.

FOREIGN AND DEFENSE POLICY OPTIONS

How are foreign and defense policies implemented? As a major power, the United States can choose from a variety of options or tools, but it usually employs the following six, or some combination of them. Whether these tools will work, either alone or in combination with others, depends on whether they fit the particular strategic situation and whether the domestic conditions for pursuing such a strategy are favorable.

Conventional Diplomacy

Much of U.S. foreign policy is conducted by the foreign service and ambassadors in face-to-face discussions in Washington and other capitals, at the United Nations, in Geneva, at North Atlantic Treaty Organization or World Trade Organization meetings, and elsewhere around the world in regional or international organizations and world conferences. International summit meetings, with their high-profile pomp and drama, are another form of conventional diplomacy. Even though traditional diplomacy appears more subdued and somewhat less vital in this era of personal leader-to-leader communication by telephone, fax, and teleconferencing, it is still an important, if slow, process by which nations can gain information, talk about mutual interests, and try to resolve bilateral and multilateral disputes.

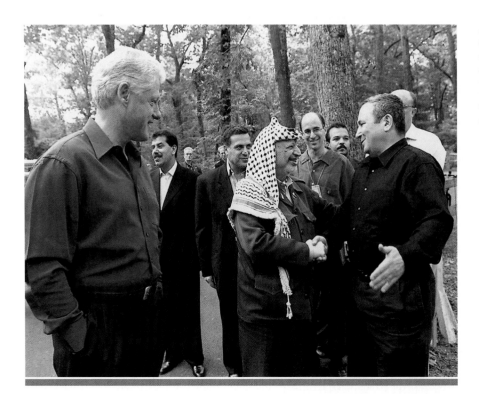

Bill Clinton engaged in strenuous personal diplomacy in trying to work out an agreement between Israeli Prime Minister Ehud Barak and Chairman Yasser Arafat at Camp David in July 2000. Arafat turned it down, and Barak was later defeated by Ariel Sharon as the new prime minister of Israel.

Some Key Foreign Policy Concepts

- *Internationalism:* A foreign policy that recognizes that concern for trade, human rights, and international peace requires not only a strong military but also the willingness to intervene where U.S. vital interests are at stake. The goal is to create an international order consistent with American values.

- *Isolationism:* A foreign policy that curtails U.S. military aid and intervention abroad as much as possible. It was the dominant policy in this country during the nineteenth century and to some degree in the 1920s and 1930s. It was put forward again by Pat Buchanan during the 1996 and 2000 presidential elections.

- *Realpolitik:* A foreign policy based on practical and self-interest factors rather than on moral, idealistic, or theoretical considerations. Realists say the United States should intervene in world affairs only if its vital interests are in jeopardy or if a dispute involves overt outside aggression, not simply internal rebellion.

- *Containment:* A foreign policy aimed at halting the spread of communism, especially the influence of the former Soviet Union. This was the underlying foreign and national security policy of the United States between 1947 and 1990.

- *Deterrence:* After World War II, the nation's primary defense against nuclear attack was a strategy of *deterrence*, the ability to threaten massive retaliation on any nation that attacked us. Effective deterrence is commonly measured by the strength of survivable second-strike force. Thus, the United States has maintained a large, diversified, and well-protected defense system so that a first strike by another nation would not cripple our ability to retaliate decisively. This strategy of *mutual assured destruction* (MAD) is still the core of American defense policy. Pentagon officials claim it works, even if it is costly. At least, it has succeeded in winning for the United States and our allies more than five decades of peace—a period twice as long as the period between World Wars I and II.

- *New World Order:* A vague and often confusing label pinned on the post–cold war period in which the United States presumably plays a vital role as the only remaining superpower in preserving peace and encouraging economic opportunity and human rights throughout the world.

Much of the conventional diplomacy carried out by the State Department may not produce important breakthroughs, yet it is difficult to measure the value of diplomatic representation. No price tag can be placed on close personal relations with foreign officials or on information gathered and arguments made to promote American interests around the world. Surely the closing of one embassy or the withdrawal from international organizations is unlikely to cause major setbacks for the United States, yet a less active diplomatic corps could mean a less effective foreign policy.

Foreign Aid

The United States offers aid to more than 100 countries directly and to a number of other nations through contributions to various United Nations development funds. Since 1945 we have provided about $400 billion in economic assistance to foreign countries. In recent years, however, foreign aid spending has amounted to around $15 billion per year, or less than 50 percent of what we spent in inflation-adjusted dollars back in 1985.[28]

Most foreign aid goes to a few countries the United States deems to be of strategic importance to our national security: Israel, Egypt, Ukraine, Jordan, India, Russia, South Africa, and Haiti. Much of what constitutes foreign aid is actually spent in the United States, where it pays for the purchase of American services and products being sent to those countries. It thus amounts to a hefty subsidy for American companies and their employees.

Ever since the United States began giving serious amounts of foreign aid after World War II, many Americans and members of Congress have opposed it. A recent Gallup poll of American citizens found only 9 percent support for increasing foreign aid, while 47 percent favored reducing it. Another 40 percent would keep it pretty much at the same level.[29] Few powerful interest groups or constituencies back foreign aid initiatives. State department officials are invariably the biggest advocates of foreign aid. Presidents also recognize the vital role foreign aid plays in advancing U.S. interests, so presidents keep asking Congress for funds for foreign aid. Successive presidents have all wanted to maintain the leverage with key countries that economic and military assistance aid provides. One of the major debates today is how much debt relief to provide for the world's poorest nations, some of which spend up to 50 percent of their budgets to service debt on old loans.

Despite the assertion by presidents and their secretaries of state that foreign aid is an investment to secure our vital national interests and a peaceful future, Congress invariably trims White House requests, saying there is too much waste. Congress doubtless is responding to polls that indicate people usually believe the United States spends too much on foreign aid. One of the problems with interpreting such polls, however, is that the average citizen often mistakenly believes we spend five to ten times more on foreign aid than we actually do. When people are informed about how little we spend relative to what they thought we spend, and how little we spend compared to other nations (of 21 industrialized countries that give the most foreign aid, the United States ranks at the very bottom), they are more supportive of having the United States provide more foreign aid.[30]

But no matter how persuasively presidents and secretaries of state preach about the virtues of foreign aid—saying that it prevents wars and instability and that it is the compassionate way—many members of Congress continue to fault foreign aid. National legislators often paint it as a "Ghana versus Grandma" case. How, they say,

can you give away taxpayers' money to some foreign country when we have poor older people who can't afford their prescription drugs and decent medical help?[31]

Critics of foreign aid say some of our foreign aid has subsidized the worst autocratic and corrupt dictators. And there are plenty of instances in which foreign aid money has been stolen or misspent. Defenders counter that some corruption is inevitable. "You can't engage in bone-poor countries that lack laws and independent journalists and elections, and expect American standards of transparency," writes *Washington Post* editorial writer Sebastian Mallaby. "Yes, many aid programs fail and will continue to do so. But you don't give up trying to educate and house people just because it's hard. And you don't give up on international engagement just because it's as daunting as it is important."[32]

Economic Sanctions

The United States has frequently applied economic pressure in response to a nation's unwillingness to abide by what we perceive to be international law or proper relations. Indeed, the United States has employed economic sanctions more than any other nation—over 100 times in the past 50 years. **Economic sanctions** entail a denial of export, import, or financial relations with a target country in an effort to change that nation's policies. Economic sanctions imposed on South Africa doubtless helped end apartheid and encourage democracy in that nation. But sanctions imposed on Iraq and Cuba have not had much effect on dislodging Saddam Hussein or Fidel Castro. The United States imposed sanctions on India and Pakistan in 1998 when both nations began a round of nuclear testing, but because of economic distress both in Pakistan and also among U.S. wheat growers, Congress and the president lifted most of these sanctions within months of imposing them.

The United States has imposed stringent economic sanctions on Burma because its repressive military regime refuses to hold meaningful talks with the democratic opposition led by Nobel Peace Prize–winner, Aung San Suu Kyi. Burma, with its government's connivance or neglect, has become the world's leading source of heroin and its region's worst area for AIDS. "Political change is essential if Burma is to transform itself into a source of stability in Southeast Asia. Sanctions may well work," said Secretary of State Madeleine Albright. "Having driven the economy into the ground, the regime desperately needs foreign investment, loans, and aid. By denying these benefits—and encouraging others to do the same—we may eventually persuade Burmese leaders to rethink where their own best interests lie."[33]

The popularity of economic sanctions has waxed and waned over the years, yet it can be an important weapon in the arsenal of diplomatic and foreign policy strategies. "Economic sanctions often emerge as the centerpiece when a balance is needed between actions that seem too soft or too strident. In these situations, sanctions are seldom regarded as the ideal weapon; rather they are seen as the least bad alternative."[34]

Sanctions are especially unpopular among farmers and corporations that have to sacrifice part of their overseas markets to comply with government controls. Indeed, business and farm lobbyists try to convince Congress and the White House that unilateral embargoes hurt our economy and produce unwanted results more often than desired ones.

Sanctions rarely work as effectively as intended. Brookings Institution scholar Richard Haass claims, "Sanctions have caused humanitarian suffering (Haiti), weakened friendly governments (Bosnia), bolstered tyrants (Cuba), and left countries with little choice but to develop nuclear weapons (Pakistan)."[35] They can also be costly to U.S. businesses and U.S. workers.

Senator Richard Lugar (R.-Ind.) believes sanctions seldom work unless they are multilateral, as opposed to being imposed by the United States alone.[36] Scholars suggest when dealing with authoritarian regimes, the United States should direct

economic sanctions
A denial of export, import, or financial relations with a target country in an effort to change that nation's policies.

sanctions at rulers, not the populace at large. "Iraqis are not our enemies. Nor are the Cubans," writes Gary Hufbauer. "Where the president imposes comprehensive sanctions on an authoritarian regime, he should view those sanctions as a prelude to the exercise of military force, not as a substitute for force. Unless we are prepared to remove bad governments with military force, we have no business heaping prolonged punishment on innocent people."[37]

Political Coercion

When relations between nations become especially strained, diplomatic relations are sometimes broken as a means of political coercion. When the United States breaks diplomatic ties, the consequences are more than merely symbolic. It greatly restricts tourist and business travel to a country and, in effect, curbs political as well as certain economic relations with a nation.

Breaking off diplomatic relations, however, is a next-to-last resort (force is the last resort), for such action undermines the ability to reason with a nation's leaders or to use other diplomatic strategies to resolve conflicts. The act also undermines our ability to get valuable information about what is going on in a nation and to have a presence in that nation.

Covert Operations

Covert activities are planned and executed to conceal the identity of the sponsor. U.S. support for the shah of Iran and the overthrow of the government in Guatemala in the 1950s are examples. During the cold war years, several presidents authorized covert operations in Vietnam and Central America. But covert activities in Cuba, Chile, and elsewhere have backfired, and support for this strategy has cooled in the post–cold war era.[38]

Military Intervention

War, it is said, is not merely an extension of diplomacy but rather the complete and total breakdown of diplomatic efforts. The United States has used military force in other nations on the average of almost once a year since 1789, although usually in short-term initiatives, such as Ronald Reagan's use of troops in Grenada, George Bush's invasion of Panama in 1989, Bill Clinton's peaceful invasion of Haiti in 1994, and NATO's military activities in Bosnia and Kosovo. Of course, these may not be

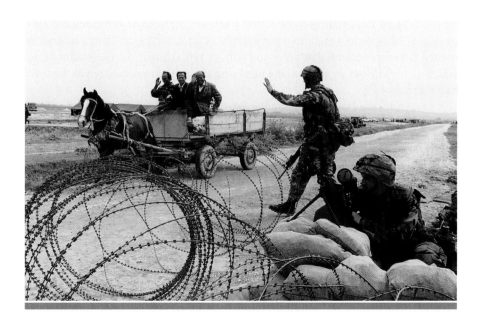

U.S. forces remained in Kosovo in an attempt to ease the confrontations between Serbs and Muslims in that divided country. Here a U.S. marine waves at a group of Albanians near a refugee camp.

considered minor events by the target nations or by the American families who lost sons and daughters in these forays.

Military action by the United States is most successful when it involves small and even medium-sized countries (Grenada, Panama, and Kuwait). But military intervention "often proves ineffective in the context of national civil wars (the United States in Vietnam; Israel in Lebanon)."[39] Lessons from past interventions are one reason Americans were reluctant, if not opposed, to U.S. military intervention in Haiti, Bosnia, and Kosovo.

United States military efforts with its NATO allies in Kosovo sought to put an end to the unacceptable ethnic cleansing in that area. After an extensive air power campaign, military forces were able to force the withdrawal of Serbian military and police forces, permit the safe return of refugees, and secure stability in the province. President Clinton had been hesitant to use the military in a decisive way in Kosovo in large part because of the apparent opposition of the American people and Congress. And many in the military were also reluctant to commit forces in a case they viewed as mainly a humanitarian initiative rather than a defense of America's vital national security interests. These opposing views prompted renewed debates about the conditions under which the United States should resort to military intervention.[40]

Kofi Annan, secretary general of the United Nations.

THE UNITED NATIONS

The United States belongs to the 189-nation United Nations and is a member of at least 200 other international organizations. The United Nations was set up in 1945 by the victors of World War II. Its main goal then and still remains to promote peace. But when the two superpowers—the United States and the former Soviet Union—became major military rivals, the United Nations was less able to achieve its central objectives.

For most of its first 45 years, the United Nations earned a reputation for ineffectiveness. Critics contend it either ducked or was politically unable to tackle crucial global issues. During much of that time, the U.N. General Assembly, dominated by a combination of Third World and communist nations, was hostile to many U.S. interests. The General Assembly often became a talk shop, passing vague resolutions. But since the cold war has ended, the five permanent members of the U.N. Security Council—the United States, China, Russia (which replaced the Soviet Union), Britain, and France—have usually worked in harmony. Moreover, the U.N.'s assumption of responsibilities in the Persian Gulf War and its extensive peacekeeping missions in Cyprus and Lebanon won it respect. U.N. efforts in Cambodia and Somalia were less successful.

Blue-helmeted U.N. peacekeeping forces are now monitoring cease-fires, elections, and human rights in several areas. These efforts are costly, and the United Nations constantly finds itself pleading with leading nations such as the United States to underwrite the required and agreed amount of the U.N. budget (based on a percentage of world GDP). Some of the U.N.'s peacekeeping missions are popular, yet as these efforts increase in number and in cost, the negotiations to raise funds for this new international peace army get harder.

Some American conservatives have long been skeptical of U.S. involvement in the United Nations, fearing that the United States risks being outvoted. Critics across the ideological spectrum question whether it makes sense to give every U.N. member an equal vote in the General Assembly, regardless of its size, population, and contribution to the U.N. budget. Critics also worry about creating a standing U.N. army with a large contingent of U.S. troops under foreign command. Some U.S. officials call this situation "taxation without representation." Critics also continue to question the efficiency of the organization's bureaucracy.

Conservatives insist Congress needs to have a greater say in how the United Nations uses taxpayers' dollars and puts our soldiers' lives at risk. "When the U.N.

TABLE 21–1 Assessing the United Nations

In general, do you think the United Nations is doing a good job or a poor job in trying to solve the problems it has had to face?

	1996	1998	2000
Good job	49%	60%	52%
Poor job	38	37	43
Don't know/Refused to answer	13	3	5

SOURCE: Gallup poll data.

Security Council votes," said former senator and Republican leader Bob Dole, "American taxpayers should grab their wallets. Once the council approves a peacekeeping operation, the United States is obligated to pay nearly one-third of the cost."[41] Several members of Congress have introduced legislation that would bar U.S. forces from any standing U.N. army and prohibit U.S. troops from serving under foreign command in U.N. operations. Some critics on both the left and right suggest that the United Nations should be allowed to wither away into irrelevance.[42]

In late 2000 the United Nations agreed to reduce the United States' share of the U.N. budget from 25 to 22 percent. The United States also won a reduction in its share of peacekeeping budget from 31 to almost 26 percent. Congress had demanded this reduction as a part of a condition to pay off its unpaid dues to the United Nations. Congress has also tied payment of the United States back debt to a streamlining of what nearly everyone derides as a bureaucracy of elephantine proportions.

Several of the specialized agencies of the United Nations—such as the World Health Organization, the United Nations High Commission for Refugees, and the World Food Program—are considered major successes. But the review is much more mixed in the United Nation's peacekeeping efforts, which have numbered more than 50 since the United Nations began in the late 1940s. Failures in Sierra Leone, Bosnia, Somalia, and Angola are offset by many successes such as in East Timor. Table 21–1 compares public attitudes toward the United Nations in 1996, 1998, and 2000.

The agency's peacekeeping operations especially in places such as Africa are plagued by inadequate and often under prepared personnel. "First-world countries with first-rate armies are usually unwilling to put their troops at risk," writes former United States Ambassador Dennis Jett. "Thus these operations are often left to third-world countries, and the United Nations sends some of the worst soldiers in the world off to situations where it can only hope they are not called on to actually do anything."[43]

Defenders of United Nations peacekeeping missions note that where the United States intervenes alone, the United States pays all of the costs and runs all the risks. When the United Nations acts, the United States only pays 26 percent of the costs and others provide the vast majority of the troops. And most Americans, when surveyed, favor multilateral more than direct United States peacekeeping actions. Still, political leaders in the United States will continue to insist that the United Nations show that the money it receives save lives and secures the peace and can do so efficiently.

NATIONAL SECURITY AND DEFENSE

The United States has a long history of military involvement in world affairs. Since 1945 more than 100,000 U.S. military personnel have died in undeclared wars; more than 400,000 have suffered battle injuries.[44] But we have formally declared war by an act of Congress on only a few occasions. Although the 1991 Persian Gulf War was not declared formally, Congress, in effect, declared war when it authorized the use of troops to repel Iraq.

Many Americans are concerned the United States will use its military clout unwisely or irresponsibly. Some believe we should resist the temptation to send our military into regional conflicts around the world when other means are available to achieve our objectives.[45] There is agreement, too, that we should not intervene in conflicts unless the action is backed by a broad public consensus at home and an alliance of nations abroad.

The "Powell Doctrine," named for the current Secretary of State General Colin L. Powell, reflects both these concerns of average Americans as well as many senior military leaders. Powell questions several of the American military interventions over the past decade. "When the United States goes to war," he says, "it should be for a clear

purpose, only when our vital national security interests are threatened and our goal should be overwhelming victory." Powell says "halfhearted warfare for half-baked reasons" is misguided defense policy.[46]

This doctrine will be vigorously debated during the George W. Bush presidency, as it was between Bush and Gore in the presidential debates of 2000, about the proper role for the United States in international affairs. And it is far more complex than a simple contest between internationalism and isolationism; it raises issues about human rights and moral leadership as well as about military effectiveness. The Powell Doctrine has widespread support. Still, most Americans believe it would be a mistake to forsake our unique leadership position and abandon responsibilities to encourage peace and human rights at this time of incredible global change.[47]

Civilian Control over the Military

One of the bedrock principles of our constitutional democracy is that a civilian, the president of the United States, is the commander in chief. Members of the military have freedom of speech, yet to ensure civilian supremacy, commissioned officers who use "contemptuous words" against a president are subject to punishment. When a popular World War II hero, General Douglas MacArthur, challenged President Harry Truman's decisions, MacArthur was removed from his command in Korea. When a two-star general made rude and critical remarks about President Bill Clinton in a speech, he was fined $7,000 and retired from the service. And military leaders, in the aftermath of the Lewinsky affair, took the unusual step of warning military personnel that they could face punishment for speaking "contemptuous words" against the president.[48]

In our entire history as a nation, we have never had any fear that the uniformed officers in command of American military forces would question the outcome of an election or question the need to respond to the commands of the president of the United States. So ingrained in our thinking and institutions is the doctrine of civil supremacy that we take for granted this fundamental principle of constitutional democracy.

Defense Organization

The president, Congress, the National Security Council, the State Department, and the Defense Department make overall defense policy and attempt to integrate U.S. national security programs. But the day-to-day work of organizing for defense is the job of the Defense Department. Its headquarters, the Pentagon, houses within its 17.5 miles of corridors 23,000 top military and civilian personnel. The offices of several

The Pentagon, headquarters for the Defense Department, is the world's largest building. It has 17.5 miles of corridors and houses nearly 23,000 workers, who tell time by 4,200 clocks, consume 30,000 cups of coffee daily, and place 200,000 calls a day on 87,000 phones connected by 100,000 miles of cable.

hundred generals and admirals are there, as is the office of the secretary of defense, who provides civilian control of the armed services.

A major issue in recent decades has been how to organize the Department of Defense to ensure that it can provide both strategic vision and practical coordination among the military services. Prior to 1947 there were two separate military departments—War and Navy. The difficulty of coordinating them during World War II led to demands for unification. In 1947 the air force, already an autonomous unit within the War Department, was made an independent department, and all three military departments—Army, Navy, and Air Force—were placed under the general supervision of the secretary of defense. The Unification Act of 1947 was a bundle of compromises between the army, which favored a tightly integrated department, and the navy, which wanted a loosely federated structure, but the act at least brought the military services under a common organizational chart.

The Joint Chiefs of Staff (JCS) serves as the principal military adviser to the president, the National Security Council, and the secretary of defense. It includes the heads of the three armed services, plus the commandant of the Marine Corps, the chair, and the vice-chair. The president, with the consent of the Senate, appoints all the service chiefs for four-year, nonrenewable terms. Note that the twice-renewable two-year term of the chair of the Joint Chiefs is part of the process of ensuring civilian control over the military.

Before 1986 the members of the Joint Chiefs of Staff were, collectively, very powerful. They advised the president and the secretary of defense. Because they functioned as a committee and could not act until unanimous agreement was reached, however, they often produced overly broad decisions. Critics, therefore, viewed much of the work of the Joint Chiefs as wasteful and even dangerous.

The Department of Defense Reorganization Act of 1986 shifted considerable power to the chair. Reporting through the secretary of defense, the chair now advises the president on military matters, exercises authority over the forces in the field, and is responsible for overall military planning. In theory, the chair of the Joint Chiefs can even make a military decision that the chiefs of the other services oppose. On paper at least, these other chiefs now serve the chair merely as advisers, and even the chair's deputy, the vice-chair, outranks the other service chiefs. The chair has a mandate to encourage "jointness" in military education and in other spheres to integrate the services for maximum effectiveness. Disputes still continue, but the chair is now much stronger than was previously the case. The chair of the Joint Chiefs today is the most powerful peacetime military officer in U.S. history. The Reorganization Act also strengthened the powers of the theater commanders who actually command forces in various parts of the world.

It is critical to appreciate, however, that the chair of the Joint Chiefs is *not* the head of the military. The chair and the JCS are advisers to the secretary of defense and the president, but the president can, and on occasion has, disregarded their advice. A president must weigh military action or inaction against the larger foreign and security interests of the nation.

The Confederational Nature of the Defense Bureaucracy

It is common to hear criticisms of the "Pentagon machine" or the "national military establishment." The defense bureaucracy is, however, best understood—as is any bureaucracy—as something less than a monolith. Insiders often stress that this policy-making structure is best thought of as a *confederation*, or bargaining arena, as opposed to a tight chain-of-command hierarchy. In fact, in recent years strong sentiment has emerged for more centralized control and direction of the nation's defense bureaucracy.

Disputes among military services involve more than professional jealousies. The technological revolution in warfare has rendered obsolete many concepts about military missions, thereby threatening the traditional roles of some of the services. In the past it made sense to divide command among land, sea, and air forces. Today defense

research and development are constantly altering formerly established roles and missions, yet the individual services are reluctant to give up their traditional functions or to serve each other's crucial needs. The navy, for example, is interested in waging sea warfare, not in running a freight service for the army. Interservice rivalries erupt when the army and air force quarrel over who should provide air support for ground troops. Each branch also supports weapons that bring it prestige. The air force and navy dispute, for example, the effectiveness of land-based versus sea-based missiles.[49]

Whether strategic policies are worked out within the Defense Department, the White House, or Congress, the decisions result from a political process in which some measure of consensus is essential. The Joint Chiefs engage in the same type of vote trading used in Congress. On budget issues the chiefs often endorse all the programs desired by each service. When forced to choose on an issue of policy, the chiefs have traditionally compromised among the different service positions rather than attempt to develop a position based on a unified military point of view.

The Draft

The Constitution authorizes Congress to do what is "necessary and proper" in order to "raise and support Armies," "to provide and maintain a Navy," and "to provide for calling forth the Militia." The problem is that the role of the United States in the world has changed dramatically since 1789, as have our military needs. Although our boundaries once defined our major national interest, U.S. interests now reach around the globe.

Military conscription (*the draft*) was first instituted in 1862, during the Civil War. It was used during World War I, when Congress passed the Selective Service Act. This act called for a draft of males between the ages of 21 and 30, with exemptions for certain public officials and for clergy. In both instances conscription ended when the conflicts ended. The first peacetime draft began in 1940, with the Selective Service and Training Act. By the time of Pearl Harbor, in late 1941, men between the ages of 18 and 35 were eligible for the draft. When World War II ended, however, the draft continued, in various forms, for almost three decades. Soon after the Vietnam war began, the *all-volunteer force* (AVF) was established by Congress. This force is charged with providing for our peacetime military personnel needs; in time of war, a draft could be reinstituted.

Since its beginning; the all-volunteer force has been much debated. Some experts contend the AVF has worked, that the quality and quantity of recruits are as good or better than under the draft, and that the social costs are much lower. Other experts say quality has dropped and that the AVF is inadequate to defend our vital interests abroad.

The military has had problems attracting the desired number of recruits. The services reported serious shortfalls; and active reserves have fewer members. Total full-time, active personnel in all services is 1.4 million. Minorities are overrepresented in the armed services, notably in the army, where blacks constitute more than 30 percent of the enlisted ranks. Women are underrepresented, although the proportion of women to men in the armed forces has grown.

Preparedness may be judged in part by the educational level of new recruits. About 80 percent of all new enlisted troops have graduated from high school, a higher level than the eligible pool. But maintaining this level requires extensive recruiting and higher pay and fringe benefits, which has been advocated by President George W. Bush.

The all-volunteer force was set up as a peacetime measure. If major emergencies came, so, presumably, would the draft. However, President Jimmy Carter asked for and won congressional approval for the resumption of draft registration. Carter's initial plan called for the registration of men and women within 30 days of their 18th birthday. Congress refused to appropriate funds for the registration of women. Later the Supreme Court upheld the men-only registration. This is the practice today. All males, by law, must report at age 18. (If college age males 18 and over have not done so, they are ineligible for federal financial aid).

Some Americans at the time opposed the draft registration because they believed it would inevitably lead to a draft. They also believed Carter was "playing politics" with

this process and that it was entirely unnecessary during peacetime. The Selective Service said registration would save less than two weeks in the event of mobilization.

Women in the Military and in Combat

Women constitute 14 percent of the total enlistment in the armed forces; 6 percent of our forces in the Persian Gulf War were female, and 10 percent of the U.S. troops serving in the NATO mission to implement the peace accords in Bosnia were women.[50] The women in Operation Desert Storm piloted troop transport and supply aircraft, helped to operate Patriot antimissile systems, and worked as tank mechanics and military police guarding Iraqi prisoners of war.

Congress has lifted any legal restrictions on air force and navy women becoming combat pilots, and the Pentagon has now opened thousands of combat-related positions in the military services for women. The military is redesigning its assignments to ensure that equal opportunity exists within its ranks.

A majority of Americans think women should be assigned to ground combat units, but others are still concerned about women in combat situations. Many women in the military have said that while they would like to have the right to serve in combat positions, most of them would not opt for these roles. The difficulty in deciding whether women should participate in combat often comes in defining what is combat.

Despite their accomplishments, women in the armed forces have faced countless problems, including sexual harassment, and women officers have complained of men refusing to take orders from them and of being given inappropriate assignments. Female navy combat pilots complain about "the silent treatment" and gender prejudice.[51] Still, women are generally winning acceptance in the military at all levels and will continue to play significant roles in virtually all aspects of the armed forces.

THE POLITICS OF DEFENSE SPENDING

The U.S. defense budget, as noted, is approximately $315 billion a year. About half the people employed by the national government work in the Defense Department. About three-quarters of federal purchases of goods and services originate in the defense budget; several thousand defense installations are scattered across the country. Contracts in excess of $100 billion result in defense-related civilian employ-

THE "DON'T ASK, DON'T TELL" CONTROVERSY

Controversy persists over whether the military has the right to expel homosexuals because of their sexual orientation. In the mid-1990s, the U.S. military expelled about 1,000 men and women every year because of sexual preference. The Pentagon defended the ban by saying that homosexuals in a military setting create difficulty because there is no privacy, no choice of association or living quarters, and no provision for those who prefer gay and lesbian lifestyles.

Many leaders in Congress and elsewhere criticized the ban, calling it the final bastion of discrimination in the military and saying it reminded them of the army's former official opposition to African Americans in uniform. Bill Clinton called for a complete end to the ban when he campaigned for his first term as president. Once in office, however, he had to settle for a compromise that merely modified the ban. Under a "Don't Ask, Don't Tell," policy, military officials are now not permitted to question recruits about their sexual orientation, and gays and lesbians are required to refrain from sexual practices while on duty or assignments. Those who commit homosexual acts are still subject to discharge.

The "Don't Ask, Don't Tell" plan was intended to provide more humane treatment for gays by permitting them to serve in the military if they did not disclose their sexual orientation or engage in homosexual practices. "It has, instead, forced gays to lie, and has resulted in more harassment and a near doubling in the number of people being discharged annually on the basis of

"This one's for not asking and this one's for not telling."

homosexuality."[*] Critics say the policy may well be as bad or worse than the previous policy.

Gay and homosexual groups have turned to the courts to try to get the new regulations overruled as unconstitutional. Some U.S. district courts have ruled that the military may not discharge a person simply because of declared sexual orientation. Various federal court rulings have upheld the regulations set by the Clinton White House, saying they were properly based on a law enacted by Congress and that courts are traditionally obligated to defer to the other branches of government, especially when the matter involves military policy.[**]

The U.S. Supreme Court has never ruled definitely on the "Don't Ask, Don't Tell" policy. But several federal appeals courts have upheld the policy, and the Supreme Court has on several occasions rejected a challenge to the policy.[†]

Americans are divided over this issue. Many conservatives would like an unambiguous rejection of gays in the military. They claim it discourages both military enlistment efforts and unit cohesion. However, as former Republican presidential candidate Barry Goldwater said, "You don't need to be straight to fight and die for your country. You just need to shoot straight."[††]

[*]"The Pentagon's Anti-Gay Policies," editorial, *The New York Times*, July 27, 2000, p. A26.

[**]See Neil A. Lewis, "Court Upholds Clinton Policy on Gay Troops," *The New York Times*, April 6, 1996, pp. 1, 7.

[†]Richard Carelli, "'Don't Ask, Don't Tell' Survives First Test in Supreme Court," *USA Today*, October 20, 1998, p.A4.

[††]Barry M. Goldwater, "The Gay Ban: Just Plain Un-American," *The Washington Post National Weekly Edition*, June 21–27, 1993, p. 28.

ment of nearly 2 million workers. More than 1.5 million retired Defense Department personnel draw pensions and other fringe benefits. The defense budget also includes more than $12 billion dedicated to nuclear weapons research and maintenance and environmental cleanup that actually is run by the Department of Energy.

Reflecting the end of the cold war, the demise of the Soviet Union, and the lack of support for maintaining defense spending at the 1980s level, defense spending

decreased during most of the 1990s. Weapons systems were canceled or postponed, bases closed, ships retired, and large numbers of troops brought home from Germany, the Philippines, and elsewhere. A number of major weapons systems whose primary justification was to fight the former Soviet Union were canceled or their production greatly curtailed. All the services lost personnel. The army was cut over 30 percent, and the National Guard and the military reserve have been cut back about 25 percent. Defense spending now represents about 16 percent of the federal budget, where in 1980 it averaged about 25 percent of federal spending.

George W. Bush campaigned for the presidency saying the American military must be supported better, modernized, and revitalized. He pledged a $1 billion pay raise for the military and increased research and development spending of at least $20 billion in the next few years. Perhaps Bush's biggest and most expensive commitment is to a national missile defense program that had earlier been championed by Ronald Reagan. On this issue, however, he will "face resistance from U.S. allies, arms experts, scientists, Democrats, and even some senior Pentagon officials."[52] This will be one of the biggest tests of Bush's leadership abilities.

Most military analysts agree that an increase in weapons procurement will be essential during the George W. Bush presidency. Much of the projected spending increases will be for replacing old weapons with more modern yet more expensive equipment, such as the air force's F-22 fighter aircraft and the navy's DD-21 destroyer ship. The marines had been aggressively pushing for procurement of hundreds of V-22 Osprey helicopters but that hope has been dashed by several crashes and a scandal over extensive falsified maintenance records in the marine squadron that had been test-flying the V-22.[53]

It is no secret in Washington, however, that the Pentagon's top military brass would like to see Congress appropriate significantly more funds for new weapons systems, higher pay scales, and new technologies. The 1990s saw constant U.S. involvement in international peacekeeping and humanitarian relief operations that military officials believe strained the nation's resources. Some in the military view such humanitarian tasks as "peripheral" or diversionary from the Pentagon's main mission; others view these peacekeeping activities as a primary mission (see Table 21–2).

Resistance to Making Cuts

One of the problems with cutting defense spending is that it immediately eliminates jobs in the home districts of members of Congress, and weapons systems continue to be protected by members more concerned with jobs and reelection hopes than with strategic needs.[54] The B-52 Stealth bomber is often pointed to as notable case. The Pentagon has not asked for more of these billion-dollar planes, yet Congress often approves funds for them because cuts in weapons systems and plant closings mean not only that people in the Defense Department and on bases lose their jobs but also that local shopkeepers, bankers, lawyers, doctors, contractors, housekeepers, babysitters—the list goes on and on—are put out of work.

Weapons are, in fact, a major American industry, an industry that members of Congress work hard to promote and protect. The agreement that operates in other pork-barrel areas works here as well: "You help me in my district, and I'll help you in yours." Even the most ardent, balance-the-budget conservatives change their tune when a contract termination hits close to their district. Similarly, vigorous antiwar doves in Congress often shout the loudest when a base closing is proposed for their home region.

This is not to say that members of Congress cast their votes on military spending solely on whether their district would profit from the decisions. An analysis of the relationships between campaign contributors and votes on weapons systems con-

TABLE 21–2 Public Opinion and Defense Spending

Question: Is the U.S. spending too much, about right, or too little on defense?

Year	Too Much	About Right	Too Little	No Opinion
2000	22%	44%	31%	3%
1998	22	45	26	7
1995	42	40	15	3
1993	42	38	17	3
1991	50	36	10	4
1989	49	37	11	3
1987	44	36	14	6
1986	47	36	13	4
1980	14	24	49	13
1976	36	32	22	10
1974	44	32	12	12
1971	49	31	11	9
1969	52	31	8	9

Source: The Gallup Organization, November 2000.

cludes that issues of defense strategy, cost, and a legislator's political philosophy are equally important.[55]

Still, the Defense Department was repeatedly frustrated in its efforts to close unneeded military bases in the United States. Influential members of Congress sometimes went to great lengths lobbying their colleagues that bases in their districts were too important to shut down. Military officials and members of Congress eventually agreed that new procedures were needed to handle congressional approval of base closings.

To thwart efforts by legislators to block closings of military bases, Congress in 1988 set up a blue-ribbon commission to identify bases that should be closed for budgetary reasons. At least three additional commissions have been appointed in subsequent years. These commissions are appointed by Congress and the president, but they work independently of both branches. They review the base-closing suggestions made by the Pentagon and make recommendations, which have to be accepted in toto or else be rejected by the president. If the president accepts the closings, the package then goes to Congress, where each chamber is allowed 45 days to consider the entire package. Congress also has to accept the entire package or no closings take place.[56]

This procedure has generally succeeded. Dozens of bases have been closed or are in the process of being shut down, and the savings will run into billions of dollars. While there have been predictable grumbling from the big losers and some lawsuits, the federal courts have upheld these procedures, and more bases are being closed as we begin the twenty-first century. Many members of Congress tried in recent years to delay base closings. Former Secretary of Defense William Cohen has said that at least another $20 billion could have been saved in recent years if more obsolete bases could have been closed. President George W. Bush's military budget calls for further base closings.

PROSPECTS FOR THE FUTURE

American foreign policy from 1945 through 1990 was shaped by tensions with its superpower rival, the Soviet Union. That opposition ended abruptly in the early 1990s, yet the rise of several Asian nations and the formation of the European Community have increased the importance of economic and trading issues in international relations.

Foreign and defense policy debates today address issues such as reducing the risk of nuclear and biochemical war, protecting energy supplies, creating jobs, encouraging free trade, and trying to reduce the proliferation and intensity of ethnic and religious conflicts both between and within nations.

The George W. Bush administration has indicated support for a broad range of United Nations activities. It has tried to establish closer ties with Mexico, has deemphasized the use of economic sanctions, and is trying to make sure that the military does not waste the defense budget preparing for yesterday's wars. The Bush administration spent its first year reviewing military threats the United States is likely to face in the future, how to fight such wars, and what will be required to pay for and provide adequate personnel and weapons.

Bush advocates a national missile defense shield. The next years will see fierce disputes over whether such a system will really work and whether this country would be more or less secure with such a system.

POLITICS ONLINE

NAFTA: Does Free Trade Work?

The United States and Canada forged a free trade alliance in the 1980s, the North American Free Trade Agreement (NAFTA). The trade pact developed economic interdependence in both nations. In 1994 the pact was expanded to include Mexico. Ratification of NAFTA engendered a major debate over free trade. Now, several years into NAFTA we can ask, does free trade work? To begin to answer this question, it is important to first learn what NAFTA is and how it came about. You can consult the NAFTA Secretariat website at: **http://www.nafta-sec-alena.org/**.

NAFTA was modeled on other free trade alliances like the European Union, comprising most western European states, and MERCOSUR, between Argentina, Brazil, Paraguay, and Uruguay. NAFTA ought to be assessed in the context of other free trade areas around the globe. More information on these free trade agreements can be found at their respective sites: **www.europa.eu.int/**, and **www.mercosur.org/**.

Supporters of free trade and specifically NAFTA argue such agreements would result in economic growth. To better understand these arguments for free trade, consult: **www.freetrade.org/** or **www.uscib.org/**. Indeed, devotees of free trade now want to expand NAFTA to include most of the Western Hemisphere under a new agreement called Free Trade Agreement of the Americas (FTAA). FTAA's official website is: **www.ftaa-alca.org/**.

Free trade and NAFTA have been criticized for costing some Americans their jobs, and that free trade agreements like the proposed FTAA do not help economically because they can hurt small domestic firms that need protection from international competition in order to be competitive in the long run. Critics also argue that free trade agreements create too much dependence on imports and pose dangers to the environment. To access arguments against the FTAA and other free trade agreements, look at: **www.stopftaa.com/** or **www.citizen.org/pctrade/tradehome.html**.

SUMMARY

1. New foreign policy challenges include nuclear and biological arms control; population growth in the face of poverty; a serious trade imbalance with Japan and the relationship of trade status to human rights violations, especially in relations with China; the Chemical Weapons Convention; aid to former Soviet-bloc nations; the European Economic Union and the future of NATO; drug traffic; and the degradation of the global environment; and budget issues.

2. The president has the primary responsibility to shape foreign policy. The principal foreign policy adviser is the secretary of state, although other cabinet secretaries are also influential. The National Security Council and the intelligence

agencies also play key roles. Public opinion, interest groups, foreign countries, political parties, and Congress also affect the politics of making foreign policy.

3. Presidents, Congress, and the American people all become involved in defining our vital national security interests, but they often have contradictory views. Presidents must sometimes act swiftly and decisively. Plainly, the role of the president in foreign affairs was strengthened during the cold war years as the United States developed an enormous standing military capability and an extensive intelligence network. Presidents are often in a good position to see the nation's long-term interests above the tugging of bureaucratic and special interests. But in our constitutional democracy, presidents and their advisers must consult with Congress and inform the American people. The media and special interests also play a role.

4. U.S. foreign policy interests are advanced by one or a combination of the following strategies: diplomacy, foreign aid, economic sanctions, political coercion (including the breaking off of diplomatic relations), covert action, and military intervention.

5. The United States is an active participant in numerous international organizations, especially the United Nations. The United Nations is likely to play an even greater role in the post–cold war world, even if many Americans, especially conservatives, are highly critical of the way the U.N. works. The primacy of the nation-state is not in question, yet more and more of our global policy problems will be solved through international organizations of one type or another.

6. Our system is designed to provide civilian control over the military. Although the military in any society has enormous potential for direct political involvement, this has not occurred in the United States. The president, Congress, the secretary of defense, the Joint Chiefs of Staff, and cabinet officers continually weigh national security against competing claims.

7. Although the past decade witnessed major reductions in the size of the military and major cuts in military spending, some critics say the defense budget can be cut much further. Critics on the right, however, claim we have weakened our defense preparedness. The nature of warfare and the preventing of wars are changing but in ways that are hard to predict.

KEY TERMS

permanent normal trade relations status (PNTR) 480

bipartisanship 488

economic sanctions 491

FURTHER READING

GEORGE BUSH and BRENT SCOWCROFT, *A World Transformed* (Knopf, 1998).

WARREN CHRISTOPHER, *In the Stream of History: Shaping Foreign Policy for a New Era* (Stanford University Press, 1998).

IVO H. DAALDER and MICHAEL E. O'HANLON, *Winning Ugly: NATO's War to Save Kosovo* (Brookings Institution Press, 2000).

JOSEPH G. DAWSON III, ed., *Commanders-in-Chief: Presidential Leadership in Modern Wars* (University Press of Kansas, 1993).

LOUIS FISHER, *Presidential War Power* (University Press of Kansas, 1995).

JOHN LEWIS GADDIS, *The United States and the End of the Cold War* (Oxford University Press, 1992).

RICHARD N. HAASS, *The Reluctant Sheriff: The United States After the Cold War* (Council on Foreign Relations, 1997).

RICHARD N. HAASS and MEGHAN L. O'SULLIVAN, eds., *Honey and Vinegar: Incentives, Sanctions and Foreign Policy* (Brookings Institution Press, 2000).

OLE HOLSTI, *Public Opinion and American Foreign Policy* (University of Michigan Press, 1996).

SAMUEL HUNTINGTON, *The Clash of Civilization and the Remaking of World Order* (Simon & Schuster, 1996).

LOCH K. JOHNSON, *Secret Agencies: U.S. Intelligence in a Hostile World* (Yale University Press, 1996).

HAROLD HONGJU KOH, *The National Security Constitution: Sharing Power After the Iran-Contra Affair* (Yale University Press, 1990).

STEVEN KULL and I. M. DESTLER, *Misreading the Public: The Myth of a New Isolationism* (Brookings Institution Press, 1999).

THOMAS W. LIPPMAN, *Madeleine Albright and the New American Diplomacy* (Westview Press, 2000).

ROBERT S. LITWAK, *Rogue States and U.S. Foreign Policy: Containment After the Cold War* (Johns Hopkins University Press, 2000).

WILLIAM PERRY, *Preventive Defense: A New Security Strategy for America* (Brookings Institution Press, 1999).

JOHN PRADOS, *Keepers of the Keys: A History of the National Security Council from Truman to Bush* (William Morrow, 1991).

ROSEMARY RIGHTER, *Utopia Lost: The United Nations and World Order* (Twentieth Century Fund, 1995).

JOSEPH ROMM, *Defining National Security: The Nonmilitary Aspect* (Council on Foreign Relations, 1993).

GEORGE SHULTZ, *Turmoil and Triumph: My Years as Secretary of State* (Scribner's, 1993).

RONALD STEEL, *Temptations of a Superpower* (Harvard University Press, 1995).

ROBERT W. TUCKER and DAVID C. HENDRICKSON, *The Imperial Temptation: The New World Order and America's Purpose* (Council on Foreign Relations, 1992).

STEPHEN R. WEISSMAN, *A Culture of Deference: Congress's Failure of Leadership in Foreign Affairs* (Basic Books, 1995).

GEORGE C. WILSON, *This War Really Matters: Inside the Fight for Defense Dollars* (Congressional Press, 2000).

22

STATE AND LOCAL POLITICS WHO GOVERNS?

CHAPTERMEDIA

 POLITICS ONLINE
*What's Happening in Local
Government?*
www.prenhall.com/burns

WHO PAVES OUR ROADS, RUNS OUR SCHOOLS, SHAPES WELFARE POLICY, DECIDES WHO GOES TO PRISON OR GETS PROBATION, AND LEVIES PROPERTY AND SALES TAXES?

Elected and appointed officials in our states and localities determine most of these public policies. Many of the most critical domestic and economic issues facing the United States today are decided at the state and local level of government. And as welfare and other programs have been transferred from the federal government to the states, state and local governments now oversee the transition from welfare to work. Over 90 percent of the more than 1.2 million people in prisons or jails are in state and local facilities, not federal prisons. Another major challenge—how to bring the residents of the inner city in our large metropolitan areas into the economic mainstream—requires imaginative leadership and thoughtful public policy making at the state and local levels of government as well as in Washington.

State and local governments flourished on this continent long before there was a national government. Indeed, the framers of our Constitution shaped the national government largely according to their practical experience with colonial and community governments. What happens today in state and local governments continues to influence the policies of the national government. The reverse, of course, is also true: the national government and its policies have an important impact on local and state government. The national government's activities—dramatic military or diplomatic maneuvers, key Supreme Court decisions, major congressional debates and investigations—receive such great publicity that we often overlook the countless ways governments closer to home affect our lives.

Studying state and local governments to find out how they operate and who governs them is a challenge. It is one thing to study our national system, vast and complex as it is; it is something else to study 50 separate state governments, each with its own legislature, executive, and judiciary, each with its own intricate politics and political traditions. Moreover, state and local governments are only part of a much larger picture. To discuss the government of the state of Mississippi or of the city of Detroit without mentioning race, the government of New York City or of Los Angeles without noting the politics of ethnic groups, or the government of Texas without referring to the cattle and oil industries would be to ignore the real dynamics of the political process. State and local governments, like the national government, are more than organizational charts. They are systems of politics and people. And the great variations among the states and

localities—in population, economic resources, environment—make comparisons and generalizations difficult.

Every government system is part of a larger social system. A government is a structure and a process that resolves, or at least manages, conflicts. It regulates, distributes, and sometimes redistributes income and property. It is also a means for achieving certain goals and performing services desired both by those who govern and by those governed. It operates in the context of an economic system, class structure, and lifestyle that are often more important than the structure of the government itself or even the nature of its political processes. The interrelations among the economic, social, and political systems are complex, and it is often difficult to unscramble them, and to decide which is cause and which is effect.[1]

This already complex picture is complicated still further by the fact that more than 87,500 cities, counties, towns, villages, school districts, water-control districts, and other governmental units are piled one on top of another within the states. If all states or cities or towns were alike, the task might be manageable. But of course they are not. Each city, like each state, has distinct characteristics.[2]

WHO HAS THE POWER?

How can we grasp the operations and problems of state and local government without becoming bogged down in endless detail? We can do so by calling attention to the core components of democratic governance: citizen participation, liberty, constitutional checks and balances, representation, and responsible leadership. Further, we can attempt to answer several questions that throw light on all these problems: Who governs? How much influence or control is in the hands of the business community? Does political power tend to gravitate toward a relatively small number of people? If so, who are these people? Do they work closely together, or do they oppose each other? Do the same people or factions shape the agenda for public debate and dominate all decision making? Or do some sets of leaders decide certain questions and leave other questions to other leaders or simply to chance?

In 1924 two sociologists from Columbia University, Robert and Helen Lynd, studied a typical American city as though they were anthropologists investigating a tribe in Africa or Indonesia. For two years they lived in Muncie, Indiana—at that time a city of 38,000 residents—asking questions and watching how people made their living, raised their children, used their leisure time, and joined in civic and social associations. The Lynds reported that despite the appearance of democratic rule, a social and economic elite actually ran things.[3] Their work stimulated studies in all kinds of communities to find out whether power is concentrated in the hands of the few, is dispersed among the many, or operates in some other way.

Relying on a mix of research methods, social scientists since the Lynds' time have studied patterns of power in communities and arrived at a variety of findings. Floyd Hunter, a sociologist who analyzed Atlanta in the 1950s, found a relatively small and stable group of top policy makers drawn largely from the business class. This elite operated through secondary leaders who sometimes modified policy, but the power of the elite was almost always important.[4] In contrast, Robert Dahl and two of his graduate students at Yale studied New Haven at that same time and concluded that although some people had a great deal of influence, there was no permanent elite. There were, instead, shifting coalitions of leaders who sometimes disagreed among themselves but who always had to keep in mind what the public would accept when making decisions.[5]

Rule by a Few or Rule by the Many?

One group of investigators, chiefly sociologists such as Hunter, have been concerned with **social stratification** in the political system—how politics is affected by divisions among socioeconomic groups or classes in a community. These social scientists

social stratification

Divisions in a community among socioeconomic groups or classes.

assume that political influence is a function of social stratification. They try to find out who governs a particular community by asking various citizens to identify the people who are most influential. Then they study those influential people to determine their social characteristics, their roles in decision making, and the interrelations among them and between them and the rest of the citizens. Those who use this technique report that the upper socioeconomic groups make up the *power elite*, that elected political leaders are subordinate to this elite, and that the major conflicts within the community are between the upper and the lower socioeconomic classes.

Other investigators question these findings and raise objections to the research techniques used. They contend the evidence in the social stratification studies does not support the conclusion that communities are run by a power elite. Rather, the notion of a power elite is merely a reflection of the techniques used and the assumptions made by stratification theorists. Instead of studying the activities of those who are thought to have "clout," these researchers insist one should study how decisions are made.

Those who conduct *community power* studies by analyzing the making of decisions usually find a relatively open, pluralistic power structure in which some people do have more influence than others, but that influence is shared among many people and tends to be limited to particular issues and areas. For example, those who decide how the public schools are run may have little influence over economic policies. In many communities and for many issues there is no identifiable group of influential people, and policies emerge not from the actions of a small group but rather from the unplanned and unanticipated consequences of the behavior of a relatively large number of people, especially from the countless contending groups that form and win access to those who make the important decisions. According to community power theorists, the social structure of the community is certainly one factor, but it is not the determining factor in how goods and services are distributed.

We have here an example of how the questions we ask influence the answers we find. If we ask highly visible and actively involved citizens for their opinions of who is powerful, we find they name a relatively small number of people as the real holders of power. But if we study dozens of local events and decisions, we find that a variety of people are involved—different people in different policy areas.

Other studies of local politics suggest that local values, traditions, and the structure of governmental organizations determine which issues get on the local agenda.[6] Thus tobacco, mining, or steel interests may be so dominant in some areas that tax, regulation, or job safety policies will be kept off the local policy agenda for fear of offending the "powers that be." And those "powers" may indeed go to great lengths to prevent what they deem to be adverse policies. This type of research alerts us to weigh carefully the possibility that defenders of the status quo can mobilize power resources in such a way that "nondecisions" may be more important than decisions. In effect, these researchers tell us not only to study who governs, but also to study the procedures and rules of the game. They urge us to determine which groups or interests would gain and which would lose by political decisions.[7]

On many economic policy matters, local corporations and business elites are involved. Studies of cities in Michigan and in Atlanta, both employing refined and contextual analysis of political decision making, conclude that business elites are indeed important, but they are not necessarily the controlling factor in city governance:

> There is, then, no controlling hand in community politics. No conspiracy of business and government exists. Business interests do not invariably dominate government policy even where a single industry dominates the community. However, the giant industrial companies do provide the backdrop against which the public policy process operates in the industrial city. They are always there, seldom intervening in specific policy matters but never far from the calculations of policy makers.[8]

Studies of states and communities have now produced enough findings that we can begin to see how formal government institutions, social structure, economic factors, and other variables interact in a working political system.

THE STAKES IN THE POLITICAL STRUGGLE

The national government has become the driving force behind the nation's economic strength and security. It assumes major responsibility for protecting civil rights, fighting inflation and unemployment, regulating sectors with great economic power, and subsidizing weaker sectors of the economy—not to mention matters of war and peace. Certainly state and local governments cannot claim so central a role, yet the role of states and localities is increasing over a range of domestic policies, not only in absolute terms but even in financial terms compared with the national government (see Figure 22–1).

Since World War II, state and local government activities have increased much faster than the nondefense activities of the federal government. In the past decade, the federal government has been downsizing while the states and local governments have been growing. Six times as many people work for state and local governments compared to federal civilian employees: 18 million state and local employees and less than 3 million federal civil servants.[9] States have had to assume greater responsibilities for raising taxes, setting economic and social priorities, and administering most welfare and job-creation programs as a result of cutbacks in federal funds and devolution of responsibilities to the states.

State and local governments deal more directly with the average person than does the national government, because neighborhood, school, and housing problems are closely regulated by state and local governments. The points at which people come into contact with government services and officials most often concern schools, streets and highways, parks and playgrounds, police and fire protection, zoning, and health care. But even in these areas, the mix of national, state, and local programs and responsibilities is such that it is often hard to isolate which level of government does what to whom. Also, there are some national-to-individual relationships that bypass state and local governments altogether, such as the Internal Revenue Service, Postal Service, and Social Security.

The Maze of Interests

Special-interest groups can be found in varying forms in every state and locality. For example, industrial Rhode Island has farm organizations, and rural Wyoming has trade unions. Influential economic pressure groups and political action committees (organized to raise and disburse campaign funds to candidates for public office) operate in the states much as they do nationally. They try to build up the membership of their organizations; they lobby at the state capitals and in city halls; they educate and organize the voters; and they support their political friends in office and oppose their enemies. They also face the same internal problems all groups face: maintaining unity within the group, dealing with subgroups that break off in response to special needs, and balancing democracy with discipline.

One great difference, however, is that group interests can be concentrated in states and localities, whereas their strength tends to be diluted in

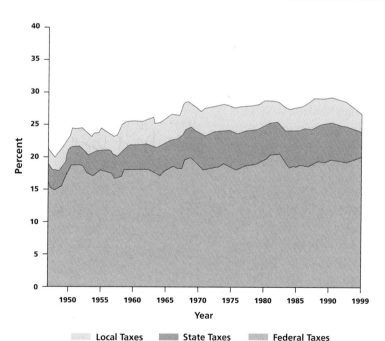

FIGURE 22–1 **Total Taxes Collected as a Percentage of the GDP**

Source: *The New York Times*, April 10, 1994, sec. 4, p. 1. Copyright © 1994 by The New York Times Co. Reprinted by permission. Updated from U.S. Bureau of the Census, *Statistical Abstract of the United States, 1999*, (Government Printing Office, 1999), pp. 349, 721. For more information, go to www.census.gov/govs/qtax/.

[handwritten note: Intrest are more dominant because the represent the majority]

the national government. Big business does not really run things in Washington, D.C., any more than Wall Street, the Catholic Church, or the American Legion do. But in some states and localities, certain interests are clearly dominant because they represent the social and economic majorities of the area. Few politicians in Wisconsin will attack dairy farmers; few candidates for office in Florida will oppose benefits for senior citizens; and few officeholders in Idaho will support gun control. In other areas, industries such as timber or energy are influential because of their role in the local economy.

It is the range and variety of these local groups that give American politics its special flavor, excitement, and challenge: auto unions and manufacturers in Michigan, corn and hog farmers in Iowa, gas and oil dealers in Texas, gun owners in New Hampshire and Idaho, tobacco farmers in North Carolina, poultry growers in Arkansas, Boeing and Microsoft in the Seattle area, cotton growers in the South, coal miners in West Virginia, and sheep ranchers in Utah. However, the power of these groups should not be exaggerated.

We have to be cautious about lumping all workers, all business-people, all teachers, all Hispanics, or all African Americans together. The union movement is sometimes sharply divided among the team-sters, building trades, machinists, auto workers, and so on. The business community is often divided between big industrial, banking, and commercial firms on the one hand, and small merchants on the other. In New England, Irish and Italian fraternal societies express the opinions of their respective groups on public issues; other organizations speak for people of French Canadian or Polish descent. New England politicians fear the power of ethnic groups to influence elections, especially primaries, yet there are examples of "Yankees" winning in heavily ethnic areas. Similarly, Asian American, Latino, and African American communities are playing an increasingly important role in elections in states such as California, Florida, and Texas.

Compared to the other considerations affecting voters' choices, the ethnic factor may be small. Still, even a small percentage voting according to their ethnic interests can have a decisive effect on an election. Much depends on the character of the candidates and their personal appeal. Any group, no matter how strong, must cope with a variety of cross-pressures, including a general sense that the voter does not vote for "one of our own" on that ground alone.

Other interests that are more specialized may also have a close relation to local government. Many businesspeople sell products to the state or perform services for it: milk dealers, printers, contractors, parking meter manufacturers, computer and communications technology firms, makers of playground equipment, and textbook publishers. They often organize formally or informally to improve their relations with purchasing officials. At the local level, developers and home builders and their lawyers press for zoning and planning commission action. Millions of dollars are often at stake, and the resulting action or inaction frequently shapes both the economic growth and the environmental quality of a community.

Business interests are inevitably involved in city and county politics and policy making. As one study of Atlanta found, the business elite is rarely a passive or reluctant partner in setting local priorities. "Atlanta's postwar political experience is a story of active business-elite efforts to make the most of their economic and organizational resources in setting the terms on which civic cooperation occurs."[10] Businesses everywhere depend on local governments for parking, good roads and transportation, safety, urban renovations, and much more. Business elites get involved in long-range community planning, are keenly interested in who gets elected, and are ever-watchful of any changes in taxation structures.

Pet Peeves

Some areas of life might seem far removed from any government—having a dog or a cat as a pet, for example. But a dog needs a license and a collar, it must be confined, and it must be inoculated. And if anyone thinks that cats are beyond the reach of the law, they should remember Adlai E. Stevenson's famous veto of the "cat bill" when he was governor of Illinois. The bill would have imposed fines on cat owners who let their pets run off their premises, and it would have allowed cat haters to trap them. Stevenson said:

I cannot agree that it should be declared public policy of Illinois that a cat visiting a neighbor's yard or crossing the highway is a public nuisance. It is in the nature of cats to do a certain amount of unescorted roaming. . . . I am afraid this bill could only create discord, recrimination, and enmity. . . . We are all interested in protecting certain varieties of birds. . . . The problem of cat versus bird is as old as time. If we attempt to resolve it by legislation, who knows but what we may be called upon to take sides as well in the age-old problem of dog versus cat, bird versus bird, or even bird versus worm.

So the governor sided with cat supporters over bird lovers, while staying neutral between bird lovers and worm diggers. Such incidents illustrate how the complex workings of modern society can lead to government intervention in or overregulation of our lives.

SOURCE: Governor Adlai Stevenson, veto message to members of the Senate Assembly, Springfield, Illinois, 1949.

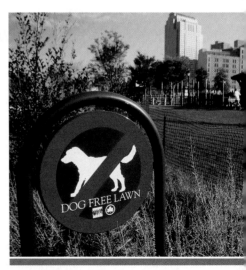

Government reaches into many trivial aspects of our lives, such as restrictions on our pets.

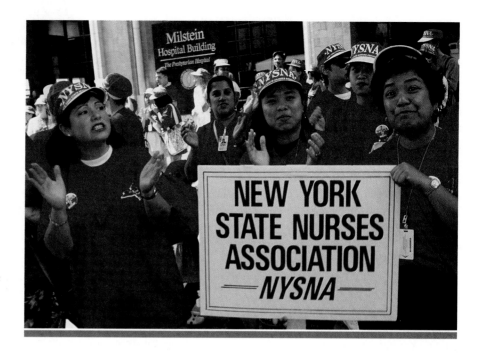

Professions and occupations of various types are regulated by the government through licensing and standards.

Another type of group intimately concerned with public policy is the professional association. States license barbers, beauticians, architects, lawyers, doctors, teachers, accountants, dentists, and many other occupational groups. You will find representatives from the Beauticians Aid Association, the Funeral Directors and Embalmers Association, the Institute of Dry Cleaning, and the Association of Private Driver-Training Schools lobbying at the statehouse. Associations representing such groups are concerned with the nature of the regulatory laws and the makeup of the boards that do the regulating. They are especially concerned about the rules for admission to their profession or trade and about the way in which professional misconduct is defined and punished. Stiffening licensing requirements for physicians will decrease the supply of new doctors, for example, and thereby raise the incomes of those in practice. Bar associations, for the same reason, closely monitor licensing standards for the legal profession and the appointment of judges.

Today other groups of citizens are also likely to organize to influence decisions at the state capital: those who are pro-life and those who are pro-choice; those who want stiffer sentences for drunken driving; and those who favor three-strikes-and-you're-out legislation to send repeat criminals to jail for life. Right to Life groups, Planned Parenthood, antismoking groups, animal rights activists, and prison guards are also well organized. Increasingly significant are environmental groups such as the Sierra Club, both in forging public policies and as forces in election contests.

Lobbyists at the Statehouse

Many businesses, especially larger corporations, employ lobbyists, public relations specialists, political consultants, or law firms to represent them.[11] One of the growth businesses in state politics is consulting, usually by specialized lawyers or former state legislators. For a fee, lobbyists push desired bills through the legislature or block unwanted ones. This kind of activity again raises the question of who has clout or who governs. Clearly, those who can hire skilled lobbyists and other experts to shape the public agenda often wield more influence than unorganized citizens, who rarely even follow state and regional governmental decision making.

Lobbyists are present in every state capital, and they are there to guide through the legislature a small handful of bills their organization wants passed or to stop those their organization wants defeated.[12] Legislators process hundreds or even thousands of bills each year, in addition to doing casework on behalf of constituents and

worrying about reelections. Shrewd lobbyists usually get a chance—sometimes several chances—to influence the fate of their few bills.

There is a widespread impression that lobbyists have freer rein in state legislatures than they do in the U.S. Congress and, what is more, that bribes or informal payoffs by lobbyists are cruder and more obvious in state legislatures. Certainly lobbying restrictions in the states are more relaxed than at the federal level, although in some of the larger states they may be even more stringent. There is less media coverage of state politics in many states than is focused on national politics in Washington.

Corruption of legislators and state officials is usually hard to prove. Exposure of scandals in several states pushed many legislatures to curb election abuses and pass ethics codes with stringent conflict-of-interest provisions.[13] Several legislatures have enacted comprehensive financial disclosure laws, and today most state governments are more open, professional, and accountable than in the past.[14] Former President Jimmy Carter, who served in the Georgia Senate and then became governor, recalled that only a "tiny portion" of the 259 members of the Georgia legislature were not good or honest people. But Carter found that "it is difficult for the common good to prevail against the intense concentration of those who have a special interest, especially if the decisions are made behind locked doors."[15]

In a few states one corporation or organization may have considerable influence; in others a "big three" or "big four" dominate politics. But in most states there is competition among organizations, and no single group or coalition of groups stands out. In no state does only one organization control legislative politics, although the powerful Anaconda Company once came close in Montana. For example, nearly 400 lobbyists are reportedly registered in Arkansas. Of these, 125 represent utilities; more than 200 represent individual businesses, industry, or professions; 9 represent labor interests; 8 work on behalf of senior citizens; and 3 lobby for environmental interests. The Arkansas Power and Light Company, the railroads, the poultry and trucking industries, the teachers, and the state Chamber of Commerce are the most effective lobbyists. "It is still true that ordinarily those with greater economic resources, greater numbers, and higher status have far more impact than those who lack these attributes," writes political scientist Diane D. Blair. "Nevertheless, an increasingly complex economy has produced many more actors in the political system, and especially when there is division among the economic elite, some of the lesser voices can be heard."[16]

In Michigan, about 1,250 lobbyists are registered with the state, including representatives of Chrysler, Ford, General Motors, the United Auto Workers, the AFL-CIO, the Michigan Education Association, the Michigan Manufacturers Association, the city of Detroit, the Michigan Chamber of Commerce, certain conservation and environmental groups, and various antitax groups.[17]

Not to be overlooked are the growing number of groups and media outlets that view themselves as "watchdogs" of the public policy process. Groups such as the League of Women Voters, Common Cause, and various citizens groups regularly monitor state politics for questionable fund-raising or lobbying practices. Their "watchdog" efforts are aided sometimes by reporters who cover the state capital.

PARTICIPATION PATTERNS IN SMALL AND MEDIUM-SIZED CITIES

Although it is widely believed that citizens feel "closer" to city and county governments than they do to the more remote national government in Washington, citizens generally take less interest in, vote less often, and are less informed about their local governments than they are about the national government. There are understandable reasons for the lower involvement in local

Comparison of Ethics Laws in the States

■ No contributions from lobbyists: 7 states completely ban lobbyists from contributing to campaigns at any time.

■ No contributions from lobbyists during legislative sessions: 23 states prohibit lobbyists from making contributions during a legislative session.

■ Gifts and expenditure limitations: 25 states restrict the monetary value of gifts a public employee may receive.

■ Investigatory authority: Agencies that may initiate an investigation of ethics violations on their own volition result in ten times the number of investigations per year as those that may only investigate in response to a formal complaint.

SOURCE: *The Book of the States, 2000–2001* (Council of State Governments, 2000), p. 397.

Drawing by Wright, *The Miami Press.*

government. Although issues about where to locate a garbage dump or a prison, or how to deal with police brutality, can arouse considerable heat, most of the time local governments are preoccupied with relatively noncontroversial routines, such as keeping the roads in shape, providing fire and police service, attracting businesses that can create more jobs, or applying for state and federal financial assistance.

Local communities want to keep their tax rates down and promote their cities as "nice places" in which to live, work, and raise a family. Mayors and city officials generally try to avoid controversy and the kind of criticism that will divide a community. Although they do not always succeed, they go to considerable lengths to be reasonable and work for the good of the community. Few aggressively seek to alter the status quo. They do not, as a rule, try to promote equality by redistributing various resources to needier citizens. **Redistributive policies** are programs to shift wealth or benefits from one segment of the population to another, usually from the rich to the poor. Local officials tend to believe this is the task of the national or state authorities—that is, if they think it should be done at all. Typically, they say their communities do not have the funds for that type of program. They might add, "Go see the governor" or "Go talk to your member of Congress." This may be good advice, because various programs (educational loans, unemployment compensation, disability assistance, and so on) explicitly designed to help the less fortunate are administered at the state or federal level.

Neighborhood groups sometimes become involved in protecting their neighborhoods and petitioning for improvements. One concern that often activates neighborhood groups is the possibility that "undesirable" facilities might be located in their neighborhood, such as drug rehabilitation clinics, prisons, dumps, or homeless shelters. Attendance at local government meetings is usually low. However, the announcement of a land-fill area or a prison construction project often stimulates the reaction that local officials call NIMBY, an acronym for "Not In My Back Yard!"

The Role of Local Media

Most communities have only one newspaper, and in small communities it is often a weekly. Some newspapers and local radio and television stations do a good job of covering city and county politics, but this is the exception rather than the rule. Reporters assigned to cover local politics are often inexperienced beginners, yet they provide the only news that citizens get about their city council or zoning board. Even the best of them cannot convey the full complexities of what is going on in a column or two of newsprint.

Some local newspapers have a cozy relationship with elected local officials. Sometimes the owners or editors are social friends or golfing buddies of local officials. Friendships and mutual interests develop, and close scrutiny of what goes on in city hall takes a back seat to city boosterism. In effect, "newspapers boost their hometown, knowing that its prosperity and expansion aid their own. Harping on local faults, investigating dirty politics, revealing unsavory scandals, and stressing governmental inefficiencies only provide readily available documentary material to competing cities."[18]

Editors and station managers recognize that their readers or listeners are more interested in state or national news, and especially in sports, than in what is going on at municipal planning meetings or county commission sessions. Much of what takes place in local government is rather dull. It may be important to some people, yet it strikes the average person as decidedly less exciting than what goes on at the White House, or whether Congress has finally solved the Social Security problem, or whether their stocks have gone up or down recently, or whether the New York Jets, the Cleveland Indians, or the Los Angeles Lakers won last night. We have dozens of ways to find out about Congress and the goings-on at the White House, but we usually have only one source to give us the story on the mayor or sheriff or

redistributive policies
Governmental tax and social programs that shift wealth or benefits from one segment of the population to another, often from the rich to the poor.

school board. Of course, we could attend board meetings or even talk with our mayor, but this is not what most people are likely to do.

Apathy in Grass-Roots America

Voter apathy in local elections is summed up in the bumper sticker, "Don't Vote. It Only Encourages Them." Many important political and economic transactions in communities are ignored by the press and citizens. Charter revision and taxation often galvanize only those directly affected by the new taxes or regulations. Even New England town meetings have difficulty getting people to participate—despite the fact that decisions made at these meetings have major consequences for the local tax rate and the quality of the schools, the police force, and the parks and recreational areas. Thomas Jefferson once proclaimed the town meeting to be the noblest, wisest instrument yet devised for the conduct of public affairs, yet today most towns find that only about 2 or 3 percent of the population cares enough to come.[19]

Meetings of the Austin, Texas, school-board do not usually draw a crowd, but when the topic of sex education was discussed, a vocal and concerned crowd turned out.

The major reason for grass-roots apathy is that the average person is just not interested in local politics. Most people are content to leave politics and political responsibilities to a relatively small number of activists while they pursue their own private concerns—their bowling leagues, their children's Little League or soccer games, golf, or fishing. In a healthy democracy we can expect most people will be involved with their families and jobs, and other than voting occasionally, they will leave civic responsibilities to a relatively small number of their fellow citizens. This is probably a reasonable choice. It may also be an indication of satisfaction with the state of the community.

Cynicism about the effectiveness and fairness of local political processes is sometimes reflected in the politics of protest—mass demonstrations, economic boycotts, even civil disorders—to make demands on government. When certain issues become intense, people become politically active. African Americans, Hispanics, gays, and others form political organizations to present their grievances and marshal their votes. Neighborhood organizations work for better housing and enforcement of inspection ordinances and to prevent crime and drug dealing.

Civic Initiatives in Local Governments

Just as there will always be indifference toward politics and apathy about government, so too will there always be creative, entrepreneurial people who are willing to step forward and find new ways of solving problems. States such as Oregon and Minnesota seem to encourage a climate of innovation and civic enterprise, and a wider look at the United States finds buoyant, optimistic, creative problem solvers in nearly every corner of the nation.

Enterprising local activists have advocated and implemented cost-saving energy programs, environmental cleanup campaigns, recycling and solar energy initiatives, job-training centers, AIDS prevention efforts, housing for the elderly, tutoring for the illiterate, housing for the poor, and hundreds of other problem-solving and opportunity-enhancing community efforts.[20] In almost every case, they create partnerships with elected officials at city hall, sometimes with the Urban League or Chamber of Commerce, and often with local foundations and business corporations.

Sometimes it takes a tragedy to get community groups mobilized. Such a tragic event happened in Boston in 1992 when gang members burst into the funeral of a young man. "In the presence of the mourners, the gang killed one of those in attendance," writes the Reverend Eugene Rivers of the Azusa Christian Community. "That brazen act told us we had to do more. Now."

Not all citizens are apathetic. These young people are spending their free time rehabilitating a community center.

That young man's death galvanized us, and soon the Ten Point Coalition was reaching out to at-risk youth. Our mission was to pair the holy and the secular, to do whatever it took to save our kids. The black churches worked hand-in-hand with the schools, courts, police, and social service agencies. We called on anyone

and everyone who had the means to help our children. We formed programs for teens, neighborhood watches, and patrols. . . . We established ourselves in the neighborhood, standing on the same street corner where the drug dealers once stood. We tracked down the thieves, dealers, and gangs. We tried to give people a chance but if they wouldn't take it, we staked our claim and ran them out of our neighborhood.[21]

WE THE PEOPLE

What One Person Can Accomplish

Urban League leader T. Willard Fair is a committed problem solver for his Liberty City community in Miami. He is recognized as a one-man force trying to rid Liberty City of drug dealers. In the late 1980s Fair started a private-public collaboration to improve the quality of life in this inner-city community. Among many other results, his efforts led to 3,500 arrests, the breakup of 27 crack houses, the towing of many abandoned vehicles, and the trimming of trees to expose shaded areas where drug deals were made. But above all, Fair was able to get his neighbors in Liberty City to band together and have faith that their neighborhood could be rid of its pushers.

"Fair started the program after reading about a young woman who had been shot. Residents were too fearful of drug dealers to cooperate with police." Fair became a catalyst for change, enlisting the help of government and school officials, police and fire officers, churches, residents, and local businesses. He also per-

T. Willard Fair

suaded the national drug program to share some funds, and he raised other funds by whatever means he could. By 1992 he could declare, along with the Liberty City residents, that their 70-square-block, drug-free zone was "off limits" to what he calls "the drug boys."

SOURCE: Catherine Foster, "One Man Rallies a Neighborhood Against Pushers," *Christian Science Monitor*, June 11, 1992, p.7.

There are persistent debates about how to solve social, economic, and racial problems in our large metropolitan areas. Some contend government can't undertake this task, and that private initiatives can be more effective. Others insist that state and local governments are best suited to deal with these challenges. Still others contend that imaginative public-private collaboration is needed to fashion the strategies and mobilize the resources to revive our cities and bring about greater opportunity. Whatever the merits of such contending interpretations, it is clear that neighborhood organizations and spirited civic renewal are critical to the vitality of local government.[22]

CHALLENGES FOR STATE AND LOCAL GOVERNMENTS

The last decade has been a time of testing in many states and communities. One-third of our inner-city governments and school systems face financial distress. The cycle of poverty in the inner cities remains one of the greatest threats to the economic health of the country. These cities often cannot raise enough funds through local taxes to create jobs and housing. Federal and state initiatives have attempted to create economic opportunities for inner-city residents. Community reinvestment programs, community development banks, "empowerment zones," Head Start, charter schools, and the national service corps (Americorp) programs have all been tried in an attempt to bring residents of depressed inner cities into the economic mainstream. But these efforts have been inadequate.

The following central issues in the states and local communities command the attention of the country. They vary depending on location, of course, yet these urgent challenges are part of the unfinished business of a government by the people:

1. *People want more services*, yet at the same time would like to see their taxes cut. City and state officials are constantly trying to do more with less and introduce efficiencies into city and state operations. Voters in many communities have enacted spending limitations that constrain growth in public budgets.

2. *Racism still exists in many communities.* The burning of dozens of black churches a few years ago was distressing evidence of racial hatred. As our

Local residents often form citizen patrols to keep the streets safe and watch over the young people in the community.

nation has become more diverse, most Americans have learned to appreciate the strength that comes from multiple cultures and races. Yet the Ku Klux Klan and other racist groups still thrive in many areas, and bigotry and discrimination persist.

3. *Drugs, gangs, and drug-related crime impose tough policy challenges.* The costs of corrections and prisons have skyrocketed in recent years, yet gangs and drugs and crime are still a menace in our urban areas. Most state and local "wars on drugs" have failed, and the ravages of drug abuse are enormously costly to the nation. Drug abusers lose their jobs; they make our streets, schools, and neighborhoods unsafe; they add to our welfare rolls; and in numerous ways they undermine the vitality of a great many cities and towns.

4. *Poverty in the inner cities persists.* We have extremes of rich and poor within metropolitan regions, and often the wealthier suburbs turn their backs on the problems and poverty of the older cities. Indifference to these inequalities and lack of opportunities may undermine a sense of community and fairness in America.

5. *We need to guarantee the best possible education for all our young people.* Parents are demanding better education and more parental involvement. There is considerable talk about educational choice and competition, and about school vouchers and charter schools. Improving the public schools is necessary, but the salaries of public school teachers are often too low to attract and retain the best-qualified teachers. State and local governments have the responsibility to pay for public education, so educational reform and the search for excellent teachers and learning processes must remain a top state and local priority.

6. *Environmental regulation, land use, and recycling are also major challenges at the local level.* Every city and state wants economic growth and economic opportunities for its workers and businesses, but many forms of economic development impose costs in terms of the quality of air, water, landscapes, and health. Local officials are faced with tough decisions about the need to balance economic and environmental concerns.

7. *Health care costs and delivery are challenges to all levels of government.* Health care reform has been an important policy issue for many years. Some states have experimented with universal health care; others have worked to control costs. Many of the uninsured end up obtaining health

care in emergency rooms in local public hospitals, which in turn seek funding from the local and state governments.

For more information on these and other issues confronting state and local governments go to our home page (**www.prenhall.com/burns**) or to the website of the Council of State Governments at **www.csg.org** or that of the National Conference of State Legislatures at **www.ncsl.org/**.

POLITICS ONLINE

What's Happening in Local Government?

Americans like local government. Opinion surveys consistently show that a majority of Americans hold positive attitudes towards their state and especially their city or town governments. The problem is that there is not one local government but several. Governmental units below the state level include counties, cities, towns, special purpose districts like water, sewer, and power districts, school districts, and then possibly regional transportation agencies. A first step in relating to your local government is to identify which of these governments tax you and impact your life. To learn what your local government is, go to:

wwwpiperinfo.com/state/index.cfm.

Once you identify your local governments, find your city and state on a web browser to see if your city or other unit of local government has a home page. This is the first step in learning what is happening in these governments and determining if you are comfortable with local policies. After surveying what is happening at city council meetings, you might want to learn more about what other local governments are doing regarding the things that interest you. For example, you might be concerned with transportation, managing growth, air pollution, or crime. The Library of Congress maintains a "meta-site" for state government resources at:

lcweb.loc.gov/global/state/stategov.html.

The Council of State Governments maintains an "Issue Alert" bulletin for state government policy materials. You can access it at:

www.csg.org.

Another excellent policy resource for state governments is the National Conference of State Legislatures (NCSL), which has a useful website at:

www.ncsl.org.

To learn more about your local government, visit the National League of Cities and Towns and click on your state:

www.nlc.org/nlc-leag.htm.

SUMMARY

1. Many of the most critical domestic and economic issues facing the United States today are decided at the state and local level of government.

2. Studies of states and communities have investigated how formal government institutions, social structure, economic factors, and local traditions interact to create a working political system. Special-interest groups operate in every state and locality.

3. Although it is widely believed that local governments are "closer" to the people than the national government, voting and other forms of participation at the local level are low.

4. Innovative programs at the local level address problems in the environment, gang violence, illiteracy, and other areas to improve community life. Local civil action is a form of politics.

KEY TERMS

social stratification   506   redistributive policies   512

FURTHER READING

THAD L. BEYLE, ed., *State Government: CQ's Guide to Current Issues and Activities, 2001–2002* (Congressional Quarterly Press, 2001).

BUZZ BISSINGER, *A Prayer for the City* (Random House, 1997).

PAUL BRACE, *State Government and Economic Performance* (Johns Hopkins University Press, 1993).

ALLAN CIGLER and BURDETT LOOMIS, eds., *Interest Group Politics*, 5th ed. (Congressional Quarterly Press, 1998).

FRANK J. COPPA, *County Government* (Praeger, 2000).

THOMAS E. CRONIN and ROBERT D. LOEVY, *Colorado Politics and Government: Governing the Centennial State* (University of Nebraska Press, 1993).

E. J. DIONNE, JR., ed., *Community Works: The Revival of Civil Society in America* (Brookings Institution Press, 1998).

THOMAS D. DYE, *Politics in States and Communities*, 10th ed. (Prentice Hall, 2000).

ROBERT S. ERIKSON et al., *Statehouse Democracy: Public Opinion and Policy in the American States* (Cambridge University Press, 1993).

JOEL GARREAU, *Edge City: Life on the New Frontier* (Doubleday, 1991).

STEPHEN GOLDSMITH, *The Twenty-First Century City* (Regnery, 1997).

VIRGINIA GRAY, RUSSELL HANSON, and HERBERT JACOB, eds., *Politics in the American States*, 7th ed. (Congressional Quarterly Press, 1999).

JONATHAN HARRIS, *A Civil Action* (Vintage, 1996).

DENNIS R. JUDD and PAUL KANTOR, eds., *Politics of Urban American: A Reader* (Addison-Wesley, 1997).

DANIEL KEMMIS, *The Good City and the Good Life* (Houghton Mifflin, 1995).

DAVID L. KIRP, JOHN P. DWYER, and LARRY A. ROSENTHAL, *Our Town: Race, Housing and the Soul of Suburbia* (Rutgers University Press, 1997).

MADELEINE KUNIN, *Living a Political Life* (Vintage, 1995).

TOM LOFTUS, *The Art of Legislative Politics* (Congressional Quarterly Press, 1994).

JOHN O. NORQUIST, *The Wealth of Cities* (Addison-Wesley, 1998).

TODD SWANSTROM and DENNIS R. JUDD, eds., *City Politics: Private Power and Public Policy*, 2d ed. (Addison-Wesley, 1997).

JOSEPH F. ZIMMERMAN, *The New England Town Meeting: Democracy in Action* (Praeger, 1999).

See also the journal of the State Politics and Policy Section of the American Political Science Association, *State Politics & Policy Quarterly*.

23

STATE CONSTITUTIONS: CHARTERS OR STRAITJACKETS?

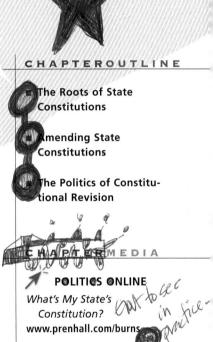

CHAPTER MEDIA

➤ **POLITICS ONLINE**

What's My State's Constitution?
www.prenhall.com/burns

Out to see in practice~

T HE STATE OF NEW YORK HAS HAD FOUR CONSTI-

TUTIONS SINCE 1777. EVERY 20 YEARS THE PEOPLE OF

NEW YORK ARE ASKED ON A GENERAL ELECTION BALLOT IF THEY

would like to convene a constitutional convention to propose a new constitution. They held such a convention in 1967, but its work was rejected. When voters were asked in 1977 if they wanted to convene another convention, they said no. The question came before them again in 1997.

In preparation for the 1997 vote, a Temporary Commission on Constitutional Revision was set up to identify issues and to inform voters about the need for a new constitution. The commission called for a convention of ordinary citizens and suggested that New Yorkers take advantage of new technology such as cable television and electronic town meetings to observe convention proceedings. The commission targeted the budget process, state-local relations, education, and public safety as being of special importance.[1] A constitutional convention, commission members argued, could write a new constitution in clear English, simplify voter registration, improve voting rules and ballot access, regulate campaign finance and lobbying, reform the legislative process, restore confidence in the courts, rethink the tax structure, improve government, and protect the environment.[2]

Opposing the calling of a constitutional convention were the AFL-CIO, the Conservative party, the Sierra Club, the National Abortion Rights Action League, some antitax groups, and some legislative leaders from both parties. Labor unions saw a convention as a threat to their right to organize; trial lawyers worried about limits on lawsuits; environmentalists feared that a convention might jeopardize provisions protecting open spaces; some women's groups were fearful that the convention might restrict abortion rights; and some conservatives feared that liberal interests would control the convention.

There was little interest in the campaign for a constitutional convention. Two weeks before the election, polls indicated that voters, upset by the apparent inability of the state government to get anything done, were overwhelmingly in favor of calling for a constitutional convention to make government work better. Then opponents of constitutional revision got busy. Unions and other anticonvention groups launched television advertisements, direct-mail operations, and phone banks, arguing that the convention was a waste of money and would open the door to dangerous changes. On November 5, 1997, 62 percent of New York voters rejected the call for the convention.[3]

New York's experience is not unusual. In recent years voters in several states have rejected calls for a constitutional convention. For example, in Michigan in November 1994, voters rejected the call for a convention by almost 3 to 1 in all 183 counties; Arkansas voters in December 1995 rejected the call by 4 to 1 in all 75 counties.[4] We have not had any constitutional conventions since Rhode Island had one in 1986, and it won approval of the voters for only 8 of 14 proposed revisions.

You might give some thought now to your own state constitution. Like the U.S. Constitution, state constitutions are both instruments of government and limitations on government. However, unlike the federal one, state constitutions are not popular symbols. On a trip to your state capital you are unlikely to find the state constitution "displayed as is the federal Constitution, in a setting similar to a Shinto shrine."[5]

In this chapter we examine the roots of state constitutions and some of the ways we work around constitutional rigidity. Then we look at methods of amending state constitutions, ending with a few case studies of states that have tried, for the most part unsuccessfully, to adopt new constitutions.

THE ROOTS OF STATE CONSTITUTIONS

The first state constitutions were outgrowths of colonial charters. Massachusetts and New Hampshire can boast of charters still in effect that are older than the federal document. Virginia added a bill of rights to its constitution in 1776—13 years before the national one was proposed by Congress. In 1787 the framers of the U.S. Constitution drew heavily on their experience with these state charters. "What is the Constitution of the United States but that of Massachusetts, New York, and Maryland!" remarked John Adams. "There is not a feature in it," he said, "which cannot be found in one or the other."[6]

Subject only to the broad limitations of the U.S. Constitution, the people of each state are free to create whatever kind of republican government they wish. All state constitutions are similar in general outline (see Figure 23–1). A state constitution typically consists of a preamble, a bill of rights, articles providing for separation of powers, a two-house legislature (although the Supreme Court of Rhode Island recently ruled that there is no separation of powers in that state, leading for calls by the governor and the *Providence Journal* for a constitutional convention to overrule the decision[7]), an executive department (usually consisting of a governor, a lieutenant governor, and a half dozen or more statewide elected officials), an independent judiciary with the power of judicial review, a description of the form and powers of local units of government, an article on how to amend the constitution, and miscellaneous provisions dealing with election procedures, corporations, railroads, finances, education, and other specific topics.

The bills of rights in state constitutions are, in general, similar to the federal Bill of Rights, although they sometimes use different language and cover different rights. For example, "Twenty-seven states have speech and press guarantees quite different from the First Amendment's, thirty-eight have equality guarantees dissimilar to the equal protection clause, and thirty-nine have guarantees of a separation of church and state that differ from the federal establishment clause." Fourteen states adopted the Equal Rights Amendment even though it was never ratified to become part of the U.S. Constitution.[8]

Constitutional Rigidity and Evasion

State constitutions contain more details than does the U.S. Constitution. They are longer and less flexible, and they require more frequent amendment (see Figure 23–2).[9] States frequently adopt entirely new constitutions, although a careful

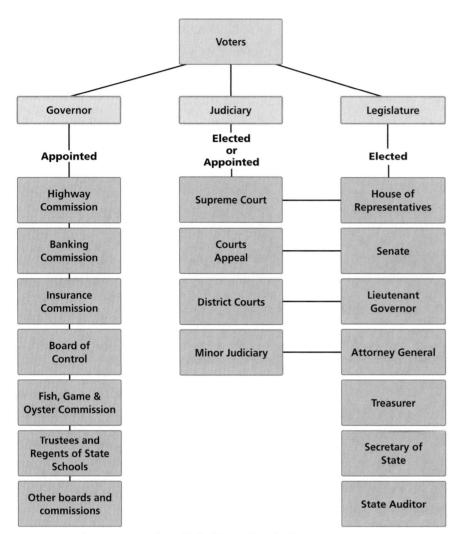

FIGURE 23–1 Government under a Typical State Constitution

empirical study shows that short constitutions that avoid detail do not last longer than those that are lengthy and more statutory in content. In fact, "longer and more detailed design of state constitutions actually enhances rather than reduces their longevity."[10] Louisiana has had 11 constitutions; Georgia has had 10; South Carolina, 7; and Alabama, Florida, and Virginia, 6.[11] State constitutions vary in length—from the 8,295 words of Vermont's (the only state constitution shorter than the Constitution of the United States as amended), to the 310,296 words of Alabama's. The U.S. Constitution has only 7,400 words; most state constitutions have around 26,000 words.[12]

Although most state constitutional provisions deal with matters of significance, some also some also deal with trivial subjects. California's much-amended constitution (500 amendments since it was adopted in 1879) goes into great detail about the taxation of fish and the internal organization of various departments. The Oklahoma Constitution proclaims, for example, "Until changed by the Legislature, the flash test for all kerosene oil for illuminating purposes shall be 115 degrees Fahrenheit; and the specific gravity test for all such oil shall be 40 degrees."[13] The South Dakota Constitution declares that providing hail insurance is a public purpose and authorizes the legislature to levy a tax to provide for it.[14] The Alabama Constitution authorizes the legislature to indemnify peanut farmers for losses incurred as a result of Aspergillus flavus (a fungus) and freeze damage in peanuts.[15]

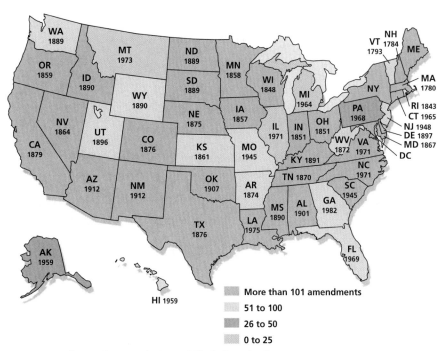

FIGURE 23–2 **States Frequently Amend Their Constitutions**

SOURCE: *The Book of the States, 2000–2001* (Council of State Governments, 2000).

Constitutions as Roadblocks

The earliest state constitutions granted authority to the legislatures without much restriction on how their powers should be exercised. But after many legislatures gave special privileges to railroads, canal builders, and other interests, constitutional amendments were adopted to prevent such abuses. Distrusting the legislatures, reform groups began to insist that certain controls be incorporated into state constitutions. In time, state constitutions became encrusted in layer after layer of procedural detail.

What does this mean for democratic government? Most simply, it means that state constitutions—intended as charters of self-government—are often like strait-jackets imposed on the present by the past. Some outdated provisions do no harm, but more often they are roadblocks to effective government. For example, fixed salaries do not reflect changing economic conditions, and a rigidly organized administrative structure is incapable of adjusting to new needs. When a constitution allocates revenues, elected officials are deprived of discretion to deal with current budget difficulties. Under such conditions the legislature cannot act, and voters then turn to constitutional amendments.

Getting Around the Constitution

Can state constitutions forever prevent the wishes of the people from being carried out? Not necessarily. The constitutional system of the states, like that of the national government, includes more than the formal written document. Unwritten rules, practices, political parties, and interest groups also shape events. When people see a need for change, they usually find ways to overcome formal barriers.

One device for constitutional change is **judicial interpretation**, whereby judges modify a constitutional provision by their interpretation of its meaning. The more complex and detailed the constitution, the easier it is for judges to redefine its meaning. Actually, one reason for the growing length of some constitutions is that amendments are often required to reverse judicial interpretations. In addition, some sections of state constitutions have been invalidated by federal action, especially in the area of civil rights and suffrage.

judicial interpretation
A method whereby judges can modify a constitutional provision's force by interpretation of its meaning.

The New Judicial Federalism

In what is called **new judicial federalism**, state constitutions have taken on greater importance. For decades state judges tended to look only to the U.S. Constitution and how it had been interpreted by the U.S. Supreme Court. But since the 1970s, as the U.S. Supreme Court has become more conservative, some states have begun applying their own state constitutions and state bill of rights to review the actions of state and local officials.

This trend takes its inspiration from the U.S. Supreme Court, which sent clear messages to state supreme court judges that they are free to interpret their own state constitution to impose greater restraints than does the U.S. Constitution. The U.S. Supreme Court and the U.S. Constitution set the floor, not the ceiling, for the protection of rights.[16] As a result, some state judges are now using their constitution to require their legislature to provide better schools for children living in poor neighborhoods, build low-income housing, provide public financing of abortions for poor women, and regulate business enterprises to protect the environment.[17]

When state judges rely on their own state constitution to protect rights beyond those required by the U.S. Constitution, they do so at some political peril, since most judges are dependent upon voter approval to keep their office. This risk has increased now that the Supreme Court requires state judges who wish to escape a review of their decisions by the Supreme Court to make it clear they have decided a case on adequate and independent state constitutional grounds.[18]

The Center for State Constitutional Studies of Rutgers University website (**www-camlaw.rutgers.edu/statecon/overview**) provides links that review a conference on "The State of State Constitutions" held in Philadelphia on May 4–6, 2000. This conference brought together experts to discuss "the strengths and weakness of contemporary state constitutions and directions for state constitutional reform." The website provides the keynote address by G. Alan Tarr, director of the center, and summarizes the workshops on all aspects of state constitutions.

AMENDING STATE CONSTITUTIONS

A mendments may be proposed by: (1) the state legislature, (2) citizen-initiated ballot petitions, or (3) constitutional conventions. After an amendment has been proposed, it must be ratified. In all states except Delaware, where the legislature can ratify as well as propose amendments, ratification is by the voters. In most states, an amendment becomes part of the constitution when approved by a majority of those voting on the amendment. In some states—for example, Minnesota—approval by a majority of all those voting in the election is required. This provision makes ratification difficult, because some people who vote for candidates do not vote on amendments. Slightly more than three-quarters of all constitutional amendments proposed by legislatures have been adopted in recent years.[19]

Legislative Proposals

All states permit their legislature to propose amendments; in fact, this is the most commonly used method. Although provisions vary, the general practice is to require the approval by two-thirds of each chamber of the legislature. Some

---

The California Revision Commission

In 1992, after the California Senate rejected a proposal asking voters if they wanted a constitutional convention (the first such convention in 113 years) to change the way the state does business, California turned to a revision commission to overcome its budgetary gridlock. Over the last several decades the people of California had amended their state consitution so frequently that amendments and federal mandates allocated 85 percent of the state's annual revenues before the governor and state legislature even started to work on the budget! For example, Proposition 13 set limits on property taxes, and Proposition 98 allocated 40 percent of the state budget to the public schools. Eventually *all* state revenues could be allocated constitutionally if the trend continued, and there would be no state funds available for programs such as higher education and health care.

A 23-member revision commission—consisting of members appointed by the governor, the Speaker, the Senate Rules Committee, and some *ex officio* officers like the chief justice—was created in 1993 to examine the budget process and the configuration of state and local government duties. Two years later, in its report to the legislature, the commission recommended:

- Reduce the number of statewide elective offices by making the state treasurer, the superintendent of public instruction, and the insurance commissioner appointive rather than elected.
- Change the initiative process to allow the legislature to amend statutory initiatives after six years.
- Require two-year state budgets.
- Allow the legislature to approve budgets by a simple majority instead of the current two-thirds.
- Allow school districts to raise additional revenue.
- Require the governor to submit to the legislature a state/local reassignment plan.
- Strengthen the home-rule powers of local governments.

The California legislature failed to act on any of the commission's recommendations, perhaps in part because they were proposed in an election year. Also, because the state Senate was Democratic and the state Assembly Republican, it was hard to work out any compromises.

---

new judicial federalism
The practice whereby state courts use the bill of rights in their state constitution to provide more protection for some rights than is provided by the Supreme Court's interpretation of the Bill of Rights in the U.S. Constitution.

DECISIONS! DECISIONS! DECISIONS!

California voters are regularly given ballots that, in addition to a long list of candidates for national, state, and local offices, contain constitutional amendments proposed by the legislature, a dozen or so highly technical amendments submitted by citizens by the initiative process, as well as numerous bond issues. In the larger California cities voters are routinely asked in general elections to decide 40–50 separate state, local, and special district ballot questions. Shown here are some of the decisions faced by California voters in the November 2000 election.

MEASURES SUBMITTED TO THE VOTERS

STATE

32 VETERANS' BOND ACT OF 2000. This act provides for a bond issue of five hundred million dollars ($500,000,000) to provide farm and home aid for California veterans. Fiscal Impact: Costs of about $858 million over 25 years (average cost of about $34 million per year); costs paid by participating veterans.

Yes	+
No	+

33 LEGISLATURE. PARTICIPATION IN PUBLIC EMPLOYEES' RETIREMENT SYSTEM. LEGISLATIVE CONSTITUTIONAL AMENDMENT. Allows Legislative members to participate in the Public Employees' Retirement System plans in which a majority of state employees may participate. Fiscal Impact: Annual state costs under $1 million to provide retirement benefits to legislators, with these costs replacing other spending from the fixed annual amount provided in support of the Legislature.

Yes	+
No	+

34 CAMPAIGN CONTRIBUTIONS AND SPENDING. LIMITS. DISCLOSURE. LEGISLATIVE INITIATIVE AMENDMENT. Limits campaign contributions and loans to state candidates and political parties. Provides voluntary spending limits; expands public disclosure requirements and increases penalties. Fiscal Impact: Additional net costs to the state, potentially up to several million dollars annually, and unknown but probably not significant costs to local government.

Yes	+
No	+

35 PUBLIC WORKS PROJECTS. USE OF PRIVATE CONTRACTORS FOR ENGINEERING AND ARCHITECTURAL SERVICES. INITIATIVE CONSTITUTIONAL AMENDMENT AND STATUTE. Amends constitution eliminating existing restrictions on state, local contracting with private entities for engineering, architectural services; contracts awarded by competitive selection; bidding permitted, not required. Fiscal Impact: Unknown impact on state spending for architectural and engineering services and construction project delivery. Actual impact will depend on how the state uses the contracting flexibility under the proposition.

Yes	+
No	+

37 FEES. VOTE REQUIREMENTS. TAXES. INITIATIVE CONSTITUTIONAL AMENDMENT. Requires two-thirds vote of State Legislature, majority or two-thirds of local electorate to impose future state, local fees on activity to study or mitigate its environmental, societal or economic effects. Defines such fees as taxes except property, development, certain other fees. Fiscal Impact: Unknown, potentially significant, reduction in future state and local government revenues from making it more difficult to approve certain regulatory charges.

Yes	+
No	+

38 SCHOOL VOUCHERS. STATE-FUNDED PRIVATE AND RELIGIOUS EDUCATION. PUBLIC SCHOOL FUNDING. INITIATIVE CONSTITUTIONAL AMENDMENT. Authorizes annual state payments of at least $4000 per pupil for private/religious schools. Permits replacement of current constitutional public school funding formula. Fiscal Impact: Near-term state costs from zero to $1.1 billion annually. Long-term state impact from $2 billion in annual costs to $3 billion in annual savings, depending on how many public school students shift to private schools.

Yes	+
No	+

39 SCHOOL FACILITIES. 55% LOCAL VOTE. BONDS, TAXES. ACCOUNTABILITY REQUIREMENTS. INITIATIVE CONSTITUTIONAL AMENDMENT AND STATUTE. Authorizes bonds for repair, construction or replacement of school facilities, classrooms, if approved by 55% local vote. Fiscal Impact: Increased bond debt for many school districts. Long-term costs statewide could total in the hundreds of millions of dollars annually. Potential longer-term state savings to the extent school districts assume greater responsibility for funding school facilities.

Yes	+
No	+

COUNTY OF ORANGE

G Should 60% of the revenues received from the tobacco litigation Master Settlement Agreement be used to fund health care services, tobacco use prevention, and public safety programs and services, with the other 40% used to reduce the County's bankruptcy-related debt?

Yes	+
No	+

H Should all revenues received from the tobacco litigation Master Settlement Agreement be used to fund health care services, tobacco use prevention, and public safety programs and services?

Yes	+
No	+

---

revision commission

A state commission that recommends changes in the state constitution for action by the legislature and vote by the voters.

states, however, permit proposal of an amendment by a simple majority in two successive legislatures.

A legislature may appoint a **revision commission** to make recommendations for constitutional change that, except in Florida, have no force until acted upon by the legislature and approved by the voters. The legislature creates a commission of a relatively small number of people—some selected by the governor and some by the legislature—and charges it with presenting proposals for constitutional revision. A commission is less expensive than a full-blown constitutional convention, does not require initial voter approval, and gives the legislature final control of what is presented to the electorate.

Constitutional commissions have been used frequently. Florida, Virginia, and Louisiana have used the commission procedure to bring about significant constitutional change. Mississippi has tried, so far unsuccessfully, to use it for changing its 1890 constitution—a constitution that had been designed to keep African Americans out of the political process.[20] The Utah Constitutional Revision Commission is a permanent body, required by law to submit recommendations for constitutional revision to the legislature 60 days before each regular session.[21] It has initiated revisions relating to rights of crime victims as well as to changes in revenue and taxation.[22] Florida has a Taxation and Budget Reform Commission that is called into session every ten years. Unlike other such commissions, in addition to making recommendations to the legislature, it may propose constitutional amendments directly to the voters.[23] In 1998 the Commission recommended nine amendments; Florida voters approved eight.

The recommendations of revision commissions are seldom implemented quickly, perhaps because the commissioners have not been responsive to political currents or are not representative of broad enough interests. Still, a commission may provide less partisan consideration of amendments and be more resistant to single-interest groups than either the legislature or a convention.

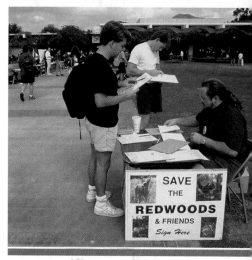

Initiative petitions deal with a great variety of reforms.

Initiative Petitions

At the end of the nineteenth century, revelations of corruption pushed the prestige of state governments, especially state legislatures, to a new low. Out of this disillusionment came a variety of reforms as part of the Progressive movement. Among them was the **constitutional initiative petition**, a device that permits voters to place specific constitutional amendments on the ballot by petition. Eighteen states allow amendments to their constitutions to be proposed by initiative petitions.

The number of signatures required on petitions varies from 4 to 15 percent of either the total electorate or the number of voters who voted in the last election.[24] Although it takes more signatures to propose a constitutional amendment than to place other kinds of initiatives on the ballot, "the higher threshold is no longer a significant impediment to well-financed special interest groups."[25]

Once the appropriate state official (attorney general or secretary of state) approves the precise wording of a petition, the amendment is placed on the ballot at the next general election. (California allows initiatives to appear on primary election ballots.) The number of votes required to approve a constitutional amendment is typically a majority vote, although a few states have a more demanding requirement. Illinois requires a majority of those voting in the election or three-fifths of those voting on the amendment, and Nevada requires a majority vote on the same measure in two successive elections.

In some states initiative proposals are limited to *amending* the state constitution, not to *revising* it. The distinction between a revision and amendment is that revision refers to a comprehensive change to the basic governmental plan, or a substantial alteration in the basic governmental framework,[26] or a substantial alteration of the entire constitution, rather than to a less extensive change in one or more of its provisions.[27] Some states exclude certain subjects from amendment by initiative. Massachusetts, for example, does not allow amendments by popular initiative that concern religion, the judiciary or judicial decisions, that are restricted to a particular town, city, or political division, that appropriate money from the state treasury, or that restrict rights such as freedom of speech.[28]

In recent years, voters have approved about 50 percent of amendments proposed by initiative petitions. This figure compares with a slightly more than 75 percent approval rate for amendments proposed by state legislatures.[29] A variety of factors may account for the lower adoption rate of initiative measures. Initiatives tend to be used for controversial issues that have already been rejected by the legislature. Initiatives are also often proposed by narrow-based groups or by reform-minded

constitutional initiative petition
A device that permits voters to place specific amendments to a state constitution on the ballot by petition.

You Decide...

Who should propose constitutional amendments?

Of the 24 states that have the popular initiative, only 18 permit constitutional amendments by initiative. Are states well served by having citizens propose amendments, or is it a bad idea? Should all states be required to permit constitutional alteration by the initiative process? What do you think?

*[handwritten notes in margin: 233 CC's 144 in 19th / 63 in 20th. / *American idea / Bring it Back to People]*

elites who lack broad support for their views. Sometimes initiatives are proposed to launch educational campaigns rather than to win adoption.

People anxious to limit the power of state and local governments are using the initiative process in more states. Since California adopted Proposition 13 in 1978, which limited the state government's right to raise property taxes, other states have followed suit. In addition, these "new reformers" have produced "a series of state constitutional amendments that, taken together, fundamentally altered the character and powers of state governments by limiting the tenure of governmental officials, reducing their powers, and transferring policy making responsibilities to the people."[30] In addition, to "the focus of constitutional initiatives . . . has shifted from questions of governmental structure . . . to questions of substantive policy," such as initiatives on tort liability, rights of gays, affirmative action, the rights of immigrants.[31]

Constitutional Conventions

Americans love constitutional conventions (or at least we used to); we have had 233 of them—144 in the nineteenth century but only 63 in the twentieth century.[32] One scholar noted that calling conventions of the people is a uniquely American idea, emphasizing that legislators cannot be trusted and that the supreme power belongs to the people.[33]

Forty-one state constitutions authorize their legislature to submit the calling of a convention to the voters; the other states assume the legislature has the power to do so. Fourteen state constitutions require the legislature to question voters about a convention at fixed intervals, varying from every 9 to every 20 years. For example, Missouri is required to submit the question to the voters every 20 years; Hawaii raises the issue every 9 years; Michigan, every 16 years.

If the voters approve, the next step is to elect delegates to a convention. Some state constitutions contain elaborate procedures governing the number of delegates, the method of election, and the time and place of the convention. Others leave the details to the legislature. The way convention delegates are selected seems to affect the kind of document the convention proposes. Selection by nonpartisan, multimember districts is more likely to result in a reform convention that makes major changes than one in which political parties play a major role.[34]

After delegates have been chosen, they usually assemble at the state capital. When the convention has prepared a draft of the new constitution, the document is submitted to the voters. But first the convention delegates have to make a difficult choice: Should the voters be asked to accept or reject the new constitution as a whole? Or should they vote on each section separately?

The advantage of the first method is that each provision of a constitution ties in with another, and to secure all the advantages of revision, the entire constitution should be adopted. The disadvantage is that those who oppose a particular provision may vote against the entire constitution. When convention delegates know that a particular provision is controversial, they may decide to submit that provision separately. Whichever method they choose, the supporters of change must rally their forces to gain voter approval of their work.

THE POLITICS OF CONSTITUTIONAL REVISION

[handwritten note in margin: Constitutions determine who gets what?]

Constitutions are not a neutral set of rules perched above the world of everyday politics. Rather, they significantly affect who gets what from government. Therefore, how a constitution is changed can help or hinder various groups.

Although there are campaigns for constitutional reform under way in Alabama, Oklahoma, and Texas, most people simply do not care.[35] It is difficult to work up enthusiasm for revising a state constitution except among those with special interests, and they are more likely to oppose than to favor adoption. Supporters of the status quo thus have a built-in advantage, which, combined with obstacles to the

amending process in the constitution, helps explain the lack of action. "Revision is time consuming, requiring sophisticated legal and drafting skills of the highest order, and involves negotiation and compromise. To be successful, revision requires gubernatorial as well as legislative leadership. . . . An effective political campaign is essential. . . . Success at the polls is not assured. Constitutional revision can be a high-risk endeavor and will continue to be."[36] Following are some case studies that illustrate the risky nature of constitutional revision.

Rhode Island Amends Its Constitution

Rhode Island's constitutional convention produced 14 separate propositions for amending its 1843 constitution. On November 4, 1986, voters approved 8 of the 14 provisions, rejecting attempts to increase compensation of state legislators, to provide for merit selection of judges, and to create a "paramount right to life without regard to age, health, function, or condition of dependency," which would have banned abortions or public funding of them. The voters approved provisions strengthening free speech, due process, and equal protection rights, and expanding fishing rights and access to the shore, as well as a statement that the rights protected by the Rhode Island Constitution "stand independent of the U.S. Constitution."

The Rhode Island Constitution calls for voters to be asked every ten years if they want to convention a constitutional convene. In November 1994 the voters rejected a convention by a vote of 173,693 to 118,545.[37]

Louisiana Revises Its Constitution

The Louisiana Constitutional Revision Commission set out during 1973 and 1974 to write a streamlined "people's constitution"—one the average person could understand.[38] The AFL-CIO, National Association for the Advancement of Colored People, League of Women Voters, Committee for a Better Louisiana, National Municipal League, and many other lobbying groups became involved in shaping the new constitution. It took well over a year to write, and it cost approximately $4 million. In the end, a readable 26,000-word document replaced the existing 265,000-word document that contained some 536 amendments. In April 1974, Louisiana voters approved the new charter by a large margin.

The Louisiana Constitution can no longer be cited as the prime example of an unworkable state constitution, although 107 amendments have been added since 1974, and the length has inched back up to 54,112 words. "Indeed," according to one commentator, constitutional amendment in Louisiana is "sufficiently continuous to justify including it with Mardi Gras, football, and corruption as one of the premier components of state culture."[39]

Changing the Hawaii Constitution

More than 800 proposals for constitutional changes were submitted to the Hawaii state constitutional convention of 1978. The League of Women Voters and other groups conducted extensive information and discussion meetings, and the convention held many public hearings on key issues. The 102 delegates to the convention met for nearly three months during the summer of 1978. After extensive debate, the convention narrowed the proposals to 34 questions to be placed on the fall ballot. Convention delegates rejected proposals for the initiative, referendum, and recall; for a unicameral legislature; and for an elected (instead of an appointed) attorney general.

The delegates were not opposed to all government reforms, however, for they endorsed a two-term limit for governor and lieutenant governor, moved to make Hawaii party primaries more open by allowing voters to cast ballots without declaring party preference, and authorized the state legislature to provide partial public funding for election campaigns and to establish spending limits. The convention reflected concern over government spending by setting tougher debt and spending

Thinking It Through . . .

Critics charge that when several complex initiatives are on the ballot, voters are asked to make decisions for which they are not well prepared. Others contend that the use of the initiative petition prevents elected representatives from exercising their proper authority. Still others hold that the initiative process encourages detailed and frequent amendment of a constitution, which should be a blueprint of enduring principles and not be too specific about how government operates on a day-to-day basis. Critics also charge that the initiative process has recently become the tool of well-organized, single-interest groups that present voters with simplistic choices of yes or no on complex matters.

Defenders of the constitutional initiative petition contend it is a valuable safety valve against an unresponsive legislature. When a legislature is tied so closely to special interests that it refuses even to acknowledge the real needs of a majority of citizens, the initiative process can be a corrective. Defenders also contend that voters are much smarter than critics say and that they have, in fact, acted rather prudently when asked to decide most constitutional questions.

limits for the state. It also strengthened environmental safeguards and gave further constitutional and financial protection to the special status of native Hawaiians.

On November 7, 1978, 74 percent of the voters went to the polls; all 34 amendments were adopted; 20 percent of the voters had accepted the amendments as a package.

In 1986 Hawaiians rejected the periodic question of whether to call a convention by a vote of 173,977 to 139,236. Again in 1996 the question of calling a convention was put to the voters, and the vote was 163,869 in favor and 160,153 against, but 45,245 people left the question unanswered. Blank ballots were tallied as a no, in response to a decision of the state supreme court that the Hawaii Constitution required approval by a majority of all ballots cast. The Ninth U.S. Circuit Court of Appeals, which refused to order a new election, sustained this decision.

Proposals for a convention had been backed by several interests, including those who wanted to overturn a decision of the Hawaii Supreme Court favoring the legalization of same-sex marriages, by those who wanted to impose term limits, and those who wanted to limit the power of state courts to restrict police searches.[40]

Hawaii's experiences with the revision process are reminders that constitution making is not just an exercise in abstract argument or logical reasoning but flows directly from a state's political life.

Texas Keeps Its Old Constitution

Texas has a lengthy constitution. Adopted in 1876, it has been amended more than 370 times. The most recent effort to thoroughly revise it was in 1972, after political scandals brought in a new governor, Dolph Briscoe, and a reform-oriented state legislature. After pushing through a variety of reforms dealing with the ethics of office-holders, campaign practices, and registration of lobbyists, the legislature did an unconventional thing by calling into being a constitutional convention consisting of members of the legislature rather than a specially elected body.

After working for 17 months, the legislator-delegates came up with a much-revised and shortened document intended to modernize many obsolete governmental practices. The convention deadlocked, however, over whether to give constitutional status to the state's right-to-work law, which prohibits labor contracts that require union membership as a condition of employment, so this issue was referred to the voters. In the end, neither the AFL-CIO nor Governor Briscoe supported all of the convention's recommendations. The governor was especially opposed to the proposal for annual legislative sessions, rather than every two years, which he argued

After three years of preparation and deliberation, the proposed Texas Constitution of 1974 failed by three votes in the final hectic session of the Constitutional Convention.

would cause higher taxes. Advocates of the revised constitution tried to salvage their work by offering substantial parts of the new charter to the voters as amendments to the existing constitution.

Conservatives praised the old constitution, claiming it had served Texas well for 100 years. Progressives complained that the old constitution was elitist, permitted only the narrowest governmental objectives, and made real change nearly impossible. In November 1975, amid charges and countercharges, Texas voters rejected the amendments by a 2 to 1 vote.[41] Since then, Texans have approved 143 amendments and rejected 33 but have not held another convention.

The Arkansas Constitution

Arkansas's eighth constitutional convention was a protracted affair. The 100 delegates who were elected in 1978 held their organizational session in the winter of that year but did not get down to work until the spring of 1979. Then, having reconvened in June 1980 to revise the final draft, they submitted the proposed constitution to the voters in November 1980.

Opposition developed to a provision in the new constitution allowing the legislature, by a two-thirds vote, to set interest rates rather than limit them, as in the current constitution. Others opposed a provision enlarging the taxing powers of local governments. Even though then Governor Bill Clinton, the Democratic party, and the Arkansas Education Association endorsed the new constitution, the voters rejected it by a 2 to 1 margin.

As we have noted, the question of a constitutional convention was again put to the voters of Arkansas in December 1995. Those planning the 1995 convention structured the convention call in such a way that the convention would avoid addressing "issues which were not critical to state government but which would inflame folks" and would concentrate on "issues of pure governance."[42] Nonetheless, the call for the convention was decisively rejected.

Statehood for the District of Columbia?

In the 1790s, when the U.S. capital was moved to a ten-mile-square enclave known as the District of Columbia, the framers of the Constitution gave control of its local government to the federal government and denied its residents the right to vote for members of Congress. They did so because crowds in Philadelphia had threatened the Congress of the young Republic. In 1971, however, D.C. residents won the right

"We must try to bring democracy to the rest of the world."

From *The Washington Post* April 9, 2000.

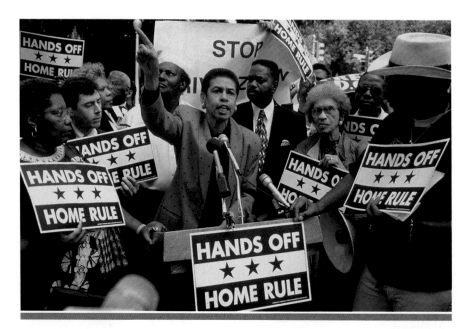

Eleanor Holmes Norton, the official representative of the District of Columbia in Congress, leads a demonstration against proposed restrictions on District self-government.

to elect a nonvoting delegate to Congress, and in 1974 the right to elect the mayor and city council. Ever since, activists have lobbied unsuccessfully for full representation in Congress. Claiming "no taxation without representation," advocates for statehood eventually filed lawsuits aimed at forcing Congress to give residents the right to vote for statehood, or to unite with another state, or to elect full senators and representatives. But in 2000 a federal appeals court dismissed the suits, holding that the matter was for Congress and the political process, not the judiciary, to decide.

POLITICS ONLINE

What's My State's Constitution?

You probably have a good knowledge of our U.S. Constitution but to many citizens, state constitutions are unknown and inaccessible. As we have demonstrated, state constitutions are different from the federal constitution because of their much greater specificity and length. Moreover, several states have abandoned their original constitutions and adopted new ones. To access your state constitution go to any state government home page through servers like Yahoo by "state constitutions" in the search feature.

An interesting way to learn about state constitutions is to compare provisions of your home state's constitution with those of three or four other states. Take provisions for state legislatures and compare your state to Nebraska, which has a unicameral legislature. For much of U.S. history the Bill of Rights in the U.S. Constitution was not applied to state governments. How then do state constitutions address freedom of religion, press, and speech? Also, what differences can you think of between the U.S. Bill of Rights and the various state bills of rights? To compare the U.S. Bill of Rights to that of any state, you can go to www.harbornet.com/rights/states.html. Be sure to note the details contained in the state bills of rights versus the U.S. Bill of Rights. A good example of the detail in state constitutions is that several states have articles guaranteeing specific rights to victims of crimes. Should the U.S. Bill of Rights include a similar provision? And in what ways are the states laboratories for the federal government? In your survey of state constitutions, be sure to select states that have different political cultures, such as Massachusetts and Louisiana.

SUMMARY

1. State constitutions attempt to spell out the fundamental laws of the states. Although they vary considerably in detail, each outlines the organizational framework of the state, vesting powers in the legislature and other departments. Each includes a bill of rights, sets procedures for holding elections, provides for local governments, and contains a variety of provisions dealing with finances, education, and other state issues.

2. Most state constitutions are cumbersome documents containing more detail than the U.S. Constitution. Although reformers may have introduced such detail to prevent abuse, most constitutional scholars believe such matters are better left to statutory law.

3. In the past 20 years there has been a flurry of renewed interest in state constitutions as they have been discovered to be additional instruments for protecting and expanding rights in what is known as the new judicial federalism.

4. State constitutions can be amended by ratification by the voters of proposals submitted by the legislature, by popular initiative petitions, or by constitutional conventions. Conventions tend to revise the entire constitution rather than just amend portions of it.

5. In recent decades there has been an expanded use of the initiative process to bring about narrowly targeted constitutional change.

6. Despite the considerable constitutional change brought about during the last half-century through amendments, voters have often been resistant to sweeping constitutional revision.

KEY TERMS

judicial interpretation 522   new judicial federalism 523   revision commission 524   constitutional initiative petition 525

FURTHER READING

The Greenwood Publishing Group has commissioned reference guides for the constitution of each state, written by an expert on the state. As of 2000, guides for Alaska, Indiana, Iowa, Kentucky, Michigan, Montana, Oklahoma, Texas Utah, Wisconsin, and West Virginia are available.

BURTON C. AGATA and ERIC LANE, eds., *State Constitutions: Competing Perspectives* (Hofstra Law and Policy Symposium, 1996), vol. 1.

BRUCE E. CAIN and ROGER G. NOLL, eds., *Constitutional Reform in California* (Institute of Governmental Studies Press, University of California, Berkeley, 1995).

CONGRESSIONAL INFORMATION SERVICE, *State Constitutional Conventions, Commissions and Amendments, 1979–1988: An Anno-*

tated Bibliography (U.S. Congressional Information Service, 1989).

ELMER E. CORNWELL, JR., JAY S. GOODMAN, and WAYNE R. SWANSON, *State Constitutional Conventions: The Politics of the Revision Process in Seven States* (Praeger, 1975).

PAUL FINKELMAN and STEPHEN E. GOTTLIEB eds., *Toward a Usable Past: Liberty Under State Constitutions* (University of Georgia Press, 1991).

JOHN KINCAID, ed., "State Constitutions in the Federal System," *Annals of the American Academy of Political and Social Science* 496 (March 1988).

SANFORD LEVINSON, ed., *Responding to Imperfection: The Theory and Practice of Constitutional Amendment* (Princeton University Press, 1995).

BERNARD D. REAMS, JR., and STUART D. YOAK, *The Constitutions of the States: A State by State Guide and Bibliography to Current Scholarly Research* (Oceana Publications, 1988).

ALAN G. TARR, *Constitutional Politics in the States: Contemporary Controversies and Historical Patterns* (Greenwood Press, 1996).

ALAN G. TARR, *Understanding State Constitutions* (Princeton University Press, 1998).

ROBERT F. WILLIAMS, *State Constitutional Law: Cases and Materials*, Teachers Edition (Michie, 1993).

See also the quarterly review, *State Constitutional Commentaries and Notes*, published by the Edward McNail Burns Center for State Constitutional Studies at Rutgers University.

24

PARTIES AND ELECTIONS IN THE STATES

DESPITE THE CHAOTIC AND DISPUTED OUTCOME OF THE PRESIDENTIAL ELECTION OF 2000, MOST CITIZENS OF THE UNITED STATES TAKE FOR GRANTED THAT ELECTIONS will be fairly administered and that power will be peacefully transferred to the winner of the election. In stark contrast to these fundamentals of our electoral democracy is what happened in the 2000 presidential election in Yugoslavia. Incumbent President Slobodan Milosevic, indicted for war crimes for his actions in Bosnia, was defeated by challenger Vojislav Kostunica by at least 10 percentage points. Neutral observers estimated that Kostunica had received 51 percent of the vote.[1] Milosevic, in a desperate move to retain power, claimed that Kostunica fell short of the 50 percent needed to win the election and called for a runoff election. Kostunica refused to participate in the runoff, claiming he had won a majority in the first election. He cited instances of election fraud, including 350 "phantom" polling stations and an extra 150,000 votes for Milosevic in Kosovo.[2]

The citizens of Yugoslavia took matters into their own hands through protest demonstrations, civil disobedience, and widespread strikes. Schools and businesses closed, and some shopkeepers hung signs in their windows that read "Closed Because of Robbery"—a reference to Milosevic's election theft. Blackouts started throughout the country when an estimated ten thousand coal miners went on strike.

Hundreds of thousands of protesters took to the streets of Belgrade and stormed the parliament building, setting parts of it on fire. They also took control of the state-owned television stations. The coal miners, protesters, and opposition party leaders risked their lives by standing up to the government. There was no guarantee that their efforts would be successful. The military and police did not take any serious action against the protesters, and some even joined in the throng. Milosevic fled the capital to the countryside, and Kostunica claimed leadership. Within days he was recognized as the legitimate president by the international community, including Russia.[3] Clearly, it was not the election of Kostunica alone that produced these dramatic events; the opportunity to express popular discontent against a despot and an illegitimate government contributed as well.

The Yugoslav election demonstrates that honest election procedures and accurate vote counting are not universal. Nor is it always the case that the winner of an election will take office. Election fraud in other countries helps us appreciate our own democracy. We find it unthinkable that an American mayor, governor, or president

CHAPTER MEDIA

 POLITICS ONLINE
Why Not Vote on the Internet?
www.prenhall.com/burns

When presidential candidate Slobodan Milosovic refused to accept defeat in the election in Yugoslavia, the citizens of Belgrade took to the streets night after night, and some set fire to the Parliament building. Finally, Milosovic capitulated, and Vojislav Kostunica took over as president.

would annul an election when his party did not win. But if election violations do occur, people in the United States have recourse to the courts and even to the police to redress them. We expect the losing candidate to exit the office peacefully so that the winning candidate can assume power. Yet, as we Americans learned in the aftermath of the 2000 presidential election, our own ballots and election procedures are flawed, and not only in Florida. Modernizing how we vote may involve complex legislation and even constitutional amendments since U.S. elections are largely governed by state law and administered at the county level.

ELECTORAL POLITICS IN THE STATES AND LOCALITIES

The U.S. Constitution provides only the most general guidelines to the states in the regulation of elections for members of the U.S. Congress. Article I, Section 4, says, "The Times, Places and Manner of holding Elections for Senators and Representatives shall be prescribed in each State by the Legislature thereof; but the Congress may at any time by Law make or alter such Regulations, except as to the Places of choosing Senators." The constitutional language regarding presidential elections also defers to state law: "Each State shall appoint, in such Manner as the Legislature thereof may direct, a Number of Electors." The role of the state legislature in naming electors became part of the drama of the 2000 presidential election as the Florida legislature went into special session to name an alternate state of electors, in part because of uncertainty surrounding the various state and federal court rulings regarding the counting and recounting of ballots.

Amendments to the U.S. Constitution do not alter the central role of state constitutions and state law regarding voting rights. Rather, the amendments expressly forbid the states to restrict the right to vote in any election, for state and local as well as for national offices, to certain kinds of people. States cannot deny the franchise on the basis of "race, color, or previous condition of servitude" (Fifteenth Amendment), gender (Nineteenth Amendment), failure to pay a poll tax (Twenty-fourth Amendment), or age for persons over age 18 (Twenty-sixth Amendment).

Federalism and Elections

Political federalism in this country is noteworthy. State identities are important to both politicians and voters. We tend to think of ourselves not only as citizens of the United States but also as citizens of a particular state. Each state has a distinctive polit-

ical tradition and political culture. It should not be surprising, then, that state parties are in many ways more important than national parties. Indeed, national parties, aside from their congressional campaign committees, are largely federations of state parties. And since our national parties as electoral organizations have never been strong, the activities they undertake usually end up being carried out by the state parties. The independence of state parties also helps explain why, for instance, Democratic voters in one state can be so different from those in another, and why Republicans from different states can come down on opposite sides of some major issues.

The electoral process in the United States is *decentralized* in its rules and administration. All elections in the United States are administered by state and local governments, not by the national government. The president is chosen in state elections conducted according to state rules. Because of the Electoral College and the winner-takes-all rule, presidential politics focuses on winning states more than on winning individual votes. State elections also determine who will serve as members of Congress, governor, other statewide officials like attorney general, as well as the outcome of many ballot questions.

Most states prescribe the organization of the state parties, the means by which their officers are elected, and the nomination process for president and other offices.[4] In states that have some form of public financing of elections or parties, the state also regulates the distribution of public funds to the parties and the reporting of how those funds were spent.

States differ in the hours the polls are open, how close to the voting place campaigning may be conducted, and whether they require voter registration. Differences between the states in how long you need to have lived in the state before voting, and how you may register to vote, have diminished in recent years.

And as we learned in the 2000 presidential election in Florida, there is great variation in how people vote, even from county to county. Some Florida counties use ballots read by optical scanners and others use punch-card ballots. Other states use these same types of ballots as well as paper ballots, voting machines, and in the 2000 primaries, some states experimented with voting via the Internet.

We have many types of elections, including *general elections* to determine who holds office and *primary elections* to determine who will run in the general election. Most statewide elections are partisan, whereas most local elections for school boards, water districts, and city governments are nonpartisan. State legislative elections are partisan except in Nebraska, where the legislature is nonpartisan. Many local elections are nonpartisan. Voters in all states but Delaware must approve changes to the state constitution in a referendum. Roughly half of the states allow votes on initiatives to be put on the ballot by petition. The initiative and referendum also are found in many local governments.

THE ROLE OF POLITICAL PARTIES

Although political parties are not mentioned in the U.S. Constitution, they are vital not only to our national government but also to the functioning of the electoral system within the states. Parties organize the competition by recruiting and nominating candidates, function as the loyal opposition when out of power, unify and organize the electorate, and provide a link between the people and their government. The existence of political parties is acknowledged in many state constitutions.

Election rules favor the two major parties over minor parties. The Republican and Democratic parties have a "preferred position"—that is, their candidates will definitely be placed on the ballot. But ballot access for minor party and independent candidates is less certain. State law typically requires that to be on the ballot, minor parties must have garnered a minimum number of votes in the previous election or must submit a prescribed number of signatures of registered voters. States vary in the difficulty of ballot access for minor parties depending on three factors: the

WE THE PEOPLE

A Demographic Profile of Local Government Officials, January 1992

Number of local elected officials	494,093
Gender	
Male	76.3%
Female	23.7
Race	
White	96.7
Black	2.8
American Indian and Alaskan Native	0.4
Asian and Pacific Islanders	0.1
Hispanic	1.4

SOURCE: U.S. Bureau of the Census, "Popularly Elected Officials in 1992," *1992 Census of Governments* (Government Printing Office, 1992).

---

number of signatures required, the time allowed to collect them, and whether signatures must be distributed across several counties.

States election ballots are of two kinds. The **party column** or **Indiana ballot**, which encourages party-line voting, is organized by parties, with the party name and symbol at the top of a column that lists all the party's candidates running for offices in that election (see Figure 24–1). Typically, there is a spot at the top of the column to make a single mark or pull a single lever on the voting machine to cast votes for all candidates of that party. When voters make such a mark or pull the party lever, they cast a **straight ticket**. Voters may also have to work their way through state constitutional amendments, referendums, and initiatives on the ballot, one by one.

Partly to discourage straight-ticket voting, some states use the **office block** or **Massachusetts ballot**, which lists all the candidates running for an office together in one block, all those running for another office in another block, and so on (see Figure 24–2). If voters want to cast a straight-party ticket, they have to hunt through each column for their preferred party candidate. Office block ballots encourage **split-ticket** voting, or voting for candidates from more than one party.

Party Organization and Officers

Although state party organizations are not all alike, in all states there is a *party chair* who is elected by the party's central committee or delegates to a party convention. Other statewide party officers include the *vice-chair*, who by state law or party bylaws generally must be of the opposite gender from the party chair, plus officers like treasurer and secretary. Party leaders generally answer to a *central committee*, which consists of 20 or more persons who are elected or otherwise chosen for specified terms.

The state party chair is the spokesperson for the party. He or she raises money for the party and its candidates. The state party chair works closely with the governor when that party controls the governorship; under these circumstances, the central committee defers to the governor in the selection of the chair. Because overt expressions of partisanship are thought to be unbecoming of a governor or a senator, it is often the party chair who defends the party and, when necessary, goes on the offensive against the opposition party.

The day-to-day operations of the party are usually carried out by the party's *executive director*, a full-time employee who oversees the staff, assists the chair, and coordinates the work of the central committee and other party officials. The executive director schedules functions and serves as a liaison with the national organizations.

At the local level, political parties generally have a structure patterned after the state party organization. In some counties party organizations are fully staffed and functioning, but in most counties they are run by volunteers and are inactive until just before an election. Local parties provide opportunities for ordinary citizens to become involved in politics, a first step that can eventually lead to running for office. Some states, like Minnesota, have congressional district parties as well.[5]

party column ballot
Method of voting in which all candidates are listed under their party designations, making it easy for voters to cast votes for all the candidates of one party. Also called the *Indiana ballot*.

straight ticket
Voting for all of one party's candidates.

office block ballot
Method of voting in which all candidates are listed under the office for which they are running. Also called the *Massachusetts ballot*.

split ticket
Voting for some of one party's candidates and some from another party.

Official Ballot for Piute County, Utah, November 7, 2000

REPUBLICAN	DEMOCRATIC	REFORM	INDEPENDENT AMERICAN	LIBERTARIAN	NATURAL LAW	GREEN / SOCIALIST WORKERS	(WRITE-IN VOTING COLUMN)
						All candidates not affiliated with a political party are listed below. They are to be considered with all offices and candidates listed to the left. Only ONE vote is allowed for each office.	*Valeen H. Brown* — County Clerk

For President of the United States
- GEORGE W. BUSH (Republican)
- AL GORE (Democratic)
- PAT BUCHANAN (Reform)
- HOWARD PHILLIPS (Independent American)
- HARRY BROWNE (Libertarian)
- JOHN HAGELIN (Natural Law)
- RALPH NADER (Green)
- JAMES HARRIS (Socialist Workers)

For Vice-President of the United States
- DICK CHENEY
- JOSEPH LIEBERMAN
- EZOLA FOSTER
- CURTIS FRAZIER
- ART OLIVIER
- NAT GOLDHABER
- WINONA LADUKE (Green)
- MARGARET TROWE (Socialist Workers)

For U.S. Senator
- ORRIN G. HATCH (Rep)
- SCOTT N. HOWELL (Dem)
- CARLTON EDWARD BOWEN (Ind Am)
- JIM DEXTER (Lib)
- LOUIE G. YOUNGKEIT (Socialist Workers)

For U.S. Representative, District #3
- CHRIS CANNON (Rep)
- DONALD DUNN (Dem)
- MICHAEL J. LEHMAN (Ind Am)
- KITTY K. BURTON (Lib)
- RANDALL TOLPINRUD (Natural Law)
- ROBERT LEO BECK (Socialist Workers)

For Governor
- MICHAEL O. LEAVITT (Rep)
- BILL ORTON (Dem)
- JEREMY FRIEDBAUM (Ind Am)
- DUB RICHARDS (Natural Law)

For Lieutenant Governor
- OLENE S. WALKER (Rep)
- KAREN HALE (Dem)
- LEE McKENZIE (Ind Am)

For Attorney General
- MARK L. SHURTLEFF (Rep)
- REED M. RICHARDS (Dem)
- W. ANDREW McCULLOUGH (Lib)

For State Auditor
- AUSTON G. JOHNSON III (Rep)
- JIM ELWELL (Lib)

For State Treasurer
- EDWARD T. ALTER (Rep)
- HUGH A. BUTLER (Lib)
- ELLIOT J. HULET (Natural Law)

For State Senator, District #28
- LEONARD M. BLACKHAM (Rep)
- DON P. FOUTZ, JR. (Dem)
- GARY R. VAN HORN (Ind Am)

For State Representative, District #70
- THOMAS HATCH (Rep)
- LOUISE EXCELL (Dem)

For County Commissioner
- W. KAY BLACKWELL (Rep)

FIGURE 24–1 A Sample Party Column Ballot

ELECTORS FOR PRESIDENT AND VICE PRESIDENT
(A VOTE FOR THE CANDIDATES WILL ACTUALLY BE A VOTE FOR THEIR ELECTORS)
(VOTE FOR GROUP)

Candidate	Party
GEORGE W. BUSH (FOR PRESIDENT) / DICK CHENEY (FOR VICE PRESIDENT)	REPUBLICAN
AL GORE (FOR PRESIDENT) / JOE LIEBERMAN (FOR VICE PRESIDENT)	DEMOCRATIC
HARRY BROWNE (FOR PRESIDENT) / ART OLIVIER (FOR VICE PRESIDENT)	LIBERTARIAN
RALPH NADER (FOR PRESIDENT) / WINONA LaDUKE (FOR VICE PRESIDENT)	GREEN
JAMES HARRIS (FOR PRESIDENT) / MARGARET TROWE (FOR VICE PRESIDENT)	SOCIALIST WORKERS
JOHN HAGELIN (FOR PRESIDENT) / NAT GOLDHABER (FOR VICE PRESIDENT)	NATURAL LAW
PAT BUCHANAN (FOR PRESIDENT) / EZOLA FOSTER (FOR VICE PRESIDENT)	REFORM
DAVID McREYNOLDS (FOR PRESIDENT) / MARY CAL HOLLIS (FOR VICE PRESIDENT)	SOCIALIST
HOWARD PHILLIPS (FOR PRESIDENT) / J. CURTIS FRAZIER (FOR VICE PRESIDENT)	CONSTITUTION

CONGRESSIONAL

UNITED STATES SENATOR (VOTE FOR ONE)
- BILL McCOLLUM (REP)
- BILL NELSON (DEM)
- JOE SIMONETTA (LAW)
- JOEL DECKARD (REF)
- WILLIE LOGAN (NPA)
- ANDY MARTIN (NPA)
- DARRELL L. McCORMICK (NPA)
- (WRITE-IN)

REPRESENTATIVE IN CONGRESS
23rd CONGRESSIONAL DISTRICT (VOTE FOR ONE)
- BILL LAMBERT (REP)
- ALCEE L. HASTINGS (DEM)
- (WRITE-IN)

STATE

TREASURER (VOTE FOR ONE)
- TOM GALLAGHER (REP)
- JOHN COSGROVE (DEM)

COMMISSIONER OF EDUCATION (VOTE FOR ONE)
- CHARLIE CRIST (REP)
- GEORGE H. SHELDON (DEM)
- VASSILIA GAZETAS (NPA)

LEGISLATIVE

STATE SENATOR DISTRICT 27 (VOTE FOR ONE)
- KEN PRUITT (REP)
- DESERE' CLABO (REF)
- (WRITE-IN)

NONPARTISAN JUDICIAL/SCHOOL BOARD

JUSTICE OF THE SUPREME COURT

Shall Justice R. FRED LEWIS of the Supreme Court be retained in office? YES / NO

Shall Justice BARBARA J. PARIENTE of the Supreme Court be retained in office? YES / NO

Shall Justice PEGGY A. QUINCE of the Supreme Court be retained in office? YES / NO

DISTRICT COURT OF APPEAL

Shall Judge JOHN W. DELL of the 4th District Court of Appeal be retained in office? YES / NO

Shall Judge BOBBY W. GUNTHER of the 4th District Court of Appeal be retained in office? YES / NO

Shall Judge FRED A. HAZOURI of the 4th District Court of Appeal be retained in office? YES / NO

Shall Judge LARRY A. KLEIN of the 4th District Court of Appeal be retained in office? YES / NO

Shall Judge BARRY J. STONE of the 4th District Court of Appeal be retained in office? YES / NO

Shall Judge CAROLE Y. TAYLOR of the 4th District Court of Appeal be retained in office? YES / NO

FIGURE 24–2 A Sample Office Block Ballot

Although party bosses and strong party machines are a thing of the past, local politics is still organized on a partisan basis in many of our largest cities. However, local politics is more often characterized by nonpartisanship. Two-thirds of cities with populations over 5,000 have nonpartisan elections.[6]

Party Activities in Elections

American politics is candidate centered. Candidates create their own campaign organizations. Yet parties serve important secondary roles in elections. They provide the structure for elections; in some places they recruit candidates, register voters, mobilize voters on election day, and supply resources and campaign help to their candidates.

STRUCTURE FOR ELECTIONS   Our election system would function in a dramatically different way if we had no political parties to organize the competition. Parties

narrow the field of candidates through a primary election or convention process, providing voters with relatively few choices in the general election. Candidates, to one degree or another, must secure the support of party members to win a place on the ballot as the party's nominees for the offices they are seeking.

CANDIDATE RECRUITMENT   Party officials traditionally recruited candidates to run for office, helped train them in how to run, and supported them financially. In many states this responsibility is now more fiction than fact.

Many offices go uncontested. The number of unopposed candidates increases as you go down the ballot. To be sure, some incumbents have done such a good job that to oppose them would be an exercise in futility. Yet lack of competition in elections violates American assumptions about democracy and is reminiscent of politics in the former communist states, where party officers ran unopposed. There would be far more unopposed candidates, especially at the local levels, were it not for the efforts of party leaders to recruit candidates.[7] One important characteristic of American parties at all levels is that they are extremely open to would-be candidates. Virtually anybody can run for any local office anywhere in the United States.

VOTER REGISTRATION   All states except North Dakota require citizens to register before permitting them to vote. In California you can register online, and some states, like Wisconsin, allow registration at the polls on election day. Voter registration became easier when Congress passed the National Voter Registration, or Motor-Voter Act, in 1993. People are now able to register to vote when they apply for or renew their driver's license or visit certain public agencies. A half-dozen states that permit election-day registration or do not require voter registration are exempt from the law. The idea behind Motor-Voter is to increase the number of registered voters and thereby increase the turnout.

What difference has Motor-Voter made? Since January 1995, when the act went into effect, almost 20 million people have been added to the voter registration rolls, reversing a decades-old trend of declining registration for Democrats and for Republicans outside the South.[8] More recently, many of the new Motor-Voter registrants are registering as Independents. In terms of party balance, Motor-Voter appears not to have made much difference.[9]

At the time of registration, 19 states ask voters to register with a political party; in 3 other states party registration is optional.[10] Voters, of course, have the option to decline to state their party at the time of registration, and a significant number of them do so. For example, in California in 2000, 7 percent of the registered voters declined to state their party preference.[11] An excellent data bank on voter registration and turnout is maintained by the National Conference of State Legislatures at **www.ncsl.org**.

Voter registration drives are sometimes run by groups independent of a party or candidate; more often, however, these drives are managed by Democrats and Republicans who target their efforts at citizens they anticipate will vote for their party's candidate. Voter registration drives targeted at African Americans and Hispanics have been especially important to the Democratic party.[12]

Political parties favor laws requiring voters to disclose their party preference at the time they register. First, this requirement permits parties to limit participation in their primaries to registered party members in states that have a closed primary system. Second, party registration creates voter registration lists, which parties find extremely useful for campaigning and fund raising. In addition, *list vending*— selling voter lists with addresses, phone numbers, and party preferences—is a multimillion-dollar industry. Third, voter registration helps the parties in the redistricting process because state legislators—using party registration, voting, and other data—can draw new legislative district boundaries in such a way as to advantage their party.

VOTER MOBILIZATION   Only about 70 percent of eligible voters are registered, and of that number only about 72 percent vote in presidential elections, meaning that *only half of the voting-age population bothers to vote in a presidential election*, and fewer still vote in a midterm election.[13] Get-out-the-vote drives are therefore a major activity of candidates and parties. Party workers, through telephone or door-to-door canvasses, identify registered voters who are likely to support their party and then contact those voters personally on election day, perhaps more than once, to encourage them to go to the polls. Where resources permit, the parties may even provide transportation to the polls or baby-sitting services.[14]

In states that permit registration by mail or by roving registrars, volunteers register voters at the same time they find voters who will support their party's candidates in the election. In states that permit absentee voting by mail, voter mobilization efforts help voters fill out the form requesting an absentee ballot and then mail the form for them. A few weeks later, a party volunteer checks to make sure a ballot has arrived and has been filled out and returned. Because most voters prefer one party over another, it makes sense for candidates from the same party to consolidate their efforts.

Party volunteers keep the phone lines humming as they urge potential voters to come out on election day and support their candidate.

CAMPAIGN RESOURCES   American political parties, with some notable exceptions, are organizationally weak. In better-organized states, parties often provide campaign funds and a significant amount of campaign help. They raise funds for their party organization and finance voter registration and mobilization efforts. A few parties raise enough money to help fund campaigns for candidates for governor or other state offices. As at the national level, control of the governorship helps in fund raising because interest groups are much more likely to contribute to the governor's party.

In states with well-organized parties, the parties train the candidates they have recruited. Wisconsin and New York have strong state legislative campaign committees that distribute resources to candidates, as the national party committee does to congressional candidates.[15] Sometimes the state parties provide polling data to state and local candidates, help establish campaign themes, or prepare generic advertising that can be used in several state legislative districts. Parties also channel money from the national congressional campaign committee to local congressional candidates.

State parties have been the beneficiaries of **soft money**, money given to them, often in large amounts, that does not have to be disclosed under federal law because it is not contributed to support the election or defeat of a *specific* candidate, but can be used for "party-building" purposes. Republican and Democratic national party committees are now raising and distributing large amounts of soft money. Because state parties largely spend the soft money for the national parties, this expenditure has not helped make state parties stronger. Controversy has surrounded the abuse of soft money in recent elections, but so far Congress has refused to close the soft money loophole, in large part because incumbents benefit from it.

Parties raise soft money, they claim, to respond to **issue advocacy**, in which an interest group attacks some political candidates and supports others but carefully avoids telling voters to vote for or against that individual. While much of the soft money and issue advocacy advertising focuses on presidential and congressional elections, both parties have also devoted these resources to gubernatorial and state legislative races, especially in anticipation of the redistricting in 2001 and 2002.

Voting Choices

Voters generally base their election decisions on three factors listed in order of importance: political party identification, candidate appeal, and issues. But in many local elections, since party labels are absent from the ballot, voters rely more on candidate appeal, issues, and factors like incumbency, media endorsements, and name recognition.

soft money
Money contributed to a state or local political party for party-building purposes that is unlimited. Once transferred to the state parties its expenditure is often undisclosed.

issue advocacy
Promoting a particular position on an issue, often funded by interest groups and designed to influence voters' choices on election day. It is unlimited and undisclosed.

PARTY IDENTIFICATION   Party identification is the most important predictor of the vote. Parties provide a party label that guides voters in making their decisions. Party labels are especially important in elections where voters have little information about candidates, like contests for attorney general, state senator, state representative, or county commissioner. The simplifying device of party labels helps voters sort through the many candidate choices they encounter on election day.

People who identify themselves as strong Democrats and strong Republicans are remarkably loyal to their party when voting for governor and other state and local offices. Independent-leaners have clear partisan preferences in the direction of one party or the other. Pure Independents have no party preference and are most inclined to vote for one party and then another with changing circumstances, but there are few pure Independents in the total electorate.[16]

CANDIDATE APPEAL   Although party identification is important, it is not decisive. Candidate appeal can be crucial. For example, in the 1998 Minnesota gubernatorial election, Reform party candidate Jesse Ventura was elected largely because his style and approach generated interest among voters, and a plurality preferred him over the established candidates in the major parties. Minnesota's system of public financing helped Ventura become visible, and he worked hard to become credible. In the end he won in a stunning upset.

In state and local elections, name identification and the advantages of incumbency are important. Incumbents generally have an advantage in candidate appeal because of greater name recognition and access to campaign resources. Candidates sometimes use creative means to generate positive name recognition. For example, when Bob Graham was governor of Florida, he often worked one day a week in different jobs around the state to demonstrate his desire to relate to his constituents.

ISSUE VOTING   Issues can be very important to the outcome of elections. Economic conditions are an important factor in state and local elections as they are in national ones. William Weld, a Republican, was able to win his first Massachusetts gubernatorial election, despite the fact that Massachusetts is a very strong Democratic state, because the economy was so bad. Former New Jersey Governor Christine Todd Whitman won election in part because her opponent had raised state taxes and she promised a 30 percent tax cut. While issues are important to state and local elections, it is fair to say that they are probably less important than at the national level.[17]

NONPARTISAN LOCAL ELECTIONS   Nonpartisan elections were intended to weaken political parties in local elections, and they have been successful. Arguing that political parties had little to contribute to administration of local government, reformers during the first half of the last century introduced nonpartisan elections. The two parties were, in effect, blocked from exerting open influence on local politics.

Some contend nonpartisan local elections make it more difficult for poor persons, minorities, and the less educated to participate effectively. For such people, the party label serves to identify politicians who share their values and perspectives on government. Better-educated and better-off voters know more about who is running and what they stand for, even without party labels. Nonpartisan elections sometimes help Republican candidates, especially in cities with populations of more than 50,000, because Republican voters tend to vote more in low turnout elections and are more likely to know which candidates are Republicans.[18]

Parties in State Government

PARTIES IN THE EXECUTIVE BRANCH   Just as winning the presidency is the big prize at the national level, so is winning the governorship at the state level. The party that controls the governorship can raise more money and build a stronger party than

the party that controls the legislature. Governors run as heads of their party and help define the party for their state. They customarily win office with the help of fellow partisans, and they know from the day they take office that the other party is planning ways to defeat them and their party in the next election.

Governors often assist in recruiting candidates for the state legislature; they sometimes campaign on behalf of their party, even when they are not on the ballot for reelection. Presidential candidates court governors. Governors raise money for campaigns as well as for the state party. They have wide latitude in appointing boards, commissions, judges, and state administrators, and they almost always take party affiliation and activity into account when making appointments.

PARTIES IN THE LEGISLATURE   Like Congress, state legislatures (excluding Nebraska, which is nonpartisan) are organized largely along party lines. The *Speaker of the house* and the *president of the senate* are elected by the majority party in most states. They preside over floor proceedings and make key assignments to standing committees and study committees. Most state legislatures have floor leaders, called *majority leaders* and *minority leaders* and majority and minority *whips*.

In most states, parties sit on different sides of the aisle in the chamber and are separated in committee meetings as well. Committee chairs in most state legislatures go to members from the majority party in that chamber, with the leaders of the majority party wielding great power in the final decision. The **party caucus** is often important in state legislatures. The caucus is where party leaders and legislators meet to discuss party policy. Because some state legislatures meet for only a few months a year, the party caucus can help hammer out agreements rapidly.

One area on which legislatures are predictably partisan is **redistricting**, or **reapportionment**. Each decade, following the national census, state legislatures are constitutionally required to realign their congressional district boundaries to make them equal in population and reflect population changes. How district lines are drawn can help or hurt a party. Where one party controls both houses and the governorship or has a veto-proof majority in the legislature, the majority party can do pretty much what it wants with district boundaries, so long as it keeps the districts equal in population and respects the rights of racial minorities. Where power is divided between the parties, the result is often a redistricting that protects incumbents.

Parties in Local Government

Political parties are still important in the politics of many cities, although they are in a much weaker position now than they were 25 or 50 years ago. Mayors often lead city party organizations and play a role in the campaigns of presidents, senators, and governors. The mayor's office is sometimes a stepping-stone to other offices. Jesse Ventura began his political career as mayor of Brooklyn Park, Minnesota; U.S. Senator Richard Lugar was once mayor of Indianapolis; Ohio Senator George Voinovich was mayor of Cleveland and became governor of Ohio before going on to the U.S. Senate; Secretary of Defense William Cohen was mayor of Bangor, Maine; and U.S. Senator Dianne Feinstein was mayor of San Francisco.

Parties rarely get involved in initiative and referendum elections at the local or state levels, but some nonpartisan local elections have partisan overtones as candidates may be identified with the parties, or the parties may want to advance the career of a local nonpartisan candidate.

PARTY BALANCE AND IMBALANCE

State politics may be classified according to how the parties share public offices. In a **two-party state**, the Republican and Democratic parties alternate in winning majorities. In a **one-party state**, one party wins all or nearly all the offices, and the second party usually receives only a small proportion of the

party caucus
Meeting of the members of a party in a legislative chamber to select party leadership and discuss party policy. Called a *conference* by Republicans.

redistricting
The redrawing of congressional and other legislative district lines following the census, to accommodate population shifts and keep districts as equal as possible in population. Also called *reapportionment*.

two-party state
A state in which the two major parties alternate in winning majorities.

one-party state
A state in which one party wins all or nearly all the offices and the other party receives only a small proportion of the popular vote.

Machines and Bosses

For many years the epitome of a political machine in the United States was Tammany Hall, the building where the Tammany Society (named after a Delaware Indian chief) met and ran New York City politics. Tammany Hall was closely identified with Democrats and was ruled by William Tweed, the boss of New York City politics.

A *boss* is a party leader who uses patronage, government contracts, and access to power to dictate policy. Some bosses, like Tweed, were never elected to office but were powers behind the scene who told the mayor and other city officials what to do. Party bosses were common after the Civil War and well into this century. Other cities with powerful political machines were Chicago, Los Angeles, Boston, Pittsburgh, Cincinnati, Philadelphia, Indianapolis, San Francisco, and Baltimore.

The principal objective of the urban reform movement in the early twentieth century was to overthrow the bosses and the political machines. Reformers advocated nonpartisan local elections, competitive bids for projects, and civil service in place of patronage. They achieved most of their goals, although it is not clear whether the power of political machines was reduced by these reforms or by other social and economic forces.

popular vote. One-party Republican states currently include Utah, Idaho, and Kansas. In the *modified one-party* state, one party wins all or almost all the offices over the years, but in some years the other party receives a substantial percentage of the votes and sometimes surprises everybody—including itself—by winning.

Since the end of World War II, there has been an accelerating trend toward two-party politics. The Democratic party lost its previously solid support in the South as more and more white southerners moved over to the Republican party. At first Republican resurgence in the South was mainly evident in presidential and congressional elections, but in recent years Republicans have regularly been elected to southern state legislatures. Since the middle 1970s the number of Republicans in southern state legislatures has increased from about 12 percent to almost 40 percent[19] and continues to increase.

Republican gains have also been evident in contests for governor. Since 1966 all southern states except Georgia have elected Republican governors, and in 2001, six southern states were led by Republican governors. In terms of the popular vote for president, the South has voted more Republican than the country as a whole in nine of the last eleven presidential elections.[20] Even with southerners like Clinton and Gore on the ballot, the Democrats carried no southern state in 2000.

Outside the South there has also been a gradual spread of two-party politics, with the rise of Democratic strength in the formerly solid Republican states of Iowa, Maine, and New Hampshire. Democrats have lost strength in parts of the Rocky Mountain area; however, the Democratic party has been gaining loyalists in the Midwest, Northeast, and Pacific Coast states.

What are the consequences of party balance? When parties and their candidates compete on an equal basis, they are more likely to be sensitive to public opinion, for the loss of even a fraction of the voters can tip the scales to the other side in the next election. Party competition tends to push leaders within each party to work together, at least as elections draw near. Any defection may throw a race to the opponents, so competition generally produces more teamwork and efficiency in government. Doubtless it also generates more service to constituents by legislators.

In a one-party state, party imbalance may have a serious effect on the dominant party. Because it is almost guaranteed a victory no matter how poor its record, the majority party may not keep itself in "fighting trim." Competition that otherwise would occur *between* the major parties occurs *within* the majority party. The most important contests in some states like Massachusetts are not between Democrats and Republicans but among Democrats in the primary; the same is true for Republicans in Utah. In these intraparty fights, personalities dominate the campaign. Voters do not participate as much as they do in two-party contests.

If party imbalance disorganizes the dominant party, it pulverizes the minority party. With faint hope of winning, minority party leaders do not put up much of a fight. They find it difficult to raise money for campaigns and to persuade people to become candidates. They have no state or local patronage to give out. Volunteers are slow to come forward. Young people wishing to succeed in politics drift into the dominant party. The second party is likely to be concerned only with national politics and the patronage that could come its way if its candidate wins the White House.

Party imbalance can be found in more extreme forms in cities and towns than at the state level. Republicans hardly ever carry Chicago, Boston, Washington, Baltimore, Albany, Hartford, Pittsburgh, and many other cities throughout the industrial North. But party balance is not always a determining factor. In heavily Democratic New York City, for example, voters elected and reelected a Republican, Rudolph Giuliani, as mayor.

ELECTIONS AT THE STATE AND LOCAL LEVEL

Each year there are thousands of state and local elections. Europeans, who are used to voting for one or two candidates at the national and local levels and voting only once every two or three years, are flabbergasted to learn that we engage in elections almost continuously. Selection of town and local officials in the late winter may be followed in the spring by primaries to choose delegates to conventions, then primaries to choose party candidates, then general elections in the fall in which the actual officeholders are chosen—all interspersed with special elections, special town or state referenda, and even, in some states, recall elections to throw an official out of office.

Even more bewildering to some Europeans is the number of offices we vote on, from president to probate judge, from senator to sheriff, from governor to member of the library board. This is the *long ballot*. Europeans are more accustomed to electing a handful of key officials, who in turn appoint career officials. Given this volume of election activity, it is fair to conclude that Americans like elections, even though most of them choose not to vote in most of those elections.

Differences in Who May Vote

Subject to constitutional constraint, states can regulate who may vote. Most, for example, do not permit prison inmates to vote. Today, if a state wanted to permit 16-year-olds to vote, it could do so. Voter registration rules can discourage people from participating in elections. States differ in the length of their residency requirement, as well as in whether they permit roving registrars, postcard registration, online registration, or election-day registration. Most states require a periodic purge of the voter registration list to remove people who have moved or died.

A common reason why people do not register is that they have moved and have not registered at their new address. About one-third of Americans change their residence within a two-year period.[21] After moving, they may not realize that they need to register at their new address until only a few days before the election, and then it is too late. Maryland, North Carolina, and the District of Columbia allow college students who have moved within a city or county to vote without registering if they notify election officials of their move. All told, a state's registration rules can lower turnout by as much as 9 percent.[22]

Voting by Mail and Absentee Ballot

Modern technology makes it possible to vote by other means than appearing in person at a voting place on election day. Cities like San Diego, Berkeley, and Vancouver first experimented with holding *elections by mail.* Voters are mailed a pamphlet that describes the questions to be decided in the election and gives instructions on how to complete the ballot and return it by mail. Voters sign the return envelope, and their signature is compared against their signature on the voter registration form. There have been no major problems in administering these local mail-ballot elections, and the response has been considerably higher than the norm for in-person special elections.[23]

In January 1996, Oregon voters elected a U.S. senator in a special election through the mail rather than in person. Oregonians had 20 days from the date the ballots were mailed to return them to county clerks, and two-thirds of those who received ballots returned them. Now all Oregon elections are conducted through the mail, including the 2000 general election, which included 25 ballot initiatives. There appear to have been few instances of fraud, and the Oregon election officials are strong advocates of vote-by-mail elections in the future.

Opponents of the vote-by-mail system worry about fraud and that voters might be pressured to vote a certain way. Supporters point to the higher turnout and lower costs in administering vote-by-mail elections.

A less dramatic reform of election laws is the *absentee ballot.* In most of the country, voters may request a ballot by mail, often without having to state a reason for doing so.[24] Absentee balloting is especially useful for initiative measures. In states

like California or Washington, where voters may face 20 or more complicated ballot questions, those who vote by absentee ballot can take their time researching and pondering how they are going to vote and do not have to decide within the few minutes they would have in a voting booth.

Ease of obtaining ballots has significantly expanded the rate of absentee voting in California. It has been used especially by Republicans to activate retired and other voters who find it difficult to get from their homes to the polling places. Absentee ballots made up nearly half of all ballots in Washington in 1998.[25] Other states have also liberalized their absentee voting provisions. Oklahoma and Texas, for instance, have *early voting*, whereby voters may vote for several days before an election at several locations in each county.

Absentee ballots also figured in the controversy in the Florida 2000 presidential voting. In two counties, absentee ballot request forms had incorrect voter identification numbers, but the county clerk permitted the Republican party to correct the mistake after the forms were returned to the county. In other Florida counties, some absentee ballots from military personnel did not have postmark dates or were otherwise technically not in compliance with the law. Initially some counties did not count these ballots, but eventually, most military ballots were counted.

Differences in Nomination Processes

State law establishes the process by which party nominees are selected. Most states use a *primary election*, but some permit the parties to nominate their candidates through a *caucus* or *convention*. In the caucus system, party delegates who are elected in local voting district meetings decide on the party nominee. In some states a convention narrows the field to two candidates if no candidate gets a set percentage of delegate votes.

The dynamics of winning a nomination in states with a caucus system are different from those in states with a primary. In a caucus system, having a grass-roots organization that can mobilize voters to attend a neighborhood meeting is essential for candidates. The state best known for the caucus system is Iowa, whose party caucuses are the first decision in our presidential election system and are covered extensively by the media. Some form of the caucus or convention system is used in about a dozen states.

There are two kinds of party primaries, closed and open. In a **closed primary**, only those voters registered in a party may vote in that party's primary. Such a primary discourages **crossover voting**—voters from outside the party helping to determine the party's nominee—which is why partisans prefer closed primaries. In an **open primary**, any voter can participate in any party's primary. Wisconsin has long had open primaries.

Some states, like Washington and California, allowed voters to vote for more than one party in the same primary election; this is called a **blanket primary**. Thus a voter could choose a Democratic nominee for governor and Republican nominees for U.S. senator and attorney general. The blanket of primary, according to those who advocated it, encouraged voters to select the best nominees regardless of party and was thought to help moderate candidates. Opponents said it further weakened parties and made our system even more candidate driven. In July 2000 the Supreme Court ruled that blanket primaries are unconstitutional because they violate the right to political association under the First Amendment.[26]

In a primary election, when all the candidates are from the same party, voters make their choices based on candidate appeal and issues. They may also vote for the candidate they perceive has the best chance of winning the general election.[27]

Louisiana has a unique system. All candidates, regardless of party, run in a single election. If no candidate gets a majority of the votes, there is a runoff election to determine the winner. It is not uncommon for both candidates in a runoff to be from the same party.

closed primary
A primary in which only persons registered in the party holding the primary may vote.

crossover voting
A member of one party voting for a member of another party.

open primary
A primary in which any voter, regardless of party, may vote.

blanket primary
A primary open to all voters, who may vote for candidates from any party for each office.

HOW WE VOTE

Although millions of Americans carry cell phones, own computers, and shop on the Internet, as a nation we still vote an antiquated way. One of the surprises of the 2000 Florida presidential election was the extent to which we are still using 1970s technology. Nearly one in five counties in the United States use punch card ballots, which are subject to problems like dangling or dimpled chads that do not clearly indicate the voter's intent. Another two in five communities use optically scanable ballots on which the voter uses a pencil to mark the ballot and a scanner records the vote. While much more reliable than punch-cards, scanned ballots are also subject to problems if voters color outside the box or do not use a pencil.

Voting machines with levers are used in 15 percent of counties and paper ballots are used in 12 percent of counties. Unlike punch cards, optical scanners, and paper ballots, voting machines do not permit an audit of the vote.

Surprisingly, less than 10 percent of counties use electronic or computer voting systems. When Congress considers election reform, there may be a move to computerized voting. Such voting could be facilitated by the fact that many high school computer labs are connected to the Internet. One concern will be the secrecy of voting by computer and another will be how to do a recount. Despite these concerns, significant changes in how we vote are certain to occur.

SOURCE: *USA Today*, November 14, 2000, p. 21A. Research by Paul Overberg and April Umminger; graphic by Frank Pampa and Dave Merril.

Voting machines in the United States vary from simple boxes to state-of-the-art computer screens.

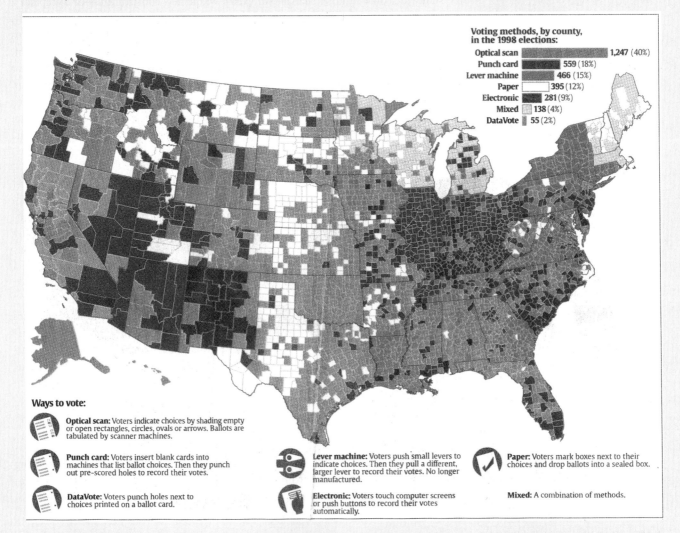

Voting methods, by county, in the 1998 elections:

Method	Count	Percent
Optical scan	1,247	(40%)
Punch card	559	(18%)
Lever machine	466	(15%)
Paper	395	(12%)
Electronic	281	(9%)
Mixed	138	(4%)
DataVote	55	(2%)

Ways to vote:

Optical scan: Voters indicate choices by shading empty or open rectangles, circles, ovals or arrows. Ballots are tabulated by scanner machines.

Punch card: Voters insert blank cards into machines that list ballot choices. Then they punch out pre-scored holes to record their votes.

DataVote: Voters punch holes next to choices printed on a ballot card.

Lever machine: Voters push small levers to indicate choices. Then they pull a different, larger lever to record their votes. No longer manufactured.

Electronic: Voters touch computer screens or push buttons to record their votes automatically.

Paper: Voters mark boxes next to their choices and drop ballots into a sealed box.

Mixed: A combination of methods.

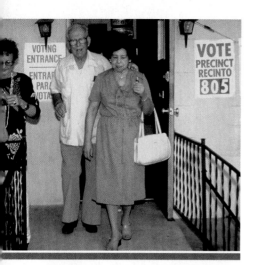
To encourage voter participation, election signs and ballots are often printed in several languages.

Differences in Timing and Frequency of Elections

Federal law sets the date of the presidential election as "the Tuesday next after the first Monday in November, in every fourth year," with similar language applying to elections for the House and Senate. States are free to determine the dates of all other elections, but for ease of administration they usually consolidate gubernatorial and state general elections on the first Tuesday after the first Monday in November. Two states elect their governor every two years. Five states conduct their elections (primary and general) for governor, other state officials, and the state legislature in odd-numbered years, leaving the even-numbered years for federal elections. Two-thirds of the states (including the two-year states) elect governors in presidential midterm years, halfway between presidential elections.

Separating state elections from presidential or federal elections permits voters to focus more closely on state issues than if they had to vote for state and federal candidates at the same time. Separating elections also means that state and local officials are not as likely to be hurt by an unpopular presidential candidate at the top of the ticket.

Some states hold their primaries in late spring, others in mid-September. Primary elections are under the control of state law. Some states have two primaries in presidential years, one for the presidency in the spring and one for other contests in the fall.

State law establishes the rules for local elections but often allows cities and towns some discretion in setting the dates of elections. Many municipal elections are held in the spring of odd-numbered years, again to avoid any positive or negative carryover from candidates running for federal or statewide office. Counties usually conduct their elections at the same time state officials are elected.

State governments can call *special elections* to vote on a ballot initiative, a statewide constitutional change—or even a whole new constitution—or to replace a U.S. senator who has died or resigned. Participation in special elections varies greatly, depending on what is being decided, but turnout is generally lower than in midterm general elections. Before states hold special elections to fill a vacated U.S. Senate seat, they often have a special primary election to determine the party nominees for that election. In these primaries, turnout is even lower than in the special general election.

The frequency of our elections and the range of choices sometimes make it hard for voters to pay enough attention to cast informed votes. For this reason, some reformers have proposed consolidating elections to once or twice every couple of years.

Participation: Who Votes?

What are the consequences of holding so many elections at so many different times? One is that Americans pick and choose which elections, if any, they participate in. States vary significantly in their rate of **turnout**, the proportion of the voting-age public that votes. Note that political scientists do not calculate turnout on the basis of *voter registration* because there is such variability in state registration rules that it is unfair to compare the turnout in a state with difficult registration laws with the turnout in a state whose laws make voting much more accessible. Rather we calculate turnout based on the Census Bureau's estimate of the voting age population in each state.

Primaries usually draw fewer voters than general elections, and in some cases the turnout is quite low. Low turnout raises concerns about whether voters in primary elections reflect the general public. Primary voters are generally better educated, earn more money, and are more likely to be white than the rest of the population.[28] Primary election turnout is also related to strength of partisan identification, the ease of voter registration, and the issues in the campaign.

Campaign Finance

In the early 1970s many states enacted campaign finance disclosure laws, a few instituted partial public financing of elections, and others provided partial underwriting of the costs of parties. **Disclosure** is a common element of campaign finance legislation at the state and local level. Candidates typically are asked to file disclosure state-

turnout
The proportion of the voting-age public that votes.

disclosure
A requirement that candidates specify where the money came from to finance their campaign.

ments specifying where the money came from to finance their campaign. Interest groups are often required to file reports on how they distribute their campaign contributions. Once elected, most state and local officials are required to file a different kind of disclosure form, one that indicates their personal wealth, investments, and other financial matters that may reveal conflicts of interest.

Roughly two-thirds of the states have enacted campaign finance reforms that limit individual contributions, and several states provide some form of public financing. State laws are often patterned after federal law, but states have experimented with lower contribution limits than those allowed in federal elections. Other states have experimented with tax credits to encourage small contributions. In 1996, Maine voters passed a ballot initiative that provided what supporters call a "clean money" option of public financing.[29] Under this system candidates who agree to take no private money and accept spending limits receive public funds for their campaigns.

Voting on Ballot Questions

Voting on ballot questions is heavily influenced by campaign spending. Presumably, greater expenditures make the most difference when there is a low level of information, as is the case with many ballot propositions. And opinions on ballot propositions are more volatile because voters' views on such matters are not deeply rooted in party affiliation, feelings toward an incumbent, or party appeal.[30]

Because many initiatives are supported by well-funded interests, and because a vote in one state can start a national movement on an issue, initiative campaigns can attract large sums of money. Some examples of heavy spending include a 1988 election in Maryland in which the National Rifle Association and other groups spent a record $6.8 million in an unsuccessful attempt to defeat a hand-gun registration referendum. The tobacco industry spent more than $21 million in California in 1988 to defeat an initiative raising the cigarette tax. More than $101 million was spent in California in that year on five initiatives that dealt with automobile insurance reform.

Voting on ballot questions is different from voting for candidates because voters do not have such simplifying factors as party and candidate appeal to rely on. More people vote for candidates than vote on ballot questions. Voters who are confused tend to vote no. "Ballot fatigue" also makes people more likely to vote no.[31]

State and Local Campaign Financing

- 36 states limit the size of individual contributions

- 21 states prohibit corporate contributions and 10 states prohibit labor union contributions

- 26 states limit contributions from PACs and 24 states limit contributions from corporations and labor unions and their respective PAC's

- Minnesota places much lower contribution limits during nonelection years

- 29 states offer limited public financing from the government to statewide candidates or political parties. Hawaii and Minnesota also give funding directly to state legislative candidates

- 5 states offer partial or total tax credits to encourage small contributions

- 3 states impose ceilings on candidates who accept partial public financing

- 8 states raise campaign money through their income tax system

SOURCE: James A. Palmer and Edward D. Feigenbaum, *Campaign Finance Law '98* (Federal Election Commission, 1998), charts 2A, 2B, 4.

THE FUTURE OF GRASS-ROOTS DEMOCRACY

Political parties are vital to the operation of our democracy. Many political scientists believe that our system would be strengthened if we had stronger political parties. The first step in the renewal of the parties would be to change their negative image and persuade citizens that political activity is essential to a healthy constitutional democracy. The next would be to give people who support parties a greater say in choosing the candidates who run under their party's label. While our candidate-centered tradition will certainly remain, it is important to moderate it with strengthened parties that can discipline candidates, at least by withholding resources that candidates cannot easily acquire elsewhere. We would do well to make ballots and elections more "voter friendly." The proliferation of elections, including special elections, turns off even the most committed citizens. Why not, many reformers argue, consolidate elections so that voters might exercise their vote only once or twice, rather than three or four times, a year?

Getting good people to run for office is another challenge. The spiraling cost of campaigns and the advantages enjoyed by incumbents have deterred many good potential candidates. Others are repelled by the nasty and negative tone of recent elections. But unless a democracy produces able citizens who are willing to run for office, it loses its ability to hold incumbents accountable.

POLITICS ONLINE

Why Not Vote on the Internet?

The 2000 ballot-counting controversies in Florida illustrate how antiquated our modes of voting are. Punch cards were the state of the art in the 1960s and 1970s, before the advent of computer terminals and personal computers. The fact that many states still employ this form of voting tells us how low a priority funding election reform is. With more and more Americans having access to the Internet , why not vote via the Internet?

One reason is that not all Americans have access to computers or the Internet. Less educated and poorer Americans, some of the groups who already turnout to vote less than others, could be further discouraged from participation in elections if this became the means of voting. Obversely, younger people who tend to vote least often are the most interested in the Internet, and this may be a means to reach and involve them.

A second reason for not switching to Internet voting is ballot security. How would election officials know if a voter was actually casting someone else's ballot? The obvious answer is a personal identification number, or PIN, much like what you use for banking purposes. While such processes are technically possible, they would impose costs on election officials to maintain lists of PINs, to be able to remind voters who forget their PIN, and to create software that handles electronic ballot submissions.

Despite these reasons, many groups still advocate Internet voting. One such organization is the Internet Voting Technology Alliance. Visit their site at: www.ivta.org/. Another source of interesting information on this topic is: www.securepoll.com. Some websites also offer sample Internet voting systems and plans for implementing the process. Some of these sites are: www.internetvoting.com, www.safevote.com, and www.election.com. Some groups, like People For Internet Responsibility, maintain that these states were too hasty, especially in light of large-scale releases of credit card numbers retrieved from major Internet vendors. To see their statement on the Internet voting, go to: www.pfir.org/.

SUMMARY

1. In the United States technically there are no national elections, only state elections. Even the presidential election is really a set of 51 different elections to choose electors who will, in turn, cast their ballots for president. Elections for U.S. senators and representatives are conducted largely under state law.

2. Political parties are essential to the functioning of democracy at all levels, but they are principally organized around the units of competition. This arrangement makes state parties vitally important. Routinely, they are patterned after the national party organization and include a chair, vice-chair, and a central committee. State parties are often run by full-time party administrators called executive directors.

3. Political parties play important roles in candidate recruitment, voter registra-tion, voter mobilization, and fund raising, and they provide a link between people and government. Parties are also important to the operation of most state legislatures. The governor is the head of the party in power. Governors consider party loyalty when appointing people to many executive and judicial openings.

4. Voters usually vote along party lines in state and local elections, although candidate appeal and issues can also be important.

5. Political parties were once strong and well organized at the local level; in some cities these organizations were called machines and were led by party bosses. Reaction to the abuses of these machines produced reform efforts. One of these reforms was to make local politics officially nonpartisan.

6. States vary in whether the two parties are competitive. In one-party states elections are always won by one party, while two-party states see the parties alternating in holding power. Modified one-party states see the less successful party win occasionally.

7. State election law is important in defining who may vote, when elections will be held, how party nominees are chosen, and which candidates will appear on the ballot. State election law also establishes a framework within which fair elections are assured.

8. State registration laws make voting more or less difficult, depending on their requirements. States may require persons to register by party to vote in primary elections; when voting is thus limited, the primaries are called closed primaries. Over the course of U.S. his-

tory states have gradually eased registration requirements. Suffrage has also been expanded by adoption of constitutional amendments that granted the right to vote to African Americans, women, and finally, all citizens 18 years of age and older. A constitutional amendment also banned the use of poll taxes.

9. Turnout varies by type of election, with turnout being higher in general than primary elections, and higher in presidential than midterm years. Turnout is higher in state than local elections, and regularly scheduled elections typically have higher turnout than special elections. Turnout in vote-by-mail elections is also higher than in in-person elec-

tions in most cases. More people vote for major candidate races than vote on ballot questions.

10. The health of a constitutional democracy may be most in evidence at the grass roots—that is, the state and local levels. American democracy remains strong, but there are important issues that if not addressed, could diminish its vitality.

KEY TERMS

party column ballot 536
straight ticket 536
office block ballot 536
split ticket 536

soft money 539
issue advocacy 539
party caucus 541
redistricting 541

two-party state 541
one-party state 541
closed primary 544
crossover voting 544

open primary 544
blanket primary 544
turnout 546
disclosure 546

FURTHER READING

THOMAS E. CRONIN, *Direct Democracy: The Politics of Initiative, Referendum and Recall* (Harvard University Press, 1989).

PAUL S. HERRNSON, *Party Campaigning in the 1980s* (Harvard University Press, 1988).

MALCOLM E. JEWELL AND DAVID M. OLSON, *Political Parties and Elections in American States*, 3d ed. (Dorsey Press, 1988).

V. O. KEY, JR., *American State Politics: An Introduction* (Knopf, 1956).

DAVID B. MAGLEBY, *Direct Legislation: Voting on Ballot Propositions in the United States* (Johns Hopkins University Press, 1984).

L. SANDY MAISEL, *Parties and Elections in America* (Random House, 1987).

A. JAMES REICHLEY, ed., *Elections American Style* (Brookings Institution, 1987).

ALAN ROSENTHAL, *Governors and Legislators: Contending Powers* (Congressional Quarterly Press, 1990).

ALAN ROSENTHAL, *Legislative Life: People, Process, and Performance in the States* (Harper and Row, 1981).

LINDA WITT, KAREN M. PAGET, AND GLENNA MATTHEWS, *Running as a Woman: Gender and Politics in American Politics* (Free Press, 1994).

25 STATE LEGISLATURES

THERE WAS ONCE A POPULAR ADAGE THAT "NO PERSON'S LIFE, LIBERTY, OR PROPERTY IS SAFE SO LONG AS THE LEGISLATURE IS IN SESSION." THINGS HAVE IMPROVED IN recent decades, yet citizens continue to complain about their state legislators. Voters have become more hostile than they were in previous decades. Some legislators blame the press or the governors for portraying state legislators as villains, but a few admit, "We're to blame." For example, Robert Jubelirer, a Pennsylvania state senator, explains, "A lot of this has been done by us to us. So many campaigns are nothing but 30-second spots making the opponent out to be less than slime"[1]

The legislative process is not easy to understand. Only those directly involved can fully comprehend its slowness and procedures, which are informal as well as formal, consensual as well as conflictual, behind-the-scenes as well as open, combative as well as collegial, and often just plain messy.[2]

State legislatures are the oldest part of our government. They were around long before the adoption of the U.S. Constitution. Legislatures were the most powerful governing institutions in the country during the Revolutionary period. Indeed, the creation of the Constitution was in part a reaction against the excessive power of the state legislatures. The framers of the Constitution imposed limits on the powers of the state legislatures (see especially Article I, Section 9).

The Tenth Amendment to the U.S. Constitution makes it clear that any power not given to the national government or denied to the states lies with the states or with the people. State constitutions, in turn, give some of this reserved power exclusively to nonlegislative agencies and specifically deny some to the legislature. What is left is inherited by the state legislatures.

Although state legislatures today do not dominate state policy making the way they did in 1787, they do play a vital role in state politics and state policy making. State legislators strive to solve problems and provide services—and do so, whenever possible, without raising taxes or creating larger bureaucracies. Legislators these days seek to make the legislature a counterbalance to powerful governors and powerful state bureaucracies.

In 2000, legislatures were involved in a great variety of activities:

• Colorado's legislature adopted stronger gun control legislation.

• New Hampshire legislators voted to prevent the use of death penalty sentencing.

- The New Hampshire House of Representatives impeached a state supreme court justice.
- Vermont voted to recognize "civil unions" between same-sex couples, granting then virtually all the benefits, protections, and responsibilities given to married couples.
- South Carolina legislators voted, by a narrow margin, to remove the Confederate flag over their statehouse dome.
- Hawaii's legislature approved the medical use of marijuana.
- The Tennessee legislature overrode the governor's veto and enacted an $18.3 billion budget without a state income tax their governor had demanded.
- California legislators passed a record-breaking budget for fiscal year 2001.
- The Minnesota legislature, at the request of Governor Jesse Ventura, considered a constitutional amendment to convert to a unicameral legislature similar to that in Nebraska, but the proposal never got out of committee.

In short, legislators everywhere make or modify policies on all kinds of issues. Although there are influential and even occasionally charismatic state legislators, strong governors generally overshadow the legislative body and its leaders. By its very nature, a legislature made up of many individuals from different parties, speaking with many voices, cannot provide unified, swift policy leadership. Even in states with well-paid and well-staffed legislative bodies, the legislature seldom is the dominant policy-making branch. Legislators rarely can compete with governors for the public's attention.

State legislatures make laws and modify and approve budgets. Perhaps as important, they help balance conflicting political pressures. Legislatures perform countless constituency services and, along with the governor and the courts, help to keep state agencies accountable to both the laws and the citizens. Legislators must constantly reconcile pressures among competing interest groups. Representing local views at the state level, they dramatize issues and bring them into the open. A state legislature serves as a lightning rod to which most of the conflicting pressures of American society are drawn.

You may know someone who has run for state legislator—about 11,000 people seek this job every two years. Sometimes there is no real contest; able and entrenched incumbents often run unopposed. About one-third of state legislative elections are uncontested; this is especially true in smaller, one-party states and in the South.[3] Moreover, about 75 percent of incumbents who are eligible run for reelection, and they have at least a 90 percent chance of winning renomination and reelection. An incumbent seeking reelection has many advantages over a challenger: name recognition, better access to campaign funds, experience in running campaigns, and a record of helping with constituent problems. Still, few legislators feel politically secure, even when they have not been opposed in the last election.

In an incumbent's mind, there seldom is such a thing as a "safe district" and a sure reelection. "Whatever their margins of victory in prior elections, however 'safe' their district may appear to the analyst, incumbents know that lightning can strike. . . . They have seen colleagues relax their efforts and subsequently lose their seats. They live in perpetual danger of casting a roll-call vote that upsets their constituency or mobilizes a key interest group to seek their defeat."[4] Incumbents also worry about scandals in their party or having to run with an unpopular candidate at or near the top of their party ticket.

Why do people seek this office? For many reasons: the excitement, the opportunity to serve their fellow citizens, personal gain, a chance to advertise themselves, the desire to make better laws, a sense of loyalty to their political party, and as a stepping-stone to higher elective office. Often the reason is a mixture of these factors as well as a desire to be where the action is.

THE LEGISLATIVE BRANCH

All states except Nebraska have a two-house, or **bicameral legislature**. Nebraska has a one-house **unicameral legislature**.[5] The larger chamber is generally called the House of Representatives. (In a few states it is called the Assembly or House of Delegates.) It contains from as few as 40 members (in Alaska) to as many as 400 members (in New Hampshire); the typical number is around 100. In all but five states, representatives serve two-year terms; in Alabama, Louisiana, Maryland, Mississippi, and North Dakota representatives serve for four years. The smaller chamber, known as the Senate, is typically composed of about 40 members. State senators serve four-year terms in most states.

Certain states, such as New Hampshire and Wyoming, have what are called part-time "citizen legislatures," whereas New York and California are sometimes characterized as full-time "professional legislatures." In the New Hampshire House of Representatives, legislators are essentially volunteers. These "citizen-legislators" represent districts of about 3,000 people. They earn $200 for the year and meet for no more than 45 days a year. In contrast, the California Assembly has 80 members, each representing a district of about 450,000 people. California legislators earn $99,000 a year in addition to expense allowances, meet nearly all year long, and consider their legislative work a full-time occupation (see Table 25–1).

Forty-four state legislatures meet every year from January through May or June. Legislatures in seven states, such as Arkansas, Montana, Nevada, and Texas, meet only every other year. Some state constitutions limit their legislatures to regular sessions of a fixed number of days, usually 60 or 90. Such restrictions reflect distrust of government, the feeling that "the faster we get it over with, the better." *Special sessions* have been developed to get around these limitations. The governor has the power to call the legislature into special session and in some states to determine the issues that may be discussed in the special session—a power governors frequently use.

The organization and procedures of state legislatures are similar to those of the United States Congress. A *Speaker*, usually chosen by the majority party, presides over the lower house. In many states Speakers have more power to control proceedings than their national counterpart has. For example, most state Speakers have the right to appoint committees and thus play a key role in determining policy. But the power of Speakers varies a lot: Speakers have great powers in West Virginia, New Hampshire, and Arizona; their powers are minimal in Alaska, Mississippi, Hawaii, and Wyoming.[6] In 26 states, lieutenant governors preside over the Senate, though they are usually mere figureheads; in other states the presiding officer is chosen by the majority party in the senate.[7]

As in Congress, the committee system prevails. In several states, such as Maine and Massachusetts, *joint committees* are used to speed up legislative action. However, state legislative committees usually do not have the same power over bills as do their national counterparts; many still lack adequate professional assistance; the seniority system is not as closely followed as in Congress; and membership turnover is somewhat higher, especially where term limits have taken effect.

Every legislature has committees on education, transportation, agriculture, and energy or natural resources. Most also have important committees on rules, appropriations, and taxes (sometimes called the Ways and Means Committee). Legislators generally specialize and become experts on one or two substantive matters, such as education, crime, taxation, or the budget process. As in any organization or

TABLE 25–1 The Diversity of State Legislatures

State legislatures across the country vary greatly in many respects. The National Conference of State Legislatures grouped them into three types based on their length of session.

Type 1
Full-Time, High-Pay, Large-Staff "Professional Legislatures"

California	New York
Florida	Ohio
Illinois	Pennsylvania
Massachusetts	Wisconsin
Michigan	
New Jersey	

Type 2
In-Between Hybrid

Alabama	Minnesota
Alaska	Missouri
Arizona	Nebraska
Colorado	North Carolina
Connecticut	Oklahoma
Delaware	Oregon
Hawaii	South Carolina
Iowa	Tennessee
Kansas	Texas
Kentucky	Virginia
Louisiana	Washington
Maryland	

Type 3
Part-Time, Low-Pay, Small-Staff "Citizen Legislatures"

Arkansas	New Mexico
Georgia	North Dakota
Idaho	Rhode Island
Indiana	South Dakota
Maine	Utah
Mississippi	Vermont
Montana	West Virginia
Nevada	Wyoming
New Hampshire	

SOURCE: National Conference of State Legislatures, cited in Charles Mahtesian, "The Sick Legislature Syndrome," *Governing*, February 1997, p. 20.

bicameral legislature
A two-house legislature.

unicameral legislature
A one-house legislature.

Members of the Texas House of Representatives gather around the Speaker's podium to iron out a disputed point.

large assembly, an individual earns respect and influence primarily by developing specialized knowledge about either policy or procedural matters.

Striking differences exist among state legislatures. Some have excellent staff and splendid information technology, and are well-run professional organizations. Yet others are no more professional than they were a generation or two ago.[8] These differences sometimes stem from historical or ethnic traditions. They can also arise from urban-rural or east-west factional splits, and sometimes from regional differences, as is the case with the "Hill people" versus the "Delta people" in Mississippi. Here is how one expert on state politics viewed some of the more distinctive characteristics shaping state politics in the United States:

> In New York professional politics, political wheeling and dealing and frantic activity are characteristic. In Virginia, one gets a sense of tradition, conservatism, and gentility. . . . Louisiana's politics are wild and flamboyant. By contrast, moderation and caution are features of Iowa. A strong disposition of compromise pervades Oregon, with politicians disposed to act as brokers and deal pragmatically rather than dogmatically. In Kansas hard work, respect for authority, fiscal prudence, and a general conservatism and resistance to rapid social change are pervasive features of the state environment. Indiana is intensely partisan. Wyoming is mainly individualistic, and Ohio is fundamentally conservative. In Hawaii the relatively recent political dominance of Japanese and the secondary status of Chinese, native Hawaiians, and Haoles (whites) makes for tough ethnic politics. Yankee Republicans used to run Massachusetts, but now the Irish dominate. Their personalized style, which blends gregariousness and political loyalty, results in a politics of the clan. Mormonism of course dominates Utah.[9]

What Do State Legislators Do?

What do the nation's 7,424 state legislators do? Among other things, they enact laws that create state parks, specify salaries for state officials, draw up rules governing state elections, fix state tax rates, set worker's compensation policies, determine the quantity and quality of state correctional, mental health, and educational institutions, and oversee welfare programs. State legislators approve all appropriations and thereby confirm or modify a governor's proposed budget. Legislators in most states are also responsible for overseeing the administration of public policy. Although they do not administer programs directly, legislators can and do determine whether programs are being carried out according to legislative intentions through hearings, investigations, audits, and the budgetary process. Figure 25–1 outlines the steps in passing state laws.

State legislatures perform various functions within the larger federal system, such as ratifying proposed amendments to the U.S. Constitution, exercising the right to petition Congress to call for a constitutional convention to propose an amendment to the U.S. Constitution, and approving interstate compacts on matters affecting state policies and their implementation. The national government has recently turned back many health and welfare responsibilities to the states.

Each state's constitution prescribes the procedures its legislatures must follow, sets limits on the rate of taxation, the kinds of taxes, the subjects that may be taxed, and the purposes of taxation. State legislatures participate in amending their state's constitutions by proposing amendments for voter ratification. Legislatures also have authority to impeach and try state officials, and they are involved in the appointive process.

State legislators help to translate public wants and aspirations into laws and regulations. In addition to their law-making functions, they also try to be service providers or ombudsmen—to listen, learn, and find solutions to problems. Invariably, state legislators wind up doing a lot of favors: getting a merchant a license to sell lottery tickets, persuading some state agency to look into safety standards at the local hospital, pushing for funds to repair county roads, arranging for a campaign supporter to be appointed to the state labor commission, and so on. State legislators

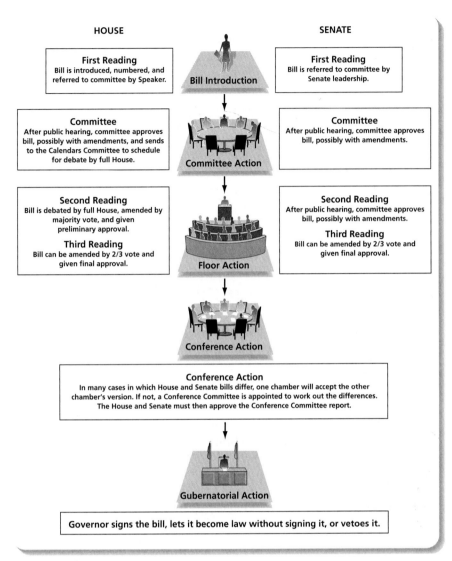

HOUSE

First Reading
Bill is introduced, numbered, and referred to committee by Speaker.

Committee
After public hearing, committee approves bill, possibly with amendments, and sends to the Calendars Committee to schedule for debate by full House.

Second Reading
Bill is debated by full House, amended by majority vote, and given preliminary approval.

Third Reading
Bill can be amended by 2/3 vote and given final approval.

SENATE

First Reading
Bill is referred to committee by Senate leadership.

Committee
After public hearing, committee approves bill, possibly with amendments.

Second Reading
After public hearing, committee approves bill, possibly with amendments.

Third Reading
Bill can be amended by 2/3 vote and given final approval.

Bill Introduction

Committee Action

Floor Action

Conference Action

Conference Action
In many cases in which House and Senate bills differ, one chamber will accept the other chamber's version. If not, a Conference Committee is appointed to work out the differences. The House and Senate must then approve the Conference Committee report.

Gubernatorial Action

Governor signs the bill, lets it become law without signing it, or vetoes it.

FIGURE 25–1 How a Bill Becomes a State Law

are accessible. Citizens and students can nearly always contact their legislators and talk with them in person or at least by telephone.

With the growth of state functions, legislators are spending increasing amounts of time on casework or constituency services. Constituent relations are often the most time-consuming aspect of a legislator's job. Local city and school officials always need the help of legislators, and interest groups back home are always pressing their views. Legislators usually try hard to perform constituent casework because they recognize its political value. The more help they give to home-district citizens and businesses, they reason, the more they will earn respect, win reelection, or perhaps gather support for election to higher office.

Who Are the State Legislators?

The typical American state legislator is a 48-year-old white male, well-educated and well-off, often a businessman or lawyer of Anglo-Saxon origin who has had some type of previous political experience—not always elective—at the city or county level. Some have worked as a staff member in the legislature or in state government.[10] Most state legislators have held some type of local party position and have been active in political campaigns. Surprisingly, about one-third were born in some other state, a reflection of our increasingly mobile population.

Slightly more than half of the nation's state legislators (53 percent) call themselves Democrats; most of the rest (47 percent) are Republicans. About 20 of the 7,424 legislators consider themselves Independents or are affiliated with a third party. All 49 members of Nebraska's unicameral legislature are nonpartisan.[11] Not long ago, Democrats dominated state legislatures in most urban and southern states, but no longer. Republicans made significant gains in the past decade, and the two parties today are often separated by only a few seats for control of one of the chambers of their statehouse.

Lawyers continue to be the largest occupational group in most state legislatures, yet the percentage of attorneys continues to drop; today attorneys constitute only about 17 percent of state legislators nationwide. There has been an increase in those who consider themselves full-time legislators, and there has been a slight increase as well of teachers, homemakers, retirees, and students.[12] Real estate and insurance dealers and sales representatives are also commonly found in legislatures (see Figure 25–2). The number of farmers continues to fall as redistricting continues to shift power away from rural areas and as the number of farms declines. Moreover, longer sessions of the legislatures make it less possible to be a farmer and a legislator. When legislatures used to meet for just a few winter months, farmers were able to fit their schedules to the legislative cycle.

More women and African Americans in recent years are winning election to state legislatures, yet both groups are still notably in the minority. Of the 7,424 state legislators, about 22 percent are women, about 600 are African American, and about 190 are Latinos. Approximately 60 Asian Americans and more than 45 Native Americans serve as state legislators as of 2001.[13]

Because legislators must have flexible schedules, the job often attracts retired people and those whose businesses or professional practices have been so successful that they can afford to take time off. Legislators used to identify themselves by their occupations outside the legislature, but this is less the case now; many refer to their occupation as legislator.

The trend in many states has been to somewhat longer annual legislative sessions with better salaries. New York legislators earn $79,500 a year plus $89 per day for expenses. Pennsylvania pays its legislators $59,245 annually plus $115 per day for expenses. A few other states pay at least $40,000. Other states, such as Maryland and Oklahoma, provide "living wages." But in most states legislators receive modest salaries: Florida pays $26,388, Texas pays $7,200, and Georgia, Indiana, and Nebraska pay about $12,000 a year.[14] In some states, legislators go to the capital for only a few months a year, and they are paid so little that many are able to serve only if they are independently wealthy, if they can live off their spouses, or if they have other jobs that can be readily combined with legislative service.[15]

Legislative salaries are most often set by the legislature. Most legislators are reluctant to increase their salaries and, as a result, lawmakers' salaries lag well behind the rate of inflation and the increases in the cost of living. Most people run for the legislature for reasons other than compensation. "No one goes into politics to get rich," notes Massachusetts state senator Tom Birmingham. 'But you can't have a system where only the rich get into politics."[16]

State legislators are better educated and are somewhat better paid than the average person. They also come from middle- and upper-income groups. They are usually hardworking, public-spirited citizens who believe being in the legislature is a good opportunity for service. Yet state legislators enjoy less prestige than do members of Congress, especially in states that have large legislatures. Discouraged by modest salaries and long hours, many serve a few terms and then either retire volun-

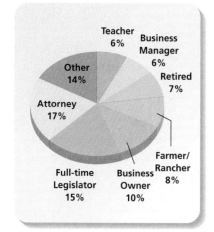

FIGURE 25–2 A Profile of State Legislators

Teacher 6%
Business Manager 6%
Other 14%
Retired 7%
Attorney 17%
Farmer/Rancher 8%
Full-time Legislator 15%
Business Owner 10%

Source: National Conference of State Legislatures.

WOMEN IN THE STATEHOUSE

In the late 1960s state legislatures were dominated by men and often had the look of a "good old boys" club. This has changed in recent years as more women have been elected, bringing the national average up from just 4 percent in 1969 to 22 percent today. In the Washington State legislature 40 percent are women, in Nevada 37 percent, in Arizona 36 percent, and in Colorado and Kansas 33 percent. In Alabama only 8 percent of the lawmakers are women.

As women have won election to state legislatures across the country, their influence has grown, and more women win election to key legislative posts. About half the states now have women's caucuses within state legislatures, which can serve as a counterpoint to the traditional caucuses. For example, all women legislators in Maryland meet once a week during legislative sessions and on an ad hoc basis when not in session. These Maryland legislators even hold an annual October retreat to discuss legislative priorities for their upcoming session. California's women lawmakers meet monthly. Illinois's Council of Women Legislators meets monthly on an issue-by-issue basis and has three volunteer staff members.[*]

Does the election of women to state legislatures make a significant difference in how women are represented? Some analysts believe female legislators are more likely to offer leadership on women, family, and children's policy issues.[**] Yet another study of legislators of the Arizona and California state legislatures found there was often little or no difference in how men and women dealt with gender policy issues.[***]

SOURCE: Sam Howe Verhovek, "Record for Women in Washington Legislature," *The New York Times*, February 4, 1999, p. A14.

[*]Rita Thaemert, "Twenty Percent and Climbing," *State Legislatures*, January 1994, pp. 24–27.

[**]Sue Thomas, *How Women Legislate* (Oxford University Press, 1996). See also Kathleen Bratton and Kerry L. Haynie, "Agenda Setting and Legislative Success in State Legislatures: The Effects of Gender and Race," *Journal of Politics* 61, no. 3 (1999), pp. 658–79.

[***]Beth Reingold, *Representing Women: Sex, Gender and Legislative Behavior in Arizona and California* (University of North Carolina Press, 2000).

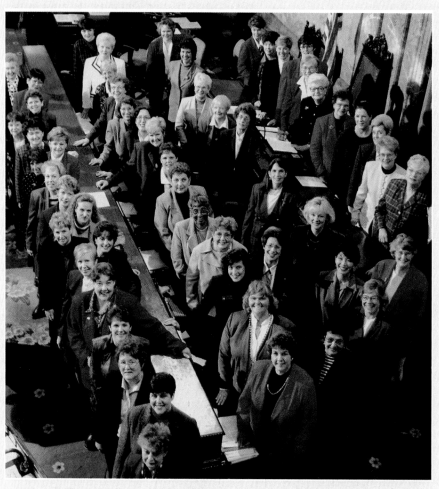

Women members of the Washington Legislature constitute the highest percentage of women in any legislature in the nation's history.

Current Percentage of Women in State Legislatures

SOURCE: Center for the American Women and Politics; reprinted from *The New York Times*, January 4, 1999, p. A18.

tarily or run for higher office. Some leave after just a couple of terms because they get bored listening to matters that frankly do not interest them. As one one-termer explained: "In short, a great deal in the political process does not—repeat does not—involve the glamorous policy issues. Most of the work is sheer routine and hardly awe-inspiring."[17] And, of course, some are now leaving because of term limits in their states that prevent more than two or three terms.

What Do Legislative Committees Do?

A legislative committee is where bills get drafted, hearings are held, and the general policy making and preliminary law making takes place. Committees vary in power and influence from state to state; in general, however, the influence of committees has increased in recent decades. They used to be pale shadows of their counterparts in the U.S. Congress, and they often still are in the less populous states because of short sessions, limited staffing, and turnover of both staff and legislators. Still, legislative committees process and shape hundreds or even thousands of bills and resolutions.[18]

Committees do the legislature's work. They consider and amend legislation, oversee the implementation of the laws, interview judges, and serve as the major access point for citizens, interest groups, and lobbyists. The functions of a legislative committee are advisory; all of its proposals are subject to review, approval, or rejection by the legislative body of which it is a part.

Some of the functions of standing committees or interim committees include:

- Studying pending legislation carefully
- Conducting public hearings on proposed bills and resolutions
- Debating and modifying initial proposals
- Screening, eliminating, or burying undesirable legislation
- Grading legislation in terms of desirability
- Confirming key administrative personnel
- Monitoring or overseeing administrative practices and regulations.

The committee system allows members to concentrate their energies on specific areas of governmental operations. Over time, legislative committees and their members develop extensive knowledge about particular activities and provide useful information to their colleagues. Since it is impossible for everybody to be an expert on all aspects of state government, committees, properly staffed and run, can evaluate the merits and faults of a proposed law more effectively than can any individual legislator.

What Influences State Legislators?

POLITICAL PARTIES   Candidates for state legislatures are nominated by political parties in primaries or by party conventions and caucuses, and they are elected *as party members*. Although the official party organization is sometimes not a dominant influence in recruiting state legislative candidates, a candidate nonetheless has to go through the party to gain the nomination. Figure 25–3 shows the current party control of state legislatures.

The role of political parties in the governance of legislatures and in policy making varies widely from state to state. In nearly half the states—especially in the urban, industrialized states and in the Northeast—the political party is a key factor in decision making. In other states—in the Southwest, for example—parties appear less significant. Instead coalitions tend to form along rural-urban, conservative-liberal, or regional lines.

Parties in most states are less influential than they used to be. Candidates welcome what help they can get from the parties, yet it's often not much. However, in some states party leaders in the legislature raise and allocate campaign contributions

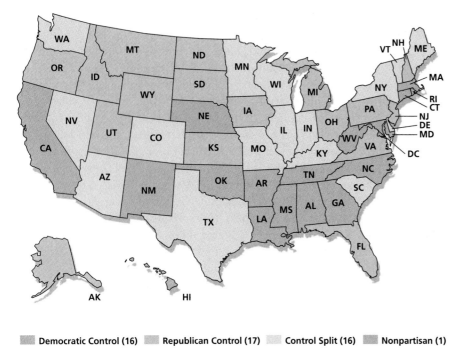

Democratic Control (16) **Republican Control (17)** **Control Split (16)** **Nonpartisan (1)**

FIGURE 25–3 **Party Control of State Legislatures, 2001**

that prove helpful to those running for the first or second time, particularly in competitive races. Party organizations and political action committees are major sources of money for many legislative candidates. Still, legislative candidates almost always have to form their own personal organization, separate from the local party apparatus, to wage a winning campaign.

In nearly every state where there are two active parties, the political party selects legislative leaders and assigns members to committees. Party leaders in many state legislatures distribute sought-after perks, ranging from committee assignments to parking spaces. **Party caucuses**—meetings of all the members of one party in the chamber—also distribute campaign funds to their members and to specifically targeted districts.

Party unity on policy matters is typically found in states with a highly competitive two-party system. Here party caucuses develop party positions, and party members are expected to support them in the legislative chambers. In a few states, binding votes in party caucuses virtually (although not legally) force party members to vote as a unified bloc on the floor of their chamber. Binding caucus votes are, however, taken on relatively few issues. Voting regularly with the party and being a member of the majority party can help legislators win discretionary grants or other favors for their districts.

The party caucus is a principal instrument for legislative decision making in about half the states, including Colorado, Delaware, Idaho, Montana, California, and Utah. In states where a party holds a slim majority of the seats in a legislative chamber, representatives are more likely to feel pressure to "toe the party line" than where a party commands a large majority.[19] Similarly, legislators are more likely to vote with their party in states where the political party plays an important role in recruiting and nominating candidates.

In legislatures in which a single party has had long-standing dominance or control, as in some southern states, parties are less important in conducting and shaping legislative business. Because of the recent rise of the Republican party in the South and Southwest, however, parties and partisanship are gradually increasing in strength in such states as Florida, Texas, and North Carolina. A rebirth of partisanship and growing attention to elections of legislators are apparently making the parties more important than they have been in the past.

party caucus
Party members in a legislative chamber who meet to select party leadership, decide policy positions, and distribute campaign funds.

lobby
To attempt to influence public officials, especially legislators and the policies they enact.

LOBBYISTS AND INTEREST GROUPS   To **lobby** is to try to influence the decisions of public officials, especially legislators. The right to lobby is secured by the First and Fourteenth Amendments to the Constitution, which protect the right of the people to petition the government for redress of grievances. State constitutions provide similar protections.

Anyone can try to influence how a state legislator votes. States usually define a professional lobbyist as someone who is paid to influence legislators on behalf of a client or clients. States now require lobbyists to register annually, either with the secretary of state's office or with an elections or lobbyist commission. In most states lobbyists must pay a fee for lobbying. In Texas, for example, professional lobbyists pay a $300 fee, although lobbyists for tax-exempt public interest groups pay only $100.

Hundreds of lobbyists openly ply their trade in the committee rooms and corridors of the state capitols. The more populated states register thousands of lobbyists. In one recent year, Texas and New York each registered as many as 1,800 professional lobbyists. Even less-populated Vermont had more than 600 lobbyists registered with the secretary of state.

Most lobbyists are regular employees of corporations, unions, or trade associations. Many are members of law firms; others are former state employees. Effective lobbyists are specialists in both subject matter and legislative procedure. Lobbyists for organized interests know the schedule of general hearings, committee meetings, floor debates, and social events. They also know as much as possible about the legislators, their electoral support, their values, their hobbies, and who has their "ear." They are present and prepared when their interests are affected. Veteran lobbyists know how to influence legislators. Two rules lobbyists live by are: It's a lot easier to kill a bill than to pass it, and work in such a way so that you have no permanent allies and no permanent enemies. Today's opponent may be your supporter on the next issue for which you are lobbying.[20]

For obvious reasons, some of the most effective lobbyists are retired state legislators. Five of the top ten highest paid lobbyists in Colorado in one recent year were former state legislators. They all have good contacts with their former colleagues, and they can be pretty effective in killing bills, which sometimes can be done in a Senate or House committee with just a handful of legislators. "If you happen to know the four people on a certain Senate committee," said one Colorado legislator, "it's pretty damn easy to kill a bill."[21]

Information is usually the key ingredient in gaining or losing a vote. Lobbyists are useful providers of such information to anyone who can influence state policy making. "Lobbyists are strategists, tacticians, builders of coalitions among groups, experts and communicators. They testify in committees, buttonhole lawmakers one-on-one, organize meetings between their members and legislators, stage rallies and demonstrations, and try to put a favorable 'spin' on media coverage of their issues."[22]

Groups that may be affected by legislative decisions seek to bend those decisions to their advantage. Bankers, insurance companies, road builders, developers, and large landholders have, on occasion, sought contracts or special rulings by illegal means. This problem challenges the integrity of representative government in the United States, especially since legislators often get the money with which they run for office from the people who have the greatest stake in pending legislation. There is sometimes a hazy line between a campaign contribution and a bribe.

Illegal use of lobbying techniques, primarily bribery, has been found in some states. Scandals were exposed in Arkansas, Arizona, Kentucky, Massachusetts, New Mexico, and South Carolina, among others, in recent years. For example, F. William Sawyer, a highly regarded veteran lobbyist who worked for the John Hancock Mutual Life Insurance Company on issues before the Massachusetts legislature, was convicted in federal court in 1995 of illegally giving gifts to a number of Massachusetts

lawmakers. Most of his gifts were meals and golf outings, yet one was a $3,200 tab for flying a legislator and his wife to a Superbowl game in New Orleans.[23]

Still, bribery is not a widespread problem in most states. Writing about his own experiences in the Vermont Senate, Frank Smallwood observed that, as a general rule, most of the lobbyists

> were articulate, hard-working, and extremely well informed in their particular areas of expertise. This last attribute—information—represented their chief weapon and gave them real clout. As far as I could find out, the lobbyists didn't offer legislators any money or other direct inducements, at least, they never offered me anything, not even a sociable drink. Instead they relied on information.[24]

How important are interest groups and state political action committees as a source of influence on state legislatures? Teacher organizations, trade associations, labor groups, trial attorneys, taxpayer associations, insurance, mining, real estate, road builders, and banking interests are often the most visible single-interest groups. In states with an obvious major economic interest, legislators pay close attention to the needs of that interest, regardless of whether the group employs lobbyists. The legislatures in these states seldom pass legislation hostile to their own state's principal economic interests.

Interest groups are usually the major financial backers of incumbent legislators, and in return the lobbyists for those groups get unusual access. As the costs of state legislative races climb, so does the dependence of legislators, legislative leaders, and political parties on organized interests.[25]

In recent years, states have sought to regulate lobbying activities, conflicts of interest, and the financing of political campaigns. Wisconsin and Minnesota ban such favors as buying meals for a legislator. In the wake of a 1992 Federal Bureau of Investigation sting, lawmakers in Kentucky are now barred from taking anything from a lobbyist except $100 per year in meals and drinks. State senators in New York voluntarily swore off the meals and gifts worth more than $25 that interest groups had routinely lavished on them.[26]

Not all these reforms have been easy to implement, nor have they all worked according to the original intentions. Laws that control lobbying and regulate how much individuals may spend to influence either elections or the legislative process are difficult to enforce. It is sometimes unclear, too, whether they infringe on the constitutional right of persons to petition their government and to spend their own money for political purposes. In some cases, states have probably overcompensated in their efforts to avoid even the appearance of having their integrity compromised.[27]

OTHER INFLUENCES ON STATE LEGISLATORS   A legislator's personality, leadership style, and conception of responsibilities influence how he or she will vote and perform constituent service.

Many legislators believe they have a responsibility to rail against wasteful government spending yet at the same time fight to see that their own district gets a fair share of state government construction projects and subsidies. Voting for one's home district makes sense to many legislators. Former state legislator John E. Brandl writes that state legislators understand that on election day their constituents who are grateful for favors received "are more apt to express positive sentiments on the ballot than those not receiving benefits from the capitol. . . . A former colleague of mine in the Minnesota House of Representatives seemed bewildered when he heard the suggestion that his first responsibility as a legislator might not be to look out for his district but rather to be concerned for the good of the whole state. 'Nobody who thinks like that could ever get elected from my district,' he maintained."[28]

Influences on Legislators' Voting

- Personal political philosophies
- Legislative colleagues
- Legislative staff specialists
- Committee recommendations
- Interest group lobbyists
- The governor
- Cabinet and agency heads
- Legislative party leaders
- Party leaders
- Local elected officials
- Local and state media
- Constituent mail and opinion
- Urban and rural splits in the state
- Regional blocs within the state
- National trends
- Programs that have worked in other states
- Family and friends

But if state legislators are elected to represent the people and their views at the statehouse, few lawmakers think they should merely mirror or "re-present" the views of their district's constituents. Most legislators like to consider themselves **trustees** of their constituents, claiming to rely on their own consciences or on their considered judgments in making decisions. Legislators who view themselves as **delegates**, on the other hand, adhere more closely to instructions from their constituents. Not surprisingly, the trustee role is not only the most popular but also the easiest and most realistic to practice. Given the complexity of government and the difficulty of finding out where citizens stand on a wide variety of issues, the trustee role is more practical in the day-to-day decision making of a legislator during legislative sessions.

Views of constituents back home are influential on matters such as taxes and major construction on highway projects, yet on most issues the people back home have little direct influence on law making. To be sure, on issues that are of keen local interest, legislators take them into account when they vote. Thus, state lawmakers act as trustees on some issues and delegates on others. Yet "conscience" and personal philosophy are seldom the only, or even the most, important guide. Colleagues, committee recommendations, party leadership, staff counsel, and lobbying by the affected interests are also important.

New legislators soon learn it makes sense to depend on friendly colleagues to inform them about issues. According to a Pennsylvania legislator, "Very early in the session, you try to find other representatives who sit on other committees and who are similar to you in their outlook politically. When a bill comes to the floor for a vote, you have to look to that person, you have to trust him."[29]

Another aspect of state politics that often fuels legislation is action taken by other states. Legislators frequently ask their staffs, "What is California, Minnesota, or Oregon doing on this problem?" Legislators are always on the lookout for innovative tax, educational, or welfare policies implemented elsewhere. Legislators are keenly interested in how their state compares to others in certain areas—on sales taxes, for example, high school dropouts, clean air, or federal monies coming to the state. The press often uses such rankings in headlines and editorials.

The National Conference of State Legislatures (NCSL), a nonpartisan professional organization funded by all 50 state legislatures, acts as an effective clearinghouse for new ideas (**www.ncsl.org**). With about 180 staff members located mainly in Denver, Colorado, it distributes its studies to legislators across the country. A rival yet smaller and more conservative group, the American Legislative Exchange Council, has developed in recent years (**www.alec.org**). The Council of State Governments is yet another group that helps state legislators (**www.csg.org**).

Actions taken by the federal government also influence state laws and regulations. Over the past 30 years, state legislatures have been burdened by **federal mandates**, which require states to allocate state funds to match federally stipulated programs such as Medicare. Funding for federal mandates was often the fastest-growing part of a state's budget, a sore point with state legislators. In the 1990s Congress began to place restraints on the growth of federal mandates.

Legislatures today face new pressures: lobbying is more intense than ever; campaign costs have increased; fewer members follow the old folkways that used to make for an almost clubhouse collegiality in most legislatures. Greater participation of women and minorities and more independent-minded legislators have meant a broader mix of agendas and ideas. The influence of legislative leaders has decreased, and the influence of the media and staff has grown.[30] According to state legislative scholar Alan Rosenthal, "Earlier, leaders were truly in command, and power was tightly held. Partly as a consequence of modernization and reform, legislatures have been democratized. Resources are more broadly distributed, and the gap between leaders and other legislators is narrower."[31]

trustee
A view of the role of legislators that holds that they should think and vote independently, based on their judgment of the facts.

delegate
A view of the role of legislators that holds that they should represent the views of their constituents.

federal mandate
A requirement imposed by the federal government as a condition of receipt of federal funds.

MODERNIZATION AND REFORM

State legislatures in the past were criticized as inefficient, ineffective, poorly staffed, boss-ridden, secretive, sexist, unrepresentative, and often dominated by rural interests. Most legislatures had little or no staff and high rates of turnover among members. Legislators had to rely primarily on information that came to them from lobbyists or the governor's office. Legislatures were often run by factions that could not be held accountable, and parliamentary procedures and inadequate committee systems either prevented action or served narrow or specially favored interests.

> Given the goals of members, the demands of groups, and the heavy workload, deliberation gives way to expediency. Members frequently are unwilling to say no to their colleagues, lest their colleagues say no to them. They also are averse to saying no to constituents, lest their constituents withdraw support. The process has become porous; much seeps through that probably should not. Standing committees do not screen the wheat from the chaff as diligently as they might.[32]

To remedy these perceived shortcomings and to strengthen the policy-making role of legislators in state governments, legislatures have implemented reforms. Thus most legislatures now have longer annual sessions, expanded and more competent staffs, more effective committee systems, streamlined procedures such as automated bill status and statute retrieval systems, higher salaries, and modern information systems.[33] Every legislature now has a colorful website with detailed information about the workings of the lawmaking body. Hawaii has a fully equipped and staffed "public access room," making it easy for citizens to lobby their state legislators.[34] Prodded by federal court rulings, legislatures have become more representative, and legislative districts are now approximately equal in population.

In short, the largely amateur, part-time state legislatures are a thing of the past in most states. A new professionalism reflects a determination on the part of most legislators—especially the leaders—to take charge of their own branch as major players in shaping state public policy.

Legislative Term Limits: Problem or Solution?

Although the complexity of state problems may well require professional legislators who devote full-time attention to legislative issues, this development "runs counter to the traditional theory of American politics in which citizens come together, conduct the public's business and return to their other occupations."[35] In the 32 states where there are no term limits, many legislators are now viewed as career politicians—less like the people they represent.

The movement to encourage full-time professional legislatures with impressive staffs has not been universally praised. In fact in recent years some political scientists and many citizens have argued that we were better off when we had part time "citizen legislators." The groundswell in the early 1990s to enact term limits was a voters' revolt against professionalized legislators who were making their work into a career.

Term limits were the most talked about legislative "reform" in the 1990s. It began in 1990 when voters in California, Colorado, and Oklahoma approved the first term-limit restrictions through citizen-instigated ballot initiatives. Two years later another 11 states enacted voter initiatives along the same lines. Overall, voters in 19 states approved term-limit provisions of some type for their constitutions, while voters in three states rejected them. However, state supreme courts struck down term limits in three states: Massachusetts, Nebraska, and Washington. In addition, state legislators in Utah and Louisiana voted to impose term limits on themselves; in Louisiana it was then passed on to the voters for their approval. A term limit initiative failed in Mississippi in 1999.

What Makes a Good Legislator?

There are many ways to be an effective legislator. Some legislators specialize in issues, others in procedures or helping their districts through casework, and still others become chamber or party leaders. Nearly everyone learns that there is more to the job than making a lot of speeches or trying to get more bills passed than colleagues.

Legislators themselves say they admire colleagues who are confident but not arrogant, cooperative but not spineless, principled but flexible, and humorous but not silly. Retired lawmakers suggest these rules:

- Keep your word.
- Be patient.
- Be honest.
- Don't promise too soon.
- Make friends with the staff.
- Never surprise a politician.
- Learn how to build alliances.
- Learn the procedures.
- Think beyond party labels.
- Know how to count votes.
- Know that timing is often the key.
- Don't hog the credit.

"Yes, I think some officials should be limited to one or two terms, and others to none."

Dunagin's People by Ralph Dunagin. © Tribune Media Services, Inc. All rights reserved.

Should term limits be imposed on state legislators?

Proponents of term limits contend the principle of rotation is an old and cherished one in the United States and that we should encourage citizen-legislators and discourage career politicians. Supporters also say incumbents have voted too many perks and advantages for themselves and that term limits may be the only way to restore real competition to legislative races. They argue that *permanent incumbency*—legislators and state officials staying on for multiple terms, sometimes decades—is creating a kind of professional ruling class that is out of touch with ordinary citizens. The term-limits movement is a manifestation of public frustration with what is viewed as a failure of government. Would placing limits on how long legislators can serve solve the problem?

Although the U.S. Supreme Court ruled in 1995 that it was unconstitutional for any state to impose term limits on the members of Congress, a poll showed that 80 percent of American voters favored the idea.

Term limits provisions now exist in 19 states (see Table 25–2). These new rules limit state legislators to legislative service of 6 to 12 years. In some states lawmakers are banned from serving in the same office beyond a set number of years. In 11 other states they must skip one term (or more, depending on the state) before running for the same office.

Voters in California went even further and enacted a measure that slashed legislative staffs and curbed legislative pension benefits as well as limited the number of terms legislators could serve. This citizen-sponsored and citizen-enacted law also prohibited legislators from ever running again for the legislature.

Voters, of course, can dispatch legislators from office by voting for challengers. But voters seem to want the added constitutional device of doing for them what most voters do not do themselves—throw the rascals out! All the hoopla about term limits diverts attention from other serious problems, such as weak parties, too many safe-seat districts where one party virtually always wins, and neglect of educational investment and economic development in the states.

Term limits will definitely bring about changes. In California, novice lawmakers now chair committees, and there are signs in California and elsewhere that term limits discourage legislative cooperation, decrease institutional expertise, and generally weaken legislatures relative to governors, bureaucrats, and lobbyists. Term limits thus far have not, however, brought a different type of person to the legislatures that are affected by term limits.[36]

THE POLITICS OF DRAWING LEGISLATIVE DISTRICT LINES

State legislatures are required by constitutions and court rulings to draw district boundaries for both their state legislature and U.S. House of Representative seats. Legislatures must redraw these boundaries after each population census. The 2000 census once again triggered redistricting of congressional and state legislative seats in almost every state.

redistricting
The redrawing of congressional and other legislative district lines following the census. Also called *reapportionment*.

gerrymandering
The drawing of legislative district boundaries to benefit a party, group, or incumbent.

malapportionment
Legislative districts of unequal populations.

TABLE 25–2 States with Term Limits

State	Year Enacted	House Limit (years)	House Year of Impact	Senate Limit (years)	Senate Year of Impact	Percent Voted Yes
Maine	1993	8	1996	8	1996	67.6
California	1990	6	1996	8	1998	52.2
Colorado	1990	8	1998	8	1998	71
Arkansas	1992	6	1998	8	2000	59.9
Michigan	1992	6	1998	8	2002	58.8
Oregon	1992	6	1998	8	1998	69.6
Florida	1992	8	2000	8	2000	76.8
Missouri*	1992	8	2002	8	2002	75
Ohio	1992	8	2000	8	2000	68.4
South Dakota	1992	8	2000	8	2000	63.5
Montana	1992	8	2000	8	2000	67
Arizona	1992	8	2000	8	2000	74.2
Idaho	1994	8	2004	8	2004	59.4
Oklahoma	1990	12	2004	12	2004	67.3
Nevada	1996	12	2008	12	2008	70.4
Utah	1994	12	2006	12	2006	leg. passed
Wyoming	1992	12	2006	12	2006	77.2
Louisiana	1995	12	2007	12	2007	76
Nebraska**	2000	8	2008	—	—	55.82

SOURCE: National Conference of State Legislatures.

*Because of special elections, term limits became effective in 2000 for eight current members of the House and one Senator in 1998.

**Note—Nebraska is a unicameral body.

Redistricting is the action of a state legislature or other body in redrawing legislative electoral district lines following a new census. Ten states delegate these responsibilities to independent redistricting or reapportionment commissions. In Alaska, the governor's office draws the legislative districts. Most legislatures, however, consider these once-a-decade responsibilities so important that they are unwilling to turn control of this task over to anybody else.

The drawing of legislative district boundaries has always been controversial, in large part because redistricting decisions are made by partisan majorities in legislatures. The highly political nature of the undertaking is usually reflected in the results. "Redistricting is the political equivalent," says one observer, "of moving the left field fence for a right-handed pull hitter. By changing the boundaries, redistricting helps some, hurts others—and leaves just about everyone else scrambling."[37]

The politics and debate about redistricting are most intense in the years immediately after a census is taken. Drawing district boundaries to benefit a party, group, or incumbent is called **gerrymandering**. The term was first used in 1811 to describe a strange, salamander-shaped legislative district drawn in northeastern Massachusetts when Elbridge Gerry was governor. A district does not need to be odd in shape, however, to be gerrymandered.

Another problem with state legislative districts used to be **malapportionment**, or districts of unequal populations. Major redistricting battles came to the courts in the 1960s, when critics charged that state legislatures for decades had given rural and small-town voters more votes in the legislature than they were

Thinking It Through . . .

Support for term limits comes from both Republicans and Democrats, yet organized support and financial aid have generally come from conservative antitax and antigovernment groups. *The Wall Street Journal* has frequently editorialized in support of term limits. Consumer activist and Green party presidential candidate Ralph Nader has also been among its most vocal supporters. He and like-minded populists on the left believe only the bludgeon of term limits will motivate legislators to give reforms like public funding of political campaigns a serious chance. Many term limits were aimed at the U.S. Congress as the primary target, but that restriction was struck down by the U.S. Supreme Court.

Legislators and most political scientists have opposed this reform. They contend term limits are a solution in search of a problem that does not exist. Most state legislators, they note, stay in the legislature for only three or four terms anyway. Indeed, most states have more of a problem nurturing and retaining experienced leadership than they have in bringing in new blood. The expertise and institutional memory once available from veteran members and longtime leaders, critics say, will be diminished by term limits.*

Critics of term limits think this reform will have the unintended consequence of increasing the power of various unelected officials, such as lobbyists, legislative staffers, and bureaucrats. Power resides somewhere, critics say, and you don't get rid of it so much as shift it. "I calculate that term limits is costing the legislature 694 years of collective experience," complained Ohio state legislator Jo Ann Davidson. "Now the institutional memory vote will be in the hands of the lobbyists and the legislative staff when it should rest with the elected policy makers."**

*See David S. Broder, *Democracy Derailed: Initiative Campaigns and the Power of Money* (Harcourt, 2000), p. 223.

**Quoted in Francis X. Clines, "Term Limits Bring Wholesale Change into Legislatures," *The New York Times*, February 14, 2000, p. A19. See also the criticism in Peter Schrag, *Paradise Lost: California's Experience, America's Future* (New Press, 1998), p. 3. See also John M. Carey, Richard G. Niemi, and Lynda W. Powell, *Term Limits in the State Legislatures* (University of Michigan Press, 2000).

entitled to on the basis of their declining share of the population. In Georgia, for instance, the 1960 reapportionment gave the largest county, with 556,326 inhabitants, no more representation than the three smallest counties, whose combined population was 6,980.[38] City officials complained bitterly that small-town and farm-dominated legislators were unsympathetic to their problems and had different legislative priorities.

Enter the Federal Courts

But no matter how much they protested, people who were underrepresented in the state legislatures made little progress. Legislators from small towns and farm areas naturally did not wish to reapportion themselves out of jobs, and their constituents did not wish to lose their influence. Even though the failure of state legislatures to reapportion often violated express provisions of state constitutions and raised serious questions under the U.S. Constitution, state and federal judges took the position that issues having to do with legislative districting were "political questions" and outside the scope of judicial authority.

Finally, the U.S. Supreme Court stepped in. In 1962, in *Baker v Carr*, the Court held that voters do have standing to challenge legislative apportionment and that such questions should be considered by the federal courts. Arbitrary and capriciously drawn districts deprive people of their constitutional rights of representation, and federal judges may take jurisdiction over such cases.[39] *Baker v Carr* started a small tidal wave.

One Person, One Vote

In *Wesberry v Sanders* (1964) the U.S. Supreme Court announced that as far as congressional representation is concerned, "as nearly as practicable one man's vote in a congressional election is to be worth as much as another's."[40] The Court extended this principle to representation in the state legislatures, although it subsequently modified this decision.

In *Reynolds v Sims* (1964), the Court held that "the fundamental principle of representative government in this country is one of equal representation for equal numbers of people, without regard to race, sex, economic status, or place of residence within a state." In the Court's view, this principle applied not only to the more numerous house of the state legislature, which was usually based on population, but also to the state senate, where representation was often based on area, such as the county or some other governmental unit. Defenders of this pattern had argued that as long as the more numerous chamber represented population, the senate could represent geographical units. Look at the federal system embodied in the U.S. Constitution, they said. Isn't representation in the U.S. Senate based on area? Although many thought this a compelling argument, a majority of the Court did not. Chief Justice Earl Warren explained: "Legislators represent people, not trees or acres. Legislators are elected by voters, not farms or cities or economic interests. . . . The right to elect legislators in a free unimpaired fashion is a bedrock of our political system."[41] The U.S. Senate analogy, in short, did not hold.

The Supreme Court has been especially strict about how states draw districts for the U.S. House of Representatives. A state legislature must justify any variance from mathematical equality by showing it made a good-faith effort to come as close as possible to the standard. The Supreme Court is, however, less insistent upon absolute equality for state legislative districts. Thus the Court, in 1983, upheld a Wyoming plan that allocated at least one state legislative seat per county, saying that Wyoming's policy was rational and appropriate to the special needs of that sparsely populated state.[42] This ruling was a rare exception to the general principle of allowing at most a 10 percent deviation between state legislative districts. The requirement that the districts be established in accordance with the one-person, one-vote principle still remains.

New Rules for Redrawing the Districts

Even though the one-person, one-vote principle is firmly established, many issues affecting the nature of legislative representation continue to be hotly debated. In northern metropolitan areas, for instance, the general pattern has been for the center city to be Democratic and the outlying suburbs Republican. If legislative district lines in these areas are drawn like spokes from the center city to the suburbs, fewer Republicans will probably be elected than if the district lines are drawn in concentric circles.

In recent decades African Americans and Hispanics have begun to charge that state legislatures have an obligation under the Voting Rights Act of 1965 to redraw legislative districts to avoid dilution of the influence of minorities at the ballot box. They have gone to court to force legislators to create **majority-minority districts**. The U.S. Supreme Court, however, has put restraints on such implementation of the act. The Court has held that although legislatures may take race into account in drawing state and federal legislative district lines and must act to avoid diluting the voting strength of minorities, a legislature violates the constitutional rights of white voters if race becomes the overriding motive.[43]

Controversy continues to surround reapportionment, no matter what processes are used. No one ever doubts the ability of incumbents in the majority to rig elections through reapportionment. In the words of the old-time politicians: "You tell me the results you want, and I'll draw the district map to do it." Today computers are shaping the districts, and those who control the computers, their programming, and their data can influence the outcome.

DIRECT LEGISLATION: POLICY MAKING BY THE PEOPLE?

Does "We the People" in our Constitution mean the people themselves should govern directly? Around the turn of the century, Populist and Progressive reform movements fought to "return the government to the people" through the initiative, referendum, and recall. Give the voters the power to make or veto laws and to recall officials, they said, and the political machines will be destroyed and the special interests beaten.

Populists and Progressives had good reason between 1890 and 1912 to want to bypass their legislatures, for the legislatures in several states were either incompetent or under the domination of the political machines. For example, the Southern Pacific Railroad's political machine in California had dominated the selection of state legislators, governors, and U.S. senators for years.[44] The Progressives placed enormous trust in the wisdom of the people, assuming that voters would inform themselves about issues and make responsible decisions on a variety of policy questions put before them.

Initiative

The **initiative** permits a designated minimum number of voters to propose a law or constitutional amendment by petition. It becomes law if approved by a majority of the voters at a subsequent election. Twenty-four states, mostly in the West, authorize the making of laws by means of the initiative petition (see Figure 25–4). In California, Oregon, Washington, North Dakota, Arizona, Colorado, Michigan, and Massachusetts, the initiative has become an important feature of state political life.

In some states the *direct initiative* applies to constitutional amendments and to legislation; in others it can be used only for one or the other. Thus in Florida the direct initiative can only be used to change the state constitution, while in Idaho direct initiative can only be used for statutory law making. In a

majority-minority district
A congressional district created to include a majority of minority voters; ruled constitutional as long as race is not the only factor.

initiative
Procedure whereby a certain number of voters may, by petition, propose a law or constitutional amendment and have it submitted to the voters.

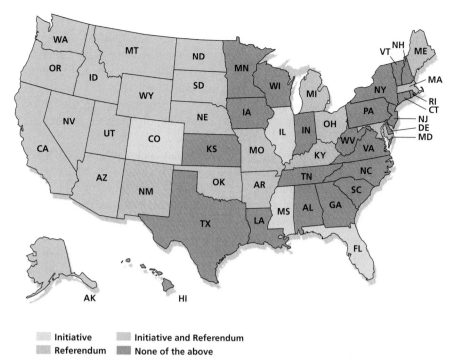

Initiative   Initiative and Referendum
Referendum   None of the above

FIGURE 25–4 Citizen-Initiated Initiative and Referendum at the State Level

state that permits the direct initiative, any individual or interest group may draft a proposed law and file it with a designated state official—usually the secretary of state. Supporters have only to secure a certain number of signatures (between 2 and 15 percent of the vote in the last election) to place the measure on the next general election ballot. Only California permits initiatives on primary election ballots.

The *indirect initiative* is used in a few states, such as Alaska, Maine, and Massachusetts. After a certain number of petition signatures have been collected, the state legislature is given an opportunity to act on the measure without alteration; if approved, the law simply goes into effect. If not approved, the proposed legislation is then placed on the ballot, although in some states additional signatures are required before the proposal can be placed before the voters.

Referendum

A **referendum** permits a majority of the voters to vote on, and possibly overturn, recently passed laws or legislatively proposed amendments to a state's constitution. It is required in every state except Delaware for the ratification of constitutional amendments.

Legislation may be subject to mandatory or optional referenda. The *mandatory referendum* calls for a waiting period, usually 60–90 days, before legislation goes into effect. If during this period a prescribed number of voters sign a referendum petition requesting that the act be referred to the voters, the law does not go into effect unless a majority of the voters give their approval at the next election. The *optional referendum* permits the legislature, at its discretion, to provide that a measure shall not become law until it has been approved by the voters at an election. This second kind is the most common.

Although statewide initiatives and referenda get the most attention, the same processes also flourish at the local level in many states. The annual volume of measures presented to voters in school districts, cities, and counties runs to several thousand, and many are on topics of considerable importance and controversy:

referendum

Procedure for submitting to popular vote measures passed by the legislature or proposed amendments to a state's constitution.

bonds for school buildings, fluoridation of water, banning of glass bottles, restrictions on nuclear power facilities, and approval or rejection of convention facilities or sport stadiums.

Recall

Recall is the means by which voters may remove elected public officials before the end of their term. Eighteen states, mostly in the West, provide for recall of state officers, but many others permit the recall of local officials (see Figure 25–5). Recall also requires a petition, but it needs more signatures (typically 25 percent of voters in the last election for the position in question) than the initiative and referendum. There are various kinds of recall elections. In some the official must stand on his or her record; in others candidates are permitted to file and run against the incumbent.

In effect, recall is like impeachment by the public. But unlike impeachment, formal charges of wrongdoing against the incumbent are not required. Rather, recall permits throwing people out of office merely because of policy differences. For recall, voters need only circulate petitions and obtain the required number of signatures. Recall is seldom used at the state level, although one governor and several state legislators have been recalled. In 2000, a recall effort was mounted in California against Insurance Commissioner Chuck Quackenbush. His critics faulted him for being too generous to donors he was supposed to be regulating. Although the recall is rarely used successfully in the 18 states that now permit it, even the threat of a recall serves to remind legislators and other state officials of their obligations to the voters.[45]

A few years ago New Jersey voters were asked to approve the right to recall for local, state, and federally elected officials. Taxpayer and antipolitician groups argued passionately in favor of passage. *The New York Times* vigorously opposed the recall, saying it would discourage public officials from making unpopular decisions that nevertheless bring about long-term public benefits. The *Times* also editorialized that the recall authority was unnecessary: "If voters are unhappy with someone they have elected, they can vote that person out the next time! If an official breaks the law, prosecutors can deal with it."[46] But over 70 percent of New Jersey voters voted in favor of adopting the recall.

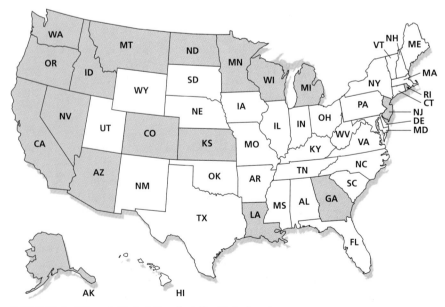

FIGURE 25–5 Citizen-Initiated Recall at the State Level

recall

Procedure for submitting to popular vote the removal of public officials from office before the end of their term.

The Debate over Direct Democracy

Hundreds of issues have been placed on state election ballots by citizen initiative in recent years. Citizens have turned to the initiative process to try to regulate handguns in California, to protect the moose in Maine, to encourage the death penalty in Massachusetts, to approve the sale of wine in local grocery stores in Colorado, to abolish daylight savings time in North Dakota, and in several states to allow marijuana to be used for specific medicinal purposes. Voters in Oregon approved the so-called Death with Dignity law that allows legally assisted suicide, and voters in Washington state approved a measure mandating that criminals convicted of three felonies be sentenced to life in prison without parole. Voters in California and Washington voted to overturn affirmative action programs in state hiring and college admissions programs.

In Oregon's November 2000 election, voters had to vote on 26 ballot measures, most of which were placed there by citizen initiatives. The voters had to decide on initiatives proposing huge tax cuts, repealing the death penalty, banning animal trapping, requiring background checks to buy firearms at gun shows, limiting the amount of money spent on political campaigns, and forbidding public school teachers to speak favorably of homosexuality.

Two hundred and four ballot measures were voted on in 42 states in November 2000. Of the 71 citizen-initiated proposals (the others were initiated by the state legislatures), about 48 percent were approved by the voters, a slightly higher passage rate than is usually the case.[47]

Political scientists, law professors, and lawmakers are often critical of direct legislation.[48] Early opponents had argued that such measures would undermine the legitimacy of representative government and open the way for radical or special-interest legislation. Critics of the initiative and referendum believe the Progressives who advocated direct legislation were naively idealistic and that these mechanisms are more likely to be used by special interests. Only well-organized interests can gather the appropriate number of signatures and mount the required media campaigns to gain victory. Critics of direct democracy say this is generally what happened in California.[49]

In addition to giving advantages to well-organized interests, direct legislation often introduces confusion because some petitions are not so much worded for clarity but to win votes. Moreover, the 30-second ads that support or oppose many initiatives also tend to confuse rather than clarify.

What have been the results of these populist devices? Historically, direct legislation by initiative has resulted in progressive victories on many consumer and economic issues, and conservative victories on social issues. Direct democracy has not weakened our legislatures; seats in state legislatures are still valued, sought after, and competed for by able citizens. Nor, with some exceptions, has unwise legislation generally been enacted. The overall record suggests that voters reject most unsound ideas that get on the ballot. However, voters in California, Colorado, Oregon, and Washington have adopted budget and tax measures in recent years that have had considerable impact on state taxes and spending. These measures have pleased many conservatives, upset liberals, and made life difficult for governors and state legislators.

A problem in a few states is the number of issues on the ballot. California and Oregon voters often have had to decide on a dozen or more ballot issues, some initiated by interest groups and the rest placed on the ballot by the legislature. States are now seeing multiple initiatives on a single topic, with counterinitiatives sponsored by people who actually oppose one of the measures but have decided that the best way to defeat the undesirable initiative is by sponsoring a watered-down version of their own.

Another serious problem has arisen in western states. Political consulting firms, for a price, will gather signatures and put nearly anything you want on the

ballot. Deceptive pitches are sometimes made to get people to sign petitions. It takes a small fortune to do this, and only well-organized, well-financed, single-interest groups can afford it.[50]

Still another problem with the initiative process is that it can be used to target minorities, as did California's limitations on illegal immigrants in 1994 and affirmative action in 1996. Similarly, Colorado's controversial Measure 2 in 1992 targeted gays and lesbians. How far can the majority go in using the initiative process against minorities? The courts have generally reversed part or all of discriminatory initiatives that were successful at the polls, yet such reversals put the courts in the awkward position of opposing a vote of the people.

The initiative process has become a powerful tool used by interest groups, politicians, and ideologues. "A vote on an issue in a single state can propel an issue onto the national agenda because of the widespread media attention given to some controversial initiatives." Interest groups have set state policy by means of the initiative and have used it to reduce local government options in taxing, zoning and planning, and related matters. "One reason for this tendency to take on matters that were previously local and decide them at the statewide level is interest group efficiency. It is easier to restrict local taxing powers, strike local rent control laws, and eliminate ordinances protecting gays and lesbians by mobilizing a single statewide vote" rather than by campaigning to reverse or defeat local initiatives.[51]

Viewed from another perspective, most of the perceived flaws of the populist processes of direct democracy are also the flaws of democracy. When we vote in an election, we often wish we had more information about issues and candidates. Delegates at constitutional conventions or national party conventions frequently have similar misgivings when they are forced to render yes and no votes on complicated issues. So, too, members of state legislatures—especially in those frantic days near the end of their sessions—yearn for more information, more clarity about consequences, and more discussion and compromise than time will permit.

Critics lament the rise in what they call "public policy-making by bumper sticker." Opponents of direct legislation fear the very fabric of legislative processes and representative government is at stake. To be sure, lack of faith in legislative bodies has sometimes prompted the use of direct legislation devices, but the best way to restore faith in the legislature is not to bypass it, but to elect better people to it.

Supporters of populist democracy say they have not given up on the legislative process. Rather, they wish to use direct legislation primarily when legislatures prove unresponsive. If our legislature will not act, they say, give us the opportunity to debate our proposals in the open arena of election politics. Supporters further contend the people are capable of making decisions on complex matters.

Voters throughout the country say that citizens ought to have the right, at least occasionally, to vote directly on policy issues. Surveys find that both voters and nonvoters say they would be more likely to become interested in politics and vote if some issues appeared along with candidates on their ballots.[52] Moreover, Californians, who have had to deal with more ballot issues than voters in any other state, continue to say statewide ballot propositions elections are overall "a good thing for California" (74 percent), even as they acknowledge limits to their own grasp of the process.[53]

The legislative process is never perfect. Even with larger professional staffs, hearings, new technologies, bicameralism, and other distinctive features of constitutional democracy, mistakes are made and defective bills are enacted into law in our legislatures. The Supreme Court has overturned hundreds of laws passed by state legislatures as unconstitutional, and state legislatures often spend much of their time amending or otherwise improving measures they passed in previous years. As a practical matter, both the legislative and the citizen-initiated processes can stand improvement.

POLITICS ONLINE

Citizens as Legislators?

Slightly less than half of the states permit citizens to petition to place laws or constitutional amendments before the voters by the initiative process. This device literally makes it possible for citizens to act as lawmakers, and some draft legislation as if they were themselves the legislature. The text of a proposed law or constitutional amendment drafted by these individuals is put before the legislature in some states, or directly before the voters in others if the proponents can meet a specified petition signature threshold.

In order to understand the various procedures followed by the states, you can compare the basic steps in the initiative and referendum process by accessing the Initiative and Referendum Institute (I & R) at: www.iandrinstitute.com/. Go to the heading of the statewide I &R, and then click on I&R requirement. Arizona and Florida provide great sources for a summary of the process. You may also find it helpful to access the official sites for the secretary of state of active initiative states such as California (www.ss.ca.gov/) or Oregon (www.sos.state.or.us/elections/elechp.htm) to find the specific rules and regulations of the direct legislation process.

Some people have proposed integrating the Internet into the initiative process, either by allowing people to sign petitions via the Internet or by permitting them to vote on referendums via the Internet. Proponents of the Internet idea see it as encouraging more participation and greater citizen awareness of policy issues. Opponents contend that initiatives already experience widespread drop-off in voter participation, and that voters do not generally want to be legislators. Ultimately, the debate boils down to the extent to which citizens want to be legislators themselves or whether they want to delegate this task to their elected representatives.

SUMMARY

1. Although Americans value the state legislature as a vital institution in our constitutional form of government, we are quick to criticize its imperfections. Perhaps we overestimate the possibilities for responsive and representative legislatures. Yet today state legislatures are stronger than they were 40 years ago, and they play a vital role in state politics and state policy making.

2. The nation's 7,424 state legislators are called upon to represent diverse views, help formulate state public policy, oversee the administration of state laws, and mediate political conflicts that arise in the state.

3. The main influences on a state legislator's voting decisions are political parties, lobbyists and interest groups, district considerations, constituent views, colleagues, committee recommendations, the party leaders, the media, and actions taken by other states and the federal government.

4. State legislators are constantly subjected to intense lobbying by organized interests. Lobbyists and interest-group representatives are important sources of information.

5. As a result of legislative reform efforts, most states now have longer annual sessions, larger and more competent staffs, open-meeting laws, and a variety of electronic-age information systems.

6. Nineteen states have limited the number of terms legislators can serve. Most state legislators and political scientists oppose term limits for a variety of reasons, yet voters in many states have viewed them as a way of keeping their representatives accountable and encouraging the notion of citizen representation.

7. The politics of redistricting, or redrawing legislative boundaries, heats up every ten years after the census is taken. Redistricting is never easy; political careers can be ruined by redrawn boundaries. Major controversies have arisen over partisan and racially motivated drawing of legislative district lines, and the federal courts are increasingly asked to establish guidelines that will limit such outcomes.

8. Direct legislative procedures, especially the initiative petition, are a prominent part of the legislative process, particularly in the West. Other direct mechanisms, such as the referendum and the recall, are also available to voters in many states.

KEY TERMS

bicameral legislature 553

unicameral legislature 553

legislative caucus 559

lobby 560

trustee 562

delegate 562

federal mandate 562

redistricting 564

gerrymandering 564

malapportionment 564

majority-minority district 567

initiative 567

referendum 568

recall 58 569

FURTHER READING

SHAWN BOWLER AND TODD DONOVAN, *Demanding Choices: Opinions, Voting, and Direct Democracy* (University of Michigan Press, 1998).

SHAWN BOWLER, TODD DONOVAN, AND CAROLINE J. TOLBERT, EDS., *Citizens as Legislators: Direct Democracy in the United States* (Ohio State University Press, 1998).

DAVID S. BRODER, *Democracy Derailed: Initiative Campaigns and the Power of Money* (Harcourt, 2000).

WILLIAM M. BULGER, *While the Music Lasts: My Life in Politics* (Houghton Mifflin, 1996).

BRUCE E. CAIN, *The Reapportionment Puzzle* (University of California Press, 1984).

JOHN M. CAREY, RICHARD G. NIEMI, AND LYNDA W. POWELL, *Term Limits in the State Legislatures* (University of Michigan Press, 2000).

THOMAS E. CRONIN, *Direct Democracy: The Politics of the Initiative, Referendum, and Recall* (Harvard University Press, 1989).

VIRGINIA GRAY, RUSSELL HANSON, AND HERBERT JACOB, EDS., *Politics in the American States*, 7th ed. (Congressional Quarterly Press, 1999).

JOHN J. KENNEDY, *The Contemporary Pennsylvania Legislature* (University Press of America, 1999).

TOM LOFTUS, *The Art of Legislative Politics* (Congressional Quarterly Press, 1994).

BURDETT A. LOOMIS, *A Legislative Year: Time, Politics and Policies* (University Press of Kansas, 1994).

DAVID B. MAGLEBY, *Direct Legislation: Voting on Ballot Propositions in the United States* (Johns Hopkins University Press, 1984).

GARY MONCRIEF, PEVERILL SQUIRE, AND MALCOLM E. JEWELL, *Who Runs for the Legislature?* (Prentice Hall, 2001).

NATIONAL CONFERENCE OF STATE LEGISLATURES AND AMERICAN SOCIETY OF LEGISLATIVE CLERKS AND SECRETARIES, *Inside the Legislative Process* (NCSL, 1998).

ALBERT J. NELSON, *Emerging Influentials in State Legislatures: Women, Blacks and Hispanics* (Praeger, 1991).

BETH REINGOLD, *Representing Women: Sex, Gender and Legislative Behavior in Arizona and California* (University of California Press, 2000).

JAMES RICHARDSON, *Willie Brown: A Biography* (University of California Press, 1996).

ALAN ROSENTHAL, *The Decline of Representative Democracy* (Congressional Quarterly Press, 1998).

ALAN ROSENTHAL, *Drawing the Line: Legislative Ethics in the States* (University of Nebraska Press, 1996).

ALAN ROSENTHAL, *The Third House: Lobbyists and Lobbying in the States* (Congressional Quarterly Press, 1993).

PETER SCHRAG, *Paradise Lost: California's Experience, America's Future* (New Press, 1998).

FRANK SMALLWOOD, *Free and Independent: The Initiation of a College Professor into State Politics* (Stephen Greene Press, 1976).

SUE THOMAS, *How Women Legislate* (Oxford University Press, 1994).

SUE THOMAS AND CLYDE WILCOX, EDS., *Women and Elective Office* (Oxford University Press, 1998).

JOEL A. THOMPSON AND GARY F. MONCRIEF, EDS., *Campaign Finance and State Legislative Elections* (Congressional Quarterly Press, 1998).

See *State Legislatures*, published ten times a year by the National Conference of State Legislatures. *Legislative Studies Quarterly* often has articles on state legislatures; it is published by the Legislative Studies Section of the American Political Science Association. *Governing*, published monthly by Congressional Quarterly, Inc., regularly covers state politics and state legislative issues.

26

STATE GOVERNORS

W ISCONSIN'S GOVERNOR, REPUBLICAN TOMMY
THOMPSON, BEGAN HIS FOURTH TERM IN 1999. AS A YOUNG
STATE LEGISLATOR A GENERATION EARLIER, HE HAD EARNED THE
nickname "Dr. No" for his vehement opposition to most of the legislation Democrats proposed. But when he became governor he changed, becoming an activist, entrepreneurial policy leader who believes in using state government to accomplish important social and economic goals. To be sure, what he now advocates and proposes differs from the Democratic
measures he had earlier opposed.

Thompson is a conservative who discovered you have to spend money on welfare to save money on welfare. He has won widespread praise for his visionary
approach and vigorous implementation of welfare reform called "Wisconsin Works."
"Virtually all recipients are required to work, either at a regular job, a subsidized
one, or in community service. For those handicapped by disabilities or substance
abuse, there is a transition program of education, rehabilitation, or treatment."[1]
Thompson also initiated major statewide child care services for working mothers
with children under six years old, and he worked on getting affordable health insurance for all Wisconsin residents. Thompson's welfare reforms became a model for
welfare reform enacted at the national level.

"I don't get hung up on ideological dogma when I'm looking at problems," says
Thompson. "If we're going to be successful we have to put money into those resources,
and we've done that. I don't consider it liberal or conservative. I consider it common
sense."[2] Thompson, of course, has his critics. But Wisconsin voters reelected him to his
fourth term with an impressive 60 percent of the vote. In 2001 he became secretary of
Health and Human Services in George W. Bush's cabinet.

The job of governor is one of the most important and exacting in American political life today. Over the past two decades Congress and the White House decentralized
many activities to the states that were previously considered national responsibilities,
such as welfare assistance. This transfer has meant governors now have to be even more
effective managers. They have to ask the right questions and consider long-term implications and side effects of their policies.

Governors are often looked to for national leadership. Sixteen governors have
gone on to serve as U.S. presidents, and at least 17 members of the current U.S. Senate served earlier in their states. Two or three former governors are typically in the
president's cabinet.

CHAPTER MEDIA

 POLITICS ONLINE
*Why Elect Auditors,
Treasurers, and Secretaries
of State?*
www.prenhall.com/burns

In this chapter, we look at how governors come into and keep office, a typical governor's power and influence, efforts to bring modern management techniques to the governor's office, ways that governors interact with other elected state officials, and the rewards of being governor. But first, we examine the rising expectations we have for governors.

RISING EXPECTATIONS FOR GOVERNORS

How do we evaluate governors? Although the constitutional powers of governors vary from state to state, we assess and rate governors pretty much as we do presidents.[3] Governors in the large and even medium-size states are responsible for running complex enterprises that are at least as complicated as Fortune 500 corporations. Lamar Alexander, former governor of Tennessee, said a governor needs to "see the state's few most urgent needs, develop strategies to address them, and persuade at least half the people that he or she is right."[4] An effective governor also has to perform countless symbolic and ceremonial functions and win the respect of the people and the legislature in order to exercise fully the executive functions of the office.

Today a governor is expected to be, among other things, the state's chief policy maker, shaper of the state budget, a savvy political party leader, chief recruiter of the best available advisers and administrators, and an inspiring renewer of confidence in state programs. The governor must also champion the state's interests against the encroachments of federal or local governments and be the state's chief booster to attract business and tourism. In order to be effective, governors are expected to take trips abroad to encourage foreign investment in their states and promote their local products.[5] Thirty-eight states even operate some form of overseas office, including trade mission posts in Harare and Kuala Lumpur.[6] Governors also work with their legislatures to raise revenues for such programs as welfare, education, and economic development. Governors act as a crucial link among the states and between the local and the national governments.

BECOMING AND REMAINING GOVERNOR

Each state's constitution and laws spell out the rules of eligibility, tenure, and salary for its governor. In most states, to run for the office a person must be at least 30 years of age, a citizen of the United States, and a state resident for at least five years immediately preceding the election. You are constitutionally eligible to be governor in California, Ohio, South Dakota, Washington, and Wisconsin when you become 18, although your chances of being elected at such an age are not very good.[7] In theory, any qualified voter of the state who meets a state's age qualification is eligible for the office of governor; in practice, however, there are well-traveled career paths to the governor's office.

Most governors are white male attorneys about 40 to 55 years old. Only about a dozen women have served as governors in the past generation. Many governors were state legislators or held statewide elective office, and some have had law enforcement experience. For example, New York's George Pataki, Georgia's Roy Barnes, and Colorado's Bill Owens all served earlier in their state legislatures. In one recent year, 31 governors were attorneys, 2 were farmers, 1 was a dentist, and most of the rest were businesspeople.

A common path is election to the state legislature, followed by election to a statewide office such as lieutenant governor, secretary of state, or attorney general. Illinois Governor George Ryan spent nearly 30 years in state politics, first as a state legislator, then as Speaker of the House, then as two-term lieutenant governor, and then as a two-term secretary of state before becoming governor. May-

Former Governor Tommy Thompson

ors often run for governor; the mayors of Albuquerque, Phoenix, Indianapolis, Lincoln, and Las Vegas have all run for governor in their states in recent years. Minnesota Governor Jesse Ventura, who most people recall mainly as a former World Wrestling Federation TV entertainer, actually served four years as mayor of a suburban community.

Occasionally a person who has not held any elective office will win a governorship, although such individuals typically have been active in other ways in political life. George W. Bush was a Texas businessman who enjoyed widespread name recognition as the son of a former president, as did his younger brother, Jeb Bush, who went from a business career to the Florida governorship.

Two hundred years ago most states had one- or two-year terms for their governors. Today all states except New Hampshire and Vermont have four-year terms, and all states except Virginia allow governors to run for more than one term. Some governors, such as Jim Thompson in Illinois, Roy Romer in Colorado, Cecil Andrus in Idaho, Mario Cuomo in New York, Jim Hunt in North Carolina, and Tommy Thompson in Wisconsin, were elected for three or four terms as governors, but 37 states now have a two-term limit on governors, and Utah has a three-term limit.

Governors on the Spot

Once elected, governors enjoy high visibility in their states. Governors earn more than $100,000 in 24 states, such as New York, Illinois, Michigan, Texas, and California. The average is now about $95,000, ranging from $179,000 in New York to $65,000 in Nebraska.[8] In addition, governors receive an expense allowance; all but 4 are provided an executive mansion; 42 of them have regular access to a state plane or helicopter or both. Governor Jesse Ventura of Minnesota, to take a visible example, earns $122,303 a year in salary, has a state-provided residence, a state car, and enjoys access to a state plane and helicopter. He also has a staff of 45.

But just as governors have become increasingly important in recent decades, they have also had to deal with the twin problems of rising aspirations and scarcity of resources. People want better schools, highways that do not spoil the

WE THE PEOPLE

Women Governors

Nellie Taylor Ross, Wyoming	1925–27
"Ma" Ferguson, Texas	1925–27, 1933–35
Lurleen Wallace, Alabama	1967–68
Ella Grasso, Connecticut	1975–80
Dixie Lee Ray, Washington	1977–81
Martha L. Collins, Kentucky	1983–87
Madeleine Kunin, Vermont	1985–91
Kay Orr, Nebraska	1987–91
Rose Mofford, Arizona	1988–91
Joan Finney, Kansas	1991–95
Ann Richards, Texas	1991–95
Barbara Roberts, Oregon	1991–95
Christine Todd Whitman, New Jersey	1994–2001
Jeanne Shaheen, New Hampshire	1997–
Jane Dee Hull, Arizona	1998–
Judy Martz, Montana	2001–
Ruth Ann Minner, Delaware	2001–
Jane Swift, Massachusetts	2001–

Governor Jane Swift (Massachusetts)

Governor Jeanne Shaheen (New Hampshire)

Governor Jane Dee Hull (Arizona)

environment, adequate welfare programs, protections for civil rights, safe streets, and clean air and streams. But citizens seldom if ever want higher taxes.

Former New York Governor Mario Cuomo (who served from 1983 until 1995) used to say he was always running into people who wanted him to expand programs. He would look them in the eye and say: "Now what are you going to give me so that I can pay for it? Do you want to wait longer in line at the Motor Vehicle office to get your license renewed? Do we stop paving the road in front of your home? Do you mind if we plow the snow less often?" Typically, of course, he heard that the people requesting additional spending did not want to forgo any of those things, which prompted him to say, "Well, then, I don't understand. Where do I get what I need to do what you want?" His point is simple. Given limited resources, choices must be made. Elected officials cannot afford to do everything people would like. Politicians are elected to negotiate trade-offs. You must "give to get."[9]

Governors and state legislators face the challenge of administering federally mandated welfare programs with fewer federal dollars. They have campaigned for the federal government to give more dollars to the states—without strings. The Republican-controlled Congress in recent years responded by terminating many federal mandates and shifting several federal programs to the states. Governors and state legislators now face the challenge of reworking old federal welfare programs as state welfare programs with cutbacks in federal grants.

Reelection and Raising Taxes

About 75 percent of incumbent governors who run for reelection are reelected.[10] Nearly three-quarters of elections for governor are scheduled for nonpresidential or midterm election years (for example, 2002 or 2006); New Jersey and Virginia elect governors in odd-numbered years. Reformers have successfully argued that presidential and gubernatorial elections should be separated so that governors are not subject to the tides of national politics.

But not every governor is reelected; sometimes running after four years of making tough decisions, generating controversy, and incurring opposition is a disadvantage. Governors in Arizona, Alabama, Arkansas, and Oklahoma left office in recent years because of personal scandals. Governors in Oregon and Kansas left because they had such low approval ratings in the polls that they chose not to run again. Incumbents sometimes lose because of a depressed state economy or because they increased state taxes and became unpopular. In 1993, for example, New Jersey Governor James Florio was narrowly defeated by Christine Todd Whitman, due in part to a recession but mostly because Florio had recommended, and the legislature had enacted, a major tax increase. That tax increase came back to haunt Florio when he ran for senator in the New Jersey Democratic primary in 2000. His opponent, Jon Corzine, ran ads stressing Florio's role as a big spender and won the primary.

Circumstances often dictate what a governor can or cannot do. The health of the state's economy and the public's attitude toward proposed programs are critical factors. The good economic times in the late 1990s plainly helped most governors who ran for reelection. Thus in 1998 all but 2 of the 25 incumbents who ran for reelection were victorious; in 2000 all but 1 of the 6 who ran for reelection won another term.

Some candidates for governor effectively campaign on promises to cut taxes. Thus, Republican James Gilmore in Virginia won a landslide victory in his race for governor by repeatedly saying "No Car Tax"—a reference to a highly unpopular personal property tax on cars, trucks, and motorcycles. George Pataki became governor in New York by pledging a property tax reduction.[11]

Because voters reward frugality and sometimes punish elected officials for tax increases, most governors go to considerable lengths to avoid having to raise taxes,

especially with an election approaching. Indeed, many politicians believe that a governor who proposes new taxes will face defeat in the next election, although some studies cast doubt on this fear.[12] Voters and legislatures often go along with governors who can make a compelling case for new revenues and new investments. When governors request a tax increase targeted for a specific worthy cause (for example, improving the schools), voters often support them. This is especially true if "political leaders are candid about why they need the money, sensible and fair in how they intend to spend it and courageous enough to lead the fight themselves. Americans are neither selfish nor short-sighted on taxes—they just want assurance that their money will be spent wisely."[13] Several governors around the country have proposed and campaigned for *investment taxes* (that is, taxes that could be invested in building better highways or increasing teachers' salaries) and became popular because of their targeted efforts to improve their state.

A GOVERNOR'S FORMAL POWERS

B efore the American Revolution, royal governors, appointed by and responsible to the British Crown, had broad powers, including extensive veto power over the voter-elected colonial legislatures. As anti-British sentiment increased, royal governors became more and more unpopular. The position of state governor in the new Republic was born in this atmosphere of distrust. Initially, state legislatures elected state governors, a method that ensured that governors would remain under the control of the people's representatives. The early state constitutions also limited governors to few powers and terms of just a year or two.

Gradually, however, the office of governor grew in importance. In New York the position of chief executive was sufficiently developed and effective by 1787 that it became one of the main models for the proposed American presidency. If we compare the formal sources of authority in the U.S. Constitution and in a typical state constitution, we see significant differences. "The executive Power," says the Constitution, "shall be vested in a President of the United States of America." Compare this statement with its counterpart in a typical state constitution: "The executive department shall consist of a Governor, Lieutenant Governor, Secretary of State, Treasurer, Attorney General," and perhaps other officials. Unlike the president, the governor *shares* executive power with other elected officials. Most state constitutions go on to say, however, that "the supreme executive power shall be vested in the Governor, who shall take care that the laws be faithfully executed." Thus the public looks to the governor for law enforcement and the management of bureaucracies. In some states the governor has been given authority to supervise the activities of local prosecutors.

Twenty-four states have strengthened the governorship by making the lieutenant governor run with the governor as a team, so that the chief executive is less likely to be faced with a hostile lieutenant governor. In 39 states the lieutenant governor, like the U.S. vice president, takes over executive office responsibilities if for any reason the governor cannot fulfill the duties. Most important, in almost all states the governor presents the state budget to the legislature and controls spending after the budget has been approved. Thus state officials must look to the governor as well as the legislature for funds.

It is difficult to specify exactly the powers of a typical governor because they vary widely from state to state (see Table 26–1). But regardless of a governor's formal constitutional authority, a governor's actual power and influence depend on his or her ability to persuade.[14] This power, in turn, usually depends on the governor's

TABLE 26–1 Rankings of States According to the Formal Powers of the Governor

Strong	
Maryland	Ohio
New Jersey	Pennsylvania
New York	Utah

Moderately Strong	
Alaska	Nebraska
Colorado	North Dakota
Connecticut	South Dakota
Iowa	Tennessee
Kansas	West Virginia
Michigan	Wisconsin
Minnesota	Wyoming
Montana	

Moderate	
Arizona	Louisiana
California	Maine
Delaware	Massachusetts
Florida	Missouri
Hawaii	Nevada
Idaho	New Mexico
Illinois	Oregon
Indiana	Texas
Kentucky	Virginia

Weak	
Alabama	Oklahoma
Arkansas	Rhode Island
Georgia	South Carolina
Mississippi	Vermont
North Carolina	Washington
New Hampshire	

Source: Adapted from Thad L. Beyle, "The Governors," in *Politics in the American States: A Comparative Analysis*, ed. Virginia Gray, Russell Hanson, and Herbert Jacob, 7th ed. (Congressional Quarterly Press, 1999), pp. 210–11.

Note: Rankings are based on budget powers, appointive and organizational powers, tenure potential, veto powers, and party control.

Califorinia Governor Gray Davis

reputation, popularity, knowledge of what should be done, and, of course, ability to communicate. Governors must have political skills as well as constitutional authority if they are to provide leadership.

To supplement their formal constitutional powers, governors may hold town meetings around the state, appear on radio and television talk shows, or invite legislators and other influential party and policy leaders to the executive mansion for lobbying and consultation sessions. Remember, however, that not all states vest great constitutional power in the governor. Whether the state constitution defines a strong role is just one of the factors in determining the effectiveness of a governor.

Most governors have the following constitutional authority:

- To make appointments
- To prepare the state budget
- To veto legislation and to exercise an item veto over appropriations measures
- To issue executive orders
- To command the state National Guard
- To pardon or grant clemency
- To help establish the legislature's agenda

Appointive Power

Perhaps a governor's most important job is to recruit talented leaders and managers to head the state's departments, commissions, and agencies.[15] Through recruitment of effective people and prudent delegation of responsibilities to them, a governor can provide direction for the state government.

In most states the governor is one executive among many, with only limited authority over elected officials, whom the governor can neither appoint nor dismiss. And if these officials are political enemies of the governor, they may not accept the governor's leadership. Governors have greater, yet still limited, power over officials they appoint. Some governors appoint hundreds of key officials; others, such as those in Mississippi, South Carolina, and Texas, have severe restrictions on their appointive power. Moreover, in most states governors must share their appointive power with the state senate and may remove people only when they have violated the law or failed in their legal duties. State administrators whose programs are supported by federal funds also have a measure of independence from the governor.

Governors face other problems as well. First, salaries for cabinet and agency administrators are modest in many states, especially in the smaller ones, and it is often hard to get people to leave better-paying jobs in private industry. The situation is even worse when the state capital is in a remote or rural section of the state. Second, powerful politicians may demand that their friends be appointed to certain top posts, and they may threaten to be uncooperative if the governor does not go along with their "suggestions." Finally, relatively high turnover in many state positions often hampers a governor's efforts to carry out programs.

Fiscal and Budgetary Power

A governor's financial planning and budgetary powers are usually key weapons in getting programs passed. Purchasing, budgeting, and personnel matters are frequently centralized under the governor. When implemented by a strong staff and backed by a strong political base, a governor's fiscal powers are extremely important.

In almost all states the governor has responsibility for preparing the budget and presenting it to the state legislature. This takes place every year in 30 states and every second year in 20 states. The art of budget making involves assessing requests from various departments and agencies and balancing them against available resources. Governors and their staffs have to calculate the costs of existing and newly proposed programs and weigh those costs against estimated revenues for the state.

veto
Rejection by a president or governor of legislation passed by a legislature.

This is how the budget process typically works in most states. In May and June the governor's budget office, which may be called Office of Management and Budget or Department of Administration, sends request forms to the various executive agencies. From July to October the agencies complete their detailed requests and send them back for consideration. Their requests are invariably 10–15 percent higher than what is probably available and also much higher than the governor's proposed guidelines. The governor's budget chief evaluates all requests, sometimes holds internal administrative hearings, and then makes recommendations to the governor. Finally, the governor presents the recommendations to the legislature at the beginning of the new year.

Although the governor and chief budget officials may appear to control the budgetary process, considerable budgeting influence remains in the hands of the executive branch agencies. Further, a governor's budget reflects to a very high degree budgetary decisions made over the years (costs such as prisons or state universities that will not be shut down), so what governors end up doing in practice is tinkering or adjusting at the edges of the overall budget. (See Figure 26–1 for the proposed general budget put forward by California Governor Gray Davis for Fiscal Year 2001, and compare it with Figure 26–2, the budget adopted several months later by the California legislature. Note that in this uncommon case the booming economy in California that year greatly raised revenue estimates and allowed the legislature to approve a much more generous state budget.)

The final budget document is presented to the legislature for adoption as an *appropriations measure*. State monies cannot be spent without legislative appropriations. Legislators can, and usually do, make a number of alterations in a governor's budget. In theory, a legislature controls all state activities through the budget process because it has the final say in approving the budget. In practice, however, most legislatures do not review every budgetary item; they merely trim or make additions at the margins. Hence, budgets usually reflect the policy views of those responsible for their preparation—namely, the governor and the governor's budget office. A governor who has control over the budget and uses this power effectively has an important asset.

Most states spend at least 40 percent of their state's budget on education. Welfare assistance, highways, prisons and criminal justice programs, health and rehabilitation efforts, and state parks and recreation consume other large portions of the budget. Fifty percent of a state's revenue usually comes from taxes; another 20 percent comes from federal sources. When state revenues do not match expenses, governors have to cut or delay programs, since state constitutions as a rule require a balanced budget.

Veto Power

Among the most useful gubernatorial powers is the power to **veto**, or conditionally reject legislative bills, especially appropriations measures. For example, Governor Jeanne Shaheen in New Hampshire vetoed a bill in 2000 that would have repealed the death penalty in her state, and in 1997

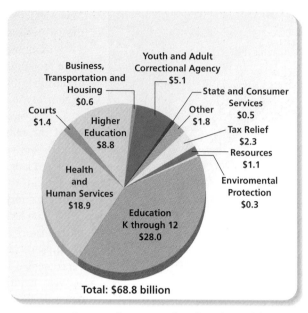

FIGURE 26–1 Governor's Proposed Budget for California for FY 2001 (in Billions of Dollars)

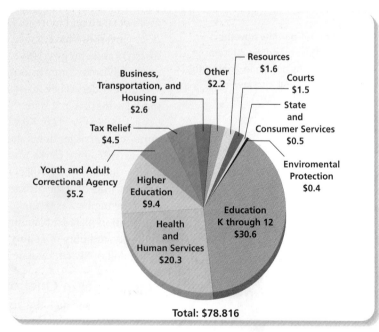

FIGURE 26–2 Legislature's Approved Budget for FY 2001 (in Billions of Dollars)

New York Governor George Pataki

New Mexico's Governor Gary Johnson vetoed legislation that would have allowed the early release of some nonviolent criminals.[16]

In all but eight states governors have the **item veto**, a provision that permits them to veto individual items in an appropriations bill while signing the remainder of the bill into law. Thus they can influence the flow of funds to, and thereby attempt to control the activities of, the executive departments.

In several states a governor can reduce particular appropriations; this power is called the **reduction veto**. In 19 states governors can exercise what is called an **amendatory veto**, which allows a governor to return a bill to the state legislature with suggested language changes, conditions, or amendments. In this last case, legislators must decide to accept the governor's recommendations or attempt to pass the bill in its original form over the veto.

State legislatures can override a governor's veto; in most states it takes a two-thirds majority of both legislative chambers. Some governors, like Wisconsin's Tommy Thompson, vetoed thousands of legislative measures. New York Governor George Pataki vetoed 1,379 provisions the legislature sent him in 1998.[17] Governors on average veto about 4 percent of the bills sent to them, but only about 2 percent of gubernatorial vetoes are overridden by legislatures.[18] Most governors believe the veto power should be used sparingly. Indeed, some observers think too frequent use of the veto is a sign of gubernatorial weakness because an effective governor usually wins the battle through negotiations rather than confronting state legislators.[19]

Legislators in several states have established a *veto session*—a short session following adjournment—so they can reconsider any measures vetoed by their governor. This is clearly an effort to reassert the legislature's check-and-balancing authority in relation to the governor. Most states using veto sessions have legislatures that meet for a limited time; in full-time legislatures a veto session would be unnecessary.

Executive Orders

One long-standing power of governors is their authority to issue **executive orders** that have the force of law. Even though executive orders differ from statutes or formal acts passed by the legislature, they have almost the same binding effect. Governors get their authority to issue executive orders from their implied powers as chief executive of the state, from specific constitutional grants, or from delegations of authority by the state legislature. Executive orders supplementing a law are both more detailed and more important than the general guidelines contained in legislation. Governors have issued executive orders during such emergencies as natural disasters and energy crises, in compliance with federal rules and regulations, and to create advisory commissions. State legislators are sometimes angered by sweeping executive orders. They insist they, not the governors or the courts, should be the primary lawmakers in a state.

In 1996 Governor Kirk Fordice of Mississippi issued an executive order banning same-sex marriages in his state. The intended effect of Fordice's executive order was to prevent county clerks from issuing marriage licenses for gays or lesbians after a similar measure had failed to win passage in the state's legislature.[20] Gay rights activists, joined by the Mississippi American Civil Liberties Union, criticized the governor, saying he was trying to circumvent the state legislature, adding that the state's constitution makes it plain that it is the legislature, not the governor, who defines the authority and duty of county clerks. In this instance, this governor's executive order brought about what the state legislature had not been able to approve.

Commander in Chief of the National Guard

Emergencies enhance the authority of an executive because they call for decisive action. As commander in chief of the state's National Guard when it is not in federal service, a governor may use this force when local authorities are inadequate—in case of riots, floods, and other catastrophes. The National Guard has played a role in the

item veto
A provision that permits governors in some states to veto individual items in an appropriations bill while signing the remainder of the bill into law.

reduction veto
The power of governors in a few states to reduce a particular appropriation.

amendatory veto
The power of governors in a few states to return a bill to the legislature with suggested language changes, conditions, or amendments. Legislators then decide either to accept the governor's recommendations or to pass the bill in its original form over the veto.

executive order
An order issued by a president or governor that has the force of law.

aftermath of floods in midwestern states, riots and earthquakes in California, fires in Florida, and hurricanes throughout the southeastern states. In most states the state police are also available for emergencies.

Congress provides most of the money to operate the National Guard. This fact, along with the supremacy clause of the U.S. Constitution, gives Congress and the president the power to take charge of a state's National Guard even against the wishes of a governor. In 1990 the Supreme Court unanimously ruled that Congress can authorize the president to call National Guard units to active duty and send them outside the United States despite the objections of the governors, several of whom had tried to keep President Ronald Reagan from calling their respective National Guards to training exercises in Honduras.[21] States could if they wish (but none has done so) provide and maintain from their own funds a defense force exempt from being drafted into the armed forces of the United States.

Pardon Power

In half the states, governors may pardon violators of state law; in the other states, they share this duty with a pardoning board. Except in cases of impeachment or certain specified crimes, the governor may pardon the offender, commute a sentence by reducing it, or grant a reprieve by delaying the punishment. The governor is normally assisted by pardon attorneys or pardon boards that hold hearings and determine whether there are sufficient reasons for a pardon.

A Tennessee governor, Ray Blanton (1975–79), caused considerable controversy and sparked a federal investigation when he pardoned or paroled several dozen convicts just before leaving office in 1979. Critics charged that some of these convicts allegedly "purchased" their releases. Blanton's misuse of his pardon powers created such a ruckus that his elected successor, Lamar Alexander, was sworn in early and the locks to the governor's office were quickly changed so Blanton was not able to enter the office, let alone grant any additional pardons. Seldom, however, is the pardon power the subject of such controversy, because it is generally administered with appropriate care.

Similar to the governor's pardon power is the authority for a governor to grant a stay of execution in death penalty cases. This is one of the most controversial aspects of executive power in states that provide for the death penalty.[22] Former Governor George W. Bush came under attack from many people because more than 130 Texas inmates had been executed while he served as governor yet he insisted all were guilty as charged. Illinois Governor George Ryan, also a Republican, won national attention in 2000 for imposing a moratorium on executions in his state. Ryan had long been a death penalty supporter, but he became persuaded that too many mistakes had been made by the courts in sentencing innocent people to death row. Indeed, 13 Illinois inmates in the past generation had been exonerated. "A series in *The Chicago Tribune* found that of 266 capital cases that had been appealed, fully half have been reversed for a new trial or sentencing hearing. In more than 30 cases, lawyers representing death row inmates were disbarred or suspended."[23]

Policy-Making Influence

How much policy-making influence do governors have? Obviously, they can send detailed policy and program messages to their legislature and argue for their programs. In some states they can trade appointive jobs for legislative support, and they can also use their veto power to trade for votes. They can usually attract more public attention to their views than can any single legislator. Yet being the spokesperson for a policy does not guarantee success. Much depends on a governor's ability, political base, and personal popularity, as well as on the political situation in which he or she operates.

Some states have a long tradition of strong executive leadership. When governors have the support of powerful political organizations, as well as ample

constitutional authority, the chances for their success increases. The governors of Pennsylvania and New York, for example, have strong constitutional powers, and they usually have strong party organizations behind them, which enhance close ties with followers in their respective legislatures.[24] Figure 26–3 shows the current political party control of governorships.

The governor of Nevada has much less formal power than the governor of New York and carries less weight on the national political scene, yet within Nevada, control over jobs, contracts, and patronage enhance the governor's prestige. Governors of rural and smaller states generally have few other competing institutions or interests when exercising policy leadership.[25] "Powerful governors in large urbanized states have many others with whom they must compete—heads of major industries, media personalities, mayors of large cities, and even presidents of prestigious universities," comments political scientist Thad Beyle. "There are lots of big fish in a larger pond, which can mean that a governor may not be as powerful as it might first appear."[26]

Consider these two contrasting evaluations of the governorships in Maine and Mississippi:

- The governor is the central player in [Maine]. Notwithstanding the importance of legislative deliberations, the governor's place in the processes of both policy formulation and policy implementation is critical. In modern-day state government, the governor is the most visible state official, the figure most often in the news, and the person who commands the largest source of information through overseeing the state bureaucracy.[27]

- Mississippi's governor remained less powerful than the state legislature. The large number of independent boards and commissions and independently elected executive officials limits his ability to effectively manage the executive branch. It is easy for agency heads to "go native" and reflect the views of their co-workers and clients rather than those of the chief executive. . . . The office of governor in Mississippi has nevertheless become more influential in recent years.[28]

Balanced against a governor's formal powers are great obstacles, which may include a hostile legislature, cutbacks in federal funding, a depressed state economy,

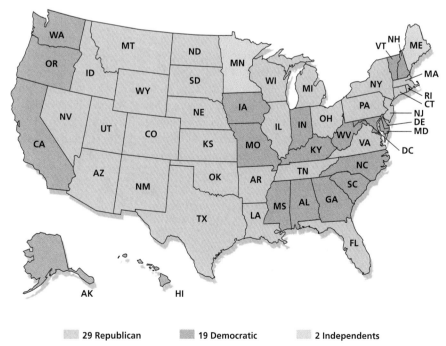

| 29 Republican | 19 Democratic | 2 Independents |

FIGURE 26–3 Party Control of the Governor's Office, 2001

corrupt party or administrative officials, regional tensions in the state (downstate versus upstate, east versus west, or urban versus rural), special interests and lobbyists, a cynical press, an indifferent or apathetic public, the sheer inertia of a vast bureaucracy, antiquated civil service systems, and the reluctance of most citizens to get involved.[29]

Some western governors complain that many of their state's problems are caused by absentee landlords or the national government, which together control much land in the West. The federal government owns 83 percent of Nevada, 68 percent of Alaska, 65 percent of Utah, and 53 percent of Oregon. This land is managed, regulated, and overseen by a score of federal agencies, such as the National Park Service, the Forest Service, the Bureau of Land Management, the Fish and Wildlife Service, and the Department of Defense. Governors of western states find they must constantly negotiate with these many federal agencies. In contrast, states east of the Rockies have only small amounts of land owned by the federal government. In Kansas and Maine, for example, less than 1 percent of the land is owned by the federal government.[30]

Governors also find they must become preoccupied with daily housekeeping tasks, and this focus often collides with their efforts to define long-range priorities. Former Vermont Governor Madeleine Kunin recalls she had to fix problems as they happened and yet simultaneously had to define her policy vision for the future. "Finding the time, energy, and perspective to carry out a dual strategy was to be the physical and mental challenge of governing."[31] Even though management duties occupy a fair amount of time, many governors consider these the least glamorous of their responsibilities (see Table 26–2).

Even though governors come to office hoping to introduce new programs and reforms, they often spend most of their time raising money just to keep things going; hence some governors are viewed as merely budget balancers rather than leaders or shapers of a state's future. The governor's role as leader of his or her political party also has an important impact on policy. The coalitions that governors form within their political parties help them put into effect the policies they desire. A governor's power increases in a state that has a competitive two-party system. In such a state, legislators of the governor's party are likely to work more closely with the governor to produce a successful legislative record.

Recent years have witnessed the election of a new breed of well-educated and able governors who have been effective in enlarging their policy-making roles: Tom Ridge in Pennsylvania, Gary Locke in Washington, Roy Barnes in Georgia, John Kitzhaber in Oregon, and Tommy Thompson in Wisconsin. Because many contemporary governors come to office with impressive legislative and administrative experience, they are more likely to be real executive heads of government, not mere figureheads. Some have initiated experimental welfare and job-training programs that have become models for others to emulate. Because states are now playing a larger role in planning and administering a wide range of social and economic programs, the managerial and planning ability of a governor is clearly important.

MANAGING THE STATE

Governors and their senior staffs perform a variety of functions:

- Provide strategic planning and vision
- Restructure ineffective programs and agencies
- Initiate policy
- Maintain a policy or position under pressure
- Settle disputes among different agencies

TABLE 26–2 How Governors Say They Spend Their Time	
Activity	Percent of Time Spent*
Managing state government	29%
Working with the legislature	16
Meeting the general public	14
Performing ceremonial functions	14
Working with press and media	9
Working with federal government	7
Working with local governments	7
Carrying out political activities	6†
Recruiting and appointing	6
Doing miscellaneous activities (staff, interstate, reading, phoning)	16

SOURCE: Thad L. Beyle, "The Governor as Chief Legislator," *State Government* (Winter 1978), p. 3.

*Totals do not add to 100 percent but are averages of the governors' estimates of the time they devoted to the particular activities. Percentages based on responses from those scheduling gubernatorial time in 40 states.

†Plainly, some governors understate time spent campaigning for reelection.

- Promote the state (attracting tourism, exports, investment)
- Recruit top state administrative and judicial officials
- Propose budget priorities and new revenue strategies
- Improve the quality of services rendered to the taxpayers
- Negotiate disputes with the federal government and with nearby states

Much recent federal legislation turning programs over to the states specifically designates the governor as the chief planning and administrative officer. This role has given governors both more flexibility and more headaches. On one hand, governors can now dispense federal funds as a form of patronage, supporting services and programs for influential professional and local communities. On the other hand, this new intergovernmental relations role requires more time, more staff, and constant negotiations both with the "feds" and with local interest group leaders vying for the money or services involved.

Who Runs the State?

Although most state civil servants are part of the executive branch, they are also subject to pressure from the legislature. Indeed, state legislators are often viewed by state employees as having more of an impact on key policy and budget decisions than governors have[32] (see Table 26–3). But as a general rule, governors enjoy a lot of influence. Some agencies are not as cooperative with their governors as governors would like. State agencies operate in a highly political culture, and sometimes bureaucrats are more responsive to interest groups, the legislature, or their own definitions of the public interest.

Some reformers have suggested that all state agencies should be accountable to the governor all the time, but others believe politics should be kept out of the day-to-day operations of a state agency. For example, how much influence should a governor have over the running of the department of corrections in a state? Should public agencies respond to fluctuations in public opinion or to a governor's political mood? Which policy decisions should be made by professionals and experts, and which should be controlled by elected officials or by partisan appointees?

Modernizing State Government

Governors in recent years have had more managerial control over their states as a result of the use of modern management techniques: strategic planning, systems analysis, and sophisticated information technology and budgeting systems. In fact, a

TABLE 26–3 Gubernatorial Versus Legislative Influence over State Administrative Agencies

		Governor	Legislature	Equal
Which exercises greater degree of control?	1984	42%	35%	23%
	1998	49	27	24
Who exercises more detailed review of agency budget requests?	1984	37	30	33
	1998	35	26	39
Who has greater tendency to reduce your budget?	1984	36	44	20
	1998	49	27	24

SOURCE: Deil S. Wright, from the 1998 data files of the American State Administrators Project, Institute for Research in Social Science, University of North Carolina.

Note: Questions were asked of top state administrators in all 50 states.

modern system of professional management has gradually replaced the old "buddy system" in which governors relied on political pals to get things done.

In urban states with competitive party systems—such as New York, Illinois, New Jersey, Pennsylvania, Washington, and California—governors have considerable formal constitutional authority to organize their administrations as they see fit. Even in more rural states, such as South Dakota, scores of agencies have been consolidated into a few comprehensive units as the result of executive orders from the governors.

A few years ago, in the wake of highly publicized scandals in the legislature, the South Carolina legislature agreed to abolish 75 state boards, folding them into 17 larger executive agencies. This restructuring also gave the governor the authority to hire and fire the directors of most of these agencies.[33]

During the past several decades various reformers have urged that the governor be made the true manager of the executive branch. The following principles of reorganization are often suggested:

1. Agencies should be consolidated and integrated into as few departments as possible, so that similar functions will be grouped together and the governor will be able to exercise real control.

2. Lines of responsibility should be fixed and definite.

3. Single executives are preferable to boards and commissions.

4. The governor should have power to appoint and remove subordinates, including officers now elected, with the possible exception of the auditor.

5. The governor should have control over budgeting, accounting, reporting, purchasing, personnel, and planning and should have the staff necessary to do these jobs.

However, attempts to reorganize state governments have not received universal praise. In some states reorganization commissions have submitted reports that were filed away and forgotten. Groups that profit from the existing structure can be counted upon to resist change. So, too, can officials who fear loss of job or prestige. Also, legislators are sometimes reluctant to approve recommendations that might make a governor too powerful.

Many critics oppose not so much the idea of reorganization as the basic principle of strengthening executive power and responsibility, which has dominated the reorganization movement. Often, they say, there is little evidence to support the adoption of these reforms, and there is a real danger that reorganizers are overlooking basic values in their concern with saving money. Intent on efficiency and economy, reformers often fail to foresee the risks involved in creating a powerful chief executive where no effective party or legislative opposition exists to keep a strong governor in check.

Reorganizers agree it is wrong to make changes without regard to local conditions and problems. However, they maintain that the basic ideas—integrated authority, centralized direction, simplified structure, clear responsibility—are sound. In fact, it is more likely that narrow special interests not responsible to the voters will take over government when the administrative structure is cumbersome, confusing, and too spread out. The legislature can more effectively supervise an administration integrated under the governor's control than one in which responsibility is split.

Effects of Reorganization

Although large savings have been realized through centralized purchasing and the adoption of modern money-management practices, it is difficult to measure the results of consolidating departments, strengthening the governor's control over the executive branch, or establishing the office of ombudsman to handle citizen complaints. However, the best-governed states do seem to be

Christine Todd Whitman, formerly governor of New Jersey, was named director of the Environmental Protection Administration by President George W. Bush.

Thinking It Through . . .

Clearly, any state agency such as a university that uses state tax revenues and provides services to citizens needs a certain amount of regulation and supervision by the people's representatives. The question is how much influence should a governor have? How much influence should a state agency have?

In the final analysis, the governor is accountable to the voters. A governor can be voted out of office, is subject to a recall (in several states), and can be impeached by the legislature. Agency heads can be removed by either the governor or the boards that supervise them. Ultimately, everyone who exercises public power is, in our complicated political system, held accountable for the way they exercise the power temporarily granted to them. It is often a seemingly messy rather than a tidy way of organizing leadership and accountability, yet generally it works.

those in which the administrative structure has been closely integrated under the governor.

Overall formal reorganization is not the only way states modify and modernize their governmental structures. Often they change in stages, copying innovations from other states. Certain states, in fact, serve as exporters of innovations. So does the federal government. When the federal government creates a Department of Housing and Urban Development, states often respond by creating similar departments; when the federal government establishes a Department of Transportation, so do several of the states; and when the federal government creates a special White House–level office for trade, many governors set up their own offices for trade and export responsibilities.

Although governors are more powerful today than they have ever been, vigorous gubernatorial direction of a state's bureaucracy is still more the exception than the rule. Some governors fail to exploit their powers of appointment or budget setting. "Governors also have other tasks than functioning as chief bureaucrat. . . . Bureaucratic complexity also discourages involvement. Given these realities, involvement with state bureaucracies is very much a matter of governors picking their spots."[34]

Several former governors—for example, Mario Cuomo in New York and Pete Wilson in California—experimented with private-sector reforms such as total quality management (TQM) and performance-based pay initiatives, but these reforms were opposed by public employee labor unions. Such proposals have also been viewed as impractical: "From TQM to vision statements to performance measurements to virtual organizations, the management theories and trends come thick and fast—faster than a lot of government employees can keep up with them."[35] Moreover, management reform often gets cast aside where one governor takes over from another, as when Republican Governor George E. Pataki replaced Democratic Governor Mario M. Cuomo in New York.

"Although the analogy between a governor and a private sector chief executive is apt," writes political scientist Thad Beyle, "governors have a distance to go before possessing comparable power of appointment and removal."[36] Many governors don't have the flexibility in hiring and firing personnel that business executives have, and they must share control with various boards, commissions, and elected officials.

In sum, governors can be influential in leading certain reforms and introducing management improvements, but they are rarely as influential and as effective as most citizens assume is the case. All kinds of constitutional, legal, and political restraints put brakes on their attempts to bring about fundamental change. Still, in good economic times, governors generally are able to begin new programs and improve the performance of existing state operations.

OTHER STATEWIDE ELECTED OFFICIALS

Other executive officials elected by the people in most states include the lieutenant governor, secretary of state, attorney general, treasurer, and auditor (see Table 26–4).

Lieutenant Governor

Forty-two states have a lieutenant governor, a post similar to vice-president at the national level. In nearly half the states the lieutenant governor is elected on the same ticket as the governor, and in those states the job is indeed like that of the vice-president—the job and its influence depend very much on the mood of the governor. In 26 states, the

TABLE 26–4 Number of State Elected Officials	
Governor	50
Attorney general	43
Lieutenant governor	43*
State treasurer	39
Secretary of state	36
State auditor	16
Superintendent of education	12
Agriculture commissioner	10
Comptroller	13
Insurance commissioner	8

SOURCE: *The Book of the States, 2000–2001* (Council of State Governments, 2000), p. 33. Copyright by the Council of State Governments. Reprinted with permission.

*In Alaska, Hawaii, and Utah, one elected official serves as both lieutenant governor and secretary of state. In Tennessee there is no lieutenant governor, but the Speaker of the state senate has the additional statutory title of "lieutenant governor."

lieutenant governor presides over the state senate. In 39 states, the lieutenant governor becomes governor or acting governor in case of the death, disability, or absence of the governor from the state. Doubtless for this reason, more governors have sprung from this office than from other statewide elective offices. For example, in 2000 two lieutenant governors were elected governor: Judy Martz of Montana and Ruth Ann Minner of Delaware. And the lieutenant governor in Texas, Rick Perry, became governor there when George W. Bush moved to the White House.

In states where the governor and lieutenant governor are elected on the same ticket, the lieutenant governor is likely to be given some significant responsibilities. Still, many lieutenant governors have no statutory duties, and in some smaller states, being lieutenant governor is really a part-time job. In the states where the lieutenant governor is elected independently of the governor, the lieutenant governor can sometimes be a member of the opposition party, and he or she can become a thorn in the side of the chief executive. In states like Texas, where the lieutenant governor is elected separately, the lieutenant governor is sometimes as politically powerful as the governor.[37]

Are lieutenant governors really necessary? Eight states are doing without one. If the job they perform best is assuming the governor's job in case of death, resignation, or impeachment, the replacement function could be performed by a state's attorney general, secretary of state, or the ranking member of the governor's party in the legislature.

Although the position of lieutenant governor has worked well in some states, the view persists that lieutenant governors are often in search of job assignments that make them look important. The staffs and cabinets that are currently growing up around governors make the governor's chief of staff more of a deputy governor than most lieutenant governors. Moreover, many candidates for lieutenant governor appear to seek the post primarily for the name recognition and statewide experience to advance their political careers. In sum, the value to the state of the often obscure office of lieutenant governor is debatable.[38]

Attorney General

The attorney general—the state's chief lawyer—gives advice to state officials, represents the state before the courts, and in some states supervises local prosecutors. Some have real authority over local prosecutors and may prosecute cases on their own initiative, although in most states prosecution of criminals remains under the control of the local county prosecutor. In many states, attorneys general have taken the lead as champions of the consumer and protectors of the environment. They have launched major investigations into the insurance industry and into business practices. They have also led the fight against the tobacco companies and have waged antitrust investigations against corporations such as Microsoft. The office is sometimes a stepping-stone to the governorship.[39]

Disputes between attorneys general and governors can be partisan if they belong to different parties or have conflicting ambitions, but disputes can also be issue oriented. Thus governors in many states have their own staff lawyers to represent them in contests with attorneys general.

Secretary of State

The secretary of state publishes the laws, supervises elections, and issues certificates of incorporation. In some states the secretary issues automobile licenses and registers corporate securities. Voters in 36 states elect secretaries of state. In eight states governors appoint people to this position. In three states secretaries of state are elected by the legislature. And three states don't have this position at all.

This office is sometimes the dumping ground for jobs that do not seem to belong to any other office and are not important enough to justify setting up a new agency. Yet several secretaries of state in recent years have modernized voter registration procedures or sponsored campaign finance and disclosure reforms. For example, former Illinois Secretary of State Jim Edgar (whose office regulated motor vehicles) used a campaign against drunk driving to help propel himself into the governor's office.

Treasurer and Auditor

The treasurer is the guardian of the state's money. Although in some states the job is largely ministerial, state treasurers generally have the responsibility of ensuring that cash is available to meet the obligations of the state and that all available funds are invested to maximize interest return. Texas recently abolished the position.

The auditor in most states has two major jobs: to authorize payments from the state treasury and to make periodic audits of officials who handle state money. In Montana the state auditor serves as an insurance commissioner. Before money can be spent, the auditor must sign a *warrant* certifying that the expenditure is authorized by law and that the money is available in the treasury. This job is more accurately called the *preaudit* and is increasingly being assigned to a comptroller appointed by and responsible to the governor. Auditing *after* money has been spent, however, is a job that most believe should be given to an officer responsible to the legislature. Even advocates of much more centralized administration believe the auditor should not be responsible to the governor.

Other Officials

This category may include superintendent of public education, agriculture commissioner, public utilities commissioner, comptroller, and insurance commissioner. These positions are less likely to be elected than treasurers or auditors. Putting positions like these on the ballot results in a longer ballot and voter fatigue; in one instance as many as 50 percent of those who went to the polls failed to vote for superintendent of public instruction. Proliferation of elected officials also makes it more difficult for governors to manage and lead state government. Think of the kinds of challenges a president of the United States would face if the secretary of defense and the head of the Environmental Protection Agency were elected rather than appointed!

As part of the trend toward integrated administration, the duties of elected state officials have generally been limited to those specified in the state constitution. Some important functions have been given to officials appointed by the governor. In many states the budget director appointed by the governor has a more important role than the elected treasurer or secretary of state. Yet elected officers can often control patronage, attract a following, and thus develop a political base from which to attack the governor's program and administration.

Sometimes progressive and controversial initiatives in state governments come from elected officials. An attorney general in Texas helped design and pass the Texas Open Records Act, one of the broadest and most strictly enforced freedom-of-information statutes in the country. A secretary of state in Massachusetts modernized election laws, helped enact campaign finance laws, and championed conflict-of-interest reforms. A state treasurer in Colorado battled to transfer some of his state's revenue deposits from a few large Denver banks to smaller banks around the state and devised incentives for these banks to loan money to students and small businesses and to support low-income housing and family farms.

A Closer Look

JESSE VENTURA ON GOVERNING

Jesse Ventura—former Navy seal, former wrestler, former radio talk-show host, and former mayor of Brooklyn Park, Minnesota—was elected governor of Minnesota in November 1998 on the Reform party ticket. He expressed his sometimes outrageous opinions on life in general and politics in particular in a book titled *I Ain't Got Time to Bleed:*

"I didn't need this job. I ran for governor to find out if the American dream still exists. . . . I'm happy to say that it does. I'm living proof that the myths aren't true. The candidate with the most money isn't always the one who wins. You don't have to be a career politician to serve in public office. . . . You don't even have to be a Democrat or Republican. . . . The will of the people is still the most powerful force in our government. We can put whomever we choose into office, simply by exercising that will."

"I'm under constant scrutiny by the people, by the press, and by security. From the moment capitol security came in and encircled me on election night, I've felt a little bit like a prisoner.

I've never had this many restrictions in my life. I can't leave my home without my 'protection.'. . . I had no idea how much it would change my life on a daily basis."

"I've kept all of my promises: I got Minnesotans their tax rebate, I lowered taxes for working folks, I cut classroom size and increased education funding, and I started laying the groundwork for long-term plans like a unicameral legislature, a law-review year every four years, and Minnesota's Big Plan of smart government and self-sufficiency."

"I'm no political science major, but I don't believe that government has to be that complicated. If it did, there could be no such thing as a government of, by, and for the people. Frankly, I think working-class people haven't had enough folks in office who can understand their needs and can speak with them instead of speaking down to them."

"The American media are suffering from very serious problems, and now I've seen them first-hand. They have the most

Governor Jesse Ventura

twisted set of biases I've ever seen. . . . As their whipping-boy-of-choice, I've been in a unique position to see what the media have become. There are a few honorable exceptions, but for the most part, they're corrupt, shameless, and irresponsible as hell."

SOURCE: Jesse Ventura, *I Ain't Got Time to Bleed* (Signet, 2000), pp. 1, 239, 280–81, 296–97.

THE REWARDS OF BEING A GOVERNOR

No one thinks governors have an easy job. Yet most governors earn praise for their leadership, and most governors enjoy solid public approval ratings.[40] Recent governors—Zell Miller of Georgia, Robert Ray of Iowa, Bob Graham of Florida, Dan Evans of Washington, Richard Riley of South Dakota, and Cecil Andrus of Idaho—became popular despite the political "heat" and the need to make tough decisions. "A governor achieves his personal best by being honest and by staying in touch with the people who elected him to serve them," says former Governor Lamar Alexander of Tennessee.[41] Former Governor Tom Kean of New Jersey echoed similar thoughts: "I have tried to show during my political career, and especially my years as governor, that responsible government can meet people's needs and bring them together, that government can make a difference in the way we live."[42]

Who are the best governors? A popular former governor of Utah, the late Scott Matheson, wrote that they have been the men and women who have the right combination of values "for quality service, the courage to stick to their convictions, even when in the minority, integrity by instinct, compassion by nature, leadership by perception, and the character to admit wrong, and when necessary, to accept defeat."[43]

POLITICS ONLINE

Why Elect Auditors, Treasurers, and Secretaries of State?

One of the distinctive features of American politics is our penchant to elect officers in the executive branch at the state level. Unlike the federal level, where we elect only the president and vice-president, at the state level we elect lieutenant governors, auditors, treasurers, attorneys general, and secretaries of state. In some states, like Washington, voters elect a state insurance commissioner, while in California voters elect the superintendent of public instruction. What do all these people do? Why do voters elect them at the same time they elect a chief executive—the governor?

To learn more about each of these positions, go to the home page of one or more of these officers in your state. You can do this by going to: www.yahoo.com and then proceed to: regional, U.S. States, chose a state, government, elected and appointed officials. From here you can choose the officer—governor, attorney general, etc. Compare the home page of your state's governor by going through the same steps for your home state. Many of these officers have national associations, such as the national association of attorneys general. You can learn about these national associations by going to: www.nga.org/ for governors, www.naag.org for attorneys general, www.nass.org for secretaries of state, and www.nast.org for state treasurers.

As you read about these different positions, assess the implications for politics and policy of having so many independently elected state executives. An example of a topic you might examine is the tobacco litigation brought by several attorneys general. Having won a $368 billion settlement, governors and legislators now want some say in how this money will be spent. You will get different perspectives on the tobacco settlement and other issues as you study these different state executives.

SUMMARY

1. The job of governor is one of the most important and exacting in American political life. Governors are usually white male lawyers in their 40s. At least three out of four governors who run again win reelection.

2. Today a governor is expected to be the state's chief policy maker, the architect of the state budget, the chief manager of the state administration, and the political and symbolic leader in the state. The governor also plays an increasingly complex role as the crucial link between the national and local governments. In short, governors are asked to accomplish miracles in this era of scarce resources and rising demands.

3. Governors have many formal powers. The most important are their appointive

and budgetary powers. Governors also have veto and pardon powers and the power to issue executive orders. They are commanders in chief of the national guard. But a governor's formal powers mean little if he or she is not a persuasive communicator with good judgment and the capacity to focus simultaneously on daily tasks and long-range priorities. Governors who are effective help set the policy agenda and frame the debate on important public issues. Yet governors, as a general rule, have more responsibility than power.

4. Over the past generation, reforms in management and organization have strengthened most governorships. Most governors have gained powers that enable them to achieve more of their goals. But constitutional, legal, and

political restraints continue to limit their efforts. Thus few governors have an easy tenure, and it is generally agreed that public demands and expectations on governors today are higher than ever.

5. In addition to a governor, the voters in most states also elect other statewide officials such as a lieutenant governor, secretary of state, attorney general, and state treasurer. In about half of the states the governor and lieutenant governor run as a team ticket, but elsewhere this is not the case and all other statewide elected officials run separately. Many of the officials play important political and policy roles in their states, and about a third of the current governors previously served in some other statewide elected capacity.

KEY TERMS

veto 580

item veto 582

reduction veto 582

amendatory veto 582

executive order 582

FURTHER READING

LAMAR ALEXANDER, *Steps Along the Way: A Governor's Scrapbook* (Thomas Nelson Publishers, 1986).

CECIL ANDRUS AND JOEL CONNELLY, *Cecil Andrus: Politics Western Style* (Sasquatch Books, 1998).

THAD L. BEYLE, ED., *Governors and Hard Times* (Congressional Quarterly Press, 1992).

THAD L. BEYLE AND LYNN R. MUCHMORE, EDS., *Being Governor: Views from the Office* (Duke University Press, 1983).

THOMAS M. CARSEY, *Campaign Dynamics: The Race for Governor* (University of Michigan Press, 2000).

THOMAS E. CRONIN AND ROBERT D. LOEVY, *Colorado Politics and Government* (University of Nebraska Press, 1993).

ROBERT S. ERIKSON ET AL., *Statehouse Democracy: Public Opinion and Policy in the American States* (Cambridge University Press, 1993).

EARL H. FRY, *The Expanding Role of State and Local Governments in U.S. Foreign Affairs* (Council on Foreign Relations Press, 1998).

VIRGINIA GRAY, RUSSELL HANSON, AND HERBERT JACOB, EDS., *Politics in the American States: A Comparative Analysis*, 7th ed. (Congressional Quarterly Press, 1999).

THOMAS H. KEAN, *The Politics of Inclusion* (Free Press, 1988).

MADELEINE M. KUNIN, *Living a Political Life* (Vintage, 1995).

GERALD C. LUBENOW AND BRUCE E. CAIN, EDS., *Governing California* (Institute of Governmental Studies Press, University of California, 1997).

SARAH M. MOREHOUSE, *The Governor as Party Leader* (University of Michigan, 1998).

DAVID OSBORNE, *Laboratories of Democracy: A New Breed of Governor Creates Models for National Growth* (Harvard Business School Press, 1988).

GEORGE PATAKI WITH DANIEL PAISNER, *Pataki: An Autobiography* (Viking, 1998).

ALAN ROSENTHAL, *Governors and Legislatures: Contending Powers* (Congressional Quarterly Press, 1990).

LARRY SABATO, *Goodbye to Good-Time Charlie: The American Governor Transformed*, 2d ed. (Congressional Quarterly Press, 1983).

SUE THOMAS AND CLYDE WILCOX, *Women and Elective Office* (Oxford University Press, 1998).

TOMMY G. THOMPSON, *Power to the People: An American State at Work* (HarperCollins, 1996).

JESSE VENTURA, *Do I Stand Alone?* (Pocket Books, 2000).

JESSE VENTURA, *I Ain't Got Time to Bleed* (Signet, 2000).

See also the quarterly *Spectrum: The Journal of State Government; Governing; State Policy Reports;* and *State Government News;* see also the valuable University of Nebraska Press series on state politics in the individual states, each of which has a chapter on governors.

The National Governors' Association publishes a variety of surveys, reports, and studies, including a weekly *Governors' Bulletin* and the *Proceedings of the National Governors' Association* annual meetings. These and related documents can be purchased by writing to the National Governors' Association, 444 N. Capitol Street, NW, Washington, D.C. 20001.

27

JUDGES
AND JUSTICE
IN THE STATES

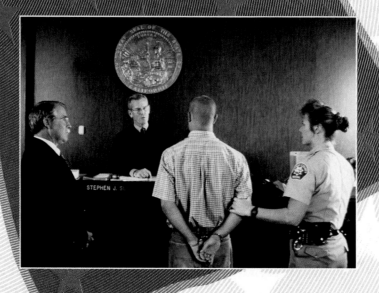

DO YOU KNOW THE NAME OF THE CHIEF JUSTICE OF YOUR STATE SUPREME COURT? PROBABLY NOT. YOU ARE NOT ALONE—ABOUT 99 PERCENT OF YOUR FELLOW CITIZENS don't either! Although you hear more about federal judges than about their state counterparts, the 28,000 state and municipal judges conduct most of the nation's judicial business. Most of these judges are white males, but this imbalance is changing rapidly. Nationwide there are about 5,000 women state court judges, about one in five.[1] State judges preside over most criminal trials, settle most lawsuits between individuals, and administer most estates. They also interpret state laws and play a vital role in determining who gets what, where, when, and how. Thus they have a crucial role in making public policy.

State judges have the final say—most of the time. Through **writs of *habeas corpus***—petitions to federal courts alleging that petitioners are being held by a state as the result of a proceeding that denies them due process of law in violation of the U.S. Constitution—criminal defendants may occasionally get federal district judges to review the actions of state courts. Or if state judges have to interpret the meaning of the U.S. Constitution, or a national law, or a national treaty—that is, if the case raises a *federal question*—the losing party may request the U.S. Supreme Court to review the decision of the highest state court to which it may be taken under state law. Of the hundreds of thousands of decisions by state judges each year, however, only a few are reviewed by the United States Supreme Court.

In recent decades, state courts have become more prominent in the political life of their state. In many states, in what is called **new judicial federalism**, judges have interpreted the bill of rights in their state constitution more rigorously than has the U.S. Supreme Court in applying the national Bill of Rights, for example, with respect to the rights of gays and lesbians.[2] There has also been a revolution in **tort law**—law relating to injuries to person, reputation, or property. This "tort revolution" has flooded state courts as more people sue more often about more disputes: for example, *product liability suits* brought by people who believe they have been injured as the result of faulty products, and *malpractice suits* brought by people who believe they have been injured as the result of mistakes by doctors, hospitals, lawyers, and other professionals. And there have been notable increases in cases relating to property rights and to breach of contract cases. However, there has recently been a reaction against the explosion of tort filings, and in many states legislative tort "reform" has made it more difficult to bring lawsuits.

CHAPTERMEDIA

 POLITICS ONLINE
Electronic Justice
www.prenhall.com/burns

There has also been a significant increase in criminal cases as people press for tougher action against criminals. Many states have passed so-called "three-strikes-and-you're-out" laws, which result in the mandatory imposition of life sentences after three felony convictions. These felony cases are threatening to overwhelm our courts and our prisons.

As state courts have become more active in our political life, state judges have become embroiled in controversial issues. And as the public has grown more sophisticated about the importance of judges as policy makers, judicial politics in the states has become a significant feature of the political landscape.

THE STRUCTURE OF STATE COURTS

Each state has its own court system. Because the 50 systems vary, it is difficult to generalize about them. For convenience we categorize and discuss state courts as (1) minor courts of limited jurisdiction, (2) trial courts of general jurisdiction, and (3) appellate courts (see Figure 27–1).

Minor Courts

In most states minor courts handle **misdemeanors**—the less serious violations of state and local laws—traffic cases, and civil suits involving relatively small amounts of money. In some places they also hold preliminary hearings and set bail for more serious charges. **Felonies** are serious crimes, the penalty for which can range from death to imprisonment in a penitentiary for more than a year. Decisions of these courts may be appealed and in most instances tried *de novo*—that is, tried all over again without reference to what happened in the minor court. In most places these courts are financed and administered by the local unit of government: the township, the city, or the county. In cities, these minor courts are known as *municipal courts* and are often divided into traffic courts, domestic relations courts, small claims courts, and police courts. Paid *magistrates* trained in the law preside over most of these courts.

writ of *habeas corpus*
Court order directing any person having a person in custody to produce the prisoner and explain to a judge why the prisoner is being held.

new judicial federalism
The practice whereby state courts use the bill of rights in their state constitution to provide more protection for some rights than is provided by the Supreme Court's interpretation of the Bill of Rights in the U.S. Constitution.

tort law
Law relating to injuries to person, reputation, or property.

misdemeanor
A minor crime; the penalty is a fine or imprisonment for a short time, usually less than a year in a local jail.

felony
A serious crime, the penalty for which can range from death to imprisonment in a penitentiary for more than a year.

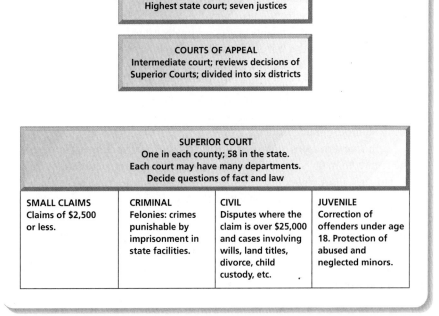

CALIFORNIA SUPREME COURT
Highest state court; seven justices

COURTS OF APPEAL
Intermediate court; reviews decisions of Superior Courts; divided into six districts

SUPERIOR COURT
One in each county; 58 in the state.
Each court may have many departments.
Decide questions of fact and law

SMALL CLAIMS	CRIMINAL	CIVIL	JUVENILE
Claims of $2,500 or less.	Felonies: crimes punishable by imprisonment in state facilities.	Disputes where the claim is over $25,000 and cases involving wills, land titles, divorce, child custody, etc.	Correction of offenders under age 18. Protection of abused and neglected minors.

FIGURE 27–1 The California State Courts

SOURCE: Guide to California Courts: www.courtinfo.ca.gov/reference/guide.

Although traditional justices of peace courts are being phased out, the *justice of the peace* system survives in some states (Arizona, Arkansas, Delaware, Louisiana, Montana, Texas, and Wyoming), especially in rural areas. Justices of the peace are elected for short terms. They need not be trained in the law, and they usually serve from two to six years. Their authority is limited to performing marriages, notarizing papers, handling traffic violations, and hearing misdemeanors, usually those involving fines of less than $200. They also hear minor civil disputes. Because plaintiffs can often choose among several justices of the peace in a county, they may pick the one most likely to decide in their favor. Thus it has been said JP stands for "Judgment for the Plaintiff."

Courts handling minor crimes are often so crowded that cases are "processed" with little time for individual attention. While many critics of the legal system contend that judges are too lenient and those accused of crime are back on the streets too quickly, others charge that poor and ignorant defendants often spend days in jail waiting for their cases to come to trial.

A new and apparently effective reform is the establishment of *court-watching groups*. In some cities these groups are sponsored by organizations concerned with seeing that the courts treat those charged with crimes fairly. In other cities, groups are sponsored by organizations concerned that judges are too easy on defendants. Prosecutors, public defenders, and judges, it is alleged, become a comfortable work group, with little or no public scrutiny. Court watchers make these professionals more sensitive to the views of the general public.

Trial Courts of General Jurisdiction

Trial courts where cases first appear (**original jurisdiction**) are called county courts, circuit courts, superior courts, district courts, and common pleas courts. They administer common, criminal, equity, and statutory law. Some states maintain separate courts for criminal and civil matters. States generally also have special *probate courts* to administer estates and handle related matters. These courts are all *courts of record* in which trials take place, witnesses are heard, and juries render verdicts, although most cases are heard and decided by a judge. *Appellate courts* may review decisions of trial courts; most decisions of trial judges are not reviewed, however, and become final. There is growing recognition that these courts do more than apply the law; they also participate in the never-ending process of shaping the law.[3]

Appellate Courts

In a few states—Delaware, Montana, New Hampshire, Nevada, North Dakota, Rhode Island, West Virginia, and Vermont—appeals from trial courts are carried directly to the state supreme court. (In North Dakota the Supreme Court can assign cases to a court of appeals composed of three judges chosen from among the trial judges.) Most states, however, have intermediate appeals courts that fit into the system in much the same way that the United States courts of appeals fit into the federal structure.

All states have a *court of last resort*, usually called the Supreme Court. In Maine the court of last resort is called the Supreme Judicial Court; in Maryland and New York this court is called the Court of Appeals; in West Virginia it is the Supreme Court of Appeals. And, if that is not confusing enough, in New York the trial courts are called Supreme Courts. Texas and Oklahoma have two courts of last resort—a Supreme Court that handles civil matters and a Court of Criminal Appeals.

Unless a federal question is involved, state supreme courts are the highest tribunal to which a case may be carried. State courts of last resort have from five to nine judges; most have seven. Each state court has developed its own method of operating, with the pattern and practices varying widely among the states. Of the more than

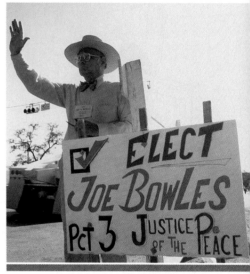

In some states, justices of the peace still run for office. They handle many lesser legal transactions and need not be trained lawyers.

original jurisdiction
The authority of a trial court to hear a case "in the first instance."

Due to an overcrowded prison system, I'm sentencing you to stand in that corner for the next six months."

The Wall Street Journal.

60,000 decisions by state supreme courts, only 2 percent are appealed to the U.S. Supreme Court, which reviews even fewer of them.[4]

All state judges of all state courts take an oath to uphold the supremacy of the U.S. Constitution, and all state judges have the power of **judicial review**. That is, they may refuse to enforce, and may restrain state and local officials from enforcing, state laws or regulations or actions if they conclude that these conflict with the state constitution or the U.S. Constitution. State judges may also declare actions of federal officials or federal laws or regulations to be in conflict with the U.S. Constitution, subject to final review by the U.S. Supreme Court.

State Courts and State Politics

Judges are a much more prominent part of the American political scene, at both the national and state levels, than are judges in any other democracy. But state courts differ from federal courts in the following ways:

1. State judges are more involved in the affairs of their legislative and executive branches than the U.S. Supreme Court is involved in congressional and presidential matters.[5] State judges are likely to be part of the state's legal culture since most such judges have been educated in the state's law schools.[6]

2. State judges are unconstrained by the doctrine of federalism in dealing with local units of government.

3. State judges are much less constrained than federal courts from hearing cases brought by taxpayers. In federal courts persons lack *standing to sue*—the legal right to sue—unless they show some immediate injury. In fact, in nine states the state supreme court can give advisory opinions at the request of the governor or state legislature. An **advisory opinion** is an opinion unrelated to a particular case that gives a court's view about a constitutional or legal issue.

4. State judges have greater freedom than do most federal judges. Unlike federal judges, most state judges serve for limited terms and stand for election, so they can claim to be representatives of the people. "As elected representatives, like legislators, they feel less hesitant to offer their policy views than do appointed judges."[7] In addition, if there is dissatisfaction with a decision of a state supreme court, it can be more readily set aside than can a decision of the U.S. Supreme Court.[8]

HOW JUDGES ARE CHOSEN

Judges are selected in four different ways (see Figure 27–2):

1. Appointment by the governor
2. Election by the legislature
3. Popular election
4. A modified appointment plan known as the Missouri Plan.

Appointment by the Governor and Election by the Legislature

In Delaware, Hawaii, Maine, New Jersey, New York, and Vermont, judges are appointed by the governor and confirmed by the state senate. In Delaware and Massachusetts, governors select appointees from names submitted by judicial nominating commissions. Election by the legislature is the constitutional practice in Connecticut, Rhode Island, South Carolina, and Virginia. However, we need to look beyond the formal election procedures. "A majority of the judges serving in states utilizing an elective judiciary . . . are in fact initially appointed by the governor to fill mid-term vacancies, usually occasioned by the retirement or death of sitting

judicial review
The power of a court to refuse to enforce a law or a government regulation that in the opinion of the judges conflicts with the Constitution, or, in a state court, that conflicts with the state constitution.

advisory opinion
An opinion unrelated to a particular case that gives a court's view about a constitutional or legal issue.

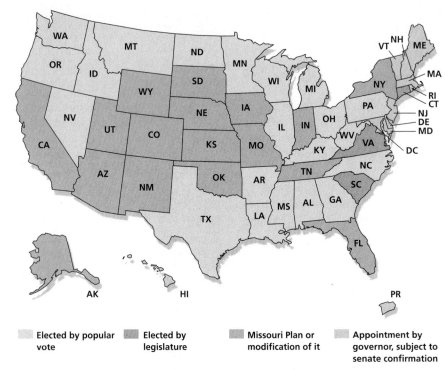

Elected by popular vote

Elected by legislature

Missouri Plan or modification of it

Appointment by governor, subject to senate confirmation

FIGURE 27–2 Method for Selection of Judges of the Court of Last Resort

SOURCE: *The Book of the States, 2000–2001.*

judges . . . and these appointed judges are overwhelmingly favored in their first electoral bids following appointment."[9]

In addition to the formal process of nomination and selection, there is an informal process with some combination of the following: lawyers interested in becoming judges make their interest known either directly or indirectly to party officials; leaders of the local bar associations often promote favored members; various members of the bar seek out candidates and recruit them; political leaders and interest groups also participate. Following such suggestions, the names go through the formal process of appointment.[10]

Check out **www.constitutionproject.org** for the website of a nonpartisan group dedicated to protecting the independence of courts from partisan political attacks, for a list of events in states, and for attempts to establish standards of conduct for judicial candidates. See also the site of the Brennan Center's Project on Judicial Independence at the New York University Law School, **www.brennancenter.org**. You can also subscribe to its biweekly e-mail list to get summaries of news stories relating to judicial independence, judicial elections, and judicial appointments. Another valuable site for information about courts is that of the American Judicature Society: **www.ajs.org**.

Popular Election

Judges are chosen by elections in which the voters choose among judicial candidates in nearly half the states, some of which, mostly in the West and upper Midwest, hold *nonpartisan* primaries for nominating judicial candidates and elect them on nonpartisan ballots. That a ballot is nonpartisan does not necessarily mean that political parties are not involved. In at least half the nonpartisan elections, parties actively campaign on behalf of candidates. Some states try to isolate judicial elections from partisanship by holding them separately from other elections. However, more than 80 percent of state judges face elections, these days increasingly contentious ones.[11]

A Closer Look

STANDARDS OF CONDUCT FOR JUDICIAL CANDIDATES

Citizens for Independent Courts (a program of the Constitution Project) has developed standards that will encourage judicial candidates to seek the "higher ground" in their campaigns. The Higher Ground Standards create a yardstick against which all candidates can be judged. The standards were developed with the assistance of former judges, legal scholars, and good government groups. Almost all of them can be found in judicial canons that govern the behavior of judges. However, the Higher Ground Standards distill volumes of "legalese" into a few concise and easy-to-understand principles.

Judges Are Not Politicians

Judicial candidates should not be political candidates in the traditional sense. Political candidates are expected to represent the interests of a geographically defined group of people. They are expected to be partisan and favor a political party and certain interest groups. As a qualification for election, voters expect them to declare their positions on controversial public policy issues in advance. As surprising as it may sound to some, judges do not, or at least should not, do any of these things.

Judges do not represent constituents. They represent the law. Their decisions must be based upon an informed and good faith interpretation of the law and the Constitution, not popular opinion or special interests. Judicial candidates should not support any political or ideological agenda. They should not declare in advance how they would decide a case, since the facts are different in each case. Such a declaration would be the equivalent of an umpire calling a pitch before it's thrown.

The Right to Impartial Justice

If you enter a courtroom as a litigant, you have a right to expect three things:

- That the judge is impartial.
- That the judge is fair.
- That the judge is knowledgeable about the law.

Wouldn't it be distressing if you had a case before a judge who had expressed an opposing position on cases such as yours during his or her campaign? Wouldn't it be equally disconcerting to know that your opponent in the case was a major campaign contributor to the judge? Of course it would. Justice that is absolutely impartial is a cornerstone of democracy. And yet these scenarios are played out in many courtrooms daily. If justice is to remain impartial, the rulings of judges must be independent of popular opinion and political pressure.

Higher Ground Standards for Judicial Candidates

Courts are often the last and best hope for the redress of grievances and the realization of justice. They protect the general welfare from those seeking privileged advantage and preserve individual rights from the heavy hand of government. Our courts can decide cases fairly only when judges are free to make decisions according to the law and constitutional principles, without regard to political or public pressure.

Because of the unique role of judges in our democratic system, candidates for judicial offices must be held to higher standards than are candidates for other elected offices. Thus, judicial candidates must not only be unbiased and impartial; they must avoid any appearance of bias or impropriety. Therefore:

1. Candidates should refrain from making promises about how they will decide issues that may come before them as judges, since it would be improper for them to prejudge a case.

2. Candidates should solicit or accept campaign funds only through an official campaign committee.

3. Candidates should disclose publicly each contributor's name, occupation, and the amount of any contribution of $100 or more (or the amount specified by state law if it is lower) within five days of the donation.

4. Candidates should take responsibility for all advertising, statements, and other campaigning done on their behalf by staff and supporters, and should condemn all campaigning on their behalf that is misleading or unfair.

5. Candidates should not make misleading or unfair references to opponents or misrepresent their records.

6. Candidates should conduct themselves in a manner that promotes public confidence in the integrity, independence, and impartiality of the judiciary.

A judge's position is one of great and sacred trust. Judicial candidates should adhere to these and all principles that uphold the dignity of the courts, promote judicial independence, and avoid even the appearance of partiality.

For more information contact: the Constitution Project, 50 F Street, NW, Suite 1070, Washington, D.C. 20001 (www.constitutionproject.org).

In 1986 California amended its constitution to forbid political parties from endorsing candidates for judicial offices. Since then the federal courts have declared the proposition unconstitutional, and California political parties are once again endorsing judicial candidates. These courts apparently endorsed the view of Justice Thurgood Marshall that "the prospect that voters might be persuaded by party endorsements is not a *corruption* of the democratic political process; it *is* the democratic political process."[12]

JUDICIAL CAMPAIGNS AND ISSUES   Most states have adopted provisions similar to the American Bar Association's code of judicial conduct that banning judicial candidates from telling the electorate anything about their views on legal and political matters—whether they are in favor, for example, of punishing criminals harshly or of expanding privacy rights. This restriction is designed to keep judges from making promises on how they will decide future cases. Other states have gone further; the Minnesota Supreme Court, for example, issued Canon 5, which prohibits judicial candidates from soliciting campaign contributions, declaring their political affiliation, seeking party endorsement, or attending precinct caucuses.[13] The Minnesota Republican party's challenge to this canon is currently before the courts, as candidates and others have begun to object to these laws as limiting their constitutional right to speak and restricting the voter's right to know how candidates stand on legal and political questions. "Rulings by state and federal courts in Alabama, Georgia, Michigan, Ohio, and other states have become a roadblock for efforts to curb the increasingly raucous nature of judicial politics."[14]

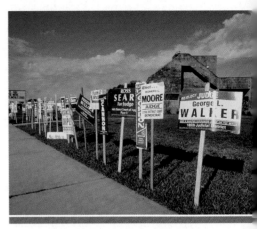

In states with elected judges, campaigns can become very competitive.

Until recently, there was little interest in judicial elections, and voter turnout tended to be low. But judicial elections are becoming increasingly spirited.[15] Special interest groups are focusing attention on judges whose decisions they find objectionable. The issues vary from election to election and from state to state. In some states the issue has been the death penalty. In Texas and California, efforts to limit liability lawsuits and damage awards led to campaign clashes over judicial candidates, with trial lawyers, consumers, and union groups on one side and business interests on the other. In Idaho one candidate for the Supreme Court campaigned on a platform that the theory of evolution could not be true—and won. In Wisconsin the chief justice won reelection, although she had to fight for her seat and felt compelled to explain why she had once allowed an aerobics class in the court's hearing room. An Illinois judge was unseated because of his decisions in abortion cases. In Ohio a Republican "traditional-conservative" candidate and a more liberal Democratic incumbent battled for a seat on a court in which the ideological balance on many issues had been split 4 to 3. The campaign drew national attention and major spending by business groups on one side and union groups on the other.[16] Judges now have to act like politicians and "feel they are under increasing pressure to be accountable to public opinion."[17] "The image of impartiality in the courts" may well be "a casualty of the new judicial politics."[18]

The costs of judicial elections have escalated. Critics charge that this need to raise large sums for their campaigns compromises judges and judicial candidates. Judicial campaigns have been especially expensive in Texas, North Carolina, and Pennsylvania. In Ohio more than $5 million was spent for a bitterly contested seat for the state supreme court, and the trend is even visible in relatively rural states such as Arkansas.[19] Nevada features attack ads and increasingly expensive campaigns, with judicial candidates turning to the gambling casinos for campaign contributions.[20] In many states that continue to elect judges, it is increasingly clear that judicial candidates are dependent on a small number of law firms or special interests for their campaign funds.

MINORITY REPRESENTATION   The one-person, one-vote rule that applies to legislative elections does not apply to judicial elections.[21] States may create judicial districts so that one judge "represents" many more voters than another judge. However, although there is no requirement that states elect judges, if they choose to do so, the federal Voting Rights Act of 1965 applies to these judicial elections.[22]

Because the Voting Rights Act of 1965 forbids any practice or procedure that dilutes the voting power of minorities, it raises the question about the constitutionality of at-large judicial elections. When judges are elected at-large for a city or a state, African American and Hispanic candidates sometimes find it difficult to

Since the passage of the Voting Rights Act of 1965, minorities have had greater opportunities to be elected judges.

WE THE PEOPLE

Minority Judges in the United States, 1997

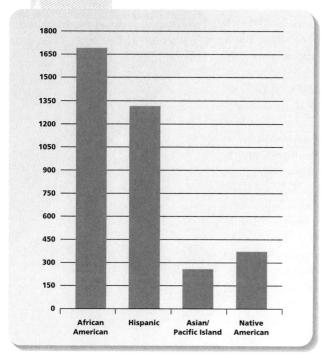

| | African American | Hispanic | Asian/Pacific Island | Native American |

SOURCE: *The Directory of Minority Judges of the United States*, 2d ed. (American Bar Association, 1997).

get elected. African American and Hispanic voters tend to be concentrated in the inner cities or in certain geographic areas; thus their impact is diluted in citywide or statewide elections. For example, in a state in which the population consists of 20 percent African American voters, 20 percent Hispanic voters, and 60 percent Anglo voters, with five judges to be elected on a statewide basis, few if any African American judges or Hispanic judges will be elected. Spokespersons for Hispanics and African Americans argue that the solution is to divide such a state into five districts, with one judge elected in each district, and draw district lines in such a way that African Americans and Hispanics make up a majority of voters in as many districts as possible, giving them a chance to elect at least one of their own.

Merit Selection: The Missouri Plan

Many lawyers and political scientists have argued in favor of some kind of selection procedure in which there is a screening process before judges are appointed or elected to ensure that only candidates of merit will be considered. One such merit plan is the Missouri Plan.[23] The **Missouri Plan**, as used in most states, provides that when a judicial vacancy occurs, a special *nominating commission* (usually composed of three lawyers elected by the bar, three citizens appointed by the governor, and the chief justice) nominates three candidates.[24] The governor selects one, who then serves as a judge for at least a year. At the next general election the voters are asked: "Shall Judge X be retained in office?" If a majority of the voters agree, the judge serves a new full term (typically 6 to 12 years); if not, another person is selected by the same procedure. At the end of his or her term, the judge certifies a wish to have his or her name placed on the ballot, and the voters are again asked whether they want to retain that judge in office.[25] These uncontested elections, in which judges run against their own record, are called *retention elections*.

In California the governor appoints judges of the Supreme Court and appellate court for twelve-year terms with the approval of the Commission on Judicial Appointments. The commission consists of the attorney general, chief justice and senior appellate presiding justice in case of supreme court appointments or the senior presiding justice in the appellate district in case of appellate court appointments. In the next statewide election, the judge runs against his or her own record. The governor appoints trial judges for six-year terms who may be challenged when seeking reelection, but his or her name does not appear on the ballot if no one else runs for the position.

Even more of a hybrid is the system used in New Mexico, where a judicial nominating commission sends names to the governor, who selects a judge. Then at

Missouri Plan

A system for selecting judges that combines features of the appointive and elective methods. The governor selects judges from lists presented by panels of lawyers and laypersons, and at the end of their term the judges may run against their own record in retention elections.

the next general election an opponent nominated in the other party's primary may challenge the judge in a partisan election. If no opponent is nominated, the incumbent gets a "free ride." Whoever wins that election then serves one term and thereafter runs against his or her own record in a retention election.

Until recently retention elections generated little interest and low voter turnout.[26] In all, of the almost 4,600 judicial retention elections since 1960, fewer than 60 judges have been removed as the result of retention elections, although a few judges have decided not to run when they realized they might face disapproval.[27] Recently some state supreme court justices have been vigorously challenged in retention elections, especially when their decisions differed appreciably from the mainstream of public opinion and aroused the hostility of significant special interests. Frequently the charge was that the judge was "soft on crime." A Republican group, the Emergency Florida State Supreme Court Project, is raising funds to oppose three Florida Supreme Court justices in their 2002 retention election because these judges had ruled in favor of Al Gore's request for a hand recount of some ballots in the 2000 presidential elections. Florida limits what justices can say in public and how they may campaign for retention.[28] Interest groups have learned that it is relatively easy to target incumbents, but because of constraints on the way judicial candidates are expected to campaign, it is "difficult for targeted judges to defend themselves."[29]

Most voters know little about judges, and what information they get comes from interested parties and persons, especially those who dislike what the judges have done. To provide a more balanced picture, a few states—Alaska, Utah, Colorado, Arizona, Tennessee—have tried to supply more neutral information about judicial performance. In Colorado an *evaluation committee* in each judicial district—jointly appointed by the chief justice, governor, president of the Senate, and Speaker of the House—disseminates information through newspaper supplements, including a final recommendation of "retain" or "do not retain."[30] In Alaska a judicial council composed of three lawyers, three nonlawyers, and the chief justice provides evaluations that are widely publicized.[31] In Utah the Judicial Council—consisting of the chief justice and 12 members elected by judges, assisted by a committee of lawyers and members of the public—certifies incumbents, and this certification, or lack of it, is included on the ballot.

Even though contested retention elections are the exception, sitting judges are aware that if they make decisions that offend organized interest groups, they may face opposition the next time their names are placed on the ballot. Whether these pressures threaten the independence of the courts or are an expected part of our political system in which judges play such an important role is part of the political debates.[32]

The Appointive versus the Elective System

For more than 200 years, people have debated the merits of an appointive versus an elective system for the selection of judges. Those who favor the appointive method contend voters are generally uninformed about candidates and are not competent to assess legal learning and judicial abilities. Popular election, they assert, puts a premium on personality, requires judges to enter the political arena, and discourages many able lawyers from running for office.

Proponents of the appointive system contend the elective process conceals what is really going on. Absent name recognition, voters go for party labels, which are increasingly less significant as indicators of ideology.[33] In addition, because retirement and death create many vacancies, it is often the governor who selects the judges. The governor makes an interim appointment until the next election, and the temporary appointee usually wins the election.

What are the arguments of those who favor the elective method? Judges, they argue, should be directly accountable to the people; when judges are appointed they

Should judges be elected or appointed?

Which method produces better judges? The first problem is to define a "good judge." Most people define a good judge as one who makes decisions they like. Even if the desirable features are defined more precisely—ability to maintain neutrality between parties, knowledge of the law, writing ability, personal integrity, physical and mental health, and ability to handle judicial power sensibly—these are still factors that are hard to measure.

Are judges selected by appointment more likely to make decisions of a certain kind than judges chosen by election? Are judges of greater legal knowledge and probity more likely to be selected by one method rather than by another?

are apt to lose touch with the general currents of opinion of the electorate. Moreover, the appointive process gives governors too much power over judges. And even if judicial elections do not result in the defeat of many sitting judges, elections serve to foster accountability because judges do not want to be defeated and will try to maintain popular support.

In general, bar associations, corporate law firms, and judges tend to favor some kind of merit selection system; plaintiffs, attorneys, women's associations, minority associations, and labor groups are skeptical or opposed.

How Judges Are Judged

Unlike federal judges, who hold office during "good behavior," most state judges are selected for fixed terms, typically 6 to 12 years. In Massachusetts, New Hampshire, and Puerto Rico, judges serve to age 70; in Rhode Island they serve for life. Thirty-seven states and the District of Columbia mandate the retirement of judges at a certain age, usually 70.[34]

The states, rather than the national government, have taken the lead in establishing procedures to judge the judges. Because impeachment has proved to be an ineffective means to remove judges, today each of the 50 states has a board, commission, or court to handle allegations of judicial misbehavior. Despite the objections of many judges, these commissions are most often composed of both nonlawyers and lawyers. They investigate complaints and hold hearings for judges who have been charged with improper performance of their duties or unethical or unfair conduct. Establishment of these commissions appears to have helped restore public confidence in the state judicial systems.[35]

THE JUDICIAL REFORM MOVEMENT

Many reforms—court unification, centralized management, state financing, and merit selection—have been adopted, but waste and delay continue to plague our courts. We are, many charge, a "litigious society." Dockets are crowded, relief is costly, and inordinate delays are common.[36]

Some of the reforms for improving the administration of justice include:

- Judges should be selected by some kind of merit system that screens candidates in terms of their qualifications.

- Judges should be paid adequately so that they have the financial independence to concentrate on their work and so that successful lawyers will be willing to serve on the bench. In most states, judges' salaries are considerably less than the average incomes of practicing attorneys of the same age and experience. Judges are unable to earn anything beyond their salaries, and they must be cautious about investments in order to avoid conflicts of interest.

- Judges should serve for long terms so that they can make decisions without fear of losing their jobs.

- Rule-making powers should be given to the state supreme court or its chief justice. States are permitting judges to adopt procedural rules and codes of professional conduct. Some rules even require lawyers to continue their education by taking refresher courses.

- Although no person should be appointed or elected to a court solely because of race or sex or ethnic background, our courts need to become more representative of the communities they serve.[37]

- States should provide for alternative dispute resolution.

Alternative dispute resolution (ADR) refers to procedures that serve as alternatives for formal trials. These procedures include mediation, arbitration, conciliation,

private judging, and advisory settlement conferences. From time to time Congress has made grants to encourage states and localities to develop alternative dispute resolution mechanisms, especially for domestic relations issues. ADRs can be part of the established court system or separate from it in neighborhood justice centers or arbitration and mediation forums. Half the states are operating arbitration programs as part of their court system.

Despite the trendy nickname of "rent-a-judge," the rather old practice of hiring private decision makers is being revived. These decision makers are paid by the parties to the dispute, who agree in advance to abide by the outcome. In some states appeals courts can review these decisions. There is some concern that these alternative practices are drawing the best lawyers into the private system, resulting perhaps in one system for the rich, a private one, and one for the poor, a public one.

The judicial reform movement has been successful, but like most reform movements, it has its critics and skeptics. Some observers maintain that court delay is not as serious a problem as has been charged and that the remedies may undercut our checks and balances system. Delay, for example, often works to the advantage of defendants and their attorneys, who wish to postpone trials. At other times prosecutors want delays in order to put pressure on defendants to accept guilty pleas. Lawyers may seek delays so that they can accept more clients.

No matter how "modernized" the management of court business, the flow of legal business grows continuously. Some people have proposed that traffic violations, automobile injury cases, and so-called "victimless crimes" be handled by some procedure other than a court trial. New York has led the way in removing from the courts minor traffic offenses that do not involve serious moving violations; other states are following this lead. No-fault insurance programs could reduce the large number of cases stemming from automobile accidents. Because half the people in prison, as well as half the trials that are held, involve victimless crimes such as using marijuana, *decriminalization* could substantially reduce the load on the courts. Six states, for example, have already repealed statutes on public drunkenness and now consider alcoholism a disease rather than a crime.

The reform of state judicial systems is enmeshed in partisan, ideological, and issue politics. Judges are but one part of the total justice system, and their operations are best studied in the context of the entire justice system.

THE JUSTICE SYSTEM

Justice is handled in the United States by a series of institutions that are only loosely connected to each other. In addition to judges, there are juries, prosecutors, defense counsels, public defenders, victims, and defendants. Parole, probation, and prison officials are also part of the justice system.

The Jury

Although most of us will never be judges or serve as professionals in the administration of justice, all adult citizens have an opportunity—even an obligation—to be jurors. Trial by jury in civil disputes is used less often these days; people make settlements prior to trial, elect to have their cases decided by a judge alone, or have their cases referred to a mediator or arbitrator. Furthermore, only a small fraction of criminal cases are actually disposed of by a trial before a jury. Still, jury trials, or the threat of them, remain a key feature of our justice system.[38]

We have moved from a jury system in which service was restricted to white male property owners to one in which jury duty is the responsibility of *all* adult citizens. Today more time and energy are spent in trying to persuade (or coerce) people to serve on juries than in trying to exclude them. Because jury service is time consuming and burdensome, many busy people do their

Thinking It Through...

1. Some studies point to judicial elections as working against women and minorities. One study found: "Judicial elections . . . have a built-in bias for men. . . . Quite simply, few women, blacks, Hispanics, or Asians have the political connections, financial resources, and campaign sophistication to overcome the stereotype that has the blindfolded woman holding the scales of justice, but a white man sitting at the bench dispensing it."* Other studies show that more women are chosen by gubernatorial appointment and merit methods, but that African Americans fare as well in judicial elections and nearly as well in legislative ones. Another study found that merit systems tend to produce higher proportions of Protestant judges, in contrast to Catholic and Jewish judges.

2. There is some evidence that elected judges are more likely to impose the death sentence than either appointed judges or juries.**

3. Democratic judges tend to make more liberal decisions than their Republican colleagues do.***

4. Courts to which judges are nominated and elected on a nonpartisan ballot show less partisan division than those whose judges are nominated by party conventions and elected in partisan elections.

*John H. Culver, "Politics and the California Plan for Choosing Appellate Judges," *Judicature* (September/October 1982), p. 158.

**Stuart Taylor, Jr., "Taking Politics for a Fatal Ride," *The Recorder*, October 30, 1995, p. 6. See also Justice John Paul Stevens, dissenting in *Harris v Alabama*, 513 US 504 (1995).

***Sheldon Goldman, "Voting Behavior on the U.S. Courts of Appeals Revised," *American Political Science Review* (June 1975), pp. 491–506.

best to avoid serving. In the past, judges were often willing to excuse doctors, nurses, teachers, executives, and other highly skilled persons who pleaded that their services were essential outside the jury room. As a result, juries were often selected from panels consisting in large part of older people, those who were unemployed or employed in relatively low-paying jobs, single people, and others who were unable to be excused from jury service. Most states have reacted to these problems by making it more difficult to be excused.

Jury trials take more time than bench trials (trials before judges). They also cost more. As a result, some states are using juries of fewer than 12 people for some criminal trials, and a few states are permitting verdicts by less than a unanimous vote. The Supreme Court has approved these practices, provided the juries consist of at least 6 persons.[39]

Only a handful of those accused of committing a crime actually stand trial, and only 10–15 percent of those who are convicted are declared guilty as the result of a formal trial before either a judge or a jury. Most people who go to prison or who have to pay a criminal fine do so because they plead guilty.

The Prosecutor

The 18,000 prosecutors in the United States are usually county officials, locally elected and subject to little supervision by state authorities. In Connecticut they are appointed by judges, in the Virgin Islands by the attorney general, and in New Jersey by the governor with the consent of the state senate. A prosecutor has "more control over life, liberty, and reputation than any other person in America."[40] (Incidentally, the prosecutor is largely an American invention, one of the few governmental positions we did not inherit from England.)

When presented with a case by the police, the prosecutor must decide first whether to file formal charges. He or she may: (1) divert the matter out of the criminal justice system and turn it over to a social

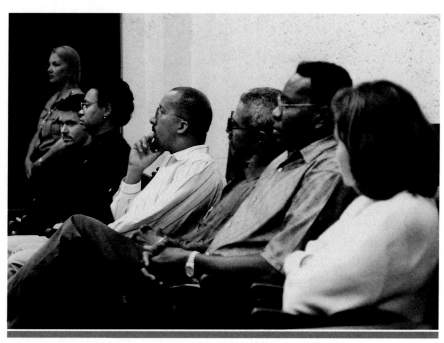

All citizens have an obligation to serve on juries, and lawyers develop skills in selecting people they think may be sympathetic to their client.

welfare agency; (2) dismiss the charges; (3) take the matter before a grand jury, which almost always follows the prosecutor's recommendation; (4) in most jurisdictions file an **information affidavit**, which serves the same function as a grand jury **indictment**.

A prosecutor who decides not to charge a person accused of some notorious crime is often subject to political pressure and public criticism. But for routine crimes, the prosecutor is politically in a better position to dismiss a charge than are the police. Police are supposed to enforce every law all the time. Of course, it is impossible for them to do so, and they must exercise discretion.[41] But officers who fail to arrest a person alleged to have committed a crime could well be charged with failing in their duty. The prosecutor, however, has more leeway. In fact, the prosecutor is less likely to be criticized for dropping a case because of insufficient evidence than for filing a charge and failing to get a conviction.

Defense Counsel, Public Defenders, and Others

Many defendants cannot afford the legal counsel to which they are constitutionally entitled. The **assigned counsel system** is the oldest system to provide such defendants with an attorney, and it continues to be used, especially in rural areas. Judges appoint attorneys to represent defendants who cannot afford them. Most such attorneys are paid from the public treasury, but sometimes they are expected to do the work *pro bono*—for the public good. Seldom are they given funds to do any investigatory work on behalf of their clients. Often judges pick young lawyers just beginning their careers or old ones about to retire. Some less scrupulous lawyers make their living as assigned counsel and because it is often to their financial advantage to do so are quick to plead their clients guilty. They are known contemptuously as members of the "cop-out bar."[42]

Dissatisfaction with the assigned counsel system led to the creation of the **public defender system**, first started in Los Angeles in 1914 and now used in most big cities. Under this system, the government provides a staff of lawyers whose full-time job is to defend those who cannot pay. This system provides experienced counsel and relieves the bar of an onerous duty. Critics—including some defendants—protest that because public defenders are paid employees of the state, they are not likely to work as diligently on behalf of their clients as they would if they were specifically assigned to them. But most observers consider the defender system superior to the assigned counsel system. Steps are being taken to increase the pay of public defenders, protect their independence, and see that they win the confidence of those they represent.

Victims and Defendants

When we talk about our criminal justice system, we sometimes forget the two most important parties in any criminal case—the victim of the crime and the person accused of it.

> The rights of victims or potential victims are not of the same order as the rights of the accused; the rights of the accused are constitutional rights spelled out in amendments, but nowhere in the Constitution is there any mention of the rights of victims or the public. The framers of the Constitution apparently were much more worried about protecting citizens against the government than about protecting citizens from each other.[43]

In general terms, defendants are likely to be "younger, predominantly male, disproportionately black, less educated, seldom fully employed, and typically unmarried. By the time the sorting process has ended, those sent to prison will consist of an even higher proportion of young, illiterate, black males."[44] Victims, too—compared to the rest of the population—tend to be young, black or another minority, and uneducated. A substantial number of victims—either because of lack of

A disproportionate number of prisoners tend to be young, poorly educated, black males.

information affidavit
Certification by a public prosecutor that there is evidence to justify bringing named individuals to trial.

indictment
A formal charge issued by a grand jury against an individual for a specified crime.

assigned council system
Arrangement whereby attorneys are provided for persons accused of crime who are unable to hire their own attorneys. The judge assigns a member of the bar to provide counsel to a particular defendant.

pro bono
Term used to describe the work lawyers (or other professionals) do to serve the public good and for which they either receive no fees or decline to receive fees.

public defender system
Arrangement whereby public officials are hired to provide legal assistance to those persons accused of crimes who are unable to hire their own attorneys.

You Decide...

Will mandatory life sentences deter criminals?

In many states there is a movement toward three-strikes-and-you're-out legislation, which imprisons people who have committed three felonies for life. In some states it must be three violent felonies; in others, it is any three felonies. Is this good public policy?

knowledge of what to do or fear of doing it, or because, as in the case of rape victims, they believe they have little chance of proving their attackers to be guilty—never report crimes to police and prosecutors.

Our system puts the responsibility for prosecuting criminals on the government. In most instances, victims have no role other than as witnesses. They are not consulted about what the charge should be or asked what they think might be an appropriate penalty. The matter is strictly between the state, represented by the prosecutor, and the accused, represented by an attorney.

Plea Bargaining

A common practice is for the prosecution to offer to reduce the seriousness of the charge if a defendant will enter a plea of guilty to a lesser crime. This practice is called a **plea bargain**. In many places "between 95 and 99 percent of felony convictions are by plea."[45] At one time this practice was universally condemned. Many people still consider there is something "dirty" about it, like bartering away justice.

Critics say plea bargaining forces people to give up their rights; moreover, defendants often do not get off much more leniently by pleading guilty to lesser offenses than if they stood trial.[46] Defenders of plea bargaining contend it works, producing "a result approximating closely, but informally and more swiftly, the results which ought to ensue from a trial, while avoiding most of the undesirable aspects of that ordeal."[47] Many experts and investigators who have looked into the matter have endorsed plea bargaining.

Plea bargaining offers something to all involved. Prosecutors are able to dispose of cases quickly, avoid long and drawn-out trials, eliminate the risk of losing cases, and build up better "election-worthy" conviction records. Those who are accused avoid the danger of being sentenced for more serious charges by pleading guilty to lesser offenses. Defense attorneys avoid "the dilemma of either incurring the expense of going to trial with a losing case or appearing to provide no service whatever to their clients."[48] By being able to handle more clients, they can also make more money. Judges are able to dispose of cases on their dockets more rapidly. In fact, were every case tried, it would overwhelm the judicial system.

Once the bargain between the prosecutor and the defendant's attorney has been accepted, the matter is taken before a judge. The judge goes through a series of questions to the defendant: "Are you pleading guilty because you are guilty? Are you aware of the maximum sentence for the crime to which you are entering a guilty plea? Were you coerced into pleading guilty or offered anything in return for it? Are you satisfied with the representation afforded by your attorney?" Following appropriate responses, the plea is accepted.[49] As long as defendants know what they are doing and enter into the bargain intelligently, they waive their constitutional rights to trial by pleading guilty and may not subsequently back out of the arrangement. Prosecutors must also live up to their side of the bargain.[50]

Sentencing

Due process must be observed in sentencing, which takes place in open court. The prisoner must be present and represented by counsel. In many places, social workers are assigned to help the judge determine the proper sentence. The judge also receives recommendations from the prosecution (and in some jurisdictions from the victim as well), hears the arguments of the defense, and then sets the sentence within the limits prescribed by the state.

The judge sets the sentence, but concerns about sentencing permeate the judicial system. One writer has put it this way:

plea bargain

Negotiations between prosecutor and defendant aimed at getting the defendant to plead guilty in return for the prosecutor's agreeing to reduce the seriousness of the crime for which the defendant will be convicted.

Because police and prosecutors screen out a large proportion of the doubtful cases, most left to be dealt with by the courts are those in which there is no serious dispute over the guilt or innocence of the defendant. . . . This fact sets the tone for the process. . . . Everyone concerned—the defense lawyers, the prosecutor, the judge, the probation officer—becomes aware of the fact that he or she is involved in a process where the primary focus is on deciding what to do with the people who are in fact guilty.[51]

Early in our national history, retribution, deterrence, and protection of society were the primary purposes of sentencing. Then rehabilitation became the major goal, and many thought it was a more humane approach. The indefinite sentence became popular, motivated by the idea that each prisoner should be considered an individual suffering from an "illness." Each prisoner should be diagnosed; a course of treatment should be prescribed; and if and when such experts as psychologists and social workers could certify a "cure," the prisoner should be released.

Most political leaders and many scholars have become disillusioned about our ability to bring about "cures."[52] Others are disillusioned about the deterrent effect of imprisonment. A comprehensive study of rehabilitative efforts inside prisons, although rejecting the conclusion that "nothing works," nonetheless stated: "We do not know of any program or method of rehabilitation that could be guaranteed to reduce the criminal activity of released offenders."[53]

Judicial discretion remains broad, however. Penal codes usually do not set specific terms of punishment. Different judges issue different sentences to defendants convicted of the same crime.[54] To reduce such disparities, several reforms have been suggested, including establishing more precise legislative standards, creating advisory sentencing councils, and adopting the British practice of allowing appellate courts to modify sentences.

This disillusionment with rehabilitation, combined with growing concerns about crime in the streets and mounting criticism about alleged judicial leniency, has fueled legislative action for mandatory minimum sentencing requirements and for narrowing judicial discretion.[55] State after state has adopted mandatory prison terms for more and more crimes. As noted earlier, a three-strikes-and-you're-out requirement is being adopted by many states.

Probation and Prisons

Prison populations in the United States are skyrocketing. Today the United States, including juvenile facilities, has about 2 million people behind bars, about 135,000 in federal custody, 1.2 million in state custody, 600,000 in local jails, and more than 100,000 in juvenile facilities[56] (see Table 27–1). (*Prisons* are for committed criminals serving long sentences; *jails* are for short-term stays for persons awaiting trial and those with sentences of a year or less.)

> The United States now imprisons more people than any other country in the world—perhaps half a million more than Communist China. The American inmate population has grown so large that it is difficult to imagine: imagine the combined population of Atlanta, St. Louis, Pittsburgh, Des Moines, and Miami behind bars.[57]

In addition to those in prison or jails, there are almost 4.5 million adult men and women on probation or parole. (*Probationers* are offenders courts have placed in community supervision rather than putting them in prison; *parolees* are people released after serving a prison term who are under supervision and are subject to being returned to prison for rule violations or other offenses.)

State and federal prison populations in the United States actually declined during the 1960s, but public demands for tougher sentences caused them to climb after

Thinking It Through . . .

Pro

Fear of a lifetime in prison will deter people from committing violent crimes.

It will reduce public fears about crime.

People who commit one crime usually will commit another. Between 1991 and 1994, for example, approximately 43,000 Florida convicts who were released early because of prison overcrowding were arrested again.

Con

Lifetime imprisonment is very expensive, and in some states it could lead to reduced funding for other socially desirable programs. In California, for example, it has been estimated that the cost of keeping a felon in prison for a year is about $22,300—more than the cost of keeping seven students at a California community college for a year.

It results in keeping people in prison in their 50s, 60s, and 70s, when there is little evidence they are dangerous to society.

It reduces judges' flexibility in tailoring the sentence to the crime.

SOURCES: ". . . And Throw Away the Key," *Time*, February 4, 1994, pp. 54–58; "Will Your Children's College Chances Be Struck Down by 'Three Strikes and You're Out'?" California Postsecondary Education Commission, April 12, 1994.

TABLE 27-1 Prisoners under the Jurisdiction of State or Federal Correctional Authorities, 2000

U.S. total	1,385,492	Delaware	7,043
Federal	142,530	Dist. of Columbia	8,575
State	1,242,962	Florida	71,233
		Georgia	43,626
Northeast	177,965	Kentucky	15,444
Connecticut	18,616	Louisiana	34,734
Maine	1,715	Maryland	23,704
Massachusetts	11,150	Mississippi	18,379
New Hampshire	2,254	North Carolina	31,110
New Jersey	31,081	Oklahoma	23,009
New York	71,691	South Carolina	22,154
Pennsylvania	36,617	Tennessee	22,566
Rhode Island	3,186	Texas	163,503
Vermont	1,655	Virginia	29,890
		West Virginia	3,800
Midwest	236,820		
Illinois	44,819	**West**	272,062
Indiana	19,874	Alaska	4,025
Iowa	7,646	Arizona	26,287
Kansas	8,780	California	164,490
Michigan	47,317	Colorado	16,319
Minnesota	6,219	Hawaii	5,051
Missouri	27,292	Idaho	5,465
Nebraska	3,663	Montana	3,039
North Dakota	1,004	Nevada	9,920
Ohio	46,838	New Mexico	5,277
South Dakota	2,571	Oregon	10,313
Wisconsin	20,797	Utah	5,450
		Washington	14,704
South	556,115	Wyoming	1,722
Alabama	25,786		
Arkansas	11,559		

SOURCE: U.S. Department of Justice, Bureau of Justice Statistics Bulletin, *Prison and Jail Inmates at Midyear 2000* (March 2001), p. 3.

TABLE 27-2 Number of Persons Held in State or Federal Prisons or in Local Jails, 1990–2000

Year	Total inmates in custody
1990	1,148,702
1991	1,219,014
1992	1,295,150
1993	1,369,185
1994	1,476,621
1995	1,585,586
1996	1,646,020
1997	1,743,643
1998	1,816,931
1999	1,875,199
2000	1,931,859

SOURCE: Bureau of Justice Statistics Bulletin, *Prison and Jail Inmates at Midyear 2000* (March 2001), p. 2.

1969. The prison population has increased by 77 percent since 1990 (Table 27–2). "If the current trend continues … the number of Americans behind bars or on probation or parole will approach the 6 million students enrolled full-time in four-year colleges and universities nationwide."[58]

The increase in prison population has resulted in serious overcrowding. In most states, conditions are so bad that in recent years federal judges have issued orders calling for either immediate improvement or the release of persons being held in conditions that violate the Eighth Amendment prohibition against cruel and unusual punishment. Most states are responding to judicial intervention by spending millions to build new prisons and renovate old ones. It costs at least $60,000 to build each cell, and on average $20,000 a year must be spent to guard and feed each prisoner.[59]

Relatively few people commit most violent crimes. One out of every three persons let out of prison returns in three years. If we could identify these "career criminals" (**recidivists**) and keep them in prison, while at the same time releasing offenders who are not likely to commit other crimes, we might be able to cut down on

the overcrowding in the prisons and better protect the public. The trouble with this idea is that it is not easy to determine in advance who are career criminals and who are not. For this reason, some argue that requiring every criminal convicted of a second offense to stay in prison for five years would cut down the crime rate by 16 percent.

Some cities and counties have even resorted to **privatization**, turning over the responsibility for operating jails to private firms on a contractual basis. Except for New Jersey and Wisconsin (and the District of Columbia), privatization of prison facilities is concentrated among southern and western states. Texas has 42 and California 24 prisons managed by private, independent businesses.[60] Correctional peace officers are strongly opposed to privatization and have become a potent interest group making major contributions to gubernatorial elections.

The high cost of corrections may lead some states to rethink the wisdom of mandatory sentencing and to reconsider the need to create such alternatives for nonviolent offenders as halfway houses, intensive probation, work release programs, and other community corrections facilities, even home confinement, first pioneered in New Mexico in 1983, where prisoners are observed by a variety of monitoring devices.[61] The problem is that these alternative solutions are subject to political attack for being "soft on criminals." Even so, the pressure to find places to hold prisoners is so great that correction officials believe that these alternative procedures, including home confinement, will become an increasingly important part of the criminal justice system.[62]

COURTS IN CRISIS

Crime is a national issue confronting all those involved in the criminal justice system in America. The nation's attention has been focused on drive-by shootings, random killings—especially in schools—and other forms of violence. Critics claim courts are "overwhelmed by the huge volume of cases" and that "career criminals beat the system," defense attorneys "shop" for judges known for lenient sentences, prosecutors are "blackmailed" into accepting lenient plea bargains, and many career criminals are out of jail in a few months.[63]

The American Bar Association has prepared a series of recommendations for state legislatures and Congress. The president of the association, in announcing its concerns, stated: "Justice in the United States takes too long, costs too much and is virtually inaccessible and unaffordable for too many Americans.... Our courts are grossly overburdened ... and woefully underfunded.... The justice system is no longer a 'court of last resort' ... but is becoming an emergency room for every social trauma."[64]

There is widespread agreement that our justice system, both on the civil and the criminal side, is in crisis. There is less agreement on what to do about it. The problems are complex, and the issues are political in the best sense of the word; that is, each suggested reform has costs and benefits. Change and reform are likely to come slowly, and perhaps this is as it should be, for our justice system has been created over the centuries, built on the accumulated wisdom of the past. How best to administer justice is likely to be high on our political agenda.

Victim's Rights

The victim's rights movement, initiated originally by liberals (chiefly feminists concerned about the difficulty of winning prosecutions for rape and about the harsh treatment of women witnesses), gained the support of conservatives who considered the judicial system unfair to victims. In the 1984 Victims of Crime Act, Congress authorized federal funds, which are distributed by the Office of Crime Victims in the Department of Justice, to support state programs compensating victims and provide funds to some victims of federal crimes as well.

More than 30 states and Congress have adopted "Son of Sam" laws. They are named after multiple-murderer David Berkowitz, who referred to himself as Son of Sam. Such laws seek to take from convicted criminals any financial gain they might earn from selling the rights to their stories and make these funds available to compensate their victims.

About 30 states have amended their constitutions to provide for a "victim's bill of rights," which makes it easier for victims to recover their stolen property held in police custody. It also gives victims a chance to be heard when prosecutors file formal charges, when judges set bail and impose sentences, and when parole boards consider releasing prisoners.* These victim's bills of rights are not without constitutional problems. The U.S. Supreme Court, after first holding to the contrary, has upheld the right of a prosecutor to make statements to a jury in a murder trial about the personal qualities of the victim and to allow such a jury to consider evidence relating to the personal characteristics of the murder victim and the emotional impact of the crime on the victim's family.**

Congress is considering a Victim's Rights Amendment to the U.S. Constitution. It would give victims the right to be informed of and given the opportunity to be present at every proceeding, to be heard at any proceeding involving sentencing, to be informed of any release or escape, and to receive full restitution from the convicted offender.

Under the stimulus of federal matching funds, most states now provide a victims' compensation program. Almost all states now compensate victims or permit victims and their families to sue for civil damages. Yet even if victims win the right to collect damages from the defendants, defendants seldom have the resources to pay for damage awards.

*Naftali Bendavid, "Victims Strike Back," *The Recorder*, July 3, 1996, p. 14.

**Payne v Tennessee, 501 US 808 (1991), overruling *Booth v Maryland*, 482 US 496 (1987) and *South Carolina v Gathers*, 490 US 805 (1989).

†Katharine Qeelye, "Gore Seeks Constitutional Guards for Crime Victims," *The New York Times*, national ed., July 19, 2000, p. A21.

recidivist
A repeat offender.

privatization
The contracting out to the private sector of services that are usually provided by government.

SUMMARY

1. State and local courts are important arenas for the making and carrying out of public policy. As they have become more active in political life, state judges have become embroiled in controversial issues and the public has recognized their importance as policy makers.

2. Each state has its own court system. Although the systems vary, they can generally be described as including minor courts of limited jurisdiction, trial courts of general jurisdiction, and appellate courts.

3. Judges are selected in four different ways: appointment by the governor, election by the legislatures, popular election, and a modified appointment plan known as the Missouri Plan. Most legal reformers and political scientists appear to favor the Missouri Plan, or

some merit selection system instead of judicial elections.

4. Judicial reforms are aimed at eliminating the waste and delay that plague courts. Among those suggested are alternative dispute resolution mechanisms. Other reforms include merit systems that screen candidates for judgeships, higher pay and longer terms for judges to increase their judicial independence, rule-making powers for state supreme courts, and the appointment of judges more representative of the communities they serve.

5. Judges, together with jurors, prosecutors, defense counsel, public defenders, and correctional officials, make up a loosely interrelated justice system. Many believe this system is not properly dispensing justice to individual defen-

dants or protecting the public from career criminals.

6. In recent years more attention has been paid to the rights of victims at both the national and state level, including amendments to state constitutions giving victims and their families the right to participate in the trial and providing for compensation to victims and their families.

7. There are about 2 million persons in our prisons, and the number continues to rise. Prisons are overcrowded. Imprisonment has been justified as retribution, deterrence, protection of society, and, most recently, rehabilitation. Disillusionment with rehabilitation has led to calls for mandatory minimum sentencing requirements, including three-strikes-and-you're-out legislation.

KEY TERMS

writ of *habeas corpus* 596
new judicial federalism 596
tort law 596
misdemeanor 596
felony 596

original jurisdiction 597
judicial review 598
advisory opinion 598
Missouri Plan 602
information affidavit 607

indictment 607
assigned council system 607
pro bono 607
public defender system 607
plea bargain 608

recidivist 611
privatization 611

FURTHER READING

NATHAN AASENG, *The O. J. Simpson Trial: What It Shows Us About Our Legal System* (Walker, 1996).

STEPHEN J. ADLER, *The Jury: Trial and Error in the American Courtroom* (Times Books, 1994).

LAURENCE BAUM, *American Courts: Powers and Policy* (Houghton Mifflin, 1994).

ANTHONY CHAMPAGNE AND JUDITH HAYDEL, EDS., *Judicial Reform in the States* (University Press of America, 1993).

DAVID COLE, *No Equal Justice: Race and Class in the American Criminal Justice System* (The New Press, 1999).

GEORGE F. COLE, *Criminal Justice in America* (Brooks/Cole, 1996).

NORMAN J. FINKEL, *Commonsense Justice: Juror's Notions of the Law* (Harvard University Press, 1995).

SUSAN P. FINO, *The Role of State Supreme Courts in the New Judicial Federalism* (Greenwood Press, 1987).

JULIA FIONDA, *Public Prosecutors and Discretion* (Oxford University Press, 1995).

JOHN B. GATES AND CHARLES A. JOHNSON, *The American Courts: A Critical Assessment* (Congressional Quarterly Press, 1991).

JOSEPH R. GRODIN, *In Pursuit of Justice: Reflections of a State Supreme Court Justice* (University of California Press, 1989).

DAVID HEILBRONE, *Rough Justice: Days and Nights of a Young D.A.* (Pantheon Books, 1990).

JAMES P. LEVINE, *Juries and Politics* (Brooks/Cole, 1992).

MARILYN D. MCSHANE AND FRANK P. WILLIAMS III, EDS., *Encyclopedia of American Prisons* (Garland, 1996).

DAVID W. NEUBAUER, *America's Courts and Criminal Justice System*, 6th ed. (Wadsworth, 1999).

DAVID W. NEUBAUER, *Judicial Process: Law, Courts, and Politics in the United States*, 2d ed. (Harcourt Brace, 1997).

WALTER K. OLSON, *The Litigation Explosion: What Happened When America Unleashed the Lawsuit* (Dutton, 1991).

ELLIOT E. SLOTNICK, ED., *Judicial Politics: Readings from Judicature*, 2d ed. (American Judicature Society, 1999).

HARRY P. STUMPF AND JOHN H. CULVER, *The Politics of State Courts* (Longman, 1992).

G. ALAN TARR AND MARY CORNELIA ALDIS PORTER, *State Supreme Courts in State and Nation* (Yale University Press, 1988).

PAUL B. WICE, *Court Reform and Judicial Leadership* (Praeger, 1995).

See also *Judicature, The Journal of the American Judicature Society*, published monthly. The National Center for State Courts does not publish a regular journal but is an independent, nonprofit organization dedicated to the improvement of justice. Its materials can be obtained from its headquarters at 300 Newport Avenue, Williamsburg, Virginia 23185; its home page is: oyez.ncsc.dni.us/about.htm.

28

LOCAL GOVERNMENT AND METROPOLITICS

How many counties in Portland? Question on test

LOCAL GOVERNMENTS IN THE UNITED STATES EMPLOY ABOUT 12 MILLION PEOPLE IN 87,500 DIFFERENT JURISDICTIONS (SEE TABLE 28–1). FOR EXAMPLE, ILLINOIS HAS

6,800 units of local government, made up of 102 counties, 1,288 municipalities, 1,433 townships, 3,068 special districts, and 944 school districts.[1] North Carolina has 953 units of local government, including 100 counties, 518 municipalities, 335 special districts, and 192 school districts of one type or another.[2] The Chicago metro area has about 1,200 different jurisdictions. Local government is not only a very big deal; it is costly and overlapping, and it affects nearly every one of us every day.

Counties, cities, suburban communities, school districts, townships, metropolitan planning agencies, water control districts—all are crowded together and piled on top of one another. Citizens typically live under several layers of government. They pay taxes to nearly all of them, and they also elect most of their leaders.

Why do we have such a labyrinth of government in this country? The basic pattern was imported from England, as were many of our governmental forms. As time passed, new governments were created to take on new jobs when existing units proved either too small or unequal to the task. Also, people kept moving into, or at least near, the large cities. The past two generations have seen millions of Americans moving from the cities to the suburbs, and a steady migration to urban and suburban areas continues from rural areas as well. Decades of compromise and struggle among conflicting groups have given us our present system. It creaks and groans. It costs a lot of money. People claim it is inefficient. But it's here.

THE NATURE OF STATE AND LOCAL RELATIONS

Local governments vary in structure, size, power, and relation to one another. But in a *constitutional* sense, they all rely on power "borrowed" from the state. Most state constitutions create a **unitary system** in which power is vested in the *state* government, and *local* units exist only as agents of the state. Local government is not mentioned in the U.S. Constitution. Local units exercise only those powers expressly given to them by their respective state governments.

Although dispersion of governmental power among various local units and the state government produces many of the same problems that flow from the relationship of states and the national government, there is a crucial difference. Most local units of

CHAPTER MEDIA

 POLITICS ONLINE
Taking on City Hall via the Internet
www.prenhall.com/burns

government, unlike states, do not have constitutional status. State-local relations are generally unitary in nature, in contrast to the federal nature of nation-state relations.

Because local governments are typically created by the state legislatures and usually have no constitutional authority in their own right, there are fewer obstacles to state interference in local matters than there are to national interference in state matters. State officers participate in local government to a much greater extent than federal officers do in state politics. When doubts arise about the authority of local governments, courts generally decide against them.

In the beginning state legislatures were given almost unlimited constitutional authority over their local governments, and they ran them pretty much as they wished. They granted, amended, and repealed city charters, established counties, determined city and county structure, set debt limits, and passed laws for the local units. But by the end of the nineteenth century, many state constitutions forbade state legislatures to pass laws dealing with local governments, and constitutional provisions determined the structure, and in some cases even the process, of local governments.

Constitutional home rule granted constitutional independence to some local units, primarily larger cities, giving them constitutional authority to choose their form of government as well as constitutional authority over a whole range of subjects. With the protection of constitutional home rule, state legislatures no longer determined the structure and powers of local units.

At the same time that voters were adopting state constitutions that curtailed the power of the state legislature, the power of state administrative officials was being expanded. Problems once thought to be local came to be viewed as statewide, especially problems relating to law enforcement, finance, health, highways, welfare, and election procedures. Because many local governments had notoriously ineffective administrative practices, state officials sometimes took over responsibilities previously handled by local people. At other times the states offered local governments financial assistance with certain strings attached. Gradually, state officials were given more authority to supervise what local officials do.

The extent of state control over local units today varies from state to state and also among the different kinds of local government within each state. At one extreme, local officials merely have to file reports with specified state officials. At the other extreme, state officials have the authority to appoint and remove some local officials, thus exerting considerable control over local affairs.

State officials are genuinely conscious of local problems. This heightened concern is acknowledged by mayors and city managers, who regularly work with both state and federal officials. In recent years, the direct ties between national and local officials,

unitary system
A constitutional arrangement in which power is concentrated in a central government.

constitutional home rule
State constitutional authorization for local governments to conduct their own affairs.

especially in the larger urban areas—ties that used to ally them against state officials—have weakened as federal assistance has been cut back.

COUNTIES IN THE UNITED STATES

Counties are the largest jurisdiction within a state, yet they get a lot less attention from citizens and the media than do cities or school districts. However, a few counties are better known than the cities or local municipalities within them: for example, Westchester County, New York; Montgomery County, Maryland; Marin and Orange Counties, California; Dade County, Florida (which includes Miami); and Cook County, Illinois (which includes Chicago). Some cities, such as Boston, New York, Denver, Baltimore, Philadelphia, San Francisco, and Honolulu, are simultaneously cities and counties.

States are divided into counties (in Louisiana they are called *parishes* and in Alaska they are known as *boroughs*). With a few exceptions (such as Connecticut and Rhode Island, where counties have lost their governmental function), county governments exist everywhere in the United States. There are 3,043 of them, and they vary in size, population, and functions. Loving County, Texas, for example, has fewer than 150 inhabitants; Los Angeles County, California, has nearly 10 million. (Table 28–2 lists the 15 largest counties.)

Counties were originally organized on the idea that a county seat would be no more than a day's journey for everyone within the county's borders. Farm families could pile into their wagons and head for the county seat, and while farmers were attending to business, their families could shop and pick up the local gossip. Then they could all get home in time to do the evening chores. Today, of course, a farmer can drive across a whole state or several states in a day.

There are two major types of counties: large urban ones and nearly 2,400 rural ones. Urban counties have many of the same structures as their rural counterparts, but they are more intertwined with their urban centers.

The traditional functions of counties are law enforcement, highway construction and maintenance, tax collection and property assessment, recording of legal papers, and welfare. Until recently, counties were convenient subdivisions; they spent most of their time merely carrying out policies established elsewhere. Over the past generation, however, counties have taken on more tasks than they have lost. Counties in a few states have given up some of their responsibilities, but in most other states, especially in the South, they are taking over from the states such urban functions as transportation, water and sewer operation, and land-use planning.[3] Elsewhere, cities are contracting with counties to provide such joint services as personnel training, law enforcement, and correctional facilities. County governments are least active in the New England states, where the county is little more than a judicial and law enforcement district; county officials do some road building but not much else.

County Government

Most counties have little legislative power. The typical county has a central governing body, variously titled but most frequently called *county commission* or *board of supervisors*. Most boards have from three to seven members, with a median size of six. They administer state laws, levy taxes, appropriate money, issue bonds, sign contracts on behalf of the county, and handle whatever jobs the state laws and constitution assign to them (see Figure 28–1).

Layers of Governance in a Typical Small Town

1. Borough of Whitehall
2. Baldwin-Whitehall School District
3. Baldwin-Whitehall Schools Authority
4. Pleasant Hills Sanitary Authority
5. South Hills Regional Planning Commission
6. South Hills Area Council of Governments
7. City of Pittsburgh
8. Allegheny County Sanitary Authority
9. Allegheny County Soil and Water Conservation District
10. Allegheny County Criminal Justice Commission
11. Allegheny County Port Authority
12. Allegheny County
13. Western Pennsylvania Water Company
14. Southwestern Pennsylvania Regional Planning Commission
15. Air Quality Control Region
16. Commonwealth of Pennsylvania
17. United States of America

TABLE 28–2 The 15 Largest U.S. Counties (by Population)

1. Los Angeles Co., Calif.
2. Cook Co., Ill.
3. Harris Co., Tex.
4. San Diego Co., Calif.
5. Orange Co., Calif.
6. Maricopa Co., Ariz.
7. Wayne Co., Mich.
8. Dade Co., Fla.
9. Dallas Co., Tex.
10. King Co., Wash.
11. Santa Clara Co., Calif.
12. San Bernardino Co., Calif.
13. Cuyahoga Co., Ohio
14. Middlesex Co., Mass.
15. Broward Co., Fla.

SOURCE: U.S. Bureau of the Census, *Statistical Abstract of the United States, 2000* (Government Printing Office, 2000).

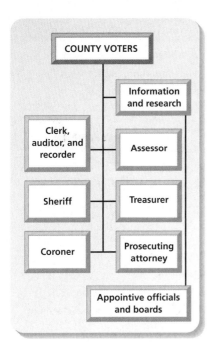

COUNTY VOTERS

Information and research

Clerk, auditor, and recorder

Assessor

Sheriff

Treasurer

Coroner

Prosecuting attorney

Appointive officials and boards

FIGURE 28–1 The Commission Form of County Government

County boards are of two types: the larger boards are usually composed of township supervisors or other township officials; the smaller boards are usually, though not always, elected in at-large elections. At-large elections make it difficult for minorities to be elected to office, especially when they are concentrated in a few areas. Minorities usually win more seats in a district election than in an at-large system.

The county board shares its powers with a number of other officials, most commonly the sheriff, the county prosecutor or district attorney, the county clerk, the coroner, and the auditor, who are generally elected rather than appointed. Sometimes county treasurers, health officers, and surveyors are also found on the ballot.

In general, counties are administered by an unwieldy collection of relatively independent agencies, and until recently there was seldom a single executive responsible for coordinating such activities. However, today about 800 counties appoint a chief administrative officer who serves at the pleasure of the county commissioners. Approximately 400 counties now elect a *county executive* who is responsible for most administrative functions (see Figure 28–2).

County Performance

How well do counties do their job? The picture is mixed. The existence of counties adds to the fragmentation of authority and responsibility among a variety of elected officials, often producing needless jurisdictional conflicts, inefficiencies in purchasing, duplication of costs, and resistance to developing modern purchasing and personnel systems.

Although counties have often been the forgotten government within the states, this is changing. Their jurisdictional boundaries give them great potential for solving complex problems that are difficult to solve at the city level or have been decentralized to local levels of government by the states.[4] The growing professionalization of county work forces and the trend to electing or appointing professional county executives are improving efficiency. "City-county functional consolidation in areas such as emergency medical services and natural-disaster planning is growing throughout the United States. . . . Increasing cooperation is likely to occur in the future as cities and counties struggle to provide more services to a tax-resistant public."[5]

TOWNS, CITIES, SUBURBS

Since the 1940s the areas around the cities have been the fastest-growing places in the United States (see Figure 28–3). At least 50 percent of Americans now live in suburban communities. Suburbs grew at the expense of cities for a variety of reasons: inexpensive land, lower taxes, cleaner air, more open space for recreational purposes, less crime, better highways, and the changing character of the inner cities. There is no one explanation for the exodus to the suburbs. In part it was because people desired to escape the deteriorating central cities. Resistance to mandatory busing to achieve integrated schools in the 1960s and 1970s also contributed to so-called "white flight." But it was just as much a matter of class as of race, with middle and upper-middle income level whites, Asians, and African Americans fleeing to the suburbs to escape urban crime and to seek more attractive environments in terms of class, religion, race, and lifestyle.[6]

Young families who could afford it left the crowded and blighted cities in search of a house with a lawn and a backyard. Parents wanted good school systems with modern facilities. Industries moved from the central cities in search of cheaper land, lower taxes, and less restrictive building and health codes. Businesses followed the people and the industries, and a myriad of shopping centers grew in outlying communities. Much of this exodus was accelerated by federal policies, such as new interstate highways, mortgages insured by the Federal Housing Administration, and the construction of public housing. Most of the new jobs created in the United States continue to be located in the suburbs or newer cities on the fringe of the central cities.

In most counties, the sheriff is an elected official.

The major tasks of suburban government are often bound together with those of the metropolis.[7] Larger cities usually maintain an elaborate police department with detective bureaus, crime-detection laboratories, and communications networks, but its jurisdiction stops at the city line. Criminals, however, seldom stop at the city line. Suburbs have fewer police, and they are often untrained in criminology, so they call on urban police expertise. Cities and suburbs are also tied together by highways, all of which have local access roads. In matters of health, too, there are often wide differences in services between city and suburb, but germs, pollution, and smog do not notice city signposts.

Older suburbs from Long Island to California's Bay Area are now experiencing some of the problems long associated with disinvestment and population decline. Some suburbs, too, are challenged by sprawling growth that creates crowded schools, traffic congestion, loss of open spaces, and a lack of affordable housing.[8] Many people believe there is a need for collaborative city-suburb strategies to address sprawl and the structural challenges facing older suburbs and inner cities. We'll return to this topic later in this chapter.

The Rise of "Edge Cities"

In recent decades, cities have been built on the edge of cities. Writer Joel Garreau calls these "edge cities" and suggests that virtually every expanding American city grows in the fashion of Los Angeles, with multiple urban cores.[9] Thus we have Tysons Corner, Virginia, outside Washington, D.C., the Perimeter Center at the northern tip of Atlanta's Beltway, the Galleria area west of downtown Houston, and the Schaumburg area outside of downtown Chicago.

Edge cities are defined as places with 5 million or more square feet of office space, 600,000 or more square feet of retail space, and more jobs than bedrooms. More often than not, these edge cities were empty spaces or farmland just 30 years ago. New freeways appeared first, then a shopping mall or two, and then industrial parks.

Some of the problems of the inner city have caught up with edge cities, just as they have with suburbs: traffic congestion, parking problems, crime, pollution, and urban blight. Political problems have cropped up as well. Most edge cities are in unincorporated areas of counties and are subject in varying degrees to control by county governments. These edge cities are sometimes run by "shadow governments"—private

FIGURE 28–2 The Council with Elected Executive Form of County Government

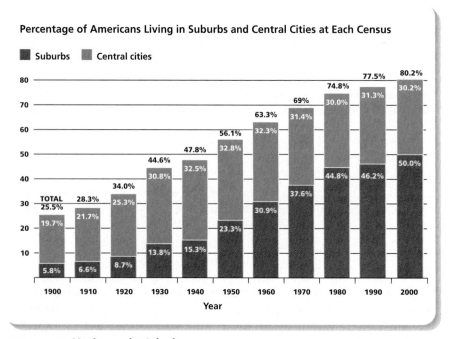

FIGURE 28–3 Moving to the Suburbs

A Closer Look

THE NEW ENGLAND TOWN MEETING

The New England town meeting has long been a celebrated institution. The traditional picture of sturdy, independent citizens coming together to settle public affairs and speak their minds is a stirring one. The New England town is sometimes pointed to as the one place in the United States where there is no elite, and where participatory democracy really exists. The town meeting is our most obvious example of *direct democracy*; voters participate directly in making rules, passing new laws, levying taxes, and appropriating money. Despite this idealized picture, it is generally a veteran group of activists that provides political and policy-making leadership.

At least 1,000 New England towns (especially those with populations under 20,000) still hold annual town meetings open to all voters. Maine has nearly 400 towns that use the town meeting system of democracy; Vermont has about 200 towns using the town meeting process.

The assemblies at town meetings usually choose a board of executive officers, historically called *selectmen*. These boards, which generally have three to five members, carry on the business of the town between meetings. The selectmen are in charge of town property; they also grant licenses, supervise other town officials, and call special town meetings. A town treasurer, assessor, constable, and the school board, as well as others, are elected by the voters or appointed by the selectmen. A town

administrator often functions as a city manager and reports to the board of selectmen.

Some state and local officials in New England say the town meeting is on the decline. Derry, New Hampshire, for example, held its last town meeting in 1985; then it switched to a mayor-council system. The town meeting had served Derry well for most of its 158-year history, but it proved unable to deal with rapid growth and an influx of people who commute long distances to work. In 1996 nearly 60 communities or school districts in New Hampshire modified their town meeting process so that meetings are for discussion purposes only, with final decisions on proposed laws made by the voters at the polls one week later. In Rhode Island, 13 towns abandoned the town meeting, and 18 towns utilize the meeting only to adopt the town budget.

Many larger communities in New England with populations of more than 25,000 have modified the town meeting by moving to a *representative* town meeting. At representative town meetings, between 50 and 300 local residents from various town precincts are elected to serve three-year terms representing their neighborhoods at their annual town meetings. This is a popular format in many

The New England town meeting, like this one in Sandwich, New Hampshire, has long been a celebrated American institution.

suburbs of Boston with 25,000 to 50,000 residents.

The New England town meetings are tenacious institutions that continue to work well. Crucial to their success is a committee system. "Committee members become subject matter experts and provide advice to the town meeting which is followed most of the time."* Thus the open town meeting, at least in small towns in New England, still proves to be a rather vital way for people to participate in the policy making of their communities.

*Joseph F. Zimmerman, "The New England Town Meeting: A De Facto Representative Assembly," paper presented at the American Political Science Association Annual Meeting, Boston, September 5, 1998, p. 25.

---

charter
A city "constitution" that outlines the structure of city government, defines the authority of the various officials, and provides for their selection.

mayor-council charter
The oldest and most common form of city government, consisting of either a weak mayor and a city council or a strong mayor and council.

owners who set the fees for policing, transportation, and various other services that are normally financed by taxes. There is not much room for government by the people in a community that is essentially a business.

CITY GOVERNMENT TODAY

What does the word "city" call to mind? Bright lights and crowded streets? A city is not merely improved real estate; it is also people—men and women living and working together. Aristotle observed that people came together in the cities for security, but they stayed there for the good life.

The "good life" is defined differently by different people, yet it often includes these attractions:

- Employment opportunities
- Cultural centers, museums, performing arts centers, theaters
- Diverse educational institutions
- Entertainment and night life
- Professional sports teams
- Wide variety of stores and specialty shops
- Good restaurants
- Diversity of people, architecture, and lifestyles

Although a few cities existed when the U.S. Constitution was written, the nation was overwhelmingly rural in 1787, and seven out of ten people worked on farms. People clustered mainly in the villages and small towns scattered throughout the 13 states and neighboring territories. The villages and cities were the indispensable workshops of democracy, the places where democratic skills were developed, where grand issues were debated, and, above all, where the people resolved to fight the British to secure their fundamental rights.

The United States is now a nation of about 19,300 cities, and although some cities have just a few hundred people, others have millions. Three American supercities and their suburbs (New York, Los Angeles, and Chicago) have populations larger than the total population of the Republic in the 1780s (see Table 28–3).

Every municipality has two major purposes. One is to provide government within its boundaries: to maintain law and order, keep streets clean, educate children, purify water, create parks, and make the area a good place in which to live.[10] As an instrument of the state, the city has a second major purpose: to carry out state functions.

The **charter** is to the city what a constitution is to the national or the state government. It outlines the structure of the government, defines the authority of the various officials, and provides for their selection. Although charters are good sources of information on how the people in our cities are governed, they can be misleading. Different structures are not neutral in their impact, for different forms encourage different kinds of participation and responsiveness. In short, power and clout and who gets what, where, and how can definitely be shaped by a city's structural arrangements.

The Mayor-Council Charter

The **mayor-council charter** is the oldest and most popular charter (see Figure 28–4). Under this type of charter, the city council is usually a single chamber. The size of the council varies from as few as 2 members to as many as 50, though 7 is the median size in cities with more than 5,000 people.

Many methods are used to select council members: nonpartisan and partisan elections, elections by large and small wards, or elections from the city at-large. Large cities that elect members affiliated with political parties generally choose them by small districts or wards rather than at-large. This arrangement tends to support strong party organizations. Nonpartisan at-large elections make party influence difficult. The larger the election districts, the more likely citywide considerations will affect the selection of council members, and the greater the influence of citywide institutions such as local newspapers.

The difference between at-large citywide elections and elections based on small, single-member districts within a city can be significant for racial and ethnic representation on the city council. The at-large system tends to produce councils made up of the city's elite and middle classes. The small district gives minorities and

TABLE 28–3 The 15 Largest U.S. Cities

Rank/City

1. New York, N.Y.
2. Los Angeles, Calif.
3. Chicago, Ill.
4. Houston, Tex.
5. Philadelphia, Pa.
6. San Diego, Calif.
7. Phoenix, Ariz.
8. San Antonio, Tex.
9. Dallas, Tex.
10. Detroit, Mich.
11. San Jose, Calif.
12. San Francisco, Calif.
13. Indianapolis, Ind.
14. Jacksonville, Fla.
15. Columbus, Ohio

SOURCE: U.S. Bureau of the Census, *Statistical Abstract of the United States, 2000* (Government Printing Office, 2000).

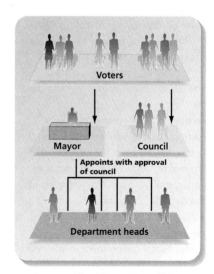

FIGURE 28–4 The Mayor-Council Form of City Government

the less advantaged a somewhat better chance for representation where neighborhoods may have high concentrations of one minority.

The Voting Rights Act of 1965 forbids cities with a past history of discrimination against minority voters from adopting the at-large systems for electing council members if the effect would be to dilute the voting strength of these minorities. In fact, no local government in regions spelled out in this act can make a change in its voting system without the approval of the U.S. attorney general. But what of cities or counties that have long had at-large elections? Can they be forced to give them up because at-large elections virtually ensure that minorities will never be elected? The mere fact that no African American is elected under a certain system does not by itself constitute a violation of the Fourteenth or Fifteenth Amendment. The Constitution forbids only practices adopted or maintained *with the purposeful intent to discriminate*.

When Congress debated the extension of the Voting Rights Act in 1982, civil rights advocates urged it to outlaw at-large systems. They contended city officials are not so foolish as to admit that they want to keep minorities from being elected. Others argued that cities should be free to adopt whatever election system they wished; after all, the Constitution guarantees that no person will be denied the right to vote because of race, not that candidates of the voter's own race will win an election.

The Voting Rights Act as interpreted by the Supreme Court has made it easier to prove that at-large systems violate civil rights. Discriminatory intent need not be proved by direct evidence; it may be inferred from the following facts: (1) a city or county has a past history of discrimination designed to keep minorities from voting; (2) minorities make up a large majority of the population; and (3) no member of a minority has ever been elected to office under an at-large system.[11]

Weak Mayor Councils and Strong Mayor Councils

The powers of the mayor-council form of government vary from charter to charter and even more widely from city to city and mayor to mayor. There are, however, two basic variations of the mayor-council form: weak mayor-council and strong mayor-council.

In **weak mayor-council** cities, mayors are often chosen from members of the elected city council rather than elected directly by the people. The mayor's appointive powers are usually restricted, and the city council as a whole generally possesses both legislative and executive authority. The mayor must usually obtain the council's consent for all major administrative decisions. Often weak mayor-council cities permit direct election by the voters of a number of department heads, such as police chief or controller. In weak mayor-council cities, there is no single administrative head for the city, and power is fragmented. The weak mayor-council plan was designed for an earlier era, when cities were smaller and government simpler. It is ill-suited to large cities, where political and administrative leadership is vital.

Under the **strong mayor-council** form, the mayor is elected directly by the people and given fairly broad appointment powers. The mayor, often with the help of his or her staff, prepares and administers the budget, enjoys almost total administrative authority, and has the power to appoint and dismiss department heads. This system obviously calls for a mayor to be both a good political leader and an effective administrator—qualities not always found in the same person.

Many people believe the strong mayor-council system is the best form of government for large cities because it gives the cities strong political leaders and makes responsive administration possible. Further, by centering authority in the hands of a few individuals, it makes less likely the growth of "invisible government" by people who have power but are not publicly accountable for its use.

The Council-Manager Charter

Reformers in the early 1900s acclaimed the **council-manager plan** (also known as the *city-manager plan*), in which the city council hires a professional administrator to manage city affairs. It was indeed a significant governmental innovation. In 1908

weak mayor-council
Form of local government in which the members of the city council select the mayor, who then shares power with other elected or appointed boards and commissions.

strong mayor-council
Form of local government in which the voters directly elect the city council and the mayor, who enjoys almost total administrative authority and appoints the department heads.

council-manager plan
Form of local government in which the city council hires a professional administrator to manage city affairs; also known as the *city-manager plan*.

the small city of Staunton, Virginia, appointed a general manager to direct the city's work. Little note was taken of the step, but the council-manager plan soon became the darling of both reformers and the business elite. They liked the idea that the council would serve as a sort of "board of directors" in the business sense of setting broad policies, while a professional executive would see that these policies were carried out with businesslike efficiency (see Figure 28–5).

Under the council-manager charter, the council is usually elected in nonpartisan primaries and elections, either on a citywide basis or by election districts much larger than the wards in mayor-council cities. The council appoints a city manager and supervises the manager's activities. The council still makes the laws and approves the budget, and although it is not supposed to interfere in administration, the council often supervises city government through the manager. The mayor is expected to preside over the council and represent the city on ceremonial occasions, but many mayors in fact do a good deal more than this. Contrary to what some textbooks imply, the mayor in council-manager cities can sometimes be a strong policy and political leader as well as a dominant influence in exercising political power.[12] This has surely been the case in cities as different as Cambridge, Massachusetts, San Antonio, Texas, and Colorado Springs, Colorado.

The city manager advises the council on policy and supervises the administration of city business. Because council-manager cities try to attract the best available persons, few of their charters require the councils to select managers from among local citizens, nor do they prescribe detailed qualifications. Although city-manager charters seem to call for a nonpolitical city manager who merely carries out policies adopted by the council, and for council members who refrain from interfering with the administration of city affairs, it is often difficult to distinguish clearly between making and applying policy.

Today over 2,700 cities, located in virtually every state, operate under a council-manager charter. It has, in fact, become the most popular form of local government in medium-sized cities of more than 10,000 citizens. It is especially popular in California, where about 98 percent of the cities now use it, as well as in other western and sun belt cities. The largest cities operating under a city manager are Dallas, San Antonio, San Diego, Phoenix, Kansas City, Cincinnati, Oakland, and Fort Worth.

How has the city manager plan worked? In cities characterized by low social diversity and high consensus about community goals, the council-manager form has met with success. Such cities have generally enjoyed improved standards of public employment, reduced costs, and better services. But some observers say this plan has also weakened political leadership in these cities and has confused citizens as to who really provides policy leadership.

In an effort to become more responsive, some council-manager cities have expanded the size of their councils and have abandoned at-large elections for district elections. More than 60 percent of the city-manager cities now also directly elect their mayors in an effort to provide greater political accountability and leadership.[13]

THE ROLE OF THE MAYOR

Two hundred years ago the notion of a strong mayor providing vigorous leadership was nonexistent. The need for strong mayoral leadership developed in the late nineteenth century. It was seen as a means to deal with the social revolution brought on by urbanization, massive waves of immigration, and mounting economic problems of growing cities. In the larger cities, gradually and often grudgingly, the office of mayor became a key position for political leadership.

The typical mayor is a college graduate, an experienced grass-roots politician, a business or a legal professional, and is usually 40–50 years old. Mayors in the largest cities earn $90,000 to $160,000, and in middle-sized cities between $40,000 and

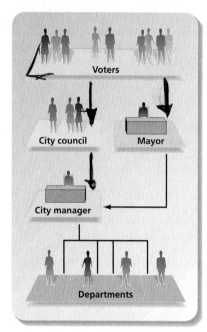

FIGURE 28–5 The Council-Manager Form of City Government

Special Districts

The sheer complexity and fragmentation of government administrations in suburbia often create confusion and frustration. With few exceptions, each suburb has its own government, fire and police departments, school system, street-cleaning equipment, and building and health codes. *Special districts* piled one on top of the other further complicate the situation.

Special districts are units of government typically established to provide one or more specific services, such as sewage disposal, fire protection, water supply, or pollution control for a local or regional area. They are often created to enable an existing unit of government to evade established tax and debt limits and to spread the tax burden over an area wider than individual municipalities or counties. Many smaller special districts are formed in suburban areas to obtain urban services without having to create a city government or be annexed by one.

Special districts usually have governing boards appointed by officials of other governments or elected by the general public. Special districts are useful for dealing with urgent problems that overlap boundaries of existing units of government. Many urban and regional problems defy city and county boundaries, and special districts offer economies of scale that make sense.

Some critics say that the rapid increase in special districts in the past 30 years has prevented comprehensive planning. Critics also lament that few citizens know who runs these special districts, and even fewer know how these officials make decisions.

$80,000. City managers, chief city administrators, and top appointees sometimes make more than the mayors.

Although most mayors are male, several of the nation's largest cities have recently had women mayors, including Pittsburgh, Houston, Dallas, San Diego, San Antonio, Portland, and Washington, D.C. In fact, about 20 percent of municipal governments in the United States with a population of 30,000 or more are headed by women, and the number is growing. Many of them worked their way up through service on school boards and city councils and in the League of Women Voters. An increasing number of African Americans also serve as mayors. Currently more than 300 cities have African American mayors, including Atlanta, Philadelphia, Denver, Detroit, Houston, San Francisco, Newark, Richmond, and Washington, D.C.

The main job of the mayor is administrative in the broadest sense of the term. Mayors supervise the line agencies—police, fire, public safety, traffic, health, sanitation—as well as a host of special agencies, such as the board of elections, the city planning agency, and commissions that regulate particular occupations and professions. Big-city mayors usually have staffs that carry out typical executive office functions such as personnel, management, budgeting, scheduling, and public relations. In this respect mayors face the same tasks as corporate executives: coordinating a variety of different activities, assigning responsibilities, checking that projects are carried out, finding the ablest people to take charge, and allocating money through control of the budget.

Usually mayors become involved with the private sector in an effort to promote economic opportunities. They try to secure additional jobs, increase the tax base, make the city more attractive to certain kinds of businesses, and coordinate public service expansion with private sector requirements. The private sector becomes involved in economic development because its success depends upon having an educated labor base with appropriate skills, a constant consumer population, stable communities, and increasing property values.

Many mayors, such as those in New York, San Francisco, Seattle, Atlanta, Chicago, and Miami, have their own "foreign policies." That is, they play host to foreign dignitaries and business delegations and travel abroad seeking foreign investments as they sing the praises of local exportable goods.[14]

Sometimes a mayor must depend on the party organization to ensure support in the council, as in Chicago, where the huge city council consists of 50 members. Other mayors may have to deal with smaller councils, but they are likely to be weak unless they have enough political support to win cooperation.

Although partisan politics is waning as a feature of city government, mayors as party leaders still often dominate the party's city organizations. Mayors help recruit candidates for office, deal with revolts and opposition within their parties, and represent their parties in Washington or the state capitals. As chief legislator, mayors draw up proposed legislation and also make many specific policies. As chief fundraiser, mayors bargain for more money for their cities before state and national legislatures.[15] Mayors often climb the political ladder to run for governor or sometimes even president. For example, Ohio's former governor and now U.S. senator, George Voinovich, had previously been mayor of Cleveland, and former California governor Pete Wilson had been mayor of San Diego. U.S. Senator Richard Lugar of Indiana had been mayor of Indianapolis.

Mayors are expected to help revitalize the economy and attract investors, sports teams, tourists, and conventions. It takes courage and missionary zeal to overcome the pessimism and decay that beset most inner cities. But several mayors—such as Ed Rendell in Philadelphia, Rudolph Giuliani in New York City, Richard Riordan

in Los Angeles, Steve Goldsmith in Indianapolis, Wellington Webb in Denver, Norm Rice in Seattle, and both Richard J. Daley and Richard M. Daley in Chicago—have succeeded.[16] These cities have reduced crime, increased economic opportunities, and revitalized downtown businesses and residential areas.

In recent decades, mayors, like presidents and governors, have grown in power and importance. Most cities have altered their charters to give their mayors power to appoint and remove heads of departments, investigate departmental activities, send legislative messages to the city councils, prepare budgets, and veto council ordinances. In other words, mayors have been given a share in policy making, and city administration has been centralized under the mayor's direction.

WHO INFLUENCES LOCAL POLICY MAKING?

Most Americans, most of the time, leave the responsibility of running the cities and counties to local officials and people willing to serve on boards and in local civic organizations. This does not mean that Americans rave about the quality of services received from local governments. Although they generally respond favorably to the services they get from city government and local public transportation agencies, they often rate them less favorably than they do the services provided by commercial organizations.

But if most people do not choose to be leaders in their communities, that does not mean they do not care about tax rates, the quality of schools in the community, and the availability of services. Hundreds of local people can be mobilized quickly if city hall mishandles local affairs or makes unpopular decisions. Indeed, activism has increased in recent years. It is now common for people to form groups to protect their communities from waste landfills, toxic dumps, shopping malls, and highways. With dogged perseverance and shoestring budgets, grass-roots protest groups have often successfully taken on city hall or won victories for their neighborhoods in the courts.

A sure way to involve people in city government is to propose a policy that threatens the value or safety of the homes of middle- or upper-middle-class taxpayers. The slightest hint that a correctional facility, a freeway, a garbage dump, or a toxic disposal site is coming to their neighborhood will swiftly mobilize citizens who are otherwise happy to be passive spectators in local government. Similarly, the firing of a popular school principal, the closing of a neighborhood school, or a major increase in the property tax will produce a volley of citizen protests that can change the policy-making process at city hall.

Elected and appointed officials try to sense the mood of the local citizenry. They want to avert marches on city hall, recall elections, and citizen dissatisfaction. Their desire to be reelected and respected keeps them reasonably accountable.[17]

Interest Groups in Cities

The stakes and prizes in city politics are considerable: city jobs and commissioner posts, tax breaks, city contracts, regulations, licenses, and much more. Local politicians must deal with the kinds of interest groups found in any industrial society: organized workers, business leaders, neighborhood associations, professional associations, good government associations, home builders and developers, consumers, taxpayers, environmentalists, and various racial and ethnic groups.

The most powerful groups in most cities are typically business groups. Employers provide the economic base for taxes and for jobs, and mayors know they will win or lose the next election in large part on how well they promote the local economy.

Investors and businesses are free to locate wherever they please. Thus they may move from a central city to a nearby suburb or from one city to another. City policy makers, therefore, must follow an "economic logic" that requires them to adopt policies that persuade businesses and investors to remain as participants in the local economy, either by keeping tax rates relatively low or by increasing the quality of

- Neighborhood associations
- Chambers of Commerce
- Local trade and manufacturing associations
- Business leaders of major local concerns (bankers, department store owners, publishers, managers of local high-tech or steel companies)
- Small merchants' associations (downtown merchants' groups, Main Street associates, shopping mall owners)
- Taxpayers' associations
- Civic associations
- Utilities (power, electricity, and fuel companies)
- Real estate and home builders' associations
- Local contractors
- Local unions
- League of Women Voters
- Public employee groups (teachers, police, and fire fighters)
- Civil and human rights groups (Urban League, National Association for Advancement of Colored People, Hispanic and Asian American groups)
- Parents' groups (PTA, Mothers Against Drunk Driving)
- Environmental groups (Sierra Club)
- Farmers' groups (Farm Bureau, Farmers Union)
- Religious organizations
- Ethnic and fraternal organizations
- Single-interest groups (NIMBY—Not In My Back Yard; PUKE—People United for a Klean Environment)

service and amenities. If successful, this kind of growth politics enhances the prospects of city officials for reelection because economic growth, especially business investment, boosts the tax base and increases economic opportunities.[18]

But business groups have to share political power and influence with unions, environmentalists, ethnic groups, and many others. Most business officials learn that they can influence city political decision making by cultivating allies.[19] City politics generally involves informal alliances of public officials working together with private-sector individuals and institutions.[20]

Police, fire fighters, street cleaners, teachers, and other public employees have organized into unions, many of which are affiliated with national unions. Such unions are often a major influence in larger cities. They fight for improved pay, working conditions, and job security. Although strikes by city employees providing vital services are prohibited by law in most states, enforcement is difficult. Teachers and municipal workers use the strike, or the threat of a strike, to force cities to increase wages and provide better benefits. Mayors complain that public employee unions are sometimes so powerful they make the old-fashioned political machine look tame.

In addition, nonprofit groups such as the League of Women Voters, cultural foundations, local nonpartisan civic city clubs, independent local planning groups, and arts leagues exist in most urban areas, and they, too, want to be heard in the policy-making discussions of their cities.

Americans would like to believe that every citizen has a say in local government. We know, however, that prominent families and local business leaders have more influence than the rest of us. Nursing home residents, the unemployed, migratory workers, young drifters, and the homeless are unlikely to have much influence. Participation in community affairs is often a middle-class and upper-middle-class practice. Low-income residents and the homeless are often ignored when mayors and business elites pursue aggressive economic development policies. "For renters and low-income residents, . . . a booming economy with rising land values may put affordable housing out of reach."[21] This is true in New York City as well as in places like Aspen, Colorado. There are costs as well as benefits to urban growth. Economic development can destroy neighborhoods and drive cities into debt.

THE CENTRAL CITY AND ITS POLITICS

Today most Americans live in *metropolitan areas*, which include large cities and their suburbs, rather than the farm or small town so beloved in American fact and fiction. A metropolitan area is, in the minds of most people, a big city and its suburbs. But the Census Bureau, which counts 284 metro areas, uses a more formal definition:

> A metro area is built around one or more central counties containing an urban area of at least 50,000 people. It also includes outlying counties with close ties—economic and social—to the central counties. To be considered part of the metro area, the outlying counties must meet certain criteria, including numbers of commuters, population density and growth, and urban population.[22]

About 75 percent of the American people live on about 5 percent of the land; 80 percent live in metropolitan areas; 55 percent live within 60 miles of coastal shoreline (Atlantic, Pacific, Gulf of Mexico, or along the Great Lakes or the St. Lawrence River); and 30 percent live in central cities.

In the nineteenth century masses of new immigrants arrived from Europe; in the twentieth century migrants came from the rural areas, especially from the South; and more recently this country experienced waves of newcomers from Cuba, Korea, Vietnam, the Philippines, Nicaragua, Haiti, Mexico, and other Latin American countries. The majority of newcomers settled first in the inner cities—usually in the poorest, most decayed sections—which inevitably put great stress on the schools and sometimes on community safety as well. Overcrowding and substandard housing in these areas increased health and fire hazards.

Any picture of central cities as composed exclusively of huddled, starving, homeless youth gangs and unemployed masses, however, is misleading. Nor is it fair to say simply that central cities have all the problems and suburbs have all the resources. Central cities do have more "high-cost citizens" (truly needy, handicapped, and senior citizens), and most aging cities are losing population. They are losing businesses, too, because land, rents, utilities, and taxes are often less expensive in the outer suburbs, and businesses move to lower their operating costs. But their departure means cities have smaller tax bases. Higher operating costs in the cities also result from aging public works.

The city of Hartford, Connecticut, illustrates the challenge many cities face. It is home to many of the nation's wealthiest insurance companies, the capital city of the nation's most affluent state. It boasts excellent colleges and universities. And yet, as journalist Alan Ehrenhalt wrote, it has serious problems:

> [Hartford's] residential neighborhoods are riddled by crime and drugs. It has lost more than 20 percent of its population in the past four decades. In a metro area that is 90 percent white, Hartford itself is 70 percent Hispanic and black. More than a quarter of its residents—36,000 in all—live below the official poverty line.[23]

Somewhat in contrast to Hartford, Rhode Island's capital city, Providence, is thriving these days. City leaders there crusaded for downtown development, historic preservation, arts and athletic complexes, and all kinds of public-private partnerships that have enriched Providence and attracted considerable state and federal aid.[24]

As the income gap between city and suburban residents widens, central cities find it hard to raise new revenues or to force suburbanites to pay a larger share of the bill for the city services they use. This is the economic problem. The legal problem is

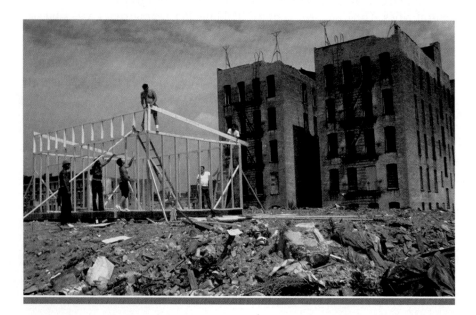

Urban renewal in many communities is replacing large apartment houses with smaller individual homes.

that most of the states have not permitted their cities to raise funds in any meaningful way with a local income tax.[25]

In an effort to recapture part of the tax base that escapes to the suburbs in the evenings, some cities have imposed local payroll or other types of *commuter taxes* to obtain revenue from people who work in the central cities and make frequent use of city facilities yet live in the suburbs. Some city officials say the payroll or commuter tax is an effective way to shift some of the burden to those who benefit from the city but live beyond its borders. But others say it is unlikely to provide significant long-term revenue growth, and they think it encourages even more businesses to leave the city.

Today, however, many of the once down-and-out central cities are showing signs of rejuvenation. Several cities such as Boston, Cleveland, and Washington, D.C., that had lost population a decade ago are now gaining new residents. Gentrification and "yuppy" development have attracted some suburbanites to come back to central cities. The reasons for the rebound of many central cities varies from city to city, yet analysts believe the sustained economic boom of the 1990s grew local tax revenues, which were then invested heavily in local infrastructure to make cities more appealing. The boom and investment in cities also helped to create more jobs.[26]

MEETING THE CHALLENGES OF GROWTH AND ECONOMIC DEVELOPMENT

Until recently everybody, or at least almost everybody, wanted to see his or her city grow. Everybody was a city booster. The local newspaper, the television stations, the radio stations, the Chamber of Commerce, the union leaders, the business community, the developers, the teachers, and proud citizens worked together to attract new industries. Such industries would bring, they hoped, new jobs, more amenities, increased land values, and more opportunities for the young. The consensus was that a city with a growing population was a healthy one; one with a decreasing population was a sick one.

Local politicians found it risky to oppose economic development and economic growth; those who did feared they would not be reelected. However, beginning two decades ago, an *antigrowth* movement developed in many cities. There had always been restraints in the wealthy suburbs outside of the central cities; in fact, many suburbs were created to escape the growth taking place in central cities. These suburbs adopted building and zoning codes and land-use regulations to make it difficult, if not impossible, for industries to be located there and to keep out people who could not afford large houses on large lots. New suburbs were carefully planned to ensure they would not become too crowded. These zoning regulations were attacked in the courts as strategies to keep the poor and minorities out, but as long as they were racially neutral on their face, the courts left them undisturbed.

By the 1980s environmental awareness spread, and coalitions formed to fight unregulated growth. Disturbed by noise, pollution, and traffic jams, and fearful that developers would build too many houses too close together and overload the infrastructure of roads, sewage disposal, and schools in the community, opponents of growth joined together.

Strategies to Govern Metro Regions

Divided executive authority, fragmented legislative power, splintered and noncompetitive political parties, the absence of strong central governments, and the necessity to bargain with national, state, and local officials—all these factors suggest that metro regions, where about 80 percent of Americans now live, are shapeless

giants with nobody in charge. Metro regions, of course, typically encompass many cities, counties, towns, and suburbs so they too are complicated and often splintered.

At the turn of the century, reformers were afraid of domination by political bosses. But in the modern metropolis, political machines do not run the central city. Urban bureaucracies may wield a lot of power, but they do not offer metropolitan leadership. Special interests seldom really control the metropolis, nor does a business elite. Who, then, governs the metropolis? It's typically a "nobody's in charge" arrangement.

Growing fragmentation of government in large metropolitan areas has brought about a variety of reform movements and structural innovations aimed at improving efficiency, effectiveness, and performance. Political scientists and public administration specialists have never been bashful about proposing remedies. Here are the better-known ideas, all of which have been tried somewhere, yet none of which has been adopted nationwide.

ANNEXATION   In the South, West, and Southwest, large central cities have absorbed adjacent territories. Oklahoma City, for example, added almost 600 square miles. Houston, Phoenix, San Antonio, El Paso, Colorado Springs, and Kansas City, Missouri, also expanded their boundaries. The now-extended cities serve almost as regional governments.[27]

But annexation has not proved helpful to cities in the Northeast and Midwest because these cities are ringed by entrenched suburban communities that seldom want to be annexed, and state laws make it difficult for the central city to do so against the wishes of the suburbs. Even in such places as the Houston metropolitan area, the annexation option is plagued by legal obstacles and political jealousies.

AGREEMENTS TO FURNISH SERVICES   The most common solution to the problems of overlapping and duplicating jurisdictions is for the units of government to contract for services. This reform is applauded by many economists, who say it comes close to providing a market that operates according to laws of supply and demand. Most of these agreements involve a few cities sharing a single activity. For example, a city may provide hospital services to its neighbors or contract with the county for law enforcement. Especially popular in the Los Angeles area, the contract system is used with increasing success in many parts of the country.

REGIONAL COORDINATING AND PLANNING COUNCILS   Just about all metro regions have some kind of *council of government* (COG). COGs began in the 1950s and were encouraged by the national government. Congress, in fact, mandated that certain federal grants be reviewed by regional planning groups. In essence, these councils bring locally elected officials together. They devote most of their time and resources to physical planning; rarely do they tackle problems of race, poverty, and the financial inequities in metro regions. Councils are set up, moreover, in such a way as to give suburbs a veto over virtually any project that would threaten their autonomy. In a few regions the councils assume operating responsibilities over such regional activities as garbage collection, transportation, and water supply. Critics say these councils rarely provide for creative area-wide governance, yet they provide an important common ground for elected

People Helping People

Countless people are coming together in their own neighborhood to tackle common problems or to form neighborhood cooperatives. Some of these self-help groups simply handle baby-sitting arrangements or organize charity events or golf tournaments; others are involved in neighborhood crime watches or Little League field construction. Local nonprofit groups in New York have built award-winning apartment complexes amid burned-out inner-city tenements. Other groups have mobilized to bring about storefront revitalization, street improvement, and area beautification programs by initiating farmers' markets, mini-parks, and gardens.*

The contemporary self-help movement is rooted in an American past that has long been marked by volunteerism and local associations. In former times the whole community often rallied when a neighbor's barn burned down; volunteer fire departments emerged out of this tradition. But as the nation has become more mobile and impersonal, we have drifted away from these traditions. Today, most Americans shop at shopping malls rather than on Main Street or in the old downtown area. At the same time, they resent the fact that public institutions have become remote and overly professionalized. Thus people across the country are joining together to do in an informal and decentralized way what extended families or small villages of the past used to do. Simply, they come together and lend a hand.

Many local groups seeking help from city hall or from county officialdom give up after running into a maze of building codes, zoning rules, and countless regulations that inhibit innovation in local government. The alternative to despair is to do it yourself. And this is exactly what is happening at the grass-roots level right now. The more successful experiments are watched carefully by the professionals at city hall, and some of the innovations are copied by those in office.

Sometimes progress or justice comes about because some activists take issues to court. Such was the case in bringing in alternative housing for lower income residents in Mount Laurel, New Jersey. And it was also the case in addressing the fatal effects of toxic dumping by businesses in Woburn, Massachusetts.**

*See the related stories in E. J. Dionne, Jr., ed., *Community Works: The Revival of Civil Society in America* (Brookings Institution, 1998).

**See David L. Kirp et al., *Our Town: Race, Housing, and the Soul of Suburbia* (Rutgers University Press, 1997); and Jonathan Harr, *A Civil Action* (Vintage, 1996).

officials to talk about mutual problems, and they help solve some problems in many of the regions.

CITY-COUNTY CONSOLIDATIONS One traditional means of overcoming the fragmentation of metro regions is to merge the city with the county. This is a pet reform of business elites, the League of Women Voters, and Chambers of Commerce. It is viewed as a rational, efficient way to simplify administration, cut costs for taxpayers, and eliminate duplication.

About 30 city-county mergers have taken place. Occasionally, one city joins with another, as Sacramento and North Sacramento did in the 1960s. Such mergers can usually be brought about only by a referendum approved by the citizens of the region. Although efforts have been made to consolidate cities with counties, few have been successful in recent decades. Other than St. Louis, Nashville, Jacksonville, and Indianapolis, consolidations have occurred in only a handful of smaller urban areas.

What happened in Indianapolis is typical of these consolidations, most of which are in the South and West. In 1970 Indianapolis combined with Marion County to create UNIGOV. This merger required special permission by the legislature. UNIGOV provides many services, but the school systems remain separate, as do the police and sheriff departments.

The era of city-county consolidation appears over. Only about ten consolidations have taken place since 1970, and only one—Athens and Clark Counties in Nevada—occurred in the 1990s. Proposed mergers are usually defeated by county voters. But it is no longer unusual to find counties running what used to be city jails, zoos, libraries, and similar services. Formal and informal agreements abound as cities and counties remedy overlap and fragmentation by shifting responsibilities for providing specific services among themselves.

FEDERATED GOVERNMENT This strategy attempts to take into account political realities by building on existing governments but assigning some crucial functions to an area-wide metro government.[28] One of the few attempts—and there have been only a few—to create a federated government is the Twin Cities Metropolitan Council for the Minneapolis–St. Paul region. This regional organization, established by the legislature in 1967, consists of a 17-member council. Sixteen members are appointed by the governor to represent equal population districts, and the seventeenth is a full-time executive who serves at the pleasure of the governor.

Today the Metropolitan Council, in essence a new layer of government superimposed on top of existing units, serves as a metropolitan planning and policy-making as well as policy-coordinating agency. It reviews applications for federal funds from the region. It guides regional planning and development and opposes local actions that would endanger the overall welfare of the region. It also has taxing authority for the region. The Twin Cities model would appear to be a ready candidate for transfer elsewhere, yet this has not happened except in the Portland area.

In 1992, Portland area voters adopted a bold new charter for the Portland Metropolitan Services District that had been created by the state legislature several years earlier. It is a directly elected regional government serving three counties and 24 cities. Its nonpartisan commission members and elected executive officer have an impressive budget and more than 1,200 employees. They oversee waste collec-

tion, a zoo, recycling, waste disposal, transportation planning, and regional air- and water-quality programs, and they constructed Oregon's new Convention Center. They have also created a greenbelt around the metro area that preserves extensive open areas.

THE POLITICS OF METROPOLITAN REORGANIZATION

In most metropolitan regions, to combine city and suburbs would be to shift political power to the suburbs. In most northern centers, this would give suburban Republicans more control of city affairs. In other cases it would enable Democrats to threaten the one-party Republican systems in the suburbs. Under these circumstances, neither Democratic leaders in the central cities nor Republicans in the suburbs show much enthusiasm for metropolitan schemes. African Americans and Hispanics often oppose area consolidation or similar reform proposals that would invariably dilute their political power, often severely.

Some people believe solutions to metropolitan problems are beyond the capacity of the metropolis itself. They favor a strengthened role for the national government, with special emphasis on ensuring "equity" or on relating services directly to needs. Some advocate reviving federal revenue sharing. Others believe the job must be done by the states, which hold the fundamental constitutional power. Still others put forward bold proposals to establish regional planning and governance arrangements that would embrace "citistate" areas that include two or more metropolitan clusters, like Baltimore and Washington, D.C.[29]

Today's aging central cities unquestionably face problems: congestion, slums, smog, tension, rootlessness, loss of community, drugs, unsafe streets, neglected children, and sprawl and visual pollution. They live with racial and ethnic tensions, not just white-black rivalry but rivalry among Latinos, Koreans, and a host of other racial and ethnic rivalries. Gangs, poverty, broken families, drive-by shootings, and drug-related crimes make life miserable for many who live in the inner cities. Yet is this new? Writers and critics since Thomas Jefferson have projected an unflattering image of the city as a cold, impersonal, and often brutal environment in which crime flourishes and people lose their dignity.

Supporters, on the other hand, contend the big city is not just a place of smog and sprawl; it is the center of innovation, excitement, and vitality. The city offers social diversity and puts less community pressure on the individual to conform. The large community is a meeting place for talent from all over the nation and the world: dancers, musicians, writers, scholars, actors, and business leaders.

Some dismiss the notion of an "urban crisis." They contend most city dwellers live more comfortably than ever before, with more and better housing, schools, and transportation. By any conceivable measure of material welfare, the present generation of urban Americans is better off than other large groups of people anywhere at any time. Most cities, especially in the West and South, are thriving, and older cities such as Boston, Pittsburgh, and Indianapolis are generally viewed as revived and vital, not decaying.

Throughout history cities have been threatened by political, social, and environmental catastrophes. Urban decay, in one form or another, has always been with us.[30] Cities thrive because over time they respond to crises and because they are an economic necessity. The economy, transportation systems, past investments, as well as cultural contributions all make cities inevitable. How well cities survive, and with what mix of people, will depend on the tides of the national economy, the way our regions are organized, the way our social and economic policies are designed, the vision and leadership individual cities muster to build their future, and the degree to which our national leaders promote policies that can help our central cities.[31]

The Times Square area of New York City has undergone major redevelopment, with new theatres and hotels replacing porno movie houses and rundown buildings.

SUMMARY

1. Local governments in the United States come in a variety of shapes and structures and perform various functions. However, since constitutional power is vested in the states, most counties, cities, and towns act as agents of the state.

2. The most common governmental form at the county level is a board of county commissioners, although larger urban counties are moving to council-administrator or council–elected executive plans.

3. There is no typical suburb. Although many suburbs are homogeneous, suburban United States is highly heterogeneous. Suburbs are confronting the same problems as the urban areas they surround. In fact, big cities and their suburbs are now described as metropolitan areas.

4. The most common governmental forms at the city level are the mayor-council and the council-manager (city-manager) plans. Mayor-council governments generally have a strong mayor elected by voters, though some plans have a weaker mayor elected by the council. Council-manager plans appoint a professional administrator. In general, council-manager cities are found in medium-sized to large cities and in western, especially sun belt, cities. Mayors and managers are key political leaders.

5. While local governments are run by officials, business interests and interest-group activism are also influencing policy.

6. The standard of living in the central cities of the United States may be much better than it was 50 years ago, but the inequalities between many central cities and their middle and outer rings of affluent suburbs are increasing. Central cities are often faced with economic hardships, intense racism, and drug-related gangs and criminals. Fragmentation and dispersal of political authority in the metro areas and even in many of the central cities themselves often make it difficult not only to govern the big cities but also to respond with adequate policies and funds to treat the problems of the metropolis.

7. Cities, suburbs, and metro areas all face problems related to growth, uneven tax bases, environmental concerns, and fragmented authority. A variety of strategies have been used in an effort to solve them—annexation, agreements to furnish services, regional coordinating and planning councils, city-county consolidations, federated government, and multipurpose special districts. Almost all proposals for metropolitan reorganization involve shifts in political power.

KEY TERMS

unitary system 616

constitutional home rule 616

charter 620

mayor-council charter 620

weak mayor-council 622

strong mayor-council 622

council-manager plan 622

FURTHER READING

BARBARA ACKERMANN, *"You the Mayor?" The Education of a City Politician* (Auburn House, 1989).

ROGER BILES, *Richard J. Daley: Politics, Race and the Governing of Chicago* (Northern Illinois University Press, 1996).

BUZZ BISSINGER, *A Prayer for the City* (Random House, 1997).

MICHAEL BRIAND, *Practiced Politics: Five Principles for a Community That Works* (University of Illinois Press, 1999).

ALAN EHRENHALT, *The Lost City: Discovering the Forgotten Virtues of Community in the Chicago of the 1950s* (Basic Books, 1995).

JOEL GARREAU, *Edge City* (Doubleday, 1991).

STEPHEN GOLDSMITH, *The Twenty-first Century City* (Regnery, 1997).

JONATHAN HARR, *A Civil Action* (Vintage, 1996).

JOHN J. HARRIGAN, *Political Change in the Metropolis*, 5th ed. (HarperCollins, 1993).

DENNIS R. JUDD AND TODD SWANSTROM, *City Politics: Private Power and Public Policy*, 2d ed. (Longman, 1998).

DANIEL KEMMIS, *The Good City and the Good Life* (Houghton Mifflin, 1995).

DAVID L. KIRP ET AL., *Our Town: Race, Housing, and the Soul of Suburbia* (Rutgers University Press, 1997).

PAUL G. LEWIS, *Shaping Suburbia: How Political Institutions Organize Urban Development* (University of Pittsburgh Press, 1996).

TOM MCENERY, *The New City-State: Change and Renewal in American Cities* (Roberts Rinehart Publishers, 1994).

DONALD C. MENZEL, ED., *The American County: Frontiers of Knowledge* (University of Alabama Press, 1996).

JOHN O. NORQUEST, *The Wealth of Cities: Revitalizing the Centers of American Life* (Addison-Wesley, 1998).

MYRON ORFIELD, *Metropolitics: A Regional Agenda for Community and Stability* (Brookings Institution, 1997).

NEAL R. PEIRCE, WITH CURTIS W. JOHNSON AND JOHN STUART HALL, *Citistates: How Urban America Can Prosper in a Competitive World* (Seven Locks Press, 1993).

GARY RIVLIN, *Fire on the Prairie: Chicago's Harold Washington and the Politics of Race* (Holt, 1992).

DONALD N. ROTHBLATT AND ANDREW SANCTON, EDS., *Metropolitan Governance: American-Canadian Intergovernmental Perspectives* (Institute of Governmental Studies, University of California, 1993).

DAVID RUSK, *Cities Without Suburbs*, 2d ed. (Woodrow Wilson Center Press/Johns Hopkins University Press, 1995).

CLARENCE N. STONE, *Regime Politics: Governing Atlanta, 1946–1988* (University Press of Kansas, 1989).

JON C. TEAFORD, *Post-Suburbia: Government and Politics in the Edge Cities* (Johns Hopkins University Press, 1996).

ROBERT J. WASTE, *Independent Cities: Rethinking U.S. Urban Policy* (Oxford University Press, 1998).

WILLIAM JULIUS WILSON, *When Work Disappears: The World of the New Urban Poor* (Harvard University Press, 1996).

JOSEPH F. ZIMMERMAN, *State-Local Relations: A Partnership Approach* (Praeger, 1995).

See also *Governing: The Magazine of States and Localities*, published monthly by Congressional Quarterly, Inc.; *The National Civic Review*, published by the National Civic League; and *The Municipal Yearbook*, published annually by the International City Management Association.

29

MAKING STATE AND LOCAL POLICY

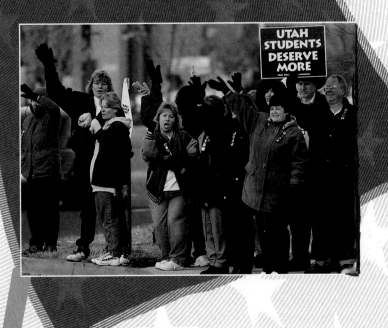

W

HEN YOU LISTEN TO DEBATES IN STATE LEG-
ISLATURES, ATTEND CITY COUNCIL MEETINGS, OR OBSERVE
STATE AND LOCAL CANDIDATES, YOU FIND CIVIC-MINDED PEOPLE
dealing with difficult policy decisions. Should the town close one of its schools? Will voters
approve a bond issue to construct a new hospital? Should the state superintendent of schools
establish merit pay for teachers? What can be done about the traffic jams on Main Street?
Should commercial growth be encouraged because of the jobs it will bring, or discouraged
because of the traffic and pollution it will generate? Hundreds of people—mayors, legislators, judges, county commissioners, union officials, commercial and residential developers,
and leaders of Chambers of Commerce—have to come up with workable answers to questions like these. The decisions of these policy makers are not as well publicized as those made
in Washington, D.C., but their effect on our lives is often more important.

PUBLIC EDUCATION

I n ancient Greece, Plato and Aristotle saw education as a vital task of government.
Thomas Jefferson, too, was convinced that an educated citizenry was essential to
democratic government. But only in the twentieth century did the idea that government
should provide tax-supported education for everyone become generally accepted.

For a long time many people opposed "free" education. They feared it would lead
to social unrest, undermine the family, give government control over the minds of the
young, require huge bureaucracies, and result in a fatal mixture of education and politics. And was it fair, they asked, to make people who could afford to educate their own
children in private schools pay taxes to educate other people's children? Despite these
objections, today free compulsory public education for grades 1 through 12 is an established practice in the United States.

Education is now the number one priority for most states. State and local governments have the primary responsibility for education and put up most of the funds. In
recent years there has been a decline in the federal contribution to education; however,
this has not deterred the federal government from pushing federal goals for education.

Approximately one-third of all state and local government expenditures are for education—more than for any other function of government[1] (see Figure 29–1). The federal
government's contribution to education is fairly constant across states, but since 1979 state
funding has surpassed that of local governments, though in New Hampshire and some

CHAPTERMEDIA

 POLITICS ONLINE

*Should Public Education Be
Privatized?*
www.prenhall.com/burns

PUBLIC SCHOOLS IN JAPAN

Students in both the United States and Japan attend 12 years of school at the elementary, junior high, and high school level, but that is where the similarities end. Japanese high school students spend 50 percent more time in the classroom than their American counterparts. One out of eight Japanese seniors has taken calculus, compared to only one in one hundred in the United States. Eighty-six percent of Japanese students report attending *juku*—evening prep schools or Saturday tutorial schools. This added study helps them prepare for the extremely difficult qualifying exams necessary to matriculate into the best junior high and high schools.

Japanese entrance exams are so competitive that more than half of all college-bound seniors fail the first time around and spend additional years preparing to take the test again. Students have been known to take three and even four years

between high school and college to pass the exams to get into top universities like Tokyo University. This additional effort does pay off. The average international high school achievement test scores for Japan are 67/100, with the United States far behind at only 48/100.

This high level of competition and achievement is not without a price, though. Some Japanese educators have argued that the system is too rigid and ruthlessly competitive. Students who do not perform well as early as age 13 can be labeled and classified. These second-class students will be called "salarymen" and will spend their lives working at low-paying jobs without serious chance for advancement.

SOURCE: Edward R. Beauchamp, *Windows on Japanese Education* (Greenwood Press, 1991); Merry White, *The Japanese Educational System: A Commitment to Children* (Free Press, 1987).

other states revenues for education continue to come primarily from local government.[2] The state role in financing education has increased over the last several years as a result, at least in part, of pressure from the courts to equalize expenditures on education across local school districts. There is also wide variation between states in the total amount of state and local spending per student, from a high of almost $10,000 in New Jersey to a low of under $4,000 in Utah, with an average of roughly $6,360.[3]

Administration

Unlike most other democracies, which administer and fund education at the national level, the basic unit responsible for public elementary and secondary education in the United States is the local school district, of which there are nearly 14,000.[4] In almost all districts, the voters elect a board of education that usually sets the school tax rate, appoints a superintendent of schools and other personnel, hires teachers, and runs the schools from kindergarten or grade 1 through grade 12.

Each state has a state superintendent of public instruction or commissioner of education. In about a third of the states, this official is popularly elected; in almost all states he or she shares authority with a state board of education.

Although actual operation of the public schools is the responsibility of the local community, state officers have important supervisory powers and distribute financial assistance to the communities. Many policies are established at the state level, and it is up to local authorities to enforce them. Local authorities must ensure that new school buildings meet the minimum specifications set by the state. In some states officials have the authority to set the course of study in schools—that is, to determine what must be taught and what may not be taught. In several states, especially in the South and Southwest, state authorities determine which textbooks will be used as well. State money is distributed according to many formulas, but, as noted, the trend is toward giving more money to poorer communities to equalize education spending.

The Role of the National Government

After the Soviet Union's successful launch in 1957 of *Sputnik*, the first satellite put into orbit,[5] Congress responded by increasing federal funding for education to strengthen math and science education.[6] The national government's share in financing local education rose from about 2 percent in 1940 to about 9 percent in 1980. In the next two decades, however, the trend was reversed, and the federal share of spending on local education declined and stabilized at about 6 percent.[7]

Through the national Department of Education (created in 1979) and other agencies, the federal government makes grants to the states for facilities, equipment, scholarships, loans, research, model programs, and general aid at the elementary, secondary, and higher education levels. But federal control over how the money may be spent comes with these federal dollars. Today federal regulations cover school lunch programs, employment practices, admissions, record keeping, care of experimental animals, and many other matters. Indeed, school authorities complain that there are often more regulations than dollars.

FIGURE 29–1 Typical State Government Expenditures

Police and Corrections 4.6%
Health and Hospitals 7.7%
Highways 7.6%
Other 20.0%
Education 35.0%
Public Welfare 25.1%

SOURCE: Council of State Governments, *The Book of the States, 2000–2001* (Council of State Governments, 2000), p. 284.

Educational Issues

What shall be taught and who shall teach it are hotly contested questions. Schools are favorite targets for groups eager to have children taught the "right" things. Religious groups want family values and morality emphasized, and some want constraints imposed on the teaching of evolution. Others want the schools to teach facts only, without regard for values, especially in areas like sex education. Labor leaders want students to get the right impression about labor and its role in society. Business leaders are eager for children to see the free enterprise system in a favorable light. Minorities and women's groups want textbooks to present diversity issues from the perspective they consider correct. Professional educators and civil libertarians try to isolate schools from the pressures of all outside groups—or at least the ones they do not agree with. They say decisions regarding what textbooks should be assigned, what books should be placed in school libraries, and how curricula should be designed are best left to professionals.[8]

It has long been an American tradition that education should be kept free from partisan political influences. The separation of schools from politics is strongly supported. Most local school boards are nonpartisan and are often elected when no partisan races are on the ballot. Elaborate attempts have been made to isolate educational agencies from the rest of government. This separation is strongly supported by parent-teacher associations, the National Education Association, the American Federation of Teachers, the American Association of University Professors, the American Council on Education, and other educational groups. Most citizens also believe that education should be kept out of the hands of mayors and city councils. However, education is of such concern to so many people, and there are so many different ideas about how schools should be run, that it cannot be divorced from politics.

PUBLIC SCHOOL INTEGRATION During the 1970s and 1980s, battles were fought in many cities over how to overcome racial segregation in the public schools. One method, which became very contentious, was to bus students from one neighborhood to another to achieve racial balance in the schools and overcome the effects of past segregation. By the 1990s, battles over school busing were ending, but, despite the efforts of the federal courts, de facto racial segregation is still the pattern for the inner-city schools of most large cities, in parts of the North, South, and West[9] (see Figure 29–2).

EDUCATIONAL REFORM In recent years a series of blue-ribbon reports on education helped focus national attention on educational reform.[10] A 1990 meeting between President George Bush and many of the nation's governors laid the foundation for Goals 2000: Educate America Act, which seeks to achieve many of the goals identified as important since the 1960s. With the aid of federal money, states are encouraged to set educational standards in order to achieve a number of goals, including:

1. All children will start school ready to learn.

2. The high school graduation rate will be at least 90 percent.

3. Students will have mastered a challenging curriculum by grades 4, 8, and 12.

4. Teachers will have access to professional development opportunities.

5. U.S. students will rank first in the world in science and math achievement.

6. All adults will be literate.

Violence in the Public Schools

Under the guidance of local police, students at Columbine High School escaped the terror inside their school when two fellow students went on a killing and bombing spree.

Violence in the public schools increased in the 1990s, as has the number of youths arrested for violent crimes. In a survey of school administrators, 97 percent indicated that they believed school violence had increased, and more than 25 percent of middle school principals reported an increasing number of acts of violence. As many as 35 percent of male students in some urban areas carry guns, and 45 percent of all students claim to have been threatened with a gun or shot coming from or going to school. Some students even bring semi-automatic rifles to school. In several incidents students were killed or wounded before their attackers were subdued.

In response, federal, state, and local governments increased spending on student and teacher protection. School districts increased surveillance to identify students bringing weapons to school. Many schools installed metal detectors and surveillance cameras to discourage students from bringing guns and knives into the classroom. There are also more closed campuses, more police officers patrolling hallways, and more undercover police working in schools to address problems of violence and drugs. Some schools have adopted "zero tolerance" (meaning you are expelled on the first offense) for students who bring a weapon to school or are found in possession of drugs.

These efforts to combat school violence appear to be slowly paying off. According to the Department of Education, the number of student expulsions for weapons violations was declining by the end of the decade. For more information and resources, visit the website of Safe Schools at www.stwnews.org.

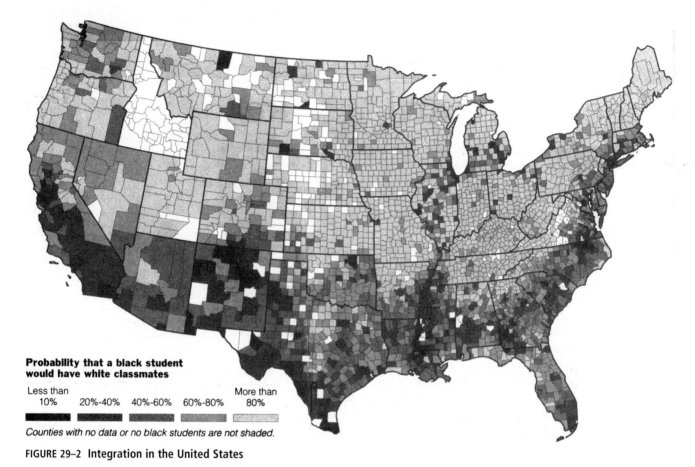

Probability that a black student would have white classmates

Less than 10% | 20%-40% | 40%-60% | 60%-80% | More than 80%

Counties with no data or no black students are not shaded.

FIGURE 29–2 Integration in the United States

Source: "School Is Out on Desegregation in the Classroom," *The New York Times*, April 2, 2000, p. WK5.

7. Schools will be free of drugs, violence, and firearms.

8. Every school will promote parental involvement in education.[11]

Several states initially objected to Washington's setting goals and standards for public education, an activity that has traditionally been a local function. Additionally, some thought it unfair to "hold students to nationwide standards if they have not had the equal opportunity to learn" due to unequal resources among communities.[12] These concerns, however, did not deter states from setting goals and standards. The autonomy of local and state authorities is also protected, with the federal government's role defined in terms of general goals.

Education was a key theme in the 2000 elections, national as well as state and local, with candidates from both major parties and all ideologies insisting that we must improve the quality of public education. However, there was little agreement on how it should be done. Three proposed reforms are especially contentious: vouchers, charter schools, and national student testing.

VOUCHERS   Some reformers argue that we will not see real progress in public education until we inject competition into the system by permitting parents to shop for schools the way they shop for goods and services in the economy. One way to do this would be to provide parents with a set amount of money—a **voucher**—that they could use to pay for part or all of their child's education in a public or private school of their choice. This reform has been labeled "choice in education" because it would give parents the freedom to choose where to send their children to school.[13]

Voucher programs have been tried since the mid-1980s in New York, Indianapolis, San Antonio, and Milwaukee. Some programs were directed at low-income students, a plan that, according to one observer, meant some poor families

voucher

A school reform program whereby a set amount of money is provided by government to parents for their use in paying for their child's education, in a public or private school of their choice.

formed political alliances with conservative Republicans, not their more natural liberal Democratic allies. As Terry Moe argues:

> In the new politics of education, the conservatives have become the progressives, pushing for major change, promoting the causes of the disadvantaged, and allying themselves with the poor. The progressives of yesteryear, meantime, have become the conservatives of today, resisting change, defending the status quo against threats from without, and opposing the poor constituents they claim to represent.[14]

Among the most vigorous opponents of vouchers are teachers unions, like the National Education Association (NEA) and the American Federation of Teachers (AFT), which, understandably, see vouchers as a threat to their jobs and benefits because they could drain off financial support from the public schools.

Some have proposed that voucher programs should include religious schools. Well over 80 percent of those receiving vouchers in places like Milwaukee or San Antonio attend religious schools, with most of those students going to Catholic schools.[15] Opponents of vouchers for religious schools argue that such an arrangement violates the constitutional separation of church and state. They fear that in some parts of the country, vouchers would be used for schools that practice racial segregation.

Others oppose the voucher system, even for public schools, on the grounds that such a system would have a negative impact on efforts to reform the public schools. Some argue that it would promote "skimming," meaning the higher achieving students would opt out of public schools, leaving behind the underachievers and the discipline problems and creating an increasingly negative atmosphere in public schools.

Proposals for school vouchers that have been put before the voters have been defeated in Oregon, Colorado, and Washington, as well as in California and Michigan. In the 2000 election in the latter two states, voters turned down initiatives that would have established vouchers, in spite of well-financed campaigns supporting their adoption. The political movement pushing vouchers lost some of its steam because of these defeats, the opposition of the teachers unions, and court rulings that said poor families do not have the right to demand vouchers from state and local governments to allow their children to attend better schools.

CHARTER SCHOOLS   One educational reform that does not go as far as vouchers but still provides publicly funded alternatives to standard public schools is the **charter school**. Some states now grant charters to individuals or groups to start schools

In many poorer communities, classes are conducted in overcrowded, poorly equipped buildings.

charter school
A publicly funded alternative to standard public schools in some states, initiated when individuals or groups receive charters; charter schools must meet state standards.

In East Los Angeles sits Vaughn Street School, California's first charter school, established in 1992. Most of the children at this elementary school speak English as their second language and live in dangerous neighborhoods. Once the children had to step around a dead body as they approached the school's entryway. It was not a healthy learning environment.

In 1992 Vaughn Street's pupils ranked in the 9th percentile in reading (91 percent of public school students in America could read better than they) and the 14th percentile in math. Now their reading and math scores rank in the 47th and 59th percentile, respectively. Today these students experience hands-on learning about computers in the $1.6 million learning center, and parents from more wealthy neighborhoods want to send their kids to Vaughn. Principal Yvonne Chan attributes these changes to freedom from bureaucracy.

During the last decade, the number of charter schools has grown steadily because of concerns about students' poor academic performance and high dropout rate. About a fifth of all high school students do not graduate. For more state-by-state information, visit the website of the Center for Education at edreform.com/pubs/chglance.htm.

Would Parents Choose Charter Schools?

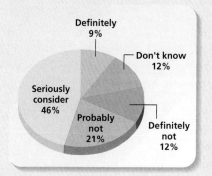

- Definitely 9%
- Don't know 12%
- Seriously consider 46%
- Probably not 21%
- Definitely not 12%

SOURCE: Public Agenda, as reported in "Issues 2000: Education," *The Economist*, September 30, 2000, p. 20.

and receive public funds if they can meet standards specified by law. Unlike vouchers, which provide funds to the parents, charter schools deal directly with the local school boards. There are about two thousand charter schools, with a half million students. "The vast majority of the schools are operated by local nonprofit organizations, and the educational theories that guide them are as various as the communities they serve."[16]

An Arizona law that permits any person or organization to found a charter school has not fostered a wide variety of schools with different emphases. Most of Arizona's charter schools have been for secondary education, with several targeting at-risk students. An early study in Arizona found that 67 percent of students attending charter schools came mostly from public schools. Charter schools did not result in a brain drain from the public schools, as the average test scores of students entering were lower than state and national averages. The ethnic mix and income distribution of families of charter school students were broadly representative of Arizona public school students.[17]

As with privatization in other government services, charter schools are intended to interject the competition of the marketplace into elementary and secondary education. Charter schools generally have more flexibility to hire and fire teachers and are not subject to the collective bargaining arrangements that prevail in many public school systems. Proponents of charter schools want to remove these schools from state and local regulation as much as possible. Some of their teachers may not have training in education, but proponents of charter schools maintain that classroom performance is more important than the undergraduate major of the teacher.

The biggest opponent of charter schools are teachers unions, which stand to lose their collective bargaining position with school boards if charter schools take off. Other opponents contend that in school systems already strapped for money, it does not make sense to invest public funds in such an untested idea. Concerns about what will be taught in charter schools and the level of teacher competence are often expressed. Also at issue is whether religious schools should qualify for public funds as charter schools.

Spending on charter schools remains small compared to the billions spent on public education, but it has been growing in recent years. As charter schools become more visible, they are likely to become more controversial. Yet individuals and groups appear to be willing to give the idea of charter schools a try, and even the National Education Association has indicated that it plans to set up some charter schools itself, albeit with less autonomy from school boards than many charter school supporters favor.

NATIONAL STUDENT TESTING   Standardized testing is not new or controversial. What is new and controversial is *statewide* standardized testing. At the beginning of the last decade only 14 states had standards for their core curriculum, but by 2000–2001, 49 states had adopted standards. After adopting standardized testing for students, Oregon rejected a ballot initiative that would have amended the state constitution to require annual testing of math and verbal skills of public school students in grades 4 through 12.

Even more controversial are *national* tests and *national* norms or goals. Such tests would be administered to students periodically to permit parents, administrators, and legislators to assess how individual students, classes, schools, school districts, and states compare with one another. Moreover, once such testing is established, it could be expanded to include year-to-year measurement of individual students as they progress through the public schools.

Some critics of standardized national tests contend it is unfair and misleading to use such tests to measure learning. Minority students and students in districts in impoverished areas may not do well on these tests, and their low scores will reinforce cultural bias. Other critics worry that the use of such tests will force teachers to "teach to the test." Sensitive to the fact that their students will be compared with students in other classes, teachers will attempt to "beat the test" by emphasizing certain topics and ignoring others. This strategy might work for some students but would limit the learning of others. The main contention of the opponents of national testing, however, is that such measurement will not produce positive changes in education.

HIGHER EDUCATION

Until the 1950s, most local school districts provided only elementary and secondary education, although some larger cities also supported junior colleges and universities. Since the end of World War II, however, there has been a major expansion of *community colleges*. Now students may attend the first two years of college or receive a technical education within their own communities. The trend is to create separate college districts to operate and raise funds for local community colleges; in a few areas these colleges are part of the local public school system.

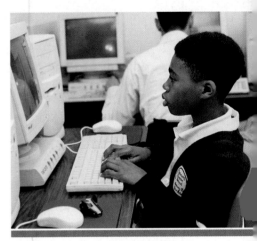

This charter school in Jersey City, New Jersey, provides a computer lab for its science classes.

Administration

States support many kinds of universities and colleges, including land-grant universities created by the Morrill Act of 1862. State colleges and universities are governed by boards appointed by the governor in some states and elected by the voters in others. These boards are designed to give public institutions of higher education some independence, even though they depend on the state legislature and governor for their funding. A few states have gone so far as to protect the independence of their universities in the state constitution.

With over 78 percent of our nearly 15 million college students now attending publicly supported institutions, the control and support of higher education have become significant political questions. States have created boards with varying degrees of control over operations and budgets. In addition, governors have tried to impose controls on universities and colleges that many university administrators insist are inappropriate. Yet institutions of higher education have greater independence from political oversight than any other tax-supported institution. Publicly funded colleges and universities usually can control teaching loads, internal procedures, areas of teaching emphasis, who shall be hired and promoted, and how to allocate funds among internal units.

Funding Higher Education

In the twenty-first century, we face questions of access and funding for our colleges and universities due to increasing enrollments (see Figure 29–3). Who should go? Only those who can afford it? What about minorities who are underrepresented in our colleges and universities? Access to colleges and universities for all students who wish to go has long been the declared goal in many states, but is this goal realistic? Should students be required to pay higher tuition to cover the cost of their education? And is our higher education system training people for jobs that will exist ten years after they graduate, or for soon-to-become-obsolete jobs?

Tuition at state universities and colleges has gone up in most states. Since 1975 tuition has increased 500 percent, or twice the rate of inflation. Professors' salaries have not kept pace with tuition increases and have grown only slightly more than the rate of inflation (see Table 29–1). Although many people agree that we need an infusion of new money to update college laboratories, improve libraries, and recruit and keep first-rate college professors, there is no consensus about who should pay for these efforts. The federal government is the chief supplier of student

1998	14.6%
2010	17.4%
	Percent change +19.2

FIGURE 29–3 College and University Enrollments (in Millions)

Source: "Statistics 101," *The Washington Post*, October 10, 2000, p. A11.

TABLE 29–1 **Tuition and Professors' Salary Increases, 1975–1998 (in 1998 Dollars)**

| | Tuition/Required Fees* | | Professors' Salaries** | |
	Public	Private	Public	Private***
1975	$1,787	$7,798	$49,522	$49,522
1980	1,636	7,423	43,047	43,047
1985	2,067	10,207	46,539	49,224
1990	2,499	12,707	51,453	55,383
1991	2,544	13,409	51,850	55,385
1992	2,757	13,947	51,822	57,199
1993	2,892	14,501	51,093	57,314
1994	3,054	15,025	51,226	58,265
1995	3,135	15,310	51,710	58,344
1996	3,223	15,963	51,556	58,819
1997	3,321	16,531	52,000	59,300
1998	3,489	17,197	53,600	61,500

SOURCE: U.S. Bureau of the Census, *Statistical Abstract of the United States, 1999* (Government Printing Office, 1999), p. 318.

*Annual average in-state tuition for a four-year degree.

**Annual average salary and benefits for full-time professors of all ranks in four-year institutions.

***Excludes church-related colleges and universities.

financial aid, and many states are now making major efforts to expand their programs of student aid.

Most institutions of higher education—both private and public—receive some kind of government subsidy, through a variety of devices, so that students do not pay the full cost of their education. The national government and most states provide need-based financial assistance in the form of loans and grants, with students in the greatest financial need at the higher-cost institutions eligible for the most aid. Thus higher education has what is in effect a voucher system; students receive funds and can choose the kind of college or university that best serves their needs. It also means that in the United States, we have avoided a *two-track system*—one set of colleges and universities for the poor and another for the rich. Poor students can be found in most high-cost private colleges and universities along with students from higher-income families.

Funding for the public universities must compete with the rising costs of other state services, notably the criminal justice system and prisons. There is generally an inverse relationship between the rising levels of state spending on corrections and the declining state spending on higher education, although, with the prosperity of the last decade, state spending on both prisons and colleges has increased.

SOCIAL SERVICES

What role should state and local governments play in making sure all citizens have their basic housing, health, and nutritional needs met? How important are these social services compared to government's obligation to provide police and fire protection, education, parks and recreation, and other services? For much of our history, human service needs were left to private charities that ran orphanages, old-age homes, hospitals, and other institutions. Philosophically, this reliance on private charity fit well with the American notions of limited government and self-reliance. That view changed dramatically during the Great Depression of the 1930s, when poverty, unemployment, and homelessness affected such large numbers of people that the government could no longer act as if these were private matters.

Then in the 1960s, with Lyndon Johnson's Great Society agenda, the nation embarked on a second major wave of social service programs, which Johnson labeled a War on Poverty. Today, we continue to debate whether such programs accomplish their goals and whether alternatives would prove more successful.

Welfare

Pressure to reform the welfare system increased among both Democrats and Republicans in the last decades of the twentieth century. The number of Americans on welfare soared from about 2 million households in 1950 to close to 6 million in the early 1990s[18] (see Figure 29–4). Why such growth? Some said that this country had finally recognized its obligation to care for the truly poor. Others charged that "government handouts" robbed recipients of the self-confidence they need to go to work and succeed; in this sense, dependence on welfare becomes a curse.

Welfare policy was a complex web of federal, state, and local programs that shared or matched financial responsibilities. Most of the administrative burden, however, fell on state and local governments. Every state had a department of human services or welfare that either administered welfare programs directly or supervised local officials who administered these programs. County welfare departments determined who was entitled to assistance and dealt directly with recipients.

In 1996, fundamental changes were made in the role of the federal government in providing welfare. Most of the responsibility for welfare programs was shifted to the states, with national guidelines for administration. The landmark legislation that ended the Aid to Families with Dependent Children (AFDC) program

Hope Scholarships

During the last decade a number of states have established HOPE Scholarships modeled after Georgia's Helping Outstanding Pupils Educationally (HOPE) program. Under the leadership of former Governor Zell Miller, in 1993 Georgia instituted Hope Scholarships providing any high school graduate with a B average or better full tuition, all mandatory fees, plus a book allowance of $100 a quarter or $150 a semester if he or she attends a state public college, university, or technical institute. The program was later expanded to provide up to $3,000 per year for students meeting the same standards who attend a private Georgia university. Students can keep their scholarship so long as they maintain their B average.

Thirteen states currently have versions of HOPE Scholarship programs. For more state-by-state information, go to the website of the Education Commission of the States at www.ecs.org.

FIGURE 29–4 Percentage of the U.S. Population on Welfare Since 1960

SOURCE: U.S. Department of Health and Human Services, June 2000. For more information on welfare statistics, go to www.acf.dhhs.gov/news/stats/6090_ch2.htm.

This welfare-to-work trainee is learning skills that will enable her to find employment at a steady, well-paid job.

responsibility contract

A welfare strategy adopted by some states in which recipients sign a written agreement specifying their responsibilities and outlining a plan for obtaining work and achieving self-sufficiency.

workfare

A welfare strategy adopted by some states that gives able-bodied adults who do not have preschool-aged children the opportunity to learn job skills that can lead to employment.

enterprise zone

Inner-city areas designated as offering tax incentives to companies that invest in plants there and provide job training for the unemployed.

police powers

Inherent powers of state governments to pass laws to protect public health, safety, and welfare; the national government has no directly granted police powers, but accomplishes the same goals through other delegated powers.

was named Temporary Assistance for Needy Families (TANF).[19] States would now receive federal block grants that require state matching funds. Each state files a plan with the secretary of health and human services every two years that: (1) explains how it will ensure that recipients engage in work activities within two months of receiving benefits; (2) establishes goals to prevent and reduce out-of-wedlock pregnancies; (3) describes treatment of families moving into the state; and (4) explains whether it intends to provide aid to noncitizens. Money is distributed to states based on the highest amount of federal funding they received in the previous three fiscal years. To continue receiving federal funds, states must spend at least 75 percent of the amount they spent in 1994. Federal money is disbursed through the state legislatures, not controlled by the governors. Additional federal funds are available to states as incentives for high performance and as loans in times of financial hardship for the state.

States are encouraged to experiment with welfare programs. Their experiments are evaluated by the federal government to ensure they meet policy goals. Some states had previously started to cut back on welfare payments. For example, Wisconsin's Governor Tommy G. Thompson had proposed capping welfare payments for unwed teenage mothers, regardless of the number of children they have. Larger grants were paid to those who were married.[20] This option is now included in the national legislation. Previously, federal laws had unintentionally encouraged fathers to leave the family by making it easier for single-parent families to receive benefits. Current law seeks to overcome this disincentive by offering higher benefits to two-parent families.

Other states have developed **responsibility contracts**, requiring recipients to sign a written agreement specifying their responsibilities and outlining a plan for them to obtain work and achieve self-sufficiency. Some states provide child care and Medicaid benefits beyond the federal one-year extension for families who lose benefits due to unemployment.

About half of the states, including Massachusetts, New York, Wisconsin, and California, have experimented with **workfare** programs designed to help welfare recipients develop the self-confidence, skills, and habits necessary for regular employment. Workfare gives able-bodied adults who do not have preschool-aged children the opportunity to learn job skills that can lead to employment. Another government program creates **enterprise zones** in large cities that give tax incentives to companies that provide job training for the unemployed in depressed neighborhoods.[21]

As a result of the 1996 welfare reform, the percentage of people on welfare was reduced by more than half—from close to 6 million families in the early 1990s to about 2.3 million by the end of the decade. Federal and state welfare expenditures also declined by over $10 billion to from $22.4 billion to $12.4 billion. A number of states—including Hawaii, New York, Kentucky, and West Virginia—set aside unspent TANF funds as "rainy day" reserves to invest in benefits and services to help needy families overcome transportation and child-care barriers to staying employed.[22]

States are now the prime laboratories for making and implementing social policy. The federal government originally became involved in welfare programs because states had been unwilling or unable to tackle these problems on their own. When confronted with competing demands in other policy areas, will states give the needs of poor people a lower priority? And what will happen if the current economic boom goes bust? How will the states cope with larger numbers of needy people?

Health

During the hot summer of 1794, a yellow-fever epidemic ravaged Philadelphia. The streets were deserted. All who could afford to do so had fled with their families to the country. Every night the sounds of the death cart echoed through the

nearly empty city. Most families that remained behind lost a child, a father, or a mother. Only when cool weather returned did the city resume normal activity.

Yellow fever, dysentery, malaria, and other diseases periodically swept American cities in the eighteenth and nineteenth centuries. As late as 1879, yellow fever struck hard in the South. Memphis was nearly depopulated. Following the lead of Louisiana and Massachusetts, state after state established a board of health to deal with such epidemics. Spurred by the medical discoveries of Louis Pasteur and other scientists, authorities undertook additional efforts to protect public health. Open sewers were covered, and hygienic measures were instituted.

Prevention and disease control are still major public health activities today. Doctors are required to report cases of communicable disease. Health department officials then investigate to discover the source of the infection, isolate the afflicted, and take whatever action is called for. Most state health departments give doctors free vaccine and serum, and many local departments give free vaccinations to those who cannot afford private physicians. Mobile units take free x-rays of schoolchildren, teachers, and the general public; county health departments provide free or low-cost inoculations, vision tests, and hearing tests. Public health officials try to protect water supplies and ensure the safe disposal of waste and sewage. They protect the community's food supply by inspecting hotels, restaurants, and food markets.

Today the overwhelming public health issues are smoking, pollution, and AIDS. Like the contagious and infectious disease issues of prior times, they require concerted efforts and public health policies. Thousands of local governments—counties, cities, townships, and special health districts—have some kind of public health program. Every state has an agency, usually called a Department of Health, that administers the state program and supervises local health officials. At the national level, the U.S. Public Health Service conducts research, assists state and local authorities, and administers federal grants to encourage local agencies to expand their programs. Every state also administers various federal medical benefit programs for the needy, such as Medicaid. As usual, however, wealthier states tend to take advantage of or match these programs more liberally than poorer states.

The health care crisis in the United States involves access—who gets care—and the dramatic rise in costs. Access and costs are related, of course. Wealthy people can afford the costs and gain the access; poor people on welfare usually have access to health care, although the quality of their care may be lower. It is the people in the middle who are worried about whether their insurance will be adequate to cover their health care needs.

Governors and state legislators have to deal with federal mandates in health care. In recent years Congress has passed legislation setting minimal length of a maternity stay in hospitals, requiring parity in mental health care, and mandating insurance portability—all of which will affect state budgets. If costs continue to skyrocket, federal mandates could bankrupt many states.

LAW ENFORCEMENT

Many state and local government powers stem from their **police powers**, the inherent power of states to use physical force if necessary to protect the health, safety, and welfare of their citizens. This power is among those not delegated to the federal government by the Constitution and reserved to the states. It is on this basis that mayors or governors impose curfews, as they have in some urban riots. But

AIDS

For almost two decades, Acquired Immune Deficiency Syndrome (AIDS) received more media attention than even perennial killers such as cancer and heart disease. Certainly the high rate of growth of HIV-positive infections (the virus that leads to AIDS) justified labeling the disease an "epidemic." The government responded to the crisis with increased funding to various research programs, both public and private. The federal government spent billions of dollars on AIDS research, and there are some signs of success in dealing with the deadly virus, as AIDS-related deaths have dropped in recent years. Yet the treatment of AIDS is costly, and some poor people cannot afford the treatment.* Although medication is extending the lives of people with the virus, no cure has been found.

The AIDS epidemic reminds us of the role of public health agencies in educating the public about health hazards, urging precautions, and seeking cures. Health officials predict that there are more than 40,000 preventable cases of AIDS, reinforcing the point that the message of "safe sex" is not getting through to teenagers and others. Public schools have adopted different approaches to educating students about AIDS, including the distribution of condoms in some public schools. Other public health issues surrounding AIDS have to do with the regulation of health care professionals and records kept on persons infected with the disease.

*Michael Ellison, "Living with It," *The Guardian*, November 19, 1998, p. 18.

Public health clinics provide free vaccinations and other health services to children whose families cannot afford medical insurance.

the police power extends to other activities of government, such as regulating public health, safety, and morals.

The State Police

In 1835 the famous Texas Rangers were organized as a small border patrol. In 1865 Massachusetts appointed a few state constables to suppress gambling, a job the local police had proved unwilling or unable to do. But not until 1905, with the organization of the Pennsylvania State Constabulary, did a real state police system come into being. It was so successful that other states followed Pennsylvania's example.

The establishment of the Pennsylvania State Constabulary marked a sharp break with traditional police methods. This was a mounted and uniformed body organized on a military basis; centralized control was given to a superintendent directly responsible to the governor. The Pennsylvania pattern was followed by other states, and these forces are now among the most respected police organizations in the world. They are well equipped and maintain high standards of conduct and discipline.

State police became a part of our law-enforcement system for a variety of reasons. The growth of urban and metropolitan areas, the coming of the automobile (and the resulting demand for greater protection on the highways and the creation of a mobile force for catching fleeing criminals), and the need for a trained force to maintain order during strikes, fires, floods, and other emergencies all promoted the creation of state police.

Other Police Forces

State police are not the only law enforcement agencies maintained by state governments. There are liquor law enforcement officials, fish and game wardens, fire wardens, detective bureaus, and special motor vehicle police. This dispersion of functions has been widely criticized, but each department insists it needs its own law enforcement agency to handle its special problems.

At the local level, almost every municipality maintains its own police force; the county has a sheriff and deputies, and some townships have their own police officers. In fact, there are more than 40,000 separate law enforcement agencies in the United States employing more than 600,000 men and women.

With crime continuing to be an important issue to many voters, the importance of crime control has been on the minds of elected officials. State and local governments spend more than $35 billion on police protection. Local governments pay for over 70 percent of all law enforcement costs, including such routine activities as controlling traffic and patrolling neighborhoods but also maintaining court security and preventing juvenile crime. The number of police officers increased by 10 percent during the 1990s and may increase even more with recent state and federal legislation.[23]

Federal-State Action

The national government has gradually moved into law enforcement, a field traditionally reserved for state and local governments, although the main cost of local law enforcement is still borne by local governments. Today, for example, it is a federal offense to transport kidnapped individuals or stolen goods across state lines. Taking firearms, explosives, or even information across state lines for illegal purposes is also a federal offense. Federal law enforcement agencies include the Federal Bureau of Investigation (FBI), the Bureau of Alcohol, Tobacco and Firearms (ATF), and the Drug Enforcement Administration (DEA).

Perhaps due to increased national and state expenditures, crime rates have been declining. Despite these positive trends, politicians in both parties continue to press for government to do more about crime. Some advocate more strict laws regu-

A Closer Look

RACIAL PROFILING

Racial profiling—state police stopping and arresting minorities—made news in New Jersey but was also found to occur in other states as well. An extensive review based on interviews with troopers, state officials, and victims revealed a pattern of selective enforcement that had gone on for more than a decade.

"The story begins in the mid-1980's, when the federal Drug Enforcement Administration responded to the street violence of the crack epidemic by enlisting local police forces to catch smugglers who were importing drugs from Latin America, often to Florida, and moving them to major American cities by car.

By 1989, the New Jersey State Police had become such a successful part of "Operation Pipeline" that D.E.A. officials hailed the troopers as exemplary models for most other states.

But on New Jersey roadways, black and Hispanic drivers were subjected to such frequent, unjustified traffic stops and searches that they complained of a

new, unwritten violation in the state's traffic code: "driving while black." In state police barracks, some black and Hispanic troopers bitterly acknowledged that even though the state officially prohibited racial profiling, senior troopers trained them to single out drivers on the basis of their ethnicity or race. . . .

On April 22, 1998, troopers shot and wounded three unarmed black and Hispanic men during a traffic stop on the turnpike, propelling the controversy to the center of the state's political stage. State officials, including Gov. Christie Whitman, at first clung to their insistence that there was no pattern of profiling. But under unrelenting pressure from civil rights leaders and the federal Justice Department's Civil Rights Division, the Whitman administration ultimately acknowledged racial profiling, revamped its narcotics strategy, and agreed to let a federal judge monitor the force."

A 2001 court decision wiped out most of these arrests and paid compensation to the victims.

State police in New Jersey and other states have been stopping and arresting minority drivers because they fit a profile of potential drug dealers.

Source: David Kocieniewski and Robert Hanley, "An Inside Story of Racial Bias and Denial," *The New York Times*, December 3, 2000, pp. 53 and 56.

---

lating guns, while others favor more police on the street or more prisons to keep criminals off the streets. Because politicians fear appearing "soft on crime," taking action on crime is a high priority at all levels of government.

PLANNING THE URBAN COMMUNITY

Are our cities good places in which to live and work? Crime, pollution, garbage, crowded shopping areas, dented fenders, shattered nerves, slums and blighted areas, inadequate parks, impossible traffic patterns—are these the inevitable costs of urban life?

For many decades American cities were allowed to grow unchecked. Industrialists were permitted to erect factories wherever they wished; developers were allowed to construct towering buildings that shut off sunlight from the streets below; commuters, bicyclists, and pedestrians all ended up with transportation systems that did not meet their needs.

Zoning Laws

The most common method of assuring orderly growth is *zoning*—creating specific areas and limiting property usage in each area. A community may be divided into areas for single-family, two-family, or multifamily dwellings, for commercial purposes, and for light and heavy industry. Regulations restrict the height of buildings

or require that buildings be located a certain distance apart or a certain distance from the boundaries of the lot.

Zoning regulations attempt to enable the city or county government to coordinate services with land use and to stabilize property values by preventing, for example, garbage dumps from being located next to residential areas. Day-to-day enforcement is usually the responsibility of a building inspector, who ensures that a projected building is consistent with building, zoning, fire, and sanitary regulations before granting a building permit. A zoning ordinance, however, is no better than its enforcement. In most cases a zoning or planning commission or the city council can amend ordinances and make exceptions to regulations, and these officials are often under tremendous pressure to grant exceptions. But if they go too far in permitting special cases, the whole purpose of zoning is defeated.

Zoning is only one kind of community planning. Until recently, city planners were primarily concerned with streets and buildings. Today many are concerned with the quality of life. Consequently planning covers a broad range of activities, including methods to avoid air pollution and to improve water quality. Planners collect all the information they can about a city and then prepare long-range plans. Can smaller-scale communities be devised within urban centers? Can downtown areas be revitalized, and if so, how? Where should main highways or mass-transit facilities be constructed to meet future needs? Will the water supply be adequate for the population 10, 20, or 50 years from now? Is a larger or new regional airport needed? Are hospitals and parks accessible to all? Does the design of public buildings encourage crime or energy waste?

Controlling Growth

Critics of urban and state planning are skeptical whether governors, mayors, or state and local legislators can prevent what they sometimes call the "Los Angelization" of the United States, by which they mean urban growth without much planning for transportation, environmental protection, or management of water and other resources. Unregulated market forces can cause severe harm to residents, and "politics as usual" does not ensure sensible growth patterns or protect the air, water, and beauty of most states and communities.

Seattle and San Francisco residents voted to limit the height and bulk of downtown buildings in an effort to protect these cities from excessively fast growth. Maryland and many other states have passed "Smart Growth" legislation aimed at

Repair of deteriorating infrastructure, a nuisance to residents, is necessary to maintain the quality of life in the cities and also attract business and consumers.

preserving large blocks of contiguous land and ensuring that the necessary roads, sewers, and schools are in place before development proceeds. This legislation is implemented in two ways: (1) the state gives priority funding to development in areas designated by counties as having the proper infrastructure and meeting other local guidelines; (2) state funds are allocated to local governments and private land trusts to purchase the development rights to land "rich in agricultural, forestry, natural, and cultural resources."[24]

Obviously, planning and sensible growth depend upon public support. They also depend on market forces. No plan will be effective, however, unless it reflects the interests and values of major groups within the community. Planning is clearly a political activity. Different groups view the ends and means of planning differently, and agreements on tough policy options are often hard to reach. Moreover, one of the barriers to successful planning is the general fear of government power. Thus effective planning requires imaginative collaboration between planners, community leaders, and the popularly elected officials who must bear the responsibility for implementing the plans.[25]

Environmental Regulation

State and local governments have long been concerned about managing land use and protecting the environment. In such heavily polluted places as Pittsburgh, smoke abatement ordinances were enacted as early as 1860, but aggressive action on air pollution did not come until after World War II.[26] By the 1950s, states had established agencies to deal with resource management issues, but it was the federal legislation of the early 1970s that pushed environmental protection onto their agendas.[27] One important reason for the expanded federal role is the reality that pollution does not recognize state boundaries. Air and water pollution are particular examples of the interstate nature of environmental problems.

As states became more involved in toxic waste regulation and air pollution in the 1960s and early 1970s, pressure on the national government to develop national environmental standards increased. Part of the pressure for federal legislation was due to the inconsistent state policies being considered and enacted. Not only did environmental activists want a single national approach to these problems, so did many of those who were being regulated. Automobile manufacturers, for instance, preferred one national standard for automobiles rather than dozens of differing state standards. Businesses operating in several states also pressed for uniform federal environmental standards.[28]

In the 1950s and 1960s, the federal government provided grants to state and local governments for research and assistance in developing and implementing their own environmental standards. The key piece of legislation in the transition to a greater role for the federal government was the Federal Environmental Protection Act, passed in 1970, which created the Environmental Protection Agency (EPA). Other acts dealing with specific environmental problems followed: the Clean Air Act of 1970, the Clean Water Act of 1972, the Safe Drinking Water Act of 1974, and the Toxic Substances Control Act of 1976. Most of these acts have been amended one or more times.

The basic model of environmental regulation has been for the federal government to set national standards in water quality and air quality. State and local governments are then charged with implementing these standards and monitoring compliance. States have long argued that these unfunded mandates impose a heavy financial burden on them. Water and sewage services are the largest local government expenditure, at $43 billion a year nationally.[29] Some states have been aggressive in correcting pollution. In 1996, for example, New York voters approved a bond to spend $1.75 billion over the next three decades on clean water and clean air projects.[30]

Another area in which states are increasingly responsible for environmental policy is waste management. Not unexpectedly, states where the economy is growing

Few aspects of government are more enmeshed in politics than highway building and maintenance. Groups such as the American Automobile Association (AAA) support highway development. Automobile and tire manufacturers, oil companies, motel and restaurant associations, automobile and tourist clubs, trucking associations, and others join hands to advance their common cause. In most states, they have been strong enough to persuade legislatures to allocate gasoline taxes, drivers' license fees, trucking fees, and other user taxes for road purposes. But there is always conflict over where the money should be spent. Farmers want secondary roads developed; truckers and tourists favor the improvement of main highways; and merchants prefer that roads come through their towns. Do you favor increased gasoline taxes to provide better roads?

eminent domain

Power of a government to take private property for public use; the U.S. Constitution gives national and state governments this power and requires them to provide just compensation for property so taken.

have regulated waste management more aggressively than states where this is not the case. Economically hard-pressed states may fear driving industries away.[31] Fears about nuclear waste, acid rain, and hazardous wastes have sparked extensive efforts at regulation within states, as well as court battles with nearby states over the export of unwanted by-products of energy development.

Despite the fact that the national Environmental Protection Agency (EPA) gets lots of headlines, state and local governments have more people working to control pollution.[32] States can and do experiment with ways to improve air quality. California, for instance, has been a leader in testing automobile emissions. One innovation being considered is *remote sensing*, which uses roadside devices that shoot an infrared beam across a road to detect the emissions of passing cars. This device has also a video camera that records the license plates of vehicles in violation of emissions standards. Such a system could replace the periodic state inspections now required for all vehicles.

Environmental interest groups in many states have taken the lead in pressing for stronger environmental regulation, demanding that stiff penalties be imposed for violations of environmental laws. And some of the effort has shifted to individual action—recycling, conservation, saving and planting trees, and using public transportation.

Transportation

Before the automobile, canals and railroads were the major methods of long-distance commercial travel. Local roads were built and repaired under the direction of city, township, and county officials. Able-bodied male citizens were required either to put in a certain number of days working on the public roads or to pay taxes for that purpose. By the 1890s, bicycle clubs began to urge the building of hard-surfaced roads, but it was not until the early 1900s and the growing popularity of the automobile that road building became a major industry. This function was gradually transferred from the township to larger units of government, but counties and townships still have important building and maintenance functions.

Although much of the money comes from the federal government, it is the state and local governments that build the highways, public buildings, airports, parks, and recreational facilities. State and local governments, in fact, spend more money on transportation than on anything else except education and welfare. Because highways and bridges around the nation are aging, a federal tax on gasoline was levied to help rebuild these public facilities.

The national government has supported state highway construction since 1916, and through various federal highway laws passed over the last 85 years, federal aid has increased. States do the planning, estimate the costs, and arrange for the construction work, even when they receive federal assistance. In order to receive support, however, states must submit their plans to, and have their work inspected by, the U.S. Department of Transportation (DOT). All federally funded highways must meet DOT standards governing the engineering of the roadbed, employment conditions for construction workers, and weight and load conditions for trucks.

Under the Federal Highway Act of 1956, states planned and built the National System of Interstate and Defense Highways. The Interstate System consists of 43,000 miles of superhighways linking almost all cities with a population of 50,000 or more. The federal government paid 90 percent of the cost of this system, with most of the money coming from taxes on gasoline, tires, and trucks that are placed in a trust fund designated for that purpose.

In 1998 Congress passed a $216 billion, six-year surface transportation bill that included $173 billion in funding for highways as well as $2 billion for highway safety. The bill funds repairing cracked asphalt, increasing safety reinforcements on bridges, and expanding the network of highways. One billion dollars is dedicated to state programs that increase the percentage of drivers who use safety belts and prevent drunk driving. The legislation also provides $41 billion for mass transit.[33] This massive federal investment is funded by continuing the 18.3 cents-per-gallon tax on gas. The full

amount will now be devoted to transportation, including the 4.3 cents that was formerly used for deficit reduction.

Economic Development

A primary concern of governors and mayors, as well as other state and local officials, is providing jobs for their citizens. It is not uncommon for governors to spend a significant amount of time encouraging companies to relocate within their borders, courting corporate officials, going on trade missions to other countries to promote their state's products, and negotiating favorable tax and other incentives with new businesses. This interest is not new. What is new is the international proportions of these activities. Former Utah Governor Norman Bangerter was fond of saying, "The one thing you will always see on an economic development trip to Tokyo is another governor."

States compete with one another because economic development is the key to increasing the tax base that funds government services. But states face a dilemma, because satisfying the demands of new businesses can be expensive, and tax incentives can reduce the tax return the new companies will generate. Competition among states has intensified to the point that localities are worried about keeping the jobs they have, not just persuading new companies to move to their area. New York City has offered billions of dollars in incentives to influence several companies not to leave. Critics of these "bidding wars" argue that states should spend tax money on rebuilding infrastructure and strengthening education rather than offering public funds to selected large private companies.

REGULATION

States and local communities adopt safety regulations on the assumption (sometimes mistaken) that the benefits to the general public will outweigh the costs to the individuals and groups being regulated. Thus laws requiring drivers' licenses, compelling motorists to stop at red lights, mandating seat-belt use, or imposing severe penalties on people caught driving under the influence of alcohol or drugs are intended to protect the safety and freedom of innocent pedestrians or occupants of other motor vehicles. Most such laws are accepted as both necessary and legitimate. States have raised the drinking age and stiffened the punishments for drunk driving, in most cases because the federal government tied federal funds to the passage of such legislation. An interest group, Mothers Against Drunk Driving (MADD), helped to force the issue.

Public Utilities

Corporations receive their charters from the states. Banks, insurance companies, securities dealers, doctors, lawyers, teachers, barbers, and various other businesses and professions are licensed by the states, and their activities are supervised by state officials. Farmers and industrial and service workers are also regulated. But of all businesses, public utilities are the most closely monitored.

It is easier to list than to define public utilities. They include (among others) water plants, electric power companies, telephone companies, railroads, and buses. Public utilities are distinguished from other businesses because government gives them special privileges, such as the power of **eminent domain** (power to take private property for public use), the right to use public streets, and protection from competition (monopoly). In return, utilities are required to give the public adequate service at reasonable rates.

Public utilities supply essential services in fields in which market competition may be counterproductive. In the United States, private enterprise—subject to public regulation rather than public ownership—has been the usual method of providing essential services. Nevertheless, more than two-thirds of our cities own their own waterworks, about a hundred operate their own gas utilities, and many are taking

Thinking It Through...

With only one exception, federal and state taxes on motor fuels (gasoline and diesel) go directly to pay for highway construction. The exception is a gasoline tax that was part of President Bill Clinton's 1993 deficit-reduction package. The trucking industry and others strongly objected to the tax because it broke with the tradition of gasoline taxes paying for highway construction and maintenance. Republican congressional leaders vowed to repeal the tax.[*]

Not everyone is pleased by the heavy commitment of public funds to highways. These roads, some say, are a massive subsidy for automobile users and makers; without highways, autos would not be so popular or so widely used, and mass transit would be used more. Some people use the highways far more than others, yet everyone must contribute to the taxes that pay for highway construction. Why not tax people in proportion to their actual use of the highways? Some people advocate installing a meter in every vehicle at a cost of less than $20 to measure usage of roadways in order to extract adequate federal user fees. Others favor incentives or restrictions on employers to foster mass transit and car pools, such as limiting parking space as part of a building permit for a new business.

[*]Alissa J. Rubin and Andrew Taylor, "GOP Goes for a Gas Tax Repeal," *Congressional Quarterly Weekly Report*, May 11, 1996, p. 1276.

over the operation of their transit systems. But other services—intercity transportation, airlines, telephone—are almost everywhere provided by private enterprise subject to government regulation.

Every state has a utilities commission (usually called the Public Utilities Commission, or PUC) to ensure that utilities operate in the interest of the public. In about 31 states, utility commissioners are appointed by the governor with the consent of the state senate. In Virginia they are chosen by the legislature, and in about a dozen other states they are elected by the voters.[34] Formerly, PUC posts were considered political plums, and commissioners used them as stepping-stones to higher elective office.

Public Utilities Commissions must strike a balance between fair rates for consumers and adequate profits for the utility companies. "The tremendous work load on these commissions," writes one observer, "finds commissioners constantly walking a tightrope between helping a regulated industry get a decent return on investment, and making sure consumers get good service at a fair price."[35] Utility commissioners raise or lower utility rates—perhaps the most visible part of their job—but they are also involved in toxic waste disposal, nuclear power, and truck regulation, as well as telephone, cable television, and other energy-related disputes. The average tenure for commissioners is only about three and a half years, a statistic that suggests the burnout and fatigue involved in the job.

Utility commissioners operate under the assumption that their decisions are not political, yet nearly every decision they make comes under political attack or stirs political reaction. Several states have enacted laws prohibiting conflict of interest, limiting commissioners' affiliations with the utilities they regulate, and, for at least a year after they resign from the PUC, prohibiting them from accepting employment with any company that was under their regulation. Other states have established a separate office of consumer advocate to encourage even greater responsiveness to consumer needs.

Technology and innovation are driving the deregulation of utilities across the nation. The deregulation of utilities is a controversial topic in virtually every state legislature, as telephone and power companies seek to influence the new rules for competition. Telephone communication is no longer limited to communication transmitted by telephone lines but includes cellular and satellite communications. Gas turbines now make it possible for some consumers of electricity to generate their own power rather than depend on power from public utility companies. Much of the political pressure for deregulation of utilities comes from consumers.

State legislatures and utility regulators are adopting a marketplace model in which competition between providers is encouraged rather than restricted. In the past, state utility regulators structured rate systems to provide a subsidy to rural and low-income consumers of telephone and electricity services. It is likely that these subsidies will continue, but it is more difficult to identify who pays the subsidy with so many firms now providing telephone and electricity services.

The politics of regulation, especially regulation of public utilities, is of growing interest to citizens and consumers. In many areas citizens' groups make presentations to the PUC and regularly monitor PUC operations. There has been an increasing interest in PUC activity all across the country, especially in regulating nuclear power and monitoring the cost of energy. For example, after many years of citizen concern over the environmental impact of the San Onofre Nuclear Generating Station, the California Coastal Commission adopted a plan that will mitigate, but not prevent, the destruction of fish and kelp.[36] In Virginia, the water in the Chesapeake Bay was found to contain high levels of pollutants that cause an increased risk of cancer, and that discovery led the public utilities director to impose a strict monitoring program and stiff fines for violations.

Employers and Employees

Despite the expanded regulations of the national government, state and local governments still have much to say about working conditions.

- *Health and Safety Legislation*: States require proper heating, lighting, ventilation, fire escapes, and sanitary facilities in work areas. Machinery must be equipped with safety guards. Some standards have also been established to reduce occupation-related diseases. Health, building, and labor inspectors tour industrial plants to ensure compliance with the laws.

- *Workers' Compensation*: Today all states have workers' compensation programs based on the belief that employees should not have to bear the cost of accidents or illnesses incurred because of their jobs. The costs of accidents and occupational diseases are borne by employers and passed on to consumers in the form of higher prices. In the past, employees had to prove their employers were at fault if they suffered an accident on the job. Today if people are injured or contract a disease in the ordinary course of employment, they are entitled to compensation set by a pre-arranged schedule. Workers' compensation is a controversial issue, with employers arguing that employee claims of workplace stress are excessive and will make American firms uncompetitive.

- *Child Labor*: All states forbid child labor, yet state laws vary widely in their coverage and in their definition of child labor. Many states set the minimum age for employment at 14. Higher age requirements are normal for employment in hazardous occupations and during school hours. Many of these regulations are now superseded by federal laws.

- *Consumerism*: This movement, which became prominent in the 1960s, maintains that consumers should be provided with adequate safety information and should have their complaints heard. Most states have offices to hear consumer complaints, including lawyers working in the offices of the state attorney general. State governments often establish professional standards and handle complaints about legal and medical services or insurance practices.

Recent state activity in protecting consumers has focused on fraud, especially "guaranteed prize schemes," which are mailed to more than 54 million Americans and to which roughly one-third respond. When the prize is not exactly what was promised or the method for selecting winners is deceptive, the public often turns to the state government for help. Other areas in which state governments have been active in attempting to protect consumers include charitable solicitations by telephone, "900" telephone numbers, credit card promotions, and guaranteed loan scams.

THE IMPORTANCE OF STATE AND LOCAL POLICY

Over the past decade the focus of American politics has shifted toward domestic politics and policy as a result of the end of the cold war and the fall of communism as a threat to national security. Divided government in Washington has meant neither party could have its way with domestic policy, so Congress, especially with the Senate evenly divided as a result of the 2000 elections, must take a moderate approach on such issues as welfare reform, health care, and education. State governments have also been important in the domestic policy debate, and their role has been significantly strengthened as the national government turned to them for leadership and assistance in implementing a decentralized social policy agenda. Recently, dynamic

Workplace Safety

Americans take it for granted that the safety of their workplaces is guaranteed by the government, but a fire in a North Carolina chicken-processing plant served as a reminder that basic safety features are not always checked by government authorities. In this 1991 case, the plant operators had chained the fire exit doors closed. When the fire started, employees were unable to use them to get out of the building, and 24 people were killed. Most were found near locked or blocked doorways where they had unsuccessfully attempted to escape. In addition to the locked doors, the plant's lack of fire extinguishers (there was only one), lack of an automatic heat detection sprinkler system, and lack of a contingency plan for such a crisis contributed to the tragedy.

The state officials responsible for inspecting such plants admitted that they had not been able to inspect the plant regularly because of a shortage of money and staff. They also pointed to the federal government's failure to hold them to stricter standards as a factor contributing to the plant's unsafe conditions.

Many of the surviving workers expressed great bitterness toward their employers for their seeming lack of care for worker welfare. There is now a heightened sense of awareness about plant safety in the South, where poultry plants are numerous, and support for increased regulation is growing. State and local authorities will have to deal with these demands, along with the unwillingness of taxpayers to pay higher taxes to finance their implementation.

SOURCE: "Fire Victims Died Trying to Open Shut Exits," *The New York Times*, September 7, 1991, p. A9.

state policies have been aided by a robust national economy. In addition, strong and innovative governors have proposed changes such as welfare reform, educational testing, and regulation of health maintenance organizations. Clearly, in the twenty-first century, states will remain important partners in American public policy.

POLITICS ONLINE

Should Public Education Be Privatized?

By any measure, public education is one of the most important issues at state and local levels. Presidential candidates have made it a centerpiece of their platforms, as both Al Gore and George W. Bush did in 2000. State and local governments invest large amounts of money in public schools, yet the quality of those schools and the ability of American students to compete in a global economy are serious problems.

One suggested reform is to infuse competition into public education through vouchers or parental choice options. Enabling parents to send their children to private or charter schools is thought by some to be the kind of privatization that might force the public schools to do better. One example is Proposition 38, which was on the ballot in California in 2000 and provided a $4,000 voucher to parents that would be accepted at the school of their choice. To read either a summary of this measure or the complete proposal, go to: vote2000.ss.ca.gov/VoterGuide/text/text_title_summ_38.htm. To learn about other proposals in favor of school choice or parental vouchers, as well as to read the arguments of opponents, go to: www.ksg.harvard.edu/pepg/papers/htm.

Some people oppose these ideas, maintaining that governments are already under-funding public education, and diverting tax dollars to these experimental schools will further reduce the available dollars to fund public schools for most of America's youth. The most visible and powerful opponent of school vouchers has been the National Education Association (NEA), a union of teachers. To learn their position on vouchers, charter schools, and improving public education, go to: www.nea.org/issues/vouchers/.

SUMMARY

1. We ask our state and local governments to do many things for us, and what we request in the areas of education, public welfare, health and hospitals, public safety, and transportation are the most costly, accounting for most state and local expenditures.

2. In addition, we ask states and communities to keep our streets safe, protect our natural resources, provide parks and recreation, encourage job opportunities, and protect consumers. There are, of course, great differences in how states and communities set their priorities in these areas. Some communities are so concerned about environmental quality that they are settling for selective growth at the expense of job opportunities. Other communities favor attracting jobs and industry despite the environmental costs.

3. Education has been a major area of state and local government activity and concern. It moved to center stage because of a growing concern that our system was not keeping pace with our needs or our global competitors. Several reform efforts originating at the state and local levels have sought to improve our system.

4. Concern about the U.S. system of higher education has also grown as states attempt to balance budgets and meet pressing demands in corrections, health, welfare, and other areas. Few people question the need for a major investment in laboratories, computer instruction, and libraries at colleges and universities, but the federal government has not offered to pay for these things, and most states do not have the resources to do more than stay afloat in this policy area.

5. The huge national welfare overhaul legislation in 1996 eliminated any federal implementation of programs, transferring all responsibility to the states, supported with block grants of federal money. It was prompted by a desire to trim the federal budget and to eliminate disincentives for self-sufficiency and responsibility that the former welfare system seemed to create. Before the national legislation was passed, many states had experimented with limiting their caseload, placing time limits on welfare, implementing a work requirement, and placing special requirements on teenage mothers. Most of these ideas were then included in the 1996 federal law. This state experimentation and innovation in addressing pressing social problems may set a precedent for the future.

6. States play an important role in setting policies relating to public health. States

have long sought to eradicate disease and foster practices conducive to a healthy population. The challenges for states today include the administration of federal outlay programs such as Medicare and Medicaid, reforming health care services, and controlling the AIDS epidemic.

7. Law enforcement is a traditional responsibility of state and local governments. After several decades of rising crime rates, that trend has recently been reversed, in part due to increased national and state expenditures.

8. Some state and local governments have taken the lead in protecting the environment, but more generally it has been the federal government that sets the policy standard in environmental matters.

Businesses operating in several states often are most involved in pressing for national standards of air and water quality and policies on toxic wastes. While the federal government typically sets environmental standards, the states have enforced them.

9. Transportation is a major area of state and local government activity. Although the federal government provides some financial assistance with the construction of roads and highways as well as urban mass transit, the responsibility of planning, building, and maintaining these transportation systems lies with the states. Federal and local fuel taxes have been used to help pay for transportation.

10. States openly compete with one another in the area of economic development by

offering tax incentives, waiving environmental regulations, and giving other enticements to businesses to locate or stay within their boundaries.

11. The primary purpose of regulation is to protect the health and safety of individuals and to promote fairness in the marketplace. Among the most regulated industries are public utilities because they enjoy a monopoly. Government usually gives these companies special privileges, specifically eminent domain—the power to take private property for public use. Public utilities, like other industries, are being deregulated as state and federal governments permit competition in these areas. States regulate other economic activities by conducting inspections, granting licenses, and limiting land uses.

KEY TERMS

voucher 638
charter school 639

responsibility contract 644
workfare 644

enterprise zone 644
police powers 644

eminent domain 650

FURTHER READING

BURT S. BARNOW, THOMAS KAPLAN, AND ROBERT A. MOFFITT, EDS., *Evaluating Comprehensive State Welfare Reforms* (Brookings Institution, 2000).

JOHN D. DONAHUE, *Disunited States* (Basic Books, 1997).

DENNIS DRESANG AND JAMES GOSLING, *Politics and Policy in American States and Communities*, 2nd ed. (Prentice Hall, 1998).

THOMAS DYE, *Politics in States and Communities*, 10th ed. (Prentice Hall, 2000).

CHESTER E. FINN, BRUNO V. MANNO, AND GREGG VANOUREK, *Charter Schools in Action: Renewing Public Education* (Princeton University Press, 2000).

VIRGINIA GRAY, RUSSELL HANSON, AND HERBERT JACOB, EDS., *Politics in the American States:*

A Comparative Analysis, 7th ed. (Congressional Quarterly Press, 1999).

JOHN J. HARRIGAN, *Politics and Policy in States and Communities*, 6th ed. (HarperCollins, 1997).

KIM QUAILE HILL, *Democracy in the Fifty States* (University of Nebraska Press, 1994).

NORMAN R. LUTTBEG, *The Grassroots of Democracy: A Comparative Study of Competition and Its Impact in American Cities in the 1990s* (Lexington Books, 1999).

DAVID C. NICE, *Policy Innovation in State Government* (Iowa State University Press, 1994).

MICHAEL A. PAGANO AND ANN O. M. BOWMAN, *Cityscape and Capital: The Politics of*

Urban Development (Johns Hopkins University Press, 1997).

DIANE RAVITCH, *Left Back: A Century of Failed School Reforms* (Simon & Schuster, 2000).

C. EUGENE STEUERLE, VAN DOORN OOMS, GEORGE PETERSON, AND ROBERT D. REISCHAUER, EDS., *Vouchers and the Provision of Public Services* (Brookings Institution, 2000).

R. KENT WEAVER, *Ending Welfare As We Know It* (Brookings Institution, 2000).

JOHN F. WITTE, *The Market Approach to Education: An Analysis of America's First Voucher Program* (Princeton University Press, 1999).

30

STAFFING AND FINANCING STATE AND LOCAL GOVERNMENTS

D EVASTATING WILDFIRES BURNED 6.7 MILLION ACRES ACROSS 11 WESTERN STATES DURING THE SUMMER OF 2000. IDAHO WAS HARDEST HIT, WITH 1.2 MILLION ACRES burned. Some 852 buildings were destroyed by the fires, which cost $878 million to put out. Governments at all levels assisted in fighting the fires and in providing disaster relief. Democratic and Republican governors forged a bipartisan partnership to persuade Congress and the White House to increase federal funding for fire fighting and to revise fire prevention policies.[1]

Emergencies like this one remind us how much we rely on government for basic services. When an earthquake hits, a tornado strikes, or a forest fire forces large-scale evacuations, we expect governments to come to the rescue. Things as simple as working traffic lights, accessible roads and highways, and safe drinking water all come under the purview of state and local governments.

CHAPTERMEDIA

 POLITICS ONLINE
Betting on the Internet?
www.prenhall.com/burns

PUBLIC EMPLOYEES: ESSENTIAL TO GOVERNMENT

G overnment involves many intangibles—legal authority, popular consent, shared values—but it is also very much a matter of people and money. People must be elected and hired, salaries must be negotiated and paid, and materials must be purchased. Some 18 million people work in our state and local governments.[2] They include doctors, lawyers, teachers, accountants, engineers, construction workers, secretaries, administrators, and persons with training in many different areas. The cost and quality of government depend partly on the ability and performance of these public employees and partly on the adequacy of the resources they use.

Merit Systems

More than one-third of the cost of state and local government is for people. How are these people chosen? A few of them are elected. The rest are generally hired through some kind of **merit system** in which selection and promotion depend on demonstrated performance (merit) rather than on political patronage. Although in many jurisdictions it still helps to know the right people and belong to the right party, patronage is not as prevalent as it once was. Affirmative action requirements call for recruitment through open procedures. The fact that many public employees now belong to unions has also reduced patronage.

Deeply embedded in our civic ethic is the idea that civil servants should not strike, especially those (like police and fire fighters) on whom the public depends for vital services. Many state and local elected officials, and certainly many ordinary citizens, believe it is wrong and dangerous for police, fire fighters, and hospital workers to strike. In 1919, Massachusetts Governor Calvin Coolidge became famous for opposing the Boston police strike with these words: "There is no right to strike against the public safety by anybody, anywhere, anytime."

At the national level, Ronald Reagan's decision to fire all eleven thousand air traffic controllers who engaged in an illegal strike in 1981 was supported by most of the public. When serious problems arise, like the Idaho and Montana wildfires, residents don't want their local fire fighters to be in the middle of a public employee strike.

Should public employees be allowed to strike? If you would limit the right of public employees to strike, would you limit all public employees? Would you feel differently if you were a public employee yourself?

merit system

A system of public employment in which selection and promotion depend on demonstrated performance rather than on political patronage.

spoils system

A system of public employment based on rewarding party loyalists and friends.

collective bargaining

The process of negotiation between unions and management to determine wages, hours, and conditions of employment.

binding arbitration

A collective bargaining situation in which both parties agree to adhere to the decision of the arbitrator.

Throughout much of the nineteenth century, governments at all levels were dominated by political patronage, a political **spoils system** in which employment was a reward for partisan loyalty and active political support in campaigns and elections. However, in 1939 Democratic Senator Carl Hatch of Arizona pushed through Congress the first Hatch Act, which promoted the merit principle and limited the political activities of federal and state and local employees whose salaries were supported with federal funds. Subsequently, state and local governments enacted "little Hatch Acts" that enforced merit principles and restricted the political activities of their employees. Merit testing is now used in 30 states for hiring or promoting employees.[3] Moreover, in 1976 the Supreme Court declared it unconstitutional for all but a few top policy-making public employees to be dismissed for political reasons.[4]

Merit systems are generally administered by an office of state personnel, which prepares and administers examinations, provides lists of job openings, establishes job classifications, and determines salary schedules. It also serves as a board of appeal for those who are discharged. State personnel offices are concerned with training those already employed, bargaining with labor unions, administering affirmative action programs, and filling top-level executive positions.

How well do state personnel offices do their job? Critics complain they are too slow because they are hampered by red tape and clumsy rules; since job lists are not kept up-to-date, it often takes weeks to fill vacancies. A more serious charge is that their hiring and firing rules deprive responsible officials of authority over their subordinates. It is argued that there is so much emphasis on insulating public employees from political coercion that employees enjoy too much job security. Administrators cannot get rid of incompetents; sometimes it takes months and several elaborate hearings to dismiss public employees unwilling or unable to do their jobs. Although merit systems are supposed to emphasize ability and minimize political favoritism, they sometimes discourage able people from seeking public sector jobs.

Public Employee Unions

Public employee unions grew rapidly over the past generation as government workers organized to demand better wages, hours, working conditions, and pensions. These unions now wield considerable political clout in most states and cities. In places such as New York City, they are viewed as one of the most powerful forces in political life. In dealing with unions, state and local governments participate in **collective bargaining**—the process of negotiating disputes between unions and management—and **binding arbitration**—the process of settling disputes by agreeing to adhere to the decision of an arbitrator.

More than half of all state and local public employees are unionized. The American Federation of State, County, and Municipal Employees (AFSCME), representing over 1.3 million members, has been one of the fastest growing unions in the country in recent decades.[5] Other large public employee unions are the American Postal Workers Union, with approximately 366,000 members;[6] Service Employees International Union (SEIU), with more than 600,000 of its 1.4 million members working in the public sector;[7] and the American Federation of Teachers (AFT), which represents 940,000 teachers.[8] The fire fighters' union, often considered one of the most effective political organizations among public employee unions, sometimes engages in door-to-door and telephone campaigning to elect city officials. Unions often raise funds for candidates and sponsor letter-writing campaigns to influence local and national elections. Union pressure in the 1970s and 1980s was a major reason the average pay of public employees, including benefits, rose faster than that of workers in private industry. However, since 1995 employees in private businesses have done better than public employees.[9]

The failure of the merit system to meet many of the needs of public employees encouraged the growth of public sector unions. Growth was also spurred by the example of the success of collective bargaining in the private sector (see Table 30–1).

TABLE 30-1 Comparison of Merit and Collective Bargaining Systems

	Merit System	Collective Bargaining
Management rights	Extensive	Minimal
Employee participation and rights	Union membership not required	Union membership required
Recruitment and selection	Open competitive exam; open at any level	Union membership and/or occupational license
Promotion	Competitive on basis of merit (often including seniority)	On basis of seniority
Classification of position	Based on objective analysis	Classification negotiable
Pay	Based on balanced pay plan or subject to prevailing rates	Negotiable and subject to bargaining power of union
Hours, leave, conditions of work	Based on public interest as determined by legislature and management	Negotiable
Grievances	Appeal through management with recourse to civil service agency	Appeal by union representation to impartial arbitrators

SOURCE: Adapted from *Classics of Public Administrations*, 3d ed., by Jay M. Shafritz and Albert C. Hyde. Copyright © 1992 by Harcourt, Inc. Reproduced by permission of the publisher.

But much of the success of public employee unions has come about because government workers learned how to become a political force in government. Most public employees are educated, intelligent people who can deliver two of the most valuable components of campaigns—money and labor (not to mention the votes of their members, members' families, and friends).

Surveys show that the general public thinks public workers have more job security and better wages and fringe benefits than people working in the private sector. Critics point out that public employees seem to have the best of both worlds: job protection coupled with the bargaining power of a labor union. Although collective bargaining and unionization have been generally accepted in the private sector, these rights were not as widely accepted in the public sector.

Because the public sector provides services almost everyone wants and perceives as necessities, demand is relatively constant. Also, public employee unions are an effective political force, so they can influence crucial decisions that affect taxation and the allocation of revenue. Some believe these two factors may result in policies that favor public employees. Awareness of this political clout of the unions has stiffened the spines of some city and state officials. Today it is not uncommon for mayors in large cities to fight the unions and win support from taxpayers and business groups who think the unions have overstepped their bounds.

Mayors as Collective Bargainers

In dealing with labor unions, mayors differ from presidents of private corporations in several ways. First, they have a responsibility to the voters. Second, union members' votes helped put them in their job; so, in a sense, mayors are employees of their own employees.

Public services are primarily monopolistic in character. Usually no one else supplies the services governments provide, and many are so vital to public health and survival that a stoppage would be catastrophic. These factors place great pressure on

Thinking It Through . . .

Strikes by all public unions are illegal in most states, and even states that permit them prohibit strikes by those who provide "vital and essential services." Nevertheless, such strikes do occur, and in most instances local and state officials are more concerned with getting people back to work than with sending them to jail for violating the law. Thus amnesty for the strikers has usually been the rule. Union organizers, for their part, refuse to consider such strikes as defying the law; instead, they believe the strike is a legitimate and useful weapon in a labor dispute. Still, the strike is generally viewed as a weapon of last resort, to be used only under intolerable conditions.

Moreover, striking has political risks for the public employee unions. Adverse public reaction may strengthen the hand of governors, mayors, or other politicians who oppose the unions. Many union leaders now favor compulsory arbitration over the strike, and more than 20 states have enacted laws providing for some form of arbitration. In binding arbitration, a neutral third party or mediating board hears the arguments of both sides in the dispute and devises what it considers to be a fair settlement. The arbitrator's verdict is final. Union leaders who favor arbitration hope that it will gain them something they might not get at the bargaining table, but without arousing the public backlash that usually accompanies strikes. Binding arbitration is used in several states, mostly in such public safety areas as police and fire protection.

Although binding arbitration does not guarantee there will be no public employee strikes, the number of such strikes has been reduced in states where it is practiced. However, the settlements that result from binding arbitration are often expensive. Each decision in a binding arbitration case has a ripple effect on the rest of a city or state administration. A pay raise for one group sets the standard for other public workers.

You Decide . . .

Can private companies do a better job of providing services than government agencies do?

Governments at all levels have experimented with privatization of some of their services. Examples of state and local government privatization include:

- *Prisons:* North Carolina hired private profit-making companies to build and manage prisons in hopes of reducing prison overcrowding. Bay County Jail in Panama City, Florida, one of the few privately operated jails in the country, is being watched carefully by other public officials.

- *School lunches:* Many school districts now contract with private corporations to provide lunches in public schools.

- *Sanitation:* Many localities now contract out trash collection. Atlanta Mayor Bill Campbell claimed to have saved his city $20 million a year by privatizing water and sewer systems.*

- *Public schools:* A private firm was hired to run Minneapolis public schools and was promised bonuses of nearly $500,000 a year if educational and administrative goals were met.

*Charmagne Helton, "Focus on Privatization," *The Atlanta Journal and Constitution*, February 8, 1997, p. O2E.

privatization
The contracting out to the private sector of services that are usually provided by government.

the bargainer. Then, too, because of the public nature of government operations, bargaining often takes place in a goldfish bowl of publicity. Mayors are also more restricted than executives in private industry in dealing with labor unions because the results must be accepted by their legislative bodies. This is particularly true wherever a strong city council can exert a check on executive power. It may then look upon any independent actions taken by the mayor during negotiations as usurping its legislative powers.[10]

Providing Public Services for a Profit?

To make government more efficient and curb the growing influence of public employee unions, many communities have "contracted out" certain public services to the private sector. This practice, called **privatization**, can mean governments save money while the private sector providers still make a profit. Today virtually every community service is contracted out somewhere in the United States, and this trend is expected to continue.[11] While states and localities vary widely in the extent to which they privatize, public-private partnerships have grown during the last two decades in order to reduce the costs of government services and to improve economic development. One frequently cited example of privatization is Indianapolis; under the leadership of Mayor Stephen Goldsmith, the city claims to have saved $230 million over a decade by privatization.[12]

As cities and states have become hard pressed for cash, efforts to encourage entrepreneurs to provide public services at a profit have increased. Delegation of emergency and police powers to profit-making corporations, however, raises questions of liability and protection of individual rights. It also raises fears that private contractors will hire transient help at less pay, undermining merit systems and public employee morale.

For successful privatization to occur, the contract between the government and the private company providing the service must define that service to the satisfaction of both parties. Because of the wide range of services provided by local police departments or health departments, it may be difficult to word such a contract. On the other hand, garbage collection and snow removal can easily be defined and specified in a contract, making these services attractive for privatization, so the trend toward outsourcing municipal services like these will continue.

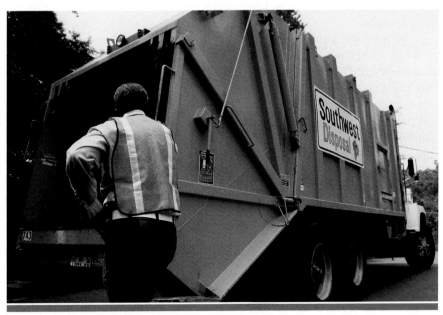

Many communities have turned over garbage collection and other services to private companies.

PAYING FOR STATE AND LOCAL GOVERNMENT

State and local governments get most of their money from taxes. Yet unlike the federal government, they are more likely to share control of the process of raising taxes with the voters through referenda, which are sometimes required before they can levy new or higher taxes. In addition, state and local governments frequently have to meet responsibilities mandated by higher levels of government, which do not always provide the funding for those mandates.

The politics of reducing the federal budget deficit and the antitax mood of the public in recent decades have meant that Congress and the president often enacted policies and expected state and local governments to pick up the tab. At the same time, citizens had high expectations for services provided by their state and local governments—and wanted even more services. This combination of increasing demand and decreasing federal funding made state and local governments the fiscal "stress joints" of American government. When the economy is thriving, states often have surplus revenue and enact tax cuts; but when times are not as good, they have to raise taxes and cut spending. Because most states are constitutionally forbidden to use deficit spending for general government programs, they have to balance their budgets and respond to shortfalls by strengthening and diversifying their revenue bases.[13]

The overlapping layers of government in the United States complicate the tax picture. Tax policies at different levels of government often conflict. While the national government is reducing taxes, states may be raising them. Indeed, when the federal government cuts both taxes and federal grants, state and local governments have little choice but to raise taxes. This is precisely what happened in the late 1970s and early 1980s.[14] But the ability of states to respond to changing economic circumstances was hampered by the tax revolt of the late 1970s, which lowered taxes and made it harder to raise them in the future. Many states enacted spending limits, which reduced the discretion of state and local elected officials. The economic growth of recent years has meant that tax cuts rather than tax increases have been more the norm at both state and federal levels.

The ability of different levels and units of government to make their own tax policy has made tax collection more complicated and expensive. For example, national officials, state officials, and some local officials collect taxes on gasoline, and each level of government maintains its own tax-collecting office. Taxpayers are

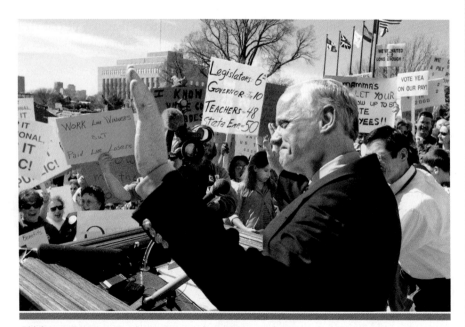

Oklahoma Governor Frank Keating speaks to state employees gathered at a rally on the steps of the state capitol asking for higher wages.

Thinking It Through...

Privatization of public services has been hotly debated. Advocates— including those who bid on contracts, some academics, some city managers, and city and state elected officials—say privatization keeps taxes down and increases productivity. Opponents—including public employee unions, other academics, and other city and state officials—contend that privatization raises serious issues of accountability, quality, flexibility, and integrity.

Public employee groups say privatization:

- Masks hidden costs to government, including the expenses of contract preparation and monitoring contractor performances

- Emphasizes the profit motive, making contracted services neither cheaper than publicly provided services nor of comparable quality

- Locks public officials into inflexible contracts that prevent responses to unforeseen circumstances

- Increases opportunities for corruption

- Diminishes government accountability to citizens.

Source: Thomas B. Darr, "Pondering Privatization May Be Good for Your Government," *Governing*, November 1987, p. 47.

allowed to deduct certain business expenses and state income taxes from their federal income tax. Texas, Florida, South Dakota, New Hampshire, Nevada, Washington, and Wyoming have no personal income tax and rely on sales taxes. In those states, taxpayers lose the deduction for state income taxes on their federal tax returns. By contrast, in Alabama, Iowa, Louisiana, Missouri, Montana, North Dakota, Oklahoma, Oregon, and Utah, taxpayers may deduct their federal income tax from their state taxes.[15] Thus, changes in state laws can affect the amount of federal and state taxes a person must pay. Although there is little coordination in setting tax policy, there is cooperation between state and federal tax administrators.

No matter who collects the taxes, all the money comes out of a single economy. Although each level of government has a different tax base, and each tax hits some groups rather than others, all taxes ultimately depend on the productivity of the American people. And that productivity is affected by many of the activities of government.

Who Pays the Taxes?

Who bears the cost of state and local services is decided in the United States by politics. State and local governments are free to extract whatever taxes they wish from whomever they wish, as long as their taxing practices meet the stipulations of the U.S. Constitution. The Constitution has been interpreted to forbid states:

> To tax exports or imports or to levy tonnage duties without the consent of Congress
>
> To use their taxing power to interfere with federal operations
>
> To discriminate against interstate commerce, unduly burden it, or directly tax it
>
> To use their taxing power to deprive persons of equal protection of the law
>
> To deprive individuals of their property without due process.

Constitutional lawyers and judges spend much of their time applying these principles to concrete situations. Out of hundreds of disputes, courts have decided that states may collect sales taxes from interstate sales and income taxes from persons and corporations within the states, even if the income was earned from interstate business. However, states may not tax the privilege of engaging in interstate commerce or the profits made through interstate transactions that cannot be apportioned to a single state.

State constitutions also restrict state taxing power. Certain kinds of property, such as that used for educational, charitable, and religious purposes, are exempt from taxation. State constitutions frequently list the kinds of taxes that may be collected and stipulate the amount of tax that may be collected from various sources.

General Property Tax

Widely criticized as "one of the worst taxes known to the civilized world," the **general property tax** is a chief revenue source for local governments. The property tax is difficult to administer, leads to favoritism and inequities, and takes little account of ability to pay.[16] Forty years ago it provided 45 percent of the revenues for state governments and an even higher percentage of the revenues for local governments. But during the last two decades reliance on property taxes has declined. Today it provides less than one-third of total state and local government revenues. But some states remain acutely dependent on property taxes. New Hampshire, for instance, raises nearly two-thirds of its state and local revenues from the property tax. At the other end of the scale, Alabama and New Mexico raise only about one-tenth of their state and local tax dollars from the property tax.[17]

ADMINISTRATION OF THE PROPERTY TAX   A hundred years ago, wealth was primarily *real property*—land and buildings—that was relatively easy to value. Assessors could guess the value of the property a person owned, and that assessment was a good indicator of his or her ability to pay taxes. Today wealth takes many

general property tax

Tax levied by local and some state governments on real property or personal, tangible property, the major portion of which is on the estimated value of one's home and land.

forms. People own varying amounts of personal property—both *tangible* (furniture, jewels, washing machines, rugs, paintings) and *intangible* (stocks, bonds, money in the bank). It is possible to concentrate a large amount of wealth in a small rented apartment. The nature of real property has also changed. It no longer consists mainly of barns, houses, and land but rather of large industrial plants, huge retail stores, and office buildings whose values are hard to measure. In addition, property ownership is less likely these days to reflect ability to pay taxes. An elderly couple with a large house valued at $300,000 may be living on Social Security payments and a small allowance provided by their children. But they have to pay higher property taxes than a young couple with two healthy incomes who live in a rented apartment.

Although many communities stipulate that the general property tax be imposed on all property, this is not what actually happens. Significant amounts of real property are exempted from property taxes because they are owned by tax-exempt groups, such as churches and charitable organizations. Local governments often waive the tax as an economic development inducement or for other reasons. As a result, two taxpayers may own similar property, but one is assessed at a higher rate, and the principle of horizontal equity is violated. Intangible personal property is also seldom taxed. Some communities deliberately impose a lower rate on intangible property to induce owners to declare ownership. In addition, tangible personal property such as watches, rings, and other jewelry often escapes taxation or is grossly undervalued.

The general property tax is hard to adjust to changing circumstances. This tax is typically administered by an assessor, who attempts to place a value on property—an **assessment**. The assessment may or may not reflect the real market value of the property. In some states the assessment is legally required to be a percentage of market value—say, 25 percent. The property tax rate is usually a tax per $100 or $1,000 of assessed valuation or some other such measure. Local and state governments can do very little to change the assessment, but they can raise or lower the tax rates.

During times of rising prices, assessed values increase much more slowly than the general price level does. Thus when governments need more money, the lagging tax bases fail to provide it. When prices fall, valuations do not drop at the same rate. When people cannot pay taxes, property may be sold on the market to cover tax delinquency, but such occurrences are rare. In some areas, property taxes are already so high that to increase them may discourage businesses and lower-income families from moving into the locality.

A property tax bill typically includes fees or taxes charged by three, four, or more governmental units like the city, county, school board, or the water, utility, and other special districts. The lump-sum payment aspect of the property tax is one reason for its widespread unpopularity and has prompted some places to permit tax payers to pay their taxes in installments, often collected with their mortgage payments.

PROPERTY TAXES AND PUBLIC EDUCATION   In recent years controversy has been stirred up by reliance on the local property tax to support public schools. The amount of money available to finance education varies tremendously from area to area; rich suburban areas with a high property valuation per pupil are able to spend much more than poor areas like the central cities, which need the money most. Reformers have urged the states to take over the financing of public education, or at least to assume a greater share of the burden, in order to equalize differences from community to community. Although this is not a popular idea, most states do distribute funds to local districts in an attempt to ensure more equitable expenditures.

Those hoping for greater state support for the public schools have often turned to the courts. Several state courts have ruled that wide differences between school districts in per pupil expenditures are inconsistent with the equal protection clause of the Fourteenth Amendment.[18] The California Supreme Court, for example, saw such differences as violating the California Constitution.[19] However, in 1973 the U.S. Supreme Court held that there is no federal constitutional requirement that the

assessment
The valuation a government places on property for the purposes of taxation.

amount spent per pupil in each school district must be the same.[20] The Supreme Court's 1973 decision temporarily slowed the push toward equalization of school expenditures, but the controversy and the issues remain. Several state courts have now handed down rulings similar to that of the California Supreme Court. Kentucky, New Hampshire, New Jersey, New York, Ohio, Texas, and Wyoming courts, for example, have held that their state constitutions require that education be financed in a way that avoids differences in funding due to differences in wealth among local school districts.[21]

Despite its weaknesses, the general property tax remains an important source of revenue for local government. Supporters of the tax say it is a practical and suitable tax because real rather than personal property is the chief beneficiary of many local services, such as fire protection. Alternatives are few, and each has disadvantages. Moreover, some of the bad features of the general property tax can be corrected by improving assessment and administration methods.

One effort to reform the general property tax is the *circuit-breaker exemption* (sometimes called a *negative income tax*) by which most states and certain cities give a form of tax relief to lower-income families and the elderly. The idea is to protect family income from property tax overload in the same way an electrical circuit breaker protects a family home from an electrical current overload: "When the property tax burden of an individual exceeds a predetermined percentage of personal income, the circuit breaker goes into effect to relieve the excess financial pressure."[22] The circuit-breaker property tax exemption seems to be most popular in the Great Lakes and Plains states and least popular in the Southeast, where property tax burdens are low.

TAX REFORM AND REVOLT   Hostility to the property tax spawned the tax revolts of the last three decades of the twentieth century. The watershed event in the politics of tax cutting was passage of California's Proposition 13, which set a 1 percent limit for property taxes and limited increases to a maximum of 2 percent a year. Throughout the 1970s, California property taxes had risen dramatically, until voters passed an initiative in 1978 to cut them. Such direct citizen involvement in making fiscal pol-

Citizen rebellions against the large tax bite of local taxes have been occurring in states all over the country.

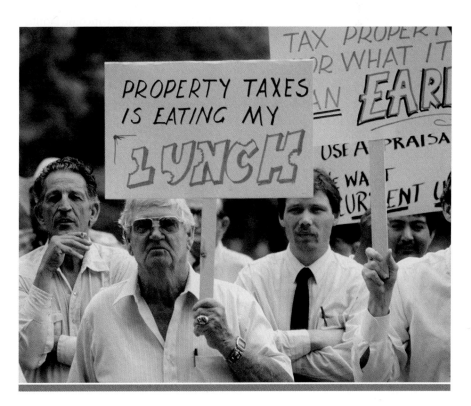

icy is not uncommon in the United States, and there has been a resurgence of initiative and referendum activity in recent decades.[23]

Passage of Proposition 13 made tax reduction an important issue nationwide. Heralded as the start of a modern tax revolt, it triggered taxing and spending limits in more than a dozen states and helped spur movements for constitutional amendments setting federal spending limits, requiring a balanced federal budget, and **indexing** income tax brackets (automatic adjustment of income tax rates to rise with inflation so that, in effect, income tax rates remain constant). Tax reduction was not limited to ballot initiatives but spread to state legislatures, most of which reduced income, sales, or property taxes.

The importance of California's example grew as Proposition 13 received national attention. Political commentators frequently observed that its passage signified a new move toward conservatism, the resurgence of the middle class, a general tendency toward tax cutting, and a strong message to government. Indeed, one of the most important consequences of Proposition 13 was that it gave rise to a new conventional wisdom that the public had become more conservative and desired less government.[24] The impact of this ballot proposition was profound. Proposition 13 prompted leaders in both parties to speak in more fiscally conservative tones.

Cutting taxes, either at the state or local level, is one way of attempting to limit government spending. Loss of revenue from taxes, however, can be made up temporarily by taking money from some other source or drawing on budget surpluses if available. More permanent solutions may involve creating new revenue sources. Thus tax cuts do not necessarily achieve the end of reducing or limiting government spending. Recognition of this fact has fostered a wide variety of more direct limitations on government spending. In their simplest form, such limitations restrict future spending to current levels; more typically, they provide for an annual increase in spending that is either limited to a fixed percentage or tied to increases in personal income or inflation. Spending limitations can be enacted without tax cuts and, unlike tax cuts, can incur few political costs since no services are being reduced in the short run.

New Jersey was the first state to enact spending limits that applied to both the state and local governments. Passed in 1976, the New Jersey law limited the growth in state expenditures to the annual percentage increase in per capita personal income and restricted localities to increases of no more than 5 percent without voter approval. Nearly half of the states have followed New Jersey's example and imposed limits on state expenditures.[25]

One consequence of the tax revolt is that the property tax has become a less significant part of the tax base of local governments. As a result local governments have had to develop other sources of funding. See Table 30–2 for a summary of the various revenue sources and expenditures.

Other Taxes

State and local governments employ a wide range of other taxes that have become increasingly popular since the property tax revolts of the 1970s and 1980s (see Figure 30–1). States and localities seek to diversify their taxes to "spread the pain" of taxes as much as possible.

SALES TAXES   Born during the Great Depression, the **sales tax** is now the most important source of revenue for states. The 45 states with such taxes annually collect over $150 billion.[26] Almost all states impose some kind of general sales tax, normally

TABLE 30–2 State and Local Revenues and Expenditures, 1997

	Percentage of Total Revenues
Taxes	
Property	0.9%
Individual income	13.9
Corporate income	2.9
Vehicle licenses	1.2
Motor fuels	2.6
Other	20.9
Intergovernmental revenue	
From federal government*	$215,421,000,000
Education	15.6%
Public welfare	57.1
Highways	8.9
Other	12.8
From local governments	1.4
Utilities and liquor stores	.70
Insurance trust revenue	20.9
Charges and miscellaneous	13.5
Total Revenues	**$1,039,422,000,000**
	Percentage of Total Expenditures
Education	29.4%
Public welfare	21.7
Hospitals and health programs	6.7
Highways	6.4
Police protection	.80
Correction (prisons)	3.1
Utilities and liquor stores	1.2
Insurance trust expenditures	10.1
Debt redemption	4.4
Other	15.9
Total Expenditures	**$935,208,000,000**

SOURCE: U.S. Bureau of the Census, *Statistical Abstract of the United States, 2000* (Government Printing Office, 2000), p. 324. See also www.census.gov/ftp/pub/govs/www/state.html.

*Percentages are based on state revenues from the federal government and not on state revenues as a whole.

indexing
Automatic adjustment of income tax rates to rise with inflation so that, in effect, income tax rates remain constant.

sales tax
General tax on sales transactions, sometimes exempting food and drugs; the most important source of revenue for states.

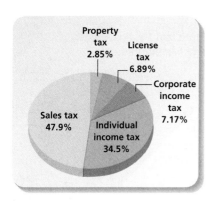

FIGURE 30–1 State Revenues by Type of Tax (Percent)

SOURCE: U.S. Bureau of the Census, State Government Tax Collections, reported in *The New York Times Almanac, 2000* (Penguin, 1999), p. 217.

value-added tax (VAT)

A tax on increased value of a product at each stage of production and distribution (rather than a sales tax just at the point of sale); commonly used by governments in Europe to raise revenues.

on retail sales. Local sales taxes were uncommon until after World War II, but now 34 states also allow cities to impose sales taxes. Sales taxes are unpopular with local merchants, who fear they drive business away. In most cases, this is a minor issue that arises only along state borders where consumers can drive into another state with a lower sales tax to make their purchases. Most consumers do not pay that much attention to the sales tax on most items.

Sales taxes are easy to administer and produce large amounts of revenue. Many consumers consider sales taxes relatively painless because they can avoid paying a large tax bill at one time. But labor groups and low-income consumers remain opposed to sales taxes, favoring wider use of the income tax instead. They argue that people with small incomes spend larger percentages of their budgets on food and clothing than do the wealthy, so sales taxes fall heaviest on those least able to pay. Hence many states exempt food and drugs from the sales tax.

States continue to search for ways to tax services, both because they are under acute pressure to find new revenues and because the service sector of the economy continues to expand. All states tax some services, but none has a broad-based tax on services. Among the kinds of services taxed are cable television, landscaping, income-tax preparation, pest control, videotape rental, laundry and dry cleaning, and photocopying.

State and local officials listen with concern to talk about the federal government's imposing a **value-added tax (VAT)** like that used in many Western European countries. This tax is imposed on whatever value is added to a product at each stage of production and distribution. Should the federal government impose such a tax, state and local officials fear their ability to use the sales tax will be reduced.

There is a running battle about whether states can tax mail-order catalog and Internet sales. Opponents contend taxing this activity violates the constitutional protection of interstate commerce. The Supreme Court, in general, has left the issue to be decided by Congress. The stakes are high. Online retail sales are estimated to rise to $184 billion by 2004.[27] Billions in revenues could go to states and localities if they taxed these purchases at the same rate they tax merchants operating within their states.

But there is a question of fairness. Local merchants who have to collect sales taxes are put at a disadvantage if mail-order and Internet firms can escape these taxes. Mail-order merchants and their lobbyists claim it would be an administrative nightmare to collect and reimburse all the sales taxes, and they argue that they should not be obligated to collect taxes for a state in which they do not have a physical presence. But this position does not reduce complexity. It means if there is an Eddie Bauer store in your state and you buy a shirt from the Eddie Bauer catalog, you are charged a sales tax, while a similar shirt from a Land's End catalog would escape the tax in every state except Wisconsin, where Land's End is located.

The large volume of commerce conducted electronically suggests some more sensible and consistent policy will have to be developed. Congress enacted the Internet Tax Freedom Act of 1998, creating the Advisory Commission on Electronic Commerce to study the matter. In the meantime, the federal government imposed a moratorium on state and local taxes on e-commerce. State and local governments contend that the moratorium unfairly preempts their authority and will erode the tax base of many governments. The issue of taxation of e-commerce is becoming more controversial and significant as the size of e-commerce grows. How can retailers avoid multiple taxation, overregulation, and conflicting state regulations? On the other hand, is it fair to require bricks-and-mortar firms to collect sales taxes but not their electronic competitors? And as e-commerce grows and is exempted from state taxes, state sales tax revenues will decline and schools and other institutions supported by such taxes will suffer, or other taxes will have to be increased.

INCOME TAXES   The state income tax has been one of the fastest-growing revenue sources for most states. Several states impose a tax on personal income, and income

tax revenue is higher than general sales tax revenue in more than 20 states. Personal income taxes are generally **progressive taxes**; that is, the rate goes up with the size of the income. State income tax rates, however, do not rise as sharply as the federal income tax and seldom go above 10 percent of taxable income. Corporation incomes are frequently taxed by states at a flat rate. In some states exemptions are generous.

States generally do not allow local governments to levy income taxes. However, some cities—following the lead of Philadelphia and Toledo—now collect a *wage tax*, and most cities in Ohio and cities, towns, and school districts in Pennsylvania levy a similar *payroll tax* on all persons. For instance, visiting professional athletes who compete in Philadelphia are subject to the city's earned income tax. The Toledo tax also applies to corporate profits. A municipal income tax enables hard-pressed cities to collect money from citizens who use city facilities but live in the suburbs. Similar taxes are collected by New York City, Detroit, and Louisville.

Governments impose excise taxes on cigarettes to generate revenue but also to discourage smoking and to fund the cost of treating smokers.

EXCISE TAXES   Almost all states tax gasoline, alcohol, and cigarettes; taxes on specific items are known as **excise taxes**. Because many cities also tax these items, the combined local, state, and federal levies often double the cost of these "luxury" items to the consumer. Gasoline taxes are sometimes combined with the funds collected for automobile and driver's licenses and are earmarked for highway construction and maintenance. Liquor taxes often consist of both license fees to manufacture or sell alcoholic beverages and levies on their sale or consumption; they are often used for general government spending.

Some states own liquor stores, with the profits going to the state treasury. High taxation of liquor is justified on the grounds that it reduces the amount of alcohol consumed, falls on an item that is not a necessity of life, and eases the task of law enforcement. Some states, like North Carolina, set aside part of their alcohol taxes for mental health programs and the rehabilitation of alcoholics. If the tax is raised too high, however, liquor purchases tend to be diverted into illegal channels and tax revenues fall off.

The rationale for taxing cigarettes is similar. High tobacco taxes in states like Alaska, New Jersey, and Hawaii, which do not grow tobacco, compared with low tobacco taxes in tobacco-growing states like Virginia and the Carolinas, have led to interstate smuggling. Some states levy a general sales tax on top of the excise tax, especially on tobacco taxes.

SEVERANCE TAXES   In several states **severance taxes** have been a key source of revenue. This is a tax on the privilege of "severing" such natural resources as coal, oil, timber, and gas from the land. In recent years the severance tax accounted for more than 20 percent of tax collections in eight states: Alaska, Louisiana, Montana, New Mexico, North Dakota, Oklahoma, Texas, and Wyoming. Although more than 30 states rely on some type of severance tax, significant revenues from this tax are not available to most states. Tax revenues from severance taxes go up and down with the price of oil, gas, and coal.

The state and local taxes described here do not begin to exhaust the kinds of taxes collected by state and local governments. Admission taxes, stock transfer taxes, inheritance taxes, parimutuel taxes, corporate franchise taxes, and taxes on utilities and insurance are common.

Nontax Revenues

In addition to taxation, states derive revenue from fees and special service charges. At least 10 percent of the money collected by state and local governments comes from inspecting buildings, recording titles, operating courts, licensing professions, disposing of garbage, and other services. Parking meters have become an important revenue source for some cities. Municipal governments frequently operate water-supply and local transit systems. City-operated liquor stores are administered by, and turn a

progressive tax

A tax graduated so that people with higher incomes pay a larger fraction of their income than people with lower incomes.

excise tax

Consumer tax on a specific kind of merchandise, such as tobacco.

severance tax

A tax on the privilege of "severing" such natural resources as coal, oil, timber, and gas from the land.

A Closer Look

SELLING HOPE: LOTTERIES AS A SOURCE OF REVENUE

Lotteries are state-sponsored and state-administered gambling used to raise money for public purposes. Along with the District of Columbia and Puerto Rico, 37 states operate lotteries to generate revenue without raising taxes. Lotteries are not entirely new; the Continental Congress ran a lottery to help finance the Revolutionary War. Indeed, all 13 states used lotteries as a form of voluntary taxation in the 1780s. Lotteries also helped to establish some of the nation's earliest colleges, notably Princeton, Harvard, and Yale. In 1964 New Hampshire was the first state to revive the practice in modern times to help balance its budget.

In recent decades state lotteries increased in popularity, and gross receipts have generally grown over time. State-run lotteries provide less than 3 percent of all state tax revenues, but few states that have lotteries would want to increase other taxes to make up for lottery income. States pay out between 50 and 70 percent of their gross receipts from lotteries in prizes and roughly 6 percent in administration. The remaining revenues are used for public purposes.

Elected officials like lotteries because they raise revenue without raising taxes. Critics contend that lotteries take advantage of poor people: "You're seven times more likely to be killed by lightning than to win a million in the state lottery."[*] Despite these economic arguments, Americans are hooked on gambling. They gamble an average of $300 per year per family. "Washington, D.C., is the lottery capital of the nation, with spending of about $1,000 per household."[**]

Revenues from lotteries are used for a variety of purposes. About half of the states with lotteries earmark most or all of their proceeds for education; a significant number of the remaining states commit their proceeds to the state general fund. Some states, like Kansas and Oregon, designate lottery profits for economic development; Minnesota commits part of what it makes through the lottery to the environment; Pennsylvania and West Virginia designate senior citizens programs to receive lottery profits.

Proponents of lotteries identify a popular cause like education, the environment, or senior citizens as the beneficiaries of lottery profits in hopes of getting popular support for passage of the lottery. Opposition to the lottery often comes from church groups, which contend that state lotteries are immoral because they are a form of legalized gambling. Proponents counter that churches often raise funds through raffles, bingo, and other games of chance. Opponents also argue that lotteries are a bad investment because they yield a poor rate of return. Proponents respond that tickets are purchased more for their entertainment value than as an investment.

To find out more about lotteries go on the website of the Multi-State Lottery Association at www.musl.com/

A Texas lottery winner collects over $21 million dollars.

lotterylinks.htm or the North American Lotteries at www.interloto.com. You may find more about the history of lotteries at www.scigames.com/block9.htm.

SOURCES: Peter Passell, "Maybe the Lottery Raises a Lot of Revenue, But As an Investment, It's Chancier Than You Might Think," *The New York Times*, August 6, 1998, p. D2.

[*]Susannah Calkins, "State Lotteries: Has a Growth Industry Faltered?" *Tax Notes*, March 23, 1992, p. 1563.

[**]James K. Glassman, "Lottery Madness," *The Washington Post*, July 28, 1998, p. A15.

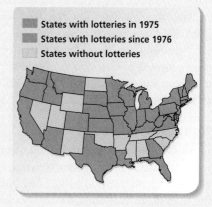

■ States with lotteries in 1975
■ States with lotteries since 1976
□ States without lotteries

SOURCE: *Roper Center for Public Opinion Research.*

profit in, certain cities in Alaska, Minnesota, North Carolina, and South Dakota. The city of Dallas owns and operates an FM radio station (WRR), which plays classical music. Some states and cities run other business enterprises, such as cable television services, from which they make money (and sometimes lose it, too). North Dakota, for example, operates a state-owned bank. Municipally owned gas and power companies often contribute to city treasuries. In some cases, utility profits are large enough to make other city taxes unnecessary.

LEGALIZED GAMBLING   Recent years have seen a dramatic increase in legalized gambling in the United States. Only Hawaii and Utah do not permit some form of legalized gambling. For many years, only Nevada permitted legalized casino gambling, but now 37 states, the District of Columbia, and Puerto Rico have legalized gambling, including lotteries, and 20 states allow casinos. This increase occurred because American Indian tribes asserted their right to self-rule on reservations and brought casinos to states like California, Michigan, Connecticut, and South Dakota. In addition, gambling companies asserted that prohibitions against land-based casinos did not apply to floating ones, and they promoted gambling on riverboats and dockside casinos. A casino is estimated to be within a four-hour drive for 95 percent of all Americans. "The Bible Belt might as well be renamed the Blackjack Belt, with floating and land-based casinos."[28]

As more states permit legalized casinos, neighboring states rush to follow their lead to avoid losing the possibility of these tax revenues. Opponents of gambling assert that lotteries and legalized gambling have not produced as much revenue as promised and see negative social consequences flowing from expanded gambling opportunities.

USER FEES OR CHARGES   State and local collection of **user fees**—fees paid directly by individuals to use public services such as parks and municipal golf courses—has grown rapidly in recent years. In some cities these fees account for more than one-third of total local tax revenue.[29] Examples of services for which users pay fees are toll roads, higher education, hospitals, airports, parks, sewerage, and solid waste management. It is harder to impose fees on other kinds of services because such charges would raise questions of fairness and access. The cost of libraries could be paid entirely by library users, for instance, but most localities seek to encourage library use by the disadvantaged through heavy subsidies.

It is not always easy to distinguish between individual and community benefits. Public schools obviously benefit the families who use them more than the families who do not. Yet education is generally thought to yield considerable benefits for the community at large, so it is financed by taxes rather than user fees. Similarly, it would not be fair to support fire departments by charging people whose homes or businesses experienced fires in a given year.

GRANTS   Grants from states to local governments have become increasingly important during the last several decades. The national government once allocated large sums to cities, but that stopped in the 1980s. Local governments now go to the states to get more than $237 billion in assistance. State officials return revenues collected from certain taxes to local governments, often without specifying the purposes for which the money should be used. Local governments receive state and federal grants in a wide range of areas, including education, transportation, corrections, law enforcement, housing, welfare, community development, and health care. One reason local governments receive so much money in the form of grants is that they are the unit of government closest to the people and most experienced at providing services.

Local governments often see state and federal grants as enhancing the services they provide. In return for a modest investment of local tax revenue, local

User fees, like the tolls collected at this tunnel entrance in New York City, contribute to the maintenance of such facilities.

user fees
Fees charged directly to individuals who use certain public services on the basis of service consumed; also called a user charge.

governments can get grant money from state or federal governments. But grant money may not be available for some pressing local priorities, or the strings attached to the money may permit state and federal governments to set local priorities. In such cases, are local governments wise to pursue the grants, or should they put their money into their most pressing priorities? Local governments also worry about depending on grant money if state or federal money may dry up in a year or two.

Borrowing Money

State and local governments collect large sums of money to pay for current operating expenses—garbage collection, police protection, and social services. To fund long-term projects—so-called *capital expenditures*—cities and states often have to borrow money. This long-term borrowing is necessary for building schools, constructing roads, and clearing slums—projects whose costs are so large that it is not feasible to pay for them out of current revenue. Moreover, because these improvements have long lives and add to the wealth of the community, it is reasonable to pay for them over time. For this purpose, governments issue bonds, often with voter approval.

During the early years of the nineteenth century, states and cities subsidized railroad and canal builders. The money for these and other public improvements came from bonds issued by the cities or states and purchased by investors. Provision for payment of these debts was inadequate, and citizens were burdened with debts long after the improvements had lost their value. As a result, default on obligations was frequent. Aroused by the legislatures' abuse of their authority, voters insisted on constitutional amendments restricting legislative discretion to borrow money. The National Tax Reform Act of 1986 restricted the ability of states and localities to issue tax-exempt debt, and the power to borrow money for the long term now routinely requires voter approval.

Increasingly important since the passage of the National Tax Reform Act are special purpose governments or special districts: airport authorities, bridge and highway authorities, water and wastewater districts, public transit authorities, and community college districts. Their creation has resulted in turning more and more to *revenue bonds* to help finance their operations. The repayment and dividends due investors come from tolls and fees charged by the facility. In most cases, revenue bonds do not require voter approval, making it much easier to issue this kind of debt and also to spend more on services like public transportation.[30]

State and local bonds are attractive to investors because the interest is exempt from federal income tax. State and local governments can borrow money at a lower interest rate than can private businesses, and although credit ratings differ sharply according to economic health, the credit of most cities and states is good. Hence, they can easily find buyers for their bonds. Because governments are often permitted to issue bonds beyond the limitations on their general indebtedness, they use them whenever possible. However, as New York City learned in the 1970s, excessive reliance on bonds can be detrimental to the fiscal health of a state or city.

DOING MORE WITH LESS

John Shannon, an authority in the field of public finance, has written that there were three "R's" that shocked state and local governments in the recent past. The first "R" was the revolt of the taxpayers, which started with California's Proposition 13 and quickly became a national phenomenon. The second "R" was the recession of the late 1980s and early 1990s, which placed demands on state and local governments to care for the unemployed and needy. And the third "R" was the reduction in federal grants, which meant state and local governments were on

their own.[31] States had to search for ways to make ends meet and to live within their revenue projections.

As discussed in Chapter 29, welfare reform in the mid-1990s encouraged states to experiment and modify welfare funding within broad parameters. The federal government would still pay for most of welfare, but with far fewer strings attached. Whether this division of responsibility between the national and state governments will become a model for other areas of public policy is not yet clear.

Another area where policy is in flux is telecommunications. The Telecommunications Act of 1996 opened local telephone markets to competition, set conditions for the powerful telephone companies to enter new markets, and regulated competition between telephone and cable companies. States were allowed to continue regulating telephone company profits. The act stresses that there shall be no barriers to entry and assigns the Federal Communications Commission (FCC) regulatory power over that of the states. Many cellular and satellite services are provided by out-of-state companies that traditionally have not been taxed by the states. Property taxes may need to be adjusted in several states as utilities contest their tax assessments.

Intergovernmental Competition

State and local governments exist in a competitive environment in which they seek to enhance their own economy and overall reputation. They have become more competitive in courting business and economic growth because of the increasing mobility of business and the stagnant growth in some sectors of the economy and in some regions of the country. One way governments compete in this marketplace is in the use of *tax incentives* that offer reduced tax rates to promote business investment in the local community. Government officials assume that a pro-growth policy is good politics because voter confidence increases when new jobs and businesses move into a community or state.

Local governments that are successful in luring businesses to locate within their boundaries also assume that in the long run these new businesses will add to the tax base by stimulating sales taxes and property taxes. In the case of large shopping malls that attract shoppers from surrounding communities, the revenues from the sales tax may actually lower the tax burden for residents of the city because of sales taxes paid by nonresidents.

Developers of shopping malls or office complexes who are thinking about relocating often play one local government off against another in an effort to drive down their tax burden. Established businesses in the community then cry foul about the tax incentives offered to attract new businesses or keep those who threaten to leave. Economists are skeptical about how important these incentives really are. Some believe that such factors as space availability, cost of land, cost of labor, and quality of life are at least as important in decisions about where businesses locate.[32]

Another example of intergovernmental competition for tax incentives and subsidies concerns sports teams and stadiums or arenas. In recent years competition between cities, especially larger cities, has drawn them into funding the construction of major sports facilities for professional football, basketball, hockey, or baseball teams. Because the teams are identified with the city or state and are perceived to enhance the community's reputation, local and state governments have been responsive to the demands of team owners. Some cities have offered team owners "sweetheart deals" to keep the team or build them a new stadium.[33] The New York Yankees threatened to leave their historic location in the Bronx for New Jersey's Meadowlands, but agreed to stay put after getting concessions from local government. Often the building of new facilities requires a referendum, but other arrangements like the proceeds from parking and vendors are open to negotiations between the owners and government officials.[34]

SUMMARY

1. Wages for public employees constitute more than one-third the cost of state and local government. These public employees are hired through merit systems.

2. One of the most controversial aspects of state and local government in recent years has been the unionization of over 50 percent of public employees at the state and local levels. Public employee unions have been increasingly successful in recruiting new members and bargaining for better wages, hours, working conditions, and pensions. Their success has caused some public backlash.

3. One response to growing costs has been outsourcing of public services to the private sector. Garbage collection, recreation, and even emergency services are now contracted out in some cities. Arguments in favor of privatization include lower cost and better services. But others argue that this movement reduces government accountability and may lead to corruption in the awarding of contracts.

4. State and local governments get most of their money from taxes. Decreasing federal funding has made state and local governments the "stress joints" of American government.

5. The general property tax, despite its unpopularity, remains the most important source of revenue for many local governments. Property is generally thought of as real estate but can include other personal property like automobiles or boats. Administration of the tax is generally handled at the local level, but several states provide oversight. The property tax is a major revenue source for public schools.

6. The tax revolts in the 1970s and 1980s resulted in limits on property taxes in several states and often made it more difficult to raise property taxes. The property tax is now a less significant part of the tax base of local governments.

7. State and local governments have traditionally received revenues primarily from property taxes but also from sales taxes, income taxes, excise taxes, and severance taxes. Recently, they have diversified their revenue sources by turning to such devices as lotteries, legalized gambling, user fees, other fees and special service charges, and taxes not previously used at the state and local level. This diversification was made necessary by economic downturns and by cutbacks in federal support. Intergovernmental grants from states to cities and school districts have increased in importance as local governments have had to deal with rising costs and expectations but limited revenues. In addition, the growth in special district governments has led to greater reliance on revenue bonds to finance local services.

8. States and local governments have also become more competitive in courting business and economic growth, especially through tax incentives and subsidies.

KEY TERMS

merit system 658	privatization 660	sales tax 665	severance tax 667
spoils system 658	general property tax 662	value-added tax (VAT) 666	user fees 669
collective bargaining 658	assessment 663	progressive tax 667	
binding arbitration 658	indexing 665	excise tax 667	

FURTHER READING

J. RICHARD ARONSON AND JOHN L. HILLEY, *Financing State and Local Governments*, 4th ed. (Brookings Institution, 1986).

TERRY N. CLARK AND LORNA C. FERGUSON, *City Money: Political Processes, Fiscal Strain and Retrenchment* (Columbia University Press, 1983).

RONALD C. FISHER, *Intergovernmental Fiscal Relations* (Kluwer, 1997).

KATHRYN A. FOSTER, *The Political Economy of Special-Purpose Government* (Georgetown University Press, 1997).

STEVEN D. GOLD, ED., *The Fiscal Crisis of the States: Lessons for the Future* (Georgetown University Press, 1995).

CHARLES T. GOODSELL, *The Case for Bureaucracy*, 3d ed. (Chatham House, 1994).

ROY T. MEYERS, ED., *Handbook of Government Budgeting* (Jossey-Bass, 1999).

NATIONAL CONFERENCE OF STATE LEGISLATURES, *Legislative Budget Procedures in the 50 States* (National Conference of State Legislatures, 1998).

MICHAEL PAGANO AND RICHARD MOORE, *Cities and Fiscal Choices* (Duke University Press, 1985).

B. GUY PETERS, *The Politics of Taxation: A Comparative Perspective* (Blackwell, 1991).

JOHN E. PETERSEN AND DENNIS R. STRACHOTA, EDS., *Local Government Finance, Concepts and Practices* (Government Finance Officers Association, 1991).

HENRY J. RAIMONDO, *Economics of State and Local Government* (Praeger Publishers, 1992).

HARVEY S. ROSEN, *Public Finance*, 5th ed. (Irwin, 1994).

E. S. SAVAS, *Privatization: The Key to Better Government*, 2d ed. (Chatham House, 1998).

RONALD SNELL, ED., *Financing State Government in the 1990s* (National Conference of State Legislatures and National Governors' Association, 1993).

THOMAS R. SWARTZ AND JOHN E. PECK, EDS., *The Changing Face of Fiscal Federalism* (M. E. Sharpe, 1990).

Also, the U.S. Bureau of the Census regularly publishes reports on state and municipal finances.

34

THE DEMOCRATIC FAITH

AMERICA'S FOUNDING GENERATION FOUGHT AN EIGHT-YEAR REVOLUTION TO SECURE THEIR RIGHTS AND LIBERTY. THEN THEY FACED THE CHALLENGE OF CREATING A government, first at the Constitutional Convention in 1787 and later in the first Congress, writing a Constitution, and drafting a Bill of Rights that would protect the rights to life, liberty, and self-government for themselves and for those who would come later. But they knew, as we also know, that passive allegiance to ideals and rights is never enough. Every generation must see itself as having a duty to nurture these ideals by actively renewing the community and nation of which it is a part.

The framers knew about the rise and decline of ancient Athens. They were familiar with Pericles and his famed funeral oration in which he said that the person who takes no part in public affairs is a useless person, a good-for-nothing. The city's business, as Pericles and many Athenians saw it, was everyone's business. Athens had flourished as an example of what a civilized city might be, but it foundered when greed, self-centeredness, and smugness set in. As time went on, the Athenians wanted security more than they wanted liberty; they wanted comfort more than they wanted freedom. In the end they lost it all—security, comfort, and freedom. "Responsibility was the price every man must pay for freedom. It was to be had on no other terms."[1]

If we are to be responsible citizens of the United States in the truest meaning of the term, our dreams must transcend personal ambition and the accumulation of material goods. Our country needs citizens who understand that our well-being is tied to the well-being of our neighbors, community, and country.

The theme in this last chapter is simple: elected leadership and constitutional structures and protections are important, yet an active, committed citizenry is equally important. Freedom and obligation go together. Liberty and duty go together. The answer to a nation's problems lies not in producing a perfect constitution or a few larger-than-life leaders. The answer lies in encouraging a nation of citizen-leaders who will, above and beyond their professional and private ambitions, care about the common concerns of the Republic and strive to make democracy work.

I dream of a republic that is independent, free, and democratic; a republic with economic prosperity yet social justice; a humane republic that serves the individual and therefore hopes that the individual will serve it in turn; a republic of well-rounded people, because without such people, it is impossible to solve any of our problems.

Vaclav Havel
New Year's Day Speech, January 1, 1990

*We have awakened the people
We have seeded democracy
We will win
Our next generation will continue.
It doesn't matter
If we don't succeed.*

Poem by an anonymous
democracy demonstrator in China's
Tiananmen Square, Spring 1989

During my lifetime I have dedicated myself to this struggle of the African people. I have fought against white domination, and I have fought against black domination. I have cherished the ideal of a democratic and free society in which all persons live together in harmony and with equal opportunities. It is an ideal I hope to live for and to achieve. But if needs be, it is an ideal for which I am prepared to die.

Nelson Mandela
Statement at the Rivonia Trial, 1964

This participant in a Black Voter Awareness Rally urges citizens to accept responsibility for perpetuating democracy.

THE CASE FOR GOVERNMENT BY THE PEOPLE

More people today live under conditions of political freedom rather than under authoritarian governments than at any previous time. Throughout history, most people lived in societies in which a small group at the top have imposed their will on the others. Authoritarian governments justify their actions by saying people are too weak to govern themselves; they need to be ruled. Thus, neither in Castro's Cuba nor in the military regime of North Korea, neither in the People's Republic of China nor in Saudi Arabia, do ordinary people have a voice in the type of decisions we Americans routinely make: Who should be admitted into college, or serve in the military? Who should be allowed to immigrate into the country? How much money should be spent for schools, economic development initiatives, health care, or environmental protection?

The essence of our Constitution is that it both grants power to and withholds power from government. Fearing national weakness and popular disorder, the framers wanted to limit the powers of the national government to what it might need to carry out its responsibilities, such as maintaining national defense. They also wanted to limit state governments in order to keep them from interfering with civil rights and property rights. Valuing above all the principle of individual liberty, the framers wanted to protect the people from too much government. They wanted a limited government—yet one that would work. The solution was to divide up the power of the national government, to make it ultimately responsive, if only indirectly, to the voters.

Most Americans want a government that is efficient and effective but also promotes social justice. We want to maintain our commitment to liberty and freedom. We want a government that acts for the majority yet also protects minorities. We want to safeguard our nation and our streets in a world full of change and violence. We want to protect the rights of the poor, the elderly, and minorities. Do we expect too much from our elected officials and public servants? Of course we do!

Constitutional democracy is a system of checks and balances. It balances values against competing values. Government must balance individual liberties against the collective security and needs of society. The question always is: Which rights of which people are to be protected by what means and at what price to individuals and to the whole society?

PARTICIPATION AND REPRESENTATION

No political problem is more complicated than working out the proper relationship between voters and elected officials. It is not just a simple issue of being sure that elected officials do what the voters want them to do. Every individual has a host of conflicting desires, fears, hopes, and expectations, and no government can represent them all. But even if millions of voters could be represented in their many interests, the question of how they would be represented would remain. Through direct representation, such as a traditional New England town meeting or ballot initiatives and referenda? Through economic or professional associations, such as labor unions or political action committees? Through a coalition of minority groups? All these and other alternatives can be defended as proper forms of representation in a constitutional democracy. Yet all also have limitations.

Some propose to bypass this thorny problem of representation by vastly increasing the role of direct popular participation in decision making. What many people regard as the most perfect form of democracy would exist when every person

has a full and equal opportunity to participate in all decisions and in all processes of influence, persuasion, and discussion that bear on those decisions. Direct participation in decision making, its advocates contend, will serve two major purposes. It will enhance the dignity, self-respect, and understanding of individuals by giving them responsibility for the decisions that shape their lives. And it will act as a safeguard against undemocratic and antidemocratic forms of government and prevent the replacement of democracy by dictatorship or tyranny. This idea rests on a theory of self-protection that says interests can be represented, furthered, and defended best by those they concern directly.

New technologies present ways in which governments can appeal directly to voters, and voters can speak directly to public officials. We now have voting by mail in Oregon and other places, and some people advocate voting on the Internet. Digital town halls may be next. Some applaud these developments; others are appalled by them.

The average American citizen has access to an abundance of information about public affairs: the number of cable television news programs has increased enormously in recent years; talk radio regularly airs diverse views on every political controversy; newspapers and magazines do a fine job of covering national politics, although they do less well at covering state and local public affairs. In half the states, people can vote on many citizen-initiated ballot issues. We also have polls nearly every day on nearly every subject, fascinating technologies that encourage interactive video conferencing, and groups who advocate electronic town meetings.

But we still need institutions such as elected legislatures, which can take the time to digest complicated information and conduct impartial hearings to hear competing points of view. The average citizen rarely has the time or experience to digest all the available information. We are only now beginning to learn how to harness our new electronic technologies to infuse more deliberation into our leadership and public policy making programs.

Experience with many forms of participatory democracy also suggests its limitations as a form of decision making. In an age of rapidly growing population, increasingly complex economic and social systems, and enormously wide-ranging decision-making units of government, direct participation can work only in small communities or at the neighborhood level. As a practical matter, people simply cannot put in endless hours taking part in every decision that affects their lives.

Participatory democracy can still play an important role in smaller units—in neighborhood associations, local party committees, and the like. And perhaps the idea of participation could be greatly extended, for example, to greater influence of workers in the running of factories and corporations. But we must distinguish between democracy as direct participation and as citizen participation. One course of action would be to enlarge the role of participation in representation—that is, to broaden the power of all people to take part in choosing their representatives in larger units of government. This brings us back to the hard questions of indirect representation.

If we must have representatives, who shall represent whom? By electing representatives in a multitude of districts, it is possible to build into representative institutions—the U.S. Congress, for example—most minority interests and attitudes. In the United States we generally have election processes in which only the candidate with the most votes wins. But there are other ways. For example, one way widely used in European nations is proportional representation—a system in which each party running receives the proportion of legislative seats corresponding to its proportion of votes.

Representation can also be influenced by whether there is only one party, or two, or several. Ours is a generally strong two-party system that knits local constituencies into coalitions that can elect and sustain national majorities.

To Protect the Dissenter

"... we have devised a variety of ways to protect the dissenter. Our civil liberties are a part of that system, and so are Robert's Rules of Order, and grievance procedures, and the commonly held view that we should hear both sides of an argument. In short, we have a tradition, a set of attitudes and specific social arrangements designed to ensure that points of view at odds with prevailing doctrine will not be rejected out of hand.

But why be so considerate of dissent and criticism? To answer this question is to state one of the strongest tenets of our political philosophy. We do not expect organizations or societies to be above criticism, nor do we trust the men who run them to be adequately self-critical. We believe that even those aspects of society that are healthy today may deteriorate tomorrow. We believe that power wielded justly today may be wielded corruptly tomorrow. We know that from the ranks of the critics come cranks and troublemakers, but from the same ranks come the saviors and innovators. And since the spirit that welcomes nonconformity is a fragile thing, we have not depended on that spirit alone. We have devised explicit legal and constitutional arrangements to protect the dissenter."

SOURCE: John W. Gardner, *Self-Renewal*, rev. ed. (Norton, 1981), pp. 71–72.

Proud to Be a Politician

Must a politician gain public office by denouncing the profession? From the tone of many recent congressional races, it would appear that this is a growing trend. Journalist Charles McDowell of the *Richmond Times-Dispatch* noted this trend on the PBS series *The Lawmakers* and suggested that such a tactic "demeans an honorable and essential profession—that of the politician." McDowell proposed that every member of Congress be required to take the following oath:

> I affirm that I am a politician. That I am willing to associate with other known politicians. That I have no moral reservations about committing acts of politics. Under the Constitution, I insist that politicians have as much right to indulge in politics as preachers, single-issue zealots, generals, bird-watchers, labor leaders, big business lobbyists, and all other truth-givers.
>
> I confess that, as a politician, I participate in negotiation, compromise, and tradeoffs in order to achieve something that seems reasonable to a majority. And, although I try to be guided by principle, I confess that I often find people of principle on the other side, too.
>
> So help me God.

Which is better: elected officials who represent coalitions of minorities, or officials who represent a relatively clear-cut majority and have little or no obligation to the minority? The answer depends on what you expect from government. A system that represents coalitions of minorities usually reflects the trading, competition, and compromising that must take place in order to reach agreement among the various groups. Such a government has been called *broker rule;* elected officials act essentially as a go-between, as a mediator among organized groups that have definite policy goals. Under broker rule, leaders cannot get too far ahead of the groups; they must tack back and forth, shifting in response to changing group pressures. Instead of acting for a united popular majority with a fairly definite program, either liberal or conservative, the government tries to satisfy all major interests by giving them a voice in decisions and sometimes a veto over actions. In the pushing and hauling of political groups, the government is continually involved in delicate balancing acts.

Some critics point out that fair representation has not been achieved in the American system. They point to the extent of nonvoting and other forms of nonparticipation in politics; the fact that low-income persons are less well organized than upper-income persons; the bias of strong organized groups toward the status quo; the domination of television and the press by a few corporations; and the virtual monopoly of party politics by the two major parties, which do not always offer the voters meaningful alternatives. Critics are concerned that our system of government builds in procedures designed to curtail legislative majorities—for example, the filibuster in the Senate or the power of the Supreme Court to declare laws unconstitutional. Critics also point to the many mistakes made by voters and election machines in the 2000 Florida elections as yet another weakness of our democratic system.

Such charges may be exaggerated, yet they cannot be denied. Those who believe governments should be more directly responsive to political majorities can point to steady improvement in recent years. There have been changes in election laws to simplify voter registration, expand and improve voting procedures, and enforce one-person, one-vote standards. Pressure has been building to limit the ability of rich people and well-financed interests to influence elections. Pressure has also been building to streamline voting systems and pass campaign reform measures. And some progress has been made in Congress to strengthen majority rule.

By this point, you undoubtedly appreciate that democracy has to mean much more than popular government and unchecked majority rule. A democracy needs competing politicians with differing views about the public interest. A vital democracy, living and growing, places its faith in the voters, faith that they will elect not just people who will mirror their views but leaders who will exercise their best judgment—"faith that the people will not condemn those whose devotion to principle leads them to unpopular courses, but will reward courage, respect honor, and ultimately recognize right."[2]

The Role of the Politician

Americans today have decidedly mixed views about elected officials. They realize that at their best politicians are skillful at compromising, mediating, negotiating, brokering—and that governing often requires these qualities. But they also suspect politicians of being ambitious, conniving, unprincipled, opportunistic, and corrupt. Compared to people in other professions, Americans hold politicians in low esteem.

Still, we often find that individual officeholders are bright, hardworking, and friendly (even though we may suspect they are simply trying to get our vote). And our liking sometimes turns into reverence after these same politicians die. George

Washington, Abraham Lincoln, Dwight D. Eisenhower, and John F. Kennedy are acclaimed today. Harry Truman liked to joke that a statesman is merely a politician who has been dead for about ten years.

Of course, we must put the problem in perspective. In all democracies the public probably expects too much from politicians. Further, people naturally dislike those who wield power. Public officeholders, after all, tax us, regulate us, and conscript us. We dislike political compromisers and ambitious opportunists—even though we may need such people to get things done.

Politics is a necessity. Politics is a vital and—at critical times—a noble leadership activity. Politicians are essential for running the American Republic, whose fragmented powers require them to mediate among factions, build coalitions, and compromise among and within branches of government to produce policy and action.

Leadership for a Constitutional Democracy

Even though one of the most universal cravings of our time is a hunger for creative and compelling leadership, defining leadership is a challenge in itself. Leadership can be understood only in the context of both leaders and followers. A leader without followers is a contradiction in terms. Leadership is also situational and contextual; a person is often effective in only one kind of situation. Leadership is not necessarily transferable. James Madison, for example, was a brilliant political and constitutional theorist; he was also a superb politician. Still, he was not a brilliant president. The leadership required to lead a marine platoon up a hill in battle is different from the leadership needed to change racist or sexist attitudes in city governments. The leadership required of a campaign manager differs from that required of a candidate. Leaders of thought are not always effective as leaders of action.

Although leaders are often skilled managers, they need more than just managerial skills. Managers are concerned with doing things the right way; leaders are concerned with doing the right thing. Managers are concerned with efficiency and process, especially routines and standard operating procedures. Leaders, on the other hand, concentrate on goals, purposes, and a vision of the future.

Some leaders have indispensable qualities of contagious self-confidence, unwarranted optimism, and dogged idealism that attract and mobilize others to undertake tasks they never dreamed they could accomplish. In short, they empower others and enable many of their followers to become leaders in their own right. Most of the significant breakthroughs in our nation, as well as in our communities, have been made or shaped by people who, while seeing all the complexities and obstacles ahead of them, believed in themselves and in their purposes so much that they refused to be overwhelmed and paralyzed by self-doubts. They were willing to gamble, to take risks, to look at things in a fresh way, and often to invent new rules.[3]

Leaders recognize the fundamental—unexpressed as well as expressed—wants and needs of potential followers. By bringing followers to a fuller consciousness of their needs, they help convert their hopes and aspirations into practical demands on other leaders, especially leaders in government. A leader in a democracy consults and listens while educating followers and attempting to renew the goals of an organization.

RECONCILING DEMOCRACY AND LEADERSHIP

Americans are fond of saying, "It is all politics, you know." This greatly oversimplified insight is offered as profound. More important, it is intended as a negative judgment, as if things somehow would be improved if we did not have politics and politicians.

But politics is the lifeblood of democracy, and without politics there is no freedom. To conclude that politicians are interested in winning elections is about as profound as to conclude that businesspeople are interested in profits. Of course they are! We do not expect our economy to operate because the shoe store owner is motivated

only by a desire to see that people have dry, warm feet. Rather, we harness the store owner's desire to make a living as a way to see to it that the largest number of people get the shoes they want at the lowest possible price. So also we harness the elected official's desire for reelection as the way to ensure that elected officials do what most of the voters want them to do. It is the politician's need to serve and please the voters that is the indispensable link in making democracy work.[4]

One of our major political challenges is to reconcile democracy and leadership. In the past we often have held a view of leaders as all powerful. Yet a nation of subservient followers can never be a democratic one. A democratic nation requires educated, skeptical, caring, engaged, and conscientious citizen-leaders. It also requires citizen leaders who will recognize when change is needed and have the courage to bring about necessary reforms and progress.[5]

Such democratic citizen-leaders appreciate that power wielded justly today may be wielded corruptly tomorrow. Democratic citizen-leaders are moved to protest when they know a policy is wrong or when the rights of other citizens are diminished. Such leaders appreciate that criticism of official error is not unpatriotic criticism of our country. Citizen-leaders recognize as well that democracy rests solidly upon a realistic view of human nature. Our capacity for justice, as theologian and philosopher Reinhold Niebuhr observed, makes democracy possible. But our "inclination to injustice makes democracy necessary."[6]

Democratic politics is the forum for excellence and responsibility, where, by acting together, citizens become free. In this sense, politics is not a necessary evil; it is a realistic good. It is the preoccupation of free people, and its existence is a test of freedom.[7]

Leadership thought of as an engagement among equals can empower people and enlarge their opinions, choices, and freedoms. The answer for our Republic lies not in producing a handful of great, charismatic, Mount Rushmore leaders, but in educating a citizenry who can boast that we are no longer in need of superheroes because we have become a nation of citizens who believe that each of us can make a difference, and that all of us should regularly try.[8]

Leaders will always be needed. However, our system of government is, in many ways, designed to prevent strong and decisive action, lest too much political power be placed in the hands of too few people. Thus, while we have emphasized the role of leadership in constitutional democracies in these last few pages, the potential for abuse is checked not only by an involved citizenry but also by the very structure of our constitutional system—separation of powers, checks and balances, federalism, bicameral legislatures, and the rule of law.

The ultimate test of a democratic system is the legal existence of an officially recognized opposition. A cardinal characteristic of a constitutional democracy is that it not only recognizes the need for the free organization of opposing views but positively encourages this organization. Freedom for political expression and dissent is basic—even freedom for nonsense to be spoken so that good sense not yet recognized gets a chance to be heard.[9]

THE DEMOCRATIC FAITH

Crucial to the democratic faith is the belief that a constitutional democracy cherishes the free play of ideas. Only where the safety valve of public discussion is available and where almost any policy is subject to perpetual questioning and challenge can there be the assurance that both minority and majority rights will be served. To be afraid of public debate is to be afraid of self-government. "Rulers always have and always will find it dangerous to their security to permit people to think, believe, talk, write, assemble, and particularly to criticize the government as they

please," said former Supreme Court Justice William J. Brennan, "but the language of the First Amendment indicates the framers weighed the risk involved in such freedoms and deliberately chose to stake this government's security and life upon preserving liberty to discuss public affairs intact and untouched by government."[10]

Your authors hold with Thomas Jefferson that there is nothing in the country so radically wrong that it cannot be cured by good newspapers, sound schoolmasters, and a critical reading of history. Inform and educate the citizenry, and a major hurdle is overcome. Jefferson had boundless faith in education. He believed people are rationally endowed by nature with an innate sense of justice; the average person has only to be informed to act wisely. In the long run, said Jefferson, only an educated and enlightened democracy can hope to endure.

Education is one of the best predictors of voting, participation in politics, and knowledge of public affairs. People may not be equally involved or equally willing to invest in democracy, but the attentive public—frequently those like yourself who have gone to college—has the willingness and self-confidence to see government and politics as necessary and important. An educated public has an understanding of how government works, how individuals can influence decision makers, and how to elect like-minded people.

Recent years have sadly witnessed an increase in racial and ethnic tensions in the United States. These tensions sometimes encourage separation and antagonism toward the larger and more dominant culture. When carried to the extreme, these tensions promote various ethnicity cults that exaggerate differences, intensify resentments, and drive deep wedges between nationalities and races. "The genius of America" writes historian Arthur M. Schlesinger, Jr., "lies in its capacity to forge a single nation from peoples of remarkably diverse racial, religious, and ethnic origins." Schlesinger acknowledges that our government and society have been more open to some than to others, "but it is more open to all today than it was yesterday and it is likely to be even more open tomorrow than today."[11]

We are a restless, dissatisfied, and searching people. We are often our own toughest critics. Our political system is far from perfect, but it still is an open system. People *can* fight city hall. People who disagree with policies in the nation can band together and be heard. We know only too well that the American Dream is never fully attained. It must always be pursued.

Millions of Americans visit the great monuments in our nation's capital each year. They are always impressed by the memorials to Washington, Jefferson, Lincoln, Franklin D. Roosevelt, and the Vietnam and Korean War veterans; they are awed by the beauty of the Capitol, the Supreme Court, and the White House. The strength of the nation, however, resides not in these official buildings and monuments but in the hearts, minds, and behavior of citizens. If we lose faith, stop caring, stop participating, and stop believing in the possibilities of self-government, the monuments "will be meaningless piles of stone, and the venture that began with the Declaration of Independence, the venture familiarly known as America will be as lifeless as the stone."[12]

The future of democracy in America will be shaped by those citizens who care about preserving and extending our political rights and freedoms. Our individual liberties will never be assured unless there are people willing to take responsibility for the progress of the whole community, people willing to exercise their determination and democratic faith. Carved in granite on one of the long corridors in a building on the Harvard University campus are these words of American poet Archibald MacLeish: "How shall freedom be defended? By arms when it is attacked by arms, by truth when it is attacked by lies, by democratic faith when it is attacked by authoritarian dogma. Always, in the final act, by determination and faith."

Why People Shy Away from Running for Office

- Invasion of privacy
- Less time to spend with families or favorite pastimes
- Less income than in many business or professional occupations
- Exposure to partisan and media criticism
- Involvement in many things most people would rather not do—like marching in countless parades, attending county fairs, and going to endless political dinners, banquets, and service club meetings
- Fear that one may have to compromise principles because of the complexity of our adversarial system
- Expense of campaigning
- Aversion to conflict, divisiveness, and ambition
- Concern that the constitutional structure and party system make it nearly impossible to exercise meaningful leadership

APPENDIX

THE DECLARATION OF INDEPENDENCE

Drafted mainly by Thomas Jefferson, this document adopted by the Second Continental Congress, and signed by John Hancock and fifty-five others, outlined the rights of man and the rights to rebellion and self-government. It declared the independence of the colonies from Great Britain, justified rebellion, and listed the grievances against George the III and his government. What is memorable about this famous document is not only that it declared the birth of a new nation, but that it set forth, with eloquence, our basic philosophy of liberty and representative democracy.

IN CONGRESS, JULY 4, 1776
(The unanimous Declaration of the Thirteen United States of America)

Preamble
When, in the course of human events, it becomes necessary for one people to dissolve the political bands which have connected them with another, and to assume, among the powers of the earth, the separate and equal station to which the laws of nature and of nature's God entitle them, a decent respect to the opinions of mankind requires that they should declare the causes which impel them to the separation.

New Principles of Government

We hold these truths to be self-evident; that all men are created equal, that they are endowed by their Creator with certain unalienable rights, that among these are life, liberty, and the pursuit of happiness.

That, to secure these rights, governments are instituted among men, deriving their just powers from the consent of the governed.

That whenever any form of government becomes destructive of these ends, it is the right of the people to alter or to abolish it, and to institute new government, laying its foundation on such principles, and organizing its powers in such form, as to them shall seem most likely to effect their safety and happiness. Prudence, indeed will dictate that governments long established should not be changed for light and transient causes; and accordingly all experience hath shown that mankind are more disposed to suffer while evils are sufferable, than to right themselves by abolishing the forms to which they are accustomed. But when a long train of abuses and usurpations, pursuing invariably the same object, evinces a design to reduce them under absolute despotism, it is their right, it is their duty, to throw off such government, and to provide new guards for their future security.

Reasons for Separation

Such has been the patient sufferance of these colonies; and such is now the necessity which constrains them to alter their former systems of government. The history of the present king of Great Britain is a history of repeated injuries and usurpations, all having in direct object the establishment of an absolute tyranny over these states. To prove this, let facts be submitted to a candid world.

He has refused his assent to laws, the most wholesome and necessary for the public good.

He has forbidden his governors to pass laws of immediate and pressing importance unless suspended in their operation till his assent should be obtained; and when so suspended, he has utterly neglected to attend to them.

He has refused to pass other laws for the accommodation of large districts of people, unless those people would relinquish the right of representation in the legislature, a right inestimable to them, and formidable to tyrants only.

He has called together legislative bodies at places unusual, uncomfortable, and distant for the depository of their public records, for the sole purpose of fatiguing them into compliance with his measures.

He has dissolved representative houses repeatedly, for opposing, with manly firmness, his invasions on the rights of people.

He has refused, for a long time after such dissolutions, to cause others to be elected; whereby the legislative powers incapable of annihilation, have returned to the people at large for their exercise; the state remaining, in the meantime, exposed to all the dangers of invasion from without and convulsions within.

He has endeavored to prevent the population of these states; for that purpose obstructing the laws of naturalization of foreigners, refusing to pass others to encourage their migration hither, and raising the conditions of new appropriations of lands.

He has obstructed the administration of justice, by refusing his assent to laws for establishing judiciary powers.

He has made judges dependent on his will alone for the tenure of their offices, and the amount and payment of their salaries.

He has erected a multitude of new offices, and sent hither swarms of officers to harass our people and eat out their substance.

He has kept among us, in times of peace, standing armies, without the consent of our legislature.

He has affected to render the military independent of, and superior to, the civil power.

He has combined with others to subject us to jurisdiction foreign to our constitution and unacknowledged by our laws, giving his assent to their acts of pretended legislation:

For quartering large bodies of armed troops among us;

For protecting them, by a mock trial, from punishment for any murders which they should commit on the inhabitants of these states;

For cutting off our trade with all parts of the world;

For imposing taxes on us without our consent;

For depriving us, in many cases, of the benefits of trial by jury;

For transporting us beyond seas, to be tried for pretended offenses;

For abolishing the free system of English laws in a neighboring province, establishing

therein an arbitrary government, and enlarging its boundaries, so as to render it at once an example and fit instrument for introducing the same absolute rule into these colonies;

For taking away our charters, abolishing our most valuable laws, and altering, fundamentally, the forms of our governments;

For suspending our own legislatures, and declaring themselves invented with power to legislate for us in all cases whatsoever.

He has abdicated government here, by declaring us out of his protection and waging war against us.

He has plundered our seas, ravaged our coasts, burned our towns, and destroyed the lives of our people.

He is at this time transporting large armies of foreign mercenaries to complete the works of death, desolation, and tyranny already begun with circumstances of cruelty and perfidy scarcely paralleled in the most barbarous ages and totally unworthy of the head of a civilized nation.

He has constrained our fellow-citizens, taken captive on the high seas, to bear arms against their country, to become the executioners of their friends and brethren, or to fall themselves by their hands.

He has excited domestic insurrections among us, and has endeavored to bring on the inhabitants of our frontiers the merciless Indian savages, whose known rule of warfare is an undistinguished destruction of all ages, sexes, and conditions.

In every stage of these oppressions we have petitioned for redress in the most humble terms; our repeated petitions have been answered only by repeated injury. A prince whose character is thus marked by every act which may define a tyrant is unfit to be the ruler of a free people.

Nor have we been wanting in attention to our British brethren. We have warned them, from time to time, of attempts by their legislature to extend an unwarrantable jurisdiction over us. We have reminded them of the circumstances of our emigration and settlement here. We have appealed to their native justice and magnanimity; and we have conjured them, by the ties of our common kindred, to disavow these usurpations, which would inevitably interrupt our connections and correspondence. They, too, have been deaf to the voice of justice and of consanguinity. We must, therefore, acquiesce in the necessity which denounces our separation, and hold them, as we hold the rest of mankind, enemies in war, in peace, friends.

We, therefore, the representatives of the United States of America, in General Congress assembled, appealing to the Supreme Judge of the world for the rectitude of our intentions, do, in the name and by authority of the good people of these colonies, solemnly publish and declare, that these united colonies are, and of right ought to be, free and independent states; that they are absolved from all allegiance to the British crown, and that all political connection between them and the state of Great Britain is, and ought to be, totally dissolved; and that, as free and independent states, they have full power to levy war, conclude peace, contract alliances, establish commerce, and do all other acts and things which independent states may of a right do. And, for the support of this declaration, with a firm reliance on the protection of Divine Providence, we mutually pledge to each other our lives, our fortunes, and our sacred honor.

THE FEDERALIST, NO. 10, JAMES MADISON

The Federalist, No. 10, written by James Madison soon after the Constitutional Convention, was prepared as one of several dozen newspaper essays aimed at persuading New Yorkers to ratify the proposed constitution. One of the most important basic documents in American political history, it outlines the need for and the general principles of a democratic republic. It also provides a political and economic analysis of the realities of interest group or faction politics.

To the People of the State of New York: Among the numerous advantages promised by a well-constructed union, none deserves to be more accurately developed than its tendency to break and control the violence of faction. The friend of popular governments, never finds himself so much alarmed for their character and fate, as when he contemplates their propensity of this dangerous vice. He will not fail, therefore, to set a due value on any plan which, without violating the principles to which he is attached, provides a proper cure for it. The instability, injustice, and confusion introduced into the public councils, have, in truth, been the mortal diseases under which popular governments have everywhere perished; as they continue to be the favorite and fruitful topics from which the adversaries to liberty derive their most specious declamations. The valuable improvements made by the American constitutions on the popular models, both ancient and modern, cannot certainly be too much admired; but it would be an unwarrantable partiality, to contend that they have as effectually obviated the danger on this side, as was wished and expected. Complaints are everywhere heard from our most considerate and virtuous citizens, equally the friends of public and private faith, and of public and personal liberty, that our governments are too unstable; that the public good is disregarded in the conflicts of rival parties; and that measures are too often decided, not according to the rules of justice, and the rights of the minor party, but by the superior force of an interested and overbearing majority. However anxiously we may wish that these complaints had no foundation, the evidence of known facts will not permit us to deny that they are in some degree true. It will be found, indeed, on a candid review of our situation, that some of the distresses under which we labor have been erroneously charged on the operations of our governments; but it will be found, at the same time, that other causes will not alone account for many of our heaviest misfortunes; and, particularly, for that prevailing and increasing distrust of public engagements, and alarm for private rights, which are echoed from one end of the continent to the other. These must be chiefly, if not wholly, effects of the unsteadiness and injustice, with which a factious spirit has tainted our public administrations.

By a faction, I understand a number of citizens, whether amounting to a majority of the whole, who are united and actuated by some common impulse of passion, or of interest, adverse to the rights of other citizens, or to the permanent and aggregate interests of the community.

There are two methods of curing the mischiefs of faction: the one, by removing its causes; the other, by controlling its effects.

There are again two methods of removing the causes of faction: the one, by destroying the liberty which is essential to its existence; the other, by giving to every citizen the same opinions, the same passions, and the same interests.

It could never be more truly said, than of the first remedy, that it was worse than the disease. Liberty is to faction what air is to fire, an aliment without which it instantly expires. But it could not be a less folly to abolish liberty, which is essential to political life, because it nourishes faction, than it would be to wish the annihilation of air, which is essential to animal life, because it imparts to fire its destructive agency.

The second expedient is as impracticable, as the first would be unwise. As long as the reason of man continues fallible, and he is at liberty to exercise it, different opinions will be formed. As long as the connection subsists between his reason and his self-love, his opinions and his passions will have a reciprocal influence on each other; and the former will be objects to which the latter will attach themselves. The diversity in the faculties of men, from which the rights of property originate, is not less an insuperable obstacle to an uniformity of interests. The protection of these faculties is the first object of government. From the protection of different and unequal faculties of acquiring property, the possession of different degrees and kinds of property immediately results; and from the influence of these on the sentiments and views of the respective proprietors, ensues a division of the society into different interests and parties.

The latent causes of faction are thus sown in the nature of man; and we see them everywhere brought into different degrees of activity, according to the different circumstances of civil society. A zeal for different opinions concerning religion, concerning government, and many other points, as well of speculation as of practice; an attachment to different leaders ambitiously contending for preeminence and power; or to persons of other descriptions whose fortunes have been interesting to the human passions, have, in turn, divided mankind into parties, inflamed them with mutual animosity, and rendered them much more disposed to vex and oppress each other, than to cooperate for their common good. So strong is this propensity of mankind, to fall into mutual animosities, that where no substantial occasion presents itself, the most frivolous and fanciful distinctions have been sufficient to kindle their unfriendly passions and excite their most violent conflicts. But the most common and durable source of factions, has been the various and unequal distribution of property. Those who hold, and those who are without property, have ever formed distinct interests in society. Those who are creditors, and those who are debtors, fall under a like discrimination. A landed interest, a manufacturing interest, a mercantile interest, a moneyed interest, with many lesser interests, grow up of necessity in civilized nations, and divide them into different classes, actuated by different sentiments and views. The regulation of these various and interfering interests forms the principal task of modern legislation, and involves the spirit of the party and faction in the necessary and ordinary operations of the government.

No man is allowed to be a judge in his own cause; because his interest will certainly bias his judgment, and, not improbably, corrupt his integrity. With equal, nay, with greater reason, a body of men are unfit to be both judges and parties at the same time; yet what are many of the most important acts of legislation, but so many judicial determinations, not indeed concerning the right of single persons, but concerning the rights of large bodies of citizens? And what are the different classes of legislators, but advocates and parties to the causes which they determine? Is a law proposed concerning private debts? It is a questions to which the creditors are parties on one side, and the debtors on the other. Justice ought to hold the balance between them. Yet the parties are, and must be, themselves the judges; and the most numerous party, or, in other words, the most powerful faction, must be expected to prevail. Shall domestic manufacturers be encouraged, and in what degree, by restrictions on foreign manufacturers? Are questions which would be differently decided by the landed and the manufacturing classes; and probably by neither with a sole regard to justice and the public good. The apportionment of taxes, on the various descriptions of property, is an act which seems to require the most exact impartiality; yet there is, perhaps, no legislative act, in which greater opportunity and temptation are given to a predominant party to trample on the rules of justice. Every shilling, with which they overburden the inferior number, is a shilling saved to their own pockets.

It is in vain to say, that enlightened statesmen will be able to adjust these clashing interests, and render them all subservient to the public good. Enlightened statesmen will not always be at the helm, nor, in many cases, can such an adjustment be made at all, without taking into view indirect and remote considerations, which will rarely prevail over the immediate interest which one party may find in disregarding the rights of another, or the good of the whole.

The inference to which we are brought is, that the causes of faction cannot be removed; and that relief is only to be sought in the means of controlling its effects.

If a faction consists of less than a majority, relief is supplied by the republican principle, which enables the majority to defeat its sinister views, by regular vote. It may clog the administration, it may convulse the society; but it will be unable to execute and mask its violence under the forms of the Constitution. When a majority is included in a faction, the form of popular government, on the other hand, enables it to sacrifice to its ruling passion or interest, both the public good and the rights of other citizens. To secure the public good, and private rights, against the danger of such a faction, and at the same time to preserve the spirit and the form of popular government, is then the great object to which our inquiries are directed. Let me add, that it is the great desideratum, by which alone this form of government can be rescued from the opprobrium under which it has so long laboured, and be recommended to the esteem and adoption of mankind.

By what means is this object attainable? Evidently by one of two only. Either the existence of the same passion or interest in a majority, at the same time, must be prevented; or the majority, having such coexistent passion or interest, must be rendered, by their number and local situation, unable to concert and carry into effect schemes of oppression. If the impulse and the opportunity be suffered to coincide, we well know that neither moral nor religious motives can be relied on as an adequate control. They are not found to be such on the injustice and violence of individuals, and lose their efficacy in proportion to the number combined together; that is, in proportion as their efficacy becomes needful.

From this view of the subject, it may be concluded, that a pure democracy, by which I mean a society consisting of a small number of citizens, who assemble and administer the government in person, can admit of no cure for the mischiefs of faction. A common passion or interest will, in almost every case, be felt by a majority

of the whole; a communication and concert, results from the form of government itself; and there is nothing to check the inducements to sacrifice the weaker party, or an obnoxious individual. Hence, it is, that such democracies have ever been spectacles of turbulence and contention; have ever been found incompatible with personal security, or the rights of property; and have in general been as short in their lives, as they have been violent in their deaths. Theoretic politicians, who have patronized this species of government, have erroneously supposed, that by reducing mankind to a perfect equality in their political rights, they would, at the same time be perfectly equalized and assimilated in their possessions, their opinions, and their passions.

A republic, by which I mean a government in which the scheme of representation takes place, opens a different prospect, and promises the cure for which we are seeking. Let us examine the points in which it varies from pure democracy, and we shall comprehend both the nature of the cure and the efficacy which it must derive from the union.

The two great points of difference, between a democracy and a republic, are, first, the delegation of the government, in the latter, to a small number of citizens, elected by the rest; secondly, the greater number of citizens, and greater sphere of country, over which the latter may be extended.

The effect of the first difference is, on the one hand, to refine and enlarge the public views, by passing them through the medium of a chosen body of citizens, whose wisdom may best discern the true interest of their country, and whose patriotism and love of justice, will be least likely to sacrifice it to temporary or partial considerations. Under such a regulation, it may well happen, that the public voice, pronounced by the representatives of the people, will be more consonant to the public good, than if pronounced by the people themselves, convened for the purpose. On the other hand the effect may be inverted. Men of factious tempers, of local prejudices, or of sinister designs, may by intrigue, by corruption, or by other means, first obtain the suffrages, and then betray the interest of the people. The question resulting is, whether small or extensive republics are most favourable to the election of proper guardians of the public weal; and it is clearly decided in favour of the latter by two obvious considerations.

In the first place, it is to be remarked that, however small the republic may be,

the representatives must be raised to a certain number, in order to guard against the cabals of a few; and that however large it may be, they must be limited to a certain number, in order to guard against the confusion of a multitude. Hence, the number of representatives in the two cases not being in proportion to that of the constituents, and being proportionally greatest in the small republic, it follows, that if the proportion of fit characters be not less in the large than in the small republic, the former will present a greater option, and consequently a greater probability of a fit choice.

In the next place, as each representative will be chosen by a greater number of citizens in the large than in the small republic, it will be more difficult for unworthy candidates to practice with success the vicious arts, by which elections are too often carried; and the suffrages of the people being more free, will be more likely to centre in men who possess the most attractive merit, and the most diffusive and established characters.

It must be confessed, that in this, as in most other cases, there is a mean, on both sides of which inconveniences will be found to lie. By enlarging too much the number of electors, you render the representatives too little acquainted with all their local circumstances and lesser interests; as by reducing it too much, you render him unduly attached to these, and too little fit to comprehend and pursue great and national objects. The federal constitution forms a happy combination in this respect; the great and aggregate interests being referred to the national, the local and particular to the state legislatures.

The other point of difference is, the greater number of citizens, and extent of territory, which may be brought within the compass of republican, than of democratic government; and it is this circumstance principally which renders factious combinations less to be dreaded in the former, than in the latter. The smaller the society, the fewer probably will be the distinct parties and interests composing it; the fewer the distinct parties and interests, the more frequently will a majority be found of the same party; and the smaller the number of individuals composing a majority, and the smaller the compass within which they are placed, the more easily will they concert and execute their plans of oppression. Extend the sphere, and you take in a greater variety of parties and interests; you make it less probable that a majority of the whole will

have a common motive to invade the rights of other citizens; or if such a common motive exists, it will be more difficult for all who feel it to discover their own strength, and to act in unison with each other. Besides other impediments, it may be remarked, that where there is a consciousness of unjust or dishonourable purposes, communication is always checked by distrust, in proportion to the number whose concurrence is necessary.

Hence, it clearly appears, that the same advantage, which a republic has over a democracy, in controlling the effects of faction, is enjoyed by a large over a small republic—is enjoyed by the union over the states composing it. Does this advantage consist in the substitution of representatives, whose enlightened views and virtuous sentiments render them superior to local prejudices, and to schemes of injustice? It will not be denied that the representation of the union will be most likely to possess these requisite endowments. Does it consist in the greater security afforded by a greater variety of parties, against the event of any one party being able to outnumber and oppress the rest? In an equal degree does the increased variety of parties, comprised within the union, increase the security? Does it, in fine, consist in the greater obstacles opposed to the concert and accomplishment of the secret wishes of an unjust and interested majority? Here, again, the extent of the union gives it the most palpable advantage.

The influence of factious leaders may kindle a flame within their particular states, but will be unable to spread a general conflagration through the other states; a religious sect may degenerate into a political faction in a part of the confederacy; but the variety of sects dispersed over the entire face of it, must secure the national councils against any danger from that source: a rage for paper money, for an abolition of debts, for an equal division of property, or for any other improper or wicked project, will be less apt to pervade the whole body of the union than a particular member of it; in the same proportion as such a malady is more likely to taint a particular county or district, than an entire state.

In the extent and proper structure of the union, therefore, we behold a republican remedy for the diseases most incident to republican government. And according to the degree of pleasure and pride we feel in being republicans, ought to be our zeal in cherishing the spirit, and supporting the character of federalists.

THE FEDERALIST, NO. 51, JAMES MADISON

The Federalist, No. 51, also written by Madison, is a classic statement in defense of separation of powers and republican processes. Its fourth paragraph is especially famous and is frequently quoted by students of government.

To what expedient, then, shall we finally resort, for maintaining in practice the necessary partition of power among the several departments as laid down in the Constitution? The only answer that can be given is that as all these exterior provisions are found to be inadequate the defect must be supplied, by so contriving the interior structure of the government as that its several constituent parts may, by their mutual relations, be the means of keeping each other in their proper places. Without presuming to undertake a full development of this important idea I will hazard a few general observations which may perhaps place it in a clearer light, and enable us to form a more correct judgment of the principles and structure of the government planned by the convention.

In order to lay a due foundation for that separate and distinct exercise of the different powers of government, which to a certain extent is admitted on all hands to be essential to the preservation of liberty, it is evident that each department should have a will of its own; and consequently should be so constituted that the members of each should have as little agency as possible in the appointment of the members of the others. Were this principle rigorously adhered to, it would require that all the appointments for the supreme executive, legislative, and judiciary magistracies should be drawn from the same fountain of authority, the people, through channels having no communication whatever with one another. Perhaps such a plan of constructing the several departments would be less difficult in practice than it may in contemplation appear. Some difficulties, however, and some additional expense would attend the execution of it. Some deviations, therefore, from the principle must be admitted. In the constitution of the judiciary department in particular, it might be inexpedient to insist rigorously on the principle: first, because peculiar qualifications being essential in the members, the primary consideration ought to be to select that mode of choice which best secures these qualifications; second, because the permanent tenure by which the appointments are held in that department must soon destroy all sense of dependence on the authority conferring them.

It is equally evident that the members of each department should be as little dependent as possible on those of the others for the emoluments annexed to their offices. Were the executive magistrate, or the judges, not independent of the legislature in this particular, their independence in every other would be merely nominal.

But the great security against a gradual concentration of the several powers in the same department consists in giving to those who administer each department the necessary constitutional means and personal motives to resist encroachments of the others. The provision for defense must in this, as in all other cases, be made commensurate to the danger of attack. Ambition must be made to counteract ambition. The interest of the man must be connected with the constitutional rights of the place. It may be a reflection on human nature that such devices should be necessary to control the abuses of government. But what is government itself but the greatest of all reflections on human nature? If men were angels, no government would be necessary. If angels were to govern men, neither external nor internal controls on government would be necessary. In framing a government which is to be administered by men over men, the great difficulty lies in this: you must first enable the government to control the governed; and in the next place oblige it to control itself. A dependence on the people is, no doubt, the primary control on the government; but experience has taught mankind the necessity of auxiliary precautions.

This policy of supplying, by opposite and rival interests, the defect of better motives, might be traced through the whole system of human affairs, private as well as public. We see it particularly displayed in all the subordinate distributions of power, where the constant aim is to divide and arrange the several offices in such a manner as that each may be a check on the other—that the private interest of every individual may be a sentinel over the public rights. These inventions of prudence cannot be less requisite in the distribution of the supreme powers of the State.

But it is not possible to give to each department an equal power of self-defense. In repub-lican government, the legislative authority necessarily predominates. The remedy for this inconveniency is to divide the legislature into different branches; and to render them, by modes of election and different principles of action, as little connected with each other as the nature of their common functions and their common dependence on the society will admit. It may even be necessary to guard against dangerous encroachments by still further precautions. As the weight of the legislative authority requires that it should be thus divided, the weakness of the executive may require, on the other hand, that it should be fortified. An absolute negative on the legislature appears, at first view, to be the natural defense with which the executive magistrate should be armed. But perhaps it would be neither altogether safe nor alone sufficient. On ordinary occasions it might not be exerted with the requisite firmness, and on extraordinary occasions it might be perfidiously abused. May not this defect of an absolute negative be supplied by some qualified connection between this weaker department and the weaker branch of the stronger department, by which the latter may be led to support the constitutional rights of the former, without being too much detached from the rights of its own department?

If the principles on which these observations are founded be just, as I persuade myself they are, and they be applied as a criterion to the several State constitutions, and to the federal Constitution, it will be found that if the latter does not perfectly correspond with them, the former are infinitely less able to bear such a test.

There are, moreover, two considerations particularly applicable to the federal system of America, which place that system in a very interesting point of view.

First. In a single republic, all the power surrendered by the people is submitted to the administration of a single government; and the usurpations are guarded against by a division of the government into distinct and separate departments. In the compound republic of America, the power surrendered by the people is first divided between two distinct governments, and then the portion allotted to each subdivided among distinct and separate departments. Hence a double security arises to the rights of the people. The different governments will control each

other, at the same time that each will be controlled by itself.

Second. It is of great importance in a republic not only to guard the society against the oppression of its rulers, but to guard one part of the society against the injustice of the other part. Different interests necessarily exist in different classes of citizens. If a majority be united by a common interest, the rights of the minority will be insecure. There are but two methods of providing against this evil: the one by creating a will in the community independent of the majority—that is, of the society itself; the other, by comprehending in the society so many separate descriptions of citizens as will render an unjust combination of a majority of the whole very improbable, if not impracticable. The first method prevails in all governments possessing an hereditary or self-appointed authority. This, at best, is but a precarious security; because a power independent of the society may as well espouse the unjust views of the major as the rightful interests of the minor party, and may possibly be turned against both parties. The second method will be exemplified in the federal republic of the United States. Whilst all authority in it will be derived from and dependent on the society, the society itself will be broken into so many parts, interests and classes of citizens, that the rights of individuals, or of the minority, will be in little danger from interested combinations of the majority. In a free government the security for civil rights must be the same as that for religious rights. It consists in the one case in the multiplicity of interests, and in the other in the multiplicity of sects. The degree of security in both cases will depend on the number of interests and sects; and this may be presumed to depend on the extent of country and number of people comprehended under the same government. This view of the subject must particularly recommend a proper federal system to all the sincere and considerate friends of republican government, since it shows that in exact proportion as the territory of the Union may be formed into more circumscribed Confederacies, or States, oppressive combinations of a majority will be facilitated; the best security, under the republican forms, for the rights of every class of citizen, will be diminished; and consequently the stability and independence of some member of the government, the only other security, must be proportionally increased. Justice is the end of government. It is the end of civil society. It ever has been and ever will be pursued until it be obtained, or until liberty be lost in the pursuit. In a society under the forms of which the stronger faction can readily unite and oppress the weaker, anarchy may as truly be said to reign as in a state of nature, where the weaker individual is not secured against the violence of the stronger; and as, in the latter state, even the stronger individuals are prompted, by the uncertainty of their condition, to submit to a government which may protect the weak as well as themselves; so, in the former state, will the more powerful factions or parties be gradually induced, by a like motive, to wish for a government which will protect all parties, the weaker as well as the more powerful. It can be little doubted that if the State of Rhode Island was separated from the Confederacy and left to itself, the insecurity of rights under the popular form of government within such narrow limits would be displayed by such reiterated oppressions of factious majorities that some power altogether independent of the people would soon be called for by the voice of the very factions whose misrule had proved the necessity to it. In the extended republic of the United States, and among the great variety of interests, parties, and sects which it embraces, a coalition of a majority of the whole society could seldom take place on any other principles than those of justice and the general good; whilst there being thus less danger to a minor from the will of a major party, there must be less pretext, also, to provide for the security of the former, by introducing into the government a will not dependent on the latter, or, in other words, a will independent of the society itself. It is no less certain that it is important, notwithstanding the contrary opinions which have been entertained that the larger the society, provided it lie within a practicable sphere, the more duly capable it will be of self-government. And happily for the *republican cause*, the practicable sphere may be carried to a very great extent by a judicious modification and mixture of the *federal principle*.

THE FEDERALIST, NO. 78, ALEXANDER HAMILTON

The Federalist, No. 78, written by Alexander Hamilton, explains and praises the provisions for the judiciary in the newly drafted Constitution. Notice especially how Hamilton asserts that the courts have a key responsibility in determining the meaning of the Constitution as fundamental law. Hamilton is outlining here the doctrine of judicial review as we now know it.

We proceed now to an examination of the judiciary department of the proposed government.

In unfolding the defects of the existing Confederation, the utility and necessity of a federal judicature have been clearly pointed out. It is the less necessary to recapitulate the considerations there urged as the propriety of the institution in the abstract is not disputed; the only questions which have been raised being relative to the manner of constituting it, and to its extent. To these points, therefore, our observations shall be confined.

The manner of constituting it seems to embrace these several objects: 1st. The mode of appointing the judges. 2nd. The tenure by which they are to hold their places. 3rd. The partition of the judiciary authority between different courts and their relations to each other.

First. As to the mode of appointing the judges: this is the same with that of appointing the officers of the Union in general and has been so fully discussed in the two last numbers that nothing can be said here which would not be useless repetition.

Second. As to the tenure by which the judges are to hold their places: this chiefly concerns their duration in office, the provisions for their support, the precautions for their responsibility.

According to the plan of the convention, all judges who may be appointed by the United States are to hold their offices *during good behavior*, which is conformable to the most approved of the State constitutions, and among the rest, to that of this State. Its propriety having been drawn into question by the adversaries of that plan is no light

symptom of the rage for objection which disorders their imaginations and judgments. The standard of good behavior for the continuance in office of the judicial magistracy is certainly one of the most valuable of the modern improvements in the practice of government. In a monarchy it is an excellent barrier to the despotism of the prince; in a republic it is a no less excellent barrier to the encroachments and oppressions of the representative body. And it is the best expedient which can be devised in any government to secure a steady, upright, and impartial administration of the laws.

Whoever attentively considers the different departments of power must perceive that, in a government in which they are separated from each other, the judiciary, from the nature of its functions, will always be the least dangerous to the political rights of the Constitution; because it will be least in a capacity to annoy or injure them. The executive not only dispenses the honors but holds the sword of the community. The legislature not only commands the purse but prescribes the rules by which the duties and rights of every citizen are to be regulated. The judiciary, on the contrary, has no influence over either the sword or the purse; no direction either of the strength or of the wealth of the society, and can take no active resolution whatever. It may truly be said to have neither FORCE NOR WILL but merely judgment; and must ultimately depend upon the aid of the executive arm even for the efficacy of its judgments.

This simple view of the matter suggests several important consequences. It proves incontestably that the judiciary is beyond comparison the weakest of the three departments of power; that it can never attack with success either of the other two; and that all possible care is requisite to enable it to defend itself against their attacks. It equally proves that though individual oppression may now and then proceed from the courts of justice, the general liberty of the people can never be endangered from that quarter; I mean so long as the judiciary remains truly distinct from both the legislature and the executive. For I agree that "there is no liberty if the power of judging be not separated from the legislative and executive powers." And it proves, in the last place, that as liberty can have nothing to fear from the judiciary alone, but would have everything to fear from its union with either of the other departments, that as all the effects of such a union must ensue from a dependence of the former on the latter, notwithstanding a nominal and apparent separation; that as, from the natural feebleness of the judiciary, it is in continual jeopardy of being overpowered, awed, or influenced by its co-ordinate branches; and that as nothing can contribute so much to its firmness and independence as permanency in office, this quality may therefore be justly regarded as an indispensable ingredient in its constitution, and, in a great measure, as the citadel for the public justice and the public security.

The complete independence of the courts of justice is peculiarly essential in a limited Constitution. By a limited Constitution, I understand one which contains certain specified exceptions to the legislative authority; such, for instance, as that it shall pass no bills of attainder, no *ex post facto laws*, and the like. Limitations of this kind can be preserved in practice no other way than through the medium of courts of justice, whose duty it must be to declare all acts contrary to the manifest tenor of the Constitution void. Without this, all the reservations of particular rights or privileges would amount to nothing.

Some perplexity respecting the rights of the courts to pronounce legislative acts void, because contrary to the Constitution, has arisen from an imagination that the doctrine would imply a superiority to the judiciary to the legislative power. It is urged that the authority which can declare the acts of another void must necessarily be superior to the one whose acts may be declared void. As this doctrine is of great importance in all the American constitutions, a brief discussion of the grounds on which it rests cannot be unacceptable.

There is no position which depends on clearer principles than that every act of a delegated authority, contrary to the tenor of the commission under which it is exercised, is void. No legislative act, therefore, contrary to the Constitution, can be valid. To deny this would be to affirm that the deputy is greater than his principal; that the servant is above his master; that the representatives of the people are superior to the people themselves; that men acting by virtue of powers do not authorize, but what they forbid.

If it be said that the legislative body are themselves the constitutional judges of their own powers and that the construction they put upon them is conclusive upon the other departments it may be answered that this cannot be the natural presumption where it is not to be collected from any particular provisions in the Constitution. It is not otherwise to be supposed that the Constitution could intend to enable the representatives of the people to substitute their *will* to that of their constituents. It is far more rational to suppose that the courts were designed to be an intermediate body between the people and the legislature in order, among other things, to keep the latter within the limits assigned to their authority. The interpretation of the laws is the proper and peculiar province of the courts. A constitution is, in fact, and must be regarded by the judges as, a fundamental law. It therefore belongs to them to ascertain its meaning as well as the meaning of any particular act proceeding from the legislative body. If there should happen to be an irreconcilable variance between the two, that which has the superior obligation and validity ought, of course, to be preferred; or, in other words, the Constitution ought to be preferred to the statute, the intention of the people to the intention of their agents.

Nor does this conclusion by any means suppose a superiority of the judicial to the legislative power. It only supposes that the power of the people is superior to both, and that where the will of the legislature, declared in its statutes, stands in opposition to that of the people, declared in the Constitution, the judges ought to be governed by the latter rather than the former. They ought to regulate their decisions by the fundamental laws rather than by those which are not fundamental.

This exercise of judicial discretion in determining between two contradictory laws is exemplified in a familiar instance. It not uncommonly happens that there are two statutes existing at one time, clashing in whole or in part with each other and neither of them containing any repealing clause or expression. In such a case, it is the province of the courts to liquidate and fix their meaning and operation. So far as they can, by any fair construction, be reconciled to each other, reason and law conspire to dictate that this should be done; where this is impracticable, it becomes a matter of necessity to give effect to one in exclusion of the other. The rule which has obtained in the courts for determining their relative validity is that the last in order of time shall be preferred to the first. But this is a mere rule of construction, not derived from any positive law but from the nature and reason of the thing. It is a rule not enjoined upon the courts by legislative provision but adopted by themselves, as consonant to truth and propriety, for the direction of their conduct as interpreters of the law. They thought it reasonable that between the interfering acts of an equal authority that which was the last indication of its will should have the preference.

But in regard to the interfering acts of a superior and subordinate authority of an original and derivative power, the nature and reason of the thing indicates the converse of that rule as proper to be followed. They teach us that the prior act of a superior

ought to be preferred to the subsequent act of an inferior and subordinate authority; and that accordingly, whenever a particular statute contravenes the Constitution, it will be the duty of the judicial tribunals to adhere to the latter and disregard the former.

It can be of no weight to say that the courts, on the pretense of a repugnancy, may substitute their own pleasure to the constitutional intentions of the legislature. This might as well happen in the case of two contradictory statutes; or it might as well happen in every adjudication upon any single statute. The courts must declare the sense of the law; and if they should be disposed to exercise WILL instead of JUDGMENT, the consequence would equally be the substitution of their pleasure to that of the legislative body. The observation, if it prove anything, would prove that there ought to be no judges distinct from that body.

If, then, the courts of justice are to be considered as the bulwarks of a limited Constitution against legislative encroachments, this consideration will afford a strong argument for the permanent tenure of judicial offices, since nothing will contribute so much as this to that independent spirit in the judges which must be essential to the faithful performance of so arduous a duty.

This independence of the judges is equally requisite to guard the Constitution and the rights of individuals from the effects of those ill humors which the arts of designing men, or the influence of particular conjunctures, sometimes disseminate among the people themselves, and which, though they speedily give place to better information, and more deliberate reflection, have a tendency, in the meantime, to occasion dangerous innovations in the government, and serious oppressions of the minor party in the community. Though I trust the friends of the proposed Constitution will never concur with its enemies in questioning that fundamental principal of Republican government which admits the right of the people to alter or abolish the established Constitution whenever they find it inconsistent with their happiness; yet it is not to be inferred from this principle that the representatives of the people, whenever a momentary inclination happens to lay hold of a majority of their constituents incompatible with the provisions in the existing Constitution would, on that account, be justifiable in a violation of those provisions; or that the courts would be under a greater obligation to connive at infractions in this shape than when they had proceeded wholly from the cabals of the representative body. Until the people have, by some solemn and authoritative act, annulled or changed the established form, it is binding

upon themselves collectively, as well as individually; and no presumption, or even knowledge of their sentiments, can warrant their representatives in a departure from it prior to such an act. But it is easy to see that it would require an uncommon portion of fortitude in the judges to do their duty as faithful guardians of the Constitution, where legislative invasions of it had been instigated by the major voice of the community.

But it is not with a view to infractions of the Constitution only that the independence of the judges may be an essential safeguard against the effects of occasional ill humors in the society. These sometimes extend no farther than to the injury of the private rights of particular classes of citizens, by unjust and partial laws. Here also the firmness of the judicial magistracy is of vast importance in mitigating the severity and confining the operation of such laws. It not only serves to moderate the immediate mischiefs of those which may have been passed but it operates as a check upon the legislative body in passing them; who, perceiving that obstacles to the success of iniquitous intention are to be expected from the scruples of the courts, are in a manner compelled, by the very motives of the injustice they mediate, to qualify their attempts. This is a circumstance calculated to have more influence upon the character of our governments than but a few may be aware of. The benefits of the integrity and moderation of the judiciary have already been felt in more States than one; and though they may have displeased those whose sinister expectations they may have disappointed, they must have commanded the esteem and applause of all the virtuous and disinterested. Considerate men of every description ought to prize whatever will tend to beget or fortify that temper in the courts; as no man can be sure that he may not be tomorrow the victim of a spirit of injustice, by which he may be a gainer today. And every man must now feel that the inevitable tendency of such a spirit is to sap the foundations of public and private confidence and to introduce in its stead universal distrust and distress.

That inflexible and uniform adherence to the rights of the Constitution, and of individuals, which we perceive to be indispensable in the courts of justice, can certainly not be expected from judges who hold their offices by a temporary commission. Periodical appointments, however regulated, or by whomsoever made, would, in some way or other, be fatal to their necessary independence. If the power of making them was committed either to the executive or legislature there would be danger of an improper complaisance to the branch which possessed

it; if to both, there would be an unwillingness to hazard the displeasure of either; if to the people, or to persons chosen by them for the special purpose, there would be too great a disposition to consult popularity to justify a reliance that nothing would be consulted by the Constitution and the laws.

There is yet a further and a weighty reason for the permanency of the judicial offices which is deducible from the nature of the qualifications they require. It has been frequently remarked with great propriety that a voluminous code of laws is one of the inconveniences necessarily connected with the advantages of a free government. To avoid an arbitrary discretion in the courts, it is indispensable that they should be bound down by strict rules and precedents which serve to define and point out their duty in every particular case that comes before them; and it will readily be conceived from the variety of controversies which grow out of the folly and wickedness of mankind that the records of those precedents must unavoidably swell to a very considerable bulk and must demand long and laborious study to acquire a competent knowledge of them. Hence it is that there can be but few men in the society who will have sufficient skill in the laws to qualify them for the stations of judges. And making the proper deductions for the ordinary depravity of human nature, the number must be still smaller of those who unite the requisite integrity with the requisite knowledge. These considerations apprise us that the government can have no great option between fit characters; and that a temporary duration in office which would naturally discourage such characters from quitting a lucrative line of practice to accept a seat on the bench would have a tendency to throw the administration of justice into hands less able and less well qualified to conduct it with utility and dignity. In the present circumstances of this country and in those in which it is likely to be for a long time to come, the disadvantages on this score would be greater than they may at first sight appear; but it must be confessed that they are far inferior to those which present themselves under the other aspects of the subject.

Upon the whole, there can be no room to doubt that the convention acted wisely in copying from the models of those constitutions which have established *good behavior* as the tenure of their judicial offices in point of duration, and that so far from being blamable on this account, their plan would have been inexcusably defective if it had wanted this important feature of good government. The experience of Great Britain affords an illustrious comment on the excellence of the institution.

Presidential Election Results 1789–2000

Year	Candidates	Party	Popular Vote	Electoral Vote
1789	George Washington			69
	John Adams			34
	Others			35
1793	George Washington			132
	John Adams			77
	George Clinton			50
	Others			5
1796	John Adams	Federalist		71
	Thomas Jefferson	Democratic-Republican		68
	Thomas Pinckney	Federalist		59
	Aaron Burr	Democratic-Republican		30
	Others			48
1800	Thomas Jefferson	Democratic-Republican		73
	Aaron Burr	Democratic-Republican		73
	John Adams	Federalist		65
	Charles C. Pinckney	Federalist		64
1804	Thomas Jefferson	Democratic-Republican		162
	Charles C. Pinckney	Federalist		14
1808	James Madison	Democratic-Republican		122
	Charles C. Pinckney	Federalist		47
	George Clinton	Independent-Republican		6
1812	James Madison	Democratic-Republican		128
	DeWitt Clinton	Federalist		89
1816	James Monroe	Democratic-Republican		183
	Rufus King	Federalist		34
1820	James Monroe	Democratic-Republican		231
	John Quincy Adams	Independent-Republican		1
1824	John Quincy Adams	Democratic-Republican	108,740(30.5%)	84
	Andrew Jackson	Democratic-Republican	153,544(43.1%)	99
	Henry Clay	Democratic-Republican	47,136(13.2%)	37
	William H. Crawford	Democratic-Republican	46,618(13.1%)	41
1828	Andrew Jackson	Democratic	647,231(56.0%)	178
	John Quincy Adams	National Republican	509,097(44.0%)	83
1832	Andrew Jackson	Democratic	687,502(55.0%)	219
	Henry Clay	National Republican	530,189(42.4%)	49
	William Wirt	Anti-Masonic		7
	John Floyd	National Republican	33,108(2.6%)	11
1836	Martin Van Buren	Democratic	761,549(50.9%)	170
	William H. Harrison	Whig	549,567(36.7%)	73
	Hugh L. White	Whig	145,396(9.7%)	26
	Daniel Webster	Whig	41,287(2.7%)	14
1840	William H. Harrison	Whig	1,275,017(53.1%)	234
	Martin Van Buren	Democratic	1,128,702(46.9%)	60
1844	James K. Polk	Democratic	1,337,243(49.6%)	170
	Henry Clay	Whig	1,299,068(48.1%)	105
	James G. Birney	Liberty	63,300(2.3%)	
1848	Zachary Taylor	Whig	1,360,101(47.4%)	163
	Lewis Cass	Democratic	1,220,544(42.5%)	127
	Martin Van Buren	Free Soil	291,163(10.1%)	
1852	Franklin Pierce	Democratic	1,601,474(50.9%)	254
	Winfield Scott	Whig	1,386,578(44.1%)	42
1856	James Buchanan	Democratic	1,838,169(45.4%)	174
	John C. Fremont	Republican	1,335,264(33.0%)	114
	Millard Fillmore	American	874,534(21.6%)	8
1860	Abraham Lincoln	Republican	1,865,593(39.8%)	180
	Stephen A. Douglas	Democratic	1,381,713(29.5%)	12
	John C. Breckinridge	Democratic	848,356(18.1%)	72
	John Bell	Constitutional Union	592,906(12.6%)	79
1864	Abraham Lincoln	Republican	2,206,938(55.0%)	212
	George B. McClellan	Democratic	1,803,787(45.0%)	21
1868	Ulysses S. Grant	Republican	3,013,421(52.7%)	214
	Horatio Seymour	Democratic	2,706,829(47.3%)	80
1872	Ulysses S. Grant	Republican	3,596,745(55.6%)	286
	Horace Greeley	Democratic	2,843,446(43.9%)	66
1876	Rutherford B. Hayes	Republican	4,036,571(48.0%)	185
	Samuel J. Tilden	Democratic	4,284,020(51.0%)	184
1880	James A. Garfield	Republican	4,449,053(48.3%)	214
	Winfield S. Hancock	Democratic	4,442,035(48.2%)	155
	James B. Weaver	Greenback-Labor	308,578(3.4%)	
1884	Grover Cleveland	Democratic	4,874,986(48.5%)	219
	James G. Blaine	Republican	4,851,931(48.2%)	182
	Benjamin F. Butler	Greenback-Labor	175,370(1.8%)	
1888	Benjamin Harrison	Republican	5,444,337(47.8%)	233
	Grover Cleveland	Democratic	5,540,050(48.6%)	168

Presidential Election Results 1789–2000

Year	Candidates	Party	Popular Vote	Electoral Vote
1892	Grover Cleveland	Democratic	5,554,414(46.0%)	277
	Benjamin Harrison	Republican	5,190,802(43.0%)	145
	James B. Weaver	Peoples	1,027,329(8.5%)	22
1896	William McKinley	Republican	7,035,638(50.8%)	271
	William J. Bryan	Democratic; Populist	6,467,946(46.7%)	176
1900	William McKinley	Republican	7,219,530(51.7%)	292
	William J. Bryan	Democratic; Populist	6,356,734(45.5%)	155
1904	Theodore Roosevelt	Republican	7,628,834(56.4%)	336
	Alton B. Parker	Democrat	5,084,401(37.6%)	140
	Eugene V. Debs	Socialist	402,460(3.0%)	0
1908	William H. Taft	Republican	7,679,006(51.6%)	321
	William J. Bryan	Democratic	6,409,106(43.1%)	162
	Eugene V. Debs	Socialist	420,820(2.8%)	0
1912	Woodrow Wilson	Democratic	6,286,820(41.8%)	435
	Theodore Roosevelt	Progressive	4,126,020(27.4%)	88
	William H. Taft	Republican	3,483,922(23.2%)	8
	Eugene V. Debs	Socialist	897,011(6.0%)	0
1916	Woodrow Wilson	Democratic	9,129,606(49.3%)	277
	Charles E. Hughes	Republican	8,538,211(46.1%)	254
1920	Warren G. Harding	Republican	16,152,200(61.0%)	404
	James M. Cox	Democratic	9,147,353(34.6%)	127
	Eugene V. Debs	Socialist	919,799(3.5%)	0
1924	Calvin Coolidge	Republican	15,725,016(54.1%)	382
	John W. Davis	Democratic	8,385,586(28.8%)	136
	Robert M. La Follette	Progressive	4,822,856(16.6%)	13
1928	Herbert C. Hoover	Republican	21,392,190(58.2%)	444
	Alfred E. Smith	Democratic	15,016,443(40.8%)	87
1932	Franklin D. Roosevelt	Democratic	22,809,638(57.3%)	472
	Herbert C. Hoover	Republican	15,758,901(39.6%)	59
	Norman Thomas	Socialist	881,951(2.2%)	0
1936	Franklin D. Roosevelt	Democratic	27,751,612(60.7%)	523
	Alfred M. Landon	Republican	16,681,913(36.4%)	8
	William Lemke	Union	891,858(1.9%)	0
1940	Franklin D. Roosevelt	Democratic	27,243,466(54.7%)	449
	Wendell L. Wilkie	Republican	22,304,755(44.8%)	82
1944	Franklin D. Roosevelt	Democratic	25,602,505(52.8%)	432
	Thomas E. Dewey	Republican	22,006,278(44.5%)	99
1948	Harry S. Truman	Democratic	24,105,812(49.5%)	303
	Thomas E. Dewey	Republican	21,970,065(45.1%)	189
	J. Strom Thurmond	States' Rights	1,169,063(2.4%)	39
	Henry A. Wallace	Progressive	1,157,172(2.4%)	0
1952	Dwight D. Eisenhower	Republican	33,936,234(55.2%)	442
	Adlai E. Stevenson	Democratic	27,314,992(44.5%)	89
1956	Dwight D. Eisenhower	Republican	35,590,472(57.4%)	457
	Adlai E. Stevenson	Democratic	26,022,752(42.0%)	73
1960	John F. Kennedy	Democratic	34,227,096(49.9%)	303
	Richard M. Nixon	Republican	34,108,546(49.6%)	219
1964	Lyndon B Johnson	Democratic	43,126,233(61.1%)	486
	Barry Goldwater	Republican	27,174,989(38.5%)	52
1968	Richard M. Nixon	Republican	31,783,783(43.4%)	301
	Hubert H. Humphrey	Democratic	31,271,839(42.7%)	191
	George C. Wallace	American Independent	9,899,557(13.5%)	46
1972	Richard M. Nixon	Republican	46,632,189(61.3%)	520
	George McGovern	Democratic	28,422,015(37.3%)	17
1976	Jimmy Carter	Democratic	40,828,587(50.1%)	297
	Gerald R. Ford	Republican	39,147,613(48.0%)	240
1980	Ronald Reagan	Republican	42,941,145(51.0%)	489
	Jimmy Carter	Democratic	34,663,037(41.0%)	49
	John B. Anderson	Independent	5,551,551(6.6%)	0
1984	Ronald Reagan	Republican	53,428,357(59%)	525
	Walter F. Mondale	Democratic	36,930,923(41%)	13
1988	George Bush	Republican	48,881,011(53%)	426
	Michael Dukakis	Democratic	41,828,350(46%)	111
1992	Bill Clinton	Democratic	38,394,210(43%)	370
	George Bush	Republican	33,974,386(38%)	168
	H. Ross Perot	Independent	16,573,465(19%)	0
1996	Bill Clinton	Democratic	45,628,667(49%)	379
	Bob Dole	Republican	37,869,435(41%)	159
	H. Ross Perot	Reform	7,874,283(8%)	0
2000	George W. Bush	Republican	50,456,169(48%)	271
	Al Gore	Democrat	50,996,116(48%)	266
	Ralph Nader	Green	2,767,176(3%)	0

GLOSSARY

adversary system   A judicial system in which the court of law is a neutral arena where two parties argue their differences.

advisory opinion   An opinion unrelated to a particular case that gives a court's view about a constitutional or legal issue.

affirmative action   Remedial action designed to overcome the effects of past discrimination against minorities and women.

amendatory veto   The power of governors in a few states to return a bill to the legislature with suggested language changes, conditions, or amendments. Legislators then decide either to accept the governor's recommendations or to pass the bill in its original form over the veto.

American Dream   The widespread belief that individual initiative and hard work can bring economic success and that the United States is a land of opportunity.

amicus curiae **brief**   Literally, "friend of the court" brief, this document is filed, with permission of the court, by an individual or organization to present arguments in addition to those presented by the immediate parties to the case.

Annapolis Convention   A convention held in September 1786 to consider problems of trade and navigation, attended by five states and important because it issued the call to Congress and the states for what became the Constitutional Convention.

Antifederalists   Opponents of ratification of the Constitution and of a strong central government generally.

antitrust legislation   Federal laws (starting with the Sherman Act of 1890) that try to prevent monopolies from dominating an industry and restraining trade.

antitrust regulation   Federal laws and regulations that try to prevent one or a few businesses from dominating a particular market through monopoly or restraint of trade.

appellate jurisdiction   The authority of a court to review a decision of a lower court.

Articles of Confederation   The first constitution of the American states, drafted in 1777, ratified in 1781, and replaced by the present Constitution in 1789.

assigned council system   Arrangement whereby attorneys are provided for persons accused of crime who are unable to hire their own attorneys. The judge assigns a member of the bar to provide counsel to a particular defendant.

attentive public   Those who follow public affairs carefully.

Australian ballot   A secret ballot printed by the state.

bad tendency doctrine   Interpretation of the First Amendment that would permit legislatures to forbid speech that has a tendency to cause people to engage in illegal action.

bicameral legislature   A two-house legislature.

bicameralism   The principle of a two-house legislature.

bill of attainder   Legislative act inflicting punishment, including deprivation of property, with-out trial on named individuals or members of a specified group.

binding arbitration   A collective bargaining situation in which both parties agree to adhere to the decision of an arbitrator.

bipartisanship   A policy that emphasizes a united front and cooperation between the major political parties, especially on sensitive foreign policy issues.

blanket primary   A primary open to all voters, who may vote for candidates from any party for each office.

bundling   A tactic of political action committees whereby they collect contributions from like-minded individuals (each limited to $2,000) and present them to a candidate or political party as a "bundle," thus increasing their influence.

bureau   The largest subunit of a government department or agency.

bureaucracy   A professional corps of officials organized in a pyramidal hierarchy and functioning under impersonal, uniform rules and procedures.

bureaucrat   Career government employee.

cabinet   Loosely designated advisory body for the president, consisting of the heads of the executive departments, the vice-president, and a few others the president considers cabinet-level officials.

capitalism   An economic system characterized by private property, competitive markets, economic incentives, and limited government involvement in the production and pricing of goods and services.

caucus   Meeting of local party members to choose party officials and/or candidates for public office and to decide the platform.

caucus (legislative)   Meeting of the members of a party in a legislative chamber to select party leadership and discuss party policy. Called a conference by Republicans.

centralists   Those who favor national action over action at the state and local levels.

charter   A city "constitution" that outlines the structure of city government, defines the authority of the various officials, and provides for their selection.

charter school   A publicly funded alternative to standard public schools in some states, initiated when individuals or groups receive charters; charter schools must meet state standards.

checks and balances   Constitutional grant of powers that enables each of the three branches of government to stop some acts of the others and therefore ensure that no branch can dominate.

civil disobedience   Deliberate refusal to obey a law or requirement one believes is unjust in the hopes of calling forth public pressure to change it.

civil liberties   Rights of freedom of conscience, religion, and expression.

civil rights   Rights protecting against discrimination because of race, religion, gender, ethnic origin, or sexual orientation.

class action suit   Lawsuit brought by an individual or a group of people on behalf of all those similarly situated.

clear and present danger doctrine   Interpretation of the First Amendment that holds govern-ment cannot interfere with speech unless the speech presents a clear and present danger that it will lead to acts that are evil or illegal. To shout "Fire!" falsely in a crowded theater was Justice Oliver Wendell Holmes's famous example.

closed primary   A primary in which only persons registered in the party holding the primary may vote.

closed rule   A procedural rule in the House of Representatives that prohibits any amendments to bills or provides that only members of the committee reporting the bill may offer amendments.

closed shop   A company with a labor agreement whereby union membership is a condition of employment.

cloture   Procedure for terminating debate, especially filibusters, in the Senate.

coattail effect   The boost candidates of the same party as the president receive in a presidential election from the president's popularity.

collective bargaining   Method whereby representatives of the union and employer determine wages, hours, and other conditions of employment through direct negotiation.

commerce clause   The clause of the Constitution giving Congress the power to regulate all business activities that cross state lines or affect more than one state, and also prohibiting states from unduly burdening or discriminating against the business activities of other nations or states.

commercial speech   Advertisements and commercials for products and services that receive less First Amendment protection, primarily false and misleading ads.

community policing   Recent programs to move police from patrol cars into neighborhoods, where they walk the beat and work with churches and other community groups to reduce crime and improve relations with minorities.

comptroller general   Head of the General Accounting Office, appointed by the president with the approval of the Senate for a 15-year term.

concurrent powers   Powers the Constitution gives to both the national and state governments, such as the power to levy taxes.

concurrent resolution   A resolution passed in the same form by both houses of Congress that expresses the "sense" of Congress on some question. It is not sent to the president and does not have the force of law.

concurring opinion   An opinion that agrees with the majority in a Supreme Court ruling but differs on the reasoning.

confederation   A constitutional arrangement in which sovereign nations or states, by compact, create a central government but carefully limit its power and do not give it direct authority over individuals.

conference committee   Committee appointed by the presiding officers of each chamber to adjust differences on a particular bill passed by each but in different forms.

Congressional Budget Office (CBO)   An agency of Congress that analyzes presidential budget rec-

ommendations and estimates the costs of proposed legislation.

Connecticut Compromise Compromise agreement by states at the Constitutional Convention for a bicameral legislature with a lower house in which representation would be based on population, and upper house in which each state would have two senators.

conservatism A belief that limited government ensures order, competitive markets, and personal opportunity.

Constitutional Convention The convention in Philadelphia, May 25–September 17, 1787, that framed the Constitution of the United States.

constitutional democracy A government that enforces recognized limits on those who govern and allows the voice of the people to be heard through free and fair elections.

constitutional home rule State constitutional authorization for local governments to conduct their own affairs.

constitutional initiative petition A device that permits voters to place specific amendments to a state constitution on the ballot by petition.

constitutionalism The set of arrangements and processes—checks and balances, federalism, separation of powers, rule of law, due process, and a bill of rights—that disperses and limits the power of government officials. Constitutionalism provides for the granting as well as restraining of powers and seeks to ensure that a government's leaders and representatives are accountable to the citizens.

contract clause Clause of the Constitution that was originally intended to prohibit laws that adversely affect the value of property and to maintain the status quo at the expense of the power of the states to guard the public welfare; it now allows states to make reasonable modifications of contracts to protect public health and safety.

council-manager plan Form of local government in which the city council hires a professional administrator to manage city affairs; also known as the city-manager plan.

court of appeals A court with appellate jurisdiction, which hears appeals from the decisions of lower courts.

cross-cutting cleavages Divisions within society that make groups more heterogeneous or different.

crossover voting A member of one party voting for a candidate of another party.

de facto segregation Segregation that arises as a result of social practices, such as housing patterns.

de jure segregation Segregation sanctioned by law.

dealignment Dramatic change in the composition of the electorate or its partisan preferences that points to a rejection of both major parties and a rise in the number of Independents.

debt The accumulated total of federal deficits, minus surpluses, over the years.

decentralists Those who favor state or local action rather than national action.

defendant In a criminal action, the person or party accused of an offense.

deficit The difference between the revenues raised from sources of income other than borrowing and the expenditure of government, including paying the interest on past borrowing.

delegate A view of the role of a member of Congress which holds that legislators should represent the views of constituents even when personally holding different views.

demagogue Leader who gains power by appealing to the emotions and prejudices of the masses.

democracy Government by the people, either directly or indirectly, with free and frequent elections.

democratic consensus Widespread agreement on fundamental principles of democratic governance and the values that undergird them.

demographics The study of the characteristics of populations.

deregulation A policy promoting cutbacks in the amount of federal regulation in specific areas of economic activity.

devolution revolution The effort to slow the growth of the federal government by returning many functions to the states.

direct democracy Government in which citizens come together to discuss and pass laws and select rulers.

direct primary Election open to all members of the party in which voters choose the persons who will be the party's nominees in the general election.

discharge petition Petition that, if signed by a majority of the members of the House of Representatives, will pry a bill from committee and bring it to the floor for consideration.

disclosure A requirement that candidates specify where the money came from to finance their campaign.

dissenting opinion An opinion that conflicts with the majority in a Supreme Court ruling.

divided government Governance divided between the parties, as when one controls the executive branch and the other the legislative branch.

double jeopardy Trial or punishment for the same crime by the same government; forbidden by the Constitution.

dual citizenship Citizenship in two or more nations.

due process Established rules and regulations that restrain those in government who exercise power.

due process clause Clauses in the Fifth and Fourteenth Amendments stating that the national (Fifth) and state (Fourteenth) governments shall not deprive any person of life, liberty, or property without due process of law.

economic sanction A denial of export, import, or financial relations with a target country in an effort to change that nation's policies.

Electoral College The electoral system used in electing the president and vice-president, in which voters vote for electors pledged to cast their ballots for a particular candidate.

eminent domain Power of a government to take private property for public use; the U.S. Constitution gives national and state governments this power and requires them to provide just compensation for property so taken.

enterprise zone Inner-city areas designated as offering tax incentives to companies that invest in plants there and provide job training for the unemployed.

entitlement program Programs such as Social Security, Medicare, and unemployment insurance that provide a specified set of benefits as a matter of right to all who meet the criteria established by law.

environmental impact statement A statement required by federal law from all agencies for any project using federal funds that assesses the potential effect of the new construction or development on the environment. Many states also require these statements.

environmentalism An ideology that is dominated by concern for the environment but also promotes grass-roots democracy, social justice, equal opportunity, nonviolence, respect for diversity, and feminism.

equal protection clause Clause in the Constitution that forbids any state to deny to any person within its jurisdiction the equal protection of the laws. By interpretation, the Fifth Amendment imposes the same limitation on the national government. This clause is the major constitutional restraint on the power of governments to discriminate against persons because of race, national origin, or sex.

establishment clause Clause in the First Amendment that states that Congress shall make no law respecting an establishment of religion. It has been interpreted by the Supreme Court to forbid governmental support to any or all religions.

ethnicity A social division based on national origin, religion, language, and often race.

ethnocentrism Selective perception based on individual background, attitudes, and biases that leads one to believe in the superiority of one's nation or ethnic group.

ex post facto law Retroactive criminal law that works to the disadvantage of an individual; forbidden in the Constitution.

excise tax Consumer tax on a specific kind of merchandise, such as tobacco.

exclusionary rule Requirement that evidence unconstitutionally or illegally obtained be excluded from criminal trial.

Executive Office of the President The cluster of presidential staff agencies that help the president carry out his responsibilities. Currently the office includes the Office of Management and Budget, the Council of Economic Advisers, and several other units.

executive order A directive issued by presidents or governors that has the force of law.

executive privilege A long-recognized doctrine with some constitutional standing that permits a president to withhold sensitive documents and information from Congress and the courts.

express powers Powers specifically granted to one of the branches of the national government by the Constitution.

extradition Legal process whereby an alleged criminal offender is surrendered by the officials of one state to officials of the state in which the crime is alleged to have been committed.

faction A term used by James Madison and other founders of this country to refer to political parties as well as what we now call special interests or interest groups.

fairness doctrine Doctrine interpreted by the Federal Communications Commission that imposed on radio and television licensees an obligation to ensure that differing viewpoints were presented on controversial issues or persons; repealed in 1987.

federal mandate A requirement imposed by the federal government as a condition of receipt of federal funds.

Federal Register Official document published every weekday that lists new and proposed regulations of executive departments and regulatory agencies.

Federal Reserve System The public-private banking regulatory system created by Congress in 1913 to establish banking practices and regulate

currency in circulation and the amount of credit available. It is comprised of 12 regional banks, and its major responsibilities are supervised by a seven-member presidentially appointed Federal Reserve Board of Governors in Washington, D.C.

federalism Constitutional arrangement whereby power is distributed between a central government and subdivisional governments, called states in the United States. The national and the subdivisional governments both exercise direct authority over individuals.

Federalists Supporters of ratification of the Constitution whose position promoting a strong central government was later voiced in the Federalist party.

fee for service System of health care payment in which patients can choose their own physician, whose bills are then covered by insurance companies.

felony A serious crime, the penalty for which can range from death to imprisonment in a penitentiary for more than a year.

fighting words Words that by their very nature inflict injury upon those to whom they are addressed or cause acts of violence by them.

filibuster A procedural practice in the Senate whereby a senator holds the floor and thereby delays proceedings and prevents a vote on a controversial issue.

fiscal policy Government policy that attempts to manage the economy by controlling taxing and spending.

free exercise clause Clause in the First Amendment that states that Congress shall make no law prohibiting the free exercise of religion.

free rider An individual who does not join an interest group representing his or her interests, yet receives the benefit of the influence the group achieves.

full faith and credit clause Clause in the Constitution requiring each state to recognize the civil judgments rendered by the courts of the other states and to accept their public records and acts as valid documents.

gender gap The difference between the political opinions or political behavior of men and women.

General Accounting Office (GAO) An independent investigative arm of Congress established in 1921 to check on receipt and disbursement of public funds and review the performance of government agencies.

General Agreement on Tariffs and Trade (GATT) An international trade organization with 125 members, including the United States, that seeks to encourage free trade by lowering tariffs and other trade restrictions.

general property tax Tax levied by local and some state governments on real property or personal, tangible property, the major portion of which is on the estimated value of one's home and land.

gerrymandering The drawing of legislative district boundaries to benefit a party, group, or incumbent.

government corporation Cross between a business corporation and a government agency; created to secure greater freedom of action and flexibility for a particular program.

grand jury A jury of 12 to 23 persons who, in private, hear evidence presented by the government to determine whether persons shall be required to stand trial. If the jury believes there is sufficient evidence that a crime was committed, it issues an indictment.

gross domestic product (GDP) An estimate of the total output of all economic activity in the nation, including goods and services.

habeas corpus See Writ of *habeas corpus*.

Hatch Act Federal statute barring federal employees from active participation in certain kinds of politics and protecting them from being fired on partisan grounds.

health maintenance organization (HMO) Alternative means of health care in which people or their employers are charged a set amount and the HMO provides health care and covers hospital costs.

hold A procedural practice in the Senate whereby a senator temporarily blocks the consideration of a bill or nomination.

honeymoon A period at the beginning of a new president's term in which the president enjoys generally positive relations with the press and Congress, usually lasting about six months.

ideology One's basic beliefs about political values and the role of government.

immunity An exemption from prosecution for a particular crime in return for testimony pertaining to the case.

impeachment Formal accusation against a public official and the first step in removal from office.

implied powers Powers inferred from express powers that allow Congress to carry out its functions.

impoundment Presidential refusal to allow an agency to spend funds authorized and appropriated by Congress.

independent agency A government entity that is independent of the legislative, executive, and judicial branch.

independent expenditures Money spent by groups or individuals not associated with candidates to elect or defeat candidates for office.

independent regulatory agency A government agency that exists outside the three branches of government and is responsible for enforcing particular statutes. Generally a regulatory agency has quasi-legislative and quasi-judicial functions as well as executive powers.

independent regulatory board An independent agency with regulatory power whose independence is protected by Congress. Some are independent regulatory commissions.

indictment A formal written statement from a grand jury charging an individual with an offense.

inflation A rise in the general price level (and decrease in dollar value) owing to an increase in the volume of money and credit in relation to available goods.

information affidavit Certification by a public prosecutor that there is evidence to justify bringing named individuals to trial.

inherent powers Those powers of the national government in the field of foreign affairs that the Supreme Court has declared do not depend upon constitutional grants but rather grow out of the very existence of the national government.

initiative Procedure whereby a certain number of voters may, by petition, propose a law or constitutional amendment and have it submitted to the voters.

initiative petition A device that permits voters to place specific amendments to a state constitution on the ballot by petition.

interest group A collection of people who share some common interest or attitude and seek to influence government for specific ends. Interest groups usually work within the framework of government and employ tactics such as lobbying to achieve their goals.

interested money Financial contributions by individuals or groups in the hopes of influencing the outcome of an election and subsequently influencing policy.

interlocking directorate A corporation in which an officer or director sits on the board of a competitor, with the effect of restraining trade.

interstate compact An agreement among two or more states. The Constitution requires that most such agreements be approved by Congress.

iron triangle A mutually supporting relationship among interest groups, congressional committees and subcommittees, and government agencies that share a common policy concern.

issue advertising Commercial advertising on radio and television advocating a particular position on an issue, paid for by interest groups and designed to influence voters' choices on election day.

issue advocacy Promoting a particular position on an issue, often funded by interest groups and designed to influence voters' choices on election day.

item veto Authority of the president or governor of a state to veto parts of a legislative bill without having to veto the entire bill. Also known as the line-item veto.

Jim Crow laws State laws formerly pervasive throughout the South requiring public facilities and accommodations to be segregated by race; ruled unconstitutional.

joint committee Committee composed of members of both the House of Representatives and the Senate; such committees oversee the Library of Congress and conduct investigations.

judiciable dispute A dispute that grows out of an actual case and is capable of settlement by legal methods.

judicial activism Judicial philosophy proposing that judges should interpret the Constitution to reflect current conditions and values.

judicial interpretation A method whereby judges can modify a constitutional provision's restrictive force by a narrow interpretation of its meaning.

judicial restraint Judicial philosophy proposing that judges should interpret the Constitution to reflect what the framers intended and what its words literally say.

judicial review The power of a court to refuse to enforce a law or a government regulation that in the opinion of the judges conflicts with the Constitution, or, in a state court, that conflicts with the state constitution.

Keynesian economics Economic theory based on the principles of John Maynard Keynes stating that government spending should increase during business slumps and be curbed during booms.

labor injunction A court order forbidding specific individuals or groups from performing certain acts (such as striking) that the court considers harmful to the rights and property of an employer or community.

laissez-faire economics Theory that opposes governmental interference in the economy beyond what is necessary to protect life and property.

libel Written defamation of another person. In the case of public officials and public figures, the constitutional tests designed to restrict libel actions are very rigid.

liberalism A belief in the positive uses of government to bring about justice and equality of opportunity.

libertarianism An ideology that cherishes individual liberty and insists on a sharply limited government, promoting a free-market economy, a noninterventionist foreign policy, and an absence of regulation in the moral and social sphere.

literacy test Literacy requirement imposed by some states as a condition of voting; generally used to disqualify blacks from voting in the South; now illegal.

lobby To attempt to influence public officials, especially legislators, and the policies they enact.

lobbying Activities aimed at influencing public officials, especially legislators, and the policies they enact.

lobbyist A person who is employed by and acts for an organized interest group or corporation to try to influence policy decisions and positions in the executive and legislative branches.

log rolling Mutual aid and vote trading among legislators.

magistrate judge An official appointed for renewable terms who performs a variety of limited judicial duties.

majority The candidate or party that wins more than half the votes cast to win an election.

majority leader The legislative leader selected by the majority party who helps plan party strategy, confers with other party leaders, and tries to keep members of the party in line.

majority rule Governance according to the expressed preferences of the majority.

majority-minority district A congressional district created to include a substantial number of minority voters.

malapportionment Legislative districts of unequal populations.

manifest destiny A notion held by nineteenth-century Americans that the United States was destined to rule the continent from the Atlantic to the Pacific oceans.

mass media Means of communication that reach the mass public. The mass media include newspapers and magazines, radio, television (broadcast, cable, and satellite), films, recordings, books, and electronic communication.

mayor-council charter The oldest and most common form of city government; consisting of either a weak mayor and a city council or a strong mayor and council.

Medicaid Federal program that provides medical benefits for low-income persons.

medical savings account Alternative means of health care in which individuals make tax-deductible contributions to a special account that can be saved from year to year and used to pay for medical expenses.

Medicare National health insurance program for the elderly and disabled.

merit system A system of public employment in which selection and promotion depend on demonstrated performance rather than political patronage.

minor party A small political party that rises and falls with a charismatic candidate or, if composed of ideologues on the right or left, usually persists over time.

minority leader The legislative leader selected by the minority party as spokesperson for the opposition.

misdemeanor A less serious violation of state and local laws.

Missouri Plan A system for selecting judges that combines features of the appointive and elective methods. The governor selects judges from lists presented by panels of lawyers and laypersons, and at the end of their term the judges may run against their own record in retention elections.

monetarism A theory that government should control the money supply to encourage economic growth and restrain inflation.

monetary policy Government policy that attempts to manage the economy by controlling the money supply and thus interest rates.

monopoly Domination of an industry by a single company; also the company that dominates.

movement A large body of people interested in a common issue, idea, or concern that is of continuing significance and who are willing to take action on that issue. Movements seek to change attitudes or institutions, not only policies.

national party convention The national meeting of delegates elected in primaries, caucuses, or state conventions who assemble once every four years to nominate candidates for president and vice-president, ratify the party platform, elect officers, and adopt rules.

national supremacy Constitutional doctrine that whenever conflict occurs between the constitutionally authorized actions of the national government and those of a state or local government, the actions of the national government take priority.

natural law God's or nature's law that defines right from wrong and is higher than human law.

natural rights The rights of all citizens to dignity and worth; also called human rights.

naturalization A legal action conferring citizenship upon an alien.

necessary and proper clause Clause of the Constitution setting forth the implied powers of Congress. It states that Congress, in addition to its express powers, has the power to make all laws necessary and proper for carrying out all powers vested by the Constitution in the national government.

New Jersey Plan Proposal at the Constitutional Convention made by William Paterson of New Jersey for a central government with a single-house legislature in which each state would be represented equally.

new judicial federalism The practice of some state courts of using the bill of rights in their state constitutions to provide more protection for some rights than is provided by the Supreme Court's interpretation of the Bill of Rights in the Constitution.

news media That part of the mass media that emphasizes the news.

nonpartisan election A local or judicial election in which candidates are not selected or endorsed by political parties.

nonprotected speech Libel, obscenity, fighting words, and commercial speech, which are not entitled in all circumstances to constitutional protection.

North American Free Trade Agreement (NAFTA) Agreement signed by the United States, Canada, and Mexico in 1992 to form the largest free-trade zone in the world.

obscenity Quality or state of a work that taken as a whole appeals to a prurient interest in sex by depicting sexual conduct as specifically defined by legislation or judicial interpretation in a patently offensive way and that lacks serious literary, artistic, political, or scientific value.

office block ballot Method of voting in which all candidates are listed under the office for which they are running.

Office of Management and Budget (OMB) Presidential staff agency that serves as a clearinghouse for budgetary requests and management improvements for government agencies.

Office of Personnel Management Agency that administers civil service laws, rules, and regulations.

one-party state A state in which one party wins all or nearly all the offices and the other party receives only a small proportion of the popular vote.

open primary A primary in which any voter, regardless of party, may vote.

open rule A procedural rule in the House of Representatives that permits floor amendments within the overall time allocated to the bill.

open shop A company with a labor agreement whereby union membership cannot be required as a condition of employment.

opinion of the court An opinion explaining the decision of the Supreme Court or any other appellate court.

original jurisdiction The authority of a trial court to hear a case "in the first instance."

outsourcing The contracting out to the private sector of services that are typically provided by government; also called privatization.

override An action taken by Congress to reverse a presidential veto that requires a two-thirds majority in each chamber.

party column ballot Type of ballot that encourages party-line voting by listing all a party's candidates in a column under the party name. Also called Indiana ballot.

party convention A meeting of party delegates to pass on matters of policy and in some cases to select party candidates for public office.

party identification An informal and subjective affiliation with a political party that most people acquire in childhood.

party platform The official statement of party policy.

party registration The act of declaring party affiliation; in some states required when one registers to vote.

patronage Dispensing government jobs to persons who belong to the winning political party.

permanent normal trade relations status (PTNR) Trade status granted as part of an international trade policy that gives a nation the same favorable trade concessions and tariffs that the best trading partners receive.

petit jury A jury of 6 to 12 persons that determines guilt or innocence in a civil or criminal action.

plea bargain An agreement between a prosecutor and defendant aimed at getting the defendant to plead guilty to a lesser offense to avoid having to stand trial for a more serious offense.

plurality A candidate or party wins the most votes cast, not necessarily more than half.

pocket veto A veto exercised by the president after Congress has adjourned; if the president takes no action for ten days, the bill does not become law and is not returned to Congress for a possible override.

police powers Inherent powers of state governments to protect the public health, safety, welfare, and morals; in the United States, the states, but not the national government, have these powers.

political action committee (PAC) The political arm of an interest group that is legally entitled to raise funds on a voluntary basis from members, stockholders, or employees in order to contribute funds to favored candidates or political parties.

political culture The widely shared beliefs, values, and norms concerning the relationship of citizens to government and to one another.

political party An organization that seeks political power by electing people to office so that its positions and philosophy become public policy.

political predisposition A characteristic of individuals that is predictive of political behavior.

political question A dispute that requires knowledge of a nonlegal character, or the use of techniques not suitable for a court, or explicitly assigned by the Constitution to Congress or the president; judges refuse to answer constitutional questions that they declare are political.

political socialization The process by which we develop our political attitudes, values, and beliefs.

poll tax Payment required as a condition for voting; prohibited for national elections by the Twenty-fourth Amendment (1964) and ruled unconstitutional for all elections in *Harper v Virginia Board of Elections* (1966).

popular consent The idea that a just government must derive its powers from the consent of the people it governs.

popular sovereignty A belief that ultimate power resides in the people.

pork-barrel legislation Government benefits or programs that may help the economy of a member of Congress's district.

preemption The right of a federal law or regulation to preclude enforcement of a state or local law or regulation.

preferred position doctrine Interpretation of the First Amendment that gives freedom of expression a preferred position in the constitutional hierarchy as it is essential to the political process.

president pro tempore Officer of the Senate selected by the majority party to act as chair in the absence of the vice-president.

prior restraint Restraint or censorship imposed before a speech is made or a newspaper published; usually presumed to be unconstitutional.

privatization The process of contracting public services to private organizations.

procedural due process Constitutional requirement that governments proceed by proper methods; places limits on how governmental power may be exercised.

progressive tax A tax graduated so that people with higher incomes pay a larger fraction of their income than people with lower incomes.

property rights The rights of an individual to own, use, rent, invest in, buy, and sell property.

proportional representation An election system in which each party running receives the proportion of legislative seats corresponding to its proportion of the vote.

protectionism Policy of erecting trade barriers to protect domestic industry.

public defender system Arrangement whereby public officials are hired to provide legal assistance to those persons accused of crimes who are unable to hire their own attorneys.

public opinion The distribution of individual preferences or evaluations of a given issue, candidate, or institution within a population.

race A grouping of human beings with common characteristics presumed to be transmitted genetically.

racial gerrymandering The drawing of election districts so as to ensure that members of a certain race are a minority in the district; ruled unconstitutional in *Gomillion v Lightfoot* (1960).

racial or religious restrictive covenants A provision in a deed to real property excluding its sale to persons of a particular race or religion; judicial enforcement of such deeds is unconstitutional.

racial profiling Police target racial minorities as potential suspects of criminal activities.

realigning election An election that proves to be a turning point, redefining the agenda of politics and the alignment of voters within parties during periods of historic change in the economy and society.

reapportionment The assigning by Congress of congressional seats after each census. State legislators reapportion state legislative districts.

recall Procedure for submitting to popular vote the removal of officials from office before the end of their term.

recidivist A repeat offender.

reconciliation Process by which Congress, by a budget resolution, sets ceilings on what appropriations subcommittees can appropriate.

redistributive policies Governmental tax programs that shift wealth or benefits from one segment of the population to another, often from the rich to the poor.

redistricting The redrawing of congressional and other legislative district lines following the census, to accommodate population shifts and keep districts as equal as possible in population.

reduction veto The power of governors in a few states to reduce a particular appropriation.

referendum Procedure for submitting to popular vote measures passed by the legislature or proposed amendments to a state's constitution.

regressive tax A tax whereby people with lower incomes pay a higher fraction of their income than people with lower incomes. In other words, a regressive tax is one that weighs most heavily on those least able to pay.

regulation The attempt by government to control the behavior of corporations, other governments, or citizens through altering the natural workings of the open market to achieve some desired goal.

regulatory taking Government regulation of property so extensive that government is deemed to have taken the property and thus exercised the power of eminent domain, for which it must compensate the property owners.

reinforcing cleavages Divisions within society that reinforce one another, making groups more homogeneous or similar.

representative democracy Government that derives its powers indirectly from the people, who elect those who will govern; also called a republic.

responsibility contract A welfare strategy adopted by some states in which recipients sign a written agreement specifying their responsibilities and outlining a plan for obtaining work and achieving self-sufficiency.

revenue sharing Program from 1972 to 1987 whereby federal funds were provided to state and local governments to be spent largely at the discretion of the receiving governments, subject to few and very general conditions.

revision commission A state commission that recommends changes in the state constitution for action by the legislature and vote by the voters.

revolving door The employment cycle in which individuals work, in turn, for governmental agencies regulating interests and then for the interest groups or businesses with the same policy concern.

rider A provision that may have little relationship to the bill it is attached to in order to secure its passage.

right of expatriation Right of an individual to choose his or her own nationality.

safe seat An elected office, usually in a legislature, that is predictably won by one party or the other, so reelection is almost taken for granted.

sales tax General tax on sales transactions, sometimes exempting food and drugs; the most important source of revenue for states.

search warrant A warrant issued by a magistrate that authorizes the police to search a particular place or person, specifying the place to be searched and the objects to be seized.

sedition Attempting to overthrow the government by force or to interrupt its activities by violence.

select or special committee A congressional committee created for a specific purpose, sometimes to conduct an investigation.

selective exposure The process by which individuals screen out those messages that do not conform to their own biases.

selective incorporation The process by which provisions of the Bill of Rights were bought within the scope of the Fourteenth Amendment and so applied to state and local governments.

selective perception The process by which individuals perceive what they want to in media messages and disregard the rest.

senatorial courtesy Presidential custom of submitting the names of prospective appointees for approval to senators from the states in which the appointees are to work.

seniority rule A legislative practice that assigns the chair of a committee or subcommittee to the member of the majority party with the longest continuous service on the committee.

separation of powers Constitutional division of powers among the legislative, executive, and judicial branches, with the legislative branch making law, the executive applying and enforcing the law, and the judiciary interpreting the law.

severance tax A tax on the privilege of "severing" such natural resources as coal, oil, timber, and gas from the land.

Shays' Rebellion Rebellion by farmers in western Massachusetts in 1786–87, protesting mortgage foreclosures, led by Daniel Shays, and important because it highlighted the need for a strong national government just as the call for a Constitutional Convention went out.

single-member district An electoral district in which in any given election the voters choose one representative or official.

social capital Participation in voluntary associations that reinforce democratic and civic habits of discussion, compromise, and respect for differences.

Social Security A combination of entitlement programs, paid for by employer and employee taxes, that includes retirement benefits, health insurance, and support for disabled workers and the children of deceased or disabled workers.

social stratification Divisions in a community among socioeconomic groups or classes.

socialism An economic and governmental system based on public ownership of the means of production and exchange.

socioeconomic status (SES) A division of population based on occupation, income, and education.

soft money Money contributed to a state or local political party for party-building purposes that does not have to be disclosed under federal law.

Speaker The presiding officer in the House of Representatives; formally elected by the House but actually selected by the majority party.

split ticket Voting for some of one party's candidates and some from another party.

spoils system System of public employment based on rewarding party loyalists.

standing committee A permanent committee established in a legislature, usually focusing on a policy area.

stare decisis The rule of precedent, whereby a rule or law contained in a judicial decision is commonly viewed as binding on judges whenever the same question is presented.

statism The idea that the rights of the state (meaning nation) are supreme over the rights of the individual.

straight ticket Voting for all of one party's candidates.

strong mayor-council Form of local government in which the voters directly elect the city council and the mayor, who enjoys almost total administrative authority and appoints the department heads.

substantive due process Constitutional requirement that governments act reasonably and that the substance of the laws themselves be fair and reasonable; places limits on what a government may do.

tariff Tax levied on imports to help protect a nation's industries, labor, or farmers from foreign competition. It can also be used merely to raise additional revenue.

tax expenditure Loss of tax revenue due to federal tax laws that provide special tax incentives or benefits to individuals or businesses.

The Federalist Series of essays promoting ratification of the Constitution, written by Alexander Hamilton, John Jay, and James Madison in 1787 and 1788.

theocracy Government by religious leaders, who claim divine guidance.

three-fifths compromise Compromise agreement between northern and southern states at the Constitutional Convention in which the slave population would be counted at three-fifths for determining direct taxation and representation in the House of Representatives.

tort law Law relating to noncontractual injuries to person, reputation, or property.

trade deficit An imbalance in international trade in which the value of imports exceeds the value of exports.

trust A monopoly that controls goods and services, often in combinations that reduce competition.

trustee A view of the role of a member of Congress that holds that legislators are elected to think and vote independently for the general welfare, and not as their constituents direct.

turnout The proportion of the voting-age public that votes.

two-party state A state in which the two major parties alternate in winning majorities.

unicameral legislature A one-house legislature.

union shop A company in which new employees must join a union within a stated time period.

unitary system A constitutional arrangement in which power is concentrated in a central government; also called a unitary government.

user fee Fees charged directly to individuals who use certain public services on the basis of service consumed; also called a user charge.

value-added tax (VAT) A tax on increased value of a product at each stage of production and distribution (rather than a sales tax just at the point of sale), commonly used by governments in Europe to raise revenues.

veto Rejection by a president or governor of legislation passed by a legislature.

Virginia Plan Proposal at the Constitutional Convention made by the Virginia delegation for a strong central government with a bicameral legislature, the lower house to be elected by the voters and the upper chosen by the lower.

voter registration System designed to reduce voter fraud by limiting voting to those who have established eligibility by submitting the proper form.

voucher A school reform program whereby a set amount of money is provided by government to parents for their use in paying for their child's education, in a public or private school of their choice.

weak mayor-council Form of local government in which the members of the city council select the mayor, who then shares power with other elected or appointed boards and commissions.

whip Party leader who is the liaison between the leadership and the rank-and-file in the legislature.

white primary Primary operated by the Democratic party in southern states that, before Republicans gained strength in the "one-party South," essentially constituted an election; ruled unconstitutional in *Smith v Allwright* (1944).

winner-take-all An election system in which the candidate with the most votes wins.

women's suffrage The right of women to vote.

workfare A welfare strategy adopted by some states that gives able-bodied adults who do not have preschool-aged children the opportunity to learn job skills that can lead to employment.

World Trade Organization (WTO) International organization derived from the General Agreement on Tariffs and Trade (GATT) it promotes free trade around the world.

writ of *certiorari* A formal writ used to bring a case before the Supreme Court.

writ of *habeas corpus* Court order directing any official having a person in custody to produce the prisoner in court and explain to the judge why the prisoner is being held.

writ of *mandamus* Court order directing an official to perform an official duty.

yellow-dog contract Contract by an anti-union employer that forces new workers to promise they will not join a union as a condition of employment.

NOTES

CHAPTER 1

1. See Jackie Calmes, "State of the Union: Ambivalence," *The Wall Street Journal*, December 14, 2000, p. 12.
2. Garry Wills, *A Necessary Evil: A History of American Distrust of Government* (Simon & Schuster, 1999), pp. 306–7.
3. John W. Gardner, speech to the White House Fellows Association, Corcoran Gallery of Art, Washington, D.C., October 1, 1999.
4. Robert H. Jackson, *West Virginia State Board of Education v Barnette*, 319 US 624 (1943).
5. Robert Dahl, *On Democracy* (Yale University Press, 1998), p. 145.
6. Harold Stanley and Richard Niemi, *Vital Statistics on American Politics, 1999–2000* (Congressional Quarterly Press, 2000), pp. 25–29.
7. For a major theoretical work on the principle of majority rule, see Robert A. Dahl, *Democracy and Its Critics* (Yale University Press, 1989).
8. Seymour Martin Lipset, "The Social Requisites of Democracy Revisited," *American Sociological Review* 59 (1994), pp. 1–22.
9. For a discussion of the importance for democracy of such overlapping group memberships, see David Truman's seminal work, *The Governmental Process*, 2d ed. (Knopf, 1971).
10. See Robert D. Putnam, *Bowling Alone: The Collapse and Revival of American Community* (Simon & Schuster, 2000), p. 19. See also Pippa Norris, ed., *Critical Citizens: Global Support for Democratic Governance* (Oxford University, 1999), and for a somewhat different point of view, Everett Carll Ladd, *The Ladd Report* (Free Press, 1999).
11. Michael Schudson, *The Good Citizen: A History of American Civic Life* (Harvard University Press, 1998), p. 296.
12. Quoted in D. W. Miller, "Perhaps We Are Bowling Alone, But Does It Really Matter?" *Chronicle of Higher Education*, July 16, 1999, p. A17.
13. Joyce Appleby, "The American Heritage: The Heirs and the Disinherited," *Journal of American History* (December 1987), p. 808.
14. Richard L. Hillard, "Liberalism, Civic Humanism and the American Revolutionary Bill of Rights, 1775–1790," paper presented at the annual meeting of the Organization of American Historians, Reno, Nevada, 1988.
15. Quoted in Charles L. Mee, Jr., *The Genius of the People* (Harper & Row, 1987), p. 51.
16. Seymour Martin Lipset, "George Washington and the Founding of Democracy," *Journal of Democracy* (October 1998), p. 31.
17. See the essays in Thomas E. Cronin, ed., *Inventing the American Presidency* (University Press of Kansas, 1989). See also Richard J. Ellis, ed., *Founding the American Presidency* (Rowman and Littlefield, 1999).
18. Charles A. Beard and Mary R. Beard, *A Basic History of the United States* (New Home Library, 1944), p. 136.
19. See Herbert J. Storing, ed., abridgment by Murray Dry, *The Anti-Federalist: Writings by the Opponents of the Constitution* (University of Chicago Press, 1985).
20. On the role of the promised bill of rights amendments in the ratification of the Constitution, see Leonard W. Levy, *Constitutional Opinions* (Oxford University Press, 1986), chap. 6.

CHAPTER 2

1. Max Lerner, *Ideas for the Ice Age* (Viking, 1941), pp. 241–42. See also *The American Public's Knowledge of the U.S. Constitution: A National Survey of Public Awareness and Personal Opinion* (Hearst Corporation, 1987).
2. Sanford Levinson, *Constitutional Faith* (Princeton University Press, 1988), pp. 9–52.
3. Richard Morin, "We Love It—What We Know of It," *The Washington Post National Weekly Edition*, September 22, 1997, p. 35.
4. Thomas Jefferson, quoted in Alpheus T. Mason, *The Supreme Court: Palladium of Freedom* (University of Michigan Press, 1962), p. 10.
5. James Madison, *The Federalist*, No. 47, ed. Clinton Rossiter (Mentor Books), p. 301.
6. James L. Sundquist, "Needed: A Political Theory for the New Era of Coalition Government in the United States," *Political Science Quarterly* (Winter 1988–89), pp. 613–35; Robert A. Godwin and Art Kaufman, eds., *Separation of Powers: Does It Still Work?* (AEI Press, 1986).
7. Charles O. Jones, "The Separate Presidency," in Anthony King, ed., *The New American Political System*, 2d ed. (AEI Press, 1990), p. 3.
8. Morris P. Fiorina, "An Era of Divided Government," *Political Science Quarterly* 107, no. 3 (1992), p. 407.
9. David R. Mayhew, *Divided We Govern: Party Control, Lawmaking, and Investigations, 1946–1990* (Yale University Press, 1991), p. 4. See also James A. Thurber, ed., *Divided Democracy: Presidents and Congress in Cooperation and Conflict* (Congressional Quarterly, 1991).
10. Charles O. Jones, *Separate But Equal Branches: Congress and the Presidency* (Chatham House, 1995).
11. Robert C. Vipond, *Liberty and Community: Canadian Federalism and the Failure of the Constitution* (State University of New York Press, 1991), p. 192.
12. Alec Stone, "Governing with Judges: The New Constitutionalism," in Jack Hayward and Edward C. Page, eds. *Governing the New Europe* (Polity Press, 1995), pp. 286–313; Donald P. Kommers, "The Federal Constitutional Court in the German Political System," *Comparative Political Studies* 26 (January 1994), pp. 470–91; Martin J. Shapiro, "The European Court of Justice," in Alberta M. Sbrdagia, ed., *Euro-Politics*, (Brookings Institution, 1992); Martin J. Shapiro and Alec Stone, "The New Constitutional Politics," *Comparative Political Studies* 26 (January 1994), pp. 397–420; Alec Stone, *The Birth of Judicial Politics in France* (Oxford University Press, 1993).
13. *Marbury v Madison*, 1 Cranch 137 (1803).
14. Dumas Malone, *Jefferson the President: First Term, 1801–1805* (Little, Brown, 1970), p. 145.
15. J. W. Peltason, *Federal Courts in the Political Process* (Random House, 1955).
16. See Eleanore Bushnell, *Crimes, Follies, and Misfortunes: The Federal Impeachment Trials* (University of Illinois Press, 1992); Michael J. Gerhardt, *The Federal Impeachment Process: A Constitutional and Historical Analysis* (Princeton University Press, 1996).
17. Richard E. Neustadt, *Presidential Power* (Free Press, 1990), pp. 180–81.
18. Ronald L. Goldfarb, "The 11,000th Amendment: There's a Rush to Amend the Constitution, and It Shows No Signs of Letting Up," *The Washington Post National Weekly Edition*, November 25–December 1, 1996, p. 22.
19. See Committee on the Constitutional System, *A Bicentennial Analysis of the American Political Structure: Report and Recommendations of the Committee on the Constitutional System* (1987), for recommendations of a committee co-chaired by Senator Nancy L. Kassebaum, C. Douglas Dillon, and Lloyd Cutler. For critical comments, see Mark P. Petracca, "To Right What the Constitution Has Wrought or To Wrong What Is Right," paper presented at annual meeting of the American Political Science Association, Washington, D.C., 1988.
20. Ann Stuart Diamond, "A Convention for Proposing Amendments: The Constitution's Other Method," *Publius* (Summer 1981), pp. 113–46; Wilbur Edel, "Amending the Constitution by Convention: Myths and Realities," *State Government* 55 (1982), pp. 51–56.

21. Russell L. Caplan, *Constitutional Brinksmanship: Amending the Constitution by National Convention* (Oxford University Press, 1988), p. x. See also David E. Kyvig, *Explicit and Authentic Acts: Amending the U.S. Constitution, 1776–1995* (University Press of Kansas, 1996), p. 440.
22. Samuel S. Freedman and Pamela J. Naughton, *ERA: May a State Change Its Vote?* (Wayne State University Press, 1979).
23. Kyvig, *Explicit and Authentic Acts*, p. 286; *Dillon v Gloss*, 256 US 368 (1921).
24. Gregory A. Caldeira, "Constitutional Change in America: Dynamics of Ratification Under Article V," *Publius* (Fall 1985), p. 29.

25. Mark R. Daniels, Robert Darcy, and Joseph W. Westphal, "The ERA Won—At Least in the Opinion Polls," *PS: Political Science and Politics* (Fall 1982), p. 583.
26. Ibid.
27. Janet K. Boles, *The Politics of the Equal Rights Amendment: Conflict and Decision-Making Powers* (Longman, 1979), p. 4.
28. Gilbert Y. Steiner, *Constitutional Inequality: The Political Fortunes of the Equal Rights Amendment* (Brookings Institution, 1985), p. 64. See also Mary Frances Berry, *Why the ERA Failed: Politics, Women's Rights, and the Amending Process of the Constitution* (Indiana University Press, 1986).

CHAPTER 3

1. For background, see Samuel H. Beer, *To Make a Nation: The Rediscovery of American Federalism* (Harvard University Press, 1993).
2. The term "devolution revolution" was coined by Richard P. Nathan in testimony before the Senate Finance Committee, as quoted by Daniel Patrick Moynihan, "The Devolution Revolution," *The New York Times*, August 6, 1995, p. B15.
3. See Michael Burgess, *Federalism and the European Union: Building of Europe, 1950–2000* (Routledge, 2000).
4. *United States v Lopez*, 514 US 549 (1995).
5. *Alden v Maine*, 119 S.Ct. 2240 (1999); *Kimel v Florida Board of Regents*, 120 S.Ct. 631 (2000); and *Vermont Agency of Natural Resources v United States ex rel. Stevens*, 120 S.Ct. 1858 (2000).
6. *Saenz v Roe*, 119 S.Ct. 1518 (1999). See also Roderick M. Hills, Jr., "Poverty, Residency, and Federalism: States' Duty of Impartiality Toward Newcomers," in Dennis J. Hutchinson, David A. Strauss, and Geoffrey R. Stone, eds., *The Supreme Court Review—1999* (University of Chicago Press, 2000), pp. 277–336.
7. *Reno v Condon*, 120 S.Ct. 666 (2000).
8. Martha Derthick, "American Federalism: Half-Full or Half-Empty," *Brookings Review* (Winter 2000), pp. 24–27.
9. William H. Stewart, *Concepts of Federalism* (Center for the Study of Federalism and University Press of America, 1984). See also Edward L. Rubin and Malcolm Feeley, "Federalism: Some Notes on a National Neurosis," *UCLA Law Review* 41 (April 1994), pp. 903–52.
10. Morton Grodzins, "The Federal System," in *Goals for Americans: The Report of the President's Commission on National Goals* (Columbia University Press, 1960).
11. Thomas R. Dye, *American Federalism: Competition Among Governments* (Lexington Books, 1990), pp. 13–17.
12. Michael D. Reagan and John G. Sanzone, *The New Federalism* (Oxford University Press, 1981), p. 175.
13. Gregory S. Mahler, *Comparative Politics: An Institutional and Cross-National Approach* (Prentice-Hall, 2000), p. 31.
14. Frederick K. Lister, *The European Union, the United Nations and the Revival of Confederal Governance* (Greenwood Press, 1996).
15. William H. Riker, *The Development of American Federalism* (Academic Publishers, 1987), pp. 14–15. Riker contends that not only does federalism not guarantee freedom but that the framers of our federal system, as well as those of other nations, were not animated by considerations of safeguarding freedom but by practical considerations of preserving unity.
16. The Court, however, ruled in several recent cases that Congress exceeded its power to regulate interstate commerce. See *Printz v Mack*, 117 S.Ct. 2365 (1997); *United States v Lopez*, 514 US 549 (1995); *New York v United States*, 505 US 144 (1992); and *United States v Morrison*, 120 S.Ct. 1740 (2000).
17. *Heart of Atlanta Motel v United States*, 379 US 241 (1964).
18. See *United States v Morrison*, 120 S.Ct. 1740 (2000), striking down the Violence Against Women Act, and discussed later in this chapter.
19. *New York v United States*, 505 US 144 (1992); *Printz v United States*, 117 S.Ct. 2365 (1997).
20. *Seminole Tribe of Florida v Florida*, 517 US 44 (1996); *Alden v Maine*, 119 S.Ct. 2240 (1999); and *Kimel v Florida Board of Regents*, 120 S.Ct. 631 (2000).
21. *California v Superior Courts of California*, 482 US 400 (1987).

22. David C. Nice, "State Participation in Interstate Compacts," *Publius* 17 (Spring 1987), p. 70. See also Council of State Governments, *Interstate Compacts and Agencies* (1995), for a list of compacts by subject and by state with brief description.
23. *McCulloch v Maryland*, 4 Wheaton 316 (1819).
24. Joseph F. Zimmerman, "Federal Preemption Under Reagan's New Federalism," *Publius* 21 (Winter 1991), pp. 7–28.
25. Oliver Wendell Holmes, Jr., *Collected Legal Papers* (Harcourt, 1920), pp. 295–96.
26. *U.S. Term Limits, Inc. v Thornton*, 514 US 779 (1995).
27. *Garcia v San Antonio Metro*, 469 US 528 (1985).
28. See, e.g., *United States v Lopez*, 514 US 549 (1995). Also see Richard A. Brisbin, Jr., "The Reconstitution of American Federalism? The Rehnquist Court and Federal-State Relations, 1991–1997," *Publius* (Winter 1998), pp. 189–217.
29. *U.S. Term Limits v Thornton*, 514 US 779 (1995).
30. *Seminole Tribe of Florida v Florida*, 517 US 44 (1996).
31. *Alden v Maine*, 119 S.Ct. 2240 (1999); *Kimel v Florida Board of Regents*, 120 S.Ct. 631 (2000); and *Vermont Agency of Natural Resources v United States ex rel. Stevens*, 120 S.Ct. 1858 (2000).
32. George Will, "A Revival of Federalism?" *Newsweek*, May 29, 2000, p. 78.
33. See *Jones v United States*, 120 S.Ct. 2236 (2000).
34. *United States v Morrison*, 120 S.Ct. 1740 (2000).
35. John E. Chubb, "The Political Economy of Federalism," *American Political Science Review* 79 (December 1985), p. 1005.
36. Paul E. Peterson, *The Price of Federalism* (Brookings Institution, 1995), p. 127.
37. Donald F. Kettl, *The Regulation of American Federalism* (Johns Hopkins University Press, 1987), pp. 154–55.
38. See Paul J. Posner, *The Politics of Unfunded Mandates: Whither Federalism?* (Georgetown University Press, 1998).
39. Advisory Commission on Intergovernmental Relations, *Restoring Confidence and Competence* (ACIR, 1981), p. 30.
40. Cynthia Cates Colella, "The Creation, Care and Feeding of the Leviathan: Who and What Makes Government Grow," *Intergovernmental Perspective* (Fall 1979), p. 9.
41. Aaron Wildavsky, "Bare Bones: Putting Flesh on the Skeleton of American Federalism," in Advisory Commission on Intergovernmental Relations, *The Future of Federalism in the 1980s* (ACIR, 1981), p. 79.
42. Peterson, *Price of Federalism*, p. 182.
43. "GOP Confounds Expectations, Expands Federal Authority," *Congressional Quarterly Weekly Report*, November 2, 1996, p. 3117.
44. Eliza Newlin Carney, "Power Grab," *National Journal*, April 11, 1998, p. 798. See also Joshua Wolf Shenk, "Washington's Counter-Devolutionaries," *U.S. News and World Report*, November 24, 1997, p. 34.
45. Luther Gulick, "Reorganization of the States," *Civil Engineering* (August 1933), pp. 420–21.
46. David E. Osborne, *Laboratories of Democracy* (Harvard Business School Press, 1988), p. 363.
47. Dye, *American Federalism*, p. 199.
48. Edward Felsenthal, "Firms Ask Congress to Pass Uniform Rules," *The Wall Street Journal*, May 10, 1993, p. B4.
49. John J. DiIulio, Jr., and Donald F. Kettl, *Fine Print: The Contract with America, Devolution, and the Administrative Realities of American Federalism* (Brookings Institution, 1995), p. 60.

CHAPTER 4

1. Robert D. Putnam, "Bowling Alone: America's Declining Social Capital," *Journal of Democracy* 6, no. 1 (January 1995), pp. 65–78. See also Robert D. Putnam, *Bowling Alone: The Collapse and Revival of American Community* (Simon & Schuster, 2000).

2. Clinton Rossiter, *Conservatism in America* (Vintage, 1962), p. 72.

3. See Ronald Dworkin, *Taking Rights Seriously* (Harvard University Press, 1977).

4. *Marbury v Madison*, 1 Cranch 137 (1803).

5. For an analysis of one aspect of the underclass, see Paul M. Sniderman and Michael Hagen, *Race and Inequality: A Study in American Values* (Chatham House, 1985).

6. When adjusted using the consumer price index (CPI), the percent of households earning over $75,000 a year has risen from 9.0 percent in 1970 to 18.4 percent in 1997. U.S. Bureau of the Census, *Statistical Abstract of the United States, 1999* (Government Printing Office, 1999), table 742.

7. Bernard Bailyn, *The Ideological Origins of the American Revolution* (Harvard University Press, 1967).

8. Robert A. Dahl, "Liberal Democracy in the United States," in *A Prospect of Liberal Democracy*, ed. William Livingston (University of Texas Press, 1979), p. 64.

9. Ibid., pp. 59–60.

10. Franklin D. Roosevelt, State of the Union Address, January 11, 1944, *The Public Papers of the President of the United States, 1944* (Government Printing Office, 1962), pp. 371–94.

11. Harry S Truman, State of the Union Address, 1949, *The Public Papers of the President of the United States, 1949* (Government Printing Office, 1964), pp. 1–7.

12. E. J. Dionne, Jr., *They Only Look Dead: Why Progressives Will Dominate the Next Political Era* (Simon & Schuster, 1996), p. 13.

13. David Brooks, "Need a Map? The Right," *The Washington Post*, October 31, 1999, p. B1.

14. Warren B. Rudman, *Combat: Twelve Years in the U.S. Senate* (Random House, 1996), p. 270.

15. David B. Magleby, "Issue Advocacy in the 2000 Presidential Primaries," in David B. Magleby, ed., *Getting Inside the Outside Campaign* (Center for the Study of Elections and Democracy, Brigham Young University, 2000), p.13. Also at www.byu.edu/outsidemoney.

16. Kathleen Day, *S & L Hell: The People and the Politics Behind the $1 Trillion Savings and Loan Scandal* (W.W. Norton & Co., 1993).

17. Sylvia Nasar, "Even Among the Well-Off, the Rich Get Richer," *The New York Times*, March 5, 1992, p. A1.

18. Irving Howe, *Socialism and America* (Harcourt, 1985); Michael Harrington, *Socialism: Past and Future* (Arcade, 1989).

19. Daniel Yergin and Joseph Stainslaw, *The Commanding Heights: The Battle Between Government and the Marketplace That is Remaking the Modern World* (Simon & Schuster, 1998).

20. www.gp.org/fullplatform.htm

21. Charles Murray, *What It Means to Be a Libertarian* (Broadway Books, 1997); see their 2000 platform at www.lp.org/issues/campplat

22. Center for Political Studies, University of Michigan, *American National Election Study, 1990: Post-Election Survey* (April 1991).

23. Michael Kranish, "Discord Replaced by Desire to Win," *The Boston Globe*, July 31, 2000, p. A10.

24. Nat Hentoff, "Liberal Trimmers of the First Amendment," *The Washington Post*, January 17, 1998, p. A25.

25. Dinesh D'Sousa, *Illiberal Education: The Politics of Race and Sex on Campus* (Free Press, 1991), p. 313.

CHAPTER 5

1. George W. Bush Campaign, "Governor Bush Proposes 6-Month Standard for All Immigration Applications," press release, July 5, 2000, at the Annual Conference of the National Council of La Raza, San Diego, Calif., at www.georgewbush.com/News.asp?FormMode=NR&Search=1&ID=829, August 15, 2000.

2. Albert Einstein, quoted in Laurence J. Peter, *Peter's Quotations* (William Morrow, 1977), p. 358.

3. Alexis de Tocqueville, *Democracy in America*, ed. J. P. Mayer, trans. George Lawrence (Doubleday and Company, 1969), p. 278.

4. *Handbook of International Statistics* (Central Intelligence Agency, Directorate of Intelligence, February 1999), Table 41: "Big Seven: Exports by Commodities," pp. 52–53.

5. U.S. Bureau of the Census, *Statistical Abstract of the United States, 1999* (Government Printing Office, 1999), p. 300.

6. V. O. Key, Jr., *Politics, Parties, and Pressure Groups*, 5th ed. (Thomas Y. Crowell, 1964), p. 232.

7. Earl Black and Merle Black, *The Vital South: How Presidents Are Elected* (Harvard University Press, 1992), p. 4.

8. Joseph A. Pika and Richard A. Watson, *The Presidential Contest*, 5th ed. (Congressional Quarterly Press, 1996), pp. 80–81.

9. www. census.gov/population/cen2000/tab01.pdf./

10. Robert S. Erikson, Gerald C. Wright, and John P. McIver, *Statehouse Democracy: Public Opinion and Policy in the American States* (Cambridge University Press, 1993).

11. U.S. Bureau of the Census, *Statistical Abstract of the United States, 1997* (Government Printing Office, 1997), p. 28.

12. Holly Idelson, "Count Adds Seats in Eight States," *Congressional Quarterly Weekly Report* 48 (December 29, 1999), p. 4240.

13. *Statistical Abstract, 1999*, p. 40.

14. Ibid., p. 46.

15. U.S. Bureau of the Census, www.census.gov/population/socdemo/race/black/tabs99/tab16.txt.

16. Kevin M. Pollard, "America's Racial and Ethnic Minorities," *Population Bulletin*, September 1999.

17. *Statistical Abstract, 1999*, p. 48.

18. Ibid., p. 34.

19. Robert D. Ballard, "Introduction: Lure of the New South," *In Search of the New South: The Black Urban Experience in the 1970s and 1980s*, ed. Robert D. Ballard (University of Alabama Press, 1989), p. 5; *Statistical Abstract*, 1999, p. 34.

20. U.S. Bureau of the Census, www.census.gov/hhes/income/histinc/f05.html, August 2000.

21. *Statistical Abstract, 1999*, p. 484.

22. Joseph Dalker and Bernadette D. Proctor, U.S. Census Bureau, Current Population Reports, "*Poverty in the United States, 1999*," September 2000 (www.census.gov/hhes/www/povty99.html).

23. *Statistical Abstract, 1999*, p. 475.

24. U.S. Bureau of the Census, www.census.gov/hhes/www/wealth/wlth93f.html.

25. U.S. Bureau of the Census, *Household Wealth and Asset Ownership, 1991*, Current Population Reports P-70, no. 34 (Government Printing Office, 1991), table H.

26. Ibid., p. 169.

27. Ibid., p. 191.

28. Ibid., p. 23.

29. Mark R. Levy and Michael S. Karmer, *The Ethnic Factor: How America's Minorities Decide Elections* (Simon & Schuster, 1973). See also Mark Stern, "Democratic Presidency and Voting Rights," in *Blacks in Southern Politics*, ed. Lawrence W. Mooreland, Robert P. Steed, and Todd A. Baker (Praeger, 1987), pp. 50–51.

30. David Bositis, *Blacks and the 1992 Republican National Convention* (Joint Center for Political and Economic Studies, 1992), p. 5; "Portrait of the Electorate," *The New York Times*, November 10, 1996, p. 16.

31. *Statistical Abstract, 1999*, p. 39.

32. See Frank R. Parker, *Black Votes Count: Political Empowerment in Mississippi After 1965* (University of North Carolina Press, 1990).

33. "Number of Black Elected Officials in the United States, by State and Office, January 1998," Joint Center for Political and Economic Studies, at www.jointcenter.org/databank/graphs/98_beo.pdf.

34. Ibid.

35. Rodolfo O. de la Garza, Louis DeSipio, F. Chris Garcia, John Garcia, and Angelo Falcon, *Latino Voices: Mexican, Puerto Rican, and Cuban Perspectives on American Politics* (Westview Press, 1992), p. 14.

36. Todd S. Purdum, "Shift in the Mix Alters the Face of California," *The New York Times*, July 4, 2000, p. A1.

37. *Statistical Abstract, 1999*, p. 54.

38. de la Garza et al., *Latino Voices*, p. 14.

39. *Statistical Abstract, 1999*, p. 38.

40. U.S. Bureau of the Census, *The Foreign-Born Population in the United States, March 1999*. Issued August 2000 (www.census.gov/prod/2000pubs/p20–519.pdf), p. 1.

41. *Statistical Abstract, 1999*, p. 169.

42. *Statistical Abstract, 1999*, p. 10.

43. Martha Farnsworth Riche, "America's Diversity and Growth: Signpost for the 21st Century," *Population Bulletin*, January 2000.

44. James West Davidson, William E. Gienapp, Christine Leigh Heyrman, Mark H. Lytle, and Michael B. Stoff, *Nation of Nations* (McGraw-Hill, 1990), pp. 833–34.

45. G. Thomas Edwards, *Sowing Good Seeds: The Northwest Suffrage Campaigns of Susan B. Anthony* (Oregon Historical Society Press, 1990), p. 136.

46. Paul Kleppner, *Continuity and Change in Electoral Politics, 1893–1928* (Greenwood Press, 1987), p. 172.

47. Margaret C. Trevor, "Political Socialization, Party Identification, and the Gender Gap," *Public Opinion Quarterly* 63 (Spring 1999), p. 62.

48. Diane L. Fowlkes, "Feminist Theory: Reconstructing Research and Teaching About American Politics and Government," *News for Teachers of Political Science* (Winter 1987), pp. 6–9. See also Sally Helgesen, *Everyday Revolutionaries: Working Women and the Transformation of American Life* (Doubleday, 1998); Karen Lehrman, *The Lipstick Proviso: Women, Sex and Power in the Real World* (Anchor Books and Doubleday, 1997); Tanya Melich, *The Republican War Against Women: An Insider's Report from Behind the Lines: Updated Edition* (Bantam Books, 1998); and Virginia Valian, *Why So Slow? The Advancement of Women* (MIT Press, 1998).

49. Barbara C. Burrell, *A Woman's Place Is in the House: Campaigning for Congress in the Feminist Era* (University of Michigan Press, 1994).

50. Marjorie Connelly, "The Election; Who Voted: A Portrait of American Politics, 1976–2000," *The New York Times*, November 12, 2000, p. D4.

51. Arlie Russell Hochschild, "There's No Place Like Work," *The New York Times*, April 20, 1997, p. 51.

52. Alexis Simendinger, "Why Issues Matter," *National Journal*, April 1, 2000, based on data from a Pew Center Poll conducted March 15–19, 2000.

53. *Statistical Abstract, 1999*, p. 481.

54. June O'Neill and Solomon Polachek, "Why the Gender Gap in Wages Narrowed in the 1980's," *Journal of Labor Economics* 11 (1993), pp. 225–29.

55. Jeffrey Schmalz, "Survey Stirs Debate on Number of Gay Men in U.S.," *The New York Times*, April 16, 1993, p. A20.

56. Tamar Lewin, "So, Now We Know What Americans Do in Bed. So?" *The New York Times*, October 9, 1994, sec. 4, p. 3.

57. Adam Clymer, "Senate Expands Hate Crimes Law to Include Gays," *The New York Times*, June 21, 2000, p. A1.

58. *Boy Scouts of America and Monmouth Council et al. v James Dale*, 120 S. Ct. 2446 (2000).

59. *Statistical Abstract, 1999*, p. 111.

60. Ibid., p. 110.

61. www.icpsr.umich.edu/GSS99/codebook/pework.htm.

62. For a discussion of the Holocaust, see Leni Yahil, *The Holocaust: The Fate of European Jewry* (Oxford University Press, 1990).

63. Stephen C. LeSuer, *The 1838 Mormon War in Missouri* (University of Missouri Press, 1987), pp. 151–53.

64. John Conway, "An Adapted Organic Tradition," *Daedalus* 117 (Fall 1988), p. 382. For an extended comparison of the impact of religion on politics in the United States and Canada, see Seymour Martin Lipset, *Continental Divide: The Values and Institutions of the United States and Canada* (Routledge, 1990), pp. 74–89.

65. Robert N. Bellah, *Beyond Belief: Essays on Religion in a Post-Traditional World* (University of California Press, 1991), pp. 168–90.

66. National Opinion Research Center, General Social Survey, 1972–94.

67. William H. Flanigan and Nancy H. Zingale, *Political Behavior of the American Electorate*, 9th ed. (Congressional Quarterly Press, 1998), p. 118.

68. *Statistical Abstract, 1997*, p. 69.

69. www.cnn.com/ELECTION/2000/results.

70. Ibid.

71. Lyman A. Kellstedt and John C. Green, "Is There a Culture War: Religion and the 1996 Election," paper presented at the American Political Science Association Annual Meeting, Washington, D.C., 1997, at www.wheaton.edu\polsci\kellstedt.

72. Telephone survey of 113,000 households in the 48 contiguous states, April 1989–April 1990, Graduate School of the City University of New York.

73. Organization for Economic Cooperation and Development (OECD), *National Accounts*, vol. 1, *Main Aggregates, 1960–89* (OECD, 1991), p. 145.

74. Raymond E. Wolfinger, Fred I. Greenstein, and Martin Shapiro, *Dynamics of American Politics*, 2d ed. (Prentice Hall, 1980), p. 19.

75. Thomas Jefferson, "Autobiography," in *The Life and Selected Writings of Thomas Jefferson*, ed. Adrienne Koch and William Peden (Modern Library, 1944), p. 38.

76. U.S. Department of Education, *Digest of Education Statistics, 1997* (Government Printing Office, 1997), p. 324.

77. Harold W. Stanley and Richard G. Niemi, *Vital Statistics on American Politics 1999–2000* (Congressional Quarterly Press, 2000), p. 115.

78. Stanley Fischer, "Symposium on the Slowdown in Productivity Growth," *Journal of Economic Perspectives* 2 (Fall 1988), pp. 3–7.

79. U.S. Bureau of the Census: www.census.gov/hhes/poverty/threshld/thresh99.html.

80. *Statistical Abstract, 1999*, p. 486.

81. Ibid., p. 487.

82. W. Michael Cox and Richard Alm, "Why Decry the Wealth Gap?" *The New York Times*, January 24, 2000, p. A24.

83. U.S. Bureau of the Census: www.census.gov/hhes/income/incineq/p60tb3.html.

84. *Statistical Abstract, 1999*, p. 459. "Real" means that inflation has already been taken into account.

85. Daniel Bell, *The Coming of Post-Industrial Society: A Venture in Social Forecasting* (Basic Books, 1973), p. xviii.

86. *Statistical Abstract, 1999*, pp. 424–34.

87. Ibid., p. 460.

88. Ibid., p. 428.

89. Mattei Dogan and Dominique Pelassy, *How to Compare Nations: Strategies in Comparative Politics*, 2d ed. (Chatham House, 1990), p. 47.

90. Responses for subjective social class vary somewhat with wording of the question. The data on Great Britain are from the *Index to International Public Opinion, 1991–92* (Greenwood Press, 1992), p. 462.

91. Lipset, *Continental Divide*, p. 170.

92. www.bls.gov/csx/1999/Aggregate/age.pdf.

93. *Statistical Abstract, 1999*, p. 484.

94. U.S. Bureau of the Census: www.census.gov/population/socdemo/voting/history/vot23/txt, May 1998.

95. www.cnn.com/election/2000/results/index.epolls.html.

96. Seymour Martin Lipset, *Political Man* (Doubleday, 1963), pp. 283–86.

97. Thomas Jefferson to P. S. du Pont de Nemours, April 24, 1816, *The Writings of Thomas Jefferson*, ed. Paul L. Ford (G. P. Putnam's Sons, 1899), 10:25.

98. *Statistical Abstract, 1999*, p. 163.

99. Ibid., p. 170.

100. Ibid., p. 169.

101. Herbert McClosky and John Zaller, *The American Ethos: Public Attitudes Toward Capitalism and Democracy* (Harvard University Press, 1984), p. 261.

102. John Gunther, *Inside U.S.A.* (Harper & Brothers, 1947), p. 911.

103. Carl N. Degler, *Out of Our Past: The Forces That Shaped Modern America*, 3d ed. (Harper & Row, 1984), p. 322.

CHAPTER 6

1. Richard M. Stevenson, "The 2000 Campaign: The Tactics—Wealthy Texan Bought Anti McCain Ads," *The New York Times*, March 4, 2000, p. A1.

2. David Rogers, "Lobbyist Funded Mailing That Hurt McCain Campaign," *The Wall Street Journal*, July 11, 2000, p. A28.

3. See David B. Magleby, "Getting Inside the Outside Campaign: Issue Advocacy in the 2000 Presidential Primaries," report released at the National Press Club, Washington, D.C., July 17, 2000, www.byu.edu/outsidemoney.

4. James Parks, "COPE Endorsements, 1968–1992," AFL-CIO, Department of Information, personal communication, January 6, 1994.

5. U.S. Bureau of the Census, *Statistical Abstract of the United States, 1997* (Government Printing Office, 1997), pp. 398, 400.

6. James MacGregor Burns and Stewart Burns, *A People's Charter: The Pursuit of Rights in America* (Knopf, 1991).

7. William R. Donohue, *The Politics of the American Civil Liberties Union* (Transaction, 1985).

8. See NEA home page: www.nea.org/index.html.

9. Robert Salisbury, "Interest Representation: The Dominance of Institutions," *American Political Science Review* 78 (March 1984), p. 66.

10. V. O. Key, Jr., *Public Opinion and American Democracy* (Knopf, 1961), pp. 504–507.

11. R. Kenneth Godwin, *One Billion Dollars of Influence: The Direct Marketing of Politics* (Chatham House, 1988).

12. Lucius J. Barker, "Third Parties in Litigation: A Systemic View of the Judicial Function," *Journal of Politics* 29 (February 1967), pp. 41–69; Jethro K. Lieberman, *Litigious Society*, rev. ed. (Basic Books, 1983).

13. Gregory A. Calderia and John R. Wright, "Organized Interests and Agenda Setting in the U.S. Supreme Court," *American Political Science Review* 82 (December 1988), pp. 1109–27. See also Gregory A. Calderia and John R. Wright, "Amici Curiae before the Supreme Court: Who Participates, When, and How Much?" *Journal of Politics* 52 (August 1990), pp. 782–806.

14. Karen O'Connor, *Women's Organizations' Use of the Courts* (Lexington Books, 1980).

15. Steven Preston Brown, "Restoring Faith: The New Christian Right, Religious Liberty and the Courts" (University of Virginia, May 1998), Ph.D. diss.

16. Lee Epstein and C. K. Rowland, "Debunking the Myth of Interest Group Invincibility in the Courts," *American Political Science Review* 85 (March 1991), pp. 205–17.

17. For a discussion of the 1998 New Mexico race, see Lonna Rae Atkeson and Anthony C. Coveny, "The 1998 New Mexico Third Congressional District Race," in David B. Magleby, ed., *Outside Money: Soft Money and Issue Advocacy in the 1998 Congressional Elections* (Rowman & Littlefield, 2000), pp. 135–52.

18. Ethan Bronner, *Battle for Justice: How the Bork Nomination Shook America* (Norton, 1989), pp. 50–55.

19. David Mayhew, *Congress: The Electoral Connection* (Yale University Press, 1974), p. 45.

20. John R. Wright, "Contributions, Lobbying, and Committee Voting in the U.S. House of Representatives," *American Political Science Review* 84 (June 1990), pp. 417–38.

21. For evidence of the impact of PAC expenditures on legislative committee behavior and legislative involvement generally, see Richard L. Hall and Frank W. Wayman, "Buying Time: Moneyed Interests and the Mobilization of Bias in Congressional Committees," *American Political Science Review* 84 (September 1990), pp. 797–820.

22. Edwin M. Epstein, "Business and Labor Under the Federal Election Campaign Act of 1971," in Michael J. Malbin, ed., *Parties, Interest Groups, and Campaign Finance Laws* (American Enterprise Institute for Public Policy Research, 1980), p. 112. See also Gary Jacobson, *Money in Congressional Elections* (Yale University Press, 1980).

23. Senator Charles C. Mathias, statement in *The New York Times*, February 27, 1986, p. A31.

24. Brody Mullins and Charlie Mitchell, "Soft Money Unleashed," *National Journal*, February 7, 2001, pp. 500–501.

25. Amy Dockster, "Nice PAC You've Got Here . . . A Pity If Anything Should Happen to It: How Politicians Shake Down the Special Interests," *Washington Monthly*, January 27, 1987, p. 24, quoted in Margaret Cates Nugent and John R. Johannes, eds., *Money, Elections, and Democracy: Reforming Congressional Campaign Finance* (Westview Press, 1990), p. 1.

26. Hall and Wayman, "Buying Time," pp. 797–820. A different study of the House Ways and Means Committee found campaign contributions to be part of the representatives' policy decisions, but even more important was the number of lobbying contacts. See Wright, "Contributions, Lobbying, and Committee Voting," pp. 417–38.

27. Ronald Reagan, "Remarks to Administration Officials on Domestic Policy," December 13, 1988, *Weekly Compilation of Presidential Documents*, vol. 24 (December 1988), pp. 1615–20.

28. Sylvia Tesh, "In Support of Single-Interest Politics," *Political Science Quarterly* 99 (Spring 1984), pp. 27–44.

29. Report and Recommendations of the California Commission on Campaign Financing, *The New Gold Rush: Financing California's Legislative Campaigns* (Center for Responsive Government, 1985), pp. 177–97. For a study of state lobby regulation, see Cynthia Opheim, "Explaining the Differences in State Lobby Regulation," *Western Political Quarterly* 44 (June 1991), pp. 405–21.

30. Adam Clymer, "Congress Sends Lobbying Overhaul to Clinton," *The New York Times*, December 16, 1995, sec. 1, p. 36.

31. David B. Magleby and Candice J. Nelson, *The Money Chase: Congressional Campaign Finance Reform* (Brookings Institution, 1990), pp. 72–97.

32. Factors that predict the formation of PACs include company size and the degree of regulation for corporations. See Craig Humphries, "Corporations, PACs and the Strategic Link Between Contributions and Lobbying Activities," *Western Political Quarterly* 44 (June 1991), pp. 353–72.

33. Harold W. Stanley and Richard G. Niemi, *Vital Statistics on American Politics* (Congressional Quarterly Press, 2000), p. 100.

34. ftp.fec.gov/fed.

35. Greg Hitt, "Democrats Move Ahead in Soft-Money Race," *The Wall Street Journal*, August 17, 2000, p. A24.

36. www.opensecrets.org/industries/indus.asp?Ind+H04.

37. Marianne Holt, "Stealth PAC's Revealed: Interest Group Profiles." Press release from the Center for Public Integrity, February 5, 2001.

38. David B. Magleby, ed., *Election Advocacy: Soft Money and Issue Advocacy in the 2000 Congressional Elections* (Center for the Study of Elections and Democracy, 2001) at www.byu.edu/outsidemoney.

CHAPTER 7

1. John E. Mueller, "Choosing Among 133 Candidates," *Public Opinion Quarterly* 34 (Fall 1970), pp. 395–402.

2. E. E. Schattschneider, *Party Government* (Holt, Rinehart and Winston, 1942), p. 1.

3. See Scott Mainwaring, "Party Systems in the Third Wave," *Journal of Democracy* (July 1998), pp. 67–81.

4. Joseph A. Schlesinger, *Political Parties and the Winning of Office* (University of Michigan Press, 1994).

5. Lizette Alvarez, "Senate to Divide Power and Money Equally in Panels," *The New York Times*, January 6, 2001, p. A1.

6. See David B. Magleby, ed., *Outside Money: Soft Money and Issue Advocacy in the 1998 Congressional Elections* (Rowman & Littlefield, 2000).

7. Nick Anderson and Jonathan Peterson, "China Trade Vote: House OK's China Trade Bill," *Los Angeles Times*, May 25, 2000, p. A1.

8. David W. Brady and Craig Volden, *Revolving Gridlock: Politics and Policy from Carter to Clinton* (Westview Press, 1998); James A. Thurber, ed., *Divided Democracy: Cooperation and Conflict Between the President and Congress* (CQ Press, 1991); James A. Thurber, ed., *Rivals for Power: Presidential-Congressional Relations* (CQ Press, 1996); Charles O. Jones, *Separate But Equal Branches: Congress and the Presidency* (Chatham House, 1995), chaps. 5, 6; Jon R. Bond and Richard Fleisher, *The President in the Legislative Arena* (University of Chicago Press, 1990).

9. *California Democratic Party et al. v Jones*, 120 S.Ct. 2402 (2000).

10. Arthur Sanders and David Redlawsk, "Money and the Iowa Caucuses," in *Getting Inside the Outside Campaign*, ed. David Magleby (Center for the Study of Elections and Democracy, 2000), pp. 20–29.

11. *The Book of the States, 1998–1999* (Council of State Governments, 1998), pp. 159–60.

12. www.cnn.com/ELECTIONS/2000/results, November 27, 2000.

13. William H. Riker, "The Two-Party System and Duverger's Law: An Essay on the History of Political Science," *American Political Science Review* 76 (December 1982), pp. 753–66. For a classic analysis, see Schattschneider, *Party Government*.

14. See Paul S. Herrnson and John C. Green, eds., *Multiparty Politics in America* (Rowman and Littlefield, 1997); J. David Gillespie, *Politics at the Periphery: Third Parties in Two-Party America* (University of South Carolina Press, 1993).

15. Steven J. Rosenstone, Roy L. Behr, and Edward H. Lazarus, *Third Parties in America: Citizen Response to Major Party Failure*, 2d ed. (Princeton University Press, 1996). See also Xandra Kayden and Eddie Mahe, Jr., *The Party Goes On: The Persistence of the Two Party System in the United States* (Basic Books, 1985), pp. 143–44.

16. On the impact of third parties, see Howard R. Penniman, "Presidential Third Parties and the Modern American Two-Party System," in William J. Crotty, ed., *The Party Symbol* (W. H. Freeman, 1980), pp. 101–17. See also Frank Smallwood, *The Other Candidates: Third Parties in Presidential Elections* (University Press of New England, 1983).

17. Benjamin Franklin, George Washington, and Thomas Jefferson, quoted in Richard Hofstadter, *The Idea of a Party System* (University of California Press, 1969), pp. 2, 123.

18. For concise histories of the two parties, see two studies by Robert A. Rutland, *The Democrats: From Jefferson to Clinton* (University of Missouri Press, 1996), and *The Republicans: From Lincoln to Bush* (University of Missouri Press, 1996).

19. See V. O. Key, "A Theory of Critical Elections," *Journal of Politics* 17 (February 1955), pp. 3–18; Walter Dean Burnham, *Critical Elections and the Mainsprings of American Politics* (Norton, 1970), pp. 1–10; and E. E. Schattschneider, *The Semisovereign People: A Realist's View of Democracy in America* (Holt, Rinehart and Winston, 1975), pp. 78–80.

20. William E. Gienapp, *The Origins of the Republican Party, 1852–1856* (Oxford University Press, 1987).

21. David W. Brady, "Elections, Congress and Public Policy Changes: 1886–1960," in Bruce A. Campbell and Richard Trilling, eds., *Realignment in American Politics: Toward a Theory* (Texas University Press, 1980), p. 188.

22. Gerald Pomper, "Classification of Presidential Elections," *Journal of Politics* 29 (1967), p. 538.

23. www.cnn.com/ELECTION/2000/results/index.epolls.htm.

24. Federal Election Commission, "15-Month Summary on Political Party Finances," June 8, 1998 (www.fec.gov/press/pty1598.htm).

25. Paul Allen Beck, *Party Politics in America*, 8th ed. (Longman, 1997), chap. 2.

26. See L. Sandy Maisel, *From Obscurity to Oblivion: Running in the Congressional Primary*, rev. ed. (University of Tennessee Press, 1986).

27. The early Republican efforts and advantages over the Democrats are well documented in Thomas B. Edsall, *The New Politics of Inequality* (Norton, 1984); Gary C. Jacobson, "The Republican Advantage in Campaign Finances," in John E. Chubb and Paul E. Peterson, eds., *New Direction in American Politics* (Washington, D.C.: Brookings Institution, 1985), p. 6.

28. John F. Bibby, *Politics, Parties, and Elections in America*, 3d ed. (Nelson-Hall, 1996). For further data on these roles, see Cornelius P. Cotter, James L. Gibson, John F. Bibby, and Robert J. Huckshorn, *Party Organizations in American Politics* (Praeger, 1984).

29. See James L. Gibson, Cornelius P. Cotter, John F. Bibby, and Robert J. Huckshorn, "Assessing Party Organizational Strength," *American Journal of Political Science* 27 (May 1983), pp. 193–222; Cotter et al., *Party Organizations in American Politics*.

30. Paul S. Herrnson, *Party Campaigning in the 1980s: Have the National Parties Made a Comeback as Key Players in Congressional Elections?* (Harvard University Press, 1988), p. 122.

31. Jonathan S. Krasno and Daniel E. Seltz, *Buying Time: Television Advertising in the 1998 Congressional Elections*, report of a grant funded by the Pew Charitable Trusts (1998).

32. On the influence of local parties, see Kayden and Mahe, *Party Goes On*. See also John C. Green and Daniel M. Shea, eds., *The State of the Parties: The Changing Role of Contemporary Parties*, 2d ed. (Rowman and Littlefield, 1996), which presents their recent case studies of parties at the local level.

33. Bob Nash, director, White House Office of Personnel, interview with David Magleby, October 26, 1998. A listing of many of these positions is presented in *Policy and Supporting Positions* (Government Printing Office, November 9, 1988). For a general discussion of this topic, see G. Calvin Mackenzie, "Partisan Presidential Leadership: The President's Appointees," in Maisel, ed., *Parties Respond* pp. 316–37.

34. *Marbury v Madison* I Cranch 137 (1803).

35. See Angus Campbell, Philip E. Converse, Warren E. Miller, and Donald E. Stokes, *The American Voter* (Wiley, 1960); Norman A. Nie, Sidney Verba, and John R. Petrocik, *The Changing American Voter*, enlarged ed. (Harvard University Press, 1979); Warren E. Miller and J. Merrill Shanks, *The New American Voter* (Harvard University Press, 1996).

36. "At the Races: A Weekly Review of Campaign 2000," *National Journal* 39 (September 2000), p. 2991.

37. Campbell et al., *American Voter*, pp. 121–28.

38. Keith et al., *Myth of the Independent Voter*.

39. See Byron E. Shafer, *The End of Realignment: Interpreting American Electoral Eras* (University of Wisconsin Press, 1991).

40. Hedrick Smith, *The Power Game: How Washington Works* (Random House, 1988), p. 671.

41. Nine percent of all voters were Pure Independents in 1956 and 1960. Keith et al., *Myth of the Independent Voter*, p. 51. In 1992 the same percent were Pure Independents. *1992 American National Election Study*, Center for Political Studies, University of Michigan.

42. For the "optimistic view," see Ralph M. Goldman, *Search for Consensus: The Story of the Democratic Party* (Temple University Press, 1979), pp. 366–73; Kayden and Mahe, *Party Goes On*; Larry Sabato, *The Party's Just Begun: Shaping Political Parties in America's Future* (Scott, Foresman, 1988); Joseph A. Schlesinger, "The New American Political Party," *American Political Science Review* 79 (December 1985), pp. 1152–69; David E. Price, *Bringing Back the Parties* (Congressional Quarterly Press, 1984).

43. "Party Unity Background," *Congressional Quarterly Weekly Report* 57 (December 1999), p. 2993.

44. Ibid.

45. Barbara Sinclair, "Evolution or Revolution?" in *Parties Respond*, ed. Maisel, pp. 263–85.

46. Herrnson, *Party Campaigning in the 1980s*, pp. 80–81.

CHAPTER 8

1. David B. Magleby, ed., *Election Advocacy: Soft Money and Issue Advocacy in the 2000 Congressional Elections* (Brigham Young University, Center for the Study of Elections and Democracy, 2001), monograph presented at the National Press Club, Washington, D.C., February 5, 2000, available at www.byu.edu/outsidemoney/2000general.

2. See Todd Donovan, "Campaign Spending and Activity in the 2000 Washington 2nd Congressional District Race," in David B. Magleby, ed., *Election Advocacy*, pp. 261–76. See also Drew Linzer and David Menefee-Libey, "Campaign Spending and Activity in the 2000 California Twenty-Seventh Congressional District Race," in ibid., pp. 132–47.

3. www.gallup.com/poll/releases/pr001107.asp.

4. www.cnn.com/ELECTION/2000/results/index.html.

5. Robert Coles, *The Moral Life of Children* (Atlantic Monthly Press, 1986); Robert Coles, *The Political Life of Children* (Atlantic Monthly Press, 1986).

6. Coles, *Political Life of Children*, pp. 59–60.

7. Pamela Johnston Conover, "The Influence of Group Identifications on Political Perception and Evaluation," *Journal of Politics* 46 (August 1984), pp. 760–85; Henry E. Brady and Paul M. Sniderman, "Attitude Attribution: A Group Basis for Political Reasoning," *American Political Science Review* 79 (December 1985), pp. 1061–78.

8. Shawn W. Rosenberg, "Sociology, Psychology, and the Study of Political Behavior: The Case of the Research on Political Socialization," *Journal of Politics* 47 (May 1985), pp. 715–31.

9. Russell J. Dalton, "Reassessing Parental Socialization: Indicator Unreliability Versus Generational Transfer," *American Political Science Review* 74 (June 1980), pp. 421–31.

10. Suzanne Koprince Sebert, M. Kent Jennings, and Richard G. Niemi, "The Political Texture of Peer Groups," in M. Kent Jennings and Richard G. Niemi, *The Political Character of Adolescence* (Princeton University Press, 1974), p. 246.

11. Edgar Litt, "Civic Education Norms and Political Indoctrination," *American Sociological Review* 28 (February 1963), pp. 69–75. See also Elizabeth Leonie Simpson, *Democracy's Stepchildren* (Jossey-Bass, 1971); Jennings and Niemi, *Political Character of Adolescence*; Stanley Allen Renshon,

"Personality and Family Dynamics in the Political Socialization Process," *American Journal of Political Science* 19 (February 1975), pp. 63–80; Frances Fitzgerald, *America Revised* (Atlantic–Little, Brown, 1979).

12. Kenneth Feldman and Theodore M. Newcomb, *The Impact of College on Students*, vol. 2 (Jossey-Bass, 1969), pp. 16–24, 49–56.

13. Everett C. Ladd and John Benson, "The Growth of News Polls in American Politics," in Thomas Mann and Gary Orren, eds., *Media Polls in American Politics* (Washington, D.C.: Brookings Institution, 1992), pp. 19–31.

14. Benjamin I. Page and Robert Y. Shapiro, *The Rational Public: Fifty Years of Trends in Americans' Policy Preferences* (University of Chicago Press, 1992), p. 237.

15. George J. Church, "What in the World Are We Doing?" *Time*, October 18, 1993, p. 42.

16. David Mayhew, *Congress: The Electoral Connection* (Yale University Press, 1974); Richard F. Fenno, Jr., *Home Style: House Members in Their Districts* (Little, Brown, 1978).

17. Robert S. Erikson and Kent L. Tedin, *American Public Opinion: Its Origins, Content and Impact*, 5th ed. (Allyn and Bacon, 1995), p. 279.

18. Thomas E. Mann and Raymond E. Wolfinger, "Candidates and Parties in Congressional Elections," *American Political Science Review* 74 (September 1980), pp. 617–40.

19. Erikson and Tedin, *American Public Opinion*, p. 304.

20. Neil S. Newhouse and Christine L. Matthews, "NAFTA Revisited: Most Americans Just Weren't Deeply Engaged," *Public Perspective* 5 (January/February 1994), pp. 31–32.

21. Center for Political Studies, *American National Election Studies, 1960–90* (University of Michigan, 1990).

22. www.umich.edu/~nes/nesguide/gd-index.htm and interview by Christopher Rees with Ian Stirton, Federal Election Commission Clearinghouse on Election Administration, March 5, 2001.

23. Frank R. Parker, *Black Votes Count: Political Empowerment in Mississippi After 1965* (University of North Carolina Press, 1990), p. 3.

24. Bernard Grofman and Lisa Handley, "The Impact of the Voting Rights Act on Black Representation in Southern State Legislatures," *Legislative Studies Quarterly* 16 (February 1991), pp. 111–28.

25. G. Bingham Powell, Jr., "American Voter Turnout in Comparative Perspective," *American Political Science Review* 80 (March 1986), p. 38.

26. Raymond E. Wolfinger and Steven J. Rosenstone, "The Effect of Registration Laws on Voter Turnout," *American Political Science Review* 72 (March 1978), p. 24.

27. Raymond E. Wolfinger and Steven J. Rosenstone, *Who Votes?* (Yale University Press, 1980), pp. 78, 88.

28. www.fec.gov/votregis/nvrasum.htm. See also www.essential.org/human_serve.html.

29. See Raymond E. Wolfinger and Ben Highton, "Estimating the Effects of the National Voter Registration Act of 1993," *Political Behavior* (June 1998), pp. 79–104; Raymond E. Wolfinger and Jonathan Hoffman, "Registering and Voting with Motor Voter," *PS: Political Science and Politics* (March 2001), pp. 85–92.

30. "Voter Turnout Drops in 1998 Primaries," *The New York Times*, June 30, 1998, p. A18.

31. For a discussion of the differences in the turnout between presidential and midterm elections, see James E. Campbell, "The Presidential Surge and Its Midterm Decline in Congressional Elections, 1868–1988," *Journal of Politics* 53 (May 1991), pp. 477–87.

32. David E. Rosenbaum, "Democrats Keep Solid Hold on Congress," *The New York Times*, November 9, 1988, p. A24; Louis V. Gerstner, "Next Time, Let Us Boldly Vote As No Democracy Has Before," *USA Today*, November 16, 1998, p. A15; for 2000, see www.cnn.com/2000/ALLPOLITICS/stories/12/19/election.turnout.ap.

33. Paula Ries and Anne J. Stone, eds., *The American Women, 1992–93: A Status Report* (Women's Research and Education Institute, 1992), p. 415.

34. Congressional Research Service, "Voter Turnout in the Presidential Election of 1992: The States," January 26, 1993, pp. 4–5. See also Powell, "American Voter Turnout," pp. 17–43.

35. Wolfinger and Rosenstone, *Who Votes?* p. 102.

36. Howard W. Stanley and Richard G. Niemi, *Vital Statistics on Politics, 1999–2000* (Congressional Quarterly Press, 2000), pp. 120–21; and www.cnn.com/ELECTION/2000/results/index.my.html.

37. See Angus Campbell, Philip E. Converse, Warren E. Miller, and Donald E. Stokes, *The American Voter* (Wiley, 1960). This volume is a foundation of modern voting analysis despite much new evidence and reinterpretation. See also Norman H. Nie, Sidney Verba, and John R. Petrocik, *The Changing American Voter* (Harvard University Press, 1976); Ruy A. Teixeira, *Why Americans Don't Vote: Turnout Decline in the United States, 1960–1984* (Greenwood, 1987).

38. David E. Rosenbaum, "Democrats Keep Solid Hold in Congress," *The New York Times*, November 9, 1988, p. A24.

39. Austin Ranney, "Nonvoting Is Not a Social Disease," *Public Opinion*, October/November 1983, pp. 16–19.

40. Thomas Byrne Edsall, *The New Politics of Inequality* (W. W. Norton, 1984), p. 181.

41. Frances Fox Piven and Richard A. Cloward, "Prospects for Voter Registration Reform: A Report on the Experiences of the Human SERVE Campaign," *PS: Political Science and Politics* 18 (Summer 1985), pp. 582–92.

42. Wolfinger and Rosenstone, *Who Votes?* p. 109.

43. E. E. Schattschneider, *The Semisovereign People* (Dryden Press, 1975), p. 96.

44. Stephen Earl Bennett and David Resnick, "The Implications of Nonvoting for Democracy in the United States," *American Journal of Political Science* 84 (August 1990), pp. 771–802.

45. Bruce E. Keith, David B. Magleby, Candice J. Nelson, Elizabeth Orr, Mark C. Westlye, and Raymond E. Wolfinger, *The Myth of the Independent Voter* (University of California Press, 1992), pp. 60–75; 2001 American National Election Study, Center for Political Studies, University of Michigan, Ann Arbor.

46. Martin P. Wattenberg, *The Rise of Candidate Centered Politics: Presidential Elections of the 1980s* (Harvard University Press, 1991), p. 1.

47. Barry Goldwater, quoted in Theodore H. White, *The Making of the President, 1964* (Athenaeum Publishers, 1965), p. 217.

48. William H. Flanigan and Nancy H. Zingale, *Political Behavior of the American Electorate*, 8th ed. (Congressional Quarterly Press, 1994), p. 173.

49. Kevin Sack, "The 2000 Campaign: The Democrats; Gore Surrogates Bluntly Question Bush's Competence," *The New York Times*, October 20, 2000, p. A27.

50. See Alton Mitchell, "The 2000 Campaign: The Credibility Issue; A Sustained G.O.P. Push to Mock Gore's Image," *The New York Times*, October 15, 2000, pp. 1–28; Melinda Henneberger, "The 2000 Campaign: The Gun Lobby; Rallying Voters and Relishing a Leading Role," *The New York Times*, November 3, 2000, p. A25.

51. www.cnn.com/ELECTION/2000/results/index.epolls.html.

52. J. Merrill Shanks and Warren E. Miller, "Policy Direction and Performance Evaluation: Complementary Explanations of the Reagan Elections," *British Journal of Political Science* 20 (1990), pp. 143–235; Warren E. Miller and J. Merrill Shanks, "Policy Direction and Performance Evaluation: Comparing George Bush's Victory with Those of Ronald Reagan in 1980 and 1984," paper presented at the American Political Science Association Annual Meeting, Atlanta, August 31–September 2, 1989.

53. Amihai Glazer, "The Strategy of Candidate Ambiguity," *American Political Science Review* 84 (March 1990), pp. 237–41.

54. Robert S. Erikson and David W. Romero, "Candidate Equilibrium and the Behavioral Model of the Vote," *American Political Science Review* 84 (December 1990), p. 1122.

55. Morris P. Fiorina, *Retrospective Voting in American National Elections* (Yale University Press, 1981).

56. www.cnn.com/ELECTION/2000/results/index.epolls.html.

57. Gerald H. Kramer, "Short-Term Fluctuations in U.S. Voting Behavior, 1896–1964," *American Political Science Review* 65 (March 1971), pp. 131–43. See also Edward R. Tufte, "Determinants of the Outcomes of Midterm Congressional Elections," *American Political Science Review* 69 (September 1975), pp. 812–26.

58. John R. Hibbing and John R. Alford, "The Educational Impact of Economic Conditions: Who Is Held Responsible?" *American Journal of Political Science* 25 (August 1981), pp. 423–39; Morris P. Fiorina, "Who Is Held Responsible? Further Evidence on the Hibbing-Alford Thesis," *American Journal of Political Science* (February 1983), pp. 158–64.

59. Robert M. Stein, "Economic Voting for Governor and U.S. Senator: The Electoral Consequences of Federalism," *Journal of Politics* 52 (February 1990), pp. 29–53.

CHAPTER 9

1. *1994 Census of Governments* (Government Printing Office, 1995), vol. 1, no. 2, p. 1.

2. Washington voters enacted term limits in 1992 after defeating them in 1991.

3. In the 1992 and 1994 National Election Studies, 77–78 percent of Americans favored term limits. Center for Political Studies, University of Michigan.

4. *U.S. Term Limits Inc. v Thornton*, 514 U. S. 799 (1995).

5. For an insightful examination of electoral rules, see Bernard Grofman and Arend Lijphart, eds., *Electoral Laws and Their Political Consequences* (Agathon Press, 1986).

6. Arend Lijphart, "The Political Consequences of Electoral Laws, 1945–85," *American Political Science Review* 84 (June 1990), pp. 481–95.

7. One of Al Gore's electors abstained, reducing his vote from 267 to 266. www.cnn.com/2001/ALLPOLITICS/stories/01/06/electoral.vote/index.html.

8. Dany M. Adkison and Christopher Elliott, "The Electoral College: A Misunderstood Institution," *PS: Political Science and Politics* 30 (March 1997), pp. 77–80.

9. George Rabinowitz and Stuart Elaine MacDonald, "The Power of the States in U.S. Presidential Elections," *American Political Science Review* 80 (March 1986), pp. 65–87.

10. See, as examples, David Mayhew, *Congress: The Electoral Connection* (Yale University Press, 1974); Richard F. Fenno, Jr., *Home Style: House Members in Their Districts* (Little, Brown, 1978); James E. Campbell, "The Return of Incumbents: The Nature of Incumbency Advantage," *Western Political Quarterly* 36 (September 1983), pp. 434–44.

11. Gary King and Andrew Gelman, "Systemic Consequences of Incumbency Advantage in U.S. House Elections," *American Journal of Political Science* 35 (February 1991), pp. 110–37.

12. See Gary C. Jacobson, *The Politics of Congressional Elections*, 4th ed. (Longman, 1997), chap. 6; Alan I. Abramowitz, "Economic Conditions, Presidential Popularity, and Voting Behavior in Midterm Congressional Elections," *Journal of Politics* (February 1985), p. 130.

13. See Edward R. Tufte, *Political Control of the Economy* (Princeton University Press, 1978); see also his "Determinants of the Outcomes of Midterm Congressional Elections," *American Political Science Review* 69 (1975), pp. 812–26. For a more recent discussion of the same subject, see Jacobson, *Politics of Congressional Elections*, pp. 123–78.

14. Alan I. Abramowitz and Jeffrey A. Segal, "Determinants of the Outcomes of U.S. Senate Elections," *Journal of Politics* 48 (1986), pp. 433–39.

15. This includes the postelection switch of Alabama Senator Richard Shelby to the Republican party.

16. Linda L. Fowler and Robert D. McClure, *Political Ambition: Who Decides to Run for Congress* (Yale University Press, 1989); David T. Canon, "Political Conditions and Experienced Challengers in Congressional Elections, 1972–1984," paper presented at the American Political Science Association Annual Meeting, New Orleans, August 29–September 1, 1985.

17. Keith Krehbiel and John R. Wright, "The Incumbency Effect in Congressional Elections: A Test of Two Explanations," *American Journal of Political Science* 27 (February 1983), p. 140.

18. Roll Call, "Roll Call Casualty List," *Roll Call Politics*, November 5, 1998, p. 15; "Senate, House, Gubernatorial Results," *Congressional Quarterly Weekly Report*, November 11, 2000, pp. 2694–2703.

19. "Financial Activity of Senate and House General Election Campaigns," Federal Election Commission: ftp.fec.gov/fec.

20. D. Cover, "One Good Term Deserves Another: The Advantages of Incumbency in Congressional Elections," *American Journal of Political Science* 21 (August 1977), pp. 523–42; Morris P. Fiorina, *Congress: Keystone of the Washington Establishment* (Yale University Press, 1978); Mayhew, *Congress*, pp. 52–53.

21. Mayhew, *Congress*, p. 61; Richard F. Fenno, Jr., *Congressmen in Committees* (Little, Brown, 1973); Steven S. Smith and Christopher J. Deering, *Committees in Congress*, 3d ed. (Congressional Quarterly Press, 1997).

22. Candice J. Nelson, "Campaign Finance in Presidential and Congressional Elections," *Political Science Teacher* (Summer 1988), p. 6.

23. Jonathan S. Krasno, *Challengers, Competition, and Reelection: Comparing Senate and House Elections* (Yale University Press, 1994).

24. Alan I. Abramowitz, "Explaining Senate Election Outcomes," *American Political Science Review* 82 (June 1988), pp. 385–403.

25. David B. Magleby, "More Bang for the Buck: Campaign Spending in Small State U.S. Senate Elections," paper presented at the Western Political Science Association Annual Meeting, Salt Lake City, March 30–April 1, 1989.

26. The Green Papers, "2000 Primary and Caucus Results," at www.thegreenpapers.com/PCC/Tabul.html.

27. Paul T. David and James W. Caesar, *Proportional Representation in Presidential Nominating Politics* (University Press of Virginia, 1980).

28. For a discussion of the 1996 primary rules, see Rhodes Cook, "GOP's Rules Favor Dole, If He Doesn't Stumble," *Congressional Quarterly Weekly Report*, January 27, 1996, pp. 228–31.

29. The descriptions of these types of primaries are drawn from James W. Davis, *Presidential Primaries*, rev. ed. (Greenwood Press, 1984), chap. 3. See pp. 56–63 for specifics on each state (and Puerto Rico). This material is used with the permission of the publisher.

30. *The Book of the States, 2000–2001* (Council of State Governments, 2000), pp. 164–65.

31. David B. Magleby, *Getting Inside the Outside Campaign: Issue Advocacy in the 2000 Presidential Primaries* (Center for the Study of Elections and Democracy, Brigham Young University, 2000).

32. The viewership of conventions has declined as the amount of time devoted to conventions dropped. In 1988, Democrats averaged 27.1 million viewers and Republicans 24.5 million. By 1996 viewership for the Democrats was 18 million viewers on average and Republicans averaged 16.6 million viewers. See John Carmody, "The TV Column," *The Washington Post*, September 2, 1996, p. D4. In 2000, Democrats only averaged 20.6 million viewers and Republicans 19.2 million. See Don Aucoin, "Democrats Hold TV Ratings Edge," *The Boston Globe*, August 19, 2000, p. F3.

33. Stephen J. Wayne, *The Road to the White House, 2000: The Politics of Presidential Elections* (St. Martin's Press, 2000), chap. 5.

34. Jeff Fishel, *Presidents and Promises* (Congressional Quarterly Press, 1984).

35. CNN, "Burden of Proof," August 9, 2000.

36. www.ballot_access.org/2000/status.html.

37. Jules Witcover uses the image of a marathon to describe the 1976 presidential campaign in *Marathon: The Pursuit of the Presidency, 1972–1976* (Viking, 1977).

38. Sidney Kraus, *The Great Debates: Kennedy vs Nixon, 1960* (Indiana University Press, 1962). See also Myles Martel, *Political Campaign Debates* (Longman, 1983).

39. Tom Shales, "Round 1: Candidates with Their Hats, But Not Their Hearts, in the Ring," *The Washington Post*, October 4, 2000, p. C1.

40. www.debates.org/pages/history.html.

41. Robert S. Erikson, "Economic Conditions and the Presidential Vote," *American Political Science Review* 83 (June 1989), pp. 567–75. Class-based voting has also become more important. See Robert S. Erikson, Thomas O. Lancaster, and David W. Romers, "Group Components of the Presidential Vote, 1952–1984," *Journal of Politics* 51 (May 1989), pp. 337–46.

42. David B. Magleby, ed., *Election Advocacy: Soft Money and Issue Advocacy in the 2000 Congressional Elections* (Center for the Study of Elections and Democracy, Brigham Young University, 2001) www.byu.edu/outsidemoney/2000general.

43. David B. Magleby and Candice J. Nelson, *The Money Chase: Congressional Campaign Finance Reform* (Brookings Institution, 1990), pp. 13–14.

44. *Buckley v Valeo*, 424 US 1 (1976).

45. For a discussion of recent legislation, see Herbert E. Alexander and Monica Bauer, *Financing the 1988 Election* (Westview, 1991); Frank J. Sorauf, *Money in American Elections* (Scott, Foresman, 1988).

46. Including federal funding, Federal Election Commission reports show that George W. Bush raised just over $193 million. "2000 Presidential Race: Total Raised and Spent," Center for Responsive Politics, 2001, at www.opensecrets.org/2000elect/index/AllCands.htm, February 12, 2001.

47. Federal Election Commission, Public Disclosure Office, interview by author, January 9, 2001.

48. Beth Donovan, "Parties Turned Soft Money Law into Hard and Fast Spending," *Congressional Quarterly Weekly Report*, May 15, 1993, pp. 1196–97; David E. Rosenbaum, "In Political Money Game, the Year of Big Loopholes," *The New York Times*, December 26, 1996, p. A1 fecwebl.fec.gov/press/01120/partyfunds.htm.

49. See Joseph Pika, "Campaign Spending and Activity in the 2000 Delaware U.S. Senate Race," in Magleby, ed., *Election Advocacy*, pp. 51–61.

50. Ibid.

51. Ibid.

52. Ibid.

53. See David B. Magleby, *Dictum Without Data: The Myth of Issue Advocacy and Party Building* (Center for the Study of Elections and Democracy, Brigham Young University, 2000), available on the web at www.byu.edu/outsidemoney/dictum.

54. Rick Hampson, "Former Banker Was Big Spender," *USA Today*, November 9, 2000, p. A9.

55. Sorauf, *Money in American Elections*, pp. 64–65.

56. Federal Election Commission, "Congressional Financial Activity Soars for 2000," press release, January 9, 2001.

57. Federal Election Commission: ftp.fec.gov/fec.

58. See Robert Hunter, ed., *Electing the President: A Program for Reform, Final Report of the Commission on National Election* (Center for Strategic and International Studies, 1986); James L. Sundquist, *Constitutional Reform* (Brookings Institution, 1986); Edward N. Kearny, "Presidential Nominations and Representative Democracy: Proposals for Change," *Presidential Studies Quarterly* 14 (Summer 1984), pp. 348–56.

59. Barbara Norrander and Greg W. Smith, "Type of Contest, Candidate Strategy, and Turnout in Presidential Primaries," *American Politics Quarterly* 13 (January 1985), p. 28.

60. John G. Geer, "Voting in Presidential Primaries," paper presented at the American Political Science Association Annual Meeting, Washington, D.C., September 1984. See also Albert R. Hunt, "The Media and Presidential Campaigns," in A. James Reichley, ed., *Elections American Style* (Brookings Institution, 1987), pp. 52–74.

61. Ben White, "After Drama Left the Primaries, Voter Turnout Fell Dramatically," *The Washington Post*, September 1, 2000, p. A5.

62. George S. McGovern, "Considerations on Our Political Processes," *Presidential Studies Quarterly* 14 (Summer 1984), pp. 341–47.

63. Mark Sandalow, "Gore, Bush Sweep Six Southern Primaries–Nominations Cinched," *The San Francisco Chronicle*, March 15, 2000, p. A1.

64. *A National Agenda for the Eighties*, Report of the President's Commission for a National Agenda for the Eighties (Government Printing Office, 1980), p. 97, proposes holding only four presidential primaries, scheduled about one month apart.

65. Nelson Polsby, *Consequences of Party Reform* (Oxford University Press, 1983), p. 118.

66. Thomas E. Cronin and Robert Loevy, "The Case for a National Primary Convention Plan," *Public Opinion*, December 1982/January 1983, pp. 50–53.

67. Neal R. Peirce and Lawrence Longley, *The People's President: The Electoral College in American History and the Direct-Vote Alternative*, 2d ed. (Yale University Press, 1981), describes and advocates the direct-vote alternative. Nelson W. Polsby and Aaron B. Wildavsky, *Presidential Elections: Contemporary Strategies of American Politics*, 9th ed. (Chatham House, 1995), favors the present system.

CHAPTER 10

1. Howard Kurtz, "Errors Plagued Election Night Polling Service: VNS Report Also Faults Networks in Florida Blunder," *The Washington Post*, December 22, 2000, p. A1.

2. Marvin Kalb, "Financial Pressure Doomed Networks on Election Night," *Deseret News*, December 3, 2000, p. AA7.

3. www.cnn.com/2000/ALLPOLITICS/stories/11/16/tauzin.networks/index.htm.

4. Pew Research Center for the People and the Press, "Media Seen as Fair, But Tilting to Gore," press release, October 15, 2000.

5. Pew Research Center for the People and the Press, "Internet News Takes Off," press release, June 8, 1998, p. 1.

6. James Fallows, *Breaking the News: How the Media Undermine American Democracy* (Pantheon Books, 1996), p. 3.

7. Paul Starobin, "Heeding the Call," *National Journal*, November 30, 1996, pp. 2584–89.

8. William Rivers, *The Other Government* (Universe Books, 1982); Douglas Cater, *The Fourth Branch of Government* (Houghton Mifflin, 1959); Dom Bonafede, "The Washington Press: An Interpreter or a Participant in Policy Making?" *National Journal*, April 24, 1982, pp. 716–21; Michael Ledeen, "Learning to Say 'No' to the Press," *Public Interest* 73 (Fall 1983), p. 113.

9. Leslie G. Moeller, "The Big Four: Mass Media Actualities and Expectations," in *Beyond Media: New Approaches to Mass Communication*, ed. Richard W. Budd and Brent D. Ruben (Transaction Books, 1988), p. 15.

10. Andrew Kohut, "Internet Users Are on the Rise; But Public Affairs Interest Isn't," *Columbia Journalism Review*, January/February 2000, p. 68. One service that e-mails customized news and reminders to subscribers is infobeat.com.

11. U. S. Bureau of the Census, *Statistical Abstract of the United States, 1999* (Government Printing Office, 1999) Tables 910, 920.

12. David B. Magleby, "Direct Legislation in the American States," in David Butler and Austin Ranney, eds., *Referendums Around the World: The Growing Use of Direct Democracy* (AEI Press, 1994), pp. 218–57.

13. "Media and Evaluation," *The Gallup Organization 2000*, at www.gallup.com/poll/indicators/indmedia2.asp.

14. See Ray Hiebert, Donald Ungarait, and Thomas Bohn, *Mass Media VI* (Longman, 1991), chap. 11.

15. U. S. Bureau of the Census, *Statistical Abstract of the United States, 2000* (Government Printing Office, 2000) Table 932.

16. James Flanigan, "Newspapers Aren't Dying, They're Just Turning a Page," *Los Angeles Times*, March 19, 2000, p. C1.

17. Darrell West, *The Rise and Fall of the Media Establishment* (Bedford/St. Martin's Press, 2001).

18. Inktomi, press release, "Web Surpasses One Billion Documents," at www.inktomi.com/new/press/billion.html, January 18, 2000.

19. Kohut, "Internet Users Are on the Rise," p. 68.

20. J. Scott Orr, Newhouse News Service, "Internet Becomes New Source of Untapped Campaign Cash," *The Times-Picayune*, April 5, 2000, p. A10.

21. See Robert A. Rutland, *Newsmongers: Journalism in the Life of the Nation, 1690–1972* (Dial Press, 1973).

22. Quoted in Frank Luther Mott, *American Journalism*, 3d ed. (Macmillan, 1962), p. 412.

23. During the 1930s, more than one thousand speeches were made by members of Congress on one network alone. See Edward W. Chester, *Radio, Television and American Politics* (Sheed and Ward, 1969), p. 62.

24. Frances Perkins, quoted in James MacGregor Burns, *Roosevelt: The Lion and the Fox* (Harcourt Brace, 1956), p. 205.

25. www.gannett.com/map/gan/007.htm.

26. "California; Southland Focus; Tribune Gets Antitrust Approval in *Times* Deal," *The Los Angeles Times*, April 7, 2000, p. C2.

27. Stephanie Storm, "Mergers for Year Approach Record," *The New York Times*, October 31, 1996, p. A1.

28. Geraldine Fabrikant, "The Media Business," *The New York Times*, October 11, 1996, p. D2.

29. Saul Hansell, "Media Megadeal: The Overview," *The New York Times*, January 11, 2000, p. A1.

30. Ben H. Bagdikian, *The Media Monopoly* (Beacon Press, 1983).

31. See Doris A. Graber, *Mass Media and American Politics*, 5th ed. (Congressional Quarterly Press, 1997); Gina M. Garramone and Charles K. Atkin, "Mass Communication and Political Socialization: Specifying the Effects," *Public Opinion Quarterly* 50 (Spring 1986), pp. 76–86.

32. Shanto Iyengar and Donald R. Kinder, *News That Matters* (University of Chicago Press, 1987).

33. Steven J. Simmons, *The Fairness Doctrine and the Media* (University of California Press, 1978).

34. *Christian Science Monitor*, October 17, 2000, p. 10.

35. Alliance for Better Campaigns, *The Political Standard*, Vol. 4, no. 1, p. 6.

36. Harvey G. Zeidenstein, "News Media Perception of White House News Management," *Presidential Studies Quarterly* 24 (Summer 1984), pp. 391–98.

37. See, for example, Jack Dennis, "Preadult Learning of Political Independence: Media and Family Communications Effects," *Communication Research* 13 (July 1987), pp. 401–33; Olive Stevens, *Children Talking Politics* (Martin Robertson, 1982).

38. Elihu Katz and Paul Lazarsfeld, *Personal Influence: The Part Played by People in the Flow of Mass Communications* (Free Press, 1955).

39. See the classic, Angus Campbell, Philip E. Converse, Warren E. Miller, and Donald E. Stokes, *The American Voter* (Wiley, 1960).

40. See other classic works: Paul Lazarsfeld, Bernard Berelson, and Hazel Gaudet, *The People's Choice: How the Voter Makes Up His Mind in a Presidential Campaign*, 3d ed. (Columbia University Press, 1968); Bernard

Berelson, Paul Lazarsfeld, and William McPhee, *Voting: A Study of Opinion Formation in a Presidential Campaign* (University of Chicago Press, 1954).

41. Pew Research Center for the People and the Press, "Scandal Reporting Faulted for Bias and Inaccuracy: Popular Policies and Unpopular Press Lift Clinton Ratings," press release, February 6, 1998, p. 6.

42. www.gallup.com/poll-archives/980926.htm.

43. Stuart Oskamp, ed., *Television as a Social Issue* (Sage Publications, 1988); James W. Carey, ed., *Media, Myths, and Narratives: Television and the Press* (Sage Publications, 1988).

44. Doris A. Graber, *Processing the News: How People Tame the Information Tide*, 2d ed. (Longman, 1988), pp. 107–13.

45. Times Mirror Center for the People and the Press, "Times Mirror News Interest Index," press releases, January 16 and February 28, 1992.

46. John K. Robinson and Mark R. Levy, eds., *The Main Source: Learning from Television News* (Sage Publications, 1986).

47. Graber, *Processing the News*, p. 115.

48. Rush Limbaugh, *See, I Told You So* (Pocket Books, 1993), p. 326.

49. See Nelson Polsby, *Consequences of Party Reform* (Oxford University Press, 1983), pp. 142–46. See also Stanley Rothman and S. Robert Lichter, "Media and Business Elites: Two Classes in Conflict!" *Public Interest* 69 (Fall 1982), pp. 119–25.

50. Michael Parenti, *Inventing Reality: The Politics of the Mass Media* (St. Martin's Press, 1986), p. 35.

51. Rick Lyman, "Multimedia Deal: The History; 2 Commanding Publishers, 2 Powerful Empires," *The New York Times*, March 14, 2000, p. C16.

52. David Broder, "Beware of the 'Insider' Syndrome: Why Newsmakers and News Reporters Shouldn't Get Too Cozy," *The Washington Post*, December 4, 1988, p. A21; see also Broder, "Thin-Skinned Journalists," *The Washington Post*, January 11, 1989, p. A21.

53. Robert Lichter, "Consistently Liberal: But Does It Matter?" *Forbes Media Critic* 4 (Fall 1996), pp. 26–39. These data are essentially the same as data reported a decade earlier. See David Shaw, "The Times Poll: Public and Press—Two Viewpoints," *Los Angeles Times*, August 11, 1985, pt. 1, p. 1.

54. Daniel P. Moynihan, "The Presidency and the Press," *Commentary* 51 (March 1971), p. 43.

55. S. Robert Lichter, Stanley Rothman, and Linda S. Lichter, *The Media Elite* (Adler and Adler, 1986).

56. See Thomas Patterson, *Out of Order* (Knopf, 1993); Paul Weaver, *News and the Culture of Lying* (Free Press, 1993); Anthony Munro, "Yet Another Conspiracy Theory," *Columbia Journalism Review* 33 (November 1994), p. 71.

57. Among others researching this topic, see Doris A. Graber, "Say It with Pictures: The Impact of Audio-Visual News on Public Opinion Formation," paper presented at the Midwest Political Science Association Annual Meeting, Chicago, April 1987; Benjamin I. Page, Robert Y. Shapiro, and Glenn R. Dempsey, "What Moves Public Opinion?" *American Political Science Review* 76 (March 1987), pp. 23–43.

58. Shanto Iyengar, Mark D. Peters, and Donald R. Kinder, "Experimental Demonstrations of the 'Not-So-Minimal' Consequences of Television News Programs," *American Political Science Review* 76 (December 1982), pp. 848–58.

59. Ibid.; Maxwell E. McCombs and Donald L. Shaw, "The Agenda-Setting Function of the Mass Media," *Public Opinion Quarterly* 36 (1972), pp. 176–87; Maxwell E. McCombs and Sheldon Gilbert, "News Influence on Our Pictures of the World," in Jennings Bryant and Dolf Gillman, eds., *Perspectives on Media Effects* (Lawrence Erlbaum, 1986), pp. 1–15; Iyengar and Kinder, *News That Matters*.

60. Quoted in Robinson and Sheehan, *Over the Wire and on TV*, p. xiii.

61. David B. Magleby, *Direct Legislation: Voting on Ballot Propositions in the United States* (Johns Hopkins University Press, 1984).

62. Peter Marks, "Costly Prescriptions: One Issue That Fits All," *The New York Times*, October 1, 2000, p. A22.

63. Paul T. David, Ralph M. Goldman, and Richard C. Bain, *The Politics of the National Party Conventions* (Brookings Institution, 1960), pp. 300–301.

64. Richard Davis, *The Press and American Politics: The New Mediator*, 2d ed. (Prentice Hall, 1996), p. 279.

65. Frank I. Lutz, *Candidates, Consultants, and Campaigns* (Basil Blackwell, 1988), chap. 7.

66. Larry J. Sabato, *The Rise of Political Consultants* (Basic Books, 1981).

67. Tina Cassidy, "Tipper Marches to Own Beat on Campaign Trail," *The Boston Globe*, July 11, 2000, p. C1.

68. See, in general, ibid.; James David Barber, *The Pulse of Politics: Electing Presidents in the Media Age* (Norton, 1980); Fred Barnes, "The Myth of Political Consultants," *New Republic*, June 16, 1986, p. 16.

69. Quoted in Sabato, *Rise of Political Consultants*, p. 144.

70. Thomas E. Patterson, *The Mass Media Election: How Americans Choose Their President* (Praeger, 1980), chap. 12.

71. John H. Aldrich, *Before the Convention* (University of Chicago Press, 1980), p. 65. This book is a study of candidates' choices and strategies. See also Patterson, *Mass Media Election*.

72. John Foley et al., *Nominating a President: The Process and the Press* (Praeger, 1980), p. 39. For the press's treatment of incumbents, see James Glen Stovall, "Incumbency and News Coverage of the 1980 Presidential Election Campaign," *Western Political Quarterly* 37 (December 1984), p. 621.

73. Priscilla Southwell, "Voter Turnout in the 1986 Congressional Elections: The Media as Demobilizer?" *American Politics Quarterly* 19 (January 1991), pp. 96–108.

74. William Glaberson, "A New Press Role: Solving Problems," *The New York Times*, October 3, 1994, p. D6.

75. Patterson, *Mass Media Election*, pp. 115–17.

76. Raymond Wolfinger and Peter Linguiti, "Tuning In and Tuning Out," *Public Opinion* 4 (February/March 1981), pp. 56–60.

77. Lewis Wolfson, *The Untapped Power of the Press* (Praeger, 1985), p. 79.

78. Stephen Hess, *The Government/Press Connection* (Brookings Institution, 1984), p. 106.

79. Lloyd Cutler, "Foreign Policy on Deadline," *Foreign Policy* 56 (Fall 1984), p. 114.

80. Michael B. Grossman and Martha Joynt Kumar, *Portraying the President* (Johns Hopkins University Press, 1981), pp. 255–63; Fredric T. Smoller, *The Six O'Clock Presidency: A Theory of Presidential Press Relations in the Age of Television* (Praeger, 1990), pp. 31–49.

81. Michael J. Robinson and Kevin R. Appel, "Network News Coverage of Congress," *Political Science Quarterly* 94 (Fall 1979), pp. 407–18; Charles Tidmarch and John C. Pitney, Jr., "Covering Congress," *Polity* 17 (Spring 1984), pp. 463–83.

82. Susan Heilmann Miller, "News Coverage of Congress: The Search for the Ultimate Spokesperson," *Journalism Quarterly* 54 (Autumn 1977), pp. 459–65.

83. See Stephen Hess, *Live from Capitol Hill: Studies of Congress and the Media* (Brookings Institution, 1991), pp. 102–10.

84. Richard Davis, "Whither the Congress and the Supreme Court? The Television News Portrayal of American National Government," *Television Quarterly* 22 (1987), pp. 55–63.

85. For a discussion of the Supreme Court and public opinion, see Thomas R. Marshall, *Public Opinion and the Supreme Court* (Unwin Hyman, 1989); Gregory Caldiera, "Neither the Purse nor the Sword: Dynamics of Public Confidence in the Supreme Court," *American Political Science Review* 80 (December 1986), pp. 1209–28.

86. For a discussion of the relationship between the Supreme Court and the press, see Richard Davis, "Lifting the Shroud: News Media Portrayal of the U.S. Supreme Court," *Communications and the Law* 9 (October 1987), pp. 43–58; Elliot E. Slotnick, "Media Coverage of Supreme Court Decision Making: Problems and Prospects," *Judicature*, October/November 1991, pp. 128–42.

87. Times Mirror Center, "Campaign '92," January 16, 1992.

88. Quoted in Herbert Schmertz, "The Making of the Presidency," *Presidential Studies Quarterly* 16 (Winter 1986), p. 25.

CHAPTER 11

1. From a poll by Opinion Dynamics, Inc., for Fox News Channel, cited in *National Journal*, September 20, 1998, p. 1856.

2. John R. Hibbing and Elizabeth Theiss-Morse, *Congress as Public Enemy: Public Attitudes Toward American Political Institutions* (Cambridge University Press, 1995), p. 147.

3. Richard F. Fenno, Jr., *Home Style: House Members in Their Districts* (Little, Brown, 1978), p. 168.

4. For an examination of this practice, see Michael Lyons and Peter F. Galderisi, "Incumbency, Reapportionment, and U.S. House Redistricting," *Political Research Quarterly* (December 1995), pp. 857–71.

5. *Davis v Bandemer*, 478 US 109 (1986).

6. *Baker v Carr*, 369 US 186 (1962).

7. See *Wesberry v Sanders*, 376 US 1 (1964).

8. *Shaw v Reno*, 509 US 630 (1993).

9. *Miller v Johnson*, 512 US 622 (1995); *Bush v Vera*, 517 US 952 (1996).

10. Frances E. Lee and Bruce I. Oppenheimer, *Sizing Up the Senate: The Unequal Consequences of Equal Representation* (University of Chicago Press, 1999).

11. Daniel Patrick Moynihan, introduction to Monica Friar and Herman Leonard, *The Federal Budget and the States: Fiscal Year 1994* (Kennedy School of Government, 1994).

12. For a brief discussion of the speakership in the 1990s, see Barbara Sinclair, "House Majority Party Leadership in an Era of Legislative Constraint," in Roger H. Davidson, ed., *The Postreform Congress* (St. Martin's Press, 1992), pp. 91–111. See also Ronald M. Peters, Jr., ed., *The Speaker: Leadership in the U.S. House of Representatives* (Congressional Quarterly Press, 1995).

13. Quoted in Adam Clymer, "Firebrand Who Got Singed Says Being Speaker Suffices," *The New York Times*, January 22, 1996, p. 1.

14. Newt Gingrich, *To Renew America* (HarperCollins, 1995) and *Lessons Learned the Hard Way* (HarperCollins, 1998).

15. Quoted in Greg Hitt, "Hastert Is Tapped as House Speaker to Fill Vacuum Created by Livingston," *The Wall Street Journal*, December 21, 1998, p. A20.

16. Richard E. Cohen and David Baumann, "Speaking Up for Hastert," *National Journal*, November 13, 1999, pp. 3298–3303.

17. For insightful memoirs by three recently retired U.S. Senators, see Bill Bradley, *Time Present, Time Past: A Memoir* (Knopf, 1996); Warren B. Rudman, *Combat: Twelve Years in the U.S. Senate* (Random House, 1996); and Alan K. Simpson, *Right in the Old Kazoo: A Lifetime of Scrapping with the Press* (Morrow, 1997). See also the reflections of Joseph I. Lieberman, *In Praise of Public Life* (Simon and Schuster, 2000), and Adam Clymer, *Edward M. Kennedy: A Biography* (William Morrow, 1999).

18. Barbara Sinclair, "Unorthodox Lawmaking in the Individualist Senate," *Extensions: A Journal of the Carl Albert Congressional Research and Studies Center* (Fall 1997), p. 11. See also Sinclair, *Unorthodox Lawmaking: New Legislative Processes in the U.S. Congress* (Congressional Quarterly Press, 1997), chap. 3.

19. Norman J. Ornstein, "Prima Donna Senate," *The New York Times*, September 4, 1997, p. A17. See also Carroll J. Doherty, "Senate Caught in the Grip of Its Own 'Holds' System," *Congressional Quarterly Weekly Report*, August 15, 1998, pp. 2241–43.

20. For an insightful set of essays on Senate leadership, see Richard A. Baker and Roger H. Davidson, eds., *First Among Equals: Outstanding Senate Leaders of the Twentieth Century* (Congressional Quarterly Press, 1991).

21. Nicol Rae and Colton Campbell, "The Changing Role of Political Parties in the U.S. Senate in the 104th and 105th Congresses," paper presented at the American Political Science Association Annual Meeting, Boston, September 3–6, 1998, p. 21.

22. Sarah A. Binder and Steven S. Smith, *Politics or Principles? Filibustering in the United States Senate* (Brookings Institution, 1997).

23. David Baumann, "The Collapse of the Senate," *National Journal*, June 3, 2000, p. 1759.

24. For a criticism of recent confirmation hearings and various reform proposals, see Stephen L. Carter, *The Confirmation Mess: Cleaning Up the Federal Appointments Process* (Basic Books, 1994). See also G. Calvin Mackenzie and Robert Shogan, eds., *Obstacle Course: The Report of the Twentieth Century Fund Task Force on the Presidential Appointment Process* (Twentieth Century Fund Press, 1996).

25. Norman Ornstein, Thomas Mann, and Michael Malbin, *Vital Statistics on Congress, 1999–2000* (AEI Press, 2000), p. 129.

26. Robert C. Byrd (D.-W.Va.), quoted in David J. Vogler, *The Politics of Congress* (Allyn and Bacon, 1983), p. 77.

27. See the case studies in Richard F. Fenno, Jr., *Senators on the Campaign Trail: The Politics of Representation* (University of Oklahoma Press, 1996), p. 331. See also Benjamin Bishin, "Constituency Influence in Congress: Does Subconstituency Matter?" *Legislative Studies Quarterly* (August 2000), pp. 389–415.

28. www.senate.gov, www.house.gov. See also thomas.loc.gov.

29. See a fascinating comparison of two Rhodes Scholars, one a liberal from Maryland and the other a conservative from Indiana, and what has shaped their votes over several terms in the U.S. Senate: Karl A. Lamb, *Reasonable Disagreement: Two U.S. Senators and the Choices They Make* (Garland, 1998).

30. See Richard Morrin, "Tuned Out, Turned Off: Millions of Americans Know Little About How Their Government Works," *The Washington Post National Weekly Edition*, February 5–11, 1996, pp. 6–7.

31. A 1999 CBS survey reported in "Poll Readings," *National Journal*, October 9, 1999, p. 2917.

32. Bradley, *Time Present, Time Past*, chap. 4.

33. Mary Lynn F. Jones, "For Top Hill Aides, Raising Money Is Part of the Job," *The Hill*, May 24, 2000, pp. 1, 30.

34. Jackie Clames, "House Divided: Why Congress Hews to the Party Line on Impeachment," *The Wall Street Journal*, December 16, 1998, p. 1.

35. *Congressional Quarterly Weekly*, January 6, 2001.

36. For reflections from a leading member of the Black Caucus, see Ronald V. Dellums, *Lying Down with the Lions* (Beacon, 2000).

37. Ornstein et al., *Vital Statistics on Congress, 1999–2000*, pp. 103–106.

38. Lieberman, *In Praise of Public Life*, p. 109.

39. Constance Ewing Cook, *Lobbying for Higher Education* (Vanderbilt University Press, 1998). See, too, Ken Kolman, *Outside Lobbying* (Princeton University Press, 1998).

40. Lieberman, *In Praise of Public Life*, p. 118.

41. Carroll J. Doherty, "Clinton's Big Comeback Shown in Vote Score," *Congressional Quarterly Weekly Report*, December 21, 1996, pp. 3427–30.

42. See Jeffrey S. Peake, "Presidential Agenda Setting in Foreign Policy," paper presented at the American Political Science Association Annual Meeting, Boston, September 3–6, 1998.

43. "Resumé of Congressional Activity," 105th Congress, *Congressional Record, Daily Digest*, January 19, 1999, p. D29.

44. Editorial, *Kansas City Star*, June 25, 2000, p. B10.

45. Sinclair, *Unorthodox Lawmaking*, p. 58. For a defense of riders as a means to cut wasteful spending, see Slade Gorton and Larry E. Craig, "Congressional Riders Rein in Excesses," *Walla Walla Union-Bulletin*, July 31, 1998, p. 4.

46. See David W. Brady and Craig Volden, *Revolving Gridlock: Politics and Policy from Carter to Clinton* (Westview Press, 1998). For two case studies on the way bills get treated in Congress, see Janet M. Martin, *Lessons from the Hill: The Legislative Journey of an Education Program* (St. Martin's Press, 1993); Steven Waldman, *The Bill—How Legislation Really Becomes Law: A Case Study of the National Service Bill* (Penguin, 1996).

47. Woodrow Wilson, *Congressional Government* (Houghton, Mifflin, 1885; reprint, Johns Hopkins University Press, 1981), p. 69.

48. Christopher J. Deering and Steven S. Smith, *Committees in Congress*, 3d ed. (Congressional Quarterly Press, 1997).

49. Karen Foerstel, "Chairman's Term Limits Already Shaking Up House," *Congressional Quarterly Weekly*, March 24, 2000, p. 628.

50. Joel D. Aberbach, *Keeping a Watchful Eye: The Politics of Congressional Oversight* (Brookings Institution, 1990).

51. "Resumé of Congressional Activity, 105th Congress," *Congressional Record, Daily Digest*, January 19, 1999, p. D29.

52. For an example of intense bargaining on a major defense appropriation bill, see Pat Towell, "Camouflage-Green Defense Bill Poised for President's Signature," *Congressional Quarterly Weekly*, July 22, 2000, pp. 1819–22.

53. William S. Cohen, "Why I Am Leaving," *The Washington Post National Weekly Edition*, January 28–February 4, 1996, p. 29. Four years later, as secretary of defense, Cohen allowed that he enjoyed generally positive relations with members of Congress except when it came to their resistance to closing more military bases. Quoted in "The Hill Interview," *The Hill*, May 17, 2000, p. 41.

54. James Madison, *The Federalist*, No. 57, in *The Federalist*, ed. Jacob E. Cooke (Meridian Books, 1961), p. 385.

55. See Kenny J. Whitby, *The Color of Representation: Congressional Behavior and Black Interests* (University of Michigan Press, 1998); Barbara Mikulski, Kay Bailey Hutchison et al., *Nine and Counting: The Women of the Senate* (Morrow, 2000).

56. See Clymer, *Edward M. Kennedy*.

57. See Charles Lewis and the Center for Public Integrity, *The Buying of the Congress: How Special Interests Have Stolen Your Right to Life, Liberty and the Pursuit of Happiness* (Avon, 1998).

58. For an excellent treatment of ethical problems faced by members of Congress and what has been and might be done about them, see Dennis F. Thompson, *Ethics in Congress* (Brookings Institution, 1995).

59. Brady and Volden, *Revolving Gridlock*, p. 178.

CHAPTER 12

1. Charles O. Jones, *The Presidency in a Separated System* (Brookings Institution, 1994), p. 295. See also Jean Reith Schroedl, *Congress, the President, and Policymaking* (M.E. Sharpe, 1994).
2. William E. Leuchtenburg, "The Twentieth Century Presidency," *Miller Center Report* 16, no. 1 (Spring 2000), pp. 15–23.
3. Glenn A. Phelps, *George Washington and American Constitutionalism* (University Press of Kansas, 1993).
4. It is difficult for the average citizen to assess systematically the health and character of presidential candidates, but voters still try to do so. For various efforts, see Fred Greenstein, *The Presidential Difference* (Free Press, 2000); David Gergen, *Eyewitness to Power: The Essence of Leadership—Nixon to Clinton* (Simon & Schuster, 2000); and Stanley A. Renshon, *The Psychological Assessment of Presidential Candidates* (New York University Press, 1996).
5. For a penetrating and realistic analysis of Abraham Lincoln, see David H. Donald, *Lincoln* (Simon and Schuster, 1995). See also, on the paradoxes and the heightened expectations we place on presidents, Thomas E. Cronin and Michael A. Genovese, *The Paradoxes of the American Presidency* (Oxford University Press, 1998).
6. See, in general, Joseph G. Dawson III, ed., *Commanders in Chief: Presidential Leadership in Modern Wars* (University Press of Kansas, 1993).
7. See Thomas J. Weko, *The Politicizing Presidency: The White House Personnel Office, 1948–1994* (University Press of Kansas, 1995).
8. See G. Calvin MacKenzie and Robert Shogan, eds., *Obstacle Course: The Report of the Twentieth Century Fund Task Force on the Presidential Appointment Process* (Twentieth Century Fund Press, 1996).
9. See James P. Pfiffner, *The Strategic Presidency: Hitting the Ground Running*, 2d ed. (University Press of Kansas, 1996).
10. *United States v Curtiss-Wright Export Corp.*, 299 US 304 (1936).
11. For those who believe the *Curtiss-Wright* ruling was too sweeping, see Harold H. Koh, *The National Security Constitution* (Yale University Press, 1990); Louis Fisher, *Presidential War Power* (University Press of Kansas, 1995); David Gray Adler and Larry N. George, eds., *The Constitution and the Conduct of Foreign Policy: Essays on Law and History* (University Press of Kansas, 1996).
12. On the president's major involvement in the budget process, see Allen Schick, *The Federal Budget: Politics, Policy, Process* (Brookings Institution, 1995).
13. Albert R. Hunt, "Clinton Ends His Tenure on High Note," *The Wall Street Journal*, December 14, 2000, p. A9.
14. See Kenneth T. Walsh, *Feeding the Beast: The White House Versus the Press* (Random House, 1996). See also Richard Morris, *Behind the Oval Office* (Random House, 1997).
15. See Howard Kurtz, *Spin Cycle: Inside the Clinton Propaganda Machine* (Free Press, 1998).
16. See also the vigorous criticism of the Washington media and their biases by former U.S. Senator Alan K. Simpson, *Right in the Old Kazoo* (Morrow, 1997).
17. See Sidney M. Milkis, *The President and the Parties: The Transformation of the American Party System Since the New Deal* (Oxford University Press, 1993); James W. Davis, *The President as Party Leader* (Praeger, 1992).
18. See Bradley H. Patterson, Jr., *The White House Staff: Inside the West Wing and Beyond* (Brookings Institution, 2000).
19. For the views on presidents and the White House staff of a highly placed White House aide in several administrations, see Gergen, *Eyewitness to Power.*
20. See Shelley Lynne Tomkins, *Inside OMB: Politics and Process in the President's Budget Office* (M. E. Sharpe, 1998).
21. See Cronin and Genovese, *Paradoxes of the American Presidency*, chap. 9.
22. Information provided to Thomas E. Cronin in a letter, February 1997, from Kathryn Hughes, secretary of the cabinet in the Clinton White House. See also Robert B. Reich, *Locked in the Cabinet* (Knopf, 1997).
23. There has been a certain amount of controversy about the Twenty-fifth Amendment. See Herbert L. Abrams, *The President Has Been Shot: Confusion, Disability and the Twenty-fifth Amendment* (Stanford University Press, 1994); Laura Myers, "Transfer-of-Power-Rules Urged for Impaired Presidents," *Seattle-Post Intelligencer*, December 4, 1996, p. A3.
24. Former Vice-President Dan Quayle's views are of interest: *Standing Firm* (Harper Paperbacks, 1995). Three useful general treatments on the vice-presidency are Jules Witcover, *Crapshoot: Rolling the Dice on the Vice Presidency* (Crown, 1992); Paul Light, *Vice Presidential Power* (Johns Hopkins University Press, 1984); Joel Goldstein, *The Modern Vice Presidency* (Princeton University Press, 1982).
25. Mark Hertsgaard, *On Bended Knee: The Press and the Reagan Presidency* (Farrar, Straus, Giroux, 1988). See also John A. Maltese, *Spin Control: The White House Office of Communications and the Management of Presidential News* (University of North Carolina Press, 1992).
26. Political scientists are unsure of these relationships. See Jeffrey E. Cohen et al., "State-Level Presidential Approval and Senatorial Support," *Legislative Studies Quarterly* (November 2000), pp. 577–90; Lyn Ragsdale, "Studying the Presidency," in Michael Nelson, ed., *The Presidency and the Political System*, 6th ed. (Congressional Quarterly Press, 2000), pp. 29–63; Paul Gronke and Brian Newman, "FDR to Clinton . . . : A 'State of the Discipline' Review of Presidential Approval," paper prepared at the American Political Science Association Annual Meeting, Washington, D.C., August 31–September 3, 2000.
27. These points are more fully developed in Cronin and Genovese, *Paradoxes of the American Presidency*, chap. 3.
28. Clinton Rossiter, *The American Presidency* (Harcourt, Brace and World, 1956), p. 257.
29. Harold J. Laski, *The American Presidency: An Interpretation* (Harper and Brothers, 1940), p. 38.

CHAPTER 13

1. David S. Broder, "A Weak Hand," *The Washington Post National Weekly Edition*, December 25, 2000–January 1, 2001, p. 4.
2. George C. Edwards, "Building Coalitions," *Presidential Studies Quarterly* (March 2000), pp. 60–61.
3. See the arguments in David Gray Adler and Michael A. Genovese, eds., *The Presidency and the Law: The Clinton Legacy* (University Press of Kansas, 2002); Louis Fisher, *Congressional Abdication on War and Spending* (Texas A & M Press, 2000).
4. James A. Thurber, "An Introduction to Presidential-Congressional Rivalry," in James A. Thurber, ed., *Rivals for Power: Presidential-Congressional Relations* (Congressional Quarterly Press, 1996), p. 6.
5. Sarah A. Blinder, "Going Nowhere: A Gridlocked Congress?" *Brookings Review* (Winter 2000), p. 18.
6. See, for example, former Republican Senator Warren G. Rudman's memoir, *Combat* (Random House, 1996), chaps. 2, 3. See also former Democratic Congressman Timothy Penny and Major Garrett, *Common Cents* (Little, Brown, 1995).
7. John R. Hibbing and Elizabeth Theiss-Morse, *Congress as Public Enemy: Public Attitudes Toward American Political Institutions* (Cambridge University Press, 1995).
8. David W. Brady and Craig Volden, *Revolving Gridlock* (Westview Press, 1998), p. 176.
9. Abraham Lincoln to his Illinois law partner W.H. Herndon, February 15, 1848, in *Abraham Lincoln, Speeches and Writings, 1832–1858* (Library of America, 1989), p. 175.
10. Leonard C. Meeker, "The Legality of U.S. Participation in the Defense of Vietnam," *Department of State Bulletin*, March 28, 1966, pp. 448–55.
11. Madeleine Albright, in *Congressional Record*, July 30, 1998.
12. David Gray Adler, "The Clinton Theory of the War Power," *Presidential Studies Quarterly* (March 2000), p. 167.
13. Fisher, *Congressional Abdication*, p. 184.
14. Ibid., p. 170. See also Louis Fisher and David Gray Adler, "The War Powers: Time to Say Goodbye," *Political Science Quarterly* (Spring 1998), pp. 1–20.

15. Lee Hamilton, "The Role of the Congress in U.S. Foreign Policy," speech delivered to the Center for Strategic and International Studies, Washington, D.C., November 19, 1998, p. 1.

16. See Henry J. Abraham, *Justices, Presidents, and Senators: A History of U.S. Supreme Court Appointments from Washington to Clinton*, 4th ed. (Rowman and Littlefield, 1999); Sheldon Goldman, *Picking Federal Judges* (Yale University Press, 1997).

17. Orrin G. Hatch, "Senate Isn't Guilty of Racism in Confirming Judges," *The Wall Street Journal*, September 5, 2000, p. A34.

18. William Bradford Reynolds, "Etiquette for the Senate," *The New York Times*, January 12, 2001, p. A23.

19. Raoul Berger, *Executive Privilege: A Constitutional Myth* (Harvard University Press, 1974).

20. Mark J. Rozell, "The Law: Executive Privilege—Definition and Standards of Application," *Presidential Studies Quarterly* (December 1999), p. 924.

21. *U.S. v Nixon*, 418 U S 683 (1974).

22. See Mark J. Rozell, "Something To Hide: Clinton's Misuse of Executive Privilege," *PS: Political Science and Politics* (September 1999), p. 551. See also Mark J. Rozell, *Executive Privilege: The Dilemma of Secrecy and Democratic Accountability*, 2d ed. (University Press of Kansas, 2000).

23. See Richard A. Posner, *An Affair of State: The Investigation, Impeachment and Trial of President Clinton* (Harvard University Press, 1999); Mark J. Rozell, "Executive Privilege and the Modern Presidents: In Nixon's Shadow," *Minnesota Law Review* (May 1999), pp. 1069–1126. See also Mark J. Rozell, "An Old (or New) Understanding of Executive Privilege," in Adler and Genovese, eds., *The Presidency and the Law*.

24. www.nara.gov/fedreg/eo.

25. See Nancy Kassop, "A New (or Old?) Understanding of the Separation of Powers: The Expansion and Contraction of Presidential Power under Clinton," paper presented at the American Political Science Association Annual Meeting, Washington, D.C., August 31–September 3, 2000. See also Christopher J. Deering and Forrest Maltzman, "The Politics of Executive Orders: Legislative Restraints on Presidential Power," *Political Research Quarterly* (December 1999), pp. 767–83.

26. Terry Moe and William Howell, "Unilateral Action and Presidential Power: A Theory," *Presidential Studies Quarterly* (December 1999), p. 856.

27. Ibid., p. 856.

28. For a useful history of the veto power, see Robert Spitzer, *The Presidential Veto: Touchstone of the American Presidency* (State University of New York Press, 1988).

29. *Clinton v City of New York*, 521 US 811 (1998).

30. Fisher, *Congressional Abdication*, p. 124.

31. Donald F. Kettl, "Presidential Management of the Economy," in James Pfiffner and Roger H. Davidson, eds., *Understanding the Presidency*, 3d ed. (Addison, Wesley, Longman, 2000), p. 363.

32. Adapted from Edwards, "Building Coalitions."

33. Ibid., pp. 49–58.

34. Ibid., p. 63.

35. See Charles Walcott and Karen Hult, *Governing the White House: From Hoover through LBJ* (University Press of Kansas, 1995); Bradley H. Patterson, Jr., *The White House Staff: Inside the West Wing* (Brookings Institution, 2000).

36. James MacGregor Burns, *Roosevelt: The Lion and the Fox* (Harcourt Brace, 1956), p. 186.

CHAPTER 14

1. Alexis de Tocqueville, *Democracy in America*, ed. Phillips Bradley (Knopf, 1944), 1:278–80.

2. Harold J. Laski, *The American Democracy* (Viking, 1948), p. 110.

3. Jerome Frank, *Courts on Trial: Myth and Reality in American Justice* (Princeton University Press, 1949), pp. 80–103.

4. *Chicago Grand Trunk Railway Co. v Wellman*, 143 US 339 (1892).

5. Philip J. Cooper, *Hard Judicial Choices: Federal District Court Judges and State and Local Officials* (Oxford University Press, 1988), p. 15.

6. *Luther v Borden*, 7 Howard 1 (1849).

7. Quoted in Paul E. Freund, *Understanding the Supreme Court* (Little, Brown, 1949), p. 3.

8. For one of the great classics, see Benjamin N. Cardozo, *The Nature of the Judicial Process* (Yale University Press, 1921).

9. Quoted in H.L.A. Hart, *The Concept of Law* (Oxford University Press, 1961), pp. 121–22.

10. David M. O'Brien, *Storm Center: The Supreme Court in American Politics*, 5th ed. (W.W. Norton, 2000), p. 30, and as updated by the author through the 1999–2000 term.

11. C. K. Rowland, "The Federal District Courts," in *The American Courts: A Critical Assessment*, ed. John B. Gates and Charles A. Johnson (Congressional Quarterly Press, 1991), pp. 61–80.

12. Quoted in Christopher E. Smith, *United States Magistrates in the Federal Courts: Subordinate Judges* (Praeger, 1990), p. 183.

13. *Peretz v United States*, 501 US 923 (1991).

14. See Donald R. Songer, "The Circuit Courts of Appeals," in Gates and Johnson, eds., *American Courts*, pp. 35–37; Deborah J. Barrow and Thomas G. Walker, *A Court Divided: The Fifth Circuit Court of Appeals and the Politics of Judicial Reform* (Yale University Press, 1988); Arthur D. Hellman, ed., *Reconstructing Justice: The Innovations of the Ninth Circuit and the Future of the Federal Courts* (Cornell University Press, 1991).

15. John Gruhl, "The Impact of Term Limits for Supreme Court Justices," *Judicature*, September/October 1997, pp. 67–68.

16. *Bordenkircher v Hayes*, 434 US 357 (1978). See also James Eisenstein, *Counsel for the United States: U.S. Attorneys in the Political and Legal Systems* (Johns Hopkins Press, 1978).

17. Joan Biskupic, "For Court Advocate, a Nominee Who Seeks 'Different Solutions,'" *The Washington Post*, April 19, 1993, p. A21.

18. For a critical analysis, see Lincoln Caplan, *The Tenth Justice: The Solicitor General and the Rule of Law* (Knopf, 1987). For a defense, see former Solicitor General Charles Fried, *Order and Law: Arguing the Reagan Revolution—A Firsthand Account* (Simon & Schuster, 1991). For a more neutral account, see Rebecca Mae Salokar, *The Solicitor General: The Politics of Law* (Temple University Press, 1992).

19. *Legal Services Corporation v Velazquez*, 120 S. Ct.(2001).

20. Neil D. McFeeley, *Appointment of Judges: The Johnson Presidency* (University of Texas Press, 1987), p. 1.

21. Harold W. Chase, *Federal Judges: The Appointing Process* (University of Minnesota Press, 1972), pp. 3–47; and Sheldon Goldman, *Picking Federal Judges: Lower Court Selection from Roosevelt Through Reagan* (Yale University Press, 1998).

22. Lettie McSpadden Wenner and Lee F. Dutter, "Contextual Influences on Court Outcomes," *Western Political Quarterly* 41 (March 1988), pp. 115–34; Ronald Stidham and Robert A. Carp, "Exploring Regionalism in the Federal District Courts," *Los Angeles Daily Journal* 18 (Fall 1988), pp. 113–25.

23. See Amy Goldstein, "Bush Curtails ABA Role in Selecting U. S. Judges," *The Washington Post*, March 23, 2001, p. A1.

24. Lisa M. Holmes and Roger E. Hartley, "Increasing Senate Scrutiny of Lower Federal Court Nominees," *Judicature*, May/June 1997, p. 275.

25. George Watson and John Stookey, "Supreme Court Confirmation Hearings: A View from the Senate," *Judicature*, December 1987/January 1988, p. 193. See also John Massaro, *Supremely Political: The Role of Ideology and Presidential Management in Unsuccessful Supreme Court Nominations* (State University of New York Press, 1990).

26. Barbara A. Perry and Henry J. Abraham, "A 'Representative' Supreme Court? The Thomas, Ginsburg, and Breyer Appointments," *Judicature*, January/February 1998, pp. 158–65.

27. Goldman, *Picking Federal Judges*, pp. 161, 327–36.

28. Sheldon Goldman, "Bush's Judicial Legacy: The Final Imprint," *Judicature*, April/May 1993, p. 291.

29. Robert A. Carp and C. K. Rowland, *Politics and Judgment in Federal District Courts* (University Press of Kansas, 1996).

30. Sheldon Goldman, "Reagan's Judicial Legacy: Completing the Puzzle and Summing Up," *Judicature*, April/May 1989, pp. 318–30.

31. Leo V. Hennessy, "Redrawing the Political Map? An Impact Analysis of the Reagan Appointments on the U.S. Courts of Appeals," paper presented at the Southern Political Science Association, Tampa, Florida, November 7–9, 1991.

32. Robert A. Carp, Donald Songer, C. K. Rowland, Ronald Stidham, and Lisa Richey-Tracey, "The Voting Behavior of Judges Appointed by President Bush," *Judicature*, April/May 1993, pp. 298–302.

33. Naftali Bendavid, "Diversity Marks Clinton Judiciary," *The Recorder*, December 30, 1993, p. 11.

34. Dan Carney, "Battle Looms Between Clinton, GOP over Court Nominees," *Congressional Quarterly Weekly Report*, February 8, 1997, p. 369.

35. David M. O'Brien, "Judicial Legacies: The Clinton Presidency and the Courts," in Colin Campbell and Bert A. Rockman, eds., *The Clinton Legacy* (Chatham House, 2000), pp. 96–117; and http://afj.org/jsp/home.html.

36. William Howard Taft to Horace Taft, November 14, 1929; quoted in Henry Pringle, *The Life and Times of William Howard Taft* (Farrar, 1939), 2:967.

37. Sue Davis, "Federalism and Property Rights: An Examination of Justice Rehnquist's Legal Positivism," *Western Reserve Political Quarterly* 39 (June 1986), pp. 250–64.

38. David M. O'Brien, *Judicial Roulette: Report of the Twentieth Century Fund Task Force on Judicial Selection* (Priority Press Publications, 1988), pp. 10–11.

39. White Burkett Miller Center of Public Affairs, *Improving the Process of Appointing Federal Judges* (Miller Center, University of Virginia, 1996).

40. Donald Santarelli, quoted in Jerry Landauer, "Shaping the Bench," *The Wall Street Journal*, December 10, 1970, p. 1. See also J. W. Peltason, *Federal Courts in the Political Process* (Doubleday, 1955), p. 32.

41. Michael A. Kahn, "The Appointment of a Supreme Court Justice: A Political Process from Beginning to End," *Presidential Studies Quarterly* 25 (Winter 1995), pp. 26, 39.

42. Ex parte *McCardle*, 74 U S 506 (1869).

43. Barry Friedman, "Attacks on Judges: Why They Fail," *Judicature*, January/February 1998, p. 152.

44. Tony Mauro, "Yipes! Stripes!" *The Recorder*, February 8, 1995, p. 8.

45. Tony Mauro, "Supreme Court Calendar Begs for More Arguments," *The Recorder*, February 13, 1996, p. 1.

46. David M. O'Brien, "The Rehnquist Court's Shrinking Plenary Docket," *Judicature*, September/October 1997, p. 58.

47. O'Brien, *Storm Center*, p. 63. See also Tony Mauro, "Jumping into the Pool," *The Recorder*, September 14, 1993, p. 6.

48. Sidney Ulmer, "The Supreme Court's Certiorari Decisions: Conflict as a Predictive Variable," *American Political Science Review* 78 (December 1984), pp. 901–11.

49. Quoted in John R. Vile, "The Selection and Tenure of Chief Justices," *Judicature*, September/October 1994, p. 98.

50. Robert J. Steamer, *Chief Justice: Leadership and the Supreme Court* (University of South Carolina Press, 1986).

51. Sue Davis, "The Supreme Court: Rehnquist's or Reagan's," *Western Political Quarterly* 44 (March 1991), p. 98.

52. David G. Savage, "The Rehnquist Court," *Los Angeles Times Magazine*, September 29, 1991, p. 13; David W. Rohde and Harold J. Spaeth, "Ideology, Strategy and Supreme Court Decisions: William Rehnquist as Chief Justice," *Judicature*, December 1988/January 1989, pp. 247–50. See also Joseph F. Kobylka, "Leadership on the Supreme Court of the United States: Chief Justice Burger and the Establishment Clause," *Western Political Quarterly* 42 (December 1989), pp. 545–68.

53. David Danelski, "The Influence of the Chief Justice in the Decisional Process of the Supreme Court," in Thomas P. Jahnige and Sheldon Goldman, eds., *The Federal Judicial System: Readings in Process and Behavior* (Holt, Rinehart and Winston, 1968), p. 148.

54. Edward Lazarus, *Closed Chambers: The First Eyewitness Account of the Epic Struggles Inside the Supreme Court* (Times Books, Random House, 1998), p. 423.

55. Gregory A. Caldeira and John R. Wright, "Organized Interest and Agenda Setting in the U.S. Supreme Court," *American Political Science Review* 82 (December 1988), p. 1110; Donald R. Songer and Reginald S. Sheehan, "Interest Groups' Success in the Courts: *Amicus* Participation in the Supreme Court," *Political Research Quarterly* 46 (June 1993), pp. 339–54.

56. *Webster v Reproductive Health Services*, 492 US 490 (1989); *Roe v Wade*, 410 US 113 (1973). See also Susan Behuniak-Long, "Friendly Fire: *Amici Curiae* and *Webster v Reproductive Health Services*," *Judicature*, February/March 1991, pp. 261–70.

57. *United States v Lopez*, 514 US 549 (1951).

58. Karen O'Connor, "The *Amicus Curiae* Role of the U.S. Solicitor General in Supreme Court Litigation," *Judicature*, December 1982/January 1983, pp. 256–64; Jeffrey A. Segal, "*Amicus Curiae* Briefs by the Solicitor General During the Warren and Burger Courts," *Western Political Quarterly* 41 (March 1988), pp. 134–44.

59. Tony Mauro, "The Supreme Court as Quiz Show," *The Recorder*, December 8, 1993, p. 10.

60. Joyce O'Connor, "Selections from Notes Kept on an Internship at the U.S. Supreme Court, Fall 1988," *Law, Courts, and Judicial Process* (Department of Political Science, Purdue University) 6 (Spring 1989), p. 44.

61. Tony Mauro, "No Comfort for Counsel After Court Review," *The Recorder*, November 10, 1997, p. 8.

62. Mauro, "Yipes! Stripes!" p. 8.

63. Joan Biskupie, "Supreme Court Film Offers Glimpse Behind Justices' Closed Doors," *The Washington Post*, June 17, 1997, p. A15.

64. William H. Rehnquist, *The Supreme Court: How It Was, How It Is* (William Morrow, 1987), pp. 289–90.

65. Daniel M. Berman, *It Is So Ordered: The Supreme Court Rules on School Segregation* (Norton, 1986), p. 114; Walter F. Murphy, *Elements of Judicial Strategy* (University of Chicago Press, 1964), p. 66; O'Brien, *Storm Center*, pp. 262–72.

66. Charles Evans Hughes, quoted in Donald E. Lively, *Foreshadows of the Law: Supreme Court Dissents and Constitutional Development* (Praeger, 1992), p. xx.

67. *Brown v Board of Education*, 347 U S 483 (1954).

68. *United States v Nixon*, 418 US 683 (1974).

69. Gerald N. Rosenberg, *Hollow Hope: Can Courts Bring About Sound Change?* (University of Chicago Press, 1991).

70. J. W. Peltason, *Fifty-eight Lonely Men: Southern Federal Judges and School Desegregation* (University of Illinois Press, 1971), p. 19.

71. Cooper, *Hard Judicial Choices*, pp. 347–50.

72. Arthur S. Miller, "In Defense of Judicial Activism," in Stephen C. Halpern and Charles M. Lamb, eds., *Supreme Court Activism and Restraint* (Heath, 1982), p. 177. See also, by the chief justice of the West Virginia Supreme Court, Richard Neely, *How Courts Govern America* (Yale University Press, 1981).

73. *United States v Carolene Products*, 304 US 144 (1938). Variations on this basic position have been restated in dozens of books. Halpern and Lamb, eds., *Supreme Court Activism and Restraint*, and Mark Tushnet, *Red, White, and Blue: A Critical Analysis of Constitutional Law* (Harvard University Press, 1988), provide analysis from all perspectives. For another analysis of this great debate, see Lief H. Carter, *Contemporary Constitutional Lawmaking* (Pergamon Press, 1985). See also Terri Jennings Peretti, *In Defense of a Political Court* (Princeton University Press, 1999); Stephen Macedo, *The New Right v the Constitution* (Cato, 1986). Leslie F. Goldstein, "Judicial Review and Democratic Theory: Guardian Democracy vs. Representative Democracy," *Western Political Quarterly* 40 (September 1987), pp. 391–412, also contains a bibliography.

74. J. W. Peltason, "The Supreme Court: Transactional or Transformational Leadership," in Michael R. Beschloss and Thomas E. Cronin, eds., *Essays in Honor of James MacGregor Burns* (Prentice Hall, 1988), pp. 165–80; Mark Silverstein and Benjamin Ginsburg, "The Supreme Court and the New Politics of Judicial Power," *Political Science Quarterly* 102 (Fall 1987), pp. 371–88.

75. *Planned Parenthood v Casey*, 505 US 833 (1992).

76. Thomas R. Marshall, *Public Opinion and the Supreme Court* (Unwin Hyman, 1989), p. 193. See also Thomas R. Marshall, "The Supreme Court and the Grass Roots: Whom Does the Court Represent Best?" *Judicature*, June/July 1992, pp. 22–28; Michael Comiskey, "The Rehnquist Court and American Values," *Judicature*, March/April 1994, pp. 261–67; William Mishler and Reginald S. Sheehan, "The Supreme Court as a Counter-Majoritarian Institution? The Impact of Public Opinion on Supreme Court Decisions," *American Political Science Review* 87 (1993), pp. 87–101; along with Mishler and Sheehan response, Helmut Norpoth and Jeffrey A. Segal, "Popular Influence on Supreme Court Decisions," *American Political Science Review* 88 (September 1994), pp. 711–24.

77. Rosenberg, *Hollow Hope*, p. 343.

78. Rehnquist, *Supreme Court*, p. 98.

79. Chief Justice Edward White, "The Supreme Court of the United States," *American Bar Association Journal* 7 (1921), p. 341.

CHAPTER 15

1. Data on U.S. budget projections and employment can be located at www.whitehouse.gov/omg and www.gpo.gov/usbudget and in *Statistical Abstract of the United States*, 2000.
2. Barry Bozeman, *Bureaucracy and Red Tape* (Prentice Hall, 2000), p. xi.
3. See data provided in Andrew Kohut, ed., *Deconstructing Distrust: How Americans View Government* (Pew Research Center for the People and the Press, 1998), p. 124.
4. An exception is a useful book of essays in praise of innovations by federal agencies, John D. Donahue, ed., *Making Washington Work: Tales of Innovation in the Federal Government* (Brookings Institution, 1999).
5. Shelley L. Davis, *Unbridled Power: Inside the Secret Culture of the IRS* (Harper Business, 1997).
6. Philip K. Howard, *The Death of Common Sense: How Law Is Suffocating America* (Random House, 1994), p. 9.
7. Many of these ideas are reported in Al Gore, *The Best Kept Secrets in Government: How the Clinton Administration Is Reinventing the Way Washington Works* (Random House, 1996). See, too, Donald F. Kettl, *Reinventing Government: A Fifth Year Report Card* (Brookings Institution, 1998).
8. Bush's campaign promises were discussed and quoted in Gerald F. Seib, "A Big Bush Idea Rises Amid Fluff, But It Is Private," *The Wall Street Journal*, August 2, 2000, p. A24.
9. Adapted from Dennis Palumbo and Steven Maynard-Moody, *Contemporary Public Administration* (Longman, 1991), p. 26.
10. For an analysis of the use and abuse of the civil service system in the early twentieth century, see Stephen Skowronek, *Building a New American State* (Cambridge University Press, 1982).
11. A history of the old Hatch Act is provided in James Eccles, *The Hatch Act and the American Bureaucracy* (Vantage Press, 1981).
12. For the 1994 revisions of this act, see Jeanne Ponessa, "The Hatch Act Rewrite," *Congressional Quarterly Weekly Report*, November 13, 1993, pp. 3146–47.
13. Paul C. Light, *The New Public Service* (Brookings Institution, 1999), p. 25.
14. Ibid., p. 2.
15. Donahue, ed., *Making Washington Work*, chaps. 12, 14.
16. Gore, *Best Kept Secrets in Government*, p. 24.
17. See the discussion in Alvin Felzenberg, ed., *The Keys to a Successful Presidency* (The Heritage Foundation, 2000), chaps. 3, 4.
18. See David E. Lewis, "The Presidential Advantage in the Design of Bureaucratic Agencies," paper presented at the American Political Science Association Annual Meeting, Boston, September 3–6, 1998.
19. Morris P. Fiorina, "Flagellating the Federal Bureaucracy," *Society* (March/April 1983), p. 73.
20. Francis E. Rourke, "Whose Bureaucracy Is This, Anyway?" *PS: Political Science and Politics* (December 1993), p. 691.
21. Surveys discussed in Bozeman, *Bureaucracy and Red Tape*, p. 39.
22. For the general philosophy of the congressional Republican leadership in the 1990s, see Newt Gingrich, *To Renew America* (HarperCollins, 1995); Dick Armey, *The Freedom Revolution* (Regnery, 1995).
23. Jonathan Weisman, "Republicans Showing Less Zeal to Cut Cabinet Departments," *Congressional Quarterly Weekly Report*, January 18, 1997, p. 171.
24. Ibid., p. 172.
25. The strategies used in these places and elsewhere are detailed in David Osborne and Ted Gaebler, *Reinventing Government: How the Entrepreneurial Spirit Is Transforming the Public Sector* (Addison-Wesley, 1992); and in David Osborne and Peter Plastrik, *Banishing Bureaucracy: The Five Strategies for Reinventing Government* (Addison-Wesley, 1997).

CHAPTER 16

1. *Felker v Turpin*, 518 US 651 (1996); *Winthrow v Williams*, 507 US 680 (1993); *McCleskey v Zant*, 499 US 467 (1991); and *Stone v Powell*, 428 US 465 (1976).
2. Neil H. Cogan, ed., *The Complete Bill of Rights: The Drafts, Debates, Sources, and Origins* (Oxford University Press, 1997); Robert A. Rutland, *The Birth of the Bill of Rights, 1776–1791* (University of North Carolina Press, 1955).
3. *Barron v Baltimore*, 7 Peters 243 (1833).
4. *Gitlow v New York*, 268 US 652 (1925).
5. Richard C. Cortner, *The Supreme Court and the Second Bill of Rights: The Fourteenth Amendment and the Nationalization of Civil Liberties* (University of Wisconsin Press, 1981).
6. Dorothy Toth Beasley, "Federalism and the Protection of Individual Rights: The American State Constitutional Perspective," in *Federalism and Rights*, ed. Ellis Katz and G. Alan Tarr (Rowman & Littlefield, 1996).
7. *Witters v Washington Department of Services for the Blind*, 474 US 481 (1986); *Zobrest v Catalina Foothills School District*, 509 US 1 (1993).
8. *Everson v Board of Education*, 333 US 203 (1947).
9. *Lemon v Kurtzman*, 403 US 602 (1971).
10. *Capital Square Review Board v Pinette*, 515 US 753 (1995).
11. *Lynch v Donnelly*, 465 US 669 (1984).
12. *Allegheny County v Greater Pittsburgh ACLU*, 492 US 573 (1989).
13. *Bowen v Kendrick*, 487 US 589 (1988); *Lee v Weisman*, 505 US 577 (1992); *Board of Education of Kiryas Joel Village School District v Grumet*, 512 US 687 (1994).
14. *Agostini v Felton*, 521 US 74 (1997).
15. *Lee v Weisman*, 505 US 577 (1992); *Santa Fe Independent School District v Doe*, 120 S.Ct. 2266 (2000).
16. *Engel v Vitale*, 370 US 421 (1962).
17. *Edwards v Aguillard*, 482 US 578 (1987).
18. *Marsh v Chambers*, 463 US 783 (1983).
19. *Employment Division of Human Resources of Oregon v Smith*, 494 US 872 (1990).
20. *City of Boerne v Flores*, 117 S.Ct. 2157 (1997).
21. *Rosenberger v University of Virginia*, 515 US 819 (1995).
22. *Board of Regents of the University of Wisconsin System v Southworth*, 120 S.Ct. 1346 (2000).
23. Oliver Wendell Holmes, in *Abrams v United States*, 250 US 616 (1919).
24. John Stuart Mill, *Essay on Liberty (1859)*, in Arthur Burtt, ed., *The English Philosophers from Bacon to Mill* (Random House, 1939), p. 961.
25. Robert Jackson, in *West Virginia State Board of Education v Barnette*, 319 US 624 (1943).
26. *Brown v Hartlage*, 456 US 45 (1982), reversing a decision of the Kentucky Court of Appeals based on the bad tendency test.
27. Oliver Wendell Holmes, in *Schenck v United States*, 249 US 47 (1919).
28. *Dennis v United States*, 341 US 494 (1951).
29. *The New York Times v Sullivan*, 376 US 254 (1964).
30. *Yates v United States*, 354 US 298 (1957).
31. *Brandenburg v Ohio*, 395 US 444 (1969).
32. *The New York Times v Sullivan*, 376 US 254 (1964).
33. *Hustler Magazine v Falwell*, 485 US 46 (1988).
34. *Masson v New York Magazine, Inc.*, 501 US 496 (1991).
35. *Gertz v Robert Welch, Inc.*, 418 US 323 (1974).
36. Potter Stewart, concurring in *Jacobellis v Ohio*, 378 US 184 (1964).
37. John Marshall Harlan, in *Cohen v California*, 403 US 15 (1971).
38. *Miller v California*, 413 US 15 (1973).
39. *Young v American Mini Theatres*, 427 US 51 (1976); *Renton v Playtime Theatres, Inc.*, 475 US 41 (1986).
40. *Barnes v Glen Theatre, Inc.*, 501 US 560 (1991); *City of Erie v Pap's A.M.*, 120 S.Ct. 1382 (2000).
41. *New York v Ferber*, 458 US 747 (1982).
42. *General Media Communications v Cohen*, 118 S.Ct. 2367 (1998).
43. See Catharine A. MacKinnon, *Only Words* (Harvard University Press, 1993), and compare another feminist, Nadine Strossen, *Defending Pornography: Free Speech, Sex, and the Fight for Women's Rights* (Scribner's, 1995).
44. *Butler v Her Majesty the Queen*, 1 S.C.R. 452 (1992).
45. *Chaplinsky v New Hampshire*, 315 US 568 (1942).
46. *Cohen v California*, 403 US 115 (1971).

47. *R.A.V. v St. Paul*, 505 US 377 (1992). See also *Wisconsin v Mitchell*, 508 US 476 (1993); *Apprendi v New Jersey*, 120 S.Ct. 2348 (2000).
48. *44 Liquormart, Inc. v Rhode Island*, 517 US 484 (1996).
49. *New York Times Company v United States*, 403 US 670 (1970); *Near v Minnesota*, 283 US 697 (1930).
50. *Hazelwood School District v Kuhlmeier*, 484 US 260 (1988).
51. *R.A.V. v St. Paul*, 505 US 377 (1992). See also *Wisconsin v Mitchell*, 508 US 476 (1993).
52. *Branzburg v Hayes*, 408 US 665 (1972).
53. *Richmond Newspapers, Inc. v Virginia*, 448 US 555 (1980). See also David M. O'Brien, *The Public's Right to Know: The Supreme Court and the First Amendment* (Praeger, 1981).
54. Oliver Wendell Holmes, dissenting in *Milwaukee Pub. Co. v Burleson*, 255 US 407 (1921).
55. *Lamont v Postmaster General*, 381 US 301 (1965).
56. *Rowan v Post Office Department*, 397 US 728 (1970).
57. *McIntyre v Ohio Election Commission*, 514 US 334 (1995).
58. *Southeastern Promotions, Ltd. v Conrad*, 420 US 546 (1975).
59. *Federal Communications Commission v Pacifica Foundation*, 438 US 726 (1978).
60. *Turner Broadcasting System v Federal Communications Commission*, 518 US 180 (1997).
61. *United States v Playboy Entertainment Group*, 120 S.Ct. 1878 (2000); *Denver Area Educational Television v Federal Communications Commission*, 518 US 727 (1996).
62. See and compare *Federal Communications Commission v Pacifica Foundation*, 438 US 726 (1978), and *Sable Communications v Federal Communications Commission*, 492 US 115 (1989).
63. *Reno v American Civil Liberties Union*, 117 S.Ct. 2329 (1997).
64. Freedom Forum Online: www.freedomforum.org/assembly/1998/9/2/march.asp.
65. Lee C. Bollinger, *Images of a Free Press* (University of Chicago Press, 1991).
66. *Walker v Birmingham*, 388 US 307 (1967).
67. *Madsen v Women's Health Center*, 512 US 753 (1994); *Schenck v Pro-Choice Network*, 519 US 357 (1997); *Hill v Colorado*, 120 S.Ct. 2480 (2000).
68. *West Virginia State Board of Education v Barnette*, 319 US 624 (1943).

CHAPTER 17

1. *Vance v Terrazas*, 444 US 252 (1980).
2. G. Pascal Zachary, "Dual Citizenship Is Double-Edged Sword," *The Wall Street Journal*, March 25, 1998, pp. B1, B15, quoting T. Alexander Aleinikoff of the Carnegie Endowment for International Peace. See also Mark Fritz, "Dual Citizenships Create Dueling Family Allegiances," *Los Angeles Times*, April 6, 1998, p. A1; William Branigin, "Pledging Allegiance to Two Flags," *The Washington Post National Weekly Edition*, June 8, 1998, p. 14.
3. *Plyler v Doe*, 457 US 202 (1982).
4. *Sale v Haitian Centers Council, Inc.*, 509 US 155 (1993).
5. *Chicago Home Building & Loan Assn. v Blaisdell*, 290 US 398 (1934).
6. *Chicago, Burlington & Quincy Railway Co. v Chicago*, 166 US 226 (1897).
7. *First English Evangelical v Los Angeles County*, 482 US 304 (1987). See Richard A. Epstein, *Taking: Private Property and the Power of Eminent Domain* (Harvard University Press, 1985).
8. *United States v 564.54 Acres of Land*, 441 US 506 (1979).
9. *Mathews v Eldridge*, 424 US 319 (1976), restated in *Connecticut v Doeher*, 501 US 1 (1991).
10. *Meyer v Nebraska*, 262 US 390 (1923).
11. *Griswold v Connecticut*, 381 US 479 (1965).
12. Philip B. Kurland, *Some Reflections on Privacy and the Constitution* (University of Chicago Center for Policy Study, 1976), p. 9. A classic and influential article about privacy is S. D. Warren and L. D. Brandeis, "The Right to Privacy," *Harvard Law Review*, December 15, 1890, pp. 193–220.
13. *Roe v Wade*, 410 US 113 (1973).
14. *Planned Parenthood of Southeastern Pennsylvania v Casey*, 505 US 833 (1992).
15. *Stenberg v Carhart*, 120 S.Ct. 2597 (2000).
16. *Bowers v Hardwick*, 478 US 186 (1986).
17. *Baker v Vermont*, 744 A.2d 864 (1999); *Powell v Georgia*, 510 S.E. 2d 18 (1998); *Kentucky v Wasson*, 842 S.W. 2d 487 (1992).
18. *Boy Scouts of America v Dale*, 120 S.Ct. 2446 (2000).
19. Antonin Scalia, dissenting in *Romer v Evans*, 517 US 620 (1996).
20. *Tennessee v Garner*, 41 US 1 (1985).
21. *Katz v United States*, 389 US 347 (1967).
22. *County of Riverside v McLaughlin*, 500 US 44 (1991).
23. *California v Hodari D.*, 499 US 621 (1991).
24. *Terry v Ohio*, 392 US 1 (1968).
25. *Minnesota v Dickerson*, 508 US 366 (1993).
26. *Almeida-Sanchez v United States*, 413 US 266 (1973); *United States v Ortiz*, 422 US 891 (1975).
27. *United States v Ramsey*, 431 US 606 (1977).
28. *Coolidge v New Hampshire*, 403 US 443 (1971); *Arizona v Hicks*, 480 US 321 (1987).
29. *United States v Ross*, 456 US 798 (1982).
30. *Pennsylvania v Mimms*, 434 US 110 (1977), reaffirmed in *Ohio v Robinette*, 519 US 33 (1997).
31. *Michigan v Tyler*, 436 US 499 (1978); *Mincey v Arizona*, 437 US 385 (1978).
32. *Chandler v Miller*, 520 US 305 (1997).
33. *Treasury Employees v Von Raab*, 489 US 656 (1989); *Skinner v Railway Labor Executives' Assn.*, 489 US 602 (1989); *Vernonia School Dist. 47J v Action*, 515 US 646 (1995); *Chandler v Miller*, 520 US 305 (1997).
34. *Mapp v Ohio*, 367 US 643 (1961).
35. Senate Committee on the Judiciary, *The Jury and the Search for Truth: The Case Against Excluding Relevant Evidence at Trial: Hearing before the Committee*, 104th Cong., 1st sess., 1997.
36. *United States v Leon*, 468 US 897 (1984); *Arizona v Evans*, 514 US 1 (1995).
37. *Miranda v Arizona*, 384 US 436 (1966).
38. *Dickerson v United States*, 120 S.Ct. 2326 (2000).
39. Justice Felix Frankfurter, dissenting in *United States v Rabinowitz*, 339 US 56 (1950).
40. *United States v Enterprises, Inc.*, 498 US 292 (1991).
41. *Williams v Florida*, 399 US 78 (1970); *Burch v Louisiana*, 441 US 130 (1979).
42. *J.E.B. v Alabama ex rel T. B.*, 511 US 127 (1994); *Batson v Kentucky*, 476 US 79 (1986); *Powers v Ohio*, 499 US 400 (1991); *Hernandez v New York*, 500 US 352 (1991); *Georgia v McCollum*, 505 US 42 (1990).
43. *Benton v Maryland*, 395 US 784 (1969). See also *Kansas v Hendricks*, 117 S. Ct. 2072 (1997).
44. *Graham v Collins*, 506 US 461 (1993).
45. Jerome Frank, *Courts on Trial* (Princeton University Press, 1949), p. 122. See also Steven Brill, *Trial by Jury* (American Lawyer Books/Touchstone, 1989).
46. Harry Kalven, Jr., and Hans Zeisel, *The American Jury* (University of Chicago Press, 1971), p. 57. See also Jeffrey Abramson, *We, The Jury: The Jury System and the Ideal of Democracy* (Basic Books, 1994).
47. George Edwards, *The Police on the Urban Frontier* (Institute of Human Relations Press and the American Jewish Committee, 1968), p. 28. See also Jerome G. Miller, *Search and Destroy: African-American Males in the Criminal Justice System* (Cambridge University Press, 1996).
48. Sandra Bass, "Blacks, Browns, and the Blues: Police and Minorities in California," *Public Affairs Report* (IGS, University of California, Berkeley) 38 (November 1997), p. 10.
49. See David Cole, *No Equal Justice: Race and Class in the American Criminal Justice System* (New Press, 1999); and Randall Kennedy, *Race, Crime, and the Law* (Pantheon, 1997).
50. See "Understanding Community Policing" (Bureau of Justice Administration), at www.community_policy.org.
51. Robert H. Jackson, *The Supreme Court in the American System of Government* (Harvard University Press, 1955), pp. 81–82.

CHAPTER 18

1. Michael R. Belknap, *Federal Law and Southern Order: Racial Violence and Constitutional Conflict in the Post-Brown South* (University of Georgia, 1987), pp. 128–204.

2. Taylor Branch, *Parting the Waters: America in the King Years, 1954–1963* (Simon & Schuster, 1988). See also Harris Wofford, *Of Kennedys and Kings: Making Sense of the Sixties* (Farrar, Strauss and Giroux, 1980).

3. See Robert D. Loevy, *To End All Segregation: The Politics and Passage of the Civil Rights Act of 1964* (University Press of America, 1990).

4. Aldon D. Morris, *The Origins of the Civil Rights Movement: Black Communities Organizing for Change* (Free Press/Macmillan, 1985); James Farmer, *Lay Bare the Heart: An Autobiography of the Civil Rights Movement* (Arbor House, 1985).

5. National Advisory Commission on Civil Disorders, *The Kerner Report* (Washington, D.C.: Government Printing Office, 1968), p. 1.

6. Ellen Carol DuBois, *Feminism and Suffrage: The Emergence of an Independent Women's Movement in America, 1848–1869* (Cornell University Press, 1978); Joan Hoff-Wilson, "Women and the Constitution," *News for Teachers of Political Science* (American Political Science Association), Summer 1985, pp. 10–15.

7. Susan M. Hartmann, *From Margin to Mainstream: American Women and Politics since 1960* (Temple University Press, 1989); Susan Gluck Mezey, *In Pursuit of Equality: Women, Public Policy, and the Federal Courts* (St. Martin's Press, 1992).

8. Celia W. Dugger, "U.S. Study Says Asian-Americans Face Widespread Discrimination," *The New York Times*, February 29, 1992, p. 1, reporting on U.S. Civil Rights Commission, *Civil Rights Issues Facing Asian Americans in the 1990s*.

9. Won Moo Hurh, *Korean Immigrants in America* (Fairleigh Dickinson University Press, 1984).

10. Antonio J. A. Pido, *The Filipinos in America: Macro/Micro Dimensions of Immigration and Integration* (Center for Migration Studies of New York, 1986).

11. Harold L. Hodgkinson, *The Demographics of American Indians: One Percent of the People, Fifty Percent of the Diversity* (Institute for Educational Leadership/Center for Demographic Policy, 1990), pp. 1–5. See also *New York Times Almanac–2000* (Penguin, 1999), p. 289.

12. Charles F. Wilkinson, *American Indians, Times, and the Law* (Yale University Press, 1987), p. 62; Vine Deloria, Jr., and Clifford M. Lytle, *The Nations Within: The Past and Future of American Indian Sovereignty* (Pantheon Books, 1984).

13. *County of Yakima v Yakima Indian Nation*, 502 US 251 (1992).

14. Theodora Lurie, "Shattering the Myth of the Vanishing American," *The Ford Foundation Letter* 22 (Winter 1991), p. 5.

15. Spencer Rich, "Native Americans, They Can Still Get Free Health Care If They're Indian Enough," *The Washington Post National Weekly Edition*, July 14, 1986, p. 34, quoting the Office of Technology Assessment.

16. *Idaho Employment v Smith*, 434 US 1 (1974).

17. *San Antonio School District v Rodriguez*, 411 US 1 (1973).

18. *Frontiero v Richardson*, 411 US 677 (1973).

19. *Califano v Webster*, 430 US 313 (1977).

20. *Mississippi University for Women v Hogan*, 458 US 718 (1982); *United States v Virginia*, 518 US 515 (1996).

21. *San Antonio School District v Rodriguez*, 411 US 1 (1973).

22. Sandra Day O'Connor, in *Kimel v Florida Board of Regents*, 120 S.Ct. 631 (2000).

23. Ibid.

24. *Washington v Davis*, 426 US 229 (1976). See also *Hunter v Underwood*, 471 US 522 (1985).

25. Justice Sandra Day O'Connor, concurring in *Hernandez v New York*, 500 US 352 (1991).

26. *Personnel Administrator of Massachusetts v Feeney*, 442 US 256 (1979).

27. *Smith v Allwright*, 321 US 649 (1944).

28. *Gomillion v Lightfoot*, 364 US 339 (1960).

29. *Harper v Virginia Board of Elections*, 383 US 663 (1966).

30. Harold W. Stanley, *Voter Mobilization and the Politics of Race: The South and Universal Suffrage, 1952–1984* (Praeger, 1987).

31. Abigail M. Thernstrom, *Whose Votes Count? Affirmative Action and Minority Voting Rights* (Harvard University Press, 1987), p. 15.

32. *Report of the United States Commission on Civil Rights* (Government Printing Office, 1959), pp. 103–104.

33. Thernstrom, *Whose Votes Count?* For a contrary view, see Bernard Grofman, Lisa Handley, and Richard G. Niemi, *Minority Representation and the Quest for Voting Equality* (Cambridge University Press, 1992).

34. *Morse v Republican Party of Virginia*, 517 US 116 (1996).

35. *Shaw v Reno*, 509 US 630 (1993). See also *Shaw v Reno*, 509 US 874; *Johnson v De Grandy*, 512 US 997 (1994).

36. *Abrams v Johnson*, 518 US 74 (1997); *Miller v. Johnson*, 515 US 900 (1995).

37. Orlando Patterson, *The Ordeal of Integration: Progress and Resentment in America's "Racial" Crisis* (Civitas/Counterpoint, 1997), p. 67.

38. *Plessy v Ferguson*, 163 US 537 (1896).

39. *Brown v Board of Education of Topeka*, 347 US 483 (1954). See also J. W. Peltason, *Fifty-eight Lonely Men: Southern Federal Judges and School Desegregation* (University of Illinois Press, 1971), p. 248.

40. *Brown v Board of Education*, 349 US 294 (1955).

41. William Celis III, "Study Finds Rising Concentration of Black and Hispanic Students," *The New York Times*, December 14, 1993, p. A1.

42. *Missouri v Jenkins*, 495 US 33 (1990).

43. See Gary Orfield, Susan E. Eaton, and the Harvard Project on School Desegregation, *Dismantling Desegregation: The Quiet Reversal of Brown v Board of Education* (New Press, 1996). See also Peter Appelbome, "Schools See Reemergence of 'Separate But Equal,'" *The New York Times*, April 8, 1997, p. A8.

44. Raymond Hernandez, "NAACP Suspends Yonkers Leader After Criticism of Usefulness of School Busing," *The New York Times*, November 1, 1995, p. A13.

45. Quoted by Peter Applebome, "Opponents' Moves Refueling Debate on School Busing," *The New York Times*, September 26, 1995, p. A1.

46. Justice William O. Douglas, dissenting in *Moose Lodge No. 107 v Irvis*, 407 US 163 (1972).

47. *New York State Club Association v New York City*, 487 US 1 (1988).

48. *Boy Scouts of America v Dale*, 120 S.Ct. 2446 (2000).

49. *Civil Rights Cases*, 109 US 3 (1883).

50. *Heart of Atlanta Motel v United States*, 379 US 421 (1964).

51. Darryl Van Duch, "Plagued by Politics, EEOC Backlog Grows," *The Recorder*, August 18, 1998, p. 1; David Rovella, "EEOC Chairman Casellas, 'We Are Being Selective,'" *The National Law Journal*, November 20, 1995, p. 1.

52. Charles M. Lamb, "Housing Discrimination and Segregation," *Catholic University Law Review* (Spring 1981), p. 370.

53. *Shelley v Kraemer*, 334 US 1 (1948).

54. Timothy Noah, "Housing Report Says Racial Bias Remains Prevalent," *The Wall Street Journal*, August 30, 1991, reporting on findings of report prepared by the Urban Institute commissioned by the Department of Housing and Urban Development.

55. Daniel Mitchell, quoted in CQ Researcher, *Housing Discrimination* 5 (February 24, 1995), p. 174.

56. Justice John Marshall Harlan, dissenting in *Plessy v Ferguson*, 163 US 537 (1896).

57. *University of California Regents v Bakke*, 438 US 265 (1978).

58. Sandra Day O'Connor, in *Richmond v Croson*, 488 US 469 (1989).

59. See *Adarand Constructors, Inc. v Pena*, 515 US 2000 (1995).

60. *Shaw v Reno*, 509 US 630 (1993); *Miller v Johnson*, 515 US 900 (1995).

61. *Hopwood v Texas*, 518 US 1016 (1996).

62. "Affirmative Action in California Passed," *The Economist*, April 8, 2000, p. 29.

63. Romel Hernandez, "Universities Will End Offers of Scholarships Based on Race," *The Oregonian*, March 21, 1998, at www.oregonlive.com/todaynews.

64. Carol M. Swain et al., "When Whites and Blacks Agree: Fairness in Educational Opportunities," Institute of Governmental Studies, University of California at Berkeley, Working Paper 98-11, 1998, p. 6. See also Lee Sigelman and Susan Welch, *Black Americans' Views of Racial Inequality: The Dream Deferred* (Cambridge University Press, 1994); Peter Skerry, "The Affirmative Action Paradox," *Society* 35, no. 6 (September/October 1998), p. 11.

65. James Farmer, quoted in Rochelle L. Stanfield, "Black Complaints Haven't Translated into Political Organization and Power," *National Journal*, June 14, 1980, p. 465.

66. National Academy of Science, *A Common Destiny: Blacks and American Society* (National Academy Press, 1989).

67. Gary Orfield, "Separate Societies: Have the Kerner Warnings Come True?" in Fred R. Harris and Roger W. Wilkins, eds., *Quiet Riots: Race and Poverty*

in the United States—*The Kerner Report Twenty Years Later* (Pantheon, 1988), p. 103. See also Madeline Landau, "Race, Poverty and the Cities: Hyperinnovation in Complex Policy Systems," *Public Affairs Report* (Bulletin of the Institute of Governmental Studies, University of California, Berkeley) 30 (January 1989), p. 1; Margaret C. Simms, ed., *Black Economic Progress: An Agenda for the 1990's* (Joint Center for Political Studies, 1988); Nicholas Lehmann, *The Promised Land* (Knopf, 1991).

68. Patterson, *Ordeal of Integration*, p. 54.
69. Gary Orfield and Carole Ashkinaze, *The Closing Door: Conservative Policy and Black Opportunity* (University of Chicago Press, 1991), p. 26.
70. William J. Wilson, *The Truly Disadvantaged: The Inner City, the Underclass, and Public Policy* (University of Chicago Press, 1987), esp. chap. 5.
71. Orfield and Ashkinaze, *Closing Door*, pp. 221–34.

CHAPTER 19

1. Robert A. Dahl, *On Democracy* (Yale University Press, 1998), p. 158.
2. See "National Debt," at http://www.jeffords.senate.gov/debt.html.
3. For a discussion of the budgetary cycle, see Allen Schick, *The Federal Budget: Politics, Policy, Process*, rev. ed. (Brookings Institution, 2000).
4. Efforts at past tax reform are described by Jeffrey H. Birnbaum and Alan S. Murray, *Showdown at Gucci Gulch: Lawmakers, Lobbyists, and the Unlikely Triumph of Tax Reform* (Vintage, 1988). See also Timothy J. Conlan, Margaret T. Wrightson, and David R. Beam, *Taxing Choices: The Politics of Tax Reform* (Congressional Quarterly Press, 1990).
5. John R. Wilke, "Showing Its Age: Fed's Huge Empire, Set Up Years Ago, Is Costly and Inefficient," *The Wall Street Journal*, September 12, 1996, p. 1.
6. Arthur Rolnick, research director at the Minneapolis Fed, quoted in ibid., p. 2.
7. Quoted in Frederick Lewis Allen, *Since Yesterday* (Harper, 1940), p. 64.
8. W. H. Beveridge, *The Pillars of Security* (Macmillan, 1943), p. 51.
9. The debate over Keynes and his economic theories is still alive in the United States. See Donald E. Moggridge, *Maynard Keynes: An Economist's Biography* (Routledge, 1992).
10. See "Who Owns the Knowledge Economy?" *The Economist*, April 8, 2000.
11. Gary Burtless, Robert J. Lawrence, Robert E. Litan, and Robert J. Shapiro, *Globaphobia: Confronting Fears About Open Trade* (Brookings Institution, 1998), p. 29. For more information about GATT and the World Trade Organization, go to www.wto.org.
12. Burtless et al., *Globaphobia*, p. 126.
13. Robert W. Crandall et al., *An Agenda for Federal Regulatory Reform* (American Enterprise Institute and Brookings Institution, 1997), p. 1.

14. See Robert Kuttner, *Everything for Sale: The Virtues and Limits of Markets* (Knopf, 1997); Gary Bryner, *Blue Skies, Green Politics: The Clean Air Act of 1990 and Its Interpretation*, 2d ed. (Congressional Quarterly Press, 1995).
15. Harold W. Stanley and Richard G. Niemi, *Vital Statistics in American Politics, 1999* (Congressional Quarterly Press, 1999), p. 258.
16. Stephen Moore, ed., *Restoring the Dream: The Bold New Plan by House Republicans* (Times Books, 1995), p. 156.
17. But more progress is encouraged by Crandall et al., *Agenda for Federal Regulatory Reform*, pp. 12–16.
18. *United States v E. C. Knight Company*, 156 US 1 (1895).
19. On the origins of the Federal Trade Commission and the role of Louis D. Brandeis, see Thomas K. McCraw, *Prophets of Regulation* (Belknap, 1984), chap. 3.
20. Don L. Boroughs with Betsy Carpenter, "Cleaning Up the Environment," *U.S. News and World Report*, March 25, 1991, p. 46.
21. For a useful history of airline deregulation, see Steven A. Morrison and Clifford Winston, *The Evolution of the Airline Industry* (Brookings Institution, 1995).
22. See the book on Southwest Airlines and its longtime chief executive Herb Kelliher by Kevin Freiberg and Jackie Freiberg, *Nuts!* (Bard Press, 1996).
23. *Reno v American Civil Liberties Union*, 521 U.S. 844 (1997).
24. See Robert W. Crandall and Harold Furchtgott-Roth, *Cable TV: Regulation or Competition?* (Brookings Institution, 1996); Richard Klinger, *The New Information Industry: Regulatory Challenges and the First Amendment* (Brookings Institution,1996); Lawrence Lessig, *Code and Other Laws of Cyberspace* (Basic Books, 2000).

CHAPTER 20

1. www.georgewbush.com.
2. www.algore2000.com.
3. Michael B. Katz, *In the Shadow of the Poorhouse: A Social History of Welfare in America* (Basic Books, 1986).
4. www.ssa.gov/statistics/fast_facts/index.html.
5. Martha Derthick, "No More Easy Votes for Social Security," *Brookings Review* 10 (Fall 1992), pp. 50–53.
6. www.cbo.gov.
7. Peter Francese, "Social Security Solution," *American Demographics* 15 (February 1993), p. 2. See also Terry Savage, "Can Social Security Find Its Way Back to Stability?" *Chicago Sun Times*, December 8, 1998, p. 6.
8. For a pessimistic view of the viability of Social Security, see Neil Howe and Richard Jackson, "The Myth of the 2.2 Percent Solution," at www.cato.org/pubs/ssps11es.html. Robert D. Reischauer of the Brookings Institution testified before the House Committee on Ways and Means, November 19, 1998, that by 2021 Social Security will start running deficits and that by 2032 "reserves will be depleted."
9. Lyndon Johnson, speech at the University of Michigan, May 1964, in *Congress and the Nation, 1965–1968: A Review of Government and Politics During the Johnson Years* (Congressional Quarterly Press, 1969), 2: 650.
10. *Congress and the Nation, 1945–1964: A Review of Government and Politics* (Congressional Quarterly Press, 1965), 1:49.
11. For examples on both sides of this debate, see John E. Schwartz, *America's Hidden Success: A Reassessment of Twenty Years of Public Policy* (Norton, 1983); Charles Murray, *Losing Ground: American Social Policy, 1950–80* (Basic Books, 1984).
12. Robert Pear, "House Sends Senate an Overhaul of Welfare System" *The New York Times*, December 22, 1995, p. Ap. 37.
13. William J. Clinton, State of the Union Address, January 23, 1996, *House Document 104–168* (Government Printing Office, 1996).
14. William J. Clinton, acceptance speech at the Democratic National Convention, Chicago, 1992, printed in *Los Angeles Times*, July 7, 1992, p. A10.
15. "Household Income at Record High: Poverty Declines in 1998," at www.census.gov/PressRelease.htm.
16. Gertrude Schaffner Goldberg and Eleanor Kremen, eds., *The Feminization of Poverty: Only in America?* (Greenwood Press, 1990).
17. U.S. Bureau of the Census, Historical Tables—People, Table P-40, at www.census.gov/hhes/income/histinc/p40.html.
18. June O'Niel and Solomon Polachek, "Why the Gender Gap in Wages Narrowed in the 1980s," *Journal of Labor Economics* 11 (1993): 225–229.
19. Robert Pear, "Judge Rules States Can't Cut Welfare," *The New York Times*, October 14, 1997, p. A1.
20. Administration for Children and Families web site: www.acf.dhhs.gov/news/stats/aug-sep.htm.
21. See www.oecd.orglels/health/software/fad13.htm for a description of issues surrounding Medicaid, see Kathleen N. Lohr and M. Susan Maquis, *Medicare and Medicaid: Past, Present and Future* (Rand Corporation, 1984); Congressional Research Service, *Medicaid Source Book* (Library of Congress, 1993). For a discussion of Medicare generally, see Theodore R. Marmor,

Jerry L. Mashaw, and Philip L. Harvey, *America's Misunderstood Welfare State: Persistent Myths, Enduring Realities* (Basic Books, 1990), p. 97.

22. "Health Spending in 1998: Signals of Change," *Health Affairs in the Business of Health Finance* 19, no. 1 (January–February, 2000), p. 131; also www.projhope.org.

23. U.S. Bureau of the Census. *Statistical Abstract of the United States, 1999* (Government Printing Office, 1999), p. 194.

24. www.cdc.gov/nechs/fastats/hinsure.htm.

25. www.census.gov/press.release/www/1999/clo99-189.html.

26. *Statistical Abstract, 1999*, p.404.

27. www.hcfa.gov/stats/nhe-oact/tables/t1.htm.

28. John Greenwald, "Ouch!" *Time*, March 8, 1993, p. 53.

29. *Statistical Abstract, 1999*, p. 448.

30. Health Care Financing Administration home page, October 4, 1998, table 11: www.hcfa.gov/stats/nhe-oact/tables/t11/htm.

31. *Statistical Abstract, 1999*, p. 93.

32. Campbell, "Health Insurance Coverage."

33. Laurene A. Graig, *Health of Nations: An International Perspective on U.S. Health Care Reform* (Congressional Quarterly Press, 1993), p. 20.

34. According to the Public Citizens Research Group, the optimal number of c-sections is 12 percent of total births. But in the most recent year for which we have data 21 percent of births were by c-section, producing an estimated 330,000 unnecessary c-section deliveries. National Center for Health Statistics (NCHS) home page: www.cdc.gov/nchs/datawh/statab/pubd/4611s39h.htm.

35. Health Care Financing Administration, Office of the Actuary, National Health Statistics, December 15, 1997, at www.hcfa.gov/stats/nhe-oact/tables/t11.htm.

36. Mark M. Hagland, "Physicians Using Computers Show Lower Resource Utilization," *Hospitals*, May 5, 1993, p. 17.

37. Michael D. Lemonick, "Doctors Deadly Mistakes," *Time*, December 13, 1999, p. 74.

38. Jennifer Steinhauer, "At Beth Israel, Lapses in Care Mar Gains in Technology," *The New York Times*, February 15, 2000, p. B1.

39. Associated Press, "Medicare Funds Going Up in Smoke," *Deseret News*, May 17, 1994, p. A1.

40. www.Washingtonpost.com/wp-srv/natinal/longterm/tobacco/overview.htm.

41. www.medicarehmo.com/mcmnu.htm.

42. "Measuring the HMOs," *Los Angeles Times*, October 3, 1998, p. B7.

43. Mary Agnes Carey and Rebecca Adams, "Managed-Care Conferees Agree on Appeals Principles; Key Details Remian Unresolved," *Congressional Quarterly Weekly Report*, April 15, 2000, p. 903.

44. For more information on HMO reform, consult the Bush and Gore home pages at www.georgewbush.com and www.algore2000.com.

45. James A. Klein, "Should Employers Select Health-Insurance Options for Workers?" *The Dallas Morning News*, August 2, 1998, p. J1.

46. Institute of Medicine, Committee on Employer-Based Health Benefits, *Employment and Health Benefits: A Connection at Risk*, ed. Marilyn J. Field and Harold T. Shapiro (National Academy Press, 1993), p. 5.

47. The amount permitted for a medical savings account is 75 percent of the maximum total deduction for medical expenses for an individual or couple. See www.irs.ustreas.bov/prod/forms_pubs/pubs/p96901.htm.

48. Philip B. Kurland and Ralph Lerner, eds., *The Founders' Constitution* (University of Chicago Press, 1987).

49. U.S. Department of Education, Office of Educational Research and Improvement, National Center for Education Statistics, *Federal Support for Education: Fiscal Years 1980 to 1998*, National Center for Education Statistics 98–115 (1998), p. iii.

50. nces.ed.gov/pubs99/digest98/d98t319.html.

51. B. Guy Peters, *American Public Policy: Promise and Performance*, 4th ed. (Chatham House, 1996), p. 338.

52. www.uscharterschools.org/gen_info/gi_main.htm.

53. Center for Education Reform, charter school highlights and statistics, updated November 18, 1996, edreform.com/pugs/chglance.html.

54. Stephen E. Gorrie, president of the Massachusetts Teachers Association, quoted in Andrea Billups, "Massachusetts Teachers Face Competency Tests," *The Washington Times*, June 2, 2000, p. A1.

55. "House Passes Bill Clarifying Gun-Crimes Law," *Congressional Quarterly Weekly Report*, February 28, 1998, p. 498.

CHAPTER 21

1. Christopher S. Wren, "U.N. Report Maps Hunger Hot Spots," *The New York Times*, January 9, 2001, p. A8.

2. Vernon Loeb, "Future Threats," *The Washington Post National Weekly Edition*, December 25, 2000–January 1, 2001, p. 16.

3. Condoleeza Rice, "Promoting the National Interest," *Foreign Affairs*, January/February 2000, pp. 46–47.

4. William J. Broad, "27 Countries Support New Atom Accord," *The New York Times National Edition*, May 3, 1992, sec. 1, p. 9.

5. Michael Mandelbaum, "Lessons of the Next Nuclear War," *Foreign Affairs*, March/April 1995, pp. 22–37. See also Paul H. Nitze, "A Threat Mostly to Ourselves," *The New York Times*, October 28, 1999, p. A25.

6. "The Future of Warfare," *The Economist*, March 8, 1997, p. 15.

7. Harold Brown, Melvin R. Laird and William J. Perry, "Ratify, But Review," *The New York Times*, January 7, 2001, p. 17.

8. Nitze, "Threat Mostly to Ourselves,"p. A25.

9. "A Dangerous Treaty," editorial, *The Wall Street Journal*, February 19, 1997, p. A16. But see Pat Towell, "Clinton Pressures GOP to Act on Chemical Arms Ban," *Congressional Quarterly Weekly Report*, March 11, 1997, pp. 545–50.

10. Warren Christopher, *In the Stream of History: Shaping Foreign Policy for a New Era* (Stanford University Press, 1998), p. 533.

11. The case for continued reliance on vital and well-supported U.S. embassies abroad is well made in Mary Locke and Casimir A. Yost, eds., *Who Needs Embassies? How U.S. Missions Abroad Help Shape Our World* (Georgetown University School of Foreign Policy, 1997).

12. Jane Perlez, "As Diplomacy Loses Luster, Young Stars Flee State Department," *The New York Times*, September 5, 2000, pp. 1, 12.

13. For a fascinating history of U.S. intelligence operations, see Christopher Andrew, *For the President's Eyes Only: Secret Intelligence and the American Presidency from Washington to Bush* (HarperCollins, 1995). See also

Rhodri Jeffreys-Jones, *The CIA and American Democracy*, 2d ed. (Yale University Press, 1998).

14. Chuck McCutcheon, "Tenet Gives CIA Credibility on the Hill," *Congressional Quarterly Weekly*, January 22, 2000, pp. 139–42.

15. For President Bush's recollections and surprise, see George Bush and Brent Scowcroft, *A World Transformed* (Knopf, 1998), pp. 302–33.

16. See Loch K. Johnson, *Secret Agencies: U.S. Intelligence in a Hostile World* (Yale University Press, 1996).

17. Daniel Patrick Moynihan, *Secrecy: The American Experience* (Yale University Press, 1998), pp. 221, 227.

18. Johnson, *Secret Agencies*, p. 201.

19. James Kitfield, "What Now for the Spooks?" *National Journal*, March 1, 1996, p. 597.

20. The full report of this commission headed by Les Aspin and Harold Brown is *Preparing for the 21st Century: An Appraisal of U.S. Intelligence*, Report of the Commission on the Roles and Capabilities of the U.S. Intelligence Community (Government Printing Office, March 1, 1996).

21. Steven Kull, "What the Public Knows That Washington Doesn't," *Foreign Policy* (Winter 1995–96), p. 115. See also Steven Kull and I. M. Destler, *Misreading the Public: The Myth of a New Isolationism* (Brookings Institution Press, 1999).

22. John E. Rielly, ed., *American Public Opinion and U.S. Foreign Policy, 1995* (Chicago Council of Foreign Relations, 1995), p. 40.

23. For an examination of how Japanese companies try to influence foreign policy and trade officials in Washington, see Pat Choate, *Agents of Influence* (Knopf, 1990).

24. "G.O.P. Returns $100,000 Gift," *The New York Times*, January 20, 2001, p. A.8.

25. For a useful review of how Congress has occasionally challenged and even more often failed to challenge the White House when it comes to

the war power, see Louis Fisher, *Presidential War Power* (University Press of Kansas, 1995).

26. For an analysis that asserts U.S. foreign policy is almost entirely shaped by self-appointed elites, see Eric Alterman, *Who Speaks for America? Why Democracy Matters* (Cornell University Press, 1998). More generally, see Ole Holsti, *Public Opinion and American Foreign Policy* (University of Michigan Press, 1996).

27. See Robert S. McNamara, *In Retrospect: The Tragedy and Lessons of Vietnam* (Times Books, 1995).

28. "U.S. Foreign Aid Spending Since World War II," data presentation in *The Public Perspective* 8, no. 5 (August/September 1997), p. 11.

29. Gallup poll data, May 2000.

30. See Kull and Destler, *Misreading the Public*, pp. 113–33.

31. See Sebastian Mallaby, "Why So Stingy on Foreign Aid?" *The Washington Post National Weekly Edition*, July 3, 2000, p. 27.

32. Ibid., p. 27. But see Doug Bandlow, "The Case Against Foreign Aid," *The Christian Science Monitor*, September 29, 1999, p. 9; Eric Schmitt, "Helms Urges Foreign Aid Be Handled by Charities," *The New York Times*, January 12, 2001, p. A4.

33. Madeleine Albright, "Testing of American Foreign Policy," *Foreign Affairs*, November/December 1998, p. 57.

34. Gary Hufbauer and Jeffrey J. Schott, "Economic Sanctions and Foreign Policy," *PS: Political Science and Politics* (Fall 1985), p. 727.

35. Richard N. Haass, "Sanctions Almost Never Work," *The Wall Street Journal*, June 19, 1998, p. A14. See also Richard N. Haass and Meghan L. O'Sullivan, eds., *Honey and Vinegar: Incentives, Sanctions and Foreign Policy* (Brookings Institution Press, 2000).

36. Cited in Gerald F. Seib, "Capital Journal," *The Wall Street Journal*, June 17, 1998, p. A18.

37. Gary Hufbauer, "Foreign Policy on the Cheap," *The Washington Post National Weekly Edition*, July 20–27, 1998, p. 22.

38. John Prados, *The President's Secret Wars: CIA and Pentagon Covert Operations Since World War II* (Morrow, 1986); Moynihan, Secrecy.

39. Hufbauer and Schott, "Economic Sanctions," p. 278.

40. Ivo H. Daalder and Michael E. O'Hanlon, *Winning Ugly: NATO's War to Save Kosovo* (Brookings Institution Press, 2000), esp. chap. 6.

41. Bob Dole, "Peacekeepers and Politics," *The New York Times*, January 24, 1994, p. A11. Dole reiterated this general theme in Robert Dole, "Shaping America's Global Future," *Foreign Policy* (Spring 1995), pp. 29–43. See also Miles A. Pomper, "Helms Gives Blunt Message to U.N. Security Council: Don't Tread on U.S.," *Congressional Quarterly*, January 20, 2000, p. 144.

42. See, for example, Michael Lind, "Twilight of the U.N.," *The New Republic*, October 30, 1995, pp. 25–33; Rosemary Righter, *Utopia Lost: The United Nations and World Order* (Twentieth Century Fund, 1995).

43. Dennis C. Jett, "The U.N.'s Failures Are Everyone's Fault," *The New York Times*, May 22, 2000, p. A23. See also Christopher S. Wren, "Era Waning: Holbrooke Takes Stock," *The New York Times*, January 14, 2001, p. 8.

44. Norman A. Graebner, "The President as Commander in Chief: A Study in Power," in *Commander-In-Chief: Presidential Leadership in Modern Wars*, ed. Joseph G. Dawson III (University Press of Kansas, 1993), p. 31.

45. See the arguments in Robert W. Tucker and David C. Hendrickson, *The Imperial Temptation: The New World Order and America's Purpose* (Council on Foreign Relations, 1992). See also Ronald Steel, *Temptations of a Superpower* (Harvard University Press, 1995).

46. Colin Powell, quoted in Steven Mufson, "From Soldier to Diplomat," *The Washington Post National Weekly Edition*, December 25, 2000–January 1, 2001, p. 6.

47. Kull and Destler, *Misreading the Public*. (Brookings Institution Press, 1999).

48. Steven Lee Myers, "Military Warns Soldiers of Failure to Hail Chief," *The New York Times*, October 21, 1998, p. A22.

49. See George C. Wilson, *This War Really Matters: Inside the Fight for Defense Dollars* (Congressional Quarterly Press, 2000).

50. Dana Priest, "Peacekeeping Is Putting Women in the Trenches," *The Washington Post National Weekly Edition*, January 26, 1998, p. 9; Mark Thompson, "Boys and Girls Apart," *Time*, January 5, 1998, p. 104.

51. Evan Thomas and Gregory L. Vistica, "Falling Out of the Sky," *Newsweek*, March 17, 1997, p. 26.

52. Gus Fenoglio and Carl M. Cannon, "What Bush Promised," *National Journal*, January 6, 2001, p. 18.

53. Elizabeth Becker and Steven Lee Myers, "Pentagon Says Commander Admits He Altered Records," *The New York Times*, January 20, 2001, p. A7.

54. See, for example, James Kitfield, "Ships Galore!" *National Journal*, February 10, 1996, pp. 298–302.

55. Kenneth R. Mayer, *The Political Economy of Defense Contracting* (Yale University Press, 1991), p. 223.

56. On the bureaucratic and congressional politics of these panels, see Robert Scott Dering, "The Politics of Military Base Closures, 1988–1995," paper presented at the American Political Science Association Annual Meeting, Boston, September 3–6, 1998.

CHAPTER 22

1. For a discussion of what factors improve economic performance and state policy effectiveness, see Paul Brace, *State Government and Economic Performance* (Johns Hopkins University Press, 1993); Susan E. Clarke and Martin R. Saiz, "Economic Development and Infrastructure Policy," in *Politics in the American States*, ed. Virginia Gray, Russell Hanson, and Herbert Jacob, 7th ed. (Congressional Quarterly Press, 1999), pp. 540–43.

2. Readers interested in understanding the enormous variety of political cultures within our states would do well to read books in the fascinating University of Nebraska series called Politics and Governments of the American States. About 18 of planned volumes on the 50 states have been published, including studies of Arkansas, Colorado, Illinois, Kentucky, Michigan, New Jersey, North Carolina, and West Virginia. We rely on several of these studies in our chapters on state politics.

3. Robert S. Lynd and Helen M. Lynd, *Middletown* (Harcourt, 1929). See also their analysis of Muncie ten years later in *Middletown in Transition* (Harcourt, 1937).

4. Floyd Hunter, *Community Power Structure* (University of North Carolina Press, 1953). For a reassessment and rebuttal of Hunter's findings, see M. Kent Jennings, *Community Influentials: The Elites of Atlanta* (Free Press, 1964).

5. Robert A. Dahl, *Who Governs? Democracy and Power in an American City* (Yale University Press, 1961).

6. See the interesting study of San Jose, California, by Phillip J. Troustine and Terry Christensen, *Movers and Shakers: The Study of Community Power* (St. Martin's Press, 1982). See also Clarence N. Stone, *Regime Politics: Governing Atlanta, 1946–1988* (University Press of Kansas, 1989).

7. See, for example, Peter Bachrach and Morton S. Baratz, *Power and Poverty: Theory and Practice* (Oxford University Press, 1970); Matthew A. Crenson, *The Unpolitics of Air Pollution: A Study of Non-Decision Making in Two Cities* (Johns Hopkins University Press, 1971); John Gaventa, *Power and Powerlessness: Quiescence and Rebellion in an Appalachian Valley* (University of Illinois Press, 1980).

8. Bryan D. Jones and Lynn W. Bachelor, *The Sustaining Hand: Community Leadership and Corporate Power*, 2d ed. (University Press of Kansas, 1993), p. 254. See also Stone, *Regime Politics*.

9. U.S. Office of Management and Budget, *Budget of the United States, FY 2000* (Government Printing Office, 1999); *New York Times Almanac 2000* (Penguin, 1999), p. 155. See also stats.bls.gov/news.release/pdf/empsit.pdf.

10. Stone, *Regime Politics*, p. 232.

11. For a detailed analysis of how the W. R. Grace Company and Beatrice Foods Company had to rely on law firms to fight legal actions surrounding their operations in Woburn, Massachusetts, see Jonathan Harr, *A Civil Action* (Vintage Books, 1996).

12. See Clive S. Thomas and Ronald J. Hrebenar, "Interest Groups in the States," in *Politics in the American States*, ed. Gray et al., pp. 122–58; and *The Book of the States, 2000–2001* (Council of State Governments, 2000), p. 397.

13. For a general discussion of ethics reform and enforcement efforts, see *Spectrum: The Journal of State Government* (Winter 1993).

14. On various efforts to improve ethical practices and professionalism in the state legislatures and the limits of these efforts, see Alan Rosenthal, *Drawing the Line: Legislative Ethics in the States* (University of Nebraska Press, 1996).
15. Jimmy Carter, *Why Not the Best?* (Bantam Books, 1976), p. 101. See also the memoir by Tom Loftus, a former speaker of the Wisconsin State Assembly, *The Art of Legislative Politics* (Congressional Quarterly Press, 1994), chap. 3.
16. Diane D. Blair, *Arkansas Politics and Government* (University of Nebraska Press, 1988), p. 118.
17. William P. Browne and Kenneth VerBurg, *Michigan Politics and Government* (University of Nebraska Press, 1995), pp. 241–45.
18. Paul Peterson, *City Limits* (University of Chicago Press, 1981), p. 124. See also the useful discussion of the challenge of covering state legislative politics in Browne and VerBurg, *Michigan Politics and Government*, pp. 242–45.
19. Joseph F. Zimmerman, *The New England Town Meeting: Democracy in Action* (Praeger, 1999).
20. See for example, Daniel Kemmis, *The Good City and the Good Life* (Houghton Mifflin, 1995); David L. Kirp, John P. Dwyer, and Larry A. Rosenthal, *Our Town: Race, Housing and the Soul of Suburbia* (Rutgers University Press, 1997).
21. Eugene F. Rivers III, "High-Octane Faith," in *Community Works: The Revival of Civil Society in America*, ed. E. J. Dionne, Jr. (Brookings Institution Press, 1998), p. 61.
22. For the efforts of a big-city mayor and his team of advisers, see Buzz Bissinger, *A Prayer for the City* (Random House, 1997). See also the example of Milwaukee's mayor, John O. Norquist, *Wealth of Cities* (Addison-Wesley, 1998).

CHAPTER 23

1. *Effective Government Now for the New Century: Final Report of the Temporary New York State Commission on Constitutional Revision* (Nelson A. Rockefeller Institute of Government, 1995).
2. Mario M. Cuomo, "Real Reform: It's Time for a People's State Constitutional Convention," *Rockefeller Institute Bulletin* (1993), pp. 41–46, an article taken from a special message the governor released at the time Cuomo appointed the Temporary Commission on Constitutional Revision in 1993.
3. Richard Perez-Pena, "Voters Reject Constitutional Convention: Last-Minute Campaign Appears to Sway Ballot," *The New York Times*, November 5, 1997, p. B1.
4. Michigan Department of State, Bureau of Elections: www.sos.state.mi.us/law; Arkansas Government Relations home page: http://www.uark.edu/~govinfo/PAGES/History/del.html; gopher://gopher.sos.state.mi.us/00 and _elect/genres1994/d90E90000000.
5. Gerald Benjamin, "The Functions of State Constitutions in a Federal System," paper presented at the American Political Science Association Round Table, Washington, D.C., 1984.
6. John Adams, quoted in Judith S. Kaye, "Federalism's Other Tier," *Constitution* 3 (Winter 1991), p. 50.
7. *The Providence Journal*, July 7, 2000, as reported on www.projo.com.
8. G.Alan Tarr, *Understanding State Constitutions* (Princeton University Press, 1998), p. 47.
9. Donald S. Lutz, "Toward a Theory of Constitutional Amendment," in *Responding To Imperfection: The Theory and Practice of Constitutional Amendment*, ed. Sanford Levinson (Princeton University Press, 1995), pp. 237–274.
10. Christopher W. Hammons, "Was James Madison Wrong? Rethinking the American Preference for Short, Framework-Oriented Constitutions," *American Political Science Review* 93 (December 1999), p. 838.
11. *The Book of the States, 2000–2001* (Council of State Governments, 2000 p. 3; John Kincaid, "State Constitutions in the Federal System," *Annals of the American Academy of Political and Social Science* 496 (March 1988), p. 14.
12. *Book of the States 2000–2001*, p. 3; Hammons, "Was James Madison Wrong?" p. 838.
13. Jack W. Strain, *An Outline of Oklahoma Government*, ed. Leroy Crozier and Carl F. Reherman (Bureau of Local Government Services, Department of Political Science, Central State University, 1984), p. 21.
14. South Dakota Constitution, Article XI, Section 8.
15. Alabama Constitution, Amendment 383 (1901), cited by Hammons, "Was James Madison Wrong?" p. 839.
16. Kaye, "Federalism's Other Tier," p. 54. Judith Kaye is chief judge of the Court of Appeals of the State of New York.
17. Miranda S. Spivack, "How States' Rights Can Rectify the Wrongs of the Supreme Court," *Los Angeles Times*, June 16, 1991, p. M2.
18. *Michigan v Long*, 463 US 1032 (1983). "Our Judicial Federalism," *Intergovernmental Perspective* 15 (Summer 1989), pp. 8–15; William M. Wiecek, "Some Protection of Personal Liberty: Remembering the Future," and Kermit L. Hall, "Mostly Anchor and Little Sail: The Evolution of American State Constitutions," both in *Toward a Usable Past: Liberty Under State Constitutions*, ed. Paul Finkelman and Stephen E. Gottlieb (University of Georgia Press, 1991), pp. 371–417.
19. According to the *Book of the States, 2000–2001*, p. 11, in 1998–99, of the 266 legislative proposed amendments in the 49 states that require submission to the voters for ratification, 210 were adopted, or 78.8 percent.
20. "Mississippi Begins Analyzing Its Racist Constitution of 1890," *The New York Times*, December 12, 1985, p. B2. See also Janice C. May, "State Constitutions and Constitutional Revision: 1988–89 and the 1980s," in *The Book of the States, 1989* (Council of State Governments, 1990), p. 23; and Tip H. Allen, Jr., "The Enduring Traditions of the State Constitutions," in Dale Krane and Stephen D. Shaffer, *Mississippi Government and Politics: Modernizers versus Traditionalists* (University of Nebraska Press, 1992), pp. XX–XX.
21. *The Book of the States, 2000–2001*, p. 10.
22. *The Book of the States, 2000–2001*, p. 11.
23. *The Book of the States, 2000–2001*, p. 11.
24. David B. Magleby, "Direct Legislation in the American States," in *Referendums Around the World: The Growing Use of Direct Democracy*, ed. David Butler and Austin Ranney (American Enterprise Institute Press, 1994), p. 225.
25. California Commission on Campaign Financing, *Democracy by Initiative: A Summary of the Report and Recommendations of the California Commission on Campaign Financing* (Center for Responsive Government, 1992), p. 25.
26. Katherine M. Mauk, "Approaches to Altering State Constitutions," research report of the Public Law Research Institute at Hastings College of the Law, 1995, p. 5. See also www.uchastings.edu/piri/spring95/statecon.html.
27. *Amador Valley Joint Union High School District v State Board of Equalization*, 22 Cal. 3d 208, 1978, California Supreme Court, quoted in Eugene C. Lee, "The Revision of California's Constitution," *CPS Brief: A Publication of the California Policy Seminar* 3 (April 1991), p. 1.
28. Mauk, "Approaches to Altering State Constitutions," p. 5.
29. *Book of the States, 2000–2001, p. 11*. See also Magleby, "*Direct Legislation in the American States*," p. 251.
30. *Tarr*, Understanding State Constitutions, p.158.
31. Ibid., pp. 160–61.
32. Gerald Benjamin and Thomas Gais, "Constitutional Conventionphobia," in *State Constitutions: Competing Perspectives*, ed. Burton C. Agata and Eric Lane (Hofstra Law and Policy Symposium, 1996), 1:69; Tarr, *Understanding State Constitutions*, p. 25
33. Caleb Nelson, "Majorities, Minorities, and the Meaning of Liberty: A Reevaluation of Scholarly Explanations for the Rise of the Elective Judiciary in Antebellum America," Yale Law School, 1991, p. 51, elaborating the thesis of Gordon Wood, *The Creation of the American Republic, 1776–1787* (University of North Carolina Press, 1969), pp. 306–25.
34. Elder Witt, "State Supreme Courts: Tilting the Balance Toward Change," *Governing*, August 1988, p. 33.
35. G. Alan Tarr, Keynote Address, conference on State Constitutional Reform, May 4, 2000, at www.camlaw.rugers.edu/statecon/keynote.html.
36. Lee, "Revision of California's Constitution," p. 7. See also Lutz, "Toward a Theory of Constitutional Amendment," pp. 355–70.
37. Re Jan Ruggiero, Director of Elections, Elections Division, Office of the Secretary of State, Providence, R.I., at www.state.ri.us.

38. Cecil Morgan, "A New Constitution for Louisiana," *National Civic Review*, July 1974, pp. 343–56.

39. Mark T. Carleton, "Elitism Sustained: The Louisiana Constitution of 1974," *Tulane Law Review* 54 (April 1980), p. 560, Tarr, *Understanding State Constitutions*, p. 143.

40. Bob Egelko, "Court Rejects New Vote on Constitutional Convention," March 27, 1998, at www.sfgate.com/cgi-bin/art.

41. Beryl E. Pettus and Randall W. Bland, *Texas Government Today* (Dorsey Press, 1979), pp. 34–36. See also Janice C. May, "Texas Constitutional Revision and Laments," *National Civic Review*, February 1977, pp. 64–69.

42. Andre Henderson, "Selling a Constitution: California Desperately Needs a New Charter, That Doesn't Mean It Will Get One," *Governance*, December 1995, pp. 30–31.

CHAPTER 24

1. Steven Erlanger, "Milosevich Pledges Harsh Crackdown on Strike Leaders," *The New York Times*, October 4, 2000, p. A1.

2. "Serb Strikers Foil Police to Occupy Mine," cnn.com, October 4, 2000, at europe/cnn.com/2000/WORLD/europe/10/04/yugo.protest.03/index.html.

3. Steven Erlanger, "Yugoslavs Claim Belgrade for a New Leader: Police Join Crowd," *The New York Times*, October 6, 2000, p. A1.

4. John Bibby, *Politics, Parties, and Elections in America* (Nelson Hall, 1987), pp. 94–95.

5. See Cornelius P. Cotter, James L. Gibson, John F. Bibby, and Robert J. Huckshorn, *Party Organizations in America* (Praeger, 1984).

6. William Crotty, *The Party Game* (W. H. Freeman, 1985), pp. 105–6.

7. Ibid., pp. 196–97.

8. Curtis Gans, Interview with authors. December 28, 2000.

9. Steven A. Holmes, "The World: Heads Up; The Melting Pot Politics of 2000 Are Truly Soupy," *The New York Times*, February 13, 2000, sec. 4, p. 1.

10. www.fec.gov/votregis/pdf/nvra.pdf.

11. California Secretary of State Office, *Report of Registration—General Election 2000*, October 2000, pp. 175–76.

12. See A. James Reichley, "The Rise of National Parties," in *The New Directions in American Politics*, ed. John E. Chubb and Paul E. Peterson (Brookings Institution, 1985), pp. 193–94.

13. Federal Election Commission, *Federal Election Statistics*, technical report 1, (National Clearinghouse on Election Administration, 1992).

14. For a discussion of coordinated campaigns, see Paul Herrnson, "National Party Organizations and the Postreform Congress," in *The Postreform Congress*, ed. Roger Davidson (St. Martin's Press, 1992), pp. 65–67.

15. See Cotter et al., *Party Organizations in America*.

16. See Bruce E. Keith, David B. Magleby, Candice J. Nelson, Elizabeth Orr, Mark C. Westlye, and Raymond E. Wolfinger, *The Myth of the Independent Voter* (University of California Press, 1992), p. 52.

17. William H. Flanigan and Nancy H. Zingale, *Political Behavior of the American Electorate*, 8th ed. (Congressional Quarterly Press, 1994), p. 171.

18. Willis D. Hawley, *Nonpartisan Elections and the Case for Party Politics* (John Wiley and Sons, 1973), pp. 81–82.

19. John J. McGlennon, "Party Competition in Southern State Legislatures, 1976–1996: The Last Block of the Solid South Crumbles," *American Review of Politics* 17 (Summer 1996), p. 218.

20. Harvey L. Schantz, "Sectionalism in Presidential Elections," in *American Presidential Elections: Process, Policy, and Political Change*, ed. Harvey L. Schantz (SUNY Press, 1996), pp. 106–7. See www.cnn.com.election/2000/results/index.epolls.html.

21. Peverill Squire, Raymond E. Wolfinger, and David P. Glass, "Residential Mobility and Voter Turnout," *American Political Science Review* 81 (March 1987), pp. 45–65. See also Thad A. Brown, *Migration and Politics* (University of North Carolina Press, 1988).

22. Raymond E. Wolfinger and Steven J. Rosenstone, *Who Votes?* (Yale University Press, 1980), p. 130.

23. David B. Magleby, "Participation in Mail Ballot Elections," *Western Political Quarterly* 40 (March 1987), pp. 79–91.

23. www.absenteeballot.net

25. Diane Morgan, Office of the Washington Secretary of State, interviews with authors, March 22, 1999.

26. Case; Linda Greenhouse, "Split Decisions: The Court Rules, America Changes," *The New York Times*, July 2, 2000, sec. 4, p. 1. *California Democratic* Party et al v. Jones, Secretary of State of California, et al. no. 00–401. Decided June 26, 2000.

27. Malcolm E. Jewell and David M. Olson, *Political Parties and Elections in American States*, 3d ed. (Dorsey Press, 1988), p. 121; Flanigan and Zingale, *Political Behavior of the American Electorate*, p. 195.

28. James I. Lengle, *Representation and Presidential Primaries: The Democratic Party in the Postreform Era* (Greenwood Press, 1981). For more on primary elections, see Larry M. Bartels, *Presidential Primaries and the Dynamics of Public Choice* (Princeton University Press, 1988); Jeane J. Kirkpatrick, *The New Presidential Elite: Men and Women in National Politics* (Basic Books, 1976); Barbara Norander, "Ideological Representativeness of Presidential Primary Voters," *Journal of Politics* 51 (November 1989), pp. 977–92.

29. Edward Zuckerman, "Maine Campaign Reform: Were Voters 'Hoodwinked' by Outside Groups?" *Political Finance and Lobby Reporter*, December 24, 1996, pp. 1–4.

30. David B. Magleby, "Campaign Spending and Referendum Voting," paper presented at the Western Political Science Association Annual Meeting, Albuquerque, N.M., March 1994.

31. David B. Magleby, *Direct Legislation: Voting on Ballot Propositions in the United States* (Johns Hopkins University Press, 1984), chaps. 7–9.

CHAPTER 25

1. Quoted in David S. Broder, "Legislatures Under Siege," *State Legislatures*, July 1991, p. 21. And see also David S. Broder, "States of Renewal," *The Washington Post National Weekly Edition*, September 13, 1999, p. 4.

2. William M. Bulger, *While the Music Lasts: My Life in Politics* (Houghton Mifflin, 1996), pp. 316–18. See also former Wisconsin legislator Tom Loftus, *The Art of Legislative Politics* (Congressional Quarterly Press, 1994), and former Minnesota legislator John E. Brandl, *Money and Good Intentions Are Not Enough* (Brookings Institution, 1998).

3. See Peverill Squire, "Uncontested Seats in State Legislative Elections," *Legislative Studies Quarterly* 35 (February 2000), pp. 131–46.

4. Alan Rosenthal, "The Legislative Unraveling of Institutional Fabric," in Carl E. Van Horn, ed., *The State of the States*, 3d ed. (Congressional Quarterly Press, 1996), p. 118.

5. For a useful look at Nebraska's unique legislature see Jack Rodgers, Robert Sittig, and Susan Welch, "The Legislature," in Robert Miewald, ed., *Nebraska Government and Politics* (1984), pp. 57–86.

6. Richard A. Clucas, "Exercising Control: The Power of State House Speakers," table 6. Paper presented at the Western Political Science Association Annual Meeting, Los Angeles, March 1998. See also Malcolm E. Jewell and Marcia Lynn Whicker, *Legislative Leadership in the American States* (University of Michigan, 1994).

7. *The Book of the States, 2000–2001* (Council of State Governments, 2000), p. 46.

8. See James D. King, "Changes in Professionalism in U.S. State Legislatures," *Legislative Studies Quarterly* 15, no. 2 (May 2000), pp. 327–43.

9. Alan Rosenthal, *Legislative Life: People, Process and Performance in the States* (Harper and Row, 1981), pp. 112–13.

10. Gary F. Moncrief, Peverill Squire, and Malcolm E. Jewell, *Who Runs for the Legislature?* (Prentice Hall, 2000).
11. As of Spring 2000. *Book of the States, 2000–2001*, p. 70.
12. See Sue Thomas, *How Women Legislate* (Oxford University Press, 1994). See also Lesley Dahlkemper, "Growing Accustomed to Her Face," *State Legislatures*, July/August 1996, pp. 37–45; Kathleen Dolan and Lynne Ford, "Change and Continuity Among Women State Legislators," *Political Research Quarterly* (March 1997), pp. 137–51.
13. Data from National Conference of State Legislatures.
14. See *Book of the States, 2000–2001*, pp. 83–84.
15. See Richard Perez-Pena, "Lawyers Abandon Legislatures for Greener Pastures," *The New York Times*, February 21, 1999, p. 3; Karen Hansen, "Legislator Pay: Baseball It Ain't," *State Legislatures*, July/August 1997, pp. 20–24.
16. Quoted in ibid., p. 20.
17. Frank Smallwood, *Free and Independent: The Initiation of a College Professor into State Politics* (Stephen Greene Press, 1976), p. 223.
18. For fascinating comparative data, see *Inside the Legislative Process: A Comprehensive Survey by the American Society of Legislative Clerks and Secretaries* (National Council of State Legislatures, 1998).
19. Hamm and Moncrief, "Legislative Politics in the States," p. 184.
20. Practical lobbying strategies are outlined in Judith C. Meredith, *Lobbying on a Shoestring*, 2d ed. (Auburn House, 1989). Other lobbying realities are discussed in Loftus, *Art of Legislative Politics*, chap. 10, and Alan Rosenthal, *Drawing the Line: Legislative Ethics in the States* (University of Nebraska Press, 1996).
21. Thomas Frank, "Ex-Legislators Use Contacts," *The Denver Post*, July 5, 1996, p. 16A. See also Loftus, *Art of Legislative Politics*.
22. Samuel K. Gove and James D. Nowlan, *Illinois Politics and Government* (University of Nebraska Press, 1996), p. 53.
23. Garry Boulard, "Lobbyists as Outlaws," *State Legislatures*, January 1996, p. 20. See also David Fireston, "Arkansas Lawmakers Indicted in Vast Corruption Case," *The New York Times*, April 28, 1999, p. A14.
24. Smallwood, *Free and Independent*, p. 165. See also Alan Rosenthal, *The Third House: Lobbyists and Lobbying in the States* (Congressional Quarterly Press, 1993). But see Associated Press, "State Legislators Mix Public and Private Business, Study Says," *The New York Times*, May 21, 2000, p. 26.
25. Joel A. Thompson and Gary F. Moncrief, eds., *Campaign Finance in State Legislative Elections* (Congressional Quarterly Press, 1998).
26. Winnie Hu, "Lobbying Code Puts an End to Lawmakers' Gravy Train," *The New York Times*, April 11, 2000, pp. A1, A27.
27. Charles Mahtesian, "The Ethics Backlash," *Governing*, October 1999, pp. 39–41.
28. Brandl, *Money and Good Intentions Are Not Enough*, p. 58.
29. Quoted in David Ray, "The Sources of Voting Cues in Three State Legislatures," *Journal of Politics* (November 1982), p. 1081. See also John J. Kennedy, *The Contemporary Pennsylvania Legislature* (University Press of America, 1999).
30. Karl T. Kurtz, "The Old Statehouse, She Ain't What She Used to Be," *State Legislatures*, January 1994, pp. 20–23. See also Alan Rosenthal, *The Decline of Representative Democracy* (Congressional Quarterly Press, 1998).
31. Alan Rosenthal, "The Legislative Institution," pp. 136–37. See also Alan Ehrenhalt, "An Embattled Institution," *Governing* (January 1992), pp. 28–33; Karen Hansen, "Our Beleaguered Institution," *State Legislatures*, January 1994, pp. 12–17.
32. Alan Rosenthal, "The Legislative Institution: In Transition and at Risk," in Carl E. Van Horn, ed., *The State of the States* 2nd ed. (Congressional Quarterly Press, 1993), p. 144.
33. See, for example, Christopher Conte, "Laptop Legislatures," *Governing*, November 1999, p. 36.
34. Carrie Koch, "A Room for a View," *State Legislatures*, May 1997, pp. 32–34.
35. Rich Jones, "The State Legislatures," in *The Book of the States, 1992–1993* (Council of State Governments, 1992), p. 125.
36. See Carey et al., *Term Limits in the State Legislatures*. Briefings by Gary F. Moncrief of Boise State University also make this point.
37. Jack Quinn et al., "Redrawing the Districts, Changing the Rules," *The Washington Post National Weekly Edition*, April 1–7, 1991, p. 23.
38. Gordon E. Baker, *The Reapportionment Revolution* (Random House, 1966), p. 47.
39. *Baker v Carr*, 369 US 186 (1962).
40. *Wesberry v Sanders*, 376 US 1 (1964).
41. *Reynolds v Sims*, 377 US 533 (1964).
42. *Brown v Thomson*, 103 S Ct 2690 (1983).
43. *Shaw v Reno*, 509 US 630 (1993); *Abrams v Johnson*, 138 L Ed 2d 285 (1997). For a summary of state and federal judicial cases on drawing legislative district lines, see *Redistricting Case Summaries from the '90s* (National Conference of State Legislatures, 1998); additional updates can be found at www.ncsl.org.
44. See Spencer C. Olin, *California's Prodigal Sons: Hiram Johnson and the Progressives, 1911–1917* (University of California Press, 1968).
45. See Joseph F. Zimmerman, *The Recall: Tribunal of the People* (Praeger, 1997).
46. Editorial, *The New York Times*, October 29, 1993, p. A16.
47. Jennie Drage, "A Smorgasbord of Ballot Measures," *State Legislatures* (December 2000), p. 16.
48. See, for example, Eugene C. Lee, "The Initiative Boom: An Excess of Democracy," in Gerald C. Lubenow and Bruce E. Cain, eds., *Governing California* (Institute of Governmental Studies, University of California, 1997), pp. 113–36. See also David S. Broder, *Democracy Derailed: Initiative Campaigns and the Power of Money* (Harcourt, 2000). But see Elisabeth Gerber et al., "Minorities and Direct Legislation: Evidence from California Ballot Proposition Elections," paper presented at American Political Science Association Annual Meeting, Washington, D.C., September 1–3, 2000. See also Elisabeth Gerber, *The Populist Paradox* (Princeton University Press, 1999).
49. See Peter Schrag, *Paradise Lost: California's Experience: America's Future* (New Press, 1998).
50. David Magleby and Kelly D. Paterson, "Consultants and Direct Democracy," *P.S.*, June 1998, pp. 160–61. See also Broder, *Democracy Derailed*.
51. David B. Magleby, "Ballot Initiatives and Intergovernmental Relations," paper presented at the Western Political Science Association Annual Meeting, Los Angeles, March 1998, pp. 2, 13.
52. Thomas E. Cronin, *Direct Democracy: The Politics of the Initiative, Referendum, and Recall* (Harvard University Press, 1989).
53. Michael G. Hagen and Edward L. Lascher, Jr., "Public Opinion About Ballot Initiatives," paper presented at the American Political Science Association Annual Meeting, Boston, September 3–6, 1998.

CHAPTER 26

1. Ellen Perlman, "The Welfare Risk-Taker," *Governing*, December 1997, p. 32.
2. Quoted in ibid., p. 32. See also Tommy G. Thompson, *Power to the People: An American State at Work* (HarperCollins, 1996).
3. See Thad Beyle, "Enhancing Executive Leadership in the States," *State and Local Government Review* (Winter 1995), pp. 18–35; Thad Beyle, "The Governors," in Virginia Gray, Russell Hanson, and Herbert Jacob, eds., *Politics in the American States: A Comparative Analysis*, 7th ed. (Congressional Quarterly Press, 1999), pp. 191–231.
4. Lamar Alexander, *Steps Along the Way: A Governor's Scrapbook* (Thomas Nelson Publishers, 1986), p. 112. Similar views can be found in former Vermont Governor Madeleine M. Kunin's memoir, *Living a Political Life* (Vintage, 1995).
5. See Earl H. Fry, *The Expanding Role of State and Local Governments in U.S. Foreign Policy* (Council on Foreign Relations Press, 1998). See also, for example, Alan Johnson, "Taft Shows He's Up to the Job on Foreign Grounds," *Columbia Dispatch*, February 14, 2000, editorial page.
6. *The Book of the States, 1998–99* (Council of State Governments, 1998), p. xxiii.
7. *The Book of the States, 2000–2001* (Council of State Governments, 2000), table 2.2, p. 17.
8. Ibid., table 2.3, p. 18.
9. This story is adapted from Robert S. McElvaine, *Mario Cuomo: A Biography* (Scribner's, 1988), pp. 337–38. See also the assessment of Governor Pete Wilson's turbulent first years as governor of California in

Robert Reinhold, "The Curse of the Statehouse," *The New York Times Magazine*, May 3, 1992, pp. 27–28, 54, 58–59.

10. Thad L. Beyle, "Being Governor," in Carl E. Van Horn, ed., *The State of States*, 3d ed. (Congressional Quarterly Press, 1996), pp. 90–91.

11. James M. Perry, "Virginia's New Governor Joins a GOP Trend," *The Wall Street Journal*, February 11, 1998, p. A24.

12. Richard F. Winters, "The Politics of Taxing and Spending," in Gray et al., eds., *Politics in the American States*, p. 329.

13. Fred Branfman and Nancy Stefanik, "Who Says Raising Taxes Is Political Suicide?" *The Washington Post National Weekly Edition*, February 13–19, 1989, p. 24. See also the excellent case studies of governors in Michigan, Massachusetts, Pennsylvania, Arizona, and elsewhere who pushed through economic development programs in the 1980s, in David Osborne, *Laboratories of Democracy: A New Breed of Governor Creates Models for National Growth* (Harvard Business School Press, 1988).

14. In some cases a governor's style and strategy alienates legislators. See, for example, Charles Mahtesian's analysis of Minnesota's Jesse Ventura, "Can He Govern?" *Governing*, May 2000, pp. 36–42. In contrast Governor Bruce Babbitt worked effectively even with a legislature controlled by the opposition party. See David R. Berman, *Arizona Politics and Government* (University of Nebraska Press, 1998), pp. 116–17.

15. For a lighthearted commentary by a member of Governor Pete Wilson's Electronic Commerce Advisory Council, see Stewart Alsop, "Helping the Governor Figure Out E-Commerce," *Fortune*, June 8, 1998, p. 269.

16. "N.H. Veto Saves Death Penalty," *The New York Times*, May 20, 2000, p. A16; Alan Rosenthal, *The Decline of Representative Democracy* (Congressional Quarterly Press, 1998), p. 297.

17. Cited in a profile of New York in *Governing* (February, 1999), p. 66.

18. Beyle, "Being Governor," p. 89. See also Beyle, "Governors."

19. But see Governor Thompson's defense of using frequent vetoes, *Power to the People*, and the view of one of his main critics in the Wisconsin legislature, Tom Loftus, *The Art of Legislative Politics* (Congressional Quarterly Press, 1994), chap. 5. On the varied effectiveness of the item veto as a tool for fiscal responsibility, see Glenn Abney and Thomas P. Lauth, "The Item Veto and Fiscal Responsibility," *Journal of Politics* (August 1997), pp. 882–92. On how a governor's rash use of the item veto can infuriate legislators, see Mahtesian, "Can He Govern?" p. 40.

20. Ronald Smothers, "Mississippi Governor Bans Same-Sex Marriages," *The New York Times*, August 24, 1996, p. 6.

21. *Perpich et al. v Department of Defense*, 110 L Ed 312 (1990).

22. For background on this controversy, see Jonathan Alter, "The Death Penalty on Trial," *Newsweek*, June 12, 2000, pp. 26–34.

23. Quoted in an editorial, "Governor Ryan's Brave Example," *The New York Times*, July 3, 2000, p. A20. See also Judy Keen, "Death Penalty Issue Looms over Bush Campaign," *USA Today*, June 16, 2000, p. 17A.

24. For a scholarly analysis of the role political parties play in nominating and assisting governors, see Sarah McCally, *The Governor as Party Leader: Campaigning and Governing* (University of Michigan Press, 1998).

25. See Don W. Driggs and Leonard E. Goodall, *Nevada Politics and Governments* (University of Nebraska Press, 1996), chap. 7.

26. Beyle, "Governors," p. 230.

27. Kenneth Palmer, G. Thomas Taylor, and Marcus LiBrizzi, *Maine Politics and Government* (University of Nebraska Press, 1992), pp. 92–93.

28. Thomas Hardy, "The 'Weak' Governor," in Dale Krane and Stephen Shaffer, eds., *Mississippi Government and Politics* (University of Nebraska Press, 1992), p. 152.

29. See, for example, how hard it is for a governor to control the economic fortunes of a state, especially during a recession, in Paul Brace, *State Government and Economic Performance* (Johns Hopkins University Press, 1993).

30. Data from *State Legislatures*, June 2000, p. 7.

31. Kunin, *Living a Political Life*, p. 382.

32. Richard C. Elling, *Public Management in the States* (Praeger, 1992).

33. Alan Ehrenhalt, "Reinventing Government in the Unlikeliest Place," *Governing*, August 1993, pp. 7–8.

34. Richard C. Elling, "Bureaucracy: Maligned Yet Essential," in Virginia Gray and Herbert Jacob, eds., *Politics in the American States: A Comparative Analysis* (Congressional Quarterly Press, 1996), p. 308.

35. Jonathan Walters, "Fad Mad," *Governing*, September 1996, pp. 48–50.

36. Beyle, "Being Governor," in Carl E. Van Horn, ed., *The State of the States*, 2d ed. (Congressional Quarterly Press, 1993), p. 106.

37. See the discussion of Governor George W. Bush and his relationship with his lieutenant governor in Jonathan Walters, "The Taming of Texas," *Governing*, July 1998, p. 20. See also "The Future of the Texas Lieutenant Governor," *Comparative State Politics*, October 1995, pp. 21–24.

38. But see Charles N. Wheeler III, "Why Illinois Still Needs Lieutenant Governor's Position," *Illinois Issues*, September 1994, pp. 6–7.

39. On the recent fate of attorney generals who have aspired to become governors, see Charles Mahtesian, "Blocked Path to the Big Job," *Governing*, March 1996, p. 47.

40. Professor Thad Beyle at the University of North Carolina at Chapel Hill tracks state polls on governors' job performances and finds that Democratic, Republican, and Independent governors alike all averaged about 60 percent public approval in the 1990s. Data supplied to author by Professor Beyle, June 6, 2000.

41. Alexander, *Steps Along the Way*, p. 141.

42. Thomas H. Kean, *The Politics of Inclusion* (Free Press, 1988), p. 248.

43. Scott Matheson with James Edwin Kee, *Out of Balance* (Peregrine Smith Books, 1986), p. 186. See also the reflections of another popular western governor in Cecil Andrus and Joel Connelly, *Cecil Andrus: Politics Western Style* (Sasquatch Books, 1998).

CHAPTER 27

1. www.uslaw.com/library/article/ABA/women.justice.

2. Mark S. Pulliam, "State Courts Take Brennan's Revenge," *The Wall Street Journal*, January 4, 1999, p. A11.

3. Lynn Mather, "Policy Making in State Trial Courts," in John B. Gates and Charles A. Johnson, eds., *The American Courts: A Critical Assessment* (Congressional Quarterly Press, 1991), pp. 119–57.

4. Based on research and samples reported by Henry R. Glick, "Policy Making and State Supreme Courts," in ibid., pp. 87–88.

5. Robert F. Williams, "In the Supreme Court's Shadow: Legitimacy of State Rejection of Supreme Court Reasoning and Results," *South Carolina Law Review* (Spring 1984), p. 353.

6. Harry P. Stumpf and John H. Culver, *The Politics of State Courts* (Longman, 1992), pp. 8–11.

7. Hans A. Linde, "Observations of a State Court Judge," in Robert A. Katzmann, ed., *Judges and Legislators: Toward Institutional Comity* (Brookings Institution, 1988), p. 118.

8. Peter J. Galie, "The Other Supreme Courts: Judicial Activism among State Supreme Courts," *Syracuse Law Review* 33 (1982), pp. 731–93.

9. Philip L. Dubois, "State Trial Court Appointments: Does the Governor Make a Difference?" *Judicature* (June/July 1985), pp. 20–21.

10. Charles H. Sheldon and Nicholas P. Lovrich, Jr., "State Judicial Recruitment," in Gates and Johnson, ed., *American Courts*, pp. 172–73.

11. William Glaberson, "Fierce Campaigns Signal a New Era for State Courts," *The New York Times*, June 5, 2000, p. A22.

12. Thurgood Marshall, in *Renne v Geary*, 501 US 312 (1991).

13. Robert Whereatt, "Republicans Deny Endorsement for Supreme Court Justices," June 11, 2000, at www.startribune.com.

14. William Glaberson, "Court Rulings Curb Efforts to Rein in Judicial Races," *The New York Times*, October 7, 2000, p. A8.

15. Edwin Chen, "For Judges, the Stakes Are Rising," *The Los Angeles Times*, March 4, 1988, p. 1; Glaberson, "Fierce Campaigns," pp. 1, 22.

16. William Glaberson, "A Spirited Campaign for Ohio Court Puts Judges on New Terrain," *The New York Times*, national ed., July 7, 2000, p. A11.

17. See report of survey conducted in July 1997 by the American Judicature Society, reported in "Judges Say Political Influence Threatens Independence of Judiciary," *Press & Dakotan* (www.pressandakotan.com/stories/101797/judges.html); Jerome J. Shestack, "The Risks to Judicial Independence" (www.abanet.org/journal/june98/06PP.html); Henry Weinstein, "Forum Airs Questions of Jurist Independence," *The Los Angeles Times*, November 22, 1998, p. A18.

18. Jerome J. Shestack, "The Risks to Judicial Independence," www.abanet.org/journal/june98/06PP.

19. Peter D. Webster, "Selection and Retention of Judges: Is There One 'Best' Method?" *Florida State University Law Review* 23, no. 1 (Summer 1995), p. 8.

20. Toddy Woody, "Gambling with Justice," *The Recorder*, October 6, 1997, p. 12.

21. *Wells v Edwards*, 409 US 1095 (1973).

22. *Chisom v Roemer*, 501 US 400 (1991); *Houston Lawyer's Assn. v Texas Attorney General*, 501 US 419 (1991). See also Tracy Thompson, "The New Front in the Battle for Civil Rights' Judgeships," *Washington Post National Weekly Edition*, December 18–24, 1989, p. 34.

23. J. W. Peltason, *The Missouri Plan for the Selection of Judges* (University of Missouri Studies, 1945). The plan was previously known as the Nonpartisan Plan for the Selection of Judges or the Kales Plan until called the Missouri Plan by this monograph. See also Webster, "Selection and Retention of Judges." The author is a judge of the Florida First District Court of Appeals. The Internet address is: law.fsu.edu/lawreviewissues/231/webster/html.

24. Beth M. Henschen, Robert Moog, and Steven Davis, "Judicial Nominating Commissioners: A National Profile," *Judicature* 73 (April/May 1990), pp. 328–34.

25. Philip L. Dubois, "The Politics of Innovation in State Courts: The Merit Plan of Judicial Selection," *Publius* 20 (Winter 1990), p. 40.

26. Warren K. Hall and Larry T. Aspin, "What Twenty Years of Judicial Retention Elections Have Told Us," *Judicature* 70 (April/May 1987), pp. 340–47; Susan B. Caron and Larry C. Berkson, *Judicial Retention Elections in the United States* (American Judicature Society, 1980).

27. Larry Aspin, "Trends in Judicial Retention Elections, 1964–1968," *Judicature* 83 (September/October 1999), p. 79; "Evaluating the Performance of Judges Standing for Retention," edited transcript of panel at the American Judicature Society Annual Meeting, 1995, printed in *Judicature* 79 (January/February 1996), pp. 190–95.

28. Dexter Filkins, "Republican Group Seeks to Unseat Three Justices," *The New York Times*, December 20, 2000, p. A17.

29. Traciel Reid, "The Politicization of Retention Elections," *Judicature* 83 (September/October 1999), p. 68.

30. Thomas E. Cronin and Robert D. Loevy, *Colorado Politics and Government* (University of Nebraska Press, 1993), pp. 251–53.

31. "Evaluating the Performance of Judges Standing for Retention"; "The Need for Judicial Performance Evaluations for Retention Elections," *Judicature* 75 (October/November 1991), p. 124.

32. Weinstein, "Forum Airs Questions of Jurist Independence."

33. Anthony Champagne and Greta Thielemann, "Awareness of Trial Court Judges," *Judicature* 74 (February/March 1991), p. 276.

34. Jeffrey Shaman, Steven Lubet, and James Alfini, *Judicial Conduct and Ethics*, 3d ed. (Lexis Law Publishing, 2000), sec. 15.07.

35. Jolanta Juskiewicz Perlstein and Nathan Goldman, "Judicial Disciplinary Commissions: A New Approach to the Discipline and Removal of State Judges," in Phil Dubois, ed., *The Analysis of Judicial Reform* (Lexington Books, 1982), pp. 93–106.

36. Franklin M. Zweig et al., "Securing the Future for America's State Courts," *Judicature* 73 (April/May 1990), pp. 297–98.

37. Beverly Blair Cook, "Women Judges in the Opportunity Structure," in Laura L. Crites and Winfred L. Hepperle, eds., *Women, the Courts and Equality* (Sage, 1987), pp. 143–71.

38. John Guinther, *The Jury in America* (Facts-on-File Publications, 1988).

39. *Burch v Louisiana*, 441 US 130 (1979); *Ballew v Georgia*, 435 US 223 (1978). See Reid Hastie, Steven D. Penrod, and Nancy Pennington, *Inside the Jury* (Harvard University Press, 1983), for a study showing that nonunanimous verdicts are more likely to bring in convictions than those requiring unanimity. Federal courts often use juries of fewer than 12 for civil cases. For federal criminal trials the Supreme Court still requires both the common law jury of 12 and unanimous verdicts.

40. Robert H. Jackson, *Journal of the American Judicature Society* (1940), p. 28, quoted in Jack M. Kress, "Progress and Prosecution," *Annals of the American Academy of Political and Social Science* (January 1976), p. 100.

41. William K. Muir, *Police: Streetcorner Politicians* (University of Chicago Press, 1977).

42. Charles E. Silberman, *Criminal Violence, Criminal Justice* (Random House, 1978), p. 303.

43. Jay Livingston, *Crime and Criminology* (Prentice Hall, 1992), p. 474.

44. Silberman, *Criminal Violence*, p. 218.

45. John H. Langbein, "Torture and Plea Bargaining," *Public Interest* (Winter 1980), p. 48. See also Malcolm M. Feeley, *The Process Is the Punishment* (Russell Sage, 1979).

46. Thomas M. Uhlman and N. Darlene Walker, "A Plea Is No Bargain: The Impact of Case Disposition on Sentencing," *Social Science Quarterly* 60 (September 1979), pp. 218–34.

47. Thomas Church, Jr., "Plea Bargains, Concessions and the Courts: Analysis of a Quasi-Experiment," *Law and Society Review* 14 (Spring 1976), p. 400. For a contrary view, see National Advisory Commission on Criminal Justice Standards and Goals, *Report of the Task Force* (Government Printing Office, 1979).

48. Church, "Plea Bargains, Concessions and the Courts," p. 400.

49. Jonathan D. Casper, *American Criminal Justice: The Defendant's Perspective* (Prentice Hall, 1972), pp. 52–53. Abraham S. Goldstein, *The Passive Judiciary: Prosecutorial Discretion and the Guilty Plea* (Louisiana State University Press, 1981), is critical of judges for not supervising plea bargains more actively.

50. *Santobello v New York*, 404 US 257 (1971).

51. Edward Barrett, "The Adversary Proceeding and the Judicial Process," lectures to the National College of State Trial Judges, quoted in Lynn M. Mather, "Some Determinants of the Method of Case Disposition: Decision-Making by Public Defenders in Los Angeles," *Law and Society Review* 12 (Winter 1974), pp. 187–88.

52. Henry N. Pontell, *A Capacity to Punish* (Indiana University Press, 1985).

53. Lee Sechrest, Susan O. White, and Elizabeth D. Brown, eds., *The Rehabilitation of Criminal Offenders: Problems and Prospects*, panel on Research on Rehabilitative Techniques of the National Research Council (National Academy of Sciences, 1979), pp. 3–6.

54. John Hagan and Kristin Bumiler, "Making Sense of Sentencing: A Review and Critique of Sentencing Research," in Alfred Blumstein et al., eds., *Research on Sentencing*, vol. 2 (National Academy Press, 1983); Susan Welch, Michael Combs, and John Gruhl, "Do Black Judges Make a Difference?" *American Journal of Political Science* 32 (February 1988), pp. 126–35.

55. William B. Eldridge, "Shifting Views of the Sentencing Functions," *Annals of the American Academy of Political and Social Science* (July 1982), pp. 104–11.

56. Bureau of Justice Statistics, press release, August 9, 2000, "The Nation's Prison Population Growth Rate Slows"; Bureau of Justice Statistics Bulletin, *Prison and Jail Inmates at Midyear 2000* (March 2001).

57. Eric Schlosser, "The Prison-Industrial Complex," *The Atlantic Monthly*, December 1998, p. 52.

58. Fox Butterfield, "More in U.S. Are in Prisons," *The New York Times*, August 9, 1998, p. 14.

59. *The New York Times*, December 4, 1993, p. 21.

60. www.web.cim.ufl.edu/pep/census/1999Chart3.

61. Barbara Fink, "Opening the Door on Community Corrections," *State Legislatures*, September 1984, pp. 24–31.

62. Gary Enos, "Despite New Technology, Home Confinement Faces Risks, Public Opposition," *City and State*, May 21, 1990, p. 14.

63. Arlen Specter and Paul R. Michel, "The Need for a New Federalism in Criminal Justice," *Annals of the American Academy of Political and Social Science* (July 1982), pp. 67–69.

64. Quoted in Associated Press, "ABA 'Public Jurist' Considers Reforms in Legal System," December 1993.

CHAPTER 28

1. U.S. Census Bureau, *Statistical Abstract of the United States, 1999* (Government Printing Office, 1999), p. 338.

2. Jack D. Fleer, *North Carolina Government and Politics* (University of Nebraska Press, 1994), p. 198.

3. The best overview of counties available is Donald C. Menzel, ed., *The American County: Frontiers of Knowledge* (University of Alabama Press, 1996).

4. See, for example, the story about Cuyahoga County (Ohio) Commissioner Jane Campbell, Ellen Perlman, "Polite Tenacity," *Governing*, November 2000, p. 34.

5. Ibid., p. 214.

6. For a history of suburban development, see Rosalyn Baxandall and Elizabeth Ewen, *Picture Windows: How the Suburbs Happened* (Basic Books, 2000).

7. See Paul G. Lewis, *Shaping Suburbia: How Political Institutions Organize Urban Development* (University of Pittsburgh Press, 1996).

8. For further discussion, see U.S. Department of Housing and Urban Development, *The State of the Cities 1999* (June 1999). See also Rob Gurwitt, "The Quest for Common Ground," *Governing*, June 1998, pp. 16–22.

9. Joel Garreau, *Edge City* (Doubleday, 1991).

10. For the views of three mayors on the good city, see Stephen Goldsmith, *The Twenty-first Century City* (Regnery, 1997); Daniel Kemmis, *The Good City and the Good Life* (Houghton Mifflin, 1995); John O. Norquist, *The Wealth of Cities: Revitalizing the Centers of American Life* (Addison-Wesley, 1998).

11. *Rogers v Lodge*, 458 US 613 (1982); *Thornburg v Gingles*, 478 US 30 (1986).

12. For the experience of one mayor in a council-manager city, see the memoir by Cambridge, Massachusetts, Mayor Barbara Ackermann, *"You the Mayor?" The Education of a City Politician* (Auburn House, 1989).

13. See James H. Svara and Associates, *Facilitative Leadership in Local Government: Lessons from Successful Mayors and Chairpersons in the Council-Manager Form* (Jossey-Bass, 1994).

14. See Earl H. Fry, *The Expanding Role of State and Local Governments in U.S. Foreign Affairs* (Council on Foreign Relations, 1998), esp. chap. 4.

15. For a vivid portrait of Philadelphia's Mayor Ed Rendell and his efforts to govern and revitalize that city, see Buzz Bissinger, *A Prayer for the City* (Random House, 1997). For an analysis of Providence, Rhode Island's Mayor Buddy Cianci, see Charles Mahtesian, "Buddy's Town," *Governing*, October 1998, pp. 28–32.

16. For general interest, see David A. Kaplan and Patricia King, "City Slickers," a cover story on influential and effective big city mayors, in *Newsweek*, November 11, 1996, pp. 30–36. See also Rob Gurwitt, "In Recovery," an essay on Detroit's mayor Dennis W. Archer, *Governing*, November 2000, p. 25.

17. It is fascinating to examine how mayors of different cities view their roles and responsibilities. Excellent books about important mayors are Roger Biles, *Richard J. Daley: Politics, Race and the Governing of Chicago* (Northern Illinois University Press, 1995); Adam Cohen and Elizabeth Taylor, *American Pharaoh: Mayor Richard J. Daley: His Battle for Chicago*

and the Nation (Little, Brown, 2000), and Robert A. Dahl, *Who Governs? Democracy and Power in an American City* (Yale University Press, 1961), a classic study of Mayor Richard Lee of New Haven. See also two reflective books by mayors in medium-sized or smaller cities: Kemmis, *Good City and Good Life*, and Ackermann, *"You the Mayor?"*

18. David R. Judd and Todd Swanstrom, *City Politics: Private Power and Public Policy*, 2d ed. (Longman, 1998), p. 7.

19. See, for example, the analysis of other groups such as the African Americans in Atlanta in Clarence N. Stone, *Regime Politics: Governing Atlanta, 1946–1988* (University Press of Kansas, 1989). See also Bryan D. Jones and Lynn W. Bachelor, *The Sustaining Hand: Community Leadership and Corporate Power*, 2d ed. (University Press of Kansas, 1993).

20. For suggestions on how to form community groups and effective alliances seeking progress in cities, see Michael Briand, *Practical Politics: Five Principles for a Community That Works* (University of Illinois Press, 1999).

21. Judd and Swanstrom, *City Politics*, p. 7.

22. For greater detail, see Standards for Defining Metropolitan Areas, www.census.gov.

23. Alan Ehrenhalt, "The Underclass and the Suburban Solution," *Governing*, June 1993, p. 6. Mayor Mike Peters tried to turn things around, but it has been a constant challenge. See also Rob Gurwitt, "Rudderless in Hartford," *Governing*, September 2000, pp. 75–78.

24. Mahtesian, "Buddy's Town."

25. The legal constraints on Baltimore, as an example, are outlined in David Rusk, *Baltimore Unbound: A Strategy for Regional Renewal* (Abell Foundation/Johns Hopkins University Press, 1996).

26. D'Vera Cohn, "A New Millennium for America's Cities," *The Washington Post National Weekly Edition*, October 30, 2000, p. 34.

27. David Rusk, former mayor of Albuquerque, makes this case well in *Baltimore Unbound* and in *Cities without Suburbs*, 2d ed. (Woodrow Wilson Center Press/Johns Hopkins University Press, 1995).

28. See Alan Ehrenhalt, "Cooperate or Die," *Governing*, September 1995, pp. 28–32. See also Myron Orfield, *Metropolitics: A Regional Agenda for Community and Stability* (Brookings Institution, 1997).

29. See the recommendation often prescribed by a major proponent of regionalism, Neal Peirce, in Charles Mahtesian, "The Civic Therapist," *Governing*, September 1995, pp. 24–27. See also Neal R. Peirce, "Visions of a New Urban Policy," *National Journal*, October 26, 1996, p. 2302.

30. "The End of Urban Man? Care to Bet?" *The Economist*, December 31, 1999, pp. 25–26.

31. See the thoughtful recommendations in Robert J. Waste, *Independent Cities: Rethinking U.S. Urban Policy* (Oxford University Press, 1998).

CHAPTER 29

1. John W. Wright, ed., *The New York Times Almanac, 2000* (Penguin, 1999), p. 217.

2. Ibid., p. 368.

3. Thomas R. Dye, *Politics in States and Communities*, 10th ed. (Prentice Hall, 2000), p. 472.

4. Ibid., p. 469.

5. John E. Chubb and Terry M. Moe, *Politics, Markets, and America's Schools* (Brookings Institution, 1990), p. 5.

6. For a discussion of the deficiencies in American math and science education in the 1950s, see James Bryant Conant, *The American High School Today: A First Report to Interested Citizens* (McGraw-Hill, 1959).

7. U.S. Office of Management and Budget, *Budget of the United States Government, FY 2000* (Government Printing Office, 1999).

8. Harmon Zeigler and M. Kent Jennings, *Governing American Schools: Political Interaction in Local School Districts* (Duxbury Press, 1974). See also George Kaplan, *Who Runs Our Schools? The Changing Face of Educational Leadership* (Institute for Educational Leadership, 1989).

9. See Gary Orfield, Susan E. Eaton, and the Harvard Project on School Desegregation, *Dismantling Desegregation: The Quiet Reversal of Brown v. Board of Education* (New Press, 1996).

10. National Commission on Excellence in Education, *A Nation at Risk: The Imperative for Educational Reform, An Open Letter to the American*

People (Government Printing Office, 1983). Ernest L. Boyer, *High School: A Report on Secondary Education in America* (Harper and Row, 1983), based on observations of high schools, contains a detailed series of recommendations. See also the National Science Board Commission on Precollege Education, *Mathematics, Science, and Technology: Educating Americans for the 21st Century* (Government Printing Office, 1983); Carnegie Forum on Education and the Economy, *A Nation Prepared: Teachers for the 21st Century* (Carnegie Forum, 1986).

11. James B. Steman and Wayne C. Riddle, *Goals 2000: Educate America Act Implementation Status and Issues* (Congressional Research Service, October 1, 1996), pp. 2–4.

12. Rochelle L. Stanfield, "Learning Curve," *National Journal*, July 3, 1993, pp. 1688–91.

13. C. Eugene Steuerle, Van Doorn Ooms, George Peterson, and Robert D. Reischauer, eds., *Vouchers and the Provision of Public Services* (Brookings Institution, 2000).

14. Terry M. Moe, "Private Vouchers," in Terry M. Moe, ed., *Private Vouchers* (Hoover Institution Press, 1996), p. 35.

15. Ibid., p. 22. See also John F. Witte, *The Market Approach to Education: An Analysis of America's First Voucher Program* (Princeton University Press, 1999).

16. Elizabeth Kolbert, "Unchartered Territory," *The New Yorker*, October 9, 2000, p. 36.

17. Mary Gifford, "Arizona's Charter Schools: A Survey of Parents," in Arizona Issue Analysis (Goldwater Institute, April 1996). See also Chester E. Finn, Bruno V. Manno, and Gregg Vanourek, *Charter Schools in Action: Renewing Public Education* (Princeton University Press, 2000).

18. Ed Lazere, "Welfare Balances After Three Years of TANF Block Grants," Center on Budget and Policy Priorities, January 12, 2000, p. 1.

19. R. Kent Weaver, *Ending Welfare As We Know It* (Brookings Institution, 2000).

20. See Tommy G. Thompson, *Power to the People: An American State at Work* (HarperCollins, 1996).

21. See Burt S. Barnow, Thomas Kaplan, and Robert Moffitt, eds., *Evaluating Comprehensive State Welfare Reforms* (Brookings Institution, 2000); Carol W. Weissert, ed., *Learning from Leaders: Welfare Reform Politics and Policy in Five Midwestern States* (Brookings Institution, 2000).

22. For more information go to the website of the Center on Budget and Policy Priorities at www.cbpp.org.

23. U.S. Bureau of the Census, *Statistical Abstract of the United States, 1998* (Government Printing Office, 1998), pp. 222, 308.

24. Larry Morandi, "Growing Pains," *State Legislatures* 24 (October/November 1998), pp. 24–28.

25. See Robert B. Albritton, "Subsidies: Welfare and Transportation," in Virginia Gray, Herbert Jacob, and Kenneth Vines, eds., *Politics in the American States: A Comparative Analysis*, 7th ed. (Congressional Quarterly Press, 1999); E. J. Dionne, Jr., ed., *Community Works: The Revival of Civil Society in America* (Brookings Institution, 2000).

26. For a discussion of the evolution of environmental policy in a particularly interesting place, see Charles O. Jones, *Clean Air: The Policies and Politics of Pollution Control* (University of Pittsburgh Press, 1973).

27. Jacqueline Vaughn Switzer and Gary Bryner, *Environmental Politics*, 2nd ed. (St. Martin's Press, 1998), pp. 64–66.

28. Bruce A. Williams, "Economic Regulation and Environmental Protection," in Gray et al., eds., *Politics in the American States*.

29. John Holusha, "Cities Enlisting Private Companies for Sewage Treatment," *The New York Times*, May 5, 1996, p. A18.

30. James Dao, "Governor Claims Victory for Environment Bond Act," *The New York Times*, November 6, 1996, p. B14.

31. Bruce A. Williams and Albert R. Matheny, *Democracy, Dialogue, and Social Regulation: The Contested Languages of Environmental Disputes* (Yale University Press, 1995), p. 148.

32. See B. Dan Wood, "Federalism and Policy Responsiveness: The Clean Air Case," *Journal of Politics* 53 (August 1991), p. 852.

33. Alan K. Ota, "Congress Clears Huge Transportation Bill, Restoring Cut-Off Funding to States," *Congressional Quarterly Weekly Report*, May 23, 1998, pp. 1385–86.

34. *The Book of the States, 2000–2001* (Council of State Governments, 2000), p. 394.

35. Nancy M. Davis, "Politics and the Public Utilities Commissioner," *State Legislatures*, May 1985, p. 20. See also William T. Gormley, Jr., "Policy, Politics, and Public Utility Regulation," *American Journal of Political Science* 27 (February 1983), pp. 86–105.

36. Amy Wallace, "San Onofre Mitigation Plan Wins Approval," *Los Angeles Times*, July 17, 1991, p. A3.

CHAPTER 30

1. Michael Janofsky, "West's Governors Back Clinton Plan for Fighting Fires," *The New York Times*, September 9, 2000, p. A1; Edward Walsh, "U.S. to Resume 'Prescribed Fires,'" *The Washington Post*, October 27, 2000, p. A33.

2. *The Book of the States, 2000–2001* (Council of State Governments, 2000), p. 362.

3. Ibid., p. 350.

4. *Elrod v Burns*, 427 US 347 (1976).

5. www.afscme.org.

6. www.apwu.org.

7. www.seiu.org/index.html.

8. Bureau of Labor Statistics, Employment Cost Index, October 27, 2000, at 146.142.24/cgi-bin/surveymost.

9. Ibid.

10. Former Milwaukee Mayor Henry W. Maier, "Collective Bargaining and the Municipal Employer," in Sam Zagoria, ed., *Public Workers and Public Unions* (Prentice Hall, 1972), pp. 108–18.

11. Edwin Blackstone and Simon Hakim, "Private Ayes: A Tale of Four Cities: New York, Philadelphia, Indianapolis, and Phoenix," *American City and County* 112 (February 1997), pp. 4–8.

12. Stephen Goldsmith, *The Twenty-first Century City* (Regnery Publishing, 1997), p. 10.

13. John Shannon, "The Deregulation of the American Federal System: 1789–1989," in Thomas R. Swartz and John E. Peck, eds., *The Changing Face of Fiscal Federalism* (M. E. Sharpe, 1990), pp. 17–34.

14. Roy W. Bahl, Jr., "Changing Federalism: Trends and Interstate Variations," in ibid., p. 59.

15. *The Book of the States, 2000–2001*, p. 295.

16. For a brief history of the property tax, see Dennis Hale, "The Evaluation of the Property Tax: A Study of the Relation Between Public Finance and Political Theory," *Journal of Politics* 47 (May 1985), pp. 382–404. See also C. Lowell Harris, ed., *The Property Tax and Local Finance* (Academy of Political Science, 1983).

17. National Conference of State Legislatures, *Critical Issues in State-Local Fiscal Policy: A Guide to Local Option Taxes* (November 1997), p 10.

18. See Roy Bahl, David L. Sjoquist, and W. Loren Williams, "School Finance Reform and Impact on Property Taxes," *Proceeding of the Eighty-third Annual National Tax Association Conference, 1990* (National Tax Association, Tax Institute of America, 1991), pp. 163–71.

19. *Serrano v Priest*, 5 Cal. 3d 487, 96 Cal. Rptr. 601 (1971).

20. *San Antonio Independent School District v Rodriquez*, 411 US 1 (1973).

21. David L. Kirp, "New Hope for Failing Schools: State Courts Are Remedying the Shame of Inadequate Education Funding," *The Nation*, June 1, 1998, p. 20. See also *Board of Education, Levittown, Etc. v Nyquist*, 439 N.E. 2d 359 (1982); *Washakie County School District Number One v Herschler*, 606 Pacific 2d 310 (1980); *Edgewood Independent School District v Kirby*, 34 Tex. Sup. Ct. J. 386 (1991).

22. J. Richard Aronson and John L. Hilley, *Financing State and Local Governments*, 4th ed. (Brookings Institution, 1986), p. 138. See also U.S. Advisory Commission on Intergovernmental Relations, *Property Tax Circuit-Breakers: Current Status and Policy Issues* (Government Printing Office, 1975); Steven D. Gold, "Circuit Breakers and Other Relief Measures," in Harris, ed., *Property Tax and Local Finance*, pp. 119–32.

23. David B. Magleby, *Direct Legislation: Voting on Ballot Propositions in the United States* (Johns Hopkins University Press, 1984), pp. 61–76.

24. See "Is There a Parade?" *The Nation*, October 14, 1978, pp. 363–64; Tom Bethell, "The Changing Fashions of Liberalism," *Public Opinion* 2 (January/February 1979), pp. 41–46.

25. National Conference of State Legislatures, *Survey of Legislative Fiscal Officers*, April 1996; telephone interview with Mandy Rafool, NCSL tax specialist, September 15, 1998.

26. *The Book of the States, 2000–2001*.

27. Ibid.

28. Popkin and Hetter, "America's Gambling Craze," *U.S. News and World Report*, March 14, 1994, p. 43.

29. David Brunori, "An Essay on the Future of Urban Taxation," *State Tax Notes*, June 15, 1998, p. 1943.

30. Kathryn A. Foster, *The Political Economy of Special-Purpose Government* (Georgetown University Press, 1997); Robert L. Bland and Wes Clarke, "Budgeting for Capital Improvements," in Roy T. Meyers, ed., *Handbook of Government Budgeting* (Jossey-Bass, 1999), pp. 653–77.

31. John Shannon, "The Deregulation of Fiscal Federalism," in Swartz and Peck, eds., *Changing Face of Fiscal Federalism* p. 31.

32. For a thorough discussion of issues related to intergovernmental competition in attracting business and related tax issues, see Robert L. Bland, *A Revenue Guide for Local Government* (International City Managers Association, 1989), chap. 9.

33. Charles Mathesian, "The Stadium Trap," *Governing*, May 1998, p. 22.

34. See Mark Rosentraub, *Major League Losers: The Real Cost of Sports and Who's Paying for It* (Basic Books, 1997).

CHAPTER 31

1. Edith Hamilton, *The Echo of Greece* (W.W. Norton, 1957), p. 47.
2. John F. Kennedy, *Profiles in Courage* (Pocket Books, 1956), p. 108.
3. See Warren Bennis and Patricia Ward Biederman, *Organizing Genius: The Secrets of Creative Collaboration* (Addison-Wesley, 1997).
4. See Lawrence R. Jacobs and Robert Y. Shapiro, *Politicians Don't Ponder* (University of Chicago Press, 2000); Christopher Beem, *The Necessity of Politics* (University of Chicago Press, 1999); and John E. McDonough, *Experiencing Politics* (University of California Press, 2000).
5. See Kareem Abdul-Jabar and Alan Steinberg, *Black Profiles in Courage* (Morrow, 1996).
6. Reinhold Niebuhr, *The Children of Light and the Children of Darkness* (Charles Scribner's Sons, 1944), p. xi.
7. See Bernard Crick, *In Defense of Politics*, rev. ed. (Pelican Books, 1983); Stimson Bullitt, *To Be a Politician*, rev. ed. (Yale University Press, 1977).
8. See the essays in Benjamin R. Barber, *A Passion for Democracy* (Princeton University Press, 1998).
9. See Nat Hentoff, *Free Speech for Me—But Not For Thee: How the American Left and Right Relentlessly Censor Each Other* (Harper Perennial, 1993).
10. William J. Brennan, commencement address, Brandeis University, Waltham, Mass., May 18, 1986.
11. Arthur M. Schlesinger, Jr., *The Disuniting of America* (W.W. Norton, 1993), p. 134.
12. John W. Gardner, *Self-Renewal*, rev. ed. (Norton, 1981), p. xiv.

PHOTO CREDITS

Chapter 1: 1 Library of Congress **2** S.E. McKee/AP/Wide World Photos **3** Corbis Digital Stock; White House Collection, courtesy White House Historical Association **6** Bob Daemmrich/Corbis/Sygma **7** Jeffrey Markowitz/Corbis/Sygma **15** *(left)* The Granger Collection; *(right)* Corbis **16** Liaison Agency, Inc. **21** Courtesy Louise Turner Arnold

Chapter 2: 25 The Granger Collection **31** The Granger Collection **32** Theo Westerbenger/Liaison Agency, Inc. **34** *(top)* The Granger Collection; *(middle)* Fabian Bachrach/FPG/International LLC; *(bottom)* Ron Edmonds/AP/Wide World Photos **39** AP/Wide World Photos

Chapter 3: 51 Mike Williams, Preamble, 1987; painted metal on vinyl and wood; National Museum of American Art, Smithsonian Institution; Gift of Nissan Motor Corporation; Art Resource, N.Y. **52** *(top)* Greg Baker/AP/WideWorld Photos; *(bottom)* Donald McLeod/AP/Wide World Photos **60** Jim Wilson/New York Times Pictures **66** AP/Wide World Photos

Chapter 4: 73 Spencer Grant/Photo Reseaachers, Inc. **76** *(top)* Richard Shock/Liaison Agency, Inc; *(left)* Stephen McBrady/Photo Edit: *(right)* Michal Heron/Pearson Education/PH College **78** Jean Catuffe/SIPA Press **80** UPI/Corbis **84** Richard Ellis/Liaison Agency, Inc. **85** Librado Romero/New York Times Pictures **86** Greg Gibson/AP/Wide World Photos **87** Courtesy of Libertarian National Committee, Inc. **88** SIPA Press **89** Mitchell Cohen

Chapter 5: 95 Jake Schoellkopf/AP/Wide World Photos **97** Library of Congress **98** LouKrasky/AP/WideWorld Photos **105** Liaison Agency, Inc. **107** *(left)* Liaison Agency Inc., courtesy of National Archives/Newsmakers; *(center)* Les Stone/Corbis/Sygma; *(right)* Laura Rauch/AP/Wide-World Photos

Chapter 6: 117 John Chiasson/Liaison Agency, Inc. **123** Liaison Agency, Inc. **124** Celano Lee/Liaison Agency, Inc. **125** Susan Hunt/SIPA Press **126** Bob Daemmriach/Stock Boston **127** Cynthia Howe/Corbis/Sygma **132** *(left)* Corbis; *(right)* Roswell Angier/Stock Boston **134** © Sam Mircovich/Reuters New Media Inc./Corbis **135** Crandall/The Image Works

Chapter 7: 143 Daniel MacDonald/Stock Boston **146** Bob Daemmmrich/The Image Works **149** John Harrington/Black Star **150** Ed Betz/AP/Wide-World Photos **153** Paul Conklin/PhotoEdit **154** Dennis Paquin/AP/Wide-World Photos **155** *(top)* Ron Edmonds/AP/Wide World Photos; *(bottom)* Mark HumphreyAP/WideWorld Photos **164** Dennis Cook/AP/Wide World Photos **165** AP/Wide World Photos

Chapter 8: 171 Joe Raedle/Liaison Agency, Inc. **172** Bob Daemmrich/Stock Boston **176** UPI/Corbis **178** Bob Daemmrich/Stock Boston **179** Alexis DCLOS/Liaison Agency, Inc. **183** Julia Malakie/AP/Wide World Photos **184** Liaison Agency, Inc. **186** Walter Michot/AP/Wide World Photos

Chapter 9: 193 © Brian Snyder/Reuters New Media Inc./Corbis **196** Liaison Agency, Inc. **199** Richard Drew/AFP/Corbis **205** Mike Fiala/SIPA Press **206** *(left)* © Don Emmert/AFP/Corbis; *(right)* © Jeff Mitchell/Reuters New Media Inc./Corbis **212** *(top)* AP/Wide World Photos; *(bottom)* Charles Rex Abrogast/AP/Wide World Photos **216** Lawrence University **217** AP/Wide World Photos

Chapter 10: 223 Lisa Quinones/Black Star **225** © AFP/Corbis **227** Geostock/PhotoDisk, Inc. **229** UPI/Corbis **230** © Mitchell Gerber/Corbis

Chapter 11: 243 L. Mark/UPI/Corbis **244** © Mike Theiler/Reuters New Media Inc./Corbis **246** *(top)* Corbis; *(bottom)* Corbis **249** Robert Trippett/ SIPA Press **251** *(top)* J. Scott Applewhite/AP/Wide World Photos; *(bottom)* Robert Trippett/SIPA Press **253** Robert Trippett/SIPA Press **257** AP/Wide World Photos

Chapter 12: 273 Reuters/Jeff Mitchell Archive Photos **280** Dennis Brack/Black Star **282** Liaison Agency, Inc. **284** Bruce Chambers/SABA Press Photos, Inc. **285** Beaudenon/SIPA Press **289** © Reuters New Media Inc./Corbis

Chapter 13: 297 AP/Wide World Photos **298** The Nashua Telegraph/SIPA Press **303** AP/Wide World Photos **305** Alex Wong/AP/Wide World Photos **306** AP/Wide World Photos **311** Joe Marquette/AP/Wide World Photos

Chapter 14: 317 Brad Markel/Liaison Agency, Inc. **324** *(left)* Clary/UPI/Corbis; *(center)* Carol T. Powers/AP/Wide World Photos; *(right)* Reuters/Corbis **325** *(left)* Reuters/Gary Hershorn/Corbis; *(right)* Reuters/Steve Jaffe/Corbis **328** Susan Walsh/AP/Wide World Photos **329** Supreme Court Historical Society **333** Reuters/Gary Hershorn/Corbis

Chapter 15: 343 © Roger Ressmeyer/Corbis **344** Sue Klemens/Stock Boston **357** Robert Trippett/SIPA Press **359** © Gail Mooney/Thomas A. Kelly/Corbis

Chapter 16: 363 Rob Crandall/The Image Works **367** Joe Raedle/Liaison Agency Inc. **369** LM Otero/AP/Wide World Photos **371** Charles Tasnadi/AP/Wide World Photos **372** Tom Uhlman/AP/Wide World Photos **377** Jean Catuffe/SIPA Press **379** *(left and right)* Adam Nadel

Chapter 17: 383 Andrew Lichtenstein/Stock Boston **384** David McNew/Liaison Agency, Inc. **386** Corbis **390** Joe Marquette/AP/Wide World Photos **392** *(top)* Chris Hondros/Liaison Agency, Inc.; *(bottom)* Blair Seitz/Photo Researchers, Inc. **393** Bob Daemmrich/Stock Boston **394** James Wilson **398** Seth Perlman/AP/World Wide Photos **399** Damian Dovarganes/AP/Wide World Photos

Chapter 18: 403 Raynor/SIPA Press **406** AP/Wide World Photos **407** *(top)* AP/Wide World Photos; *(bottom)* L.P. Winfrey/Woodfin Camp & Associates **408** Corbis **409** AP/Wide World Photos **410** Eric Haase/Contact Press Images Inc. **415** UPI/Corbis **416** AP/Wide World Photos **419** AP/Wide World Photos **420** McKinney & McDowell Associates **421** Curiale Dellaverson Hirschfield/Kelly & Kraemer

Chapter 19: 427 Robert Visser/AP/Wide World Photos **431** Joe Marquette/AP/Wide World Photos **434** Bob Daemmrich/Stock Boston **435** Mike Theiler/Reuters/Corbis **439** Peter DeJong/AP/Wideworld Photos **441** AP/Wide World Photos **444** Mark Wilson/Newsmakers Inc./Liaison Agency, Inc.

Chapter 20: 455 Steve Schneider/SIPA Press **456** AP/Wide World Photos **457** AP/Wide World Photos **459** Official White House Photo **460** AP/Wide World Photos **461** AP/Wide World Photos **472** John Ficara/Corbis/Sygma **473** Chris MartinezLiaison Agency, Inc.

Chapter 21: 477 Jake Rajs/Stone **482** *(top to bottom)* UPI/Corbis; Corbis; UPI/Corbis; UPI/Skingley/Corbis; UPI/Corbis **483** *(top to bottom)* UPPI/Don Rypka/Corbis; Reuters/Mark Caldwell/Corbis; Reuters/Jeff Mitchell/Corbis; Joe Marquette/AP/Wide World Photos; Howard Sachs/Liaison Agency, Inc. **486** SIPA Press **487** Jake Schoellkopf/AP/Wide World Photos **489** Corbis/Sygma **492** Wade Goddard/Corbis/Sygma **493** UN-DPI, John Isaac/AP/Wide-World Photos **495** UPI/Corbis **498** T. Campion/Corbis/Sygma

Chapter 22: 505 Alden Pellett/AP/Wide World Photos **509** Margaret Ross/Stock Boston **510** Steven Rubin/The Image Works **513** *(top)* Bob Daemmrich/Stock Boston; *(bottom)* J. Wilson/Woodfin Camp & Associates **514** Courtesy of the Urban League of Greater Miami **515** Bob Daemmrich/The Image Works

Chapter 23: 519 Nubar Alexanian/Woodfin Camp & Associates **525** Andy Levin/Photo Researchers, Inc. **528** The Senate of the State of Texas/Senate Media Services **529** Rick Reinhard/Impact Visuals Photo & Graphics, Inc.

Chapter 24: 533 R. Jenkins/SIPA Press **534** Yukad/SIPA Press **539** David Sams/Stock Boston **545** Tony Freeman/PhotoEdit **546** Alan Reininger/Contact/Woodfin Camp & Associates

Chapter 25: 551 Bob Daemmrich Photography, Inc. **554** Bob Daemmrich/Stock Boston **557** Larry Davis/New York Times Pictures **564** Randy Hampton Photography

INDEX

B

Bad tendency test, 370, 371
Baker v Carr, 245, 566
Bakke, Allan, 419
Balanced Budget and Emergency Deficit
 Control Act (1985), 310
Balanced government, 16
Ballot questions, voting on, 547
Ballot types
 absentee, 543–44
 Australian, 181
 Indiana, 536
 long, 543
 Massachusetts, 536
 office block, 144
 party column, 144
Bangerter, Norman, 651
Bankruptcy judges, 322
Baptists, 107, 108
Barnes, Roy, 576
Bauer, Gary, 84
Beard, Charles, 20
Beauty contests, presidential primaries as,
 202
Bernstein, Carl, 229
Beyle, Thad, 588
Bicameralism, 246, 553
 consequences of, 246–47
 defined, 17
 in Germany, 246
Big government, growth of, 68–69
Billboards, constitutional protection of,
 377
Bill of Rights, 9
 Second, 80
 state bills of rights, 364, 366
 in state constitutions, 13
 states and, 364–66
Bills of attainder, 363, 364, 365
Binding arbitration, 654
Biological arms control, 479
Bipartisanship, foreign policy and, 486
Blanket primaries, 147, 544
Blanton, Ray, 583
Blinder, Sarah, 301
Block grants, 66, 463
Board of county commissioners, 617
Border searches, 392
Bork, Robert, 131, 305, 324, 326
Borrowing
 by state/local governments, 666
 by U.S. government, 429
Bosnia, 481, 492
Bowers v Hardwick, 390
Boy Scouts of America v Dale, 391, 417
Brady Bill, 473
Brandeis, Louis, 55
Brandl, John E., 561
Brennan, William J., Jr., 326, 328, 330, 412
Breyer, Stephen, 7, 65, 281, 325, 367
Briscoe, Dolph, 528

Broadcasting
 constitutional protection of, 377–78
 impact of, 228–29
Broder, David, 233, 297
Broker rule, 678
Browne, Harry, 87
Brown v Board of Education of Topeka, 405,
 471
Buchanan, Patrick, 149, 205–6
Buckley v Valeo, 209
Budde, Bernadette, 130
Budget
 defense, 498–501
 process, 430–32
 steps in, 431
Budget Act (1974), 310
Budget and Accounting Act (1921), 430
Budget Reform Act (1974), 431
Bull Moose Party, 149
Bundling, 135
Bureaucracy, federal, 343–60
 accountability, 356–58
 to Congress, 357–58
 to president, 356–57
 bureaucrats in, 346–47
 case study, 353–56
 Clinton-Gore reform efforts, 344
 congressional oversight of, 248
 defined, 344, 345
 evolution of, 345–46
 operating procedures, 350–53
 bureaucratic realities, 352–53
 hiring practices, 351, 352
 management principles, 351
 reform efforts, 352
 regulation of employees, 351–52
 organization, 347–49
 formal, 347–49, 350
 informal, 349–50
 policy implementation by, 347
 as political issue, 344–45
 privatization and, 356, 357
 public opinion of, 358–60
Bureaucrats, 346–47
 defined, 344
 drug testing issue, 352, 353
Bureau of Alcohol, Tobacco and Firearms,
 443, 473
Bureau of Indian Affairs, 410
Bureaus, 348
Burger, Warren, 306, 330, 334
Burns, James MacGregor, 313
Burr, Aaron, 196
Bush, George, 64, 439
 judicial appointments, 324–25, 326, 327,
 331, 480
Bush, George W., 1, 6–7, 137, 153, 187–88,
 206, 208, 297, 477, 577
 cabinet, 287
 Comprehensive Test Ban Treaty, 479
 education reform, 455
 faith-based social service initiative, 107

 on federal bureaucracy, 344–45
 immigration issues, 95
 judicial selection, 325
 military budget, 500
 traditional conservatism and, 84
Bush, Laura, 293
Bush v Gore, 1, 6–7
Business
 government promotion of, 437–38
 as interest group, 119
 regulation of, 445–46
Business and Industrial Political Action
 Committee (BIPAC), 130
Business Higher-Education Forum, 119
Business-Industry Political Action
 Committee, 134

C

Cabinet, 287
Cable communications, constitutional protection of, 377–78
Cable television, 229
 regulation of, 444–45
Calhoun, John C., 64
California
 ballot questions in, 524
 economic/political importance of, 100
 Proposition 13, 660–61
 Proposition 187, 408
 Proposition 209, 422–23
Campaign finance, 207–13
 in Canada, 219
 candidates' personal wealth, 211
 current, consequences of, 211–13
 in Great Britain, 219
 independent expenditures, 211
 issue advertising, 210–11
 reform efforts, 208–9
 scandals involving, 207–8
 at state and local level, 547
Campaigns
 for House of Representatives,
 199–200
 presidential, 206–7
 for Senate, 201
 state judicial, 601
 state parties and, 539
Campbell, Ben Nighthorse, 411
Canada
 campaign financing, 219
 constitution, 31
 federalism, 61
 gun control, 474
 multiparty system, 149
Candidate activists, 159
Candidate appeal, voting on basis of,
 187–88, 540
Candidate-centered party system, 145
Candidates
 appeal, voting on basis of, 187–88
 media's role in choice of, 235
 personal wealth of, 211

Candidates (*continued*)
reasons for and against becoming, 670, 671
recruitment of state/local, 538
Cantwell, Mary, 193
Capitalism, defined, 78
Carson, Rachel, 440
Carter, Jimmy, 187, 206, 287
draft registration, 497
judicial appointments, 326
Categorical-formula grants, 66
Caucus/convention system, 144, 146, 203
Cavazos, Laura F., 103
Census, controversy over, 96, 97
Central cities, 626–28
Central Intelligence Agency (CIA), 484–85
Centralists, decentralists *vs.*, 63–64
Certiorari, writ of, 333
Chamber of Commerce of U.S., 119, 131
Charters, 620–23
council-manager, 622–23
mayor-council, 621–22
Charter schools, 471, 472, 639–40
Chavez, Linda, 287
Checks and balances, 9, 27–30
modifications of, 28–29
Chemical Weapons Convention, 480
Cheney, Dick, 205, 262, 289
Chicago Tribune, The, 229
Chief Justice of Supreme Court, 333–34
Child Care and Development Block Grant (CCDBG), 67
Child labor, 653
regulation, 446
Child Online Protection Act (1998), 373
Child pornography, 373
China, trade with, 480
Chinese Americans, 409
Christian Coalition, 84–85, 92, 107, 117, 123
Cisneros, Henry G., 103
Cities
African Americans in, 101
antigrowth movement, 628
central, 626–28
charters for, 620–23
council-manager, 622–23
mayor-council, 621–22
city-county consolidations, 630
edge, rise of, 619, 621
enterprise zones, 644
mayor's role, 623–25
participation patterns, 511–14
apathy and, 513
civic initiatives and, 513–14
media role, 512–13
policy making, interest groups and, 625–26
purposes of, 621
Citizenship rights, 383–87
City-county consolidations, 630
City-manager plan, 622

Civic initiatives, in local governments, 513–14
Civic organizations, political culture and, 76
Civil disobedience, 379
Civilian Conservation Corps (CCC), 457
Civil law, 318, 364
Civil liberties, 364, 403
Supreme Court and, 400
Civil rights, 364, 403, 404–23
affirmative action and, 404, 419–23
African Americans and, 405–7
Asian Americans and, 408–9
Chinese Americans and, 409
contemporary issues, 423–24
education and, 415–16
equality and, 404
Hispanics and, 408
Japanese Americans and, 409
Native Americans and, 410–11
racial justice and, 405–7
voting and, 413–15
women and, 407–8
Civil rights acts
1957, 414
1964, 58, 63, 406, 414, 462
Title II, 417–18
Title VI, 416
Title VII, 418
1991, 414
list of, 414
Civil Service Commission, 346
Civil Service Reform Act (1978), 346, 349
Civil War, rise of Republicans and, 151
Class action suits, 318, 319, 418
Classifications, Constitutional
quasi-suspect classifications, 412
suspect classifications, 411–12
tests for, 411–12
Clay, Henry, 196
Clayton Act (1914), 445–46
Clean Air Act (1990), 448, 649
Clean Water Act (1972), 649
Clear and present danger test, 370, 371
Cleveland, Grover, 196
Clinton, Bill, 28–29, 206, 232, 234, 258, 287, 376, 439, 462
Chemical Weapons Convention, 480
confirmation politics, 304–5
executive orders, 307
executive privilege, 306
federal mandates, 67
impeachment of, 34, 311
judicial appointments, 325, 326, 327, 330
public opinion and, 284–85
use of implied powers by, 300
welfare reform, 67, 459
Clinton, Hillary Rodham, 293
Closed primaries, 147, 544
Closed rule, 250
Closed shop, 121, 447

Cloture rule, 251
CNN, 13, 30
Coalition builder, president as, 283–84
Coalition for a Democratic Majority, 154
Coalition government, 148
Coattail effect, 197
Cohen, Mitchell, 89
Cohen, William, 265–66, 501, 541
Collective bargaining, 447, 654
mayors and, 655–56
merit systems compared with, 655
Commerce clause, 58, 416, 417
Commerce Department, 437
Commercial speech, 374
Commission on Presidential Debates, 206
Committee of the whole, 248
Committee on Political Education (COPE), 120–21, 134
Commodity Futures Trading Commission (CFTC), 443
Common law, 318, 364
Communications Decency Act (1996), 373, 378
Communist party, 149
Community colleges, 641
Community Mental Health Centers Act (1964), 462
Community policing, 400
Community power, 507
Commuter taxes, 628
Competitive federalism, 53
Comptroller general, 432
Concurrent powers, 59
Concurrent resolutions, 431
Concurring opinion, Supreme Court, 336
Confederate flag, controversy over, 98
Confederation, 54
federalism compared to, 54, 55
Confederations, 54
Conference Board, 119
Conference committees, 260, 264–65
Confirmation politics, 304–5
Confirmation power of Senate, 28, 251–52, 254, 326
Congress, 243–69. *See also* Congressional-presidential relations
accountability of bureaucracy to, 357
assessment of, 265–69
budget process and, 431–32
committees, 261–65
choosing members of, 262–63
conference, 264–65
investigation/oversight by, 264
joint, 261–62
select, 262
seniority rule, 263–64
Connecticut Compromise and, 18
Constitutional powers of, 247–48
criticisms of, 266–68
defense of, 268–69
elections for, 197–201, 244–46
50/50 split in, 263

Monopolies, 79, 445
Montesquieu, Charles, 26
Montgomery, Alabama, bus boycott, 406
Morale builder, president as, 281
Moral Majority, 107
Mormons, 108
Morrill Land Grant Act (1862), 471
Morris, Dick, 236
Mothers Against Drunk Driving (MAAD), 92, 651
Motion pictures, constitutional protection of, 377
Motor-voter registration, 181–82
Movements
    antigrowth, 628
    anti-international trade/globalization, 125
    antitax, 660–61
    defined, 118
    Green, 86–87
    judicial reform, 604–5
    MAAD, 92
    self-help, 629
    social, 116–17
Moynihan, Daniel Patrick, 217, 247, 485
Muhammad, Khallid Abdul, 378
Multiparty systems, 147, 148
    in Canada, 149
    in Israel, 148
Municipal courts, 596
Murdoch, Rupert, 230
Murphy, Mike, 236
Murray, Patty, 253
Mutual assured destruction (MAD), 490

N

Nader, Ralph, 87, 123, 147, 149, 197, 207, 440
National Abortion and Reproductive Rights Action League (NARAL), 117, 171
National Aeronautics and Space Administration (NASA), 376
National Association for the Advancement of Colored People (NAACP), 130
National Association for the Self-Employed, 119
National Association of Arab Americans, 124
National Association of Government Employees, 352
National Association of Manufacturers, 119
National Association of Secretaries of State, 186
National chair, of major political parties, 154, 155
National committees, of major political parties, 154
National Education Association (NEA), 117, 122, 639
National Environmental Policy Act (1969), 448

National Federation of Federal Employees, 352
National Guard, 582–83
National Highway Traffic Safety Administration, 444
National Institute of Standards and Technology (NIST), 437
National Institutes of Health (NIH), 464
Nationalism
    as American value, 77
    political socialization and, 174
Nationality interest groups, 126
National Labor Relations Act (1935), 447
National Labor Relations Board (NLRB), 447
National Oceanic and Atmospheric Administration, 437
National Organization for Women (NOW), 39, 130
National party conventions, 154, 203–6
    decline in importance of, 203–4
    role of, 204
    value of, 205
    vice-presidential nominee and, 205–6
National Rifle Association (NRA), 123, 473
National Right to Life, 117
National Security Council (NSC), 482–83
National security policy, president and, 282–83
National supremacy
    article, 57
    doctrine, 63
National Tax Reform Act (1986), 666
National Treasury Employees Union, 352
National Voter Registration Act (1993), 181
Native American Rights Fund (NARF), 410
Native Americans, 102, 410–11
    welfare reform and, 417
Naturalization, 384–85
Natural law, U.S. Constitution as, 25
Natural Law party, 151
Natural rights, 74, 403, 404
Necessary and proper clause, 57
Necessary Evil: A History of American Distrust of Government, A (Wills), 83
Negative advertising, 237
New conferences, presidential, 239
New Deal
    major programs of, 457
    Social Security, 458–59
New England town meeting, 620
New federalism, 53
New Jersey Plan, 17, 18
New judicial federalism, 366, 523, 595
New Right, 84
News media, 223–40
    bias in, 233–34
    changing role of, 227–30
    conglomerates, 229–30
    defined, 224

    elections and, 235–38
        campaign coverage, 235–36
        choice of candidates, 235
        image making, 236
        media consultants, 236–37
        voter choice, 237–38
    governance and, 238
    influence on politics, 224–27, 230–31
        factors limiting, 231–32
    in Japan, U.S. media compared to, 228
    local, role of, 512–13
    newspapers, 226–27
    public opinion and, 231–32
    radio, 226
    regulation of, 230
    sex scandal reporting by, 234, 235
    television, 225–26
    2000 presidential election and, 223–24
    World Wide Web, 227
Newspapers, 226–27
New World Order, 490
New York Times, The, 29, 226
New York Times v Sullivan, 372
NIMBY (Not In My Back Yard), 512
Nineteenth Amendment, 180, 408, 413
Ninth Circuit court of appeals, debate over dividing, 320, 321
Nitze, Paul H., 479
Nixon, Richard M., 287, 293, 337
    executive privilege, 306
    impoundment policy, 310
    resignation, 34
Nominating process
    political parties and, 146–47
    presidential, 201–3, 205–6
    reform of, 215
    state, differences in, 544, 546
Nonmajor committees, 262
Nonpartisan elections, 144, 540
Non-Partisan Political League, 134
Nonpreferentialist test, 367
Nonprotected speech, 370, 371–72
    commercial speech, 374
    fighting words, 374
    libel, 371, 372–73
    obscenity, 373
    pornography, 373
Nonpublic forums, freedom of assembly in, 379
Nontax revenues, 663–66
    grants, from states to local governments, 665–66
    legalized gambling, 665
    long-term borrowing, 666
    lotteries, 664
    user fees, 665
Nonvoters, 178
Nonvoting, seriousness of, 184–85
Norris, Pippa, 13
Norris-LaGuardia Act (1932), 446
North American Free Trade Agreement (NAFTA), 121, 439–40

North Atlantic Treaty Organization (NATO)
future of, foreign policy and, 481
Nuclear arms control, 479
Nuclear Regulatory Commission (NRC), 443, 444
Nurses Training Act (1964), 462

O

Objective journalism, 228
Obscenity, 371, 373
Occupation, political diversity and, 109–10
Occupational health, regulation of, 446
Occupational Safety and Health Act (1970), 446
Occupational Safety and Health Administration (OSHA), 443, 444
O'Connor, Sandra Day, 64, 65, 367, 422
Office block ballot, 144, 536
Office of Management and Budget (OMB), 286, 309, 349, 430
Office of Personnel Management (OPM), 346
Office of Surface Mining, 444
Off-year elections, 182
Oklahoma City bombing case, press and, 376
Old Age, Survivors, and Disability Insurance Trust Fund (OASDI), 458
Older Americans Act (1965), 462
Omnibus Crime Control and Safe Streets Act (1968), 462
Omnibus Housing Act (1964), 462
O'Neal, Shaquille, 102
One-party state, 541–42
One-person one vote principle, 566
Open primaries, 147, 544
Open rule, 250
Open shop, 121
Opinion makers, 486
Opinion of the court, 336
Oppenheimer, Bruce, 247
Optimism, as American value, 77
Optional referendum, 568
Original intent/originalism, 273–74, 328–29
Original jurisdiction, 319
state courts and, 597
Osborne, David, 357
Override of presidential veto, 260
Oversight function, congressional, 248, 264
Owens, Bill, 576

P

Pacific Legal Foundation, 327
PACs (Political Action Committees), 145
defined, 133
effectiveness of, 135
growth of, 134
investment of money by, 134–35
regulation/reform of, 136–38
Panama invasion, 492

Pardon power
gubernatorial, 583
presidential, 281
Parenti, Michael, 233
Parks, Rosa, 406
Parliamentary systems, 147–48, 274
Partial preemption, 68
Participation, political
in constitutional democracy, 179–80, 676–79
local, patterns of, 511–14
apathy and, 513
civic initiatives and, 513–14
media role and, 512–13
protest as, 179
voting and, 180–85
Partisan dealignment, 162
Partisan realignment, 161–62
reasons for slowness of, 162–63
Part-time citizens, 179
Party activists, 159
Party caucus
in House of Representatives, 249
in state legislatures, 541, 559
Party column ballot, 144, 536
Party conventions, 144, 146
Party identification
political ideology and, 82
voting choice and, 160–61, 540
Party leader, president as, 285–86
Party registration, 158, 159
Party unity score, 166
Pataki, George, 576
Patent and Trademark Office, 437
Paterson, William, 17
Patronage, 145
Payroll taxes, 429
Peace Corps, 486
Peace Corps Act (1961), 486
Peña, Frederico, 103
Pendleton Act, 346
Pennypacker, Samuel W., 578
Pentagon Papers, 229
People for the American Way, 131, 324
Percy, Charles, 211
Peremptory challenges, 395
Pericles, 675
Permanent Normal Trade Relations (PNTR) status, 480
Permissive federalism, 53
Perot, Ross, 30, 147, 149, 205
Persian Gulf War, 494
Personal liberty, as democratic value, 5
Personal Responsibility and Work Opportunity Reconciliation Act (1996), 67, 463
Petit juries, 320
Plain-view exception, searches/seizures and, 392
Planned Parenthood v Casey, 338, 390
Platforms, national party, 156–57, 204
Plays, constitutional protection of, 377

Plea bargaining, 322, 395, 608
Plessy v Ferguson, 415
Plurality rule, 9, 148
in British system, 33
Pocket veto, 260, 308
Poland, in NATO, 481
Polarization of public opinion, 173
Police powers, 388, 645
Policy clarification, congressional function of, 248
Policy committees, Senate, 251
Political Action Committees. *See* PACS
Political activities, political culture and, 76
Political bosses, 542
Political coercion, 492
Political correctness (PC), 176
Political culture, 73–81. *See also* Ideology
American Dream, 78–79
American values, 74–75, 77
overview, 73
political/economic change and, 79–81
sources of, 76
Political institutions, news media and, 239
Political landscape, diversity in, 95–113. *See also* specific racial, ethnic groups
age, 101, 110–11
education, 111–12
ethnicity, 101–4
family structure, 106
gender, 104–5
geography, 97–100
national identity, 97–98
sectional differences, 98–99
state and local identity, 99–100
occupation, 109–10
population shifts and, 100–101
race/ethnicity, 101–4
religion, 106–8
sexual orientation, 105
social class, 110
unity out of, 112–13
wealth/income, 108–9
Political machines, 542
Political parties, 143–67. *See also* Democrats/Democratic party; Republicans/Republican party
American
congressional-presidential relations and, 301
decline of, debate over, 163, 166
defined, 154
divided government and, 152–53
in electorate, 159–60
in executive branch, 158
foreign policy and, 487–88
functions of, 144–46
history of, 149–50
influence on Congress, 256–57
as institutions, 154–58
interest group formation of, 131
in judicial branch, 158–59
judicial selection and, 326

Public employees, 653–56. *See also* Bureaucracy
    collective bargaining for, 654, 655–56
    merit system for, 653–54
    privatization and, 656
    strikes by, debate over, 654, 655
    unions of, 654–55
Public forums, freedom of assembly in, 379
Public Health Service (PHS), 464
Public interest groups, 123–24
Public Interest ResearchGroups (PIRGs), 123
Publicity, as interest group technique, 128
Public opinion, 171–90. *See also* Participation, political; Voting
    abortion and, 173
    awareness/interest and, 177–79
    of bureaucracy, 358–60
    congressional-presidential relations and, 301
    defense spending and, 501
    defined, 172
    factors in formation of, 174–76
        family, 175
        mass media, 176
        schools, 175–76
    foreign aid and, 490
    foreign policy and, 486–87
    intensity of, 174
    latency of, 174
    media effect on, 231
        agenda setting and, 234
        factors limiting, 231–32
        issue framing and, 234–35
    president as molder of, 284–85
    presidential accountability and, 291–92
    as presidential constraint, 291–92
    public policy and, 177
    salience of, 174
    stability/change in, 176–77
    trust in federal government and, 345
Public opinion polls, 236
Public policy, 427–28
    public opinion and, 177
    stages in making of, 428
Public utilities, state/local regulation of, 651–52
Public Works Administration (PWA), 457
Puerto Rican immigrants, 102–3
Putnam, Robert D., 12, 13, 73

Q

Quackenbush, Chuck, 569
Quasi-suspect classifications, 412
Queer Nation, 92

R

Race
    judicial selection and, 326
    political diversity and, 101–4
    political ideology and, 82
Racial covenants, 418

Racial gerrymandering, 413–14
Racial profiling, 399, 647
Racism, 514
Radio
    impact of, 228–29
    pervasiveness of, 226
Random sampling, 172
Ranney, Austin, 184
Ratification
    of U.S. Constitution, 19–21
Ratification of U.S. Constitution, 19–21
Rational basis test, 411
Ray, Robert, 591
Reagan, Michael, 226
Reagan, Ronald, 64, 187, 231, 234, 287
    judicial appointments, 324, 326, 327, 330
Reaganomics, 434
Realigning elections, 150–52
Realignment, partisan, 161–62
Realpolitik, 490
Reapportionment, 245, 345, 541
Recall of elected officials, 29, 569
Recidivists, 610
Reconciliation, budget, 432
Recruiter, president as, 281–82
Redistributive policies, 512
Redistricting, 200, 245, 541
    politics of, 564–67
Red tape, 344
Reduction veto, 582
Referendum, 29, 568–69
Reform
    of bureaucracy, 352
    campaign finance, 155
    of Congress, 264, 265
    Democratic party, 166
    education, 472
    of Electoral College system, 218
    of interest groups, 136–40
    of judicial selection process, 331–32
    welfare, 67
Reform party, 147, 149
Regional coordinating/planning councils, 629–30
Regional primaries, 215
Registration
    party, 158, 159
    voter, 181–82, 538
Regressive taxes, 429, 433
Regulation, 440–51
    debate over, 444–45
    defined, 442
    deregulation debate, 448–50
    economic, 443
    environmental, 447–48, 649–50
    of interest groups, 136–38
    labor-management, 446–47
    of lobbying, 137
    social, 443
    state/local policies, 651–53
Regulatory federalism, 65–67
Regulatory takings, 388

Rehabilitation Act (1973), 414
Rehnquist, William H., 34, 64, 65, 330, 333, 334, 339, 367
Reid, Whitelaw, 228
Reinforcing cleavages, 96
Religion
    political diversity and, 106–8
    political ideology and, 82
    political socialization and, 176
    as shared identity, 106
Religious covenants, 418
Religious Freedom Restoration Act (1993), 369
Religious organizations, political culture and, 76
Religious Right, 154
Reno, Janet, 232
Reno v ACLU, 373, 378
Representation. *See also* specific types
    congressional function of, 248
    in constitutional democracy
        leadership and, 679
        politician's role, 678–79
    defined, 254
Representative democracy, defined, 4, 8
Republic. *See* Democracy
Republicans/Republican party, 99, 150, 151, 156–57
    ideological diversity, 154
    midterm elections, 198
    1998 midterm election, 189
    reform among, 166
    social policy and, 456
    southern resurgence of, 542
    2000 presidential election, 189
Respect for individual, as democratic value, 5
Responsibility contracts, 644
Responsible party system, 145
Retrospective issue voting, 188
Revenue bonds, 666
Revenue sharing, 66
Reverse discrimination, 419
Revision commissions, 524
Revolving door, 132, 133
Reynolds v Sims, 566
Rhode Island, constitutional revision in, 527
Rice, Condoleeza, 478
Richardson, Bill, 103
Richmond v Croson, 422
Riders, 258–59
Ridge, Tom, 154
Rights. *See also* Civil rights
    of access, 375
    of aliens, 386
    citizenship, 383–87
    of expatriation, 385
    in original Constitution, 366
    of persons accused of crimes, 364, 391–96
    political, 364

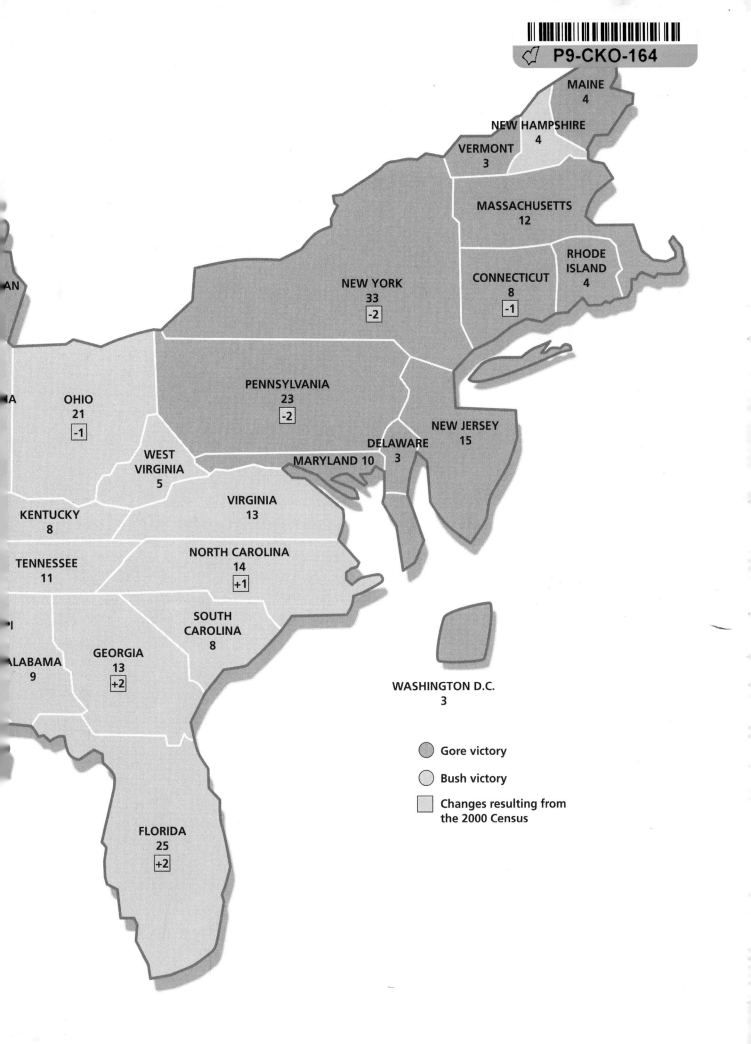

P9-CKO-164

MAINE
4

NEW HAMPSHIRE
4

VERMONT
3

MASSACHUSETTS
12

NEW YORK
33
-2

CONNECTICUT
8
-1

RHODE ISLAND
4

PENNSYLVANIA
23
-2

OHIO
21
-1

NEW JERSEY
15

DELAWARE
3

MARYLAND 10

WEST VIRGINIA
5

VIRGINIA
13

KENTUCKY
8

NORTH CAROLINA
14
+1

TENNESSEE
11

SOUTH CAROLINA
8

GEORGIA
13
+2

ALABAMA
9

WASHINGTON D.C.
3

FLORIDA
25
+2

● Gore victory

○ Bush victory

☐ Changes resulting from the 2000 Census